THE COMPLETE

PC Upgrade & Maintenance Guide

Fifteenth Edition

THE COMPLETE

PC Upgrade & Maintenance Guide

Fifteenth Edition

Mark Minasi

SYBEX®

San Francisco   London

Associate Publisher: Neil Edde

Acquisitions and Developmental Editor: Maureen Adams

Production Editor: Erica Yee

Technical Editor: Jim Kelly

Copyeditor: Kim Wimpsett

Compositor: Happenstance Type-O-Rama

Graphic Illustrator: Happenstance Type-O-Rama

CD Coordinator: Dan Mummert

CD Technician: Kevin Ly

Proofreaders: Laurie O'Connell, Nancy Riddiough

Indexer: Nancy Guenther

Book Designer: Maureen Forys, Happenstance Type-O-Rama

Cover Designer and Illustrator: Richard Miller, Calyx Design

To the people who have helped me and continue to help me over the years, the people who gave me a chance or gave me a hand: Ludwig Braun, Andy Kydes, Nancy Denkhe, Pete Moulton, John, Doug, Julie, and the other Data-Tech folks, Maureen Quinn, all of the thousands of students who've read this book and helped make it better, Fred Langa, Steve Levy, Wayne Rash, the Sybex gang (Dianne, Rudy, Rodnay, Gary, Neil, Ellen, Guy, Barbara, and many others), Donna Cook, Stan Altman, and everyone else I've overlooked. Thank you all very much!

—Mark Minasi

To Kara, Abbie, and Lauren.

—Quentin Docter

To Margaret, for the usual reasons.

—Faithe Wempen

Acknowledgments

SINCE THIS BOOK'S FIRST incarnation in 1986, I've had help from many people. I can't thank them all here, but let me mention a few. My apologies to anyone I miss. Over the years, I've gotten plenty of editorial assistance and suggestions from Sheila Walsh, the biggest, baddest Tae Kwon Do black belt to ever open up a PC; Pete Moulton, my old partner and good buddy; and Rob Oreglia and Scott Foerster, more instructors emeriti. I continue to get good feedback from the staff of Tech Teach International: Kris Ashton, Peter Brondos, Shawn Caison, Patrick Campbell, David Costow, Eric Christiansen, Bob Deyo, Ceen Dowell, Brandi Dunnegan, Paul Eve, Scot Hull, Lisa Justice, Andrew McGoff, Ellen O'Day, Nicole Price, Holliday Ridge, David Sheridan, Marc Spedden, Frederick Thornton, and Steven Wright. And you, too, can give me feedback at help@minasi.com on the Internet. And speaking of my e-mail address, thanks to all of you who have taken a few minutes to tell me how much you liked the book.

A hearty thanks to Faithe Wempen and Quentin Docter for their hard work on this edition. Faithe Wempen, M.A., A+, MOUS Master Instructor, is the author of over 70 books on computer hardware and software. She also teaches Computer Information Technology at Indiana University Purdue University at Indianapolis (IUPUI) and owns and operates Sycamore Knoll Bed and Breakfast (www.sycamoreknoll.com). Faithe is a contributing editor and A+ certification and MOUS author/reviewer for CertCities.com, and is on the advisory panel for the A+ Technician training program at Training, Inc. in Indianapolis. Quentin Docter, Sun Certified System Administrator, Sun Certified Security Administrator, CCNA, MCSE, CNE, Server+, and A+, is a 10-year IT industry veteran. He has worked as a Master Technical Instructor and Curriculum Developer, a consultant, senior Network Administrator, and Webmaster. He is now working as a part-time author and consultant while pursuing his Master of Business Administration at Purdue University in West Lafayette, Indiana.

These books don't get into your hands unless some publisher who thinks they're worth it puts them there. The first such person was Stephen Levy, the publisher of the first version of this book, and my thanks go to him. Dianne King at Sybex arranged for Sybex to start publishing this; Dianne's goofing off somewhere, but we miss her. Gary Masters, the Maxwell Perkins of the computer press, remains this book's guardian angel. Thanks also to this edition's Sybex editors Neil Edde, Maureen Adams, and Erica Yee; the technical editor Jim Kelly; copyeditor Kim Wimpsett; page compositor and illustrator Happenstance Type-O-Rama; CD coordinator Dan Mummert; CD technician Kevin Ly; Proofreaders Laurie O'Connell and Nancy Riddiough; and, of course, indexer Nancy Guenther.

—Mark Minasi

I'd like to thank the Sybex staff for their exceptional dedication and understanding.

—Quentin Docter

Thanks to the staff at Sybex for another job well done.

—Faithe Wempen

Contents at a Glance

Contents

Introduction

THIS NEW EDITION OF *The Complete PC Upgrade & Maintenance Guide* brings tons of new information. Over the years, each edition has seen chapters yanked out and completely rewritten, and that's true in this edition in spades.

What's New in the 2003 Edition

In some ways, the PC hardware world doesn't change much. After 12 years, Video Graphics Array (VGA) is still the baseline video standard and floppies still hold only 1.44 megabytes (MB) of data. But in other ways, it's moving all the time, and that has motivated this latest overhaul of *The Complete PC Upgrade & Maintenance Guide*.

As I do each year, I've updated this edition to cover the latest technologies that affect users. Among the new topics included in this edition are the Pentium 4 processor and the newest technologies including flash memory, all-in-one printers, satellite dish Internet access, video capture cards, and all of the new DVD recordable technologies.

In addition to updating the chapters to include the latest technologies, I've added handy Quick-Steps sections to the beginning of many chapters—these sections get straight to the point by providing step-by-step instructions for many major upgrade and repair procedures. The QuickSteps sections also list the items you'll need on hand and preparations you'll need in place before you begin.

In this edition, I've continued to include a Visual Upgrades section that'll guide you through many of the common upgrades quickly and easily. As their name implies, the Visual Upgrades walk you through the process visually.

The combination of QuickSteps, Visual Upgrades, and the videos included on the CD will provide the confidence you need as you work through a particular procedure.

Finally, I've updated the troubleshooting sections at the end of many chapters. You'll find workarounds to many common problems concentrated in these distinct sections. These sections also alert you to gotchas lurking within major hardware components and upgrading scenarios.

Why This Book?

I've been programming computers since 1973. But for years I wasn't a "hardware guy." After moving from mainframe programming to the early PCs that came out in the mid-'70s, I watched the microcomputer market, waiting for a computer that was useful and didn't require any soldering to get it up and running.

That's why I liked the IBM PC from the beginning. Just take it out of the box, plug some stuff together, and *voilà!* A completely usable computer—and *no soldering*.

That was, of course, until I had it for nine months. Then, right in the middle of doing some work, all of a sudden, the floppy drive light came on for no apparent reason, the system rebooted itself, and the number 601 appeared on the screen. Nothing else happened—the machine refused to do any more. I turned it on and off again, and it did the same thing.

"What now?" I thought. It was 1982. Replacing *everything* was expensive. Floppy drives cost $500 apiece. A PC motherboard cost $1400. A floppy controller cost $275. Of course, all of this happened shortly *after* the warranty on my PC expired. I had an all-IBM machine, but some of the parts came from a dealer who wasn't an authorized IBM dealer, so IBM wouldn't even talk to me. I went to a service department of a large computer store chain seeking help. I looked at their hourly rates and *knew* from their high prices that they must know what they were doing (I was younger and dumber), so I confidently left my machine with them. They kept the machine for two months, said they couldn't find anything wrong with it, and charged me $800.

The problem, of course, persisted. I was scared. I mean, I had just spent some big bucks for this computer and then spent $800 on some nonrepairs, and it still didn't work. So I figured, "What the heck, I can't make it any worse," and took the top off.

What I saw was that the drive was connected with a ribbon cable to a circuit board, a board I later learned was called the *floppy controller board*. The controller board was new, the drive was new (the repair shop had already replaced them)—but what about the cable? You guessed it; $35 bought a new cable from a local computer supply place, and the problem went away forever.

I found out that I wasn't the only person with PC repair needs. On average, seven out of ten PCs suffer a breakdown of some kind. It takes an average of five days to fix, and the fix costs an average of $257. (This is according to a survey from the Business Products Consulting Group. The results were based on a survey of 500 business users. Besides, it was about time to throw in a statistic.) Even if you pay a maintenance company lots of money to keep your machines in shape, you should *still* do whatever repairs you can. That's because the big cost of machine failures isn't the cost of the machine—it's the cost of the lost employee time because employees must wait in line to use machines or forgo the services of a PC altogether. You may have to wait four hours for a service person only to find that the fix was a simple five-minute operation. The result: four hours of lost employee time. Furthermore, and perhaps more important, service bureaus don't repair hard disks; they throw them away—along with your data. It's not hard to bring dead hard drives back to life, as you'll learn in this book.

Emboldened by my success, I read what few references existed about microcomputer repair, and I tried fixing a lot of things. Some things got fixed, some got "smoked." I asked a lot of questions and made a lot of mistakes, and I finally got to the point where at worst I didn't do any damage and usually succeeded. I'd like to accelerate *you* to that point with this book. (But you'll still "smoke" the occasional device—everybody does.) Once I figured out how simple it was to fix PCs, I developed a series of seminars on PC repair that I conduct in the United States, Canada, and Europe.

That's why you're reading this. (Unless you're thumbing through it in the bookstore. If you are, then *buy* the silly thing. Hundreds of thousands of people already have, so it's a good bet that you'll like it.)

This book won't teach you to fix *all* problems. Not all problems *can* be fixed—for instance, leaving your hard disk out in the rain will probably render your erstwhile data storage medium usable for little more than a paperweight. Nevertheless, even if you've never opened up a PC or installed an expansion board, this book can help you.

It'll also help with terminology. Part of your job may involve talking to technical types. Some of those folks are good at talking to ordinary mortals, but some (and I'm sure you know a few of them) can't seem to speak a single sentence without a liberal sprinkling of TLAs (you know, Three-Letter

Acronyms). Thoroughly reading this book will enable you to speak fluent "PC-ese," and the index will point you to definitions of most PC terms. The glossary also has scores of definitions to help your geek-speak.

You'll also see a fair amount about installation in this book. Installing new equipment often brings headaches: understanding how to do it and why it doesn't work once installed, testing the new equipment, and ensuring that it doesn't adversely affect already installed equipment. I'll also talk about how to take a tired old PC and soup it up to get better performance from it.

In the process of working with IBM PCs since 1981 and microcomputers since 1976, I've picked up or written a number of useful utilities that assist in the diagnosis of PC problems, and I'll discuss them in this book.

Who Is This Book For?

I'm writing this for the needy and the curious. Some of you *must* understand the machines you depend on so that you can better keep them in top shape. Others may just wonder what's going on under the hood. Whoever you are, dig in and try something!

Don't let that useful little gray box on your desk control *you* when it goes down. Take control of *it*. (Remember who's supposed to be boss.) Even if you never take the machine apart (coward!), you'll still learn a lot about what goes on under the hood of your machine and how to make it work faster and live longer.

Terminology

There are so many machines that it's hard to know how to refer generically to PCs. So here's the informal convention I'll use in this book: when I say *PC* in this text, I include all PC-compatible machines—anything from an 8088 Central Processing Unit (CPU) to a Pentium 4, a laptop to a desktop, big to small—unless otherwise specified. Where necessary, I'll use *XT* to refer to XTs and XT clones—the 8088-based machines that you may have hanging around. I'll use *AT* to refer to 286, 386, 486, or Pentium machines in general. More specifically, an *AT-type machine* is a desktop machine using a processor of 286 or later vintage. Most nowadays use a combination of expansion slots called Industry Standard Architecture (ISA) and Peripheral Component Interconnect (PCI) slots, but you may come across other kinds such as Extended Industry Standard Architecture (EISA) and Video Electronics Standards Association (VESA) bus slots (and don't worry, I'm going to explain what those are in greater detail in Chapter 2, "Inside the PC: Core Components"). Examples of those machines include not only the common clone but also big names such as Compaq, Hewlett-Packard (HP), Sony, Dell, and Gateway.

My goal in developing this book is to include material of use to "techies" as well as to those who've never even opened up a PC. I'm not going to try to make an electrical engineer out of you; I'm not one myself. All it takes to do most PC maintenance is a screwdriver and some patience. I've made every effort to keep the jargon to a minimum and to define unusual PC terms when I use them. I *am* going to use jargon, however, because it'll get you used to the "industry-speak;" this will equip you to read industry journals, Web sites, and other books.

Structure of This Book

First, you'll take a minute to survey the machines out on the market and look at the features that sep-arate one type of PC from another. Second, you'll look under the hood and see what's inside a PC. After that, you'll step back and examine some preventive maintenance techniques and troubleshooting approaches. Next, you'll look in detail at circuit boards, PC memory, and power supplies. Then you'll learn all about hard disks and CD and DVD drives: how they work, how to install them, and how to do data recovery on them. The book then takes a look at floppy drives, printers, and multimedia essentials (modems, video capture boards, and sound cards). Next you'll learn about managing hard-ware, using the Internet for support, and networking. There's even a whole chapter on tapping into the vast sea of resources and information available on the Internet. You'll also get some great tips about buying a PC and all the latest on laptops.

Safety Notes and Cautions

Before you get started, a few words of disclaimer: please heed the warnings you see in the text. Read *all* of a chapter before trying surgery. The reason for this is simple. If I've put something in an order that isn't clear, you could damage the computer or yourself.

I mention many products in this text. I'm not endorsing these products. Where I make note of them, they have been of value to me. However, manufacturer quality can vary, and goods can be rede-signed.

In general, it's pretty hard to hurt yourself with a PC, short of dropping it on your toe. But there are a few exceptions:

◆ There's a silver or black box with a fan in it in the back of your machine. It's the power supply; it converts Alternating Current (AC) from the wall socket into Direct Current (DC) for the PC's use. You can't miss the label, in five languages, that says, "If you open me, I'll kill you." *Don't open it.*

If you were to open the top of the power supply while the machine was plugged in, or even if the power was off, you could get a full 120 volts (220–240 for those of you on the other side of the Atlantic) through you if you touched the wrong things. Even if the power supply isn't plugged in, power-storing devices called *capacitors* can give you a good shock even after the machine has been unplugged and turned off. The same, by the way, goes for monitors: don't open them.

*WARNING   Let me reiterate this: do not open the power supply or the monitor. Under the wrong circumstances **this could kill you**. There's always somebody who doesn't pay attention to the important stuff, but PAY ATTENTION TO THIS WARNING.*

◆ It's certainly safe to *replace* a power supply, but when doing such a replacement, again, be double sure it's unplugged before removing the original power supply. More important, why go into the power supply in the first place? The only possible user repair I can imagine is to replace the fuse in the box, and again, don't even think of trying it unless you know how to discharge large capacitors safely.

◆ Another power supply item: never connect a power supply to the wall socket and turn it on *when it isn't connected to a PC motherboard*. Only turn on a power supply when the motherboard power connectors are in place.

Why? Back in the original PC days, some of the power supplies on the market would literally *explode* if you ran them like this (called "running it without a load"). Power supplies aren't glamorous things; no one touts the quality of their power supplies when selling PCs. The result? The cheapest power supplies get put into PCs. Your modern power supply is almost certainly not one of the explosive kinds, but I'd avoid the risk, myself. Besides, there isn't anything you can test with a power supply just standing alone.

◆ Unless it's an emergency procedure, *back up* your data before doing anything drastic. What if something goes wrong and the machine never comes back?

◆ You can damage circuit boards by removing them with the power on. Don't do it. Turn the machine off before removing a circuit board.

◆ Take static electricity precautions; they're discussed in Chapter 4, "Avoiding Service: Preventive Maintenance."

The rest of the components you'll find in the PC are safe, but don't ignore these warnings.

Having said all of that, welcome! It's time for you to get to know your PC better and have some fun in the process.

Part 1

Core Components

Chapter 1

Five Easy Pieces: PC Hardware in a Nutshell

- ◆ CPUs, Peripherals, and Controllers
- ◆ Buses and Interfaces
- ◆ The Sixth Piece: Drivers
- ◆ Other PC Components and Issues

Introduction

If you have any experience buying, using, or fixing PCs, you've no doubt heard a bushel of strange terms—RAM, CPU, USB, PCI, FireWire, Athlon, Duron, Pentium, Itanium, Centrino, you name it. And believe me, it's not going to get any better because this business *loves* jargon.

Since their introduction in the '80s, PCs have evolved nonstop. The most recent changes are bringing them more closely in line with consumer hardware such as video cameras, DVD players, and televisions. Standards seem less chiseled in stone and more written in shifting sand. Until recently, consumer electronics and PCs didn't really talk to one another. But technology is rapidly moving toward a wired world. With the advent of wireless technology, your notebook computer will automatically link up to your desktop computer, and while you're trying to figure out what's for dinner, your laptop will update the files on your desktop. You'll also be able to turn on the television with a single keystroke on the PC keyboard, and your PC's hard drive or recordable DVD drive will automatically record a television show while you work on a Microsoft Excel worksheet. Different companies are coming up with different ways to implement this type of technology, fueling a rapid-pace change in hardware and increasing the number of "standards."

There's also a trend to put add-on hardware boards, such as video and sound cards and even modems, right on the motherboard to save a little extra money in production. Consolidation seems to be a major theme; some major computer manufacturers sell computers with no expansion slots. Their reasoning is that any add-on hardware that's required can be attached via the Universal Serial Bus (USB) port.

If you don't know already, the motherboard is the central board in a PC to which everything else ultimately connects. The motherboard has a socket or slot for the Central Processing Unit (CPU), expansion slots to add other hardware boards that control features such as video and audio, ports to which devices such as your mouse connect, sockets for adding extra Random Access Memory (RAM), USB and FireWire ports for attaching a multitude of peripherals, and connectors called Integrated Drive Electronics (IDE) channels for plugging in hard drives, CD-ROM drives, and DVD drives. You'll learn a lot more about them in Chapter 2, "Inside the PC: Core Components."

PC hardware *can* be confusing because there are so many parts to a PC—and some of these parts change pretty quickly. I wish I could write this book so that it completely avoids the geeky details such as, "The standard keyboard port uses I/O addresses 60 hex through 64 hex and IRQ1," but ultimately you'll *have* to know some of that stuff or you won't really be effective as a buyer, upgrader, or fixer. (A *keyboard port*, by the way, is the connector and circuitry in the computer that makes it possible for you to attach a keyboard to your PC.) And until they get those direct neural interfaces working in the next century or two, keyboards will remain kind of essential. (I'll explain that I/O and IRQ stuff in Chapter 5, "Installing New Circuit Boards.") Jumping in at that level right now, however, would probably convince the average reader that quantum physics would be a simpler course of study.

Knowledge really *is* power where computers are concerned. What you need, then, is some structure, along with a bird's-eye view of PC hardware. It's a lot easier to understand some new term if you have a classification system. What I'm going to explain in this chapter is the mental model that I use to understand PC hardware. It's not perfect—not *everything* will fit into this model—but I think you'll find it useful in your hardware education.

CPUs, Peripherals, and Controllers

Basically, PC hardware boils down to three kinds of devices: the CPU (or, as more and more machines offer multiprocessor capabilities, the CPUs), *peripherals* (the input, output, and storage devices that make a computer functional and user-friendly), and in-between devices that I'll generically call *controllers* or *adapters*.

For example, consider what makes it possible for the PC to put images on your video monitor. Every PC has a video monitor, and every PC also has a chip inside it called the CPU, often called the *processor*, which is essentially the "engine" of the PC. When you hear people say they have a "Pentium 4 computer," they're describing the particular model name of the CPU around which their computer is built. Common CPU names you might hear are Pentium (in various flavors, such as II, III, or the non-Roman numeric 4), Celeron, or Pentium M (which is the CPU brain of the popular mobile Centrino chipset) all of these are CPUs made by Intel. At one time, Intel had a monopoly on this market until other companies decided they could make CPUs faster and cheaper. These competitors include Advanced Micro Devices (AMD) with its Athlon, Duron, and Opteron processors, and VIA Technologies, which markets the Cyrix MII and C3 chips.

In between the CPU and the monitor is a kind of diplomatic device—a circuit that knows how to talk to both the CPU and the video monitor—called the *video adapter* or *video controller*. If you ever see a reference to an S3 graphics adapter, a Super VGA (SVGA) adapter, or a 3D adapter, it's a reference to a video adapter. Video adapters contain memory that they use to retain the current video image, as well as onboard electronics that know how to do many useful graphical tasks such as drawing lines, circles, and polygons. Why is this important? Well, if you're ever in the middle of a World War II dogfight fighting for your life (in a PC game, of course), you really want your graphics to be smooth. One of the most important specifications today for 3D video cards is how fast they can draw a simple geometric shape called a *polygon*—measured in millions of polygons per second.

Interestingly, a large number of companies used to build video controllers, as well as components for other manufacturers' video controllers. With the price erosion of high-performance graphics controllers in the latter part of the '90s, however, many of these companies either quit making graphics controllers or made them only to sell to computer manufacturers for integration into motherboards. The result: fewer third-party video adapter boards for sale at the consumer level.

You'll see this CPU-adapter or controller-peripheral connection throughout all PC hardware; for example:

- Figure 1.1 shows speaker connections on a motherboard, and Figure 1.2 shows a Creative Labs Sound Blaster Live sound card. These illustrate the two kinds of speakers used on computers since the early '90s. The first one is the small PC speaker that's attached directly to your motherboard. It doesn't make any cool noises, just simple beeps. The other is attached to special stereo sound circuitry that might also be built on the motherboard or on a separate circuit board that you plug into your motherboard. Once just cheap multimedia components, PC sound systems have risen in technology and performance, rivaling consumer audio.

- Most motherboards today have built-in circuitry to control Enhanced Integrated Drive Electronics (EIDE) hard drives, CD-ROM drives, and DVD drives. In fact, 80–85 percent of all drives being used in PCs today use the EIDE interface. Because of the prominence of the EIDE interface (which is discussed in more detail later in this chapter), you might have to install a special adapter if you want to connect another kind of drive to your system. For example, if you want to install a Small Computer System Interface (SCSI) hard drive, you'll need to install a special SCSI adapter (also called a host adapter) in one of the expansion slots on your motherboard.

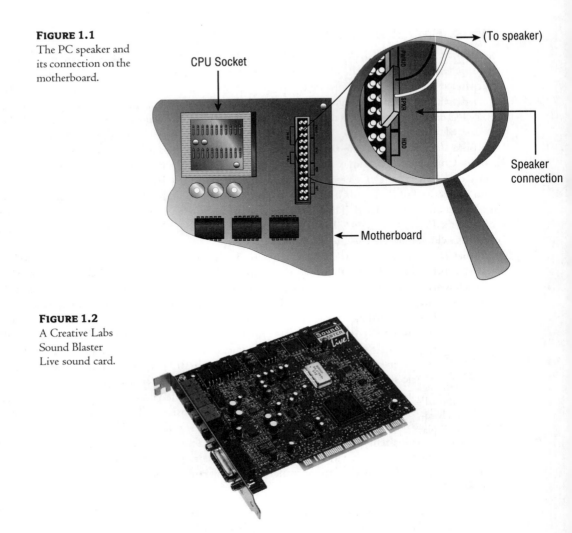

FIGURE 1.1
The PC speaker and its connection on the motherboard.

FIGURE 1.2
A Creative Labs Sound Blaster Live sound card.

- To connect a printer to the PC, you'll need a parallel port or USB port.

- If you're connecting a scanner or a digital camera to your computer, you'll probably use one of your PC's USB ports.

- To use your computer as a video-editing bay, you connect your digital video camera to your PC's FireWire port—which is an ultra-fast way to transmit digital data from one device to another.

These are just a few examples of the different types of electronic components; you'll see tons more in this book.

Buses and Interfaces

But wait, you're not done yet. You have three parts of my PC model down—CPUs, peripherals, and controllers/adapters. I'd better explain two more pieces that I've already mentioned: *buses* and *interfaces*.

Let's say you're talking to a friend who just bought a new computer. Lapsing into fluent computerese, your friend says, "Hey, I just got this 2.53-gigahertz Pentium 4 with 1024 megabytes of RAM, an 80-gig ATA 100 hard disk, and AGP 8 video." Notice how your friend describes the computer—the first thing mentioned was a "2.53-gigahertz Pentium 4." As you've already read, "Pentium 4" describes the CPU, the chip around which the entire computer is built. Some people compare it to a car's engine—not a terrible analogy, with gigahertz being vaguely analogous to horsepower—but I'll take up CPUs in greater detail in Chapter 2.

The next part of the statement, "1024 megabytes of RAM, 80-gig hard disk, and AGP 8X video," refers to hardware *other than* the CPU—hardware that helps to make the computer useful. RAM is the computer's memory, a bunch of electronic chips that the CPU uses to store the program and data on which it's currently working. (RAM isn't a very useful acronym. What we ought to call it is "chips that the CPU can both store data to and read data from," but I suppose that would make for far too long an acronym.) I'll introduce RAM in Chapter 2 and discuss it in some detail in Chapter 6, "System Memory." What about "80-gig hard disk"? Well, "80 gigs" (gigabytes, or a billion bytes) describes the amount of data-storage space the computer has on its hard drive. This is memory that will remain intact even after the computer has been shut down. Many explanations of computers show simple block diagrams that look something like Figure 1.3.

FIGURE 1.3
The CPU is logically connected through the motherboard to its memory, hard disk, video display, and printer.

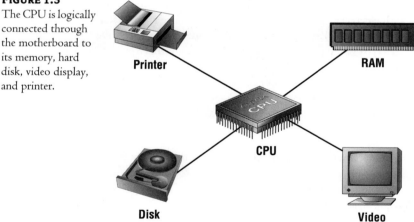

So that PCs can be easily upgraded, PC manufacturers put empty electronic connectors inside each PC; most people call them *expansion slots*. The expansion slots are the easily visible part of the *bus*, which communicates with the CPU. Over the years, several bus types have become popular. The most common bus nowadays is Peripheral Component Interconnect (PCI); don't worry about this now—I'll take it up in detail in Chapter 2. Most motherboards today have these PCI expansion slots; some also include another (older) type of bus, called Industry Standard Architecture (ISA). Figure 1.4 shows a motherboard with both of these kinds of slots. Fortunately, their designs make it impossible to plug an expansion card into the wrong type of socket. But you still need to know what types of cards your motherboard will accept before going out and buying that great video card upgrade!

FIGURE 1.4

Notice the PCI and ISA expansion slots on this Pentium motherboard.

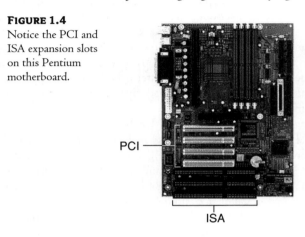

Why are there PCI and ISA bus connectors in this computer? Because they're both standards on which computer system designers and computer expansion board designers can agree. This is important because, just as the standard electrical sockets in your home's walls make it easy for you to buy appliances with electrical plugs and immediately use those appliances, a standard bus connector such as PCI or ISA means you can buy your PC from one vendor and your sound card, display board, or internal modem (to name just a few examples) from another vendor and still be pretty sure they'll work on your PC.

The mildly tentative tone of the previous sentence reflects that hardware compatibility in the PC world is sadly not a sure thing, and even the biggest names in the PC business sometimes sell hardware that just plain doesn't do what it's supposed to do. However, the industry is continually evolving, and few hardware incompatibility issues remain.

TIP   One piece of trivia you might find helpful to remember: the newer the PC motherboard, the fewer the number of ISA devices that will be supported by it. Most new motherboards have just one dual ISA/PCI slot (along with lots of PCI slots) or no ISA connections at all. ISA has been provided all along for backward compatibility, but it's on its way out because it's being replaced by faster buses.

By now you might be wondering exactly *who* sets the standards for how PCs are designed. Sadly, the answer in most cases is that there are a lot of cooks in the kitchen, and that makes standards seem less than…well, *standard*. Two of the most important cooks are Microsoft and Intel (sometimes referred to together as *WinTel*); almost every year, the companies issue a set of design guidelines that spell out the minimum requirements that a PC must have to carry the label "Microsoft Windows compatible."

Although most current video boards connect to the CPU through a PCI interface, one of the main features that drives innovation in the computer business is speed: the faster the CPU and video controller can blast pictures onto the screen, the more popular the computer is likely to be. So when some in the industry became impatient with PCI's top speed (not fast enough!), Intel decided to add another bus—for graphics boards only—that the computer could use instead of PCI. This ushered in the Accelerated Graphics Port (AGP) standard. Thus, when you read an ad saying that a computer has "AGP video," it means there's a connector inside the PC that's designed to offer higher speed than PCI, and the system uses an AGP-compatible video controller.

NOTE *The first AGP controllers offered a speed of 1 or 2, but the faster 8 controllers are now on the market, along with the motherboards that support them. The fastest AGP specification is currently 3.0. The original AGPs weren't a lot faster than using a PCI video board, but using AGP video meant you freed up a PCI slot. The 8 refers to a much faster rate of transfer from the video to the CPU and back again, something that's finally helping to end some of the video-speed bottlenecks that most people have experienced.*

You've learned about CPUs, peripherals, controllers, and buses; now what about interfaces?

Just as standard buses such as PCI make it easy for one vendor to offer a PC and another a disk controller, there's also a standard interface between the disk controller and the disk. For historical reasons, there's more than one way to connect a disk to a disk controller. The most common disk interface used today is the EIDE interface. EIDE is so popular, in fact, that virtually all motherboards have two EIDE controllers built right into them. Each EIDE controller can accommodate up to two EIDE drives (either hard drives or CD-ROM/DVD drives).

The EIDE standard for the past several years has been a parallel bus structure called Ultra ATA. Although it's been serviceable for most users, today's computers require faster data transfers to and from the hard disk. Because of the physical limitations of the Ultra ATA design, a newer standard called Serial ATA has been developed. It's fast and self-configuring, supports hot plugging, uses less power, and is easy to configure. I'll talk about more Serial ATA specifics in Chapter 10, "Understanding and Installing ATA Drives."

How are CPUs, buses, adapters, interfaces, and peripherals connected? Does one have to go with another? For example, will you find that SCSI adapters are available only for PCI? Not at all. As far as I know, SCSI adapters are available for every bus around, with the exception of AGP. Five easy pieces, then: CPUs, buses, controllers/adapters, interfaces, and peripherals. The CPU does the thinkin', the peripherals do the doin', and the controllers/adapters help them communicate. Buses and interfaces are just the glue that sticks them all together.

Actually, There's a Sixth Piece

Buying all of this hardware is of no value if you can't make it all work. As you probably know, computer hardware is of no value if there isn't *software* to control it. So, in a sense, there's a *sixth* piece to my five-piece model: software that's designed to control specific pieces of hardware. These pieces of software are called *drivers*.

The best hardware in the world is no good if your operating system and applications don't support it. The question of whether a particular piece of hardware has drivers for, say, Windows XP, Windows Millennium Edition (Me), Windows 2000, Windows Server 2003, or Linux is of vital importance when you're buying new hardware. Most newer operating systems offer formal or informal hardware compatibility lists—a roster of hardware directly supported by that operating system version. At the least, they'll have notes about devices known to have problems when used with that operating system (sometimes they include suggested workarounds, too). You should find this information for your operating system before you shop for any new piece of hardware. Buying and trying unsupported hardware can make for a long walk down a lonely road—such hardware might work just as well as one that's supported, but it might also require a lot more work on your part. So check with your software vendor before falling in love with some new doodad.

NOTE   *You can access Microsoft's Hardware Compatibility List for the entire family of Windows operating systems at* www.microsoft.com/whdc/hcl/default.mspx.

Typical PC Components and Issues

At this point, you might be thinking, "Yes, I've heard of Pentium 4, gigahertz, EIDE, and AGP, but that's not *all* I've heard of—what about BIOS, Ethernet, or FireWire connections?"

The intention of this chapter is to introduce you to several basic PC terms and help you start to organize the concepts of PC hardware in your mind—but first I needed to explain the five-part model. Now that you're comfortable (I hope!) with the terms *CPU, bus, adapter/controller, interface,* and *peripheral,* I can round out the chapter with five-second explanations of the PC terms I see as the most significant.

I'll present most of these terms again in greater detail later in the book. For now, though, Table 1.1 will serve as a good warm-up of terms you need to know.

What you'll see in Table 1.1 are PC features, a few common examples of each feature, and a brief bit of "why you should care." Following the table, Figure 1.5 identifies some of the connectors you'll see on the back of your PC.

TABLE 1.1: PC PIECES

FEATURE	TYPICAL EXAMPLES	BRIEF DESCRIPTION
AGP bus	Brown expansion slot on the motherboard for video adapters.	This bus is designed specifically for use with video boards.
Basic Input/Output System (BIOS) manufacturer	American Megatrends Incorporated (AMI), IBM, Compaq, Phoenix, Award.	BIOS is the most basic control software for your computer. The BIOS is what makes a PC IBM compatible. It tells the computer how to look at the bus, memory, and floppy drive and how to read other programs. The BIOS isn't a plug-in card; it's a chip that's mounted right on the motherboard.
Bus type	PCI, PC Card (formerly known as PCMCIA), CardBus, PC bus (8-bit ISA), AT bus (16-bit ISA), proprietary 32-bit, 16- or 32-bit Micro Channel Architecture (MCA), EISA, Local or VESA bus, AGP, FireWire.	The bus determines what kind of expansion circuit boards will work in the machine. As with a CPU, a major bus characteristic is speed. Boards built for one bus generally will not work on other buses, so the second main bus characteristic is compatibility. (Having a PC with the fastest bus in the world is no good if no one makes boards that work in that bus.) PC Card and CardBus are mainly used in laptops; most current desktops use PCI and AGP. You'll find that most controllers come in versions for any kind of bus.

TABLE 1.1: PC Pieces *(continued)*

FEATURE	TYPICAL EXAMPLES	BRIEF DESCRIPTION
Cache	256 kilobytes (KB), 512KB, 1 megabyte (MB).	RAM is slower than most CPUs, making memory speed an important system bottleneck. Faster memory exists, but it's expensive. PCs compromise by including just a small amount of faster memory, called *cache*. If it's on the motherboard, it's called Level 2 (L2) cache. Many processors include their own cache, which is called Level 1 (L1) cache.
Cartridge storage device	Iomega Jaz, Zip drives, Shark drives, Syquest drives, Castlewood Orb drives.	These work like hard disks but are usually a bit slower. Their main feature is that they're reasonably priced backup devices. Some attach to a parallel port, some to EIDE, and others to SCSI or USB.
CD-ROM drive speed, interface	EIDE, SCSI.	CDs are the basic means for distributing programs and data today. For less than $1/CD, a vendor can provide the equivalent of about 600 books of text. CD-ROM drives are the peripherals that make it possible to read those CDs. With a CD-ROM drive, speed is a relative thing. If you're using it to read text files or load software, a slower drive (around 16 by today's standards) will do. But if you're using it to play games, then you want the fastest CD-ROM drive you can get (52 plus).
CD Recordable (CD-R)/CD Rewritable (CD-RW) drive, also called CD burner	IDE, EIDE, SCSI, USB, FireWire.	A CD-R drive permits the one-time (recorder) writing of a CD, and a CD-RW drive permits the multiple (rewritable) writing of a CD. Both are usually used for data storage or writing a program or music for distribution. A CD can hold more than 720MB, but most CD-Rs write no more than 650MB (and CD-RWs even less, 440–550MB). These drives can also be used like a regular CD-ROM drive to install software and play audio CDs. USB versions are external and can easily be shared between multiple PCs (as long as all have at least one USB port).
Configuration method	Typically built into the system startup software.	Computers won't work until you tell them about themselves, or *configure* them—which you do by changing the BIOS configuration operation for your system. Today, virtually all computers configure themselves using built-in software in the BIOS. In some cases, you might need to set a few jumpers to configure CPU voltage levels, bus frequency, and cache memory on the motherboard.

Continued on next page

TABLE 1.1: PC PIECES *(continued)*

FEATURE	TYPICAL EXAMPLES	BRIEF DESCRIPTION
CPU type	Pentium, Pentium Pro, Pentium II, Pentium III, Pentium 4, Celeron, Centrino, Itanium, K5, K6, Athlon, Duron, Alpha.	The CPU determines how much memory the system can address, what kind of software it can run, and how fast it can go. The main difference in modern processors is speed, but newer ones have other capabilities, such as better graphics handling and multiprocessor support.
CPU speed	100 megahertz (MHz)–3.20 gigahertz (GHz) and getting faster every day!	MHz and GHz are rough measures of system speed. All other things being equal, a 1GHz processor would run twice as fast as a 500MHz processor. Because so many other components affect the speed of your computer, however, doubling the CPU speed never actually doubles the system speed.
DVD drive	IDE, EIDE, SCSI, USB, FireWire.	As far as computers are concerned, a DVD drive is basically the next step after a CD-ROM drive. DVDs look like CDs, but DVDs can store more than 26 times as much data as CDs. [DVDs can store as much as 17 gigabytes (GB), depending on the model drive and DVD you use.
DVD Recordable (DVD-R) drives, also called DVD burners	DVD-R, DVD-RAM, DVD-RW, DVD+RW.	DVD-RAM drives are similar to CD-R drives but are for the higher-capacity DVD format. DVD-RAM lets you record as much as 4.7GB of data per DVD side.
Floppy disks	$5^{1}/_{4}$": 1.2MB; $3^{1}/_{2}$": 1.44MB, 2.88MB (unusual); LS-120.	Floppy disks (also called floppies) are low-capacity removable media used to make your data portable. Today, because files are getting larger and larger, many computers aren't shipping with a floppy drive but instead with a Zip drive or some other high-capacity drive. The most common floppy drive today holds 1.44MB (just under a million and a half bytes) of data. Zip drives, by contrast, hold 100 or 250 MB—about the same as hundreds of floppy disks. Floppies are driven by circuits called *floppy controllers*, and they interface with these controllers through a standard connector on a 34-pin ribbon cable.

TABLE 1.1: PC Pieces *(continued)*

FEATURE	TYPICAL EXAMPLES	BRIEF DESCRIPTION
Hard disk/storage adapter	Advanced Technology Attachment (ATA)/IDE, EIDE, SCSI.	The interface controller allows your computer to communicate with your hard drive, CD-ROM drive, and DVD drive. Most systems today use EIDE because it's inexpensive, easy to install, and fast. EIDE uses a 40-pin cable to interface with drives. The terms IDE and EIDE are often replaced by ATA in common terminology, but they're all the same. An ATA-33 drive with 33MB per second (MBps) throughput (simply put, how fast data moves to and from the drive) is the same as an Ultra DMA/33 drive, which is the same as an Ultra ATA/33 drive. ATA/100 drives offer 100MBps throughput, and the newer Serial ATA standard can transfer data at 150MBps.
IEEE 1394 (FireWire)	Typically available as a built-in port.	FireWire is a new external bus standard that's much faster than traditional bus options, allowing for a maximum data transfer speed of more than 400Mbps (megabits per second). FireWire has many possible uses, but it seems to be most popular for connecting digital video cameras where fast real-time transfer of huge amounts of digital data is necessary.
ISA bus	Older, black expansion slots on the motherboard.	Used for old expansion cards, including modems, sound cards, and port expanders (additional serial and parallel ports).
Keyboard	Various input typing devices.	Keyboards have a controller on the PC's main board, and most use either a mini-DIN (PS/2) or a USB. Some old keyboards use a full-sized DIN interface called an *AT-style connector*—a reference to the original IBM AT. Most new keyboards are compatible, and you have a choice about what kind of shape, color, size, and ergonomics you prefer.
Local Area Network (LAN) board	Ethernet, Token Ring, FDDI, ATM, Attached Resource Computer Network (ARCNet).	LANs allow PCs to communicate with each other and share data and printers. To do this, each PC on a LAN needs a Network Interface Card (NIC). There are several types of NICs, including Ethernet, Token Ring, Fiber Distributed Data Interface (FDDI), and Asynchronous Transfer Mode (ATM). Ethernet is the most common. Most businesses have LANs, and more and more homes are adding LANs as they acquire two or more PCs. Home and small-business LANs are often *wireless*, which means that the LAN card connects to the network without cables—typically via Radio Frequency (RF) signals or your home phone line.

Continued on next page

TABLE 1.1: PC PIECES *(continued)*

FEATURE	TYPICAL EXAMPLES	BRIEF DESCRIPTION
Memory (RAM)	64MB, 96MB, 128MB, 256MB, 512MB, 1024MB (1GB).	This is the workspace PC's use for the software they're currently processing. Newer software generally requires more RAM than older software.
Memory (RAM) type	Dynamic RAM (DRAM), Extended Data Out (EDO), Synchronous DRAM (SDRAM), Rambus DRAM (RDRAM), Double Data Rate SDRAM (DDR SDRAM).	Although RAM *is* slower than most CPUs, memory chip vendors have been working hard to try to bridge that gap. The fastest current kind of main memory is called SDRAM. It's preferable in new systems. Although traditional RAM operates at 100MHz, newer forms operate at 200MHz to match faster motherboard clock speeds. Current forms of RAM are expected to be replaced by still-faster types, such as the RDRAM standard or the less-expensive (but still fast) DDR SDRAM. By the way, memory usually connects to the CPU through a proprietary bus, rather than PCI or some other standard.
Modem	300 baud, 9600 bits per second (bps), 33.6 kilobits per second (kbps), 56kbps.	Analog communications devices, allowing computers to connect to each other. Modem speeds are pretty much maxed out, and newer types of connections—such as a cable modem and Digital Subscriber Line (DSL)—are becoming more popular.
Mouse	A variety of rolling devices, including mice and rollerballs.	Designed to make computing easier by allowing people to "point and click." A key part of the Windows Icon Mouse Pointer (WIMP) interface.
Number of Direct Memory Access (DMA) channels supported	Four or eight (only very old PCs have just four).	Usually, the only thing talking to your memory is the CPU. Information stored in RAM is read by the CPU, and the CPU uses RAM to store information. Some devices, however, such as hard drives, take a (relatively) long time to move data back and forth. And if the computer needs to act as the go-between for this data, the CPU can get bogged down in the process. DMA lets certain devices to communicate directly with RAM (main memory), allowing the CPU to attend to other processes while the hard drive, for instance, transfers data to RAM. Using DMA to handle data transfer between many of the external devices and RAM really improves the overall processing speed of your computer.

TABLE 1.1: PC Pieces *(continued)*

FEATURE	TYPICAL EXAMPLES	BRIEF DESCRIPTION
Number of expansion slots	3–10.	The more the merrier. Many big-name computers sport only three expansion slots. As the popularity of USB devices increases, expect to see fewer and fewer expansion slots.
Number of peripherals supported	8 or 16 (only very old PCs have 8).	For the computer to use its peripheral devices, it needs to know when a device has information for it. For example, if you press a key, the keyboard has to have a way to get that information to the computer. In the past, computers would get this information by *polling* their external devices (looking first at one device, then the next, and so on, repeating the process many times per second). The trouble is, this takes up a lot of computing time, and early microcomputers had little power to spare. So the engineers who developed the microcomputer changed to a new system that uses interrupts. Interrupts (also called Interrupt Requests IRQ) are associated with the external devices. When a device has information for the computer, it signals the CPU through its interrupt line. The problem is, generally no two devices can share an interrupt. This means when you're configuring your system, you need to make sure you don't assign the same interrupt to two or more devices. Doing so will cause those devices to have a conflict and can make the system crash—or at least not recognize the devices.
Parallel port	Unidirectional, bidirectional, Enhanced Parallel Port (EPP), and Enhanced Capabilities Port (ECP).	The parallel port is the basic adapter for printers and external drives (such as Zip and CD-R/RW drives). The interface uses a connector called a *Centronics connector* at the printer end and what's known as a *DB25 connector* on the computer end. In its simplest form, the parallel port is unidirectional (data goes from the computer to the printer and not the reverse). Most current parallel ports now also support bidirectional data flow (data can go back and forth between the computer and the parallel device) and higher data transmission speeds.
PCI bus	White expansion slots on the motherboard.	Used for a variety of peripherals, including video cards, sound cards, modems, and SCSI host adapters.

Continued on next page

TABLE 1.1: PC PIECES *(continued)*

FEATURE	TYPICAL EXAMPLES	BRIEF DESCRIPTION
Plug and Play (PnP) compatibility	PC systems are identified as being either PnP compatible or not. (Only ancient computers, called *legacy systems*, don't support PnP.)	PnP is a standard that allows a computer to automatically identify and configure devices you want to add to the system. To have PnP work, your BIOS and operating system must support it (most new ones do), and you must have PnP hardware. Also, a newer type of PnP, called *Universal PnP*, is available in Windows XP; Universal PnP extends the PnP concept to the network, enabling automatic discovery and control of network devices and services.
Printer control language	Epson codes, HPPCL (LaserJet commands), PostScript, others.	Printer control languages tell your printer how to underline words, put pictures on the page, and change typefaces.
Serial port	COM1, COM2, COM3, COM4.	Serial ports are adapters that support a wide variety of low-speed peripherals, including modems, serial mice, digital cameras, Personal Digital Assistants (PDAs) such as the 3Com PalmPilot, and some kinds of scanners. They connect to peripherals using an interface called *RS-232*, which most commonly uses a male DB25 or DB9 connector. Generally regarded as old and slow.
Serial port Universal Asynchronous Receiver/ Transmitter (UART)	8250, 16450, 16550, 16650, 16750, 16950.	The UART is the main chip around which a serial port or internal modem is built. The 16550 UART is no longer the fastest, but it's still commonly used for high-speed communications and communications in multitasking environments. Software supports fast serial ports through a First In First Out (FIFO) buffer. The 16550 UART offers 16-byte FIFO, the 16650 offers 32-byte FIFO, the 16750 offers 64-byte FIFO, and the 16950 offers 128-bit FIFO.
Sound card	8-bit, 16-bit, 32-bit, 64-bit, 128-bit, Frequency Modulation (FM), Musical Instrument Digital Interface (MIDI), wavetable audio interface.	Sound cards support music and sound reproduction on your PC, but music and sound are represented in an 8-bit, 16-bit, 32-bit, 64-bit, or 128-bit format. The 32-bit format is better, but it takes up more space. The sounds are recorded and reproduced either with FM synthesis, MIDI control, or wavetables. Additionally, with the right audio interface cable, a sound card in combination with the right software can play music on your PC. The newest sound cards even support Dolby 5.1, so you can watch your favorite movie using your computer's DVD drive and have the same heart-pounding sound you hear in the theater.

TABLE 1.1: PC PIECES *(continued)*

FEATURE	TYPICAL EXAMPLES	BRIEF DESCRIPTION
System clock/calendar	Built-in on the motherboard or added on an expansion board on really old PCs.	The system clock keeps the proper time and date and is used to "clock" various system operations.
USB	Available as a built-in port or an add-on interface card.	This adapter was first introduced in 1995. It features both speed and flexibility; one USB interface can support up to 127 devices, including keyboards, mice, scanners, digital cameras, printers, and modems. USB adapters use a small proprietary connector as their interface to USB-compliant peripherals and can often be daisy chained together—although using multiple USB devices might require the use of one or more USB hubs (a central connectivity device). Virtually all new computer systems and all current operating systems now support the main USB standard. The current version of the standard, USB 2, is much faster (480Mbps versus USB1.1 at 12Mbps) and beats out SCSI and FireWire for drive throughput.
Video board	Video Graphics Array (VGA), SVGA, 8514 Adapter, Extended Graphics Array (XGA).	The video board determines how images are displayed on your monitor. This in turn affects what kind of software you can run and how quickly data can appear on the screen. Video boards vary in the number of colors and *pixels* (the dots on the screen) they can display. Most important in modern video boards, however, is whether they hold video data as a simple "dumb frame buffer," which requires that the CPU do all the video work, or they contain circuitry that can help with the grunt work of graphical screens. (Boards such as this are called *bitblitter* boards.) The main issues in video nowadays are speed, resolution, and color depth (the number of colors the system can display at one time). The interface between most video boards and their monitors is called an *analog RGB interface*, where RGB stands for *red, green,* and *blue*. Although some of the newer video boards interface with the new flat-panel displays with analog boards, more and more of the new flat-panel displays use a faster digital interface. Among today's fastest video boards are those including the 256-bit graphics-processing unit for optimum 3D graphics performance.

FIGURE 1.5

The connectors you'll see on the back of your computer

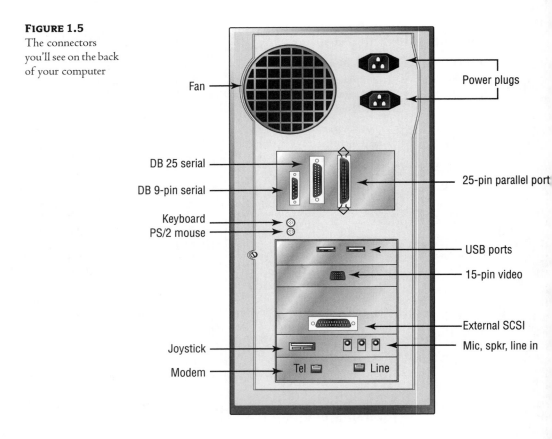

Fan

Power plugs

DB 25 serial

DB 9-pin serial

25-pin parallel port

Keyboard

PS/2 mouse

USB ports

15-pin video

External SCSI

Joystick

Mic, spkr, line in

Modem

Tel

Line

Whew! Look like a lot of stuff? Well, of course, it *is* a lot of stuff! If there weren't a whole bunch of things to learn in PC hardware, this would be a pretty short book, right? But fear not, I promise I'll cover it all. In fact, right now is a good time to dive into more details about the innards of your computer.

Chapter 2

Inside the PC: Core Components

- ◆ QuickSteps: Installing a CPU
- ◆ Motherboard
- ◆ CPU Specifications and Applications
- ◆ PC Memory
- ◆ PC Expansion Buses and Controllers
- ◆ CMOS
- ◆ Identifying Common Connectors

Introduction

The PC is a modular device—that is, it consists of a number of standard modules such as video cards, disk drives, and so on. This modularity is convenient to users and manufacturers because it enables computer systems to be compatible with each other and (as a result of standardization) inexpensive. All of the separate components are connected together through a common point—the motherboard

The PC's modularity also makes troubleshooting, repairing, and upgrading much easier than if a computer was simply one device. Because everything "comes apart," you can simply upgrade the part you need. You just need to know where to plug it. If you want to upgrade the core of your system, it's likely that you'll upgrade the motherboard itself, along with the processor, memory, and whatever else you desire.

Before jumping into all of the components found within a PC, it's important to understand this central connectivity monster and what you can and can't do with it. In addition, you must also understand processors and how they work. Only after that can you dive into the individual expansion cards that plug into the motherboard and make a computer user-friendly. Although PCs have traditionally consisted of separate components, the push over the past five to ten years has been toward integration, or bringing more of the work of the additional expansion cards (such as those for audio and video) onto the motherboard itself. For example, your PC's motherboard may include a sound or video chip in place of the separate cards discussed in later chapters.

A motherboard usually contains or has connections for the following:

◆ Central Processing Unit (CPU)

◆ Main memory, such as Dynamic RAM (DRAM), Extended Data Out (EDO), and Synchronous Dynamic RAM (SDRAM)

◆ Expansion slots attached to Peripheral Component Interconnect (PCI), Industry Standard Architecture (ISA), or Accelerated Graphics Port (AGP) bus connectors

◆ System Basic Input/Output System (BIOS), which contains the system clock/calendar

◆ Keyboard and mouse adapters (interfaces)

◆ Floppy disk controller

◆ Primary Enhanced Integrated Drive Electronics (EIDE) interface, mainly for hard disks and CD-ROM drives

◆ Secondary EIDE interface

In addition, some motherboards contain the following:

◆ Heat sink unit for the CPU

◆ Serial port (RS-232C) or COM port

◆ Parallel (printer) port

◆ Static cache memory

◆ FireWire connections

◆ Universal Serial Bus (USB) connections (usually two or more on a desktop PC and one on a portable PC)

◆ Integrated video card

◆ Integrated sound card

◆ Integrated network card

◆ Integrated modem

◆ Cooling fan(s)

In this chapter, you'll look at processors, motherboards, and the exciting world of core computer connectivity.

QuickSteps: Installing a CPU

All in all, CPUs can be one of the easier things to install and remove. The tricky part is making certain that the CPU and the motherboard you're installing it into are compatible. Try to install a Pentium III (PIII) CPU into a Pentium motherboard—it won't fit.

BE PREPARED

Before you start, there are some things you may need on hand. These include:

◆ Documentation related to both your new CPU and your motherboard for referencing. Diagrams (often found on the manufacturer's Web site) are also helpful for understanding orientation.

◆ Screwdriver(s) for opening the PC.

◆ Container for holding the screws.

◆ Antistatic wrist strap.

◆ Slender, flat bracket or similar tool for extracting the CPU (if you have an old pin package CPU.

1. Turn off the PC, disconnect the power, and remove any screws holding the PC cover in place

2. Ground yourself using the antistatic wrist strap.

3. Locate your current CPU on the motherboard, and remove it carefully. If still usable, it should be stored in an antistatic bag.

4. Consult the documentation for your motherboard and the new CPU (make sure they're com patible, see whether any adjustments need to be made for multipliers, and so on), and then gen tly seat the CPU into its place on the motherboard.

5. Replace the cover and screws, reconnect the power, and turn on the PC.

6. Go into BIOS Setup (during boot, your screen will likely report To enter Setup, press <key>), and make certain that the new CPU is seen.

The System Board/Motherboard

Since their creation in 1971, microcomputers of all kinds have usually included most of their essential electronics on a single printed circuit board, called the *motherboard*. There are other ways of designing a computer, but the put-most-of-it-on-one-board approach is most popular although even that goes through fads.

The first IBM PC in 1981 had a relatively simple motherboard and lots of expansion boards; modern computers tend to have more complex motherboards and a smaller number of expansion boards. (Integrating more components on the motherboard helps the manufacturer cut costs.) Eventually, the majority of PCs will have no expansion boards at all because the functions that most of us need will be completely incorporated into the motherboard. In fact, that's the case with some laptops, such as the Dell Inspiron 8100, which has a motherboard that includes a 56K modem, a 10/100-megabit (Mb) Ethernet card, 16-bit sound, a joystick interface, and a Digital Versatile Disc (DVD) drive.

Heavily integrated motherboards can be good and bad: on one hand, they're tremendously convenient, but on the other hand, there's a "take it or leave it" aspect to them. Some integrated motherboards have components you can't disable in order to install a separate card. As an example of the perils of overly integrated motherboards, a colleague of mine is having a devil of a time with hang-ups in his Web browser because of an integrated video chipset on his motherboard that refuses to be disabled so that a free-standing video card can be used. Get in that situation, and when the video adapter fails, you don't toss the video card and buy a new one—you have to replace the whole motherboard.

The 1981 motherboards had room for a processor chip, 64 kilobytes (KB) of memory, a keyboard connection, and some expansion slots. The 2004 motherboards on the typical desktop PC also include a serial port, parallel port, hard and floppy drive interfaces, keyboard and mouse ports, 1 gigabyte (GB) or more of memory on some models, some USB ports, and probably a FireWire port and a Serial ATA connector. Some manufacturers go even further by putting sound and video graphic accelerators, network adapters, and modems on the motherboard, as well.

One unique form factor is called the *backplane* design. In the backplane design, the basic computer has *only* expansion slots, and the CPU sits on one of them. When vendors go through these backplane phases, they claim it makes their PCs *modular*. By that, they mean you could upgrade your PC's CPU simply by removing the circuit board that contains the CPU and replacing it with a new CPU board— a five-minute bit of brain surgery that would instantly transform your PC from, say, a Pentium II (PII) to a PIII computer. What? You haven't heard of such a thing? Although this design briefly appeared in the personal computing world back in the early '90s, it's almost entirely restricted to industrial computers that are mounted in 19-inch racks and are usually found inside of seismic trucks, remote radar stations, and such. Why didn't this easy approach to upgrades catch on? Although the concept sounds appealing, the reality is less attractive: because the board that the machine's CPU is on isn't built to any kind of standard, you can't just buy a faster CPU board from anyone—you have to buy it from the original vendor. And in my experience, those vendors price their proprietary CPU upgrade boards quite high, often more expensive than just buying a new, *faster* system!

If you want modularity, the ultimate upgradable computer is a generic clone. It's based on a standard-sized motherboard that fits into a standard-sized case and takes standard boards and drives. When you want to upgrade it, all you do is buy a new motherboard and swap it for the old one. Motherboard prices are usually high only when a new board is first introduced. Many Pentium 4 (P4) motherboards sell in the $100–$200 range, depending on the make and model and special features such as extra slots, faster front-side bus, or jumper-less for fewer hardware hassles).

NOTE *Motherboards have gone by a variety of different names over the years. You might hear it called a system board, a planar board, or a mainboard.*

But enough talking about them—what do they look like? Figures 2.1, 2.2, and 2.3 show three different types of motherboards, and Figure 2.4 shows a P4 CPU.

FIGURE 2.1
Pentium
motherboard

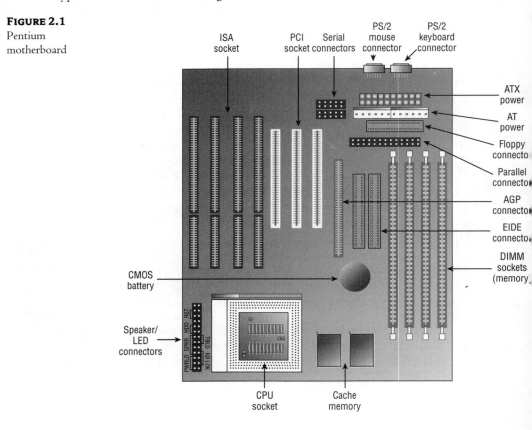

FIGURE 2.2
Pentium II
motherboard

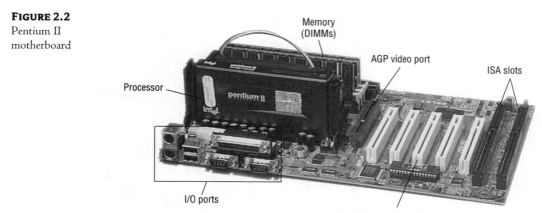

Memory
(DIMMs)

AGP video port

ISA slots

Processor

I/O ports

PCI expansion slots

FIGURE 2.3
Pentium III
motherboard

FIGURE 2.4
Pentium 4 CPU

Now that the brief introduction to motherboards is over, it's time to look at what's on them. I'll start with the most important component, the processor. After that, you'll poke around and see what else you can find.

Central Processing Unit (CPU)

There are a lot of chips on those motherboards, and they all kind of look alike, don't they? They may look equal, but some are more critical to the PC's operation than others. The big boss is the CPU. It's the part of the computer that knows how to do mathematics (and it's pretty smart; it can even do logarithms, cosines, and that sort of thing) and logic, the two parts of all computer programs.

Since the first IBM PC in 1981, most PCs have been built around CPUs designed by Intel Corporation. Today, two other manufacturers produce microprocessors that have made considerable inroads into the PCs we buy: Advanced Micro Devices (AMD) and VIA Technologies, which bought chipmaker Cyrix several years ago. But both of these manufacturers' chips were based upon the processors that Intel developed.

Because all these processors are able to run Microsoft Windows, they have been nicknamed *Wintel* computers. In truth, though, they're also able to run other operating systems such as DOS, Unix, and Linux.

Intel has designed and created many microprocessors over the years, but the ones that interest us here are members of a family of chips starting with the 8086 and progressing to the P4 and M chips. Why is there a family? Why aren't people still using the 8086? In a word, *performance*. CPU performance determines, in large part, computer performance. A modern P4 is thousands of times faster than the original 8086, and differences of speed on that order change how you use computers. Back in the early '80s, people started using spreadsheet programs, and those programs strained the power of then-contemporary chips such as the 8088. It wasn't unusual for a complex spreadsheet to require hours to recalculate. Nowadays, even the cheapest PC is so fast that recalculating spreadsheets is usually instantaneous.

Intel has been improving CPU performance in two main ways. First, they improved some micro components quantitatively by just taking an old circuit and making it run faster. Simple CPU speed, measured in megahertz (MHz) or gigahertz (GHz), is an example. The second way that CPUs get snappier is through qualitative improvements, such as new manufacturing techniques that improve chip quality.

Whether improvements come quantitatively or qualitatively, CPUs vary in several ways that affect their performance. Table 2.1 introduces these variations by CPU property. Take a minute to look over this table so that later you'll understand where a lot of PC limitations come from.

CPU Speeds (Megahertz/Gigahertz)

Computers are a little like clockwork devices. A clock strikes a beat, and a certain small amount of work gets done. Just like a beginning piano player plays to the beat of a metronome, computers run to the beat of a clock. If you set the metronome too fast for the beginning piano player, they'll become confused and the music won't come out right; the player won't have enough time to find the next piano key, and the rendition will probably fall apart. Similarly, if you set the clock rate of a CPU too high, it'll malfunction, but the result isn't discordant music; it's a system crash.

TABLE 2.1: CPU PROPERTIES

PROPERTY	DESCRIPTION
CPU speed	The number of operations that can happen per second
Microcode efficiency	The number of steps required to multiply two numbers (for example)
Number of instruction pipelines	The number of processes that can run simultaneously on this chip
Pipeline management	Enables the CPU to "look ahead" to future instructions so as to make the best of its power
Word size	The largest number that can be operated on in one operation
Data path	The largest number that can be transported into the chip in one operation
Internal cache Random Access Memory (RAM)	The amount of internal, high-speed memory that the chip includes
Numeric coprocessor	Enables the CPU to directly perform floating-point numerical computations
Maximum memory	The largest amount of memory that the chip can use.
Connection type	How the CPU connects to the motherboard (there are several standards)

Normally, running a CPU too fast can damage the chip; at the least, the computer may not func tion properly, and the problems may not seem directly related to the CPU—for example, drive read and write errors. Part of the design of a PC entails determining a clock rate. This clock rate has a con siderable effect because many chips in the PC work to the beat of the computer's clock.

CPU clocks generally "tick" millions of times per second. A clock that ticks at exactly one million times per second is said to be a 1MHz clock. The Apple II used a 2MHz clock. The early PCs and XTs (the first PCs with hard drives using an 8088 processor) used a 4.77MHz clock. IBM followed the PC with the AT, whose original model used a 6MHz clock, and later IBM offered a version that ran at 8MHz.

Modern PCs run so fast they have to be measured in gigahertz; one gigahertz (1GHz) is equal to 1,000 megahertz.

Because the speed of a computer is used as a means of measuring how well it operates, the mega hertz/gigahertz value of a computer is an important measure of its power. It's similar to looking at horsepower as an approximate measure of a car's power. All other things being equal, a faster clock means faster execution and better performance.

It's worth mentioning, however, that all things usually *aren't* equal. The CPU is only part of what makes a computer fast. A really fast CPU paired with an amazingly slow hard disk would turn in a mediocre performance. This is because your computer can only work as fast as the slowest component will allow it to work. And with the speed of today's processors, that won't be the bottleneck.

My advice, then, is this: when buying a computer on a budget, you might have to choose between a faster CPU and faster peripherals. I'd take the faster peripherals. That's because even the slowest new CPU sold today is plenty fast for just about anything you could think of doing with your PC. The bottleneck, then, comes in the other components.

Having said that, however, realize that as processor speeds continue to skyrocket, CPU manufac turers stop making the older chips in favor of the newer ones. So, even though an older (cheaper) chip might be adequate, you probably won't have the option to buy a really out-of-date, slow CPU anyway.

Nowadays, the slowest new computer you're likely to come across will be somewhere in the 1GHz range. The fastest computers will run at 4GHz—or faster. That's nearly 1,000 times faster than the first IBM PCs!

A QUICK TREATISE ON THE HISTORY OF CPU SPEED

For many years, the maximum possible CPU speed determined a lot about the rest of the computer. Usually a PC manufacturer would design the entire motherboard to operate at the same speed as the CPU. When CPUs rose in speed from 5MHz to 8MHz, motherboards had to change in speed from 5MHz to 8MHz. *All* the chips on the motherboard, including complex chips such as memory chips, had to operate at 8MHz to support an 8MHz motherboard. At the time, this turned out to be pretty difficult for speeds beyond 8MHz, so since about 1984, motherboards have been designed so that their different parts could run at different speeds. Coupling slowpoke components with speed demons means that some of the speed demons' power is wasted, but it's the only way to build eco nomical systems.

From 1984 on, the section of the motherboard that supported memory was decoupled from the rest of the motherboard, speed-wise, as were the expansion slots or *bus slots*. But memory and bus slots constituted only a fraction of the motherboard real estate. Most of the chips and circuits on the motherboards of the mid-to-late '80s had to match the CPU's speed, so every time Intel came out with a faster chip, the motherboard designers had to go back to the drawing boards and design faster motherboards.

Building faster and faster motherboards is like climbing a mountain that gets steeper and steeper as you climb. Moving from 5MHz to 8MHz was easy; moving from 8MHz to 12MHz was harder. And moving from 12MHz to 20MHz was even harder, as was the move around 1989 to motherboards that ran most of their components at 33MHz. In the closing months of the '80s, however, Intel started talking about producing 50MHz and 66MHz chips. Building motherboards that fast would have been extremely costly or impossible—so it was time to disconnect the processor speed from the motherboard speed. *Clock doublers* accomplished that.

Clock Doubler Chips

Intel needed to address several issues with their 50+MHz chips in 1989/1990. First was the motherboard question: what good is a 66MHz chip if no one knows how to build a motherboard that can use it? The second question came from the owners of existing systems: How do you upgrade easily? Weary of buying systems that seemed obsolete as soon as they were purchased, people wanted the ability to upgrade their systems without major surgery. So Intel came up with an alternative way to speed up CPUs: clock doublers.

The original clock doubler was a special 80486 that could plug into a CPU socket on a standard 25MHz motherboard. This special processor was designed to operate at 25MHz from the motherboard's point of view, but to operate internally at *twice* that rate—50MHz. Any internal action in the CPU, such as numeric calculations or moving data from one internal area of the CPU to another, was accomplished at 50MHz. But external instructions, such as loading data from memory or storing data to memory, happened more slowly, at 25MHz.

NOTE *Intel has names for these two clock rates by the way. The external speed (25MHz, in the case of the preceding example) is called the system bus frequency, or front-side bus. The internal clock rate (50MHz, in the preceding example) is called the processor core frequency.*

Now, given that this chip ran at 25MHz for external instructions and 50MHz for internal instructions, what should Intel have called this chip—a 25MHz chip or a 50MHz chip? It's all about marketing. So the new chip got the name 80486DX2-50—the *2* referring to the clock doubling, the *50* referring to its higher speed. They also offered an 80486DX2-66, a chip that plugged into a 33MHz motherboard but ran at 66MHz internally. *DX*, in those days, referred to a fuller, more capable system compared to its SX counterparts that were an interim upgrade (a 486SX was midway between a 386 and a 486).

At the time, Intel made an 80486DX-25 (a chip that ran both inside and out at 25MHz) and an 80486DX-50 (a chip that ran both inside and out at 50MHz), in addition to the 80486DX2-50. People often asked, "How fast is the DX2 *really*—is it more like the 'straight 25' or the 'straight 50'?" The answer was that it depended on what you were doing. CPU-intensive operations such as calculating spreadsheets or drawing complex graphics probably looked more like 50MHz, and input/output-oriented programs such as databases probably looked more like 25MHz. An in-between application, such as a word processor, fell somewhere in between. And, remember, Intel *also* offered the 80486DX-50 mentioned previously. Many people *thought* they were buying a 50MHz DX but actually bought a "50MHz" DX2, and the difference in performance could be significant.

Clock Tripler Chips

In 1994, Intel introduced yet another variation on the 486 line, an 80486DX that was a *clock tripler.* Offered in 75MHz and 100MHz versions, these chips operated on motherboards that were 25MHz and 33MHz, respectively.

NOTE *Why does 33MHz tripled equal 100MHz? Why not 99MHz? Marketing reality again. After all, round up 99MHz, and you get 100MHz. Well, kind of.*

Intel also took the opportunity to spruce up the internal workings of this new 486, and they added a bit more fast internal memory (called *internal cache*), raising the amount inside the chip from 8KB (which the 80486 previously contained) to 16KB. That small amount of internal memory did indeed speed up the computer a bit in addition to the clock tripling, leading Intel to explore new realms of salesmanship by calling the new chip the *DX4.* That name is just DX4 by the way; there's no *8048C* in the name. There's also a clock-tripled Pentium 200MHz chip that ran on a 66MHz motherboard.

NOTE *You might have noticed another stroke of marketing genius. The clock triplers were called DX4 chips, making them sound like they were four times faster than the original, not three times. People were often confused as to why a DX4-100 wasn't compatible with a 25MHz board when the math seemed to indicate it should be.*

Multiplying by Really Big Numbers

We've seen clocks doubled and tripled. Are there clock-quadrupled chips? Yes, and quintupled chips too: the 333MHz PII ran 66MHz externally and 333MHz internally, a fivefold increase. While figuring out how to build the 4*x* and 5*x* systems, Intel started playing around with noninteger multiples. Some CPUs had their clocks increased by *50 percent,* kind of a *one-and-a-half clock.* The original Pentium models were offered in speeds of 60MHz and 66MHz. Later Pentium chips, code-named the P54C by Intel, were rated at 90 and 100MHz. They used 60MHz and 66MHz motherboards and increased their internal clock rates by half.

Which begs the question of why exactly there were two Pentium models with two clock rates so close. Why bother offering both a 60MHz model and a 66MHz model? It's an old story now, but it's worth telling to underscore the physical feature that often makes or breaks the newest, fastest, and smallest systems—*heat.*

It's Not the Humidity, It's the Heat

The original Pentium was a really tough chip to design. Every Intel chip design team is extremely limited in that no matter what the new chip is able to do, the one thing it *must* do is run old software. This demand for backward compatibility makes for complex chips. *Complex* means lots of little components go into the chip, or, as insiders would say, the backward compatibility "needs a lot of silicon." Now, all that silicon generates heat. Put too much silicon in too small a place, and it starts to damage itself. Make the clock run faster, and the silicon gets even hotter. The Intel folks were just running up against some physical design barriers.

The Pentium's heat generation standards appeared in its technical specifications. According to Intel documents at the time, the 66MHz Pentium generated enough heat to bring the chip to 85 degrees. *Centigrade.*

That's about 185 degrees Fahrenheit. Good grief, you could've toasted marshmallows on that thing! Intel tried its hardest to make a 66MHz Pentium chip work, but it was just so difficult that they ended up making Pentium chips that were mostly rejects. They *weren't* rejects, however, if they ran at a somewhat slower, *cooler*, rate such as 60MHz. So the 60MHz chips were, unfortunately, the rejects; Intel just lowered the standards to make them sellable.

Besides clock speed, however, another determining factor in chip heat is in the voltage that the chip operates on. The heat created by a chip is related to the square of the voltage. For a long time, most CPUs ran at 5 volts.

Intel decided to build the clock with one and a half P54C chips with 3.3-volt power supplies. Five squared is 25; 3.3 squared is about 11. A 3.3-volt chip runs a lot cooler, which is why Intel uses 3.3 volts for the DX4, the newer Pentiums, and some later chips. Pentium Pros use 1.5 volts. The DX4's use of 3.3 volts meant that, paradoxically, it was the fastest 80486 chip, but it was also the coolest.

Although this story is of course about a quite old chip, its point applies to every new chip you'll see. The only ways to make chips more powerful is to stuff more circuits in them and build them to run at higher clock rates, both of which present heat problems. Add to that the fact that more people buy laptops than desktops, and you get the third heat problem—size. A modern laptop processor *might* run a lot cooler if its circuitry could be spread across an area the size of a pie plate, but then it wouldn't be very portable!

So What Is the Fastest Chip?

Once they figured out they could disconnect motherboard speeds from CPU speeds, CPU speeds skyrocketed. At the time of this writing, I couldn't find a single system available with anything slower than a 1GHz processor, and the fastest ran just faster than 3GHz, with 10GHz chips on the drawing board. Virtually all CPUs generate so much heat that even laptops have fans. (Have you ever noticed that your laptop's fan turns on and off periodically? That's because your system's power management programs keep track of your system's temperature via the multiple temperature sensors in the system— even most modern hard disks have temperature sensors—and use those temperature readings to determine when to turn on the fan.)

When you're buying a PC, don't be bedazzled by the fastest chip. The difference in speed between the fastest CPU available and the second-fastest is often tiny—but the difference in price can be significant. And remember that Intel offers entire families of CPUs all with different gigahertz ratings, but *the same speed on the front-side bus*. Think of it this way: eventually Intel will be selling a "Whizbangium" CPU, offering it in 100, 200 and 300GHz speeds—but they'll all have a front-side bus of 50GHz. They might also offer a Whizbangium XL CPU in 150, 300 and 450GHz speeds with a 75GHz front-side bus. (I made those numbers up, but they're plausible.) In other words, when your CPU needs to speak to something on the motherboard, such as your drive, memory, or whatever, then the Whizbangium CPU speaks at a mere 50GHz no matter whether you paid reasonable money for the 100GHz model or big bucks for the 300GHz model, and the Whizbangium XL CPU speaks at 75GHz to memory and disk. Which is faster? Well, if you're mainly running a database program that spends its entire day reading and writing the disk, you probably don't give a hoot what the CPU speed is—you'll likely find that the front-side bus is the more important item, and in fact the *slowest* Whizbangium XL delivers better database performance than the *fastest* Whizbangium. Clearly in that case a 300GHz Whizbangium isn't an investment with a great return. The bottom line is that I wouldn't sweat the processor speed; instead, look at what you're trying to do with the computer, look at all of its characteristics, and remember that processor speed is just one of those characteristics.

Before I move along, was your curiosity piqued by the mention of the 10GHz chips? Those won't be seen for some time although the rapid pace at which processor speeds are increasing makes this more of a *when* than an *if*. We're already at the point where you may not appreciate a great deal of difference between 1GHz and 3GHz in your usual day-to-day work at your PC. More times than not, you're more likely to get bottlenecked by your online communications speed (especially if you're using a dial-up connection on a traditional modem over analog phone lines) long before you feel your CPU is too slow for the task at hand.

A WORD ON OVERCLOCKING AND MATCHING CLOCK SPEEDS

Clock rates on chips and clock rates on motherboards are related. If the motherboard is built for 166MHz, then you should get a CPU that can handle a 166MHz clock. (Note I'm talking about the external or *system bus frequency*, not the internal rate.) Similarly, it's not a good idea to get a chip that's designed to run at a higher clock rate than the motherboard. The fit between motherboard and chip should be "just right."

Why is this true? Well, consider what happens if you get a chip that's too slow for the motherboard. For example, the Intel Pentium 150MHz chip had an external clock rate of 50MHz and was tripled. If you put it on a motherboard that's designed to provide a 66MHz clock signal to the processor, then the processor wouldn't be able to keep up with that rate. The result is that the chip would fail and overheat, possibly permanently damaging it. In the reverse situation, suppose you had a motherboard that put out a 66MHz clock signal, and you installed a 400MHz Xeon, which can handle an external clock rate of 100MHz. You wouldn't be driving the "400MHz" chip at 100MHz, you'd be driving it at 66MHz. It's a clock quadrupler, so the chip would dutifully quadruple that value, giving you a 266MHz Xeon. (Okay, again, we have a case where 66×4 isn't quite 266, but welcome to PC hardware!) That would be a waste of money.

This underscores a critical point about chips and sockets: put a chip in that's too slow, and it'll overheat and fail. Install a chip that's too fast, and it'll work fine, but you're throwing your money away.

That all sounds logical, but some people point out that the difference between slow chips and fast chips is often luck anyway because chip manufacturers just build a few thousand chips and then test them to see which ones are fast and which are slow. When testing, chip makers are conservative, goes the argument, so they might rate a chip at *x*MHz that could actually work at 1.3*x* or the like. Modern motherboards let you dial in any clock rate you want, so people buy a middle-rated chip and dial up a high clock rate. If the system doesn't crash immediately, they figure they've gotten lucky and bought a fast chip for the price of a slow one.

This is called *overclocking*. I don't recommend it, and basically here's why: you run a significant risk of ruining your chip or causing other problems. The symptoms of overclocking can be quite subtle and masquerade as problems with a hard disk or keyboard or even cause problems with your expansion boards. In addition, overclocking by its nature invalidates your product warranty, so you're on your own. Also, you should be aware that Intel has now locked down the ability to overclock in most of its product line, driving true overclocking fans to other makes of processor.

Microcode Efficiency and Pipelines

As you just read, one way to make a chip faster is to simply drive it faster by running up its clock in some way. Another way is to design the chip to make better use of each clock cycle.

MICROCODE IMPROVEMENTS

Microcode was a big advancement in that it allowed the CPU's instruction set to be implemented as a series of microinstructions. It's also called microprogramming. Microcode improvements have been an important part of Intel's strategy for ever-faster chips over the years; for example, the 8088 chip was succeeded by the 80188 chip, a chip that seemed to do all the same things that the 8088 does. Where's the difference?

In the case of the 8088 versus the 80188 (and also in the case of the 80386 versus the 80486), a lot of the difference lived in its *microcode efficiency*. Put simply, microcode efficiency just asks, "How many clock ticks does it take a CPU to get a particular task done?" For example, an 8088 could calculate an integer division—that is, a division without any decimal places; divide 7 by 2 on an 8088 and you get 3, not 3.5. And to make matters worse, it could take the 8088 up to 70 clock cycles to get that done. The 80188, in contrast, could do it in only 25 clock cycles. If you compared two early '80s PCs that were identical except that one ran an 80188 and the other ran an 8088, the 80188 would be able to do some things faster than an 8088. This has continued right up to the current time—newer processors continuously include better microcode.

PIPELINING INSTRUCTIONS

By now, the folks at Intel had squeezed a lot of the "juice" out of improving microcode efficiency. So they needed some other tricks to continue to beat better speed out of newer chips. So starting with the Pentium, Intel has designed CPUs with smarter and smarter *pipelines.*

What's a pipeline? Well, if you peek inside the workings of a CPU, you'll see that it looks somewhat like an assembly line—much like one that builds cars. Instead of turning out cars, however, CPUs turn out executed instructions, and they don't call it an assembly line; they call it a pipeline. With pipelining, a bit of data goes to the first station in the pipeline; then, after that bit moves on to the next station, another bit takes its place at the first station. With pipelining, there's a bit along every station of the process. So instead of each bit of data having to wait for the preceding bit to go through the entire pipeline before starting off, a bit moves to each station along the way immediately after its predecessor leaves.

Now, if you wanted to assemble more cars per hour, you could approach it in two ways. The obvious way is to just try to get all of the workers to do their jobs faster, enabling you to run the assembly line faster. That would be like taking an existing CPU and increasing its clock rate, upping its megahertz/gigahertz. It's not a bad approach to speed, but there's another way. Instead of just trying to do the same old thing, only faster, you could reengineer the entire process, streamlining the steps along the way.

What happens along a CPU's pipeline? It varies from chip to chip, but basically you can break down the execution of any instruction into five basic steps:

Fetch   Get the next program instruction.

Decode   Instructions differ in length; some are 1 byte long, and some are several bytes long. A given instruction, such as a MOVE command, may come in several different flavors: move from one location inside the CPU chip to a location outside the CPU chip, move from one place inside the CPU to another place inside the CPU, and so on. Even though the instruction differences are subtle, they're important. The decode section handles that.

Get the operands   Most instructions require data to work on. Simply saying MOVE means nothing; the CPU must know *what* you want to move *where*. The *what* and *where* are operands. Similarly, if you tell the CPU, "Add 34 and 22," then *34* and *22* are the operands.

Execute   As the Nike guys say, "Just do it." Whatever the instruction said to do—add, move, divide, compare, or whatever—now's the time to get it done.

Write back results   After the operation has been done, the results of the operation—both the values created and any status information—get written to registers inside the computer.

By breaking up the task of executing an instruction into smaller subtasks, chip makers can divide the job of chip design into smaller chunks, and that in turn makes it possible to build these subsystems faster and faster. In other words, it's easier to build a CPU made up of five fast subpieces than it is to build a CPU out of one fast piece. This process of fetch, decode, get operands, execute, and write back results is called the *CPU pipeline*. Some CPUs even use multiple pipelines.

REINVENTING THE WHEEL: THE PENTIUM PIPELINE STRUCTURE

Before the Pentiums, Intel CPUs had just one pipeline in each chip, which is a techie way of saying, "The 486 and predecessors could do only one thing at a time."

In contrast, all Pentium chips essentially have several CPUs within them. The first one is like a 486DX, a CPU with floating-point capabilities built right into it. The others are like a 486SX, lacking a floating-point unit. (Why didn't they put two floating-point units in? It would have made the thing bigger, hotter, and more expensive.) That means the Pentium is essentially a parallel-processing CPU, with the capability to do two or more things at once. Those two CPUs-within-a-CPU are called the *U and V pipelines*, and having more than one pipeline makes the Pentium a *super-scalar* CPU.

The neat part of this multiple pipelining is that the Pentium uses each pipeline *automatically*. It takes a simple non-Pentium-aware program, reads it, and divides it into its pipelines. Now, that's not always possible because of the way some programs contain internal *dependencies* (meaning that one command needs to finish before a second one can begin, so having two pipelines don't do much good), but the Pentium does the best it can.

THE PENTIUM PRO/II/III/4/CELERON/XEON PIPELINE STRUCTURE

If two pipelines sound like a lot, then hold onto your hat because the Pentium Pro/II/III/4/Celeron/Xeon chips contain an even more complex system (depending on how you look at it) with three or five pipelines. How does it work?

Think of the Pentium Pro family pipelines as being organized in three major pieces: decode, execute, and clean up.

The decode section works as it does on earlier chips, just mainly fetching an instruction and figuring out what it needs to do—integer math, floating-point math, a memory read or write, or something else. There are three decoding pipelines, which means the Pentium Pro can get three instructions ready at the same time. There aren't any interdependency problems with the decode phase.

The second phase executes the actual instruction. Because this takes the most time, Intel included *five* execution pipelines. Any one of them can perform simple operations, but for more demanding (or time-consuming) tasks, there are specialists. Two of the pipelines can do only integer computations, such as the V pipeline on a Pentium. Two of the pipelines can do both integer computations and floating-point computations, such as the U pipeline on a Pentium. And one of the pipelines specializes in transferring data to and from memory. As with the Pentium's two-pipeline system, there's no guarantee that all five pipelines will remain active at all times because interdependent code may, once again, make that impossible.

The P4 has made major improvements to the Pentium's two-pipeline system. Called the *NetBurst microarchitecture*, its features include hyper-pipelined technology, a rapid execution engine, a 400MHz system bus, and an execution trace cache. The hyper-pipelined technology doubles the pipeline depth in the P4 processor, allowing the processor to reach much higher core frequencies. The rapid execution engine allows the two integer Arithmetic and Logic Units (ALUs) in the processor to run at twice the core frequency, which allows many integer instructions to execute in half a clock tick.

The older Pentium had to examine the incoming stream of program instructions and determine the dependencies within that stream; the Pentium Pro and later chips have the same need. For non-optimized code, the Pentium Pro family has often proven to be fast but not amazingly so. In fact, in February 1996, *BYTE* magazine reported that the Pentium Pro ran 16-bit applications (including the 16-bit parts of Windows 95) *slower* than the Pentium did because the Pentium Pro was "tuned" to run 32-bit applications better than the Pentium. That's why if you're still running Windows 3.1 or DOS programs, *or* if you're running several of those older programs such as WordPerfect 5.1 for DOS under Windows 95/98/NT, then you may not see particularly impressive behavior. You need *truly* 32-bit code (and code optimized for the Pentium Pro family) to see the performance improvements in the Pentium Pro, the PII/III, the Celeron, and the Xeon (although the Celeron's lack of cache or limited cache makes it a pretty lame performer no matter what you do). And it's sadly true that there's not all that much code around that's really tuned to use 32 bits; even newer 32-bit software such as Office XP and even Windows 2003 still contains a lot of old 16-bit code. In my experience, the programs that are best tuned to use 32 bits are the high-end stuff—such as SQL database engines and file/print servers—and what some might call the low end—such as games. Personal productivity programs don't seem to be a priority for performance tuning; instead, the vendors seem more intent on adding thousands of features.

The P4 has almost three times the theoretical processor bus bandwidth of a PIII. A 400MHz system bus and hyper-pipelined technology (a 20-stage pipeline compared to the 10-stage pipeline in the PIII) increase overall CPU bandwidth to a theoretical maximum of about 3.2GB per second and raise the ceiling for clock speeds.

Another enhancement of the P4 is the introduction of *hyper-threading*. It sounds a lot like hyper-pipelined, but it's a little different. Hyper-threading enables multithreaded applications to execute threads (lines of executable code) in parallel. So there's reduced wait time for processes to finish. The P4 with HT technology and Xeon chips are currently the only ones that support hyper-threading.

Word Size

Every computer uses internal work areas, kind of like workbenches. These workbenches are called *registers*.

Any computer can be programmed to manipulate any size number, but the bigger the number, the longer it takes. The largest number that the computer can manipulate in one operation is determined by its *word size*. This is 8, 16, or 32 bits.

Think of it this way: if I ask you, "What is 5 times 6?" you'd answer "30" immediately—you did it in one operation. If I ask, "What is 55 times 66?" you'll do a series of steps to arrive at the answer. That's because 55 is larger than your word size and 5 isn't. If you had a bigger "workbench" (a bigger word size), then you could get complex calculations done in fewer steps and therefore more quickly. That's one reason why a 386, with 32-bit registers, is faster than a 286, with 16-bit registers.

The 8088 through 80286 chips used 16-bit words. The 80386 through Pentium Pro/II and PIII/Celeron/Xeon systems used 32-bit words. The P4 also uses 32-bit words, but the floating-point and multimedia registers of the chip have been increased to 128 bits to increase the speed of data transfers.

Data Path

No matter how large the computer's word size, the data must be transported into the CPU. This is the width of the computer's "loading door," or the *data path*. It can also be 8, 16, 32, or 64 bits. Obviously, a wider door will allow more data to be transported in less time than will a narrower door.

Consider, for example, an 8MHz 8088 versus an 8MHz 8086. The *only difference* between the 8088 and the 8086 was that the 8088 had an 8-bit data path, and the 8086 had a 16-bit data path. But both the 8088 and the 8086 had 16-bit registers, so a programmer would issue the same command to load 16 bits into either one—the command MOV AX,0200 moves the 16-bit value 200 hex into a 16-bit register called AX. That would take twice as long on the 8088 as it would on the 8086 because the 8086 could do it in one operation while the 8088 took two. Note what's going on— although they're both 8MHz computers, the 8088 machine computed more slowly for some operations.

In 1985, Intel introduced its next-generation chip, the 80386, with a 32-bit data path. Included in the 80386 series was the 386SX, which had a 16-bit data path to remain backward compatible with the existing 16-bit motherboards on the market. The 386DX was a true 32-bit chip.

The Pentium, MMX, Pentium Pro, PII, PIII, P4, Celeron, and Xeon chips actually have a data path *larger* than the word size; these chips have a 64-bit data path and 32-bit word sizes. What good is it having a front door that's twice the size of the workbench? Again, Pentium and later chips aren't so much faster because of higher megahertz but because of internal design—to use an old phrase, you might say that "they don't work harder, they work smarter." Once Intel figured they could only do so much with a single 32-bit system, they decided to speed up the process by essentially giving the Pentium a *second* workbench, or a second pipeline. That second pipeline needs feeding, hence the value of a larger data path.

Internal Cache Memory

When people talk of RAM on a computer, they're talking about chips that the CPU uses to store its programs and data as it works, chips external to the CPU. The increasing speed of CPUs has driven a corresponding need for faster RAM. Computers can also use ultra-fast memory called *cache*, which can be located internally (on the CPU package) or externally (on the motherboard).

Why Cache Is Used

RAM is commonly designed to be *dynamic*, a simpler and cheaper design than its alternative, *Static* RAM (SRAM). Incorporating RAM onto a motherboard presents a fundamental tradeoff to system designers:

◆ DRAM is relatively cheap, but it's also relatively slow. In fact, no one makes DRAM that's fast enough to match speeds of modern CPUs.

◆ SRAM is fast—it can be as fast as any of Intel's or AMD's chips. But it's expensive, up to 10 to 20 times as expensive for a given amount of memory as DRAM.

At this point, the only way to build RAM that's as fast as the CPU is to populate the entire PC with static RAM, but that would be much too expensive. So PCs use a lot of DRAM, which unfortunately sacrifices speed. To get back some of that speed, Intel puts a small amount of fast SRAM right into the CPU. That way, oft-used data needn't be accessed via the relatively slow DRAM; instead, the CPU can keep the most important data right by its side, in this small cache of storage. In fact, that's what it's called—*cache RAM*. It first appeared in some of the faster 386-based systems because designers included space on the motherboards of high-performance systems for a bit of SRAM.

L1 Cache, L2 Cache, and the 80486 Family

Many computers designed since about 1987 have included cache RAM on their motherboards. The 80486 took the idea of cache a step further, however, in that the 80486 line of chips was the first in the *x*86 family to include cache RAM right on the CPU. With the exception of the DX4, they all contained 8KB of internal cache. The DX4 doubled that amount to 16KB. But even that small amount of extra fast memory significantly improved CPU performance. Of course, although a few kilobytes of cache is *nice*, it'd be nicer to have even more.

Most desktop computers today add from 64KB to 2MB more static RAM cache to the processor itself instead of the motherboard. It's commonly called *L2 cache*.

NOTE *In the old days, cache that was built into the processor was called L1, or internal cache, and cache built into the motherboard was L2 or external cache. The new P4 (and other current Intel chips) have L2 cache built into the processor package, so it's technically still external cache. It's just now on the processor package instead of on the motherboard. This makes accessing the L2 cache faster.*

The internal cache in the 80486 and later processors is called *L1 cache*. L1 cache is built into the processor and usually runs at a speed nearly equaling or equaling the internal processor speed (the *core processor frequency* in Intel-ese).

Some Systems Are "Broke"

L2 cache is terrific for speed, but manufacturers can cut costs by eliminating the costly cache. That's *very* important to anyone trying to compare the power of two computers. It used to be that laptops were particularly hurt by their lack of cache. This is less true today, of course, although the mechanics of a laptop still affect speed compared to desktop units with much fuller hardware.

By the same token, many inexpensive *store clones* (clones you could buy off the shelf when you buy your garden tools at Sears or your barbecue at Price Club) of the original Pentium era also eliminated the L2 cache as a cost-saving measure. Some enabled you (for a considerable price) to add an L2 cache later, if desired, and others did not.

TIP   Removing the L2 cache temporarily (on older systems that permit it) can sometimes help resolve problems. For example, on problematic installations or upgrades of Windows on PCs with an L2 cache, the short-term disabling of the L2 cache will let you install or upgrade Windows, and you can then re-enable the L2 cache.

When shopping for a computer, it's important to not only note the processor speed and amount of RAM, but also how much cache is installed. Having that extra cache can make a world of difference in performance.

ORIGINAL PENTIUM CACHE

Part of how the first generation of Pentiums produced better-than-486 performance was through their cache. The Pentium's cache system was better than the 486's in four ways. First, the Pentium had twice as much cache, with two 8KB caches—one for data, one for program code. (A later variation of the Pentium, the MMX chip, had double that amount, a 16KB data cache and a 16KB instruction cache.) Second, the cache's method of organizing its cached data was more efficient, using a *write-back* algorithm. The opposite of a write-back algorithm, a *write-through* algorithm (used by the 486), forces data written to the SRAM cache memory to be immediately written to the slower DRAM memory. That means that memory *reads* can come out of the cache quickly, but memory *writes* must always occur at the slower DRAM time. Reasoning that not every piece of information written to memory *stays* in memory very long, the Pentium's cache algorithm puts off writing data from SRAM to DRAM for as long as possible. Third, the cache controller wasted time in searching to see whether an item is in the cache—the Pentium reduced that time by dividing the cache into smaller caches, each of which could be searched more quickly; that technique uses a *two-way set-associative cache*.

To explain the fourth way in which the Pentium's cache was better than the 486's, I have to first make an important point about what a cache must do. You may know that a cache must guess what data and program code the CPU will need soon and then go get that data before the CPU asks for it. But guessing what the CPU will need isn't a straightforward task, particularly when there are decisions to be made. For example, suppose the cache sees that the CPU is currently executing some instructions that mean, "Compare value A with value B. If A is greater than B, then set the value *maximum* to A; otherwise, set the value *maximum* to B." That simple statement boils down to a bunch of instructions—instructions in memory that had better be in the cache if the Pentium is going to be able to continue running without delays. But because the cache controller can't know whether the CPU will take the "A is greater than B" or the "B is greater than A" fork in the road, it doesn't know which result's code to go grab and put in the cache. For years, *mainframe* cache controllers have used a technique called *branch prediction* to guess which way the CPU will go, and now the Pentium and later PC chips have cache controllers built into them with branch prediction capabilities. So that's *four* ways the Pentium line of chips makes better use of your memory than the 486 did.

THE PENTIUM PRO, PENTIUM II, PENTIUM III, PENTIUM 4, CELERON, XEON, ITANIUM, AND PENTIUM M CACHES

What about the Pentium Pro and its more recent cousins, the PII and PIII, Celeron, Xeon, P4, Itanium, and Pentium M chips? Well, there's some good news and some bad news.

With the Pentium Pro, Intel introduced the revolutionary step of making a sort of double-sized chip, a chip that looked like two Pentium chips side by side. The second "chip," however, was 512KB

L2 memory, a built-in cache RAM. This cache was terrific in that it could talk to the CPU at half of the CPU's full internal speed (the core processor frequency), not the external bus speed. Motherboards could be designed with even more external cache, however, and some Pentium Pro systems sold with as much as 1024KB of external cache, a mix of the built-in L2 cache and some chips on the motherboard. The Pentium Pro has 16KB of L1 cache, as did the original Pentium.

With the PII, PIII, and P4, Intel created a larger rectangular package called a Single Edge Cartridge (SEC) that no longer allows external cache. You can see a PIII in Figure 2.5.

FIGURE 2.5
Pentium III
in SEC package

The result is that you couldn't design a motherboard for a PII or PIII that contains any cache. The PII/III had its built-in 512KB of L2 cache, but that's it. (The PII/III also had more L1 cache than the Pentium Pro, 16KB of data, and 16KB of instruction cache, for a total of 32KB.) And that leads to an interesting comparison of the older Pentium Pro versus the PII/III. Some of the Pro motherboards had room for 1MB of cache. Therefore, you could benchmark a Pentium Pro at 200MHz (the fastest they were built) versus a PII at 333MHz—the Pentium Pro can actually be faster because it's got 1024KB of cache versus the PII and PIII's half megabyte of cache!

The PII/III Xeon chip addressed that problem and offered considerably improved performance for two reasons. First, the Xeon communicated between its built-in L2 cache and its processor at full-core processor speed—a 600MHz Xeon talked to its L2 cache at a full 600MHz. Second, the Xeon came with up to 1024KB of built-in L2 cache.

But I haven't mentioned the Celeron. What kind of L2 cache does it have? Originally it had none. But Intel's customers weren't very happy about the Celeron's missing cache, so current models of the Celeron also have cache memory, albeit not much. The 1.2GHz–1.4GHz chips have 256KB cache, and the 1.7GHz–2.6GHz chips only have 128KB L2 cache.

Memory Addressable by a CPU

Megabytes are a unit of storage size—just about the amount of space needed to store a million characters. People use this term to talk about the size of primary memory, or RAM. This is the working memory in your computer, the kind of memory that goes in expansion boards and the kind of memory that Excel can run out of if you have a large spreadsheet. Your computer also has another type

---

ITANIUM: NOW WE'RE TALKING L3 CACHE

You've already learned a little bit about the Itanium IA-64 processor. Not only does the Itanium have the power of the Xeon—level L1 and L2 cache on board the chip itself—it adds up to 4MB of L3 cache (with an option for an L4 cache that can be added by an Original Equipment Manufacturer (OEM). The L3 cache, smaller than a 3-by-5-inch index card, isn't on the chip itself but is contained in the processor package. The Itanium also has its own unique form factor, Slot M. Both the 733MHz and 800MHz editions will operate on a 100MHz motherboard. The Itanium 2 chip runs on a 400MHz board and supports up to 6MB of L3 cache (in addition to its built-in L1 and L2 caches).

---

of memory, which is a disk drive. Sometimes disk drives are referred to as secondary memory. But when most people say *memory*, they're talking about *primary* memory, so memory means chips or RAM. Folks usually just call disk drives *disks* and skip the memory part.

Disk memory is also not *volatile*, which means that when you shut it off, it retains its data. Remove power from a memory chip (which happens whenever you turn the machine off), and it forgets whatever it contained. That's why you have to save your work to disk before shutting off the machine.

Although there is old adage, "You can never have too much memory," you can't just keep adding memory to your PC indefinitely. A particular chip can *address* only a certain size of memory. For the oldest CPUs, this amount was 16,384 bytes—16KB of memory. The original IBM PC's CPU could address 1024KB, or 1MB. As you might expect, newer chips can address more. Modern CPUs can address several gigabytes of RAM.

Slots and Sockets

Are you feeling a bit confused about slots and sockets? If so, don't feel alone. The past few years, whenever a different approach to computer processors is taken, we end up with a different way in which the CPU is packaged for installation.

In recent modern CPU history, a *socket* was simply the place on the motherboard where the CPU plugged in—pins into holes. The Socket 7 standard created for the original Pentium-class PCs allowed for a simple insertion (or plug-in) of a CPU into the motherboard. Such CPUs feature 321 pins set in five staggered rows. A *slot* allows the CPU to slide into place, something like plugging an expansion card into a PCI slot.

Socket-type CPUs are cheaper to produce overall, and a slot-type CPU is an attempt to pack more speed and power into a CPU package. Put another way, the closer you bring the cache to the processor, the better the system should perform, and the slot-type CPU helps you accomplish that.

Although Intel moved away from the Socket 7 standard as it moved to the Pentium Pro (Socket 8, with 387 pins in five dual-pattern pin rows and the cache built into the processor package) and the Pin Grid Array (PGA) 423-pin socket used by the P4, Socket 7 has lingered because alternative CPU manufacturers, particularly AMD, adopted it and used it for their line of K6 processors. Only with the Athlon did AMD begin to break stride, giving it a completely different Socket A insertion.

Intel, meanwhile, was shifting again. With the introduction of the PII came the Single Edge Contact Cartridge (SECC), wherein the processor and cache are mounted on a *daughterboard* (secondary board) on the chip and then inserted into the motherboard. PIIs and PIIIs use Slot 1 technology, which has 242 pins set in two rows of 121 pins each. When Intel introduced the Itanium, change happened again, going from Slot 1 technology to Slot M.

Socket 370 was introduced during the PII reign as alternative packaging for Celerons (which in the beginning, had no L2 cache). But as Celerons were minted that included a 128KB L2 cache, the packaging turned to Slot 1, like the PII itself, with an adapter available to fit a Socket 370 Celeron into a PII Slot 1–style motherboard. Table 2.2 lists CPUs and their slots or socket types.

TABLE 2.2: DESKTOP CPUS AND THEIR REQUIRED SOCKET/SLOT TYPES

CPU	SOCKET/SLOT FORM FACTOR
Pentium (classic)	Socket 7
AMD K6 series	Socket 7
Pentium Pro	Socket 8
Celeron (original)	Socket 370
Celeron (current)	Slot 1
Pentium II	Slot 1
Pentium III	Slot 1 or Socket 370
Pentium 4	Socket 478
Pentium 4 Mobile	732-pin Micro Flip-Chip Ball Grid Array (Micro-FCBGA)
Pentium M	732-pin Micro-FCBGA
Athlon	Socket A
Duron	Socket A
Opteron	Socket A
Xeon	Slot 1
Itanium	Slot M

TIP   When upgrading a computer or purchasing a new motherboard and CPU, it's critical to ensure that your pieces will fit together. Look at the motherboard's documentation to see which processor(s) it supports before buying it!

Details on CPU Chips

Although I've talked a lot about various CPU chips in this part of the chapter, there are a few odds and ends I haven't covered yet. I'll tie up those things here. Table 2.3 starts by listing all the Intel and Intel-compatible CPUs and summarizing their characteristics.

TABLE 2.3: CPU SPECIFICATIONS AND APPLICATIONS

Model	External Clock Frequency (ECF), in MHz	Internal Clock Frequency ICF (in MHz)	Word Size and Data Path (in Bits)	Instruction Pipelines (how many)	Physical Memory (in MB)	Math Coprocessor	Internal Cache (in KB)	Voltage (in Volts)	Intel Compatibility
Intel									
8088	8	8	16/8	1	1	No	0	5	
8086	8	8	16/16	1	1	No	0	5	
80c86	8	8	16/16	1	1	No	0	5	
80186	16	16	16/16	1	1	No	0	5	
80286	20	20	16/16	1	16	No	0	5	
80386DX	40	40	32/32	1	4096	No	0	5	
80386SX	25	25	32/16	1	16	No	0	5	
80486SLC	25	25	32/32	1	64	No	8	5	
	33	33							
80486DX	25	25	32/32	1	4096	Yes	8	5	
	33	33							
	50	50							
80486SX	20	20	32/32	1	4096	No	8	5	
	25	25							
	33	33							
80486DX2	20	40	32/32	1	4096	Yes	8	5	
	25	50							
	33	66							
80486DX4	25	75	32/32	1	4096	Yes	16	5	
	33	100							
Pentium	60	100	32/64	2	4096	Yes	16	5	

TABLE 2.3: CPU Specifications and Applications *(continued)*

Model	External Clock Frequency (ECF), in MHz	Internal Clock Frequency ICF (in MHz)	Word Size and Data Path (in Bits)	Instruction Pipelines (How Many)	Physical Memory (in MB)	Math Coprocessor	Internal Cache (in KB)	Voltage (in Volts)	Intel Compatibility
	66	133–200						3.3	
MMX	66	200–266	32/64	2	4096	Yes	32	1.5	
Pentium Pro	60	166	32/64	3	65,536	Yes	32	1.5	
	66	200							
Pentium II	66	233	32/64	3	65,536	Yes	32	1.5	
	100	266–450							
Pentium III	66	500	32/64	3	65,536	Yes	32	1.5	
	100	450–1000							
	133	533–1400							
Pentium 4	400	2000–2600	32/128	3	65,536	Yes	32	1.5	
	533	2260–2800	32/128	3	65,536	Yes	32	1.5	
	800	2400–3200	32/128	3	65,536	Yes	32	1.5	
Pentium 4 Mobile	533	2400–3060	32/128	3	65,536	Yes	32	1.2–1.3	
Pentium M	400	900–1700	32/64	3	65,536	Yes	32	1.1–1.3	
Celeron	66	233–1200	32/64	3	65,536	Yes	32	1.5	
	100	850–1400	32/64	3	65,536	Yes	32	1.5	
	400	1700–2600	32/64	3	65,536	Yes	32	1.5	
Xeon	100	350–800	32/64	3	65,536	Yes	32	2	
	400	1400–3000	32/64	3	65,536	Yes	32	2	
	533	2000–3060	32/64	3	65,536	Yes	32	2	
Itanium	266	733–800	64/64	3	65,536	Yes	32	1.5	
Itanium 2	400	1300–1500	64/64	3	131,072	Yes	32	1.3	

TABLE 2.3: CPU Specifications and Applications (continued)

Model	External Clock Frequency (ECF), in MHz	Internal Clock Frequency ICF (in MHz)	Word Size and Data Path (in bits)	Instruction Pipelines (how many)	Physical Memory (in MB)	Math Coprocessor	Internal Cache (in KB)	Voltage (in volts)	Intel Compatibility
NEC									
V20	10	10	16/8	1	1	No	0	5	8088
V30	10	10	16/8	1	1	No	0	5	8086
VIA/Cyrix									
80486SLC	25 33	25 33	32/32	1	16	No	1	5	386SX
80486SLC	25	50	32/32	1	16	No	1	5	386SX
80486DLC	33	33	32/32	1	4096	No	1	5	386DX
80486DX	33 40 50	33 40 50	32/32	1	4096	Yes	8	5	486DX
80486DX2	25 33 40	50 66 80	32/32	1	4096	Yes	8	5	486DX2
586		100–120	32/64	1	4096	Yes	16	3.45–5	Pentium
6x86	50 55 60 66 75	100 110 120 133 150	32/64	2	4096	Yes	16	3.3–5	Pentium
C3 (Cyrix III)	400	700–800	32/64	1	4096	Yes	64	1.6	Celeron

TABLE 2.3: CPU Specifications and Applications *(continued)*

MODEL	EXTERNAL CLOCK FREQUENCY (ECF), IN MHZ	INTERNAL CLOCK FREQUENCY ICF (IN MHZ)	WORD SIZE AND DATA PATH (IN BITS)	INSTRUCTION PIPELINES (HOW MANY)	PHYSICAL MEMORY (IN MB)	MATH COPROCESSOR	INTERNAL CACHE (IN KB)	VOLTAGE (IN VOLTS)	INTEL COMPATIBILITY
AMD									
386SE	25, 33	25, 33	32/16	1	16	No	0	3–5	386SX
386DE	33, 40	33, 40	32/32	1	4096	No	0	3–5	386DX
486DXLV	33	33	32/32	1	4096	Yes	8	3.0–3.6	486DX
486SXLV	33	33	32/32	1	4096	No	8	3.0–3.6	486SX
486DX	33, 40	33, 40	32/32	1	4096	Yes	8	5	486DX
486SX	33, 40	33, 40	32/32	1	4096	No	8	5	486SX
486DX2	25, 33	50, 66	32/32	1	4096	Yes	8	5	486DX2
486DX2-80	40	80	32/32	1	4096	Yes	8	5	486DX2
486DXL2	25, 33	50, 66	32/32	1	4096	Yes	8	5	486DX2
486SX2-50	25	50	32/32	1	4096	Yes	8	5	486SX
Am5x86	33	133	32/32	1	4096	Yes	16	3.45	Pentium 75
Duron	200	600–1200	32/64	3	4096	Yes	64	1.6/1.75	Celeron
Athlon	266	500–1600	32/64	3	65,536	Yes	128	1.6	Pentium III/4
Opteron	200	800–2600	64/64	3	4096	Yes	128	1.55	Itanium

Most of these are outdated because of how fast CPU speeds are updated these days.

You'll see a bit of repetition in the following pages as I detail each processor, but that's intentional. I've thrown an awful lot of concepts at you so far; the intent in the following sections is to tie up all the CPU concepts before progressing on to memory, buses, and other motherboard-related topics.

8088 AND 8086

The 8088 was the "Grand Old Man" of PC CPUs although the 8086 came before it and was arguably a better design. It came in what was called a 40-pin Dual Inline Pin (DIP) package, which means a rectangular plastic case with two rows of 20 pins. Older 8088s were called 8088-1s because they could run at only low speeds (5MHz or slower). Turbo PC/XT clones ran at 6.66, 7.16, or 8MHz. To do this, they used the 8088-2, which was rated at up to 8MHz. The 8088 was the equivalent of about 29,000 transistors.

The 8086 predated the 8088 by a year and was actually more powerful than it, but the 8086 was not as well known. The 8086 was different from the 8088 in that the 8086 not only had internal 16-bit registers (a 16-bit word) but also a 16-bit data path, the doorway to the outside world. Because that required 16-bit motherboards, however, the 8086 never really caught on. The 8088 was essentially a hobbled 8086 because it had only an 8-bit data path. But that made for a cheaper motherboard, so IBM went with the 8088—and the rest is history. But a few clone makers opted for 8086-based systems because the 8086 was 100-percent compatible with the 8088 *and* faster; one example was Compaq, with a tremendously successful computer called the *Deskpro*.

80186 AND 80188

You don't hear much about the 80186 and 80188 chips, but they were souped-up versions of the 8086 and 8088. They didn't really have much in the way of new capabilities; they were just a polished version of the old chips, sort of similar to the way that the 80486 wasn't a big leap from the 80386 but rather a mildly improved version. The main differences were that the 186 and the 188 were manufactured in a PGA package (see the "80286" section for more on this) and had more efficient microcode. Tandy sold a computer called the Tandy 2000 that was 80186 based. It could've been a high-performance competitor to the Deskpro, but Tandy unwisely opted to make it only about 60 percent compatible with the IBM PC, forcing Tandy 2000 users to buy special versions of software. There weren't too many titles developed for the Tandy 2000, and it went nowhere.

The 80186 was the last member of what might be called the first family of PC CPUs, a family that started with the 8086.

80286

Introduced in 1981, the 80286 was a major step forward for x86 technology. It was packaged in a square ceramic PGA package. It also came in a cheaper package called a Plastic Leadless Chip Carrier (PLCC). The PLCC is the more durable of the two and is mainly found in laptops because of its lower profile. The PGA package has an inner and an outer square of solid pins; the PLCC has curved-under legs around its perimeter. The PGA "stands" on its legs. The PLCC is surrounded by its legs. You can see chip package types in Figure 2.6.

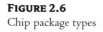

FIGURE 2.6
Chip package types

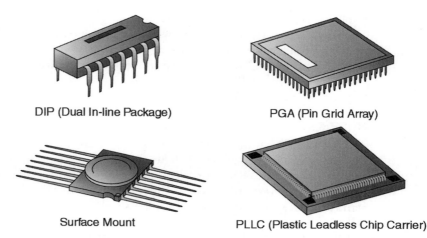

DIP (Dual In-line Package)

PGA (Pin Grid Array)

Surface Mount

PLLC (Plastic Leadless Chip Carrier)

The 286 packed a lot more power into a small package than the 8088 did: the 80286 was the equivalent of about 130,000 transistors in about the same volume. Because of this, the 80286 ran hotter, and some models required extra cooling provisions such as a heat sink. *Heat sinks* are small metal caps with metal cooling fins that fit on top of a chip and enable the chip to better dissipate the heat it generates. You see them on modern CPUs, such as Pentiums, which produce even greater amounts of heat.

The 80286 was the sole member of the second family of PC-compatible CPUs. In many ways, it was a rough draft for the 386 family, the third family of PC CPUs.

80386DX AND 80386SX

The 80386—or as it was officially called by Intel, the 80386DX—was another quantum leap for the x86 family. Introduced in 1985, it came in a PGA package and was the equivalent of about 250,000 transistors. It incorporated a wealth of programming features, including the capability to multitask DOS programs with the help of operating systems such as Windows. The 32-bit data path sped up data access, leading to the design of buses such as the Micro Channel, EISA, VESA, and PCI buses (see the upcoming section on buses). It also differed from previous x86 designs in that it could address 4096MB of RAM.

The 386SX was identical to the 386DX except that it had a 16-bit data path to enable it to be more easily incorporated into AT-type hardware designs (recall that the AT's 286 had a 16-bit data path also). It was contained in a PLCC package.

The 80386 family brought a new set of instruction codes and a 32-bit programming model to PC CPUs that's essentially unchanged to this day. Look at the most modern PC programs not written specifically for a 32-bit Windows environment (32-bit Windows being Windows 95/98, Windows 2000, and Windows XP), and many of them will run on a circa-1985 386-based system, albeit slowly.

80386SL

The SL was part of a two-chip set that was basically a combination of a 386SX and a motherboard. The two chips together constituted almost all of what's needed to build an SX computer. What made it particularly interesting was that the chipset included power management. For example, the SL system could shut down the CPU between keystrokes, saving power. The SL mainly appeared in laptops; they were in PLCC packages.

80486DX

The 80486 (officially the 80486DX) was sort of an upgraded 386. Code-named during development *P4*, it combined a tuned-up 386 with two chips that sped up a 386 system: the 385 cache controller and the 387 numeric coprocessor. The microcode was larger and faster—there were the equivalent of 1.25 *million* transistors in this chip. Depending upon what the computer was doing, a 25MHz 386 with a 385 and a 387 (cache controller and external math coprocessor) would sometimes execute only half as many instructions per second as a 25MHz 486.

Better yet, the 486 chip was actually cheaper than a 386, 385, and 387 together, so eventually 486 computers were cheaper than fully loaded 386 machines. The DX appeared in PGA packages.

80486SX

The 80486SX was more of a marketing tool than a new chip. Intel took the 486DX chips that failed the math coprocessor analysis during product testing and sold them in a new package they called a 486SX. It had a specified maximum clock speed of 20MHz and no math coprocessor. Intel then offered a math coprocessor called the 487SX that was, believe it or not, a fully functional 486DX— a CPU chip with coprocessor and all. Once the 487SX was planted in its socket, it instructed the 486SX to just go to sleep; the 487SX then handled everything, including both general computing and numeric coprocessing, just as if it were a normal 486DX system running at 20MHz.

80486DX2, DX4, AND THE OVERDRIVE CHIP

The 80487SX, as it turns out, was a mere harbinger of the wide variety in CPUs that was to follow. With the 486, Intel first started experimenting with product diversification, taking a basically good product (the 486DX) and repackaging it in a variety of ways.

Recall that the 80487SX was *not* a floating-point coprocessor. It was a fully functional 80486DX but packaged a bit differently—the pins on the bottom of the chip were arranged differently from the way they were arranged on the 80486DX, so you couldn't just pop an 80486DX in the 80487SX socket. Furthermore, unlike the floating-point coprocessors of yore (the 8087, 187, 287, and 387 families), the 80487SX didn't work with the erstwhile main processor—*it took over altogether*, effectively disconnecting the 80486SX. A bit of clever marketing, eh? Buy a "cheap" 486SX and then end up buying a whole 486DX disguised as a coprocessor, with the result that Intel gets to sell more chips than if you'd bought a 486DX in the first place.

The next stop in the 486-marketing universe was the original OverDrive chip. ("Original" because the term *overdrive* has since been recycled by Intel a number of times.) The OverDrive chip was a 486DX built for a 487SX socket, as usual, *except* that they made it a clock doubler like the 486DX2.

The net effect was that the OverDrive chip did everything at least as quickly as a 25MHz 80486DX and many operations twice as fast! So the OverDrive chip would speed up your PC by about one-third to one-half. Was it worth it? An OverDrive chip cost around $300, not a small amount but then not a budget-buster either.

Intel then took on the market of folks who had a 486DX and wanted more speed by offering the clock doubler 486DX2. Recall that the 80486DX2, like the OverDrive chip, ran outwardly at *x*MHz but worked internally at *2x*MHz. Thus, a so-called 66MHz 80486DX2 worked in a mother-board designed for a 33MHz chip but ran internally at 66MHz. The value was, again, that a PC vendor needed only take one of its already-existing 33MHz 80486DX models and replace the 33MHz 80486DX processor with a 66MHz 80486DX processor to instantly get a "66MHz 486."

The last in the Intel 486 line was the DX4, a clock tripler 486 that contained power management right on the chip, combining 386SL-like technology and clock tripling to produce a nice processor. Its main role was in laptops, where it functioned extremely well.

486SLC AND 486DLC

This one wasn't an Intel chip. It wasn't even a 486. A 486SLC was a 386SX (no numeric coprocessor, recall) with just *1KB of cache* and, of course, a *16-bit data path*. The resulting chip was somewhere between a 386SX and a 486SX in performance. The 1KB was pretty measly, so you'd have to say that the performance was closer to the 386SX than to the 486. There was also a 486DLC, a 386DX with 1KB of cache memory added and no coprocessor. These chips were pin compatible with the 386SX and 386DX, not the 486 line. My main gripe with them was the marketing baloney that went with them: people were told they were getting 486 technology when they bought one of these chips, but they actually got only 386 technology.

Micro technology improvement, macro sales pitches. Yup, you can always tell when a technological industry matures: the guys in the wheelhouse are marketing guys rather than engineers.

386DRU2

This is another Intel competitor. It had an odd-looking name, but that was how it came to be known internally at the company. This Cyrix chip was a 386 clone, save that it was a clock doubler: you could make a 25MHz 386 into a 50MHz 386 with one of these.

That, in general, has been Cyrix's modus operandi: take what Intel does and do it better. It has not served them badly.

PENTIUM

In 1993, Intel introduced the processor they had code-named *P5*, known now as the Pentium processor. In some ways, it was just a souped-up 486—and, in fact, many in the industry expected Intel to follow their 80286/80386/80486 naming convention and call this new model the 80586. In other ways, it was much more, as you've seen from the earlier parts of this chapter. The following sections provide a quick look at Pentium features besides the ones you've already examined.

Greater Raw Speed

The Pentium came in a variety of flavors: 60, 66, 75, 90, 100, 125, 133, 150, and 166MHz, and, in the newer MMX flavor, was available up to 266MHz. Intel offered an OverDrive upgrade for chips 100MHz and under that increased the chip's speed by about half.

The 120/133MHz OverDrive processor upgrade was designed to reduce the voltage used by the 60MHz and 66MHz chips from 5 volts to the 3.3 used by the more recent chips that took advantage of Intel's Voltage Reduction Technology.

NOTE *Counterintuitively, you might get better performance from a 133 than a 150 because the 133 is a doubled 66MHz chip, and the 150 is a two-and-a-halved 60.*

The Pentium was more difficult to make than its predecessors because, for one thing, it was much bigger than the 486. The 486 contained 1.2 million transistors; the Pentium contained 3.1 million— more than two-and-a-half times as many.

Fault Tolerance

The Pentium was designed to be used in conjunction with another Pentium on a motherboard specifically suited for fault tolerance (meaning, it'd try to stand up to and operate under situations that might crash a less-tolerant system). The second Pentium constantly monitored the first; if the main Pentium malfunctioned, the other one jumped right in and took up without skipping a beat.

Another purpose for two CPUs on one motherboard is Symmetric Multiprocessing (SMP), the ability to divide the workload between multiple processors. Most dual CPU implementations are designed for SMP and not for fault tolerance.

First MMX Implementation

Another Pentium first was its so-called multimedia support, the matrix functions in the MMX. The MMX was just a Pentium with MMX instructions included and a larger cache.

THE PENTIUM PRO FAMILY: PENTIUM PRO, PENTIUM II, III, 4, CELERON, AND XEON

The Pentium Pro, PII, PIII , Celeron, and Xeon chips are known as the *P6 line* of chips. The P6s differ from their predecessors for many reasons. But are they *faster* chips? Well, yes, kind of—but, like their predecessors, the P6 family is largely limited by its heritage: it's got to be *x*86 compatible.

Just looking at the P6 family shows how it's different. With the exception of the Celeron, the P6s are fairly large chips because they contain lots of memory. The Pentium Pro chip, for example, is actually *two* chips. Inside the Pentium Pro, there is one chip (*die* is the actual word; it refers to the silicon wafer that's the actual electronics of a chip), which is the main processor. It has about 5.5 million transistors. Alongside it is a built-in 256KB external or L2 cache, about 15 million transistors' worth of static memory. You can see that in Figure 2.7.

The Pentium Pro incorporates three pipelines rather than the two of the Pentium. By breaking up instruction execution into 14 steps, Intel has made it possible to do what they call *dynamic execution*. Dynamic execution works by using three parallel units to fetch and decode instructions; once prepared for execution, those instructions are tossed into a "pool" of waiting instructions. There's not much waiting, however, because the P6s have five execution units working side by side to try to shove instructions through at top speed. That helps because the Pentium Pro can handle groups of instructions *out of their original order*, which keeps as many of the fetch, decode, and execution units working at the highest capacity possible.

FIGURE 2.7
L2 cache on the
Pentium Pro chip

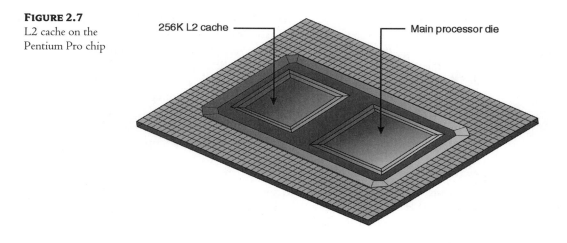

256K L2 cache   Main processor die

Oddly enough, the Pentium Pro has an L1 cache of only 16KB, the same as the standard Pentium and in fact less than the Pentium MMX chips. That's offset by the large L2 cache incorporated into the chip. By putting the L2 cache on the chip, the Pentium Pro can more quickly access that memory, making it a faster "external" cache than the external caches found on Pentium and earlier chips. But 20 million transistors! That sucker is a bit toasty, so make sure there's a decent CPU fan on your Pentium Pro. Most come with a fan, as you see in Figure 2.8.

FIGURE 2.8
Pentium II
package with fan

The other P6ers—Celeron, Xeon, and PII—all have 32KB of L1 cache and can also suffer from heat exhaustion (the Xeon even has a sensor on-chip to detect overheating).

The later P6s' heat problems weren't as terrible as they could be, however, because Intel again reduced the size of the transistors that make up the chip. Whereas the Pentium was built with 0.8-micron and 0.6-micron components, the Xeon is built with 0.25-micron components. That helps make the Xeon work at a decent reliability factor when running at 600MHz.

The PIII processors are similar to the PIIs; however, the PIIIs run faster (450MHz–550MHz), support 70 new instructions, and run on the 100MHz system bus with the original version and 133MHz on the newer Coppermines (more to come about Coppermines in just a bit).

Pentium II

The PII made some impressive improvements to the original Pentium processor. Ranging in speeds from 233MHz to 450MHz, the PII improves not only speed but also performance. The PII incorporates a 100MHz *front-side bus* interface (for the 350MHz, 400MHz, and 450MHz chips), allowing the processor to achieve greater speeds in interfacing with system resources.

The PII also has MMX technology built into the processor, thereby satisfying the new demands by users and software for faster graphics. The original PII came with 32KB of L1 cache (16KB for data and 16KB for instructions) and 512KB of L2 cache.

Pentium II Xeon

The PII processor was further enhanced by the creation of the Xeon family. The Xeon PII is designed for business applications and high-speed processing; up to eight processors can be combined to work together. The processor functions at 400MHz or 450MHz and can handle higher L2 cache. The 400MHz and 450MHz are available with 512KB or 1MB of L2 cache, but the 450MHz can handle up to a whopping 2MB.

Celeron

The Intel Celeron processor has become quite popular with home PC users. The reason for its increase in sales is because of its relatively low cost. Intel made a decision to lower processor costs (which in turn lowered PC costs) by making some changes to its existing processor families.

Recall that standard Pentium chips had 32KB of L1 cache and 512KB of L2 cache. The L2 cache is the expensive kind, so it makes sense that if you reduce its size, you reduce the cost of the processor, right? Well, that's what Intel did. The Celeron processor comes in speeds ranging from 300MHz to 2.6GHz (which can operate at up to 400MHz bus speed and still have 32KB of L1 cache). But these processors come with only 128KB to 256KB of L2 cache. Although this is a drastic cut in L2 cache size, the reduction in price for the processor and the PCs that use it make it a favorable choice for buyers looking to save money on a new PC.

The Celeron also has a built-in booster market. As Intel sought to make it tough for ambitious overclockers to push PIIs and PIIIs to higher-than-rated speeds, the Celeron became the default preference of the overclocking crowd. If overclocking techniques fail, it hurts a lot less to burn up a cheaper CPU than a much more expensive PIII or P4.

Pentium III

Intel released its PIII processor with a marketing blitz no one will soon forget. But was the new chip worth all the hype? Let's see.

First, the speeds offered by the PIII were higher than anything Intel offered before. Starting out at 450MHz–550MHz and ending up with chips in the 1GHz range, PIII chips also come with the MMX technology and (typically) 512KB of L2 cache. But other than the increase in speed, what was the big deal? Well, the PIII's strength lay in its capability to handle graphics faster and smoother than previous chips. Remember MMX? The PIII did MMX processing 70 instructions better! These new instructions were designed for real-time video, streaming video, and better graphics capabilities.

It's important to understand that the differences between a PII and a PIII are largely speed (the PII line stopped at 450MHz) and the 70 extra instructions already discussed. For the most part, the PIII CPU will drop right into a PII socket as a replacement on a motherboard, same as with the Xeon II/III.

The extra instructions included are useful in specific areas: streaming content delivered from the Internet (where the user doesn't have to sit and wait to receive *all* of a file before the audio and/or video begins to play) and in PC gaming. Depending on whose analysis you favor, performance with a PIII jumps about 10 to 15 percent over a PII in the areas where the extra instruction set counts.

However, the PIII isn't linear—there are actually two types of PIII. The original one was based on the same technology as the PII, but with those extra instructions. A change came about with Intel's Coppermine chipset in 1999, replacing traditional connectors with copper, altering the process used from 0.25-micron to 0.18-micron, and offering a 133MHz system bus (original was 100MHz), as well as a 256K L2 cache on-chip, which runs at the same speed as the processor itself. One important difference with Coppermine is that it should finally support 4X AGP, critical to helping video performance hop forward. Before this, AGP video was limited to a 1–2 data path, which fell short of allowing AGP to truly excite the serious gaming crowd that needs speed in video. All too often, AGP was chosen not because it was wildly faster and better than PCI video cards but because it freed up a PCI slot for another type of expansion board.

Pentium 4

The P4 was the first truly new processor design from Intel since the Pentium Pro debuted at under 200MHz. Believe it or not, the Pentium Pro, PII, PIII, Xeon, and Celeron processors were all based on the same P6 microarchitecture. Intel added some goodies such as MMX, SSE, and integrated cache over the years, and they changed the way the processors were made, but they were all the same basic design.

The P4 is based on Intel's radical new NetBurst microarchitecture, and it's a different animal altogether. Remember that the P6 microarchitecture topped out at about 1GHz; the P4's NetBurst microarchitecture is built to run comfortably at high clock speeds (1GHz and higher). Not only that, but Intel's engineers had another hurdle to leap with this design. If NetBurst is going to stick around for as many years as P6 has, it'll need to provide substantial performance gains as the years pass and clock speeds rise. So headroom and scalability were the orders of the day.

Intel's design philosophy gives the NetBurst microarchitecture a distinct character. For example, clock-for-clock performance, or the number of instructions per clock (IPC) the chip can process, should be relatively low. But clock speeds are very high.

The P4 adds an execution trace cache. Contemporary *x*86 processors such as the PIII and Athlon decode *x*86 instructions into smaller, bite-sized operations before processing them. (Intel calls them *micro-ops*.) This practice allows *x*86 processors to have much more Reduced Instruction Set Computing (RISC)–like designs, but decoding *x*86 instructions takes time. NetBurst's execution trace cache takes the place of a conventional L1 instruction cache, and it caches micro-ops instead of *x*86 instructions. Intel is coy about the exact size of the trace cache, but they claim it can store about 12,000 micro-ops.

Smaller is faster. The P4 incorporates a small, low-latency L1 data cache. At only 8KB, the Net-Burst L1 data cache is only half the size of the PIII's, and just a fraction of the size of the AMD Athlon's 64KB data cache. Intel chose this small cache size because smaller caches have lower latencies. Although the Athlon and PIII data caches have a three-cycle latency, the P4's L1 data cache latency is two cycles. It's all part of the plan to keep that deep pipeline well fed.

The P4's L2 cache is 256K, just like the Athlon and PIII, but it's much, much cooler. The P4's L2 cache interface is 256 bits wide, and it sends data on every clock cycle. On a 1.4GHz P4, that works out to 44.8GB per second of bandwidth. That's almost four times the bandwidth of the L2 cache on a 1GHz PIII. As for the Athlon, its L2 cache is even slower still, but then I've seen AMD engineers claim the Athlon's L2 cache isn't really bandwidth limited. Whatever the case, the P4's L2 cache is scary fast.

The NetBurst bus sends data four times per clock cycle, and you're going to hear everyone talk about it as a "400MHz bus" from here to eternity. It can also be referred to as a "100MHz, quad-pumped bus," just to keep things confusing. Whatever you call it, though, don't call it slow. This deeply pipelined, split-transaction bus is capable of transferring data at 3.2GB per second at 400MHz.

Intel has added a set of 144 new instructions to the P4, dubbed Streaming SIMD Extensions 2 (SSE2). Like the original SSE, SSE2 involves simultaneously executing a single instruction on multiple data targets (hence SIMD). Most importantly, SSE2 handles 128-bit, double-precision, floating-point math. The ability to handle more precise floating-point numbers makes SSE2 just the ticket for accelerating a host of multimedia, 3D, engineering, and workstation-type tasks—once software is properly optimized to take advantage of it.

The P4's floating-point unit isn't as capable as the Floating-Point Processor Unit (FPU) in the PIII, and it's quite a bit less capable than the Athlon's FPU. To put it simply, the P4's FPU can't do as much work at once, and it has higher latencies in some cases. Programs optimized for SSE2 will be able to bypass the P4's FPU in many cases, but without special optimizations, the P4 will have a hard time keeping up.

Taken together, these design decisions are really radical. The depth of the P4's pipeline, combined with its less-than-stellar FPU, will keep its IPC—or clock-for-clock performance—relatively low. In legacy applications, especially those that lean heavily on conventional *x*86 ALUs and FPUs, the P4's performance may not be so exciting. But the P4 platform itself is impressive, with gobs of bandwidth available all over the place. With the right optimizations for SSE2, multimedia apps positively scream on the P4.

Pentium 4 Mobile and Pentium M

The vast majority of this processor section has focused on the desktop, which is appropriate considering the history of the PC. But every once in a while a new processor comes out specifically designed for laptops and warrants notice. One such example is the 386SL; new examples are the P4 Mobile and the Pentium M.

Mobile computing is where it's at these days. It seems as though the desktop computer is starting to go the way of the dinosaur. Intel is aware of this and has put a lot of research into chips specifically designed for laptops. Both mobile CPUs have similar design features to the desktop version of the P4; just they're a bit slower in clock speed. The P4 Mobile has a faster clock speed than the M but also has less L2 cache (512KB as opposed to 1MB).

You've heard of the Pentium before, to be sure. But the Pentium M is specifically designed for mobile computing. Its top internal clock speed won't blow you away—it's only 1.7GHz, but it operates on a 400MHz external bus. In addition, the M comes with 1MB of L2 cache, which really is quite a bit for a laptop. The cache includes advanced power management to save battery life.

NOTE   *You might not have heard of the Pentium M specifically. It's generally packaged as part of Intel's Centrino chipset, which is actually a combination of three separate chipsets: the Pentium M processor, the Intel 855 chipset, and the Intel PRO/Wireless 2100 network connection.*

Intel's 855 chipset family augments the Pentium M by managing memory (up to 2GB of DDR 266/200 RAM), USB 2.0 devices, graphics, and other Input/Output (I/O) features. And, as the name implies, the PRO/Wireless 2100 handles wireless network connectivity.

Which is better for your mobile computing needs? That's a good question. And I'll talk about the answer in some detail in Chapter 31, "Notebook/Laptop Computers."

Itanium and Itanium 2: The 64-Bit Giants

The Itanium is Intel's first high-end, 64-bit central processor. Formerly code-named Merced, the Itanium is the flagship of Intel's IA-64 processor family, developed to go head to head with major professional server players such as IBM and Sun Microsystems' highly popular UltraSparc III—which are high-end RISC-based processors capable of performing some of the hardest tasks computers are called upon to do. In testing, this processor worked well with eight operating systems, including Windows NT 4, Linux, and various flavors of Unix. It's the capability to handle other than a strictly Windows-environment platform that makes Itanium a serious first entry for Intel into the powerhouse market. Intel processors have usually—intentionally or not—been designed around the Microsoft Windows platform, whether it was lower-end consumer Windows such as Windows 95/98 or higher-powered Windows NT/2000/XP. Itanium's multiplatform support has gained the interest of major Linux distributors, for example, who formed a group called the Trillium Project to help bolster Itanium's roll-out.

To this end, the Itanium isn't really designed for the typical home or corporate desktop PC. It's great for servers and processor-intensive tasks—as long as the software is written to take advantage of the Itanium's 64-bit processing. Windows XP and Windows 2003 are designed to do just that. Intel's theory is this: with processing demand growing at an infinite pace, we need to find ways to wed the economics (lower cost) and the workhorse-usability of personal computers with the power of server technology. Their initial market is e-business, a market where the current choices are either to invest heavily in the RISC-based processor environment or to settle for a much less powerful server.

With all this said, you may be surprised to hear that this powerhouse, next-generation CPU isn't a lot faster than the PIII—and, when running existing 32-bit applications, is actually slower than a P4 or Athlon XP. But that's okay because in a large, professional environment handling tens of thousands, if not millions, of records and files and performing many functions, processor speed itself takes a back seat to parallel processing, whereby multiple processors work together to push through the work. Thus, an Itanium can process large databases and work with much larger amounts of memory than the 32-bit Intel chips commonly used in regular desktop systems.

PC vendors initially offered the Itanium machines in two basic configurations: workstation and server (both high end, meaning a lot of processing power). Workstations were fitted with a dual processor (two processors), whereas servers had four or more processors.

As for technical specs, the Itanium comes in 733MHz and 800MHz varieties. Those speeds seem slow, but with their 64-bit architecture they work just fine. Their external bus frequency is 266MHz, and they support up to 4MB of L3 cache in addition to the standard L1 (32KB) and L2 (96KB) caches. Perhaps the best feature of the Itanium is scalability (needed for large servers); it can scale to 512 processors.

The Itanium 2 is the bigger cousin of the Itanium. It's the same core design, with a few major improvements. Bus speed has been increased to 400MHz, allowing for a bandwidth of 6.4GB/s. Current speeds are 1.3 to 1.5GHz, and the Itanium 2 supports up to 6MB of L3 cache in addition to having 32KB L1 and 256KB L2 caches. This processor is designed to do one thing: eliminate the need for RISC chips.

Non-Intel Pentium Challengers: M1/M2, Nx586, K5/K6, C3, Athlon, Duron, and Opteron

For many years, chip companies competed with Intel by making clones of its chips. But the Pentium was a different story because its difference from the 486 wasn't tremendous—it's a fast chip, but it's not staggeringly faster than a 486. Add that to Intel's public relations disaster back in November 1994 over the Pentium's floating-point division problems (it was noted that math computations weren't being handled correctly), and computer manufacturers soon became more open to putting a non-Intel chip in their computers.

That was the opening needed to create Cyrix's M1, NexGen's Nx586, and AMD's K5. All three of these chips were intended to be "what the Pentium should have been." They were backward compatible with 486 software, but they all departed from the Pentium in slightly different ways.

Cyrix's 6x86

In October 1995, Cyrix announced the shipment of its rival to the Pentium, the 6x86 (formerly the M1). Although the 6x86 was a two-pipeline superscalar chip like the Pentium, the 6x86 offered a number of other features that were also offered by the Pentium Pro (released after the 6x86). However, the Cyrix 5x86, formerly known as the M1sc, wasn't a rival to the Pentium although the numbering scheme made it sound like it was. 5x86s were pin compatible with an Intel 486, 6x86s with a Pentium.

The 6x86 was a clock doubler or tripler, depending on the model. It stored calculation instructions and their results in a 16KB cache so that they could be called back into memory quickly, if necessary.

Cyrix also released the M2 processors, which were supposed to rival the Intel's Celeron processor line in power—but never rivaled them in terms of *selling* power.

AMD's K5/K6

The K5 was a fifth-generation processor offered by AMD. The K5 was distinct from AMD's 5x86, a souped-up version of the 486. The K5, a 64-bit version more like the Pentium, started shipping in June 1996. The K5's most salient feature was its four instruction pipelines, which are twice as many as the Pentium.

The biggest difference between the K5 and the Cyrix 6x86 was that the Cyrix chip was a Complex Instruction Set Chip (CISC) (an older approach to designing CPUs), whereas the K5 was a RISC chip (a newer approach). As such, the K5 had to translate the complex instructions it received to simpler ones that could execute more quickly.

The K6 series offered some substantial gains over the K5 and has proved to be AMD's most popular chip design thus far, particularly after AMD introduced 3DNow! Technology to enhance Web surfing and game playing, much as the PIII did (AMD released sooner). Because the K6 could be pushed in ways the PII and the PIII couldn't, and because it was priced below the PII/III, the K6-II and K6-III represented a major alternative for many users as well as PC manufacturers.

NexGen's Nx586

This chip was the oddball of the crowd. First of all, it didn't support floating-point operations, which made it incompatible even with some programs that ran on an 80486DX. Second, it wasn't pin compatible with the Pentium, which required designers to create a whole new motherboard to use it. Third, it ran at 4 volts, which didn't match the Pentium's 3.3-volt requirement.

NexGen rates chips not by their speed but by equivalent speeds for the Pentium. (The other non-Intel manufacturers do likewise.) For example, the 6x86 that was rated at 100MHz actually ran at 93MHz, but Cyrix claimed it performed equally to a Pentium at that speed, and some benchmarks bore that out.

NOTE *AMD now owns NexGen.*

VIA's C3

After several disappointing years (in terms of both chip development and sales), Cyrix looked to be down for the count. While AMD CPUs began to gain in overall popularity, Cyrix began to fade until 1999, when it was announced that VIA Technologies (the chipset manufacturer) would acquire the company and focus on making inexpensive alternatives to Intel chips. The latest VIA chip is the C3, formerly called the Cyrix III. (This chip was originally code-named Gobi, or Joshua.) The C3 builds upon the foundation Cyrix (pre-VIA) established with the M1 and M2.

The C3 is a Celeron-compatible chip with 128KB of L1 cache and a skimpy 64KB L2 cache. It uses a Socket 370 type connection, like the Celeron. Unlike the Celeron, the C3 supports enhanced 3DNow! Technology and has a much faster 133MHz front-side bus. The initial units that shipped ran at 533KHz, and VIA claims that the C3 is the "coolest processor on the market." (I assume they're talking about low heat radiation, as opposed to really fab looks!)

AMD's Athlon (K7)

The Athlon, first introduced in 1999, has sometimes been called the first PC processor AMD didn't design wholly in Intel's shadow. Like a few new processors before it, the Athlon CPU was available in some supply before the motherboards needed to support it.

Oh, there are big similarities to Intel's PII, PIII, and P4, and these are necessary, too, because you need to be able to run the same programs regardless of which PC processor is being used. Like the Pentiums, the Athlon is mounted on a module containing separate SRAM chips making up the L2 cache, with special connectors uniting the two. Also like the Pentiums, the Athlon offers a 512KB L2 cache that runs at half the speed of the processor itself.

But the differences are notable. First, the Athlon was designed around an entirely new processor core, uses a Socket A (rather than a Slot 1) socket, and offers a 200MHz front-side bus. The L1 cache is four times the size of what's available on a PIII, and an Athlon can decode any three x86 instructions at any given time. It also has the capability to dispatch up to nine internal instructions to its execution units per clock cycle, whereas a PIII can do just five. The Athlon is also credited with offering a better floating-point multiplying and adding capability for improved application and server performance, as well as enhanced gaming.

With the introduction of the new copper-interconnected Athlon, dubbed the Thunderbird, the integrated 256KB L2 cache runs at the full speed of the processor, instead of just half-speed. Thunderbird Athlons are smaller and faster than previous models, at a similar or slightly reduced cost.

AMD calls its latest Athlon chip the Athlon XP. The XP features what AMD calls *QuantiSpeed architecture*, which includes a fully pipelined microarchitecture and FPU, hardware prefetch, and Translation Look-Aside Buffers (TLBs), that prevents the processor from waiting when future data is requested. The XP is able to perform more calculations per second, thus boosting overall productivity from Thunderbird levels. (The XP designation is because AMD says the Athlon XP is ideally suited to run Windows XP—which means it's as much a marketing gimmick as anything else; AMD also changed the way they market their XP chips, no longer designating them by speed but instead by how they compare to similarly fast Intel chips.)

AMD's Duron

AMD's Duron chip is their competitor in the price-sensitive low end of the PC market. Price-wise, it competes directly with Intel's Celeron CPU although performance-wise it's right up there, in many ways, with the P4 and AMD's higher-priced Athlon chip.

Like the Athlon, the Duron fits into the Socket A socket. Its architecture is similar to the Athlon Thunderbird, except for a smaller 64KB L2 cache. It runs at a slightly lower voltage than the Thunderbird, so it runs a lot cooler than its big brother.

Comparing the Duron to Intel's Celeron, the Duron has a faster clock speed (200MHz versus 66MHz), larger L1 cache (128KB versus 32KB), and slightly smaller L2 cache (64KB versus 128/256KB). Its performance is actually closer to the Athlon/PIII/P4 level than it is to the Celeron, which makes it an excellent choice for budget-conscious consumers.

AMD's Opteron

Intel is desperately trying to crack the RISC market with its Itanium chip, so you'd expect the second largest PC chip manufacturer to follow suit. And they have. The Opteron is the latest offering from AMD, designed to go head to head with the Itanium in the battle to crush the RISC empire.

It's a true 64-bit processor that's backward compatible with existing 32-bit software. Here are some more of its features:

◆ Sixteen 64-bit integer registers

◆ Sixteen 128-bit SSE/SSE2 registers

◆ Three HyperTransport I/O links, each of which supports 6.4GB/ per second (3.2GB per second each way)

◆ 128KB L1 cache (64KB data cache and 64KB instruction cache)

◆ 1MB L2 cache

This powerhouse can perform two 64-bit operations per cycle with a three-cycle latency and is packaged in a 940-pin PGA package.

The battle is on between Opteron and Itanium; it remains to be seen who will come out on top.

PC Memory

If the processor is the most important component that plugs into the motherboard, then the memory is the second-most important. The processor does all of the thinking for a computer, and the memory holds information so that the processor can readily retrieve it.

Some people wonder why a computer has memory. After all, when you turn the power off, all information stored in memory is gone. Hard disks don't do that. Besides, for a comparable price, hard disks can store tons more data.

The answer is speed. RAM is measured in nanoseconds (billionths of seconds) whereas hard disk access times are measured in milliseconds (millionths of seconds). This might not seem like a huge difference; after all, humans can't really detect that small of a difference in time. But when it comes to computing, and considering that processors are capable of performing billions of steps per second, the time differential is huge. Without sufficient memory, applications will run slowly, if at all.

Memory is so important, in fact, that I've dedicated an entire chapter to it. Chapter 6, "System Memory," will give you more details about RAM than you ever probably wanted to know. But because this chapter is focusing on motherboards, it's a good idea to present the most important RAM/motherboard advice there is: make sure your RAM is compatible with your motherboard.

As you've learned by reading about processors, motherboards run at a certain frequency called a *bus speed*. Processors have to match the motherboard's speed (the processor's external bus speed) or they won't work together. The same holds true for RAM. If you have a 100MHz motherboard, you need 100MHz RAM.

To that end, many newer motherboards will support several speeds of RAM (such as 100MHz, 133MHz, 166MHz, 200MHz, 266MHz, 333MHz, 400MHz, and 533MHz). Check your motherboard's documentation to be sure. Even if your motherboard can support multiple speeds of RAM, however, you can't mix RAM in a computer. So if your board supports 400MHz and 533MHz, you can use one or the other, but not both at the same time.

Expansion Buses

"Pentium III 128MB system with 18GB drive and AGP video for sale," reads a computer ad. The Pentium part is clearly the processor. The 128MB is the RAM part, as you've just read, and everybody (well, anybody reading *this* book) knows what a hard disk is. But what's AGP? AGP is the name of one kind of *expansion bus*. What exactly an expansion bus *is*, why you want one, and why you have to worry about buses is the next topic.

What Is a Bus?

In order to be useful, the CPU must talk to memory, expansion boards, keyboard, and the like. It communicates with other devices on the motherboard via metal *traces* in the printed circuit, the copper lines that you'll see running around a board. That's how the Single Inline Memory Modules (SIMMs) or Dual Inline Memory Modules (DIMMs) that probably live on your computer's motherboard communicate with the CPU, which is *also* probably on your computer's motherboard—they talk back and forth by shooting electrons along these thin metal traces.

But how can *expansion boards*, which aren't part of the motherboard, be connected to the CPU, the memory, and so on? Through the *bus*—or rather, through one of the buses—modern computers may have multiple expansion buses. And what are buses? Buses relate back to electrical engineering (as a lot of computer terminology does), and the term refers to a set of wires, tracks, or conductors used to connect various parts of the PC.

Back in the early days of microcomputers, some computers didn't allow easy expansion. Take, for example, the early Macintosh computers. To expand a 128KB or 512KB Mac, you had to do some extensive engineering—which is why most people didn't mess around inside those computers. Any circuit boards that you wanted to add usually had to be mounted haphazardly inside the Mac's case; installing a hard disk required disassembling the computer, soldering connections onto the Mac motherboard, and reassembling the machine.

You don't have to do such brain surgery on a PC, thankfully. PCs have expansion slots that allow easy upgrades. (By the way, today's Macs also have expansion slots, fortunately; in fact, Macs built after 1995 have the same bus as some PCs, the PCI bus I'll discuss soon.)

Another disadvantage of the old Macintosh approach was that the average Joe/Jane couldn't do the modifications themselves. This would be like you having to cut a hole in the wall of your house to find a main power line every time you want to use an appliance. Without standard interface connectors (that is, an outlet), you'd have to find the power line and then splice the appliance into it to get power for the appliance.

This scenario, as you know, is silly because you have standard outlet plugs. But it wasn't always unthinkable; when electricity first arrived, adding every new appliance entailed some fancy wiring work. Nowadays, however, you have an easy, standard way to add appliances. Any manufacturer that wants to sell you a device requiring electrical power needs only to ensure that the device takes standard U.S. current and add a two-prong or three-prong plug. "Upgrading" your house (adding the new appliance) is then a simple matter: just "plug and play."

Many computers adopt a similar approach. Such computer manufacturers have issued a connector standard: any vendor desiring to offer an expansion board for this computer need only follow the connector specifications, and the board will work in the computer. Even the earliest computers included such a connector, first called the *omnibus connector*, because it gave access to virtually all important circuits in the computer. *Omnibus* was quickly shortened to *bus*, and *bus* it has remained.

So, a computer bus is an intrinsic part of a computer's hardware communication standard, an agreement about how to build boards that can work in a standard PC. For various reasons, however, there are more than a six such standards in the PC world.

The First "PC" Bus

The PC wasn't the first computer based on a chip, not by about eight years. The first commercially available microcomputer was a computer called the Altair. It consisted of a case and a row of expansion slots. It was a backplane computer, with even the CPU on an expansion card. The bus that the Altair used became a standard in the industry for years, and it's still used in some machines: it was called the S-100 or Altair bus.

Although it was a standard, it wasn't ever true that every microcomputer used the S-100. The Apple II used a bus of its own, called the *Apple bus*. The original 1981 PC model used yet another bus, with 62 wires called *lines*. It came to be known as (you can see that this is something of a pattern although a dull one) the *PC bus*.

The 62 lines are offered to the outside world through a standard connector, as mentioned previously. These connectors are also called *expansion slots* because expansion boards must plug into these slots. Some PCs have had no slots at all, so they aren't expandable; other machines have three, and most clone-type machines have eight slots. Some machines offer 10 slots. The more slots, the better: expansion slots equal flexibility and *upgradability*. Let's take a minute, however, and look at what those 62 lines do.

DATA PATH

Now, remember that the original PC and XT were based on the 8088 chip. The 8088 had a data path (the "front door," recall?) of just 8 bits, so the PC bus included only eight data lines. That means this bus was *8 bits wide*, and so data transfers could occur only in 8-bit chunks. Expansion slots on a computer with this bus were called *8-bit* slots. Eight of the 62 wires, then, transported data around the computer.

Consider the importance of data path in bus design. The 8 data bits supported by the original PC bus would be pretty inadequate for a Pentium-based system; recall that the Pentium uses a 64-bit data path.

Could someone actually *build* a Pentium computer with 8-bit expansion slots? Sure. But every time that the Pentium wanted to do a full 64-bit read of data, it would have to chop that request into eight separate 8-bit reads. *Really* slow. But it could be done, and in fact there are, as you'll learn later, designs almost as bad, including most P5- and P6-based systems (which incorporate a 16-bit bus to this day), the ISA bus you'll read about in a page or two, and a 32-bit bus called PCI.

MEMORY SIZE

The original PC bus included 20 wires to address memory. What did that mean to regular user types? Well, given that each one of those address wires can carry either a 0 or a 1 signal, then each wire can carry only one of two possible values. Because there are 20 of the address lines, the total number of possibilities is 2 2 2...20 times. That's 2 to the 20th power, or just more than 1 million. However, in a sense, you already knew that because the 8088 could address only 1MB of RAM. All those address lines are duplicated on the PC bus, accounting for another 20 of the 62 bus lines.

MEMORY OR I/O ADDRESS?

The 20 address lines actually did double duty because there are two kinds of addresses: the memory's addresses and *I/O addresses*. I'll discuss I/O addresses in greater detail in Chapter 5, "Installing New Circuit Boards." However, at this point I'll mention that the computer must be able to tell when the address lines are transmitting a memory address versus when the address lines are transmitting an I/O address; one line on the bus designates which one it is.

Additionally, there are several other lines on the bus that tell whether the data on the bus has been read from memory (or an I/O device) or whether data is to be written to memory or I/O.

ELECTRONIC OVERHEAD

Some bus wires just transport simple electric power; there are +5 volts, −5 volts, +12 volts, and electric ground lines as part of the bus. Why are those lines there? Simple: to power a board plugged into a bus slot.

There are also a few control lines, such as Reset (which, as you'd imagine, resets the processor), clock signals, and Refresh, which controls memory refresh (more on that in Chapter 6, "System Memory").

INTERRUPTS AND DIRECT MEMORY ACCESS CHANNELS

Add-in cards sometimes need to demand the attention of the CPU; they do that via hardware interrupts or Interrupt Request (IRQ) levels. There are six IRQ levels on the PC bus, labeled IRQ2 through IRQ7. Each gets a wire on the bus. There are also IRQ0 and IRQ1, but they're not available on the bus.

Some of those add-in cards also need to transfer data to the system's memory quickly; they can do that via a Direct Memory Access (DMA) channel. There are three DMA channels on the bus, labeled DMA1 through DMA3. There's also DMA channel 0, but, like IRQs 0 and 1, it's not accessible through the bus.

DMA and IRQs are both *extremely* important topics in PC upgrades, and I'll cover them in detail in Chapter 5.

I've given a somewhat in-depth look into the first PC bus so that you're ready to see why the many buses that followed are improvements on the original and to help you decide which bus is right for any of the machines that you buy.

The first enhancement to the PC bus came with the IBM AT; let's take a look at that bus.

The AT (ISA) Bus

When developing the AT, IBM saw that it had to upgrade the bus. One reason was because the 80286 is a chip with a 16-bit data path. They certainly *could* have designed the AT with an 8-bit bus, but it'd be a terrible shame to make a 286 chip transfer data 8 bits at a time over the bus, rather than utilize its full 16-bit data path. So they thought it'd be nice to have a 16-bit bus.

On the other hand, there was backward compatibility with the PC and XT to think of: it would be tough to sell a lot of ATs if they couldn't use the hardware (and software) of the existing, established PC/XT world. So IBM came up with a fairly good solution: they kept the old 62-line slot connectors and *added* another 36-wire connector, placing it in line with the older 62-line connector to provide some of these features:

◆ Eight more data lines, bringing the data bus to 16 bits in width.

◆ Four more address lines, bringing the address bus to 24 bits in width. Two to the 24th power is about 16 million, so the AT's 16-bit slots could support up to 16MB of RAM, in theory.

◆ Four more DMA channels, 4 through 7.

◆ Five more IRQ levels: IRQ10, 11, 12, 14, and 15. I'm getting a little ahead of myself, but I know that some of you will have an immediate question. You may know—and if not, you'll learn in Chapter 5—that there are *eight* more IRQs on a machine of this type, so why do you see only five on this newer bus slot? First, IRQ9 is wired where IRQ2 previously was, saving a bus line. What about IRQ2? It's off the bus now because it's the line that makes possible the new IRQ lines. Second, IRQ13 is dedicated to the math coprocessor, so there's no point in giving it any of the bus's wires. Finally, IRQ8 is connected to the system's clock/calendar, so it also does not require a line on the bus.

These two-part connectors are called, as you'd expect, *16-bit slots*. You can see these two kinds of connectors in Figure 2.9.

For a while, this 16-bit bus was called the AT bus, and you'll still hear some people use that name. Since 1988, however, most people have referred to these types of bus slots as *Industry Standard Architecture (ISA)* slots. You can tell the difference between an 8-bit and a 16-bit ISA board by looking at the edge connector on the bottom of it. Take a look at an 8-bit board, as you see in Figure 2.10.

FIGURE 2.9
8-bit and 16-bit bus slots

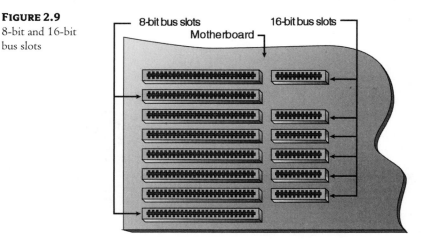

Notice that it has a single edge connector on the bottom. In contrast, look at a 16-bit board, like the one in Figure 2.11.

Because the 16-bit slots are just a superset of the 8-bit bus, 8-bit boards work just fine in 16-bit slots, which is a good thing—no modern PCs I know of have the simple 8-bit slots. However, almost all *do* have the 16-bit slots, making 8-to-16 compatibility good in the unlikely case you have an old 8-bit board around that you want to use.

Years ago, you'd sometimes see a motherboard with both 8-bit slots and 16-bit slots. If the 16-bit slots can use 8-bit boards, why have any 8-bit slots on an AT-type machine at all? The reason isn't an electrical reason but a physical reason. Some older 8-bit boards have a *skirt* that extends down and back on the circuit board, making it physically impossible to plug an 8-bit board with a skirt into a 16-bit connector. You can see a board with a skirt in Figure 2.12.

ISA has continued on systems for backward compatibility. Even if you use some of the latest equipment on your PC, some of you still have ISA sound cards and even modems and network cards either installed or sitting around as a backup.

But all reigns must come to an end, and ISA's time has come. ISA is being eliminated in an effort to finally move away from the antiquated slowness of the bus and to make room for USB and FireWire, but design specifications continue to support slower serial and parallel ports.

FIGURE 2.10
8-bit board

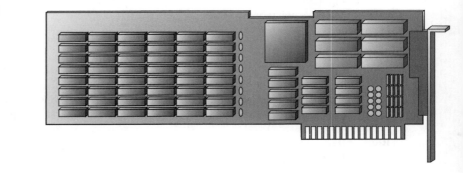

FIGURE 2.11
16-bit board

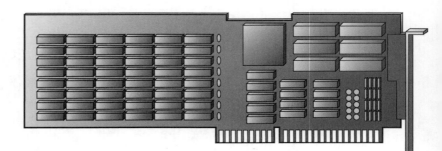

FIGURE 2.12
8-bit board
with a skirt

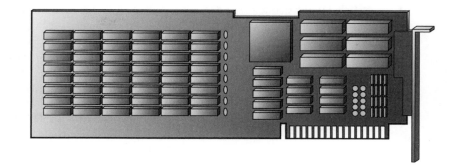

Since January 1, 2000, ISA slots can't be manufactured into a motherboard on a system that will bear the "certified Windows compatible" logo, as pronounced by the Microsoft-Intel PC design specifications. Even as Linux becomes more of a player in the PC world, Windows certification is important if you want to sell PCs.

JUST HOW FAST IS THAT BUS?

You learned back in the CPU section that different CPUs run at different speeds. You can't take a CPU rated to run at 25MHz and run it at 66MHz; it will fail. (You can *try*—recall that it's called *overclocking*—but it's not a good idea.)

Buses have clocks, as well, and those clocks drive the boards inserted into their expansion slots. That suggests a question: how is it that any board pretty much works in any kind of computer? Why does an ISA video board built for a 12MHz computer still work in a 400MHz PII?

Part of the answer, you'll recall, is that the 400MHz PII looks like a 100MHz chip from the motherboard's point of view; the 400MHz part is internal to the CPU chip. So the fastest bus you'd need for a 400MHz Pentium would be 100MHz. But for the rest of the story, let's return to 1985.

EARLY BUSES EQUALED CLOCK RATES

Prior to 1985, buses ran at the same speed as their CPUs. The PC ran at 4.77MHz, and so did the PC bus. Turbo XT clones that ran at 7.16MHz had buses that ran at 7.16MHz. When IBM released the 6MHz AT, then its bus ran at 6MHz, and so on.

But all this variation in bus speeds led to a major headache for expansion board buyers. A board designed for the 4.77MHz PC might not (and often *did* not) work in the faster machines. Part of a PC upgrader's job was to know which PC bus speeds a particular board would work in.

COMPAQ TRIES NOT TO MISS THE BUS

Then Compaq released its Deskpro 286/12.

In 1985, IBM was selling the AT, as you've already read. The fastest version ran at 8MHz. Compaq, as the number-one IBM cloner, decided to seriously outpace IBM with their new Deskpro 286/12—the 12 stood for 12MHz.

Now, okay, 12MHz isn't such a big deal nowadays. But back then, it was like Compaq today offering a Pentium that runs at 80GHz. Nobody else even came close. But what to do about the bus? If they built a 12MHz 286 computer with a 12MHz bus, then in all probability no existing boards would work. Who'd buy a fast computer that wouldn't work with any of the add-in boards on the market?

Compaq's answer: decouple the main clock from the bus clock. They ran the CPU and much of the motherboard at 12MHz but ran the bus at only 8MHz. Expansion boards sitting in slots would see only an 8MHz environment, so the new Deskpro could be both fast *and* compatible. And ever since, that's how everybody has built their ISA slots, at 8MHz. That's why you never have to worry about whether your computer is too slow for a particular board; from the board's point of view, every computer—including yours—runs at 8MHz. This *sounds* good, but....

The big drawback in having the expansion bus run at a separate clock speed than the external CPU bus is that some boards *should* run at CPU speed, such as memory boards. Imagine that you have a 100MHz Pentium. It communicates with its motherboard at 66MHz because it's a clock-and-a-half-fer. Suppose you want to put more memory on this system, so you buy an ISA memory card. (You can't, actually—they've been obsolete for ages. This is just an example.) You pop it into one of the computer's 16-bit slots, and you'll extend your memory, but *all memory accesses will be at 8MHz, not 66MHz*; every time you access memory on that board, your system will slow down to 8MHz. Yuck. And many of us use ISA boards on a daily basis to talk to our hard disks, video monitors, and Local Area Networks (LANs). This is a major reason why we need something other than the ISA bus as a standard and why there are so many kinds of alternative buses available.

ISA's Not Enough: Local Bus

The first folks to try to set a new bus standard were, again, Compaq, a year later.

In 1986, Compaq introduced one of the first 80386-based desktop computers. Because the 80386DX is a 32-bit chip, Compaq wanted to exploit that power with a new bus slot. Remember, *they* were the ones who saddled us with the 8MHz bus slots in the first place. Standard-speed bus slots were still a good idea, but how do you offer memory expansion boards that were 32-bit in data path and 16MHz (the computer's clock rate) in speed, unless by building an entirely new bus?

Compaq decided to just include a new 32-bit slot on the motherboard, a slot solely for use with a specific memory card that Compaq (and later, third-party vendors) sold. Some 386 cloners adopted this new bus format, but it never really caught on. Instead, each vendor developed its own 32-bit "standard." Intel had one it pushed for a while in the late '80s, AT&T had another, Micronics a fourth, and so on.

These buses all had several things in common:

♦ They had a 32-bit data path.

♦ They ran at the clock speed of the 386 computer—usually 16MHz, 20MHz, 25MHz, or 33MHz.

♦ They supported only one particular board, sold by the motherboard's manufacturer.

These buses came to be known as *private* buses or, later, *local* buses, because they were "local" to the processor because there was no extra clock circuitry between them and the CPU. From 1986 to 1991, the main value of local bus boards and slots was, again, to accommodate memory for their specific computer. These were the remote ancestors of what we now call the VESA Local Bus (VLB) standard.

The PS/2 Bus: Micro Channel Architecture (MCA)

Not to be outdone by Compaq in the trend-setting department, IBM attempted to change the rules again in 1987 when they announced the PS/2 line. The PS/2 models 50 to 80 (*not* the 25 or 30) got a new bus called the Micro Channel Architecture (MCA) bus in order to facilitate faster data transfer within the computer and to lower noise levels. (ISA is a *very* noisy standard, which is another reason why it hasn't gotten faster over the years.) It didn't catch on, but IBM pushed it doggedly for years before surrendering in the mid-'90s.

Introducing a new bus was a bold move (although perhaps not a bright one) in that the MCA bus was completely *incompatible* with the old ISA bus. ISA expansion boards didn't (and *don't*) work in the PS/2 line. PS/2 buyers had to be sure when buying a board that it was an MCA board, not an ISA board, because the ISA boards were completely useless in MCA machines.

What prompted this bold move? Well, some of the things I've already discussed and a few others. MCA never really caught on that strongly (and I'll talk about why that's true in a minute), but some of the features it offered have become essential for any advanced bus.

BETTER SPEED AND DATA PATH

As you'd expect, MCA tried to better ISA by hitting its weak points. MCA ran at 10MHz, not 8MHz. This isn't a great improvement but an improvement. MCA also supported either a 16-bit data path or a 32-bit data path. It actually had a streaming mode, wherein it could transfer 64 bits at a time.

SOFTWARE BOARD CONFIGURATION

Anyone who has installed an older ISA board (installation of boards is, again, the main topic for Chapter 5) has almost certainly struggled with small DIP switches and jumpers. These small hardware devices are used to configure older ISA boards. They're a pain in the neck because they're often hard to change around, and you have to remove the PC's cover to get to them in the first place.

Micro Channel boards, in contrast, were software configurable—no jumpers and no DIP switches. You just ran one central configuration program, and you could set up a computer by clicking with the mouse, rather than rooting around in the machine. This is a feature that was useful when it came out, but it's *essential* now—which is why Plug and Play (PnP) hardware is today's standard.

BOARDS CAN SHARE INTERRUPTS

Once you start configuring boards, you'll find the thing you're running out of most is interrupt levels. You can't put a mouse card on the same IRQ level as your LAN board, or your network connection could crash the first time you move the mouse. That's because of how ISA was designed.

With MCA, it was *possible* to design a board that shares its interrupts with other boards. Very few Micro Channel boards *did* share interrupts, but it's possible. Why? Blame the people who write drivers. Even though several buses now support interrupt sharing, it's still almost unheard of, even in the most modern systems.

BUS MASTERING IMPROVES UPON DMA

I haven't explained DMA in detail yet, but it's basically a way for expansion boards to quickly transfer data from themselves to the system's RAM or from the RAM to the boards.

DMA's main goal in life is speed: it makes the PC faster.

DMA can't do one thing, however. Boards can transfer data directly to RAM or from RAM to boards, but *not* from boards to boards. That's handled by a kind of "super" DMA called *bus mastering*. Bus mastering wasn't really supported by ISA (you can have one, but only one, bus master card in an entire ISA machine), but MCA supported bus mastering.

Bus mastering is another one of those features that first appeared with MCA but is *de rigueur* for any modern advanced bus.

MCA was neat because it was cleaner, as I said before, so it could transfer data at higher speeds than the ISA machines of a few years back. (I said "could" because it has the capability, but that capability never became important in its market.) It also included something called Programmable Option Select (POS). It allowed circuit boards to be a lot smarter about how they interact with the computer. For one thing, DIP switch and configuration problems lessened considerably. You'll find more on this in Chapter 5.

Extended Industry Standard Architecture (EISA)

Unfortunately, MCA turned out to be pretty unimportant in the market, mainly because IBM locked it up six ways to Sunday, patent-wise. Companies couldn't clone the MCA without paying a Draconian *5 percent* of their *gross* to IBM as fealty (oops, that's supposed to be *royalties*) for use of MCA. Five percent of gross is probably more than most companies are making as *profits*. For the 5 percent, you didn't even get the plans for MCA. *First* you had to spend hundreds of thousands of dollars figuring out how to clone MCA—IBM offered no help—*then* you got to pay Big Blue the 5 percent.

So Compaq talked eight other compatible makers (a group called Watchzone—Wyse, AST, Tandy, Compaq, Hewlett-Packard, Zenith, Olivetti, NEC, and Epson) into forming a joint venture to respond to MCA. They created yet another new bus, the Extended Industry Standard Architecture (EISA), which was intended to have MCA's good features without sacrificing compatibility with the old AT (ISA) bus. Presumably, building it cost less than 5 percent of profits. It appeared in 1989 and still shows up on the motherboards of some systems that include both PCI and EISA slots.

EISA never got amazingly popular, but it was a kind of well-designed, solid bus that found its way into a lot of high-end servers. It was gaining some momentum around the mid-'90s, but it was overtaken by the newer, more powerful PCI standard.

What about EISA's features? Summarized, they include the following:

- 32-bit data path

- Enough address lines for 4GB of memory

- More I/O addresses, 64KB of them

- Software setup capability for boards, so no jumpers or DIP switches—similar to POS

- 8MHz clock rate (unfortunately)

- No more interrupts or DMA channels

- Supports cards that are physically large, making them cheaper to build (smaller cards cost more to design)

- Bus mastering

Note that EISA *isn't* a local bus because it runs at 8MHz. It runs at that poky speed because it must be, recall, hardware compatible with ISA, hence the need for slow bus slots. EISA will also run DMA at higher speeds than will ISA. The lack of local bus means, however, that EISA memory boards aren't a possibility. EISA machines need enough SIMM space on the motherboard for sufficient memory, or the motherboard vendor must design a proprietary expansion slot for a proprietary memory card. EISA boards remain supported for use, but it's not a future standard.

Local Bus

In the XT and AT days, you expanded memory just by buying a memory expansion card, putting memory chips on it, and inserting the card into one of the PC's expansion slots. But by the time that PCs got to 12MHz, that easy answer disappeared. As I've already said, no matter how fast your PC is, the expansion slots still run at only 8MHz.

Now, I've been kind of beating up on slow buses, but they're not all *that* bad, in reality. Most boards in expansion slots communicate with components that are fairly slow anyway, such as floppy drives, printer ports, modems, and the like.

Only a handful of boards benefit from really high speeds. I've mentioned memory. Another board that really needs to be able to blitz data around is a video graphics board. Take a moment and calculate how many pixels (dots on the screen) you have on a 1024 768 video screen. Then consider that the CPU must shove them around perhaps dozens of times per second, and you can see that having fast access to the video board is a good thing.

Hard disk interfaces benefit from high speed and, in particular, Small Computer System Interface (SCSI) hard disk interfaces. Video capture boards are another type of fast board, and LAN cards are yet another candidate for local busing.

PCI: Today's Bus

The PC world needed a better bus because without a better bus, there wasn't all that much sparkle in new CPUs. Intel was aware of this and was worried. Less sparkly new systems meant fewer new systems *sold*, and that meant fewer CPUs sold. Whatever hurts the PC world hurts Intel sales, so Intel designed an even newer, faster bus slot called PCI. PCI is a good bus for several reasons, which are outlined in the following paragraphs. You can see a PCI board in Figure 2.13 and a PCI bus slot in Figure 2.14. The smaller and lighter-colored (usually white or cream or gray) slots are the PCI slots; the larger and darker (black or charcoal gray) slots next to them are ISA slots.

PROCESSOR INDEPENDENCE

The PCI bus doesn't directly interface with the CPU. Rather, it communicates with the CPU via a *bridge circuit* that can act as a buffer between the specifics of a particular CPU and the bus. If you've ever looked at Device Manager in Windows and wondered what the heck a PCI bridge is, this is it.

What does that mean? It means really good news for non-PC computer users. Macintosh PCs and RISC-based machines such as the DEC Alpha are now coming out with PCI slots. That means a bigger market for PCI boards and an avenue for board makers to reach the PC, Mac, and RISC markets with a single board.

FIGURE 2.13
PCI board

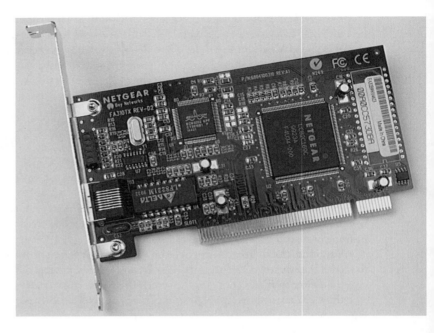

FIGURE 2.14
PCI and ISA
bus slots

WIDER DATA PATH

PCI distinguishes itself first because it's a 64-bit bus. PCI supports a data path appropriate for the newer Pentium-based computers, which require 64 bits at each clock cycle. PCI also supports a 32-bit data path, however, so it was used in some of the last 486 systems to be manufactured.

HIGH SPEED

Like VLB, PCI originally was developed to run to 33MHz. This made the net throughput of a PCI bus as large as 132Mbps with a 32-bit board or 264Mbps with a 64-bit board. That's one of the bonuses of PCI: it can be configured as both a 32-bit as well as a 64-bit bus, and both 32-bit and 64-bit boards can be used in either.

In 1998, with the adoption of a new specification, the PCI bus moved to 66MHz. When 64-bit PCI devices are used at 66MHz, the throughput increases to 524Mbps. For the most part, 32-bit PCI devices and 64-bit devices are interchangeable (some types of BIOS types differentiate between the two under CMOS setup). (CMOS stands for *complementary metal oxide semiconductor*.) Some nonstandard equipment, usually off brand, has presented some difficulties in configuration and use for the common user, but it has been, overall, one of the smoother transitions. The 66MHz PCI cards fit fine into the older PCI buses; they just won't operate at 66MHz. Meanwhile, 33MHz PCI boards go right into the newer motherboards, operating as their standard 32-bit selves.

Part of the changes in hardware over the past few years have centered around how to leave behind some of the slower buses and architecture to more adequately embrace faster technology and devices. Both USB and FireWire/IEEE 1394 are part of that move.

PC manufacturers also wanted to extend the PCI bus to give it more longevity and usefulness (and at lower cost than FireWire), in a specification referred to as *PCIx*, or PCI Extended. However, don't look for PCIx devices (with their estimated throughput of up to 1Gbps) to appear in your next bargain PC system. PCIx is pretty much reserved for more serious business use, on servers and high-end workstations. It may filter down to the more modest system at a later time, but by then, you'll probably all be using FireWire and USB 2.

BACKWARD COMPATIBILITY

Although ISA or EISA boards can't fit in PCI slots, the common chipsets that support PCI also support ISA and EISA. That means it's easy to build a PC with PCI, ISA, and EISA slots all on the same motherboard. Typical motherboard configurations either support PCI and ISA or PCI and EISA. For some reason, the PCI/ISA motherboards support only a single processor, and in general the PCI/EISA motherboards support multiple processors. There's no engineering reason for that; it's just that the Intel chipsets for single-processor systems support PCI/ISA, and the Intel chipsets for multiprocessor systems support PCI/EISA. Nowadays, almost all motherboard makers use the Intel chipsets.

BUS MASTERING

Like EISA and Micro Channel—and *unlike* VLB—PCI supports bus master adapter boards, paving the way for the "community" of processors I referred to earlier.

Non-bus-mastered data transfers require a lot of the CPU's time. For example, a coworker of mine reported that a file transfer via an Ethernet network required more than 40 percent CPU utilization when the Ethernet card was ISA but only 6 percent with a similar setup and a PCI Ethernet card. Bus mastering is a good idea, and it's discussed in more detail in Chapter 6.

SOFTWARE SETUP

PCI supports the PnP standard developed in 1992 by hardware vendors. There are, in general, no jumpers or DIP switches on PCI boards. There usually isn't even a board-specific configuration program. PCI setup is terrific on a PnP system, but it can be a bit challenging on a non-PnP system. There's an extensive discussion of that in Chapter 5.

PCI is a good architecture, and building PCI boards is relatively cheap. That's no doubt why it has become the premier PC bus.

Accelerated Graphics Port (AGP): Local Bus Returns

The original 33MHz bus was the VLB bus. And what created the driving need for a fast bus? Video. The two things that *always* seem to drive demand for faster buses are memory and video. For example, 33MHz was a pretty fast speed for a video board back when CPUs ran at 50MHz and 66MHz. Of course, they soon ran faster than that, so it shouldn't be any surprise that video is again screaming for more speed.

This time, however, Intel wanted to be out in front and so, before some competitor could come up with a faster bus for graphics, Intel did. The AGP bus accomplishes two things:

◆ It's four to eight times faster than PCI for transferring data. CPUs on systems with AGP video boards can, then, blast video images to their video board pretty quickly.

◆ It enables a video board to supplement its own video memory with some system memory.

Think of AGP as just the latest local bus. In addition to speed, AGP allows a CPU to put a bitmap into regular old system memory and then be able to directly use and display that bitmap for the video board. You can see an AGP bus slot in Figure 2.15. The AGP slot is the one that's darker (usually brown) and slightly "offset" from the other, lighter PCI slots.

FIGURE 2.15
AGP slot

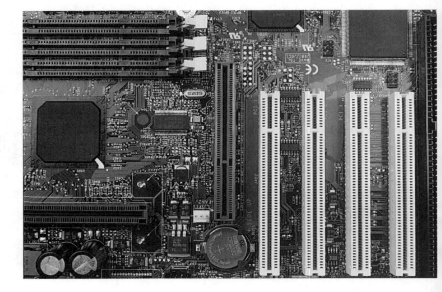

Intel clearly wants this bus to be a special-purpose bus. AGP motherboards have only one AGP slot, and as far as I can see, the chipsets allow only one AGP board. That's kind of a shame. In the past, new local buses *started* out as video or memory buses, but then SCSI host adapter vendors or other clever folks used the faster slots to do new and interesting things. More and more "interesting things" created a demand for faster buses, and soon large manufacturers responded with a new general-purpose bus. (That's how PCI appeared.) Because there's only one AGP slot essentially by definition, I suppose AGP won't turn out to be an intermediate step to a faster general-purpose bus.

When AGP first came out in wide market distribution in 1998, its speed (1 or 2) was limited by other components on a PC system. The greatest issue was overall bandwidth. But changes to overall system speed, and the new forms of memory I've discussed, have finally allowed the production of 8 AGP cards. These new 8 AGP cards fit fine into existing AGP ports for 1 and 2 cards, but you won't have the speed and features over 1/2 unless you have a sufficient system—including a motherboard/ BIOS updated for 8—to handle it.

NOTE   *The AGP 8 standard supports data transfers of up to 2.1 GB per second.*

PC Card (PCMCIA): The Portable Bus

Laptop computers are an absolute must for traveling professionals and are now being sold more frequently than desktops. Laptops are great because they're almost 100-percent software compatible with their bigger cousins, the desktop machines.

Thankfully, lower prices on laptops have allowed more people to become mobile with their computers, but laptops still generally have a fairly short life expectancy because they're much more likely to break (being dropped, jarred in transit, you name it) and because laptop theft has become a significant issue. However, the PC Card (called PCMCIA before 1995) helps to remove objections relating to upgradability, and the big 17-inch Liquid Crystal Display (LCD) screens on some laptops make working on a laptop not much different from working on a desktop system.

Over the years, it's been customary to add memory, modems, network adapters, FireWire adapters, and other communications extensions to laptops. But, because laptops never had standard expansion slots, laptop owners had to buy proprietary memory from laptop vendors—often an expensive proposition. But cost wasn't the worst part of this lack of a standard bus; in fact, cost was less important than the fact that lack of a standard bus led to the lack of a *market* for add-in boards for laptops.

Japanese vendors of memory products tried to address this problem in the late '80s by founding the Personal Computer Memory Card Industry Association, or, in its hard-to-remember acronym form, PCMCIA. (The head of the group once said, "If we'd have known how important the acronym would be, we would have picked another name." Some people just remember People Can't Memorize Computer Industry Acronyms.) After a few years of apologetic wincing, the association renamed the bus the "PC Card" bus; people still say PCMCIA, however, so you'll hear both names. A PC Card/ PCMCIA board is about the size of a credit card, but a bit thicker.

TYPE 1, TYPE 2, AND TYPE 3 PC CARD SLOTS

The standard proved extremely popular—so popular, in fact, that hardware vendors said to the PCMCIA, "Why not also support modems or hard disks?" So the memory card interface became a "PC Card Type 1 slot." A Type 1 (or *release 1* in some references) slot is 3.3-millimeters (mm) thick, with a 68-pin connector. Many Type 1 cards are memory cards, either standard RAM or "flash" memory cards loaded with a piece of software.

The need for internal modems drove the Type 2 slots. While developing Type 2, an important software standard called Card Services and Socket Services was developed—more on that later. Type 2 cards can be designed to act as an object placed directly into the PC's memory address space. Why is this different from Type 1 cards? If you bought a software-on-a-card Type 1 card, then the PC would have to copy the data from the Type 1 card into the PC's memory before it could run the software on the card. That took time *and* used up some of the PC's memory. With Type 2, that's not necessary, making startup faster and increasing the amount of free memory available. Type 2 cards are 5mm thick, allowing more space for more complex circuitry. Type 1 cards will work in Type 2 slots. Figure 2.16 shows some PC Cards.

FIGURE 2.16
PC Cards

Shortly after, the PCMCIA defined a Type 3 specification, one flexible enough to support removable hard disks. The main difference of Type 3 is that it's a lot thicker—Type 3 cards can be 10.5mm thick. Most laptops have room for either two Type 2 cards or a single Type 3. When purchasing Type 3 cards, be sure that what you're buying meets the standard—there are so-called "Type 3" hard disks that are 13mm thick. Xircom has also made a cool combination modem/Ethernet card that has the connectors right on it. The connectors made it thicker, so they went to a Type 3 form factor. Yes, it takes up both slots, but it's convenient not to have to carry cables around to attach to the card.

SOCKET AND CARD SERVICES

The PC Card standard supports the capability to remove and install a PC Card *on-the-fly*. All other buses require that you power down the computer before installing or removing a card, but PC Card supports *hot swapping*—the capability to swap a card while the computer is running. The computer supports this capability with two levels of software support:

Socket services   The PCMCIA name for the BIOS-like software that handles the low-level hardware calls to the card. They're loaded like a device driver. The latest version of the PC Card Standard (8.0) allows you to swap cards without powering down.

Card services   A higher-layer set of routines that manage how the PC Card memory areas map into the CPU's memory area. They also provide a high-level interface supporting simple commands that are common to almost all PC Cards, commands such as ERASE, COPY, READ, and WRITE data.

In Windows 3.*x* and Windows NT, you usually have to reboot in order to enable or disable a PC Card. Starting with Windows 95, however, you can change most PC Cards at will, using them and removing them without rebooting.

PC CARD FEATURES

Let's compare PC Cards to the other buses I've discussed, feature for feature (see Table 2.4).

TABLE 2.4: PC CARD FEATURES

FEATURE	RELATIONSHIP TO PC CARD
Memory address space	The PC Card supports a 64MB addressing capability. (This is because the bus uses 26 bits for addressing, and two to the 26th power is about 64 million.) This will be adequate for current machines but will look sparse in a few years as more demanding operating systems such as Windows 2003 become more popular.
Bus mastering	The PC Card doesn't support bus mastering or DMA.
PnP setup	The PC Card not only allows—but requires—that hardware setups be done with software. Because of the physical size of a PC Card, you'll never see jumpers or DIP switches.
Number of PC Card slots possible in a single system	Most of the other buses support no more than 16 slots. The PC Card standard can, theoretically, support 4080 PC Card slots on a PC. In reality, most laptops have only two Type 2 slots.
Data path	The data path for the PC Card is only 16 bits, a real shame, but one that's fixed in a later version of the PC Card is the CardBus.
Speed	Like other modern bus standards, the PC Card is limited to a 33MHz clock rate.

Years ago, it seemed to me that the smaller size of PC Cards, coupled with their low power usage, made the new bus quite attractive not only for laptops but also for the so-called "green" PCs, desktop computers designed to use as little power as possible. I figured that for that reason, PC Cards could become an important *desktop* standard as well as a laptop standard. That didn't happen in the desktop world, but in the laptop world, be *sure* that whatever new laptop you buy has at least two Type 2 PC Card slots. Or, even better, if it's a relatively new laptop, make sure it's got two CardBus slots.

Mini PCI (Portable PCI)

Are you asking yourself, "Okay, why are we going back into PCI when we're in the middle of discussing PC Card information?" Because this is a special form of PCI device, with a much smaller form factor (actually, multiple small form factors), designed specifically for laptops and other portable devices.

Mini PCI devices are small (for example, 45-by-70-by-5.5mm for Type IB) internal expansion cards used for communications—either a modem or a network interface card. You won't see Mini PCI video cards, for instance.

This technology offers some nice advantages over the PC Card. First, because they're smaller, they're cheaper to manufacture (PC Card technology still isn't cheap). Second, with such limited PC Card expansion in laptops, using Mini PCI frees up a PC Card slot for other needs. The Mini PCI specification also eliminates the need for dongles and proprietary I/O connectors.

Best of all, however, Mini PCI doesn't need any special extras in order to be recognized by, or work with, your PC operating system. Your operating system should recognize the Mini PCI card as any other PCI device and work with it without a hitch. This is because Mini PCI is the functional equivalent of standard PCI, using the 32-bit PCI local bus and the same PCI BIOS/driver interface.

CardBus

First specified back in 1994, this is *PC Card: The Next Generation*. CardBus slots' main claim to fame is that they have a 32-bit data path rather than a 16-bit data path. They're also backward compatible: a CardBus slot can accommodate a PC Card without trouble. Other features include the following:

- They run at lower voltage—3.3 volts and lower, compared to 5 volts and lower for PC Cards.

- They can transfer data at up to 133Mbps (megabits per second)—they're 4 bytes wide and run up to 33MHz.

- In theory, you can do bus mastering and actually have a CPU on the CardBus card although I haven't seen that in any cards yet.

If your laptop supports CardBus, buy CardBus cards when possible. I've run 100Mb Ethernet with both PC Card and CardBus boards, and the CardBus is noticeably faster. But be sure your operating system supports CardBus. (Fortunately, just about all CardBus cards work under Windows 98/2000/XP.)

Table 2.5 summarizes the differences between the buses.

TABLE 2.5: BUS TYPES

BUS TYPE	MAXIMUM SPEED	NUMBER OF DATA BITS	NUMBER OF ADDRESS BITS	SOFTWARE SETUP?	BUS MASTER?
PC bus	10MHz (on some clones)	8	20	No	No
ISA bus	8MHz, faster on some clones	16	24	No	Only on one board
MCA	8MHz	32	32	Yes	Yes
VESA	33MHz	32	32	No	No
EISA	8MHz	32	32	Yes	Yes
PC Card	33MHz	16	26	Yes	No
PCI	33MHz	32	32	Yes	Yes
CardBus	33MHz	32	32	Yes	Yes
AGP	66MHz	32	32	Yes	Yes
Mini PCI	33MHz	32	32	Yes	No

System Controllers

Closely related to buses are controllers. While the bus refers to the path taken by data going between components, the *controller* is the device that allows the peripheral to communicate with the rest of the computer. In most cases, the term *controller* also refers to the place you plug something in. For example, most people refer to an Integrated Drive Electronics (IDE) controller as the IDE connector on the motherboard, even though most IDE hard disks have their controllers built in. The term is a common way to designate connectors, and there's nothing really wrong with that.

Along the same lines, there tends to be a blurred differentiation between buses and controllers. For example, take the USB standard. Is it a bus or a controller? Obviously, its name indicates it's a bus, which it is. But at the same time, you plug your USB devices into the USB controller, so in a way it's both. The same holds true for the FireWire/IEEE 1394 standard.

Don't worry so much about the semantics, though. You can tell someone to plug a keyboard into the USB port, the USB controller, the USB bus, or the "little USB thingy"; all the terms pretty much refer to the same thing—colloquially, at least.

Without further ado then, this section dovetails with the bus section and examines controllers you need to know about.

What's a Controller?

Every peripheral device, whether internal or external, needs something to handle communications between it and the computer. These items are called *controllers*, *interfaces*, *ports*, or *adapters*. For example, a hard disk needs a hard disk controller, the keyboard needs a keyboard controller, and the video display needs a video adapter (controller). The main reason that controllers exist is to perform these tasks:

◆ Allow for well-defined industry standards (well, *fairly* well-defined industry standards) by creating a specification that all controller boards are designed to fit and operate in

◆ Match data transfer speeds between peripherals and the CPU

◆ Convert data from the CPU's format to what the peripheral uses, as well as amplify the electronic signals between CPU and peripheral

Adaptec's 2942W PCI SCSI bus mastering host adapter is as different from IBM's original XT-type hard drive controller as a Corvette is from a Chevette, but 99 percent of the software that was written to work with the latter works just fine (or better) with the former. The underlying hardware is a lot better, and a lot *different*, so you'd imagine there would be big compatibility problems, but the hardware has been configured to respond to CPU requests in the same manner (although faster) as the old Xebec-designed IBM controller. Ditto video controllers designed by ATI or Paradise: they respond to the same software as IBM's original CGA, EGA, or VGA but are cheaper and generally work faster. Using controllers with well-defined interfaces makes building compatible hardware possible.

Remember that notion of well-defined interfaces: together, all these interfaces define what is called *PC compatible*.

Most peripherals are considerably slower than the CPU in transferring data. Even the hard disk, for example, is thousands of times slower than the CPU. Most microcomputers (such as the PC) have been designed to control everything in their systems, to do *all* the computing work, but that's not necessary. One of the first examples of an all-encompassing microcomputer appeared with a company named Cogent Data Systems. Years ago, they made a hard disk controller for AT-class machines with memory and a microprocessor right on it: the main CPU just makes a request of the hard disk controller, then (with the right software) goes off to do something else while waiting for the controller to do the job. Eventually, the controller informs the CPU that it's finished with the data request and that in fact the controller has already transferred the data into the CPU's memory. Truthfully, the "speed matching" benefits of controllers haven't been really exploited in the PC world yet because intra-PC *distributed computing* doesn't really exist yet—again, *yet*. The power of advanced buses such as PCI was supposed to change that, but the change is coming slowly—partially because board designers tend to keep doing the same thing over and over again and partially because Intel encourages people to put work on the CPU's shoulders. That way, consumers will demand faster and faster CPUs or multi-CPU systems.

Another controller function is simple amplification. The CPU speaks its own electrical language to other chips on the motherboard. But it's a language without too much power—a CPU wouldn't be able to "shout" loudly enough to be heard any appreciable distance on a LAN. Devices such as video monitors need signals massaged into forms they can use. Again, controllers serve this function.

A typical system will have a controller for the keyboard, a controller for the video display, controllers for the disk drives, and interface controllers for a keyboard and mouse, parallel and serial ports, and perhaps even a network adapter.

Controllers Aren't Always Separate Boards

Here's a common misconception: a controller must be on a board all its own.

Not at all. The keyboard controller is generally not a board; it's just a chip on the motherboard. The hard and floppy disk controllers *used* to reside on separate boards in XT-type machines. Then, the earliest AT-class machines put the hard disk controller and the floppy controller on the same board. Another board held the parallel port, another the serial ports, yet another the joystick, and so on. Nowadays, motherboards incorporate nearly all of those functions and more in a single extremely integrated circuit board. These integrated motherboards can be terrific values in terms of price and performance.

Let's take a quick look at the common controllers in the system.

Video Adapter

To allow the computer to communicate with a display monitor, either an integrated display adapter is used or an adapter card must be inserted in one of the PC's expansion slots. Also, you'll hear *video adapter, display adapter,* and *video card* used interchangeably. They all mean the same thing.

The basic kind of video board you find in the PC world even to this day is an enhancement of an old 1987 video standard called the Video Graphics Array, (VGA). It can display information either in a text-only form or in a graphical form.

Why is a 15-plus-year-old standard still current? Mainly because of the lack of a market leader. For years, graphical standards were created by IBM, video boards with names such as MDA, CGA, PGA, 8514, EGA, and the now-common VGA. You can see a video board in Figure 2.17.

FOR THOSE WHO'VE READ EARLIER EDITIONS...

You may be raising your eyebrows at that previous comment. What am I doing singing the praises of integrated motherboards? Didn't I once warn readers away from them? Yes, that's true: I *used* to be very much opposed to putting everything on the motherboard. So why the change?

Well, I *like* integrated motherboards now for the same reason I disliked them before: compatibility. Nowadays there's an informal standard for these "do-it-all" motherboards; you can easily find a replacement motherboard for your Acme Clones computer from the Zudak Clones company. My old objection stemmed from the fact that the folks who used integrated motherboards (Compaq, Dell, Gateway, and those folks) all built integrated motherboards that weren't interchangeable. Hence, if a Dell motherboard went bad, you were stuck buying a replacement from Dell, at a higher price than you would have paid had the motherboard been a more generic item. New manufacturing techniques have improved the quality of these motherboards, reducing the risk of failure of one or more of the integrated components.

However, there still is a downside: many in the PC industry see this as a cost-cutting measure and not satisfactory for those of us more inclined to upgrade our PCs and customize them rather than buy the same unit as those belonging to neighbors and coworkers. The percentage of motherboards including integrated components is on the rise right now, but it's being tempered by a large dissenting audience who still feels this is a poor way to go.

FIGURE 2.17
Generic video
adapter

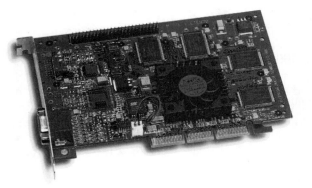

But the lack of industry centralization has left us with no new standards; instead, there are a lot of video boards that exceed VGA's capabilities, boards generically called Super VGA (SVGA) boards. Even though they're all lumped under the SVGA designation, they're all different, making it difficult sometimes to find *drivers* (the software that controls the video board) for a particular board.

Despite their variation, video boards all have several distinct components, as you see in Figure 2.18.

FIGURE 2.18
Video board
components

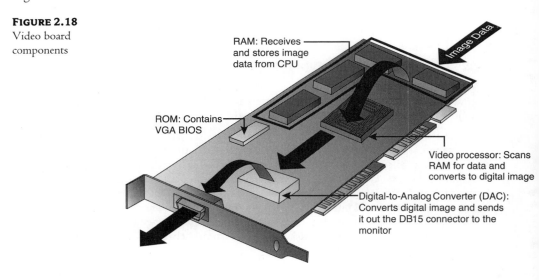

RAM: Receives and stores image data from CPU

ROM: Contains VGA BIOS

Image Data

Video processor: Scans RAM for data and converts to digital image

Digital-to-Analog Converter (DAC): Converts digital image and sends it out the DB15 connector to the monitor

The video board contains video memory, into which the CPU places the video image. A video chip on the video board then examines the data in the video memory and creates a digital image signal. That digital signal is then converted to an analog signal by the Digital-to-Analog Converter (DAC), another chip on the video board, and the resultant signal goes out the connector on the back of the board and into your monitor.

Video boards are distinguished by their *resolution*, which is the number of dots (pixels) they can put on the video screen, and their *color depth* (the number of colors they can display at one time). More dots means sharper pictures. They're also distinguished by how many colors they can display on those dots and by how much work the CPU must do in order to create images.

You see, on older video boards, the CPU had to do all the work of picture creation; it had to place each and every one of the pixels on the computer's screen. Nowadays, however, video boards include special circuitry called *accelerator* or *bitblitter* chips that can speed up video operations considerably. Many video boards also have hardware support for 3D rendering, allowing games to have a real-time realism that quite literally couldn't have happened in a under-$1 million machine 10 years ago. Other video boards include television tuner support and/or video capture hardware.

Of all components that can be integrated into a motherboard, the video card is the one that causes the most consternation. This is because most people think a separate video adapter gives them increased flexibility—and it does. If you have a separate card and want to upgrade it, you simply remove the old card, add the new card, and install the drivers. If the video chipset is built into the motherboard, it might be more difficult to upgrade.

In most cases where there's a video card built into the motherboard, the motherboard manufacturer will tell you that all you have to do is install a new video adapter into an expansion slot (more than likely PCI because many motherboards with built-in video forego AGP slots), and the motherboard will detect it and disable the onboard video. In a lot of cases, this works well in theory but not so great in practice. This automatic detection/disabling feature has gotten better over the years, but it can still cause problems if you have integrated video.

Video cards and their all-important terminal devices (monitors) will be covered in extensive detail in Chapter 20, "Video Adapters and Displays."

Floppy Disk Controller and Disk Drives

The floppy disk drive is an ancient peripheral, but it's still included for backward compatibility. The 1.44MB format has existed since the mid-'80s and has improved not a whit since then. Why? As with video, there's no market leader in the PC hardware area that can simply put a stake in the ground and say, "This *is* the new floppy standard." There are some great floppy technologies that store upward of 250MB on a removable disk, including the popular Zip drives, but none has really caught on and created a critical mass. And sadly, there may *never* be an industry consensus about high-capacity floppy drives because most modern machines can boot from CDs, allowing firms to bypass floppies altogether for distribution purposes and ship CDs instead, even for operating systems (which require the distribution media to be bootable). In addition, with the advancement of recordable CDs and DVDs (which can hold a *lot* more data), floppy disks are quickly becoming outdated as storage media.

Because they're peripherals, floppies require an interface, called a *floppy disk controller*. In general, these will not give you many problems. They *do* fail occasionally, however, so you need to know how to recognize this and address it because virtually all PCs have the floppy drive circuitry on the motherboard. In the case of a floppy drive controller failure, you'd have to either get a new motherboard (the excuse you've been looking for to upgrade to a newer processor!) or disable the floppy controller circuit and try to find a stand-alone board that can act as a floppy controller. (You can find more information about this in Chapter 14, "Understanding, Installing, and Repairing Floppy Drives.")

The much more fertile ground for failure lies in the floppy disks and floppy disk drives themselves. Floppy drives can require speed adjustment, head alignment, and head cleaning. Speed adjustment and head cleaning can be done simply and cheaply. Alignment can require some specialized equipment and isn't cost effective. Floppy drives are so cheap these days that it's pointless to do anything but replace them, but it never hurts to know a bit about a component's innards.

Beyond adjustment is the problem of compatibility among drive types. There are three kinds of 3 1/2-inch floppies, something you'll need to know if you're working with old floppies; for the past decade or so, the standard floppy has been the 1.44MB version. Chapter 14 talks about floppy installation and the kinds of maintenance you can do on a floppy drive.

IDE Controller

IDE controllers have been in computers for a long time and, aside from occasional speed increases, have remained pretty much the same. The primary devices you'll hook to an IDE controller are hard disks, but IDE also readily supports CD-ROM drives, DVD drives, Zip and Jaz drives, and tape backup devices.

HARD DISKS

Most of your system's software and most of the data you've created lives on your system's *hard disk*. Years ago, you bought a hard disk by its size and by its interface. Normal-duty hard drives used an interface called ST-506. High-performance drives used a drive interface called the *Enhanced Small Device Interface*, or *ESDI*.

Nowadays, you still choose a hard disk by its size (see, some things never change) and by its interface; but the interface will either be the SCSI or EIDE interface, usually called just IDE today. The vast majority of PCs currently use IDE because virtually all PC motherboards haven't one but *two* IDE interfaces built right on them. Each IDE interface can support two drives. As there are two IDE interfaces, then, the average PC can support four drives right out of the box. Most folks have at least one CD-ROM drive and a hard disk drive, so they have two free spots for more hard disk drives, a CD-R/RW or DVD drive, or perhaps a tape drive or Zip drive for backups.

When a hard disk fails, your main concern shouldn't be the hard disk. Hard disks are easy to replace and install, as you'll learn in "Part II: Devices."

CD-ROMs AND DVDs

Once a nice add-on, a CD-ROM drive is now a necessity for any home machine and a recommended peripheral for a business machine. Not only are CD-ROM drives basic equipment today, but more and more, CD-ROM drives that can write and even rewrite CDs (not just any CDs; the media has to be specifically rewrite capable) are common hardware in many offices and homes. In the time it takes me to get a cup of coffee, I can burn about 700MB of data to my CD Rewriteable (CD-RW) drive. (Traditionally, CD-ROM drives are IDE or SCSI, but USB and FireWire drives are the de facto standard now.)

DVD drives are the next technology level for CDs. Whereas CDs can store up to 700MB on a 4 1/2-inch disk, DVDs theoretically can store up to 17GB (17 *billion* bytes).

DVDs use the same kind of interfaces as CDs, either IDE (as is most common) or SCSI. They're backward compatible, which means you can read CDs in DVD drives (but not vice versa).

Relatively new to the market are DVD recorders, in various formats. There are two record-only formats (DVD-R and DVD+R), and at least three rewritable formats (DVD-RAM, DVD-RW, and DVD+RW). As of this writing, no single format has become a standard, so you're likely to see recordable/rewritable DVD drives from different manufacturers embracing different, mostly incompatible formats.

Chapter 9, "CD-ROM and DVD Drives," covers CD-ROM and DVD drives, so turn there for more information.

TAPE DEVICES

If your computer doesn't have a backup device, then ask yourself: Can I really afford to lose all this data? If the answer is *no*, then think about getting a tape drive. Tape drives install in the same kind of slot that you'd put a floppy drive into. Some tape drives run off an IDE or SCSI host adapter; others connect to the floppy disk controller; and a few have their own proprietary controller. Or consider the Jaz drive from Iomega, a tool I like and use quite a bit. It's a backup system that uses removable hard disk cartridges. The benefit to this drive is that if you have a hard disk failure, you can reboot with any drive, and run your programs and read your data directly from the Jaz drive the same way you would with a hard drive.

Whatever your situation is, if you can't afford to lose the data, then you better back it up.

SCSI Host Adapter

SCSI is a general-purpose interface that allows you to install just one circuit board in your system and use it to act as the "manager" for hard disks, tape drives, optical disks, CD-ROM drives, DVD-ROM drives, digital cameras, scanners, and even a few kinds of printers. As you'll learn in Chapter 11, "Understanding and Installing SCSI Devices," basic SCSI standards can support up to seven devices per controller, and newer SCSI standards can support 15 per controller. Generally speaking, SCSI devices will give you better performance than comparable IDE devices, but you'll also pay more for the performance.

Keyboard and Mouse

The PC is useless without an input device, and the keyboard is one of the two input devices (the other being a mouse) used by most of us. The keyboard is subject to a number of hazards, however, so it needs maintenance—and sometimes replacement. The PC's keyboard actually contains a microprocessor of its own, called the Intel 8041, 8042, or 8048. Taking apart a keyboard isn't hard—but reassembling it *is*, and truthfully there's little point in it nowadays because keyboards are cheap. You can get a regular 101-key enhanced keyboard for less then $10 or an ergonomic "broken" keyboard for under $40. You can even add wireless keyboards to your system; the RF receiver connects to your PC's keyboard connector, and the keyboard itself acts as the radio transmitter.

Most keyboards have either a PS/2 (also called a mini-DIN) or a USB connector. Older keyboards used a larger DIN connector, but you can get an adapter to convert the DIN to a PS/2.

Nearly every computer is equipped with a *mouse*, an input device used for pointing and selecting. The Graphical User Interfaces (GUIs) on modern operating systems can work with just a keyboard, but they're cumbersome without some kind of dedicated pointing device, and the most common is a mouse.

Mice come in the mechanical and optical variety. The mechanical is the traditional (and lower-cost) wheel-equipped type, but improvements in optical technology may change that within the next few years. Mice interface with the computer via a serial port (very old), a PS/2 port (old), or a USB port. Trackballs and pointing sticks are also becoming popular choices that use the mouse interface

You can learn more about the keyboard and the mouse in Chapter 19, "Keyboards and Mice."

Parallel (Centronics) Interface/IEEE 1284

The most common use for a parallel connector over time has been to attach a printer to a computer (although now USB printers are standard). The interface was named after Centronics, the company that invented it in 1976. It's more commonly known today as the *parallel port*. Other ways to connect printers to PCs include the serial port and USB port, and I'll cover them in the next few sections.

PCs can support up to three parallel ports. They're named LPT1, LPT2, and LPT3; the name refers to Line PrinTer 1, 2, or 3.

Originally, parallel ports were unidirectional. They transported data only from the PC to the printer. *Control* lines led status information from the printer back to the PC, but data flowed in only one direction. For years, some parallel ports have had the option to move data backward, from the printer to the PC. That's important for two reasons:

- ◆ Printers can send textual status information to the PC. Thus, it's possible for the printer to tell the PC, "I'm low on toner," or "I'm a LaserJet 6."

- ◆ Modern PCs put things on the parallel port that aren't printers. Removable media drives, CD-ROM drives, and scanners are examples of peripheral hardware devices that can have parallel port options.

Parallel ports not only support bidirectional data flow, but they also support increased data transfer speed. These ports are called Enhanced Parallel Ports, or EPP interfaces. Parallel ports use a direct memory access channel and become Extended Capabilities Ports (ECPs), offering even more speed. The IBM PC's parallel port was originally a proprietary interface, but it's become so widely used that there's now an "official" standard describing it, IEEE 1284. You'll sometimes see parallel ports or parallel cables referred to not as *parallel* but as *IEEE 1284 compliant*.

Most printers require only a simple unidirectional parallel port. But if you have a bidirectional, EPP, or ECP port, then those more advanced ports work fine with any kind of printer.

Parallel ports won't usually pose much of a problem, once you have them installed and configured. But the printers themselves, well, that's another story.

The actual printer is the greater source of failures: printers employ a large number of moving parts. Although printers are much more reliable nowadays than they were in the bad old days of daisy-wheel printers, there's always the odd paper feed or black page problems.

Serial Port

Besides parallel ports, the other common printer interface is the *serial port*. Serial ports are also known as *async ports, comm ports,* or *RS-232 ports*. They're bidirectional interfaces for low- to medium-speed data transfer; most serial ports can't transfer data faster than 115,000 bits per second, but there are some serial ports that can transfer data at 345,000 bits per second.

A serial port's main job isn't usually printers, however. The two most common uses for serial ports are to attach mice or modems to your PC. Modems enable your PC to communicate remotely with other computers via phone lines and to act as a fax machine.

The standard over the years has been for computers to support four serial ports, named COM1 through COM4. COM1 and COM3 share IRQ4, and COM 2 and COM4 share IRQ3, though; so on older machines you might run into some conflicts if you want to use all four COM ports (which usually isn't a problem).

RS-232 is a source of many cable problems: either the wrong cable is configured, or environmental problems (electronic noise) cause communication errors. Figure 2.19 depicts an IBM RS-232 adapter. Data communications troubleshooting is an entire book in itself—several books, in fact—but I cover the essentials in Chapter 29, "Modems and Other Internet Connection Devices."

FIGURE 2.19
IBM RS-232
adapter

Serial ports have been the PC's general-purpose I/O devices, but now USB has taken over because it's faster and cheaper. But you can occasionally still find hand-held machines such as the PalmPilot that attach to the PC via serial ports, as well as digital cameras, some scanners, modems, mice, and printers…it seemed on many systems that there were too many things to attach to a serial port and not enough serial ports. *That's* why they invented USB. Well, that and because serial ports are so *slow*.

Universal Serial Bus (USB)

It's used to be far too easy to run out of serial ports. For instance, say you had a serial mouse and a modem. No problem, right? The mouse went on COM1, and the modem went on COM2. But what happened when you added a smart Uninterruptible Power Supply (UPS), a device that could communicate with your computer for diagnostics and software control, to the mix? At that point, you had the choice of either losing your mouse (it's possible to navigate a graphical operating system with the arrow and Tab keys, but it's no fun), losing some of the UPS's capabilities, or adding another COM port with an add-in card and hoping that one set of software will function with a nonstandard interrupt. If you didn't set up COM3 to use another interrupt, then it would conflict with COM1, but not all software is prepared to deal with that. All in all, it was a royal pain.

It was a puzzle, and the problems associated with adding serial ports kept people from using some devices that need them. That's why the USB was invented. All new PCs come with one or more (usually two or four) USB ports.

WHAT IS USB?

USB, developed by Microsoft, Compaq, National Semiconductor, and 25 other USB members, was designed to take the place of the keyboard port, parallel ports, game port, and serial ports by replacing them with a single connection from which you can daisy-chain *more than 100* USB-compatible devices. This single connection is even simpler than a nine-pin serial port because it has only four pins. Physically, it looks either like one device (such as a keyboard) plugged into the computer, with everything else plugged into a hub on the keyboard, or like a hub plugged into the computer, with everything plugged into the hub. As in SCSI, each device can be plugged into up to seven devices and/or hubs at a time.

Either way, it's designed to be much simpler to put together; rather than installing cards for many of these devices, you plug them into a hub and call it a day. If they're true PnP devices (which they'd better be), then your operating system will recognize them with little help from you.

NOTE   *Windows 98, Me, 2000, XP, and 2003 have USB support with device drivers built into them.*

USB is much, much faster than serial ports, as well. The original standard transmits up to 12Mbps, as opposed to the 100+ kilobits per second of a serial interface. Between the speed and the ease of configuration, it's no wonder USB took flight in such a hurry.

USB recognizes four types of data transfer, divided by the type of peripheral device that uses them: bulk, interrupt, asynchronous, and control. Printers, scanners, and digital cameras, which must send a great deal of information to the PC at one time, are bulk transmitters. Keyboards and joysticks, which people use to sporadically transmit small amounts of data that must be processed immediately, use interrupt transmittal. Telecom applications, which must be delivered in a steady stream and in a certain order, use asynchronous transmissions.

The hub detects which devices are plugged into it at any given time, and from that it deduces how much bandwidth each needs, based on the kind of data transmittal the device is trying to perform.

WHAT'S IT GOOD FOR?

Just about anything you want to be good for. The ability to plug in a number of devices with only one port is particularly useful to laptop owners because laptops have limited real estate into which to plug additional devices. You don't need lots of available ports, and the hub should be easier to get to than the back of your computer. It's intended to work for just about anything you can plug into a port in your computer: speakers, modems, keyboards, and the like.

One of the things I like most about USB, besides the single IRQ use and the transportability, is the fact that I can happily shelve my printer or my scanner or graphics tablet when I'm not using it. When I need the device again, I just plug it in, and it's instantly found and available for use.

USB 2: THE NEW FRONTIER

If you liked USB version 1, the newer installment—USB 2—is about 40 times faster than the original USB implementation. To be exact, USB 2 runs at up to 480Mbps. USB 2 nearly equals high-end SCSI and FireWire/IEEE 1394 for throughput although the difference in speed is practically inconsequential. As the standard has matured, the availability of USB 2 devices has increased substantially. The other good news about USB 2 is that it is backward compatible with the two previous versions (USB 1.0 and USB 1.1). This means you can use USB 2 devices with existing USB ports in your computer.

Slower devices such as mice, keyboards, and simple digital cameras won't need that kind of speed (in fact, they use a 1.5Mbps subchannel, leaving the real bandwidth open for the high-speed devices), but USB 2 makes an attractive option for those doing video editing or using high-speed drives, providing close to the same performance as FireWire. Oh, and USB is a lot cheaper, too.

But wait, there's more! There are also adapters made for USB to EIDE, USB to SCSI-2, and USB to Ethernet. In addition, you can connect two PCs together with USB, provided you have a USB bridge. (Do *not* connect two PCs together directly with an "A to A" USB cable, or you could fry each computer!) If you need to network a lot of computers, though, a regular LAN connection is still recommended.

All in all, USB will obviate the need for serial and parallel ports in computers. It'll likely take some time (after all, some of us are still hanging onto our 5^1/4-inch floppies), but it'll happen.

FireWire/IEEE 1394

Apple created the FireWire interface to replace serial ports, parallel ports, SCSI ports, and any other port you'd use to connect a device to your computer. Apple owns the term *FireWire* and is protective of it, so this interface on a PC must be referred to by its IEEE specification number. (Which doesn't stop everybody and their brother—and me!—from referring to PC-based IEEE1394 connections by the FireWire name.)

Like USB, FireWire is based on a daisy-chain physical topology, meaning that devices will be able to cascade from hubs attached to the card in the computer. FireWire supports 63 devices, however, instead of the 127 that its cousin interface, USB, supports. This isn't a major issue because the chance you'd want to actually connect that many devices is remote. Although it's not required that a FireWire expansion card be PCI, all the FireWire cards released to date *are* PCI. The FireWire bus needs all the speed it can get because it's designed to work with devices that require a lot of bandwidth, such as scanners, video cameras, and the like. Although, as I said, FireWire is designed to replace all other ports; it's also designed to cope with devices that require high and variable amounts of bandwidth. The standard is designed to support speeds of 100Mbps, 200Mbps, and 400Mbps, varying the path the signal takes in order to avoid traffic problems.

FireWire (IEEE 1394) is the interface of choice for digital camcorders and is now appearing as an option on several high-end scanners and digital still cameras. Intel wants USB 2 to replace the need for IEEE 1394, but given that FireWire has been almost universally adopted for consumer electronics products (such as camcorders), it looks as if FireWire is here to stay. In addition, although USB 2 does offer excellent performance, FireWire will still transfer slightly more data in the same amount of time.

FireWire (IEEE 1394) is positioned to be an important component in the integration of consumer electronics with PC desktops, and that also might be a big part of the direction in which PC hardware is heading. The home and office of the future is likely to have the PC and its functions built into or connected into a whole complex of devices, not separate from them.

Configuring for FireWire may sound simple, but how about *powering* those dozens of devices? Well, two of the six wires in the cable are power lines, so your add-in devices can technically use your computer's main power supply. However, providing many devices their own power supplies is probably a good idea in order to keep the strain on the system power supply to a minimum.

System Clock/Calendar and Configuration (CMOS) Chip

You've probably heard someone talking about *CMOS* (pronounced *sea-moss*, and no one really cares what it stands for) before. You might have even entered into the CMOS configuration to set up hard disks or modify other hardware settings on your computer. But the confusing part to most people is, what is CMOS or BIOS or even the Setup?

Technically speaking, the CMOS is the physical chip on the motherboard that stores information on the hardware configuration of your computer, as well as the system date and time. CMOS is powered by a battery, which looks a lot like a watch battery.

CMOS holds a firmware program called the BIOS. Now wait a minute, you might think. Doesn't the BIOS handle input and output for the computer? Yes it does, and as a program it's located on the CMOS chip. (Incidentally, you might also hear the BIOS called *firmware* because it's truly neither software nor hardware but something in between.) So when you go to make sure your computer recognizes your hard disks (or disable ports or set your processor speed), you're in the BIOS configuration screens. A lot of people will also call this interface *the Setup*, as in, "Go into the Setup, and make sure the CPU speed is right." You can substitute the word BIOS or CMOS as well, and get the same point across.

BATTLE OF THE PERIPHERAL TITANS: USB VERSUS FIREWIRE/IEEE 1394

The big question on everyone's minds is, "which one of these standards is going to win?" The answer might not be very simple.

Both USB and FireWire have been around for a while now; as I mentioned earlier, they're both old hat to Macintosh users. In terms of speed, they're both about equal. High-speed USB 2 devices can run at 480Mbps, whereas IEEE 1394 currently tops out at 400Mbps. Even though this is the case, IEEE 1394 is still considered the better solution for high-speed data transfers (such as video editing) because it can sustain higher throughput than can USB.

Most new PCs have at least one USB connection. Built-in FireWire ports are more hit and miss. Although desktops usually have four or more USB ports, some have FireWire and others don't. As for laptops, again, it depends on the make and model, but USB is guaranteed, and FireWire is likely. This might be the decisive difference. And currently, USB devices are generally cheaper than their FireWire counterparts.

It's still too early to tell if one of the standards will win over the other. But for now, you can get great performance from either, and you should go with the one you feel most comfortable using.

Technically, they're all different things. In practice, though, they all refer to the same functional part of your computer.

The Clock/Calendar and CMOS Battery Issues

The clock/calendar is built on the same chip as the configuration memory circuit, already introduced as the CMOS. Another way to view it is as a small amount of memory that holds information that the computer needs in order to get started in the morning.

When you first turn your computer on, it must figure out what hardware it contains so that it can control that hardware. There's a list of the hardware in your system in the configuration memory. Most memory, however, is *volatile*, a 75-cent word meaning, "When you remove power from the memory, the memory forgets whatever was sitting in it." That's why the memory has a battery attached to it, so the memory doesn't lose power, so it can remember while the rest of the PC slumbers.

Of course, with time, that battery will run down in power, the configuration memory will forget what kind of hardware is in your system, and the clock/calendar will no longer keep correct time. You'll have to install a new battery, of course, to fix the problem; but there's a common question about batteries and the clock.

People will tell me that their computer can no longer remember its configuration information, forcing them to re-enter the configuration information into the computer every time they turn the computer on. (They should just replace the battery, but, for whatever reason, they haven't.) I explain they've got to replace the battery, but they disagree, saying, "No, the battery's fine."

"How do you know that?" I ask.

"Because the computer keeps correct time," they respond. They're arguing that because the clock circuit still runs, the configuration memory circuit should still run. It's a good argument, but it misses the fact that running the clock requires less power *by far* than does running the configuration memory. As you may have learned from painful experience, it's possible for your car's battery to have enough power to run the interior lights and the radio, but not to crank the starter.

The vast majority of the time, the only problem from the clock will be with the battery or the software to use it.

The battery causes problems, of course, when it runs down and no longer keeps time. Replacement is no problem (usually $3–$10 at any decent electronics counter), save for some clock/calendar boards that *solder* the battery on the board. Many motherboard manufacturers nowadays have a soldered battery, but that may not be terrible news because some of those motherboards also support a standard external battery; you just move a jumper on the motherboard to disable the soldered battery and enable the connection for the external battery.

Other Common Controllers

Depending on your motherboard, you might have one or more of the following types of devices built in:

◆ Network adapter

◆ Sound card

◆ Modem

A network adapter allows you to communicate with other computers on a network, or even get on the Internet. You'll take a long look at network adapters (as well as how to set up a basic network) in Chapter 27, "Networking Concepts and Hardware," and Chapter 28, "Installing and Trouble-shooting Networks."

Sound cards give you audio but not that cheesy little beep sound when your computer boots. That comes from a piezoelectric speaker. Sound cards give you the real sound you want to hear, such as the intense noises of your favorite game or the calming influence of your relaxation music CD. Sound cards will be covered in detail in Chapter 21, "Play It Loud: Sound Cards."

You've already looked a little at modems earlier, and you'll see them again in Chapter 29. Some motherboards have them integrated, others don't.

With each of these types of devices, if your motherboard doesn't have one, it's not a big deal. You can simply purchase an expansion card and add it as you need it. And of course, as you read the rest of this book, you'll find out how exactly to do that.

Locating and Identifying Components

You probably already know what a lot of devices, such as the CD-ROM drive, hard disk, and power supply look like. If not, don't worry because after tearing your computer apart during the next chapter, you will. Once everything is out, all you'll have left is the motherboard: the big green board bolted to your case.

In the first part of this section, you'll be able to see where all of the things discussed in this chapter (PCI, ISA, CPU, memory, and so on) plug into on the motherboard. After that, you'll get a visual show of some connectors you'll need to be able to identify—there's a quiz later.

Finding Things on the Motherboard

Your system's motherboard, once you remove it, will have a few points worth noting. I'll use a typical PII motherboard for examples.

THE POWER CONNECTION

Be sure to note where the power cables from the power supply go to the motherboard. Putting the old-style XT connectors back together backward will smoke the motherboard. You see the power connection in Figure 2.20.

FINDING THE CPU

The CPU on your system is often easily identifiable because many of them have a prominent Intel logo painted on them. If you're working with a much older system, look also for the distinctive names 80386, 80486, Pentium, and the like. Nowadays, finding a PIII or 4 is a snap; they're sitting upright in black plastic cases. You usually can't see the actual CPU, though, because it's surrounded by metal fins. Those fins are the heat sink that helps keep the chip from catching fire. (No, I'm not kidding.)

Older CPUs are also often socketed. But no matter what generation of PC you own, one good method for finding the CPU is to look for the largest chip in the box; that's often it.

FIGURE 2.20
Motherboard
power connection

REMEMBERING THE MEMORY

Your PC's motherboard has both RAM and Read-Only Memory (ROM) on it.

RAM memory is usually easy to spot because it's typically in the form of a SIMM, DIMM, or RIMM (long thin sticks). If you have an older computer that uses separate chips, then the memory looks like uniform rows of small socketed chips. You see the memory in Figure 2.21.

FIGURE 2.21
SDRAM in
Pentium III
motherboard

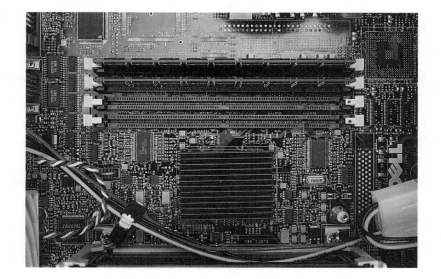

ROM memory is usually a large chip or pair of chips in sockets, *often with a label on the top* indicating a software version number. Newer systems don't have socketed ROM because they're flash memory and don't need physical replacing—you just download new versions of the BIOS programs.

SLOTS

The only other parts you'll be sure to want to find are the expansion slots in the computer. They're obvious, in that they're relatively long, narrow electrical connectors. Refer to the bus discussion earlier in this chapter to get an idea about the differences between bus slot types. Figure 2.22 shows (from right to left) two ISA slots, four PCI slots, and an AGP slot.

FIGURE 2.22
Expansion slots
on a motherboard

CMOS BATTERY

Keep a computer long enough, and you'll have to replace the battery or it won't be able to hold its configuration. Figure 2.23 shows that this motherboard uses a coin-type battery.

DRIVE INTERFACES

Every motherboard I know of these days has the floppy drive controller and two EIDE host adapters integrated into its electronics. You'll have to attach and detach drive ribbon cables, so it's a good idea to locate the floppy and EIDE connectors, as you see in Figure 2.24.

Identifying Connectors

This is going to sound silly, but I use two basic approaches to identifying strange connectors.

The first rule is the "What is it connected to?" rule. Suppose you're trying to figure out what a connector does. You notice that it's connected to a cable that goes to the video monitor. Heck, even a nonphysicist such as me can figure out that the board must have something to do with video, so it's probably a video adapter.

The second rule of connector identification is the "What does it look like?" rule. There are different kinds of connectors on the back of a PC. Take a minute to become familiar with them.

FIGURE 2.23
CMOS battery on a motherboard

FIGURE 2.24
Floppy and EIDE connectors on motherboard

Floppy
connector

EIDE
connectors

THE D-SHELL CONNECTOR

The *D-shell connector* is called that because if you look at it the right way, it looks like a capital *D*. You can see a D-shell connector in Figure 2.25.

FIGURE 2.25

A D-shell connector

D-shell connectors come in male and female varieties. They also vary by the number of pins or sockets in their connectors. You'll see DB9 (nine pins or sockets), DB15, DB25, and DB37 connectors. They're used in serial ports, parallel ports, video adapters, joystick interfaces, and some LAN interfaces.

HP OR MINIATURE D-SHELL CONNECTOR

The *miniature D or HP connector* looks a lot like a D-shell connector, but the pins are all placed next to one another. The HP connector puts 50 pins in the same space that a normal D-shell puts only 25 pins. You can see an HP connector in Figure 2.26.

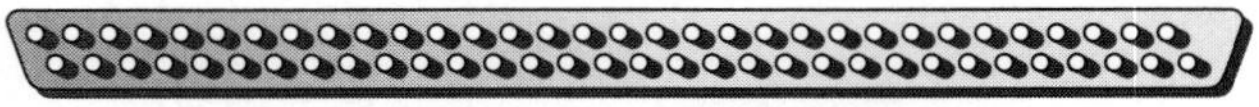

FIGURE 2.26

An HP connector

As I said, it looks like a D-shell connector. The main application I've seen for HP connectors is in SCSI interfaces. A 50-pin version shows up on SCSI-2 interfaces, and SCSI-3 (a later version of the SCSI standard) uses a 68-pin HP connector.

Sometimes you'll hear people call the 50-pin HP connector a Centronics 50-pin because the pin configuration is similar to the Centronics connector discussed next.

CENTRONICS CONNECTOR

Made popular by its first big use in an interface created by a company of the same name, the *Centronics connector* looks like Figure 2.27.

Don't confuse the Centronics connector with the Centronics interface, another name for the parallel port. The connector, which looks like an edge connector surrounded by a metal shell, is used on printers and in SCSI devices. In addition to parallel ports, Centronics connectors are used by some SCSI host adapters.

FIGURE 2.27

A Centronics connector

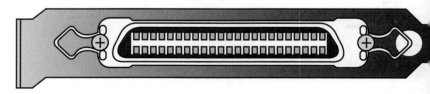

MINIATURE DIN CONNECTOR

As the name implies, these are smaller versions of DIN connectors. You see a couple of variations on this in Figure 2.28.

FIGURE 2.28
Miniature DIN
connectors

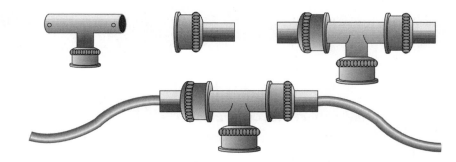

You'll see these used for bus mouse interfaces, InPort mouse interfaces, keyboard interfaces, and some serial port applications.

USB CONNECTOR

USB systems have a *USB connector*—a kind of flat connector with a tongue in its middle, as you see in Figure 2.29. That's the end that plugs into the motherboard, or the A end. The B end goes into the device. Figure 2.30 shows both ends of a USB cable.

FIGURE 2.29
USB connector
(in center; mini-
DINs on left,
D-shells on right)
on a motherboard

FIGURE 2.30
USB A connector
(left) and USB
B connector (right)

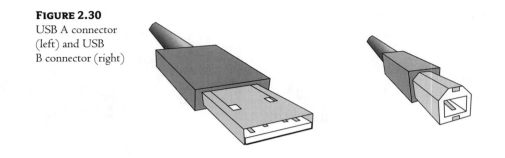

FireWire/IEEE 1394 Connectors

FireWire must also have its own connectors installed on the machine or provided by an adapter installed into an expansion slot on the PC itself. FireWire connectors come in both four-pin and six-pin varieties. The six-pin connector is the standard because the four-pin one doesn't provide power to the device. Figure 2.31 shows the ends of four-pin and six-pin FireWire cables.

FIGURE 2.31
FireWire/IEEE
1394 connectors

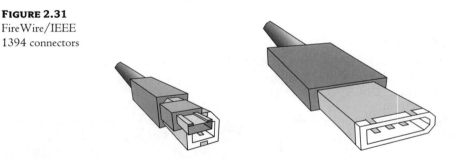

RJ-45 Connector

These connectors look like the so-called *modular jacks* that you use to plug a phone into an answering machine or a wall jack. As a matter of fact, the connector you use for a standard phone is a Registered Jack Type 11 (RJ-11) connector. Many networks use the slightly larger *RJ-45 connector*, which looks similar. The RJ-11 has four wires in it. The RJ-45 has eight wires in it.

RJ-45 is used in 10Base-T Ethernet connections, as well as LocalTalk connectors such as you'd see in a Macintosh network.

BNC Connector

A *BNC connector*, or *Bayonet Naur connector* (a bayonet is what they supposedly look like, and Naur is the guy who invented them), looks like a cylinder about 1 centimeter across with a thin tube down its center and two small bumps on its periphery. You can see several BNC connectors in Figure 2.32.

FIGURE 2.32
BNC connectors

In Figure 2.32, you see (clockwise, from upper left) a T connector, used to connect a single BNC connector to two other BNC connectors. Next, you see a BNC plug and then a T connector with two plugs. At the bottom of the diagram, you see two cables with BNC plugs connected to a T connector. The T connector would then be attached to a BNC connector on the back of a circuit board.

BNCs are most typically used in a kind of LAN called *Ethernet* although they're rarely used any more because of RJ-45. Ethernet attaches in several ways, known as *thick*net, *thin*net, and *10Base-T*. It's the thinnet implementation of Ethernet that uses BNC connectors. Thinnet is also known as *10Base-2*.

BNC connectors have also been used in ARCNet and 3270 (a mainframe terminal interface) connectors.

DIN Connector

The DIN connector comes from Germany; roughly translated, its name means *German national connector*. The DIN connector is a round, notched connector about an inch across, with from three to seven pins in it. DIN connectors were most commonly used in the PC world to connect keyboards to a motherboard. You'll rarely see them anymore.

Miniplug

A *miniplug connector* is the kind of connection that enables a set of headphones to attach to a Sony Walkman. You see these on CD-ROM players (not always, but often) or on the backs of sound cards for microphone inputs or line input or output.

RCA Plug

RCA plugs are the kind of connectors you might see on the back of your VCR labeled Audio In or Video In. They were used years ago for simple video output on an old kind of video board called the Color/Graphics Adapter and a later board called the Enhanced Graphics Adapter. Nowadays, you usually see them only for sound inputs or outputs on some sound cards or for video inputs on a video capture board.

Other Connectors

Sometimes you'll see these connectors on the back of your motherboard, and other times on the back of an expansion card. Regardless, you should be able to identify them. Take a look at Figure 2.33.

In Figure 2.33, you see the backs of some common interface boards. As I said earlier, note the extensive use of D-shell connectors.

Originally, video boards used a female DB9 connector to pipe out color images, via what was called an RGB connector, or high-resolution monochrome images, via a digital monochrome video interface. That led to confusion because it was possible to plug an RGB color monitor into a digital output; when that happened, little wisps of smoke would soon issue from atop the color monitor, and it would cease to function. Color video boards also output a kind of signal called *composite video*, which you can read more about in Chapter 23, "Digital Video." If you see a female DB9 on a modern system, the board is most likely a Token Ring network card.

Nowadays, however, virtually all video adapters use a D-shell that's the same size as the old DB9, except that this D-shell has *three* rows of pins, not two, housing 14 or 15 pins. I say "14 or 15" because there's room for 15 pins, but some boards fill in one of the holes. You'll see those connectors on just about every video board, and *very* rarely you'll see a video board with several RCA connectors on the back; such a board is sending video out in multiple signals as is done on some high-end video equipment.

The parallel port usually employs a 25-socket female D-shell connector. I say "usually" because Tandy used a DIN connector for their parallel port for a while. And, just to confuse the issue a bit, some older SCSI host adapters use a female DB25 for attaching external SCSI devices.

Serial ports also use D-shell connectors—two kinds, in fact. Some serial ports use a male DB25. Others use a male DB9 connector. Note that oddity: most connectors you'll find on a PC *aren't* male connectors, so the fact that serial ports use either 9-pin or 25-pin males is unusual. (My former girl-friend Sheila—she's mentioned in the acknowledgments—told me she remembered that male 25s and male 9s were serial ports because most serial killers were male. A rather graphic way of remembering, for sure, but then again, Sheila is 6'1" and was rated number one in the country in Tae Kwon Do, so I didn't argue with her about the little things, if you know what I mean.)

NOTE   *Why are most connectors on a PC female? Well, designers of some kinds of interfaces have to put a connector of one gender on the PC and a connector of the opposite gender on the cable that the interface uses. Male connectors have a bunch of little pins, and pins break. Female connectors have a bunch of little sockets, and sockets don't, in general, break. Now, in the case of pin breakage, would you rather have to replace a cable ($) or an interface board ($$$)? That's why the female connectors go on the PC side rather than the cable side.*

Let's look at some more boards, as you see in Figure 2.34.

FIGURE 2.33
Common connectors

25-pin male:
generally a serial port.

25-pin female:
a parallel port.

EGA: 9-pin female,
two RCA connectors,
DIP switches.

Fifteen pins in three
rows indicates VGA
(Video Graphics
Array) and graphics
accelerators.

As I mentioned earlier, Ethernet comes in three guises: thicknet, thinnet, and twisted-pair versions. Thicknet is the oldest variety of Ethernet, and it's also called 10Base-5 Ethernet. It interfaces via a DB15 female connector and is sometimes called an Adapter Unit Interface (AUI) or DEC-Intel-Xerox (DIX) connector. Thinnet uses a BNC connector; in the board pictured in Figure 2.34, you can use either the thicknet connector or a thinnet connector. The board next to it shows the third kind of Ethernet connection, a twisted-pair, or 10Base-T, connection, with an RJ-45 connector.

Next to that board is a modem. Modems have RJ-11 jacks for interfacing to phone lines, and the RJ-11s look like RJ-45s, so it might be easy to confuse an Ethernet card with a modem card. But modems have two connectors, and Ethernet cards often have an LED or two on their backs.

FIGURE 2.34
Additional boards

| A BNC connector helps give this away as an Ethernet LAN board. Here, the female 15-pin connector is for Thick Ethernet cable, not games. | A 10baseT Ethernet card has an RJ-45 connector with a few LEDs. Some combination Ethernet boards include BNC and 15-pin connectors, too. | Two RJ-11 phone jacks: an internal modem. |

| Joysticks and standard Ethernet (Thicknet) use 15-pin connectors. This may be a game card or an Ethernet LAN board. | Not all mice use a 9-pin serial connection; PS/2s use a round 6-pin mouse port. | A round port with nine holes identifies this as a bus mouse interface card. |

Below those cards is a VGA, mentioned earlier, a joystick interface (a female DB15), and two types of miniature DIN connectors used to create a mouse interface.

Let's wrap up our look at the connectors on the backs of common boards with a third group of boards, shown in Figure 2.35.

The top three boards in Figure 2.35 are varieties of SCSI interfaces, as I've mentioned earlier. Video capture boards take video inputs and convert them into digital data, and they can accept either simple composite video (like the kind that comes out the back of common VCRs), or they'll usually take the higher-quality super VHS–type connector, a miniature DIN. Below them are some backsides of some sound cards. Note that many sound cards have a joystick interface built right onto them.

Well, that was a long chapter, but now you're a motherboard and processor expert! In the next chapter, you get to tear apart your computer and look at a lot more parts.

FIGURE 2.35

Common boards

Centronics 50, 50 HP, and 68 HP connectors are all used for SCSI host adapters.

Sound cards typically have a joystick port, volume control, and audio input/output jacks.

Playback-only sound cards have headphone output jacks, line-out jacks, and volume control.

Interface cards for add-in CD-ROM drives have two audio output jacks for speakers.

Chapter 3

Taking Apart and Rebuilding the PC

- ◆ QuickSteps: Disassembling the PC
- ◆ Tools to Use, Tools to Avoid
- ◆ Disassembly Advice
- ◆ Successful Reassembly
- ◆ Upgrading Computers
- ◆ Troubleshooting Tips

Introduction

In this chapter, you'll take a look at how to disassemble a PC so that you can reassemble it. Sounds like fun, eh? Even more fun is putting it back together and actually having it work.

Now, it might seem that I ought to give you all of the details about PCs and PC repair before actually taking the thing apart. But that's *not* what I'm going to do—well, other than the whole motherboard and Central Processing Unit (CPU) discussion we've already had. You see, in teaching PC repair to thousands of people, I've found that understanding PC repair and upgrade requires *two* kinds of knowledge.

The first kind of knowledge is a sort of "how it all fits together" knowledge—an understanding of topics such as how extended memory is different from conventional memory or what a superscalar CPU is. It's this knowledge of the components and interfaces—the connections between those components—that enables you to diagnose a problem or select the correct upgrade part. You've already learned about some of this stuff, and you'll get the rest of it throughout the book.

The second sort of knowledge you'll need is a different kind; it's a familiarity with tools and with some simple rules of disassembly. Some of us are naturally better with tools than others. Personally, I'm the kind of guy who forgets to put the plug in the bottom of the oil pan before I start refilling my car engine with oil. That won't be true for all of you—if you're already someone who is comfortable with tools, then you probably *don't* have to be reminded that screwdrivers go "lefty loosey, righty tighty"—but some of us do, at least sometimes, and that's what this chapter is about. There are right ways to take a machine apart and there are wrong ways; this chapter shows you one of the right ways and talks about some of the wrong ways.

QuickSteps: Disassembling the PC

Here's a rundown of the procedure for taking apart your PC that I'll discuss in detail in this chapter, plus a list of the tools you'll need to get the job done right.

BE PREPARED

Before you start, there are some things you may need on hand. These include the following:

- ◆ Documentation for your PC or its separate components (including warranty information).

- ◆ Container for holding screws between removal and reinstallation.

- ◆ Appropriate screwdriver(s), such as a Phillips-head. (Today's machines offer a lot of diversity in the types of screws—and even the hard plastic retaining pins used in place of screws—that keep the cover in place and mount expansion cards inside the case. You may need to put a little effort into finding the right screwdriver—and it's possible you'll need more than one size.)

- ◆ Paper and pen for taking notes and diagramming, or the ability to record information on another PC until you're done with the one you're fixing.

- ◆ Antistatic wrist strap.

- ◆ Chip extraction tool or L-shaped, slim piece of metal for removing the CPU if it's in other than a Zero Insertion Force (ZIF) socket.

- ◆ Adequate room to work (with sufficient lighting).

WARNING *Make sure the PC and externals aren't only turned off but that the power cord is disconnected.*

Now you're ready to get started. The following are the *general* steps you need to take to disassemble your PC's system unit. For more specific instructions (to back up the system configuration, for example), read the rest of the chapter. Follow these steps:

1. Determine whether your PC is still under warranty. If it is, call your vendor first—they have more experience, and you may invalidate your warranty by opening it yourself. Next, determine whether you actually need to take apart your PC.

2. Find adequate clean space on a tabletop, with good lighting in the work area.

3. Have the proper tools available, including a container in which you can store screws (or you can replace the screws in their holes in the part once it's fully removed) and other small hardware pieces. Also, be equipped with an antistatic wrist strap.

4. Back up the configuration before disassembly, noting the following regarding your hard drive(s):

   - ◆ Some PCs don't permit the user to set the drive type in the Basic Input/Output System (BIOS), so you don't need to worry about storing the configuration because it should reset itself during the next boot.

◆ For most PCs that do let you set the drive type in the BIOS, record any information available on drive type and drive parameters (including cylinders, heads, and sectors per track)—you'll need this if your system can't be or isn't set to autodetect the drive(s).

◆ The controllers of SCSI drives have their own BIOS that stores the configuration information, so you may see that (a) the PC BIOS doesn't see a drive of that type listed at all, and/or (b) you need to tell your BIOS not to worry about the SCSI drive.

5. Turn off the PC and anything attached to it.

6. Remove the monitor and put it aside.

7. Unplug the PC and remove the cover, setting screws into the container discussed in step 3.

WARNING   *Be careful you don't rip cables when removing the top; the metal cases used on most PCs can have sharp edges.*

8. Diagram the setup and internals before you begin removing anything, and then rediagram as necessary to add information you couldn't see when you first began, noting in particular:

◆ Types and placement of cables

◆ Location and status of Dual Inline Package (DIP) switches and jumpers

◆ Motherboard connections, including power supply, power, speaker, and keyboard (detach the battery only if it's really necessary)

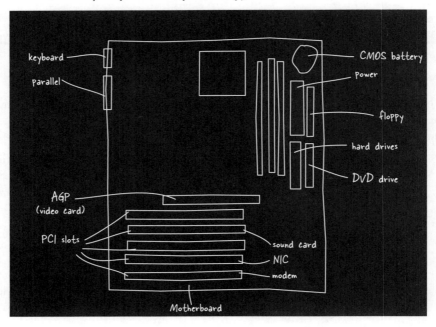

9. Start detaching connections.

10. Remove the boards. Set the boards in a clean, safe location.

WARNING   *Don't force things. If a part won't come out, stop and look again. Did you miss a screw that's holding it in?*

11. Remove the drives, along with their various drive screws and cables. Set them in a clean, safe location and store the screws in a container.

12. Remove the power supply. (See the section "Understanding Advanced Power Management" in this chapter for information on the different types.)

13. Carefully remove the CPU. If it's a slotted CPU, removing it is just like removing an expansion card, except that most CPU slots have braces on the end to hold the CPU card upright. Pull the brace back on one side, and rock that end of the CPU out. Then pull the other side out using the same method. Don't forget to unplug the CPU fan! If you've socketed chip, then remove it by unlocking the locking lever on the ZIF socket.

14. Carefully remove the motherboard as necessary for the type of case in use, being cautious not to bend it or exert undue pressure on it. Put this aside in a clean place where it can't be jostled or knocked to the floor.

15. Evaluate the removed components, as desired.

16. Begin reassembling the PC while checking to make certain you're not making a common error, such as reversing the way a cable should connect, forgetting to reconnect a wire, or failing to seat a board. This is a great time to upgrade your PC if that's one of your goals.

Choose Your Weapons: PC Repair Tools

Most PC problems can be fixed with nothing more complex than a screwdriver. But if you do a *lot* of PC work, you'll no doubt want to add other tools to your toolkit.

What's the best kind of PC to work on? Ask me at different times, and I'll give you different answers. If I'm fixing a PC when you ask me, then I'll tell you, "A PC sitting on the middle of a table, which is sitting in the middle of a room on a nice, low-static wood floor." Fixing PCs is a lot of fun; getting at the PC to work on it, however, is usually a pain. Computers are frequently shoved into corners—dark corners; connectors, if they're labeled at all, are labeled in the smallest print possible, and every year it seems the machines get more and more tightly packed inside.

Screwdrivers

The basic tool.

Screwdrivers come in straight-slot, Phillips-head, and Torx varieties. You may also occasionally need a tool called a *nut driver*, which is a sort of screwdriver that has a hex drive at the end instead of a blade. The most common size nut driver for computers is 1/4-inch. The *straight-slot screw* has, as its name implies, a single metal slot across its top. Be careful with these—it's easy for the screwdriver to slip from the slot, which makes it hard to bear down on a straight-slot screw and easy to jab yourself in the hand.

That's probably why Phillips screws were invented. *Phillips screws* have two slots at right angles to one another that taper in toward the center of the two slots. A corresponding peak in the Phillips-head screwdriver's tip fits nicely into that indentation, helping the screwdriver to stay centered and not slip as easily.

Or at least that's the idea.

There are two problems with Phillips screws, at least in the PC business. First, the screws that PC makers use are often made of some kind of soft, presumably cheap steel. And to make matters worse, the slots aren't very deep, making it easy to strip the heads of the screws. So be careful when removing Phillips screws from your computer.

The second problem is related to the first. It seems that half of the computers I work on have previously been worked on by Ignatz the Strong Man, apparently on loan from the circus. People tighten PC case screws as if their data will leak out of the seams otherwise. It's a dumb practice for two reasons—first, it's unnecessary, and second, you'll strip the heads of the screws. Tighten screws to a snug fit; don't cinch them down as if they'll be subjected to a vibration test.

Another thought along those lines: there are several sizes of Phillips-head screwdrivers. I'm aware of sizes 000, 00, 0, 1, 2, and 3, and I'm sure there are more. Most PC screws are size No. 1. However, you may come across a case screw (one of the screws that secures the case to the chassis) that's a No. 2. The important point is to use the correct size screwdriver for the screw with which you're working. Don't try to remove a No. 2 screw with a No. 1 Phillips-head; again, you'll strip the head. By the way, if you should happen to come across a screw that *has* a stripped slot, get out the 1/4-inch nut driver I mentioned earlier. You can screw it in (or out) with that because virtually all PC screws these days also have hex heads instead of round heads (see Figure 3.1).

Personally, I like electric screwdrivers. The Black & Decker I got for Christmas was just about the most useful present I've received.

FIGURE 3.1
The typical hex head/Phillips PC screw can be turned with either a Phillips-head screwdriver or a $1/4$-inch nut driver.

Compaq, just to be difficult, sometimes builds their computers using a third type of screw, called a *Torx screw*. The Torx uses a six-sided, star-shaped hole in the head of the screw. Torx screwdrivers come in at least 15 sizes, which is a major pain for support people. You'll probably use only sizes T-10 and T-15. Why do manufacturers use Torx screws? Well, it's certainly not because of convenience—whatever they are, they aren't *convenient*. I think it's because until about 10 years ago, most people couldn't easily buy Torx screwdrivers. The idea was probably that a computer company that used Torx screws could keep casual users from attempting to work on their computers. This was, however, a dumb idea. Things sometimes go wrong with PCs. Also, you may want to upgrade yours or replace a battery. If you can't get inside it, a PC can become useless junk before its time.

NOTE *What about magnetic tip screwdrivers? They might seem handy because they can essentially pick up dropped screws. But around computers, which include devices that store data as magnetically coated information, you shouldn't use these types of screwdrivers. Instead, use a regular screwdriver and have a retrieving tool handy in case you drop something.*

Antistatic Wrist Straps

Repairing your PC can do more harm than good if you're not careful. I'll say this again in Chapter 4, "Avoiding Service: Preventive Maintenance," but it's worthwhile to mention it here (even if it *will* end up being a bit redundant). Remember the following:

◆ Static electricity can damage chips and other sensitive components.

◆ You generate static all the time.

◆ In order for you to *feel* a static charge, it must be in excess of 2,000 volts.

◆ You can destroy a chip with 200 volts or less!

We're all aware of static electricity on dry winter days, when walking across a carpet and touching a metal doorknob results in an annoying shock. But you're probably not aware that you generate static almost all the time—static you don't even feel. It's entirely possible that you can reach over and pick up a board or a chip, not feel any tingle at all, and destroy the board or chip.

The answer to this problem is an *antistatic wrist strap*. It's an elastic, fabric band that fits over your wrist and then attaches to an electrical ground. Some antistatic wrist straps attach to a ground by plugging into a wall socket; they've actually got a plug on them! Because it *is* possible that a badly wired outlet could shock you, don't plug yourself in until you've read Chapter 7, "Power Supplies and Power Protection." In it, you'll find information about an outlet-wiring tester that you can use to check an outlet before hooking yourself up to it. Other antistatic wrist straps have alligator clips on them, which you connect to a piece of unpainted metal on your computer's case.

No matter what kind of antistatic strap you get, be sure to get *something* or you could end up breaking more things than you fix.

Now that you know the right way to handle the possibility of static, let's discuss the most common way people ground themselves to work on a PC: touching their hands to the outer frame of the PC before beginning to work inside the case. Why shouldn't you use this method? Because it's too easy to forget to ground yourself each time you go back in. It's also not foolproof. And, quite frankly, the wrist strap reminds you that you need to focus on the task at hand. So, use it.

TIP *While I'm at it, here are two tips that don't apply only to women: first, remove any jewelry from fingers or wrists. Rings can catch on objects inside the case, as can watch straps, bracelet links, and long necklaces. Scratches may result on either internal components or the jewelry itself. Better to remove such items and pocket them while you work. Second, if you have long hair (or, heaven forbid, have to wear a tie), pull it back before getting into the case. Everyone with long hair knows how much fun static is and how much of it long hair attracts.*

Interestingly, although newer computers use smaller and denser components, most current components are actually less susceptible to static damage than older ones because they're designed with buffers on the input and output lines. Although this can save you if you happen to make a mistake, don't use it as an excuse to be careless with your system and components—they can still be destroyed by static. Also, don't be fooled into thinking you'll see a big zap if this happens. As I said earlier, you may not even feel the kind of discharge that can ruin a piece of delicate electronics.

TIP *Here's something else you might not think about: if you happen to be wearing a loose bandage, rewrap it so it's snug and less likely to catch on something. If you're not wearing a bandage yet, you might want to have one handy. The edges of some of these frames and controller cards are razor sharp.*

Retrieving Tools

Here's the scenario: you're putting a PC back together, and you're mostly done. You're threading one of the last screws into the back of an expansion board, and the screw slips…and drops into the bowels of the PC.

Arggh!

What do you do? Well, one approach is to pick up the PC, hold it upside down, and give it a shake. C'mon, admit it—you've done it. (*I* have.) In Information Technology (IT) circles, this is called the "spit it out!" technique. But it's not a good idea. First, the silly screw will end up hitting the floor and rolling under something, so you'll never find it. Second, you'll probably rearrange something inside the cabinet of the PC.

Some people have screwdrivers with magnetic tips that they use to retrieve lost screws. This method works, but I'm awfully leery of having magnets around PCs. It's far too easy to forget that the screwdriver is magnetic and to lay it on top of a floppy disk or a tape cassette. Doing any of those things might erase data on the disk or tape (and that's why you shouldn't put refrigerator magnets on your PC case).

Instead, pick up a little gadget called a *retrieving tool* (also known as a pickup tool or a multifinger tool). They look kind of like giant hypodermic needles, with a button or a plunger at one end and a set of little spring-loaded fingers on the other end (see Figure 3.2). Push the plunger, and the fingers pop out like a tiny hand; let go of the plunger, and the little fingers retract, grabbing anything within their grasp. Retrieving tools come in different sizes, ranging from the "too short" version, which doesn't quite reach as far as you need it to, to the "way too long" version, usable for oil refinery part retrieval, presumably. There are also versions with flexible shafts to aid with retrieval in hard-to-reach corners. You can find them in hardware stores.

TIP   *If you're careful, you can also retrieve small parts with a long screwdriver and a bit of two-sided tape. Just fasten the tape on the end of the screwdriver, and poke at the part until it sticks to the tape. Just be careful not to become too attached to any other parts inside the case in the event they're not as firmly fastened down as you'd like.*

WARNING   *Once again, avoid using tools with magnetic coatings. They might be tempting to use, but they can damage your data.*

FIGURE 3.2
Retrieving tool

Hemostats

Some people call these *forceps*; they look somewhat like a pair of skinny pliers. Their tips are narrow, allowing you to grab things in hard-to-get-to spaces (like the extractors, mentioned later in this chapter). Additionally, this tool has a little clamp, so you can use it to hold things together. And, if you went to college in the early '70s as I did, then, hey, you may even have one of these around from those days.

The retrieving tool (mentioned previously) is smaller, so it can get into a wider range of places. On the other hand, hemostats can grip better, making them ideal for removing things jammed into the wrong place, like the narrow space between your internal CD-ROM and disk drives.

Pliers and Diagonal Cutters

Retrieving tools, hemostats, and pliers make a kind of hierarchy. Pliers aren't nearly as good at reaching difficult places as the other two are, but their gripping power is wonderful.

Another incredibly useful tool is known to techies as *diagonal cutters* or, for reasons I've never heard explained, *dikes* (see Figure 3.3). This tool is shaped a bit like a pair of pliers, but it has diagonal cutters at the business end instead of grippers. So, when someone says they're going to "dike that chip off the board," they're not talking about water control devices, they're just saying that they'll use the diagonal cutters to remove a chip.

FIGURE 3.3
Pliers and diagonal
cutters (dikes)

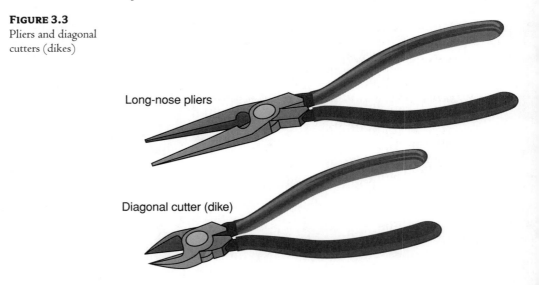

Long-nose pliers

Diagonal cutter (dike)

Chip Extractors (PLCC and PGA)

As you learned in Chapter 2, "Inside the PC: Core Components," there are many types of integrated circuits (chips). Some are rectangular, and others are square. The square chips come in two varieties. One is a Plastic Leadless Chip Carrier (PLCC), and the other is a Pin Grid Array (PGA). PLCCs are pretty tough to remove from their sockets without breaking them unless you have the right tool; they require a special extractor. Ever since about 1993, most socketed PGAs (such as Pentium processors) are in ZIF sockets and don't require a tool. All you do is lift the locking lever and lift out the chip.

For the older PGAs, you'll need a different extractor than for the PLCCs. Where do you get those tools? You can find them at just about any computer parts store. The good news is that it's rare to have to pull chips to fix computers these days. Although you can still find the tools, it's unlikely you'll ever need to use them.

Lights and Mirrors

You can make poking around inside the dark, cramped quarters of a typical PC system unit a little easier with improved lighting. For that reason, one of the best tools to add to your toolkit is a little flashlight such as the Mini-Maglite. Flexible flashlights, such as the SnakeLight, can be useful, too. You can find both types of flashlights at any good hardware store.

For peering into those hard-to-see places, you can't beat a small dental mirror. If you can't steal one from your friendly dental hygienist, you can probably buy one at a drug store or a hobby store.

Tools to Avoid

Many PC repair types start their tool collections with one of those 10-piece sets that you can pick up at computer stores for 10 bucks or so. Some of these are better than others—some super-cheap kits may not survive their first job. Overall, however, they're not a bad start, and they usually contain a few straight-slot, Phillips-head, and Torx screwdrivers, as well as a multifinger retrieving tool and the "chip-mangler twins"—DIP chip extractors and chip inserters. The manufacturers of these devices think they're useful extraction/insertion tools, but they're not. If you get them in a kit, throw them away. They do more damage than good and are to be avoided.

Rectangular-shaped chips with two parallel sets of "legs" are called *DIP chips*. Older computers had several of these that you could remove to perform upgrades and such, but most chips on today's motherboards are soldered on. But while you're out looking for a PLCC extractor for your museum, you might as well get a DIP extractor (and inserter) as well.

The DIP *chip extractor* has two hooks that you snag under the DIP chip and then pull up to remove the chip. The first problem with these tools is their inaccuracy. It's just as easy to yank a chip's socket off the motherboard as it is to yank the chip itself. The second problem is the lack of control they offer. When removing a DIP chip with this extractor, you end up grabbing the tool as you would a pair of pliers, a hand/muscle configuration better suited to pulling *teeth* than to pulling delicate chips. You'll get the chip out, all right—or, at least, you'll get *most* of it out.

It's better to use a flat-blade screwdriver to remove DIP chips. Just pry up one end of the chip a bit, then go to the other end of the chip and pry up the other end a bit, then return to the first end, and so on. Gradually work it out of the socket, and it'll come out whole and reusable.

The DIP *chip inserter* is a small cylindrical tool with a plunger in it. The idea is that you put a chip into the slot at the end of this tool, position the tool over the chip socket, push the plunger, and the chip slides right into the socket. The reality is that the chip smashes against the socket, mashing all the chip's legs and generally rendering the chip unusable. *Stay away from this tool.*

NOTE *Fortunately, DIP chip extraction and replacement has mostly gone the way of 8-inch floppy disks. It's not likely you'll need these tools anyway.*

Now that you have the right tools (and have gotten rid of the wrong ones), let's see what to do with them.

TIP *Whatever kind of tool set you start with, make certain you can manage it in your hands and you can work both within and outside the case with the tools. Tools too large or too small for the job or your hands are ill advised. Check the grip, too. Some ultra-cheap kits have slippery handles—you don't want to drop a screwdriver on the card below—and tools that won't withstand much stress.*

General PC Disassembly Advice

It's quite important to keep a few basics in mind when disassembling computers. Something as simple as not having enough elbow room could cause you physical discomfort, and losing all your data because you forgot to back up your hard drive would certainly cause another type of discomfort!

Be Sure That Disassembly Is Necessary

New troubleshooters are always trigger-happy with their electric screwdrivers, but, as I'll discuss in Chapter 25, "Troubleshooting PC Problems," the vast majority of PC problems *aren't* hardware problems.

The most important thing you can do before opening the PC is to consider what else might be causing the problems aside from the hardware within the case. Although going inside the PC isn't a big deal, it can be a hassle, and each trip inside increases the chances you might unseat a cable or short out a board. So you want to avoid opening the machine when it's not necessary.

Here are some common things to check first:

◆ Is everything plugged in and otherwise connected as it should be? Is everything plugged into a wall socket; is the socket live (test it by plugging in something that you know is working)? Always, always check your connections first. It can save you a lot of time and headaches.

◆ Anything you added, removed, or modified just before the problem developed—this can be hardware, software, or drivers. Try to reverse the changes you made to see if the current problem "disappears."

◆ Outdated hardware drivers—particularly after upgrading your operating system, Web browser, or other major application. Updated drivers can usually be obtained from the manufacturer's Web site.

Even if you *do* have a hardware problem, you should stop before opening the machine and ask yourself an important troubleshooter's question: Is this thing still under warranty? If you can make the problem Somebody Else's Problem (SEP), then by all means do. If you're sure it's a printer that's dead out of the box, don't try to fix it—just send it back. Stuff that's dead right out of the box usually can't be fixed because it never worked originally. (There *are* a few exceptions to that rule, but it's true in general.) Always ask: Is this trip necessary?

Make Sure You Have Adequate Workspace

You'll need a lot of room—most of a tabletop would be good; all of it would be better. Reduce the potential for static electricity. Raise the air humidity to 50 percent or so, use a commercial antistatic remedy, or at least touch something metal before you touch any PC component. Chapter 4 has more ideas for handling static electricity.

Keep the Small Parts Organized

Get a cup or a bag in which to store screws and small pieces of hardware. If you leave the screws on the table, you'll eventually end up accidentally sweeping the screws off the table and onto the floor, where they'll roll down a floor register or under the heaviest object available.

NOTE *An important goal of good PC maintenance is to end up without any spare parts.*

Because there will be at least two kinds of screws, it's not a bad idea to steal a page from car mechanics' books and use an egg carton to store them. Screws to secure the case, for example, tend to be a different size from the rest of the screws in the system, and sometimes you'll run across hard disks or CD-ROM drives that require short screws. Anyway, egg cartons have a bunch of compartments, and you can label each compartment to correspond to the screw(s) you put there. Or if you want something even more secure, many hardware and sporting goods stores sell small, plastic, compartmentalized boxes with hinged lids. They aren't very expensive, and you can close the lid on each compartment as you fill it. That way, you'll know what goes where when you go to put the computer back together.

Or use yet another approach: After you've removed a part, put all the screws into the holes where they came from. You'll have to remove them again before replacing the part in its original location, so there's a bit of extra work with this method, but the chances of losing screws or getting them mixed up are much slimmer this way. This is particularly true because now and then you'll see a drive mounted in some kind of bracket in such a way that you *must* use the very short screws that came with the drive and bracket. If you use standard-length PC mounting screws instead, you'll end up driving the screw into the housing of the drive itself, making the drive unusable.

Back Up the Configuration

Virtually every modern PC stores a small bit of vital configuration information in a special memory chip called *CMOS memory*. (Remember from Chapter 2 that CMOS stands for Complementary Metal Oxide Semiconductor.) That memory chip can't work—to be more specific, it won't "remember" its settings—unless it's hooked up to a working battery. If you end up removing the battery, the system will complain about not being configured when you reassemble it.

Let's take a minute and be sure you understand what I'm talking about here because there's a pretty common error that you may see when you reassemble your PC. When your computer's CMOS memory loses its information, your computer announces that with an error message on bootup. The message will say something such as, "I've lost my configuration information, so I don't know what kind of hardware I've got. Please reload the setup information in my CMOS."

On some older computers, you'll see some pretty cryptic messages, ranging from 162 (accompanied by two beeps) to `Invalid CMOS information-run SETUP` and the like. I'll cover this later, in Chapter 5, "Installing New Circuit Boards," but the Setup program is usually built into your computer and is accessed with different combinations of keystrokes. For example, on a computer with an AMI BIOS, you press the Delete key (Del) while the computer is booting. On an Award or Phoenix BIOS, you usually start Setup by pressing Ctrl+Alt+Esc while the system boots; it's Ctrl+Alt+Ins for some other machines. You make a Dell computer run Setup by pressing Ctrl+Alt+Enter at any time. Some computers (such as Compaq) flash a rectangular-shaped cursor in the upper-right or upper-left corner of the screen for a brief period while booting up; the computer will enter its Setup if you press F1, F2, or F10 (depending on the computer model) during that time.

By the way, do you see the extreme variation in methods of accessing Setup? That's only the first of many, many reasons why it's essential to keep your computer's documentation someplace handy, something I'll harp on throughout this book.

TIP   *Note that if you're running utility programs such as Norton Utilities, you may need to create and use special startup / system recovery disks to properly boot up your system and use the utilities. Refer to your software documentation for more information.*

No matter how you get into Setup, seeing this error message is pretty unsettling for first-time PC explorers. Relax; if you end up getting this message when you reassemble your system, it's probably not something you did wrong. More than likely, your computer lost its CMOS because you disconnected the battery while disassembling, or it may just be that the battery was failing. All you have to do is run Setup and restore the PC's values.

In general, a PC that has lost its CMOS information can make pretty good guesses about what the correct values for the CMOS parameters should be. In many cases, it'll beep at you and make you look over what it comes up with, and you'll be content with its choices. But one place where the computer might need a bit of help is in identifying your hard disk. This is more often true on earlier systems because post-1995 PCs are pretty good at figuring out what kind of hard disk or disks they have. Still, even the newest PC might get confused, so it's a good idea to note the hard disk information on your PC before disassembling it. Run your PC's Setup program and look in the "basic configuration" screen; you'll see information on up to four disks there.

NOTE   *It may be obvious, but I'll say it anyway: write down the configuration information before you disassemble the PC. That way you can easily reset the configuration to the way it was before—no guessing required.*

On older systems, the hard disk type is represented as a number between 1 and 47 or as Autodefined. Write down either the type number, or if it's Autodefined, write down the number of cylinders, heads, and sectors. Most newer systems are able to autodetect the hard drive type. Just boot up, and the computer will autodetect the hard drive(s) although it still may beep and give you an error asking you to verify the configuration.

Also, beware that Small Computer System Interface (SCSI) hard disks are sufficiently unusual in that the basic software that's built into the PC can't handle them. As a result, these unusual drives have their own built-in software (BIOS) to support themselves. However, because the basic BIOS that comes with the PC is of no use, you must tell the PC's BIOS to not worry about the hard disk. That leads to this seeming paradox: if you have a SCSI disk drive, your computer's Setup program will probably indicate that you have no hard disks.

When you have all of that information written down, you'll be set in case you find that the CMOS data has dissolved.

TIP   *If you own Norton Utilities, then take a look at the utility named DISKTOOL. Among other things, it'll save CMOS information to a file as part of making what it calls a rescue disk.*

Again, recording the CMOS information is important; you never know when you're going to need this information.

TIP *I'll mainly cover hardware here, but you also need to be aware of a pesky little operating system matter. Whenever doing anything of this nature, it's wise to have a* system boot disk, *also called a startup disk or system recovery disk, updated for whatever version of the operating system you're using. This helps you to boot the system even if the operating system is having a problem that precludes it from starting normally. Make sure you have created a startup disk before you disassemble your computer. To create a startup disk in Windows, choose Start ➤ Settings ➤ Control Panel. Then choose Add/Remove Programs, and select the Startup Disk tab. Follow the directions in each dialog box.*

Turn the PC and Associated Peripherals Off

This should be a relatively straightforward step. Just turn everything off!

By the way, when I say turn the peripherals off, I mean *all* peripherals—everything that's connected to the system unit. That includes printers, monitors, modems, you name it.

Take the Monitor off the PC and Set It Aside

If you don't have much workspace, it's not a bad idea to put the monitor on the floor *with the tube facing into the room.* This might seem like exactly the wrong thing to do because you might think you could accidentally kick in the picture tube. In fact, just the opposite is true. It's very difficult to kick in the front of a picture tube. The glass in front is usually between ¹/₂ and ³/₄ of an inch thick! Kick the front, and you're more likely to break your foot than the picture tube. The most vulnerable part of a monitor is the little stem that's at the rear of the picture tube. It's usually protected by only a thin wall of plastic, and the glass stem is only about ¹/₁₆ of an inch or so thick.

If you have a Liquid Crystal Display (LCD) monitor, you do need to be careful of the screen. Gone are the days of impenetrable thick glass; LCD screens are much thinner and a lot less hearty. When working on your computer that has an LCD display, you still need to take the monitor off of the table and set it aside. The question is, where do you put it? I recommend placing it in another room—or at least far away from your working area. The good news is that LCD displays are usually a lot lighter than old bulky monitors, so you won't strain yourself carrying it into the next room.

Unplug the Computer and Remove the Cover

First things first. Now that you have everything turned off, take the extra step of unplugging your PC. This protects you when you start messing around with all the electrical stuff inside.

Next, it's time to start taking things apart. Now, I don't know about you, but whenever I look at the back of a PC that I'm trying to disassemble for the first time, all I see are screws.

The problem then becomes knowing which screws help get the top off the computer and which screws will, when loosened, cause something in the computer to go "thunk!" (if the screw was supporting something big) or "dink!" (if the screw was supporting something small). You'll see case support screws on the back and sometimes on the sides of PC cases. There are typically two to four screws on the back of a PC that don't hold the cover in place—they fasten the power supply to the inside of the PC. Usually they're located near a fan, so they're somewhat easy to identify. So look carefully, and make sound decisions when removing PC screws.

TIP *The screws holding the case together aren't always screws. Sometimes they're larger thumbscrews that you can loosen and tighten by hand, with no tools required. These thumbscrews are sometimes located on the sides of tower PCs.*

PC cases come in several styles and sizes. There are basically two types: desktop cases and tower cases. *Desktop cases* are typically located on top of your desk (hence, the name) and come in two basic sizes— regular and slimline. Slimline cases usually have one or two removable faceplates for adding devices such as CD Recordable (CD-R)/CD Rewriteable (CD-RW) or Zip drives. Regular desktop cases can have as many as five or six removable faceplates for additional internal devices. Desktop cases aren't as expandable as tower cases, and the slimline desktop is less expandable than the regular desktop case.

Tower cases are the more popular choice with PCs. Full-size tower cases offer the most expandability and are ideal for servers. Smaller towers are more popular for consumers and are available in mid-, mini-, and micro sizes. Some PC cases are specially designed for quick and easy access, and others can be a bit more cumbersome.

I can't detail how to get into every kind of PC case, but let's take a look at these two common case types. Let's start with a desktop case (see Figures 3.4 and 3.5).

Note that on the back of the PCs in Figures 3.4 and 3.5, there are four to six screws that hold the case in place and four others that hold the power supply in place. When you remove the screws, remember that you have to keep track of them somehow, so store them in one of the ways I recommended earlier (or use your own storage method if you're feeling adventuresome). Be careful not to knock the screws onto the floor.

If you have a case like the one shown in Figure 3.5, slide the cover carefully forward and set it aside. And I mean *carefully*—don't rip the thin ribbon cables when you remove the top. The part of the case that mates with the middle screw is often a piece of unsmoothed sheet metal, and those of us who've met it before know it as the *cable ripper*. So be careful because it's *very easy* to scratch a cable with the ripper. Just a nick can make your floppy or hard disk (the peripherals that use these cables) misbehave. I once saw a cable that had gotten the "rip the top open and scratch the cable" treatment, and although floppies could read and write fine, it caused them to refuse to format.

WARNING   *If the edge of a case is sharp enough to rip a cable, it's also sharp enough to rip your flesh. Be careful when handling these cases—or keep a box of bandages nearby, just in case!*

Now let's look at how to remove the cover on a tower case, like the one in Figure 3.6.

This is a full-sized tower, but all sizes come apart basically the same way. You remove some screws from the back and swing the cover off. Note that the power supply screws are on the inside of the back of the computer. The case screws, in contrast, sit outside of the metal lip that runs around the outside of the back of the computer.

FIGURE 3.4
Desktop case

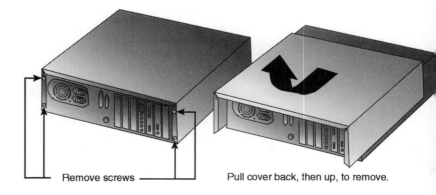

Remove screws ⎯⎯⎯⎯⎯⎯⎯   Pull cover back, then up, to remove.

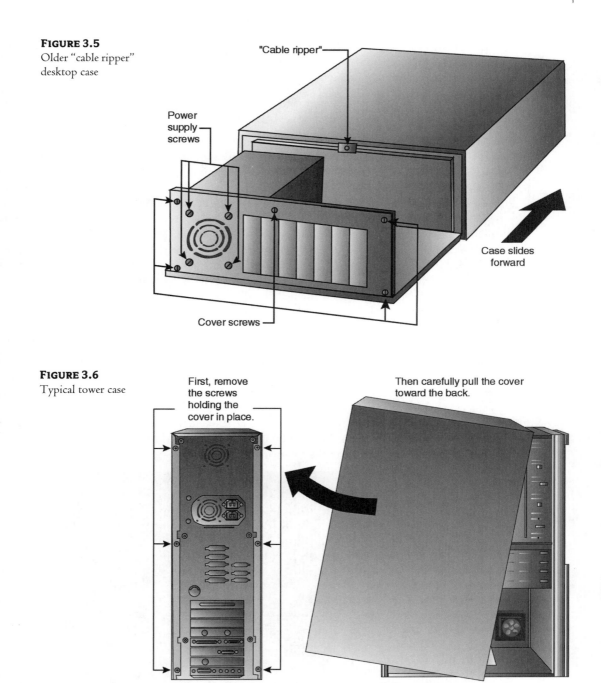

FIGURE 3.5
Older "cable ripper" desktop case

"Cable ripper"

Power supply screws

Case slides forward

Cover screws

FIGURE 3.6
Typical tower case

First, remove the screws holding the cover in place.

Then carefully pull the cover toward the back.

It's usually tougher getting the cover back onto a tower than it is removing the cover in the first place, so keep an eye on how the cover comes *off* so that you can figure out how it goes back *on*. Expect that the worst part of reassembling the computer will be convincing the cover to fit nicely on the case.

NOTE   *The newest trend in tower cases are cases where the top comes off and then each side comes off independently. These cases only have two screws to hold the top in place and are generally easy to put back together.*

Now that you have the top off, take this opportunity to write your name on the inside of the case with an indelible marker, as a small extra bit of security. By the way, in desktop cases, the most important screw in the back is the top center screw—it holds the weight of the monitor. In normal usage, it's best to ensure that all five screws are in place. However, if you're going to be lazy, the one screw *you must have* in place is the center screw. When you're reassembling, however, *don't* be lazy. Every one of those screws has a job.

Today's machines offer a lot of diversity in the types of screws—and even in the hard plastic retaining pins used in place of screws—to keep the cover in place and to mount expansion cards inside the case. So you may need to put a little effort into finding the right screwdriver—and it's possible you'll need more than one size. A good tip is to set aside any tools you find to be a good match so you can use them exclusively for doing PC hardware repairs. This helps ensure not only that you have the tools ready for troubleshooting but also that they're clean and in good condition (and didn't just come in from repairing the lawnmower).

Diagram!

Ensure that you have some paper and a pen so you can diagram what you disassemble. What order were the boards in? When you unplug something, it may not be simple to see how to reconnect it *unless* you have a good diagram. If there's no distinct marking on a cable, take a marker and *make* one. These machines aren't library books—it's okay to write on them. Remember that the game plan is to at least leave the machine the way you found it. You may not be able to fix the system, but you certainly don't want to leave it any *worse* off than you found it. If you're new in the business, pay special attention to the problem sources discussed in the following sections.

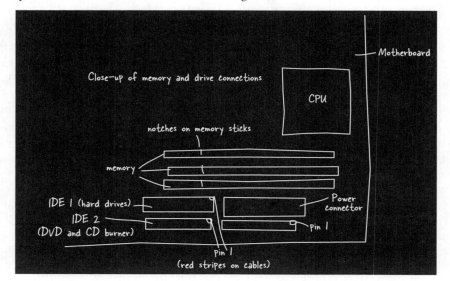

RIBBON CABLES

Ribbon cables (also called *data cables*) are flat cables connected to upright pins on circuit boards. There's a definite correct way to put them on a connector. As you can see in Figure 3.7, the ribbon cables have a dark stripe on one edge (usually red). Some manufacturers use fine red speckles along one edge of the ribbon cables, so look carefully if you don't see the stripe at first.

The stripe on the ribbon cable corresponds to the position of pin 1 on the connector. Trouble is, often the connector you're plugging the cable into will not be labeled. Therefore, it's a good idea to closely look at how the cable is connected to the board/device. A few landmarks can be useful. For example, does that dark stripe go up on the board? Down? Toward the speaker? Toward the power supply? (Note that I didn't say *left* or *right*—those can get you into trouble.) Make sure to note the current position of the cables in your diagram.

TIP Using left and right as directions in computer diagrams can get you into trouble if you get turned around. Instead, one idea is to use north as referring to the back of the computer and then reference the other directions as you would if you were using a map.

FIGURE 3.7
Ribbon cable

Dark red stripe on this edge

And while you're diagramming cables and cable placement, remember to not only diagram what cables are there but diagram what cables *aren't* there. I know this sounds sort of like a Zen koan, but what I mean is this: suppose there's a ribbon connector on one of your computer's circuit boards, but you're not using it. For example, many sound cards nowadays have a connector on them for a proprietary CD-ROM drive interface. If you're not using the interface—for instance, if you don't have a CD-ROM drive, or if you have a SCSI CD-ROM drive—then you probably won't notice the connector when you disassemble the computer. When you reassemble the computer, however, you'll say to yourself, "Hmmm...a connector. I wonder what goes on it...."—and then you'll get creative, usually with bad results. (Plugging a floppy drive into a CD-ROM drive interface will toast the floppy drive. It might even toast the CD-ROM interface.)

I recently removed a motherboard from a system that had two rows of 15 pins on the corner of the motherboard. Small wires connected to the pins for power control, reset, status lights, and the like, as usual. But the connectors seemed to have been put on randomly: one connector sat across three pins, then four pins were unused, then another connector covered two pins, then six pins were unused in the first row. The second row was just as bad. Now, if I hadn't written these connections down, try to imagine how many different possibilities I'd have had to try when I reinstalled the mother-board—it boggles the mind. So remember: noting which connections are *unused* is as important as noting which connections are *used*.

Some enterprising souls have noted the inherent inefficiency of the traditional ribbon cable and created a round Integrated Drive Electronics (IDE) cable. I like 'em—they take up a lot less space than the old flat cables, and they're easier to deal with inside the case. Plus, they come in a variety of colors, so you can color coordinate if you want to (which could be really important if you have a clear case); see Figure 3.8.

FIGURE 3.8
Round IDE cable

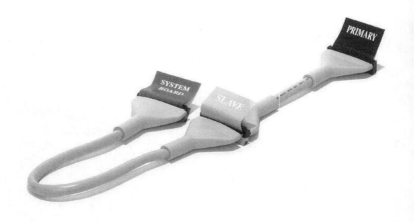

BOARD AND CABLE PLACEMENT

Students often ask, "Does it matter which slot you put a board into?" Well, it depends, but in general the answer is "yes." It's good practice to put the board back in the original slot it came from. For one reason, as you learned in the previous chapter, there may be several different types of slots on your motherboard. You have to put boards of type X into slots of type X. For example, AGP cards won't fit in PCI slots, which really is a good thing.

Furthermore, more advanced bus types require that you note which slot you took a board from and restore the board to that slot. Plug a board into the wrong slot, and the PC will either emit lots of error messages or fail to work altogether when you put it back together. In other words, if you took a board out of the second slot over from the power supply, then put the board back into the third slot over from the power supply, you may encounter problems.

Some boards require you return them to their original slot for electronic reasons. Other boards require you return them to their original slot for more pedestrian reasons: their slot may be the only slot in which they fit. You may not be able to get cables routed to and from the boards unless you put the boards in particular slots. Or a board may sit a bit higher than the others, and only one slot offers enough vertical clearance to accommodate that board; or some slots may be effectively truncated by memory modules, rendering them useless for longer boards.

And speaking of cables, you should be able to tuck cables out of the way when reassembling—take note of how it's done on the machine before you take it apart.

DIP Switches

Before you remove a board, check whether the board has any DIP switches. Odds are that it doesn't, but if you have an old card still in service, it might have some. If it does, make a note of the DIP switch settings (see Figure 3.9). I've spent 20 minutes setting a DIP switch bank only to find that I set the *wrong* bank! I messed up a perfectly good configuration and made my reassembly task all the more difficult.

FIGURE 3.9
Typical DIP
switches

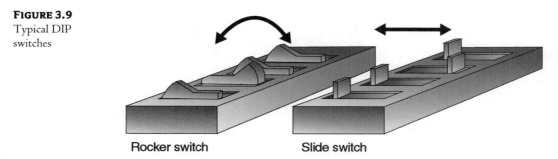

Rocker switch   Slide switch

Jumpers

These have the same story as DIP switches. Write them down, take a picture of them, try putting the board on a copying machine, whatever works—but document the things.

Motherboard Connections

After you have the case open, you'll see the motherboard. It'll be the biggest board, and it'll have a bunch of things connected to it, including the following:

Power supply connections The current power connection standard is the ATX form factor. It uses only one big 20-pin connector, as shown in Figure 3.10, rather than two smaller ones like the old AT standard did.

Speaker connection This connects the timer (which generates the sound signal) to the speaker. It's generally a connector with yellow and black wires.

Power connection Computers have "soft power" switches to allow software to control whether the computer is powered up. There's a button on the front of the PC that tells the power management software that it's okay to completely power up the computer. But the button must be connected to the motherboard for that to happen. Forget to reconnect the button, and the PC will look awfully dead, which is the sort of thing that can panic your clients—or you, if it's your PC and it's the first time you're disassembling it.

NOTE *If you do run across an old AT power supply, be careful not to plug the connectors in backward because you'll fry the motherboard. Keep the black wires together, and you'll be okay.*

FIGURE 3.10

An ATX power connector

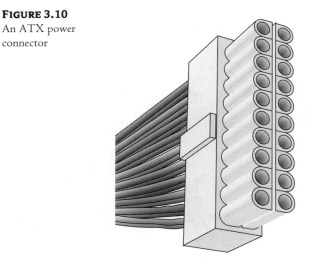

Remove the Boards Correctly

First, detach all connectors from the board. When you do that, again, please be sure to diagram which connector went where. Don't just assume you can check the circuit board's schematic or diagram later, if needed, on the vendor's Web site. These diagrams are sometimes mislabeled or poorly displayed, so you want to be able to depend on your eyes and your diagram. Be very careful about forcing anything open or off. Remove the board's retaining screw (put the screw in the cup, remember) and grasp the board front and back with two hands. Rock the board back and forth (*not side to side!*), and it'll come out. *Don't* touch the gold edge connectors on the bottom part of the board. Oil and dirt on your fingers can corrode the connector or, at the least, make the connection less efficient.

If you've never removed a circuit board, take a look at Figure 3.11 and Figure 3.12.

FIGURE 3.11

Removing a circuit board

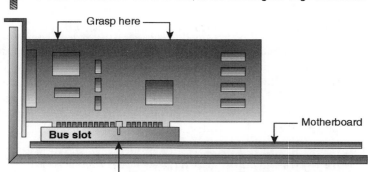

1. Remove any connectors (diagramming them first).
2. Remove the board's mounting screw.
3. Grasp the board along its top edge and rock it *gently* up and out.
4. Once the board is out of its slot, avoid touching the edge connector.

Grasp here

Bus slot

Motherboard

Edge connector (obscured in bus slot connection)

FIGURE 3.12
Rocking an
expansion board

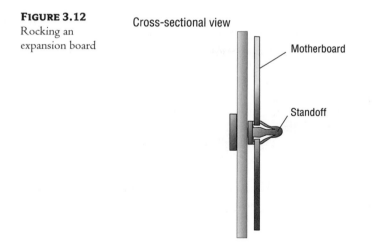

Cross-sectional view

Motherboard

Standoff

Now that you have those boards out, you may notice how similar boards are. How do you keep track of the fact that *this* green-and-black circuit board with lots of jumpers goes into the first slot, but *that* green-and-black circuit board with lots of jumpers goes into the *third* slot? Take a look at Figure 3.13 for some hints.

FIGURE 3.13
Various identifica-
tion marks on boards

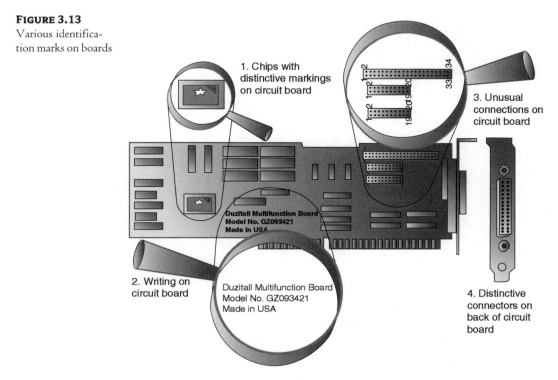

1. Chips with distinctive markings on circuit board

3. Unusual connections on circuit board

Duzitall Multifunction Board
Model No. GZ093421
Made in USA

2. Writing on circuit board

Duzitall Multifunction Board
Model No. GZ093421
Made in USA

4. Distinctive connectors on back of circuit board

When you get started in the PC disassembly business, all boards look the same. But after a while you'll see that they have quite distinguishable characteristics.

As you know, circuit boards are covered with chips. And those chips may have a distinctive look such as a company logo or the like. It's hard, for example, to miss Intel's logo on their CPUs.

Boards may also have some kind of writing on them. Sometimes it's a copyright or patent notice or the logo of the board designer. Sometimes it's even a label on the board that actually tells you what the thing does. Use these things to distinguish various boards.

Other boards have connectors that stand out, either on the board's face or on the back of the board. Use them, chip logos, and writing on the board to differentiate boards. You don't have to know yet what a board does; you've only got to be able to document where it came from and what it was connected to.

Of course, if there's no other way to differentiate boards, you can always just put a paper label on the boards—printer-ready mailing labels are just fine, as long as you don't tape over any of the circuitry.

Remove the Drives

After you've removed the boards, you may want to take a bit of a breather—you've done some real work there, especially if it's your first time inside a system unit. As a matter of fact, in some classes we stop here, put the boards back in, power the system up, and verify that it still works. A gradual approach to exploration isn't a bad idea. (Remember, we *did* orbit the earth for practice for eight years before going to the moon....

When you *are* ready to remove some drives, you'll find up to six main types in your computer:

- Floppy disk drives

- Hard disk drives

- CD-ROM drives

- DVD-ROM drives

- Tape drives

- Removable cartridge storage drives (Zip, Jaz, SuperDisk)

Of course, your computer probably doesn't have all six types of drives. But no matter what kind of drives you have, they all come out roughly the same way:

- They're secured to the chassis in some way.

- They have at least two cables attached to them: a power connector and a data (ribbon) cable. Some devices, such as CD-ROM and DVD-ROM drives, will also likely have a cable from the sound card.

DISCONNECTING CABLES

Your drive will have a power cable and a data cable connected to it. Your CD-ROM drive will probably also have an audio cable. Remove those first. (Are you remembering to add these to your diagram?)

The first, and easier, cable to find and remove is the power cable. Power cables extend, as you'd imagine, from the power supply (the silver box with the big thick power cable on the back of it) to the drive. You'll see one of two types of power connectors, as shown in Figure 3.14.

FIGURE 3.14
Two types of
power connectors

Molex connector   Berg connector

Most drives use the larger, more common Molex connector (named for the company that makes them). It's a milky white plastic connector with four relatively thick wires extending from its back; it has one yellow, one red, and two black wires. Just work the connector from side to side to remove it. $3^1/_2$-inch floppy drives use the smaller Berg connector. On some machines, the drive power cables are labeled P10, P11, or P12. Remove them from the drive's circuit board *carefully* because the connector tends to be a bit balky about coming loose from some drives. Now and then, I see some would-be Hercules who ends up breaking the connector right off the drive altogether. Just grasp the power connector and gently rock it from side to side. It'll come loose.

NOTE   *Incidentally, no one uses the names of the connector types. They're usually referred to as* big *and* little *power connectors.*

After you have the power connector off, take the data cables off. These are usually flat ribbon cables. Floppy drives and tape drives have 34-wire cables. IDE CD-ROM drives (the most common type) have 40-wire cables, as do IDE hard disks. CD-ROM drives can also have a three-wire CD audio cable that attaches to your sound card. SCSI drives have 50-wire cables. Again, diagramming is important. Replace one of these cables backward, and you could permanently damage something. One of the top mistakes that troubleshooters make is to blithely remove cables without first noting where they should go upon reassembly or in what configuration—red line up, red line down, or whatever.

REMOVING DRIVE SCREWS

After the cables are out of your way, free the drives from the PC's chassis. Most drives come out something like in Figure 3.15.

Part of the PC chassis is usually a metal cradle with holes drilled on either side of it. Screws threaded through the holes secure the drive to the chassis. Usually four screws hold a drive in place, two on either side (there are exceptions, but most computers work this way). Remove the screws, and you'll be able to move the drive around; that'll make removing the cables easier. After you have removed the screws, pull out the cables from the back of the drive and remove the drive.

In most newer cases, the bay that the hard drive is mounted in is also removable. For example, if you look at Figure 3.13 again, you'll notice the drive bay in the left pane has conveniently been made to look transparent. That transparent bay might have screws that specifically hold it to the rest of the case. Remove the bay first, and it'll be a lot easier to remove the drive from the bay.

FIGURE 3.15
Removing the
hard drive

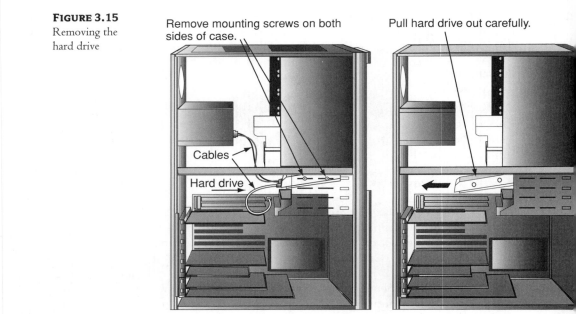

Remove mounting screws on both sides of case.

Pull hard drive out carefully.

Cables

Hard drive

Notice that most modern hard drives remove from the back. The floppy, CD-ROM, and DVD-ROM drives on most machines can usually be removed from the front or the back; do whatever is easiest for you.

NOTE *Some cases will only allow you to remove a drive from the front if you remove the plastic faceplate from the case.*

Remove the Power Supply

By now, the boards are out of the machine, and the drives are also gone. That'll make removing the power supply simple. At this point, the power supply's drive connections are detached, so you needn't worry about them. What you *haven't* yet detached, however, are the power connections to the motherboard. Some computers have two motherboard power connectors that must be detached. Others (those with advanced power management abilities) have just one big power connector.

UNDERSTANDING ADVANCED POWER MANAGEMENT

Before 1990 or so, most computers had a single power switch, located on the back of the computer. The power switch was inconvenient there, but it was simple for the PC designers: the power supply was back there, and it was just easier to put the switch on the power supply.

Around 1990, PC designers decided that people wanted power switches on the fronts of their computers, so they routed a big thick cable from inside the power supply to the front of the PC, and the switch controlled that. It's a bit cumbersome for anyone building a new PC (as you'll read in a bit), but at least the switch was in a convenient place.

Around 1997, PCs got a whole new level of power management. If you're running Windows 98/Me/2000/XP/2003 (or even a late version of Windows 95), the operating system can shut down your computer or sort of put it into a light sleep when you're not using it.

These computers also have a power switch on their front panels—but it's not a *real* power switch. Follow the wires from the "power" switch, and you'll see that it doesn't go to the power supply; it connects to the motherboard. The front power switch is a "soft" power switch. You can power up your computer with it, or you can turn the computer off—but it doesn't *really* go off. It goes into a low-power suspended state. That way, when you turn on your computer, it doesn't have to go through the entire boot process; it needs only to "wake itself up" and it's ready to go. The *real* power switch is on the back of the PC.

REMOVING THE POWER SUPPLY OF A FRONT POWER SWITCH PC

If you have a PC with only one power switch located in the front (which most are), here's what you'll need to do.

First, remove any connections and remove the power supply case. But there's a middle step that doesn't exist on the power supplies with rear switches. A thick black cable extends from inside the power supply all the way to the front switch. There are four wires inside the thick black cable: a black, a blue, a white, and a brown wire. Now, Alternating Current (AC) power doesn't include positive and negative wires—there's a *hot* wire and a *return* wire instead. Ordinarily, the black is the hot, and the white is the return; older power supplies just ran a white and black into the power supply from the wall socket, and that was all that was needed—but the needs of the new power supply's front panel switches change all that. In order to build a front-panel switch, power supply/case makers decided to drag both the hot *and* the return out to the *front* of the case, and then send the hot and return *back* into the power supply. This is now the case:

- The *black* wire connects the *hot* side of the wall outlet to the switch.

- The *brown* wire connects the *hot* side of the power supply's power input to the power switch. When you push the switch on, you connect white and brown, providing a *hot* AC connection for the power supply.

- The *white* wire connects the *return* side of the wall outlet to the power switch.

- The *blue* wire connects the *return* side of the power supply's power input to the power switch. When you push the switch on, you connect black and blue, providing a return AC connection for the power supply.

If you disconnect the black, blue, white, and brown wires from the front panel switch, you should be able to see from the previous discussion how important it is to diagram your connections. This is one case where if you reconnect things backward, you could end up directly connecting *hot* from the wall socket right into *return* from the wall socket. That would cause a short circuit that could make your computer catch fire!

If you look at the front panel switch, you'll see four flat connection points called *spade lugs* where you can connect or disconnect the white, black, brown, or blue wires. You'll notice a low ridge on the connector and that there are two spade lugs on either side of the ridge. Before disconnecting the wires from the switch, notice that the black and the blue are on one side of the ridge, and the white and the brown are on the other side. The ridge is just a "reminder" about which wires go with which other wires. Just keep the white and the brown on one side and the black and the blue on the other side, and all will be well. The way I remember it is that one side is "black and blue."

I've been beating the drum of "diagram" for the entire chapter, but there's no more important place to diagram than this. Put simply, these wires run directly from the AC line current to the power supply. Mix them up when you put them back together, and you'll create a direct short circuit on your house or office wiring. If you don't diagram this, don't put it back together.

Remove the CPU and RAM

Just how you remove the CPU depends to some degree on the type of motherboard you have, but it depends more on the type of socket the CPU is situated in. Most CPUs these days are on card edge packages, meaning that you remove them just as you would an expansion card. The other type of connector is a pin package, and those connectors are called *ZIF sockets*.

A ZIF socket features a small locking lever. Gently push up on the lever, and the CPU is freed and ready to be carefully removed—you can just use your fingers. (Push down on the lever to lock the CPU back into place.)

Pulling the Random Access Memory (RAM) is usually pretty simple. It sits in slots and has clips on either side to hold it in place. Pull the clips back and remove the RAM.

WARNING   The CPU and RAM are the most likely components to get fried while working on a computer. Place them in a safe spot. On or in an anti-static bag is the best place.

Remove the Motherboard

Finally, the motherboard comes out. (Recall that the motherboard is the circuit board lying flat on the bottom of the case.)

Before you remove it, look on the motherboard for small wires and flat rectangular connectors; they usually lead to the keylock, speaker connections, status LEDs, a reset switch, and the front panel power switch, if you haven't removed them already. Take these connectors off, but, again, be *very, very very sure* to diagram those connections before removing them.

You could also remove the battery from the motherboard (assuming it has one), but if possible, remove the motherboard with the battery attached. It saves you the trouble of reconfiguring the system when you reassemble it.

DRAWER-TYPE CASES

If you have a system with the drawer-type case, look around the back of the case near the peripheral connections and see if you can find the latch that holds the drawer in place. It's usually a sheet metal tab you slide to the side that lets you then smoothly slide out the motherboard. *Smoothly*, if you've remembered to disconnect everything, that is—keep a watchful eye out for wires you've forgotten; it's easy to sever them with the often-sharp edges of the sheet metal of the PC case. If you're replacing the motherboard, you unbolt it from the drawer and bolt the new one in.

You can remove the motherboard from the drawer by removing two to six screws. They attach the motherboard to the drawer with metal standoffs.

STANDARD CASES

With standard PC cases, you'll have to unbolt the motherboard from the bottom of the PC case to remove it (or the side, if you have a tower case). You'll see from one to six small plastic connectors or screws, depending on the make of the case.

Although different motherboards are held in place in different ways, the most common method involves a couple of screws and some plastic spacers to keep the motherboard from directly touching the case. Remove the screws and store them.

NOTE   Instead of screws, some motherboards are secured to the case with plastic spacers only, which have tab-like clips on top of them to keep the board from moving. If your motherboard is held on by these, use a pair of needle-nosed pliers to pinch the tabs together and remove the board. You'll need to do it one tab at a time. Figure 3.16 shows you how.

FIGURE 3.16

Pinching the spacers to release them from the motherboard

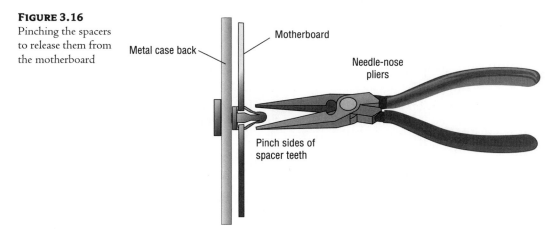

After you've removed the screws, you still might not be able to just pull out the motherboard. It sometimes sticks to the spacers that keep it off of the metal case. In most cases, you don't need to remove the spacers. Instead, grab the board and carefully move it away from the power supply. The motherboard should slide over and out of the case. If it doesn't, work it *gently* until it does. Applying pressure or force will damage the motherboard.

Some motherboards use metal standoffs instead of plastic spacers. In that case, you'll remove from three to six screws, and the motherboard will lift right out of the case.

Did you get this far? Then congratulations! You've completely disassembled a PC. (And you've remembered to diagram everything, right?)

Reassembly Hints

A rock-climber friend once explained to me some of the ins and outs of rock climbing. The thing that surprised me most was that people get into the most trouble when climbing *down* mountains, not *up*. I guess that shouldn't have been all that surprising, though, because PC disassembly is pretty similar. It's during the reassembly that the mistakes get made.

Basically, when reassembling machines, just reverse the order of disassembly. Plan ahead. Don't be afraid to pull some things out and start over if you're in a corner. The important thing is to *take your time*. Follow these steps:

1. If you removed the spacers for the motherboard, set them in their original positions. Then reinstall the motherboard, using the original screws to hold it in place. If the motherboard sits directly on the case (in other words, no spacers), it'll fry the board when you try to power the computer up. Not a good thing.

2. Reinstall the CPU and RAM onto the motherboard, and verify that you've seated them correctly in their sockets.

3. Replace the power supply. Support it with your hand until you have enough screws in place to support its weight. Then, reconnect the wires to the motherboard according to the diagrams you made during disassembly.

4. Reinstall the drives and reconnect them to the power supply. Verify that you've inserted the power plugs in the right direction and orientation.

5. Reinsert the circuit boards into their original slots, taking care not to touch the gold edge connectors at the bottom of the boards. Use the diagrams you made during disassembly to reconnect all connectors back to each board, including any connectors to the drives you reinstalled in step 4. Secure the boards in place with the retaining screws.

6. Verify you have no spare parts and that all items have been reassembled according to the diagrams you made before you began to disassemble your computer.

The following sections highlight a few tips for putting your computer back together.

Connecting Cables and Edge Connectors: The Pin 1 Rule

Earlier, I mentioned the ribbon cables that attach drives to their controller card (or motherboard). Most ribbon connectors can plug in either of two ways. Plugging in a connector upside down will usually not damage the device or the controller board, but it'll keep it from working. Many cables are *keyed*—that is, a connector is modified so that it can't be plugged in incorrectly. However, many aren't, so the following bit of information is valuable.

A ribbon cable consists of many small wires laid out flat in parallel to form a flat cable, hence the *ribbon* name. One of the wires on the extreme outside of the cable will be colored differently than the others. For instance, ribbon cables are usually blue, white, or gray. The edge wire's color is often darker, such as dark blue or red. As you learned earlier, this wire—the colored edge—connects to pin 1 of the connector. This is the Pin 1 Rule. (Some cables are multicolored, looking like small rainbows. Use the brown wire for pin 1 there.) This information has saved me more times than I care to recount.

How do you find pin 1 on the circuit board? Many labels are stenciled right onto the board—very nice. Others label only pin 2 because pin 1 is on the back of the board. So look for a 1, and if you can't find it, look for a 2. In the absence of a 1 to indicate pin 1, some manufacturers will place a small, painted circle or short line next to pin 1 (see Figure 3.17). If you can't find either, turn the circuit board over. Notice the round blobs of solder where chips are secured to the circuit board. These are called *solder pads*. On some circuit boards, all the solder pads are round except for pin 1—they're square.

FIGURE 3.17
Finding pin 1 on
a circuit board

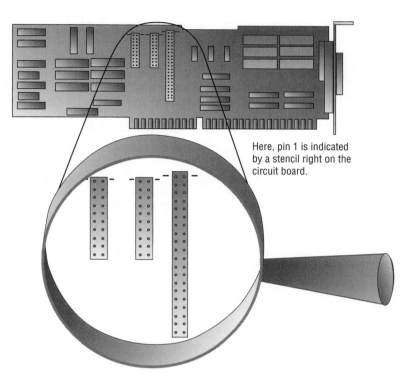

FIGURE 3.17
Finding pin 1 on
a circuit board

Here, pin 1 is indicated
by a stencil right on the
circuit board.

You'll find pin 1 on the circuit board of a hard or floppy disk, on disk controllers, or anywhere a ribbon cable connects to a circuit board.

Like most other convenient rules, there are exceptions. You may not find any indication of pin 1. Not all boards are labeled. Sadly, there is no Pin 1 Police. That's why diagrams are so important.

With ribbon cables comes one of the most common—and most dangerous—reassembly mistakes; you can see it in Figure 3.18.

FIGURE 3.18
Examples of
ribbon cables
installed incorrectly

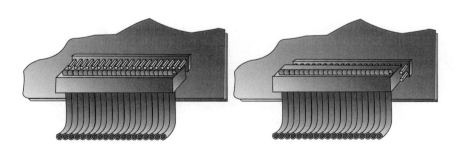

Unfortunately, it's remarkably easy to put a ribbon cable back on and accidentally offset it by one pin or a row of pins, either vertically or horizontally. On one motherboard I worked with, offsetting the pins by one destroyed the motherboard.

Figure 3.18 shows the missed pins as being nicely visible, but bear in mind it's just as easy to leave the naked pins *below* the connector, where it'll take close inspection to find them. Besides, it can be difficult to see exposed pins inside dark cases. So check your pin header connections closely.

Avoiding Common Reassembly Mistakes

In general, all you need for a good reassembly is patience and a good diagram. But here's what people tend to do wrong. Most of this stuff isn't fatal to your system *in the long term*, but it'll make you sweat until you figure it out.

SEATING THE MOTHERBOARD INCORRECTLY

Pay special attention when reseating the motherboard on its plastic or metal spacers. Make sure the motherboard isn't sitting directly on the metal case; there must be a bit of air space between it and the case, or you'll short-circuit the board for sure. I tend to come across a lot of cheap cases whose screw holes don't line up exactly right, and I worry that some stray piece of metal on the (cheap) case will short out the (expensive) motherboard. So I tuck a sheet of cardboard between the motherboard and the case, punching holes in the cardboard to allow the screws and plastic spacers to pass through.

REVERSING DATA OR CONTROL CABLES

"Let's see, which side *does* this blue line go on?" That's a common question. If you don't diagram carefully, you may find yourself having trouble trying to figure out how a ribbon cable connects to, say, a drive. Well, if you didn't diagram carefully, use the Pin 1 Rule to help you.

MISHANDLING BOARDS

Don't stack boards. Lay them out separately. Occasionally, rough handling can scratch and remove a circuit board trace. You can repair this by soldering a short wire across the cut in the trace. But why would you want to have to do this? If you're unsure whether there's been a cut or scratch significant enough to make a difference (traces can be faint or thin to begin with), use your ohmmeter. Set to low ohms (R1 on the dial), then put the probes on either side of the suspected cut. The meter should read 0 if everything's okay.

TIP   When a board comes in an antistatic bag, inspect the board but then put it back in the bag until you're ready to install it. This will prevent misfortune from finding the board before you need it.

FORGETTING TO ATTACH POWER

This one's good for a heart attack. You forget to attach that Molex or Berg power connector to the hard disk, and—arggh!—you get disk boot failure.

NEGLECTING TO PLAN CABLING

Novice troubleshooters stuff the cables any which way to get them in the box. Then, the next time they open the box, the cables pop up and get caught on the tab for the center screw. Cables rip and bend, teardrops flow—you get the picture. Stuffed cables also impede airflow in the case and heat up the inside of the machine.

Put the drives part way in, attach their cables, then look and ask, "How can I route these cables so they'll be out of the way?" Sometimes the best way is to move the drives around, so don't hesitate to be creative.

As I mentioned, there's another good reason for watching your cables: heat. Fans in your PC try to remove warmer air from the hot components and circulate the cooler air drawn in through the vents. If a cluster of cables is allowed to block airflow within the case, you'll end up with a PC running hotter, and this makes delicate components more inclined to fail or report strange errors.

FORGETTING THE SPEAKER CONNECTION, KEYLOCK CONNECTION, AND BATTERY

The first two are minor, the last annoying. Forget to reconnect the battery, and your computer won't remember the configuration you set up. This can be frustrating because the system will run when you set it up, but the next time you try to boot you'll get the `Invalid Configuration` error.

PANICKING WHEN IT DOESN'T POWER UP IMMEDIATELY

I've seen students do this sometimes. They can't get the computer to boot up, so they tear it apart again, ripping cables and forcing boards out before removing their screws. Stay calm. If necessary, take a break and come back to it when you can evaluate the situation more objectively—you're more likely to catch something you've missed if you don't stare at it. No matter how important the machine is, you can't fix it by rushing.

Upgrading Your Computer

Now is the perfect time to upgrade your existing, slow system. Why you ask? The computer is already apart, and you need to put it back together, right? Why not put some newer gadgets in while you're at it?

I'll caution you against upgrading just for the sake of upgrading, though. Just because your friend has a cool video card or the salesperson said that the sound card will make you think you're at the concert doesn't mean you need it. Right? But if you do need the increased functionality that an upgrade can provide, go ahead and do it.

Just like anything else in computing, though, you should probably plan your upgrade before you begin. Planning includes making backups (which you should have done before you tore the machine apart in the first place) and deciding which items you want to upgrade.

Deciding What to Upgrade

First, make a checklist of what you need the computer to do. Should it be faster? I know the answer to this is always "yes." But you need to ask yourself how much you're willing to pay for increased speed. Do you need new capabilities? Components that can provide these include modems, networks, printers, scanners, and video cameras...you get the idea.

The following list includes most traditional computer hardware and peripherals; use it as a guide to create your own checklist for planning your upgrade. You may choose to add other unusual or esoteric components to your own list.

- Case
- Motherboard
- Processor

- Memory
- Hard drive and floppy drive
- CD-ROM and DVD-ROM drives
- Removable media or tape drive
- Video card
- Sound card
- Modem
- Networking components
- Extra interfaces
- Scanners, printers, and cameras

Some of these components will obviously derive more benefit from an upgrade than others. For example, a processor and motherboard upgrade will likely do you a lot more good than a floppy drive upgrade. Unless your floppy drive is dead, you should probably just leave well enough alone.

Making Decisions on Parts

I know we haven't talked about all of the parts in a computer yet—that will come later. For now, we'll just stick to general advice regarding getting cool new stuff. The following sections talk about some things to look for when choosing what to upgrade.

COMPUTER CASES

There's more to this important item than meets the eye. The case provides a framework for your whole system. It's the main part of the computer that you'll see, and it includes the power supply that will run your computer. So choose one that looks nice (if that's important to you), has lots of room to work in, and is sturdy and solidly built. You can choose from a wide variety of case styles these days. There are even cases with translucent plastic case covers and built-in neon lights. You gotta love vanity.

Depending on your personal taste and needs, you can purchase several different types and sizes of cases. Above all, make sure you match the case with the motherboard you plan to purchase and get a case with enough bays to hold all the equipment you plan to install, such as hard drives, floppy drives, and a CD/DVD-ROM drive.

MOTHERBOARDS

The motherboard serves as the basis of your PC, so it's important you choose one with the features you need to put everything else in place. Here are some factors to consider when choosing a motherboard:

Processors accepted This is your primary decision factor. Choose the processor model and speed you want to build your system around first and shop only for motherboards that accept that processor. Both the AMD and Intel Web sites offer listings of approved motherboards for their processors.

Motherboard versus case   Make sure the motherboard matches up with the case. ATX is the standard case and power style, but you need to be sure your motherboard can be mounted in the case. Most of the time, this isn't a problem because cases have several mounting holes available. Still, it doesn't hurt to check.

Type of memory used   If you want to reuse memory from an old system, make sure the motherboard will support it. Many new motherboards support only a certain memory form factor and speed of memory, such as 100 megahertz (MHz) or 133MHz; your old Single Inline Memory Module (SIMMs) and Dual Inline Memory Module (DIMMs) may not work in such a motherboard. Remember that your goal is to build the ultimate computer, so don't downgrade the computer too much to accommodate your old memory. The cost of memory, like everything else, has plummeted in the past few years.

Number of expansion slots   Newer motherboards have phased out Industry Standard Architecture (ISA) slots. That's fine, unless you have old ISA devices, such as a modem, network card, or sound card that you were planning to reuse in this system. Instead of reusing your ISA cards, it's time to get modern and upgrade to Peripheral Component Interconnect (PCI). So, make sure the computer has adequate slots for all of your cards. Also, make sure the motherboard has an Accerlerated Graphics Port (AGP) slot for your AGP video card.

USB support   This is almost a no-brainer these days—all motherboards have it. But some motherboards offer more Universal Serial Bus (USB) ports than others. More is better, obviously. Try to get a motherboard that supports the newest version of USB, version 2.0.

Built-in video   Some motherboards come with a built-in video card. If the motherboard is made by Intel, the integrated graphics card is excellent. If you buy a cheaper off-brand motherboard, ask about the graphics capability of the integrated graphics chip. If it's really poor, you can usually disable it in the BIOS if you want to use a third-party video card. Many motherboards with built-in video forego AGP slots, which can be a problem if you want to upgrade later. Remember that unless you're upgrading this computer to play really high-end 3D graphic games, the integrated video is usually more than adequate.

Built-in sound   Some motherboards have a built-in sound card, often an Ensoniq model (a division of Creative Labs, the Sound Blaster people). It's good enough for casual use, but those with serious sound demands, such as gamers or musicians, may find it inadequate. Like with the built-in video, you can install a high-end card and usually disable the integrated sound in the BIOS if you don't want it.

Don't forget that when you upgrade your motherboard, you'll most assuredly need to upgrade your CPU and RAM, too. In fact, most people start off wanting a faster processor and then end up needing a new motherboard to support that new ultra-fast CPU. Make sure to coordinate your motherboard, CPU, and RAM upgrade purchases.

HARD DRIVES AND FLOPPY DRIVES

The hard drive holds the most valuable thing in your computer—your data. Choose your new drive carefully. The drive should be fast, reliable, and large enough to handle more than double the data you'll need to store.

"Double?" you say. Yep, double. Once a drive gets half full, it starts to slow down. So, for example, if you think you'll need 60 gigabytes (GB), get a 120GB or larger drive.

NOTE   *When you get a hard drive, buy it as a complete kit. That way, you'll get all of the extra bits and pieces you need to install it easily. For example, mounting rails aren't always needed, but they're great to have on hand if you discover you need them for the slot you're trying to mount the drive into in your case.*

Hard disks have two critical performance measurements:

Average access time   The time it takes for the drive head to reach and read the average bit of data, measured in milliseconds. Lower is better. A decent speed is 8 milliseconds (ms).

Data transfer rate   How quickly data moves from the hard disk to memory is expressed as the rotational speed of the hard drive. Higher is better. At this time, the two most popular rotational speeds being offered on Enhanced Integrated Drive Electronics (EIDE) hard drives are 5400 and 7200 revolutions per minute (rpm), with 10000rpm becoming more common. Although higher rotational speed can produce higher data transfer rates, the difference in performance isn't as directly related as it may appear. As the rotational speed increases, there's an increase in latency because it's more difficult for the drive to extract the data sequentially from the faster spinning disk. The result is that the 7200rpm drive transfers data faster, but the increase isn't earthshaking

Floppy drives are being used less and less these days. Still, they're cheap, and you should have one installed if only for the purposes of having a way to boot the system up for diagnostic purposes. In most cases, though, there's no reason to upgrade this device.

CD-ROM/DVD DRIVES

Now this is something that always gets me excited. Don't ask me why. I guess I'm still a kid when it comes to movies, but the technology of DVD movies is just plain incredible.

DVD drives can hold more than two hours of high-quality, full-motion picture video as well as CD-quality, 3D stereo sound! And I can watch it on my computer (my own personal movie theater) or connect it to a big-screen TV and hi-fi stereo system and share it with my friends.

So if you get a DVD drive, you can use any of the standard-format CDs or DVDs. The kinds of things to look for when you go out to buy a DVD drive are speed and features.

Now, when I say "features," I'm not kidding. You can purchase DVD drives as a drive only or as a kit. With the speed of today's processors, it's no longer necessary to buy the kit that contains the hardware decoder. The software decoder that's included with nearly every DVD-ROM drive is more than capable of providing all of the features found in hardware decoders. In fact, hardly anyone sells the DVD hardware bundles (kits) anymore.

So, why do you need decoding? When the DVD image is put onto the disc, the information is compressed so that the manufacturer can fit more stuff on it. This stuff includes alternate languages (yes, Kermit the Frog speaks Cantonese on some DVDs) and different screen proportions, such as standard and wide screen (also called letterbox). They also usually include the promos and trailers, and sometimes feature extra goodies, such as a director's cut of the movie or behind-the-scenes information.

Anyway, the data on the DVD disc has to be decoded. Two kinds of decoders are available: software and hardware. In practice, as long as your computer is running at a speed of 200MHz or better, you'll see excellent results with the software decoders. I highly recommend the PowerDVD by Cyber-Link (`http://www.gocyberlink.com/english/index.asp`). This software application is hands-down the best you can get for your DVD drive. Of course, you can pay more and get a hardware decoder.

The hardware decoder decodes the data on the DVD with very little burden on the CPU. Remember that even though this is the ultimate computer, your computer is fast enough to produce excellent movies with software decoders.

VIDEO CARDS

Video cards are one of the hidden bottlenecks in computers. You can have the fastest system (you're building one), but if you use a slow video card, it'll still perform like it's on vacation in the Bahamas.

For your ultimate system, you'll use an AGP video card with lots of built-in video RAM. Recall that AGP is a type of system bus corresponding to a slot on the motherboard. You may see both PCI and AGP video cards for sale when you shop. If your motherboard will accept an AGP model, that's what you want; if not, PCI will do. AGP performs somewhat better because it has a faster path to the processor than PCI.

When you go to buy a video card, the three basic things you should look for initially are speed, memory, and 3D capability.

Speed on video cards is measured in lots of different ways. One is a measurement of "millions of polygons per second." Polygons are the shapes used to create 3D graphics. The more polygons per second, the faster the card can produce images.

Another speed measurement that's often listed is something called the *frame rate*. A *frame* in computer graphics terms is the same as a single frame on movie film. To get smooth, realistic, full-motion video, you should have a frame rate of at least 30 frames per second, which is comparable to the number of frames per second you see in a movie at the theater. As the frame rate goes down, the image gets jumpy. For a business system that isn't going to be playing a lot of graphic-intensive games, a rate of 15 frames per second would be minimally acceptable.

Video cards have their own built-in memory that's used for video processing. The higher the resolution and the greater the color depth, the more video memory that's required for that operating mode. For example, a video card with 2 megabytes (MB) would be able to display 16.7 million colors at 800 600 resolution, but only 256 colors at 1024 768 resolution. The amount of memory a card has nothing to do with its speed of performance.

You also need to think about inputs and outputs. The basic function of a video card is to accept data from a computer and output images to a video display. But most video cards today can do a lot more. Some accept video input from video cameras and output to television sets, and others will output to digital flat-panel displays. If you think you might be interested in any of those capabilities, make sure you shop with them in mind.

SOUND CARDS

People love for their PCs to make noise—to play music, to make game sounds, to talk back to them. And who do we have to thank for it? Creative Labs and their amazing Sound Blaster cards. Okay, there are other sound cards available today. But the Sound Blaster was the first, and for a long time, it's been the best. They made the rules for sound cards, much as Hayes made the rules for smart modems. So today, even though Hayes is long gone, their modem's AT instruction set is still the standard (along with a lot of new extensions). And, as far I can see, Creative Labs will be with us for a long time to come, and the Sound Blaster's standard will continue to be the template for all other sound cards.

When you go to buy a sound card, the first thing to look for is Sound Blaster compatibility (unless, of course, you're getting a genuine Sound Blaster of some sort). If you get a card that isn't Sound Blaster–compatible, there's a chance it won't work with some of the programs you may want to run.

The next thing to look for is the card's specifications. There are three factors to be concerned about with a sound card—its number of bits, its wavetable capability, and its input and output jacks:

Number of bits   Almost all sound cards today are 16-bit or 32-bit cards. Don't accept an 8-bit card.

Wavetable capability   There are two kinds of sound cards: Frequency Modulation (FM) synthesis and wavetable synthesis. The latter is preferable. Wavetable cards have prerecorded, built-in sounds, such as the sounds of various instruments playing different notes. (FM synthesis cards simulate those notes instead, which doesn't sound as good.) Wavetable cards commonly have 32, 64, or 128 voices that they can play at once.

NOTE   *If you hear of a sound card that has 16 in its name, it's probably referring to its bits, and it probably doesn't contain wavetable synthesis (check the box to be sure). If, on the other hand, there's 64 or 128 in the name, the numbers probably refer to the number of wavetable voices.*

Input and output   The important question is this: does the card have the jacks you want? Jacks come in many varieties, and not everyone needs every kind. You'll, at the minimum, want a speaker output, a microphone port, and line in/line out. You may also want to look for Musical Instrument Digital Interface (MIDI) input, which enables you to plug in a keyboard or other digital instrument, and an auxiliary input.

Most sound cards also have a built-in joystick port. Joysticks are primarily for games, but they can also be used for some accessibility programs that let people with disabilities use a PC.

MODEMS

Want to connect to the Internet? To get online, you need a device that will connect your computer to it. For most of us, unless you have broadband access such as a cable modem or Asymmetric Digital Subscriber Line (ADSL), this is going to be some kind of modem. You really need a fax modem if you're using your computer as a fax machine. One of my clients also needs a dial-up modem to access an older-style state service that tracks bills going through the state legislature.

If you're getting a standard modem, the things you should look for are the speed (almost all are 56K), data-translation capability (these days you should get V.92), and any extra features you may want to have, such as voice and fax. Most modems today do faxing, but not all have voice capabilities. This allows you to hook up a speaker and microphone so that the computer will operate as a speakerphone or answering machine. You may also want to get a modem that can handle a video camera so you can have two-way videophone communications.

The final decision you need to make regarding your modem is whether to get an internal or external one. External modems have LEDs on them that let you see what the modem is doing from one moment to another. They also don't use any of the system power or system slots. On the other hand, most of us don't need to know exactly what the modem is doing and rarely use up every slot in our systems. Also, an external modem uses up either a serial port (there are only two of them) or a USB port, which will cost you more money.

For these reasons, and because I don't like to have so many extra things hung on the outside of the computer, I usually recommend internal modems. But for a real Internet connection, I wouldn't go with a standard modem at all—I'd spring for a cable or Digital Subscriber Line (DSL) connection. But if that's not available, get a nice 56K modem.

NETWORKING

You may think that just because you have a home system or a small office system, you don't need networking. Well, you may want to think again.

The only people who don't really need a Local Area Network (LAN) are people with just one computer. Everyone else will benefit from it. This is true even if the other computer is your kid's computer. A second system can really save you if you ever crash. One of the best things you can do with your network is back up the data from one computer onto another. Or better yet, back it up onto a removable media drive that's connected to another computer. Then, if one of the systems goes down (I should say *when* it goes down because eventually they all do), you can go over to the other computer, download the files you need from the removable media drive, and continue working while the sick one is being revived. And, by the way, be sure to install the drivers for the removable media drive on both machines so that it can be run from either computer.

To set up a small Ethernet network, you'll need the following, most of which can be purchased together in some sort of network starter kit at your local PC store:

A Network Interface Card (NIC) for each PC   Two speeds are commonly available: 10Base-T and 100Base-T. 100Base-T is better and faster, but most of these cards support both speeds and are called 10/100. This is the best choice, and they aren't expensive.

Hub or switch   You'll need a hub to connect the various PCs and networked devices together. Be sure you get one with room for expansion. For example, if you currently have three PCs, get a five-device switch.

Cables   You'll need a network cable to run between each NIC and the hub. Check the plugs on the NIC and the hub, but you'll probably want RJ-45 plugs on the cable. The cable is referred to a Cat-5 cable.

Of course, the current trend in networking is wireless. Wireless network cards and switches have dropped dramatically in price over the past several years, and wireless provides you flexibility that wired networking doesn't. For more information on networking, see Chapter 26, "Networking Concepts and Hardware," and Chapter 27, "Installing and Troubleshooting Networks."

EXTRA INTERFACES

The idea of extra interfaces might surprise you. Don't worry, you'll use them later—for now, just get them. One is USB, which you may already have built into your motherboard. It has become the standard interface, like serial and parallel, and all of the new motherboards have them. A lot of new devices are being offered with USB connections, and they make adding other devices to the system very simple—no Interrupt Requests (IRQs) or other complications to consider. Just plug it in and the system recognizes it.

The other connection I'm recommending is FireWire, also known as IEEE 1394. This interface is quite fast, and it's the best way to get full-motion digital video from a digital video camera. If you aren't concerned about getting the video as a digital signal, you can use a standard National Television System Committee (NTSC) or S-Video interface, but neither is as sharp as digital.

PRINTERS, SCANNERS, AND CAMERAS

Printers are usually necessary for a home computer user. This kind of goes without saying. But scanners and cameras are more luxury items that can turn your computer from a functional necessity to a fun toy.

For printers, look for resolution, speed, and features. Most printers these days are color capable, and some produce great quality photo prints. The better the resolution, the better your pictures will look. Of course, if all you print are black and white text documents, then you can probably save a bit by going with a simple black and white printer.

One choice for those with limited space is an all-in-one device. These combine the features of a printer, copier, and scanner (and often fax machine, too) into one device. Most of these devices have great print quality and offer flat-bed scanning. When these types of devices first came out, their drivers were sometimes a bit problematic. Now, though, you shouldn't run into many problems.

Digital cameras can interface directly with your PC (usually through a USB port) to automatically download pictures. Web cams can also do similar things and let you do video teleconferencing if you're so inclined. Cameras will be discussed in depth in Chapter 22, "Digital Imaging."

Troubleshooting Tips

One of the major mistakes you can make in working with hardware is to assume. And you run the risk of assuming when you don't follow some of the suggestions I offer you in this chapter and in the rest of the book.

One suggestion I've offered is that you diagram as you work so you know how things were when you started and how to put them back together when you're done. Don't make the mistake of assuming you can look up the schematics for a particular motherboard or other circuit board later. Many times, you'll be able to find what you need, but sometimes you won't find the board diagram at all, or worse, it may be mislabeled. If you're new to hardware, you may not be able to spot the mislabeling

A user recently came to me, tearing out his hair because he bought a used system in which he wanted to upgrade the old ISA video adapter with a faster, better-featured AGP video adapter. He had the new adapter in hand, but with the PC apart for hours, he still couldn't find where to plug the AGP adapter in. His motherboard's age and chipset indicated he shouldn't have AGP support onboard, but his motherboard's documentation and the diagram of the motherboard on the manufacturer's Web site showed one. Indeed, the poor guy didn't have an AGP port on the motherboard despite what he'd read, so he had to go exchange his super new AGP adapter for a PCI.

With this in mind, consider these steps when you're looking at documentation and diagrams and trying to match them against the diagram you drew of the motherboard:

◆ Try to orient any diagrams and figures in the documentation to the way you're looking at the motherboard to reduce confusion—this means try to look at the diagram from the same perspective you're looking into the case to view the motherboard.

◆ Always locate major components such as the CPU and the PCI slots in the diagrams or documentation—if your motherboard and your diagram show four PCI slots but the documentation shows three or five, you're probably not looking at an accurate diagram.

◆ When your computer's innards and your diagram look different from the documentation, consult the manufacturer's Web site first. Sometimes you'll find updated and/or corrected material there that was printed incorrectly in the paper manual.

◆ If there's still a discrepancy, use other sources to try to find out whether you have a different motherboard than you thought or whether the manufacturer just provided the wrong model in the documentation. Some of the online hardware resources provided in Chapter 24, "Using the Internet for Hardware Support," are a good place to start for this information because many of these resources review motherboards new to the market and provide pictures and specifics about them.

◆ When the differences between your diagram and the printed documentation are minor, note the differences on both the diagram and the documentation. That way, if you find just one (the diagram or the documentation) for a later troubleshooting session, you'll have a record of the correct information.

Now that you know how to take your PC apart, in the next chapter you'll look at some preventative maintenance techniques. Using them might save you from having to rip your system apart in the first place!

Chapter 4

Avoiding Service: Preventive Maintenance

- ◆ QuickSteps: Checking the Environment
- ◆ QuickSteps: Preventive Maintenance
- ◆ The Menace of Heat
- ◆ Dealing with Dust
- ◆ Magnetism
- ◆ Stray Electromagnetism
- ◆ Damage Caused by Water and Liquids
- ◆ Troubleshooting Tips

Introduction

The most effective way to cut down your repair bills is good, preventive maintenance. There are things in the PC environment—some external, some accidentally created by you—that can drastically shorten your PC's life.

Some of the things that affect your PC's life are commonsense things; I don't imagine that I have to tell you not to spill soft drinks (or, for that matter, hard drinks) into the keyboard. But other PC gremlin sources aren't quite so obvious. You'll get to all the environmental hazards, obvious or not, in this chapter. These are a few of the factors that can endanger your PC's health:

◆ Excessive heat

◆ Dust

◆ Magnetism

◆ Stray electromagnetism (including that found in electrical storms)

◆ Power surges, incorrect line voltage, and power outages

◆ Water and corrosive agents

There's an additional factor, which is produced by people and seen more and more as PCs become commonplace throughout the workplace and home. This factor—believe it or not—is grease, the kind that can be found in poorly ventilated kitchens, near cooking areas, or in workshop environments such as a garage. Combine grease with dust, and you have a sort of sludge that can form on and within the PC, effectively gumming up the works.

QuickSteps: Checking the Environment

Let's quickly run through the procedures and guidelines for protecting your PC that are covered in this chapter.

BE PREPARED

Before you start, there are some things you may need on hand. These include the following:

- Nonmagnetic Phillips-head or Torx screwdriver for opening the PC case

- Container for holding the screws between removal and reinstallation

- Antistatic wrist strap for reducing the chance of stray electrostatic discharge damaging components inside the case

Some type of temperature gauge for checking PC internal temperatures
Follow these steps:

1. Check power considerations:

   - No heating elements (coffeemaker, portable heaters) in the same outlet as a PC

   - No large electric motors (refrigerators, air conditioners) on the same line as the PC

   - Some kind of power noise protection

2. Check the computer's internal temperature ranges:

   - Maximum 110 degrees F (43 degrees C). (This actually varies, but 110 is generally considered the top acceptable internal temperature.)

   - Minimum 65 degrees F (18 degrees C). (The minimum temperature can be considerably lower, as long as the computer remains *on* all the time.)

3. Prevent dust buildup—you can buy power supplies with a filtered fan that sucks air in through the *back* rather than the usual approach of pulling it in through the front.

4. Make sure there isn't a source of severe vibration on the same table as the hard disk.

5. Make sure you know or (if you're a support person) teach your users:

   - That you should leave the machines on all the time

   - That cables should be kept screwed in and out of the way

   - Basic "don't do this" things about your operating system—for example, formatting the hard disk

6. Protect against static electricity.

QuickSteps: Preventive Maintenance

Although this chapter mainly discusses the environmental problems that PCs face, I also want to talk about some preventive maintenance concerns. The fact is, preventive maintenance will save you time and headaches in the long run. These steps should take about two hours.

BE PREPARED

Before you start, there are some things you may need on hand. These include the following:

- Nonmagnetic Phillips-head or Torx screwdriver for opening the PC case and removing expansion boards and other equipment within the case, such as drives mounted in their drive bays
- Container for holding the screws between removal and reinstallation
- Antistatic wrist strap for preventing static discharges while working inside the PC
- System backup software and available medium (Zip disks, CD-RWs, or tape cartridges) for performing a full or incremental system backup of the PC to protect the data
- Diagnostics software and commercial products such as a disk tools suite, a virus scanner, and other system check utilities in case you have problems identifying the source of difficulty
- Commercial connector cleaner solution and a lint-free cloth or a hard artist's eraser for cleaning the edge connectors
- Twist ties for binding cables together to keep them out of the way
- Slender, bent piece of metal for extracting a CPU (as described in Chapter 2, "Inside the PC: Core Components")
- Can of compressed air for removing dust from components

Follow these steps:

1. Pick up the PC at its work site. (Yes, this takes more time than having it delivered to your workplace, but you'll learn a lot just from observing its working environment.) Determine the following:
   - Are the connectors screwed in?
   - Have screws disappeared from the back of the machine?
   - What else is plugged into the PC's outlet? No other computer equipment? No cell phone rechargers? No coffeemakers?
   - Is the PC on a rickety table?
   - Is the PC near a window? Is it in a location that gets direct sun at some point in the day

2. Ask if the machine is doing anything strange.

3. Ensure that the hard disk (if any) is backed up.

4. If the machine is running Windows Me or Windows XP, run System Restore to set a system restore point.

5. Run the machine's diagnostics. (If you're running a version of Windows *prior* to XP, it's a good idea to run ScanDisk; it's not included in the XP operating system.)

6. If it's a DOS computer, examine the AUTOEXEC.BAT and CONFIG.SYS files for any obvious problems—lack of a BUFFERS command, for example. If it's an older Windows machine (pre–Windows 95), look at the INI files for obvious tampering. Then run Windows and the programs a bit to ensure they don't generate a lot of error messages (stating missing devices or conflicts) or return specific notes about stacks or buffers when programs crash. (This includes ensuring that the machine can print and can communicate over your corporate network or the Internet.)

7. Disassemble the PC.

8. Ground yourself.

9. Clean the edge connectors with a connector cleaner and a lint-free cloth or a hard, white artist's eraser.

10. Push the chips back into their sockets.

11. Use canned air to remove dust from circuit boards—don't forget the circuit board under the hard disk.

12. Reassemble the PC. Ensure that all the cables are securely in place.

13. Rerun the diagnostics.

14. Ensure that all screws are present. If they're not, add the appropriate screws.

Heat and Thermal Shock

Every electronic device carries within it the seeds of its own destruction. More than half of the power given to chips is wasted as heat—and heat destroys chips. One of an electronics designer's main concerns is to ensure that an electronic device can dissipate heat as quickly as it can generate it. If it can't, heat slowly builds up until the device fails.

More and more, heat can be seen as a by-product of overclocking, methods by which power users attempt to push their PC hardware for faster or otherwise more optimal performance. This is usually done through tweaking the motherboard and Central Processing Unit (CPU), but it's increasingly being done with many video adapters, too.

You can help control your PC's heat problem in several ways:

◆ Install an adequate fan in the power supply, or add an auxiliary fan (or clean the one you have)

◆ Install a heat sink.

◆ Adjust your box design for better ventilation (including keeping cables from blocking proper air circulation within the PC case itself).

◆ Install a heat sensor device or monitor your existing one.

◆ Run the PC in a safe temperature range.

Removing Heat with a Fan

Most desktop and tower PCs will surely fail without a fan. Actually, many of today's PCs have several fans: one integrated into the power supply, one for the CPU, one for a high-performance video adapter, and sometimes more added to move heat from a hot hard drive.

NOTE *Traditionally, many laptops haven't used fans because heat buildup wasn't an issue. Today, though, a lot of laptops include fans to dissipate heat.*

When designing a fan, engineers must trade cooling power for noise. This is because the greater the capacity of the fan, the greater the noise produced—more air and more movement equal more noise. But it requires more engineering and costs more to make a very small fan that moves a fair amount of air—more than most of us would want to pay for a tiny fan. Years ago, power supplies were quite expensive, running about $300 for the cheapest power supply, so great care was exercised in choosing the right fan for protection. Nowadays, basic power supplies cost less than $25, and I doubt that most PC company engineers could even tell you what kind of fan is sitting in their machines, any more than they could tell you who makes the case screws.

Now, that's a terrible shame because the $3 fan that's sitting in most PC power supplies is a vital part. If it dies, your PC will cook itself in just a few hours.

And fans *do* die. When they die, you need to replace them immediately or run the risk of ruining your computer. Signs that your fan might have died include the following:

◆ Less noise coming from your computer (the fan is usually the loudest component)

◆ Especially warm components, such as the top or sides of the case, or removable media after you eject it

Fans range in quality, capacity, and purpose. As a general rule, the cheaper fans tend to wear out faster, sometimes in as little as six months to a year, and the more expensive variety made with bearings tend to endure. Such fans can often be removed, carefully cleaned of dust and debris (a pencil-sized paintbrush with a firm tip is ideal for this because you want to be careful to avoid damaging the fan), oiled, and returned to service without the need to replace the fan.

WARNING *Never open a power supply unless you have been specifically trained on how to repair them.*

What causes all this heat that the fan is trying to remove? The more stuff that's in your PC, the hotter it runs. The things that make PCs hot inside include the following:

◆ Most chips, including memory chips, and CPUs in particular because they have the greatest number of transistors inside them.

◆ Drive motors in some hard disks, floppy drives, and CD-ROM/DVD drives. Some CD-ROM/DVD drives run quite warm, and large hard disks can run *extremely* hot. I've seen an old Maxtor 660 megabyte (MB) ESDI drive run so hot that it almost burned my fingers. However, I saw the same thing on a more recent 1.7 gigabyte (GB) Fujitsu drive. Fortunately, drives in the 3½-inch half-height or third-height format run much cooler. Some circuit boards can run quite hot, depending on how well (or how poorly) they're designed.

Truthfully, heat buildup inside a PC is much less of a problem today than it was in the mid-1980s. In those days, every drive was a full-height drive, and every computer had 640 kilobytes (KB) of memory built up from 90 separate 64KB chips. Add one of those early hot 8087 coprocessors, and it was common to find the inside of a PC running 30 degrees F (16 degrees C) warmer inside its box than in the outside room.

Today's PCs, however, are much more energy efficient. A standard 180- or 230-watt power supply handles far more devices hooked to it than do hardware designs from times past. But that doesn't mean you can't exhaust the power supply's range if you install many additional drives, for example. This can require a power supply upgrade to 300 watts, which is designed for more professional needs.

Removing Heat with a Heat Sink

For years, electronics designers have had to struggle with hot components on circuit boards. Sometimes a fan just isn't enough, so they need more help cooling an internal chip. They do it with a heat sink. A *heat sink* is a small piece of metal, usually aluminum, with fins on it. The heat sink is glued (using a thick substance known as *heat sink compound*) or clamped to the hot chip. The metal conducts heat well, and the fins increase the surface area of the heat sink. The more area on the heat sink, the more heat that can be conducted off into the air and thereby removed from the PC.

The standard Pentium 4 processor packages have a heat sink and a fan integrated with the chip. The idea is that the heat sink pulls the heat off, and the fan disperses it. The Celeron doesn't come with a heat sink, but that doesn't mean it's not a good idea to think about putting one on a hot chip. You can find heat sinks in electronics supply catalogs. Adding a fan can really increase the heat sink's ability to cool its chip. I've noticed that many modern motherboards have connections to power a couple of auxiliary fans, and you can buy fans that attach to those connections from PC clone parts places (look in the back of one of the PC magazines for them).

Understanding Good and Bad Box Designs

It's frustrating how totally unaware of heat problems many computer manufacturers are. The first tower computer I purchased was from a company named ACMA, and they put together an impressive machine. There were two fans in the case—a very nice touch—as well as a CPU fan. I have to say that they spoiled me. A later (1994) purchase, from an outfit called Systems Dynamics Group, was somewhat less enjoyable. The back of the PC chassis had room for two fans, but the system included only one fan. There's nothing intrinsically wrong with that, except that the cutout for the second fan—which is right next to the first fan—was left empty. The result was that the fan just sucked in air from the cutout a few inches away from it and blew that air back out. It made the fan happy, I suppose, but didn't do much for the CPU.

I noticed this pointless ventilation system pretty quickly, so I took some tape and covered up the extraneous cutout. Within seconds, the air being pumped out the back of the Pentium got 10 degrees warmer—which means that the CPU itself got that much cooler. If I'd left the extra cutout uncovered, the only ventilation that my Pentium system would have gotten was the simple convection from the heated boards and drives. Even at that, however, the Pentium system—which included a 1GB drive, 80MB of Random Access Memory (RAM), a CD-ROM, video capture board, video board, SCSI host adapter, and Ethernet card—ran only 10 degrees hotter inside the box than outside the box.

Things could have been a bit worse if the case was like some I've seen, with the fan *on the bottom of the tower!* This isn't too common, fortunately, but it's worth asking about so you can avoid it when purchasing a PC. This setup puts the circuit boards on the top of the tower and the fan on the bottom. (Heat rises, remember—this means a bottom-mounted fan is cooling the coolest part of the system.) Take a minute, and look at the airflow in the box. Even if you have a good box, you can still run into heat problems.

Using Heat Sensor Devices

Heat sensors can save you a lot in repair costs, such as the 110 Alert from a company called PC Power & Cooling. They're a name to know when you're buying power supplies. The 110 Alert, shown in Figure 4.1, is a circuit board about the size of a business card that plugs into a floppy power connector. When the PC's internal temperature gets to 110 degrees F, the alert starts making an annoying squealing noise. At 118 degrees F, it just shuts the computer down. The device costs around $15, and every network server should have one or one like it.

While I'm on the subject of PC Power & Cooling, I should mention that this company also makes an interesting variety of power products for the PC, including power supplies with very quiet fans, power supplies with built-in battery backup, and high-quality PC cases. I use their stuff when I want to increase the odds that my PC will be running when I need it. If you have any questions about what rating of power supply to use, the company's Web site (`www.pcpowercooling.com`) will give you an analysis based on information you provide about your system and your needs.

Additionally, several motherboard manufacturers include a thermal sensing device onboard—meaning that it's built right into the board itself and can be enabled or disabled in the BIOS.

NOTE *Intel's Pentium III and Pentium 4 processors include a diode that monitors the temperature of the CPU and shuts down the system if the CPU temperature exceeds 135 degrees F. Some Pentium III motherboard manufacturers have incorporated a BIOS feature that allows you to check the CPU running temperature that the onboard diode reports. If your motherboard supports this feature, you'll find the CPU temperature readout in the BIOS setup screen.*

FIGURE 4.1
The 110 Alert
thermal sensor
device

Another great tool for monitoring heat (and your power supply in general) is SpeedFan. This program, produced by Alfredo Milani-Comparetti (www.almico.com/speedfan.php), monitors fan speeds, temperatures, and voltages in computers with hardware monitoring chips. In addition, SpeedFan can utilize S.M.A.R.T. hard disk technology (most newer hard disks have this) to show hard disk speeds. And based on its name, SpeedFan can control the speed of your fan to control temperatures. And best of all, it's freeware (although Alfredo does appreciate donations)!

Finally, a program called CoolMon can also monitor vital system statistics, such as motherboard and processor heat. You can find CoolMon at http://coolmon.arsware.org/.

WARNING   *The monitoring programs mentioned here have worked well for me in the past, but as always, use these apps at your own risk!*

Keeping Temperature Ranges Safe for PCs

Electronic components have an ambient (room) temperature range within which they're built to work. IBM suggests that the PC, for instance, is built to work in the range of 60 to 85 degrees F. This is because the circuit boards can run as hot as 125 degrees F, but a typical machine may be as much as 40 degrees hotter *inside* than outside. And 125 minus 40 equals 85 degrees F, the suggested maximum temperature.

Obviously, if you have a good fan, the acceptable range of room temperatures expands considerably. If you have a really good fan, the inside of the machine is close to the same temperature as the outside. You don't want the inside of the PC to get any hotter than 110 degrees—hard disks can fail at that point, but, again, circuit boards can function in higher temperatures.

Heat also aids the corrosion process. Corrosion is a chemical process, and inside a computer, corrosion can roughly *double* in speed when the temperature of the process is raised by about 18 degrees F (10 degrees C). Chips slowly deteriorate, the hotter the faster.

Because the temperature inside the PC is the ambient temperature plus some constant, there are two ways to cool the inside of the PC—either lower the constant with a good fan or lower the ambient temperature. Keep the room cooler, and the PC will be cooler. In fact, if you walk into server rooms at companies that understand this, you had better bring a parka.

How do you measure temperature and temperature changes in your PC? Simple: get a *digital temperature probe*. Several companies—including Radio Shack, other electronics retailers, and even some camping supply stores— market them for about $15 to $30.

The easy way to use the probe is to tape it over the exit vents by the fan's power supply. An indoor, outdoor switch lets you quickly view the PC's inside temperature and the ambient temperature.

You may ask yourself, "Okay, but what's the best operating temperature range for my CPU?" Intel and other chip designers and manufacturers provide optimum operating temperatures by CPU on their Web sites, along with other specific technical information.

Before leaving the subject of temperature ranges, I should mention one debate that never goes away: whether it's ever wise to leave the cover off a PC for any extended period.

Many of us leave the cover off in the short term to make sure a new piece of equipment installed will work before we put in the screws. However, a considerable number of people, including seasoned computer veterans, believe that a PC functions better, overall, without the cover. Their theory is that much better air circulation is achieved, with the bonus that you can better monitor and access the hardware.

The other side argues that today's systems were specifically optimized for overall cooling with the cover in place, and that you put the PC—and operator—at some degree of risk by leaving the cover off.

Indeed, during the summer, if you have your PC cover off for any period of time, you'll notice that the interior picks up almost as many dead insects as an outdoor light fixture. And, of course, operating a PC without a cover is ill-advised for anyone with small children, pets, or a crazy cousin who might decide to see what happens if he moves a switch or pulls a cable. As mentioned earlier, many surfaces inside the system can be razor sharp.

For peace of mind and a cleaner PC, you probably want to keep your cover on except when you're installing, removing, or checking a piece of hardware within the case.

DUTY CYCLES

I said before that a device should get rid of heat as quickly as it creates it. Not every device is that good, however. Devices are said to have a *duty cycle*. This number—expressed as a percentage—is the proportion of the time that a device can work without burning up. For example, a powerful motor may have a 50 percent duty cycle. This means it should be active only 50 percent of the time. A starter motor on a car, for example, must produce a tremendous amount of power. Powerful motors are expensive to produce, so instead cars use motors that can produce a lot of power for a very short time

If you crank the engine on your car for several minutes at a stretch, you'll likely damage or destroy the car's starter motor. Floppy drive motors are a similar example: run a floppy motor continuously, and you'll likely burn out the motor. *Hard* disk motors, on the other hand, run continuously and must be designed with a 100 percent duty cycle.

Duty cycle is used to describe active versus inactive time for many kinds of devices. For some components, you control some of the overall duty cycle. For example, you decide how much work your printer will do in a single day. But many devices have internal cycles to keep them working on their own on a system that's up around the clock, just as many of today's PCs operate continuously.

THERMAL SHOCK

Because a PC is warmer inside than outside, changes in room temperature can become multiplied inside a PC.

This problem leads to a hazard called *thermal shock*. Thermal shock comes from subjecting components to rapid and large changes in temperature. It can disable your computer because of expansion/contraction damage. The most common scenario for thermal shock occurs when the PC is turned on Monday morning after a winter weekend. Many commercial buildings turn the temperature down to 55 degrees F over the weekend; your office may contain some of that residual chill early Monday morning. Inside the PC, though, it may still be 55. Then you turn on the machine. Within 30 minutes some PCs can warm up to 120 degrees. This rapid, 65-degree rise in temperature brings on thermal shock.

This is an argument for leaving the PC on 24 hours a day, seven days a week. (You'll see some more reasons to do this soon.) The temperature inside the PC will be better regulated.

By the way, you can't leave portable PCs on all the time, so you should be extra careful with portables to avoid thermal shock. If your laptop has been sitting in the trunk on a cold February day, be sure to give it some time to warm up before trying to use it. And give it some time in a *dry* place, or water vapor will condense on the cold disk platters. Water on the disk platters is a surefire way to reduce your drive's life.

SUNBEAMS

Another heat effect is caused by sunbeams. Direct sunlight isn't a good thing for electronic equipment. A warm sunbeam feels nice for a few minutes, but sit in one for an hour and you'll understand why PCs don't like them. Direct sunlight is also, of course, terrible for floppy disks. Find a shadowy area for your PC and floppies, or use drapes or good window blinds/shades to protect them from the sun.

Dealing with Dust

Dust is everywhere. It consists of tiny sand granules, fossil skeletons of minuscule creatures that lived millions of years ago, dead skin, paper particles, and tiny crustaceans called dust mites that live off the other pieces. Dust is responsible for several evils.

First, it sticks to the circuit boards inside your computer. As dust builds up, an entire board can become coated with a fine insulating sheath. That would be fine if the dust was insulating your house, but thermal insulation is definitely bad for computers. As you've seen, you seek to minimize impediments to thermal radiation from your computer components. To combat this, remove dust from inside the computer and from circuit boards periodically. A good period between cleaning is a year in a house and six months in an office. A simpler approach is to use the "while I'm at it" algorithm—when you need to disassemble the machine for some other reason, clean the inside while you're at it. A tool that can assist you is a can of compressed air. (*Compressed air* isn't actually compressed air; it's some kind of compressed gas.)

Just as effective for the case and inside support assemblies is a dust-free cloth wetted with a little water and ammonia (just a few drops). Don't use the cloth on circuit boards—get a can of compressed air, and blow the dust off.

This should be obvious, but when you blow dust off boards, be aware of where it's going. If you can, have the vacuum cleaner nearby, or take the board to another area. *Please* don't hold the board over the PC's chassis and blow off the dust with compressed air—all this does is *move* the dust, not *remove* it.

The second dust evil is that dust can clog spaces, such as:

◆ The air intake area to your power supply or hard disk

◆ The space between the floppy disk drive head and the disk

To combat the floppy drive problem, some manufacturers offer a floppy dust cover that you put in place when the machine is turned off. The sad part of this is that you really need the cover when the machine is on. In addition, Cathode-Ray Tube (CRT) displays have an unintended, unexpected, unpleasant, and unavoidable side effect—they attract dust. Turn your screen on, and all the dust in the area drops everything (what would dust particles drop, I wonder?) and heads straight for the display. Some of the particles get sidetracked and end up in the floppy drives.

One place that creates and collects paper dust is, of course, the printer. Printers should be vacuumed or blown out periodically, *away* from the computer. (Remember, dust goes somewhere when it's blown away.)

By the way, another fertile source of dust is ash particles. Most of us don't burn things indoors, *unless* we're smokers. If you smoke, fine: just don't do it near the computer. An old (1985) study by the U.S. Occupational Safety & Health Administration (OSHA) estimated that smoke at a computer workstation cuts the computer's life by 40 percent. How true that holds today is unknown. But it's still not a good idea to put anything smoky near the PC, and it's not wise to leave cigarette or cigar ash nearby, where it can be drawn into the machine. Greasy air isn't good either, so avoid setting up a PC next to a much-used stove or in a garage right next to where a vehicle pulls in.

NOTE *Many people decide to put air cleaners/ionizers in the room where they use their PC(s). This seems to be especially true of smokers. Although that's fine to do, it's best to position the air cleaner at least several feet from the PC itself. Otherwise, smoke, dust, and other particles are apt to be drawn to the intake fan of the air cleaner. If the air cleaner is close to the PC, the PC's front vent may pick up some of the airborne debris instead.*

Magnetism

Magnets—both the permanent and electromagnetic type—can cause permanent loss of data on hard or floppy disks. Most often, the magnetism found in an office environment is produced by electric motors and electromagnets.

Don't think you have magnets around? How about:

◆ Magnets to hang notes on a file cabinet

◆ A paper clip holder with a magnet

◆ A word processing copy stand with a magnetic clip

◆ A magnetic screw extractor

TIP   A frequently overlooked electromagnet is the one found in phones that ring using a real bell (which aren't common these days). The clapper is forced against the bell (or buzzer, if the phone has one of those) in the phone by powering an electromagnet. If you absentmindedly put such a phone on top of a stack of floppy disks and the phone rings, you'll probably have unrecoverable data errors on at least the top one. It's a good idea to get a phone with a ringer that isn't a real bell to minimize the chance of erasing data inadvertently. (Plus, you'll have fewer people teasing you about your "old-fashioned" phone.)

Another source of magnetism is, believe it or not, a CRT display. I have seen disk drives refuse to function because they were situated inches from a CRT.

X-ray machines in airports similarly produce some magnetism although there's some controversy here. Some folks say, "Don't run floppies through the x-ray—walk them through." Others say the x-ray is okay, but that the metal detector zaps floppies. Some people claim to have been burned at both. Personally, I walk through an average of three to four metal detectors per week carrying $3^1/_2$-inch floppy disks and have never (knock on wood) had a problem. My laptops have been through x-ray machines everywhere, and I've never lost a byte on the hard disk because of it.

The fact of the matter is that airport metal detectors *should* be sufficiently gentle for floppies. Magnetism is measured in units called *gauss*. Metal detectors *in the U.S.* (notice the emphasis) emit far less gauss than that necessary to affect disks. I'm not sure about Europe, but the fillings in my teeth seem to set off the metal detectors in the Ottawa airport.

Another large source of magnetism is the motor in a printer—generally, it isn't shielded (the motors on the drives don't produce much magnetism, in case you're wondering).

And do you (or someone you assist) work in a word processing pool? Many word processors (the people kind, not the machine kind) use a copy stand that consists of a flexible metal arm and a magnet. The magnet holds the copy on the metal arm. The arm can sit right in front of the operator's face so that the operator can easily type the copy.

The problem arises when it's time to change the copy. I once watched a word processing operator remove the magnet to change the copy and slap the magnet on the side of the computer. It made perfect sense—the case was steel and held the magnet in a place that was easy to access. The only bad part of the whole operation was that the hard disk on that particular PC chassis was mounted on the extreme right side of the case, right next to the magnet. You can start to see why I hate magnets...

Oh, and by the way, *speakers* have magnets in them. Years ago, a friend purchased a home entertainment system that included a VCR, a stereo, and some monster speakers. That's when I noticed he had stacked his videotapes on top of the speakers. I almost didn't have the heart to tell him, but I eventually advised him that his videos were history—and, sad to say, they *were*. Modern multimedia PCs all have speakers that claim to have shielded magnets, but I have a Sony woofer/satellite speaker system that makes my monitor's image get wobbly when I put the speakers too near the monitor. No matter what the manual says, I think I'll just keep the floppies away from there.

What about preventive maintenance? My advice is to go on an antimagnet crusade. Magnets nea magnetic media are disasters waiting to happen.

Stray Electromagnetism

Stray electromagnetism can cause problems for your PC and, in particular, for your network. Here I'm referring to any electromagnetism that you don't want. It comes in several varieties:

- Radiated Electromagnetic Interference (EMI)
- Power noise and interruptions
- Electrostatic Discharge (ESD)—static electricity

Electromagnetic Interference

EMI is caused when electromagnetism is radiated or conducted somewhere that you don't want it t be. Two common types commonly related to computer problems are crosstalk and Radio Frequency Interference (RFI).

CROSSTALK

When two wires are physically close to each other, they can transmit interference between themselve called *crosstalk*. I'm not talking about short circuits here; the insulation can be completely intact. The problem is that the interfering wire contains electronic pulses. Electronic pulses produce magnetic fields as a side effect. The wire being interfered with is touched or crossed by the magnetic fields. Magnetic fields crossing or touching a wire produce electronic pulses as a side effect. (Nature is, unfortunately, amazingly symmetrical at times like this.) The electronic pulses created in the second wire are faint copies of the pulses (the signal) from the first wire. These pulses interfere with the signa that you're trying to send on the second wire.

Crosstalk isn't really a problem when applied to power lines, but I've heard of cases where the alter nating current in power lines creates a hum on a communications line through crosstalk. The large worry is when bundles of wires are stored in close quarters, and the wires are data cables.

There are five solutions to crosstalk:

- Move the wires farther apart (not always feasible).
- Use twisted-pair cable (the pairs of cable are twisted at varying rates to reduce the amount o crosstalk—it's a physics thing).
- Use shielded cable (the shield reduces crosstalk—don't even think of running ribbon cables for distances more than 6 feet).
- Use fiber-optic cable—it's not electromagnetic; it's *photonic* (is that a great word, or what?). That means it uses light instead of electricity to transmit data, so there's no crosstalk.
- Don't run cables over fluorescent lights. The lights are noise emitters.

I once helped troubleshoot a network that had been installed in a classroom. The contractor had run the wires through the ceiling, but the network didn't seem to work. I pushed aside the ceiling tiles and found that the cable installer had saved himself some time and money by forgoing cable trays and instead wrapped the cables around the occasional fluorescent lamp. On a hunch, I turned off the lights and said to the people I was working with, "Start the network up again." Sure enough, it worked.

RADIO FREQUENCY INTERFERENCE

RFI is high-frequency (10kHz) radiation. It's a bad thing for computer communications. Sources are:

◆ Nearby radio sources

◆ Cordless telephones

◆ Keyboards

◆ Power-line intercoms (intercoms that use the power line's 60Hz as the carrier wave)

◆ Motors

Worse yet, your PC can be a *source* of RFI.

RFI is bad because it can interfere with high-speed digital circuits. Your computer is composed of digital circuits. RFI can seem sinister because it seems to come and go mysteriously. Like all noise, it's an unwanted signal. How would you go about receiving a *wanted* RF signal? Simple—construct an antenna. Suppose you want to receive a signal of a given frequency. You'd design an antenna of a particular length. Now, suppose that some kind of RFI is floating around. You're safe as long as you can't receive it. But suppose the computer is connected to the printer with a cable that, through bad luck, happens to be the correct length to receive that RFI. The result: printer gremlins. Fortunately, the answer is simple: shorten or lengthen the cable.

Electric motors are common RFI-producing culprits. I recently saw a workstation in Washington where the operator had put an electric fan (to cool *herself*, not the workstation) on top of the workstation. When the fan was on, it warped the top of the CRT's image slightly. Electric can openers, hair dryers, electric razors, electric pencil sharpeners, and printers are candidates. Sometimes it's hard to determine whether the device is messing up the PC simply by feeding back noise onto the power line or whether it's troubling the PC with RFI. Either way, the answer is to put the devices on separate power lines.

Because your PC also *emits* RFI, it can impair the functioning of other PCs, televisions, and various sensitive pieces of equipment. By law, a desktop computer can't be sold unless it meets Class B specifications—that is, the Federal Communications Commission (FCC) requires that a device that's 3 meters from the PC must receive no more RFI than shown in Table 4.1.

TABLE 4.1: PERMISSIBLE RFI OUTPUT (FCC CLASS B SPECIFICATION)

MAXIMUM FIELD STRENGTH FREQUENCY	(MICROVOLTS/METER)
30–88MHz	100
89–216MHz	150
217–1000MHz	200

RFI became an issue when the personal computer was first introduced, because IBM shielded its PC line in an effort to make life a little tougher on the clonemakers. By pushing the FCC to get tough on PCs, IBM had a bit of a jump on the market. Unfortunately, getting Class B certification isn't that hard, and just about every PC qualifies these days: clonemakers now say their machines are "FCC Class B Certified." This has caused the reverse of IBM's original intent because the FCC certification seems a mark of legitimacy. In reality, FCC certification isn't a measure of good design, quality components, or compatibility; it just means that the equipment doesn't produce excessive amounts of electromagnetic interference.

Protecting your PC from the devices around it and protecting the devices from your PC are done in the same way. If the PC doesn't leak RFI, then it's less likely to pick up any stray RFI in the area. Any holes in the case provide entry/exit points. Use the brackets that come with the machine to plug any unused expansion slots. Ensure that the case fits together snugly and correctly. If the case includes cutouts for interface connectors, find plates to cover the cutouts or simply use metal tape.

A simple Amplitude Modulation (AM) radio can be used to monitor RFI field strength. A portable radio is ideal because it has light headphones and a small enough enclosure to allow fairly local signal strength monitoring. A cheap model is best—you don't want sophisticated noise filtering. Tune it to an area of the dial as far as possible from a strong station. Lower frequencies seem to work best. You'll then hear the various devices produce noises through the radio. I first noticed these noises when working ages ago on a clone computer that had an XT motherboard, a composite monitor, an external hard disk, and a two-drive external Bernoulli box. The quietest part of the system was the PC. The hard disk screamed and buzzed, the Bernoulli made low-frequency eggbeater-like sounds, and the monitor produced a fairly pure and relatively loud tone.

The PC sounded different, depending on what it was doing. When I typed, I heard a machine gun–like sound. When I asked for a text search, the fairly regular search made a "dee-dee-dee" sound. It's kind of fun (okay, I guess I don't get out much), and you might pop the top on your system and do a little "radio astronomy" on it.

NOTE *This is also a fairly effective way to "eavesdrop" on other people's PCs. Sophisticated detection devices are capable of tracking how a computer is used (and replicating a PC's monitor image) by monitoring a PC's RF emissions.*

I've also used the radio in a number of other ways. Once, I received a new motherboard, a 486 that I was going to use to upgrade a 286 system. I installed it, and nothing happened. No beeps, no blinking cursor, nothing but the fan. So I removed the motherboard and placed it on a cardboard box (no electrical short fears with a cardboard box). Then I placed a power supply next to it, plugged in the P8/P9 connectors, and powered up. I ran the radio over the motherboard and got no response, just a constant hum. Placing the radio right over the CPU got nothing. I reasoned that what I was hearing was just the clock circuit. I felt even more certain of my guess when I noticed that the CPU had been inserted backward into its socket. One dead motherboard, back to the manufacturer.

Power Noise

Wall sockets are a source of lots of problems. They basically fall into these three categories:

- Transients—spikes and surges
- Overvoltage and undervoltage
- No voltage at all—a power blackout

I'll cover these categories in depth in Chapter 7, "Power Supplies and Power Protection." Right now, however, let's look at a special problem—lightning—and then the fourth kind of power noise, the one that *you* cause: *power-up power surges*. In the process of discussing how to fix this, I'll weigh in on the Great PC Power Switch Debate.

When Lightning Strikes

In many ways, lightning fits into what you've already read about in this chapter (transient electrical charges, for example), but it's worth discussing separately because of the PC damage caused each year by it.

Anyone who lives in an area prone to serious electrical storms during warmer months knows the damage a strike can cause to a television, particularly one with an external antenna wired into it. The charge from a strike on the antenna can travel into the house, into the back of the set, and can result in an explosion (if not a fire, too).

A PC can be at least as sensitive to lightning's effects and usually costs more to replace.

With PCs, you need to worry not only about the unit itself but about anything that wires into it from a source that could be affected by an electrical storm. In the most common situation, you use a phone line connected to a modem connected to your PC, which can act much like the TV with the lead wire from the antenna coming in. When lightning strikes phone lines in your neighborhood, the shock waves can travel along the connections and potentially travel into your home or office and into the back of the PC.

External modems, which have a separate power supply, tend to isolate the effects. Lightning may blow out the capacitors in the modem, but the damage usually stops there. Internal modems, however, are connected to the PC's motherboard. A charge occurring here could ruin not just the modem, but it could perhaps fry the motherboard, as well. Think of what this means when you have a motherboard with the modem integrated into the system board itself. Electricity felt on your phone line is delivered directly.

TIP   Don't underestimate the potential damage lightning can cause when you're reading about protection methods in Chapter 7. Also take lightning into consideration if your PC develops some strange problems—a malfunctioning modem, no power up, or odd boot errors—immediately following a large storm.

Leave Your Machines On 24 Hours a Day

I'd like to discuss one power-related item here: user-induced power surges. What user-induced power surges, you say? Simple: every time you turn on an electrical device, you get a power surge through it.

Some of the greatest stresses that electrical devices receive are when they're turned on or turned off. When do lightbulbs burn out? Think about it—they generally burn out when you first turn them on or off. One study showed that when a device is first turned on, it draws as much as four to six times its normal power for less than one second. (This phenomenon is called *inrush current*.)

The answer? Leave your PCs on 24 hours a day, seven days a week. We've done it at my company for years. Turn the monitor off, turn the screen intensity down, or use one of those annoying automatic screensavers so the monitor doesn't get an image burned into it. Turn the printer off also. Modern power management techniques (check for a Power Management icon in Windows 98/2000/XP) let you put the hard drives and monitor to sleep on a set schedule. Leaving the machines on also regulates temperature and reduces a phenomenon called *chip creep*.

What? You're still not convinced? I know, it doesn't seem intuitive—most people react that way. But it really does make sense. First of all, consider the things that you keep on all the time:

- Digital clocks, which obviously run continuously, incorporate some of the same digital technology as microcomputers, and they're pretty reliable.

- Calculators—I've seen accountants who use calculators that are kept on all the time.

- Mainframes, miniframes, and your phone's Private Branch Exchange (PBX) never go off.

- TVs—part of the TV is powered up all the time so that it can "warm up" instantly, unlike older sets.

- Thermostats—the temperature-regulating device in your home or business is a circuit that works all the time.

Most of the things that I just named are some of the most reliable, never-think-about-them devices that you have.

Second of all, consider the hard disk. All disks incorporate a motor to spin them at high speeds (depending on the drive, they may spin at speeds ranging from 3600rpm to 10,000rpm). You know from real life that it's a lot harder to get something moving than it is to keep it moving. (Ever push a car?) The cost, then, of turning hard disk motors on and off is that sometimes they just won't be able to get started.

Yes, the motor's life is shortened when continuously on, but even then the expected life of the motor is beyond the reasonable life of a hard disk.

Leaving your computer on all the time heads off thermal shock, which is yet another reason to leave it on. Machines should never be power cycled quickly. I've seen people fry their power supplies by turning their computers on and off several times in a 30-second period to "clear problems" but ended up creating bigger problems.

TIP *If you do have to cycle the power on your computer, turn it off and count—slowly—to 15, and then turn it back on.*

A word of caution, however: leaving the machine on all the time is a good idea only if:

- Your machine is cooled adequately. If your machine is 100 degrees F inside when the room is 70 degrees, it'll overheat when the building management turns off the cooling in your building on summer weekends and the room goes to 90 degrees. Make sure your machine has a good enough fan to handle higher temperatures.

- You have adequate surge protection, typically in the form of a surge protector strip installed between your computer (and its peripherals) and the AC power outlet. Actually, you shouldn't run the machine at all unless you have adequate surge protection.

- You have fairly reliable power. If you lose power three times a week, there's no point in leaving the machines on all the time—the power company is turning them off and on for you. Even worse, the power that comes on just after a power outage is noise-filled. And even if you do have fairly reliable power, you may want to change your practice when there's a possibility of the kind of severe weather likely to cause temporary power problems.

Of course, if your operating system is prone to crashing, it's almost impossible to leave your system on continuously. For that reason, upgrading to a more stable operating system, such as Windows 2000 or Windows XP, will enable you to leave your system up-and-running even though individual applications may crash. In addition, older (pre–Windows XP/2000) versions of Windows are prone to "memory leakage" and need to be rebooted about once a day to free up lost memory; Windows XP doesn't have this problem, which lets you keep your system running without constant rebooting.

Before moving on, let's take a quick peek at the other kinds of power problems—the ones you'll tackle in greater detail in Chapter 7.

TIP   One more final word of caution: with broadband Internet connections through cable and Digital Subscriber Line (DSL) modems becoming increasingly popular and affordable, using a firewall to protect your PC from hack attacks is a necessity, especially if you leave your PC on 24 hours a day. Consumer and professional firewalls, such as ZoneAlarm (`www.zonealarm.com`*) and BlackICE Defender (*`www.iss.net`*), help you protect your PC or network from unwanted intrusion and virus attacks.*

TRANSIENTS

A *transient* is any brief change in power that doesn't repeat itself. It can be an undervoltage or an overvoltage. *Sags* (momentary undervoltage) and *surges* (momentary overvoltage) are transients. In brief, the transient may be of a high enough frequency that it slips right past the protective capacitors in your power supply and punches holes in your chips. (No, they're not holes that you can see, at least not without some very good equipment.) Transients have a cumulative effect—the first 100 may do nothing. Eventually, however, one of them will take its toll. I'll talk about how to protect against these transients in Chapter 7.

OVERVOLTAGE

You have an *overvoltage* condition when you get more than the rated voltage for a period of greater than $2^{1}/_{2}$ seconds. Such a voltage measurement is made as a moving average over several seconds.

Chronic overvoltage is just as bad for your system as transient overvoltage: the chips can fail as a result of it.

UNDERVOLTAGE

Summer in much of the U.S. means that air conditioners are running full blast, and the power company is working feverishly to meet the power demands they bring. Sometimes it can't meet the full needs, however, so it announces a reduction in voltage called a *brownout*, or an *undervoltage*.

Brownouts are bad for large motors, like the ones you'd find in a compressor for refrigeration. Brownouts make your TV screen look shrunken, and they confuse power supplies. A power supply tries to provide continuous power to the PC. Power equals voltage times current. If the voltage drops and you want constant power, what do you do? Simple: draw more current. But drawing more current through a given conductor heats up the conductor. The power supply and the chips get hot and may overheat.

Surge protectors can't help you here. A *power conditioner* can—it uses a transformer to compensate for the sagging voltage. An Uninterruptible Power Supply (UPS) also helps remedy a number of electrical problems that interrupted power can cause. I'll discuss power conditioners and UPSs in greater detail in Chapter 7.

Electrostatic Discharge

ESD—or, as you probably know it, *static electricity*—is annoyingly familiar to anyone who has lived through a winter indoors. The air is very dry (winter and forced hot-air ducts bring relative humidity to around 20 percent in my house, for example) and is an excellent insulator. You build up a static charge and keep it until you touch something such as a metal doorknob—or much worse, your computer. And *zap!* On the other hand, in the summer, when relative humidity can be close to 100 percent, you still build up static charges, but they leak away quickly because of the humidity of the air. Skin resistance also has a lot to do with dissipating charges. The resistance of your skin can be as little as 1000 ohms when wet and 500,000 ohms when dry. (This fun fact is courtesy of Jearl Walker's *Flying Circus of Physics*, published by John Wiley in 1977.)

You know how static electricity is built up. Static can damage chips if it creates a charge of 200 volts (sometimes even less). But for the average person to notice it, static discharge must be at least 2000 volts.

Scuffing across a pile carpet in February can build up 50,000 volts. This is an electron "debt" that must be paid. The next metal item you touch (metal gives up electrons easily) pays the debt with an electric shock. If it's 50,000 volts, why doesn't it electrocute you when you touch the metal? Simple: the amperage (which is the volume of electricity) is tiny. This is because even though the voltage is high, the resistance is up in the millions of ohms, and 50,000 volts divided by millions of ohms is a tiny amount of current. Different materials generate more or less static. Many people think that certain materials are static-prone while others aren't. As it turns out, materials have a triboelectric (the electrical discharge created when you rub two objects together) value. Two materials rubbed together will generate static in direct proportion to how far apart their triboelectric values are.

Some common materials, in order of their triboelectric values (from highest to lowest, reading the left column top to bottom, and then the right column top to bottom), are as follows:

Air	Cotton
Human skin	Steel wool
Asbestos	Hard rubber
Rabbit fur	Nickel and copper
Glass	Brass and silver
Human hair	Gold and platinum
Nylon	Acetate and rayon
Wool	Polyester
Fur	Polyurethane
Lead	Polyvinyl
Silk	Chloride
Aluminum	Silicon
Paper	Teflon

Once an item is charged, the voltage potential between it and another object is proportional to the distance between it and the other item on the table. For instance, suppose I charge a glass rod with a cotton cloth. The glass will attract things following it on the preceding list, such as paper, and it'll attract more strongly things listed after paper.

Why does static damage PC components? The chips that largely comprise circuit boards are devices that can be damaged by high voltage, even if they're at low current. The two most common families of chips are Complementary Metal Oxide Semiconductor (CMOS) chips and Transistor-Transistor Logic (TTL) chips. CMOS chips include Negative Metal Oxide Semiconductor (NMOS), Positive Metal Oxide Semiconductor (PMOS), and an assortment of newer devices that seem to appear on an almost daily basis. TTLs are an older family of chips. You can identify one common family of TTL chips by ID numbers that start with 74 (as in 7400, 7446, 74LS128, and the like). TTLs are faster-switching chips—so potentially faster chips (memories, CPUs, and such) could be designed with TTL. Ah, but TTL has a fatal flaw: it draws a lot of power. TTL chips need much more electricity than CMOS chips, so they create more heat. Therefore, although fast TTL CPUs could be constructed, CPUs are tough to justify because densely packed TTLs produce so much heat that they would destroy themselves.

CPUs and memories are generally CMOS chips. CMOS has a lower theoretical maximum speed, but it runs on a lot less power. Sadly, they're also more subject to static electricity damage. TTL chips can withstand considerably more static electricity than CMOS chips.

Even if static doesn't destroy a chip, it can shorten its life. Static is, then, something to be avoided if possible. Another effect occurs when the static is discharged: When the fat blue spark jumps from your finger to the computer case, a small Electromagnetic Pulse (EMP) is created. This isn't too good for chips. The easiest way I get rid of my static is to discharge the static buildup on something metal that isn't the computer's case, such as a metal desk or table leg.

For your business, however, you may want something a trifle more automatic. The options are to:

◆ Raise the humidity with a humidifier (evaporative, not ultrasonic—ultrasonic creates dust)

◆ Raise the humidity with plants or, perhaps, an aquarium

◆ Install static-free carpet

◆ Put antistatic "touch me" mats under the PCs

◆ Make your own antistatic spray (covered in a moment)

From the point of view of comfort, I recommend the first option strongly. Your employees won't feel dried out, and the static problem disappears. Raise humidity to just 50 percent, and the problem will go away.

You can also make inexpensive, homemade antistatic spray. Just get a spray pump bottle, and put about an inch of fabric softener in it. Fill it the rest of the way with water and shake it well, and you have a spray for your carpets to reduce static. Just spritz it on the carpet—the carpet will smell nice, and everyone will know you've been busy. (I hear you asking, "How long does it last?" Don't worry, you'll know.)

NOTE   *In a similar vein, someone from a temporary services agency once told me that they tell their word processing operators to put a sheet of Bounce under the keyboard to reduce static. Although this may make the area smell nice, it will have no effect on static around the computer.*

Technicians who must work with semiconductors all the time use an *antistatic wrist strap*, or *ground strap*, to minimize ESD. As you know from Chapter 3, "Taking Apart and Rebuilding the PC," the idea of an antistatic wrist strap is that you never create a spark—or, therefore, EMP—because you always have a nice ground connection that's draining off your charges. A good antistatic wrist strap is an elastic wristband with a metal plate built into it to provide a good electrical connection, attached to a wire with an alligator clip. You put the clip on something grounded—the power supply case is the most common place—and put the strap around your wrist. Because you're connected to a ground, you continuously drain off your charges. A resistor in the ground strap slows down the discharge process a bit (from a microsecond to a few milliseconds), so you don't end up with one of the dangerous sparks I've discussed before. If you do a lot of board work in a dry place, antistatic wrist straps are essential. Several Silicon Valley defense-contracting firms have a policy of firing employees for not wearing their ESD wrist straps when working on high-tech equipment such as satellites and military equipment.

When you must handle electronic components, take these precautions:

♦ Get an antistatic strap. They're cheap.

♦ Remember the high-tech equivalent of knocking on wood—touch unpainted metal periodically.

♦ Reduce the chances you'll have a lot of static in the air—even though you're wearing the antistatic wrist strap, you still want to avoid raising any more stray static in the area than you have to, so if you're wearing anything acrylic on a very cold day, remove it. Also, avoid standing on an acrylic carpet without a rubberized floor pad beneath your feet, and keep long hair tied behind your back.

♦ Don't handle components in areas that have high static potential, such as high-humidity environments or carpeted areas (unless the carpets are made of antistatic material).

♦ Consider what you're wearing. Don't wear an acrylic sweater when changing chips. Get leather-soled shoes. If your work environment allows it, you can really avoid static by removing your shoes and socks.

♦ Don't handle chips any more than is necessary. If you don't touch them, you won't hurt them.

♦ Use antistatic protective tubes and bags to transport and store chips.

♦ If possible, pick up components by their bodies. Don't touch the pins any more than necessary.

♦ Have I mentioned yet that you should have an antistatic strap and use an antistatic mat?

Use the proper precautions, and your PC won't get a big "charge" out of being touched by you.

Avoiding Water and Other Liquids

Water is an easy hazard to detect and avoid. You don't need any sophisticated detection devices. Shielding is unnecessary—you just keep the computer away from water.

Water and liquids are introduced into a computer system in one of several ways:

◆ Operator spills

◆ Flooding

◆ Leaks

Spills generally threaten the keyboard. One remedy—the one recommended by every article and book I've ever read on maintenance—is to forbid liquids near the computer. In most shops, this is unrealistic. Some people use clear, flexible, plastic covers on the keyboard, kind of like what some fast-food restaurants use on their cash registers. They have "normal" cash registers, but they have a plastic skin over the keys that allows the user to spill special sauce all over the keyboard without harming it. Use the plastic covers, and they can just hose down the keyboard (just kidding).

A similar disaster, flooding, sometimes occurs. Don't assume that flooded components are destroyed components. Disassemble the computer and clean the boards by cleaning the contacts and edge connectors. You can buy connector cleaner fluids; some people use a hard, white artist's eraser—don't use pencil erasers! (A Texas Instruments study showed that they contain acids that do more harm than good to connectors.) Blow out crevices with compressed air. (And if you do disassemble, clean, dry, and reassemble your computer and then find that it works, write the manufacturer a letter; they might put your face in an advertisement.)

Avoid damage caused by floods by thinking ahead. Don't store any electrical devices directly on the floor; not only are they at risk during a flood, but they'll be damaged when the floor is cleaned. Generally, flooding indoors is under 6 inches. In addition, be aware of leaking from improper roofing; when installing PCs, don't put one in directly under the suspicious stain on the ceiling. ("Oh, that— it was fixed two years ago. No problem now.")

Corrosion

Liquids (and gases) can accelerate corrosion of PCs and PC components. Corrosive agents include the following:

◆ Salt sweat in skin oils

◆ Water

◆ Airborne sulfuric acid, salt spray, and carbonic acid

Your fear here isn't that the PC will fall away to rust; the largest problem that corrosion causes is oxidation of circuit contacts. When a device's connector becomes oxidized, it doesn't conduct as well, and so the device doesn't function, or—worse—malfunctions sporadically. Salt in sweat can do this, so be careful when handling circuit boards; don't touch edge connectors unless you must. This is why some firms advertise they use gold-edged connectors; gold is resistant to corrosion.

You don't believe you have detectable traces of finger oils? Try this simple experiment. Pour a glass of soda or beer into a very clean glass—preferably a plastic cup that has never been used before. There will be a noticeable "head" of foam on the drink. (Diet soda seems particularly fizzy.) Now put your finger into the center of the head, just for a second. The head will rapidly dissolve because the oils damage the surface tension required to support the head. It's the quickest way to eliminate a large head so you can pour a larger glass of beer. Or you could try buying a nice new flat-screen Liquid Crystal Display (LCD) computer monitor and see how many of your colleagues fail to understand that it isn't a touch-screen device. You'll end up with numerous thick, oily smudge marks on your monitor that are very visible and annoying when a dark background is displayed on it.

Carbonated liquids include carbonic acid, and coffee and tea contain tannic acids. The sugar in soda is eaten by bacteria that leave behind conductive excrement—like hiring some germs to put new traces on your circuit board. Generally, try to be very careful with drinks around computers.

Don't forget cleaning fluids. Be careful with that window cleaner you're using to keep the display clean. (In fact, most commercial window cleaners will eat the surface of your monitor anyway, so use a monitor-specific cleaner.) If your PC is on a pedestal on the floor and the floor is mopped each day, some of the mopping liquid gets into the PC. Cleaning fluids are very corrosive.

Again, you can clean edge connectors with either hard, white erasers (remember, don't use the pink erasers—they're acidic!) or connector cleaner products. One of the best-known vendors of these products is Texwipe (`www.texwipe.com`).

NOTE *Although this chapter has discussed some preventive maintenance concerns, I've mainly talked about the environmental problems PCs face. But you should also do preventive maintenance, which means taking a machine off your desk at regular intervals, perhaps as often as every six months, and moving it to your "shop" to give it a good going-over so that you'll anticipate problems. If you missed the key preventive maintenance procedures listed at the beginning of this chapter, make sure you go back and check them out!*

Troubleshooting Tips

When troubleshooting PC problems, it's important not to overlook the environmental factors discussed in this chapter (as well as whether the system has been "pushed" or overclocked to try to bolster performance).

Ask yourself these questions when you're working on a perplexing problem, particularly one where the difficulties occur at certain times of the day:

◆ Is the PC in direct sunlight or positioned in such a way that strong sunlight is hitting the case or monitor for a prolonged period of time? Install a shade or blinds, close the curtains, or move the PC where sunshine won't heat up the PC case, which in turn heats up the internal components.

◆ Is the room in which the PC is located prone to severe temperature changes? For example, in the winter, is the office quite warm during the day yet only has minimal heating during the cold nights? Such fluctuation isn't good for any system. If possible, move the PC into an area where the temperature remains more even throughout the day and night. If it must stay put, then the ambient temperature needs to be normalized before turning on the PC.

◆ Is the PC in a room shared with animals? Cats and other small critters like to huddle around warm things on cold days, and the hair they shed can gum up the works faster than a Kansas dust storm. In addition, a cat jumping on your keyboard can not only cause mechanical problems but can also introduce unwanted static electricity. If at all possible, isolate the PC from the animals. (And I know how impossible this is in many home office environments!)

◆ Are the problems occurring when the room temperature is very cold or very warm but not occurring at other times? Again, moving the PC to a more climate-controlled area is a good idea.

◆ Is hardware acting flaky after a particularly bad storm or power fluctuation? If so, the system needs to be evaluated, parts need to be replaced (as necessary), and the system then needs to be equipped with some type of power protection scheme, such as an UPS or surge protector.

◆ Is the PC located in an area where large appliances cycling up or down may cause a short flux in the power (noticeable by a brief flicker of the lights)? The PC should be moved to a different circuit from any other equipment that may interfere with it or its constant power supply. A power protection scheme such as a surge protector should be used.

◆ Is the area in which the PC is located prone to dampness? Dampness can cause odd behavior in a PC and can short out electronic components. Move the PC to a dry, temperate area.

◆ Have you or the PC's user recently "pushed" the limits of the system by adjusting clock settings on the motherboard or video card? If so, such changes may cause a heat problem inside the case, as well as account for other random errors and device failures. Reverse the "overclocking" and then either leave it alone or step it up gradually.

By now, your PC is shined to a high gloss. In the next chapter, you'll learn how to add fancy new expansion cards to upgrade your system.

Chapter 5

Installing New Circuit Boards

- ◆ QuickSteps: Installing a New Circuit Board
- ◆ Configuring New Circuit Boards
- ◆ Resolving Installation Conflicts
- ◆ Understanding I/O Addresses, DMA, IRQs, and Bus Mastering
- ◆ Working with Plug and Play
- ◆ Troubleshooting Tips

Introduction

Circuit boards and chips are fairly reliable as long as you keep them above water and don't subject them to the ol' 110-volt torture test. So, most boards you handle won't be defective. Much more often, you'll be doing upgrades to existing machines, such as replacing a video board with a faster, more powerful one, adding a sound card, or adding a Local Area Network (LAN) board to a machine that isn't yet on your company's or home network.

Putting a new board into your system and making it work involves five steps:

Installing the board   Put the board in the system, and make sure all the cables are attached properly.

Configuring   Make sure the board and the rest of the system communicate.

Testing   Weed out any boards that either don't work or will soon stop working.

Loading and configuring the drivers   Load the software that will help the PC use the hardware

More testing   Try out the new device to make sure it works with the drivers.

Getting those five things done will be the focus of this chapter.

This chapter begins with a "QuickSteps" section for those of you impatient for the basic steps of circuit-board installation.

QuickSteps: Installing a New Circuit Board

Now let's run through the procedures you'll need to follow when you install or replace a new circuit board.

BE PREPARED

Before you start, there are some things you'll need to perform the operation. These include the following:

- Nonmagnetic Phillips-head screwdriver
- Documentation for the new board
- Documentation for the motherboard on which you're installing the circuit board
- Installation CD or disk for the new board

Also, before installing or removing boards, be sure that:

- You're wearing an antistatic wrist strap.
- The PC is turned off and unplugged.

To install the board, follow these steps:

1. If your board has them, set any jumpers or switches on the new board to the resources you've already determined are available.

2. Install the board in an available motherboard slot of the correct type.

3. Boot to your operating system and let Windows detect the card. Windows will install any drivers you need and might ask you for the drivers' CD (or disk) if Windows can't find an appropriate driver.

4. Test the board's operation. If it doesn't work, check for resource conflicts.

5. Test all the other devices on your system to make sure that installing the new board hasn't caused a problem with any of them.

6. Document the settings for the new board, as well as any changes you made to existing device settings.

But I Have Plug and Play, So
I Don't Have to Worry About This, Right?

For several years now, PC manufacturers have attempted to make our lives easier by designing PCs around a specification called Plug and Play (PnP). If you have a PC that was built after 1996 (and why wouldn't you?), it's almost certainly a PnP system. PnP's designers intended that PnP systems would configure themselves automatically, as you no doubt guessed from the name. You just pop a new board into your system and boot up the computer, and your PC automatically loads the drivers it needs to use the new board. And now, with Windows XP and 2003, *Universal* PnP allows your computer to discover and use network devices. In seconds, you're using your new hardware.

Older circuit boards and systems that aren't PnP are called *legacy* devices and systems. Some newer systems won't accept legacy devices and have the dubious title of being legacy free. According to Microsoft, "The term *legacy free* refers to the elimination of many elements of the original PC architecture—both hardware elements and firmware interfaces. The move to a legacy-free system architecture is impacting all of the PC industry, from component makers and IHVs to BIOS makers and PC system manufacturers." What this term generally means is that the motherboard doesn't have any Industry Standard Architecture (ISA) expansion slots, only Peripheral Component Interconnect (PCI). It can also refer to serial and parallel ports, which are quickly becoming dinosaurs as well. Compaq computers that are legacy free don't have any expansion slots at all; you add hardware through the Universal Serial Bus (USB) port.

Early PnP boards sometimes *did* work as advertised, but only if your PC met some fairly specific criteria—the right hardware, the right drivers, and the right operating system. If you *didn't* have all those pieces in place, however, you found that PnP systems were actually *harder* to configure than older systems. In fact, let's say that again, with emphasis.

WARNING *PnP needs three things: hardware, software, and Basic Input/Output System (BIOS) support. So if you're not using a PnP hardware device but are running a PnP-compliant operating system, such as Windows 95/98/ Me/2000/XP/2003, and a PnP-compatible BIOS, your PC isn't PnP; hardware configuration can still be a real pain no matter whose PnP hardware you buy.*

Installing boards in a PC of any kind isn't the toughest task in the world, but getting them to work once they're installed can a bit difficult because of a few different things. Some of the stumbling blocks are bad board documentation (and there's no shortage of that); insufficient information about the computer you're installing the board into (that's usually *your* fault); address, Interrupt Request (IRQ), and Direct Memory Access (DMA) conflicts; and PnP woes.

Those challenges are what this chapter is all about. You'll learn what all of those things are and what you need to know to get new circuit boards into your system and make them work. It's not difficult stuff, but it *does* need some explaining, and I promise I'll make the whole thing as understandable as possible. As an extra bonus, the knowledge you gain in this chapter about Input/Output (I/O), DMA, IRQ, and the like will give you a head start when troubleshooting other problems you'll learn about later in the book.

Configuring New Circuit Boards

Most circuit boards are fully functional when you take them out of the box. But many of those circuit boards seem not to work when you install them in a PC. Why? The main reason is that the new board may *conflict* with existing boards or, more specifically, with some resource on an existing board.

Put simply, you can't have two boards that claim the same identity in a system. If you were to insert two identical sound cards into the same system, neither one would work, even if both boards were in working order before you put them into the PC.

Configuration consists of the following:

◆ Assigning resources to the device, avoiding any conflicts with existing devices

◆ Providing software support for the device (through the BIOS and/or device drivers)

On older boards, you specify the resources that the device should use by setting jumpers or Dual Inline Package (DIP) switches. Newer PnP boards almost always set resources through the BIOS or the operating system.

Depending on the board, your system, and your operating system, you may need to do some (but probably not all) of the following:

◆ Tell a modem which COM port to use (COM1, COM2, COM3, COM4, or higher)

◆ Tell a printer port whether it's on LPT1, LPT2, or LPT3

◆ Select DMA channels on a board

◆ Select IRQ lines on a board

◆ Select I/O addresses on a board

◆ Select Random Access Memory (RAM) and/or Read-Only Memory (ROM) addresses on a board

◆ Load a driver for the board

In many cases, the board is preconfigured at the factory to settings that will work in your PC, but not always. That's because it's impossible for the manufacturer to know what the proper settings should be for I/O addresses, DMA channels, IRQ lines, RAM addresses, and ROM addresses in your particular machine. Some older boards, unfortunately, are hardwired to a particular configuration that you can't change. The inflexible nature of those boards may mean that you won't be able to get them to work in your PC.

That's the whole reason PnP was invented—to eliminate setup hassles and resource conflicts. But we'll get into that more later in this chapter.

Software Switch Setup Advice

Boards in today's marketplace are designed without DIP switches. Such boards are set up through software provided with them or through PnP. Software setup has a good side and a bad side. The good side is that you can change settings on a board (such as making it COM1 rather than COM2)

without having to open up the PC and mess with jumpers—you just run a program, and you're done. The bad side is that now *you have to keep the setup program disk around forever*. What's that, you say? You're not that organized? You can barely keep track of the software long enough to get the board installed once? Okay, one solution is to get a big envelope and tape it to the side of your computer. Then put all of your setup disks in that envelope so that you'll always have them if you ever need them. Still think you might lose your disks? Okay, okay, maybe you don't *have* to keep the disk around forever, but it's a real good idea because you'll need the software that it contains to reinstall the board if your system ever fails. You may also want to make a copy of the disks or copy their contents to your hard disk in a folder created for that purpose. Of course, you can always burn all those setup disks, as well as downloaded drivers and hotfixes, to a CD-R or CD-RW to keep them all in one place, too. Then you'll have just one setup CD that you'll have to keep around.

So what happens if you *do* lose the disk? Check the manufacturer's Web site. Almost every board manufacturer maintains a database of the installation software for their boards online. As long as the company is still around, you should be able to get the software from the Web site. And, by the way, it might be a good idea to check that site once in a while anyway because the companies often provide upgraded drivers there, too. Who knows—you might be able to improve your system's performance. For example, U.S. Robotics has a software upgrade for some of their 33.6K modems (if you still have one kicking around somewhere). All you have to do is download the new software for their 33.6K modem, and it becomes a 56K modem!

Avoiding Configuration Conflicts

When you install a new card, the most likely problem that will occur is that the card won't work. But malfunctions can be caused by a variety of problems, both hardware and software related.

One of the more common causes of problems is a hardware resource conflict. What does a hardware conflict *look* like? Well, the following are a few common examples. These scenarios are examples of installation woes; you'll look at the workarounds later, after you know all about the resources that cards use.

Scenario 1   You install an internal modem in a PC; the modem refuses to work. Worse, your mouse, which used to work, doesn't work anymore. What do you do?

Scenario 2   You install a sound card in your system, and it seems to work pretty well. But now you can't print from inside Windows without crashing. What do you do?

Scenario 3   You're installing an Ethernet LAN card in a system, and it doesn't work. So you try an identical one. It doesn't work either. As you watch the *fourth* identical board fail, you begin to suspect a pattern. What's going on?

Scenario 4   You want to install a video capture board into a 2 gigahertz (GHz) PnP Pentium 4 system running Windows XP, but then you realize the devices in your system have already used up all the IRQs. You need another IRQ (which I'll define later, but for now just understand it's a scarce thing). You realize that you have an internal modem in your system that you don't use and that it takes up an IRQ. So you remove the internal modem, install the video capture board, and fire up your computer. After Windows XP starts, it tells you that there's no way you can use the video capture board because there aren't enough IRQs to accommodate the board. Clearly, Windows XP is delusional, so how do you medicate it properly?

You might have an idea of what's wrong in each case, or you might not. It's not a big deal either way, but understand that each of these problems is caused by *resource conflicts*. Now it's time to look at the resources themselves, and then you can examine and understand the solutions for these four scenarios.

Understanding I/O Addresses, DMA, IRQs, RAM, and ROM Addresses

Does the mammoth list of acronyms in this industry ever end? No. But this section tries to help you take another step in understanding what each of them mean and how they relate to your computer. Even though this chapter is specifically discussing expansion cards, most of the resources listed in this section are used by other devices, as well. For example, the keyboard uses IRQ1, and the Primary IDE controller uses IRQ14, and they're certainly not classified as expansion boards.

The documentation that comes with circuit boards often tries to recommend settings but also isn't always the easiest to understand. The folks who write circuit-board documentation assume that you understand five pretty important things:

I/O addresses   Addresses the circuit board uses to communicate with the CPU.

DMA channels   Used by some devices to speed up I/O to and from the system's memory. A system has only a few DMA channels, so a system is severely limited in how many devices requiring DMA channels it can have installed at once.

IRQs   Hardware components must interrupt the CPU to force it to service them in some time-critical fashion. Each device uses an interrupt request, or IRQ, to get the CPU's attention.

ROM addresses   Many boards include some of their low-level control software in ROM. The ROM requires a memory address, which can't conflict with other ROMs or any RAM in the system.

RAM buffers   Some add-in cards maintain a little (8KB to 64KB) RAM onboard to hold data temporarily. That RAM shouldn't conflict with any other RAM or ROM in your system.

The following sections give you the scoop on these resources.

I/O Addresses

Stop and think for a minute about how the CPU talks to a piece of hardware such as a serial port, a disk controller, or a keyboard controller. You already know how the CPU talks to one kind of hardware—the memory. The CPU can determine which part of what memory chip it's talking to because each location in memory has its own unique *memory address*.

Other hardware components have addresses, as well, and although they're not memory addresses, the computer talks to them in more or less the same way it talks to memory. First, the computer puts the address of the device it wants to talk to on its bus, and then it either reads data from that location or writes data to that location. The address locations that the computer uses to talk to these devices are called I/O addresses.

There are fewer I/O addresses than there are memory addresses—a lot fewer: any computer buil
with a 386 or later processor can address 4096MB of RAM or more, but only 64KB of I/O addresses.
That's not a serious limitation, however, because most of us won't be attaching (for example) 100C
keyboards to a single PC.

I/O addresses allow a CPU to tell its peripherals apart, as you can see in Figure 5.1.

FIGURE 5.1

Distinguishing
peripherals with
I/O addresses

The CPU communicates with the RAM using memory addresses. It communicates with other
peripherals—a keyboard controller, a serial port with a mouse on it, and an Ethernet LAN card, in
this simplified example—via their I/O addresses. The keyboard controller sits at address 64, the
serial port at 3F8 (there's an F in the number because it's a hex number, which I'll get to in a minute)
and the Ethernet card is at address 300.

What this means is that when the CPU wants to send some data to the Ethernet card, it drops the
data down the tube labeled 300, rather than the one labeled 3F8 or 64. (There aren't really tubes in
a computer, of course; I just like the imagery of the CPU communicating with its minions via old-
fashioned pneumatic tubes.)

IT'S HEX, BUT THERE ARE NO SPELLS

A quick word on the hex notation: you'll see that both memory addresses and I/O addresses tend to
be reported in hexadecimal, an alternative way of writing numbers. There's no especially good reason
for this; it's just something that techies prefer. To learn the gory details of hex, take a look at a featur
on the Bonus CD, "A Short Overview on Reading Hexadecimal."

Briefly, though, hex is just another way to represent numbers. We're all comfortable with counting
in the decimal system—the "normal" way of numbering: 0, 1, 2, 3, 4, 5, 6, 7, 8, 9…but what come
next? Well, we expect the next number to be 10, which is the first number—0—with a 1 at the from
of it. We expect the number after that to be 11 (the number 1 with a 1 at the front of it), and so on
of it. We count in hex, then, like so: 0, 1, 2, 3, 4, 5, 6, 7, 8, 9, A, B

The decimal system has 10 single-character number symbols, which is why it's called *base 10*.
Hexadecimal is based not on 10, but on 16. Why do we use hexadecimal? Because it's a lot easier
for programmers to use than binary (1001101100111101110110101010101), which is the way
computers actually "think." Anyway, hex starts off with the familiar 0 through 9, so it's got the firs
10. But after 9 comes the letter A—hex uses the letter A to represent its 11th digit. As you'd imag
ine, B comes next, and so on to F. You count in hex, then, like so: 0, 1, 2, 3, 4, 5, 6, 7, 8, 9, A, B
C, D, E, F…and then 10. See, hex has a 10 just like decimal, but it arrives later and corresponds to
the number 16 in decimal.

For example, suppose I told you that the COM1 serial port uses an address range from 3F8 to 3FF. How many addresses does COM1 then take up? Well, you know that 3F8 is its first address. After 3F8 comes 3F9. Just like all the numbers you've ever known, the rightmost digit is the one that changes as the number gets bigger; 9 comes after 8, so 3F9 is the next value. You just learned that 9 is followed by A, so the next address would be 3FA, then 3FB, 3FC, 3FD, 3FE, and finally 3FF. Why *finally?* Because the range is from 3F8 to 3FF, so when you get to the 3FF, you stop. Go back and count them up, and you'll see that a serial port uses eight I/O addresses.

What does a serial port do with all of those addresses? Several things. A serial port can both transmit and receive bytes at the same time. So, one address holds received data, and one holds outgoing data. Of the other addresses, some will be used for status information, such as, "Does the modem have a connection to another modem?" Some will be wasted—because of a peculiarity in the PC hardware, it's easier for a circuit designer to take 8 or 16 addresses than the actual number a device requires.

COMMON I/O ADDRESS USES

That's probably a bit more than you actually wanted to know. What you really need to ask about addresses is, "How do you know which ones are currently taken?" Well, you can start off with Table 5.1.

TABLE 5.1: COMMON I/O ADDRESS USES IN PCS

HEX ADDRESS RANGE	USER
00–0F	DMA Controller 8237 #1
20–21	Programmable interrupt controller 8259A #1 IRQs 0–7
40–43	Timer 8253
60–63	8255 peripheral controller
60–64	Keyboard controller (8742)
80–8F	DMA page registers
A0–A1	Programmable interrupt controller #2 IRQs 8–15
A0–AF	NMI mask register
C0–DF	8237 DMA controller #2
CF8–CFF	PCI bus I/O port
F0–FF	Math coprocessor (integrated into modern processors but still reserved)
170–177	Secondary hard disk controller, if present (present in most modern systems)
1F0–1F8	Primary hard disk controller
200–20F	Joystick controller
210–217	Expansion chassis
220–22F	Frequency Modulation (FM) synthesis interface (waveform device), Sound Blaster default

Continued on next page

TABLE 5.1: COMMON I/O ADDRESS USES IN PCS *(continued)*

HEX ADDRESS RANGE	USER
230–233	Common CD-ROM I/O port
238–23B	Bus mouse
23C–23F	Alternate bus mouse
274–277	ISA PnP I/O port
278–27F	LPT2
2B0–2DF	Enhanced Graphics Array (EGA) (usually *not* used by modern video)
2E8–2EF	COM4 serial port
2F8–2FF	COM2 serial port
300–30F	Ethernet card (common location, not a standard)
320–32F	Hard disk controller (XT only)
330–33F	Musical Instrument Digital Interface (MIDI) port (common location, not a standard)
370–377	Alternative floppy controller address
378–37F	LPT1 printer port
3B0–3BF	Monochrome adapter (also used on modern video)
3BC–3BF	LPT3 (uncommon)
3D0–3DF	Color/graphics adapter (also used on modern video)
3E8–3EF	COM3 serial port
3F0–3F7	Floppy disk controller
3F8–3FF	COM1 serial port
778–77F	LPT1 I/O port

NOTE *In PnP systems, PCI boards are assigned I/O addresses higher than 1000. A common I/O address for a PCI network board, for example, might be 1060–107F.*

You can also see what I/O addresses are in use in Windows by using the Device Manager. Double click Computer in the Device Manager (at the top of the list of devices), and choose Input/Output (I/O) to see which addresses are occupied. You can also view I/O address assignments in System Information (Start ➤ Programs ➤ Accessories ➤ System Tools ➤ System Information) in Windows 98, Me/2000. (In Windows XP and 2003, you choose Start ➤ All Programs ➤ Accessories ➤ System Tools ➤ System Information.)

Many devices have only one I/O address they can use. Using the example of COM1 again, part of the very definition of COM1 is that it uses I/O addresses 3F8–3FF. Other devices may allow you to use any of a range of addresses. For example, most sound cards default to address 220 but will allow you to reconfigure them to use another address if 220 isn't available. Reconfigure a COM1 serial port, in contrast, and it's no longer a COM1 serial port.

The key to understanding why this information is important is knowing that an assigned address can't be used by any other device; only one device is used per I/O address. To understand why this is so, I'll steal an old analogy.

I/O Address Conflicts

Think of I/O addresses as being like post office boxes. Say the keyboard has P.O. Box 64. When the keyboard has data for the system, it puts the data in Box 64. When the CPU wants to read the keyboard, it looks in Box 64. Box 64 is, in a real sense, a better definition of the keyboard from the CPU's point of view than the keyboard itself is. If you plug a new device into your system and that device uses I/O address 64, then the new device won't work, and the keyboard will cease to work as well—because you can't run two devices off the same I/O address.

Now, in reality, no one is going to design a device that uses address 64 because everyone knows it's reserved for the keyboard. But what about a case where you have a conflict over an optional address?

For example, several years ago I installed a Sound Blaster 16 on a PC that was already equipped with an Ethernet card and a SCSI host adapter. The Sound Blaster 16 included a circuit called MIDI, and it happened to be set at I/O address 330. Unfortunately, 330 was the I/O address used by the SCSI host adapter, so I got a disk boot failure when I turned on my system. There actually was nothing wrong with the *disk*; it was the disk's host adapter board that couldn't work because of the conflict with the Sound Blaster 16. Checking the documentation, I found that the sound card's MIDI circuit offered either address 330, which it was currently using, or 300. I set the address to 300 (the Sound Blaster 16 uses a jumper to set its MIDI address), reinstalled the board, and had the situation shown in Figure 5.2.

Now the CPU's I/O address 300—that particular "post office box"—is shared by the MIDI circuit on the sound card and the Ethernet card. The system didn't complain when I booted up because my system doesn't need either the sound card or the Ethernet card in order to boot. But when I tried to configure the sound card, it failed. You can see why in Figure 5.3.

FIGURE 5.2

Sharing I/O addresses between an Ethernet card and a sound card

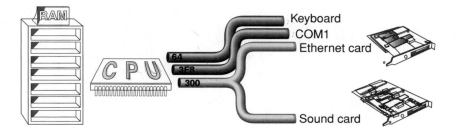

FIGURE 5.3

I/O conflict
between an
Ethernet card
and a sound card

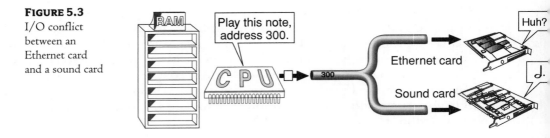

A "play this note" message went into I/O address 300. The Ethernet card has no idea how to respond to this request and indeed may not be prepared for any requests at all. Worse yet, the electrical signal from the CPU gets split up two ways, so it may not be strong enough to actually get to *either* board.

Why did Creative Labs, the creator of the Sound Blaster 16, build a deliberate conflict into its card? The answer is, they didn't. There's no official standard for SCSI host adapter I/O addresses. Adaptec uses 330 for some of their boards, Iomega offers a range from 320 through 350, and I'm sure other SCSI vendors have other options. Ethernet cards *tend* to sit at address 300, but that's not carved in stone. The problem is the lack of standardization. The most common conflicts occur between the types of boards that appeared after the mid-'80s, such as Ethernet cards and sound cards because there's been no central coordinating force in the PC hardware industry since then.

How did I solve the conflict, by the way? Well, the Adaptec board offered me 330 or 300 as my only choices, as did the sound card. The Ethernet board offered 300, 310, 320, 330, or 340. I didn't want to mess with the Adaptec board because it was the hard disk interface and if *it* became conflicted I'd lose access to the hard disk—so I left the SCSI board at 330. That meant that the Sound Blaster 16 had to go to 300. The Ethernet board then played the peacemaker because I set it to address 310.

Board manufacturers have all but moved from jumper settings to software settings, but in this case the SCSI board and the sound card set their addresses with jumpers, and the Ethernet card set its I/O address with software. Which do I prefer? Well, software is, of course, nice. But suppose the sound card came preset to 330, as it did, and required that I run some software to get it to switch addresses? That would be a real pain. Think about it: I installed the sound card at 330 initially because I had no choice. That would disable my hard disk, requiring that I juggle floppies in order to run the program that would set a different address for the sound card. To add insult to injury, the setup program for the sound card works only after it's installed on the hard disk. I just might decide that getting past *that* gauntlet wouldn't be worth it and scrap the board altogether in favor of a different brand. In contrast, all I *actually* had to do was to move a jumper. So there are pros and cons to both sides.

What would I have done, by the way, if the Ethernet card was set at 300 and wouldn't accept any other addresses? How would you resolve that problem? *You may not be able to resolve all I/O address conflicts* because not all boards even give you the chance to change I/O addresses.

NOTE   *When working with very old computers, I occasionally run across Original Equipment Manufacturer (OEM) components (that is, parts that came with the computer when it was originally built) that were designed, as a cost-cutting measure, to work with only one I/O address. Some memory expansion boards were like that in 286-based PCs, as well as some modems. If you find a device like that, the best solution is probably to replace the device if possible with one that offers more flexibility.*

PROGRAMMED INPUT/OUTPUT (PIO)

Once a hard disk controller gets some data from the hard disk, that data's got to be stored in RAM. The same thing gets done when new data comes in on a LAN card. Big blocks of sound information must be zapped out to a sound card in a smooth, reliable fashion for that card to produce pleasant-sounding voice or music sounds. The data originates in the system's memory, and it must get to the sound card.

A fundamental problem in computer design is getting data from memory (RAM) to or from a hard disk controller, LAN board, video capture card, sound card, video card—in short, to transfer data between memory and a *peripheral*. (From this point on, I'll use the term *peripheral* to mean a LAN card, disk interface, and so forth.)

The easiest way to move data between a peripheral and memory is through *programmed input/output (PIO)*. With PIO, the CPU sends commands to the peripheral through an I/O address or addresses; let's see how that's done with a simple example.

Suppose the CPU wants some data stored on one of the disk drives. Data on disks is organized into *sectors*, which are blocks of data that can be anywhere from 512 bytes to as long as 32KB (actually, 32,768 bytes), depending on the size and internal data organization of your hard drive. When a PC accesses data from a disk, it can't take it in 1- or 2-byte chunks; the smallest amount of data that the CPU can ask for is a sector of data (which, once again, can be from hundreds to tens of thousands of bytes long). Suppose the goal for the moment is to get sector 10 from the disk and to put it into RAM. The first step is for the CPU to tell the disk interface to get the data; it does that on I/O address 1F0 on many disk interfaces, as you can see in Figure 5.4.

The disk interface responds to the request, pulling all of the data in the selected sector off the disk drive. The interface then tells the CPU that it's ready, and the CPU now has the task of getting the data from the disk interface to the RAM. The CPU begins by requesting the first 2 bytes of data, as shown in Figure 5.5.

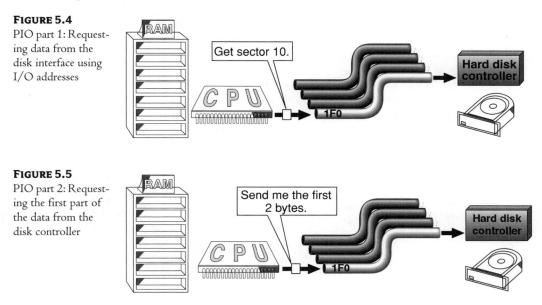

FIGURE 5.4
PIO part 1: Requesting data from the disk interface using I/O addresses

Get sector 10.

FIGURE 5.5
PIO part 2: Requesting the first part of the data from the disk controller

Send me the first 2 bytes.

The CPU then stuffs that data somewhere in RAM, as you see in Figure 5.6.

FIGURE 5.6
PIO part 3: Putting
the data into RAM

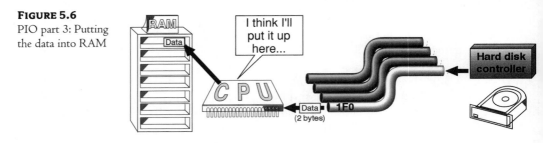

Moving those 2 bytes takes time, as does figuring out where to put the *next* 2 bytes. The CPU then requests 2 more bytes, puts them in RAM, figures out where the next bytes will go, and so on. Will this work? Yes, undoubtedly. Is it fast? Well, not always. Can we make this faster? Certainly; read on.

DMA (Direct Memory Access) Channels

Now, let's take a look at how PC CPUs access floppy disk drives. Suppose I want to read sector 20 from a floppy disk. Things start out very much the same as before, as you can see in Figure 5.7.

FIGURE 5.7
DMA part 1:
Requesting data
from the floppy
disk controller

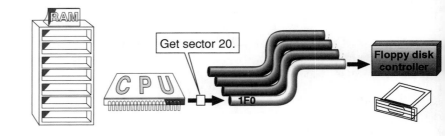

The floppy disk controller is at address 1F0, so the CPU sends the initial command out over that address. Ah, but when the disk controller has the data ready, it knows that having the CPU pick up 2 bytes and put them down and then pick up 2 more bytes and put them down (and so on) takes time. The idea is to get the data into the RAM, so why not cut out the go-between (as you can see in Figure 5.8)?

FIGURE 5.8
DMA part 2: Diver-
sion of the CPU
by the floppy disk
controller

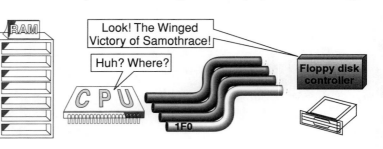

First, there's a diversionary tactic, allowing something other than the CPU to control the bus; then, as you see in Figure 5.9, the data is delivered to the RAM directly.

FIGURE 5.9
DMA part 3:
Using the DMA
channel to put data
directly into RAM

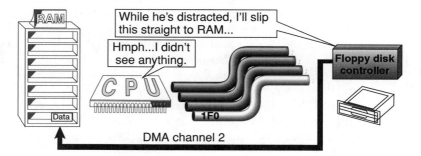

Okay, I admit that the disk controller doesn't really distract the CPU; actually, it says to the CPU, "May I have direct access to the memory?" Some of the wires on the bus are DMA request (DREQ) lines, and some are DMA acknowledge (DACK) lines. A board requests direct access to the memory bus with a DREQ line, and the CPU responds with a DACK. The idea is to allow only one peripheral at a time to control the bus. There are multiple DMA request/acknowledge lines, more commonly called *DMA channels*.

The original PC had a single DMA controller chip, the 8237. It allowed up to four DMA channels, and to this day 8-bit ISA slots have only four DMA channels available, numbered from 0 to 3, as shown in Table 5.2.

TABLE 5.2: 8-BIT ISA DMA CHANNELS

DMA	DEFAULT FUNCTION
0	Dynamic RAM refresh
1	Available
2	Floppy disk controller
3	Hard disk controller

The original PC used DMA channel 0 for "dynamic memory refresh" and, as such, wasn't associated with a bus slot. Briefly, here's how it worked: there are two kinds of memory, dynamic and static. *Dynamic* sounds better than *static*, but it isn't. When you tell static RAM (SRAM) something, it remembers it until you turn off the power or change it. Think of memory as a container of liquid, and static RAM is a ceramic mug. You put water in it, and it stays there. Dynamic RAM (DRAM), on the other hand, is like a water cup made out of a thin sheet of paper; it leaks. Put data into a DRAM, and it'll forget whatever you tell it within 4 milliseconds (ms).

As a result, old PCs had to drop everything and do a RAM refresh every 3.86ms. This took five clock cycles out of every 72, or about 7 percent of the PC's time. Of course, if the CPU was doing a lot of INs, OUTs, internal calculations, or the like, then you wouldn't notice the slowdown; the whole idea of DMA is to work in parallel with the CPU. Wouldn't static RAM make a faster computer? Yes, in fact, it'd make the computer much, much faster, but it's also much, much more costly. In more modern PCs, the RAM refresh is handled by a separate circuit. DRAM still needs to be refreshed in modern systems, but the CPU isn't involved, which means no DMA is required and channel 0 is free on most modern PCs.

On those old PCs, the hard disk controller used DMA channel 1, but most modern disk interfaces don't use DMA. Instead, they use PIO, for reasons I'll explain in a minute. As a result, channel 1 is available on modern PCs. The floppy disk controller has employed channel 2 since the old PC days, and it still does, so you shouldn't assign anything else to DMA channel 2. Channel 3 is typically unused.

Any PC built after 1985 will have 16-bit ISA, Micro Channel Architecture (MCA), Extended Industry Standard Architecture (EISA), PC Card, PCI, Video Electronics Standards Association (VESA), or AGP slots, all of which have *two* DMA controllers and thus eight DMA channels to the XT's four.

Notice that this implies you have only *one* free DMA channel on an old XT-type machine but seven available DMA channels on most modern PCs—just leave channel 2 for the floppy disk controller, and you're in good shape. However, in reality, you may not have seven free DMA channels. PCs nowadays can require two DMA channels for the sound card, and parallel ports are actually Extended Capabilities Port (ECP), which is basically just a parallel port with, uh, extended capabilities—it's bidirectional and faster than the standard parallel port—but ECP needs DMA. Table 5.3 shows the DMA channels on a 16- or 32-bit ISA/PCI system. Of these, all are associated with a bus slot except channel 4, which is a cascade to channels 0–3. As with the 8-bit system, channels 0–3 have 8-bit transfer capabilities, but the added channels, 5–7, are 16-bit.

To DMA or Not to DMA?

You're probably wondering by now what I left out of the story. I just finished explaining that DMA allows for faster transfers of data between peripherals and memory and that modern machines basically don't use DMA. (You're supposed to go "huh?" at this point.)

TABLE 5.3: 16/32-BIT DMA CHANNELS

DMA	DEFAULT FUNCTION	TYPE
0	Available	8-bit
1	Available	8-bit
2	Floppy disk controller	8-bit
3	Available	8-bit
4	Cascade to first DMA controller	N/A
5	Available	16-bit
6	Available	16-bit
7	Available	16-bit

DMA is pretty nifty, except for one thing. To assure backward compatibility, the AT's designers limited DMA operations to 4.77 megahertz (MHz)—the original PC's clock speed. Lest you skim over this because it sounds like a history lesson, *ISA bus machines still do DMA at 4.77MHz*. Honest. If you have a shiny new 3GHz Pentium 4 system on your desk and you do a DMA operation on it, the whole shootin' match slows down to slower than *1 percent* of that 3GHz clock speed. The best the other, now obsolete buses (such as EISA and MCA) do when "DMA-ing" is 8MHz. Therefore, depending on the device, using DMA with an ISA device may actually slow things down rather than speed them up.Fortunately, most modern ISA devices give you a choice about whether to DMA. Check the documentation—a device may have a jumper that turns DMA on or off, or you may be able to control DMA usage through the device's properties in Windows. You may want to try a device both ways and see which way you get better performance.

NOTE *Generally speaking, ISA buses are becoming rare to find on new systems. More and more, new systems don't have any ISA slots, so the question of whether to use DMA with an ISA·device may be moot. PCI is the newer bus, and PCI doesn't use DMA.*

So, in summary, if you have an expansion board that needs a DMA channel:

◆ On old PCs, the only one available is generally DMA channel 3.

◆ If you're installing a 16-bit board, try whenever possible to use the extra 16-bit-only DMAs, channels 4–7, so you'll leave room for the 8-bit boards in your system to use channel 3.

NOTE *Some of the first "16-bit" ISA sound cards that came out used a DMA trick. They were really only 8-bit cards, but they had software built in them to emulate a 16-bit card and therefore had to use a second 8-bit DMA channel. So, you had one card, used two DMAs, and emulated 16-bit sound.*

◆ If you're out of DMAs, see if the board offers the option to disable DMA. It may be slower, or it may be faster. Try it both ways to see.

To summarize, you can see common DMA uses in Table 5.4.

TABLE 5.4: COMMON DMA CHANNEL USES IN THE PC FAMILY

CHANNEL	USE
0	DRAM refresh (XT only)
1	Hard disk controller (XT only) or commonly used by sound cards in AT architecture
2	Floppy disk controller
3	Unused but also used on many 16-bit sound cards (they use two DMA channels) or ECP parallel ports
4–7	Available on modern PCs

BUS MASTERING

This is a slight digression, but it's important, it fits in here, and I'll keep it short.

You just learned that DMA is a neat idea that's hampered by a historical error—4.77MHz. DMA actually has another problem, but it's not one that's immediately apparent.

DMA can transfer data from a peripheral to RAM or from RAM to a peripheral, with neither transfer requiring the CPU's intervention. But DMA can't transfer data from a peripheral to a *peripheral*. Such an operation would actually be two DMA operations—peripheral 1 to RAM, followed by RAM to peripheral 2.

Many boards built for the EISA, MCA, or PCI buses can do *bus master transfers*, allowing them to bypass not only the CPU but RAM as well, transferring data between peripherals at the maximum speed that the bus supports. Bus mastering, then, can speed up a system in two ways. You see this diagrammed in Figure 5.10.

FIGURE 5.10

Bus mastering

The ISA slots in computers support bus mastering but allow only one bus master board per ISA system. The PCI slots, in contrast (as well as EISA or MCA slots, for historical sake), allow multiple bus masters. It's a feature worth exploiting. But bus mastering is useful for more than just peripheral-to-peripheral transfer; it's also terrific as a replacement for DMA. Designers of PCI-based boards use bus mastering to support fast peripheral-to-RAM transfers that aren't hobbled by the 4.77MHz limitation.

IRQ (Interrupt Request) Levels

In the DMA section, I described PIO. After the CPU made the request of the disk controller for the data, I said, "The interface then tells the CPU that it's ready..."—which was a trifle sneaky on my part. As far as the CPU is concerned, it initiates all conversations with peripherals; the peripherals "speak when they're spoken to." A peripheral gets the CPU's attention in one of two ways: *polling* or *interrupts*.

POLLING

Let's look at how DOS controls a parallel port to print data. (Don't worry; we'll get to more modern methods in a minute.) The printer is massively slower than the CPU, so there has to be some way to handshake the two. Things start off as you see in Figure 5.11.

FIGURE 5.11
Printing data
through the
parallel port

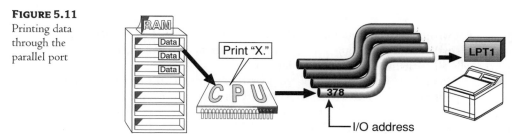

Data travels through I/O address 378, the address of LPT1, and is deposited from there into the printer. The CPU then keeps an eye on the printer, as you see in Figure 5.12.

FIGURE 5.12
The CPU watches
the printer.

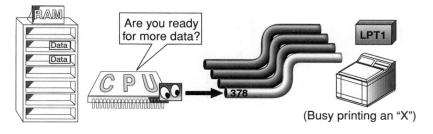

The CPU sits there at the "pneumatic tube" numbered 378, just waiting for the word from the printer, much as someone expecting a letter might run out to the mailbox every 10 minutes.

The CPU essentially sits on address 378, asking, "Are you ready now? How about *now*? How about NOW?" It's a big waste of the CPU's time, but this polling method of waiting for an I/O device to finish its work is simple to design. Besides, in a single-tasking world such as DOS, the CPU doesn't have anything else to do anyway; it's singly focused on servicing the parallel port. Eventually, as you see in Figure 5.13, the port responds.

The CPU now sends another byte to the printer, and it begins all over again. As I've said, the process is wasteful but simple, and it works fine in the single-tasking DOS world.

FIGURE 5.13
Response of the par-
allel port to polling

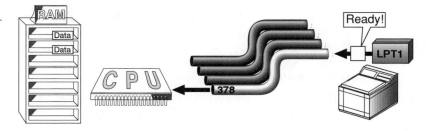

HARDWARE INTERRUPTS

But what about a multitasking world, such as the one most of us live in today? And even if you work in single-tasking mode, there are many peripherals on your PC, and the PC can't poll them all. That's why hardware interrupts are built into the PC.

You can see how interrupts work if you look back to the discussion of how the CPU gets data from the disk interface. Recall that the CPU stuffed a "get some data" request down I/O address 1F0. Now, it takes time for the disk to return the desired data. Why not let the CPU use that time to do other things? Figure 5.14 shows the CPU multitasking.

FIGURE 5.14

The CPU works on other things while waiting for the disk controller.

The disk interface is in its "own private Idaho," as is the CPU. But most modern disk controllers (I'm equivocating because some really high-performance SCSI host adapters don't do this) have a circuit running between themselves and the CPU, a circuit called an IRQ level. The disk interface wakes up the CPU, as you can see in Figure 5.15.

Once the CPU has been interrupted, it knows to start getting the information from the disk controller, as I described in the discussion of PIO a few pages back.

FIGURE 5.15

Using IRQ levels to get the attention of the CPU

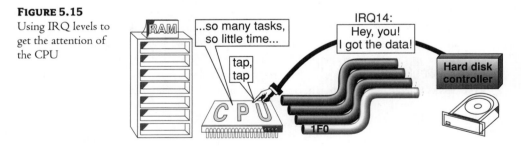

HOW INTERRUPTS WORK

PC interrupts were originally handled by an Intel 8259 Prioritized Interrupt Controller (PIC). Nowadays, though, there's no discrete 8259 on your system; it's just built into the motherboard's chipset. The interrupt controller is *prioritized* in that the interrupt levels it controls are numbered from 0 to whatever (depending on which computer you're using). Lower numbers get higher priority. That means if interrupt 3 and interrupt 7 both ring at the same time, it's interrupt 3 that gets handled first (*serviced*, in PC hardware lingo).

When an interrupt occurs, the interrupt controller forces the CPU to put its current work "on hold" and immediately execute a program that allows it to handle the interrupt. Such a program is called, appropriately, an *interrupt handler* or an *interrupt service routine*. For example, in the disk drive example, when IRQ14 occurs, the CPU jumps to a small program that tells it how to grab the data from the disk controller. The computer then stuffs the data into some RAM and returns to whatever it was doing before it was interrupted.

IRQs 2–7 in XTs (A Brief History)

The original PC had only one interrupt controller (the 8259), which had only eight interrupt lines. Interestingly, the 8259 implemented only lines 2 through 7. Lines 0 and 1 weren't even on the bus because they were preassigned. What's now IRQ8 (0 on the first 8259) was attached to a timer circuit that created an interrupt about 18 times per second, and IRQ1 was attached to the 8042 keyboard controller.

Driving the keyboard interface using interrupts is a good idea because the keyboard controller is pretty dumb. It has no memory to speak of, so every time a keystroke arrives at the controller, it must hand off that keystroke to the CPU (which then puts it in the keyboard buffer) before another keystroke comes in. Essentially, once the keyboard controller gets a keystroke, it wants to say to the CPU, "Hey! Stop everything! Come service me *now* before the user presses another key!" And so it "rings the bell"—okay, not really a bell; actually it just activates its interrupt line—and the CPU stops doing whatever it's doing and executes the program that moves the keystroke to the keyboard buffer. If it didn't do this, you would have a lot of dropped keystrokes. Someone designing an expansion slot for the XT, then, could build a board to use IRQs 2–7; but not IRQ 0 or 1 because there simply weren't any wires running from IRQ 0 or 1 to the XT expansion bus slot connector.

Suppose a floppy disk controller wired to use IRQ6 wanted to interrupt the CPU to get serviced? It would go through these steps, simplified a bit:

1. The disk controller sends a signal through IRQ6 on the bus.

2. The 8259 receives that signal on its input number 6.

3. The 8259 then looks to see if it's currently getting an interrupt signal from its higher-priority inputs—in other words, is the timer, keyboard, or anything attached to IRQs 2–5 demanding the 8259's attention?

4. Assuming there are no higher-priority interrupts, the 8259 then taps the CPU on the shoulder with the 8259's one "output" line, which is wired to the CPU's "incoming interrupt" line.

5. The CPU responds by putting a signal on the bus that says, "Okay, I'm willing to be interrupted; which interrupt number is it?"

6. The 8259 then seizes control of the *data* lines on the XT bus and uses them to transfer the value 6, the interrupt number.

7. The CPU has a table of locations where it keeps software to deal with different interrupts. There's a place there for servicing IRQ6, the floppy disk controller, so the CPU jumps to that location and executes that program, called the *floppy disk interrupt service routine.*

8. Satisfied that its work is done for the moment, the 8259 resets the IRQ6 input line and is ready for the next interrupt.

CHOOSING IRQs

Eight IRQ lines with two preallocated for the timer and keyboard made configuring XTs a bit tricky so PCs since the AT have all been equipped with a second 8259, bringing the total of interrupts on PCs up to 16. *How* they added that 8259 is another story, one I'll tell you in a minute. Before I do that, however, let's take a look at which IRQs are usually free or taken; you can see the common uses for IRQs in Table 5.5.

TABLE 5.5: COMMON IRQ USES IN THE PC FAMILY

INTERRUPT LINE	DEVICE	COMMENTS
0	Timer	Not accessible by peripherals.
1	Keyboard	Not accessible by peripherals.
2	Cascade to IRQs 8–15	Used by second 8259 to signal interrupts; not available except on XTs.
3	COM2	Can also be COM4 but only one of the two.
4	COM1	Can also be COM3 but only one of the two.
5	XT hard disk controller, LPT2	Free on most PCs. Hard disk interface used only on XTs or alternatively for LPT2 on the unusual machine with LPT2.
6	Floppy disk controller	
7	LPT1	
8	Clock	Not accessible by peripherals.
9		Generally available but can be confused with IRQ2; see text.
10		Generally available.
11		Generally available.
12	PS/2-type mouse port	If your PC/laptop has a built-in mouse port with a small circular connector, that port probably uses IRQ12.
13	Coprocessor	Interrupt required even for modern processors with integrated numeric coprocessors.
14	Primary hard disk interface	Taken in virtually all machines as the "primary PCI EIDE interface."
15	Secondary disk interface	Taken on most post-486 systems as the "secondary PCI EIDE interface."

If you're installing a board and need an IRQ, your best bet is to first look to IRQs 9, 10, 11, or 5, in that order (it's the order of descending priority, as you'll see in a minute). If they're not available, consider disabling your parallel port, if you're not using it, to recover IRQ7, or perhaps one of your COM ports if it's idle. If you're *still* in need, and you have only one hard disk and one CD-ROM drive, then you might ensure that the hard drive and CD-ROM are both on the primary EIDE interface and then disable the secondary EIDE interface, freeing up IRQ15. Be aware, however, that it can be a pain to consolidate a drive and a CD-ROM drive on the same interface if they're not already set up that way (you might have to set jumpers on one or both devices, for example), *and* not all systems even *allow* you to disable the secondary interface.

If you're configuring an XT (in a museum, perhaps?), your best bet for a free IRQ is either 2 or perhaps 7, but 7 is available only if you disable or remove your parallel port. And if you're configuring an 8-bit card in a modern system, the card can use only IRQs 0–7. Typically, 8-bit cards can use only IRQ5 because IRQ2 isn't available.

Whatever you set your boards to, *write it down!* You'll need the information later.

Earlier, I suggested taping an envelope to the side of a PC and keeping important floppies there. Here are some other things to put in there. Each time I install a board (or modify an existing board), I get a new piece of paper and write down all the configuration information for the board.

IRQs 2 AND 9: XT PROBLEMS THAT LIVE TO THIS DAY

Take a look back at Table 5.5, and you'll notice that IRQ2 isn't available except on XTs. Why did those old dinosaurs have an IRQ we don't have? Recall that I said earlier that IBM had to do some fancy designing to add more IRQs to their AT. Unfortunately, that designing built a few quirks into the AT's IRQ structure—and every PC since has been designed in the same way, even your new 3GHz Pentium 4 system.

Recall that the PC/XT systems had a single interrupt controller, an Intel 8259 chip. The 8259 could support up to eight interrupt channels, and the original PC/XT systems hardwired channels 0 and 1 to the system timer (a clock circuit that goes "tick" every 55 milliseconds) and the 8042 keyboard controller.

The system was wired with those interrupts because IBM wanted to make sure that the keyboard and the timer had high priorities; recall that on an 8259, when two interrupts occur at the same time, the one with the lower number gets priority.

In 1984, the first 16-bit PC-compatible system was released—the IBM AT. The proliferation of add-in devices on the market made it clear that eight interrupt levels just weren't enough. So, how do you add another 8259? Just slapping the extra 8259 onto the motherboard might present some backward-compatibility problems, so IBM decided to kind of slip the extra 8259 in "through the back door," as you can see in Figure 5.16.

First, IBM added another 8259 and used its eight inputs to create IRQs 8–15. Just as the old 8259 had two IRQs that never showed up on the system bus (0 and 1), so also the new 8259 had two IRQs that the system bus didn't see: IRQ8 supported the clock/calendar, and IRQ13 supported the math coprocessor chip. But how do you let the CPU know when one of the second 8259's IRQs fired? By *cascading* the 8259s: the second 8259's output—its way of saying, "Hey, I've got an interrupt!"—was connected as one of the *inputs* of the first 8259, IRQ2, in fact.

FIGURE 5.16
Adding an extra
8259 for more IRQ
levels

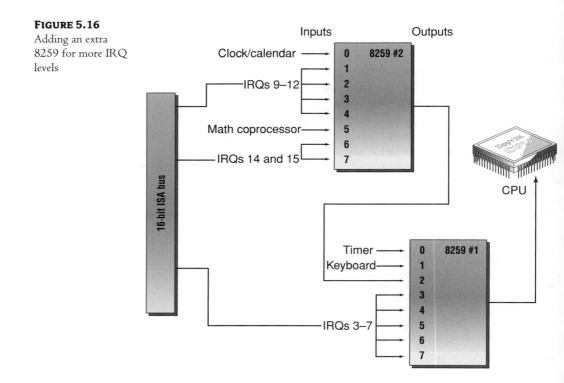

NOTE *So, if an IRQ between 8 and 15 triggers, the second 8259 activates its output line. That shows up in the first 8259 as IRQ2. The first 8259 tells the CPU, "I've got an interrupt for you," and the CPU of course asks, "Which IRQ?" When the 8259 replies, "IRQ2," the CPU knows that really means it now has to go to the second 8259 and say, "I hear from the first 8259 that you have an interrupt. Which line is it?" The second 8259 replies, and the CPU services the second 8259's interrupt. Incidentally, all this talk about IRQs will become unimportant in the years to come when ISA buses are no longer part of the average new PC. The PCI bus, when unencumbered by ISA, doesn't require each device to have its own IRQ, so this entire system will be going away when PC makers stop putting the ISA bus in their systems. In the interim, PCI buses can do a limited amount of IRQ sharing if the operating system supports it; see "IRQ Sharing in PCI Systems" later in this chapter.*

But now notice that IRQ2 is dedicated, as were IRQs 0 and 1 before. There wouldn't be any point in leaving IRQ2 available on the ISA bus, so IBM removed the wires on the motherboard, connecting the first 8259's input number 2 and the pin on the ISA bus connectors. But, they reasoned, why waste that pin—so they recycled that bus pin, giving it to the newly created IRQ9. That's fine, in general, except for one thing—if you put an old 8-bit ISA board into a 16-bit ISA slot, the 8-bit board will think that pin is IRQ2, as was the case in the 8-bit ISA days. Even the jumpers on the 8-bit board will tell you that you're using IRQ2, but you're not—you're using IRQ9. And, generally, software drivers written to go with 8-bit boards don't understand the IRQ 2/9 confusion and don't even *give* you the option to choose IRQ9. What do you do? Well, avoid IRQ2 on non-XT systems if you can;

if you can't, then play around with the driver and jumper settings. In some cases, lying to the board and/or driver ("Sure, you're IRQ2, trust me") will make it work. The best answer? Get those ancient 8-bit cards out of your system!

And here's one more thought about how this cascaded 8259 structure affects IRQs: priorities. In the vast majority of cases, you don't really care which IRQ you assign a board to, as long as the board has an IRQ. But sometimes you'll see two boards that won't work together—the system works with either one but not with both—even though they have different IRQs. In that case, try swapping the IRQ levels. If that fixes it, then the problem was priorities.

But what's the order of priorities in IRQs? Well, you read earlier that back in the 8-bit XT days, IRQ0 had the highest priority and IRQ7 the lowest. But since IRQs 8–15 snuck in through IRQ2, the priorities go from highest to lowest like so: 0, 1, 8, 9, 10, 11, 12, 13, 14, 15, 3, 4, 5, 6, 7.

So You Want a Third COM Port?

PCs were originally designed to support two RS-232 ports, which got the system names COM1 and COM2. But before the advent of the USB, serial ports were so darn useful that many people found they needed a third one—for example, on one of my PCs, I need a serial port for the mouse, another for my digital camera, one for my PalmPilot, and a fourth for an external infrared port.

If the PC was designed to support just two COM ports, how can you have more than two? By going *outside* of the basic PC design. You can add as many COM ports as you like beyond the first two, but the system treats them like any other "unusual" device—a network card, a SCSI board, or the like. What I mean is whether you're running DOS or Windows 95/98/Me/2000/NT/XP/2003, you don't need to load any drivers to configure your operating system to support things such as a standard keyboard, LPT1, COM1, COM2, a floppy drive, or a hard disk. That's because those pieces of hardware are part of the "basic PC," so to speak. But add a network card, a sound card, or something else, and you take the PC beyond the bare minimum, requiring that you load drivers for the "unusual" hardware and perhaps configure those drivers. COM3 and beyond fall into the "unusual" category of hardware.

That means you'll need to do some more configuration to make a third or higher COM port work. Each COM port needs an IRQ, so be sure you have one free before trying to install an extra COM port. It also needs a range of I/O addresses, but there are usually enough of those around. Then you have to get the operating system to play ball with your new port.

If you're running Windows 95/98/Me/2000/XP/2003, they do a pretty good job of detecting extra COM ports automatically. But if they don't, use Control Panel to tell Windows that you have a COM port. Open the System applet and choose the Device Manager Ports node (COM and LPT), then choose the particular port, and click Properties. Click the Resources tab, and deselect Use Automatic Settings. You can then tell Windows 95/98/Me/2000/XP/2003 what I/O address and IRQ your serial port is using.

IRQ Sharing in PCI Systems

Practically every system today is PCI based, and such systems can usually share a single IRQ among multiple PCI devices. For example, on my current system, IRQ11 is used for my PCI Ethernet card, my PCI sound card, and my PCI video card. PnP can set up this sharing automatically in Windows 95B (OSR2, a later OEM release) and Windows 98/Me/2000/XP/2003, and it'll report "no conflicts" even though several devices are using the same IRQ. And it's true—there are "no conflicts"—

because the devices share it peacefully without any infighting for control. Such is the beauty of PCI. On a non-PnP operating system, you must check the documentation for each device to find out whether it supports IRQ sharing and go through a trial-and-error process to see which PCI devices will share with which others.

Some CMOS setup programs have an option that enables or disables PCI IRQ sharing (sometimes called *steering*). I usually leave this turned on unless I'm experiencing problems with the sharing because it makes the whole IRQ situation a lot easier to handle. (As you learned in Chapter 2, "Inside the PC: Core Components," CMOS stands for *complementary metal oxide semiconductor.*)

THE TECHNICAL SCOOP ON PCI IRQ SHARING

For techies only, here's a behind-the-scenes look at how IRQ sharing works: almost all PCI devices share a single IRQ called INTA#. (There are three other PCI interrupts, INTB# through INTD#, but they're not used except by PCI devices that require multiple IRQs.) However, the PCI interrupts must be mapped by the BIOS to ISA interrupts in an ISA system. And because ISA interrupts aren't sharable, each PCI device must be mapped to a unique ISA interrupt, so you're back where you started—out of IRQs. When you turn on PCI IRQ sharing in the BIOS, though, it passes the interrupt assignment duty to the operating system, which (if it's capable) can map multiple PCI devices to a single ISA IRQ. Windows 95B/98/Me/2000/XP/2003 all support PCI IRQ sharing; the original version of Windows 95 and Windows 95A don't.

ROM Addresses and RAM Buffers

In addition to I/O addresses, DMA channels, and IRQ lines, there's a fourth source of potential conflict: ROM addresses. Some really, really old adapter boards require some ROM onboard to hold some low-level code; the most common examples are SCSI host adapters, video adapters, and some network cards.

Onboard ROM makes sense on some adapters. For example, the SCSI host adapters I use the most are from Adaptec, and most of those have ROM on them. A program stored in that ROM causes any computer equipped with the Adaptec adapter to show at startup a message such as "Press Ctrl+A to enter SCSI diagnostics." The diagnostics are a useful set of utilities that you can access even if your hard disk isn't working (which is a good possibility, if you're installing a new SCSI adapter).

Other boards have some RAM onboard to provide memory that's *shared* between the system CPU and the adapter's circuitry. But RAM and ROM can present a configuration problem because, as before, a possibility exists that two different boards may require some software onboard, and if the two boards *both* try to locate their ROM or RAM at the same location in the PC's memory address space, neither one will work.

Some boards let you configure the start address of the ROM/RAM (through DIP switches, jumpers, or software). However, most of the major boards that include ROM/RAM, such as the EGA, Video Graphics Array (VGA), XT-type hard disk controller, and the like, should *not* have their ROM addresses changed (if it's even possible). Too many pieces of software rely on their standard addresses. The boards you'll see that typically have ROM include the following:

◆ Video boards, which have ROM addressed at either address C0000 (yes, more hexadecimal; memory addresses are, like I/O addresses, expressed in hex) or E0000. It's usually not a good idea to move these addresses.

◆ High-performance disk interfaces, like some special EIDE host adapters or SCSI host adapters, have ROM on them, but that ROM can be safely moved if the board permits.

◆ Token Ring network adapters have some ROM on them; it's moveable.

◆ Any kind of LAN board can have ROM on it if the PC boots from the network and not from its local hard disk. It's unusual, but some companies use this "diskless workstation" approach. Some have RAM, as well.

◆ Some high-end sound cards may have ROM on them; the ROM contains images of prerecorded sounds, such as pianos, violins, or flutes.

◆ All PCs have some ROM at the top 64KB of the first megabyte, the memory range from F0000 through FFFFF. That ROM is called the BIOS ROM.

You should be concerned about two things when configuring memory on add-in cards. The first is the obvious one: make sure that two different boards don't have memory configured to the same address.

The second thing you have to be concerned about is the effect of adapter memory on memory managers. Windows-based memory managers can handle these cards without much problem, but older operating systems (pre–Windows 95) can have problems. Memory managers on these operating systems must know exactly which areas of memory are already filled up with adapter RAM or ROM, or the memory manager will overwrite the RAM or ROM, potentially causing lots of system problems.

Most adapter RAM and ROM ranges vary, so I can't document them for you here, but you can see the ranges that don't change in Table 5.6.

TABLE 5.6: COMMON ROM AND RAM BUFFER ADDRESSES

FUNCTION	ADDRESS RANGE (HEX)	ADDRESS LENGTH
XT hard disk controller	C8000–CBFFF	16KB
EGA	C0000–C3FFF	16KB
VGA	C0000–C7FFF or E0000–E7FFF	32KB

Another set of heavy users of onboard RAM is PC Card boards, which brings you to the next topic.

CONFIGURING PC CARD BOARDS

If you have a laptop, it probably has at least one expansion slot designed to support a credit card–sized adapter card called a *PC Card* or, formerly, a PCMCIA. There are PC Card–format modems, both wired and wireless network cards, hard disks, Global Positioning System (GPS) sensors, memory cards, SCSI adapters, and sound cards, just to name a few. Under some circumstances, PC Cards offer no trouble—but in certain situations you may have to struggle with them a bit.

PC CARD IS PNP

PC Card boards are PnP in that they set up their own interrupts, memory, and so on. Any system using PC Cards should have some software called a *card services manager* that examines the cards in the system and sets their resources appropriately, making sure that no IRQs, I/O addresses, or memory addresses conflict. (DMA isn't a problem because PC Cards can't use DMA.)

Of the popular operating systems available, Windows 95/98/Me/2000/XP/2003 handle PC Cards the best because they have a built-in card services management program. Older operating systems have no native PC Card support.

Handling Multiple PC Cards

But what about a system with multiple PC Cards? Again, in Windows 95/98/Me/2000/XP/2003 you probably won't have a problem—the integrated card services manager handles the conflicts if it can. But in older environments without a card services manager (such as in Windows NT 4 and earlier), you may see a situation where two PC Cards clobber each other. You can easily test this: try the system with just the first card. If that works, pull out that card and insert just the second card. If *that* works but they don't work together, then they're conflicting. What do you do about this?

Well, it's simple—just run the lame PC Card all by itself and note which IRQ, I/O, and possibly which memory it uses. Then pull that card out and insert the other one. Set its resources to give the first PC Card's desired resources a wide berth, and all will be well. And remember that whenever you configure a card to use particular resources, *write it down*. Put a mailing label on the PC Card and note to which I/O, IRQ, and memory you set the card.

Resolving Device Conflicts

Now that you know what all of those goofy resource acronyms stand for, it's time to look at resolving problems created when they're not configured properly.

First things first, though. Earlier in this chapter, I presented four scenarios that involved new circuit boards not working properly and causing problems. I promised I would talk about them more, including answers. So here are the answers.

Answers to the Scenarios

The following are some explanations of what caused the problems.

Scenario 1   You install an internal modem in a PC; the modem refuses to work. Worse, your mouse, which used to work, doesn't work anymore. What do you do?

Scenario 1 Answer   All modern computers come with two serial ports, named COM1 and COM2. But internal modems also need a communications port—in fact, they have serial interface hardware right on them, meaning that when you install an internal modem, you're *also* installing an extra COM port.

Now, that COM port built into the internal modem is probably set up at the factory to act like COM2, but you've already *got* a COM2 on your system. This means that the COM port will conflict with the existing COM2 on your system—and if your mouse isn't working anymore, then it's likely your mouse is a serial mouse on, as you've guessed by now, COM2.

What's the answer? There are two basic approaches. First, you could disable one of the serial ports that came with your PC. Second, you could configure the new COM port that's incorporated into the internal modem to be a third COM port (that is, COM3). Basically, you do that by assigning a spare IRQ to the COM port. But that can be a problem if you've run out of IRQs (an easy thing to do) or if the communications software you're running is too dumb to be able to work with any-thing but good ol' vanilla COM1 and COM2. That happens *less* with Windows 95/98/Me/2000/NT/XP/2003 software than it did with DOS software, but it happens.

Now, I hear you asking, "*How* do I disable one of the COM ports on my computer or assign a 'spare' IRQ to this internal modem?" The answer is the basis of configuration: you move a jumper (see Figure 5.17), move a DIP switch (see Figure 5.18), or run a program to shut off a COM port or assign different resources to it. Whether it's a DIP switch, a jumper, or a program depends on the hardware involved. Most modern systems configure all of the I/O ports in the BIOS, so that's prob-ably where you'll go to change the settings for your built-in COM1 and COM2.

FIGURE 5.17

Jumpers and how they work

Jumpers tend to be arranged by manufacturers in one of two ways. In the situation above, you see three sets of jumper pins. Moving from left to right, you see a jumper above the three pairs of pins, then connecting the leftmost pair, then connecting the middle pair. This might be interpreted as "jumper leftmost pins—enable BIOS" and "jumper middle pins—disable BIOS."

The alternative use of the jumpers is in triples. Here, you select an option by jumpering either pins 1 and 2, or 2 and 3. Here, you see the jumper above the pins, then jumpering pins 2 and 3, and finally jumpering pins 1 and 2. For example, jumpering pins 1 and 2 might mean "enable BIOS" and jumpering 2 and 3 might mean "disable BIOS."

FIGURE 5.18
Jumper and DIP
switches example

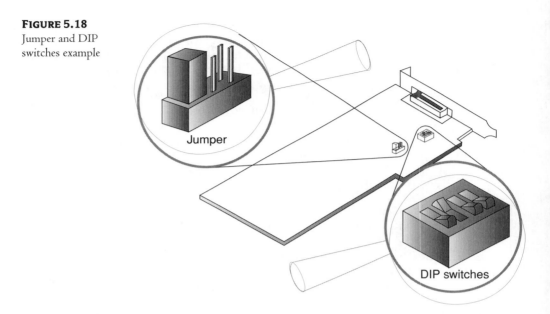

Note the symptom in that first example: you installed a new internal modem, and, all of a sudden, the mouse stopped working.

NOTE   Here's a clue to device conflicts: if you've installed a new board and it doesn't work, don't just pull it out. Test the rest of the system with the new board in place. Does something that worked yesterday not work today? That's your clue that (1) the board is probably not broken but is conflicting with something, and (2) you now know what it's conflicting with, so it's easier to track down exactly what you have to change to make the thing work.

Scenario 2   You install a sound card in your system, and it seems to work pretty well. But now you can't print from inside Windows without crashing. What do you do?

Scenario 2 Answer   The sound card needs an IRQ. Many sound cards are set to use IRQ7, but IRQ7 is preassigned to the first parallel port, LPT1. Under an operating system such as Windows 95/98/Me/2000/NT/XP/2003, you can't build a conflict such as this into your system because the operating system notices the conflict from the beginning and attempts to correct it during installation. In contrast, DOS and Windows 3.*x* don't worry about interrupt conflicts and will simply fail. The answer? Set the sound card to another interrupt.

Scenario 3   You're installing an Ethernet LAN card in a system, and it doesn't work. So you try an identical one. It doesn't work either. As you watch the *fourth* identical board fail, you begin to suspect a pattern. What's going on?

Scenario 3 Answer   In Scenario 3, the Ethernet card has some memory on it (16KB), memory that must sit somewhere in the bottom 1024KB of memory addresses. When you install the Ethernet card, you tell it where to place that 16KB of memory—if you don't tell it where to put the memory, it just uses a default value. If a whole boatload of these cards don't work, then it could be because of one of four things. First, all of your Ethernet cards could be faulty. (It's unlikely but possible.) Second, it may be that the default location of the memory is the same location that some *other* memory in your system is using; for example, you might have a SCSI host adapter that uses the same memory addresses for its BIOS. In that case, you've just got to find another location for the Ethernet card's memory. Third, if you're using DOS on your system, you may be using a memory manager such as `EMM386.EXE`, and it may have grabbed the same address range for itself. If that happens, you have a software conflict rather than a hardware conflict, but it all boils down to the same thing: a nonfunctional board. The answer in that case is to tell the memory manager to stay the heck away from the LAN board's territory with an exclude statement. Fourth, if you're running Windows 95/98/Me/2000/NT/XP/2003, then the network card driver may be looking for that 16KB window in the wrong place. In actual fact, the board's working fine; it's just the driver software that needs adjustment. You usually adjust drivers in Control Panel in Windows 95/98/ Me/2000/NT/XP/2003.

Scenario 4 You want to install a video capture board into a 2GHz PnP Pentium 4 system running Windows XP, but then you realize that the devices in your system have already used up all the IRQs. You need another IRQ (which I'll define later, but for now just understand it's a scarce thing). You realize that you have an internal modem in your system that you don't use and that it takes up an IRQ. So you remove the internal modem, install the video capture board, and fire up your computer. After Windows XP starts, it tells you that there's no way you can use the video capture board because there aren't enough IRQs to accommodate the board. Clearly, Windows XP is delusional, so how do you medicate it properly?

Scenario 4 Answer Scenario 4 illustrates why PnP is sometimes called "Shrug and Pray." You freed up an IRQ by removing the internal modem, which, by the way, was configured to behave as COM1. That freed up the IRQ associated with COM1, which is IRQ4. So why didn't PnP automatically assign the newly freed IRQ4 to the video capture board? Because the PnP system was designed to overlook IRQ4 when searching for IRQs and because all computers have a COM1 (which uses IRQ4 by default), it therefore assumes that IRQ4 must be occupied. How do you solve this? Use the Windows Device Manager to force the computer to use IRQ4 for the video capture board. Then reboot, and the video capture board will work fine.

And, in case you're wondering, yes, all four of these scenarios *are* true stories. Sadly.

More Conflict Resolving Advice

The simplest kind of installation problem is a conflict with the I/O ports: COM and LPT. (By the way, *LPT* is an acronym for *Line PrinTer.*)

You aren't allowed to have multiple COM ports with the same designation—each port must be uniquely named. For example, you can't have more than one COM1. But you can have a COM1, COM2, COM3, and so on. You can also have an LPT1, LPT2, and LPT3, but this is far less common.

A COM or LPT conflict arises when two boards have the same COM or LPT name. If two boards both want to be COM3, reconfigure one of them to be COM4. (You wouldn't want either to be COM1 or COM2 unless you had disabled the system's built-in COM ports in the BIOS, or you would create yet another conflict.) You can reconfigure a board in one of several ways, depending on how old your machine is.

On Current Systems: PnP

PnP systems attempt to take software setup a step further by actually eliminating the need for setup—in most cases you don't even have to run a setup program. The system detects new hardware every time you boot up your computer, and appropriate drivers are automatically installed. (You might be prompted to insert the Windows CD or a disk that came with the device so that the correct driver can be retrieved.) In the case of a board that wants a COM designation, it automatically picks the next available COM number and claims it for itself. So if COM1 through COM3 are spoken for, the new board automatically becomes COM4.

TIP   By the way, if you're using a PnP board under Windows 95/98/Me/2000/XP/2003 and it won't configure automatically, you may have to remove the board from the system (through Device Manager, I mean, not physically) and let Windows reinstall it for you (correctly this time, you hope). To do this, right-click My Computer on the Desktop (or on the Start menu in Windows XP/2003), and choose Properties from the shortcut menu. This will open a System Properties dialog box. Click the Device Manager tab (or click the Hardware tab in Windows XP/2003, and click the Device Manager button). Then, find the device that isn't working correctly, select it (by clicking it once), and click the Remove button at the bottom of the window. Then, press the F5 key to have the system rescan for hardware. If it doesn't find it this way, close the System Properties dialog box and restart your computer. When your computer reboots, it should reinitialize the device correctly.

On Older Systems

If you have an older machine, you'll need to assign a COM port designation to each device manually or disable the COM function altogether by doing one of the following:

- Alter the position of a jumper, as shown back in Figure 5.17.
- Alter the settings of a DIP switch.
- Run a program to adjust the board's "soft" switch settings. They operate just like physical switches but are modified via software rather than by physically moving them around.

But this really begs the tougher, more common question: how do you know which switch to move? I'm afraid there's no simple answer here; you've just gotta look at the documentation. People don't seem to believe this; they'll bring me a circuit board and ask me, "What does this do?" while pointing to a jumper. I just shrug my shoulders. There's no way to know without the documentation, so here's one of the best pieces of troubleshooting advice you'll ever get: become a documentation pack rat—but more on documentation later.

A Word About DIP Switches

Because we're discussing configuration, here are a few points about DIP switches. (It's not likely that you'll encounter any of these beasts, but if you do, it's best to know how to defend yourself.) There are two basic types, diagrammed in Figure 5.19: the rocker switch and the slide switch.

DIP switches are chip-sized things that contain 4–12 small plastic switches. You'll see them even on some of the most modern PnP-compatible systems. In a perfect world, DIP switches are easy to access and labeled On or Off. Sadly, that's not always true; some say Open or Closed. If they do, just remember that Open = Off and Closed = On. Sometimes they say 1 or 0—1 = On, 0 = Off. Sometimes (grrrr...) they don't say anything at all. In this case, play around with them until you figure it out, and then write your findings in your notebook for future reference.

FIGURE 5.19

Types of DIP switches

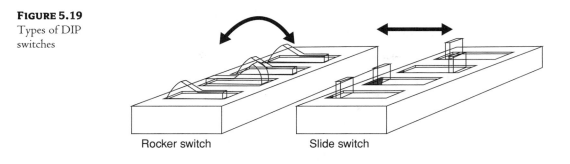

Rocker switch   Slide switch

Second, if you have set the switches correctly but the PC refuses to recognize the settings, be aware that sometimes DIP switches are defective (it's happened to me). To test this, you can remove the system board and test the switches for continuity with an ohmmeter.

Finally, remember that sometimes manufacturers mislabel DIP switches or install them upside down. It *does* happen—rarely, but it happens.

One More Conflict Resolution Example

Ready for one more real-world scenario, just for good measure? Several years ago, I needed to put some Ethernet cards into five PCs. Each PC was different and had different add-on boards installed in it.

The first LAN card I installed was in a DOS-based PC with Windows 3.1. The Ethernet board I was installing used everything we've discussed—an I/O address range, a DMA channel, an IRQ channel, and some shared RAM. I left the I/O address at 300 hex because that wouldn't conflict with the computer into which I was installing the board. The IRQ I chose was IRQ5, avoiding the more commonly used IRQ2. (I avoid IRQ2 because although it *can* be used in some systems, the fact that it cascades to IRQs 8–15 makes me a bit nervous; in the past, using IRQ2 had caused conflicts with Windows.) I set the DMA to channel 1 and put the shared RAM between CC000 and CFFFF because I knew it wouldn't then conflict with the hard disk controller ROM between C8000 and CBFFF.

When I plugged the board in, however, it refused to function. A little fiddling around made me realize that the DOS memory manager I was using was placing its memory at the same addresses as the shared memory on my LAN board, which in turn was clobbering the LAN board. I told the memory manager to exclude the range of addresses from CC000 to CFFFF. (Consult your memory manager's documentation to see exactly how to do this.) The board worked fine after that.

I set the second board identically in another DOS/Windows 3.1 PC with the same memory management software installed, and it refused to work. A quick check of my notebook reminded me that this PC had a sound card that was using IRQ5, which was causing the conflict. The LAN board offered only IRQs 2–7, and I didn't want to use any of them—I wanted to avoid 2 if I could, and 3–7 were busy—so I needed an alternative approach. A quick look at the sound card showed that it could support any IRQ up to IRQ10, so I reset the sound card to IRQ10, leaving IRQ5 free for the LAN board. Problem solved.

A third PC was a PnP system running Windows 95. I didn't worry too much about this one because I figured that when Windows started up, PnP would kick in and reassign the sound card's resources. However, as it happened, this PC had a SCSI hard drive that also wanted to use IRQ5, so when I turned it on, the LAN board and the hard drive battled it out, and neither one worked. I fixed this by removing the LAN board and rebooting and then entering the SCSI drive's setup program and changing its IRQ assignment. Then I put the LAN board back in, and things went smoothly.

I thought the fourth PC might be a challenge because it had all kinds of stuff installed—a sound card, a DVD drive, a CD-RW drive, a scanner, a printer, an internal modem—the works. A quick check in Windows 98 told me that all the IRQs were taken. So where was the LAN card supposed to go? I took a chance by installing it and booting up the system, and, amazingly enough, the Windows PnP feature set it up flawlessly. Because it was a PCI system, several PCI devices were able to share a single IRQ, making room for the new device.

Still another PC was running Windows NT 4. I knew I couldn't rely on PnP because NT 4 doesn't support it. I started by checking the current resource assignments in NT so I could avoid choosing resources for the new LAN board already in use. I did pretty well, and the LAN board installed and worked, but the user called me the next day to report that his ISDN terminal adapter was no longer working. Upon examination, I found an I/O address conflict between the two—and discovered the terminal adapter had its own setup software that needed to be run to change its resource assignments. Of course, as luck would have it, the user had no idea where that software was, so I downloaded the latest version of it from the manufacturer's Web site. I ran the ISDN terminal adapter's setup program, made a change to its I/O address, and everything worked great.

I don't want to discourage you with these stories; I just want to underscore how important it is to keep documentation of what's installed in your current machines, keep the setup disks handy for every installed device, and be aware of the differences between PnP and non-PnP systems.

Finding Diagnostic Programs

Diagnostic utilities can also help you locate problems. Some card manufacturers provide them, and some companies provide generic utilities that can detect problems regardless of the make and model of your devices. The question is, where do you get these diagnostics?

If you're looking for a diagnostic program provided by the manufacturer, the place to go is their Web site. They should have a download or support section—if they don't, you might want to go with a different producer next time.

Several generic diagnostic programs are available, including Norton Utilities or Windsor Technologies' PC-Technician. You can use those to test a board, such as a motherboard or a memory board. They're perfectly good for that, but don't do what some folks I've seen do: I know of a group who bought a lot of PS/2s. They loaded the Reference disk that came with the PS/2, told the diagnostics to run over and over, and left the machine. Hours later, they came back to see if there were any errors reported on the screen. No errors, so they shipped the machines to users. But the users complained that a lot of the machines had malfunctioning video. It turned out that the VGAs on Model 50s had a higher-than-average failure rate: I myself saw a classroom with 30 Model 50s develop video problems in about 20 percent of the machines. (If you have this problem, you might like to know that it seemed most prevalent when the room was hotter than 75 to 80 degrees F. Maybe you could turn up the air conditioning.) The support staff was puzzled. How did this slip by them? Simple. Video diagnostics often require a user to look over them. If your reds are greens and blues are blacks, the monitor doesn't know. The video board doesn't know. You need an operator to audit the video tests.

Here's a cheap memory test: build a Microsoft Excel spreadsheet that fills memory. It just consists of a single-cell A1 with the value 1, then a cell A2 with the formula A1+1. Copy that cell until you run out of memory. Choose Tools ➢ Options, and set Recalculation to Manual. Then write a short macro that loops continuously, recalculating and recalculating again. If you really want to add a level of elegance, calculate the sum of this large column of numbers and check it against the actual value. (The sum of 1, 2, 3, 4…N is equal to $N(N+1)/2$.)

If your board includes its own diagnostic testing programs, you should use them instead of the generic testing software because they'll be more likely to test the board more thoroughly. For example, Iomega supplies an RCDDIAG program that tests the controller. Alternatively, you can test a LAN board by putting a loopback connector of some kind on it to allow it to "hear" what it broadcasts.

NOTE *Windows comes with a System Configuration Utility that can help in disabling conflicting drivers and startup programs. You can run it from within System Information by choosing Tools ➢ System Configuration Utility (Windows 98 and Me) or by running the program MSCONFIG from the* C:\Windows\System *folder.*

How Plug and Play Works

All of this fiddling-with-jumpers and rooting-around-for-setup-programs gets old quick.

I mean, *really* quick.

In a perfect world, you'd just insert a board into your system and turn the system on, and the system would configure itself automatically—no muss, fuss, or greasy aftertaste. It would work something like this:

1. On bootup, the BIOS would recognize the board ("This is an Adaptec 2942W SCSI host adapter").

2. The BIOS would then ask the board what IRQs, DMAs, I/O addresses, RAM addresses, and ROM addresses it needs ("It requires an interrupt, a 256-byte block of I/O addresses, and a 16KB ROM range").

3. *Then* the BIOS would ask the board what range of IRQs, DMAs, I/O addresses, RAM addresses, and ROM addresses it *can* use ("It can use IRQ 5, 7, 9, 10, 11, or 14, any 256-byte block from address 60KB to 64KB, and any ROM address from C0000 to E0000").

4. After that, the BIOS would set the resources (IRQ and so on) so that they don't conflict with anything already in the system.

5. Once the board—and all others—were coexisting nicely, the operating system for the PC would load.

6. Early on, the operating system would note the existence of the new board and say, "Hey, this is an Adaptec 2940W, so let's load a driver for it… ah, here it is, in D:\WinDrivers…ask the BIOS what IRQs and such it set the board to…configure the driver…done!" And the new board works like a charm.

Sounds cool, doesn't it? I mean, after all, that's what *you've* got to do to make a sound card, a SCSI host adapter, or a LAN adapter card work. Why not let the computer do it? Well, that's the whole idea behind PnP.

Way back in 1993, Microsoft, Intel, and Compaq proposed a standard called PnP. The idea behind PnP was that board manufacturers would add circuitry to their add-in boards so that the automatic setup and resource query (*resource* here means IRQ, DMA, I/O address, ROM address, or RAM buffer address) capabilities of EISA and MCA would become available to machines with ISA buses. In actuality, no one ever made a PnP system that included EISA, VESA, or MCA to my knowledge; every PnP system I've ever seen used either a hybrid of PCI and ISA or just PCI. Although PC Cards aren't part of the PnP specification, most PnP systems can configure them. Laptops using just Card-Bus, a 32-bit bus, can be PnP.

PnP is a good idea, but it's a bit frustrating that you can't retrofit it on an existing system; it has to be built into a computer when you buy it. Today, fortunately, all new PCs are PnP compatible, even if the boards you add into them aren't. In fact, in some cases, you can install one or two non-PnP boards, and the computer will build the rest of the system around them (as long as they don't conflict with themselves).

Booting on PnP Systems

Let's examine how PnP works. PnP starts off with a PnP-compatible motherboard, which is hard not to find these days. This motherboard has a BIOS that understands PnP and also contains about 16KB of flash memory that's a part of the BIOS. Virtually all motherboards built in the past few years are PnP compliant; I'd hazard a guess that anything since 1995 is PnP compatible.

You also must have add-in cards that are PnP compatible, which, once again, isn't an issue anymore. These cards are configured *every time you boot*, and that configuration is done by a routine called the *Configuration Manager*. The Configuration Manager is usually part of the BIOS. It's possible to build a PnP system that loads its Configuration Manager off a disk, but I don't recommend it because you end up with an only mildly PnP system. In addition to a PnP motherboard and expansion boards, you need, as I've noted a couple of times already, a PnP-compliant operating system (such as anything Windows 95 and newer).

In the ideal world (that is, one in which everything is PnP), the system powers up, and the Configuration Manager assumes control. It asks each board what resources it needs and what range of resources it'll accept. (For example, a board might say, "I need an IRQ, and I'll take either 2, 3, 4, or 5," in the same way that the Microsoft ISA bus mouse interface does; even though there are other interrupts, its circuitry for some reason will accept an IRQ only in the range of 2 to 5.) The Configuration Manager then assigns resources to the boards, avoiding conflicts.

This means that installing one new PnP card to a PnP system potentially could cause all of the other cards to move their resources around. What does that mean for the network, SCSI, sound card drivers, and so on that must know which resources those boards use? Well, it implies that device drivers must be smart enough to figure this all out.

Once all boards are taken care of, the system boots in the usual way. The main difference with PnP is that the hardware shuffling of resources (I/O addresses, DMA channels, RAM windows, and the like) happens every time you boot the system and (one hopes) quickly and invisibly. Sometimes you install a new card, and its resources won't be assigned by the BIOS. This results from the BIOS designers trying to please impatient users who want their computers to come up to speed as soon as possible. As a result, the BIOS Configuration Manager may not be aware that a new card was installed. When this happens, check and see if there's a Reset Configuration setting in the BIOS Setup. Changing this setting to Yes forces the Configuration Manager to read all of the installed cards the next time the computer is rebooted and to assign resources accordingly. Once this occurs, Reset Configuration returns to its normal and faster setting.

Oh, by the way, can you force a particular board to a particular resource? Yes—that's called *locking* the resource. The Configuration Manager on your system should allow that, or your operating system may; Windows 95/98/Me/2000/XP/2003 lets you do it with the Device Manager, which is in the Control Panel (Control Panel ➤ System ➤ Device Manager). You can also get to it by right-clicking My Computer and choosing Properties, then clicking the Device Manager tab. In Windows XP/2003, right-click My Computer and choose Manage to open the Computer Management window. The Device Manager appears under the System Tools tree.

Be cautious in forcing your system to lock in resources. PnP systems are pretty sophisticated in accomplishing resource management, so when you lock particular resources it may make it more difficult for the Configuration Manager to assign the other resources.

Configuring ATs and Beyond: Software Setup

Answering thousands of service calls that really just stemmed from incorrectly set DIP switches convinced IBM they needed a computer that was easier to set up.

The main trouble with the XT and PC setup wasn't so much the switches as it was that the PC owner would have to take the top off the computer and pull out some boards to get to the switches. So IBM came up with software setup on the first AT back in 1984.

The AT wasn't totally set up with software; it had one DIP switch to set that configured its video. The rest of its motherboard configuration information was retained in a battery-backed memory. The add-in boards were left to fend for themselves configuration-wise; the bus was ISA, and ISA doesn't support a standard method for doing software setup on a board.

Now, this isn't just an idle history lesson: *virtually every PC since then has used the same basic approach.* Let's see how it works.

PC SETUP MEMORY: THE CMOS CHIP

The nice thing about switches was that they conveyed information—if switch 3 was on, you had a monochrome video board; if switch 3 was off, you had a color video board...that kind of thing. This information was "nonvolatile," meaning when you turned off the PC, switch 3 stayed where it was so that the PC could read its state the *next* time you turned on the PC.

Software setup wouldn't be as easy, the IBM engineers reasoned, unless they could use some kind of memory structure to store the configuration information. So, they decided to stuff the configuration data into a memory chip.

The problem with using a memory chip was that memory chips are volatile, and as soon as you turn off the computer, the data in the chip evaporates. So the AT engineers put a small low-power memory chip into the AT and attached a battery to that chip to keep it powered when the system was turned off.

Like most memory chips, it was built around the CMOS technology. The chip also contained a crude time and date/clock/calendar circuit. For some reason, the chip got the nickname "the CMOS chip," and that name stuck. It's a silly name on its face because *most* of the chips in modern machines are CMOS chips, but that's just what everybody calls it.

The CMOS memory contains 64 bytes—not 64KB, 64 *bytes*—of memory, as well as the clock/calendar. To read the data in the CMOS, your PC pushes the value's address—0 through 63—into I/O address 70 hex and then reads it back in I/O address 71 hex. The PC writes new data by storing the requested address to I/O address 70 hex and then storing the new data to I/O address 71 hex.

The CMOS chip itself is often a Motorola 146818, 24-pin chip. It's volatile, like all semiconductor memory, and so requires a battery to maintain the integrity of its data when the system is turned off. When the battery runs down, the computer starts acting aphasic (look it up, but it means what you expect it to). The most common symptom of a failing battery is the incorrect time and date. Most systems use nonrechargeable lithium batteries (the same kind used in hearing aids) that claim to have lives of 3–10 years. Others use rechargeable NiCad batteries. Some systems use a memory and battery all-in-one chip from Dallas Semiconductor. It's distinguished by the alarm clock on its face and contains a battery that Dallas Semiconductor claims is good for 10 years. When you replace it, you also replace its battery.

It's worth mentioning that, as time went on, 64 bytes just weren't enough, so EISA, MCA, and PCI machines usually have a different CMOS memory configuration.

MODIFYING THE SETUP MEMORY: RUNNING SETUP

The most important question in software setup is "How do you do it?" It depends. Since the AT's appearance in 1984, I've seen several approaches to setup programs:

◆ Early machines had a separate setup program on a $5^1/4$-inch floppy disk that you'd run to modify the CMOS chip's memory or to set the time and date.

◆ MCA and EISA systems usually require a setup program on floppy because the setup program must incorporate information about new boards. Both of these architectures are nearly obsolete, however.

◆ Most 386 machines and newer (including today's PCs) have a setup program in their BIOS, activated by pressing a certain key or key combination. Usually these keys must be pressed during startup, but on some older systems you can press them at anytime to enter the Setup utility.

◆ Pentium and higher PCI-based systems are usually a hybrid of built-in setup programs and PnP setup, wherein a system sets up at least some resources automatically with no operator intervention required.

On most modern computers, you can configure PnP settings in the CMOS or in the operating system. You just need to be careful, though, because changing the settings in one (for example, locking a resource) can cause problems in the other.

Troubleshooting Tips

For the most part, once you install a new circuit board and configure it properly, it should work normally unless it dies. Again, the key is configuration. Check, double-check, and triple-check your system configuration if a card isn't behaving properly.

If the problem isn't software (configuration), if everything's plugged in, there are no resource conflicts, and it isn't something obvious such as a burnt-out motor, a broken wire, a gummed-up printer, or an imploded display, then it's probably a defective circuit board. Step 1 is to identify the faulty part, and step 2 is repair or replacement.

The more important as well as the more difficult of these operations is the first, *identification*. How do you know which board is bad? There are several approaches you'll examine here. Next, should you fix or replace the bad board? Nowadays, replacing the board is the way to go unless you have a soldering iron, an Electrical Engineering degree, and a lot of spare time.

The following summarizes some of the problems you might have when installing a circuit board, along with some possible solutions:

◆ If an old device stops working when you install a new one, there's probably a resource conflict. Reassign resources for one of the devices.

◆ PnP devices can usually change resources through software, such as through the Windows 95/98/Me/2000/XP/2003 Device Manager. Go there first to work on resource conflict issues.

◆ IRQ conflicts are the most common resource problem, but they're not the only kind. Check also for I/O addresses, DMA channels, ROM addresses, and RAM buffers.

◆ If you run out of IRQs, it may be possible to enable IRQ sharing through the BIOS in a PCI system. You can also disable one or both internal COM or LPT ports through your BIOS, freeing up their IRQs.

◆ On all except XT systems, you should avoid assigning IRQ2 to anything because that's the IRQ used to cascade to IRQs 8–15.

◆ IRQ9 connects to IRQ2, so if you have a choice, avoid assigning IRQ9 to a device.

◆ If you're using PC Cards (formerly PCMCIA), Windows 95/98/Me/2000/XP/2003 have a built-in card services manager program to handle them. If you're using some other operating system, you should install a card services manager program if possible.

◆ If your PC forgets the date and time each time you turn it off, it may need its configuration battery replaced. Take the old one to a computer store to get an identical replacement if possible.

◆ On some systems, the old battery is soldered into place. You may be able to set a jumper on the motherboard to use an external battery instead.

◆ Be sure to get the right voltage for your replacement battery. Some motherboards allow you to select the battery voltage with jumpers; check the PC's documentation.

The following sections contain more detailed steps for fixing specific problems.

Finding the Bad Board

First, let's hunker down to the tough part—figuring out which board is the problem child.

To begin with, always follow recommended troubleshooting steps, such as those discussed in Chapter 25, "Troubleshooting PC Problems." There's no sense in being a maverick. You don't want to be ripping the machine apart to figure out why it won't boot when the last thing you did was install a new expansion board (and the machine hasn't worked since you put the board in), without first removing the new board to see if the problem goes away.

Again, just be lazy and follow the beaten path. Don't get original. Make sure you've followed the steps in Chapter 25. Also, make sure you've ruled out resource conflicts as the source of the problem. Refer to the "Avoiding Resource Conflicts" section earlier in this chapter if you need help with this. Remember, if the PC worked fine before you installed some new component, the problem is probably a resource conflict between something old and something new.

Assuming the machine *does* boot, you can use the machine to help diagnose its own problems. Run the diagnostics to find out if it's the keyboard or video and so on. That'll give you an indication of what's wrong.

Suppose the problem is clearly video. What now? Again, be lazy. Before you "remove the top and begin to swap," check the easy stuff. Swap the monitor first before the video board.

Be even lazier—is the problem specific to something such as a time of day or, more likely, a piece of software? If the video works well enough to boot the system and runs some applications but dies when you're running a particular program (games are notorious in this regard), the problem is likely software, not hardware. This may mean one of the following:

◆ You've installed the program incorrectly (easy to do).

◆ There's a bug in the program's code that talks to your video board.

◆ Your video card or its software driver isn't compatible with the program.

In this situation, if you have a second, identical computer, I'd take a copy of the program and install it there. But to find a problem such as this, it's important that the second computer be identical right down to the version of the operating system, add-in boards, and so on. If the problem shows up on the second machine, common sense tells you that it's a software problem with the program or an installation problem or that the brand of video board that both machines have isn't 100-percent compatible with the program.

Of course, this type of testing is difficult to do unless you have multiple identical systems, which is unlikely unless you're in a corporate environment.

If it's a compatibility problem, try updating the video driver, which will be available from the manufacturer's Web page. If updating the video driver doesn't help, try using a different video card. (In fact, if you have a lot of patience, you might even visit the Web site of the vendor who makes the program that's giving you the problem to see if they have a list of which video cards work and which don't.) If it's a problem with installation, try rereading the installation instructions. Maybe you made a wrong choice when you were installing the software. (Some programs require you to turn off your virus protection before installing, for example.) If you can't duplicate the problem by reinstalling the software, return to the company's Web site. Most companies have troubleshooting page(s) that list dozens or even hundreds of things that can go wrong and are easily corrected—and all of the instructions are usually right there.

TIP   *If you're having problems with a device, installing a new driver for that device is generally a great starting point.*

If the machine doesn't boot at all, consult the next section.

Night of the Living Data: Making a Dead Machine "Undead"

Suppose the computer is completely unresponsive. You can't run the diagnostics because the machine won't talk at all. The following are two approaches to bringing your machine back from the dead, along with a few other possibilities and solutions.

IDENTIFYING THE PROBLEM BOARD I: TWO MACHINES

First, assume that there's only one problem. Ideally, you have two machines, one sick and one well. A simple strategy is to swap boards one by one. Each time you swap a board, turn on *both machines* and note which machines are currently well. Ideally, you'd like to induce the problem from the originally sick PC to the originally well PC.

Second, did you check the old "intensity turned down on the monitor" trick? I'll turn down the intensity on my monitor for some reason, leave the machine, come back to the machine after a while (forgetting I've turned down the intensity), and panic, thinking that (at best) I've got a bad monitor.

Ghost in the Machine (Contagious Components)

Be careful here, however. Sometimes you end up with *two* sick machines. Why? I've seen components that, being damaged, damage other components. Suppose you've got a dead system, and you've stripped the system to the motherboard and power supply. You try to ascertain what's causing your problems, so you swap motherboards. Still no luck. So you try swapping power supplies. *Still* no response. What's happening?

You have a "demon" in the power supply: not only is it not working, but it also destroys motherboards. Originally it "ate" one motherboard, and then you fed it another one. I've seen this in two situations: bad power supplies damaging motherboards and bad keyboard interfaces on motherboards damaging keyboards.

The moral is this:

1. Swap the power supply before the motherboard.

2. Before swapping the keyboard, test the keyboard interface with a voltmeter to make sure the keyboard interface on the PC isn't the problem, as described in Chapter 19, "Keyboards and Mice."

IDENTIFYING THE PROBLEM BOARD II: JUST ONE MACHINE

If all you've got is one machine, here's a nice, minimalist approach. Some people call it the *min/max technique* (short for minimum/maximum).

Start with a machine that won't boot up at all, and assume that there's only one thing wrong with it. Break it down to the bare essentials, and then add pieces until the machine refuses to boot. *Once the machine refuses to boot, you'll know that the last item you added is the trouble board.*

Start by removing everything but the following:

◆ Power supply

◆ Motherboard

◆ Speaker

Turn it on. You should observe several things:

◆ The fan on the power supply should start right up. If it doesn't, either the power supply isn't getting power or the fan has burned out. If the fan is burned out, and it *has been* burned out, then the problem is easy—you cooked your PC the last time you used it.

NOTE *There's one other reason that the fan might not start up. The power supply is pretty smart and can sense short circuits on the motherboard. If it senses such a short, it'll shut down and refuse to do anything until the short's resolved.*

TIP *Here's a quick way to verify if a short in the motherboard is keeping the power supply from operating: with the computer shut off, unplug the power supply from the motherboard, and then turn the computer back on. If the power supply fan operates when disconnected from the motherboard, it's a good sign that the motherboard is destined for the motherboard graveyard.*

◆ The power supply might also produce a "click" on the speaker (you've probably never noticed it, but it happens each time you turn most PCs on). Another aspect of the "intelligent" power supply is that once it feels that it's up to the task of getting to work, it sends a signal to the motherboard that resets the system. The result might be a faint click. Once you hear that, you know that the power supply believes itself to be functional.

◆ Assuming that the fan starts and the power supply clicks, you'll probably get one long and two shorts beep out of the speaker—the motherboard's way of saying, "I can't find the video card." You may hear a different beep combination—different BIOS configurations respond differently to the "no video" condition.

If the three things outlined here have happened, congratulations—the machine booted. (It didn't do that before, remember?) If it didn't, there are only three possible culprits: the motherboard, power supply, or speaker. It's child's play now to figure out which is the offending component: just swap the speaker, power supply, and/or motherboard. Remember what I said before about swapping the power supply first in case it's got a demon. Remember that in the PC repair business *the cheapest and most effective piece of test equipment is a spare part.* At this point, it's a quick swap.

Assuming that the machine booted, the next step is to add the video card. Try to boot the machine Again, if it doesn't boot, try another video card. If it boots, you'll get error messages complaining about the lack of keyboard and drives. Keep adding boards until the machine fails.

When you assemble (or reassemble) your computer and apply power, sometimes the system will respond with a series of beeps. (Be sure to attach the system speaker so you can hear them.) Depending upon the system, the beeps can mean a number of different things. For example, usually a single short beep or a couple of short beeps will mean "everything's okay." On the other hand, if you get a repeating pattern of not-so-short beeps, the computer is probably trying to tell you something.

These *beep codes* will often tell you what the problem with your computer is. Because there are too many combinations of BIOS manufacturers and BIOS versions, it's impossible to list all beep codes here. Generally, though, you'll hear one of two things. The first is a series of beeps, such as seven beeps in a row. That's supposed to mean something. The second thing you might hear is a series of beeps, followed by a pause, more beeps, pause, more beeps, pause...you get the picture. It's like Morse code, only in computer lingo. For example, if you hear five beeps, pause, one beep, pause, two beeps, pause, and four beeps (with a really, really long foreboding pause at the end), that would be a 5-1-2-4 beep code. For a list of what the beep codes mean, check your motherboard manual or the motherboard manufacturer's Web site, or if you know the BIOS vendor, you can check their site, too.

Now, you may get down to the last board, the machine may be booting fine, and you insert that last board, thinking, "Aha! Gotcha. Now to prove it..." But then the machine boots fine. (Grrrr...) Why? One of the following may be true:

◆ It just wanted some attention.

◆ It fails when boards are hot, and the disassembly and reassembly cooled it to the point that it works.

◆ You didn't do the greatest job the first time you took it apart, cleaned it, and put it back together.

What Makes Boards Fail?

If you're reading this, you may already have a dead board. I've suggested you just replace it, but in case you're interested, the following are what generally zaps boards.

Most component problems boil down to environmental trouble, damage because of mishandling, or faulty manufacturing. The most common ailments (and their antidotes) are the following:

◆ Socketed chips can creep out of their sockets because of expansion and contraction. (Push them back in.)

◆ Bad solder joints can disconnect or cause short circuits. (Replace, or you can try resoldering, if you feel up to it.)

◆ Weak components can fail under heat. (Replace them, if possible.) By the way, one easy way to find a component that's failing under heat is to put a handful of cotton swabs in the freezer for an hour (keep them dry). Then put the tip of a swab on the suspected component(s). If they come back to life, you've found your culprit.

◆ PC board traces can be scratched. This is something you can usually see if you look carefully (or use a magnifying glass).

◆ Dirt and dust can build up heat. (See Chapter 4, "Avoiding Service: Preventive Maintenance.")

◆ Edge connectors or chip pins can corrode. (Clean off corrosion with a pencil eraser.)

◆ Electromagnetic interference from other devices can cause impairment. (Keep unshielded devices such as speakers well away from PC components.)

Other Problems and Solutions

The remaining chapters in this book cover peripherals in depth, but the following are some ideas for solving some kinds of problems, along with pointers to other chapters for more information.

HARD DISK PROBLEMS

If you seem to have a hard disk problem, look at the extensive discussions of drive recovery in Part II of this book.

KEYBOARD PROBLEMS

Keyboard problems are covered in detail in Chapter 19, but here are a few possibilities:

- The system board may be at fault. Test the keyboard test points.
- Is the keyboard plugged in securely? On some machines you need to push firmly to seat the keyboard plug in the socket. Never, ever remove a keyboard plug from, or insert a keyboard plug into, a computer that's energized. On older systems, this act is almost guaranteed to destroy components on the motherboard.
- Is it a PS/2 keyboard plugged into the PS/2 mouse port?
- Are you leaning on the spacebar (or any other key) accidentally, or is anything resting on a key?
- Are any keys stuck?

MANY BEEPS WHEN BOOTING, NO VIDEO

If you boot your PC and get one long beep and two short beeps and then the floppy drive light goes on but there's no display, the problem is most likely the display board. Assuming you have a bootable floppy in drive A, if the floppy drive light comes on, the system is responding—you just can't see it on the display. Swap the video board. Refer to Chapter 20, "Video Adapters and Displays."

DRIVE A LIGHT STAYS ON

You try to access drive A, and the floppy light comes on and stays on. You probably put the drive cable on backward. Check Chapter 14, "Understanding, Installing, and Repairing Floppy Drives." Ditto if the floppy drive light comes on immediately when you start the PC, and it stays on.

There's another possible reason—are you loading a program from a floppy? The problem could be insufficient memory to run your application. Try your backup disk also.

PARITY CHECK ERROR (MEMORY ERROR)

See Chapter 6, "System Memory," for more information about memory tests. Note that not all memory errors are caused by bad memory; you can also find the causes of false memory errors in that same chapter. Speaking of system memory, it's one of the most critical components in any computer, and it's covered in depth in Chapter 6.

Chapter 6

System Memory

- ◆ QuickSteps: Installing RAM
- ◆ Introducing Memory Sizes, Speeds, and Shapes
- ◆ Memory Modules
- ◆ Dynamic RAM Types
- ◆ Matching System Memory to Cache Memory
- ◆ Memory Management
- ◆ Causes of False Memory Errors
- ◆ Memory Tests
- ◆ Tips on Installing Memory Chips
- ◆ Troubleshooting Tips

Introduction

The PC must have *system memory*, or *main memory*. Main memory's job is to be the place where the PC stores the programs and data it's working on right now. It needs to be able to access these programs and data in *nanoseconds* (billionths of seconds) rather than—as in the case of secondary memory such as hard disks—*milliseconds* (thousandths of seconds).

Another name for main memory, which I've talked about before, is RAM, an acronym for the particularly unhelpful name *random access memory*. I say it's unhelpful because *random access* just means it's as easy to get to the one-millionth location as it is to get to the first location. By contrast, with *sequential access*, such as a tape drive, you have to fast-forward or rewind the tape to get to a particular location—the data is sequential. *Random* tells you very little because there's another kind of memory computers use, named *ROM*, for *read-only memory*. That too isn't sequential; the only difference between RAM and ROM is that you can both write data to RAM and read data from it, and you can only read data from ROM. Heck, even disk drives are random access. So a better name for RAM would probably be read/write memory, or RWM, but you can't pronounce RWM. You can pronounce RAM, so the term caught on.

I said in the previous chapter that you generally won't handle troubleshooting down to the chip level. Memory can be an exception to that rule. So let's talk about the chips that you *will* replace. RAM comes in a variety of flavors (sizes and speeds). Typically, you'll work with Synchronous Dynamic RAM (SDRAM), but some older computers use Static RAM (SRAM). The next few years should see SDRAM replaced by the much faster Double Data Rate (DDR) SDRAM or Rambus DRAM (RDRAM) as the most commonly used RAM in computers.

SDRAM and DDR SDRAM chips are sold mounted on several different-sized *form factors* (also called memory modules or memory sticks) that have their own unique names. Dual Inline Memory Modules (DIMMs) are, by far, the most common type of RAM memory modules sold these days. The capacity of RAM chips has increased dramatically since Bill Gates said this, his now-famous quote, in 1981: "640KB [about one-half of a megabyte] ought to be enough for anybody."

The prices of RAM have fallen dramatically in the past several years. You can likely find 128 megabytes (MB) of RAM for about $15–$20, and newer 1 gigabyte (GB) modules will only run you a few hundred dollars. For some perspective, consider the 4GB (yes, *giga*byte) RAM kit available for the Silicon Graphics (SGI) Onyx Reality. Several years ago, it was bargain priced from BuyComp.com at $19,321, a savings of more than $7,100!!! Get yours today!

This chapter acquaints you with memory characteristics and tells you how to handle and install memory chips. You'll also learn about the kinds of problems that can lead to false memory errors and the tests used to detect memory problems.

QuickSteps: Installing RAM

Installing RAM is, in theory, easy, but it's often an exercise in frustration. Why? Depending on the manufacturer of your computer, access to the part of the motherboard that contains the memory sockets can range from a simple operation to a complex process that might require dismantling the computer. I have a Packard Bell that I purchased several years ago for $700 to use as a test server. You have to remove the motherboard power coupling to install or remove RAM if you want to put anything the size of a 3½-inch hard disk in the lower drive bay, which I did. It seems that manufacturers like to make the internal workings of your computer—namely the RAM slots—difficult to access.

BE PREPARED

Before you start, there are some things you may need on hand. These include the following:

◆ Phillips-head screwdriver to remove the case screws

◆ Small cup or other receptacle to place the screws in

◆ Antistatic wrist strap to prevent zapping (a highly technical term) of the RAM, possibly causing failure

◆ Your motherboard's manual for settings, location, and jumper references

To install the RAM, follow these steps:

1. Shut down the system, and remove the power cable.

2. Place the case on a flat, stable surface. Remove the screws from the rear of the case.

3. Slide off the cover. This is different for each maker, but new machines are starting to make it easier. Place tower systems right side down. Orient desktop systems so that the ports on the rear of the case face left.

4. Locate the three DIMM or four RIMM slots. Note: RIMM is the trademarked name for a Direct Rambus memory module. RIMMs look similar to DIMMs but have a different pin count. They're approximately 4 inches long, are very close to each other, are near the Central Processing Unit (CPU), and have large white or gray tabs at each end. There should be a diagram in your computer user manual or the manual that came with your motherboard if you built your own.

   You should be wearing your antistatic wrist strap at this point; if you don't have one, touch the power supply case with your bare finger to discharge any static buildup that might be on your body.

5. Move the tabs away from the slot. They swing on sturdy hinges near the bottom of the slot.

6. Identify the pegs inside the slot. There will be two. Match those with the notches on the RAM, and orient accordingly.

7. Lower the module into the slot. Apply only slight pressure to each end. This should kick up the tabs on each end.

8. Feel the module's positioning with your fingers along the top edge. If it slides or otherwise feel loose, reseat it.

9. When you feel confident that the notches match the pegs, you think that the tabs are in the upright position from your slight pressure, and you feel comfortable that the module is ready push firmly on one end of the top edge near a tab.

10. If all things go well, which is likely, you should feel and hear a taut snap as the module enter the pin array and the tab locks over the end.

11. Repeat with the other side.

12. Start the machine.

TIP *If you have a Dell, Hewlett-Packard, Packard Bell, Micron, Gateway, Toshiba, Sony, Acer, IBM, or other big-name machine, you'll invariably view a company-specific splash screen when starting. To defeat this, tap the Delete key a few times. If this does nothing and the system enters Windows boot, reset the machine and try again with the F1 key. One of these will open the ROM Basic Input/Output System (BIOS) settings applet. Check your BIOS material for the procedures needed to turn off the vendor-specific splash screen and to turn on verbose RAM checking. Turning on RAM checking will allow you to see the RAM Power-On Self Test (POST) when the BIOS checks for faults.*

13. If the RAM isn't recognized or the system doesn't start correctly, shut down, unplug, and reseat. Verify that you have the correct replacement RAM for your computer. Next, check your documentation and verify that your computer supports the capacity of RAM you're install ing. For example, the largest memory form factor that my older Dell notebook can recogniz is 256MB Small Outline DIMM (SO-DIMM); if I were to put in a 512MB SO-DIMM, it wouldn't be detected. If everything is correct and repeated attempts to install the RAM result i failure, return the RAM for a replacement.

Introducing Memory Sizes, Speeds, and Shapes

You'll see memory referred to as *DIPs, SIPPs, SIMMs, DIMMs,* and so on. What do all these terms mean? RAM memory is classified in the following ways:

◆ By package type, which refers to the plastic coating containing the actual silicon. With today's memory modules, *package type* is a term rarely used, but in case you're working on a very old system, packaging for RAM can be any of the following:

 ◆ Dual Inline Package (DIP) is the original memory chip used back in the days when individual memory chips were inserted in sockets on the motherboard. They're little, black, plastic bricks with two rows of metal legs, one on each of their long sides, hence the name *dual inline.*

 ◆ Zigzag Inline Package (ZIP) briefly replaced DIP; all of the connectors were on one side, allowing the memory package to rest on its side rather than lying flat so that it took up less room on the motherboard. The ZIP package departed with the appearance of memory modules.

◆ By form factor, which refers to the module that contains one or more of the following packages:

 ◆ Single Inline Pin Package (SIPP) was the first attempt at a memory module. The SIPP is a small circuit board containing several memory chips and has a single row of pins across the bottom. You'll find SIPP memory on older personal computers and workstations. The SIPP memory resembles SIMMs except it has tiny pins instead of an edge connector. SIMMs eventually replaced SIPPs because the SIPP pins tended to bend or break easily.

 ◆ Single Inline Memory Module (SIMM) is a modular circuit board with memory chips soldered on it. The SIMM has an edge connector that allows the entire SIMM module to be inserted into a socket on the motherboard. The early SIMMs had 30 pins and were $3^1/_2$ inches in length; the 72-pin SIMMs that later replaced them were $3/_4$ inches longer.

 ◆ Double Inline Memory Module (DIMM) looks almost identical to the SIMM; however, the SIMM has memory chips on one side while the DIMM has memory mounted on both sides. To accommodate the extra memory, the DIMM has connectors on both sides of the module, giving it 168 pins. Another difference between the SIMM and the DIMM is the way that the modules are installed. The 72-pin SIMM installs at a slight angle to the motherboard, and the 168-pin DIMM installs straight up and down into the memory socket on the motherboard. Figure 6.1 shows you two SIMMs and a DIMM.

 ◆ Small Outline DIMM (SO-DIMM) is the module that's now in common use in notebook computers. It's much smaller than the 168-pin DIMM and is available in either 72- or 144-pin configurations.

 ◆ Rambus Inline Memory Module (RIMM) is a 184-pin module that looks a little like a DIMM. RIMMs offer faster access and transfer speed and thus generate more heat. An aluminum sheath, called a *heat spreader,* covers the module to protect the chips from overheating. The RIMM is also available in a small outline form factor (SO-RIMM).

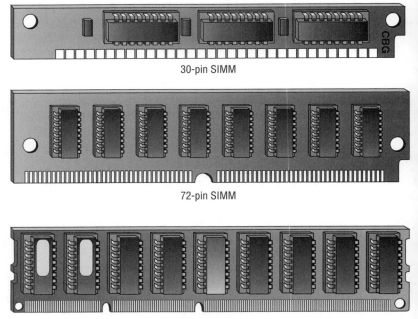

30-pin SIMM

72-pin SIMM

168-pin DIMM

- ◆ PC Cards (also known as PCMCIA cards), SmartMedia, CompactFlash, and memory sticks are small, thin modules that plug into a special socket found mostly on notebook computers, digital cameras, and Personal Digital Assistants (PDAs).

- ◆ *Stick memory* usually interfaces with your computer's Universal Serial Bus (USB) port.

- ◆ Various vendor-specific chip packages.

- ◆ By access speed (how quickly the chip fetches data), which is measured in nanoseconds (ns). Common access times are 40-, 50-, 60-, 70-, and 80ns for normal memories and as low as 8ns for expensive, high-speed memories. Lower numbers are faster.

- ◆ By memory capacity; modern DIMM/RIMM capacity generally ranges from 32MB to 1024MB for memory modules.

Memory Modules

Let's take a closer look at the more popular form factors in which you'll find memory supplied.

Modern computers use 168-pin DIMMs or 184-pin RIMMs or, rarely, some kind of proprietary memory type. Early laptops in particular have heavily used proprietary memory modules, and there's rarely any rhyme or reason to the design. Before SO-DIMMs became popular, most notebook memory was developed using proprietary designs. It's always more cost-effective for a system manufacturer to use standard components. The SO-DIMM was designed to provide a standard form factor that fit into the small confines of a laptop. (More on that a little later.)

DIMMs have replaced SIMMs (both types are shown in Figure 6.1), primarily because they're simply more efficient and they can pack twice as much memory into the same space. And before you ask: no, you can't upgrade your computer simply by installing DIMM modules into your SIMM slots because the actual package—the module board—has a different interface. Both the electronics and the connectors are different.

NOTE *The primary reason that DIMMs have a superior physical design over SIMMs is that they contain twice the contacts of SIMMs, a set on each side. This allows one DIMM to act as two SIMMs and eliminates the need to mount duplicate banks of RAM. In reality, modern systems with three physical banks for SDRAM DIMMs actually see six banks of RAM. One DIMM is already a pair. So simple, it's brilliant!*

Will you need to keep increasing the amount of memory in your computer? Silly question. Speed and capacity largely drive the computer market. More is always better, and memory sizes thought to be really spiffy last year are called "brain dead" this year. Just stay tuned. Memory chips are a hot technology area and, other than CPUs, have the most influence on what you can do with your box.

Motherboard Chipsets

Although the CPU in a computer gets a lot of attention, there's an equally important chip that determines what features and peripherals the computer will support. This all-important device is called the *chipset*, and it's this chip that ultimately determines what type and how much memory your computer supports.

Information about the chipset used in your computer is only important to those people who are purchasing motherboards to build their own computers. Although the chipset controls and provides many features on the motherboard, in this chapter you need be concerned only with the impact the chipset has on the type and amount of RAM that can be used with your computer.

Most systems being built today operate with chipsets made by Intel, VIA, or Advanced Micro Devices (AMD), with Intel controlling the lion's share of the market. When the Pentium 4 originally was released, only one chipset family would work with it—Intel's i850 series—and it only supported dual-channel PC-800 RDRAM (I'll explain RDRAM later). At the time of its release, RDRAM was very expensive to produce, and many people chose to upgrade to a faster Pentium III computer that supported cheaper SDRAM memory rather than the Pentium 4 with its expensive RDRAM. In 2001, chipsets for the Pentium 4 became available that supported the faster and cheaper alternative to RDRAM—DDR. Faced with losing market share, Intel released a chipset (the i845 series) that allowed the Pentium 4 to use DDR.

Until 2001, the most popular motherboard configurations came with three DIMM slots, and the chipset limited most of these systems to a maximum of 768MB of RAM (256MB DIMM times 3). Newer motherboards that offer support for DDR or RDRAM can accept up to a total of 4GB of RAM.

Before DIMM became the industry standard, nearly every Pentium or Pentium Pro–based motherboard used a proprietary memory module or 72-pin SIMMs. This caused confusion with many people who upgraded; you needed two 72-pin SIMMs to make a bank on these computers. This is because, as mentioned before, DIMMs are the logical representation of two SIMMs; one DIMM slot is the equivalent of two SIMM slots. Interleaving is eliminated, and because interleaving operations can be handled at the chip level and not handed off through a much slower bus, the speed increase is multifold. Many of these motherboards had four SIMM sockets, making two banks. However, the next generation of Pentium II/III/Celeron and AMD Athlon machines commonly used three banks of DIMM slots, and the DIMM slots didn't require the addition of memory in pairs.

Dynamic RAM

As computers are built faster and faster, all the components must get faster and faster to make plopping a 3GHz Pentium 4 onto a motherboard worth it. Design a system around a3GHz chip, and you need a lot of fast components—including RAM.

NOTE *SRAM is the simplest kind of memory to understand because when you put data into it, the data stays there. Now, your response might be, "Big deal—isn't that the whole idea of memory? What good is memory that doesn't hold onto the data you give it?" Well, to build that kind of memory, you have to build about six transistors into each bit storage location. That kind of memory—SRAM—can be quite fast but also quite expensive. If you used SRAM for your PC memory, then there'd be no trouble getting memory that kept up with your CPU; but, on the other hand, you wouldn't be able to afford those computers because SRAM is about 10 times more expensive than the DRAM that you're used to buying. SRAM is also physically larger than DRAM and generally runs much hotter. Of course, all these negative aspects drove the market to adopt DRAM and move SRAM into a supporting role (it's typically used for video RAM, L1 and L2 cache RAM, or other similar RAM needs). Fortunately, things have speeded up quite a bit over the past few years.*

DRAM was the economical answer to the earlier SRAM. Each DRAM bit is built of a single transistor and a capacitor, in contrast to SRAM's six transistors.

DRAM has two problems from the point of view of a PC designer. First, the *dynamic* in its name means it forgets the data you give it almost as fast as you can give it the data. This means that DRAM-based systems require refresh circuitry to get around this electronic amnesia.

Second, the way that DRAMs are built to be cheaper is that they're organized not simply into a set of addresses; rather, each bit in a DRAM has a row address and a column address. The slow part of accessing any part of a DRAM is in getting to its row. Once you're in a row, subsequent intrarow accesses can be quite fast. In fact, that's the area with the most advances recently: DRAMs that can access data quite quickly. This brings me to Table 6.1, which outlines the types of DRAM.

As you can see in this table, it took four years to get from quite slow FPM RAM to EDO RAM, which produced only a marginal increase in performance. At that time, adding 16MB of RAM to a 16MB system yielded an approximate 30 percent boost in overall performance. Going beyond that resulted in little more than an additional 5 percent, if even that.

That diminished return *ad infinitum* changed with SDRAM and its 66 megahertz (MHz) bus. This also marked the point when RAM speed became tied to the CPU speed. This is important because timing is crucial to efficient data transfer in systems that are defined by time, such as computers. Then 1998 ushered in 100MHz SDRAM, or PC-100. And 1999 showed us 133MHz SDRAM and RDRAM from a company named Rambus. The year 2001 was important because DDR became readily available, and the RAM war for market dominance between RDRAM and DDR is still being fought in earnest. Figure 6.2 shows Rambus RIMMs.

TABLE 6.1: THE MARCH OF TIME WITH DRAM

TYPE	FIRST USED	CLOCK RATE	BUS WIDTH*	PEAK BANDWIDTH	VOLTAGE
Fast Page Mode (FPM) (60ns and 70ns)	1990	25MHz	64-bit	200 megabytes per second (MBps)	5v
Extended Data Out (EDO) (50ns, 60ns, and 70ns)	1994	40MHz	64-bit	320MBps	5v
SDRAM (66MHz)	1996	66MHz	64-bit	528MBps	3.3v
SDRAM (100MHz)	1998	100MHz	64-bit	800MBps	3.3v
SDRAM (133MHz)	1999	133MHz	64-bit	1.1 gigabyte per second (GBps)	3.3v
RDRAM	1999	400MHz (∞ 2)	16-bit	1.6GBps	2.5v
DDR SDRAM (100MHz)	2001	100MHz (∞ 2)	64-bit	1.6GBps	3.3v
DDR SDRAM (133MHz)	2001	133MHz (∞ 2)	64-bit	2.1GBps	3.3v

* Indicates the maximum module data width, not its external bus width. Sixty-four-bit external pathways began with the 75MHz Pentium. Data courtesy of CMP TechWeb and Kingston Technology © 2000.

FIGURE 6.2
Rambus RIMMs

NOTE   *RDRAM is technically interesting in that instead of increasing the size of the path that the data passes through, Rambus chose to make the path smaller. Quite a bit smaller, in fact. Most RAM operates using an internal 64-bit data structure and an external 64-bit data path. RDRAM uses a 16-bit data path. Now, this yields only a 500MBps-faster performance over 133MHz SDRAM, but its internal operations move at 400MHz. RDRAM Input/Output (I/O) doubles to two paths when it operates in dual channel, which increases the effective speed to 800MHz, but that's only a theoretical speed limit and is diminished by the latency inherent with the RDRAM design.*

The current generation of RAM products includes RDRAM and DDR SDRAM (which is properly referred to as DDR). Both SDR and DDR SDRAM look like ordinary DIMM modules with a difference in the notches so as to prevent them from being installed into a system that doesn't support them. As fast as DDR is, designers are already hard at work to produce a Triple Data Rate (TDR), and there's even talk of a Quad Data Rate (QDR). After the theoretical speed of QDR is reached, designers will then need to figure out ways to increase the speed of light.

Let's look at RDRAM a little closer. RDRAM comes in a RIMM package format, and RDRAM RIMMs *must be installed in pairs*. RIMMs come in 64-, 128-, 256-, and 512MB modules, with error correction code (ECC) and non-ECC, and at speeds of 600MHz, 700MHz, and 800MHz. The other nice thing about RDRAM is that it's backward compatible. An 800MHz chip will work with together with 600MHz or 700MHz chips already in your computer.

SDRAM

SDRAM is a variant of DRAM that includes an on-chip burst counter. You can use this burst counter to increment column addresses and increase the speed of memory access.

NOTE   *SDRAM typically comes in DIMM formats, but they used to come in the SIMM format, as well. DIMM is the only format being manufactured today.*

Although faster is generally considered better and speed is pursued for its own sake, the reason behind SDRAM was that CPUs were getting faster. With their increasing speed, they required ever-faster memory to function within earshot of their potential. With SDRAM, the CPU and RAM are locked together by the same clock. Thus, the speed of the RAM and the CPU are linked, or synchronized.

FPM AND EDO DRAM

FPM and EDO DRAM types aren't used anymore. You may have one or the other in your PC that you're upgrading with the help of this book, but in the end, they'll go the way of the woolly mammoth (unless you have another old machine that could use more RAM, but then that's another set of problems).

There's one instance where EDO DRAM can still be used, but it's mostly a crutch for backward compatibility. One motherboard I have worked with, the BIOStar MicroTech M6TLC PII, is capable of handling up to 384MB of SDRAM (128MB DIMMs) but can take up to 768MB of EDO DRAM (256MB DIMMs). However, as with all pre-SDRAM DRAM types, EDO DRAM suffers from less efficient transfer speeds and reduced capabilities. If you need that much RAM, then you don't need a motherboard like this one, and you certainly don't want EDO DRAM!

NOTE   *Another solution to the problem of speeding up RAM is cached SDRAM, which boosts the overall speed of the memory by adding a SRAM area on the DRAM chip. This small amount of fast SRAM acts as a cache to the DRAM. The cached RAM briefly appeared several years ago but offered only minimal performance improvement and a chipset that supported it. Because none of the major chipset manufacturers supported it, it pretty much faded from the market.*

Normally, memory chips answer data requests. Cache memory can anticipate the CPU's needs. When the CPU asks for data, the memory already has it waiting and ready to go. Some cache memory implementations also include a pipeline. The pipelined architecture has a design in which one stage can fetch an address while other stages present the data for output. The cache memory concept has the advantage of being a simple, elegant replacement for older chips; it just plugs into the system and goes.

SDRAM modules come in 72-, 144-, and 168-pin packages and can range from 4MB to 1GB in capacity. There are generally two types of SDRAM DIMMs: *unbuffered* and *registered*. The 72-pin SO-DRAM was designed to meet the specific needs of portables and their space limitations. The problem was that upgrades required two modules, eliminating the savings in space. Thus was born the 144-pin SO-DRAM variant of the full-sized DIMM. The 168-pin packages are solely for use in systems that don't have space limitations.

NOTE   *Unbuffered memory is simple memory that relies on a controller to function predictably. This is the most common type of RAM and one of the reasons why RAM is inexpensive. Registered memory has a register array onboard, generally allowing for more orderly operations. It's also more costly to make, and that cost gets passed on to you, the buyer. Fortunately, it's really only important that you know which type your system requires. A general rule of thumb is, when in doubt, it'll probably take unbuffered memory. Don't worry. Nothing will break.*

DDR SDRAM

As noted earlier, DDR is short for *double data rate*, and DDR maximizes output by using both the leading and following edge of the clock tick to perform operations. This means that DDR can locate and pass an address in one tick as opposed to two.

TO ERROR CORRECT OR NOT TO ERROR CORRECT

You'll probably note that some types of RAM are labeled *ECC*, which is short for *error-correction code*. If you've seen this, you likely wondered why it was more expensive than non-ECC RAM. Well, the answer is simple: ECC RAM does more than conventional RAM. Of course, if you need ECC RAM, you can probably afford to buy it because it's mostly used to help prevent costly and damaging errors, faults, and mistakes. Now, if you're already buying ECC or if you already have it, then you don't need to read this sidebar and can move on. Computers that use ECC RAM automatically detect it and configure the system to use it. If you currently are using ECC RAM and add a non-ECC RAM memory module, the motherboard will detect it and disable the ECC features on both memory modules.

Good to see you stick it out. Now, how does ECC work? Good question. The answer is that ECC uses special algorithms to watch, evaluate, and fix various problems that appear in the data stream, either incoming or outgoing. This means greater stability for data-intensive applications such as Computer-Aided Design (CAD)/Computer-Aided Manufacturing (CAM) and audio and video editing, though I doubt you'll need it at home.

The physical dimensions of a DDR memory module are identical to those used by a standard DIMM except that the standard SDRAM (now called SDR, for Single Data Rate) module has two keys, or notches, where there are no pins. The DDR DIMM has only one key because it provides an additional 16 pins to the space recovered by using only one notch. This gives the DDR module 184 pins compared to the 168 pins on the standard SDR SDRAM DIMM module. This means that a SDR DIMM can't fit into a socket designed for a DDR module.

The logical names for DDR modules are PC-200, PC-266, and PC-333, which is a reference to their doubled bus speed. For example, a PC-100 doubled becomes a PC-200, right? Not exactly; for reasons that can only be attributed to blatant marketing propaganda, the new modules are labeled PC-1600, PC-2100, and PC-2700. Some have reasoned that this was so their numbers would be larger than the competing Rambus PC-800, but in fact the names are based on data transfer rates of the modules instead of their bus clock speeds.

SLDRAM

Synchronous Link DRAM (SLDRAM) is what's called a *protocol-based technology*. Unlike other RAM, a protocol-based technology works on the premise of a facilitating object being involved in the transfer of data to and from one place and another. In this case, the data being transferred is stored in RAM. Think of the CPU as a client and the SLDRAM bus as a server. When the client requests data from the server, it's sent. Requests occur in both directions. This makes for a more intelligent data manipulation interactivity. To make it as fast as possible, SLDRAM uses a multiplexed bus to move data in and out, bypassing the limitations of traditional pins. SLDRAM can currently handle I/O speeds of up to 1.6GBps with a very fast theoretical cap of 3GBps. Its potential is very strong, but with the high speeds promised by DDR and RDRAM there's little effort to make this into a commercial product.

BLAST FROM THE PAST: MEMORY INTERLEAVING

Some systems attempted to minimize the loss of speed incurred by charging capacitors by arranging the RAM into *interleaved banks*. The idea was this: memory is organized into banks, or logical groups. With interleaving, memory subsystems always have an even number of banks. Memory addresses are then *interleaved* so that when one address (in the first bank) is being accessed, the following address (which is in the second bank) is being charged up. That way, when it's time to access the second bank, it needn't be charged because the address that follows is ready to go. While reading that address in the second bank, its following address (back in the first bank) is being charged up, and so on.

Notice that this works only if the CPU's memory accesses tend to be in consecutive memory addresses. That's a pretty good assumption, but if the program running in the system jumps all around the RAM for data, then interleaving is defeated and memory accesses slow down.

Interleaving was a good idea for its time, but it was effective only for the first access in a row, and it required an even number of memory banks. It was rather awkward.

If you're upgrading an older system, keep track of whether it requires memory to be interleaved, or you might be confused as to why that old 80486 doesn't work, especially because you just put in fresh RAM.

Matching System Memory to Cache Memory

All the information mentioned earlier in this chapter on SDRAM and cache RAM points to one large problem in the personal computer industry: there's an increasing disparity in clock speeds between processors and DRAM. Combine this with an increasing degree of processor superscalability, and you get a situation in which effective cache management becomes a critical factor in obtaining optimal application performance. System main memory access now can take anywhere from tens to hundreds of CPU clock cycles. Hence, the difference between finding information in the on-chip cache instead of in main memory can completely dominate the effective speed of an application or even an entire system. There are a variety of techniques that more effectively use the processor caches. These techniques can be divided into two types: those focusing on programs and those focusing on processors.

Better Programs

An important aspect in effective data cache management is how, and how well, an algorithm accesses the data that's in the cache. Because accessing memory whose addresses are adjacent or close together speeds up cache performance, structuring program code with the memory system in mind is often the best way to increase speed. Programmers can use a couple of design strategies to improve performance, such as making greater use of large element arrays instead of arranging data in multiple, individual structures. Additionally, code can be written to use processor-specific features. For example, most CPU instruction sets provide the user with the ability to manage the data cache via software.

Better Processors

Although writing better programs is a good place to look for better matches between system memory and cache memory, what about something for those of you in the cheap seats—those of you who aren't involved in program creation? The best thing (perhaps the only thing) to do is look for systems that have already addressed this problem and look to the chip vendors to provide increasingly faster iron.

Some Pentium system designs use two or more processors with dedicated caches for each processor. The advantage of such a multiprocessor design is that each processor communicates freely with its own cache and thus provides highly efficient bus utilization. More efficient bus utilization equals more rapid cache access (equals a faster computer). Simple. The problem, of course, is that this kind of multiple-processor design tends to be expensive and complex. Each dedicated cache requires an additional cache controller and SRAMs, and each cache also requires its own data path, memory bus, and interrupt control circuitry. Big money. Big headaches.

A bit different is a design that uses two processors that share a single secondary cache. This design is simpler and less expensive. You need only one cache controller and some SRAM. It's not as fast as dedicated caches, but according to Intel, it typically improves system performance by 50 percent to 80 percent with a secondary processor installed.

Managing Memory

So far, I've probably covered many of the terms you come across when reading computer ads or tips on "powering up" your PC. Just remember the following three points, and you shouldn't have any problem distinguishing between them:

◆ RAM is volatile, meaning that it doesn't hold data when you turn a PC off, but disk drives retain the data stored on them even when the power is turned off.

◆ PCs tend to have a lot more disk space than they have RAM space.

◆ As mentioned before, RAM is a lot faster than disk memory.

You'll also encounter another bunch of terms: *conventional memory*, *extended memory*, and *expanded memory*. These are more software-oriented terms than hardware-oriented terms, but they're worth going over in case you're trying to configure software that starts asking questions about how much memory you have.

Managing Memory in the DOS World

Many of the memory-related issues that we face today have their roots in the past, a past more than 20 years ago. Trust me, this isn't just a history lesson—some things that IBM decided in the summer of 1980 affect how the latest version of Windows works today. So bear with all the DOS-era details in the sections that follow; there really is a point to all this!

Up until about a decade ago, memory management was a hot topic in the PC world. There were several reasons why:

◆ Memory chips were expensive—*very* expensive.

◆ DOS didn't do a good job of managing what memory it had.

◆ With limited memory space available, programs with a small memory "footprint" were highly valued.

◆ Many DOS programs and utilities were Terminate and Stay Resident (TSR), meaning they loaded into memory—and stayed there.

◆ The order in which programs loaded into memory affected program and system performance; if programs were loaded in the wrong order, system crashes would often result.

Memory management was *so* important that an entire subcategory of software (memory managers) was created, and several best-selling books were written about the topic. This might seem odd today, when memory is cheap and plentiful and the operating system actually does a good job of managing memory usage, but that's the way it was back then.

In the DOS world, you had to deal with the three distinct types of memory I mentioned earlier: conventional, extended, and expanded. The interaction of these different types (actually areas within the system's memory) determined what types of (and how many) programs your PC could run:

Conventional This is the first 640KB of the first 1MB (1024KB) of memory, used for configuring the DOS program environment for games and such and for loading DOS device drivers and programs that can be loaded into upper memory (640B–1024KB).

Extended   This is memory beyond the 1MB barrier. Windows does most of its work with this type of memory.

Expanded   Also called Expanded Memory Specification (EMS) or LIM, this was used by a handful of programs written in the late '80s and early '90s; it isn't a factor today. (LIM, by the way, stands for Lotus-Intel-Microsoft and was used primarily by Lotus 1-2-3 and certain Microsoft programs of the era.)

NOTE   Expanded memory is only useful in trying to support much older machines or much older software on more recent machines. Modern computer programs really don't use this any longer.

Why are there so many kinds of memory? It's worth noting something before I go any further: nobody planned this. It just kind of evolved that way. Nobody ever thought the PC would need more than 640KB of memory. (Remember Bill Gates' famous quote, mentioned earlier.)

DESIGNING A COMPUTER'S MEMORY: ZONING THE FIRST MEGABYTE

In the summer of 1980, IBM commenced the PC development project. The goal of the small design team was to build a "home computer" (that's what we called them in those days) that could compete with the Apple II. The PC had a good start in that it was based around a much more powerful chip than the Apple. The chip that IBM selected was, of course, the Intel 8088, and one of the powerful features was that the 8088 could address ("talk to") up to 1024KB—1MB, or 1,048,576 bytes—of RAM. That limit shaped DOS, the need for DOS compatibility shaped Windows 3.*x*, and Windows 3.*x* compatibility constrained much of the Windows 95/98 architecture. (Think of it as the Curse of Backward Compatibility.)

Planning a new computer is kind of like planning a new community. Before breaking ground on a new planned community, a zoning board or planning board determines what use will be made of all the land space. Thus, the planners of a new community start from some unused land, perhaps fallow farmland. After acquiring the land, the next step is to plot it out into lots and then determine which lots will hold residential buildings and which ones will hold commercial buildings, industrial buildings, local government, and so on. You could say that before any buildings are built, a planner must allocate addresses. Before any buildings get built, the planner decides that any buildings built on address *x* must be residential, and any on a given address *y* must be commercial. In the same way, planning a computer requires allocating specific contents to "addresses." Now let's take a look at how memory in IBM's first computer was designated.

IBM, too, had to worry about traffic flow (the traffic isn't cars and trucks but instructions and requests running from hardware to CPU and back), about population density (too much equipment in one place affects the heat of the unit, and overheating affects a PC's performance), and about resources (enough power to keep the drives, the video, and so on running).

INTERRUPT VECTORS AND DOS

The bottom 1KB of memory is an area used by the CPU as a kind of table of contents of hardware support programs called *software interrupts.* The table of contents is composed of pointers to those programs called *interrupt vectors.* This area is a fixed size of 1024 bytes—400 in hexadecimal. One interrupt points to the program that controls your disk drives, another to the video board, and so on. That

1KB is reserved for the interrupt vector table no matter what operating system you're running and no matter which CPU you're using. Above that is DOS itself. I can't say exactly how much space DOS takes up in memory, simply because first, there are many versions of DOS, and second, different CONFIG.SYS options use more or less space, and that space adds to the DOS space requirements.

DEVICE DRIVERS

Directly above this bottom level, DOS loads a special class of programs called *device drivers*. Virtually every DOS-based computer uses at least one of these. (Similar programs in Windows are called *Windows drivers*, and they're files with an extension of either .386 for Windows 3.*x* or .VXD for Windows 95 and newer.)

Device drivers are programs that either allow DOS to support a new piece of hardware or add new capabilities to an existing piece of hardware. Device drivers are loaded in the CONFIG.SYS file with the DEVICE= statement.

Quite often, the order in which you load device drivers is important in DOS. In any case, device drivers change the way your system reacts to information from your system's hardware. When you're trying to track down a problem, it's always a good idea to boot with as few device drivers as possible, whether it's DOS, Windows 9*x*, or Windows NT.

COMMAND SHELL

Every operating system has a program that accepts inputs from users and reformulates them in a manner that the operating system can understand. In the case of DOS, the most common command shell was and is (for those of us inclined to go to the command prompt) COMMAND.COM. It loaded after the device drivers but before TSRs.

TERMINATE AND STAY RESIDENT OR MEMORY RESIDENT PROGRAMS

Under DOS, TSR programs do much the same thing as device drivers, but they're loaded from AUTOEXEC.BAT, so they load after any device drivers.

DOS relied upon TSRs and device drivers, especially to load various types of utility programs, but they came with a price: they took up your precious 640KB conventional space that you needed to run DOS programs.

USER PROGRAMS

Above the TSRs, you find the currently loaded program. The remaining memory is then available for the program's documents. Again, the top address is 640KB minus 1, rather than 640KB, because you start counting at *zero*, not *one*.

The vast majority of DOS programs claimed they could run only in the low 640KB of your PC's memory, and that's largely true. That's why the 640KB conventional memory area is so important; if your program can live only in conventional memory, and the conventional memory is full, getting more memory won't help. One of my users once said of his computer, which had only 4MB of RAM at the time, "We need to buy more memory for my PC—I'm running out of memory." He was indeed running out of memory, but with an old application that couldn't use any more memory than 640KB. As far as that application was concerned, the memory beyond 640KB didn't even exist.

VIDEO RAM

People used to say that DOS and DOS programs had a *640KB barrier* or *640KB limitation*, but that's not actually true. DOS programs were almost all written to run on the 8088 chip (and, of course, its successors, the 286 and later). Any 8088 program could address up to 1024KB of memory—in theory. There's nothing about DOS or the 8088 (or the Pentium II, for that matter) that requires the story to end at 640KB. Nevertheless, 640KB is a real barrier for most systems. Why?

The blame for 640KB can be laid at the feet of those 1980 PC designers.

As used in the IBM world, the video board—the circuit board that acts as an interface between the CPU and the monitor—must have some memory on it. That memory is then shared between the circuitry on the video board and the CPU. The CPU "puts data on the screen" by putting data into this video RAM. The video circuitry sees the data in the memory and interprets it as graphical or textual information.

Video memory is memory used by video boards to keep track of what's to be displayed on the screen. When a program puts a character on the screen or draws a circle on the screen, it's making changes to this video memory. IBM set aside 128KB for video memory, but most video boards didn't need or use that much memory space. The answer to the original question, however ("Where does the 640KB limit come from?"), is that the video RAM must go somewhere, and the original PC designers placed it from 640KB through 768KB. Even if there were more memory for user programs above 768KB, most programs couldn't use that memory, and *here* you see the DOS limitation: in general, DOS programs needed *contiguous blocks of memory*.

Thus, DOS programs could start grabbing memory just above DOS itself and then keep going until they hit a pothole of some kind—and in this case, that pothole is the video memory—at which point they stop looking for memory. In general, DOS programs aren't smart enough to use fragmented memory. (That's not true for Windows programs, by the way.)

You may be saying, "Why doesn't someone just build a PC with the video addresses higher up? Then there'd be more space for conventional memory." Unfortunately, that wouldn't work. The reason is that a large number of programs are designed to directly manipulate the video hardware, and those programs are all written assuming that the video is where it's supposed to be—between 640KB and 768KB.

The current standard Super VGA (SVGA) still uses the addresses from 640KB through 768KB (these addresses are numbered A0000–BFFFF). This is hexadecimal (check the Bonus CD if that's new to you).

Used memory address space differs from total memory onboard because video board manufacturers use a technique called *paging* (explained further in the upcoming section "Video Memory and Paging"). Paging enables them to put lots of memory on the video board—lots of memory means better video—without taking up a lot of the CPU's total 1024KB memory address space.

Note that the video board can be convinced to disable memory usage from B0000 to B1000, the addresses that the Monochrome Display Adapter (MDA) uses. That's so your system could run two monitors. Although it's not common, some debugging systems for programmers let you test-run your program with program output going to a Video Graphics Array (VGA) monitor while displaying debugging information on a monochrome MDA monitor.

Newer PCI-based video boards are quite a bit smarter about using memory, so you can put multiple PCI-based video cards into a single computer.

Video Memory Layout

The 128KB set aside for video memory isn't just laid out as one big 128KB block; rather, there are three separate and distinct video memory areas, as shown in Figure 6.3.

FIGURE 6.3
Video memory areas

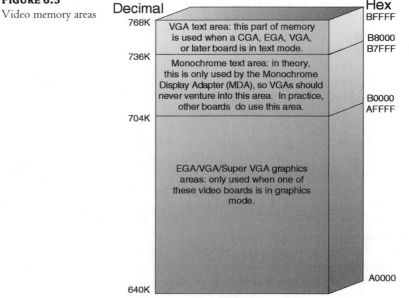

FIGURE 6.3
Video memory areas

Decimal / Hex

768K — BFFFF
VGA text area: this part of memory is used when a CGA, EGA, VGA, or later board is in text mode. — B8000 / B7FFF

736K
Monochrome text area: in theory, this is only used by the Monochrome Display Adapter (MDA), so VGAs should never venture into this area. In practice, other boards do use this area. — B0000 / AFFFF

704K

EGA/VGA/Super VGA graphics areas: only used when one of these video boards is in graphics mode.

A0000

640K

On current graphics boards, graphics activity takes place in the bottom 64KB of the video area. This is accessed only when in graphics mode. The 32KB area from B0000 through B7FFF was designated for the MDA, but IBM MDAs used only memory from B0000 through B0FFF, a 4KB area. Later MDA improvements such as the Hercules Graphics Controller and clones used the entire 32KB region.

Video Memory and Paging

As you look at the VGA area, a question may be forming in your mind. Anyone who's bought a video board recently knows that video boards come with at least 32- or 64MB of memory. Where does this memory go, given that there's only 64KB of addresses set aside for VGA graphics? The answer is in the technique I mentioned earlier, called *paging*.

Recall that the video RAM isn't on the motherboard but rather on the video board. (Of course, if the VGA is integrated into the motherboard, the video RAM will be also.) Paging hardware on the VGA board enables the video board to present only 64KB of its 256KB (the amount of memory found on a normal VGA) to the CPU at a time. There are then four 64KB pages on a standard VGA and, as it turns out, they each have a job. One page governs the blue part of the screen, another the red, another the green, and the final one the intensity of an image. The actual process of generating a complete VGA graphics screen looks something like the following:

1. Issue the command to bring in (page in) the blue 64KB.

2. Draw the blue part of the screen in the blue memory page.

3. Issue the command to page in the green 64KB page.

4. Draw the green part of the image.

5. Issue the command to page in the red 64KB page.

6. Draw the red part of the screen.

7. Issue the command to page in the intensity page.

8. Designate the areas that need high intensity and low intensity.

NOTE *Paging is a process used commonly in the computer world to shoehorn a lot of memory into just a few addresses.*

Now that you have a little insight into what's required to make *one small change* to what's visible on a VGA screen, it's easy to understand why Windows—or any graphical program—can run slowly even on a fast machine. There's just so darn much housekeeping that's got to be done every time you do so much as move the mouse! That's why a graphics accelerator (discussed in Chapter 20, "Video Adapters and Displays,") makes so much sense for today's software; in fact, most current video boards are accelerators.

THE SYSTEM RESERVED AREA

In addition to device drivers, user programs, and video, the PC needs to steal from the CPU's memory address space for the following:

◆ Small amounts of memory called *buffers* or *frames* used by some expansion boards

◆ Special memory-containing system software called ROM

Read-Only Memory (ROM)

I've talked so far about memory and RAM as if they were identical notions. As mentioned earlier, another kind of memory exists, which isn't used as much as RAM, but is important nonetheless. Unlike RAM, which the CPU can both write data to and read data from, this other kind of memory can't be altered. It can only be read, so it's called *read-only* memory. This is memory that someone (the computer manufacturer, usually) loads just once with a special device such as a PROM blaster, EPROM programmer, or the like. So you can read information from ROM, but you can't write new information. (Well, you *can* write the information, but the ROM will ignore you. Think of ROM as a chip that can *give* advice but can't *take* it.)

Why have a memory chip that you can store information in only *once*? Well, unlike normal RAM, the ROM has the virtue that it doesn't lose its memory when you turn the machine off—techie types would say it's *nonvolatile*. You use ROM to store software that won't change. In essence, you can say that ROM on a circuit board contains the software that tells the system how to use a circuit board

ROM chips are found on expansion boards such as LAN, video, or scanner interface cards, to name a few examples. ROM is also found on the system board. The ROM on the system board contains a piece of software called BIOS. You may recall from earlier in this chapter a reference to a set of low-level programs, called *software interrupts,* that directly manipulate your hardware. These programs are pointed to by the interrupt vectors at the bottom of RAM memory. Software interrupts work to help configure the working environment, and BIOS serves as something of the arbiter between the PC and DOS (or the PC and Windows). DOS relies on BIOS in that DOS doesn't communicate directly with your hardware; rather, it issues commands through BIOS. Thus, when DOS reads your floppy, it does it by calling on the BIOS routine that reads your floppy drive. That's why the BIOS is so important: the BIOS determines in large measure how compatible your PC is.

As you'd expect, IBM's BIOS is *the* standard of compatibility. Back in the early '80s, the first clone makers developed BIOS software that conformed in varying degrees to the IBM standard; so the question, "Does it run Lotus 1-2-3 and Microsoft Flight Simulator?" was the acid test of compatibility. Nowadays, I suppose it's "Does it run Windows XP?" Three companies—Phoenix Software, Award Software, and American Megatrends, Incorporated (AMI)—derive large incomes from their main business of writing *very* compatible BIOS software for clone makers. This has simplified the business of cloning considerably.

I've said that ROM contains software. As you know, software changes from time to time. Occasionally a problem can be fixed by "upgrading the ROM"—getting the latest version of the ROM-based software from the manufacturer. On older systems, it means opening the system boxes and replacing a chip. On newer systems, it's easier—all you have to do is run a program that rewrites the ROM. You do need to be careful about this, though, because the BIOS on some systems may be designed to run some specific hardware that's present on that computer only. If you replace the BIOS on a system like that, some of the devices on the computer may not function correctly (or at all).

For this reason, you have to know exactly what version of software is in the ROM chips in the computers for which you're responsible. In a maintenance notebook, keep track of the serial numbers or dates on the labels pasted on the backs of the ROM chips in your PCs, or look at the PC when it boots up for an opening message from the BIOS including the software version of the BIOS. Whenever you install a board, note any ROM identifying marks. It'll save you from having to pop the top to find out when you call for service.

ROM chips can usually be easily identified because they're generally larger chips (24- or 28-pin DIP chips), they're socketed (so they can be easily changed), and they often have a paper label pasted on them with a version number or some such information printed on it. ROM chips are memories, albeit inflexible ones, so they require a place in the memory addresses in the reserved area from 640KB to 1024KB

Flash RAM

As I just said, upgrading ROM on most modern PCs is a bit different from upgrading on older PCs. Newer PCs store their BIOS on a special kind of memory chip called *Flash RAM* or, as the chips were once more commonly known, an Electrically Erasable/Programmable Read-Only Memory (EEPROM, pronounced *double E PROM*).

Flash RAM is the same as a BIOS, with the one important exception: a *program* can modify the BIOS. BIOS upgrades can then be done by just running a BIOS update program.

Flash RAM modules are a great convenience on laptops because laptops are so crowded inside that prying them apart to change a BIOS chip is an enormous hassle. With Flash RAM, however, it's child's play: just run a BIOS update program supplied by the laptop manufacturer, and the new BIOS is installed.

Ah, but there's one caveat. With added convenience potentially comes more risk. Some motherboards of today make Flash BIOS upgrading so easy that you don't even have to open the case (a few years ago, you often had to move a jumper on the motherboard to get it to accept the "flashing"). Although this innovation is a serious time-saver, viruses have appeared that are specifically written to do damage when you upgrade your BIOS (for example, the CIH virus, a.k.a. the Chernobyl virus, set to go off on the anniversary of the Chernobyl nuclear disaster or the 26th of every month, depending on the variant). The BIOS can't discern which is a good change and which is a bad one, so encountering such a virus and leaving it unchecked could damage your BIOS. When the damage is unchecked and runs its course, replacing the motherboard—or at least the BIOS chip on the motherboard—is warranted.

Buffers and Frames

A *buffer* acts as a sort of queue, or an area for storing computer messages. A *frame* refers to one complete scan of the active area of a computer display screen, containing a set number of horizontal scan lines, with a set number of pixels in each. *Frames per second (fps)* refers to the number of times the screen updates per second.

You've seen that video boards require memory to hold the current video image. They're not the only boards that use memory addresses, however; other boards also need a little memory space reserved for them. A LAN board, for example, may require some storage space. Here are a few examples:

◆ Token Ring LAN boards have 16KB of ROM that contains a sort of network-level BIOS. They also have a RAM buffer that can be adjusted to be as small as 8KB or as large as 64KB.

◆ Many Ethernet boards these days have a 32KB RAM buffer on them; that RAM buffer must have an address within the CPU's address range.

◆ Some old ARCNet cards (which is an acronym for Attached Resource Computer Network) have up to 64KB of ROM on them.

◆ Older VGA boards had 24KB of ROM on them, but SVGA boards usually have 32KB or 40KB of ROM.

◆ Many hard disk controllers have ROM, particularly hard disk controllers that offer some kind of high-performance or unusual capabilities, such as SCSI or enhanced IDE host adapters.

◆ Scanner interface cards, such as the one supplied with the old Hewlett-Packard ScanJet, included some ROM.

◆ An expanded, or LIM, memory board contains from 16KB to 64KB of page frame memory space to buffer transfers into and out of LIM memory.

All those memory pieces must fit somewhere in the reserved area from 640KB to 1024KB in the PC memory address space. Before you leave this section, let's add reserved areas to your memory map, as in Figure 6.4.

FIGURE 6.4

Memory map with reserved areas displayed

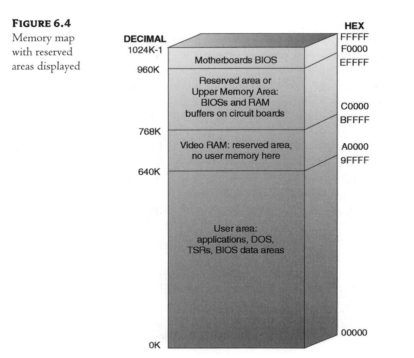

That's how the original PC designers laid out the first PC. The layout of that first 1024KB became a standard that no software or hardware designer dared violate at the cost of 100-percent PC compatibility. But with more complex PCs came more memory—and a chance to get to more space.

Believe it or not, you've only gotten as far as the 8088 in this review of how software uses memory. But don't worry—the rest goes more quickly!

EXTENDED MEMORY

Not content with the 8088/8086, Intel began in 1978 to develop processor chips with power rivaling that of minicomputers and mainframes. One thing micros lacked (then) that more powerful computers had was larger memory address space. So from the 80286's introduction in 1981 onward, Intel chips could address megabytes and megabytes. An 80286 could actually talk to ("address") 16MB. An 80386 or later could talk to 4GB (1GB is 1024MB) of RAM. The term for standard RAM above the 1MB level is *extended memory*.

Why did memory above 1024KB get a completely new name? Largely because the 286 and later chips had "split personalities": they could either address memory beyond 1024KB *or* run DOS programs. To use memory above 1024KB, the 286 and later chips had to shift to a new processor mode called *protected mode*. Protected mode had lots of virtues but one big flaw: when a chip was in protected mode, it was incompatible with an older 8088 or 8086.

You see, most early CPUs used in microcomputers were more glorified calculator chips than computers—the 4004, 8008, 8080, 8085, 8086, 8088, 80188, and 80186 all fell into this category.

Intel intended that the 80286 should have some powers that were mainframe-like and in particular should be able to talk to more memory and to *protect* that memory.

You're probably familiar with the notion that large mainframe computers can run multiple programs at the same time. Basically, the memory space of the computer gets parceled out to the applications ("Okay, text editor, you get 120KB, and database, you get 105KB, and spreadsheet, you get 150KB—no, you may *not* have more!"), and everyone's expected to stay in their places. But what about the odd program that accidentally strays from its area? If the text editor stretches a bit, it overwrites the database's area—what to do? Or, worse yet, suppose your computer was acting as a server on a LAN, and one program (a virus, or the like) tried to peek into the memory of the LAN server program itself—the *program that contains the system passwords?*

That's why memory protection is a good idea and why mainframes have memory protection. The mainframe CPU has hardware built into it that keeps track of what application gets to use what memory. It's as if the CPU can put a "force field" around each program. As long as the program stays within its force field, it's okay. But if it tries to reach out of that area, it's stopped by the force field, and the CPU's "security system" is alerted that a protection violation was attempted. The operating system can then terminate the application (with extreme prejudice). In less colorful terms, if an application tries to reach out of its space, the protection hardware senses this and stops the application, probably by ending the program and informing the user.

This memory protection is essential for any multitasking operating systems, and Linux and all versions of Windows from Windows 95 on multitask. Furthermore, they work with extended memory, so you'd think they'd exploit these "force fields."

They do, but in varying ways. The oddest approach to memory protection is the one that Windows 3.*x* used. You see, all this placing of "force fields" must be controlled by some program, which means there's got to be some control over who gets to set up force fields and who doesn't. That leads to the notion in the Intel world of *privilege rings*, as you see in Figure 6.5.

FIGURE 6.5

Privilege rings

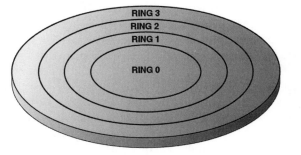

Programs in ring 0 can control anything. Programs in ring 1 can control other ring 1, 2, or 3 programs. Ring 2 programs control only ring 2 or 3 programs, and ring 3 programs can affect only other ring 3 programs. Logically, then, the operating system should be ring 0, and the applications should be ring 3. That's the way most operating systems are built.

Sadly, Windows 3.*x* didn't do that. Under that operating system, all programs were granted ring 0 privileges. *All* programs. That meant that although all programs had memory protection, all programs also had the capability to override the memory protection. No Windows 3.x program was safe from any other Windows 3.x program, leading to an unfortunately familiar error called a General Protection Fault (GPF). Other operating systems, including Windows 95/98, are built better, but Windows 95/98 really only works protection-wise when you use programs written for Windows 95/98; older Windows applications still aren't protected.

Anyway, back to the history: until 1981, none of the Intel CPUs had this built-in memory protection, but the 286 and later chips were all built with this feature. These chips could also address memory beyond 1024KB, but *only* while in protected mode. The 8088, 8086, and earlier chips couldn't under any circumstances address memory beyond 1024KB, so they couldn't ever have extended memory.

Basically, programs that run while in protected mode don't try to do *anything* with memory without first requesting memory blocks from the operating system. Then, once the operating system has granted them an area in memory, the programs load their data into their spaces and stay there.

And *that's* the problem.

The basic problem with multitasking DOS programs is that they often live up to their nickname: the "spoiled children" of PC programs. This whole notion of first asking the operating system—DOS—for permission before using memory is totally unknown in the DOS world. Programs written for DOS pretty much assume they're the only program in the system, so they just take whatever they want without asking for it. So for the 286 to have memory protection, it wouldn't only have to be a *different* chip, it'd have to be an *incompatible* chip—incompatible with DOS and DOS programs, in particular.

Now, designing and releasing a new chip that was totally incompatible with any previous Intel offerings would be suicidal. So Intel gave the 286 and subsequent chips split personalities: when they booted up, they acted just like an 8088, except faster. They could talk to 1024KB and no more: their 8088 emulation mode was called *real mode*. You'll sometimes hear people refer to DOS programs (when speaking of Windows) as *real mode programs*. That just means they were built for the 8088. Of course, despite the fact that 8088 are ancient history, software is still written for the 8088 every day because of DOS's popularity. With a few instructions, it can shift over to protected mode and talk to lots of memory beyond 1024KB. But, again, once the 286 or later chip is in protected mode, it can't run programs designed for real mode—DOS and DOS programs, that is.

You may be wondering why they didn't just write an operating system that uses this protected mode. As I suggested earlier, they have—that was the whole idea of Windows 3.x, Windows NT, and Unix. Windows 3.x programs could address 16MB; some Windows programs—the ones that used Win32s—could address even more than that, but they required a 386 or 486 computer to do so.

Does that mean DOS programs absolutely can't use extended memory? By no means. A class of DOS programs uses software called a *DOS extender* to allow them to use extended memory. Basically, a DOS extender is a tiny operating system that unlocks the door to extended memory and provides tools that programmers can exploit to use that memory. Examples include Lotus 1-2-3 version 3.x, AutoCAD, and many database programs. This use of extended memory explains why, for example, 8088-based machines could run Lotus 1-2-3 version 3.

Because XT-type machines were based on 8088/8086 chips, they *couldn't* have extended memory. ATs right up to the Pentium III and beyond *can*. When you see your computer count up to 16MB or 32MB or 64MB during the Power-On Self Test, you have some extended memory.

Let's take a simple example—an old 286 with 1024KB of memory. There's 1024KB of RAM, all of which must be given addresses. You'll recall from the earlier part of this chapter that the addresses from 0 to 640KB are intended to be filled so that conventional memory space exists. Addresses 640KB through 1024KB must be left alone because they're intended for memory from other sources, such as the video board and add-in cards. So, of the 1024KB, 640KB gets put in the 0–640KB range. That leaves 1024KB–640KB, or 384KB. Where does that memory get placed? It goes in the extended memory addresses, making it extended memory.

Figure 6.6 shows how it would look on your memory map.

FIGURE 6.6

Memory map with extended memory included

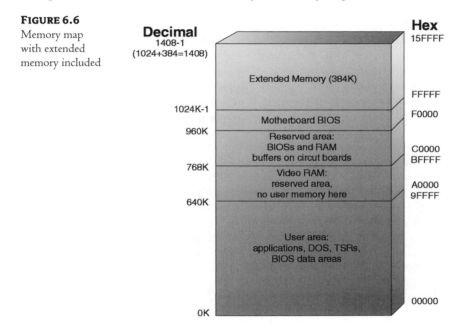

Not to belabor the point, but this breaking up of memory causes a lot of confusion for users, so let me emphasize again why the memory gets allocated this way. The key to understanding the answer is in understanding that there's a difference between *memory* and *memory addresses*.

Remember my analogy in the beginning of this section about designing a computer versus designing a town? Well, let's suppose you're designing a town built on 1024 one-acre lots (conveniently enough). Suppose you zone the first 640 lots for residential use, the next 128 for industrial, and the remaining 256 for commercial buildings. You now have addresses and purposes for those addresses but nothing in those addresses. Sure, there's now a lot called 200 First Avenue, but it's only a muddy rectangle of ground: send mail there, and it just sits outside and rots.

After the town has been zoned, you start putting houses in the residential addresses—filling your PC with memory. But suppose a vendor of prefabricated houses shows up with 1024 houses? That's the situation that a computer designer faces when building a computer with 1024KB of RAM. First, she plunks down houses in the first 640 lots, filling your "conventional" addresses. But the zoning board (that is, the requirements of PC hardware compatibility) precludes her from putting any of the houses in the top 384 addresses. (Here, the computer designer plays both the roles of the planning board and the prefabricated house vendor.) The top 384 lots don't have normal system RAM (houses) in them; rather, they have special RAM. That area is filled in for a PC with some RAM physically located on the video board and perhaps some ROM located on the motherboard or add-in boards. That, too, is worth stressing: the memory in the video area isn't taken from the system's main memory; when you buy a PC with 1024KB of memory, none of that memory is ROM or video RAM. A PC with 1024KB of RAM actually has a fair amount *more* than 1024KB of RAM, if you count the RAM on the video board and the ROM and RAM buffers on the expansion boards—and that memory is *not* counted when your system does its power-up memory count. There's simply nowhere to put the extra 384 houses, which is why XTs and PCs—8088-based computers—didn't have more than 640KB of system RAM.

Now let's move along to the 286 and later chips. They have memory limitations of 16MB or more, so now you have to zone the addresses above 1024KB. Continuing the town planning analogy, suppose that this town has been in existence for 30 years when a community springs up outside your original 1024 lots. You'd call that a suburb of the town; it might have a different tax rate, be governed differently, and have different levels of access to the privileges accorded town residents. For example, suburbanites might have to pay a fee to use the town parks whereas the town residents might be able to use the parks for free. So it is with extended memory; the addresses above 1024KB aren't accessible to the vast majority of DOS programs, as you've seen earlier in this discussion.

Return to the case of the vendor of prefab houses who finds herself with 1024 houses as she shows up in your new town. Again, she puts houses on the first 640 spaces and is then told that she can't put houses on the top 384 addresses. "What will I do with these extra 384 houses?" she wails. "Take them out to the suburbs," she's told. So she puts the remaining 384 houses in the *extended* addresses because the 384 addresses that she skipped from 640 to 1024 will be filled with buildings from another source.

So, getting back to the original question: what's happening with a 286 computer that counts up to 1024KB on power-up? First, understand that 1024KB is a count only of program memory. There's more memory in the computer—video RAM on the video board, system BIOS ROM on the motherboard, and ROM and perhaps small RAM buffers on add-in cards in the system—*that isn't counted.* The 1024KB fills up the first 640KB and can't fill up any of the addresses between 640K and 1024KB, or the PC will have program memory in the same addresses as video memory or ROM. Just as you can't put two houses on the same lot, so also two separate memories wired to the same address would both malfunction. So the extra 384KB of RAM gets addressed starting at 1024KB and going up to 1408KB.

TIP *You don't have to fill a lower memory address before filling a higher address; that's why you can have extended memory before filling the system's reserved area.*

One more point that hangs some people up: I've said that the reserved area from 640KB to 1024KB contains memory, but it's not completely full. You'll usually find plenty of unused addresses between 768KB and 1024KB, a fact that created the memory manager market in the first place. Many people seem to feel that all the addresses from 0 through 1024KB must be filled by *something* before any addresses above 1024KB can be filled. But that's not true; you *could* build a computer with 128KB of conventional memory, video RAM between 640KB and 768KB, ROM between 768KB and 1024KB, and 6MB of extended memory above 1024KB. (You'd have trouble finding software that would run on it, but you could do it.)

Extended memory is simple for programmers to use, provided those programmers are working with an operating environment that supports extended memory. But extended memory wasn't always easy to work with, which led to *expanded* memory.

EMS, LIM, PAGED, EXPANDED MEMORY

In 1985, Lotus 1-2-3 version 1A was the best-selling software package in history. People used Lotus for everything. And Parkinson's law ("work expands to fill all available resources") seemed to become an iron rule—more and more users found the 640KB limitation a chafing one. Not as chafing, however, as the 1-2-3 copy protection scheme. Copy protection was a common practice among software vendors until around 1986. Lotus 1-2-3's copy protection required that you insert a key disk into your A: drive *whenever* you wanted to run 1-2-3. No key disk, no Lotus.

So, when Lotus announced 1-2-3 version 2, people were excited. At $495 a copy, it seemed a bit pricey, but Lotus made its users an upgrade offer. "Send us $125 and your version 1A key disk, and we'll send you 2," they offered. Well, at $125, that was hard to turn down. The downside was that you had to send in the key disk, which meant you couldn't use 1-2-3 1A *or* 2 until the upgrade arrived; but Lotus shipped the upgrades, and people had only a day or so of downtime. (In case you're wondering, the world was a much different place then, and people didn't rely on PCs as heavily as they do today. Nowadays, of course, an upgrade offer that took a PC out of action for a day or two would be laughed off the market.) So hundreds of thousands of users upgraded.

This is when it became clear that there was just one little problem: 1-2-3 version 2 took up more memory space than version 1A, which meant that any spreadsheets that packed the memory up to the 640KB rafters—and there were plenty—wouldn't run under 2. Worse, the users couldn't revert to 1A (they'd turned in their 1A key disks), leaving them stranded. Lotus realized they'd better do something *fast*, so they called up Intel, the chip designers, and asked what could be done. Lotus and Intel developed a paged memory system (recall paging in the video discussion) that they called *expanded memory*. Using this memory system required the user to buy a new kind of memory board that Intel built called an *AboveBoard*.

Let's finish your memory map by adding expanded memory off to the side of the standard memory column, as in Figure 6.7.

On 8088 and most 80286 computers, you needed a specific memory board to support LIM: two common examples of this kind of memory board were, again, the Intel AboveBoard and the AST RAMPage cards. On 386 and later machines, you could achieve LIM compatibility with just software. This meant that a 386 could make extended memory behave software-wise like expanded memory. Part of what Windows 3.1 and up can do for DOS programs is to provide them with some extended memory that behaves like expanded memory. (The motherboards of some 286s could do that also, but not many.)

FIGURE 6.7

Memory map with expanded memory

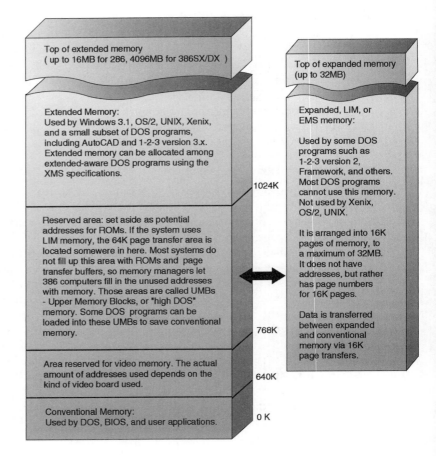

REVIEWING MEMORY TYPES

So now you've seen conventional, extended, and expanded memory and how they were used in the DOS era of personal computing. Let's review what you know so far:

- ◆ Conventional memory:
  - ◆ Available to all PCs.
  - ◆ Limited to 640KB.
  - ◆ Virtually every program can use this memory.
  - ◆ By default, DOS, device drivers, and TSRs are loaded in conventional memory.

- ◆ Extended memory:

  - ◆ Only possible with machines based on 286 and later chips; was impossible with XTs.

  - ◆ A class of DOS programs could use it.

  - ◆ Used by Unix, Linux, and Windows.

- ◆ Expanded memory:

  - ◆ Also called LIM memory or EMS memory.

  - ◆ Could be used with PCs, XTs, ATs—any PC machine.

  - ◆ Useful under DOS *with programs that can use it,* such as Lotus version 2.*x* and WordPerfect 5.1.

  - ◆ 386 and later computers can make their extended memory act like expanded, as could a few 286-based machines.

TIP   *If you have trouble distinguishing between extended and expanded memory, do what I do. I always pronounced the latter "exPanded," so I can remember that it's "Paged."*

Managing Memory in the Post-DOS World

Early versions of Windows came with the same memory constraints found on DOS machines, primarily because those operating systems were essentially built on a DOS base. For example, Windows 3.1/ Windows for Workgroups 3.11 were fairly needy of conventional memory—they wouldn't run without a certain amount of it.

Windows 95/98/Me is less dependent on the bottom 640KB—*unless* you're running old Windows 3.1 and/or DOS programs. When that happens, Windows 95/98/Me reverts to its old Windows 3.1 ways and gets needy of lower memory space. To be completely free of the need for conventional memory, you have to abandon DOS completely and move up to a 32-bit operating system, such as Windows NT, Windows 2000 and 2003, or Windows XP (which is built on Windows NT).

Different versions of Windows manage memory in different ways, but all use the Windows kernel to do the managing. The 16-bit Windows 9*x* kernel treats memory as one giant container; as you open new applications, the kernel sends data to RAM, where it's deposited in whatever memory location is available. The 32-bit WinNT kernel, on the other hand, sends the data to specific areas within RAM. This means that memory management is more efficient—and more stable—on 32-bit versions of Windows.

This may not seem like a big difference—until you have a problem. When an application develops a fatal error, Windows "fixes" the problem by pulling the entire application (and all related data) out of memory. Because the Windows 9*x* kernel crams bits and pieces of application memory anywhere there's an empty space, pulling these bits and pieces out of their holes tends to make the entire system unstable. The Windows NT kernel is much more orderly about where it puts application memory and thus can remove said memory without disturbing neighboring applications. The result is a much more stable system, where a single application crash doesn't crash the entire system.

In addition, Windows also takes advantage of *virtual memory*. By using spare hard disk space as a temporary memory storage area, Windows substantially increases your machine's effective memory—even though disk-based memory is noticeably slower than chip-based memory.

NOTE *The virtual memory space on your hard disk is called either a page file or a swap file, depending on the version of Windows you're running.*

Another factor, of course, is the shrinking price tag on memory chips. Instead of worrying about how to cram two gallons of stuff into a one-gallon container, you can now solve your problem by buying a larger container. The days of PCs with (believe it or not) 1MB of RAM are long gone; now it's not uncommon for a new PC to come with 256MB or more memory. When you have that much memory to work with, micromanaging the use of that memory just isn't necessary.

The bottom line is that if you're running any version of Windows from Windows 95 on—and especially if you're running Windows NT, 2000/2003, or XP—about the only memory-related issue you need to worry about is buying more of the stuff. Unlike the old DOS days, the easiest way to fix a memory management problem is to add more memory to your system. The more memory you have, the fewer problems you'll have, period.

MEMORY MANAGEMENT HEADACHES

After reading the previous sections on memory management, you might have a headache and rightfully so. Because of the erroneous idea that no one would ever need more than 640KB of RAM, computer users and supporters had to suffer for dozens of years, all in the name of backward compatibility.

I wanted to include this memory lesson as a historical reference for you, because it's good to see how far we've come with computing technology. The good news is that it's unlikely you'll ever need to memorize the reserved areas of conventional memory, unless you're preparing for the A+ exam, which asks arcane things such as that. The better news is that you won't have to worry about too many memory-management concepts on newer computers. These days, all you need to know is this: the more RAM the better. Headache cured.

Causes of False Memory Errors

Memory often gets blamed for problems arising from other sources. In most cases, memory that has been working for a few weeks will work forever. Although memory hardware failures were common up to the late '80s, the quality of memory chips has improved considerably since 1988. Reliability has increased substantially over the last 14-plus years, as well. Rare is the case when RAM goes bad. That said, potential problems still exist, especially in older systems that are still in use, a growing practice in today's ever-more-common multi-PC home. These older systems still need to use the older RAM and, if these systems have had RAM augmented and not replaced, these older problems can still occur.

Power Drops and Surges

Memory is often falsely accused for a simple reason: the memory is so demanding in its need for constant, clean power. If the power drops out or surges for just a few millionths of a second, the memory loses its contents, causing a memory error. This wasn't an error caused by the memory—it was a power error that just *showed up* in the memory. Think of it as the canary in the coal mine of your PC.

Along the same lines, a static electric surge looks just like a power surge. Scuff across a pile carpet on a dry day, touch your computer, and you're likely to cause a memory error—but please *don't* try this out because you may cause permanent memory damage. A failing power supply may, in the same way, cause apparent memory failures. So will noisy power being fed to a perfectly good power supply.

The telltale signs in this case are the addresses reported by the memory errors. If you've truly got a memory error, you'll see the same address reported as bad over and over. But memory errors that always report different locations—locations that test fine when tested a few minutes later—likely point to power problems.

Is there *enough* power? Insufficient power can cause parity errors. This problem can be a real pain because it waits for some large disk access to trigger the parity error—for example, when you try to save your data to disk.

You see this problem with underpowered clones: your application works fine until you want to save the file, and then you get a parity check. The trouble is that you're running the power supply to the poor thing's limits and then want to fire up the hard disk. Not enough power, the memory gets shortchanged, and, bang! A memory error happens.

And, although it's unusual, improperly shielded sources of Radio Frequency (RF) noise can alter memory, causing parity errors. I remember a certain 64KB chip made back in the early '80s; this chip was built in a chip package that was accidentally made of a ceramic material that was a low-level emitter of alpha particle radiation. Once in a while, an alpha particle would zip through the chip, causing a nonrepeatable error. I'm glad I don't have to troubleshoot *those* chips anymore.

Mismatched Chip Speeds and Manufacturers

If you need a chip that has an access speed of, say, 80ns, but you can get only a faster chip—say, one that runs at 60ns—can you use the faster 60ns chip to replace the slower 80ns chip? Yes, *but* you must replace the entire bank of chips when you do that. Putting a single 60ns chip into a bank of 80ns chips will often cause the 80s to appear to have errors.

Another issue that used to plague older memory was compatibility between manufacturers. Until the mid-'90s, whenever possible, I recommended avoiding mixing *manufacturers* in the same row. I flatly couldn't explain this, but I have seen cases where it caused problems. For instance, I had two rows of chips—one entirely Mitsubishi, another entirely Toshiba—that worked fine. Then I mixed the rows. Errors occurred. I restored the rows, and the problem disappeared. With current technology, mixing manufacturers shouldn't cause problems.

Memory Tests

Modern RAM is pretty reliable, but you may come across a RAM failure of an odd sort on some SIMMs: *soft failures*. These are failures that show up only with specific tests.

NOTE *DIMMs of SDRAM varieties rarely have faults. When they do, the faults can often be traced back to a fabrication error.*

Walking Bit Test

Years ago, a manuscript of an early edition of this book suddenly started growing typos. And odd typos they were, too: now and then, a letter would show up wrong for no reason. I first thought that the printer was failing, but checking in the file on the disk, I found that the typos were *there*, too. I thought this extremely odd because I'd proofread the text—as had many others—and these obvious typos didn't appear. I began to be certain that the problem was machine induced.

I suspected my mass storage device, a Bernoulli cartridge system, so I started saving the document on my hard disk instead. Still, the errors were cropping up. That's when I also noticed that some files were being corrupted when I copied them.

It was starting to look like the problem was in the system's memory. Whenever a piece of data passed through the system's memory, it would sometimes—very rarely, actually—become corrupt. Finally, I ran a *walking bit* test.

You see, standard memory tests just go to a particular location and test the heck out of it, stuffing different combinations of 1s and 0s into a particular byte and then reading them back. Tests of that kind were coming up zero for errors. But what about interactive problems? It turned out that there were two memory locations, at roughly 560KB and 600KB, that were in cahoots with one another, so to speak. Test either location, and there was no problem. But put a 1 into the 560KB location, and—lo!—a 1 popped up in the 600KB location.

This kind of error is called a *walking bit* error, and it's a problem on the memory address circuitry rather than the memory itself. It really doesn't matter where the error originates, however, because the answer is the same: replace the problematic memory units. You'll read more about how in a little bit. It takes software to test this properly, and several commercially available memory-testing programs test a wide range of things, including this.

Mountain/Valley and Checkerboard Tests

Here's another example of memory problems that will never be detected by single-byte testing. Consider a set of bit memory cells, as shown in Figure 6.8.

But suppose one kind of bit can "leak over" into another kind of bit, as shown in Figure 6.9.

FIGURE 6.8
Set of bit
memory cells

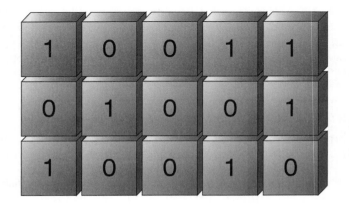

FIGURE 6.9
Set of bit memory cells with a "leak over" into another bit

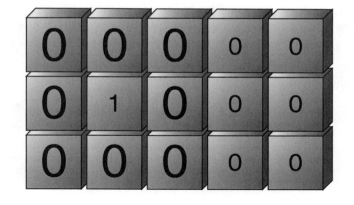

The effect is that the 0 bits leak over into the 1s, eventually turning them into 0s. Filling each bit with a 0 and then surrounding it by 1s, and vice versa, is called the *mountain/valley* test. The *checkerboard* test lays out a pattern of 1s and 0s like the light and dark squares of a checkerboard.

All of these memory tests are incorporated into the two memory tester programs (CheckIt and PC-Technician) that I recommend in Chapter 26, "Troubleshooting PC Problems." I strongly recommend running one of these programs overnight when you first install some new memory.

Tips on Installing Memory Chips

A lot of manuals include some really scary instructions for installing memory chips. I've probably installed a terabyte or so myself (512MB chips have made it easier to get to the 1GB level), so here's what works for me.

First, as always, be aware of static electricity. Your sweater and the soles of your shoes are powerful producers of it. If I'm worried about the static level of an area, and I'm not prepared with an antistatic strap, *I take my shoes and socks off.* I know it sounds a little bizarre, but I kill very few chips in my bare feet—probably fewer than a half dozen in all the time I've been installing memory.

Second, the memory chips go into slots on the motherboard. As before, don't insert a module into a board while the power is on. Push the white or gray knobs on the ends of the slot out from the center so you have room to slide in the module. Orient the module so that the notches in the pin array match the pegs in the slot on the board. Then push the chip into the socket firmly with your thumb.

TIP   *Some people who have been around it long enough call any RAM package mounted on a printed circuit board a stick of RAM. Heck, I do. I will, for the sake of clarity, not refer to them here as sticks, but as modules.*

NOTE   *Remember that patience is the keyword here: look at what you're doing and take your time if you're new to the process.*

How do I upgrade my old 486? How do I remove SIMMs? Between removing and installing, removing SIMMs can be the harder task, depending on how chintzy the motherboard manufacturer was. Figure 6.10 shows you how to remove SIMMs.

FIGURE 6.10
Removing SIMMs

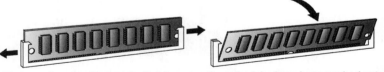

First, *gently* pull aside the plastic tabs that hold the SIMM in place. Be careful, as the tabs are easily broken.

Once the tabs have been pushed outward, rotate the SIMM forward. It then comes right out of its socket.

There's an unfortunately frequent occurrence in the classes I teach on PC repair that concerns SIMM removal. In every class, I tell students, "Don't remove SIMMs until I show you how to do it." Now and then, I'll get some prize idiot who decides he'd rather figure it out himself. So he grabs the SIMM and yanks it out—and sure enough, he *did* figure out how to remove a SIMM! Unfortunately, however, that SIMM socket will never again hold a SIMM because he has broken off the little plastic tabs that hold SIMMs in place. Even *more* unfortunately, that means memory can't be installed on the motherboard, which means someone—that student—is going to have to buy a new motherboard. So, unless you plan to exercise the old credit card when you attack SIMMs, follow this procedure.

The key to removing SIMMs (and DIMMs) is to push the little tabs outward *gently.* They hold the SIMM in place. If you push too hard, you can break them. Some SIMM sockets are better designed and use metal spring tabs to hold the SIMMs in place—it's harder to break these off—but an unfortunate number of sockets use plastic tabs. Push the tabs outward either with the blade of a small screwdriver or with your fingernails. Err on the side of caution. You'll feel the SIMM move a bit, and that will be your signal that you can try to pull it a bit forward. Once you have one tab and one side free, work on the other side.

Reinserting SIMMs is similar. You place the SIMM angled forward in the SIMM socket (don't angle a DIMM—they insert straight down), and then push it back into place. As the SIMM contacts the tabs, relieve the pressure on the tabs by helping them outward with your fingers. The SIMM will snap into place—start over if it doesn't—and all will be well. Memory is one of the most sensitive parts of your PC, both electronically and mechanically. Now that you know more about memory chips, your machine will run that much better.

Troubleshooting Tips

Before you start, this is where I get tough again. Now, I've already talked in detail about what can go wrong if you don't take the proper steps to protect yourself and your hardware before jamming your hands inside the case. I've also discussed the necessity of having any static discharge eliminated with an antistatic pad or wristband, so have your solution ready. Last, don't forget to disconnect the power cable completely. I can't stress enough the importance of these precautions unless, of course, you have money to burn on replacement parts.

TIP   *For more details on safety precautions, look over Chapter 4, "Avoiding Service: Preventive Maintenance."*

There can be only a few problems with RAM itself. Either it's bad or it's been statically "zapped." A few other problems can occur with installation. Here are some Q-and-A-type problems and solutions:

Q: I added a 128MB module to match my already installed one, but I still get only 128MB of RAM.

A: The module isn't seated correctly. First, never put the case back on and screw it tight until *after* you've verified that all systems and subsystems are working properly. Second, using your fingertip, gently wiggle the top of the module. If it moves, remove and reseat it.

Q: My system had memory modules installed in two of the four SIMM slots. I just added a third SIMM module, and the computer doesn't recognize it.

A: SIMM modules must be installed in banks of two. You will need to install a memory module in the remaining memory socket for the computer to recognize them both.

Q: I installed an additional DIMM memory module, and the computer doesn't recognize it.

A: Verify that the computer doesn't require ECC memory. When non-ECC memory is placed in a computer that expects ECC memory, the result can be that the computer turns off the ECC feature or fails to recognize the new non-ECC memory.

Q: I installed new RAM a few *weeks* ago, and everything worked fine until today, when I went from 64MB to 32MB. I reseated the DIMM several times but to no avail. What now?

A: Replace the DIMM with a new one. You can do this either through the retailer or the manufacturer. If this doesn't fix the problem, then it's likely a problem with your motherboard or another chip-level component. This is when you need to take the box in for service.

Q: I installed new RAM a few *months* ago, and everything worked fine until today, when I went from 64MB to 32MB. I reseated the DIMM several times but to no avail. What now?

A: If something is going to go wrong with RAM (or any other chip component for that matter), it'll happen in the first several weeks. Most manufacturers warrant their products for 3–12 months, others for the lifetime of the product. Make sure you keep all your warranty information in the same, easily remembered place and *register your stuff*! Once they officially know you bought it, it's hard for them to deny you service.

Chapter 7

Power Supplies and Power Protection

- ◆ QuickSteps: Replacing a Power Supply
- ◆ Power Supply Components and Form Factors
- ◆ Power Supply Maintenance
- ◆ Determining Whether You Need a New Power Supply
- ◆ Protection from AC
- ◆ What Should You Buy?
- ◆ Troubleshooting Tips

Introduction

Personal computers (at least desktop PCs) don't come with batteries included. You plug them into the wall socket, and they work. But the PC itself doesn't directly use wall current because it's 120-volt Alternating Current (AC) in North America and 220–240 volts in Europe and the U.K.

By the way, a word to European readers: everything I say here applies to you *except* for references to the mains. As I just mentioned, your mains aren't 120 volts, but more like 200+, and the power frequency is 50 hertz (Hz) (cycles per second), not 60. *Don't* try any of the tests in this chapter that refer to the actual AC unless you already know about working with the mains safely.

The PC doesn't use AC; it needs Direct Current (DC), usually 3.3 or 5 volts for its chips and 12 volts for the motors on older drives—newer drive motors run off 5 volts. But the wall sockets provide AC, so how does the PC convert the juice? With the power supply. The power supply actually doesn't *supply* power—it *converts* it from AC to DC.

There are two kinds of power supplies: *linear power supplies* and *switching power supplies.* The PC's power supply is, in every PC *I've* ever seen, a switching power supply. Both linear and switching power supplies have their positive and negative aspects.

Linear power supplies are based on transformers. That makes them hot, heavy, and impervious to changes in current levels while rendering them vulnerable to voltage swings. Linear power supplies are an older design than switching power supplies, and you still find them on monitors and some external drive cases. Even small linear power supplies generate a relatively large amount of heat, which is why you should never cover the holes atop a monitor; you can fry a monitor quickly that way.

Switching power supplies are digital in nature. They step down voltage by essentially "switching" it on and off, hence their name. Think of how they work in this way: suppose you had a 1000-watt bulb in a lamp, but you only wanted the lighting value of a 100-watt bulb. You could get 100 watts' worth out of the 1000-watt bulb by switching it on and off but leaving it off 90 percent of the time. I know it sounds goofy, but if you could switch the light on and off quickly enough, then *you'd never see it flicker.* (In fact, that's how fluorescent lights work. They're actually very bright, but they flash off and on 60 times per second, too quickly for most eyes to register—and they're off more than 90 percent of the time.)

Switching power supplies are less sensitive to fluctuations in input voltage (although that's still a problem). These power supplies generate heat—but a lot less of it than linear power supplies.

Why should you care about power supplies? Mainly because power supply troubles can be mysterious and annoying. Just as bad are similar-looking troubles with the supplied power itself. This chapter looks at both.

QuickSteps: Replacing a Power Supply

Here are the essential steps for replacing a power supply. The rest of this chapter provides more detailed coverage about power supply hardware.

BE PREPARED

Before you start, make sure you have the following handy:

- Nonmagnetic Phillips-head screwdriver
- Container to hold removed screws
- Antistatic wrist strap

To replace a power supply, follow these steps:

1. Turn everything off, and unplug the power supply from the wall outlet.

2. Unplug the power supply connectors from the motherboard and the drives.

3. Remove the four screws holding the power supply in the case, and lift the power supply out. Or, if an AT, remove the screws holding the power switch to the case.

4. Insert the new power supply and secure it with the screws you removed in step 3. Or, if an AT, attach the power switch to the case with the screws removed in step 3.

5. Connect the power supply to the motherboard:

   - In an AT system, make sure the P8 and P9 plugs connect into the motherboard with the black wires next to each other in the center.

   - In an ATX system, the single plug fits in only one direction.

6. Plug the power cord into the power supply. On an ATX system, flip the power switch on the power supply (if present).

7. Press the power button on the front of the PC. If you hear the fan(s) spinning up, the power supply is working. On newer systems, the fan(s) may not begin spinning immediately, so allow a few seconds just to make sure. Turn the power off again.

8. Connect the power supply connectors to the drives on your system. The floppy drive gets the little connector (the Berg); all other drives get the large ones (the Molex).

9. Turn the PC back on, and confirm that all devices are working.

Components of the Power Supply

The power supply is the black or silver box in the back of the PC with the large yellow label telling you in five languages not to open the box and warning you that it's dangerous to do so. Despite that I can only understand a few of the multilingual messages, I'm inclined to take them at their word.

The reason is mainly because of a thing called a *1000-microfarad capacitor,* which is inside the power supply. The capacitor is utilized to smooth out some power glitches. Big capacitors look like miniature soda cans, sized anywhere from about a couple of centimeters (about an inch) long to perhaps four times that size. Capacitors are kind of like holding tanks for electricity. If you've got some power that needs to go from point A to point B, but it tends to fluctuate a bit in the process, then an electronics designer can smooth it out a bit by putting a capacitor between A and B. The downside of a capacitor is that it's a part of a circuit that retains electricity even after you turn the circuit off. I once got a zap from a monster capacitor in a television that had been sitting unplugged in my family's attic for a few years, and I'm told I'm lucky I didn't do anything worse to myself.

The upshot of what I'm telling you is that the capacitors inside power supplies tend to argue against your trying to fix them. Power supplies can cost as little as $15 for an entire new unit, so just replace them if they're faulty. I recommend replacing and not repairing floppies just because it's a pain to repair them, but I recommend not repairing power supplies because they can hurt you.

NOTE *Another reason not to open a power supply is that they're disposable and therefore can't, in most cases, be repaired.*

Power Supply Form Factors

The motherboard needs power, and the power supply provides it. All power supplies are categorized by several characteristics, one of which is the *form factor.* This term describes the physical dimensions of the power supply and the types of power connectors it provides to power the motherboard. The form factors you'll encounter in your PC work are as follows:

PC/XT/AT form factors The original power supply form factor got its name from the IBM PC/XT. In addition to the power connectors for the peripherals, the power supply also provided a motherboard power connection using two separate connectors, P8 and P9, that plugged side by side into the motherboard. In 1984 IBM introduced the successor to the PC/XT: the AT. Although the power supply's physical dimensions changed, the AT had the same motherboard and drive connections as the PC/XT form factor. The AT also featured a remote power switch. This feature, which appeared on the first tower-style case, allowed users to power up their computers from the front rather than having to reach around to the back or the side. The AT form factor is no longer in use, except in very old computers running 286 CPUs. The Baby AT form factor replaced it.

Baby AT/LPX form factor The Baby AT form factor got its name from the simple fact that it was a smaller version of the original AT form factor. With the exception of its smaller physical size, the Baby AT had the same power connectors as the AT and was used as a replacement for AT form factor power supplies. The Baby AT was extremely popular from 1985 through 1995, which means you stand a good chance of running into this form factor when you upgrade a computer. Around the same time, another version of the Baby AT appeared under several different names, including *slimline* (because it was found in cases bearing the same name), *PS/2* (after the short-lived series of computers), and *LPX* (for *low profile*). Although the LPX is physically smaller than the Baby AT, its output connectors are the same as the AT, with one small exception: the monitor pass-through power connector at the rear of the power supply began to disappear with the LPX form factor. As popular as these two form factors were, they were eventually replaced by the ATX.

ATX/NLX form factor   The year 1995 saw the introduction of the ATX form factor, and it was the first time a genuine standard for both motherboards and their associated power supplies was created. Physically, the ATX power supply was almost identical to the Baby AT/LPX form factor, with the exception that the monitor pass-through power connector was now completely gone. Big changes occurred in both the output voltages and the connectors. A single 20-pin connector replaced the two separate connectors, P8 and P9. The ATX was the first power supply to provide 3.3 volts, and it introduced the first "soft power" switch, which allowed software to turn the computer on and off. The ATX power supply was designed for the NLX form factor motherboard, which is one of the reasons that the ATX power supply form factor is sometimes (and incorrectly) called the *NLX power supply*.

NOTE   *Some motherboards are designed for upgrading computers and have connectors for attaching to either AT or ATX form factor power supplies.*

Mini ATX/Micro ATX/SFX form factor   Mini ATX, Micro ATX, and SFX all describe a single form factor that's physically smaller than the ATX and doesn't have a −5-volt signal, which is only needed by some older expansion bus (ISA) cards.

WTX form factor   Any discussion of power supply form factors must include the WTX, which was introduced by Intel in 1998. This form factor is usually only seen on larger, more powerful systems (the *W* in WTX stands for *workstation*). The WTX is completely different from all earlier form factors. It's designed for multiple-CPU and multiple-drive systems, such as servers and high-end engineering workstations.

ATX12V form factor   The newest form factor, a superset ATX called the ATX12V, was created for systems using Pentium 4 and high-end Athlon processors. The ATX12V adds an extra +12v power connector that enables the delivery of more current to the high-end, processor-based boards. If you see a +12v four-pin connector, you have an ATX12V power supply. If you don't find a +12v four-pin connector, your power supply is an ATX version. A six-pin Aux connector provides additional +3.3v DC and +5v DC.

WARNING   *An Intel Pentium 4– or AMD Athlon processor–based PC should use at least a 250-watt ATX12V power supply and a chassis that mechanically supports the processor heat sink assembly.*

Form Factor Connectors

I've covered enough different form factors to make a large bowl of alphabet soup. Essentially, the motherboard requires either AT, ATX, or ATXV12 connectors. Table 7.1 summarizes the different form factors and their associated connectors.

AC power comes into the power supply from a wall outlet. On some systems (mostly the ATX ones), a power switch directly on the power supply turns this power influx on/off. Other systems don't have a switch on the power supply; whenever it's plugged in, it's automatically on.

However, just because the power supply is receiving juice from the wall doesn't necessarily mean it's using that power to run the PC. The PC's on/off switch is separate, and on newer systems it's usually on the front of the PC. That switch controls the "soft power" feature described earlier and has a wire running from it to the motherboard; when you press the switch, the motherboard says to the power supply, "Hey, I want to turn on now; send me some of that power!" or "Okay, I'm ready to shut down; stop sending me power now." The point is, the power supply is the master of the power coming into the system—it receives it, converts it to DC, and doles it out as needed/requested to the components plugged into it.

As I mentioned, the connectors that plug the power supply into the motherboard are different depending on whether you've got an AT, ATX, or ATXV12 system. First, let's look at the AT model. P8 and P9 are identically sized and shaped; the only difference is the colors of wires and the order in which they appear. You have to get them plugged in right or you'll irreparably smoke your motherboard. Just keep this in mind: *black together*. Both connectors have a black wire; when the connectors are plugged in properly, the black wire on P8 will be next to the black wire on P9. Figure 7.1 shows P8 and P9 connectors.

The ATX and ATXV12 design fixes the potential for confusion. On an ATX power supply, a single connector goes to the motherboard, as shown in Figure 7.2. There's no way to get it plugged in wrong because it fits in only one direction. The ATXV12 is similar, except for an additional four-pin connector for the extra power required by the newer, high-power processors.

When you buy a computer, the case, the motherboard, and the power supply work as a team: they're all AT, or they're all ATX (this includes the ATXV12). Some motherboards can go either way, so they have both AT and ATX connector sockets. Figure 7.3 shows an example of such a beast. So, if you ever buy a replacement for any of those components (a replacement power supply, for example), you need to make sure you get the right kind so it'll work with your other pieces. You also need to make sure you get a power supply with enough wattage (250 is decent for AT; 300 for ATX) to run all the devices you want to have in the system.

TABLE 7.1: FORM FACTORS AND CONNECTORS

FORM FACTOR	MOTHERBOARD CONNECTOR
PC/XT/AT	AT
Baby AT/LPX	AT
ATX/NLX	ATX
SFX	ATX
ATXV12	ATX

FIGURE 7.1
Power supply connectors to the motherboard for an AT system

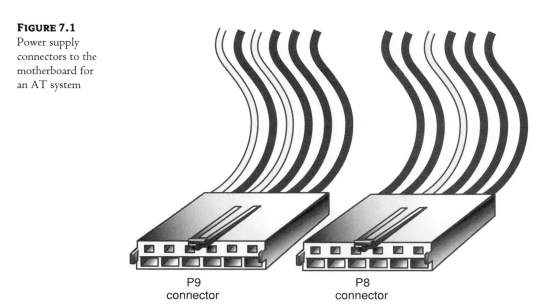

P9
connector

P8
connector

FIGURE 7.2
Motherboard connector for an ATX power supply

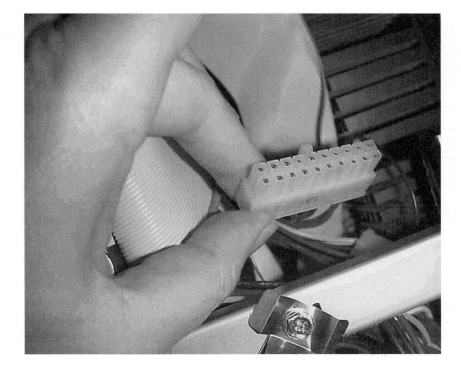

FIGURE 7.3

A motherboard with both AT and ATX power connectors

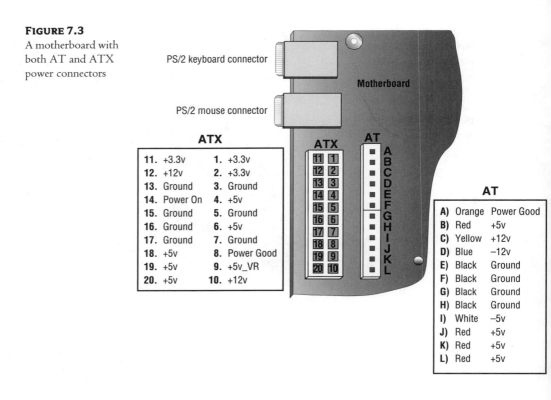

A bad power supply (either one that doesn't work at all or one that works erratically) can cause all kinds of problems in a system. If in doubt, test the power supply with a multimeter. You can test the power supply lines against a ground (any of the black wires). If you're actually testing a power supply, you should test all of the black wires.

You can then perform a resistance test of the motherboard. The tests are conducted on the power supply pins. Table 7.2 contains the *minimum* resistance for each connection. If the measured values are less than this, the motherboard is definitely faulty.

TABLE 7.2: SYSTEM BOARD RESISTANCES

COMMON LEAD (BLACK PROBE)	VOM (VOLTAGE-OHMMETER) LEAD	MINIMUM RESISTANCE (OHMS)
8	10	0.8
8	11	0.8
8	12	0.8
5	3	6
6	4	48
7	9	17

All power supplies, regardless of type, sport several identical Molex connectors for attaching to drives (hard disks, floppy disks, and tape drives). Figure 7.4 shows one of these. Most modern power supplies also include the smaller Berg connectors used to power $3\frac{1}{2}$-inch floppy drives, as shown in Figure 7.5. If your power supply doesn't have any Berg connectors, but you need one (or more), you can buy adapters at Radio Shack or a computer store that will convert a Molex to a Berg.

FIGURE 7.4

A Molex connector: your power supply has several of these.

FIGURE 7.5

A Berg connector supplies power to $3\frac{1}{2}$-inch floppy drives.

You don't need to use all of the drive power connectors. Just because you've got four drive power connectors doesn't mean that you must have four drives. (I get asked that now and then.) Just make sure that the unused power connectors are tucked out of the way. I once saw a system freeze solid because one of the ground wires (the two black wires in the middle) on an unused drive power connector made contact with a test point on a motherboard.

Maintaining and Upgrading the Power Supply

The good news here is that there isn't any maintenance required. The fan and the power switch are the only moving parts. If you suddenly notice that the PC is very quiet but still operating, your fan may have died. On newer systems, the fan(s) may be thermostatically controlled by the computer, so be sure the fan is supposed to be running before you panic. If the fan has failed, save everything and *shut down as soon as possible.* The computer's own heat can damage or destroy itself if the fan isn't working to dissipate it.

Don't block the vents that the PC uses for cooling. And take compressed air and blow the dust out of the fan now and then. (Remove the power supply from the PC case first so the dust doesn't immediately settle on the inside of computer.)

Years ago, desktop PCs lacked the power to drive all of their peripherals. It was common to find a PC start failing because it couldn't provide enough power to, well, *drive* its drives.

This experience led me to a preference for external peripherals, a preference that I retain to this day, even though today's PCs usually have power supplies with plenty of oomph. Whenever I'm buying a CD-ROM drive, large hard disk, or backup device, I buy it in an external case whenever possible. This means that every peripheral has its own fan and, as a bonus, its own power switch. Sometimes it's convenient to have the ability to disable a drive without popping the PC's top. It also means that the peripheral doesn't heat up the inside of the PC, *and* it doesn't strain the PC's power supply.

Even if you don't have my "powernoia," you'll probably never have to worry about getting a larger power supply on your machine. *But,* if you're building a server with 2 gigabytes (GB) of Random Access Memory (RAM) and several 100GB hard disks, as well as a CD-RW drive, a Small Computer System Interface (SCSI) host adapter, and two Local Area Network (LAN) cards, you might think about one of the 350-plus-watt power supplies.

Better, however, is this advice: don't just get a *big* power supply; get a *good* power supply, one of the ones made by the PC Power & Cooling people. I referred to them in Chapter 4, "Avoiding Service: Preventive Maintenance," and they really do make great products.

When buying a power supply, don't confuse "watts capacity" with "watts used." Will a 300-watt power supply use more power than a 150-watt power supply if it's put in a PC that draws only 100 watts? No. However, a 300-watt bulb uses more power than a 150-watt bulb because there, *watts* means watts used. The description "300-watt power supply" means a power supply that can convert *up to 300 watts.* Notice the *up to*—putting a 300-watt power supply on a system that only requires 50 watts will cause the power supply to convert only 50 watts. A lot of folks misunderstand that—even an IBM engineer in 1983 warned me that putting an XT's 130-watt power supply on an IBM PC would "burn up the motherboard." He was wrong, but I didn't know any better at the time.

But pushing a power supply too far isn't a good idea. How do you know how much power your machine is using? One simple way is to use a device such as the Power Meter from PARA Systems.

The Power Meter looks like a power strip with a gauge on it. You just plug it into the wall and then plug your system unit into the Power Meter. It has a wiring tester, so it tells you if your outlets are wired correctly. (See the upcoming section "Protecting the PC from the AC.") Then turn the system unit on and look at the needle on the gauge. It measures amperes of current flowing. You'll get a value between 0.5 and 3. Just multiply that ampere value by 58, and you'll get the number of watts your system unit uses. If it's close to its rated power supply, it's time to get a bigger power supply.

Why 58? You may know that Power (Watts) = Volts Amps and that you ordinarily get 120 volts from the wall outlet. Why not multiply amps by 120? Simple—this isn't direct current, where amps and volts are always in phase. Instead, you're dealing here with AC, *alternating* current. In AC, current and voltage follow a sine wave–like path, a path that can fall out of step. That means multiplying amps by 120 would overstate the total actual power requirements. To calculate the correct wattage, you need to take a kind of "average" of the power used. This is called the *RMS power.* (RMS stands for *root-mean-square.*) When buying upgrade power supplies, consider the fan. I've seen far too many tower cases that put the drives and other hot things above the fan. And for heaven's sake, don't buy those dumb plug-in boards that have a fan on them. Your PC is built to circulate air in a particular direction. Those fans may actually work *against* the system's fan!

Also avoid the newer power supplies with fans that shut down "when they're not needed." They've got a *thermocouple*—a circuit that measures heat—in them. If the heat in the system drops below some level, the fan shuts off. This is a terrible idea. PCs can suffer from "hot spots," areas that are considerably hotter than the average PC temperature. Just because the air going through the fan is, say, 100 degrees F, it doesn't mean there isn't a 130-degree section over the processor. (And speaking of processor fans, if you've got one, check it occasionally. They're made incredibly cheaply and tend to die after nine months or so, leaving you with a useless fan that actually *increases* the heat on the processor.)

Speaking of replacement power supplies, notice the first line on P8, which is called Power Good. This is a digital signal enabled by the power supply once it views itself as warmed up and ready. A flaky Power Good leads the computer to issue a long beep or short beeps or generally unusual noises. Some inexpensive replacement power supplies cause computers to emit a loud or long beep, then settle down to good service. I have experienced this myself, and I can only account for the beeps if the power supply doesn't wait quite long enough to first enable Power Good. A little initial up-and-down activity on the line induces the clock to issue a RESET command to the PC.

Determining Whether You Need a New Power Supply

You turn the computer on, and nothing happens at all. It's plugged in, so it's not that—what next?

The Power Supply Troubleshooting Trail

First, check the wall outlet. The outlet should be providing between 104 and 130 volts AC. Just set the Voltage-Ohmmeter (VOM) to read AC voltage and put one lead in each hole of the outlet. No VOM handy? Just plug in a lamp or appliance that uses AC power. In the U.S., electrical power is well regulated, so in almost all cases, if you have power at the outlet, you can assume it's within range.

Second, check the power cord. It should be firmly plugged into the power supply. If you have a spare cord, swap cords. Yes, power cords do fail.

Third, is power getting to the power supply? The fan gets it first, so if it isn't turning on, the power supply isn't getting power. When some power supplies are first turned on, the speaker emits a low click.

Fourth, check to make sure the power supply is connected to the motherboard using the right connectors, whether P8 and P9 (AT) or the single-piece, 20-pin ATX connector.

If all those things check out correctly, try swapping in a different power supply. The following section outlines how to remove and replace one.

Replacing a Power Supply

If you suspect the power supply, replace it. It's simple:

1. Open the PC case.

2. On the back of the PC, you'll see four screws bolting the power supply to the chassis. Remove these.

3. Disconnect the power cables from the motherboard and drives. Draw a picture and make notes of what connects to what. Note wire colors: the black wires on the P8 and P9 connectors (if it's an AT system) are always next to each other.

4. If it's an AT, detach the screws that hold the power switch in the front of the computer. These screws may be difficult to reach without removing drives in some cases.

5. Install the new power supply by reversing the procedure.

6. To be extra careful, strip the PC down to the minimum circuit boards. Then power up and run whatever diagnostics you use.

Protecting the PC from the AC

You can control a lot of things in your environment, but you have little control over one aspect of the PC environment: the power delivered by the electric company. For various reasons, it may not come out clean and regular like it's supposed to come out. Worse yet, you can't always blame the power company—sometimes it's your fault or your building management's fault.

Do You Have Power Problems?

Power or wiring problems can show up as any of the following:

- The computer mysteriously "freezing up"
- Random memory errors
- Lost data on the hard disk
- Damaged chips on a circuit board
- Data transmission noise and peripheral errors

Years ago, I was at a hotel doing a presentation that involved a demonstration PC. The PC did the strangest things:

◆ Once, it stopped the memory test at 128 kilobytes (KB) and froze.

◆ Another time, it gave a memory error message around 400KB.

◆ The hard disk wouldn't boot about 30 percent of the time, despite a fresh format.

◆ It stopped talking to the keyboard a few times, requiring the "Big Red Switch" (the power switch).

What was the problem? The old "hotel power problem." When the coffee machine was on, the PC did strange things. Additionally, the PC shared an outlet with two 600-watt overheads in continuous use and a slide projector. I moved it to another outlet, and the problems disappeared.

Having said that, what can you do about power problems? The four steps to power protection are as follows:

◆ Check that your outlets are wired correctly.

◆ Find out what else is on the power line.

◆ Provide a common ground for all devices.

◆ Protect against noise—surges, spikes, and undervoltages and overvoltages.

The following are the facts to "empower" you to solve your line problems.

Check Outlet Wiring

AC outlets have three wires: a large prong, a small prong, and a center cylinder. The cylinder is the safety ground; the prongs are the *hot* or *phase* line (the official term is *phase*, but anyone who has ever accidentally touched it calls it *hot*) and the *return*, also called common or neutral. The wires in the wall are supposed to be wired so that green is ground, white is return, and whatever's left (usually black) is phase.

It's not unheard of for the hot and the return to be reversed. This actually isn't a problem as long as *everything* is wired backward. But if you plug, say, the PC into a correctly wired outlet and a printer into a wrongly wired outlet, and if one of the devices connects the ground and the common—again, not an unusual occurrence—*and* there is a break in the neutral, then you'll get 120 volts across the cable from the printer to the PC. Lots of destruction will follow. Worse yet, miswired outlets can hurt you: if you touch both the PC and the printer at the same time, you're the electrical path.

You can buy circuit-wiring testers from most hardware stores. I got mine at Sears for $6 some years ago—they're probably a bit more now, but they're well worth it.

Check What Else Is on the Line

Ensure that there isn't any equipment on the same line as the PC that draws a lot of power. That includes the following:

◆ Large motors, such as the ones you find in air conditioners, refrigerators, or machine tools

◆ Heating coils, such as in small space heaters or coffee makers; "personal coffee makers" are included here

◆ Copiers and their cousins, laser printers

Anything that draws a lot of current can draw down the amount of voltage being delivered to a PC on the same breaker or fuse. Worse yet, heating coil devices such as coffee makers inadvertently create something called a *tank circuit* that can inject high-frequency spikes into the power line, noise that can slip through your power supply and go straight to the chips on the circuit boards.

One simple solution is to just get a dedicated power circuit to the computer. Another is to get an isolation transformer such as are found in a power conditioner. A Radio Frequency (RF) shield between the primary and secondary coils of the transformer removes the high-frequency noise.

Some large or old laser printers draw 15 amps all by themselves. That implies that, like it or not, you've got to put a 20-amp breaker in for *each* laser printer/PC combination. PCs *without* lasers don't draw much power and don't require a separate breaker.

Ensure Common Ground among Devices

Electrical ground is intended, among other things, to provide an electrical reference point, a benchmark value, such as sea level. A computer communicates 1s or 0s to a modem, for instance, by varying voltage relative to ground: greater than +3 volts means 0; less than −3 volts means 1. Close to 0 volts means "nothing is being transmitted."

The problem arises when the two communicating devices don't agree on the value of ground. If, in the previous example, the modem's ground is a 7-volts potential below the computer's ground, the modem and the computer each think the other is sending data when actually neither is.

Generally, it's not that bad. But if the computer's ground is 3 volts different from the modem, the occasional bit will be lost or garbled.

The answer? Simple—just ensure that all devices plugged into your PC share the same ground. A simple six-outlet power strip will do this. There's one flaw in this approach, however: what about LANs? Basically, a LAN is one big ground problem. Some people have suggested grounding the shield of the network cables every hundred feet or so. The only true solution is to use fiber-optic LANs, but they're still a wee bit expensive.

NOTE   *Ensuring that all equipment has a common ground has nothing to do with having a proper ground. A proper ground is mainly for safety, not data protection. (If someone insists you must have a good ground for proper data transfer, ask how airplanes and spaceships manage it, hmmm?) I'll discuss proper grounding soon.*

Protect against Power Noise

I've already discussed undervoltage, overvoltage, spikes, and surges in Chapter 4.

- ◆ *Undervoltage* is undesirable because the power supply reacts to too *little* voltage by drawing too *much* current. This heats up and may destroy components.

- ◆ *Overvoltage* can damage a chip because too much voltage destroys the circuits inside the chip.

When some outside force causes your power line to deliver more voltage than it's supposed to, an overvoltage condition occurs. Such conditions are, in general, dangerous to the computer.

The physics of it is this: the heart of the computer resides in its chips. A chip is a specially designed crystal. Crystals are highly structured molecules: many of them would be happier in a less structured environment. Applying electronic and heat energy to the crystals allows this breakdown in organization to occur. One spike might not do it, but it leaves damage that's cumulative. Even small spike damage is cumulative. Damage is proportional to energy. Energy is voltage, multiplied by current, multiplied by time.

Brief overvoltages of less than a millisecond in length are called *spikes*. Longer ones—milliseconds to seconds—are called *surges*. Spikes may be of high enough frequency to introduce problems similar to Radio Frequency Interference (RFI).

You (or your boss) may be skeptical about the actual seriousness of power problems. This may all be, you suspect, a tempest in a teapot. If you don't think you have power problems, spend $130 on a simple device that can monitor the quality of your power. Called the AC Monitor, you can get it from Milestek (`www.milestek.com`).

This device will continuously monitor the voltage that you're receiving at the outlet, and it'll indicate power drops, surges, or spikes (no frequency variation, sadly) with a light and an audible warning.

The big three conditions you want to avoid are these:

◆ Surges and spikes

◆ Low voltage

◆ No voltage (power outages)

Solutions to Power Problems

Solutions to power problems fall into three categories:

◆ Isolation

◆ Shielding

◆ Proper grounding

Isolation means isolating the noise (surges, spikes, and so on) from the computer—draining it off harmlessly. This is done with filters, transformers, gas discharge tubes, and Metal Oxide Varistors (MOVs). An MOV is an important part of a surge protector. When a surge comes in, an MOV shunts it off to ground. Unfortunately, the MOV is a kamikaze component—it "throws itself onto the grenade." Each MOV is only good for one big surge or a bunch of little surges. (No, there's no easy way to test to see whether an MOV is still working, at least not without a $2000 tester.) Power conditioners and surge protectors provide isolation in varying quality.

Shields minimize high-frequency noise. Shielding is evident in the filter capacitors in surge protectors, in RF shields between the primary and secondary coils in a power conditioner, in the metal case of the computer, and in the shield in shielded cable.

Some people view grounding as a magic answer to noise problems. Just run a wire from the device in question to a metal stake pounded into the ground (called a *ground stake*), and all of your ground problems go away! Not quite.

First, having a proper ground *is* important. It makes electronic equipment safer (because it keeps you out of the circuit), but, as I've mentioned, a *common* ground is important to minimize communication errors between devices. So the main reason for a proper earth ground is safety.

The idea behind a ground stake (you know, years ago, I thought ground stake was just hamburger...) is to provide a nice electrical path to earth ground. It *doesn't* eliminate noise, however: two ground stakes a few yards apart will pass current and noise between them. Ground stakes are less effective when there's a drought. I once heard of a ground stake that provided a better connection to ground than others on a particular site because it was, er, "watered" by local fauna. (No, I'm not sure I believe it, but ground *is* magic, so magical stories are appropriate.)

A final thought on grounding: some companies are careful to ground their computer rooms, thinking this will somehow protect their data. They're not so careful about the other areas in the building, however, so you've got a computer room with a cleaner ground than the rest of the building. Step back for a moment and ask what effect differential grounding would have on lightning protection. If lightning were to strike the building, it takes the easiest path to ground. If the easiest path to ground is through your computers, so be it. Basically, if you ground your computer room well and *don't* ground the rest of the building well, it's like putting a big "Eat at Joe's" sign on the computer room, as far as lightning is concerned.

Devices to Remedy Electrical Problems

Okay, now you've seen the problems and the approaches to solutions. Now you'll look at what's available on the market to solve the problems.

If you're looking for a recommendation, please understand I haven't got good news. Electric power in the 21st century in most of the Western world is getting worse because of aging equipment and lack of new capacity being pitted against ever-growing energy demands.

The PC really needs cleaner power than the stuff you feed your refrigerator, Mr. Coffee, or desk lamp. The only absolutely reliable way to get clean power is to rectify the power, put it in a battery, and then use the DC power in the battery to reconstruct the AC power. A device that does this is a Uninterruptible Power Supply (UPS). A good one will cost you about a hundred bucks, but in the long run you'll save many hundreds on new computer components and lost data. On the other hand, there are some fairly effective alternatives such as surge suppressors, Standby Power Supplies (SPSs), and power conditioners.

SURGE SUPPRESSORS AND SPIKE ISOLATORS

Many of us have purchased surge suppressors, or as they are also known, surge protectors or spike isolators.

The idea with suppression devices is that once they see a large surge coming, they redirect it out to the electric ground—kind of like opening the floodgates. The most common redirection device is an MOV, which I talked about earlier. It's an impassable barrier between the supply voltage and protective ground *until* the voltage reaches a certain level. *Gas discharge tubes* and *pellet arrestors* are slower but beefier devices. *Coaxial arrestors* fit somewhere in the middle.

The best suppressors use several lines of defense: MOVs, coax arrestors, and gas discharge tubes, for example.

Of course, an overzealous surge suppressor can redirect *too much* power for too long and create a worse surge of its own.

Another important question is, "What voltage level triggers the surge suppressor?" They're not waiting for 120.00001 volts to get going: some will pass 1000 volts before calling in the Marines. By then, your PC is toast.

PC Magazine started doing tests of surge suppression devices years ago and published the results in the magazine. They created spikes and measured how much of each spike was allowed through. Some suppressors emitted smoke and flames when subjected to a real surge. Others died quietly, not informing the owner that they are no longer protecting the PC (they still pass electricity, so there's no way to know).

The Bad News about Surge Suppressors

As I've said, the best suppressors use several lines of defense, and the heart of those are MOVs. As I've said before, MOVs are one-time-only devices. One surge, and they're history. Worse yet, you can't test them.

Some surge protectors come with a little light that goes out when the surge protector doesn't protect anymore. But those little lights can't be trusted, either. The light is in series with a fuse, and the fuse is in series with the return from the MOV—it's called a *bleeder fuse*. Given a large enough surge, the fuse will blow (along with the MOV, you recall), and the light will go out. In that case, the case of a single large surge, the light *is* effective. But a number of smaller surges can destroy an MOV. In that case, the fuse would be unaffected, and the light would stay on.

Summarizing, there's no way to know whether your surge protector is still protecting. If you've got a light on your surge protector and it goes out, you definitely have a dead surge protector. But if the light's on, that's no guarantee of surge protector effectiveness.

Meanwhile, another company has built a renewable surge protector. The company's name is Zero Surge (www.zerosurge.com), and their product is (likewise) called the Zero Surge Protector. It's a good product, but be prepared to pay a bit for it, as you would for any quality device: models range from $150 to $200.

Power Conditioners

Between a surge protector and a backup power supply is another device, also between them in price, called a *power conditioner*. A power conditioner does all the things that a surge protector does—filters and isolates line noise—and more. Rather than relying on MOVs and such, the power conditioner uses the inductance of its transformer to filter out line noise. An isolation transformer is a far superior device for removing noise to a capacitor or an MOV. Additionally, most power conditioners will boost up undervoltage so that your machine can continue to work through brownouts.

Recall that the surge protector's MOVs fail with no sign, so there's no good way to know whether your surge protector is doing any good. Power conditioners don't have that problem—when a transformer fails, you know it—the power conditioner just plain doesn't provide any power.

Which power conditioner is right for you? I've used the Tripplite LC1800. I've seen it in mail-order ads for as little as $179. One firm that sells them cheaply is Altex Electronics (www.altex.com).

The LC1800 even shows you incoming voltage via some Light-Emitting Diodes (LEDs) on its front panel. *Don't* plug your laser printer into the LC1800 because it's only rated for 6 amps. (Remember that lasers draw up to 15 amps.)

Backup Power Supplies

In addition to protection from short power irregularities, you may need backup power. I've lived in a number of places in the northeastern U.S. where summer lightning storms will kill the power for just a second—enough to erase your memory and make the digital clocks blink. You can remedy total loss of power only with battery-based systems. Such systems are in the range of $150 to $1200 and up.

SPS and UPS are the two types of backup power supplies. Figure 7.6 shows how UPSs and SPSs work. SPSs charge the batteries while watching the current level. If the power drops, they activate themselves and supply power until their batteries run down. A fast power switch must occur here, and it's important to find out what the switching time is—4 milliseconds (ms) or less is fine, and 14ms, in my experience, isn't fast enough.

A UPS constantly runs power from the line current to a battery, then from the battery to the PC. This is superior to an SPS because there's no switching time involved. Also, this means that any surges affect the battery charging mechanism, not the computer. A UPS is, then, a surge suppressor also.

FIGURE 7.6

How UPSs and SPSs work

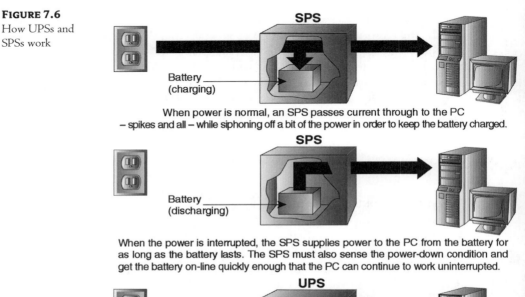

When power is normal, an SPS passes current through to the PC – spikes and all – while siphoning off a bit of the power in order to keep the battery charged.

When the power is interrupted, the SPS supplies power to the PC from the battery for as long as the battery lasts. The SPS must also sense the power-down condition and get the battery on-line quickly enough that the PC can continue to work uninterrupted.

A UPS, on the other hand, sends power from the socket right into the battery, keeping it constantly charged. The computer draws the power from the battery instead of the line.

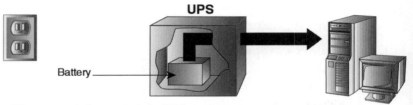

When power is interrupted, the UPS continues to supply power to the computer from the battery. Benefits: constant surge protection and zero switching time.

A UPS or SPS must convert DC from a battery to AC for the PC. AC is supposed to look like a sine wave. Older and some cheaper UPS and SPS models produce square waves (see Figure 7.7). Square waves are bad because they include high-frequency harmonics, which can appear as Electromagnetic Interference (EMI) or RFI to the computer. Also, some peripherals (printers in particular) can't handle square-wave AC. So, when examining UPSs, ask whether they use square wave or sine wave. Some produce a pseudo-sine wave. It has the stair-step look of a square wave, but it doesn't have as many harmonic problems. The good news is that most UPS and SPS models available in today's marketplace output pure sine waves.

FIGURE 7.7

UPS AC waveforms

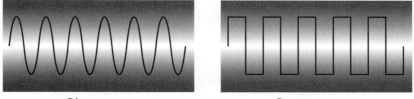

Sine wave   Square wave

Ordinarily, the purpose of a UPS is to allow you enough time to save whatever you're doing and shut down gracefully. If you're in an area where the power may disappear for hours, and may do it regularly, then you should look for the ability to attach external batteries to the UPS so that you can run the PC for longer periods.

Remember that a sine wave UPS is the only way to really eliminate most power problems. In the past, the reason *everyone* didn't have one was cost, and thanks to the advances in power conversion technology, everyone should have one.

On the other hand, remember that a UPS is *always* online, and so it must produce sine wave output. But UPSs do have the benefit that they provide surge protection by breaking down and reassembling the power, and SPSs *don't* provide this protection. You must still worry about surge protection when you buy an SPS, but that's not true if you buy a UPS. So make the choice that your budget allows.

Something to look for in backup power supplies—both UPSs and SPSs—is a serial port.

A serial port? Yes, a serial port. Most operating systems can monitor a signal from a serial port–equipped UPS/SPS. When power fails, the operating system is informed by the backup power supply of that occurrence, and the operating system can be configured to perform a graceful shutdown in the battery time remaining. This function is also called a *heartbeat*. Table 7.3 summarizes what I've covered about power problems and solutions.

TABLE 7.3: POWER PROBLEMS AND SOLUTIONS

PROTECTION METHOD	REMEDIES SURGES	REMEDIES LOW VOLTAGE	REMEDIES OUTAGE
Power conditioner	Yes	Yes	No
SPS	No	No	Yes
UPS	Yes	Yes	Yes

Before buying an SPS or a UPS, however, be aware of just one more thing—many people are selling SPSs under the name of *offline UPS*. Real UPSs are nowadays being called *online UPS*.

So, What Should I Buy?

If it sounds like you can spend a pile of money on power protection, sadly, that's true: a real, honest to-goodness UPS will set you back four figures. (As I mentioned, cheaper ones are SPSs that marketers call *offline UPS*. That's kind of like calling a car a *wingless, ground-based airplane* or calling those salespeople *honesty challenged*.) The best compromise I've come up with is a neat little combination of a power conditioner and an SPS with, of course, a serial port attached. Called the Smart-UPS 420, it's made by American Power Conversion (APC), and I've found them for about $210 (www.apcc.com). It's a complete power solution, and they've worked wonderfully for me for the past four years, through storms and power company screw-ups.

The Granddaddy of Power Problems: Lightning

When Thor's hammer falls near your site, you won't need any special equipment to note its passing. Curled-up, blackened circuit boards are pretty easy to spot.

I travel around North America and Europe teaching troubleshooting classes. You know what *every one* tells me? No matter where I am, the natives tell me they're in the "lightning capital of the world." (I know; hearing something *shocking* such as that makes you want to *bolt*.) Look at Figure 7.8 to find out where you rate.

FIGURE 7.8
Mean annual number of days with thunderstorms

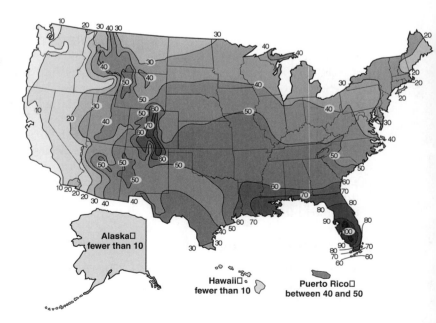

Looks like central Florida can lay claim to the "Thunderstorm Central" title in the U.S. Here's what I know about thunderstorms:

- Lightning affects your system even if it doesn't strike your building.

  If the power utilities enter your house or office building above ground, you should consider unplugging any electronic device you can't afford to lose during a severe thunderstorm. If your utilities are below ground, the chances of a direct strike to the power are greatly reduced.

- As mentioned earlier, taking special care to ground the part of the building that the big computers are in just makes those computers more vulnerable. A better-grounded path is the one that lightning will take.

- Lightning arrestors can reduce the likelihood of lightning damage.

- Newer high-tech lightning rods are being used in some sites. They look like umbrellas built of barbed wire standing about 30 feet tall.

- A cheap lightning protection: overhand knots in the power cord.

Believe it or not, some researchers discovered this last one. It makes the lightning surge work against itself and burn out the power cord, *not* the PC. And it works—Washington had the biggest thunderstorm it had in years in the summer of 1989, and the stuff with knots in the cords rode it out without a hitch. The TV didn't have knots in the cord, so I did have to buy a new TV.

The following year, a bolt hit my *telephone line*. It toasted the line from the telephone pole to my house; crispy brown little bits flaked off at the touch. But once inside, the bolt hit my five knots, and nothing inside was fried. Why did I tie the knots? I got tired of losing a modem every summer to lightning.

Because a lightning strike can send a spectacular power surge along power lines, damaging equipment that's plugged into nearby AC and phone outlets, you might want to consider something that provides a little more security than that provided by the knot-in-the-power-cord method. When it comes to lightning, the severity of these surges can only be neutralized by quality surge suppression. A good surge suppressor will provide surge protection on *all* AC outlets, not just one or two. Select models will include RJ-11 modem/fax line surge suppression as well, preventing damage to modems and phone systems. These surge suppressors also feature indicators that inform you when the protection circuit has been compromised. The best part is that the good ones come with an insurance policy that ranges from $50,000 to $100,000, covering damage that results from the surge protector failing. Although these aren't cheap, they're worth every cent you pay for them. At the time of this writing, you can expect to pay between $60 and $90 for a suppressor that offers all of the features I just described.

Power's not the sexiest part of PC hardware, but it sure can be the most troublesome. Get a Smart-UPS and a decent power supply, buy external peripherals, and you'll be electrified with the results.

Unexpected Power Outages

While lightning and too much voltage pose big problems for computers, the opposite is true too. Power sags, brownouts, and blackouts can ruin electronics just as easily. As I mentioned earlier, computer components expect a certain voltage, and expect that level consistently. If they don't get it, they might complain violently, or refuse to ever work again.

What if your power company is reliable, and you have a UPS to help? You're safe, right? Maybe, maybe not. In August of 2003 the northeastern part of the United States and Canada were treated to the biggest power outage in recorded history.

Companies stuck in that catastrophe without power protection equipment likely lost a lot of data, and probably had to reinstall several machines once power was restored. Companies with power protection were able to gracefully shut their systems down, and wait for power to be restored. I'm sure they still lost a lot of money because of the power outage, but they minimized their losses with power protection.

Troubleshooting Tips

If you're not getting any power to the PC (no fans, no nothing), do the following:

◆ Check whether power is coming from the wall outlet to the power supply.

◆ If you're using a power strip, confirm that it's on. (Most power strips have a rocker on/off switch.)

◆ Check for loose connections from the power plug to the power supply or from the power supply to the motherboard.

◆ In an AT system, confirm that the black wires of P8 and P9 are together, not at opposite ends of the power connector on the motherboard.

◆ In an ATX system, make sure that the power switch on the power supply itself is on before you press the power button on the front of the PC.

◆ If the power supply has a voltage switch (110/220), make sure that it's set for the currency in the location in which you're working (110 is standard in the U.S.).

If you're having other problems with the PC you suspect might be power-related, do the following:

◆ Check that your outlets are wired correctly.

◆ Make sure that no other high-wattage devices are sharing the power line.

◆ Make sure that your outlets are grounded and that all your devices share the same ground (plugging them all into the same power strip will accomplish this).

◆ Install equipment that can protect against surges and spikes, low voltage, and/or power outages. This might include a surge suppressor, an SPS, or a UPS.

In the next chapter, you'll take a general look at the hard drive before moving on to specific types of drives.

Part 2

Devices

Chapter 8

Hard Disk Drive Overview and Terminology

- ◆ Disk Basics
- ◆ Hard Disk Interfaces
- ◆ Disk Geometry
- ◆ Disk Capacity Barriers
- ◆ Disk Performance Characteristics
- ◆ DMA and PIO Modes

Introduction

Hard disks are important because they store most of the important data that a computer user creates, manipulates, and references in daily work. When upgrading and repairing computers, it's useful to understand the technical aspects of hard disk technology so you'll have a better picture of what can go wrong and how to fix it. This chapter presents a technical overview of hard disk technology from a hardware perspective and explains what factors separate one disk from another and why some disks may be subject to capacity limitations in certain systems.

Disk Basics

A disk is a form of *nonvolatile storage*. That means whatever is placed on the disk remains there even when the computer's power is turned off (unlike with RAM, which is *volatile storage*.) Another name for nonvolatile storage is *secondary storage*. (You'll probably see a question that asks about secondary storage if you take the A+ exam.)

There are two technologies for disk storage: *magnetic* and *optical*. Magnetic disks store data in patterns of positive and negative magnetic charge in tiny metal particles on the disk surface. Each transition between a positive and negative area is interpreted as a 1 bit; each spot that lacks a transition is interpreted as a 0. Optical disks, in contrast, store data in patterns of greater and lesser reflectivity. As with magnetic disks, a 1 bit is represented by a change (from either greater to lesser or lesser to greater), and a 0 bit is represented by a lack of change. Examples of optical discs include CD-ROM, CD-R, and DVD. Chapter 9, "CD-ROM and DVD Drives," covers optical discs in greater detail; this chapter will focus on magnetic disks.

A hard disk is called *hard* because the platters inside the disk casing are rigid and fairly thick. They're made of aluminum or glass, and they're coated with a fine dusting of iron particles. Multiple disk platters are stacked on a spindle inside the hard disk cartridge. Each platter is capable of holding billions of bits of data per square inch. A motor on the spindle drives the platters at high speeds—usually either 5400 or 7200 revolutions per minute (rpm).

Each platter is the same physical diameter as every other platter in the stack. Most desktop hard disks today use $3^1/_2$-inch platters, and most notebook computers use $2^1/_2$-inch platters. The IBM Microdrives have platters that are even smaller: 1 inch.

HARD DISK VERSUS HARD DRIVE

Hard disk versus hard drive. What's the difference?

One acceptable answer is that there *is* no difference—the terms are interchangeable. The full name is *hard disk drive*; both *hard disk* and *hard drive* are valid shortened versions. Here's why: Unlike with CD and floppy drives, the disk portion (the platters on which the data is stored) isn't removable from the drive portion (the read and write mechanisms). It's all one package. Therefore there's little occasion to refer to only the drive portion or only the disk portion. The whole thing is the hard disk or hard drive.

However, some people attempt to make a distinction between the two terms, and this distinction has to do with the way the operating system uses the hardware. When referring to the hardware—the physical hard disk drive—people tend to call that the *disk*, as in *disk partitioning utility*, *disk crash*, or *disk error*.

When that disk is partitioned into one or more drive letters, each of those drive letters is commonly referred to as a *logical drive,* or just *drive*. So a single hard disk drive is one disk, but potentially many drives. For example, you would refer to the *C: drive*, not the *C: disk*.

When speaking in general of a hard disk drive, however, either term is acceptable, and you'll hear both *hard disk* and *hard drive* thrown around synonymously in almost all techie circles. You'll notice that this book goes back and forth between the two terms at times, too.

The platters are permanently sealed inside an airtight metal casing. The sealed enclosure prevents foreign contaminants such as dust particles, fingerprints, or smoke particles from affecting the various components and operation of the disk drive. This is necessary because the read/write heads operate very close to the surface of the disk. The slightest little particle of dust can cause a *head crash*, which can occur if the head makes contact with the disk surface itself or if the head touches particles on the disk surface.

Each side of each platter has its own read/write head, which consists of a sensor that reads the magnetic charges on the disk surface and a magnet that can change the charge on specified areas to write to the disk. All of the read/write heads for the platters are connected to a single *actuator arm* that moves in and out in response to requests from its controller. Figure 8.1 shows a cutaway view of a typical hard disk drive.

FIGURE 8.1

Cutaway view of a hard disk drive

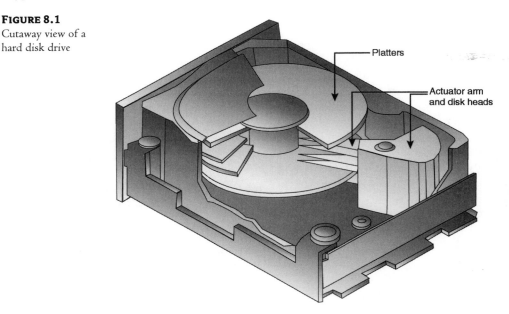

Platters

Actuator arm and disk heads

Hard Disk Interfaces

A hard disk connects to the computer via a cable connected to a disk interface. The most popular disk interfaces today are Enhanced Integrated Drive Electronics (EIDE) and Small Computer System Interface (SCSI), addressed in Chapters 10 and 11, respectively. A new, up-and-coming interface called Serial ATA will likely become the dominant interface in the next few years, and it's discussed in detail in Chapter 10, "Understanding and Installing ATA Drives," along with EIDE because they both arose from the same basic set of standards. Other possible drive interfaces include Universal Serial Bus (USB) and FireWire. A hard disk is typically designed to use only one interface, so you must choose the hard disk interface before you choose the hard disk itself. Table 8.1 briefly describes the available hard disk interfaces. EIDE is the predominant standard for hard disks at this writing, but

Serial ATA is probably going to overtake it in popularity in the next few years, and other types may be appropriate for special circumstances. Table 8.1 doesn't list exact numbers for the performance levels of each interface because they vary widely according to the variant of that interface being used and the disk drive's own capabilities.

TABLE 8.1: HARD DISK INTERFACES

INTERFACE	PROS	CONS	NOTES
EIDE	Supported almost universally by all motherboards.	Limit of two disks per EIDE channel, each EIDE channel requires an Interrupt Request (IRQ). Possible performance problems when two high-usage drives share a cable.	Faster options are becoming available, but this has been the standard for more than 10 years. Internal only.
Serial ATA	Faster than regular EIDE, easy to connect and configure.	Relatively new at this writing, so it's not the standard yet for entry-level desktop systems. You'll pay a higher price for it than for drives that work on the standard EIDE/ATA ribbon cable interface. Few motherboards support it natively, so an add-on I/O card is required.	Within the next few years will become standard on all systems, so any hardware you buy will be more likely to be usable in future systems than the ordinary EIDE.
SCSI	Fewer problems than ATA with multiple drives operating at once on the same cable, chainable such that multiple drives share a single IRQ.	Few motherboards provide SCSI support natively, so you need a SCSI interface card to which to connect the drive.	Used primarily in high-end servers, Redundant Array of Inexpensive Discs (RAIDs). Used to be faster than EIDE, but newer EIDE standards have leveled the playing field. Can be either internal or external.
USB and IEEE 1394 (FireWire)	Fast, easy to connect and disconnect, convenient to share drives between systems.	USB hard drives are currently external only. FireWire hard disks can be internal or external.	These are two competing interface standards with similar benefits and performance levels. Most motherboards natively support USB but not IEEE 1394. However, you can add an interface card for FireWire that will allow both internal and external FireWire drives to be connected. This is significant because it makes FireWire a viable competitor with Serial ATA for a mainstream hard disk connection method.

TABLE 8.1: HARD DISK INTERFACES *(continued)*

INTERFACE	PROS	CONS	NOTES
	Great for portable systems because you don't have to have an extra drive bay free to add another hard disk.		
Legacy Parallel	May be the only usable interface for an external drive on a system that lacks USB or SCSI support.	Old technology for connecting external hard disks. Slow and awkward.	Now nearly obsolete.

NOTE *EIDE and Advanced Technology Attachment (ATA) are actually two different standards that are often lumped together because of their compatibility with one another. Further, there are many variants of ATA that offer different levels of performance, including Ultra ATA (also called UATA, Ultra DMA, or UDMA) and Serial ATA (SATA). Chapter 10 covers them in detail.*

Disk Geometry

To understand how disks store data, you need to understand disk geometry. No, it's not a new kind of math! *Disk geometry* refers to the electronic organization of any type of disk drive, the actual physical number of heads, cylinders, tracks, and sectors. The following sections look at each of those items in detail.

Heads

A hard disk has an electromagnetic *read/write head* for each side of each platter, so when a specification describes the number of heads, you automatically also know the number of platters. For example, if a drive has three platters, it has six heads. The sides of the platter are also referred to as *surfaces*.

NOTE *Hard drives today have two specifications for heads: logical and physical. The physical refers to the number of platter sides. For example, a drive might have six sides and three platters. The logical refers to the way the drive is addressed by its controller. A typical number of logical heads is 16. This will become clearer later in the chapter when you learn about sector translation. For now, just know that when you see 16 as the number of disk heads in a drive's specification, it probably doesn't actually have 8 platters. It only appears to because of the way its physical specs are manipulated by its controller.*

The read/write heads mount on an actuator arm that moves the heads over the surface of the platter on a thin cushion of air to the proper track. A servo system generates feedback, which accurately positions the read/write heads. All the heads are on the same arm, so they are all at the same in-out position at the same time in relation to the stack of platters. That's okay, though, because hard disk data isn't stored in a physically contiguous way. Each of those heads can be writing data at the same time for the same file, and the operating system will still see that data as being all part of a single file.

As mentioned earlier in the chapter, the read/write heads read by looking for transitions between positive and negative magnetic charges. When a head finds a change in the polarity, it sends an electrical pulse to the disk controller that says 1. When enough time passes that it might have found a change but it did not, the disk controller interprets the silence as a 0.

NOTE *On older drives, a single read/write head performs both reading and writing functions. However, manufacturers today use Magnetoresistive (MR) heads with separate read and write elements in disk drives. These heads make it possible to place more data under a single head. Having separate heads allows the construction of wider write and narrower read heads to suit differing operating needs.*

Tracks

Like the growth rings on a tree cross-section, each side of each platter contains concentric rings called *tracks*. Each possible in-out position of the actuator arm denotes a separate track. The exact number of tracks that a disk can have per surface varies depending on the sensitivity of the drive's inner mechanical parts. On 1.44-megabyte (MB) floppy disks, there are typically 80 tracks per side, and very old hard disks might have 305 tracks per side; on modern hard disks there may be 16,000 or more tracks per side. Each track is numbered. The outermost track is 0, with the numbers increasing as you move toward the center spindle (see Figure 8.2).

FIGURE 8.2

Tracks are
concentric rings
on a platter
surface.

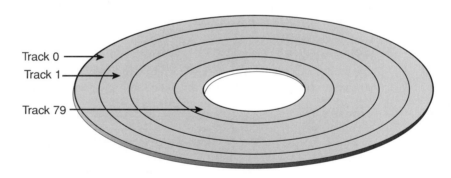

Cylinders

Remember that all the read/write heads are on a single actuator arm, so they have no choice but to move as a group? Well, all of the tracks simultaneously accessible at a single actuator arm position are known as a *cylinder*. For example, if the actuator arm has positioned the read/write heads on the outermost track on each platter, then the collection of outermost tracks are forming a cylinder there collectively. It's as if someone took a doughnut-shaped cookie cutter and sliced down through all the platters to capture all the tracks in a certain spot (see Figure 8.3).

FIGURE 8.3

The relationship between tracks and cylinders on a disk

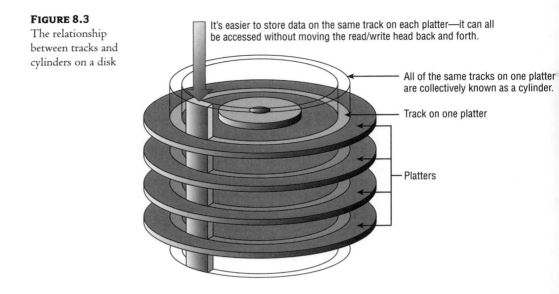

It's easier to store data on the same track on each platter—it can all be accessed without moving the read/write head back and forth.

All of the same tracks on one platter are collectively known as a cylinder.

Track on one platter

Platters

The number of tracks per surface is identical to the number of cylinders. Therefore, in the specifications for a drive, manufacturers don't report the number of tracks, but instead they report the number of cylinders. If you know the number of heads and you know the number of cylinders, you can multiply them to find out the number of tracks overall.

Sectors

Each track of a platter is further divided into individual segments called *sectors*. Sectors are created by a series of straight lines that cut the platter into pie-shaped wedges, as in Figure 8.4.

FIGURE 8.4

Sectors are sections of a track.

Cylinder 1, sector 1

Cylinder 0, sector 1

Cylinder 0, sector 9

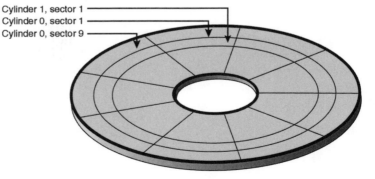

A sector is the smallest accessible unit on a disk. Sectors may vary slightly in their physical size, with the ones at the outer edges of the disk being larger than the inner ones; however, all sectors hold exactly the same amount of data: 512 bytes. In addition to containing data, each sector also contains a few extra bytes dedicated to error detection and correction and internal disk control.

The number of sectors per track varies depending on the drive, anywhere from 8 (on the oldest type of floppy disk) to 60 or more (on modern hard disks).

Zone Bit Recording

Before leaving the subject of sectors, it's worth mentioning that the diagrams you've seen in this book so far have all shown drives as having a constant number of sectors per track. That's not the case on modern drives.

The outer track on a disk is typically double or more the circumference of the innermost track. With an equal number of sectors on each track, data on the outer track is quite loose, and data on the innermost track is quite dense.

Placing differing numbers of sectors per track on a disk surface is called Zone Bit Recording (ZBR). You will also hear the terms *multiple zone recording* or even just *zoned recording* in place of ZBR. Consumer demand for greater and greater capacity on smaller and smaller drives, in combination with cheaper and faster electronics, has led to a growth in the use of ZBR.

Here's how it works: Based on their location on a disk, the ZBR program groups the tracks into zones. All tracks within a specific zone are given a constant number of sectors. Movement through the disk from the innermost zone to the outer zone passes you through multiple zones, each with a higher number of sectors than the one before.

Most software that you run on a computer won't know that your disk has ZBR. Because most computer software assumes that each track has a constant number of sectors, ZBR drives keep that software happy by pretending that this is true. One kind of disk that you'll run into that is *always* ZBR is a CD. Rather than concentric tracks, CDs have one long, continuous spiral similar to the grooves of a phonograph. CDs solve the varying numbers of sectors problem by varying the speed of the drive motor, depending on which part of the disk is being read; you'll learn more about CDs and CD-ROM drives in Chapter 9.

Logical Geometry

As mentioned previously, *physical geometry* refers to the electronic organization of any type of disk drive—the actual physical number of heads, cylinders, tracks, and sectors. In the olden days of computing (1980s), the physical and logical geometries of a drive were identical. Some problems arose with that system, however, as drives became larger in capacity and ZBR became an option.

One way to add more capacity to a drive was to add an additional platter or two. However, having a large number of platters meant using a hefty spindle motor and a fair amount of power, and made the hard disk's physical dimensions unwieldy. The ideal number of physical platters for a hard disk seemed to be three in terms of size and power consumption. Another way to eke out more capacity was to use ZBR so that there could be more sectors on the outer edges of the platters, but the BIOS couldn't grasp the concepts of certain cylinders having different numbers of sectors.

To accommodate larger drives without increasing the platter count, and to account for ZBR, *logical geometry* was introduced. It allows a drive to have two separate geometries: physical and logical. The drive manufacturer establishes the logical geometry, which is a set of bogus values for the cylinders, heads, and sectors on the disk. The disk controller gives these bogus values to the Basic Input/Output System (BIOS). The hard disk controller provides automatic translation between the logical and physical geometry. The physical geometry is totally hidden. Table 8.2 is an example of the difference between a drive's physical and logical geometry (it contains the specifications of one of my hard disks).

TABLE 8.2: SAMPLE HARD DISK'S PHYSICAL AND LOGICAL GEOMETRY

PARAMETERS	LOGICAL GEOMETRY	PHYSICAL GEOMETRY
Cylinders	7480	6810
Heads	16	6
Sectors per track	63	122–232
Total sectors	7,539,840	7,539,840

In most systems today, additional translation takes place such as Logical Block Addressing (LBA) to allow large drives to be recognized by the BIOS and operating system. You'll look at these later in the chapter.

Disk Capacity Barriers

As hard disk sizes have grown exponentially over the past 15 years, there have been some periods of "growing pains" where operating systems and PC BIOS standards haven't provided adequate support for the new larger sizes. The following sections discuss some of these obstacles and how they have been overcome, and they introduce the technology that was used to overcome them.

Sector Translation

Nearly all motherboards provide built-in support for EIDE devices, but with this support comes some limitation.

The AT BIOS command set—developed by IBM for hard disk support and implemented in EIDE—specifies some limitations on the CHS (Cylinder-Head-Sector) values for drives. Specifically, it limits a disk's logical geometry to 1024 cylinders, 16 heads, and 63 sectors per track. This adds up to a hard disk size of 528MB. This specification was later enhanced to support up to 256 heads for a maximum capacity of 8.4 gigabytes (GB). (More on that part shortly.)

NOTE   *So if the limit for EIDE is 8.4GB, how come we have 130GB and larger EIDE hard disks on the market today? Obviously that's not the limit anymore. This and subsequent barriers have been broken, and you'll learn how that was done later in the chapter. Hang in there!*

Capacity wasn't a problem until around 1994, when consumers began demanding higher-capacity drives and manufacturers became capable of delivering them.

The main problem was the cylinder limit. Drive manufacturers could make drives tens or even hundreds of thousands of tracks physically, but the PC BIOS couldn't address them. One solution has been to change the BIOS limitation—and that did happen eventually. But another solution has been to spoof the drive's CHS values reported to the BIOS so that they appear to be within the acceptable specs.

Just as the drive's inner circuitry allows it to have a different logical geometry than physical, *sector translation* allows the BIOS to see the drive's logical geometry by way of a translation table that converts its values to something it can accept. This allows the BIOS to address more of the capacity of the drive. There are two main methods of sector translation that have been used; the following sections look at some of them.

EXTENDED CHS (ECHS)

One method of CHS translation divides the number of cylinders by an integer and multiplies the number of heads by the same integer when passing CHS values from the drive to the operating system. Usually this is accomplished by multiplying the number of heads by two and dividing the number of cylinders by two. This method is sometimes called *Large* or *ECHS* in the BIOS Setup.

When a disk is set up to use ECHS, there are two translations that take place for every interaction with the PC. First the physical geometry of the drive is translated into its logical geometry through the disk's own onboard controller. Then the values passed to the system BIOS are run through a second translator to bring its request in line with the BIOS limitations.

So, for example, let's say you're running a BIOS that's been updated to support up to 1024 cylinders, 256 heads, and 63 sectors per track. You have a hard disk with a logical geometry of 1970 cylinders, 16 heads, and 63 sectors per track. The heads and sectors are okay, but there are too many cylinders. So ECHS divides the cylinders by two and multiplies the heads by two, giving a translated CHS of 985, 32, and 63. That translation is accomplished behind the scenes when you choose Large or ECHS in BIOS Setup; as the system user you'll be concerned only with the disk's standard logical geometry for setup purposes.

NOTE *Nearly every BIOS can autodetect hard disks these days, but if you ever have to manually enter the CHS values for a drive in BIOS, keep in mind that the BIOS expects you to enter the untranslated logical geometry. When you set its translation setting in BIOS to Large, it'll take care of any further translation itself.*

LOGICAL BLOCK ADDRESSING (LBA)

LBA abandons the whole notion of CHS addressing in favor of a sequential numbering scheme for all sectors, with no concern for their head or cylinder location. Such a sector-addressing scheme is a *linear addressing scheme*.

LBA assigns each sector a unique number starting at 0 and going up to the total number of sectors on the disk minus 1 (that is, if the cylinder has 18 sectors, LBA would number them 0–17). The translation is similar to ECHS translation, but instead of translating to the drive's logical geometry, translation occurs directly to a logical block number (a sector number).

LBA is the more modern, preferred translation method, and most modern drives and the BIOS will default to it.

INT13 Addressing

As you just learned, ECHS and LBA were two different ways of breaking the 528MB barrier for drive sizes. By the early '90s, however, hard disk sizes had grown to the point where there was another barrier that needed to be broken: the 8.4GB barrier imposed by INT13.

INT13 is a set of programming routines built into the Read-Only Memory (ROM) chips on the motherboard or an Input/Output (I/O) interface card. The ROM BIOS uses INT13 routines to boot from a drive. (*INT* is short for *interrupt*, but it's a different kind of interrupt than the IRQs that the operating system uses to communicate with hardware.)

The use of INT13 requires specific hard disk parameters and exact head, cylinder, and sector addressing. Conventional INT13 functions use 24 bits to represent the disk geometry, as shown in Table 8.3.

TABLE 8.3: INT13 API 24-BIT ALLOCATION OF THE HARD DISK

NUMBER OF BITS ALLOCATED	FOR THE...	FOR A TOTAL OF...
10 bits	Cylinder number	1024 cylinders (210) that the system can address
8 bits	Head number	256 heads (28) that the system can address
6 bits	Sector number	63 sectors (26 – 1) that the system can address

Therefore, for conventional CHS addressing, using the values 1024 × 256 × 63, it's possible to address up to 16,515,072 sectors. And at 512 bytes per sector, you get a theoretical disk capacity of 8.4GB. LBA views the available address bits as a single number. Larger disks require a BIOS and operating system that support INT13 extensions or an operating system that bypasses the BIOS and INT13. INT13 uses 24-bit addressing.

To circumvent the 8.4GB limitation, BIOS developers circa 1995 included extended INT13 functions that use 32 bits to represent addresses, taking the maximum capacity up to 137GB.

NOTE *No, we haven't topped out yet! ATA-6, which you'll read about in Chapter 10 (and also briefly in the "Summary of Capacity Barriers" section later in this chapter), bumps up the maximum to 144 petabytes (that is, 144 million gigabytes), blowing that 137GB limitation out of the water.*

If a disk drive has a capacity greater than 8.4GB, using INT13 extensions requires changes both to the BIOS and to the operating system. Note that later versions of Windows 95 and all subsequent versions (98, Me, XP) already support these extensions, as do most other current operating systems. Windows NT 4 and Linux don't. The Windows 2000 and 2003 setups don't determine whether BIOS INT13 extensions are enabled or available for use before allowing the creation of a system partition with more than 1024 cylinders or typically larger than 8.4GB.

Few computer systems manufactured before 1998 support the INT13 extensions, but most newer systems *do* provide this support. The easiest way to add larger hard disk support to older PCs is to update the motherboard BIOS, or to install software (such as Ontrack's Disk Manager) that links into the BIOS to add INT13 support. You can also install an intelligent host adapter with a BIOS that supports INT13 extensions, but adding this hardware to your system is probably the most complicated solution.

ATA Interface Addressing

The EIDE interface recognizes a drive and figures out its capacity by looking at the logical geometry of the drive: the number of cylinders, heads, and sectors per track that it contains. Before 1994, drives and the BIOS supported only CHS addressing. Today's drives support both CHS addressing and LBA addressing.

The EIDE interface up through ATA-5 uses 28 bits to represent the disk address, as shown in Table 8.4. The BIOS records the information in defined registers; it records the starting address of the data on the disk, the length of the data transfer, and the read or write command.

TABLE 8.4: EIDE INTERFACE DISK ADDRESSING

NUMBER OF BITS ALLOCATED	FOR THE...	FOR A TOTAL OF...
16 bits	Cylinder address in the cylinder register	65,536 cylinders (2^{16}) that the system can address
4 bits	Head address in the head register	16 heads (2^4) that the system can address
8 bits	Sector address in the sector register	255 sectors ($2^8 - 1$) that the system can address

Therefore, for CHS addressing for the EIDE interface using the values $65,536 \times 16 \times 255$, it's possible to address up to 267,386,880 sectors. And at 512 bytes per sector, you get a theoretical disk capacity of 137.4GB.

The 137.4GB limitation has recently been broken with the introduction of the ATA-6 standard, which uses 48-bit addressing and allows for hard disks as big as 144 petabytes (144 million gigabytes), 100,000 times bigger than ATA-5 could support! You'll learn more about ATA standards in Chapter 10.

Operating System Limitations on Disk Capacity

The choice of operating system can also affect the disk capacity limitations, although this is becoming less of an issue with modern operating systems such as Windows 2000 and XP. For example, the Windows NT 4 Workstation was developed before the INT13 extensions, so it isn't aware of them. Consequently, its boot process has some limitations that prevent Windows NT 4 from using a partition larger than 8.4GB as a system partition. (Other partitions can be much larger.)

There are also partition size limits depending on the file system in use. Logical drives that use the FAT16 file system are limited in size to 2.1GB because of the 16-bit addressing scheme. FAT16 is the only choice for MS-DOS and the original release of Windows 95; later releases of Windows 95 as well as Windows 98, 2000, and XP all support the 32-bit version, FAT32. (Windows 2000 and XP also support NTFS 5.0, a different 32-bit file system that's superior to FAT32 in several ways.)

Summary of Capacity Barriers

This chapter has thrown out a lot of statistics regarding drive capacities, so I'll bring it all home by running through a summary of the various barriers you might encounter:

The 528MB barrier   IDE/ATA (EIDE/ATA) disks have a limit of 16 logical heads. To compensate, these disks always have a large number of cylinders, but because of the INT13 limitation, they can see only 1024 of the cylinders and 63 sectors. When the system has a nontranslating BIOS, the capacity will be 1024 × 16 × 63 × 512, or 528MB. This is the well-known 528MB barrier.

To overcome this limit, BIOS designers implement one of two translating algorithms for converting the INT13 API address to the ATA address. The first is *BitShift translation*, which changes the cylinder and head values so that the total number of sectors remains the same. This is the most common translation method. The second algorithm is the *LBA assist translation*; a system can use this translation only if the drive supports LBA addressing.

The 2.1GB barrier   Although relatively rare, an older BIOS could have a problem translating the disk geometry if the number of cylinders exceeds 4096. A BIOS with this problem could report the disk as 2.1GB, but it could be larger. A more common reason for a 2.1GB barrier (per logical drive) is the use of a 16-bit file system such as FAT16 in MS-DOS.

The 4.2GB barrier   Some operating systems store the number of heads as an 8-bit value. This can cause a problem if the BIOS reports 256 heads and BitShift translation is in use. If this is the case, the maximum capacity is 4.2GB. Note that the LBA assist translation never reports more than 255 heads, so the problem doesn't exist where the drive and BIOS support LBA.

The 8.4GB barrier   The BIOS limitation of 8.4GB (1024 × 256 × 63 × 512) causes this barrier. New extended INT13 functions were added around 1995 to overcome this barrier. The new extension passes a 64-bit LBA address in a device address packet. Extended INT13 passes the packet through host memory rather than through host registers. If the drive supports LBA, the BIOS passes the lower 28 bits of this address directly to the ATA registers. If LBA support isn't present, the BIOS converts the LBA address to a CHS and passes that address to the ATA registers.

The 32GB barrier   In some systems, the motherboard BIOS can't address drives greater than 32GB. This is an LBA addressing limit in the particular BIOS code on the motherboard. It was an issue mostly on the pre-1999 Award BIOS. All BIOS manufacturers have now made corrections in their core BIOS, so any motherboard with a BIOS date of 2000 or higher shouldn't have this problem. Contact your motherboard manufacturer for information and for a BIOS update if necessary.

The 137GB barrier   IDE/ATA drives conforming to ATA-5 standard and lower are limited to 137GB because of the 28-bit addressing between the controller and the drive. However, ATA-6 has introduced 48-bit addressing, which has increased the maximum size for ATA disks to 144 petabytes. Just make sure the motherboard or I/O board you're using to control a drive larger than 137GB is ATA-6 compliant so that it supports 48-bit addressing.

The 144 PB Barrier   144 petabytes is the current limit on ATA-6 drives, but it's so far out there that it's almost not worth considering as a "limit" at all. A petabyte is a million gigabytes, and who on earth is going to have a hard disk larger than 144 million gigabytes? At this point, nobody even comes close. But remember that in the original IBM PC, nobody could imagine needing a hard disk bigger than 10MB, so in time this barrier too will likely become constrictive and someone will have to figure out a way around it.

So, what do all these limits mean when you're shopping for a new drive in the here and now? Most of the limits discussed so far are historical, and you don't need to worry about them. The only viable limit to consider today is the 137GB one you run up against with pre-ATA-6 drives because of the 48-bit addressing. If you're buying an EIDE drive that's larger than 137GB, match it to an ATA-6 compatible motherboard or I/O controller card and make sure your operating system supports it.

WARNING   *Don't assume your operating system supports 48-bit disk addressing. Pre–August 2002 versions of Windows XP don't, for example, unless you install Windows XP Service Pack 1. Support is enabled by default with Service Pack 1. To determine whether you have Service Pack 1, look on the General tab in System Properties. See Microsoft Knowledge Base article 303013 for more detailed help. Go to* `http://support.microsoft.com` *to access the Knowledge Base.*

A drive that's smaller than 137GB should work well in almost any fairly modern system—you have to go all the way back to 1995 to find one that won't take it (except for the few quirky Award BIOS systems I mentioned when talking about the 32GB barrier, and those can be fixed by updating the BIOS).

Disk Performance Characteristics

When shopping for hard disks, you'll encounter many different numeric statistics on the various disks you consider. The following sections present explanations of some of the most commonly shopped-for specifications.

Seeks and Latency

How quickly the disk can find and read a sector is determined in part by access time. Reading a particular sector consists of two steps: first, move the head to the correct track. Then, once the head is over that track, wait for the sector to spin under the head, and then read the sector. You see this in Figure 8.5. *Seek time* is the time required for the head to position itself over a track. The *latency period* is how long it takes the desired sector to move under the head.

Moving the head takes a lot longer than waiting for the sector to come around. So low seek times (the time to move the head) are critical to good disk performance.

Table 8.5 shows the formula you'll want to remember.

TABLE 8.5: ACCESS TIME FORMULA

ACCESS TIME	=	SEEK TIME	+	ROTATIONAL LATENCY PERIOD
Time to find a sector	=	Time to move to the sector's cylinder	+	Time to wait for the sector to rotate around and appear under the head(s)

FIGURE 8.5

Reading a sector
on a disk

Reading a particular sector involves two steps:

 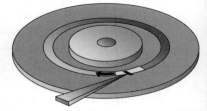

First, move the head to the desired
track. That is called seek.

Then, once the head is over that track,
wait for the sector to spin under the head
The wait is called the latency period.

TYPICAL SEEK TIMES

Of the seek time and the latency period, the seek time is usually the longer wait. Seek time is usually expressed in milliseconds (ms). It varies according to how many tracks the heads must traverse. A seek from one track to the next track is usually quick—just a few milliseconds—but most seeks aren't so convenient. Remember, the lower the seek time, the better. Note that in current PCs, a millisecond is a long period, considering that the measure for modern PC memory is in nanoseconds. This means the system may have to wait for the hard disk.

A common measure of an average seek is the time the system requires to travel one-third of the way across the disk. Most benchmark programs use this measurement. You might wonder, "Why not halfway across the disk, rather than one-third?" The reason is that most accesses are short seeks—just a few tracks.

In the dawn of PC hard drives, companies sold hard disks with seek times of almost 100ms. Today, the average seek time on a new drive is between 5ms and 10ms. In general, the low speed depends on what you're willing to spend. For example, my desktop system has an 80GB EIDE hard disk with a seek time of 8.9ms—not the worst around, but not the fastest, either. Seek times are built into a drive. There's no way for you to improve a drive's seek time, short of getting a new drive.

ROTATIONAL LATENCY/ROTATIONAL SPEED

Once a head positions itself over a track, the job's not done: now the head has to wait for the correct sector to rotate under it. How *much* time is a matter of luck: if you're lucky, the sector is already there, if you're really unlucky, you just missed it and will have to wait an entire revolution. As I mentioned before, this waiting time, whether large or small, is the *rotational latency period*. A common number cited is *average latency period*. This makes the simple assumption that, on average, the disk must make a half revolution to get to your sector. Manufacturers calculate the latency period from the spindle speed. Latency, like seek time, is normally expressed in milliseconds.

Rotational latency is directly affected by rotational speed. Depending on the model, disk drives rotate between 3600rpm and 12,000rpm. Most mainstream hard disks have a spindle speed somewhere between 5400rpm and 7200rpm; serial ATA drives are a little faster, around 7200rpm to 10,000rpm, and $2^1/_2$-inch hard disks (used in notebook PCs, for example) are a little slower, in the 4200 range.

For a disk rotating at 3600rpm, one-half revolution then takes $^1/_{7200}$ of a minute $= {}^{60}/_{7200}$ second $= 8.33$ms. This contributes to the amount of time that the system must wait for service (the rotational latency). The higher the spindle's speed (the rpm), the lower the average latency. Table 8.6 lists some standard spindle speeds and the corresponding average and worst-case rotational latency period (in milliseconds). Calculate the average latency based on a half rotation of the disk; calculate the worst-case latency on a full rotation of the disk.

Table 8.6 shows that the higher the speed of the spindle, the lower the latency. As new technologies reduce drive costs, manufacturers are increasing the spindle speeds of the newer and more expensive drives.

Data Transfer Rate

After a disk has found the data, how fast can it transfer that data to the PC? As you've already read, this is called the *data transfer rate*. Specifically, the transfer rate is a measure of the amount of data that the system can access over a period of time (typically one second). It's determined by the external data transfer rate and the internal transfer rate. The *external data transfer rate* is the speed of the communication between the system memory and the internal buffer or cache built into the drive. The *internal data transfer rate* is the speed that the hard disk can physically write or read data to or from the surface of the platter and transfer it to the internal drive cache or read buffer. Transfer rates vary depending on the density of the data on the disk, how fast the disk is spinning, and the location of the data.

TABLE 8.6: ROTATIONAL LATENCY AND SPINDLE SPEEDS

SPINDLE SPEED (RPM)	AVERAGE ROTATIONAL LATENCY (IN MS)	WORST-CASE ROTATIONAL LATENCY (IN MS)
3600	8.3	16.7
4500	6.7	13.3
5200	5.8	11.5
5400	5.6	11.1
6300	4.8	9.5
7200	4.2	8.3
10,000	3.0	6.0
12,000	2.5	5.0

Error Correction Code (ECC)

No electronic data transmission or storage system is perfect. Each system makes errors at a certain rate. Modern disks have built-in error detection and error correction mechanisms. Although this isn't really a disk performance feature, I mentioned this in passing a few pages back, and I want to give you more of the information on how disks can self-correct errors.

Disk systems are great as storage media, but they're volatile. From the first second after you lay a piece of data on a disk, it starts "evaporating." The magnetic domains on the disk that define the data slowly randomize until the data is unrecognizable. The disk itself and the media may be fine, but the image of the data can fade after *x* years. Put another image on, and it'll last for another *x* years. (If you're taking videotapes of your baby in the hopes that you can use them to embarrass her in front of her dates in 15 years or so, physics may thwart you because the videotape is magnetic.)

Disk subsystems are aware of this and so include some method of detecting and correcting minor data loss. The disk subsystem can detect but not correct *major* data loss. The controller includes *extra* data when it writes information to the disk. When the controller reads back this information (the Error Correction Code, or ECC), it lets the controller detect whether errors have arisen in the data. The basic idea is that the controller stores redundant information *with* the disk data at the time that the data is originally written to disk. Then, when the data is later read from disk, the disk controller checks the redundant information to verify data integrity.

The ECC calculations are more complex than a simple checksum. The ECC that most manufacturers implement in hard disks (and CD-ROMs) uses the Reed-Solomon algorithm. The calculations take time, so there's a tradeoff; more complex ECCs can recover more damaged data, but they take more computation time. The number of bits associated with a sector for ECC is a design decision and determines the robustness of the error detection and correction. Quite a number of modern disks use more than 200 bits of code for each sector.

Some controllers let you choose to use an *x*-bit ECC. In this example, *x* refers to the number of consecutive bad bits that the ECC can correct. The original AT hard disk controller, for instance, could correct up to 5 bad consecutive bits. That meant that it had a "maximum correctable error burst length" of 5 bits. Newer controllers can usually correct up to 11 bits. Some of the newest drives installed in the latest machines are using special high-speed controller hardware to do *70-bit* error correction.

ATA Standard Supported

In Chapter 10 you'll learn about the various ATA standards for transferring data between the motherboard and the hard disk. The ATA standards are ATA-1 through ATA-6, with the most modern drives supporting the highest standard. The higher standards support higher data throughput rates, and ATA-6 standard (the latest at this writing) supports disk sizes of larger than 137.4GB. ATA-4 and higher standards are also referred to as Ultra ATA (UATA) or Ultra DMA (UDMA), along with their theoretical maximum transfer rates: ATA-4 is UDMA/66 (for 66MB per second), ATA-5 is UDMA/100, and ATA-6 is UDMA/133.

When shopping for a hard disk for a high-performance system, it's worth paying more for support for the latest ATA standards. However, in order for the drive to take advantage of the high transfer rates afforded by the latest technology, it must be placed in a system with motherboard support for that standard (or an add-on controller board that supports it) and must be used with a special 80-wire ribbon cable. Therefore it's not worth paying extra for support for the fastest modes on an older system that will not support them. Chapter 10 explains this in much more detail.

Buffer/Cache Size

Disk drives are slow—I mean, really slow. Your computer uses RAM memory that responds to requests in tens of nanoseconds, but the disk drive responds to requests in tens of milliseconds. That's six orders of magnitude difference in speed!

Whenever you're moving data between a faster medium and a slower one, adding a cache to hold recently used or anticipated data can improve performance by reducing the amount of data that needs to travel through the bottleneck area. You've already seen this in previous chapters with the level 1 and level 2 caches on either side of the CPU, for example.

A hard disk's performance can similarly be improved by caching. Many manufacturers refer to the cache as a *buffer* in their drive specifications.

A disk cache seeks to use the speed of memory to bolster the effective speed of the disk. The cache is held in memory chips and is usually one to a few megabytes. The operating system can access data previously placed in the disk cache on an as-needed basis. Using this disk cache can cut down on the number of physical seeks and transfers from the hard disk itself. Smart caching algorithms generally mean that there is no need to change the size of the disk cache. A typical cache size for a modern hard disk is 2MB, but high-performance drives usually have more (8MB, for example).

This cache buffer acts as a holding area for one or more tracks or even a complete cylinder's worth of information in case you need it. This cache buffer can be effective in speeding up both throughput and access times.

DMA and PIO

Direct Memory Access (DMA) and Programmed Input Output (PIO) are two ways of increasing hard disk performance by bumping up the transfer rate between the drive and its interface to the motherboard.

In the BIOS Setup you may notice various DMA or PIO settings available for a hard disk. Choosing the right setting can make a difference in the disk's performance, but nearly every BIOS today can autodetect the proper DMA/PIO setting for a drive, rendering the details of this setting of interest only to technical enthusiasts.

PIO Modes

PIO modes are groups of protocols that define the speed of the connection between the disk and the PC's interface for it. The available PIO settings are 0 through 4, with 4 being the fastest and newest.

To use a particular PIO mode, the drive, the I/O controller card (if using a separate one from the motherboard) and the motherboard's BIOS must all support that mode. If you try to use a higher PIO mode than the drive is capable of, data loss may result. As I mentioned before, nearly every BIOS is able to autodetect the proper PIO mode for a drive these days. Table 8.7 lists the PIO modes and their maximum speeds.

Most modern hard disks don't use PIO modes anymore because they rely instead on DMA, explained in the following section.

TABLE 8.7: PIO MODES

PIO MODE	TRANSFER RATE IN MBPS
0	3.3
1	5.2
2	8.3
3	11.1
4	16.1

DMA Modes and UDMA

DMA is a much more effective way of speeding up the transfer of data to/from a hard disk. DMA stands for *Direct Memory Access,* meaning that it allows the disk to bypass the CPU to read/write directly to RAM. This makes the PC perform better because its CPU is less utilized by behind-the scenes operations such as disk reads and writes.

Early versions of DMA use a controller built into the chipset to make the transfer. If you see DMA modes in BIOS Setup, that setting is referring to those earlier DMA versions.

Modern DMA uses the programming built into the disk itself to make the transfer. These are expressed in new drive standards today as Ultra DMA or UDMA, and the latest versions are capable of transfer rates of up to 133MB per second.

You'll learn more about UDMA when I talk about ATA standards in Chapter 10.

Some versions of Windows don't enable UDMA/66 and higher support by default; you must go in and make some Registry changes to make that happen. I'll explain those changes in Chapter 12, "Partitioning, Formatting, and Managing Drives."

In this chapter you learned the basics of hard disk hardware and its limitations, performance factors, and interaction with BIOS. In the next chapter you'll learn the same type of information about optical discs such as CD and DVD. Then Chapters 10 and 11 will delve more deeply into the inner workings of the EIDE and SCSI interfaces, respectively.

Chapter 9

CD-ROM and DVD Drives

Introduction

Almost all software comes on Compact Disc Read-Only Memory (CD-ROM) these days, so having some type of CD drive is nearly a necessity. But which kind is best? A writeable CD drive, either CD Recordable (CD-R) or CD Rewriteable (CD-RW)? A Digital Versatile Disc (DVD) drive? A writeable DVD? Some sort of combination? And if you want a writeable DVD, which of the many competing standards will you select? This chapter attempts to provide some answers to those questions by explaining CD/DVD technology and how to install, use, and maintain optical drives and discs.

QuickSteps: Installing CD and DVD Drives

No matter what kind of CD drive you're installing (including DVD), the physical installation of the drive is basically the same. DVD drives require a little bit of extra cabling if you're also installing an MPEG decoder card (required to watch DVD movies on-screen), but other than that, they're similar.

Before you start, there are some things you may need on hand. These include the following:

BE PREPARED

- ◆ Phillips-head screwdriver for mounting the drive in the case
- ◆ Small dish to hold the screws as you work
- ◆ Any instructions that came with the drive

To install a drive, follow these steps:

1. If the drive requires a separate adapter card, install it in the PC. Most CD drives run off the motherboard's existing Integrated Device Electronics (IDE) interface, so this is probably not necessary.

2. If you're installing a DVD drive and you have an MPEG decoder card to install, install it in the PC. These are Peripheral Component Interconnect (PCI) cards.

3. Set any jumpers on the drive as needed. If it's an IDE drive you're installing, set the appropriate Master, Slave, or Cable Select (CS) settings. If SCSI, set the SCSI ID number and/or termination as needed. Refer to Chapters 10 and 11.

4. Install the drive into an open bay.

5. Attach the power cable to the drive.

6. Connect the interface cable to the drive interface (on the motherboard or adapter card) and to the drive.

7. Attach the sound cable from the CD drive to the sound card if you want to be able to play audio CDs.

8. If you're installing an MPEG decoder card as part of a DVD installation, attach a loopback cable from your computer's video board to the DVD decoder Video In port, and then connect your monitor cable to the DVD decoder Video Out connector.

How a CD Drive Works

CD and DVD drives fall into the *optical* category of drives. In Chapter 8, "Hard Disk Drive Overview and Terminology," you learned that hard disks, floppy disks, and Zip disks are all magnetic in nature—in other words, they store data in transitions between positive and negative magnetic charges on the disk surface. Optical discs and drives, on the other hand, store data in patterns of transitions between areas of greater and lesser reflectivity on the shiny surface of a disc.

When you insert a CD or DVD into a drive, a sensor detects the disc, and the spindle motor begins spinning it. A laser shines light on the surface of the disc, and the shiny surface reflects light back to a photodetector sensor. The amount of reflected light is measured, and that data is sent to the drive controller.

Data on an optical disc is stored in patterns of pits (or the appearance of pits) on the disc's surface. A *pit* is a tiny indentation in the surface that causes the light to be reflected back less strongly than in other areas. The nonpitted areas are known as *land*.

It's tempting to think that a pit stands for a binary digit, but that's not how it works. Binary digits are indicated by the patterns of transitions between pit and land areas, much like on a magnetic disk (see Chapter 8). When the sensor detects a change in the amount of light bounced back—which could be a transition from either land to pit or from pit to land—it sends an electrical pulse to the controller that indicates a 1 bit. When enough time passes that a transition could have occurred but didn't, it interprets that as a 0 bit.

Mass-manufactured CDs and DVDs have actual pits in the surface, covered by a protective clear coating. Writeable CDs and DVDs work a bit differently, as you'll learn later in the chapter. They use a writing laser to create areas of lesser reflectivity on the disc's surface that simulate the same loss of reflectivity that a pit would create. Therefore, the photodetector sees those areas as pits.

Now that you know how the drives work, you'll look at the differences between the many different optical drive and disc standards available today.

CD and DVD Drive Types

Today there are many different types of optical drives available, but the basic level is CD-ROM. Regular CD-ROM drives can read from standard data or audio CDs, but they can't read DVDs and can't write to any disc.

NOTE   *Disk or disc? When referring to optical discs, I use disc; when referring to magnetic disks, I use disk. However, not everyone uses this convention.*

All of these other types can also read standard CDs in addition to their own special capabilities:

- ◆ CD-R drives can write to write-once CD-Rs.

- ◆ CD-RW drives can write either to CD-Rs or to multirewriteable CD-RWs.

- ◆ DVD-ROM drives, also called DVD players, can read from data DVDs and can play DVD movies (with the help of an appropriate MPEG decoder).

◆ DVD-recorder drives can do everything a DVD-ROM drive can do plus they can write to DVD-R (write-once) and/or DVD-RW (multirewriteable) discs.

◆ Combination drives have the capabilities of more than one of the previous types. For example, a combination drive might include CD-RW and DVD-ROM capabilities.

When choosing a CD drive, think about how you'll use it. Do you need to be able to read DVDs? If so, choose a DVD drive. Do you need to create your own CDs? Then go with a CD-R or CD-RW drive. If you don't need either of those capabilities, go with a regular old CD-ROM drive to save yourself some money. If you need to write DVDs, there's a whole extra set of considerations because there are several competing standards; I'll address this dilemma in the "Recordable/Rewriteable DVD" section.

Regular Compact Disc Read Only Memory (CD-ROM)

You'll see some kind of CD drive in virtually every computer sold today, and in lower-end or older systems it may be a regular CD-ROM drive (that is, one that lacks any of the "special" qualities such as writing CDs, writing DVDs, or reading DVDs).

Regular CD-ROM drives read data CDs, just as you read the contents of any other disk on a PC. They also play audio CDs, provided you have a CD player program installed on your PC. They're the baseline of functionality; all DVD and CD-RW and DVD-RW drives also perform these functions, so you don't need a regular CD-ROM drive if you've got one of the other types.

So generically speaking, how does a CD store data? Well, the surface of a regular CD is arranged as a single spiral that begins at the inside of the disc and travels outward toward the edge of the disc. The commercially produced ones are made of injection-molded plastic formed from a stamper disc, coated with an aluminum film to make them reflective and then lacquered to protect the surface. (CD-Rs and CD-RWs are different, which I'll explain later.)

From 527 megabytes (MB) to 742MB will fit on a disc, depending on the number of sectors on the disc and the format used on it. Standard discs use the same-sized spiral as an audio CD (60 minutes) with 270,000 sectors and up to 99 tracks. The typical disc used in a computer-based CD-ROM drive stores 630MB using 333,000 sectors.

CDs are physically organized a little differently than hard disks. Whereas hard disks lay individual tracks in concentric circles, CDs define a track by the length of a specific file; one file equals one track. The tracks on CDs are laid sequentially on a continuous spiral. This spiral is a staggering 3 miles long and can contain more than 2 billion pits.

Commercially produced CDs are made up of a polycarbonate (plastic) wafer, about 1.2 millimeters (mm) thick. This wafer is coated with metallic film, which is then covered, for protection, by a plastic polycarbonate coating. Most CDs are single-sided; the player reads data from only one side. (In the early days of CD technology there were a few double-sided discs, but you'll seldom run into one today.)

Regular CDs store data by arrangements of pits on the CD (about 0.12 microns deep and 0.6 microns wide). The pits produce areas of less reflectivity, so when a laser hits the disc, the light doesn't bounce back as strongly. Just like with 1s and 0s in binary computer code, this "pit/no pit" system stores binary data on the CD, as I said earlier.

CD-Recordable (CD-R)

CD-R and CD-RW are two technologies for recording your own CDs. CD-R, the older technology, writes only once to a blank, writeable CD. After you write to the CD-R, you can't write to it again (except in the case of a multisession disc, which I'll get into later). It's great for data archiving or creating music CDs.

Recall from the preceding discussion that regular CD-ROMs are composed of metallic film on a plastic disc, and the disc is pitted to store the data by reflecting or not reflecting light from the pit/nonpitted areas. Commercially available CD-Rs, on the other hand, are coated with metal in a process similar to electroplating and overlaid with photosensitive organic dye. When the laser "burns" data into the CD-R media, it heats the metal and the dye together, causing the area to diffuse light in the same way that a pit would on a mass-produced CD so that CD-ROM drives are fooled into thinking that a pit exists. There's no pit, though—just a spot of less reflectivity.

CD-R has its drawbacks. If the recording process falters, you've just wasted a blank CD (they cost about 50 cents apiece these days, or less if you buy in bulk). CD-R is also not great for backing up data that changes frequently because you have to use a new CD every time something changes to make sure you have a current backup. That's where CD-RW comes in.

CD-Rewriteable (CD-RW)

A CD-RW drive can write to a blank, rewriteable CD multiple times, just like with a hard or floppy disk. You can erase files stored on a CD-RW and make changes to them, so CD-RW is an ideal format for backing up constantly changing data, such as data files from an accounting program you use daily. You can write to a typical CD-RW more than 1000 times before it "wears out." Although CD-RW blanks are more expensive, they last longer because you don't have to throw one away when the data on it becomes outdated. Most CD-RW drives sold today are dual-purpose drives that can do CD-R as well as CD-RW, depending on the type of blank you insert in them.

On a CD-R, the dye changes into a nonreflective state as a result of mixing with the underlying metal. That change is permanent, which is why you can't alter a CD-R's content. In contrast, CD-RWs also contain material that changes reflectivity when exposed to a laser, but not permanently. The CD-RW contains a silver-indium-antimony-tellurium alloy that's naturally reflective. When the CD-RW drive writes, the laser uses a high-power setting (called *Pwrite*) to heat the alloy to about 500 to 700 degrees Celsius (C), causing it to liquefy. After being liquefied, a spot loses its reflectivity when it hardens again, making an artificial pit. By reheating the area to a lower temperature (about 200 degrees C, a setting called *Perase*), the laser makes the material revert to its reflective state. In this way, it's possible to write to CD-RWs many hundreds of times.

Before you can use a CD-RW, you have to format it—much like you format a hard disk, but with a special utility that comes with the CD-RW software. Early CD-RW drives took a long time to format discs (more than 30 minutes in some cases), but modern drives can format a CD-RW in about 30 seconds. Formatting lays down a grooved spiral on the disc, ensuring accurate alignment of the burned-in data.

NOTE *Even though CD-ROM, CD-R, and CD-RW discs look similar, they store data differently as I've just explained; that's why some older CD players can't read CD-R and CD-RW discs. All the newer ones can, though.*

Digital Versatile Disc (DVD)

Like CD, DVD is known mostly by its initials. Basically, the DVD format squeezes more data onto a single disc than is possible with a regular CD. CD-ROMs can fit about 630MB onto a disc whereas DVD can fit as much as 17 gigabytes (GB). DVDs are used to distribute movies, and increasingly game manufacturers are releasing games and business applications on a single DVD that would otherwise have required multiple CDs.

A DVD is somewhat like regular CD technologically. DVDs can store more information than regular CDs because they have a smaller pit length, less space between pits, a slightly larger data area (less wasted space around the outside and inside), and a few other minor design improvements. The primary difference is that the pits are much smaller and much closer together.

There are four kinds of DVDs: single- and double-layered and single- and double-sided. You might hear certain DVDs referred to by a number, such as DVD-9 or DVD-10. That's a reference to the standard they support. The following are some of the popular standards:

◆ DVD-5: single-sided, single layered, 4.7GB capacity

◆ DVD-9: single-sided, double-layered, 8.5GB capacity

◆ DVD-10: double-sided, single-layered, 9.4GB capacity

◆ DVD-18: double-sided, double-layered, 17GB capacity

The second data layer is written to a separate substrate below the first layer, which is semireflective to allow the laser to penetrate the top layer to read the substrate below. This enables the disc to hold more than twice the data on the same surface area. On a double-layer disc, the different layers have different colors, so a double-layer disc may appear to have a gold tinge to it whereas a single-layer one looks more purely silver.

NOTE *Another term you might occasionally hear associated with DVDs is RSDL, which stands for Reverse Spiral Dual Layer. This refers to the ability for the player to automatically go to the next layer at the end of the first one. This is useful when playing a movie because it doesn't interrupt the playback, for example.*

A DVD drive can also function as a regular CD-ROM drive, so you don't need to have both in your PC; a DVD drive can replace your existing CD-ROM drive. In fact, DVD-ROM technology is on its way to replacing CD-ROM technology on the computer as a way to distribute software and high-capacity data.

Recordable/Rewriteable DVDs

If a writeable CD is good, then a writeable DVD must be even better, right? Not only can it hold hours of video footage, but it can also hold massive quantities of data, so a DVD seems like the perfect medium for large backups and data storage.

The computer industry has been enthusiastically pursuing the development of writeable DVD technology in recent years. Unfortunately, all this enthusiasm has produced many different standards. The situation you have is really similar to the early days of VCRs (remember the "Beta versus VHS" battles?), except that recordable DVDs are available in four basic physical formats: DVD-RAM, DVD-R, DVD-RW, and DVD+RW.

DVD VIDEO AND MPEG2

There are two types of DVD discs in terms of what's stored on them: DVD-video and DVD-ROM. *DVD-video* is what you buy at your local video store. These discs are optimized for the storage and playback of digital movies through a player connected to your television. These discs are analogous to audio CDs that you play in your stereo. *DVD-ROM* is the computer counterpart and, as such, is more similar to a CD that you use at your computer every day. The DVD-ROM drive in your computer will play both types of discs. However, to play DVD-video on a computer, you need either dedicated software or a special adapter card called an *MPEG2 decoder* to decode the movies.

Some DVD drives come with the needed decoder card; others make you buy it separately. Using such a decoder board is known as *hardware decoding*. The alternative is to use a software driver that does the decoding for you; this is *software decoding*. Hardware decoding results in better quality video playback, but on a powerful PC with lots of Random Access Memory (RAM) there's not much difference. The need for hardware decoding was mostly an issue in the past when PCs weren't powerful enough to handle the decoding on their own through software; however, some videophiles continue to prefer them for the highest-quality movie playback. Nearly all mainstream desktop PCs today go with software decoding.

None of these writeable formats are fully compatible with one another, and there are even compatibility problems with existing drives and players. Using the old "Beta versus VHS" VCR analogy again, you couldn't play a Beta tape in a VHS player, and you couldn't play a VHS tape in a Beta player. (Well, maybe the analogy isn't quite perfect: Beta and VHS cartridges were different sizes, so it was pretty obvious which type of cartridge you had. With the exception of DVD-RAM, which requires a caddy for handling, the other types of DVD-Rs look pretty much the same.)

When you look at the specifications for current DVD recorders, you see a mixed bag of compatibility, so you'll have to research different recorders before you make your purchase. If you want to use the DVD recorder for your own system backups and data storage, any of the following formats will probably suit your needs. However, if you intend to share or distribute your DVDs, you should select a recordable DVD format that supports the needs of your intended audience:

DVD-R   First available in the fall of 1997, this popular format comes in two versions: DVD-R for general use and DVD-R(A) for authoring. The general version uses a laser that's more compatible for the future ability to write DVD-RAM. DVD-R(A) is intended for professional development and isn't writeable in DVD-R drives. Both types, however, are readable in most DVD players and drives. Similar to CD-R technology, this format records sequentially to the disc and allows only one recording. The capacity of a first-generation disc was originally 3.9GB and later increased to 4.7GB.

DVD-RW   Introduced in Japan in December 1999, this rewriteable format was created by Pioneer. It can be rewritten about 1000 times. DVD-RW is based on the DVD-R format and can record from one to six hours of video depending on quality. DVD-RW discs have 4.7GB capacity (the same as single-layer DVD-ROMs). Though it's not usually required that you use a caddy or cartridge for the DVD-RWs, some drives may require one. DVD-RWs are playable in most DVD drives and players. However, when you insert a DVD-RW into some DVD-video players, the player may assume it's trying to read a dual-layer disc (because of the lower reflectivity of the DVD-R). This little glitch can usually be fixed with a firmware upgrade for the DVD player.

TIP   DVD-R and DVD-RW seem to be winning the standards war at this writing, so if I had to choose right now which technology to go with, that's where I'd put my money. However, what I'm actually doing is hanging back a bit and waiting until the standards war is over before I buy in. No way am I going to end up with another Betamax.

DVD-RAM   Introduced in the summer of 1998, this rewriteable format has many manufacturers behind it and is well suited for storing computer data. However, DVD-RAMs aren't compatible with most existing drives and players because of format differences. This format is also considerably more sensitive to handling than other formats. A double-sided DVD-RAM must be enclosed in a cartridge, similar to the caddy used with early CD-ROM drives. For single-sided DVD-RAMs, the cartridge is optional but recommended.

Its initial capacity was 2.6GB per side, for a total of 5.2GB. Second-generation DVD-RAMs have a capacity of 4.7GB per side and are more suitable for editing and accessing movies and music. Second-generation drives are backward compatible with 2.6GB DVD-RAMs and can read other DVD and CD formats. DVD-RAM is a rewriteable format that can handle up to 100,000 rewrites on a single disc, which is more than 100 times that of DVD-RW.

The main problem with the DVD-RAM format is with video. Most home DVD players won't play movies on DVD-RAMs. However, some DVD-RAM recorders will also record in DVD-R format as well (a write-once format) for compatibility.

DVD+RW   DVD+RW is a rewriteable format developed as a joint effort by the DVD+RW Alliance. Members include Hewlett-Packard, Mitsubishi Electric, Philips, Ricoh, Sony, and Yamaha. It offers fast access and rewriteability like DVD-RAM but without that format's incompatibility issues. DVD+RW isn't an officially sanctioned standard at this point (so buyer beware), but it does seem to offer the best of both worlds of DVD-RW and DVD-RAM. It's one to watch.

TIP   When shopping for a DVD player for your television system with homemade DVDs in mind, look for one with the DVD-Multi certification. These players should play discs in DVD-R/RW and DVD-RAM formats. When burning DVDs for use in a DVD movie player, use the write-once discs (DVD-Rs) rather than the rewriteable ones for the best chance at compatibility.

CD Drive Standards

CD drive standards used to be important in the early days of the technology because there were all sorts of competing technologies that weren't compatible with one another (just like now with the writeable DVD standards!). However, nowadays the standards for regular CD-ROM are well established—to the point where looking for compliance with particular standards is no longer significant. Nevertheless, you might find it interesting to read a brief overview of the CD drive standards that developed over the past decade or so. If not, feel free to skip this section.

A "book color" system was used to designate CD primary standards: red, yellow, orange, green, and white. The original specification was published in a book with a red cover, so that's how the naming convention originated. The next book they published with a yellow cover, and so on. Each color stood for the standards for a particular usage; therefore, they don't overlap or contradict one another.

Table 9.1 summarizes them, and the following sections examine the first two—red and yellow—in a bit more detail.

TABLE 9.1: CD STANDARDS BY BOOK COLOR

COLOR	TOPIC
Red	Audio
Yellow	Data storage
White	VideoCD (movies)
Orange	Writeable CD (CD-R and CD-RW)
Green	Combination of Red and Yellow (for kiosks)

It's important to note that these colored book standards aren't frozen in time. The Yellow Book standard isn't one single document, for example; it has been updated many times over the years to accommodate new technological improvements. Rather, each book color represents a certain functionality of CD drives.

Red Book

The Red Book was the original specification defining how digital audio information is stored and indexed. It was developed for music CDs, which were the first CDs commercially available, and almost all music CDs conform to this standard today. All CD drives available for computers today support audio CD playback by conformance to this standard.

Yellow Book

The Yellow Book, also named ISO 10149 (ISO stands for the *International Organization for Standardization*), extends the Red Book audio specifications and deals specifically with the more interactive requirements of CD-ROM: random access capability and multimedia. The specifications concentrate on storing and indexing data and error correction.

This standard supports several file formats for the different computer platforms that use CD-ROMs. These include Native Macintosh hard disk format, Digital Equipment Corporation's (DEC's) VMS, Apple's Hierarchical File System (HFS), and ISO 9660 (which you'll learn about next). As I pointed out earlier, though, these standards are a point of interest mostly for their historical value today because Yellow Book technology has become standardized.

HIGH SIERRA AND ISO 9660

In 1985, CD-ROM companies formed an alliance to produce a standard CD file structure independent of the operating system. The result is commonly known as the *High Sierra* standard. After some modifications, the standard was formally accepted by the ISO and was named *ISO 9660*. It sets forth a standard file system with a hierarchical directory structure of eight levels. This Compact Disc File System (CDFS) is similar to the File Allocation Table (FAT) architecture familiar to DOS users. It's the standard format for all data CDs produced today. When you look at a CD drive's properties in an operating system (Windows, for example), you'll see the file system reported as CDFS; now you know what that means.

NOTE *Theoretically, if a drive is an ISO 9660–compatible drive, it can, for example, read the information whether it's a Windows-based system or a Macintosh. However, this alone doesn't ensure compatibility because applications may contain instructions that use the resources of a given computing platform and that aren't available on another platform. Thus, reading data and executing the program code isn't the same; you can't execute programs written for Windows on a non-Windows machine such as a Macintosh, even if the Mac can detect the CD. Before you buy a CD, check its packaging to see what operating system it supports. Some CDs have both Mac and PC data on them; others are for one operating system or the other only. Both PCs and Macs will play audio CDs.*

CD-ROM/XA

The CD-ROM/XA standard was another extension to the Yellow Book. The *XA* stands for *Extended Architecture*, and this standard does exactly that. By defining the way in which different data types may be interleaved (that is, woven together) on a CD, the XA standard really makes multimedia CDs possible. It also allows for multisession recording.

A common application requiring the interleaving of sound and motion can be demonstrated through a multimedia presentation. Suppose you're giving a presentation with pictures of a person speaking and have sound to follow along. In order for the movement of the speaker's lips to match the spoken words, the sound and the pictures must be synchronized. To accommodate this, tracks on a CD-ROM/XA can contain interleaved video/picture, audio, and computer data.

Briefly, here's how it works: a standard CD track contains only Mode 1 data-type sectors. With CD-ROM/XA, a track contains only Mode 2 sectors. There are two form types within a Mode 2 sector: Form 1 contains user data (2048 bytes) and Error-Detection Code (EDC) and Error-Correction Code (ECC) data. Form 2 contains raw data (2324 bytes) such as audio or voice.

For a CD-ROM drive to be fully XA-compatible, it must have the following capabilities:

◆ Read data from two differently defined data streams. These streams are Mode 2, Form 1, which is static information, and Mode 2, Form 2, which is time-dependent information.

◆ Allow data from each stream to be buffered and delivered to the Central Processing Unit (CPU) and video subsystem as required.

◆ Translate the Adaptive Differential Pulse Code Modulation (ADPCM). ADPCM is a standard for audio compression, usually a 4:1 ratio. In other words, the CD-ROM drive must be able to send the audio signal to the speakers properly decoded and decompressed.

Nearly every CD drive you'll encounter today is CD-ROM/XA compatible to the point where this is a nonissue. Occasionally you may run into an old CD drive that's noncompliant, but never a new one.

MULTISESSION CAPABILITY

Recall from the earlier discussion of CD-R that you can write to a CD-R only once. *Multisession capability* provides a way out of that limitation, but at a price.

Say you have a 640MB capacity CD-R, and you write your daily backup of your data files to it. That takes up 100MB. The next day, you want to back up your data files again. You can create a second session on the same disc and write the next day's backup to the new session. The only gotcha is that once you create the second session, the first session is gone forever. In most cases you can't access multiple sessions, only the last one written to the CD-R.

A multisession CD-R drive has the capability to write multiple sessions. A multisession CD-ROM has the capability to *read* a disc that contains multiple sessions. (That is, it can read the last session written to the disc.) The most important reason an average consumer would need multisession support is to read photo CDs (such as a CD you'd get back with developed film). All modern CD-ROM drives are multisession capable, as are all DVD and CD-R/RW drives.

CD and DVD Drive Interfaces

You can connect CD drives to the rest of your computer via an Enhanced Integrated Drive Electronics (EIDE), Serial ATA (SATA), Small Computer System Interface (SCSI), legacy parallel, Universal Serial Bus (USB), or FireWire port. Although you should be familiar with these interfaces from earlier chapters, I'll briefly review them here.

Before I begin, however, I'll point out a couple of facts about CD drive interfaces. First, they work in pretty much the same way as hard disk interfaces or floppy interfaces, so if you have a handle on those, you're set. Second, most interfaces will do a credible job (with the exception of the legacy parallel port, which is extremely slow and should be avoided at all costs for external drives—if you can even find an external parallel drive anymore).

EIDE

The same EIDE interface that runs a system's EIDE hard disks will also run CD and DVD drives on most systems. I say *most* because some old systems might not support an EIDE CD drive. For it to work, the EIDE interface on the motherboard must support the AT Attachment Packet Interface (ATAPI) standard, which was introduced with ATA-3. For details about ATA-3 and the various other ATA standards, see Chapter 10, "Understanding and Installing ATA Drives."

Because EIDE interfaces are already on all PC motherboards, many CD-ROM drives use EIDE. Generally speaking, EIDE CD and DVD drives work fairly well and are less expensive than other types. However, when two EIDE devices share the same cable, latency problems (that is, delays) can result that may cause a high-speed CD-R or CD-RW drive to have errors during writing.

SATA

SATA is the bright star in high-performance drive interfaces these days, and it's expected to replace EIDE even in low-end systems in the next couple of years. When that happens, most CD drives will start coming in SATA models. For now you should be able to use a converter to get an EIDE CD drive to run on a SATA interface. It won't be any faster, but if you're trying to get rid of all the old ribbon cables, that might help.

SCSI

SCSI is a competing standard to EIDE for connecting devices to a PC. You'll learn about SCSI in Chapter 11, "Understanding and Installing SCSI Devices." SCSI can support both internal and external drives, as well as nondrive devices such as scanners.

SCSI has a reputation for being faster than EIDE in general. However, with the latest EIDE improvements and standards (see Chapter 10), the gap is closing, and CD drives run slower than hard disks on any interface anyway, so increased speed alone isn't a compelling reason to choose SCSI over EIDE for a CD drive. One thing SCSI does do exceptionally well, however, is manage the sharing of an interface among multiple devices. You could have several SCSI drives on a single interface, and each could be doing its own thing simultaneously with very little delay. That's why SCSI is the professional's choice for high-performance disk arrays.

A drawback of SCSI is that most motherboards don't support it directly. You must add a PCI-based SCSI adapter and then connect your SCSI devices to it. This adds to the overall cost by $50 to $200 if you don't already have a SCSI adapter—which isn't a problem for the high-end enthusiast but could make a difference to Joe Consumer. Furthermore, SCSI CD drives in general are more expensive than their EIDE counterparts.

Choose SCSI if high performance in a multidrive situation is important to you and you don't mind paying the extra price. SCSI is also a good choice for an external CD or DVD drive, but USB and FireWire (discussed next) are also good for that (some would say better).

USB

USB has become a popular interface in the past several years for external devices. It's fast, it's easy to connect, and you can connect/disconnect USB devices without shutting down Windows (in other words, they're *hot-swappable*).

The original USB specification to become popular was USB 1.1, which supported CD-R/CD-RW drives of only 4. (That's a speed measurement; see "Choosing the Right Drive" later in this chapter for an explanation.) Newer systems provide USB 2.0 support, which is a much faster interface and supports the newest and fastest CD reading and writing speeds.

Choose USB if you want an easy-to-connect external CD drive, but be aware of the USB standard that the drive and the motherboard's USB interface supports. If you use a USB 2.0 CD drive on a motherboard with only USB 1.1 support, it'll work but will default to USB 1.1 speed limitations.

IEEE 1394 (FireWire)

FireWire is a less common interface for CD drives than the previously mentioned ones, but FireWire drives do exist. FireWire is a competitor to USB; it's a high-speed interface for connecting external devices. Its capability is roughly equivalent to that of USB 2.0. The main drawback to FireWire is that most motherboards don't support it natively, unlike USB, so you must use an add-on PCI expansion board to insert the needed ports.

TIP   *One benefit of a FireWire drive is that you can use it with either PC or Mac.*

Choosing the Right Drive

CD drives aren't all the same. They vary in terms of their hardware interface, speed, drivers used, access to additional hardware, and where they attach to the computer. So that you can select the right one for your needs, I'll go through the details of those characteristics now.

Disc Loading

Almost all CD and DVD drives today have a tray that the disc goes directly into. Once you put the disc into the tray, it slides back into place in the drive, and the CD starts spinning.

Although you'll seldom see one today, some CD drives of yesteryear required you to place the CD in a *caddy* (a protective storage case that minimizes exposure to contaminants) for loading and then insert the caddy into the drive. Some models of writeable DVD drives also do this (mostly DVD-RAM). The advantage is that the CDs don't introduce dust particles into the drive read/write mechanism. The disadvantage, as you can imagine, is that it's awkward and time-consuming to swap CDs in and out of caddies.

Internal or External

Many CD models are available in both internal and external models. If you have an empty drive bay and don't mind opening your system to install the drive, internal drives are often the best choice. They tend to be less expensive than external drives, and more models are available. Additionally, some interfaces (such as EIDE, for example) aren't available at all in external models, so if you have an EIDE controller that you want to use with the drive, internal is your only choice.

External drives are good if you have a USB, FireWire, or SCSI interface and don't like cracking the case, don't have an extra drive bay, or are running into a bit of a power crunch from too many devices making demands on the power supply (external drives have their own power supply). They tend to be more expensive than comparable internal drives, but (assuming you have a USB port or a SCSI host adapter installed in your computer), they're much easier and faster to install. Plugging an external USB or FireWire drive into your computer is as simple as it gets. If you plug a SCSI drive into an existing SCSI chain, first make sure your computer is off (SCSI isn't hot-swappable like USB). Then, plug in its power cable, make sure it's terminated properly, power the system back on...and there's your drive. FireWire and USB drives are hot-swappable, so you wouldn't have to power down to connect or disconnect one of those.

Performance Characteristics

All CD drives look pretty much alike (within the limits of being internal or external drives), but looks aren't the measure of performance. You can buy drives with various spinning speeds, access/seek times, data transfer rates, buffering techniques, and so forth. All these features directly affect drive performance.

DATA TRANSFER RATE

Data transfer rate, measured in kilobytes per second (KBps), is the theoretical maximum amount of data that can be transferred to the PC per second. It's measured not in the actual kilobytes per second, but in "X" ratings. The original CD drives were 1, which meant they could read seventy-five 2,048-byte sectors of data per second. That comes to 150KBps. The next generation of drives were 2X, which doubled the speed by spinning the disc twice as fast past the read head. You can determine a drive's data transfer rate by multiplying its rating by 150KBps. Table 9.2 does the math for you to show some common speeds.

TABLE 9.2: CD-ROM SPEEDS AND DATA TRANSFER RATES

DRIVE SPEED	TRANSFER RATE (KBPS)
1	150
2	300
3	450
4	600
5	900
8	1200
10	1500
12	1800
16	2400
18	2700
24	3600
32	4800
36	5400
40	6000
48	7200
52	7800

In reality, the data transfer rate for a drive is seldom if ever achieved because that rating is for sustained performance. It doesn't take into account the *access time* (described in the next section), which is the time required for the disc to rotate to the correct spot to be read and the read head's arm to move to the correct position.

DVD drive speeds can't be fairly compared to CD drive speeds using ratings alone because DVD data is stored so much more compactly than CD data. If a DVD drive were a 1 drive, it'd have a theoretical maximum transfer rate of about 1.4 MBps, which is equivalent to about 9 for a CD drive.

It's not completely accurate, however, to simply multiply the X rating for a DVD drive by 9 to compare it to other drives because a DVD drive will also be used to read regular CDs. When evaluating the ability of a DVD drive to read CDs, you can approximately triple the rating to compare it to a CD drive. In other words, a 16X DVD drive would roughly compare to a 48X CD drive when reading from regular CDs.

NOTE *The speed of the DVD-ROM drive doesn't affect the quality of a DVD movie being played. For example, if you have a 2X DVD-ROM drive, replacing it with a 16X DVD-ROM drive won't improve the quality of the movie playback. The speed will impact some DVD-based interactive multimedia games, however.*

ACCESS TIME

Access time is the amount of delay between the drive receiving the command to read and the actual beginning of the reading. It's measured in milliseconds (ms). The measurement is just an average; the actual speed depends on where the data is located on the disc and how quickly the read mechanism can get to it. The closer to the center the data is, the quicker it can be accessed.

Don't expect an access time from your CD drive that even approaches the access time you see from your hard disk. I have a hard disk with an access time of 9ms, but a common CD drive access time is more than 100ms.

Table 9.3 lists some typical access times for various drive speeds. Lower numbers are better. Notice that unlike data transfer rate, the access time doesn't get better at a constant rate as the drive's X rating goes up. The access time is a function of the quality of the hardware inside the drive that moves the read/write head. It's not directly related to the rotational speed of the disc, which is what the X speed measures. The relationship between them is tangential—the faster the drive speed, the more likely it is to have modern, high-quality head movement mechanism.

TABLE 9.3: TYPICAL CD-ROM DRIVE ACCESS TIMES

DRIVE SPEED	ACCESS TIME (IN MILLISECONDS)
1X	400
2X	300
3X	200
4X	150
6X	150
8X	100
10X	100
12X	100
16X	90
18X	90
24X	90
32X	85
40X	75
48X	75
More than 48X	75

CACHE/BUFFER

Disk caching, also called *disk buffering,* temporarily stores recently accessed or frequently accessed data to the hard disk to take advantage of its higher access rates. Most CD-ROM drives have a small amount of memory in them for this purpose. Typically, the directory of the CD is cached. Caching the directory enables the computer to more quickly navigate subdirectories and makes the CD-ROM drive appear to be faster. However, the actual reading of the data is still slower.

NOTE   Some people differentiate between a cache and a buffer. Strictly speaking, a cache uses some form of logic to figure out what to store: depending on how it's set up, it'll temporarily store the most recently accessed or the most frequently accessed data on the hard disk. A buffer is just a holding area, with no logic. However, not everyone observes this distinction; many drive makers use the terms cache and buffer interchangeably in their specs.

CAV VERSUS CLV

Constant Linear Velocity (CLV) and *Constant Angular Velocity (CAV)* are two technologies for determining the spinning speed of the disc. CLV keeps the area per second constant so that the disc has to spin faster when data is being read from near the center and slower when data is being read from near the edge. CAV keeps the spinning speed constant and varies the area that's read per second.

All data is written to CD using CLV. Therefore, all writeable drives are CLV drives. You can also find CLV in older CD drives (usually slower than 16X although CLV drives are available up to 48X). The amount of data read or written per second is a constant. High-speed CLV drives tend to be noisier and more expensive than CAV drives.

High-speed nonwriteable CD and DVD drives typically use CAV because it's more efficient and allows for higher overall X ratings. For an accurate measurement of the drive's performance, such drives must report two X ratings—one for the inner areas of the disk and one for the outer. So for a regular CD drive that uses CAV, you might see a speed of 48X/52X in sales materials.

From an installation and usage perspective, there's no difference between CLV and CAV drives; the differences are purely internal and invisible to the user.

Installing a CD or DVD Drive

The installation procedure for a CD or DVD drive depends on the interface you've chosen. EIDE is different from SCSI, which differs from USB, which differs from SATA, and so on. The following sections outline the basic procedures for each interface, with some detours that apply to multiple types.

Preparing a Drive Bay

Preparing a drive bay applies to all internal drives. Decide which drive bay you'll place the drive in, and clear the way for it. That may involve removing a bezel or cover plate on the front of the PC, moving any cables out of the way, and so on.

Setting Jumpers

Setting jumpers applies to EIDE and SCSI drives. You must set jumpers on the drive to let the system know what position or role this drive fills.

For EIDE drives, you must set a jumper to the Master, Slave, or CS position. Each cable must have only one master drive on it, so if you're installing a drive on an existing EIDE cable, you must set the second drive to Slave. For more information, see the full discussion of EIDE jumpers in Chapter 10.

For SCSI drives, you must set a jumper indicating the SCSI ID number. Each device in a SCSI chain must have a unique ID number. You may also need to set a jumper for termination to indicate whether this drive is the last SCSI device on the chain. For details about SCSI jumpers, see Chapter 11.

Installing the Drive in the Bay

Again, installing the drive in the bay is for internal drives only (EIDE and SCSI). Insert the drive in the bay so that its front aligns with the front of the PC; then tighten it down with screws. On some PCs you don't use screws to attach drives; instead you use mounting rails with clips on them that snap into place. Some people prefer to attach the cables (see the next section) before tightening the drive into place.

Connecting the Cables

For an internal drive, connect a power plug from the PC's power supply to the drive. CD drives use standard Molex power connectors, which are the ones with four wires and four rather large round holes on them that plug into the four protruding cylindrical pins on the back of the drive.

Also for an internal drive, connect the ribbon cable from the EIDE or SCSI interface to the drive. The cable has a red stripe on one side; the red stripe goes toward pin 1. If you look closely at the drive, you'll see a little 1 at one end of the ribbon cable connector; that's the pin 1 end. If you can't find it, just orient the red stripe at the end closest to the power plug.

If you plan to play audio CDs on an internal CD drive, you'll need to connect the drive to the sound card with an audio cable. This is typically a thin round cable consisting of three or four thin wires, with a small plastic three or four pin connector at each end.

Okay, here's the first step for the external drives: connect its data cable to the PC using whatever interface is appropriate (SCSI, FireWire, or USB). Then connect its power cord. An external drive has its own power cord that plugs directly into a wall outlet. (Actually this is the last step for an external drive, too—they're pretty simple to connect, huh?)

BIOS Configuration

For a USB, FireWire, or SCSI drive, you don't need to do any BIOS configuration. (BIOS stands for *Basic Input/Output System.*) The operating system will handle the drive automatically. Some SCSI controllers have their own BIOS Setup routines you can access.

For an EIDE drive, on a newer system you shouldn't have to do any BIOS configuration either. The BIOS should autodetect the new EIDE device at startup. As your system boots, you'll probably see a list of detected hardware; if your new CD or DVD drive appears on that list, the BIOS has figured it out.

Even if you don't see anything indicating that the BIOS has detected the drive, go ahead and let your operating system load. If the new drive appears there, you're fine—*no worries, mon.*

On some old systems, you must enter the BIOS Setup and set the drive type for the EIDE interface to Auto for autodetection or to CD-ROM or ATAPI.

Drivers

Windows will detect and load the appropriate basic drivers for most CD and DVD drives automatically. These are protected-mode drivers. If you boot the PC to MS-DOS or boot from a startup floppy, however, you won't have access to the protected mode drivers, so you'll need a real-mode driver for the CD drive to use it from a command prompt. The startup floppies that you can create in Windows 98 and Windows Me include generic CD drivers that will work with almost all CD and DVD drives. Windows 95 startup disks don't have them, but you can add them manually to a Windows 95 startup disk. Windows NT, 2000, and XP don't allow a command-line boot from a floppy, so it's not an issue with those operating systems.

To operate a CD drive in MS-DOS or a command line outside of Windows (as in the case with a boot disk via Windows 95), you need to load the following drivers:

◆ If it's a SCSI CD drive, there needs to be a line in `CONFIG.SYS` that loads the driver for the SCSI adapter. This driver comes from the SCSI card's manufacturer. It might look like this: `DEVICE=C:\SCSI\SCSIDRV.SYS`.

◆ In `CONFIG.SYS`, there needs to be a line that installs the driver for your specific model of CD drive. This driver comes from the CD drive's manufacturer. It might look something like this: `DEVICE=C:\MYCD\NECCD.SYS /D:mscd001`.

◆ In `AUTOEXEC.BAT`, the Microsoft CD extensions need to be loaded (`MSCDEX.EXE`). That would be something like this: `C:\DOS\MSCDEX.EXE /D:mscd001` if loading from MS-DOS.

If you need a driver for a specific SCSI card or CD-ROM drive, check the manufacturer's Web site. Generic drivers are also available that might work. You see them at work on a startup disk created with Windows98 and Me, for example; they enable you to start your system and use your CD-ROM drive when you're not in Windows. In a pinch, you can copy those drivers to your hard disk and use them for running in MS-DOS mode.

Installation Troubleshooting Checklist

Having problems getting a newly installed CD or DVD drive to work? Here's a step-by-step procedure for troubleshooting:

1. If it's an EIDE drive, does the BIOS see it? Go into BIOS Setup and check. If not, check for proper cable orientation and connection and proper master/slave jumper settings. Also, make sure the EIDE channel in the BIOS isn't set to Disabled. It should be set to CD-ROM, ATAPI, or Auto.

2. If it's a SCSI drive and Windows doesn't see it, check for proper SCSI termination and ID number. See Chapter 11 for help with SCSI.

3. If the BIOS sees the drive but Windows doesn't, make sure that Windows isn't in Safe mode. Windows won't see CD drives in Safe mode. Reboot if needed.

4. If the drive isn't recognized when booting to a command prompt, make sure the CD driver is loaded in `CONFIG.SYS` and that MSCDEX is loaded in `AUTOEXEC.BAT`.

5. If data CDs will play but not music CDs, make sure you've connected an audio cable between the drive and the sound card. For external CD drives, consult the documentation to find out whether an audio cable is required.

6. If a certain CD won't work, make sure the CD is clean. Clean it with a very soft cloth. Don't scrub! If you must use liquid, use denatured alcohol. Also, make sure the CD is in a format supported by your current operating system—for example, make sure you're not trying to read a Mac CD on a PC.

7. If data DVDs will play but movie DVDs won't, make sure you have MPEG2 decoding capability. This will either be a hardware board or be a piece of software. If it's hardware, make sure the cabling for it is correct per the instructions. On some boards you must connect the monitor to the MPEG2 decoder board, then connect that board to your video card, and finally run a cable from the DVD drive to the board. Also, make sure that the correct drivers are installed and that your DVD player software is compatible with your model of DVD drive.

Recording CDs and DVDs

Windows 95 and higher will automatically recognize CD and DVD drives, but it'll see them as ordinary CD-ROM drives. If you want to access their special capabilities, you must use third-party software. (Windows XP is the exception—it recognizes and uses writeable most CD and DVD drives automatically through its own software.) You can use the software that came with your drive or some other application.

Avoiding Buffer Underruns

One of the most frustrating parts about making a CD-R is encountering an error called a *buffer underrun*. This occurs when the drive you're reading from can't keep up with the CD writer's "need for speed" and makes it wait. The problem is—it can't wait. It has to keep moving, and writing, at a more or less continuous rate. If it's ready to write but the data hasn't arrived yet, a buffer underrun occurs, and you've just wasted a blank CD.

With newer CD recorders, this is less often a problem—they have large built-in data buffers designed to prevent this. With an older system or CD burner, the following can cause the dreaded buffer underrun:

◆ Some other application is hogging the processor's attention, so the processor can't tell the source drive to send the data to the CD-R fast enough. Try not to use any other programs, or even move the mouse around, while a CD is being created.

◆ The source drive can't operate as quickly as it needs to because of its own limitation. In that case, try transferring the files for the CD to your hard disk first and then making the CD from there instead of going from CD to CD.

◆ You don't have a large enough data buffer set up. A data buffer holds information read from the data source so that even if there's a pause in the data reading, the writer can keep writing without a wait. You typically set this up in the drive properties.

- You don't have Direct Memory Access (DMA) enabled for the source drive. DMA modes transfer data with less CPU intervention. Try displaying the drive properties and turning on DMA transfer if possible.

- You're trying to record at too high a speed. Many CD-R drives advertise that they can record at up to 24X speed, but if you find you get buffer underrun errors at that speed, try a slower speed such as 8X, 6X, or even 4X, and your errors may go away.

In general, SCSI CD-R drives are less susceptible to buffer underruns than EIDE models. (But then they also cost more.)

Recording CD and Data DVDs

For CDs and data DVDs, if you're using third-party writing ("burning") software such as Roxio Easy CD Creator or Nero Burning ROM, you can choose to make an audio or data CD or DVD through that interface. Consult the software documentation.

If you're using Windows XP's built-in writing tools, the procedure for creating data versus audio CDs is different. To do an audio CD, you go through Windows Media Player; for a data CD, you use Windows Explorer to drag and drop the files to the CD and then write them.

WARNING *If you plan to use the CD or DVD on a computer with a different operating system, make sure the files have names that are recognizable in that operating system. For example, MS-DOS filenames are limited to 8.3.*

Producing and Recording DVDs

Developing a DVD content is different from creating a CD, depending on whether you want to produce a DVD-ROM or a DVD-video.

You can typically use traditional multimedia development software (Macromedia Director, Click2learn ToolBook, or other similar software programs) to develop an interactive DVD-ROM that features MPEG2 video and digital audio. Consumer and pro-level DVD-ROM formatting tools such as Adaptec Toast DVD (for the MacOS), Daikin DVD-ROM formatter (for WindowsNT and 2000), and Gear Pro DVD (for Windows95/98/NT4) will allow you to write to DVD format.

Full-quality DVD-video DVDs, however, are another matter entirely. You develop a DVD-video in three stages. First you encode the video. Then you design, configure, and test the interface. Finally, you premaster a disc image.

If you want to go the distance, you can put your home movies onto DVD-video by following these steps:

1. Use video and audio capture boards to capture your video and audio from VHS, Hi8, or DV. You can use service bureaus or scanners to transfer slides to digital format.

2. Use a software encoder to encode the video into MPEG2 format. Set the video frame rates to 29.97 frames per second (fps) for NTSC format (U.S.) or 25fps for PAL (European) format.

3. Use a software or hardware encoder to encode the audio into Dolby Digital. Format the audio as 48 kilohertz (kHz) Pulse Coded Modulation (PCM).

4. Import the video and audio clips into a DVD-video authoring program. Create menus and buttons that link to your media clips. You can also import your slides in TIF, JPEG, or Photoshop format.

5. Write your completed project to a DVD-R.

VideoCDs are easier (and cheaper) to create, especially because you can create them on CD-R or CD-RW drives. A VideoCD contains one data track that's recorded in CD-ROM XA Mode 2, Form 2. After the data track, one or more subsequent tracks contain video that's recorded in a single session. The MPEG1 standard for VideoCD is similar to VHS-quality video, and the audio is hi-fi quality. Based on the White Book standard, VideoCDs should work on PCs, Macs, VideoCD players, and CD-Interactive (CD-I) systems, provided they're equipped to handle this format. You can get MPEG1 encoding software and write up to 70 minutes of full-motion video to standard CD-R or CD-RW format. The quality won't be as good as DVD-video, but CD-R hardware, software, and discs are much cheaper than DVD.

Selecting Writeable Media

When selecting writeable CDs or DVDs, you have a wide range of choices. One blank is distinguished from another in the following ways:

Standard(s) supported   Make sure you get the right type of blanks for your drive and what you intend to do with it: CD-R, CD-RW, DVD-R, DVD+R, DVD-RW, DVD-RAM, and so on.

Rated maximum write speed   Higher-quality discs have higher maximum write speeds. If your CD-RW drive maxes out at 8X write speed for CD-R, there's no reason to spend extra to buy 32X blanks. Match the blanks to the speed at which you intend to record.

Capacity   Standard CD-R and CD-RW blanks hold 640MB of data; high-capacity ones hold 700MB. Very old writeable drives might not be able to use the high-capacity ones.

Dye and metal colors   It can be difficult to know what you're getting in this area until you open the package because most labels don't say. The standard CD-R uses green dye and gold metal; these CDs work well in most players. Gold dye/gold metal is a more sensitive combination that might not play well in an audio CD player. Blue dye and silver metal produces a longer-lasting CD, up to 100 years (or so experts believe because it hasn't been 100 years since the first one was made).

Handling CDs and DVDs

By caring for your CDs and DVDs, you're doing preventive maintenance on the drive, reducing the opportunity for contaminants to enter the drive. The following pointers will keep your CD and DVD drives up and running:

◆ Handle the CDs and DVDs only at the hub or the outer edge. Don't touch the shiny surface

◆ When you insert a CD or DVD into the drive, make sure you seat it properly in the tray.

- If a CD or DVD needs to be cleaned, use a soft, clean, *dry* cloth and wipe in a radial motion from the inner hub to the outer hub. Don't use a circular motion.

- Don't use cleaning agents—many solvents used in them can damage a disc.

- Don't use a wet cloth.

- Avoid cleaning the label side of the CD or DVD.

- Use a caddy to transport CDs and DVDs, and store them in their cases when not in use.

- Avoid exposure to extreme heat or cold.

- Avoid excess humidity.

- Avoid direct sunlight and high-intensity Ultraviolet (UV) light.

In this chapter, you learned how to select, install, and maintain CD and DVD drives. The next chapter covers the important topic of EIDE drives. EIDE is the most common interface for a variety of drive types, including CD, DVD, and hard disk.

Chapter 10

Understanding and Installing ATA Drives

- ◆ Quick Steps: Installing an EIDE Drive
- ◆ Deciphering the Acronym Soup
- ◆ Obtaining Compatible Hardware
- ◆ Setting Jumpers and Cables
- ◆ Configuring the System's CMOS

Introduction

Advanced Technology Attachment (ATA) has been the most popular interface for hard disk drives and CD drives in mainstream systems for many years, which means two things: there are lots of them around, with various specifications, and you're probably going to need to install one—if not now, then probably in the near future. In this chapter I'll address both of these points. First I'll explain what differentiates one ATA drive from another, and then I'll show you how to install them.

QUICKSTEPS: INSTALLING AN ATA HARD DRIVE

QuickSteps: Installing an ATA Hard Drive

If you're in a hurry, you're in the right place. Collected here, for your convenience, are the basic steps that you'll perform to install an ATA device.

NOTE *The terms Integrated Device Electronics (IDE), Enhanced Integrated Drive Electronics (EIDE), and ATA have become generic and are used interchangeably throughout the industry, even though there are actually subtle differences between them that you'll learn about later in this chapter. When I talk about installing an ATA drive here, I'm talking about the standard kind with a ribbon cable, not the Serial ATA kind.*

BE PREPARED

Before you start, there are some things you may need on hand. These include the following:

- Hard drive or other IDE device.

- Interface cable.

- A manual for the device and other configuration information.

- Adapter kit, if needed. Some systems come in small desktop cases and others in roomy tower cases. Regardless of which, check inside to see what drive bays you have free. All drives today are designed to fit either $5^1/_4$-inch or $3^1/_2$-inch bays. Most hard drives are $3^1/_2$-inch and CD-ROM, CD-R/RW, and DVD drives are $5^1/_4$-inch. If you have only a $5^1/_4$-inch bay free for that new hard disk drive, you'll need an adapter kit. (Those measurements, by the way, are indicative of the size of the spinning disc inside, not of the drive's outer dimensions.)

- Flashlight—if not required, at least recommended.

- Phillips-head screwdriver with a medium tip.

- Small plastic cup for holding screws. Personally, I lay out screws in a pattern so I can return them to the place I removed them from. I work left to right, top to bottom. That way, I can just repeat the process and get the right screw in the right hole.

- Antistatic wrist strap—although not exactly necessary for installing drives and other similar devices, it's a good idea to have one handy. It's best not to harbor any stray static electricity if you happen to touch a component that you're not working on, which is altogether possible.

- Toenail or fingernail clippers—also not required, but handy. These are great for cutting those hampering zip ties (those plastic little strips that bunch wires together). Just be careful not to snip a wire or two. Of course, the cutting area of nail clippers is not very big, so there's little chance of this occurring if you pay attention.

1. Gather the ingredients and open the case.

2. Jumper the drive as appropriate. If you intend for the drive to become an adjunct to the existing main drive, set it to Slave as per the drive's manual. Almost all hard drives and CD-based drives

ship with the drive jumpers set in Master mode by default. Many of the newer systems will require you to configure the drive as Cable Select (CS). Using CS means that the drive's configuration is dependent on the IDE connector to which it's attached. Although you should check the system documentation to determine which configuration you should use, you can usually tell whether the drive needs to be CS if the cable connectors are identified on the cable. Examples are connectors labeled *CD-ROM 1* and *CD-ROM 2* or labeled *Primary* and *Secondary*.

3. If you're not going to use the IDE connector on the motherboard (for whatever reason— maybe you've already used them all up, or maybe you're installing a high-performance disk drive that your older motherboard won't take full advantage of), install an Input/Output (I/O) adapter board in any free Peripheral Component Interconnect (PCI) slot.

4. Insert the drive into its intended bay. This may be easy, or it may be nigh impossible. I've dealt with both many times. The newer budget systems are the worst—they weren't designed to be upgraded. I've had to remove Random Access Memory (RAM), motherboard power taps, twisted cable, and other drives just to place a drive in a bay, sometimes all at once!

5. If you're using it, locate an IDE connector on the motherboard. The existing drive will likely be at the end of the cable, with another connector several inches behind that. If you're using an I/O adapter board instead for connecting the drive, locate the IDE connector on that board.

6. Locate an unused power connector running from the power supply. These small, white connectors have four small holes and four colored wires and can be installed in only one way.

7. Cable the drive.

8. *Now* you can put the screws in. Use the screws provided by the manufacturer. Using screws that go too deep can damage the drive. Allow the drive to be mobile while cabling or be content with the space there is between the back of a mounted drive and the power supply.

9. Leave the case open, check all your cable connections, and attach the monitor, keyboard, and mouse. The other cool stuff can come later. Power it up. You should see the drive being identified if you mounted and configured it correctly, but there are circumstances out of your control that could cause that not to happen (there's more detail further in the chapter).

10. Your system's CMOS should configure itself automatically; if it doesn't, enter Setup during boot and configure the system's CMOS so that it knows a drive is there. (CMOS stands for *Complementary Metal Oxide Semiconductor*.)

Of course, there's more to it than that, and that's why this entire chapter is devoted to the process and its details. First, though, you can work through these steps visually. That should help quite a bit. If you run into trouble, see my troubleshooting walk-through at the end of the chapter.

ATA Technology

Although the ATA interface is an excellent way to connect an internal peripheral to the computer, the many different labels by which it goes have confused many people, including IDE, EIDE, Ultra ATA (UATA), Ultra DMA (UDMA), and so on. I'll take a moment and sort it out for you.

It All Began with IDE...

Let's start with IDE. When hard drives first appeared in desktop PCs, it was necessary to install a separate controller card to connect the drive to the computer. It was an expensive and complicated arrangement that was made even more difficult by the incompatibilities of some controller and drive combinations. The hard drive industry decided there had to be a better way to attach a hard drive to a computer and, within a few years, specified a hard drive that had its own IDE.

Are IDE and ATA the same thing? Well, sort of, but not exactly. There have been three types of IDE over the years, each of which are is incompatible with the others. The first was XT IDE, used in the IBM PC XT and clones of it. XT IDE is an 8-bit interface and uses a 40-pin ribbon cable. Even though it uses the same cable as modern IDE, the interface is incompatible because it's 8-bit while modern IDE is 16-bit. Next came MCA IDE, an IBM experiment that never really caught on. MCA IDE is a 16-bit interface, using a 72-pin connector. Finally, the AT IDE was developed for the IBM AT system (the 80286), which *did* catch on and was the father (mother?) of the current standards in use today. It's a 16-bit interface, using a 40-pin connector.

When talking about modern IDE, then, yes, it's basically the same as ATA, in that ATA standards govern the modern IDE interface. Just keep in mind that there are some old, obsolete IDE versions that aren't the same as ATA.

NOTE   *The AT in ATA stand for Advanced Technology, the name that IBM gave to its PCs based on the 80286 architecture. Even though the IBM AT is long obsolete, many of the revolutionary improvements that it introduced lasted a lot longer, including AT IDE, the PS/2 mouse connector, and the AT style of motherboard.*

ATA Standards

Among the ATA standards (except for Serial ATA, which I'll address a bit later), everything is backward compatible. So basically, any ATA drive will work with any motherboard or I/O controller that supports any form of ATA. That's not to say that it'll work to its top potential, but it'll read and write at some basic level.

Therefore, when talking about systems supporting this or that ATA specification, what I'm really talking about is performance. Between the ATA controller on the motherboard and the ATA drive, you're limited in performance to the highest level they can both agree on, so it makes sense to match them as closely as possible.

Now, with that said, you'll look at the various ATA standards that have come out over the years and what each one contributed.

ATA-1

This was the original standard from 1988. It specified the 40-pin parallel ribbon cable, Master/Slave/CS configuration, and Cylinder/Head/Sector (CHS) and Logical Block Addressing (LBA) drive parameter translations. It also introduced the Identify Drive command that the Basic Input/Output System (BIOS) Setup program uses to query the drive for its settings.

ATA-2

ATA-2 can be a little confusing to talk about because several drive manufacturers introduced improvements that predated ATA-2 and were eventually rolled into its standard.

ATA-2 itself came out in 1996. Around 1994, however, Western Digital made some improvements to the original specification, and rather than wait around for the specification to be updated, they called their version EIDE. This really muddied the waters because EIDE isn't a specification and, to make matters worse, Western Digital redefines EIDE with each new release of the ATA specification. So, what EIDE meant in 1994 is different from what EIDE means today.

The next year, Seagate made improvements to the ATA specification and created their own snazzy name—*Fast ATA*, followed soon after by *Fast ATA-2*. Fortunately, Seagate and most other drive manufacturers quit coining their techno-babble names in the late 1990s (with Western Digital being the exception). Still, even though the label was a little long, drives were known as IDE/EIDE for a while

The official ATA-2 standard added support for devices other than hard disks so that manufacturers could make ATA CD drives, tape drives, and so on. This was a big deal at the time because prior to that point all other drives (except floppy) had to come with their own proprietary interface cards. A separate standard was developed to allow these other devices to use ATA called the *ATA Packet Interface (ATAPI)*.

ATA-2 also added faster Programmed Input/Output (PIO) and Direct Memory Address (DMA) transfer modes, PCMCIA support, and power management support (allowing the drives to stop spinning during periods of inactivity).

NOTE *EIDE has come to be a more or less generic term to mean an ATA-compatible IDE device that conforms at least to ATA-2 standards and uses the standard 40-pin connectors and a 40-wire or 80-wire ribbon cable. Serial ATA isn't EIDE; therefore, EIDE isn't the same as ATA.*

ATA-3

ATA-3, introduced in 1997, added a technology called *SMART*, which stands for *Self-Monitoring and Reporting Tool*. It helps the disk communicate its status to the BIOS and operating system to report possible impending failure. It also added a security mode for password protection.

ATA-4

Here's where the "ultras" make their first appearance and where hard disks start really ramping up in terms of better performance. In 1998, ATA-4 was released, providing support for a new transfer mode called Ultra DMA (UDMA). It was also called UATA by some, so you might see it either way in print

Recall from Chapter 8, "Hard Disk Drive Overview and Terminology," that DMA is a way of bypassing the Central Processing Unit (CPU) to send data directly to/from RAM for better performance. UDMA is a faster version of that, at least twice as fast as was previously available with DMA or PIO modes. The basic UDMA can transfer data at up to 33 megabytes per second (MBps) and is sometimes called UDMA/33.

NOTE *UDMA works only when both the controller (motherboard or interface card) and the drive support it. If the motherboard or interface card don't support ATA-4, the drive performs like an ATA-3 drive instead. That's an example of what I meant earlier about backward compatibility.*

ATA-4 introduced an optional 80-wire ribbon cable. It has 40 connectors at each end, but it also has a separate ground wire for every "live" wire, resulting in 80 wires in total—a pair for each signal—to improve the data transfer quality at the higher rates. Why? Well, each line needs to represent 1 or 0 values through voltages. But voltages are relative things; there's no such thing as a "universal 10 volts." It's 10 volts in comparison to something—in this case, a wire whose voltage is arbitrarily called 0 volts, or ground. Each of the 40 wires has a ground wire to compare its value to. This makes determining a 0 versus a 1 much simpler.

The final improvement in ATA-4 is that the ATAPI standard was officially rolled into the ATA standard. (They were separate standards before, but ATA supported ATAPI.) This made it easier for the BIOS Setup to work with those other drive types (such as CD-ROM).

ATA-5

ATA-5 came out in 1999. It introduced UDMA/66, which was twice as fast (in theory) as the original UDMA.

UDMA/66 mode works only when a specific set of conditions are in place, however. Not only must the drive *and* controller both support ATA-5, but you must be using an 80-wire cable. In the absence of any of those factors, performance drops to whatever ATA standard the drive and controller can agree on.

ATA-6

ATA-6, released in 2000, provides UDMA/100 support, which—you guessed it—transfers data at up to 100 megabytes per second (MBps). Like ATA-5, it requires an 80-wire ribbon cable and a drive and controller that specifically support it. It also supports 48-bit transfers, which you learned about in Chapter 8, so it breaks the 137 gigabyte (GB) barrier in capacity.

WARNING   *No matter how fast the drive interface can go, the drive can only physically move data off the platter at a maximum of approximately 60MBps. In every throughput test I've run, the difference in performance among the ATA-66, ATA-100, and ATA-133 drives is minimal or non-existent; you'll probably notice the difference only if you run a comparison test and read the results, and maybe not even then. Therefore, it doesn't make a lot of financial sense to go out and buy an I/O board to support the latest ATA-7 hard disk when the EIDE interface on your motherboard is ATA-6 compliant. Save your money for something with more bang instead!*

ATA-7

ATA-7, which came out in 2002, bumps up the speed to 133MBps and is therefore also known as UDMA/133 (or ATA-133, or Ultra ATA-133…you get the idea). At this point, the ATA standard is really pushing its technological limits. It can't get much faster and still stay on that parallel ribbon cable. But wait…here comes Serial ATA to change all that.

SERIAL ATA

The techie community is all abuzz right now about Serial ATA, the bold new improvement to ATA technology that rids us of ribbon cables and their inherent data transfer limitations and connects the motherboard/controller to the drive via a fast serial connection, somewhat akin to Universal Serial Bus (USB) or FireWire.

Serial ATA has many advantages. In addition to increased speed (150MBps) for the first generation (and hopes of 600MBps or more in the future with Serial ATA II and Serial ATA III) and the lack of any of the crosstalk issues inherent in a parallel interface, Serial ATA is self-configuring and fully Plug and Play (PnP) compatible. That means it'll be as easy to configure a new hard disk as it is to plug in a USB device (or nearly so). And because serial cables aren't subject to the harsh length limits of parallel ribbon cables (which top out at a length of 40 centimeters), cables can not only be thinner but also longer (up to one meter), so you won't have to worry about rearranging the drives in your system to make a cable reach.

NOTE *Serial ATA, like USB and FireWire, is hot-pluggable. You wouldn't normally connect a hard disk with the PC running, but it's now possible to do so with Serial ATA.*

Serial ATA is the dominant hard disk interface of the future; within a few years, most mainstream home systems will be using this technology. Right now, however, you'll mostly find it in the enterprise and enthusiast markets for a couple of reasons. One is that most low-end motherboards don't have the proper controller, so a new motherboard or I/O controller card is needed, and companies that make entry-level computers don't want to spend the extra money.

NOTE *A Serial ATA controller uses the PCI bus, so it's subject to that bus's limitations: between 133MBps and 150MBps. The only way you could practically expect to achieve 150MBps would be using multiple hard disks in a Redundant Array of Inexpensive Discs (RAID).*

Adapters are available to allow a standard ATA drive to use a Serial ATA controller. However, this is for compatibility purposes only; the drive will not enjoy any of the advantages of Serial ATA.

Really, I can't overemphasize the important benefits coming our way as PC users with Serial ATA. Just think of it—no configuration problems with SCSI settings or master/slave issues, fully hot-pluggable, instantly Plug-and-Play... If it doesn't make you want to run right out and buy one, it should.

Ironically, the very reasons that makes Serial ATA so great are the reasons why I'm not covering it in greater detail in this chapter. The installation is so simple (basically just plug it in) that I can be of better service here covering "harder" stuff like installing drives on the standard parallel ATA interface.

Summary of ATA Standards

So what do you really need to know from all this? Here's a quick rundown:

- IDE is a generic term. It refers to modern ATA types of IDE (including EIDE), plus the old MCA IDE and XT IDE that are long obsolete.

- ATA-1 through ATA-7 refer to the standard IDE technology that uses the 40-pin connector and ribbon cable.

- EIDE has become almost as generic a term as ATA or IDE. It refers to any of the standard 40 pin types of IDE that conform to ATA-2 through ATA-7. In other words, this refers to pretty much every ATA drive on the market today except Serial ATA.

NOTE *It can be argued that SATA is a form/variant of EIDE, but in this book I use EIDE to refer to the traditional 40-pin type of IDE to differentiate it from Serial ATA.*

- Any ATA drive that uses the standard 40-pin interface will work with any ATA controller, but it may not achieve its maximum performance. To achieve its top data throughput speeds, the controller and the drive must support that speed. For example, both must support UDMA/133 to operate in that mode.

- UDMA/66 and higher requires an 80-wire ribbon cable.

- Serial ATA uses a different kind of cable and interface than traditional ATA and is a little bit faster and a lot more convenient to install. In the future it promises to be a lot faster.

- When putting together a high-performance system, the latest and greatest hard disk may help a little, but in reality the maximum transfer rates are mostly theoretical and don't make that much difference because of the limitations of the mechanical portions of the hardware.

Configuration Considerations

Before you jump into the computer with your screwdriver in hand, you should take a moment to figure out your plan. What jumper settings will you use? What drive(s) will go on what EIDE controller? Trust me, these are decisions that you want to make up front, rather than after you've tightened all the screws and accessing the little jumper blocks would require a contortionist!

Master/Slave Jumpers

Before you install EIDE drives, you need to understand how two EIDE drives share a single ribbon cable and controller. They manage it by making one of the drives the boss (the "Master") and letting the other one (the "Slave") take its orders from it.

Data from the EIDE controller comes to both drives via the ribbon cable, but only the drive designated as the Master listens to it. The Master drive hears each message and is in charge of figuring out who the message is addressed to. If it's for itself, then it processes the instruction. If it's for the Slave, it passes the message along.

The Slave drive, on the other hand, doesn't listen to any incoming messages from the controller. It only listens for data being sent to it from the Master drive.

The designation as Master and Slave isn't permanent and can be changed by altering a jumper setting on the drive. This gives you more choices when you're installing a second drive; for example, you may choose to retain your old drive as Master, adding the new drive as Slave, and then use a transfer utility to move your working operating system to the new drive. Or you may opt to make your old Master a new Slave and install a fresh copy of your favorite operating system to the new drive, a freshly minted Master.

NOTE *Jumpers are little plastic blocks that have a bit of copper inside. They're formed so they can slide firmly over two posts. When you place a jumper block over two pins, you create an electrical pathway between them, altering the flow of electricity through the drive. When a jumper block is hanging off a single pin, that's the same as it not being present at all. It's simply a storage position.*

There's a third possible setting on most EIDE drives: Cable Select. This setting allows the drive's position on the ribbon cable to determine whether it's the Master or Slave. Most new PCs you buy these days will use Cable Select for drive configuration. You don't need anything special to do it, as long as the drives and motherboard (or I/O board) support Cable Select (and they all do these days). Put the Master drive at the far end of the cable, and the Slave drive in the middle, and then set the jumpers on both to Cable Select. You should not mix Cable Select and either Master or Slave on the same cable—it's an "all or nothing" proposition per cable.

Actually, there's also a fourth possible setting, but not all drives have it: Single. When an EIDE device is the only drive on the cable, it's the Master by default, but some drives have a Single jumper setting for that situation that's separate from the Master setting.

The drive will have a label on it somewhere with a diagram showing the various jumper positions. Figure 10.1 shows how some sample drawings correspond with some jumper positions.

FIGURE 10.1

Configuring drive jumpers

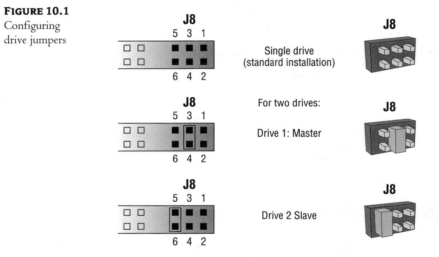

Configuring drive jumpers for a Western Digital AT-IDE hard disk drive

When installing two devices on the same cable, try to use the newer and faster of the two drives as the Master and the slower one as the Slave. That's because the Master drive has more responsibilities, so the job should be given to the more capable of the two drives.

Primary and Secondary EIDE and Add-On Boards

Nearly every motherboard has two EIDE controller channels built into it, labeled as the *primary channel* and the *secondary channel*. Each channel can support up to two devices, so you get a total of four EIDE device positions: Primary Master, Primary Slave, Secondary Master, and Secondary Slave. You can configure those four positions in the motherboard's BIOS Setup program to be set to a specific drive type, set to Auto, or disabled. (Usually this BIOS configuration happens automatically on modern systems, however.)

To support more than one drive on a cable, the cable has to have a total of three connectors: one for the motherboard (or controller) and two for drives. Figure 10.2 shows the difference between a single-drive cable and a dual-drive cable. You'll typically find the single-drive cables only on the cheapest bargain-basement PCs. New hard drives usually come with dual-drive ribbon cables, so you can replace your existing cable if needed.

FIGURE 10.2
Types of hard
drive cables

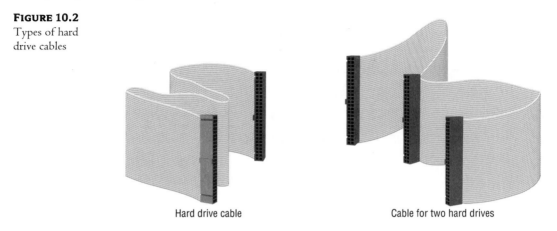

Hard drive cable   Cable for two hard drives

On systems that need more than four EIDE devices, or need to have support for one of the higher ATA standards than the motherboard's controller supports, you can add an *I/O controller board* (also called a host adapter). This is an expansion board (PCI) that fits into the motherboard and adds one or more EIDE controllers. Such controllers have their own BIOS extensions that load automatically when the PC starts up. You usually can't directly access the BIOS through a Setup program, but that's okay because they configure themselves automatically. Figure 10.3 shows a typical host adapter board running two drives.

FIGURE 10.3
Multiple EIDE
hard drives and
a host adapter
attached via a cable

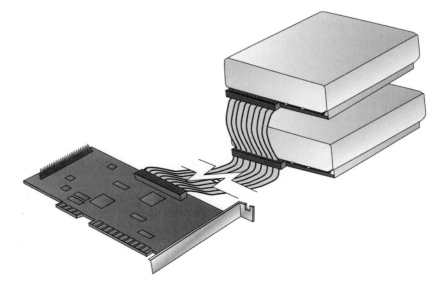

What Goes Where?

For best performance, some strategic decision making is required regarding what position each device should occupy in an EIDE-based system. Here are the general rules:

◆ If you have only two EIDE devices, put one on each channel so they don't have to share a cable. Not sharing is the best situation.

◆ A device that shares a cable with a device of a lower ATA standard than itself will default to the lower standard's performance level. Therefore, you shouldn't put a new hard disk on the same cable with an old hard disk if you can help it.

◆ An UDMA/66 and higher device won't be able to perform at its top levels on a 40-wire cable; it'll default to UDMA/33 level (or lower, as mentioned previously).

◆ A writeable CD drive shouldn't share a cable with another CD drive if you plan on doing direct disc-to-disc copying. Disc copying is a data-intensive project, and doubling the traffic on a single cable can result in error-causing delays.

◆ Match up drives that get a lot of use (such as the primary hard disk) with drives that don't get used often (such as a secondary CD drive) to minimize the amount of competing data going through the cable.

◆ Cable lengths may limit your choices in which drives connect to which controllers, but don't let this be the primary concern. Move drives to other drive bays if possible to accommodate your preferred configuration.

Installing the Drive

Now that you know which drives you want to connect where, and you've set the jumpers appropriately, it's time to do the installation.

Drive installation isn't complex. It basically involves placing the drive in a bay inside the PC's case and connecting two connectors to it: the EIDE ribbon cable and the power connector. Figure 10.4 shows the back of a typical EIDE drive.

FIGURE 10.4
Typical EIDE hard drive connections

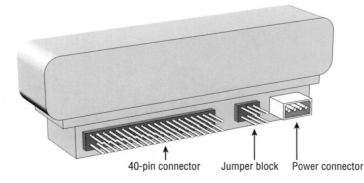

40-pin connector   Jumper block   Power connector

The Pin 1 Rule

This is a general rule for all ribbon cables, not just those for EIDE drives. The orientation of the connector is important! On some systems the EIDE connector blocks are keyed so that the connector will fit only one direction; however, on other systems there's no built-in provision for that, so you have to figure out which is the correct orientation.

Ribbon cables have a colored stripe running along one edge (usually red), and that striped end must go to pin 1. The pins on a connector are numbered, with 1 and 2 at one end and the highest numbers (39 and 40 for EIDE) at the other end. When the red stripe on the cable is nearest pin 1, the cable is properly oriented.

If you examine the circuit board on which the controller pins are mounted, you may see a very small 1 at one end or the other. That's your clue about pin 1. Alternatively, there might be a small triangle or arrow pointing at one end or the other to indicate pin 1.

If you don't see any clues about where pin 1 might be, here are two ways of guessing:

- *On a motherboard,* look at how the other cables plugged into it are oriented (such as the cable for the floppy controller or the other EIDE channel). Orient the new cable the same way.

- *On a drive,* the red stripe (pin 1) should usually be closest to the drive's power supply connector. For example, in Figure 10.4, pin1 is probably at the right end of the 40-pin connector.

Installation Steps

Okay, with all that background under your belt, the steps should be a piece of cake:

1. Open the case.

2. Jumper the drives as appropriate.

3. Insert the drive into its intended bay.

4. If needed, connect a ribbon cable to the motherboard or I/O controller board. Follow the Pin 1 Rule.

5. Connect the ribbon cable to the drive. Follow the Pin 1 Rule.

6. Connect a power connector from the power supply to the drive.

7. Reposition the drive in the bay if needed and then secure it there with screws.

This is pretty simple when you know what you're doing, huh? The hard part about installing drives isn't usually the physical installation but the mishmash of problems and errors that can occur when you don't do it properly or when the PC's BIOS doesn't want to recognize or support the drive for some reason. So let's look at BIOS issues next.

Configure the System's BIOS Setup

I could've called this section "Introducing the Hard Drive to the Computer's Hard Drive BIOS." Your computer has low-level software, a set of built-in machine language programs whose purpose it is to control your hard drive hardware. That software must be in Read-Only Memory (ROM) on your system.

Bottom line: I suggest you set all your EIDE channels to Auto in BIOS Setup and let the system handle the configuration details. The drive will report its CHS, its capabilities for LBA, DMA, and PIO modes, and other key settings to the BIOS. This works on all systems that have a PnP-compatible BIOS—that is, just about every system made after 1995 or so.

On systems made prior to PnP, the EIDE devices aren't automatically detected. However, most of them have a Detect IDE utility built into the BIOS Setup. You can execute it from within the BIOS Setup program, and it'll query each of your EIDE drives and supply its proper settings (but poor you if you still have such an ancient system!).

On a very old system, the BIOS may not be able to automatically detect certain newer drives, and in that case you'd need to set up the drive manually in the BIOS Setup by entering its CHS values and selecting all its various settings. This is becoming a non-issue as time goes by, however. Recall that ATA-1, which came out in 1988, introduced the ability for a drive to report its settings to BIOS, so any computer made after 1988 probably has a Detect IDE utility in its BIOS.

Should you need to set up a drive manually in BIOS Setup, or are just interested in exploring the settings on an FYI basis, the following are some of the key settings:

IDE Controller   This is usually set to Both, which enables both EIDE controllers on the motherboard. You can set it to Primary or Secondary to enable one or the other to free up an Interrupt Request (IRQ). If you're installing a new drive on a hitherto-unused EIDE controller and it doesn't work, check to make sure both are enabled.

LBA Mode   Enables/disables LBA, explained in Chapter 8, "Hard Disk Drive Overview and Terminology." There may be just Enable/Disable, or there may be three settings: CHS, Large, and LBA. LBA is nearly always the right choice for modern drives.

Hard Disk Pre-Delay   This is the amount of time that the system pauses at startup before it tries to read from the hard disk. It allows the hard disk the time to get up and spinning. It's useful for booting from an older hard disk.

TIP   If a system won't cold-boot but it will warm-boot, increasing the hard disk pre-delay might help. That's because with a cold boot, the drives are spinning up from a dead stop, and may need a little more time to get going than is being provided.

Multi-Sector Transfers   This specifies how many sectors are in a block that moves from hard disk to memory. Use the setting recommended in the drive's specifications. Any disk that supports multisector transfer these days should also support autodetection, so you'd seldom if ever need to set this manually.

Ultra DMA   This can be disabled or set to Mode 0, 1, or 2. Again, let the drive's autoconfiguration be your guide here. Drives that support Ultra DMA almost certainly support autodetection of their settings.

SMART   Remember from the discussion of ATA-3 that this is a monitoring capability that helps predict impending hard disk problems. Again, any drive that supports it will also support autodetection of the proper setting.

Troubleshooting Drive Installation

The following is the process I go through when installing a new drive. Work through this process to make sure your drive is working correctly:

1. Make sure all connectors are snug and all jumpers are set correctly.

2. Boot the system and watch the text scrolling by to see if the new drive is mentioned. If it is, great. You're done for now.

3. If you didn't see a message about the new drive being present, reboot and enter BIOS Setup. The exact keystroke for doing this varies, but an on-screen message will guide you—perhaps something like *Press F1 for Setup*.

4. In BIOS Setup, make sure that the EIDE channel (primary or secondary) is enabled, and make sure that the position in which the drive is installed (primary or secondary on that channel) is set to Auto.

5. If there's a Detect IDE utility built into BIOS, run it.

6. If the BIOS found the drive, great. You're done for now. If not, keep going.

7. Reboot the PC with the new BIOS settings, and look again for a message showing that it was detected. If you see one, you're done. If not, keep going.

8. Recheck the ribbon cable connectors to make sure that the red stripe is with pin 1 on both ends of all cables.

9. Recheck the power supply connectors to each drive to make sure they're snug. Try a different power connector if one is available.

10. Recheck the jumper settings on all drives.

11. Reboot with the palm of your hand on the flat surface of the drive. Do you feel any vibration? If so, it's spinning and the drive is physically okay; if not, the drive may be bad.

12. Try a different ribbon cable.

13. Try the drive in a different PC.

If those steps don't make the drive work, you've probably got yourself a bad drive; return it for replacement/refund.

Assuming that you're able to get the BIOS to recognize the new drive, you're ready for the next step: partitioning and formatting the drive. That's the subject of Chapter 12, "Partitioning, Formatting, and Managing Drives." First, though, you'll take a break from the setup process for EIDE drives look in the next chapter at the SCSI interface for hard drives.

Chapter 11

Understanding and Installing SCSI Devices

- ◆ QuickSteps: Installing a SCSI Drive
- ◆ SCSI Overview and Configuration
- ◆ SCSI-1, SCSI-2, and SCSI-3
- ◆ SCSI Physical Installation
- ◆ SCSI Software Installation
- ◆ Troubleshooting SCSI

Introduction

Small Computer System Interface (SCSI) is somewhat of the dark horse of system hardware. It's popular, especially among the enterprise crowd who use it for Redundant Array of Inexpensive Discs (RAIDs), which spread out data over multiple hard disks while making them appear to be logically a single volume, but it has always remained just behind Advanced Technology Attachment (ATA) in commonality primarily because of its higher cost and the difficulty that most people have understanding SCSI. Apple was "enlightened" for many years, having used two SCSI buses (one internal, the other external) in the vast majority of their systems. In later years, however, they too turned to the lower cost of ATA despite the somewhat weaker performance and reliability. In this chapter, you'll learn about what SCSI does, how it works, how to physically install SCSI devices, and how to set up software to support SCSI devices. Once you know that, you'll be better equipped to attack problems with SCSI.

QuickSteps: Installing a SCSI Drive

If you're in a hurry, you are in the right place. Collected here, for your convenience, are the basic steps that you will perform to install a SCSI device.

BE PREPARED

Before you start, there are some things you may need on hand. These include the following:

◆ Device's manual and other configuration information.

◆ Phillips-head screwdriver with a medium tip.

◆ Small plastic container for placing screws in. Personally, I lay out screws in a pattern so I can return them to the place I removed them. I work left to right, top to bottom. That way I can just repeat the process and get the right screw in the right hole.

◆ Antistatic wristband—though not exactly necessary for installing drives and other similar devices, it's a good idea to have one handy. It's best not to harbor any stray static electricity if you happen to touch a component that you're not working on, which is altogether possible.

◆ Hard disk drive or other SCSI device.

◆ SCSI host adapter, often referred to as a SCSI controller, if one isn't already installed in the system.

◆ Adapter kit, if needed. Not to be confused with the SCSI host adapter, an *adapter kit* refers to the hardware mounting kit used to physically mount the hard drive. You see, some systems come in small desktop cases and others in roomy tower cases. Regardless of which, check inside to see what drive bays you have free. All drives today are designed to fit either $5^1/_4$-inch or $3^1/_2$-inch bays. Most hard drives are $3^1/_2$-inch and CD-ROM, CD-R/RW, and DVD drives are $5^1/_4$-inch. If you have only a $5^1/_4$-inch bay free for that new hard disk, you'll need an adapter kit. (Those measurements, by the way, are indicative of the size of the spinning disc inside, not of the drive's outer dimensions.)

◆ Flashlight—if not required, at least recommended.

◆ Internal or external terminator, if your host adapter or SCSI device doesn't have one built in.

◆ Toenail or fingernail clippers—again, not required, but handy. These are great for cutting those hampering zip ties (those little plastic strips that bunch wires together). Just be careful not to snip a wire or two. Of course, the cutting area of nail clippers isn't very big, so there's little chance of this occurring if you pay attention.

If you went through the steps for installing an Enhanced Integrated Drive Electronics (EIDE) disk drive in Chapter 10, "Understanding and Installing ATA Drives," you'll note that I'm using pretty much the same recipe. Why? Because the installation of SCSI drives is similar to EIDE drives. The differences are in the setup and in the need to also install a SCSI host adapter card (most of the time), whereas IDE support is built into most motherboards. There are, however, some motherboards that have a SCSI bus built right in. Now, you'll get to cookin' up some SCSI stew! Follow these steps:

1. Gather the ingredients and open the case.

2. Jumper the drive as appropriate. If you intend for the drive to become an adjunct to the existing main drive, then set it to a higher SCSI ID number than the boot drive as per the drive's manual. Almost all hard disk and CD drives ship set to ID 0 or 1 by default. If you're installing a drive in an existing system, you need to ensure that you pick an ID number that isn't already in use—that includes the ID number used by the host adapter (usually 6 or 7).

3. Insert the drive into its intended bay. This may be easy, or it may be nigh impossible. I've dealt with both situations many, many times. A few of the newer budget systems can be challenging because they weren't designed to be upgraded. I've had to remove Random Access Memory (RAM), motherboard power taps, twisted cable, and other drives just to place a drive in a bay, sometimes all at once!

4. Install the SCSI host adapter board if needed. If you already have a SCSI device in the system, the new device may be able to share the same host adapter, provided it's the right type and has the right connectors on it. While you're at it, check the SCSI ID on the host adapter board just to make sure you're not setting the drive to conflict with it. If you're connecting to a SCSI interface on the motherboard, none of this is an issue.

5. Locate a SCSI cable connector on the host adapter or the motherboard. There may already be a cable connected to it; if so, look for free connectors on that cable.

6. Locate a power connector. These small, white blocks have four small holes and can be installed in only one way.

7. Cable the drive.

8. Put the screws in that secure the drive in its bay. Putting the screws in after connecting all the cables means you don't have to wedge your hand into a small space.

9. Terminate the last device on the SCSI chain if the host adapter or built-in SCSI controller doesn't provide autotermination.

10. Leave the case open, check all your cable terminal points, and attach the monitor, keyboard, and mouse. The other cool stuff can come later. Power it up. You should see the drive being identified if you mounted and configured it correctly, but there are circumstances out of your control that could cause that to not happen (there's more detail further in the chapter).

Of course, there's more to it than that. And that's why there's an entire chapter on the process and its details.

SCSI Overview

To understand how SCSI came about, you need to understand the chaos that existed in the early days of personal computers because of lack of standardization. Back in the early 1980s, there were no universal standards such as ATA, Universal Serial Bus (USB), or FireWire. Every storage device had its own proprietary controller. If you wanted to add a scanner, a hard disk, a tape backup device, and a CD-ROM drive to your computer, then you'd have to install one board into the system that would act as the interface for the scanner, another for the hard disk, one for the tape, and one for the CD-ROM drive. That meant not only four controllers, but it also meant having to *configure* four separate boards.

Most of those proprietary interface cards used a variation of a standard interface that's now known as SCSI. Designed by Shugart Associates (the people who introduced the floppy disk drive to the PC desktop), it was appropriately called the Shugart Associates Standard Interface (SASI).

Although SASI never caught on, it was modified and reappeared in the early 1990s as the proposed interface standard SCSI. Great news! There would finally be some standardization between all these proprietary storage devices and controllers so that you could use a single controller for more than one device, right?

Well, that was the idea. But the original SCSI standard (now called SCSI-1) proved to be too vague. It was possible for two devices to completely comply with the specification yet be unable to communicate with one another. During this period, SCSI earned a well-deserved reputation for being a difficult interface to work with. Sure, it was a fast, well-designed interface, but who needed the hassle? Mostly only Information Technology (IT) professionals who were willing to put up with the quirks in exchange for performance used SCSI.

Adaptec took the lead in creating a SCSI interface that could become the standard interface for all peripherals. Adaptec believed that eventually SCSI would be used for all hard drives, and they might have been right were it not for the appearance of the Integrated Drive Electronics (IDE) interface, which was inherently less expensive and less complicated. SCSI remained the interface of choice for external peripherals for a while, but then USB and FireWire came into being with their hot-pluggable Plug and Play (PnP) ease, and SCSI waned in popularity once again.

So, is SCSI going the way of the Betamax? No, not at all. Even though it costs approximately 50 percent more than the equivalent EIDE hard drive, SCSI drives still provide better data throughput than EIDE for large servers, and SCSI remains the interface of choice for servers and high-end video editing. However, Serial ATA (SATA), discussed in Chapter 10, will likely contribute to the continued dominance of ATA over SCSI in the mainstream.

Understanding SCSI requires knowing a whole new bunch of terms. I'll describe some of them in a minute, as I take you step by step through planning and configuring a SCSI installation. But next is a quick introduction to some SCSI concepts.

SCSI-1, SCSI-2, and SCSI-3

The original SCSI specification appeared in the early 1980s as a hard disk interface. It lacked agreed-upon standards, leading to a plethora of different—and incompatible—SCSI implementations. SCSI-2 made some big steps toward standardizing SCSI, improved the data transfer rate, and supported new types of devices. The original SCSI could only support eight devices (ID 0–7) per host adapter, and the host adapter itself took one of those, so in effect you were limited to seven devices per adapter. With the introduction of SCSI-2 came Wide SCSI, which supported up to 15 devices on a single SCSI cable. SCSI-3, or Ultra SCSI, increases the data transfer rate even more, increases cable lengths, and provides for simpler cable schemes. You'll see more about this later in the chapter.

Host Adapters

One nice thing about SCSI devices is that they're platform independent. SCSI devices don't know what a Macintosh, a PC, or a Sun computer is. All they know is how to communicate with a SCSI *host adapter* board that's inserted into one of those types of computers. The board then talks to the rest of the system's hardware on behalf of the SCSI device. That's where the SCSI board that you install in your system comes in. The host adapter acts as a translator that enables any SCSI device to communicate with a particular computer's bus. There are different kinds of host adapter boards, designed for different types of SCSI devices. Some are very sophisticated with their own Basic Input/Output System (BIOS) Setup programs and lots of configurable options; others are simple PnP conduits. It's important when purchasing SCSI devices to match the device's SCSI specifications with the host adapter's capabilities.

Single-Ended versus Differential SCSI

Many of the older SCSI implementations use an electronic signaling system called Single-Ended (SE) (also called unbalanced signaling). It's called *single-ended* because only one end sends—the other just receives, detecting the voltage transitions that are sent. SE SCSI systems won't work if the total length of their cables exceeds 6 meters because the signal strength isn't strong enough to overcome line noise problems. To circumvent this problem, *differential SCSI* was developed (also called balanced signaling). It uses two pairs of wires—one pair carries the original signal, and the other carries the logical opposite of that signal. The receiving device looks at the two signals and sees they're different (hence the name *differential*), and therefore it knows that the data has arrived reliably.

The original version of differential SCSI is now known as High-Voltage Differential (HVD). It could carry data up to 25 meters. However, it had a problem; it was incompatible with SE host adapters and devices. If you put an SE device on the same cable as an HVD device, you will damage the SE device. Because of this lack of backward compatibility, and the high cost of creating HVD devices and adapters, HVD never really caught on. It was implemented in the later days of SCSI-1 and also in SCSI-2, but it was removed in SCSI-3 in favor of the Low-Voltage Differential (LVD) alternative. You'll see HVD still supported in the early SCSI-3 devices (Ultra and Ultra Wide), but the switchover to LVD was complete with Ultra2 and higher.

LVD, which is a part of virtually every SCSI-3 device (Ultra2 and higher), does basically the same thing as HVD but with lower voltages (which means cheaper-to-manufacture chips). The lower voltage means that it won't damage SE devices, so they can coexist on the same cable. All LVD devices are multimode, which means that if you connect them to a cable that contains one or more SE devices, they'll function as SE, but if you connect them to an all-LVD cable, they'll use LVD instead.

The drawback of LVD is that it extends the cable maximum to only 12 meters—less than half of that of HVD. However, if you have only one device on the cable, you can use a 25-meter cable with LVD.

SCSI IDs

Because SCSI is a bus, multiple devices share it. One device is distinguished from another on the bus by its SCSI ID, a number from 0 to 7 on SCSI-1 or SCSI-2 (narrow) systems, from 0 to 15 on wide SCSI-2 or single-channel SCSI-3 systems, and from 0 to 31 on dual-channel SCSI-3 systems.

The narrow SCSI specification uses an 8-bit data bus, so I'm talking about eight wires for data. But at the same time, there needs to be a way for a signal to pass that tells which device on the chain is being addressed for each 8 bits of data. So the SCSI specification designers cleverly came up with a way of letting each wire do double duty. Each line is a SCSI ID line as well as part of the data crew. Because there are eight lines, you can have eight SCSI devices on a chain (seven plus the adapter). Wide SCSI increases the width to 16 bits, allowing up to 15 devices on the chain.

Setting a device's SCSI ID is usually accomplished via a jumper or switch, but some do it with software (especially adapters because most modern ones are entirely jumperless). As you can imagine, if two devices are set for the same SCSI ID, all heck breaks loose and neither of those devices will work.

Terminators

The electronics of SCSI require that both ends of the chain of SCSI devices contain a circuit that *terminates* the system. This stops the electrical signal at the end of the cable, preventing it from "bouncing back" down the cable and interfering with incoming data. A SCSI chain won't work unless both ends are terminated. There are a variety of termination methods and types of termination.

SE, HVD, and LVD all use different terminators. For SE, there are three terminator types: passive, active, and forced perfect.

Passive termination, the oldest and cheapest type, relies on a resistor to absorb the electricity, essentially sending it into a "black hole" where it just disappears (see Figure 11.1). If you don't speak schematic, don't sweat it: the jaggy-looking things are resistors, and the solid lines show the path of the electricity. The triangle represents the electrical ground. The main thing to notice here is that the only thing going on is resistors—there are no chips and no amplification.

FIGURE 11.1
Passive SCSI
termination

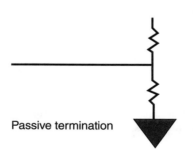

Passive termination

In contrast, *active termination* uses voltage regulators to terminate the signal. This is much more effective but also more expensive. SCSI-1 and SCSI-2 devices can use either active or passive, but SCSI-3 devices require active termination. Figure 11.2 shows a representation of active termination.

FIGURE 11.2
Active SCSI
termination

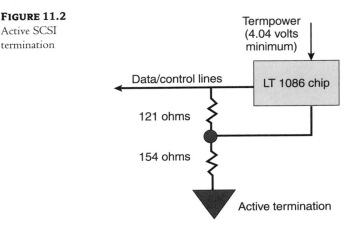

NOTE *A third kind of terminator, Forced Perfect Termination (FPT), is an improved version of the active terminator. The difference has to do with which signals the voltage regulation is performed upon. Whereas the regular active terminator terminates +5 and ground wires, the forced perfect terminator terminates the most highly active regulated voltage signals. There are several versions available, including FPT-3 and FPT-18 for 8-bit SCSI and FPT-27 bit for 16-bit SCSI. Except for in a RAID situation with special 80-pin connectors, SCSI isn't hot-pluggable like USB, FireWire, or SATA. You have to shut down the computer when adding or removing SCSI devices.*

NOTE *Yet a fourth kind is* active negation termination. *It's another improved version of the active terminator that's required on SE SCSI-3 chains. It's not common because most SCSI-3 chains use LVD, but just file it away in the back of your mind in case you ever come up against an SE SCSI-3 situation.*

LVD and HVD have their own termination methods, so if you're using LVD or HVD you simply buy the corresponding terminator. There aren't really any choices in technology among these. However, there are multimode SE/LVD terminators that can switch between the modes depending on the device configuration.

Another issue with termination is whether it's built into the device or separate. Some devices allow you to turn termination on/off with a jumper or switch. This is usually passive termination, though, so you might want to supplement it with external active termination. This involves a block-type plug that connects to the device or to the end of the cable into which the device is plugged.

WARNING *Don't let the fact that a terminator is external fool you into thinking it's automatically an active terminator because passive external terminators do exist; check the text on it or look up its model number online.*

When wide and narrow SCSI devices exist on the same chain, it works okay as long as the wide devices come first physically on the chain, followed by the narrow devices at the outer end. At the transition point between the wide and arrow is a special terminator called a *high byte terminator*. It terminates only the last eight pins of the cable, letting the first eight pins' data continue passing through.

Cables and Connectors

There are two main types of cables used in SCSI: A and P. An *A cable* is a 50-pin cable and is used with SCSI-1 and certain types of 8-bit SCSI-2 and SCSI-3. A *P cable* is 68-pin and is used with almost every other type of SCSI, including all 16-bit (wide) versions. That's the meat of what you need to know.

When I talk about A cables, I'm talking about 50 pins. However, there have been two versions over the years. The original 8-bit SCSI used a standard 50-pin Centronics connector, like the one that connects to the back of a parallel printer. SCSI-2 introduced a high-density version, called *Alternative 1*, that was smaller. It renamed the original Centronics type *Alternative 2*. The P connector is much like the high-density A connector except it has 68 pins rather than 50.

Some early SCSI-1 devices used 25-pin cables, including many of Apple's SCSI devices. You'll still see 25-pin external SCSI cables for sale today for supporting old devices that are still floating around.

There's also an 80-pin connector on some SCSI drives that are used in RAID arrays. It's called an *Alternative 4* connector, and it's a high-density Centronics type. These connectors are hot-swappable, which makes them great for RAIDs because you can take out a faulty drive without shutting down the entire RAID.

NOTE *RAIDs are commonly used in server environments to spread out data over multiple hard disks while making them appear to be logically a single volume. Depending on the RAID level (0, 1, or 5), there are different benefits and drawbacks, but let me tell you briefly about the most common one used today: RAID-5. It makes for faster disk access by spreading out data across multiple disks, and it also creates fault tolerance by using parity bits to store data. If one of the drives in the array fails, all the data it contained can be reconstructed by looking at the parity bits for it stored on the other drives. Windows 2000 and XP (both client and server versions) are able to set up and maintain RAID-5 through the Disk Management tool.*

When you see charts talking about SCSI standards on the Internet or in some other books, you may see some other cable types listed, such as B and Q. These are both obsolete, but their history is somewhat interesting.

NOTE *The B cable was an extra cable (a 68-pin cable) used with some SCSI-2 implementations to provide for higher-width data transfers. SCSI-2 was supposed to support 32-bit width, but it needed a second cable to work alongside the A cable—that is, the B cable—to achieve that. The marketplace balked, and it never really caught on. So when you see A+B in the specs for a SCSI-2 standard, that's what it's talking about. The Q cable was basically the same thing (also a 68-pin cable), except it worked in tandem with a P cable to produce 32-bit output. Note that there's a difference between the terminology used and the physical characteristics of the cable. Although Wide SCSI has more pins (68 versus 50), the cable isn't wider than a SCSI-2 cable. In fact, the SCSI-2 cable is the physically wider of the two. Wide refers to the data path—a 68-pin cable has 16 bits of data, and a SCSI-2 has only 8 bits or pins devoted to the data path.*

SCSI Technology Standards

Now you'll look in detail at each of the three major generations of SCSI technology: SCSI-1, SCSI-2, and SCSI-3. Although you'll find only SCSI-3 hardware for sale today, you may well find yourself working with the SCSI devices of yesteryear when supporting older systems so it's helpful to understand how the standards originated and built upon one another.

SCSI-1: The Beginning of a Good Idea

As I mentioned earlier, in 1981, Shugart Associates—the company that eventually became Seagate—developed a parallel block–oriented transfer protocol called SASI.

SASI became SCSI in 1984 when the American National Standards Institute's (ANSI's) X3T9 committee formalized the specification. It was later renamed SCSI-1 to differentiate between it and later SCSI-2 and SCSI-3 standards.

THE SCSI-1 INTERFACE

SCSI is an 8-bit parallel interface between a SCSI host adapter and a SCSI device. (The *8-bit* part has nothing to do—or very little to do—with your bus interface.) The standard runs at 5 megahertz (MHz), meaning a throughput of 8 bits, 5 million times a second, for a maximum data transfer rate of 5 megabytes per second (MBps).

Connector-wise, SCSI-1 uses either a 50-pin Centronics or 25-pin D-sub connector. (The latter was popular with Apple SCSI in particular.) It's limited to a maximum distance of 6 meters with SE or 12 meters with LVD.

WARNING *SCSI-1 incorporated a command set that could be only partially implemented by a vendor, but the vendor could still claim that its device was SCSI compatible. It's now obsolete, and older devices designed as SCSI-1 devices may not work with current SCSI host adapters. Even though SCSI-1 is obsolete, you'll see references to it on SCSI cable descriptions because the term is used (incorrectly) to describe the original SCSI 50-pin Centronics connector.*

SCSI-1 DEVICE TYPES

SCSI-1 defined several generic device types:

- Random access devices (hard disk)
- Sequential access devices (tapes)
- Printers
- Processors (host adapters)
- Write Once, Read Many (WORM) optical drives (the precursors to CD and DVD drives)
- Read-only random access devices

ASYNCHRONOUS AND SYNCHRONOUS SCSI

The most basic kind of data transfer over a SCSI bus is *asynchronous*. It goes something like this: the initiator requests a byte, the target responds by sending the byte over the SCSI bus, and the initiator says, "Got it," signaling to the target that the transfer went okay. That "Got it" message is called a *handshake* or an *acknowledgment.*

Each handshake takes time, however, and introduces a fair amount of overhead; in fact, one of the main failures of SCSI-1 was the amount of time spent on overhead. Therefore, in later implementations of SCSI-1, and in SCSI-2 and higher, there's a faster method whereby the initiator acknowledges big blocks of bytes, rather than every single byte. That's called *synchronous SCSI.* It's essential for high-speed disk access.

Synchronous and asynchronous SCSI devices can exist on the same host adapter. Each time a communication needs to take place, the initiating device sends out a signal asking the receiving device if it can speak synchronously. If it gets back a positive response, it initiates synchronous data transfer. If not, it transfers via asynchronous method.

NOTE   *Some SCSI-1 devices can become confused and disabled if they receive a synchronous negotiation query. Therefore, some older SCSI host adapters have an option for disabling synchronous negotiation when SCSI-1 devices are in use.*

Asynchronous versus synchronous is an issue only with SCSI-1, not with succeeding generations (which are all synchronous). Asynchronous SCSI, also known as Async, is limited to 4MBps, and synchronous SCSI, also known as Fast-5, achieves the full 5MBps of SCSI-1.

SCSI-2: The Beginning of True Standardization

SCSI-2 was being developed even prior to formalization of the SCSI-1 standard by ANSI in 1986. The point at which SCSI-1 was finalized and SCSI-2 began was rather arbitrary and had more to do with simply deciding to get the standard published on a particular date than a quantum jump in specifications. The specification simply reflects where the state of progress was at the date of publishing. SCSI-2 enhancements include new command sets, wider data paths (8 and 16 bits), and command queuing.

KINDS OF DEVICES

SCSI 2 recognizes these device types:

- Random access devices (hard disk)
- Sequential access devices (tapes)
- Printers (even though it's defined, I've never seen a SCSI printer)
- Processors (host adapters)
- WORM optical drives
- CD-ROMs and CD-R/RW (which replaced the WORM drives in the marketplace)
- Scanners
- Magneto-optical drives
- Jukeboxes (the data storage type, not the music type)
- Communications devices

FAST AND WIDE SCSI

As originally defined, SCSI is an 8-bit parallel interface between a SCSI device and a SCSI controller. Several variations have been defined in SCSI-2.

Fast SCSI doubles the data transfer rate over the existing data path. If SCSI-1 8-bit transfers are 5MBps, then Fast SCSI 8-bit transfers are 10MBps. Fast SCSI works on either SE or LVD SCSI, but if you set up Fast SCSI on SE cables, your total cable length can be only 3 meters. With LVD the maximum cable length increases to 12 meters. Fast SCSI typically uses the 50-pin A cable.

SCSI-3: Multiple High-Speed Specs

SCSI-3 isn't a single standard but a collection of standards that extends the SCSI-2 standard in various ways. There are more than a dozen major standards involved with SCSI-3, including standards for SCSI-like interfaces such as IEEE 1394 (FireWire) and Fibre Channel and support for Digital Audio Tapes (DATs) and servers. At this writing, the complete SCSI-3 specification is still not complete (Serial Attached SCSI, for example), but big pieces of it are ready to go.

The part of the SCSI-3 standard that most PC enthusiasts care about the most is SCSI Parallel Interface (SPI), which is more commonly known as Ultra SCSI. This is the part of the SCSI-3 standard that deals with SCSI hard disks.

ULTRA SCSI SPECIFICATIONS

The official SCSI-3 standards talk about various SCSI-3 types such as Fast-20, Fast-40, and so on. These numbers refer to the clock speed (in MHz) of the bus. The marketing terms for the buses, however, use the word *ultra*. So what corresponds to what?

Basically, you've got two measurements of SCSI-3 performance: the speed and the width. Speeds are measured in megahertz, and widths are measured in the number of simultaneous bits that can be sent (8 or 16; remember that 32-bit was introduced as part of the SCSI-2 standard but never implemented).

Here's the breakdown: if you don't want to read through all of this, just refer to Table 11.1, which sums it all up numerically:

- ♦ Fast-20 is the original SCSI-3. It's also called Ultra SCSI or SPI. Its narrow version (8-bit) sends data at 20MBps (that is, 1 byte per second because 8 bits is a byte, of course). It uses the standard 68-pin P cable.

- ♦ The wide version of Fast-20, also known as Ultra Wide or SPI Wide, sends data at 40BMBps (because with 16 bits you can send 2 bytes at a time).

- ♦ Fast-40, also known as Ultra2 or SPI-2, runs at 40MHz and uses LVD signaling and a smaller type of 68-pin cable called Very High Density Centronics Interconnect (VHDCI). It also supports the Single Connector Attachment (SCA-2) 80-pin cable for use on hot-swappable drive arrays.

NOTE   *You may also see VHDCI called VHDC or SCSI-5. When shopping for VHDCI cables, you may see some of them referred to as offset. When connecting a bunch of drives in a RAID, they're really close together and sometimes there's not enough room between them for the connectors to plug into the drives. An offset connector minimizes the amount of extraneous plastic on the wide surfaces of the connectors so they're more compact and work better in tight spots like that.*

◆ The wide version of Fast-40 is known as Ultra2 Wide or SPI-2 Wide, and it doubles Fast-40's throughput by adding an extra 16 bits.

◆ Fast-80DT (which stands for *Double Transition*), also known as Ultra3, Ultra160, Ultra160+, or SPI-3, runs at 40MHz, but it sends two bits of data per clock tick (one on the rising and one on the falling), so it's able to send as much data as a normal bus would at 80MHz. It's available in 16-bit width only and transfers data at up to 160MBps.

NOTE *There's an unofficial set of standards for Fast-80DT devices called Ultra160 (and an extension called Ultra160+) that drive manufacturers developed to ensure compatibility. You'll usually see Fast-80DT marketed under one of those two names.*

◆ Fast-160DT, also known as Ultra4, Ultra320, or SPI-4, is basically just like Fast-80DT except the clock speed is higher (80MHz), so it sends data twice as fast, up to 320MBps. It's more commonly used for high-performance RAIDs and servers rather than end user PCs.

TABLE 11.1: COMPARING SCSI-3 VARIANTS

OFFICIAL NAME	COMMON NAMES	SPEED	WIDTH	THROUGHPUT
Fast-20	Ultra SCSI, SPI	20MHz	8	20MBps
Fast-20/Wide	Ultra Wide, SPI Wide	20MHz	16	40MBps
Fast-40	Ultra2, SPI-2	40MHz	8	40MBps
Fast-40/Wide	Ultra2 Wide, SPI-2 Wide	40MHz	16	80MBps
Fast-80DT	Ultra3, Ultra160, Ultra160+, SPI-3	40MHz	16	160MBps
Fast-160DT	Ultra4, Ultra320, SPI-4	80MHz	16	320MBps

NOTE *Currently under development is SPI-5, also called Ultra5 or Ultra640. As you might guess from the name, it'll transfer data at up to 640MBps.*

With the higher speeds involved in Ultra SCSI, designers found that there was more sensitivity to line noise with long cables. Therefore, they halved the standard cable length limitation, and when operating under SE signaling, Ultra SCSI devices have a cable limit of only $1^{1}/_{2}$ meters when there are more than three devices on the bus (not including the host adapter). Otherwise, 3 meters is the limit. However, with HVD or LVD signaling, that increases to 12 meters.

Another side effect of the higher performance levels in Ultra SCSI is the requirement for active termination. SCSI-2 devices could use passive termination, but this isn't possible in Ultra SCSI.

OTHER SCSI-3 SPECIFICATIONS OF INTEREST

Remember when I said that SCSI-3 was more than just one set of standards? The following summarizes a few of the others.

FireWire

Almost everyone has heard of FireWire by now (also called IEEE 1394), but not everyone may realize it originated as a part of the SCSI-3 standard set. It's a technology for high-speed serial transmission between computers and external or (less commonly) internal devices such as drives, digital cameras, scanners, and backup devices. See the section in Chapter 3, "Taking Apart and Rebuilding the PC," about PC expansion buses for full details about FireWire.

NOTE *FireWire is a strong competitor to USB, the other major contender in this category. FireWire was much faster than the earlier USB standard (USB 1.1), but USB 2 leveled the playing field somewhat. The two standards will likely keep leapfrogging each other in capability and features for the next several years.*

Fibre Channel

Fibre Channel is sort of a cousin to SCSI. It's a networking technology for transferring data via fiber-optic cable (although the standard has been amended such that it also supports regular copper cable). Its main advantage is length—up to 10 kilometers with fiber optic cable! The main drawback is high price. Speeds are in the 1 to 2 Gbps range.

NOTE *The proper spelling is indeed* Fibre *in the name, not* Fiber, *which is a nod to the British roots of the technology.*

The concept of the interconnecting Fibre Channel network is called the *fabric*. Each point of connection, whether it's a hard drive or a server, is an *N-port*, also called a Node port. When Fibre Channel is used to network storage devices, it's called a Storage Area Network (SAN). Fibre Channel implementations that use a dual-loop configuration roughly analogous to Token Ring are Fibre Channel Arbitrated Loops (FC-ALs).

Clusters are groupings of servers that are accessed by a common group of clients. The main benefit of clustering is *fail-over* capabilities. If a client is running an application from a server that fails catastrophically, another server in the cluster will dynamically take over, with no disruption to the client. Some applications can also scale by using clustering technology.

Fibre Channel complements clustering technology in several ways. Because it offers the ability to add more devices than other SCSI technologies, Fibre Channel offers the capability of creating larger clusters. Further, unlike older SCSI technologies, Fibre Channel can be configured not to give priority to any node, improving cluster performance.

Serial Attached SCSI (SAS)

This is a standard for porting SCSI over to serial, much as SATA did for the ATA interface. The SCSI Trade Association began working on this in December 2001, and it's almost ready for prime time at this writing. A demo in July 2003 hosted by LSI Logic, Maxtor, and Seagate showed promise of not only greatly increased maximum cable lengths but also speeds jacked up into the heavens—1.5 gigabits per second (Gbps)!

SCSI Specifications Roundup

Whew! What a bunch of specifications I've dragged you through in the previous pages! Ready for a recap? Table 11.2 lists the specs for each of the SCSI types discussed so far in this chapter. Note that there are multiple cable maximum lengths for some depending on what type of signaling is being used.

TABLE 11.2: SCSI SPECIFICATIONS

NAME	SPEED (MHZ)	WIDTH (BITS)	TRANSFER RATE (MBPS)	MAX DEVICES	CABLE TYPE	MAX LENGTH (METERS)
SCSI-1:						
Asynchronous	5	8	4	7	A	6 (SE)/25 (HVD)
Fast-5 (Synchronous)	5	8	5	7	A	6 (SE)/25 (HVD)
SCSI-2:						
Fast-5 Wide	5	16	10	15	P	6 (SE)/25 (HVD)
Fast-10 (Fast SCSI)	10	8	10	7	A	3 (SE)/25 (HVD)
Fast-10 Wide (Fast Wide SCSI)	10	16	20	15	P	3 (SE)/25 (HVD)
SCSI-3:						
Fast-20 (Ultra SCSI)	20	8	20	7	A	1.5 or 3 (SE)/25 (HVD)
Fast-20 Wide (Ultra Wide SCSI	20	16	40	7	P	1.5 or 3 (SE)/25 (HVD)
Fast-40 (Ultra2)	40	8	40	7	A	12 (LVD)
Fast-40 Wide (Ultra2 Wide)	40	16	80	15	P	12 (LVD)
Fast-80DT (Ultra160, Ultra3)	40	16	160	15	P	12 (LVD)
Fast-160DT (Utra320, Ultra4)	80	16	320	15	P	12 (LVD)

SCSI Host Adapters

Many computers—more and more—have SCSI support right on their motherboards; others come with SCSI adapters in a slot as standard equipment. If this is true for you, then skip to the "Choosing SCSI Hardware" section. But otherwise, take a few minutes to think about the adapter that you'll choose to work with all that expensive SCSI hardware you plan to buy.

There have been host adapters for just about every type of bus that has existed, including the 8-bit (Industry Standard Architecture) ISA, 16-bit ISA, and Peripheral Component Interconnect (PCI). However, the vast majority of people buying into SCSI today will want a PCI-based adapter. Adaptec is the industry leader in SCSI adapters, so an Adaptec board is a good choice. But even if you limit yourself to a particular bus (PCI) and a particular manufacturer (Adaptec), you'll still find a dizzying array of choices. The following sections provide some selection advice.

Bus Mastering

Modern SCSI host adapters use bus mastering to improve their performance. *Bus mastering* is similar to Direct Memory Access (DMA) in that it allows the host adapter to transfer data straight into memory without having to involve the Central Processing Unit (CPU). But DMA allows only high speed transfer from peripheral to memory or memory to peripheral—not peripheral to peripheral. Bus mastering makes peripheral-to-peripheral transfers possible without CPU intervention, often leading to higher-speed data access.

Cache RAM

Some SCSI devices come with optional *cache RAM*. Although it sounds like it'll make your system really scream, what it mainly does is make the benchmarks look good. A system that provides no hurdles between the bits on the platter, and the CPU's RAM will provide pretty good data transfer rates that are real data transfer rates, not bogus ones. Bus mastering reduces the need for cache RAM on the controller.

Multichannel Host Adapters

Give a SCSI adapter an additional Input/Output (I/O) channel, and you have MultiChannel SCSI because it expands the number of I/O channels available to the system. For example, instead of a single channel supporting 15 devices, you'd have two channels, each with its own Reduced Instruction Set Computing (RISC) processor, supporting up to 30 devices.

If you need to support more than 15 devices, or if you have a slow device that's monopolizing the bus and preventing faster devices from giving you the performance you need, consider a multichannel SCSI host adapter. That way, you can put the faster devices on one channel and the devices that are slowing things down on a separate channel. There's a premium to pay in price, of course, and multichannel design is most often found in the higher-end cards such as those for Ultra320.

SCSI Standards Support

All SCSI adapters for sale today support SCSI-3 in some fashion. The question is, which variant? Ultra? Ultra Wide? Ultra2, Ultra3, or Ultra4? Match up your needs and budget—and the devices you need to connect—with the available choices. Low-cost, no-frills SCSI boards are available for $50 or so, but you can also end up spending more for a board than you did for the drive!

TIP   *One of the best ways to shop for a board is to go to the Adaptec Web site and use their Product Finder. You input your platform and operating system information and check off the various types of SCSI devices you plan to connect, and the Product Finder utility recommends a board to buy. It's not that you necessarily have to buy an Adaptec board (although they're really good), but this will help you determine the type of board you need.*

Choosing SCSI Hardware

A big part of making SCSI work is choosing the right equipment. The following sections outline some shopping tips for your SCSI adapters and devices.

Choosing the Right Host Adapter

When selecting a host adapter from a reputable manufacturer, it's not so much a question of "good" or "bad" as it's a question of whether the host adapter is appropriate for the task at hand. Consider the following factors:

◆ The host adapter must be compatible with the system's bus. For modern systems, that means it needs to be PCI. (The ISA bus is so slow that you wouldn't want a SCSI adapter running off it!) You'd be hard-pressed to find a new SCSI adapter that *wasn't* PCI these days.

◆ The host adapter must be able to support the same level of SCSI as the peripherals (SCSI-2, Ultra SCSI, Ultra2, Ultra3, Ultra4).

◆ The host adapter must have the appropriate "inny" or "outy" connectors for the devices you want to connect. Most SCSI adapters have both internal and external connectors, but some have only one or the other.

To illustrate this, you'll look at a couple of modern SCSI boards and analyze what they might be good for.

A Typical Desktop SCSI Board

I'll start with a typical SCSI host adapter designed for high-end desktop PCs (that is, a desktop PC with a SCSI hard drive and possibly some other SCSI devices). You'll look at the Adaptec 21960N, which sells for about $300 retail. It's probably more board than some people will need, but it provides a good example.

Standards-wise, it's an Ultra160 model, which you'll remember from the earlier discussion is a Fast-80DT standard that runs at 40MHz and is 16-bits wide. That means it'll be able to support both wide and narrow devices and is compatible with Ultra3 and lower devices. Its recommended usage is for high-end workstations and entry-level servers.

This board has both internal and external connectors. Its external connector is a 50-pin (narrow) Ultra SCSI. It has two internal connectors: a 50-pin connector for Ultra SCSI and a 68-pin connector that supports LVD. It's a PCI card, as should all SCSI cards be these days, so it's a 32-bit bus. It comes with a five-position 68-pin cable and a three-position 50-pin cable, both for internal use.

This board is appealing for the PC enthusiast consumer for several reasons. One is that it's a nice general-purpose board, with both 50-pin and 68-pin connectors, and both internal and external connectors. It could be used for a variety of devices, including SCSI hard drives, external SCSI tape backups, scanners, and so on.

A Typical RAID SCSI Board

Now you'll look at another—this time an Ultra320 board, the Adaptec 39320D-R board. This is a dual-channel Fast-160DT (Ultra4) board, running 16 bits at 80MHz for a total throughput of

320MBps with the dual channels. Its recommended application is mid-level servers and RAIDs. This board retails for about $400.

Because it's a dual-channel board, it supports up to 30 devices. That'll come in handy with a large RAID! It wouldn't be useful for a desktop system, but for large-scale use it's great.

Connector-wise, it has two external VHDCI connectors (68-pin) and one Ultra SCSI 68-pin internal. This tells you right away what this card is primarily designed for—it'll support an array of drives that's external to the PC in which it's installed, hence the two external connectors and only a single internal one.

The price difference between the boards is about $100, but both are fairly high-end, nice-quality boards. The main difference isn't the price but their intended purposes. One's strong point is flexibility within a desktop PC or small server; the other is focused high performance for a RAID.

Choosing the Right SCSI Peripherals

You already know a lot about SCSI peripherals (drives in particular) from the discussion earlier in the chapter. When choosing your SCSI peripherals, keep these points in mind:

◆ Each SCSI peripheral needs a compatible driver. This is a given these days because they all come with driver disks and drivers are available for download. The only time you might run into a problem would be with a very old SCSI board in a new operating system where the board's manufacturer has declined to develop a driver for the new system. For the opposite situation—a new board with an old operating system—you should be able to download the needed driver.

◆ If you put different SCSI devices on the same cable, performance of the faster one(s) may suffer. Make sure you know the SCSI standard to which a device conforms.

◆ Make sure you match the peripherals to the capabilities of the host adapter as much as possible. Performance will be limited to the lowest common denominator that both can support.

◆ Some devices have optional built-in termination, which is probably passive termination (but not always); others may have termination that's *not* optional (this is *very* bad, but fortunately not common), and still others don't include termination of any kind, relying instead on terminator blocks. So when choosing a device, find out how it's terminated and think about how you'll terminate it on your system. I'll discuss terminator selection shortly.

◆ If you're planning to connect more than one external device, you'll need to daisy chain them, so make sure an external SCSI device has two SCSI connectors: an "in" and an "out."

Choosing the Right SCSI Cabling

You know from your earlier reading in this chapter that there are several types of SCSI cabling, and even within types there are variations on connectors and differences between internal and external cables. I'll review and expand on that discussion.

For internal cables, you'll choose between 50-pin (A), 68-pin (P), or the less common 80-pin Alternative 4. Figures 11.3 and 11.4 show the A and P cables.

FIGURE 11.3

A 50-pin A cable

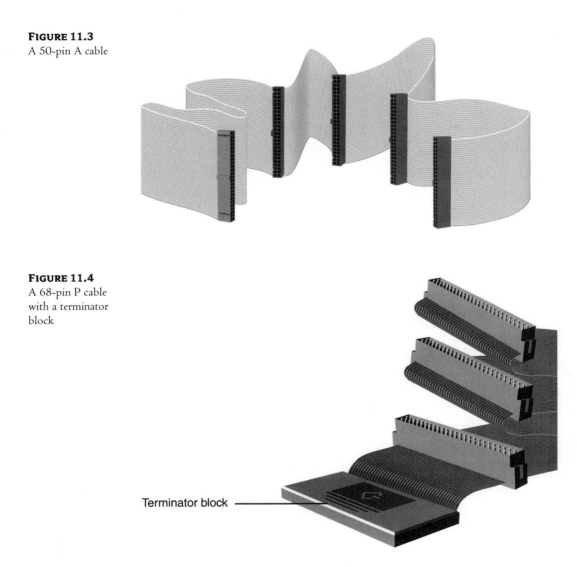

FIGURE 11.4

A 68-pin P cable
with a terminator
block

Terminator block —————

In addition, you'll choose a length. Available lengths include 26-inch, 37-inch, and 54-inch. The latter is about 1.3 meters—remember that $1^1/_2$ meters is the limit for SE SCSI-3 chains. So that's why they top out there.

NOTE   *If you've never priced SCSI cables, you'll be shocked at how much more expensive the P cables (68-pin) are than the A cables (50 pin). A good-quality internal P cable starts at about $50, and an A cable can be had for less than $10.*

Internal cables will have a certain number of connectors on them—anywhere from three (one for the host adapter and two for devices) to nine (one for the adapter and eight for devices). Generally speaking, the longer cables have more, but it's not always a completely parallel relationship.

You may have the option of buying a "terminated cable." This simply means that it comes with a terminator block (probably LVD/SE dual mode), so you don't have to buy one separately. That blocky-looking thing in Figure 11.4 is a terminator.

Cables will be rated for a specific type of SCSI, such as SCSI-2 or SCSI-3. Cables that are rated for Ultra3 or Ultra4 (that is, Ultra160 or Ultra320) will be labeled and sold as such and are usually more expensive than general SCSI-3 cables that are for Ultra SCSI and Ultra2 SCSI.

For external cables, they're commonly broken down into SCSI-1, SCSI-2, and SCSI-3 categories when for sale.

WARNING *You can use a SCSI-2 external cable with a SCSI-1 device, but not the other way around. SCSI-2 cables tend to be thicker and provide better insulation for less crosstalk, which is important as you get up into the higher speeds.*

Within those categories, you'll find different lengths (2, 3, or 6 feet) and different connectors on one or both ends. The connector categories you'll find include the following:

◆ **Centronics**: the standard 50-pin Centronics

◆ **Mini-Centronics**: the same basic shape as Centronics but smaller. This can be either 50 pin or 68 pin.

◆ **HD**: The "D" refers to the D-shaped ring around the outside of a set of pins, like on a legacy parallel or serial port connector. This can be 50 or 68 pin.

◆ **VHD**: These are the smaller versions of HD. This can be 50 or 68 pin.

Sometimes the large 50-pin Centronics is called SCSI-1 Centronics, but as you know from this chapter, that's really a misnomer. True, this connector was popular in SCSI-1, but it was also used in SCSI-2.

Pay attention to the cable's SCSI technology—1, 2, or 3, and within SCSI-3, Ultra2, Ultra3 (160), or Ultra4 (320)—and length. Connector-wise, you just shop for the cable that has the connectors to link up whatever you're trying to link up. Figure 11.5 shows a SCSI-3 to SCSI-2 cable that would be used for connecting a SCSI-2 device to a SCSI-3 host adapter, for example. It has HD connectors on both ends—one 50 and one 68.

NOTE *You may see certain external SCSI cables designed for RAID use labeled as SCSI-4. What? Did they sneak a new standard in there when you weren't looking? Nope, what this is actually referring to is Ultra4—that is, Fast-160DT or Ultra320 SCSI. It's part of the SCSI-3 standards set, as you learned earlier, but sometimes it's mislabeled as SCSI-4.*

Choosing the Right Termination

Next you need to think about how you're going to terminate your SCSI chains. You learned quite a bit about termination basics earlier in the chapter—active versus passive, internal versus external, LVD, HVD, and SE, and so on. You'll quickly review and take a look at some termination scenarios

FIGURE 11.5
External SCSI-3
to SCSI-2 cable

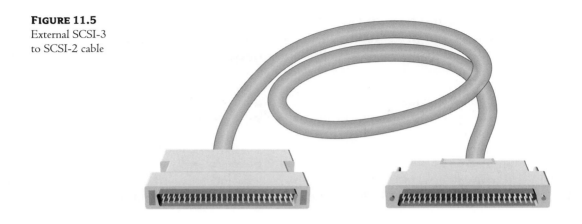

Basically, here are the choices:

◆ **SE, LVD, or HVD termination:** You've gotta match the terminator to the signaling method in use. Some terminators can do either SE or LVD.

◆ **Passive, active, or forced perfect termination:** These are an issue for SE only. Forced perfect termination is the most effective, then active, then passive. SCSI-3 requires active termination. See the discussion of these earlier in the chapter.

◆ **Built-in termination or a terminator device:** Are you going to use the built-in termination mechanism (if any) in the device or an add-on?

◆ **Internal chain or external:** There are different terminators for terminating internal SCSI chains versus external ones. If you don't want to use a device's built-in termination, you can usually disable it and add a terminator block. I say *usually* because some SCSI devices with built-in termination are boneheadedly designed without any provision for disabling termination, forcing you to not only use their built-in termination but also to place them at the end of the chain. These are few and far between anymore, though, and modern SCSI devices are never like that. Built-in termination is usually disabled via a Dual Inline Package (DIP) switch or jumper on SCSI devices or via software. Modern Adaptec adapters can be terminated and unterminated via software, for example. On an external SCSI device, there may be a switch labeled *Termination* that can be flipped on or off. *Off* means unterminated.

SCSI Installation

After all this build up and technical mumbo-jumbo, you might expect that SCSI devices are hard to install. Not at all. It's as easy as EIDE. You install the SCSI host adapter, connect the drives to it, and connect the drives to the power supply. That's pretty much it. Review the "QuickSteps: Installing a SCSI Drive" at the beginning of this chapter, and then see the following section for more details.

Installing the SCSI Host Adapter

Putting a SCSI host adapter into the PC is the same as installing any board.

Previous generations of SCSI adapters were a bit more of a pain than the average board to install because they typically required DMA channels, Interrupt Request (IRQ) levels, I/O addresses, and a Read-Only Memory (ROM) address, all of which was usually either jumper or BIOS configurable. Nowadays, however, almost everything is PnP, so you just insert the card and go. There might be a setup program to run (such as Adaptec's EZ-SCSI), but in my experience under PnP versions of Windows, it hasn't been necessary.

It's usually possible to connect SCSI devices to a host adapter both internally and externally. In Figure 11.6, which shows an Ultra Wide SCSI adapter card, you see two internal connectors (50-pin narrow and 68-pin wide) and one 68-pin external. Notice also in Figure 11.6 that there are no jumpers—this card, like all modern ones, is pure PnP with software-configurable options.

FIGURE 11.6
SCSI connectors

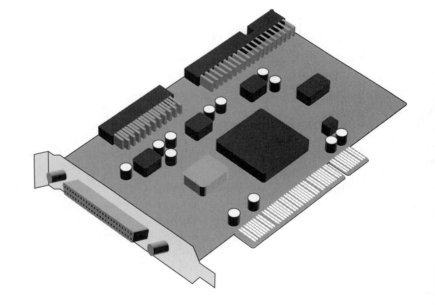

Some adapters, such as the ones shown in Figure 11.6, will allow connection to only two of the three interfaces at the same time. Thus, if you have internal wide and narrow devices, you can't use the external connector. If you think about it, that limitation makes sense because a SCSI chain is a single line of devices. Either the board itself is terminated and the chain runs out from it in one direction or the board isn't terminated (that is, it's somewhere in the middle of the chain) and the chain runs out from it in two directions. A chain doesn't run in three directions; it wouldn't be a chain anymore if it did. Therefore, if a board manufacturer wants to make all three connectors simultaneously useful, they have to do some circuit juggling inside the board. It wouldn't be that difficult if a single device were connected to the third "leg" of the chain, but remember that SCSI chains can have many devices

Assigning a SCSI ID to the Peripheral

Now consider the SCSI peripheral that you're going to install. I've talked about IDs briefly early in the chapter in a theoretical sense; these are some practical tips for setting SCSI IDs, some of which will probably be a review for you:

◆ You typically set a SCSI ID with a DIP switch, a jumper, a thumbwheel, or the like. Each device on the SCSI chain must have its own ID.

◆ The lower the SCSI ID, the higher the priority of the device. If two devices both want the bus at the same time, the one with the lower number wins. Hard drives need ID 0 or ID 1 because they should have highest priority.

◆ Don't use ID 0 or ID 1 for anything but hard disks. If you plan to boot from a SCSI hard disk, make it ID 0.

◆ Check your system documentation to see if it expects a device at a particular ID. For example, my advice to put a hard disk on ID 0 or 1 is really DOS- and Windows-based advice. Other operating systems (SCO Unix, for example) may not care about which ID you use for a boot drive. At the same time, SCO must see any CD-ROMs at ID 5.

◆ Regardless of what I recommend or what your documentation says, the only way to solve some SCSI problems is to just try different ID combinations until something works. I've never fixed anything by fiddling around with the adapter's ID, but I've fixed things by messing with other IDs.

Okay, now that I've intimidated you with all those rules about numbering, let me let you in on a little secret: SCSI is increasingly moving to PnP so you may not have to worry about SCSI ID (or termination) anymore. Newer SCSI adapters are jumperless PnP devices that can not only assign their own SCSI IDs but can also make assignments to all the other devices on the chain, as well as terminate where needed automatically. This is called SCSI Configure AutoMagically (SCAM) or SCSI Plug and Play. The catch is that it works only if all the devices on the chain are SCAM compliant. If they're not, you have to turn off SCAM mode in the adapter's software.

Enabling/Disabling SCSI Parity

On an older device, there may be a jumper, switch, or BIOS setting for SCSI parity. The short answer is: *leave it set to Parity.*

The SCSI bus can use parity signals to detect errors in transmission over the SCSI cabling. Errors can and do occur, particularly as the cable gets longer from end to end. To use SCSI parity, all devices must support it. If one device doesn't support SCSI parity in the chain, then you must disable it for all devices on the chain. However, all modern SCSI devices support parity checking so this shouldn't be an issue except in the oldest of configurations.

SCSI Daisy Chaining

Many of you will end up putting only one or two SCSI devices on a PC, but SCSI can easily support seven peripherals off a single SCSI host adapter (15 for Wide SCSI, 30 for dual channel).

Multiple devices are attached to a single SCSI host adapter via daisy chaining. With external SCSI devices, the devices typically have two SCSI ports on them—in and out. You can chain from one device to another by connecting the Out port of the first one to the In port in the next and so on. With internal SCSI devices, there's typically one long ribbon cable with multiple connectors on it, and the chain goes from device to device on this single cable.

Sample SCSI Setups

Theory is one thing, but practice is another. Now that you know about SCSI IDs and termination, you'll look at some examples.

One Internal Drive

In the setup shown in Figure 11.7, you've got just a SCSI hard disk. There must be terminators on each side, but there are only two sides, so it's simple to figure out where the terminators go. Both terminators are probably Single Inline Pin Package (SIPP) terminators. The host is ID 7, and the hard disk is ID 0; this means you're intending to boot from the hard disk.

FIGURE 11.7
SCSI setup: one internal drive

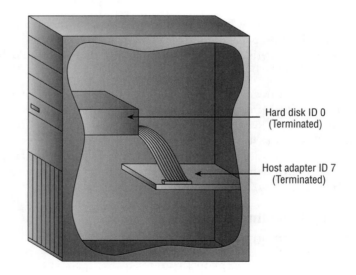

Hard disk ID 0
(Terminated)

Host adapter ID 7
(Terminated)

Two Internal Devices

Now I'll make it a bit more complex; Figure 11.8 adds an internal CD-RW. It needs a different ID, so ID 6 is good. Remember, I want to avoid the lowest ID number (ID 0) for anything other than a hard disk, and I want to have a higher number and therefore lower priority. The CD-RW isn't a high-priority device, anyway, so assigning it a higher SCSI ID versus a lower SCSI ID won't be that noticeable to a user. The hard disk terminators must be removed because the hard disk is in the middle of the chain and the CD-RW is terminated.

FIGURE 11.8
SCSI setup: two
internal devices

FIGURE 11.8
SCSI setup: two
internal devices

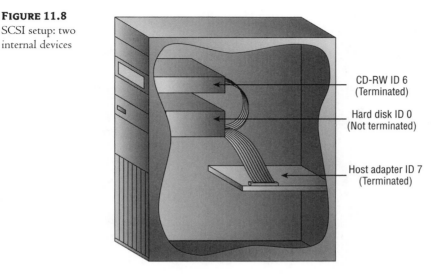

CD-RW ID 6
(Terminated)

Hard disk ID 0
(Not terminated)

Host adapter ID 7
(Terminated)

One External Device

Now let's look at the same scenario but with external devices, as shown in Figure 11.9.

FIGURE 11.9
SCSI setup: one
external device

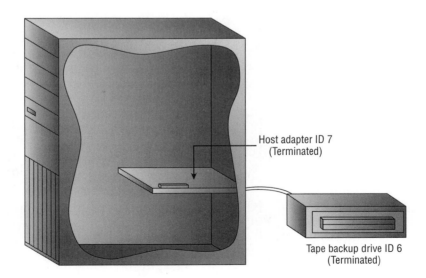

Host adapter ID 7
(Terminated)

Tape backup drive ID 6
(Terminated)

Now there's just one external device, a cartridge storage device that I won't try to boot from. I've set the tape backup drive to ID 6 and terminated it because it's the extreme end of the chain.

TWO EXTERNAL DEVICES

Continuing, I'll now add a second external device, as in Figure 11.10. This time, I'll make the CD-RW ID 5 because ID 6 is taken. The tape backup drive shouldn't be terminated because it's now in the middle of the chain and the CD-RW is terminated.

FIGURE 11.10
SCSI setup: two external devices

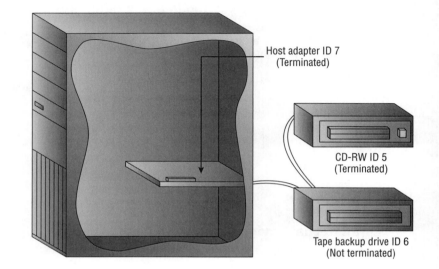

Host adapter ID 7
(Terminated)

CD-RW ID 5
(Terminated)

Tape backup drive ID 6
(Not terminated)

Internal and External Devices

For the grand finale, let's put two external devices and two internal devices on this system (see Figure 11.11).

FIGURE 11.11
SCSI setup: two external and two internal devices

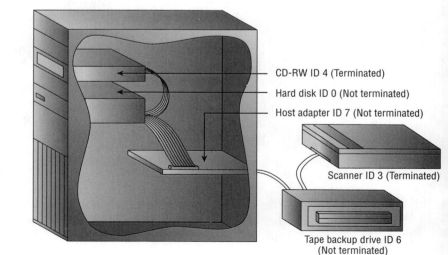

CD-RW ID 4 (Terminated)

Hard disk ID 0 (Not terminated)

Host adapter ID 7 (Not terminated)

Scanner ID 3 (Terminated)

Tape backup drive ID 6
(Not terminated)

The important point to notice about this scenario is that the termination has been removed from the host adapter because it's now (for the first time) in the middle of the chain. The external devices are attached to the external connector on the back of the SCSI host adapter, and the internal devices are hooked to the internal 50-pin header connector. Every device has a unique SCSI ID, and there's termination on the ends of the chain. Additionally, I've assigned them SCSI IDs in roughly the order that their speeds warrant—the tape backup drive is faster than the CD-RW and scanner, so you assign it a lower priority than the peripherals, resulting in equal access speeds.

SCSI Software Installation

Much of the SCSI installation process is like a normal hard disk's installation process: low-level format, partition, and high-level format. You'll learn about those in Chapter 12, "Partitioning, Formatting, and Managing Drives." Doing those things isn't much different from doing them on non-SCSI hard disks. Depending on the devices, there may be some additional software-based setup, but modern SCSI devices are PnP, so this is an issue mainly with the older stuff.

SCSI Drivers

Drivers aren't much of an issue anymore, with the wide acceptance of PnP and the ready availability of downloads from the Internet. Any devices you purchase should come with driver disks, and if they don't, you can download the drivers you need. The host adapter installs as a PnP device in Windows, and then it coordinates the communication of the various SCSI devices with the operating system.

The SCSI adapter controls the interaction of the devices with the operating system through a standard called Advanced SCSI Programming Interface (ASPI). It was developed by Adaptec as a means for standardization of SCSI device drivers. All SCSI device drivers are ASPI compatible these days, to the point where looking for a device with ASPI driver compatibility is no longer an issue.

Bootable SCSI: Onboard BIOS Support

So if the operating system (let's say Windows) needs a driver to talk to the host adapter, and the host adapter talks to the SCSI hard disk, then how can you boot from a SCSI hard disk? It seems like a chicken-and-egg conundrum, doesn't it?

The answer is that the SCSI adapter has an onboard BIOS extension that loads itself on top of the main system BIOS at boot time if you have a SCSI hard disk with an ID set to 0 or 1; this eliminates the need for the operating system to load before the drive will be recognized.

A modern adapter can detect whether a bootable SCSI hard disk exists on the chain at the proper ID, and if there isn't one, it'll not load its BIOS extension. This is good because the BIOS extension takes up some room in RAM that could be used for other things. On an older adapter you might need to set a jumper or switch to enable/disable the BIOS extension.

Troubleshooting SCSI

The SCSI of yesteryear was fraught with perils, quirks, and seemingly gratuitous incompatibilities, but with today's SCSI you'll probably encounter few problems. Here are some tips for troubleshooting:

◆ Before connecting any devices, install the SCSI adapter and make sure the operating system sees it. In Windows, go into Device Manager in the Control Panel (the System applet) and check out the adapter there. It should report that the device is working properly. If not, make sure it's physically installed correctly and that a usable driver is installed. Visit the manufacturer's Web site to download a new driver if needed.

WARNING   *Remember, except for the special 80-pin RAID situation, SCSI isn't hot-pluggable like USB, FireWire, or SATA. You have to shut down the computer when adding or removing SCSI devices.*

◆ Connect the SCSI devices one at a time, and confirm that each one works before connecting the next one. If you're having trouble with a chain containing several devices, isolate the problem by connecting each device, in turn, as the only device on the chain. If each of them works individually, then you know the problem is with relations between them.

NOTE   *If you're installing a SCSI hard drive, keep in mind that the operating system won't be able to see it until you have partitioned and formatted it. Therefore, the operating system not seeing the drive doesn't mean it isn't working. Use the host adapter's diagnostics to determine if it's working, or just look for a message scrolling by at startup that mentions it has been detected.*

◆ If a certain device won't work as an individual device on the adapter, make sure you have the right cable for it and that it's properly terminated.

◆ Make sure you're using a different ID for each device on the chain. Occasionally the ID setting mechanism on a device goes defective, such that you set one ID but it interprets it as another. So try a different ID, especially on an external device, if you're getting nowhere troubleshooting ID conflicts. One symptom of having two devices on the same ID is *phantom disks*—disks you can see but can't read or write.

◆ Watch your cable length, remembering the maximum lengths imposed by the standard you're using. Remember, it's 3 meters (or 1.5 meters for SCSI-3) for an SE chain, 12 meters for LVD, and 25 for HVD.

◆ If you have 8-bit and 16-bit devices on the same chain, make sure you use a high-byte terminator at the point where 16 switches to 8, and make sure that the 16-bit devices all are closer physically to the adapter than the 8-bit ones.

In this chapter, you learned about the SCSI standards and how to select, install, configure, and troubleshoot SCSI devices. So at this point perhaps you have a SCSI and/or EIDE or SATA hard disk physically installed and are waiting for the next step. What's the next step? Partitioning and formatting it, of course. The next chapter takes you through that process.

Chapter 12

Partitioning, Formatting, and Managing Drives

- ◆ QuickSteps: Partitioning and Formatting a Hard Disk
- ◆ Partitioning and Formatting Overview
- ◆ How to Partition and Format a Drive
- ◆ Enabling Ultra DMA Support in Windows
- ◆ Working with NTFS Compression and Encryption
- ◆ Managing Disks Under Windows 2000/XP

Introduction

Now that you've installed your hard drive, it's time to use it. If you were to boot up successfully into Windows at this point and go to My Computer, you wouldn't see your drive. To use your hard drive, you must first perform two tasks: partitioning and formatting.

Partitioning a drive means that you tell the computer how the space on the physical hard drive should be apportioned to various drive letters (*logical drives*). You might choose to make your entire hard drive one big C: drive or to break up the physical drive into C:, D:, and E:, or more. Partitioning also chooses a file storage system, such as FAT16, FAT32, or NT File System (NTFS).

Formatting your hard drive structures the drive's space into well-organized compartments that can store data. Each logical drive you create with partitioning must be formatted separately.

Take special care when using the information in this chapter on existing drives. Partitioning and formatting are "destructive" activities—they erase whatever data was stored on the disk. Once you've partitioned and formatted a drive, you'll seldom need to redo it. You'll more likely find yourself partitioning and formatting a new drive you're adding to your system or reformatting after some catastrophe (such as a virus) has trashed everything on the disk, leaving nothing left to lose.

QuickSteps: Partitioning and Formatting a Hard Disk

Whenever you install a new hard drive in your system, you'll need to partition and format it before it'll accept files. The procedure for this is radically different in MS-DOS and Windows 9*x* (that is, Windows 95, 98, and Me) than it is under NT-based Windows versions (such as 2000 and XP), so there are two separate QuickSteps sets that follow.

MS-DOS and Windows 95/98/Me

BE PREPARED

Before you start, there are some things you'll need to perform the operation. These include the following:

- ◆ A way of getting to a command prompt. If you're installing on a new PC without a hard disk, you'll need a bootable floppy disk or CD. On a system that already has MS-DOS or Windows 9*x* installed, you can boot to a command prompt.

- ◆ Access to the command-line utilities FDISK and FORMAT. If you're booting from a startup floppy that was made using Windows 9*x*, those utilities are already there. MS-DOS also includes them. Under Windows 9*x* installed on a hard disk, they're in the `C:\Windows\Command` folder.

To partition and format a hard disk in MS-DOS and Windows 9*x*, follow these steps:

1. Boot from the startup floppy if the PC doesn't already have an operating system installed.

   Alternatively, boot the operating system to a command prompt. Press F8 while booting to access a menu of boot options. If you can't boot to a command prompt, open a command prompt window after the operating system starts.

2. Run FDISK, and partition the new hard disk.

3. Exit FDISK, and reboot your computer. (You *must* reboot!)

4. Format each new partition you created in step 2. You can do this with the FORMAT command-line utility, or you can format it from within Windows if available (right-click the drive icon and choose Format).

5. Reboot your computer (which isn't necessary in all cases but is usually a good thing to do).

If you need to install your operating system, during your last reboot make sure you boot from the Setup disk required for installing your operating system. If you're partitioning and formatting a secondary drive, you won't need to reinstall your operating system.

TIP   As an alternative to FDISK and FORMAT, some hard drive manufacturers include a floppy disk with your new hard drive. This disk contains one or more utilities that help you partition and format your new hard drive quickly and easily.

Windows NT/2000/XP

If you're planning to install an NT-based Windows version on a new hard disk, you don't need the following steps because the Setup program will do it for you. Therefore, the following steps are only for setting up additional hard disks in a system that already has an NT-based Windows version installed:

1. Open Disk Management. To get to it from the Control Panel, choose Administrative Tools ➢ Computer Management ➢ Disk Management.

2. Right-click the unpartitioned space, and choose Create Partition. Then walk through the wizard that appears.

3. The wizard will ask you if you want to format the partition. Choose to do so. It'll give you a choice of file systems.

Partitioning and Formatting Overview

There are three steps involved in preparing a disk drive for use:

Low-level formatting   This happens at the factory where the disk drive is manufactured. It defines the drive's Cylinder/Head/Sector (CHS) values (see Chapter 8, "Hard Disk Drive Overview and Terminology"), dividing up the blank surface of the disk into cylinders, heads, and sectors.

Partitioning   This carves up the drive logically into one or more partitions, each of which can hold one or more logical drive letters. Partitioning is what allows a single physical disk to appear as multiple drive letters. Even if you want only a single drive letter, you must still partition.

High-Level formatting   This prepares a logical drive for use with a particular operating system by establishing a file system on the drive that the operating system can support. Common file systems are FAT16, FAT32, NTFS 4, and NTFS 5.

NOTE   *Because high-level formatting is the only kind of formatting that most end users will ever do, it has come to be synonymous with the more general term* formatting. *In this book, if I don't specifically say* low-level formatting, *you can assume I mean the high-level kind.*

You don't need to worry about low-level formatting—it's done for you long before you ever open the drive's packaging. You can partition and perform (high-level) formatting with several utilities that are either built into the operating system or separately purchased.

Before getting started with the hands-on stuff, I'll tell you a little bit about each of the three steps from a conceptual standpoint. Trust me—it'll help later.

Low-Level Formatting

Hard disks start out as blank platters with no logical organization. As part of the post-manufacturing process, the drive makers tell the built-in drive controller how many cylinders, heads, and sectors it should "see" on those blank platters, both from a physical and logical standpoint. As a consequence, when you buy a hard disk drive, it has a label on it that reports its capacity and its CHS values. I covered those values and how they're derived in detail in Chapter 8. Low-level formatting also maps any physically defective sectors on the drive and does some other fine-tuning.

If you're thinking, "Wow, it sounds like I shouldn't mess with that!" you're absolutely right. A typical disk drive shouldn't need to be low-level formatted again after it leaves the factory. If you ever decide you need to do it, make sure you get a utility that's specifically designed for that particular brand of hard disk because all the manufacturers do it a little differently.

NOTE   *In the distant past, Small Computer System Interface (SCSI) drives sometimes would come from the factory without low-level formatting, but this no longer is the case. Should you ever need to low-level format a really old SCSI drive, you'll find a utility to do so built into the SCSI adapter's Basic Input/Output System (BIOS). As you boot your PC, you'll see a message on-screen about the SCSI adapter, telling you to press some certain key to enter its Setup. Do so and then hunt around for the low-level hard disk formatting utility. But again, and I stress this strongly: don't low-level format a drive if you don't have to do so. Try partitioning it first, and if that goes okay, just forget you ever heard about low-level formatting. New SCSI drives you buy today will not require this.*

Partitioning

Partitioning a drive tells it how to allocate the available physical space among various drive letters. You must partition a drive in order to use it. Even if you're going to give the drive all to a single drive letter, you've still got to create a partition.

Most people prefer to allocate all the physical space to a single hard disk letter (C:). However, different situations may call for different configurations. For example, suppose you had a single 160 gigabyte (GB) drive. You could create two partitions, C: and D:, install Windows 98 on one of them, and install Windows XP, or Linux, or some other operating system on the other. Then each time you started the PC, you could choose which drive to work from (and which operating system to load). This is called *dual booting* or *multibooting*, and it's possible only with multiple partitions. (Well, technically there are ways around that. Some utilities do allow you to put more than one OS on a partition. But it's a really bad idea.)

NOTE *With Windows 2000, XP, and 2003, you don't need to partition manually because it's taken care of as part of the OS Setup if the drive is not already partitioned.*

WHY DO WE PARTITION?

In 1983, IBM ushered in the era of hard disks in PCs with their XT. Nobody was surprised that IBM would introduce a computer with a hard disk, but we *were* surprised by the large size of the hard disk—*10 megabytes (MB)*! Back then, that was huge.

Why did IBM put the large drive on the XT? Because they wanted to sell *two* operating systems—DOS and Xenix. For those who don't know, Xenix was a Unix variant that Microsoft was pushing for a while, back before they started selling OS/2 and *way* before Windows.

The problem with having both DOS and Xenix on the system was that they didn't get along. Xenix didn't like DOS's file format and vice versa. So the only way to get them to peacefully coexist was to draw a line down the center of the drive, saying in effect, "This is *yours*, DOS, and that's *yours*, Xenix."

So Microsoft and IBM came up with a way to essentially split a 10MB drive into two 5MB drives. (Or a 6MB and a 4MB drive, or a 2MB and an 8MB, or whatever; you can chop up a drive just about any way you like.) That "chopping up" became known as *partitioning*.

Partitioning into multiple logical drives is no longer common on the average end user PC for two reasons.

One reason is that most people stick with a single operating system, so they don't need separate partitions to support multiple operating systems. The other reason is that the limitations on a logical drive's size that some earlier operating system versions imposed are no longer in effect in the latest versions. Just like with the BIOS limitations on drive size that you learned about in Chapter 8, operating systems have also had various limitations over the years that have subsequently been broken through in later releases. For example, MS-DOS 3.3 had a limit of 32MB per logical drive. (Can you imagine?) MS-DOS 6.0 and Windows 95 had a limit of 2.1GB. The last several versions of Windows, however, have provided *large disk support*, which allows you to have a single drive letter with up to 2 terabytes (TB), which is the next step above a gigabyte, so there's virtually no operating system limitation anymore. Given that, people partition their drives into multiple logical drives for two main reasons: to support multiple operating systems or as a matter of personal organizational preference.

MASTER BOOT RECORD

The information about the disk partitions contained on a physical disk is stored in its Master Boot Record (MBR), which is contained in the first sector (0), first cylinder (0), and first head (0). When you work with a partitioning utility, it writes its data to this area of the disk. A disk has only one MBR regardless of the number of partitions or logical drives it has.

TIP   Some viruses target a disk's MBR, and occasionally the MBR on a disk just goes kablooey for no apparent reason. Therefore, I make it a practice to back up my MBR often. I use the Ranish Partition Manager (RPM) utility, which you can find at `www.ranish.com/part`*.*

PRIMARY AND EXTENDED PARTITIONS

Each hard disk has at least one primary partition. If you want to make the entire physical disk into one logical drive, you create a single primary partition out of all the space. A primary partition can be assigned only one drive letter.

Got space left on the disk that isn't being used by the primary partition? You can make an extended partition out of it. An extended partition isn't bootable, but it does have the capability of supporting multiple drive letters—*logical drives*. So, suppose you want three drive letters for a single hard disk. You could create a primary partition, which would become logical drive C:. You could then create an extended partition, which you'd then in turn carve up into two logical drives: the D: and E: drives.

NOTE   You can have more than one primary partition per physical drive (up to four), but the FDISK utility allows only one primary partition per physical disk. If you use the Disk Management tool in NT-based Windows versions or a third-party partitioning utility, it's possible to have more than one primary, but it isn't necessary in most cases. The main reason you'd want a partition to be primary rather than extended would be to be able to boot from it; Windows' multiboot capabilities enable you to boot from the primary partition and then transfer the focus to an operating system installed on an extended partition, so not every partition containing an operating system needs to be a primary one.

LOGICAL DRIVES

A lot of people tend to use the terms *partition* and *logical drive* to mean the same thing, but that's not quite correct. A logical drive appears as a drive letter in the operating system. There can be a one-to-one or one-to-many relationship between logical drives and partitions. A primary partition, as I said, can have only one logical drive. An extended partition can have one or more. Another name for a logical drive is a *volume*.

NOTE   In the official Microsoft Windows documentation, the meaning of the term volume *is inconsistent. Sometimes it means, generically, any logical drive. Other times it specifically refers to a logical drive on a dynamic disk. I'll explain dynamic disks later in this chapter.*

ACTIVE PARTITION

The *active partition* is the bootable one on a disk. Only a primary partition can be active, and only one partition can be active at a time.

You might be thinking at this point, "Wait a minute, I want to be able to multiboot between different operating systems. How can I do that if only one partition is bootable?"

The answer there is that the bootable partition isn't necessarily the one where the operating system resides that you want to load. In a multiboot situation, you start the PC, and the active partition starts the boot process and loads a menu from which you can choose the operating system you want. At that point it transfers the boot process to the logical drive containing the chosen operating system's startup files. So, yes, you're booting from only one partition—the active one—even though you're choosing your operating system and each operating system is stored on a different drive.

LARGE DISK SUPPORT

This is an issue only if you use FDISK for your partitioning needs, but it's worth mentioning. If you use a version of FDISK that comes with Windows 98 or higher, it asks if you want to enable Large Disk Support. If you specify Yes, it'll allow you to create partitions of larger than 2.1GB (which you almost certainly do want!). The other function that this setting does isn't so obvious: when the time comes to do the high-level formatting of the drive (discussed next) with the FORMAT command, if you set up the partitions with Large Disk Support turned on, the partitions will be formatted using the FAT32 file system. If you set them up with it turned off, they'll be formatted using FAT16.

High-Level Formatting and File Systems

High-level formatting establishes all the "housekeeping" needed for the disk to be addressed by the operating system. This means it sets the disk up for a particular file system. For example, FAT16 and FAT32 formatting involves creating a volume boot sector, a root directory, and a File Allocation Table (FAT)—actually, two identical copies of the FAT, for safety's sake.

NOTE *The volume boot sector is sort of like the MBR, but it's for this logical drive only. It's a reserved area that contains information about the logical drive's properties. It also contains the first file needed for booting if the disk is bootable. (For DOS and Windows 9x, for example, that would be IO.SYS.)*

High-level formatting doesn't physically manipulate each sector on the disk; it creates a table of contents for the disk. When you reformat a disk that has been formatted before, it doesn't wipe out all the data on the disk—it just wipes out the table of contents so that the disk appears to be empty. That's why it's possible in some cases to use utilities to recover the contents of a disk that has been formatted accidentally.

When a disk is formatted for the first time, each sector is checked for physical bad spots, and any bad spots are marked as "off limits." This prevents data from being written to bad spots. That's why it takes some time for formatting to occur (anywhere from a few minutes to an hour depending on the drive size and computer speed). The formatting process isn't actually changing the physical surface of the disk—it's just checking it.

If you're reformatting a disk that has already been formatted, you can specify a "quick" format. Through Windows' FORMAT interface, there's a Quick check box; at the command prompt with the FORMAT command, you can add the /Q switch. This disables the check for bad sectors, making the formatting process nearly instantaneous.

MORE ABOUT "BAD SPOTS"

You may have heard it said that reformatting a hard disk gets rid of bad areas on the disk. This isn't true—not exactly, anyway.

When you format a disk, it runs a cursory check of the disk for bad areas and excludes those bad areas from the formatting. However, not all bad areas are immediately obvious.

Bad areas have either *hard* errors or *soft* errors. Hard errors are problems in the disk surface itself, where it can't record data at all. Manufacturing defects and later abuse cause hard errors. Soft errors, in contrast, occur when some data has faded on the disk to the point where it can't be read. Disk repair programs, such as ScanDisk and Norton Utilities, fix such errors by retrieving any data they can from the area and then cordoning off the area as "bad" so it won't be used again (kind of like a hazardous waste dump for your system).

When you reformat a drive, it retains its memory of the hard errors but not the soft ones. Some of the areas previously marked as bad therefore appear to be good again, but any data you copy to them may be in peril.

Therefore, after reformatting a hard disk that contained many errors, you should run a disk utility such as ScanDisk in its Thorough mode to comprehensively check each physical sector of the disk for errors. Scan-Disk comes free with Windows 95/98/Me. An equivalent utility called Check Disk is available in NT versions of Windows (on the Tools tab in the Properties box for the drive).

When you format a drive, a file system is chosen. With the FORMAT command, a file system is chosen for you automatically (although you can override the choice with the /FS switch, as I'll explain later.) You indirectly do choose the file system that the FORMAT command automatically selects, at least in DOS/Windows 9x situations, by enabling Large Disk Support in FDISK or not. When formatting through Windows 2000/XP Setup or through Disk Management in Windows 2000/XP, you get a drop-down list of possible file systems from which to choose.

The choice of file systems is important because not all operating systems support all file systems. You won't be able to choose an unsupported file system when formatting through your operating system, but keep in mind that you might move a disk to another system that uses a different operating system at some point, or you might upgrade or switch the whole system to a different operating system.

Table 12.1 lists the most common Microsoft desktop operating system versions and file systems they can support.

NOTE There are server versions of all the NT-based Windows versions, but I don't mention them explicitly in the book every time I mention the various versions. For Windows NT 4, it's Windows NT 4 Server. For Windows 2000, it's Windows 2000 Server. For Windows XP Professional, it's Windows 2003. (Gotcha! I'll bet you thought I was going to say Windows XP Server, didn't you? But in that case the server and the desktop versions have different names.) I mention this because the server versions' file systems work the same as the desktop versions, so what's true for Windows 2000 Professional, for example, is also true for Windows 2000 Server, at least as far as talking about partitioning, formatting, and file systems.

FAT16

FAT16 is the original file system for hard disks under MS-DOS and the original version of Windows 95. It continues to be in use in situations where compatibility with one of those two operating systems is required, but its limitations on volume size make it unsuitable for use in modern systems.

TABLE 12.1: OPERATING SYSTEM SUPPORT FOR FILE SYSTEMS

OPERATING SYSTEM	FAT16	FAT32	NTFS 4	NTFS 5
MS-DOS	Yes	No	No	No
Windows 95 (Original, A, B)	Yes	No	No	No
Windows 95C (OSR2)	Yes	Yes	No	No
Windows 98	Yes	Yes	No	No
Windows 98 Second Edition (SE)	Yes	Yes	No	No
Windows Me	Yes	Yes	No	No
Windows NT 4 Workstation	Yes	No	Yes	No
Windows 2000 Professional	Yes	Yes	No*	Yes
Windows XP Professional/Home Edition	Yes	Yes	No*	Yes

* You convert NTFS 4 file systems to NTFS 5 as part of the Setup when upgrading from Windows NT 4 to Windows 2000 or XP.

As its name implies, FAT16 is a 16-bit file system. That means it must keep track of all the addressable areas on the drive using a 16-bit binary number. That's a big problem because it limits the system to 65,536 unique addresses! If each sector were addressed individually, that would mean the hard disk could be a maximum of 33,462,272 bytes in size, or about 33.5MB. No way! The situation is ameliorated considerably by the use of *clusters* (also called *allocation units*), which I'll talk about later in the chapter, that allow multiple sectors to be addressed as a single group. But even at the maximum cluster size of 64 sectors, FAT16 is still limited to 2.1GB per volume. And as you'll learn later in the "Clusters" section, having clusters that large also cause efficiency problems with the drive too, so it's less than optimal.

TIP   One minor benefit of FAT16 is that it works with some of the older disk compression utilities, such as DriveSpace in MS-DOS and Windows 95. FAT32 doesn't.

A key feature of FAT16 (and FAT32) is the use of a FAT to keep track of what's stored on the disk, including the filenames, file attributes, and physical locations on the disk of each piece of the file. Yes, I know, it's confusing to have almost the same acronym referring to the file system and the file allocation table, but there you have it.

FAT32

FAT32, as the name implies, is a 32-bit version of FAT. By increasing the number of bits used to address clusters (allocation units), it allows larger drive sizes to be supported. There can be more than 250 million addressable units. Assuming a 4KB cluster size, that comes out to 2TB of data.

If you have a choice between FAT16 and FAT32 on your operating system, by all means pick FAT32. Windows 98 comes with a FAT32 Converter utility that you can use to switch over a drive without losing its contents.

Windows 95 OSR2 also supported FAT32, but it didn't provide a converter. So in Windows 95, you can delete a partition, re-create it with large disk support, and then reformat it as FAT32, but you lose all your data.

WARNING *One place to stick with FAT16 is in a dual-boot situation between Windows 9x and Windows NT 4. As you saw in Table 12.1, Windows NT 4 doesn't support FAT32.*

However, today a more common scenario is to have a choice between FAT32 and NTFS, which is the case if you have Windows 2000 or XP (or Windows Server 2003). NTFS is so much better in so many ways (which I'll tell you about in the next section) that the only practical reason to maintain a FAT32 file system is for backward compatibility. For example, suppose you have a hard disk where you store data files on a multiboot system, where sometimes you boot Windows 98 and sometimes Windows XP. You need that hard disk to be accessible under both operating systems, so it needs to stay a FAT32 volume.

NTFS 4

NTFS was developed specifically for Windows NT and is now used as an advanced file system for Windows NT/2000/XP networks. NTFS isn't compatible with Windows 9*x* versions; you can use it only if you're running NT 4 Workstation, Windows 2000 Professional, or Windows XP or a corresponding server version.

You might encounter two versions of NTFS. NTFS 4 is used under Windows NT 4 Workstation and Server. NTFS 5 is used in Windows 2000 and higher (workstation and server versions). They're not the same file system, and they're not compatible with one another. When you upgrade from NT 4, the Setup program converts existing NTFS 4 volumes to NTFS 5 with no provision for going back. Therefore, if you need to share a volume dual booting between Windows NT 4 and Windows 2000 or XP, you'd need that volume to use a file system that both can support: FAT16.

NOTE *Would anyone still encounter Windows NT 4 these days? It's even older than Windows 95—that is to say, it's coming up on a decade old. But it was extremely popular in the corporate world in its heyday, and a lot of small businesses haven't upgraded their computers in way too long. NT Server 4 is a solid server operating system that runs on what today seems like laughably old and weak hardware, and if someone is running a business on a tight budget, that makes it look pretty good. So if you're out there in the field doing PC technical support, there's a good chance you'll occasionally see NT 4 still in use as a client, as a server, or as both.*

These are the main benefits of NTFS (both 4 and 5):

◆ Enhanced security permissions at the individual file level for local users as well as network users

◆ Support for file compression to save disk space

◆ Support for disk spanning (that is, using multiple physical disks as a single logical volume)

◆ Logging of activities in case the system goes down

Unlike FAT16 and FAT32, which are based on the idea of using FATs, NTFS is based on a tree structure. All objects, files, and directories are treated as files, or records. The Master File Table

(MFT) is the key component. The first record, or file, of the MFT is named $Mft. It's essentially an index of all the files that reside in an NTFS volume. All filenames and their time stamps are included in the $Mft file. If a file is too large to fit all of its attributes in the $Mft file, the rest of the file is allocated to other parts of the volume. This approach provides more direct means of access to files than FAT and, therefore, faster access to directories and files.

The MFT also includes a mirror file, which provides a backup index of the entire volume in case the MFT is corrupted. Another difference between NTFS and FAT is that NTFS keeps track of all changes to the disk structure. Should your system go down, NTFS is able to recover the disk back to the last valid disk structure. Note that this tracking feature can't recover user data that wasn't already written to the disk at the time a failure occurs, but the volume's structure will remain intact.

NOTE   *NTFS 4 actually predates FAT32, in that it was developed for Windows NT 4 Workstation, which predated not only the FAT32-aware versions of Windows, but even preceded the original Windows 95 itself. Microsoft knew that a better file system was needed, but they also knew that for consumers, backward compatibility was as important as performance, so that's why they chose FAT16 (and later FAT32) for the "consumer" versions of Windows (9x), leaving NTFS for the corporate versions only. It wasn't until Windows XP came out that the corporate and consumer Windows platforms merged into a single product that supports all the file systems.*

NTFS 5

NTFS 5 is an improved and enhanced version of NTFS 4. It made its debut as part Windows 2000, and with it came these features:

Disk quotas   Administrators can define the amount of space that a user is allocated. Additionally, they can define whether it's merely tracked or actually enforced by the server.

Encryption   NTFS can encrypt and decrypt data in real time as it's read and written to disk.

Reparse points   Applications are now able to capture data from open processes and perform operations on them before returning them to the system object that requested the initial operation. One of the key uses of this is for data redirection, allowing one object (that is, directory or file) to look like another. Hmmm, very Unix-like, that.

Sparse files   This is a rather interesting capability. NTFS can allocate space to a file but allow that file to remain very small. Okay, that's vague. VMWare, a virtual machine emulator, actually does this. If you tell VMWare that you want a 10GB drive container (a file that acts like a drive) to install Windows 98SE on your Windows XP computer and use up only 800MB of that space, that's all it'll use. If you look at the drive container file on your hard drive, it will say it's only 800MB. But if you look at the disk properties from within Windows 98SE inside VMWare, it reports itself as 10GB.

NTFS 5 does this a little differently. First, when an object asks for space, the system checks to see whether there's room. If there is, system then *soft allocates* that space to the object. The object can load anything into that space it wants, even if it's only a fraction of what it asked to be allocated. The system then keeps track of how much is being used of that soft allocation and will use the unused space as needed. Once the object starts asking for its requested space, the system makes sure it's available. This is a very useful feature.

USN journaling   USN journaling offers a more finely tuned way of tracking every minute operation transacted on the system. (USN stands for *Update Sequence Number*, the format that defines and localizes file system changes.) In NTFS 4, there were a finite number of operations and activities that NT could monitor before it got swamped. Journaling is a way for the system to account for itself; each operation must log its activity as opposed to the system watching everything getting done and recording it. Journaling is much less intensive for the Central Processing Unit (CPU) than *not* journaling; event traps are resource hogs.

Clusters

Okay, I've been promising for several pages now that I'd explain more about clusters, so here it is in a nutshell (get it? Nut…clusters…like the cereal…oh, never mind).

On a hard disk, each sector is 512 bytes, but almost every file you store on a disk is larger than that. Therefore, it doesn't make much sense to have each sector be individually addressable. That would just be too much overhead! Therefore, a file system addresses multiple sectors as a group. These groups are called *clusters*, and different file systems use different cluster sizes depending on the size of the volume. Microsoft calls clusters *allocation units*.

There's an efficiency versus space trade-off in cluster size. The larger the cluster, the more efficiently the file system can address the clusters because there are fewer of them to track. On the other hand, the larger the cluster, the more wasted space there may be on the drive. For example, suppose I'm working with a cluster size of 16 sectors. That's about 8KB. If I store a 2KB file in that cluster, there are 6KB remaining empty that can't be used for anything else.

There's also an issue of drive size involving clusters and the number of bytes that a particular file system has available for addressing them. For example, FAT16 uses 16-byte numbers to keep track of the individual clusters. That means there can be a maximum of 65,536 clusters on a FAT16-formatted volume. So, at maximum cluster size (64 sectors per cluster), the largest that a FAT16 drive can be is 2.1GB. This isn't really an issue with FAT32 and NTFS drives, which use 32-bit addressing for the clusters.

So what's the right answer here? What's the "correct" cluster size that balances these two factors? The answer is that there's no perfect cluster size in every situation. Depending on the drive size, different cluster sizes offer the right balance.

Luckily, the operating systems decide on the cluster size for you when you format the drive, so you don't have to worry about this unless you want to change to a different size. (You can, as I'll explain later in the chapter when you actually get down to doing it.) Table 12.2 lists the rules that Microsoft operating systems use when selecting a cluster size during high-level formatting.

TABLE 12.2: DEFAULT CLUSTER SIZES

DRIVE CAPACITY	CLUSTER SIZE
FAT16:	
16MB–127MB	4 sectors (2KB)
128MB–255MB	8 sectors (4KB)
256MB–511MB	16 sectors (8KB)

TABLE 12.2: DEFAULT CLUSTER SIZES *(continued)*

DRIVE CAPACITY	CLUSTER SIZE
512MB–1GB	32 sectors (16KB)
1GB–2GB	64 sectors (32KB)
FAT32:	
Less than 260MB	1 sector (512 bytes)
260MB–6GB	8 sectors (4KB)
6GB–16GB	16 sectors (8KB)
16GB–32GB	32 sectors (16KB)
32GB and higher	64 sectors (32KB)
NTFS:	
Less than 512MB	1 sector (512 bytes)
512MB–1GB	2 sectors (1KB)
More than 1GB	4 sectors (2KB)

How to Partition and Format a Drive

I've talked about the *why*, now you'll look at the *how* of partitioning and formatting.

But first, I'll point out that all of the drive manufacturers offer some sort of utility that will do all of the steps in the following sections for you, or at least the partitioning part. Most often, it'll be on a floppy disk or CD that comes with the drive. If you have a drive that came in an Original Equipment Manufacturer (OEM) pack (as opposed to a retail package), you can download the needed utility from the drive manufacturer's Web site.

WARNING *The utilities that come with hard disks will install a BIOS extension if needed for an old PC to support a larger hard disk than its BIOS would normally allow (see Chapter 8). However, these BIOS extensions can be quirky, so it's better to upgrade the PC's BIOS before installing the new drive if possible.*

There are many ways of partitioning and formatting, and your choices depend on your operating system version.

Under Windows 2000/XP, you can partition and format from a command line using the Recovery Console. (Get to it by booting from the Windows CD and then choosing to repair.) However, this is seldom necessary because these Windows versions provide full partitioning and formatting services as part of Windows Setup. If you already have Windows 2000/XP installed, you can use the Disk Management utility to partition/format additional disks.

If you don't have Windows installed yet, running Setup will handle the partitioning and formatting for you, and if you do have Windows installed, then you've got the Disk Management utility at your disposal. That should cover 99.9 percent of your Windows 2000/XP formatting needs. You can file that Recovery Console stuff in the back of your mind for "what if" future use, but you probably won't need it.

Under MS-DOS and Windows 95, 98, and Me, you'll need to partition and format the disk before you install the operating system. (A few versions of MS-DOS included partitioning and formatting in their Setup, but don't count on it.) To get the ball rolling, you need to boot from a startup floppy disk that contains, at the minimum, FDISK and FORMAT. After you've finished formatting the disk, you can then access the Setup program from the Windows CD to install it.

TIP *To create a startup floppy, use the utility in the Add/Remove Programs applet in the Control Panel in Windows 95, 98, or Me. If at all possible, use 98 or Me rather than Windows 95 because the resulting startup floppy disk will contain generic real-mode CD-ROM drivers that will make it possible for you to access your Windows Setup CD from the command prompt.*

If you already have MS-DOS or Windows 9*x* installed and are adding a second hard disk, you'll need to do the partitioning with FDISK from a command prompt, but then you can do the formatting either from the command prompt with the FORMAT command or from within Windows. I'll show you all these methods later in the chapter.

There's a whole category of disk partitioning/formatting third-party utilities available, and you're free to use one of those products if you like instead of following along with the material in the following sections. Some of the benefits of these utilities include the ability to adjust partition size without losing everything on the partition, the ability to switch between file systems without losing everything, and an easy-to-use GUI interface even if you don't have an operating system installed yet. The best known of these is PartitionMagic (by PowerQuest). System Commander (by VCOM) is another top-notch tool with similar capabilities. You may also want to check out Disk Manager (by Ontrack), Drive Up (by FWB Software), and EZ Drive (by MicroHouse), all of which offer a full range of partitioning and formatting utilities.

Partitioning with FDISK

You'll use FDISK to partition a drive under MS-DOS or Windows 9*x* (that is, 95, 98, or Me). It's not your only choice—you could use a third-party utility such as PartitionMagic—but FDISK is free with the operating system. Its main limitations are that it allows only one primary partition, and it sets up only DOS partitions. If you have a partition with a logical drive that uses either of the NTFS file system versions, FDISK will see it as a "non-DOS" partition and won't be able to do anything with it except ignore it or delete it.

NOTE *For NT-based Windows versions, the equivalent command-line utility is DISKPART, which can be run from the Recovery Console. You may have little reason to use it, though, because if Windows is installed you can format through a GUI interface through Disk Management and if Windows is not installed you can format through Windows Setup.*

What's this about a DOS partition? Did you think you were done with MS-DOS once and for all? Well, sort of. But Windows 9*x* uses the same file system type that MS-DOS did—FAT—so as far as FDISK is concerned, these are DOS partitions. Don't let the name throw you.

Besides setting up the partition(s) on a new drive, there are other scenarios when you might want to use FDISK. For example, suppose you have a hard disk that currently has a primary and an extended partition, each of which has a single logical drive on it. You might want to delete everything and start over with a single primary partition that encompasses 100 percent of the available space. Or you might want to go the other way, and take a system with a single logical drive and break it up into multiple logical drives.

STARTING FDISK

If you're working with an additional hard disk (not the system's main one), you can find FDISK in the C:\Windows\Command folder on your main hard disk. It's okay to run FDISK from a command prompt shell within Windows, as long as you don't tamper with the primary partition or with the logical drive that contains Windows. You can also start up a Windows 9x PC in a command prompt mode by pressing F8 at startup when you see the "Starting Windows" message and then selecting a command prompt startup from the menu that appears.

If you're setting up the primary hard disk on a PC, you'll need to boot from a startup disk that contains FDISK. If you create an emergency startup disk using Windows 95/98/Me, FDISK will automatically be included on it.

Once you get to a command prompt, do the following:

1. At a command prompt, type **FDISK** and press Enter. If the location containing FDISK isn't in the path statement, you may need to type the full path.

2. If your copy of FDISK came from Windows 95B or higher, you'll see a warning like the one in Figure 12.1 asking whether you want to enable large disk support. Choose *Y* and press Enter.

   The main FDISK Options menu appears. Figure 12.2 shows the one from the version of FDISK that comes with Windows 98. Other versions are similar.

   Figure 12.2 shows a system with multiple physical hard disks, hence option 5, Change Current Fixed Disk Drive. You won't see that if you have only one hard disk. Make sure you're working with the correct disk before making any changes, especially deleting any partitions!

3. First, check for existing partitions by choosing option 4, Display Partition Information. Existing partition information appears, if any. Figure 12.3 shows a 2GB primary partition and a 2GB extended. If you see a message that there are no partitions, then you know you'll be starting from scratch.

FIGURE 12.1

Enable large disk support if prompted.

```
Your computer has a disk larger than 512 MB. This version of Windows
includes improved support for large disks, resulting in more efficient
use of disk space on large drives, and allowing disks over 2 GB to be
formatted as a single drive.

IMPORTANT: If you enable large disk support and create any new drives on this
disk, you will not be able to access the new drive(s) using other operating
systems, including some versions of Windows 95 and Windows NT, as well as
earlier versions of Windows and MS-DOS. In addition, disk utilities that
were not designed explicitly for the FAT32 file system will not be able
to work with this disk. If you need to access this disk with other operating
systems or older disk utilities, do not enable large drive support.

Do you wish to enable large disk support (Y/N)...........? [Y]
```

FIGURE 12.2

The FDISK
Options menu

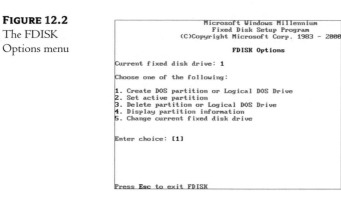

```
                    Microsoft Windows Millennium
                      Fixed Disk Setup Program
                  (C)Copyright Microsoft Corp. 1983 - 2000

                            FDISK Options

Current fixed disk drive: 1

Choose one of the following:

1. Create DOS partition or Logical DOS Drive
2. Set active partition
3. Delete partition or Logical DOS Drive
4. Display partition information
5. Change current fixed disk drive


Enter choice: [1]




Press Esc to exit FDISK
```

NOTE   Why the small disk sizes in these figures? You'll almost certainly be working with much larger physical disks and partition sizes than shown in these figures. I'm using small partitions here because I'm using a program called VMWare to create these figures, and I have a "virtual PC" set up with a 4GB hard disk for the examples. So don't feel sorry for me thinking that my poor old PC has only a 4GB hard disk! It works the same way no matter what your partition sizes are.

FIGURE 12.3

This drive has one
primary and one ex-
tended partition.

```
                    Display Partition Information

Current fixed disk drive: 1

Partition  Status    Type    Volume Label   Mbytes   System    Usage
   C: 1               PRI DOS                 2000    UNKNOWN    49%
      2        A      EXT DOS                 2094               51%



Total disk space is  4095 Mbytes (1 Mbyte = 1048576 bytes)


The Extended DOS Partition contains Logical DOS Drives.
Do you want to display the logical drive information (Y/N)......?[Y]




Press Esc to return to FDISK Options
```

DELETING EXISTING PARTITIONS

If you see from examining the partition information that the partitions are already set up the way you want them, you don't have to repartition. You can simply press Esc until you exit the program and then format the drive(s) with the existing partitions.

   If you see no existing partitions, you can skip to the "Creating a Primary Partition" section later in the chapter.

What, you're still here? That must mean you found existing partitions and you want to delete them. You must delete things in a certain order: first the logical drives on the extended partition, then the extended partition itself, and then finally the primary partition:

1. Press Esc to go back to the FDISK Options menu.

2. Choose option 3, Delete Partition or Logical DOS Drive. The menu shown in Figure 12.4 appears.

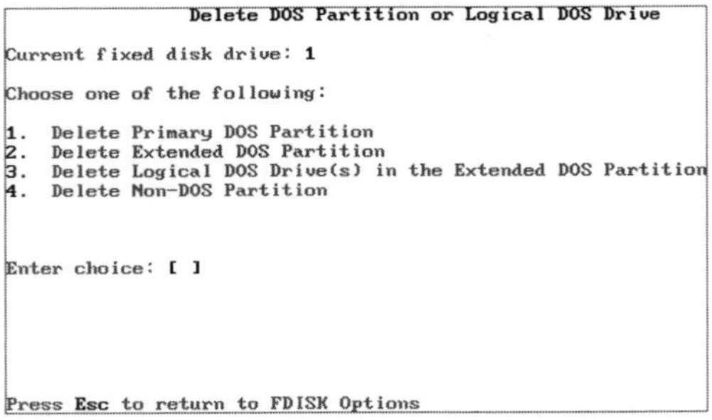

FIGURE 12.4

Delete partitions and logical drives from this menu.

```
                    Delete DOS Partition or Logical DOS Drive

Current fixed disk drive: 1

Choose one of the following:

1.  Delete Primary DOS Partition
2.  Delete Extended DOS Partition
3.  Delete Logical DOS Drive(s) in the Extended DOS Partition
4.  Delete Non-DOS Partition


Enter choice: [ ]




Press Esc to return to FDISK Options
```

3. If you have logical drives on an extended partition, delete them first. To do so, choose option 3 from Figure 12.4's menu. You can't delete an extended partition until you've first removed its logical drives. Figure 12.5 shows a logical drive being removed.

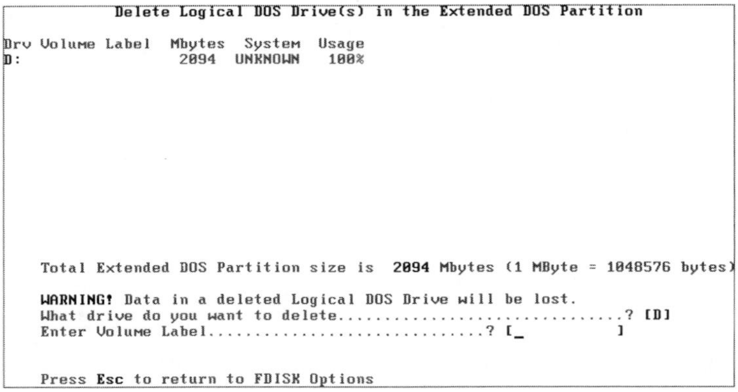

FIGURE 12.5

Delete any unwanted logical drives from the extended partition.

```
              Delete Logical DOS Drive(s) in the Extended DOS Partition

Drv Volume Label   Mbytes   System   Usage
D:                   2094   UNKNOWN   100%







    Total Extended DOS Partition size is  2094 Mbytes (1 MByte = 1048576 bytes)

    WARNING! Data in a deleted Logical DOS Drive will be lost.
    What drive do you want to delete...............................? [D]
    Enter Volume Label.............................? [_           ]

    Press Esc to return to FDISK Options
```

4. After you've deleted all the logical drives from the extended partition, delete the extended partition itself (option 2). You can't delete the primary partition until you've first deleted the extended one.

5. After you've deleted the extended partition, delete the primary partition (option 1).

6. After deleting all partitions, press Esc to return to the main FDISK Options menu (shown in Figure 12.2).

CREATING A PRIMARY PARTITION

Assuming you've deleted all the partitions, or there weren't any to begin with, you'll start by creating a new primary DOS partition:

1. From the main FDISK Options menu (shown in Figure 12.2), choose option 1, Create DOS Partition or Logical DOS Drive. The Create DOS Partition or Logical DOS Drive menu appears. See Figure 12.6.

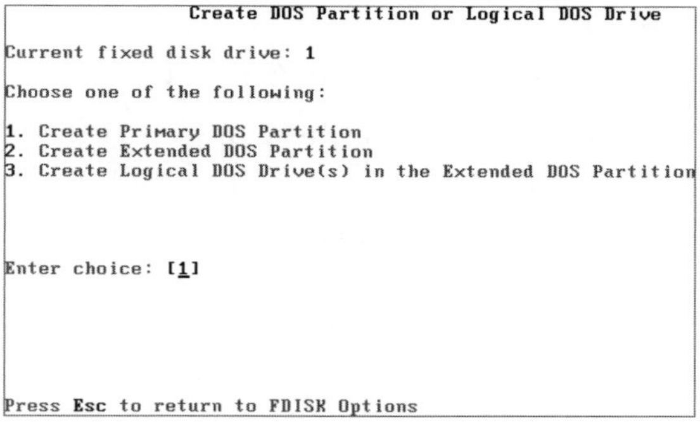

FIGURE 12.6

This menu allows the creation of partitions and logical drives.

```
                    Create DOS Partition or Logical DOS Drive
Current fixed disk drive: 1

Choose one of the following:

1. Create Primary DOS Partition
2. Create Extended DOS Partition
3. Create Logical DOS Drive(s) in the Extended DOS Partition



Enter choice: [1]




Press Esc to return to FDISK Options
```

2. Choose option 1, Create Primary DOS Partition.

3. When asked whether you want to use the maximum available size for the primary DOS partition, choose Yes or No. If you want to follow along with this example, where you create three logical drives, you'd choose No.

4. If you answered No, enter the amount of space, either in megabytes or in percentage, that you want to allocate to the primary DOS partition (that is, the C: drive). See Figure 12.7.

5. Press Esc to return to the FDISK Options menu.

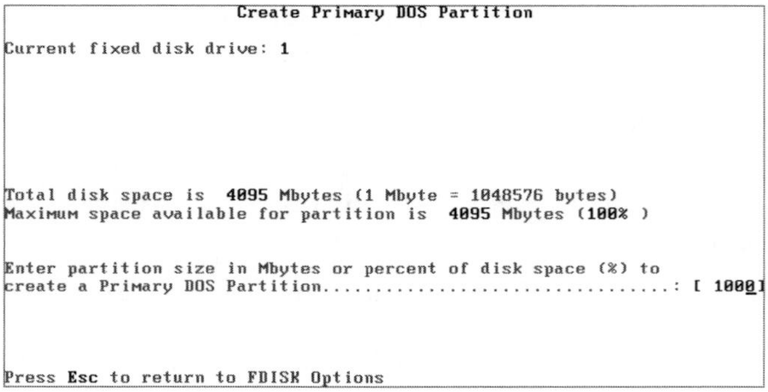

FIGURE 12.7

Allocate space for the primary DOS partition.

```
                      Create Primary DOS Partition
Current fixed disk drive: 1




Total disk space is  4095 Mbytes (1 Mbyte = 1048576 bytes)
Maximum space available for partition is  4095 Mbytes (100% )

Enter partition size in Mbytes or percent of disk space (%) to
create a Primary DOS Partition..................................: [ 1000]


Press Esc to return to FDISK Options
```

CREATING AN EXTENDED PARTITION AND ITS LOGICAL DRIVES

Next, set up your extended partition using the remaining space (assuming you have any left). If you allocated all the space for the primary partition, skip this:

1. From the FDISK Options menu, choose 1, Create DOS Partition or Logical DOS Drive.

2. Choose option 2, Create Extended DOS Partition.

3. Leave the default setting for the extended partition size, which is all of the remaining space, and press Enter.

4. Press Esc to verify the drive integrity. You're then prompted to define the logical drives.

5. Enter the amount of space to allocate to the next logical drive (D:). Leave the default to use the entire extended partition for it, or enter a specific size in megabytes or percentage. See Figure 12.8.

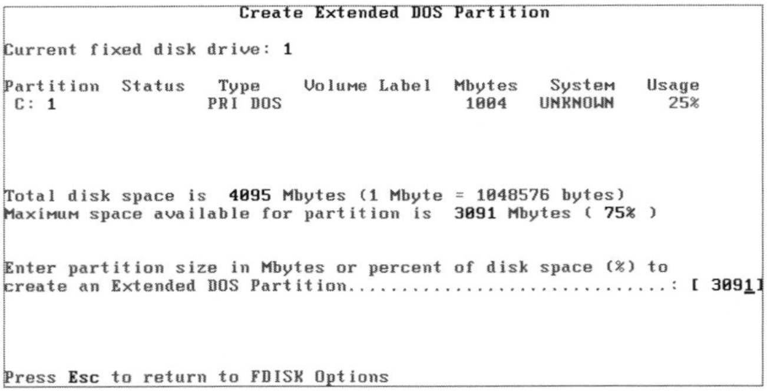

FIGURE 12.8

Allocate space for the extended DOS partition.

```
                        Create Extended DOS Partition

Current fixed disk drive: 1

Partition  Status    Type    Volume Label  Mbytes   System    Usage
  C: 1               PRI DOS                 1004    UNKNOWN     25%




Total disk space is  4095 Mbytes (1 Mbyte = 1048576 bytes)
Maximum space available for partition is  3091 Mbytes ( 75% )

Enter partition size in Mbytes or percent of disk space (%) to
create an Extended DOS Partition.............................: [ 3091]




Press Esc to return to FDISK Options
```

6. Enter the amount of space for the next logical drive (E:). For this example, leave the default to use all remaining space on the drive.

7. When you're finished assigning all the remaining space on the extended partition, press Esc to return to the FDISK Options menu.

SETTING THE ACTIVE PARTITION

If you chose not to allocate all the space to the primary partition, it isn't set automatically as the active partition. It must be active in order to be bootable. To make your primary partition active, do the following:

1. From the FDISK Options menu, choose option 2, Set Active Partition.

2. Type 1 to select partition 1 as the active one (see Figure 12.9), and press Enter.

3. Press Esc to return to the FDISK Options menu.

FIGURE 12.9
Set up the active
partition.

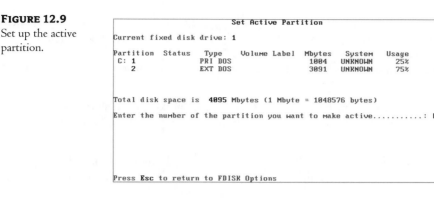

4. You're done partitioning! Press Esc to exit FDISK, and then reboot your PC.

WARNING   Don't attempt to format or use the drives until you've rebooted. That's because drive letter assignments change when you partition, and the drive letters you booted with will no longer be correct.

Formatting with FORMAT

While on the subject of MS-DOS and Windows 9*x*, I'll continue by discussing the command-line FORMAT command. You can use this command with any Windows version at a command prompt, but many people prefer the Windows Graphical User Interface (GUI) version of formatting whenever it's available. Consequently, FORMAT is used mostly when initially setting up new hard disks from a boot floppy.

CHECKING FOR EXISTING FORMATTING

You'll want to make sure you have the right drive letter if there are existing other hard disks on the system because formatting wipes out everything that a drive contains data-wise. Just to make sure, do the following:

1. Type the drive letter and a colon, and press Enter. The command prompt changes to that drive letter.

2. Type **DIR** and press Enter. If the drive is already formatted, a list of files appears, or File Not Found appears if there are no files on it yet. If the drive isn't formatted, an error appears.

If the drive is already formatted, you don't need to format it again. (However, formatting can be an easy way of deleting everything on the drive in a hurry.)

FORMATTING THE DRIVE

If the drive isn't already formatted, and you've proved it by performing the previous steps, then you're ready to format. The basic syntax is FORMAT *drive:* where *drive* is the drive letter. For example:

```
FORMAT C:
```

You'll see a warning that formatting will erase everything; type **Y** to continue. Then just let it do its thing! It takes awhile, anywhere from several minutes to an hour or more. Larger drives and slower computers take longer.

There are more options available, of course. To see the full array, type **FORMAT /?** at the command prompt. Here are a few options and switches:

/Q This does a quick format that bypasses the checking for disk errors. This one isn't possible if the drive has never been formatted before. (Not only would it be a bad idea, but the operating system won't let you.)

/A:size This lets you specify the allocation unit (cluster) size manually, in bytes (8KB and less) or kilobytes (16KB and higher). However, Microsoft strongly recommends the default sizes for general use.

/FS:filesystem This lets you specify the file system: FAT, FAT32, or NTFS. In this, FAT refers to FAT16. This switch is available only under certain Windows versions, and the file systems are limited to the ones that the operating system version supports.

/V:label This allows you to specify a volume label for the drive. A volume label is text that'll appear under the drive's icon in Windows or when you display its contents with a DIR command at a command prompt. For example, if you have several hard disks, you might want to assign volume labels such as Main, Backup, or Data to keep them straight.

NOTE *You can assign a volume label at any time through the drive's properties in Windows or with the VOL command at a prompt. Also, if you don't use the /V:label switch in your FORMAT command (where label is the label you want), you will be prompted for a volume label when the formatting process is complete.*

Formatting from My Computer

After you've partitioned a drive, you'll have access to its drive letters from within the My Computer window in Windows. (If it hasn't been partitioned yet, the only way to access it from within Windows is with the Disk Management tool, discussed later in the chapter.)

Your first clue that a drive hasn't been formatted yet is that you double-click its icon in My Computer and you get an error message. Depending on the Windows version, the message may offer to format the drive for you. You can click Yes at that point, or you can cancel the error box and do the following:

1. Right-click the drive icon, and choose Format. The Format Local Disk dialog box opens, as shown in Figure 12.10.

2. Choose any formatting options desired, such as Quick Format or a volume label.

3. Click Start. A dialog box appears, warning you that you'll lose all the data on it; click OK to continue.

4. Wait for the formatting to finish, and at the Results box at the end, click Close.

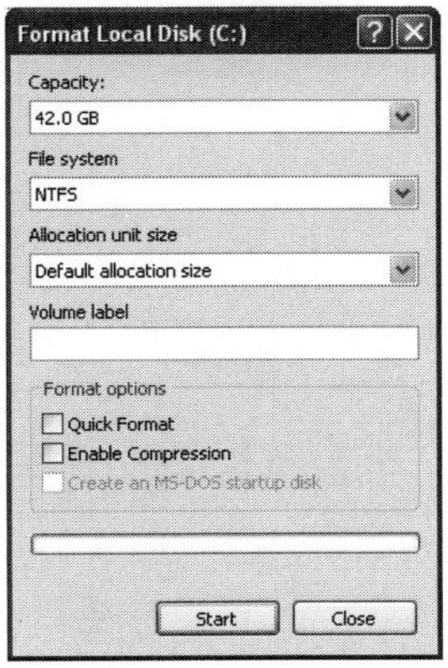

FIGURE 12.10

Format the new drive using the Format Local Disk dialog box.

After formatting the disk, it's a good idea to check it for errors with ScanDisk (Windows 9*x* and MS-DOS) or CHKDSK (Windows NT/2000/XP). I'll explain these tools in Chapter 13, "Protecting and Maintaining Hard Disks."

Partitioning While Running Windows Setup

Suppose you're installing a new hard disk on a system that you'll be installing Windows NT 4, 2000, or XP on. You're in luck; you don't have to do any special presetup work. The Setup programs for those Windows versions will offer to do the appropriate partitioning and formatting for you automatically and will even give you choices for sizes and file systems. It's pretty self-explanatory; you just follow the prompts. Figure 12.11 shows the Windows XP Setup program asking what partitions I want, for example. If I wanted a single partition containing Windows XP, I'd just press Enter at this point. If I wanted multiple partitions, I'd press C to create a partition. (I'm going to make a primary and extended partition here so I'll have something to show you in the next section, about disk management.)

FIGURE 12.11

Windows Setup has its own partitioning utility.

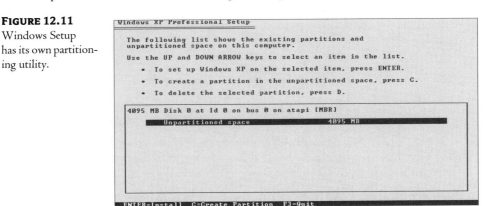

Figure 12.12 shows things after the partition(s) have been created, where it's asking what formatting I want for them. Notice the "quick" options; just as explained before, these skip the physical check of the disk for bad sectors.

FIGURE 12.12
Windows Setup has its own formatting utility too.

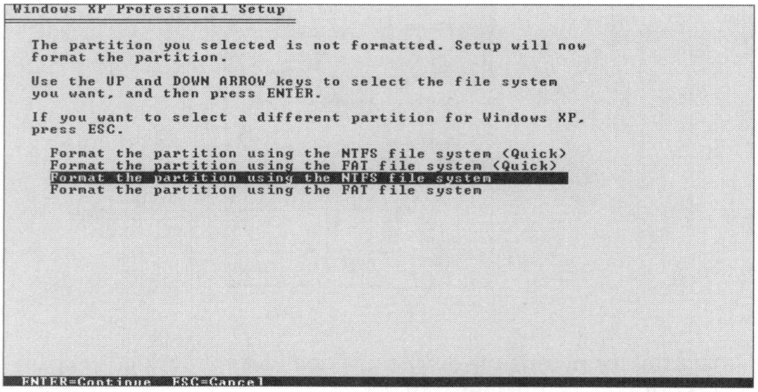

Partitioning and Formatting with Disk Management

If you're installing a second drive into a system that already has an NT-based Windows version installed, you can do the partitioning and formatting through the Disk Management utility. It's pretty slick! Versions of it have existed since Windows NT 4, but newer operating systems (2000/XP) have more options; I'll show you the XP version in this section. The same utility also exists in all the server versions (including the new one, Windows 2003).

Through Disk Management you can partition drives, create logical drives (on extended partitions), and format them separately if you want, but you can also do all of those things at once, which is the easier way to go. In each case, a wizard guides you through it. The wizards are very clear and self-explanatory, especially for people such as yourself who have a thorough grounding in the concepts behind partitioning and formatting. (See, aren't you glad you read that stuff in the first half of the chapter?)

To open Disk Management, follow these steps:

1. From the Control Panel, open the Administrative Tools folder.

2. Double-click the Computer Management icon. A Computer Management window opens. One of the items in its folder tree at the left is Disk Management.

3. Click Disk Management. After a brief pause, information about the system's hard disks and CD drives (including the DVD drive) appears, as in Figure 12.13. The Windows XP version is shown here; the 2000 and Server 2003 versions are similar.

Notice in Figure 12.13 that there are two physical hard disks. One of them has half of it devoted to an NTFS 5 partition containing Windows XP itself (the system partition). The other half is an extended partition. Half of the extended partition is occupied by a FAT32 drive, and the other half is "free," which means there's room for another logical drive.

FIGURE 12.13
Disk Management provides a graphical interface for partitioning and formatting.

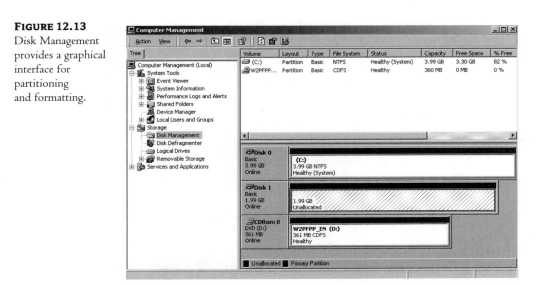

The second physical disk has all its space indicated as Unallocated. That means there are no partitions on it yet.

NOTE   When you open Disk Management in Windows XP after installing a new, empty hard disk with no partitions, an Initialize and Convert Wizard will run, offering to convert the empty disk to a dynamic disk. I'll explain more about dynamic disks shortly. They're supposedly great things, but they have given me nothing but headaches personally. If you click Cancel to avoid running that wizard, the physical disk will appear with the status of Not Initialized. That means you haven't yet chosen whether it will be a Basic or Dynamic disk. Right-click it, choose Initialize, and then choose OK to make it a basic disk. All of this will make a lot more sense after you read the "Converting to Dynamic Disks" section later in the chapter.

To create a partition out of unallocated space, right-click that space and choose Create Partition. Then just follow the prompts of the New Partition Wizard that appears. You can choose to create a primary or extended partition and to create logical drives on it. Figure 12.14 shows an example. If you choose to create an extended partition, you'll be prompted to create the logical drives on it as well.

As part of the New Partition Wizard, it asks about formatting the partition. If you choose do to so, you're prompted for a file system, allocation unit size, and volume label. You can also choose a quick format, and if you've selected NTFS as the file system, you can enable file and folder compression for the entire drive. (You'll learn more about compression later in the chapter.) Figure 12.15 shows the choices.

If you choose not to format the drive as part of the New Partition Wizard, you can format it later from within Disk Management (or My Computer, as explained earlier). To do it from Disk Management, right-click the partition and choose Format and use the Format Local Disk dialog box that appears.

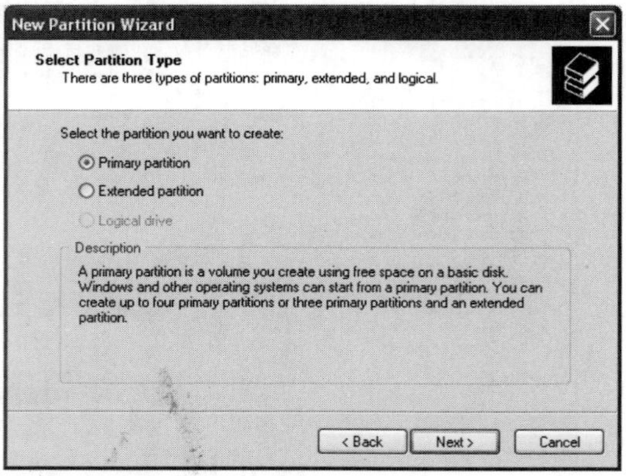

FIGURE 12.14
The New Partition
Wizard walks you
through the process
of partitioning a
new disk.

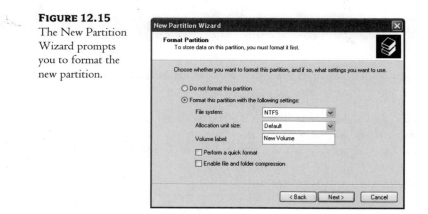

FIGURE 12.15
The New Partition
Wizard prompts
you to format the
new partition.

NOTE *It's worth saying again that the figures in this chapter show extremely small drive capacities; your drive capacities will be tens or hundreds of times the size shown here. I'm making these tiny drives using VMWare just to show you the examples.*

Partitioning and Formatting Troubleshooting Tips

Having some trouble with partitioning or formatting? Here are some possible places to start troubleshooting:

◆ If your computer won't boot from your hard drive, run FDISK again and check to see that the partition you have your operating system installed on is set as the active partition. Remember, the primary partition isn't automatically set to be active if you create more than one partition on a physical disk under FDISK.

◆ If FDISK reports a disk size that isn't true, your BIOS may be incorrectly identifying your hard drive. Run your BIOS Setup program and confirm that the size is correct, and then try running FDISK again. Return to Chapter 8 to read about the various limitations and how to overcome them.

◆ A very old BIOS may not recognize hard disks bigger than 8.4GB for the reasons described in Chapter 8. If this is the case, you should update the BIOS if possible. You may have to use special software provided by your hard disk manufacturer to fool your BIOS into recognizing the disk. This is becoming less of an issue as time goes by and the antique systems with this limitation are being taken out of service.

◆ Formatting a disk doesn't automatically make it bootable. If you've started the PC with a bootable floppy made with Windows 9x, use the /S switch with the FORMAT command (FORMAT C: /S) to copy the system files needed to boot along with the formatting operation. If you've already formatted and just need to copy the system files, use the SYS command, as in SYS C:.

Enabling Ultra DMA Support in Windows

Back in Chapters 8 and 10, I mentioned Ultra DMA, which is a generic term that refers to several different ATA standards ranging from ATA-4 through ATA-7 and offering increased performance by bypassing the CPU in the communication between Random Access Memory (RAM) and the hard disk. Depending on the type of Ultra that the controller and the disk can mutually agree on, performance levels may range from 33 megabytes per second (MBps) with Ultra DMA/33 (ATA-4) up through 133MBps with Ultra DMA/133 (ATA-7). These are sometimes called UltraATA, UATA, or UDMA instead of Ultra DMA; it's all the same thing.

However, there's a glitch. Some versions of Windows don't enable certain Ultra DMA support by default under some circumstances (such as when you upgrade Windows rather than doing a clean install). They do this to "protect" you from problems arising from incompatibilities. For example, under Windows 98/Me, shutdown, standby, and hibernation problems are known to be associated with the use of UDMA, as well as problems accessing CD drives. In addition, older versions of Windows don't support the newer Ultra DMA modes. For example, only Windows XP supports Ultra DMA/133 (ATA-7) natively, although service packs are available for Windows 2000 that bring it up to speed through Ultra DMA/100.

If you're certain that your drive and controller support a certain Ultra DMA mode, by all means enable it! You can always disable it later if you run into problems.

NOTE   *Before you start any of the following, make sure you have the latest service packs installed for your operating system. It makes a difference.*

Enabling Ultra DMA in Windows 98/Me

If you've upgraded to Windows 98/Me from Windows 95, Ultra DMA may not be enabled by default for your hard disk. This refers generically to Ultra DMA, meaning Ultra DMA/33 and higher. To check and to enable it, follow these steps:

1. Right-click My Computer, and choose Properties.

2. Click the Device Manager tab. Display the properties for the hard disk.

3. Click the Settings tab. If the UDMA check box is available but not checked, select it and click OK.

4. Restart the PC.

Enabling Ultra DMA/66 in Windows 2000

If you have an Intel-based Ultra DMA/66 Enhanced Integrated Drive Electronics (EIDE) controller on the motherboard and are running Windows 2000, Ultra DMA/66 mode won't be enabled automatically. That's because there's a bug that prevents Windows 2000 from recognizing this particular line of controllers as Ultra DMA/66 capable. To fix it, you need to edit the Registry.

NOTE *I'm sure you've heard it all before about being careful when editing the Registry. You can really screw up your Windows installation—to the point where you have to do a clean install. I'm not kidding. I've done it.*

Before you do this, make sure that the hard disk and the motherboard (or controller board) both support Ultra DMA/66, and make sure you're using the 80-wire wire ribbon cable:

1. Start the Registry Editor (Start ➤ Run and type **Regedit**).

2. Use Find to locate the following key:

   ```
   HKEY_LOCAL_MACHINE\System\CurrentControlSet\Control\Class\{4D36E96A-E325-11CE-
   BFC1-08002BE10318}\0000
   ```

3. Choose Edit ➤ Add Value, and add the following value:

   Name: EnableUDMA66

   Data type: REG_DWORD

   Value: 1

4. Exit the Registry Editor, and restart the PC.

Enabling Ultra DMA/100 in Windows 2000

Windows 2000 doesn't support Ultra DMA/100 unless you install Windows 2000 Service Pack 2. Then it will, and it'll do so automatically. Without this service pack, Ultra DMA/100 devices will run as Ultra DMA/66 devices (unless, of course, you need to do the fix described in the preceding section because you have an Intel EIDE controller). And here's a bizarre little bug: on Windows 2000 systems that don't have Service Pack 2 installed, the mode for an Ultra DMA/100 drive will appear as Programmed Input/Output (PIO), even though it's actually operating at Ultra DMA/66 levels.

TIP *Windows XP, by the way, supports Ultra DMA/66, 100, and 133 fully without any special tweaks. So does Windows Server 2003.*

Other Ultra DMA Issues and Windows

Here are a few Microsoft Knowledge Base article references that apply to specific situations involving Ultra DMA. Look them up by reference number at `http://support.microsoft.com`:

◆ 330174: "Delayed Write Failed" Error Message When You Manage Files in Windows XP

◆ 241459: HOWTO: Automate the UDMA Fix in Windows 98

◆ 317087: Computer Hangs When You Resume from Hibernation or Standby If Your Ultra Bay Has a UDMA Device

Working with NTFS File System Features

NTFS 4 and 5 both have compression features; NTFS 5 also has encryption. They're two of the benefits of using NTFS over FAT32 in an NT-based Windows version.

Compression

NTFS compression makes a file take up less space on the disk than it normally would. If you compress a folder, the compression applies to all the files you place into it. Unlike other compression utilities such as PKZIP, NTFS compression is transparent to the user. Its main disadvantage is that it slightly slows down file opening and saving.

Enabling or Disabling Compression in Windows NT 4

In Windows NT 4, compression is very simple. There's a check box for it on the General tab of every drive, folder, and file's Properties box.

Enabling or Disabling Compression in Windows 2000/XP

Under Windows 2000 and XP (and their server versions, including Windows Server 2003), you enable or disable compression by doing the following:

1. From the drive, folder, or file's Properties dialog box, display the General tab.

2. Click the Advanced button, opening the Advanced Attributes dialog box.

NOTE *No Advanced button? Then the drive doesn't use NTFS; it's probably a FAT32 volume. Encryption is only for NTFS.*

3. Mark the Compress Contents to Save Disk Space check box.

4. Click OK and then click OK again to close all open dialog boxes.

Figure 12.16 shows the Advanced Attributes dialog box; it's the same place where you turn on encryption (discussed below).

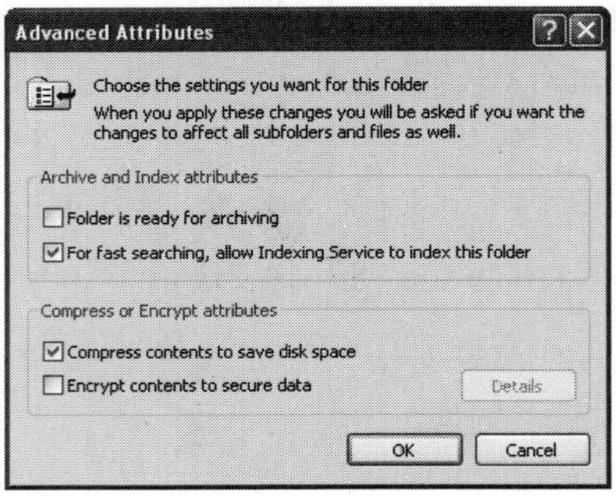

FIGURE 12.16
The Advanced Attributes is where you turn on/off compression and encryption under Windows 2000/XP.

Encryption

Encryption in NTFS is also called Encrypting File System (EFS). It allows users to set local security for files and folders so that other users logging into the same PC will not have access to them. To the user who applied the encryption, however, the files and folders look and work normally. It's available in Windows 2000 Professional and Server, in Windows XP Professional (but not the Home Edition), and in Windows Server 2003.

To encrypt a folder, simply mark the check box for encryption shown in Figure 12.16. (Get to it using the same steps as in the preceding section.)

You can encrypt files, but you shouldn't. It's easy to forget what you've encrypted. Instead, encrypt a folder and put everything in the folder that you want to be encrypted. That way, if you copy or move something out of that folder, it loses its encryption, so there's nothing that you have to remember except that one encrypted folder.

If your hard disk crashes and you need to retrieve the files from it, encryption can really leave you up a creek if you haven't adequately prepared for that possibility with good backups. NTFS encryption relies on an encryption key that's stored on the hard disk, so if anything happens to that key, you won't be able to access the files. You can back up the key to a floppy or CD, but still...be cautious.

Microsoft recommends that you not encrypt the Windows folder itself (`WINNT` on most PCs). In addition, don't encrypt general folders such as Program Files or My Documents; reserve encryption for a special corner where you stash things that are truly confidential.

TIP If you're concerned about local user privacy, one general folder you should encrypt is the `Temp` *folder. By doing this, you prevent snoops from opening up temporary files that might contain bits and pieces of your sensitive data. A wily bunch, those snoops. Gotta stay one step ahead of them.*

Using Different Colors for Compressed and Encrypted Files

You can set things up so that compressed files and folders appear with their names in different colors, so you can more easily recognize them when looking at a file listing. In Windows XP and Server 2003, you can also set up encrypted files to be a different color. You don't have a choice of the colors; compressed files are blue and encrypted ones are green.

To set this up, follow these steps:

1. From My Computer, choose Tools ➤ Folder Options.

2. On the View tab, mark one of these check boxes:

   Display Compressed Files and Folders with Alternate Color (in Windows 2000)

   Show Encrypted or Compressed NTFS Files in Color (in Windows XP/Server 2003)

3. Click OK.

Performing Disk Tasks with Disk Management

The Disk Management tool in Windows 2000/XP and their server versions is very useful for setting up, configuring, and managing disks. You've already seen how it makes the task of partitioning and formatting a drive nearly painless. Now you'll look at some of the other things it can do.

Changing Drive Letters

Be careful when changing drive letters. If you have applications installed that rely on a specific file being associated with a specific drive letter, they won't work anymore if you change the letter (well, unless you reinstall them or do some Registry editing on them). The best time to change a drive letter is when the drive is new and you haven't put anything on it yet.

Okay, that said, here's how to change one. I'll show the Windows XP version here; the other versions are similar:

1. In Disk Management, right-click the drive and choose Change Drive Letter and Paths. A Change Drive Letter and Paths dialog box appears listing the drive's current letter.

2. Click the Change button. The Change Drive Letter or Path dialog box appears. (Note the subtly different dialog box name from the previous one.)

3. Open the drop-down list, pick a different letter, and then click OK. See Figure 12.17. You'll see a warning; click Yes.

FIGURE 12.17

Change the drive letter from Disk Management.

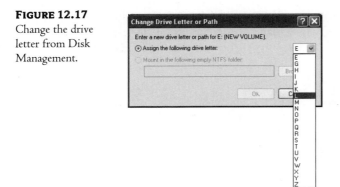

Converting to Dynamic Disks

Remember everything I explained earlier about MBRs and how disks are organized into partitions and logical drives? Well, with dynamic disks you can just throw that whole thing out the window. Dynamic disks represent an entirely new way of structuring the innards of a disk's storage system at the operating system level. It's a Microsoft-only technology that works only with Windows 2000, XP, and their associated server versions, and you can't create them with Windows XP Home Edition. (You can use dynamic disks under the Home Edition if they already exist on the system, however.)

On a traditional disk (called a *basic disk* in Microsoft-speak), the MBR stores the partition table information, which contains the number, type, and locations of the partitions. The MBR is located in the first sector of the disk. In contrast, on a dynamic disk, information about the disk organization is stored in a database file on the last 1MB of the disk.

NOTE *In the maybe-more-detail-than-you-need-to-know category: When you partition a basic disk using Disk Management in Windows 2000 or XP, it reserves the last 8MB on the disk for future use in storing the dynamic disk database should you ever convert the disk to dynamic.*

First let me tell you about the drawbacks to dynamic disks. (I'm bitter, having been dramatically screwed by a basic-to-dynamic conversion that went horrifically wrong because of a power outage, but I'll try to be fair here.) The drawbacks are as follows:

◆ Dynamic disks are completely unreadable and unusable in any other operating system besides Windows 2000 (Professional and Server), XP, and Server 2003.

◆ It's fairly easy to convert from basic to dynamic, but heaven help you if you ever want to convert back to basic. The backward conversion destroys all the data on the disk, so you need to back it all up.

◆ You can convert a disk containing data from basic to dynamic, but if something goes wrong during the conversion process, you might lose all your data.

◆ If you ever decide to mess around with a third-party set of disk tools, it probably won't work with your dynamic disks.

So why would anyone want a dynamic disk? Well, there are some benefits to them. By dumping the entire idea of partitions and logical drives, dynamic disks are able to do some tricks that basic disks (that is, ordinary ones) can't. Many of the most compelling benefits are helpful mostly in large enterprise server/ Redundant Array of Inexpensive Discs (RAID) situations, but judge for yourself:

Spanning   You can combine two or more physical disks into a single logical volume. (*Volume* is the official term for a logical drive on a dynamic disk.) So, for example, suppose you have three 30GB hard disks that are just sitting around taking up space because nobody wants a drive that small anymore. You could put them all in a PC and span them and create a 90GB volume that Windows will see as a single drive letter.

No Limit on the number of volumes   Remember that with a basic disk you can have only four primary partitions, or three plus an extended one. True, the extended one can then have multiple drive letters, but your choices of bootable partitions are limited to three (or four). With a dynamic disk, there's no more partitions—the logical drives "sit" directly on the disk. You can have an unlimited number of volumes, and any of them can be used as a system partition.

Striping   You can create striped volumes, where data is stored on 64KB stripes across separate physical disks. This can improve performance because as I discussed earlier, the main thing holding back really fast disk speeds is the physical hardware. If you can spread data out on multiple physical devices, you can access it faster. However, striping isn't fault-tolerant by itself, so if one disk goes down, it all goes down. (But see the next item.)

RAID-5   All of the previous benefits are good, but the main reason people use dynamic disks is that they enable you to use RAID-5 in a server environment. RAID-5 is a type of RAID that combines performance with data security. It starts with striping, in that it spreads data out over multiple disks, but it also adds a parity bit with each stripe and alternates on which disk it puts that parity bit. If you know the parity bit but you're missing the data on one of the physical disks, you can extrapolate what that data was and rebuild the array. That's what makes RAID-5 fault-tolerant.

If you do decide you want to convert a basic disk to a dynamic one, follow these steps:

1. Right-click the disk (the disk, not the logical drive), and choose Convert to Dynamic Disk.

2. A dialog box appears listing all the physical disks. Check the ones you want to convert. (I recommend doing only one at a time.) Then click OK.

3. A Disks to Convert box appears, confirming your selections; click Convert.

4. Another warning appears. (Turn back! Turn back!) Click Yes to continue.

5. A message appears warning you that the file systems on the disks will be dismounted. (Are you getting the idea yet that this is really serious stuff?) Click Yes to continue.

6. A box appears, letting you know that the computer will need to restart to do the conversion; click OK.

7. The computer restarts, and you'll see a message about new hardware being found, prompting you to restart again. Do so.

That's it! Nothing dramatic happens. After the PC restarts, go back into Disk Management and take a look; you'll see any logical drives that were previously on the disk have been changed to Simple Volumes. That basically just means they're stand-alone units, having not been spanned, striped, or "RAID-ed" in any way. They'll still have the same file systems they had before (NTFS, FAT32, whatever).

I don't want to turn this into a book on Windows, so I won't go into the gory details about setting up RAIDs, spanned disks, and whatnot, but you can explore these on your own, or pick up a book on Windows XP to help such as *Mastering Windows XP Professional, Second Edition* (Sybex, 2002).

Managing Disks from the Recovery Console

Throughout this chapter I've been saying that if you have Windows 2000, XP, or 2003, you don't need a boot floppy. Just to reinforce that, let's take a look at the Recovery Console, a command-line environment you can use to repair, partition, and format drives when one of those Windows versions goes to heck.

To boot to the Recovery Console, you'll need your Windows Setup CD. Do the following:

1. Insert the Windows Setup CD and boot from it. Change the boot settings in BIOS Setup if needed to be able to boot from the CD.

2. Windows Setup runs. At the Welcome to Setup screen, press R for Repair, and then C for Recovery Console. The Recovery Console loads.

3. When prompted to choose a Windows installation, press 1 (assuming you have only one copy of Windows) and press Enter. If you're prompted for the Administrator password, type it and press Enter.

Now you're in a command line, much like the one you would get by booting from a startup floppy under Windows 9x. It's not exactly the same environment, because there are some restrictions on the things you can do (you might not be able to access all folders, for example) and you can run only a limited set of commands. But the tradeoff is that you get some good utilities that aren't available anywhere else on an NT-based system.

TIP   *You can install the Recovery Console files on your hard disk if you want. This makes the Recovery Console an option on the Startup menu every time the computer starts. To do this, choose Start ➤ Run, and type* `x:\i386\winnt32 /cmdcons` *where* `X` *is the letter of your CD drive.*

To see a list of all the available commands at the Recovery Console, type HELP and press Enter. The available commands include most of the basic DOS-style file management commands like `COPY`, `DEL`, `MD`, `CD`, `ATTRIB`, `REN`, and so on, plus these special ones:

BATCH   Runs batch commands in a text file you specify.

DISABLE   Disables a Windows service or driver; useful in troubleshooting a startup problem due to a bad service or driver.

DISKPART   Runs a utility that is similar to FDISK, enabling you to manage disk partitions. Figure 12.18 shows it. It's pretty self-explanatory.

ENABLE   Enables a Windows service or driver.

FIXBOOT   Rewrites the boot sector on the boot partition; useful if a virus has trashed your boot sector.

FIXMBR   Repairs the master boot record on the disk. Again, useful if a virus has trashed it.

LISTSYS   Displays a list of all services, drivers, and startup types.

To get the syntax on a command, type it followed by /?, just like at any other command prompt. To exit, type **EXIT**.

FIGURE 12.18

The DISKPART utility in the Recovery Console

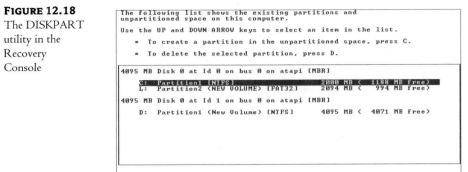

In this chapter, you learned how to partition and format hard disks using both command-line and GUI methods, and you learned about Disk Management and some of its capabilities. At this point you're ready to install an operating system on the disk, if you haven't done so already, or just to start using it as secondary storage. In the next chapter I'll tell you about some utilities that will help you keep your disks healthy and functioning well.

Chapter 13

Protecting and Maintaining Hard Disks

- ◆ Protecting Your Hard Disk
- ◆ Backing Up System and Data Files
- ◆ Preparing for Emergency Booting
- ◆ Checking a Disk for Errors
- ◆ Defragmenting the File System
- ◆ Dealing with Dead Drives

Introduction

A hard disk isn't a huge expense; if it fails, you can always replace it. But the data on the disk—now that's a different story! In most companies (and most homes, too), the data stored on the hard disk is the single valuable piece of the system in terms of how much it'd cost to replace it. Just imagine the cost of reconstructing a single spreadsheet of data that was gathered over a two-year period.

It therefore behooves all users to make sure that data is safe and to take preventive measures to make hard disk failure as unlikely as possible. That's what this chapter is about.

Protecting Your Hard Disk

There's not much to be done in the way of regular maintenance on the sealed hard disk: you can't clean the heads, and you can't align them. If the disk drive itself is fried, then about all you can do with it is toss it and buy a newer and bigger one.

Nevertheless, you can do some things to make a hard disk last longer. Eventually nearly all hard disks will conk out, but whether that happens in 2 years or 25 years can depend on how you treat it. The following are a few general things you can do to help your hard disk have a longer and more error-free life:

◆ Leave your computers on all the time (except during electrical storms and extended absences); it's easier on the drives if they don't have to start up "cold" several times a day.

◆ Get good power protection. You read in Chapter 7, "Power Supplies and Power Protection," about buying power conditioners and an Uninterruptible Power Supply (UPS) to protect your hardware—and the hard disk is no exception. Surges go through the *whole* system, including the drive heads. And if the drive heads happen to be near the File Allocation Table (FAT) or partition record...

◆ Use the proper mounting hardware for your drive, and mount it according to manufacturer's guidelines. Rattling around loose in a case is very bad for a drive.

◆ Pay attention to noises. A hard disk that suddenly makes a lot of noise when it was formerly quiet is probably on its way to failure. Now would be a good time to copy the data off onto a new disk.

Protecting Your Data

Protecting the data is different from protecting the disk itself. Although the data will be lost if the disk fails, there are other ways to lose data that leave the disk perfectly fine, such as viruses and accidental formatting.

Protecting your data includes the following:

◆ Backing up the following:

  ◆ Master Boot Record (MBR)

  ◆ System files

  ◆ User data

◆ Having an emergency boot floppy (DOS, Windows 9x) or Windows Setup CD (NT versions) handy for each system in the event that Windows won't start normally

◆ Regularly checking disks for errors in the file system with ScanDisk (DOS or Windows 9x) or Check Disk (NT-based Windows versions).

◆ Checking for physically bad spots on the disk whenever the disk encounters physical trauma or when the operating system reports disk read or write errors. ScanDisk and Check Disk both have options for doing this.

◆ Regularly defragmenting all hard disks so that data recovery will be more successful in the event of a major disk problem. The Disk Defragmenter program in Windows works fine for this.

◆ Understanding the threat posed by computer viruses and knowing how to protect yourself from them. The best way to avoid computer viruses is to use one of the many excellent anti-virus programs on the market and keep it updated. See Chapter 29, "Viruses and Other Nasty Bugs," for details.

◆ I'll explain more about many of these points in the following sections.

SMART PROTECTION

As you learned in Chapter 10, "Understanding and Installing ATA Drives,"ATA-3 and higher hard disks support a technology called Self Monitoring And Reporting Tool (SMART). This is a statistical analysis utility built into the drive that monitors things such as the average time it takes to seek, read, and write data. It knows what the drive's "normal" specifications are, and if there's a radical change, it reports the problem to the operating system as a possible sign of impending failure. That way, users can protect themselves from physically dying drives and get their data off in time. You might need to enable SMART in the Basic Input/Output System (BIOS) Setup or in the drive's properties in Windows. Also, applications such as Norton Utilities provide real-time SMART monitoring.

Backing Up the MBR

As you learned earlier in the book, the MBR is the area at the beginning of the drive (that is, near the center) that contains information about the partitions on the disk. If it gets trashed, you lose everything. Therefore, it's a good idea to back it up daily.

Windows doesn't come with an MBR backup utility, but there are good shareware and commercial ones available.

Here are some places to start:

◆ Symantec Norton Utilities at www.symantec.com.

◆ Ranish Partition Manager (RPM) at www.ranish.com/part.

◆ Active@ Partition Recovery at www.partition-recovery.com.

◆ Active@ Uneraser at www.uneraser.com.

You can also search any Web search engine for *MBR backup.*

TIP   When searching for shareware and demos, I like to start from CNET (www.cnet.com). Not only can you download from here, but you can see other people's reviews and comments on an application.

Backing Up System Files

There are several meanings to the term *system files*. It refers generically to all the files needed to start the operating system and keep it running, as one meaning. However, many of those files are standard issue with the operating system, so you could always reinstall them from the operating system CD-ROM and not have lost anything.

Therefore, when I talk about backing up system files in this case, what I'm really talking about is system *configuration* files, the files that contain the customized information about how the operating system is installed, what applications are set up, what hardware is installed, and what your display and input preferences are.

In Windows 95 and higher, the system configuration is stored in the Registry. The Registry appears to be a single database when you access it through the Registry Editor in Windows, but it actually consists of several files. Which files? That depends on the operating system: for Windows 95/98/Me, it's two files, USER.DAT and SYSTEM.DAT; for Windows NT/2000/XP/2003, it's a series of *hive* files with names such as SAM and SYSTEM, each of which describes a part of how the operating system works. You don't need to know the exact names and locations of those files to back up the Registry, though.

TIP   Windows 3.1 used two initialization files, WIN.INI and SYSTEM.INI, to store the system configuration data. If you have any old 16-bit Windows applications, they still store their settings there. So if you need to back up the system configuration files on a system that includes such apps, you should also back up those two INI files.

Backing up the Registry on a regular basis is a *very* good idea because the Registry is required to boot the operating system. If you (or an application) makes changes to the Registry that cause problems in Windows, you can always restore your most recent backup of it.

There are several ways of backing up the Registry, depending on the Windows version. Windows 98 and Windows Me have a Registry Checker utility that you can run through System Information. After it checks the Registry, it offers to make a backup of it. In Windows 2000 and XP Professional, the Backup utility includes a Registry backup option in it (called System State). The System Restore utility in Windows Me and Windows XP also backs up the Registry every day automatically plus any extra times you activate it, and it keeps several versions (about two weeks of data usually) ready in case you need to go back to an earlier configuration.

One method works in all Windows versions, and that's the Export command in Regedit, the Registry Editor. You can export the entire Registry to a backup file and then copy that backup file to a removable disk for safekeeping. If you ever need to restore it, you can once again use the Registry Editor and import the file. Run REGEDIT with the Run command on the Start menu, and then choose File ➤ Export.

Backing Up User Data

Backing up is like life insurance for your data. (Time is money, remember?) Just as every person will eventually die, every hard disk will eventually die. Backing up is like making a life insurance premium payment. Yes, you'd rather not do it, but it's a smart investment because you know that day is coming, and the consequences of *not* preparing for it are unacceptable.

TIP *Backing up your data regularly also saves you from your techie friends' condescension when your hard disk crashes and you lose everything. They'll look at you with these wide innocent eyes and say something such as, "Well, you had good backups at least, didn't you?" Even if they haven't backed up their own stuff in years, they will still roll their eyes if you admit you lost more than 48 hours of data.*

BACKUP OPTIONS

Over the years, backup options have improved dramatically. In the past, most people were stuck with floppy disks or clunky old tape backup cartridges, but these days your options include the following:

- High-speed, high-capacity tape drives

- Removable magnetic disks (floppy, LS-120, Zip)

- Writable/rewritable CDs and DVDs (see Chapter 9, "CD-ROM and DVD Drives")

- A second hard drive (hard disks are cheap now, so why not?)

- Online storage

I'll discuss these options in the next several sections.

Tape Drives

The traditional means of backing up a large hard disk is the tape drive. They're simple, they're a known quantity, and they're cheap. In addition, the high-capacity models back up a lot of data on a single tape—up to 40 gigabytes (GB), which means you don't have to baby-sit the backup job changing tapes. In contrast, backing up to a writeable CD means sitting there changing the CD every 700 megabytes (MB) or so.

When looking for a tape drive, keep the following in mind:

- Choose one with an interface that's compatible with your system. Models are available for Enhanced Integrated Drive Electronics (EIDE), Small Computer System Interface (SCSI), Universal Serial Bus (USB), and FireWire.

- An external tape drive may cost a little more, but you'll be able to use it to back up more than one system. Make sure all systems that are going to use it have the correct interface.

- Preformatted tapes can save a great deal of time because some tapes can take a long time to format.

- A good tape drive will come with compatible backup software, but more full-featured software is also available commercially.

- Not all drives are compatible with all backup software, so if you need to use a specific application, check its compatibility list before purchasing a drive.

- The same tape software that works with one operating system may not work with another. Similarly, the data on those tapes may not be readable with tape software used on another operating system.

Tape drives come in a wide range of capacities and formats: consumer models range in size from 500MB to 40GB and higher using the Digital Audio Tape (DAT) format.

Writeable CD and DVD

For backing up a small amount of data (less than 700MB) on a regular basis, CD-R and CD-RW drives are appropriate. Most mainstream computers come with a CD-RW drive these days, so there's no extra hardware to buy, and the discs themselves are inexpensive (and in the case of CD-RW, they're reusable up to 1000 times).

The downside is the relatively low capacity. If you have more than one CD of data to back up, you have to be there at the PC when it's time to swap CDs. The writing process is also much slower than with a tape backup.

This low-capacity downside can be somewhat ameliorated by going with writeable DVD drive, described in Chapter 9. This raises the maximum capacity to around 4.7GB per disc. However, you'll need to buy a writeable DVD drive (pricey) and buy blanks for it (also pricey). And if you're using two-sided blanks, you'll need to be there to flip the blank over at the proper time in the backup process, so you've really got only about 2.35GB of unattended backup capacity.

Removable Magnetic Disks

This is a big category and includes a range of disks and drives. The smallest and weakest member of this group is the lowly floppy disk (1.44MB). There's also the LS-120 (the SuperDisk), which looks just like a regular floppy but holds 120MB of data, and the Zip disk, which holds either 100MB or 250MB of data. None of these are serious contenders for large backups, of course, but they serve adequately for small amounts of data. One of these is your best bet only if you've already got the drive on your system and you have a small amount of data to back up.

NOTE   *Iomega used to make a Jaz drive that held 1GB or 2GB of data per cartridge. They no longer do. However, you may encounter one used or at a job site. They're adequate—not stellar, given the other choices available today. Most use SCSI as their interface.*

Mini USB Storage

The latest, coolest low-capacity backup devices are little USB-based keychain-sized devices that hold anywhere from 20MB to 256MB of data. True, that's not much capacity, but their USB-ness makes them extremely portable, so many people are using them as substitutes for floppies these days for shuttling data between computers. See Chapter 14, "Understanding, Installing, and Repairing Floppy Drives," for more information about them.

Another Hard Drive

Hard disk space has gotten so cheap that it's feasible to just get a second hard disk and keep a copy of your data on both disks. In Windows 9x, you can periodically drag and drop your data to the other disk, or in Windows NT, 2000, or XP Professional you can use Disk Management (or Disk Administrator in NT 4) to set up the two disks as a mirrored set. This writes all data to both disks at once, so they stay constantly synchronized.

NOTE *A mirror set is a group of two physical drives set up so that when data is written to one, it's written to the second as well.*

Of course, an extra hard drive isn't as portable as some of the other options that I've talked about here, unless you go with an external hard disk. (Iomega makes some pretty good external hard disk drives at the moment, for example.)

Other disadvantages are that, unless it's an external drive, you can't switch it to another computer easily and, if it's part of a mirror set, you'll only be able to use it on a computer that has the compatible software installed. But for a high-speed and simple backup solution, it's very workable.

Online Backups

With broadband Internet connections more affordable (and more common), you now have an offsite option for your data backup needs. Several online services will back up data from your hard disk to their storage servers via the Internet. The advantages of this kind of setup are that your data is safely stored offsite (good if your house or office burns down) and the backups can be scheduled to take place automatically. The main disadvantages are price (look to pay anywhere from $10 per month to $300 per year) and, if you have a slower connection, upload time.

Some of the more popular sites include @Backup (`www.backup.com`), BackupUSA (`www.backupus .com`), IBackup (`www.ibackup.com`), Iomega (`www.iomega.com`), and VirtualBackup (`www.virtual backup.com`). Various encryption schemes ensure your data's security. Choose a company not only by price but also by reputation—you're trusting them with your sensitive and important data, after all.

WHAT SOFTWARE DO YOU NEED?

The answer to this question depends on how you plan to do your backing up. You can either use a backup utility or simply copy files manually within the operating system (or using a CD or DVD writing utility, if your operating system doesn't include that support). For tape backup, you'll need to go the backup utility route.

Windows 2000 and XP Professional come with a decent backup utility built-in. You can access it from the Tools tab of a drive's Properties box. Windows XP Home Edition doesn't install the Backup utility, but some versions of the Home Edition do include the Backup utility on the Setup CD (although it doesn't install from Windows Setup, and you have to dig for it).

There are two types of backup software, but commercial products sometimes combine the two types to offer both functionalities:

File backup This is the "traditional" type of backup software. The Backup utility that comes with Windows 2000 and XP Professional is an example. Another is Backup Exec from Veritas. It enables you to select as few files as one, or as many as all files, from a disk and save them to a removable medium such as a disk or tape. Such programs typically compress the files as they back them up using some proprietary compression algorithm. As a result, you must use the same application to restore the files that you used to back them up.

Disk backup   This type of backup makes a clone of the entire hard disk onto another hard disk or onto high-capacity removable media. The most popular application in this category is Norton Ghost from Symantec, which has made the term *ghosting* nearly synonymous with disk backup. Another is Drive Image from PowerQuest. Cloning an entire disk creates a usable copy of it that can then be put in another PC, so its uses are not just for data backup.

BACKUP STRATEGIES

Having the tools to back up is only part of the solution. For complete data protection, you have to make sure you *use* them. I know it's a pain, but you must back up your data on a daily basis if you generate anything of importance. Even losing one day's work can be bad, so how would you re-create a week's worth?

First, centralize your data as much as possible. If you're responsible for backing up more than one networked computer, consider storing all data on a file server for backup. It's much easier to back up one computer than 10.

Second, create a schedule and stick to it. I've found that a rotating backup schedule that combines full and differential backups works quite well. On Monday, for example, you might do a full backup of the system. Then, on each day of the rest of the week, you can do a differential or incremental backup so that you only copy the files that have changed.

NOTE   *A differential backup copies those files that have changed since the last backup of any kind; an incremental backup copies only those files that have changed since the last full backup.*

Name each backup tape, disk, or cartridge with its date, the machine it belongs to, and the type of backup it is. For example, a full backup of my workstation might be labeled *3/05/04 Full backup of Workstation01.*

Finally, don't rely on your memory. Make yourself a backup schedule, and put it on the wall or someplace very visible. Posting your backup schedule in a prominent place has two advantages. First, you know at a glance when you last backed up (initial each backup after you've completed it). Second, it reminds you to back up until it gets to be a regular habit.

Preparing Boot Disks

Once you have the important bits backed up, make sure you can get your computer up and running without the help of your hard drive. This means you must make sure you have a boot method available for each of your systems.

Preparing for Emergency Boot in Windows 9x

In Windows 9x, you can create a boot floppy from the Add/Remove Programs applet (on the Startup tab) in the Control Panel. This creates a floppy that isn't only bootable but contains certain important utilities such as FDISK, FORMAT, EDIT, and ScanDisk.

If you make a boot floppy with Windows 98 or Me, it includes real-mode CD drives on it, which are necessary if you want to rerun Windows Setup after straightening out the disk problems. Windows 95 boot floppies don't, so you'll need to add the files to it that's run your CD drive. See Chapter 9 for details.

Preparing for Emergency Boot in NT-Based Windows Versions

In Windows NT/2000/XP, you can't boot directly to a command prompt from a floppy because that's not how those operating systems function. They're not based on MS-DOS the way the 9x versions of Windows are.

If you keep the Windows Setup CD handy, you're all set for boot disks because the CD is bootable. It'll start the Setup application, which then asks whether you want to repair or reinstall. If you want to repair, you can choose an automated repair process or choose to go into the Recovery Console.

Emergency Repair Disks

An Emergency Repair Disk (ERD) in Windows 2000 contains backups of certain system settings that may be helpful when the Windows Setup program is operating in its automated repair mode. It's not required, but it does increase the quality of the recovery.

To create an ERD while Windows is still healthy, use the Backup utility in Windows 2000. Start it, and then click the Emergency Repair Disk button. Then just follow the prompts.

To use an ERD when crisis strikes, insert it when prompted as part of the Windows Setup program's recovery process.

Automated System Recovery (ASR)

ASR is the Windows XP/2003 equivalent of an ERD. You create a recovery point in the Backup utility; in the Backup Utility Wizard, click Advanced Mode, then choose Tools➤ASR Wizard and follow the prompts.

To use the ASR disk, restart the computer with the Windows Setup CD in the CD drive, and press F2 when prompted during the text-only mode section of Setup. You will be prompted to insert the ASR floppy disk. Follow the instructions onscreen.

Recovery Console

The Recovery Console is a command-line environment where you can do troubleshooting and repair in a sort of ground-zero way. To boot to the Recovery Console from the Windows CD, follow these steps:

1. At the Welcome to Setup screen, press **R** for Repair.

2. Press **C** for Recovery Console.

3. Press **1** to select the first Windows installation.

4. If prompted, type the administrator password and press Enter.

You are now at the command prompt. From here you can issue many command-line commands. Table 13.1 summarizes them; you can also type **HELP** to get a list of them or type a command followed by /? to get its complete syntax rules.

TABLE 13.1: COMMANDS AVAILABLE AT THE RECOVERY CONSOLE

COMMAND	PURPOSE
ATTRIB	Changes file attributes
BATCH	Executes batch commands in a specified text file
CD	Changes the directory
CHKDSK	Checks the disk for errors
COPY	Copies files
DEL	Deletes files
DIR	Gives you a list of files in the directory
DISABLE	Disables a Windows driver or service
DISKPART	Like FDISK, creates and manages partitions
ENABLE	Enables a Windows driver or service
EXIT	Leaves the Recovery Console
EXPAND	Decompresses a file
FIXBOOT	Writes a new boot sector on the boot partition
FIXMBR	Repairs the MBR
FORMAT	Formats a logical drive
LISTSYS	Shows all available drivers, services, and startup types
MD	Makes a directory
RD	Removes a directory
REN	Renames a file or folder

You can install the Recovery Console on the hard disk so that it becomes a startup option every time you start the PC. This won't help you if the hard disk is completely trashed, but it'll allow you to boot into the Recovery Console without the Windows CD in the event that the hard disk is basically okay but Windows won't boot. To do so, follow these steps:

1. In Windows, with the Windows CD in the CD drive, choose Start ➤ Run.

2. Type *x:***i386****winnt32** /**cmdcons** where *x* is the drive letter of the CD drive.

3. Click OK. A confirmation appears. Click Yes.

4. After installation, click OK again.

From this point on, each time you start the PC, the Recovery Console will appear as one of the operating system choices on the multiboot menu. If you didn't have the multiboot menu before, you will now. It means an extra step in starting up your PC each time, which some people find annoying.

TIP *In Windows XP, you can turn the startup menu off so it doesn't appear automatically each time. From the Control Panel, choose System, then select the Advanced tab, and click Settings in the Startup and Recovery section. In the Startup and Recovery dialog box, clear the Time to Display List of Operating Systems check box.*

Checking Disks for Errors

No disk medium is perfect. Even when a disk is new, there's always the chance that a part of a platter isn't coated perfectly with magnetic particles. And as time goes by, bad treatment of the disk (such as jostling it while it's reading/writing) can cause bad spots on the disk where data can't be reliably read or written.

If a disk checking utility identifies these bad spots before anything gets written to them—great. They're cordoned off as unusable. But if data gets written there and then the area goes bad, heaven help the data! Some disk utilities can attempt to read the data and move it to a safe area, but they aren't always successful. It depends on whether the sector is completely bad or just in the process of going bad. The disk checking application tries repeatedly to read from the sector, and sometimes it succeeds. But if the sector is physically trashed completely, even the best disk utility can't bring back the data.

Physical errors are nowhere near as common in newer hard disks as they were in the old ones. The technology has gotten better for manufacturing the disks, and the shock tolerance of the average drive has greatly improved. Nevertheless, physical errors do still occasionally occur, but usually in a hard disk that's on its way to the grave anyway.

So far I've talked purely about physical errors on a disk, but there are also logical errors that occur; in fact, logical errors are more common. A *logical error* occurs when the drive's table of contents—FAT or Master File Table (MFT)—becomes out of sync with what's actually stored on the disk or contains logical errors so that the same cluster is claimed by more than one file or so that a cluster containing data isn't claimed by any file. The most common cause of a logical error is improper shutdown. When a user turns off the PC with its power button rather than going through the Shut Down command in Windows, some files remain open, and some changes might not be written to the FAT or MFT. Another cause may be improper termination of an application, such as a General Protection Fault (GPF).

Logical errors tend to build on one another—one logical error can cause another one until you have a whole mess of inaccessible files! That's why it's important to check disks for errors on a regular basis. It was more important in earlier versions of Windows (9x) than it is in Windows 2000 and XP, however, because the MFT on an NTFS drive is less susceptible to logical errors than FAT-based file systems. Still, it's a good idea at the first scent of file system problems to run a check.

Disk checking applications can find and fix both physical and logical errors, but the hunting for the physical errors takes much longer. Therefore, most applications have two modes they can run in: logical tests only or both physical and logical. The wording varies among applications; some call the physical test a *surface test.*

You already have an adequate disk checking application if you have Windows 95 and higher.

In Windows 9*x* it's called Scandisk, and you'll find it under the Start ➤ Programs ➤ Accessories ➤ System Tools menu. You can also access it from the Tools tab of a disk's Properties box. There's also a DOS-based version of ScanDisk included on the boot floppy created in Windows 9*x* versions, and ScanDisk was also included with MS-DOS 5 and higher.

In Windows NT, 2000, XP, and 2003, it's called Check Disk (run with the command CHKDSK), and there's no Start menu option for it. You can access it from the Tools tab of a disk's Properties box or by running CHKDSK with the Run command.

NOTE *Early versions of MS-DOS didn't include ScanDisk; instead, they had a utility called CHKDSK that performed logical disk checking functionality. And in the latest versions of Windows, the utility is called Check Disk, a name that's derivative of CHKDSK. So what goes around comes around. Just don't confuse the Graphical User Interface (GUI)–based Check Disk application with the command-line CHKDSK.*

Want something more powerful? Many good third-party disk checking applications are available. One of the most respected is still Symantec's Norton Utilities. In addition to its Disk Doctor utility (which is a lot like ScanDisk), it also comes with sundry other utilities for disk management.

Defragmenting the File System

After running for a while, the files on your hard drive can become *fragmented* or *noncontiguous*. This means that a given file may be stored partly in clusters 30–40 (one contiguous group) and partly in clusters 101–122 (another contiguous group). A file is said to be noncontiguous if (logically) it has more than one contiguous block of disk space.

Noncontiguous files are bad for two reasons, as demonstrated in Figure 13.1.

FIGURE 13.1

A fragmented and an unfragmented file

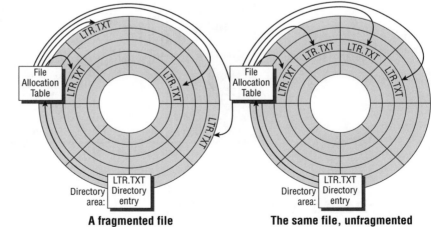

A fragmented file   **The same file, unfragmented**

First, noncontiguous files take longer to read. The fact that the disk head must go chasing all over the disk to read them slows down disk access. Putting the whole file together makes read operations quicker: move the head once, and all of the data can be read.

Second, you have a higher probability of recovering a deleted file if it isn't fragmented. Keeping disks defragmented just pushes the odds a little further in your favor. Think of it this way: suppose you have to find and piece together a file on a disk whose FAT has been zapped. Would you rather have to find a file in clusters 100, 120, and 1521 or a file in clusters 100–102? If the files are always defragmented, data recovery is easier.

How do files become fragmented? When the operating system needs a cluster, it basically grabs the first one available. When the disk is new, only a few clusters have been taken, and the rest of the disk is one large free area. New files are all contiguous. But as files are deleted, they create "holes" in the disk space. As the operating system looks for more clusters, it takes the first sector available. This can easily lead to a new file being spread out over several separate areas.

You can easily defragment files using the defrag utility included in all versions of Windows. It's located at Start ➢ (All) Programs ➢ Accessories ➢ System Tools ➢ Disk Defragmenter. Figure 13.2 shows the Windows XP version. Just fire it up, and run an analysis on the disk first to find out if it even needs it. If it does, shut down all other running programs first, and try not to use the computer while the defragmenting process is occurring. That's because if a change is detected in the disk content, the process must restart.

FIGURE 13.2

The Disk Defrag-
menter utility in
Windows XP

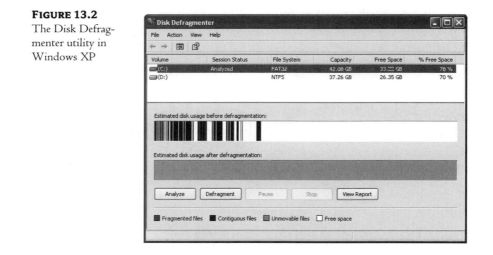

Dealing with Dead Disks

So you have an inaccessible hard disk. Maybe the PC won't start at all (in the case where it's the boot disk that's failing), or maybe one of your data disks isn't responding. What now?

Time to start troubleshooting. The following sections outline the process I use.

Step 1: Does BIOS Setup See It?

There are two kinds of "dead" in the dead drive department. First, there's the physical kind of dead. Drives can develop physical problems with the spindle or the actuator arm, their read/write heads can stop reading and writing, or the circuitry that connects the power plug to the drive mechanics gives out.

Then there's the logical kind of dead, where there's nothing really wrong with the drive mechanics but for some reason it has forgotten about all the data it was storing. It's not really dead in the permanent sense, but it's trashed until you rebuild it (new partitions, new formatting).

How can you tell if the drive is physically dead? One of the most reliable indicators is to check whether BIOS Setup continues to recognize the disk drive. If it does, the drive is probably physically still among the living. Go into BIOS Setup, and look at the drives that are listed for each of the EIDE channels (see Chapter 10). If there's a Detect IDE utility built into BIOS Setup, run it to refresh the listing.

If BIOS Setup can't see the drive, check the following:

◆ Are any of the cable connectors loose or unplugged? If you were mucking around inside the case doing something else, maybe you accidentally bumped one of them.

◆ Are other drives on the same cable working? If so, you can eliminate a bad cable and a bad EIDE connector on the motherboard as possible suspects. If it's an EIDE drive connected to the motherboard, try it on the other IDE channel. For example, if it's currently on IDE0, try it on IDE1. (Remember, of course, that EIDE is not hot-pluggable, so you have to power off between each experiment.)

◆ If you've been moving stuff around inside the PC, check that the jumper caps are still over the correct pins on the drive.

◆ If other drives on the same cable aren't working with the bad drive connected, do they start working when you disconnect the dead drive?

Step 2: Can You Read from the Drive?

If it's your boot drive that's malfunctioning, it may be difficult at first glance to distinguish between a boot problem and a drive access problem. Maybe the data is okay but the files needed to boot have somehow gotten trashed.

To check this out, boot from a startup disk and get to a command prompt, then execute a DIR (directory) command on the drive in question. If you can see a directory listing of files, you know that the data is there, and it's simply a booting problem.

At this point, if you can get a directory of files, *back up your files!* Don't start breathing normally until you've copied all the most important data files off onto floppies or other removable media. (Use the COPY command. Type COPY /? for the syntax needed.) The successful directory listing you see may be solid, or it may be tenuous and not reproducible five minutes from now. You just don't know. So retrieve your data *now*.

TIP   You won't be able to read files from an NT File System (NTFS) drive using a Windows 9x boot floppy because 9x doesn't support NTFS. However, there are utilities that do allow you to read from an NTFS drive from a DOS-based command prompt. One free one that does a nice job is NTFS Reader for DOS, available at www.ntfs.com.

BIOS AUTODETECTION

As the BIOS recognizes and registers each drive at startup, it usually prints the drive's vendor-specific information to the screen. For a typical system that has a CD-R/RW and an 80GB HDD, the BIOS POST might appear like this:

```
130,600KB RAM OK


ATA BUS0

Master - Maxtor 80GB 90845D4

Slave - None


ATA BUS1

Master - Ricoh CD-R/RW MP7040A

Slave - None
```

If you've paid attention to this over a long period of time, you'll notice immediately when something goes differently. Maybe the drive doesn't appear. Maybe it takes longer to be recognized. These two things are the biggest pointers to physical problems with a drive.

After backing up the files, start investigating the nonboot issue. Are the system files there? If you've got a Windows 9*x* boot floppy, try the command SYS C: to recopy the boot files to the hard disk (assuming your boot drive is C:). If you've got Windows NT/2000/XP, rerun Windows Setup from the CD, and if prompted to repair the installation, go with that option and follow the prompts.

If you can't read from the drive, go on to the next section.

Step 3: Try a Disk Utility

Some utility programs specialize in recovering data from unreadable hard disks. These are amazing works of programming, and if you send your disk to a professional data recovery service (see the next step), the first thing they'll do is try to use one of these utilities. So you might as well try it yourself first!

The disk utilities that do this type of recovery aren't your run-of-the-mill Norton Utilities type of program. They're specialized pieces of software, and they can be pricey. One of the best ones, EasyRecovery by Ontrack (www.ontrack.com), costs $200 for the basic version (or $89 for a "lite" version that recovers only 25 files per session). These programs painstakingly reconstruct whatever they can from any remnants remaining on the disk of the FAT, partition table, MBR, and so on. When a virus or other train wreck trashes a hard disk, it often leaves behind enough of these administrative bits and pieces that you can recover most if not all of your files.

WARNING *If you are considering using a professional service, skip right to step 4; don't try a recovery program. These programs described here can actually make it more difficult for the pros to recover your data according to my technical editor, who works at one of thos professional recovery companies.*

When shopping for a disk recovery utility program, look for one that you can "try before you buy." One reason I like Ontrack's EasyRecovery, for example, is that you can download a free version that will check your disk and let you know whether there's anything recoverable on it. If it finds something, you can then download the "pay" version to get your files back. That way, you haven't spent money for a utility that won't work. For an assortment of recovery programs that come with trial versions, search for *Recovery* at the CNET file download archives (`www.cnet.com`).

Another thing to look for in disk recovery is the ability to read from various file systems. Some of the older or "discount" recovery utilities will read only from FAT or FAT32, not NTFS 4 or 5.

Assuming that the disk recovery application does find salvageable files, you'll need a working drive to which to copy them. You can temporarily install another already-formatted hard disk for this purpose (FAT32 would be a good file system for such a disk), or you can copy them off to floppies. Most of these disk recovery programs won't work with writeable optical discs (CD or DVD) or Zip drives.

Step 4: Send It to the Pros

Not getting anywhere with the data recovery? If you *really* need that data, there is a last hope. It ain't cheap—from $500 to $20,000—but you can send the hard disk to a data recovery service. They disassemble the disk, remove the data, and then send it to you on a CD or any media you require. This is pretty much your only option if the hard disk is physically dead. An average cost would be $1500 for a 60GB drive.

These services can charge $200 to diagnose the problem, with recovery costs negotiated on top of that, ranging into the thousands. The negotiation will be colored by the time period you want it recovered in and how difficult the recovery is. It's expensive, yes, but it's cheaper than going out of business.

In this chapter, you learned about some utilities and procedures for keeping your hard disk—and more importantly, your data—safe and healthy. In the next chapter, you'll move on to the removable side of disk storage and look at the floppy drive interface and some of its modern competitors.

Chapter 14

Understanding, Installing, and Troubleshooting Floppy Drives

Introduction

The floppy disk is a very old technology, preceding even the hard disk. There have been various types over the years, each new type improving the performance and reliability levels, but I'm still talking about really, really old stuff here.

So why have floppy disks hung on this long? Mainly because until recent years there wasn't any other good way to move files between computers that everyone could agree on. Many manufacturers have come up with better ideas over the years for floppy-like storage, but none have become industry standards (although LS-120 and Zip came close). Finally, in the past several years, some compelling floppy alternatives have become mainstream, and computer manufacturers are finally phasing out the old floppy technology. In this chapter, I'll explain the basics of floppy technology and describe some modern alternatives to them. I'll also explain how to install a floppy disk drive and how to trouble-shoot floppy operation.

QuickSteps: Replacing a Floppy Drive

First, let's take a quick look at the procedures and guidelines for replacing your floppy drive.

BE PREPARED

Before you start, there are some things you'll need to perform the operation. These include the following:

- Nonmagnetic Phillips-head screwdriver
- Container to hold the removed screws
- Antistatic wrist strap
- New floppy drive

And as usual, before you work on a PC, ensure that the PC is turned off and unplugged.

WARNING   *Floppy drives aren't especially sensitive to static electricity, but installing one requires connecting it to the Input/Output (I/O) controller (usually the motherboard) with a ribbon cable, and the motherboard can be easily harmed by Electrostatic Discharge (ESD). Wear that antistatic wrist strap.*

TIP   *Before replacing a floppy drive, make sure the problem isn't with an individual disk. Try the drive with several disks.*

To replace a floppy drive, follow these steps:

1. To replace a floppy drive, first turn off the PC's power and remove the cover.

2. Disconnect the ribbon cable and the power connector from the drive. Notice which direction the red stripe on the ribbon cable points (toward the center or the outside of the drive).

3. Unscrew the screws holding the floppy drive in place (unless it's held in place by clips and drive rails; in that case, release the clips). Pull the drive out of the PC.

4. Install the replacement drive by using screws or clips, as the case requires.

5. Connect the power cable (the small Berg one).

6. Connect the ribbon cable with the red stripe going to pin 1. The drive may have a little 1 next to one end of the connector to tip you off; if not, connect it in the same way it was connected on the old drive (see step 3).

7. Turn on the PC, and test the new drive by trying to read a disk from it.

Is Floppy Technology Obsolete?

In a word: yes. Floppy drives are well on their way to being obsolete. Floppies used to be *de rigueur* in a system because they were the only removable disk type available. If you needed to "sneakernet" a file from one PC to another, a floppy was your only option. Today, however, there are writeable CDs, Universal Serial Bus (USB) Flash devices, Zip disks, the Internet, and Local Area Networks (LANs), all of which do a better job than a floppy disk and can hold more data.

However, don't expect the PC industry to let go of them just yet. New computers will probably continue to come with floppy drives for at least another couple of years, until the average Joe Consumer realizes he really doesn't need one after all.

NOTE *One reason that many people hang onto having a floppy drive is that they think they need to be able to boot from a startup floppy in the event of a system problem. And this is a valid point for people who are running 9x versions of Windows. However, the NT-based Windows versions all come on bootable CDs that kick into a Setup utility with a Repair option, so for modern Windows versions a bootable floppy isn't an issue. In addition, you can use a CD-burning application such as Roxio Easy CD Creator or Nero Burning ROM to make a bootable CD-R of your own that contains an image file of a startup floppy. When the PC boots from it, it simulates a floppy disk. So the actual physical floppy disk drive isn't a requirement.*

Alternatives to the Floppy Drive

You can probably name at least a half-dozen better ways to move data than a floppy disk, right? I'll describe a few of my favorites before getting into floppy technology in detail:

Flash Random Access Memory (RAM) devices   This is the newest, coolest thing. It's a little disk/drive combo that connects to the PC via a USB or FireWire port, and the computer sees it as a drive. When you're done with it, just disconnect it and plug it into a different computer. Instant portability!

NOTE *There are many different kinds of Flash RAM devices because this technology is in the "innovation" phase where manufacturers are getting really creative trying to capture the public's interest in the war to become the established standard. Chapter 22, "Digital Imaging," covers this in detail.*

CD-R   One-time writeable CDs—cheap, plentiful, and readable in almost every CD drive. (See Chapter 9, "CD-ROM and DVD Drives.") These hold about 700 megabytes (MB) of data.

CD-RW   These CD blanks are rewriteable up to 1000 times with packet-writing technology and hold about 700MB of data.

WARNING *The operating system must be able to read Universal Data Format (UDF) to read a CD-RW, or you have to install a UDF reader driver in the operating system. UDF is a packet-writing technology driver that allows the operating system to read the special type of data storage that CD-RWs use. Windows XP comes with it; so does the CD-RW drive's writing software.*

LS-120   This is also called SuperDisk. It's a 120MB floppy disk, which looks just like a normal floppy disk but is readable and writeable only in LS-120 drives. LS-120 drives can also read standard floppies. This was a good idea but never really caught on, and now there are better alternatives.

WARNING   Even though an LS-120 drive looks almost exactly like a regular floppy drive, it runs on the Integrated Drive Electronics (IDE) interface, not the floppy interface. Therefore, if you're setting up a system, keep in mind that going with an LS-120 drive as a floppy replacement will eat up one of the four Enhanced Integrated Drive Electronics (EIDE) positions on the motherboard.

Zip   Once the up-and-coming darling of portable storage, Iomega Zip disks have lately taken a back seat because the popularity of writeable CD. A Zip disk is a cartridge that's slightly larger than a floppy disk; it fits into a Zip drive and holds 100MB, 250MB, or 750MB of data, depending on the model. Zip drives are either SCSI or IDE. The original Zip drive also came in an external parallel model, which is now obsolete.

Jaz   Iomega used to make a larger disk/drive called Jaz that held 1 or 2 gigabytes (GB) of data, but they no longer do. You may still see such a drive in the field, however, and blank disks for it are still sold.

The Floppy Subsystem

Okay, I'm done trashing the floppy drive interface—for now, anyway. In the rest of this chapter, I'll assume you're still working with it and want to know something about it. I'll explain the mechanisms behind a floppy drive and its disks and tell you a little about troubleshooting and repairing floppy drives should you decide that it's worth your while to do so.

The floppy disk subsystem is, like the rest of the PC, modular. That's useful because you'll see that you can use this modularity to "divide and conquer" in order to solve problems. The subsystem consists of four parts: the floppy disks themselves, the drive, the disk controller, and the cable connecting the drive to the controller.

The Floppy Disk

A floppy, when extracted from its case, looks like a thin 45rpm record, only quite a bit smaller. It's a Mylar disk with iron oxide affixed to it.

We worry so much about dust getting on our hard disk surfaces that we seal up the disk drive. Should we have the same concern about floppies? Is there some way to "clean" a disk? Those of us older than, say, 30 may recall getting out the Discwasher and cleaning an album prior to playing it. For some people, a ritual such as this was comforting. For those people, I must sadly report that no such ritual occurs with floppies.

Floppies are stored inside their own Discwasher: a semirigid case lined with fleecy material. As the disk rotates inside the case, the material picks up any dust. The case has a hole cut in it so that the disk can be read/written without having to remove it from the case. In general, there's no need to clean a floppy disk. Figure 14.1 shows a typical floppy disk.

FIGURE 14.1
Floppy disk

A reasonable life expectancy for a floppy disk, according to disk manufacturers, is about three to four years. There are, of course, better and worse disks. There are different coatings on higher-density disks, generally incorporating less iron oxide (a cheap ingredient) and more cobalt or barium (expensive ingredients). Floppy disks are cheap enough these days that they're basically disposable; if a disk comes up with an error, just throw it away.

WARNING   *You shouldn't archive data on a floppy disk that you expect to need after several years because floppies tend to develop surface errors over time that make certain sectors (it's a crapshoot which ones) on the disk unreadable. Try to store important archives on CD-R, or at least Zip disks.*

There used to be different sizes and capacities of floppy disks, but nowadays there's only one: the high-density, double-sided floppy, with a formatted capacity of 1.44MB. Very occasionally you may run into other capacities and sizes; Table 14.1 summarizes the complete array.

I threw in the LS-120 in Table 14.1 because it looks and acts like a floppy disk, but technically it's not exactly a floppy disk. It uses a combination of magnetic and optical technology. The LS stands for *Laser Servo*, referring to the fact that it uses a laser for alignment in the drive. Then it writes the data using magnetic data tracks, much like an ordinary floppy does.

The Floppy Drive

For many years now, 3¹/₂-inch, 1.44MB floppy drives have been the standard; you'd be hard-pressed to find one of the old 1.2MB 5¹/₄-inch drives anymore except on the oldest PCs (we're talking XT here!). Even if you did find such a drive, finding a floppy disk for it that hasn't gone bad would be an even greater challenge! Remember, the average life of a floppy is only a few years.

TABLE 14.1: FLOPPY DISK TYPES

COMMON NAME	PHYSICAL SIZE	FORMATTED CAPACITY	NOTES
$5^1/_4$" Double-Density (DD)	$5^1/_4$"	360 kilobytes (KB)	Obsolete. Cover notch in side with a sticker to write-protect.
$5^1/_4$" High-Density (HD)	$5^1/_4$"	1.2MB	Obsolete. Can often be distinguished from $5^1/_4$" DD by a reinforcement ring around the center hole. Same write-protect .
$3^1/_2$" DD	$3^1/_2$"	720KB	Obsolete. Single square hole in corner with sliding tab for write-protection.
$3^1/_2$" HD	$3^1/_2$"	1.44MB	Current standard. Same write-protect tab as previously, plus extra square hole in adjacent corner to indicate HD capacity.
$3^1/_2$" Extra-Density (ED)	$3^1/_2$"	2.88MB	Once proposed as replacement for $3^1/_2$" HD, but it never caught on.
LS-120 SuperDisk	$3^1/_2$"	120MB	Once proposed as replacement for $3^1/_2$" ED; had limited success for a while. Write-protect tab is in different corner than on normal $3^1/_2$" floppies to protect it from accidental use in ordinary floppy drive.

The first $3^1/_2$-inch floppy drives were 720KB in capacity, rather than 1.44MB, but again, such drives will appear only on very old systems. The original 720KB floppy disk drive originated with the IBM PC AT, which was an 80286 system produced in the mid-to-late 1980s. So that gives you some idea of the age of the thing!

A $3^1/_2$-inch drive connects to the drive controller (normally built right into the motherboard) with a ribbon cable, the same as a hard drive or CD-ROM drive (except the ribbon cable the floppy drive uses is slightly narrower—34 wires instead of the 40 used for EIDE). It also requires power. Recall from Chapter 7, "Power Supplies and Power Protection," that a floppy disk uses the smaller Berg connector (also called a mini) from the power supply and not the normally chunky Molex connector.

TIP   *Most power supplies come with only one Berg connector, so if you have two floppy drives, you'll need a power cable adapter. Your computer's motherboard or power supply / case may come with such an adapter; if not, you can pick up an inexpensive one at a computer store. However, it's really rare that anyone would have two floppy drives anymore—as I said earlier, even one floppy drive is arguably too many in a modern system!*

The Disk Controller

Whenever a computer wants to interface with an outside device, it needs a controller to act as a go between to allow the outside device—a floppy, in this case—to talk with the Central Processing Unit (CPU). This functionality is handled through the motherboard's chipset (the Super I/O portion of the chipset, to be exact). A single floppy controller can handle up to two floppy drives on a single ribbon cable.

The Cable

The last piece in the floppy subsystem is the cable that connects the controller to the drive. Cables sound insignificant, but this one isn't: I've fixed a lot of floppy problems by swapping out defective cables. The drive is connected to the controller by a 34-wire ribbon cable. Most of the cables have three connectors: one for the drive controller, one for drive A:, and one for drive B: (although few computers nowadays have a second floppy drive).

NOTE   *Because the cable is 34-wires wide, you'd think that the interface between the floppy and the controller is a parallel interface—8-bits wide—but it's not. The floppy-to-controller interface is serial, transferring 1 bit at a time.*

It's important that you plug your floppy drive into the right connector on the cable. The connector that's farthest away from the other two is the one that goes to the motherboard (or I/O controller board). The one at the opposite end from that goes to the A: drive (the primary floppy drive). The middle one is optional and is used if you have a secondary floppy drive.

Why the importance of the positioning? Take a close look at the cable shown in Figure 14.2 to see why. Notice that there's a twist in part of the wires at one end of the cable. That twist changes the flow of the data between the B: drive (middle) and the A: drive (the twisted end), so the controller can distinguish between them when addressing them.

FIGURE 14.2
Floppy cable
with twist for
the A: drive

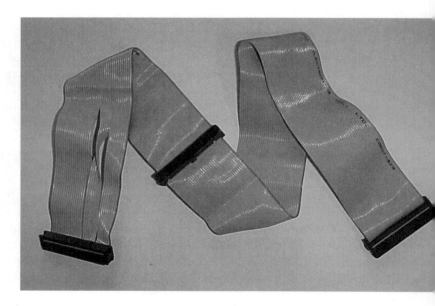

It never hurts to have a couple of extra ribbon cables around. The cables are inexpensive and available from many mail-order houses or computer discounters, so it's easy to keep an extra one around. Later in the chapter I'll tell you about some of the common problems with floppy drives, one of which is having a broken wire or two in the ribbon cable. It's fairly common and also easy to fix (just swap the cable out).

Simple Preventive Maintenance for Floppies

The failure of a floppy disk or drive can be a scary, potentially disastrous thing if you've stored some critical data on a floppy disk. (That's not a very good idea, by the way. Never put your only copy of something important on a floppy.) What can you do to lower the probability of a floppy disaster?

To Clean Heads or Not to Clean Heads?

Anyone who has a VCR and rents videotapes on a regular basis probably knows about the need to clean the VCR's heads. Something like that can be done for the floppy as well, but experts disagree as to whether it's worthwhile to do so.

Like your VCR, floppy drives have an electromagnetic read/write head that does most of the drive's work. In the process of accessing the disk, the head may rub some of the coating off the disk and onto itself. It seems reasonable, then, to assume that head-cleaning kits are good things.

When you can't see something, you get superstitious about it. We can't see the junk on floppy heads (or the data on magnetic disks, for that matter), so we play it safe and purchase a floppy head cleaner to ward off floppy evil spirits. Once we've procured the cleaner, however, our first question is, "How often should I clean the floppy heads?"

The instructions on the head cleaner say to do it every week. That doesn't seem to be a good piece of advice; shoving a floppy head cleaner in a drive could misalign a disk head. The floppy cleaner is a relatively thick piece of cotton shaped like a floppy. Worse yet, some floppy cleaners are *abrasive*— they wear away some of the floppy head with every use. (One has to look askance at this procedure. Scraping away some of the head to find a clean part seems somewhat like using sulfuric acid to clean one's teeth.)

Personally, I clean my heads only when the drive fails. I have some computers on which I've *never* cleaned the heads, and they work fine. My recommendation: clean the heads only when you start experiencing read/write errors. (Of course, for only slightly more money than a good-quality head-cleaning system, you could have a whole new floppy drive, so weigh your options.)

As I hinted before, *be careful* when choosing a floppy head cleaner! Don't buy an abrasive cleaner— make sure it uses a cotton floppy and some cleaning fluid.

NOTE *By the way, there's an issue related to cleaning the heads called* demagnetizing *them; it's done with some audio recording heads. People sometimes ask me if floppy heads need to be demagnetized—they don't.*

Defending Disks

Did you ever notice the "don't" cartoons on the back of a floppy disk jacket? Don't expose the disk to heat, cold, magnets, or dust, they warn. They lead you to believe that floppies are very fragile items. A little practical experience with disks teaches you that it isn't really true. Yes, disks must be taken care of, but you needn't get crazy about it. Don't put them on the radiator or leave them on a shelf that gets three hours of direct sunlight every day. Don't store them under the roof leak or use them as coasters. Given the choice, store them upright, stacked left to right rather than on top of each other. And keep them away from magnets.

When it comes to temperature extremes, you have to be concerned about *thermal shock* (which you read about in Chapter 4, "Avoiding Service: Preventive Maintenance"). If your portable computer has been sitting in the back of the car in freezing temperatures overnight, bring it in and let it warm up before using it. Just a little heat expansion/contraction can temporarily realign your drives or make the motors respond a little differently. In addition, condensation from rapidly warming items can build up on the electronics, and the moisture can cause electrical shorts. Extreme temperatures can damage the disks; vendors claim that disks should never be stored in weather colder than 50 degrees C or warmer than 125 degrees C. Cold isn't as much of a problem as heat.

Dust, smoke, and dirt can cause damage to the head and/or to a disk. Everybody knows smoking isn't good for you, but you may not know just how bad it is for your drives. If you're in a dusty environment, think about getting a power supply with a filtered fan. Running the air through a filter before pushing it through the system removes the vast majority of the dust particles.

As you also read in Chapter 4, magnets—both the permanent and electromagnetic type—can cause permanent loss of data on hard or floppy disks. Something I have yet to understand is the little plastic paper clip holder with the circular magnet near the opening. Why is the magnet there? Are people afraid the paper clips will get out if not magnetically restrained? (As one of the members of Monty Python might say, "Are you suggesting paper clips are migratory?") One day, you'll put a floppy on top of the paper clip holder. It'll be sad. Or you'll use one of the paper clips—now magnetized by their proximity to the magnet—to clip a document to a floppy. Arggh.

WARNING   *Watch out for less-obvious magnetic sources, too. Unshielded stereo speakers, for example, have powerful magnetic pulls. And some older telephones have magnets in them, too.*

Removing, Configuring, and Installing Floppy Drives

You generally won't repair drives; you'll replace them. That means it's most important to be able to rip 'em out and slap 'em in.

Removing Floppy Drives

You can remove floppy drives in three steps:

1. Remove screws from the mounting brackets.

2. Remove the power connection.

3. Remove the data connection.

I covered the physical extraction part pretty thoroughly in Chapter 3, "Taking Apart and Rebuilding the PC," so I won't repeat it here.

Installing Floppy Drives

Installing a floppy drive is just the reverse of removing one. To install a new floppy drive, you must follow these steps:

1. Mount it into a drive bay.

2. Connect it to the after-the-twist end of the ribbon cable if it's drive A: or to the center connector if it's drive B:. You can't have a drive B: in a system without a drive A:, so your primary floppy should always be A:, at the opposite end of the cable from the controller.

3. Attach a power connector. Again, you want the smaller power connector, the Berg (mini), for the floppy drive.

NOTE   Most PCs use a standard-sized floppy drive, but some proprietary systems (the Compaq Presario is particularly notorious in this regard) use a nonstandard floppy drive with offset positioning that requires you to buy a replacement directly from the original manufacturer (and typically at two to three times the cost of a generic replacement!). So if you're replacing a floppy drive in someone else's PC, it pays to examine the old drive before buying a replacement for it.

Troubleshooting Tips

The mechanical nature of floppy drives makes them prone to a host of ills. I'll now catalog a few of them.

A Disk Can't Be Read

Pop a disk in the drive, try to read it, and the message says `Data error reading drive A`, `Sector not found reading drive A`, or perhaps the dreaded `General failure reading drive A`. Such a message is even better than your morning coffee to get the ol' blood pumping, particularly if the disk contains your only copy of the football pool.

Do the following:

1. Press **R** for Retry. Sometimes it'll work. Ignore the painful grinding sounds. After three or four unsuccessful retries in a row, you may safely conclude that it's not going to work. But if the drive seems to read a little bit of data before repeating the error, keep trying; you may be able to kludge the drive into reading the file—perhaps just this once—before it goes kaput completely.

2. Remove and replace the floppy disk. I've seen 3^1/$_2$-inch drives that are unreadable until you take out the disk and put it back in.

3. Take out the floppy disk and try it in another drive. The read/write head on one machine may be aligned just slightly differently than on another, and that little difference might make one drive read a disk that another can't.

If one drive can read a disk that another can't, either the disk drive's head could be misaligned or the floppy disk could've been formatted by a different disk drive and *that* drive's head was misaligned. Try to find the drive that created the disk. (If it's the one you've been fooling with, obviously this advice isn't too useful.)

4. If you *still* haven't solved the problem, you're basically in the same boat as someone who's suffered a media failure on the hard disk. See Chapter 13, "Protecting and Maintaining Hard Disks," for information on data recovery from a bad disk.

The Drive Refuses to Function

When the drive won't read or write properly, there are a bunch of possible causes. I'm assuming here that this is a drive that worked fine yesterday and to which you haven't done anything that would obviously cause drive problems. Follow these steps:

1. Did you see a floppy drive controller failure error on the screen when the system booted up? Such a Power-On Self Test (POST) error message means that drive A: didn't respond. The system no longer realizes that you have a floppy drive. It means that your floppy controller has failed (in which case both floppies—A: and B:—would be dead), the floppy drive itself has failed, or the cable is bad.

TIP   If you have two floppy disk drives and only A: is recognized at bootup, not B:, it could be that the CMOS battery has died on your motherboard, resetting the BIOS Setup configuration back to factory default settings (one floppy). Try going into BIOS Setup and reinforming it that you have two floppy drives.

2. If there was no POST error, try other disks in the drive. If only one disk gives the drive fits, the problem more likely lies in the disk.

3. Clean the disk drive heads. It's easy and takes only a minute. (But see my earlier caveats about drive cleaning in the "To Clean Heads or Not to Clean Heads?" section.)

4. Try to format a disk. If you can format a disk all right but that disk is unreadable by other drives, your drive head is probably misaligned. If it's misaligned, toss it. New floppy drives are about $10 to $20 today.

5. Finally, swap the relevant components: the controller, the cable, and the drive. Swap only one component at a time, and when swapping a component doesn't solve the problem, reinstall the original component and swap another one.

Don't overlook the lowly cable. Cables can get nicked when you're installing boards, replacing drives, or just removing the cover. How bad that is depends on which line gets nicked. One cable on an old laptop that I once owned kept the change line from working; when I put in a different floppy, the file listing still showed the previous disk. It takes only a two-minute swap with another cable to find out for sure. For more information about change lines, see the next section.

Suppose you get periodic data loss and have changed the drive and controller—what next? The power supply. Malfunctioning power supplies often show up as gremlins in the system. Try swapping the power supply.

The Drive Shows Phantom Directories

Imagine that you display a file listing of a floppy disk's contents. Then you remove the disk and put a different disk in the drive. You refresh the file listing, but you see the *directory of the previous floppy, not the one in the drive now!*

If you see this symptom on a computer, this is a *red alert!* Don't use the thing until you get the problem fixed. The reason: say you put a floppy in the drive and display the listing of files on it. Then you put a different floppy in the drive and write some data to the floppy. *The PC writes data to the new floppy using the old floppy's directory!* That means the newly written file is probably okay, but everything else on the floppy is trashed. (Let me tell you about how I lost four pages out of a chapter in a book I wrote many years back...)

Where does this problem come from? It's something called the *change line signal*. I mentioned this earlier in the chapter, when I was talking about cables. Basically it means that on all modern systems, the 34th wire in the cable (the one farthest away from the red stripe) is in charge of letting the drive controller know when a new floppy has been inserted and rereading its table of contents. If there's something wrong with that wire in the cable, or with that pin on the drive connector, you get this phantom disk problem.

Suppose you find yourself with a change line problem—phantom directories. What do you do? Check the floppy cable. Try substituting a different floppy cable, and see if that doesn't clear up the problem. If it doesn't, the problem is inside the drive itself.

Floppy Troubleshooting Recap

Before you give up on a floppy drive, try these tips:

- Always try other disks in the drive before assuming the drive itself is bad.

- If the floppy drive light comes on and stays on all the time, you've installed the ribbon cable backward.

- If the floppy drive light doesn't come on at all, check the power connector.

- If you see a floppy drive controller error at startup, check the BIOS to ensure that it recognizes your floppy drive. If the CMOS battery fails, it may forget about all drives except the first floppy drive (A:).

- If you switch disks but the PC still shows the previous contents of the drive, check for a damaged ribbon cable.

- Intermittent disk access errors often indicate a bad power supply in the system.

- Data errors reading the disk can mean a bad disk. You might also try cleaning the disk heads by using a disk-cleaning kit.

◆ Try to format a disk. If it works but that disk is then unreadable by other drives, the drive head is probably misaligned. Throw the drive away, and get a new one.

◆ If replacing the drive doesn't help, try replacing the cable. If that doesn't work, the problem is probably the disk controller. If it's built into the motherboard, you may need to disable it in the BIOS and install a separate I/O controller card to use instead.

Now, let's move on to the subject of printers. In the next chapter, I'll talk about troubleshooting printers in general. Then, in the following two chapters, I'll get specific about particular printers: inkjet and laser printers.

Part 3

Supporting and Managing External Drives

Chapter 15

Printer Types and Interfaces

Introduction

Ah, printers! They're more mechanical in nature than most of the other parts of a computer and therefore more subject to failures of various kinds. Fortunately, the same few things turn out to be the problem in the vast majority of troubleshooting cases, so in that sense printer troubleshooting is rather simple—except, of course, when you run into one of those unusual cases.

I won't spend a lot of time describing the complex innards of various printer technologies here because you'll get a hefty dose of that in Chapters 16 and 17 for the two most popular technologies: inkjet and laser. Instead, this chapter eases into the topic by discussing the various classes of printers you may encounter, the interfaces they use, the general preventive maintenance you can perform on a printer, and some general printer troubleshooting tips.

QuickSteps: Connecting and Testing a Printer

This section contains the basic steps for connecting a printer. For in-depth coverage on printers and how to troubleshoot printer problems, refer to the rest of this chapter.

BE PREPARED

Before you start, there are some things you may need on hand. These include the following:

- Printer's manual.

- Computer's manual.

- Printer's setup software if you're running Windows. This may not be required if Windows has a compatible driver for the printer.

- (Optional) Extra cable to swap with, in case there's any doubt whether the current one is working. Depending on the printer interface, this may be either parallel or Universal Serial Bus (USB).

- Before you connect a printer to a PC, make sure that:

  - The computer is turned off (if parallel; this isn't necessary for USB).

  - The printer is turned off (again, if parallel; this isn't necessary for USB).

To connect a test a printer, follow these steps:

1. Set up the printer, and turn it on. Run its self-test to confirm that it's working properly.

2. Turn the printer off (if connecting with a parallel interface).

3. Connect the printer to the computer with a printer cable. This could be a parallel or USB cable depending on the printer interface. If the printer has both to choose from, USB is better.

4. Turn on the PC (if it's off). Windows may detect the new printer automatically.

5. If you have setup software for the printer, cancel any dialog box that Windows presents offering to search for a driver, and then run the setup software that came with the printer.

   Alternatively, if you don't have setup software for the printer, allow Windows to try to detect it and locate a driver for it. You can always download a driver from the Internet if this doesn't work.

6. Print a self-test using the printer's Windows driver or utility program.

Types of Printers

There have been many printer technologies developed over the years, but they all boil down to two or three factors:

Line or page printer? A line printer prints one line at a time, as the paper feeds through. Examples include inkjet and dot matrix. A page printer lays down the entire page on the paper in one swoop. Examples include laser and LED (which stands for *Light-Emitting Diode*).

Impact or nonimpact? An impact printer prints by striking something colored that's sitting next to the paper (usually an inked fabric ribbon). The impact causes the color to rub off on the paper. A nonimpact printer prints by laying down the color on the paper in some nonviolent way. Nearly all printers are nonimpact these days—which is fine, except they can't print on multipart carbon copy forms. Dot-matrix printers are the lone impact type still available.

Sheet-fed or continuous? A sheet-fed printer uses regular precut sheets of paper, feeding them through one at a time. A continuous-feed printer uses paper that's connected at the top and bottom of each sheet, one to another; it pulls the paper through with a system of sprockets that fit into little perforated holes in the sides of the paper. Most printers these days are sheet-fed except for impact printers (such as dot matrix), which are usually continuous-feed.

TIP *You can use a continuous-feed printer as a sheet-fed printer in a pinch; the only catch is that you have to insert each page individually; there's no paper tray from which to draw.*

Type of ink? Different printer types use different inks. For example, a laser printer uses toner, an inkjet printer uses liquid ink, and a dot-matrix printer uses an inked fabric ribbon. Some other less common types include colored wax, colored film, and marking pens (in the case of a plotter, for example).

THERMAL-TRANSFER PRINTERS

When you were a kid, did you ever make pictures by coloring with crayons onto a piece of heavy paper and then using an iron to transfer the colored wax to another piece of paper? (If not, just nod politely and keep reading—I'll get past the "when you were a kid" stories in a minute.) Thermal-transfer printing (known as *T-wax* printing in the trade) works something like that. Very hot pins are pressed onto a wax- or wax/resin-coated ribbon, and the wax or resin melts and transfers to the paper beneath it. The difference is that the paper has to go through the process four times, once for each color (typically cyan, yellow, magenta, and black). This kind of printer produces excellent-quality color images—better than an inkjet and arguably better than color lasers—but is rather expensive in terms of consumables. You won't find these printers for sale in the typical office-supply store—they're a specialty item. (Refills for them are also generally not available at your regular retail outlets.) Some of these also require special thermal paper, which of course is a lot more expensive than standard paper.

In the mainstream market, you'll see two types of printers for sale: laser and inkjet. Each of these has its own subtypes, but I'll save that discussion for Chapters 16 and 17. Other types of printers are either obsolete or almost obsolete, or they're designed for such a specialty audience that they aren't available in mainstream stores. Table 15.1 summarizes the printer types you may encounter.

TABLE 15.1: PRINTER TYPES

PRINTER TYPE	INK TYPE	PAPER FEED	IMPACT?	COLOR?	USED FOR	NOTES
Daisy-wheel	Ribbon	Continuous	Yes	No	Business correspondence	Thoroughly obsolete by now. Old, slow, and noisy. Works like an automated typewriter. No graphics.
Dot matrix	Ribbon	Continuous	Yes	No (usually)	Business correspondence	Mostly obsolete but still available for applications that require impact printing such as multipart forms.
Inkjet	Liquid	Sheet-fed	No	Yes (usually)	General home and business	Inexpensive and capable of color, but ink cartridges are expensive.
Laser	Powdered toner	Sheet-fed	No	Varies	General business	Excels at high-speed black-and-white printing at a low per-page cost. Color models are available but are more expensive.
LED	Powdered toner	Sheet-fed	No	Varies	General business	Very similar technologically to laser, to the point where some printers marketed as laser are actually LED.
Thermal transfer	Solid wax or resin (melted for printing)	Sheet-fed	No	Yes	Commercial art	Expensive in both initial cost and consumables but produces superior color quality.
Plotter	Pens	Varies	No	Varies	Blueprints and design	Specialty printer used in commercial art involving line drawings such as architecture.

Printer Interfaces

For years the parallel port was far and away the most common type of interface between printer and computer, but lately it has been replaced by USB, a faster and more sharing-friendly interface with hot-pluggable capability. Because you're likely to encounter both parallel and USB interfaces in the field for the next several years, it's important to understand both in relation to printers.

Parallel Ports

Most older (let's say pre-2000) printers connect to a PC via the *parallel port*, a female 25-pin connector that's typically built into the PC. The parallel port was originally devised as a high-speed, low-cost alternative to a serial port for printer interfaces, and for many years it served well in this capacity and is still in use today wherever USB isn't an option or not desirable for some reason.

The main drawbacks of the parallel port interface are as follows:

◆ It's not hot-pluggable, so you have to shut down the printer and computer before connecting or disconnecting.

◆ Cable length is limited to about 15 feet; if you go beyond that, the signal starts to break up and data errors occur. This is because of the parallel nature of the interface; see Chapter 10, "Understanding and Installing ATA Drives," for a discussion of why Serial ATA is better than standard parallel ATA to get a feel for the parallel-versus-serial thing.

◆ It's not as seamlessly Plug and Play (PnP) as USB. Windows can usually detect and identify parallel devices, if the port is set to a bidirectional mode (see the next point) and the printer is PnP, but USB does it more reliably and quickly.

◆ There are several modes that a parallel port can operate in, and you must choose the correct mode in the Basic Input/Output System (BIOS) Setup. It isn't always obvious which mode is correct to fix a problem, so a certain amount of trial and error is sometimes necessary. (See the following section for more mode discussion.)

PARALLEL PORT MODES

Parallel port technology evolved over the course of a decade or so, and in the process several different modes were introduced. Each computer's BIOS (or onboard controller for a parallel I/O card) supports all the available modes for backward compatibility:

Standard The original parallel port mode, now called Standard, was designed primarily for sending data one way: from the computer to the printer. It was asynchronous. In other words, it had different bit widths and speeds for output—8-bit, 150 kilobytes per second (Kbps)—and for input—4-bit, 50Kbps.

Bidirectional As devices became available that needed to provide input via the parallel port, a new mode was needed: *bidirectional*. It uses 8 bits and 150Kbps in both directions. It's sometimes called Extended or PS/2.

Enhanced Parallel Port (EPP) EPP speeds up the data transfer, sending and receiving at up to 2 megabits per second (Mbps). This mode was designed for nonprinter devices that needed to send a lot of data to the computer quickly, such as scanners and Zip drives.

Enhanced Capabilities Port (ECP) ECP is similar to EPP except it's designed with printers in mind rather than nonprinter devices. There are subtle differences between the two, the most noticeable of which is that ECP assigns a Direct Memory Access (DMA) channel to the port. On most modern systems there are plenty of DMA channels to go around because hardly any devices use them, so this is probably not a problem. One advantage of ECP is that it allows the printer or device to send messages to the computer, such as being low on ink or having a paper jam.

To take advantage of any of these modes other than Standard, the printer, computer, operating system, and cable all need to support that mode. This isn't an issue for any hardware made in the past 10 years—it's all good. With Windows NT 4 you can't use ECP, but other than that you shouldn't run into any operating system limitations with 32-bit Windows versions.

From the previous list, the important thing to glean is that ECP is the best choice for a parallel printer. Modern PCs ship with ECP set as the default mode for the parallel port, but you can change this in BIOS Setup if you need to (for example, to support a very old printer or to troubleshoot problems with parallel port sharing described in the following section.)

PARALLEL PORT SHARING

The biggest trouble with using the parallel port as a general-purpose port is that you have only one parallel port on most systems, so how can you have more than one parallel device at once? Well, you can continually switch cables, or you can attempt to share the port among the devices. Some nonprinter parallel devices, such as scanners, have a built-in pass-through that lets you connect the parallel devices in a sort of daisy chain, such as Small Computer System Interface (SCSI). This arrangement works poorly on some systems and worse on others. Generally speaking, inkjet printers have a harder time sharing a parallel port than do other printer types, and different BIOS mode settings for the parallel port can sometimes make the difference between sharing success (marginal at best) and failure. When troubleshooting a sharing situation in which one or both of the devices won't work, try changing the parallel port mode in BIOS Setup—try each of the four available modes to see if any of them coax the sharing to work.

ADDING PARALLEL PORTS

Most systems have only the one port, LPT1, but you can easily add expansion boards with extra ports (both parallel and serial). Back in the days when parallel was virtually the only choice for printer interfaces, it was common for high-end users to add parallel ports to a system. Today, however, USB has made it possible for a single PC to support dozens of printers on a single interface, so hardly anybody is interested in adding a parallel port Input/Output (I/O) board anymore.

Parallel ports are often referred to as LPT ports, a nod to the days of mainframes when LPT was short for *Line PrinTer*. The main built-in parallel port in a system is LPT1, and additional ports you might add are LPT2, LPT3, and so on.

NOTE *Here's some techie detail that I hope you'll never have to know, but just in case. . .the PC has a peculiar process for relating I/O addresses to LPT addresses. First, it looks for address 3BC. If there is a port at that address, it assigns it LPT1. If not, it looks for 378 and, if it exists, assigns that to LPT1. If that's not available, it finally tries for 278. Once LPT1 is assigned, it looks (in the same order) for LPT2 and LPT3. This means that if you put a first parallel port into a machine and the port has address 278, you'll end up with an LPT1, even though 278 is intended for LPT3. But install a second port at 378, and the next time you boot up, the 278 port will become LPT2.*

USB Ports

Most new printers will attach to your computer by a USB port. You learned about the USB interface in Chapter 2, "Inside the PC: Core Components." To use a USB printer with your PC, you need two things: PC support and operating system support.

First, verify that the PC has USB ports. Many Pentium II and all Pentium III/Pentium 4 motherboards (and their AMD equivalents) support USB. You may find one or two USB ports on the back of the computer, and on some computers there are also USB ports on the front. If the motherboard doesn't support USB, you can get a Peripheral Component Interconnect (PCI) USB adapter card.

Second, you need an operating system that supports the USB interface. Windows 98 and higher offer USB support, and Windows 95—except 95C, an Original Equipment Manufacturer (OEM) version—and Windows NT 4 don't. USB supports PnP installation, and you can unplug the USB cable from the printer to the PC while your PC is on. This is called *hot-swapping* or *hot-plugging*. Typically, the first time you plug the printer into your PC's USB port, Windows will automatically detect the connection and prompt you to install the printer drivers and related software. As a result, installing a USB printer is virtually painless. You have no Interrupt Request (IRQ) settings to worry about, and you can be up and running in no time.

As you learned in Chapter 2, there are two USB standards: 1.1 and 2. Although USB 2 is 40 times faster than USB 1.1, the main reason printer manufacturers continue to use USB 1.1 is that it's more than fast enough for most printers. For example, Hewlett-Packard (HP) manufactures dozens of USB-interface printers, but only certain ones support USB 2 (mostly the ones that require faster speed, such as high-speed lasers and photo-quality inkjets). Still, it's inevitable that in the future all USB devices will be 2; so, if you find yourself with a USB 2 printer and a computer with an older USB 1.1 connection, it's no sweat. Just plug the 2 device into the older USB connector, and it'll work fine. One of the wonderful features of USB 2 is its backward compatibility with the previous USB.

Serial Ports

I considered not even mentioning the serial port interface because it's so rare anymore. The original printers connected to computers via serial (RS-232) ports. It's still possible to connect printers serially today, provided the printer has a serial interface (hardly any still do). But I don't recommend it. Serial port printing can be very slow, and with today's graphics-heavy print jobs, that can mean frustration and waiting around.

Some printers used to have both a parallel and a serial interface, so, in theory, you could hook up two PCs to the same printer, each through a different interface. However, because of the speed issue with serial, I recommend instead that you share the printer through some other means—perhaps using a switch box or a network.

Infrared Ports

For members of the "virtual office" who have no desk but only a laptop to carry around and plug in as needed, there's a way to eliminate at least one of the cables you need to plug in: printers with infrared ports are available. Rather than requiring a parallel cable to connect the printer to your computer, a ray of infrared light shines between a transceiver on the computer and one on the printer.

NOTE   *There's no reason why desktop computers can't use infrared printers as well, but most desktop machines aren't equipped with infrared capabilities. In contrast, most laptops, Personal Digital Assistants (PDAs), and Pocket PCs do have this capability.*

Data travels between the computer and printer via an infrared connection. Light and electric impulses all pulse at a certain rate per second; this rate is called the *frequency*—the more pulses, the higher the frequency. Signals with higher frequencies can transmit data more quickly (each pulse can carry a bit of data). However, they have a shorter range and are more prone to interference than lower-frequency signals because anything that interferes with the signal will affect more data than it would if there were fewer pulses per second. Infrared light has a high frequency. Thus, the computer sends a beam of infrared light to the receiver on the printer. The devices have a pretty good range, but they're usually limited to line of sight. (You can't print from an office around the corner, for example.)

If you're having trouble with a wireless printer, check the following:

◆ Are the infrared ports on the printer and computer both clean and unblocked?

◆ If you're using a laptop, is the infrared port active? It's activated through the BIOS during startup. By default, it's off.

◆ Does it help to move the printer/computer to one side?

◆ Did someone stand between your printer and computer during the print job?

Other than that, troubleshooting an infrared printer is much like troubleshooting any other printer. The tricky thing about wireless printers is making the connections.

Network Printing

Most businesses don't want to be tied down to providing a printer to every single PC—or, conversely, limiting each PC to printing on only one printer. Thus was born the network printer.

There are two ways to use your Local Area Network (LAN) to print. One is to connect the printer to a PC and then share that printer on the LAN. Although the printer "belongs" to the person using that PC, anyone on the network can send printer jobs to it. The main disadvantages to this are that nobody can use the printer if that person turns his or her computer off and heavy usage of the printer can potentially cause performance slowdowns on that person's PC.

The other way to share a printer is to hook it directly into the network. This requires a network-capable printer. Some printers come network-ready; others can be made ready by installing an upgrade card in them. (This capability varies among manufacturers, but HP offers a JetDirect card for some models that make them network-capable.)

There are, however, a few caveats to networking a printer directly. First, as with any network device, you must be using the same protocols on your server that you use on the printer's network interface because the printer driver is installed on a server and then shared. The most popular protocol for a Microsoft network is Transmission Control Protocol/Internet Protocol (TCP/IP); for Net-Ware networks, it's Internet Packet Exchange/Sequence Packet Exchange (IPX/SPX). You must also be sure that the protocols are configured correctly—if you're using TCP/IP, for example, you must have an IP address and a subnet mask for the printer. This book doesn't get into the techie details of networking, and in reality most network-capable printers work pretty well right out of the box if you simply follow the directions that come with them. But it doesn't hurt to have a network administrator friend in your address book in case you run into problems.

Printer Maintenance

Keeping your printer in top condition means giving it a little maintenance attention now and then. Printer maintenance varies depending on the type of printer, so you'll now look at the upkeep for some of the most common printer types.

Dot-Matrix Printers

If you're still using a dot-matrix printer, you're either seriously strapped for cash or you need to print multipart forms. I'll assume the latter. Dot-matrix printers strike the page with small rods (called *needles* or *pins*) that protrude from the print head. Printers that use this type of technology are known as *impact* printers, as I mentioned earlier in the chapter. They can print through multiple layers of carbon (or carbonless) copies, and some businesses need that capability.

NOTE   The only kind of impact printer you'll find for sale these days is a dot-matrix printer. Daisy-wheel printers, which used to rule the marketplace 15 to 20 years ago, are all but extinct. (Okay, you might find a daisy-wheel printer at an estate sale or in a mysterious forgotten crate in a government warehouse.) Even dot-matrix printers are seriously old technology.

To clean a dot-matrix printer, use a dry, soft cloth to clean both the paper path and the ribbon path. Most manufacturers suggest cleaning every six months because the ribbon path can build up a film of inky glop that causes the ribbon to jam. Before doing this, go to a drug store and buy a dispenser box of clear latex gloves. Use them when working on the printer so that you don't have to wash your hands for hours to remove the ink. (But don't use them when you're working on chips and boards—that latex can build up some mean static.)

TIP   When you're working on a printer, it's easy to get ink on yourself and your clothes. Here's a tip that will help you clean up: a friend once told me that hairspray will remove ink from fabric. So another friend and I experimented with her hair mousse—you know, the foam you use to make your hair defy gravity? It did nothing. Then we tried some Aqua Net, a hairspray that hasn't changed since Jackie Kennedy used it in the White House. The result? We found that cheap hairspray works a lot better than the expensive stuff. Spray it on the fabric, and rinse with cold water. A little soap will pick up the rest.

You can also vacuum out the paper chaff periodically from the inside of the printer. The continuous-feed paper used in impact printers is somewhat more prone to leaving dust behind than single-sheet paper is. You may find it unwieldy to use the same vacuum on the printer as you use on the living room carpet. Purchasing a tech vacuum of some sort may be best because it's smaller and easier to use in tight areas, and it won't suck key tops right off your keyboard.

On an impact printer, the print head moves back and forth across the page, which means there's probably a drive belt. Determine if there's a belt-tightening mechanism for the printer and find the correct tension values. Keep a replacement belt on hand. (Believe me, they're no picnic to find in a hurry.)

WARNING Some dot-matrix printers have ribbon cables that carry the data to the print head. They often look like drive belts, but they are definitely not. Tighten these, and they'll usually break. If they do, you can say goodbye to your printer.

Most impact printers never need to be lubricated. In fact, oil can do considerable damage if applied to the wrong places. If you thoroughly disassemble the printer, you'll probably have to lubricate various points as you reassemble it. If you intend to do this, I strongly recommend you get a maintenance manual from the manufacturer.

Here's a tip that will extend the life of both the ribbon and the print head: put some WD-40 lubricant on a used ink ribbon. Let it soak overnight. It'll produce good output the next day, and you won't damage the print head—WD-40 is a good lubricant for print heads. Let me stress, however, that this applies only to ink ribbons. If you have any other type of printer, this won't work. So don't go soaking that laser toner cartridge in anything, okay?

The expensive part of a dot-matrix printer that dies is the print head. Luckily, almost all dot-matrix printers these days have a *thermistor* (basically, a temperature sensor) that detects when the print head is getting too hot and shuts the printer down until it cools off. To avoid excess heat buildup around a dot-matrix printer, avoid stacking things around it—leave a clear path for airflow on all sides.

Replacing the print head isn't economical on many printers because of the high price that manufacturers charge for replacements. For example, the print head replacement for a good-quality wide-carriage dot-matrix printer might cost $100 or more. The fact is, in almost every case, it makes no sense to replace a dot-matrix print head unless you need to print multipart forms or have one of the very expensive, high-speed dot-matrix printers. You can buy a new printer for about the cost of replacing a dot-matrix print head.

Inkjet Printers

Inkjet printers have come a long way since their introduction back in the '70s. At one time, inkjet printers clogged pretty regularly because the ink would dry in the tiny holes that make up the print heads. Today, the jets are designed to resist drying, and some print heads are protected by a rubber boot that keeps the holes from drying out. Also, on some models, the heads are built into the ink tanks so that when you replace an empty tank, you're also getting new jets. This keeps the print on these printers looking like new.

Still, if you let an inkjet printer sit too long without using it, the ink in the jets (and/or in the ink cartridges) will dry out, and one or more colors won't print. This can result in some odd-looking printouts with amusing (but definitely not lifelike!) colored stripes. If this happens, run the printer's built-in head-cleaning utility. You can do this by pressing certain buttons on the printer itself or in most cases through the printer's driver in Windows. (Select Start ➤ Settings ➤ Printers, or choose Printers from the Control Panel, then right-click the printer in the Printers window, and choose Properties. Look for the cleaning command, usually on the Utilities tab.) After cleaning the heads, run a nozzle test, which you might be able to do by using the printer's buttons or through its Properties box in Windows. The nozzle test prints some basic geometrical pattern of lines on the page in each of its colors, so you can see which color, if any, is failing to print. Sometimes several cycles of cleaning (up to 15 cycles on an Epson) followed by testing are required to clear out the dried-up ink residue.

One trick I recently learned for clearing up Epson ink cartridges is relatively easy. If after several cleaning cycles the pattern still doesn't print correctly, try removing the ink cartridges and immediately replacing them. This has worked for me on several occasions when the print head wasn't printing correctly after the printer hadn't been used in several months.

You may see advertisements for refilled ink cartridges, or even kits that promise to let you refill the cartridges yourself, but this is seldom a good idea. True, it can save you money, but on many models, as I mentioned, the heads are built into the ink cartridges so that you get new heads when you get new ink. This is by design. If you continue to print with the old heads tankful after tankful, the print quality will definitely suffer, and you may harm your printer.

NOTE *On some inkjet printers, moving the ink cartridges into view so you can replace them can be a real exercise in coordination. On certain Epson models, for example, you have to hold down two little tiny buttons simultaneously for several seconds and then press another button. Check the printer's manual to find out the procedure for your specific model—that's usually the only way to find out (other than visiting the manufacturer's Web site and searching for the information).*

Laser Printers

Laser printers are important enough that I'll devote an entire chapter to them later in this book. As a result, I'll limit my discussion of them here.

The laser printer is similar to a copy machine and amazingly reliable. You may be surprised to learn that many different brands of laser printers operate using the same basic innards. They need little maintenance except for a new cartridge every few thousand copies or so.

Some laser printer designs build the drum into the toner cartridge so that when you replace the toner, you also get a new photoelectric drum. Other models have separate units for them, so that you can go longer without a new drum. There are arguments to be made both ways in terms of which is best, but plan on paying more per toner cartridge for models that have a drum inside or plan on paying a lot for a new drum every several years for a printer that has them separate.

It's okay to buy recycled toner cartridges, but make sure your refill company completely rebuilds the insides, including replacing the drum (if it's in there on that model). Avoid the "drill-and-fill" vendors—they don't replace the insides, and using that kind of refill will lead to a lower-quality print image and may damage the laser printer. If you don't refill the cartridges, many manufacturers provide a way to mail in the used ones for recycling (and sometimes a rebate).

Laser printers require proper ventilation and a fair amount of power. Other than that, don't pour any Cokes in them, and they last a long time. Never ship a laser with a toner cartridge in place. It can open and cover the inside of the laser with toner. And don't take the toner cartridge out and wave it around, or toner might spill out and make a mess. You'll also want to wipe out any stray toner in the printer's insides every time you change the toner cartridge.

TIP *To get the last little bit of life out of a toner cartridge, you can take it out and shake it gently from side to side. But don't turn it on end, and don't shake it up and down, or toner might spill out.*

On some models, a new toner cartridge comes with a long, thin felt strip mounted on a piece of plastic. You drop this into some slot or other on the printer, replacing the old and cruddy strip. Not all laser printers have this, though.

Common Problems and Solutions

Printers, like any other mechanical devices, can be real maintenance headaches. Whenever you have moving parts, you have the potential for the machine to wear out, break down, or otherwise conk out.

However, it may surprise you to learn that most printer problems are *software* related. That is, the operating system or a particular program isn't sending the right information to the printer to get the desired printout. (You know the old saying—garbage in, garbage out!) For example, when a printer spits out endless sheets of paper with mysterious junk characters on them, it's a good bet that the printer driver isn't speaking the printer's language.

It's hard to discuss printer problems and troubleshooting without delving too deeply into the specifics of the thousands of models available. I don't have the space to do that (or, truthfully, the time to get to know all those printers), but I can pass along some generic pieces of advice. And, remember, I'll tell you more about lasers and inkjets in the next two chapters.

Isolate the Problem

As always, try to isolate the problem. Is it something in the computer or its software? The printer interface? The cable? The printer? Is the printer plugged in, cabled, and *online*?

The steps I use are as follows:

1. Check whether the printer is online, is plugged in, has paper, and is turned on.

2. Turn the printer off and then on again. Reboot the computer, and try it again.

3. If it's a network printer, check the network configuration (such as the IP address and subnet mask on TCP/IP).

4. Use the printer self-test to see whether the test page prints correctly. The printer's manual usually tells how to do this.

5. Check that the software is configured for the printer and that the correct drivers are loaded for it in Windows (if used).

6. Swap the printer cable to make sure your cable isn't faulty.

7. If it's a network printer, try printing from another computer.

8. Swap the printer with a different one of the same model, if possible.

These are some other things to check right off the bat:

◆ If you can get to a command prompt, do a `DIR` from the command prompt, and then try a screen print using the Print Screen key. This bypasses Windows and any Windows-based driver problems that may be occurring to see whether the basic connection between computer and printer is functioning.

◆ If you're troubleshooting a network printer, check the queue at the server to be certain there are no stuck jobs. If there are, then purge the queue.

◆ Check the printer manufacturer's Web site to see whether an updated driver is available for your version of Windows or for the particular DOS-based program form that you want to print.

Check Cable Lengths

The role of cable lengths in noise and interference has been discussed before in this text. But another problem is overly long cables. Serial cables aren't supposed to be longer than 50 feet, and older parallel cables shouldn't exceed 6 feet. Newer parallel printer cables that conform to IEEE 1284 (ECP/EPP) can go to 15 feet. If you're using long cables and getting mysterious errors, the cables may be the culprits, but it's not very likely.

There are parallel port extenders—check Black Box (`www.blackbox.com`) or the Vendor Guide on the Utilities CD for additional contact information) to find them. An extender will let you run your parallel cable up to a kilometer.

NOTE   Something I've noticed in recent years is that modern parallel port chips don't put out all that much power. I used to be able to share a printer between two computers with an A/B switch, but now it's often the case that it won't work unless the A/B switch has amplification power. The moral seems to be to keep those parallel port cables as short as possible—or better yet, use USB printers whenever possible. It's also not recommended to use an A/B switch with laser printers unless you have a powered switch.

Choose the Correct Windows Driver

If you don't have the correct driver installed for the printer, it may not work at all or it may work imperfectly or print garbage characters.

It's simple enough to say, "Use the correct driver," because it's easy to download drivers from manufacturer Web sites. But what if the correct driver isn't available for some reason? It does happen. For example, my aunt has an old Canon multifunction printer device for which Canon declined to develop Windows XP compatible software. The driver she had for Windows 2000 doesn't work.

In cases like that, the only thing to do is fall back on emulation. I won't get into a long "back in the day" story here, but basically in earlier times it was common for many different off-brand models of printers to speak the same Page Description Language (PDL) as a more popular model of printer. This was called *emulating* that printer. There were minor differences between each off-brand and the model being emulated, but the match was close enough that a driver for the popular model could be used for it.

If you need Windows to support a printer that you don't have a driver for, you need to find out what other printer models it emulates and then try kludging your way through with one of those drivers. In the case of my aunt's multifunction, we never did get it to scan or fax, but with a driver from a similar device we were at least able to get the printing functionality working.

NOTE   Windows XP uses signed drivers for devices. If you try to use an unsigned driver, Windows will give you a dire-sounding warning. Be cautious when using unsigned drivers for system-critical items such as video cards, but for a printer it doesn't hurt to try an unsigned driver if no signed one is available. The worst that can happen is the printer won't print, and that's what is happening anyway if you don't try.

Check Ports and Connections

As you know, printers can have a USB, parallel, network, serial, or infrared port. Given the choice, USB is often the best way to go. However, if you're trying to get a computer to recognize a USB printer and getting nowhere, falling back to the parallel interface if available is no disgrace.

PARALLEL PORT ISSUES

Some parallel printer cables fasten with clips; others fasten with screws. You should tighten the screws if your cable uses them; don't just plug it in and hope nobody comes along to bump it. I once saw an Okidata printer that was printing consistently incorrect characters. I tried to understand the problem by comparing the ASCII codes of the desired characters to the codes actually printed. I found in each case that bit 6 was *always 1*. It turned out that the wire for line 6 wasn't fully seated. Securing the connector did the job.

Port issues can also arise if the BIOS Setup doesn't have the parallel port set to the right mode. This is most apparent when trying to share a parallel port with multiple devices or when the printer's Windows software requires more two-way communication with the printer than the selected mode supports. As I said earlier, ECP is the best choice in most systems.

USB INTERFACE ISSUES

Because a printer that's connected to a computer using a USB interface has a few wrinkles its parallel port counterpart doesn't, here are a few tips to use when you're troubleshooting USB-related problems:

Read the manual before installing   Some of the USB printers require that you install the software before connecting the printer; others ask you to connect and power on the printer partway through the installation. On older USB devices, problems that result from not following the manual instructions for installation can be tricky to recover from. Check the manufacturer's Web site for details. Newer USB devices are less particular.

Install the printer's own software   USB printers are immediately recognized by Windows when you plug them in, and Windows may try to load its own driver for the printer. In many cases, it's better to click Cancel at that point and run the Setup utility that came with the printer. Some printers provide special management or queue programs that you won't be able to take advantage of if you run the printer from the default driver that comes with Windows.

Check the version of Windows you're using   Although most of the newer software will warn you if you're trying to install your USB printer on a version of Windows that doesn't support USB, not all installation software does. Put simply, if you're using Windows 3.*x*, Windows 95, or Windows NT 4, the USB connection won't work. Officially, Windows 95—OEM Service Release (OSR) 2.*x*, also called 95C—supports USB, but my experience has been that the USB support on any version of Windows 95 is questionable and not recommended by most printer manufacturers.

Check the USB controller in BIOS Setup   The USB controller on the motherboard can usually be enabled/disabled from BIOS Setup. It should be enabled by default on most PCs, but it's worth a check if you don't see the USB Root Hub in Device Manager in Windows. On older systems that have USB support on the motherboard, some people used to disable the USB functionality on the board to free up its IRQ if they didn't have any USB devices.

Check the USB controller in Windows   If your computer is relatively new, ignore this, but if you have one of the first computers to support USB, this step might be worth the effort. When Intel produced the first USB universal host controller chip for motherboards, they didn't have all of their ducks in a row, so to speak. As a result, the motherboard didn't support USB. At the time this chip was being used, no operating system supported USB and there were no USB-related devices, so nobody knew that the controller didn't quite work. To check it out, follow these steps

1. Right-click the My Computer icon, and open System Properties.

2. In Device Manager, open the USB and double-click the Intel 82371SB PCI to USB Universal Host Controller entry. Does the controller have a different number? If so, you're okay; that means you have a newer controller. If not, go to the next step.

3. On the General tab, see if the hardware version is 000. If it is, you have the aforementioned chip. There's no workaround; you need to upgrade the motherboard.

Consider the Weather

Everyone talks about it, but...a printer repairman told me about a day that he'd had the previous October. He said that all over town a particular model of printer was failing left and right. He couldn't figure it out. We thought about it. Around the middle of October, we turn on the heat in Washington. That dries out the air and, in turn, the items in the work area. Chips don't mind being dried, but what about capacitors? Could a paper-type capacitor be malfunctioning because it was drying beyond a certain point?

A repair memo came around from the manufacturer a couple of months later. Sure enough, a particular capacitor didn't like it too dry. The answer: either put a humidifier near the printer, or change the capacitor to a similar, less dry-sensitive replacement. Moral: be suspicious when seasons change

Troubleshooting Tips

Like a bad cable TV connection on the night of the big pay-per-view fight, printers are notorious for going on the fritz when you've got two minutes to print and fax vitally important documents. The following are some additional troubleshooting tips to help you avoid resorting to the ultimate show of frustration: whacking your printer upside its paper tray as if it were a vending machine gone bad

PRINTER WON'T PRINT AT ALL

If the printer won't print at all, use these tips:

◆ Check that the printer is getting power, is online (check the Online button), and is connected to the PC.

◆ Turn the printer off and then on again. The same goes for the computer.

◆ Look on the printer for any error codes or flashing lights that could give a clue as to the problem

◆ See that the printer has ink, toner, or ribbon and that it's installed correctly.

◆ Turn off the computer and run the printer's self-test to see if it can print as a separate entity from the computer.

◆ Check to make sure the correct driver is installed on the PC.

- Check the printer queue and purge any print jobs that appear to be hung up.
- Turn the printer off, let it sit for 10 minutes, and try again. Overheating can shut down a printer temporarily.
- Try a different printer cable.
- Try hooking up the printer to a different computer to determine whether the problem is with the printer, the computer, or the software.

PRINTOUT HAS QUALITY PROBLEMS

If the printout isn't all it should be, use these tips:

- Ensure that the correct printer driver has been installed.
- Check the printer to make sure it's using the right print emulation mode if it has more than one available.
- On a dot-matrix printer, ensure that the belt is adjusted properly.
- Replace the ink, ribbon, or toner cartridge if needed, along with any other replacement parts, such as the felt pad in some laser models.
- Clean the printer according to the instructions in its manual.
- On an inkjet, clean the nozzles by using the printer's built-in utility for that purpose.

In this chapter, I gave you an overview of various printer types and interfaces. Now, just as I promised, I'll delve more deeply into the workings of specific types of printers. Next up: inkjet printers.

Chapter 16

Troubleshooting Inkjet Printers

◆ Parts of an Inkjet Printer and How They Work

◆ Solving Common Problems

◆ Understanding Error Messages

◆ Preventive Maintenance

◆ Refilling Ink Cartridges

◆ Troubleshooting Tips

Introduction

The inkjet printer began as a "poor man's laser," producing near laser quality black-and-white output at a fraction of the cost of a real laser printer. As the technology continued to develop, affordable color inkjet printers became available (although color laser printers were still way beyond the reach of ordinary people), and inkjet printers exploded in popularity because they provided an affordable way for the average home or small-business user to get color printouts.

Today, inkjet printers still cost less than laser printers. Inkjet output isn't quite as crisp as output from a laser printer; you can tell the difference if you look closely with a magnifying glass. Inkjet output can also sometimes smear if you touch it immediately after it exits the printer. However, the difference is minor, and inkjet output looks professional enough for almost any home or business use. The drawbacks? Inkjet printing speed has traditionally been slower than that of laser printers, and the per-page cost (of the ink versus laser toner) is anywhere from slightly to significantly higher.

As with laser printers, most problems associated with inkjet printers can be attributed to either human error or ignorance. You see, inkjet printers aren't like television sets. You can't just plug them in, turn them on, and expect them to work flawlessly for their entire life without a little Tender Loving Care.

Getting the most out of your inkjet printer means getting it to work right and then maintaining it in good working order. Once you learn the ropes of regular preventive maintenance and some emergency troubleshooting, you'll be able to get quality printouts every time you hit Print.

Parts of an Inkjet Printer

Inkjet printers are fairly simple machines in concept. They all have several common pieces:

- An outer case to hold the inner parts.

- A paper-feed mechanism.

- Ink cartridges, which hold the ink.

- Inkjets (collectively called a *print head*) that control the distribution of ink on the page. In some printers, the print head is built into the ink cartridge so that when you change the ink cartridge you get a new print head; in others, the print head is separate.

- A carrier that holds the ink cartridges and moves them back and forth over the paper.

- A paper-exit tray.

Some printers are multifunction devices that also include scanning, faxing, or copying capabilities. Such units will have additional parts; check the manual to learn more about them. Multifunction devices can be either inkjet or laser.

The Case

Inkjet printer cases come in all shapes, sizes, and even a few colors. Printer cases aren't generic like PC cases. Each manufacturer has designed its case to fit a variety of design and mechanical factors, so they aren't compatible with each other.

Most printer cases have some sort of lid or hatch that lifts up to give you access to the ink cartridges. You won't need to remove the entire outer case for routine operation. Should you need to perform more drastic operations on the printer, however, you can (on most models) remove a few screws and lift off the entire outer plastic shell.

You won't find any sort of manual for removing the printer's outer casing because the manufacturer doesn't want you to do it. Instead, they want you to send your printer to an authorized repair center if there are problems that necessitate removing the case. However, I once took my Lexmark 5700 Color Jetprinter apart to clean the inner workings (it was all gunked up with ink) and was able to disassemble it and put it back together with no problems. The key is to work slowly and examine carefully how each piece fits with the others.

Did I mention that the case probably won't be just one piece? That's true. The Lexmark I took apart had something like eight pieces to its outer case. Two pieces make up the supporting base, three or four parts fit together to form the outer front of the printer, and a few more hold the paper-feed and paper-exit trays.

Whatever you do, don't force anything. Carefully note where all the screws are and remove them one at a time, putting the screws in a safe place so you don't lose them. If the screws are different sizes, write this on a piece of paper. When you try to put the case back together, this information is invaluable. After you take off one piece of the case, set it aside and move on to the next. As you remove the pieces of the case, look closely to see how they all fit together. Sometimes it seems like a jigsaw puzzle, so write some notes if you need to so you remember the details.

When you disassemble your printer, you can clean each piece of the outer case with soap and water if that doesn't work, try an alcohol-based cleaning solution and a soft cloth or paper towel. Be careful in your choice of cleaning solutions because some of them can damage the plastics used to make the case. This is a good idea if ink has sprayed on any inner surfaces or you happen to get inky fingerprints on any of the pieces (as I did).

The Paper-Feed Mechanism

The paper-feed mechanism feeds the paper into the printer, which you would guess from its name. On some printers, there's a separate, removable tray that holds the paper; on other printers, you simply stack the paper up against the feed mechanism. Most inkjet printers allow you to use different sizes of paper, including standard letter, envelope, and greeting card–sized paper. An adjustable feed guide helps you position various types of paper correctly for feeding.

Some printers have the capability of feeding paper in from either the front or the back. Hewlett Packard (HP) inkjet printers are usually front loaders, and many of the other major printer manufacturers use a gravity feed from the rear on most models. The advantage of the front loader is a smaller footprint on your desktop. The disadvantage is the limitation in the thickness of the media supported. Because the paper has to do more twisting and turning inside the printer on a front-loaded model, the printer may be less able to handle thick cardstock that doesn't bend as easily as paper.

Some printers have a manual-feed feature, which you can use to insert a single page at a time of some nonstandard paper size, such as envelopes, that the printer doesn't normally support using the standard paper-feed bin.

One of the most common problems with either type of paper-feed mechanism is in the rubber wheels that grab the paper—called *grabber wheels*. Through use, the grabber wheels begin to lose their traction because they become clogged with paper dust, resulting in misfeeds. The solution is simple—take a cotton swab and clean the wheels with denatured alcohol.

If cleaning the grabber wheels doesn't resolve the problem, the gears on the paper-feed mechanism may have become worn and are starting to fail to pull paper into the printer smoothly and evenly. With newer printers, this happens rarely. On some printers, the gears start making an annoying squeaking sound, and oiling them doesn't help much. In such cases, it's usually worth it (to me, anyway) to take the printer to an authorized service center and have the feed mechanism refurbished. It's not that you can't do it yourself, but the authorized service centers have better access to the needed parts. Of course, with good-quality color inkjet printers costing less than $100, it's probably a better use of your money to simply replace the printer.

Ink Cartridges

The ink cartridges hold the ink your printer uses. Make sure you use ink cartridges that are compatible with your make and model of printer because they come in different shapes and sizes. Most look like little boxes, and some have carefully designed nozzles and electronic contacts built in. Other more basic styles of ink cartridges are simply ink reservoirs that feed into an ink cartridge carrier, which has the more complicated parts.

Almost all color inkjet printers today have both color and black ink cartridges that you can replace separately. (On some inexpensive older models, there was no separate black ink; cyan, yellow, and magenta were combined to make black, which resulted in a somewhat muddy gray.)

Some color printers have the three primary colors in one cartridge, and other models allow you to purchase and install each of the three colors separately (magenta, yellow, and cyan). Printers that are used primarily for printing photographs may have up to five colors in the ink cartridge.

The primary disadvantage to the "all-colors-in-one-box" type of cartridge is that you may not use the colors at the same rate. If you run out of cyan, for example, you have no choice but to replace the entire cartridge to restore your color printing capability—or live with your inability to print blues. This isn't an issue that should keep you up at nights, though, because the amount of ink you lose with this method is, in most cases, insignificant.

HP ink cartridges are manufactured with a protective piece of plastic and transparent tape that covers the nozzles and contacts. Most other manufacturers have a piece of tape that covers the air vent holes to prevent them from drying out. With these types of cartridges, inserting the cartridge into the holder the first time breaks the seal and allows the ink to flow into the print head. In either case, make sure to remove the tape prior to installing.

At the end of this chapter, I'll tell you more about cartridges, including how they can be refilled (and why you may *not* want to do so).

The Ink Cartridge Carrier

The ink cartridge carrier holds the ink cartridges and moves back and forth over the paper while ink is being sprayed onto the paper. On some inkjet printers, this carrier also contains the print head. To install ink cartridges, you may have to move a lever, lift the lid, or press a button on the printer to put the carrier in a position to accept the cartridges and then snap them into place. On some printers, the cartridge carriers come out of the printer completely and then go back in with the new cartridge.

The Exit Tray

The exit tray holds the paper after it comes out of the printer. Many models of inkjet printers have sliding pieces for the exit tray, enabling you to retract the tray to save space when you're not using it. When you print, extend the tray to its full length to catch the paper.

A few printers have a lever you can flip to make the output come out at the opposite end of the printer. For example, if the output normally comes out the front, you could make it come out the back. Why would you want to do this? Primarily to get a straight path through the printer. If you're printing on some stiff medium, such as cardstock, you can avoid the otherwise-inevitable curling by allowing the paper to exit the printer in a straight line from the spot where it entered, rather than curling around a roller on its way out.

How an Inkjet Printer Works

At the most basic level, inkjet printers work by directing tiny droplets of ink onto paper. As I explained in Chapter 15, "Printer Types and Interfaces," dot-matrix printers use a mechanical print head that physically impacts a ribbon, thereby transferring ink to the paper. In contrast, inkjet printer "heads" don't physically touch the paper at all. Instead, these printers force ink through nozzles and spray the ink onto the paper. Depending on the printer and its technology, there can be between 21 and 150 nozzles for each of the four colors (cyan, yellow, magenta, and black). By mixing the colors, the printer can produce almost any color.

There are two types of inkjet printers: thermal and piezoelectric (piezo). These are two different technologies used to force the ink from the cartridge and through the nozzles.

Thermal inkjets use the older of the two technologies. They heat the ink in the cartridge (to about 400 degrees Fahrenheit), causing vapor bubbles in the cartridge that rise to the top and force the ink out through the nozzle. The vacuum caused by the expelled ink draws more ink down into the nozzles, making a constant stream. Canon calls this a *bubblejet*.

Piezo printing uses an electric charge instead of heat. It charges piezoelectric crystals in the nozzles, which vibrate in response to the electrical charge, forcing the ink out through the nozzles.

The output of both technologies is essentially the same. The primary difference between the two is that, with the thermal inkjets (such as most HP and Canon printers), every time you replace the ink cartridge, you replace the print head. Traditionally with piezo technology, only the ink cartridge is replaced, and the print head is a permanent part of the printer. The heat in a thermal model causes the print head to break down quicker, so it needs replacing more frequently.

Common Problems and Possible Solutions

Just about all printer problems can be easily fixed if you know where to look. Although I attempt in this section to give you a good general sense of what problems might occur and how to prevent them, you should read the manual that came with your printer carefully.

The list of things that can go wrong with printing is fairly large, but you can organize them into general categories to help you troubleshoot. The point is to try to remove problems that might not be affecting you to point you in the right general direction. Try thinking along these lines to categorize your printer problem:

- Your printer seems to be working, but nothing is printing.

- There are color problems.

- The printer appears dead.

- Printing seems very slow but is working.

- The quality of your printouts is smeared or generally poor.

- The output is garbled or formatted incorrectly.

- The paper is jammed or not feeding correctly.

I'll cover each of these symptoms in turn.

Printer Appears to Work but Nothing Prints

This problem may be as simple as running out of ink. Most printers come with software status controls built into their Windows driver. Right-click the printer's icon in Windows, choose Properties (it works basically the same in all Windows versions), and look for a status monitor in the printer's Properties dialog box that indicates the ink level. Replace any cartridges that indicate they're out of ink.

Be aware that most status programs are separate programs that may or may not be installed at the same time as your printer driver. With the exception of the newest ink cartridges (which have an electronic sensor in them), these status programs can only display an estimation of the amount of ink remaining. You can also manually check cartridges that have a window into the ink area or are semi-transparent. Further, most printers that have a Light-Emitting Diode (LED) panel on the printer itself will provide some ink level information through its menu system (accessed by pressing buttons on the printer).

If you have sufficient ink, try running the nozzle check and/or the print head cleaning routine that's a part of your printer control program. Your nozzles might be clogged up. This is a common occurrence if you haven't printed in a long time. A nozzle check prints a test pattern using all the jets, so you can see whether any are malfunctioning. Head cleaning self-cleans each jet. You'll want to run these two utilities, first one and then the other, to check the current nozzle functioning and to improve it. Head cleaning uses up a small amount of ink, however, so if you do it a lot, you'll end up wasting ink. Still, you'll find that if the problem is clogged jets, running the head cleaning routines—sometimes up to 10 times—may restore the printer. If you haven't used the printer in more than six months, there's a chance that the ink has dried up and you'll need to replace the cartridge(s). Piezo technology print heads are a little more susceptible to this phenomenon than thermal printers. Because thermal print heads integrate the print head and ink supply into a single unit, you get a new print head each time you replace the ink cartridge. If the ink in your piezo print head should dry up, replacing the ink cartridge won't necessarily solve the problem.

True story: one time I was working with a printer that hadn't been used in more than a year. Nearly all the nozzles were clogged, so I had to run the head cleaning routine 20 times in a row. The quality kept getting better and better, and I was feeling encouraged, but then the blue nozzles just quit. Kaput. Nothing. I panicked. Had I ruined the printer by repeated cleaning? Nope, I had just depleted all the blue ink. So I installed a new cartridge, and it worked perfectly.

If, after cleaning the print heads, you see intermittent output on the page, try cleaning them several more times; this can sometimes break loose the crud that's clogging up some of the jets. Most printers enable you to run the head cleaning routine by pressing certain buttons on the printer (check your documentation) or by choosing an option in the printer's Properties box or its Maintenance utility (as in Figure 16.1).

FIGURE 16.1
Most printers have utilities such as nozzle checking and head cleaning.

If that fails, take your ink cartridges out and check whether any obstructions might be blocking the ink. If you've recently replaced your ink cartridges, check them to make sure you removed all the protective coverings from the print nozzles and contacts.

WARNING *The documentation for some printer models claims that if you remove an ink cartridge after initially inserting it, it becomes useless and you can't reinsert it. I've reinserted a cartridge in one such printer successfully, despite the instructions, but if you have a printer that claims this, try all other troubleshooting before you resort to removing the cartridge for examination and reinsertion.*

Color Is Wrong

If the colors on your printout don't match what you see on-screen, the most likely problem is that one or more of the color jets is clogged or you're out of ink. Check the printout—do all greens look yellow, and is the blue missing? That means you're out of cyan. See the instructions in the preceding section for replacing an ink cartridge and/or cleaning the print heads.

If the color problem is subtler (all colors appear, but they look too dark, too blue, or whatever), the problem might be with your monitor's color calibration. If your video card ships with a utility that allows you to calibrate your monitor's color, you should run it. There might also be a utility built into your printer driver or video card driver; try displaying the device's properties to look for one.

Sometimes the problem lies with the color management scheme selected by the application from which you're printing. For example, if you're printing from CorelDRAW, its color management profile is active by default. So, when printing to an Epson printer (whose color management is also on by default), the result of these two color management programs trying to out-think one another can be less than desirable output. I recommend turning off all color management except the one that came with the printer—which you might not be able to turn off anyway.

Printer Doesn't Print at All

Ah, the dead printer. Fear not, the problem is usually simple.

First, check that the printer is plugged in and the power is on. Next, are any of the status lights on the printer blinking? Blinking lights can be an indication that either the printer is processing the print job or something is wrong that requires your intervention. Check your user manual to interpret the error condition. If you've ruled out any error conditions, check your printer cable connections. Try removing the printer cable and reseating it at both ends.

If these aren't causing the problem, make sure the printer appears in your operating system and that it's online and currently selected as the default printer. In Windows, check the Printers list. (In pre-Windows XP versions, use Start ➢ Settings ➢ Printers; in Windows XP, use Start ➢ Printers and Faxes). A checkmark next to the printer's icon indicates that it's the default. Right-click it, and choose Set as Default if needed. Sometimes strange things happen and this gets messed up. I've seen cases of printers disappearing or suddenly going offline.

If your default printer is a network printer, make sure your network connection is up and running. If the printer appears "faded" or "grayed out" in the Printers window, it's because the printer isn't available for some reason (usually because of a failure in the network connection to it).

Next, open the print queue for your printer (by double-clicking its icon in the Printers list or double-clicking the printer icon in the system tray) to see whether printing is currently paused. (The title bar will read Paused if it is.) Choose Printer ➢ Pause Printing to unpause it. You might have paused the printing and forgotten to reset it.

If the printer's status is User Intervention, the printer is waiting on something. If it's a network printer, there could be a warning or error message on the host computer's screen, waiting to be answered. Or the printer could be out of paper or have a paper jam, but in such events, the computer usually displays an error message indicating the nature of the problem.

Printing Is Slow or Intermittent

Slow or intermittent printing could be caused by a couple of things. First, double-check your cable connection to the printer. Second, make sure you're using a cable capable of bidirectional communications, and make sure it's connected snugly at both ends.

In Chapter 15, I told you a bit about parallel printing modes. The oldest mode is Standard (sometimes called Standard Printer Port or SPP), and the others are bidirectional, Extended Capabilities Port (ECP), and Enhanced Parallel Port (EPP). Using SPP as the mode can cause slow or intermittent printing, as can using a cable that doesn't support bidirectional, ECP, or EPP printing. Any new parallel printer cable you buy today will certainly be fine, as will nearly any of the old printer cables you may have lying around. However, if in doubt, you might try a different and newer cable. Look for IEEE 1284 in tiny writing on the cable itself. If the cable is fine, check that bidirectional printing is enabled for the port the printer is using (probably LPT1) in your PC's Basic Input/Output System (BIOS). This isn't an issue with Universal Serial Bus (USB) printing because USB is by nature bidirectional.

Slow printing could also be caused by your printer driver settings. In most cases, you can choose to print in draft, normal, or high-resolution mode. The higher the quality, the more time the printing will take. If you're printing at some really high resolution such as 2880 dots per inch (dpi), your printout may take a long time. If you want it to print faster and don't need the highest quality, lower your print quality settings through the printer's print settings. You can set these by displaying the printer's properties (right-click it and choose Properties) or, within some applications, by using a PRINT SETUP command.

TIP *When printing photographs on an inkjet printer, it isn't necessary to print at the highest resolution that the printer supports to get a good color photograph. When running some benchmark tests this year, I printed the same photograph at 720dpi, 1440dpi, and 2880dpi. Although I noticed a slight improvement in quality between the 720dpi and the 1440dpi photo, I couldn't see any difference between the 1440dpi and the 2880dpi. Yet the 2880dpi photo took three times longer to print and consumed twice as much ink. In addition, high-resolution printing is often a waste of time and ink on standard paper because the ink bleeds a bit; special photo-quality paper is often required to see any benefit from high-resolution printing.*

Finally, slow printing can be the result of using the wrong driver for your printer. If you let Windows autodetect an older printer instead of running the setup software that came with the printer, you may not be using the best possible driver. Dig through the documentation that came with the printer to find its Setup CD, and run it to install the specific driver for your printer. The autodetection of newer printers in Windows 98 and higher usually works fine. However, when given a choice between a driver provided by the Windows operating system and one provided by the printer manufacturer, always choose the one from the printer manufacturer. The one provided by the Windows operating system tends to be a no-frills version and often doesn't support many of the advanced features of the printer.

Next, never assume that the printer driver that came with the printer you just bought is the most current driver. It may have been manufactured, boxed, and sent to the distribution warehouse several driver revisions ago. Always go the manufacturer's Web site to download the most current driver for your operating system. If the newest driver isn't for your operating system, don't use it. Only use the driver for the operating system you're using with your printer. Sounds obvious, right? If I had a nickel for every time that someone had selected the newest driver without regard to the operating system, I'd have a lot of nickels.

Quality Is Poor

If the printer prints but the output isn't as good as you think it should be, you've got some investigative work to do to find out why.

First, check to see what quality mode the printer is set to operate in. As I mentioned earlier, the higher the quality, the slower the printing. Sometimes people set their printers to draft quality (the fastest, lowest-quality setting) and forget they've done so. Check the printer's Properties box to view and change the quality setting. Figure 16.2 shows an example.

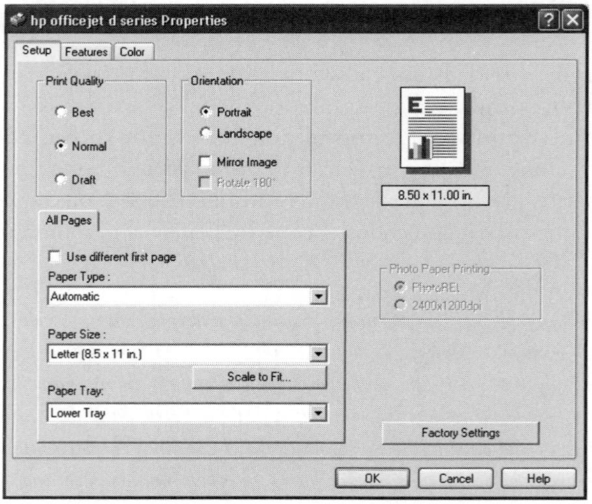

FIGURE 16.2

Most printers enable you to choose from several quality settings.

Second, while you're looking at the quality setting, see also whether there's a Media Type or Paper Type setting. With inkjet printers, plain-old copy paper doesn't produce as good an image as special inkjet paper with a shinier surface and less porous "holes." The less porous the paper, the higher the dpi setting you can use for the printout. Using a high dpi (such as 2400) with plain paper can actually result in a printout that looks *worse* than a printout at a lower resolution (720, perhaps) because the paper is too porous to handle the dots being that close together. For best results, buy paper made especially for inkjet printers because it enables you to print at higher dpi.

Next, clean your print heads through the printer control program, as described in the earlier "Printer Appears to Work but Nothing Prints" section. A clogged nozzle can result in stripes on the page (*banding*) or "bald" patches where there's no printing.

Your print heads may also be out of alignment. Run the print head alignment routine (if it exists—not all printers have alignment routines) for your printer. You'll probably find the alignment routine built into the printer driver, as with the other utilities you've seen so far in this chapter. The routine aligns the print heads and nozzles so that the black and color ink cartridges print at the same location on the page. This one does its stuff the first time, so you shouldn't have to run it multiple times for best results (as with head cleaning).

Check your ink levels. Low ink results in banding or streaking. If you're low on color ink, your printout will appear washed out or oddly miscolored. You may be out of one of the three primary colors used in color printing.

Check the brand of the ink cartridges installed in your printer. I've tested several third-party ink cartridges and found that the blacks aren't as dark and the dyes in the colors aren't as vivid as the original cartridges produced by the manufacturer.

If your HP printer appears to be smearing, remove your ink cartridges and inspect them manually to see if there's a buildup of paper debris. If there is, take a cotton swab and clean the print head portion of the cartridge and then replace it in the holder. Reinstall the cartridges and make sure they're properly seated in the carrier. Remember that not all printers allow you to reinsert the same cartridge after removing it (at least not according to the documentation; you might still be able to do so). On some HP printers, you'll be requested to run the alignment procedure again because the program thinks you've installed a new cartridge.

If you have problems at the edge of the page, such as output being cut off, you may be trying to print material outside of the effective print area of your printer. Few printers will let you print across the full width of a standard sheet of paper. This is because the edge of the paper is used to hold it in place while transporting the paper through the printer. Most modern applications that support a Print Preview function are aware of the printable area of the selected printer and media and will show you exactly what will print.

Some of the modern photo printers, such as those made by Epson, do allow edge-to-edge printing, sometimes called *full bleed*. This shouldn't be confused with earlier borderless printing, which was accomplished using a special paper with perforated edges that you removed after the printing was complete.

Output Is Garbled or Formatted Incorrectly

If you print a nicely formatted word processing document but it comes out with the wrong fonts, skewed margins, or junk characters, the problem is possibly a corrupt printer driver but more than likely it's an interrupted print job.

If you interrupt a print job, the information header for the job is often lost. When the job is restarted, the printer begins receiving the control information about the print job, but it has no way of knowing that. Rather than using this control information to set up the print job, it prints all of that code gibberish—on many sheets of paper. The solution is to take the paper out of the printer and wait for the printer, and finally the computer, to realize it is out of paper. At that time you should receive an error message, which will give you the opportunity to cancel the print jobs.

If you have a damaged driver, you can repair the driver problem by deleting the printer from the Printers list and reinstalling it using the disk that came with the printer. If you don't have such a disk download the needed setup software from the manufacturer's Web site. Windows comes with drivers for many popular printers, and you can use the Windows-provided driver in a pinch if one from the manufacturer isn't available. (The Windows version may not have as many features, so I try to always use the manufacturer-supplied drivers whenever possible.)

The driver isn't always to blame, however. One time I had a very frustrating service call, in which the printer was printing the output scrunched up on the left side of each page. The printout would appear perfectly on-screen in Print Preview, but without fail, each page came out distorted. I tried reinstalling the driver. I tried resetting the printer. I tried printing from DOS. Nothing worked. Finally, I checked inside the printer and noticed that the ink cartridges weren't completely seated in their holders. I gave them a firm push into place, and *voilà!* Problem solved. Weird but true.

Paper Is Stuck or Not Moving

If paper jams in your printer, stop what you're doing and carefully but firmly pull the paper out of the printer. Try not to rip the paper as you pull it out because you don't want to have small pieces of paper caught inside the printer. When you've removed the jammed piece of paper, throw it away and resend your job to the printer.

If paper fails to feed at all, check that the paper is seated correctly in the paper tray. If any obstructions are blocking the paper, carefully remove them. If a piece of paper is bent, it may not feed correctly You'll have to throw it away.

You should also check to ensure you haven't overloaded the paper-feed tray. Too many sheets in the tray can easily cause jams or feed problems. Sometimes using very thick or very thin paper can also cause feed problems. Try to use a standard paper weight (20-pound paper or so) whenever possible

Most printers also have paper guides that snuggle up against your paper and keep it straight as it feeds into the printer. You can set these guides for different sizes of paper. Make sure the guides are properly set and aren't loose.

Other issues that cause misfeeds or no feeds are media related. For example, most printers that can print to envelopes print one at a time or have a limit of somewhere between five and eight envelopes in the paper tray unless you have a dedicated envelope feeder. Transparency material can be difficult for some printers to pick up and may have to be fed one sheet at a time.

Finally, make sure your printer is on a flat, stable surface. If it's tilted at an angle or on a shaky table that might cause feed problems—I doubt it, but all things are possible.

Common Error Messages

Although each printer will have error messages that are unique to its particular make and model, the following are a few error messages you might encounter.

Ink Low

This signifies that your ink cartridge is running out of ink. You should replace the ink cartridge soon. Some printer manufacturers recommend that you don't change an ink cartridge until the printer reports that the ink is completely out. You can make that call yourself, but it's nice to have the advance

`Ink Low` warning so you can make sure you have a new cartridge available. This message may appear through Windows, through the LED panel on the printer itself, or through both.

WARNING   *Ink cartridges tend to dry out on the shelf. Don't stockpile ink cartridges; after six months or so, they lose their freshness.*

Out of Memory

Laser printers are page printers—they print entire pages at a time, so they must have a lot of memory in them to store a whole page. In contrast, inkjet printers are line printers—they print line by line, so they don't typically need a great deal of memory. You seldom hear of memory upgrades available for inkjet printers because it's simply not an issue. An exception might be a network-ready business inkjet printer, which would need memory for storing incoming print jobs from multiple users. I've seen such printers available with up to 48 megabytes (MB) of Random Access Memory (RAM).

Therefore, if you get an `Out of Memory` error message on-screen as you print to an inkjet printer, it most likely refers to a lack of memory on your PC, rather than on your printer. Usually it doesn't really mean you should add memory to your PC; rather, it means that either memory-hogging programs running on your PC have allocated all the available memory or you have no space left on your hard drive. In either case, there isn't enough space left for the printer driver to spool its output to the printer. It's best to restart your PC and resubmit your print job after doing so.

Out of Paper

You're completely out of paper, or if your printer has multiple paper sources, you may have designated an empty tray. You'll have to load more paper in your printer or switch to another paper tray to continue.

Paper Jam

Paper has jammed somewhere in your printer, preventing it from continuing. Carefully but firmly pull the paper out of the printer in one piece. Depending on where the paper jam occurs, you may have to pull it out of the top (or paper-feed area) or the bottom (the paper-exit tray). If you can't reach the paper easily, you might have to open the access panel to reach inside your printer.

Print Head Failure

If your ink cartridges aren't working correctly, you might receive a `Print Head Failure` error message. Dirty, fouled, or clogged ink cartridges can cause this problem. Clean your print head through your printer's built-in maintenance program, and if necessary, remove the ink cartridges and clean them with a clean cloth.

Preventive Maintenance

If you own a car, you're probably used to preventive maintenance. You change your oil every 3000 miles or every three months, check the air in the tires, check other fluid levels, and routinely put gas in it so it'll run. Printers also require some regular maintenance, but it's far less troublesome than what you need to do for a car.

Clean the Print Heads

Although you don't want to overdo it, you should clean your print heads periodically by running the head cleaning utility (as discussed earlier in the chapter). This should remove any built-up gunk or ink on the print heads and help ensure consistent high-quality printouts. Don't do it repeatedly, though, because it wastes ink.

Align the Print Heads

Every time you install new printer cartridges, you should also align your print heads. This keeps the color and black ink cartridges aligned so there are no gaps between black and color portions of your printout. Most printers do this automatically, but it doesn't hurt to do it manually by using the head alignment utility in your printer driver (covered earlier in the chapter).

Realigning print heads might also be necessary after moving your printer or bumping into it accidentally.

Refilling Ink Cartridges

Because of the cost of today's inkjet ink cartridges (usually more than $20 for black and upward of $30 to $40 for color), a cottage industry of refillable inkjet cartridges has emerged. It should be said that most manufacturers don't recommend this, but what they don't know won't hurt them. In fact, some manufacturers make their ink cartridges hard to get into by yourself, thus making it hard for you to refill them without special tools or equipment.

You should be able to purchase kits made specifically for your brand of printer and model of ink cartridges if your printer is popular enough. This method gives you some assurance that your new cartridge will contain ink with the same characteristics as the retail ink cartridge. If not, you may be stuck buying the officially designated replacement cartridges.

Refilling ink cartridges involves removing the lid of the existing ink cartridge and simply refilling it. Because of the wide variety of existing ink cartridges, you should carefully follow the instructions provided with the kit you buy.

You shouldn't refill a cartridge more than once for a thermal (bubblejet) printer because on these models, print head jets are built into the cartridges. When you replace the ink cartridge with a new one, you also give yourself a new set of jets. If you continually refill and reuse the same cartridge, you're never getting new jets, and your print quality can start to suffer. You'll get clogged jets more and more often, resulting in more head cleaning, which in turn wastes ink. Before you know it, you're caught in a vicious circle. Yes, it's okay to be a little thrifty and refill occasionally, but don't be so cheap that you cheat yourself out of decent-quality printouts.

Although all of the previous tips are possible, I don't recommend buying generic replacement cartridges or refilling them because the color inks never look as good as the manufacturer's ink—regardless of what the ads tell you. I've compared many brand-name replacements, and the results have always been noticeably inferior to the results with the manufacturer's cartridge.

Troubleshooting Tips

The following list summarizes the troubleshooting procedures covered in the chapter:

- For print quality problems, check the utilities built into the printer's driver. (Right-click the printer, and choose Properties to display the available tools and settings.)

- Use the nozzle checking utility to see whether any jets are clogged; then use the head cleaning utility to clean them. This uses ink, so balance the need for cleaning with your need not to waste ink.

- If the color is seriously off, one of the ink colors is probably out or its nozzles are clogged. If the color problem is more uniform, check the color calibration for the video card and/or the printer. One or both may have a color correction utility.

- If the printer doesn't print at all, check all your connections, and make sure the printer is installed correctly in your operating system. Look for a driver update on the manufacturer's Web site to ensure that you're using the most recent software driver.

- Make sure the printer isn't offline, isn't paused, or doesn't require user intervention (such as adding more paper).

- If the printer is accessed through a network, make sure your network connection is up and running.

- If the printer prints slowly, try decreasing the quality setting for a draft print. You can usually do this through the printer's Properties box. Slow printing may also be the result of using the wrong driver.

- Poor print quality can mean you're running out of one or more colors of ink, the print heads are misaligned or clogged, or you're using a draft-quality setting.

- Garbled output indicates a problem with the printer driver. Remove the printer from Windows (or other operating system), and reinstall.

In this chapter, you learned about inkjet printers and their troubleshooting and maintenance; in Chapter 17 you will turn your attention to the same topics for laser printers.

Chapter 17

Troubleshooting Laser Printers

Introduction

Laser printers are actually pretty reliable. Most of the printer problems you'll see aren't printer problems at all but rather problems with the humans trying to use them. As you'll learn in Chapter 25, "Troubleshooting PC Problems," you should first check the part of the equation that walks and talks. Once you've check and cleared the human component, exercise a methodical approach to test the rest of the system. Break the problem down into its possibilities/probabilities, testing and eliminating them one by one. Start with the easy stuff first. It's always possible that the only thing the printer needs is more paper.

Parts of a Laser Printer

I'll start the discussion of a laser printer by presenting its parts.

Interface Controller

Much of a laser printer is actually a computer—that is, it's composed of the same basic stuff as your desktop computer: circuit boards, memory chips, ports, and so on. As in your computer, the laser printer has a large printed circuit board that receives, modifies, and outputs data. Different manufacturers call it by different names, but in this book I'll go with the generic name *interface controller*.

The interface controller is the printer's motherboard, and it handles some pretty important tasks. This is some of what it does:

◆ It communicates with the PC that wants to print using an input interface, such as Universal Serial Bus (USB), parallel, serial, network, or infrared.

◆ It manipulates incoming data for translation to the print engine.

◆ It monitors the control panel (usually a button panel on its front) for user input.

◆ It provides information on printer status at the display and through various Light-Emitting Diodes (LEDs).

◆ It stores configuration and font information in Random Access Memory (RAM)—yes, the printer has its own RAM!

Input Interface

In Chapter 15, "Printer Types and Interfaces," I explained the various printer interfaces available (USB, parallel, and so on) and the two ways a printer can hook into a network—through a networked PC or with its own network connection. Some printers also support additional Input/Output (I/O) possibilities, such as an infrared or Macintosh connection.

CPU

Just as your computer's motherboard holds its Central Processing Unit (CPU), the printer's interface controller also holds the main brain of the printer, its CPU. No matter which port receives the data, the CPU controls its processing. Most laser printers today use a RISC processor (which, by the way, stands for Reduced Instruction Set Computer), as opposed to your PC, which uses a CISC (the C stands for *Complex*). However, the basic processing concept is the same.

Printer RAM

It's important to remember that a laser printer is a *page printer*—it composes an entire page in memory first and then transfers it to paper. So there must be enough RAM in the printer to hold an entire page, or it can't print. How much is "enough"? It depends on the page being printed. More and larger graphics, and more fonts, mean more memory required.

When laser printers first appeared on the market, they came with a measly amount of memory—often only 512 kilobytes (KB)—that wasn't enough to compose a full-page graphic. People using those printers would get an error message when printing complex pages and, naturally, they complained about it bitterly to the manufacturers.

The manufacturers responded by offering to sell memory upgrades. But these upgrades were typically a proprietary type of memory, which cost quite a bit more than normal computer memory (which, at that time, was no bargain either!). Sometimes it was actually cheaper to buy a new printer with more memory than it was to pay for one of these RAM upgrades!

Manufacturers have learned their lesson somewhat in recent years and have increased the amount of RAM in their printers to anywhere from 16 megabytes (MB) in a low-end laser printer to 128MB in a business printer. Color laser printers can have even more. In a network-enabled printer, more RAM means more print jobs can be queued inside the printer. Manufacturers of late have also been making printers that accept regular Dynamic RAM (DRAM) Double Inline Memory Modules (DIMMs)— that is, the same type of RAM that computers use. That, combined with the dropping cost of memory in general, has made it more economical to have a printer with a decent amount of memory—say, 32MB for an average home office printing at 1200 dots per inch (dpi).

Printing Mechanisms

The printer parts I've talked about so far are all computer components, but, obviously, a printer must have some mechanical parts, too. The paper needs to be taken in, printed on, and spit back out again. Different laser printers handle the paper input/output in different ways, but the process of actually creating the printed image on the page is fairly standard among laser printers. You'll learn about this printing process in the following section.

How a Laser Printer Prints

Understanding the laser printing process is more than just a techie exercise; it's essential to understanding what can go wrong and how to fix it. This information is also "must-know" knowledge if you ever decide to take the A+ Certification exams.

The following are the basic steps involved in laser printing, which are also shown graphically in Figure 17.1:

1. **Cleaning**: The drum is cleaned to remove any traces of the previous page's data.

2. **Conditioning (charging)**: A uniform negative charge is applied to the drum.

3. **Writing**: A laser partially neutralizes the negative charge in some areas, painting the entire page image on the drum in static charge.

4. **Developing**: The drum rotates past a reservoir of toner with the same negative charge as in step 1. The toner ignores the areas of the drum with the same charge as itself (that is, the unlasered areas) but sticks to the lasered areas with the lesser negative charge.

5. **Transferring**: Paper feeds into the printer and receives a positive charge. The toner on the drum jumps off onto the paper because the positive charge of the paper is more attractive than the weak negative charge of the drum.

6. **Fusing**: The paper passes through a fuser (a heater) that melts the plastic resin in the toner, affixing it to the paper.

If you include the transfer of the data to the printer from the computer, there's also a "step 0" before these wherein the data comes into the printer to be printed.

You'll now look at each of these steps in a bit more detail, focusing on what can go wrong and how to recognize a problem.

FIGURE 17.1

How a laser
printer works

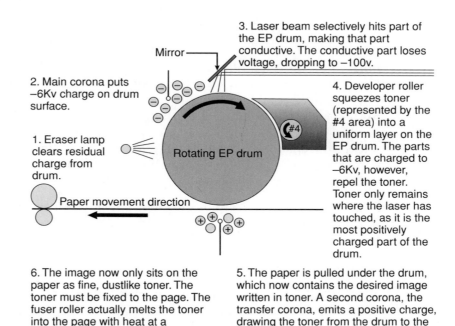

3. Laser beam selectively hits part of the EP drum, making that part conductive. The conductive part loses voltage, dropping to −100v.

Mirror

2. Main corona puts −6Kv charge on drum surface.

4. Developer roller squeezes toner (represented by the #4 area) into a uniform layer on the EP drum. The parts that are charged to −6Kv, however, repel the toner. Toner only remains where the laser has touched, as it is the most positively charged part of the drum.

1. Eraser lamp clears residual charge from drum.

Rotating EP drum

Paper movement direction

6. The image now only sits on the paper as fine, dustlike toner. The toner must be fixed to the page. The fuser roller actually melts the toner into the page with heat at a temperature of 180 degrees C.

5. The paper is pulled under the drum, which now contains the desired image written in toner. A second corona, the transfer corona, emits a positive charge, drawing the toner from the drum to the paper.

Step 1: Cleaning

The heart of the print process is the photosensitive drum, an aluminum cylinder coated with a photosensitive material. The drum's job is to pick up laser printer *toner*—a fine black dust that's the "ink" of the laser printing process—and deposit it on the paper. Another name for the drum is the Organic Photo-conducting Cartridge (OPC).

Because the same photosensitive drum is used to print every image (it actually rotates almost three times during the printing of each letter-sized page), it must be prepared for the newer image by completely purging the previous one. If the drum weren't completely purged, then subsequent pages would have ghostly images from previous pages. You know how hard it is to completely clean a blackboard when you erase it and parts of what was on the blackboard previously kind of hang around? That's what you're trying to avoid in laser printing.

The cleaning process is accomplished in two parts. Physically, excess toner is constantly wiped from the drum by means of a rubber-cleaning blade.

The drum is then cleaned electrostatically, either by another drum (in modern laser printers) or by erase lamps (in older models). On the printers with lamps, the lamps can shine onto the photosensitive drum via one of the two narrow hinged covers on the top of the cartridge, which open automatically when the cover is closed. These lamps neutralize residual charges by illuminating the photosensitive component of the drum. Lamps are obsolete technology, but printers tend to have a much longer useful life than computers in the field so you may occasionally encounter an older laser printer that uses them.

NOTE   *The photosensitive drum can be permanently damaged by exposure to light; therefore, the illumination from erase lamps is red filtered. Pop the top on certain laser printers, and you'll see red plastic; those are the filters for the lamps.*

Step 2: Conditioning

Conditioning (as known as charging) involves the application of a uniformly negative charge to the surface of the drum. In modern laser printers, another charged drum accomplishes this; in older printers, conditioning happens via the primary corona assembly. *Corona* is another name for a wire. The primary corona wire is usually located in the toner cartridge.

NOTE   *In this book, I'll generically refer to the corona wires or the charged drums that serve the purpose of corona wires as "coronas." This isn't completely accurate because technically a corona is by definition a wire; however, it'll save you some vocabulary grief because it'll help avoid confusing the main photosensitive drum with the smaller charge drums. It also reinforces the idea that the function of a corona wire and a charged drum is identical, even though their physical forms are different.*

The primary corona emits a −6000 volt (v) charge, but only 10 percent of that gets absorbed by the photosensitive drum. Therefore, the photosensitive drum ends up with a uniform charge of approximately −600v across its entire surface.

The voltage buildup on the surface of the drum is uniform because it's filtered by a grid that's attached to a *varistor* in the high-voltage power supply. A varistor is so named because it's a variable resistor. It won't conduct electricity until a specific voltage level is achieved. This, of course, is the characteristic that allows it to be useful in this particular application. See Figure 17.2.

Step 3: Writing

Now that it's conditioned, the drum is ready for the image. The laser unit scans the photosensitive drum, in a fashion similar to that of a Cathode-Ray Tube (CRT), with a repeated horizontal sweeping motion of the beam. A laser diode turns itself on and off at precise intervals to cause certain areas of the drum to be lasered and other areas to be left alone. The laser doesn't directly address the drum; it's refracted through one or more lenses and bounces off a moving mirror unit. Wherever the laser hits the drum, the charge on the drum is partially neutralized to about −100v.

On early laser printers, the on/off status of the laser diode could be changed 300 times for each inch of the beam's progress across the drum, hence the 300dpi resolution of those printers. Modern laser printers have higher resolutions; a typical modern laser printer supports 1200dpi.

NOTE   *An* LED *printer is virtually identical to a laser printer in its operation except for the writing phase. Rather than using a sweeping laser across the surface of the drum, an* LED *printer uses a set of lights positioned along the width of the drum. The lights turn on/off at specified intervals, changing the charge on the photosensitive drum just like a laser would.*

FIGURE 17.2

A varistor grid ensures that the charge applied to the drum is uniform.

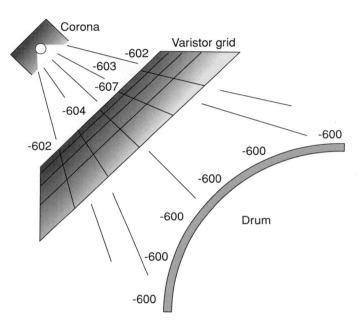

Step 4: Developing

After the image is mapped on the photosensitive drum, there's then the simple application of a basic law of nature and of magnetic properties: opposites attract.

The developer component of the cartridge contains a rotating metallic cylinder with a magnet running its length, a toner reservoir, and a toner height control mechanism. The height control is to regulate the amount of toner that may travel with the cylinder.

The metallic cylinder is situated adjacent to the photosensitive drum. Its sole purpose is to collect toner from the reservoir and present it to the drum in a usable form. This device is called the *developing cylinder*.

The developing cylinder rotates with a portion of its surface in contact with the toner in the toner reservoir of the cartridge. Its magnetic personality (not to mention that its surface is given a highly negative −600v charge by the high-voltage power supply) causes an irresistible attraction to the tiny neutrally charged particles of toner, which then cling to the cylinder.

The toner that adheres to the cylinder adopts its charge by the time it travels to the image area of the photosensitive drum. The toner is made of plastic resin particles (the part that melts) bonded to iron oxide (the part that's attracted by the electrical charges).

While the toner-laden developing cylinder rotates toward the image-ready photosensitive drum, a scraping blade removes the excess toner, thus delivering a uniform supply of it to the image process.

The electrical properties of the magnetized developing cylinder are further enhanced by a Direct Current (DC) bias and an Alternating Current (AC) potential. You can adjust the DC bias via the print density control knob on the printer. Its purpose is to regulate the density of the toner that ends up on the printed page. Counterintuitively, selecting a *higher* number on the green wheel results in *less* toner being offered to the photosensitive drum and therefore results in a lighter image being put on the page.

While the developing cylinder presents the now highly negatively charged toner to the laser-affected areas of the photosensitive drum, they're attracted to the invisible electrostatic image because it, although still negative in charge, is much less negative than the toner itself. The unlasered portions of the drum, on the other hand, are ignored because they have the same −600v charge as the toner itself.

The AC component on the developer roller affects the DC potential, thus causing the toner, in a reciprocal process, to escape the negatively charged roller at the moment of highest potential, only to be reattracted to it when the AC component swings high. This happens 60 times per second, effectively presenting a fog of toner to the laser-affected areas. Those particles of toner that find their way to the electrostatically defined image aren't drawn back to the developing cylinder. Figure 17.3 shows an overview of the process.

FIGURE 17.3

Image processing (toner)

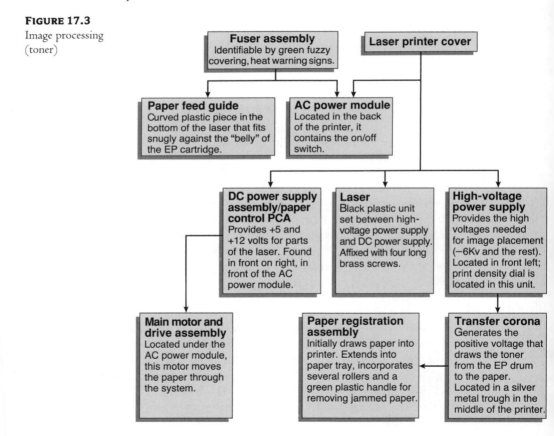

Step 5: Transferring

The desired image now exists on the drum in the form of fine toner particles. Toner is about 50 percent iron oxide and 50 percent plastic. (You can actually get toner out of fabric by rubbing a powerful magnet across the surface.) Next, the laser printer transfers the toner to paper by giving the paper a strong (+600v) *positive* charge. That charge is applied by the *transfer corona*, another important thin wire permanently mounted in the printer. The toner then jumps from the drum to the paper. The image is now transferred to the paper.

Step 6: Fusing

Once the drum has yielded the image, separating the paper from it (the drum) isn't a foregone conclusion. However, while the paper advances, its natural stiffness tends to pull it away from the drum, especially because the drum's circumference is relatively small. Thinner papers might adhere to the drum, however, so separation is also assisted by the *static charge eliminator*, a row of teeth with a highly negative charge that helps neutralize the potential between the positively charged paper and the negatively charged drum.

The paper proceeds to the fusing station with its toner image in the precarious condition of being held to the paper by only gravity and a weak electrostatic charge. The fusing station assembly is composed of a fuser roller, cleaning pad, thermistor, thermo-protector, and pressure roller.

The fuser roller is a Teflon-coated cylinder that has a high-intensity quartz lamp inside it to provide the heat for the fusing process. If the heat builds beyond acceptable levels, there's a detection/protection mechanism called a *thermistor*, located near the fuser roller, which will shut the printer down.

Just how hot am I talking about here? Well, the temperatures of the LaserJet III's fuser were 165 degrees C (330 degrees F) when on but inactive and 180 degrees C (355 degrees F) while printing. The temperatures are even higher in newer models. Given these temperatures, it's advisable to keep anything out of the printer that can be melted or damaged by heat. I've heard multiple reports of people inserting nonrated Mylar or acetate to make overhead projection display sheets. Put simply, if you try to print on something that melts below 180 degrees C, you'll probably have to buy a new fuser roller. They make special transparency film just for laser printers, so make sure you buy that kind if you need some.

The cleaning pad is positioned to remain in constant contact with the fuser roller. It collects any contaminants that seek to become part of the process and provides the already slippery fuser with a silicone film. This ensures that the paper with its now fused image will continue as planned and not have a tendency to stick around (pardon the pun).

A critical part of the toner cartridge change is the replacement of this pad. It wears out, just like your printer runs out of toner, and needs to be replaced to maintain your printer's longevity and print quality. Without the silicone film, the hot fuser will be much more likely to receive permanent contamination. The replacement toner cartridge should come with a replacement cleaning pad; if it doesn't, check your printer manual to find out what to do.

The pressure roller is a rubber roller that's situated against the fuser roller in such a way that the paper is pressed between the two rollers as it passes through. The fuser roller is one of those strong personality types that leaves a lasting impression, so every few minutes the printer will rotate this assembly to keep the rubber roller from receiving a permanent indentation in the area where the rollers are being social. That's the odd noise that your laser printer sometimes makes for no obvious reason.

NOTE *If you're unfortunate enough to get a paper jam prior to this point in the process, it'll become immediately obvious that the image on the paper hasn't yet been fused. As you remove the affected sheet, liberal amounts of toner will remain on anything it contacts.*

As the paper proceeds along its path, it's important that it doesn't wobble off to the left or right but instead cleave to the path of the straight and narrow. That's accomplished by the feed guide assembly.

Paper Exit

After the image is safely fused in place on the paper, the paper exits the printer via exit delivery rollers and guides. Some printers have only one exit tray, usually the facedown one on top. Others allow you to choose by flipping a switch or lowering a tray to exit the paper faceup at the back of the printer.

When you're printing with heavy stock or fragile items, you can spare them the final turn by using the delivery tray at the back if your printer has one; just open the door, and the paper comes out the back.

I've noticed that my envelopes don't wrinkle quite as badly if I let them exit at the back. This is because the exit delivery area at the top of the printer has the most acute angle that the paper encounters in the entire process. Unfortunately, not all printers offer an option in paper delivery.

During this whole process, the printer uses sensors located throughout it, which report to the CPU as soon as they see the paper. The printer knows how long it should take to get from one sensor to the next; if a sensor doesn't report "seeing" the paper within a particular window of time, then the printer's CPU assumes that the paper's jammed, and it stops the printing process and reports a jam.

Color Laser Printers

Many types of color printers are available to the business and home consumer these days, and color lasers are by no means the most popular. For the low-end market, color inkjets dominate. At the high end, solid-ink and dye-sublimation printers have their fans. Color lasers sit somewhere in the uncomfortable middle. They're faster and cheaper per page than most of the other color printer alternatives, but the color laser printers themselves are rather expensive.

Color laser printers work in much the same way as their cheaper black-and-white cousins. The technical details of the print process vary somewhat depending on the manufacturer. Some color lasers print each color on the page individually, making several passes (one for black and one for each of the toner colors), much like the color separation printing that's done by commercial presses. Because the printer has only one drum, the whole printing process repeats several times for each page, layering the toner.

A color printing method that's gaining more popularity is the *Direct-to-Drum*, or layering, method used by Hewlett-Packard (HP) color lasers. In this print method, the charging corona places the negative charge on the drum, and the laser then gently sweeps over the drum and creates an image for the yellow toner (the first of four primary printing colors) to attach to. After the yellow toner has made itself at home, the drum is again charged by the corona, and the laser works its art on the drum and creates an image for the next printing color, magenta. This same process happens again for the final two colors, cyan and black. After all four colors have been applied to the drum, the image is transferred onto the waiting paper. This method allows a single dot on the page to have a blended color, rather than the dithered colors of images produced on inkjet printers and cheaper color laser printers.

NOTE *An inexpensive alternative to color laser printing uses LED technology rather than lasers. Okidata's color LED printers use this technology. These printers print quickly because they make only one pass, as with an inkjet, but the quality is arguably not quite as good as with a real color laser.*

The problems people have with color laser printers are virtually identical to the problems with black-and-white models. One exception is color registration—that is, a failure of the colors to align properly on a laser printer that prints by making multiple passes over the paper. (Because fewer and fewer color lasers work that way these days, this problem is confined to only a few brands and models.) This problem is often a symptom of the paper not being fed through the printer precisely, so your difficulty is probably with the feed rollers rather than the printing process itself. Check your printer's documentation or the manufacturer's Web site to see what can be done.

Common Symptoms and Solutions

Now that you know how a laser printer works, you can see what can go wrong. There are lots of *potential* problems with lasers, but I'll confine this to the most common problems only; then you'll look at the more rigorous testing you can do.

Vertical White Streaks on the Page

Because the paper is transported top to bottom through the laser printer, the paper also passes the coronas top to bottom. If a part of the corona were covered with toner, it couldn't transmit all of its charge, leaving either the drum (if it's the primary corona) or the paper (if it's the transfer corona) with insufficient charge. That would lead to a vertical stripe with little or no charge, thereby leaving no toner—a white stripe. The answer: clean the coronas.

NOTE *Remember, as I mentioned earlier in this book, I'm using the term* coronas *to mean either actual corona wires or the charged drums that have replaced corona wires in modern laser printers.*

The primary corona is, recall, in the toner cartridge, so if you're being barraged with support calls at the time and you need a quick fix, you can just change the cartridge. But some printers come with a little brush or other cleaning tool with which you can clean your corona, and others are designed to allow for cleaning with a cotton swab. See the printer manual for details.

The transfer corona is a permanent fixture in the laser printer. Its exact position varies depending on the make and model. For models that use an actual wire, look for a row of soft bristles inside the printer; they protect the wire from damage because of paper jamming. In all models, the transfer corona is likely to be close to wherever the widest portion of the toner cartridge rests inside the printer because that's where the drum is.

If dealing with an actual wire, you can clean it with a cotton swab and some rubbing alcohol. Some printers don't let you get at the transfer corona, so check your printer manual if in doubt. And be careful with the wire! Don't break it, or your printer won't work and you're in for an expensive repair. In printers that use a roller rather than a wire, you usually don't need to clean them.

Smearing on the Page

What keeps the toner from smearing? The fusing roller. It's covered with a Teflonlike coating to keep stuff from sticking to it, but it can become scratched or junk can just get baked onto it. In either case, the heat doesn't transfer to the page. Try cleaning the roller with a soft cloth and some alcohol, but *let the thing cool down before you mess with it!* Consult the printer manual to figure out where the fusing roller is located; it's probably near the paper exit point.

NOTE *On older laser printers, smearing may occur if you print double-sided—that is, if you feed through an already-printed page to print on its backside. This is less of an issue with newer printers.*

Horizontal Streaks on the Page

If you see a regular horizontal line on your output, it's more than likely caused by an irregularity in one of the many rollers that the paper must pass by on its journey from the paper cartridge to the output bin. The key to identifying *which* roller is in measuring the distance between the lines. If the horizontal lines are always spaced the same distance apart, then *that distance is the circumference of the bad roller.*

Trouble is, how do you know the circumferences of the rollers? It's different for different printers, so there's no one master chart that will tell you. Check the Web site for the printer manufacturer to see whether a chart or table is available for the model in question.

In practical experience, however, the vast majority of problems with horizontal streaks are caused by a scratch or irregularity on the photosensitive drum itself. In a printer where the drum is built into the toner cartridge, try changing cartridges. If this clears up the problem—great. If not, get some help from the printer's manufacturer with those other rollers.

Cloudy, Faded Output

This sounds like an ad for a laundry detergent; it's what you see when the whites aren't white and the blacks aren't black. The probable cause is either low toner or a dirty or damaged corona wire (if the printer uses corona wires rather than charged rollers).

The first thing to try is replacing the toner cartridge. This will help if you're simply low on toner, of course, but it'll also give you a new primary corona/charge roller on most printers. If that doesn't help and the printer uses corona wires, clean them. (See "Vertical White Streaks on the Page" earlier in this chapter for instructions.)

Distorted Images

If your printed images look stretched, the printer's feed components are probably slipping or its gears aren't functioning properly. The gears may not be gripping on the shaft, as they should be. To restore the printer's feed capability, get new feed rollers, separator pads, and assorted bushings in a kit, and replace the worn-out components.

Black Line Down the Side of the Page

I don't know why this happens, but you'll see it when the toner is low or the toner cartridge is faulty. Replace the cartridge.

Memory Overflow Error

If you get an out of memory error, or memory overflow, or `20 MEM` message (on LaserJets), it means you asked the printer to do something that it doesn't have enough memory to do. One common reason for this is that you bought a printer without enough memory for the jobs you do. (Remember, I said earlier that many older laser printers came with only 512KB by default, which isn't enough for a full-page graphic. Most laser printers sold today come with at least 8MB of RAM.)

The answer is generally to get more memory. But another possibility is that you've filled the printer's memory with *fonts*. They take up space in memory, too. I find that I can keep the printer from running out of memory under Windows by making these modifications to the printer's properties (right-click a printer in your Printers folder and choose Properties):

- Print TrueType as graphics.
- Use raster graphics rather than HP-GL graphics.

And here's something else to try: use a different printer language if your printer supports more than one. For example, if you have a laser printer that supports both Printer Control Language (PCL) and PostScript, and you're getting memory errors using one, try installing a second instance of the printer in Windows and specifying the other type of language for it.

Printer Picks Up Multiple Sheets

Believe it or not, this usually isn't the printer's fault. You need dry paper in order to get proper feed. Is the paper sitting in the tray for weeks at a time? Not good. When paper is removed from its ream wrapper, it's supposed to be dry. So how do you keep paper dry afterward? If it gets used in a day or two, there's no problem. But if it sits in the tray for longer, particularly in a humid environment, it could pick up some humidity. And make sure you've got the correct side of the paper up when you put it in the printer (look at the package for the arrow).

If you have a newer HP laser printer, it could be that your separator pad is getting worn out. Contact HP to see if your printer is eligible to receive a free replacement pad.

Paper Jams

Trying to print double-sided can cause this. The first time you run the paper through the printer, the paper gets a slight curl imparted to it. Turn it upside down and run it through the printer again and that slight curl can sometimes translate to a paper jam. Another cause of paper jams is printing on the wrong side of the paper. There are, believe it or not, two different sides to a sheet of paper, called the *wax* and the *wire*. Paper will have a "print this side up" indication on the wrapper: pay attention to it. Paper can acquire a curl in humid environments, but the wrapper keeps the paper dry, so don't take paper out of the ream until you're ready to use it. Using cheap paper can also lead to paper jams. Also, old laser printers may have rollers that get out of round, leading to jams.

Laser printers of the "small footprint with gravity paper feed" variety occasionally suffer from paper jams because of the printer grabbing several sheets at once. This problem was especially prevalent on the HP 5L series. It was possible to get this puppy jammed enough so that a technician was required to dismantle the printer to clear the jam. If you do get a jam, resist the urge to rip out the paper. Instead, try powering the printer up and down several times. Each time the printer powers up it advances the paper a short distance. Try that to see if the printer will move the paper out for you. If your printer doesn't have a power switch, you'll need to resort to plugging and unplugging the printer.

Squeaking or Groaning Sounds

Laser printers can make some pretty bizarre sounds. Some of these sounds indicate developing problems and should, therefore, receive appropriate attention, but a perfectly healthy and properly functioning printer can also make noises that sound as though the printer is malfunctioning. The most noticeable noises are generally part of the paper-feed process.

A noise I've been asked about more than any other is the one that comes every few minutes from an idle (but powered on) laser printer. This noise sounds like the printer's electric motor beginning, as though it's about to print, and then stopping abruptly. There's a good reason for that description: that's exactly what the sound is. Because the fuser assembly remains hot even when idle, the printer needs to rotate it every so often. Otherwise, the hot metallic fuser roller would burn a permanent depression into the rubber pressure roller with which it's in constant contact.

Basic Testing

If you've got a serious laser problem, you may still be able to avoid taking the thing apart to fix it. The following are some tests to try before doing the heavy-duty screwdriver work.

Printer Power

Relative to your other office devices, laser printers are power hogs. More than seven amps of constant current draw put this device in the same league as an entire well-equipped *kitchen*. Because the printer uses this much energy, it's critical that everything related to the electrical system be in top condition.

I discussed outlet wiring in Chapter 7, "Power Supplies and Protection." With lasers, however, it's doubly important because of all the power they suck up. Ideally, you (as the technician) will have an electrical wiring diagram for each building you support, even if it's just your home. Then, when someone starts to plug a Mr. Coffee into an outlet on the same circuit as one of the workstations, you can offer appropriate and eloquent opposing arguments (all mainly consisting of "don't plug other things next to the laser unless you want to buy its replacement"), complete with documentation if necessary. You need to remember that it's a good idea to keep lasers on circuits of their own.

Resetting the Printer

Like the PC, the laser printer can become confused—it's a complex piece of equipment performing complex operations. Things go wrong. On occasion, you may find it necessary to reset the printer.

As with the PC, there are different levels of reset for a laser printer. The most severe reset of all for a PC is the power-down, or cold reboot. Cold reboots aren't usually the best way to handle PC problems because you might be using an application that must be shut down a certain way in order to start up again without problems. (Windows 95 and higher are like that.) Printers don't have the same problem. As a matter of fact, the power-down reset for the printer only clears the print buffer; it doesn't clear any downloaded fonts or other system data. This can be a useful feature, but, although it can temporarily get you past a difficulty, it won't always solve everything, and you'll still have to address the cause of the initial problem.

TIP   If you reset the printer while your computer is still spooling data to it, when the printer comes back online the data may continue flowing to it. And because the first part of the job is now gone, you're likely to get garbage characters instead of your print job. Cancel the job from your print queue first, and then reset the printer.

You can also reset some laser printers using the buttons on their front panel. (Check the documentation to find out how.) If you do this, however, you'll lose any fonts or macros you've downloaded to the printer.

On some color lasers, if the printer doesn't calibrate itself correctly at startup, the printer may work, but the colors will appear too dark. If you see this, turning the printer off and then back on again gives it another try at the color calibration routine.

Error Messages

One sure way to know you've got a problem is for your laser printer to *tell* you that you've got one. Different printers have different error codes, of course, just like different motherboards on computers have different beep codes at startup to indicate various types of low-level errors. The user manual for your printer should contain a complete listing of the error messages and their meanings, and you should also be able to find this information at the printer manufacturer's Web site.

Cables and Ports

Next, take a look at the cable and the I/O ports, both of which can be the source of printing problems.

CABLE CONNECTORS

If your printer and computer don't seem to be communicating, check the printer's power cable and the data cable to make sure they're both snugly seated. Pay special attention to the connections at both ends of the data cable. Some parallel printer cables attach to the PC via screws and to the printer via metal clips. If either aren't attached securely, it's easy to dislodge the cable, even by doing something as minor as stretching your legs under your desk and knocking the data cable aside. The same goes with USB cables; because they're not screwed in place, it's easy to dislodge them unintentionally.

CABLE LENGTH

As long as it can reach from your computer to the printer, it's not possible for a data cable to be too short. It can easily be too long, however. HP recommends a parallel cable be no longer than 35 feet. As with many manufacturer standards, I've found that to be quite conservative. I've seen printers work fine with parallel data cables well beyond twice that length.

A serial cable (including both legacy serial and USB) can be much longer than a parallel cable because the signal voltages are higher.

BAD CABLES

If the printer is printing but isn't printing what you sent it, try swapping the data cable for another one. Cables can have flaws that show up only after you've handled the cable a little. If a data pin in a parallel cable breaks, it can cause certain characters to be misrepresented in printouts. Cable flaws are less of an issue for serial cables such as USB because they either connect or don't. There's less of a possibility for one or two broken wires inside the cable to cause sporadic performance.

If the cable is fine, check to make sure you're using the right driver for the printer and for the operating system installed.

CABLE TYPE

With a USB cable, just about any pin-compatible one will work. There are two USB standards—1.1 and 2.0—but the majority of printers sold today are 1.1-compatible only, and even the 2.0-compatible ones will work with 1.1 computers and cables (although they won't achieve their top communication speeds).

Parallel cable is a different story. In Chapter 15, you learned about the various modes for a parallel port—Extended Capabilities Port (ECP), Enhanced Parallel Port (EPP), and so on. Not all parallel printer cables support these modes, so select one carefully. The original parallel printer cables weren't bidirectional, so they didn't include the needed circuitry to manage port modes in which information flows not only to the printer but also from it.

However, parallel cable technology is mature and stable by this point, and those old unidirectional parallel cables haven't been manufactured for more than a decade. Therefore, any new parallel printer cable you buy today will work with an ECP or EPP port as long as the cable is labeled as being an IEEE 1284 cable. Don't go crazy and let someone convince you that you need a special cable with gold plating. Just make sure it says either bidirectional or 1284 somewhere on the packaging. Beware, however, of old cables fished out of someone's stash of extras.

Environmental Considerations

You may not see the following concerns on Greenpeace bumper stickers, but it's important you consider them when setting up and using your printer.

HEAT

A laser printer can pump out some serious heat because of the fuser. This is one reason why it's important that it's in a well-ventilated area. Because of this, systems furniture, or any furniture that attempts to fit every part of your workstation into a neat little cubbyhole, can be bad news. It's sometimes built without regard for the fact that the equipment needs to breathe properly. While arranging a workstation, see to it that all your devices have air circulating around them so that heat can dissipate. If you use your printer when it's in an unventilated area, its heat-sensitive components are likely to cook and fail prematurely.

LIGHT

Always guard the toner cartridge from direct contact with strong light because white light will shorten the useful life of the photosensitive drum. Don't slide the toner cartridge's door open to see the photosensitive drum, unless, of course, you're planning to recycle the cartridge right away.

AMMONIA

Ammonia can be detrimental to the laser printer's ability to neutralize ozone (discussed next) and can also permanently damage the toner cartridge. The chief sources of ammonia in an office setting are the chemicals used for cleaning and those required in the blueprinting process. If you work in an office where blueprinting is done, keep a watchful eye on the fume hood fan and general ventilation in the area of the machine itself.

OZONE

In recent years, you've probably heard a lot about ozone and the ozone layer. Ozone is a pale blue gas naturally produced whenever a lightning bolt occurs. It's in the upper atmosphere as a by-product of the reaction of oxygen to solar ultraviolet rays. Ozone production doesn't require anything so dramatic as a lightning bolt, however. It's also a natural by-product of the ionization that takes place during the laser printing process in printers that use corona wires (that is, older laser printers).

Ozone is great stuff in the outer areas of the earth's atmosphere but isn't good for humans and can be anything from a minor irritant to downright dangerous in significant concentrations. If it's present in concentrations greater than one part in 20,000, it's irritating to the mucous membranes and is poisonous. You can't generally see it, but its odor is most often described as pungent. Most people can detect the presence of ozone at a concentration as low as one part of ozone per 10 million parts of air.

Not only can ozone be harmful to humans, but, as a super-effective oxidizer, it can also cause deterioration of components in the machine itself. Therefore, ozone buildup is one more reason to make sure your printer is properly ventilated. You're more likely to have problems with ozone in the following situations:

◆ There are several active laser printers and/or copiers in a small, confined area.

◆ The relative humidity is low.

◆ There's improper or nonexistent ventilation.

◆ The ozone filter is in need of replacement.

◆ Any combination of these conditions exists.

You should replace the ozone filter in the laser printer after about every 50,000 prints, if your printer has one that's replaceable (check the manual). If office ventilation leaves something to be desired, or if you've got a lot of laser printers in a small, enclosed area, I recommend that you replace the filters more frequently. Mind you, all of this only applies to printers that actually use a corona in the printing process. Newer laser printers don't.

TONER CARTRIDGE REFILLING

If you install and maintain the toner cartridge properly, you shouldn't have problems with it. In these days of environmental concern, many people wonder whether they should use recharged cartridges. You're a lot safer using retreads than you used to be: the folks recycling them are either doing a better job or are using better components (or both); the recent efforts are far superior to many of the early ones. Still, keep an eye out for unscrupulous recyclers. A properly redone cartridge includes a new photosensitive drum. Beware of what are called *drill and fill operations*, companies that drill a hole in the cartridge and refill it with toner but don't replace any of the parts inside.

Paper and Media Issues

Just think of this as an up-to-date version of "garbage in, garbage out."

PAPER TYPE

Every kind of laser printer has its own paper type and quality requirements. If you follow those requirements, you'll be less likely to run into paper jams and distortion problems. In general, the better the quality of the printer, the better the quality of paper it'll require. At the least, higher-quality paper may give you higher-quality printouts. High humidity can also affect the performance of paper in a laser printer (not to mention that it can cause the printer to seal your envelopes).

THE PAPER FEED

You'll need to inspect the feed assemblies periodically. Over time, the feed rollers become glazed and thus less efficient at picking up one sheet of paper at a time from the paper tray. Replacing the rollers isn't a major production, but many people I've talked to find immediate (but temporary—isn't that always the way?) gratification by abrading the feed rollers somehow. You might try rubbing pencil erasers or *very fine* sandpaper over the rollers.

The separation pad (it's just beneath the feed rollers) plays a major role in letting the feed roller pick up only one sheet at a time. Over time, however, it wears thin. It's a good idea to replace the feed rollers and the separation pad about every 100,000 prints. You can buy them in a kit of other like items for those heavy-duty printer maintenance sessions.

CONTAMINANTS

Laser printers are powerful, yet delicate, machines. Foreign objects in the printer can really affect their performance for the worse. Therefore, you must be careful about what you feed your laser printer: no foreign objects, only the paper recommended by the manufacturer, and no labels or other printables not intended for laser printers.

One of the nastiest things I ever heard that someone fed the laser printer was a piece of paper that had a staple in place. This is almost certain to damage the fuser assembly. If the Teflon of the roller has scratches in it, your prints will have vertical white lines on them. There's nothing to be done about this; you have to replace the fuser assembly.

Another common contaminant is any printable material not intended for a laser printer. If labels aren't specifically manufactured to be used in a laser printer, don't use them—this is one thing you really can't fudge on even if you've got extra plain labels. Also, letterhead that has raised ink may not fare well when run through the printer.

Finally, there may be partial sheets of paper buried in the rest of the ream. They won't gum up your printer, but they could cause it to jam. Also, don't use textured paper because the toner doesn't stick to it very well.

PAPER JAMS

Most laser printers have several paper jam sensors. Some of them are timing sensors, which make it highly unlikely that a jam could occur anywhere in the process without the printer alerting you. One major cause of jams is improper media; stock that's thicker or thinner than the printer is prepared to handle can cause a fair amount of difficulty.

If a jam occurs before the paper reaches the fusing assembly, you'll need to note two things:

◆ Any toner that hasn't gone through the fusing assembly will end up all over everything when the jam is fixed. The stuff is hard to get out of clothing or carpeting, so be careful when handling paper with loose toner on its surface.

◆ Be careful not to damage the transfer corona wire when removing jammed paper from a printer that uses corona wires. This isn't an issue on the newer laser printers that use charge rollers instead of wires.

PAPER CURL AND WRINKLING

The major cause of curling is the effect that the fusion heat has on the paper composition—the amount of curl is generally directly proportional to the ash content of the paper. If you follow the manufacturer's recommendation for paper type, you're less likely to have problems with curling than otherwise.

Wrinkling will usually be the result of stiff paper negotiating the tight turn at the top of the printer near the facedown tray. It's most evident with heavy stock or envelopes. If the printer is equipped for it, you can avoid the problem by allowing heavy paper to feed from the faceup tray or output faceup to the rear of the printer instead of facedown at the top.

Advanced Testing and Repair

What you've already read are the easiest to fix and most common problems. Sometimes, however, the problem requires more work than a change in paper or a tap of the Reset button.

Laser Printer Disassembly

It can be tricky to disassemble a laser printer, particularly if you're not familiar with the make and model. There's no shame in taking the printer to an authorized service center for that brand and letting someone experienced with the unit take a crack at it. However, if you're one of those do-it-yourselfers. It shows the dependencies of one part on another and can help you determine what parts you may need to disassemble in order to examine or replace a certain other part.

Voltage Tests

If, when you turn it on, the printer doesn't respond normally, the printer's power system is probably malfunctioning. To find out for sure, you'll need a voltage meter. A basic digital multimeter is a must for the printer technician; you should be able to obtain one for about $30 at your local Radio Shack or similar store.

The DC power supply provides three different DC voltages to the system's components. All three can be checked at an interface labeled J210; it's a 20-pin female interface with pin 1 located at the lower-left corner and the odd numbers along the bottom row, left to right.

Using the multimeter, check the indicated pins (every other pin along the bottom, left to right, starting at 1) for the following voltages (frame ground is the reference):

◆ Pin 1 = +5v.

◆ Pin 5 = −5v.

◆ Pin 9 = +24v.

If *none* of the voltages are present, check the fuse on the DC power supply.
If *one or more* of the voltages is missing, you'll need to do at least one of the following:

◆ Remove all optional devices, including memory.

◆ Replace the DC power supply assembly.

◆ Replace the DC controller PCA.

I/O Port Testing

Whenever there's a printing problem, the first thing you need to determine is whether the problem lies with the printer or the computer. Assuming you have checked the printer's driver in the operating system, the next thing to check is the port status on the PC. Is the port enabled? Most motherboards allow you to enable/disable both parallel ports and USB ports through Basic Input/Output System (BIOS) Setup.

If the port is enabled in BIOS, does it appear in Windows in the Device Manager? Chapter 24, "Managing Hardware Resources in Windows," explains how to check hardware in Device Manager, including ports.

On the printer side of the I/O interface, it can be more difficult to troubleshoot. Ideally, the printer will have multiple I/O interfaces, such as USB and parallel, and you can simply try the other interface to determine if one is malfunctioning. Usually the I/O ports on a printer are attached to a circuit board connected to the printer's motherboard and can be replaced if needed.

Using Diagnostic Software

If you're having output problems and want to see exactly what's going from the computer to the printer, you can capture printer output in a file by means of a utility program. Your printer may have come with its own diagnostic software, or you may be able to download a testing utility from the printer manufacturer's Web site. The printer probably also has a self-test routine built into it, and a Test Print option you can activate through its Windows-based printer driver.

NOTE *It's hard to get any information from a test print if you don't know what a good print looks like. Now, while the printer still works, you should print a test page using the self-test menu on the printer itself. Some older models may not have menus to work with; in that case, you should consult your manual to find the exact instructions because they vary from printer to printer. Keep this test print somewhere, and you can compare it with your test prints later to see how the new print compares with the baseline test print. A test print shows various gray scales, text, horizontals, and verticals. The tightest horizontals and verticals will appear to the average viewer as single heavy lines, but, if you look at them closely, you'll see multiple lines in those areas.*

Maintenance Issues

The following sections highlight a few things you should check to keep your laser printer in good working order.

Errant Toner

When, in the course of printer events, you're called upon to clean up toner, the method will depend on the amount and location. You can clean up minute amounts on the inside of the printer along the paper's path with a slightly dampened cloth or a swab dipped in alcohol. If there are larger amounts of toner, more drastic measures are required.

WARNING   Never, ever, ship a printer with a toner cartridge still inside. If a cartridge is dropped or jostled improperly during shipment, you'll likely have to clean up larger quantities of toner.

WARNING   Don't get out the Electrolux! Toner is a plastic resin bonded to iron particles, a deadly combination to hot electric motors (such as those in vacuum cleaners). If you try to vacuum the runaway toner, it'll blow straight through a normal vacuum cleaner bag and into the motor, where the plastic will melt and the iron will play havoc with the armature and brushes. The particles that don't stop in the motor will fly through the air and cover the vicinity (and you) with tiny black particles that are difficult to wash out of clothing.

If you get toner on your clothing or skin, remember its properties; use only cold water and plenty of soap. You're likely to get toner on you if you have to clear a paper jam that happened before the paper got to the fusing assembly, so be careful. If you have a large toner spill in the printer, take it outside and use a compressed air canister to clean out the printer.

Cleaning

Laser printers, especially the newer ones, don't require much cleaning. Some models are "dirtier" than others, though, and will require more of your time and energy to keep clean. I had a Canon laser printer at one point that always seemed to have a fine spray of loose toner in the bottom, no matter how many times I cleaned it up, and a client of mine has a LaserJet that gunks up a felt cleaning pad much faster than it should. The following are some tips for cleaning laser printers.

PRINTER CLEANING UTILITY

Many printers, including most of the HP LaserJets, have a self-cleaning routine you can run. One of the kindest things you can do for your printer is to run the self-cleaning routine every time you change the toner cartridge. If your printer doesn't have a cleaning utility, you might be able to download one from the manufacturer's Web site.

The self-cleaning routine will usually print a large black box on a piece of copier grade paper. This sheet of paper is then placed facedown and sent through the process again. This is the only time you should refeed a piece of paper without the luxury of a duplex unit! Sending this sheet through again will reheat the toner that was placed on the paper the first time, causing it to become slightly adhesive. Any miscreant toner particles or small pieces of paper stuck to the innards of the printer will now be pulled out. The way to tell if the self-cleaning routine has performed up to par is to check the black box that was printed on the first pass—if it's covered with shiny black specks, then you know it worked. You may need to do this more than once just to be sure you get all of the little varmints attached to your rollers.

CORONA WIRES

This is an issue only for the older printers, which use actual corona wires rather than the newer charge rollers. If your printer uses charging rollers instead of coronas, check the manual to find out what maintenance should be performed on them if any. Maintenance and cleaning on them isn't usually required.

You should clean both corona wires regularly or whenever there's a problem with the printer that might be caused by excess toner on the wire. Clean the primary corona in the toner cartridge once at the midpoint of the life of the cartridge—you've got no excuse to avoid doing so because HP and many other printer manufacturers thoughtfully provide a plastic brush for the job. Insert the suede end of the brush into the slot in the cartridge, and slide it from one end to the other.

The transfer corona is in the bottom of the printer beneath the paper path. On most printers, several monofilament lines protect it from damage in the event of a paper jam. Clean it with a cotton-tipped swab (which may come with your replacement cartridge), gently stroking it in each direction and on each side between the monofilament segments. Usually the products of your labor will be pretty innocuous: perhaps some toner or a little dust. I recommend you do this in good light, so you can see how much pressure you're putting on the corona because, if you break it, you must replace the entire corona assembly.

NOTE   *The winner in the most-disgusting-corona-problem category, however, is the time one technician reportedly found several well-done roaches in the transfer corona channel. The only reason the users discovered the cockroaches was because the insects' bodies were making the pages turn black.*

REGISTRATION AND FEED GUIDE ASSEMBLIES

Here, maintenance is pretty easy: you need only occasionally wipe with a damp cloth to clean up that errant toner (unless, of course, some foreign object happens to stop in this area). You'll need to clear paper fragments away periodically because it's here that paper fragments or partial pages will usually stop.

Troubleshooting Recap

The following is a quick review of the troubleshooting tips covered in this chapter:

- Vertical white streaks on the page can indicate a dirty transfer corona. Clean it with a cotton swab (if the printer has corona wires).

- Vertical black streaks indicate scratches on the feed rollers, perhaps caused by running staples or other hard foreign objects through the printer by mistake.

◆ Smeared ink could mean a scratched or dirty fusing roller. Clean it with a soft cloth and some alcohol (after it has cooled down). Ink sometimes also smears when you run double-sided pages on printers not designed for them.

◆ A distorted or stretched image probably means the printer's feed components are slipping or the gears aren't functioning correctly. To restore the printer's feed capability, get new feed rollers, separator pads, and assorted bushings in a kit, and replace the worn-out components.

◆ Horizontal lines are usually caused by an irregularity in one of the many rollers that the paper passes through. The most common source of such an error is the photosensitive drum itself.

◆ Cloudy or faded output usually means it's time to change the toner cartridge or you've got a dirty or damaged corona.

◆ A black line down the side of the page can indicate the toner is low or the toner cartridge is faulty.

◆ You can look up error codes that appear on the printer's LED panel in the printer's manual or on the manufacturer's Web site.

◆ A printer that picks up multiple sheets is usually fine—it's the paper that's your problem. Make sure it's dry and well fanned.

◆ Paper jams can result from trying to print double-sided or from curled or cheap paper.

◆ Many printer problems can result from using the wrong printer driver in Windows or other software you're using. Make sure you have the correct driver for both your printer and your operating system.

◆ If a printer that usually works fine gets an error or starts printing out garbage pages, try turning it off and then back on again after a few seconds.

◆ If you want the printer and computer to communicate using an ECP or EPP parallel port, make sure you have the parallel port defined in the computer's BIOS as ECP or EPP and make sure you have an ECP- or EPP-capable cable.

◆ Avoid stacking anything that blocks the airflow around a laser printer. And avoid placing it in a low-ventilation cubbyhole in a computer desk.

◆ Keep toner cartridges away from strong light; it's bad for the photosensitive drum.

◆ If your output is wrinkling, check the paper quality. You may be able to set the printer to eject the printed pages from the back, faceup, reducing the amount of turns the paper has to make to get to the exit and perhaps reducing the wrinkling.

Chapter 18

Understanding and Troubleshooting Scanners

- ◆ QuickSteps: Connecting and Testing a Flatbed Scanner
- ◆ Types of Scanners and How They Work
- ◆ Scanner Maintenance
- ◆ Solving Common Problems
- ◆ Troubleshooting Tips

Introduction

Because of their shrinking cost, scanners are becoming an integral part of most home computer sys tems. You can get a decent scanner for well under $100 these days, and they're relatively easy to hook up and use.

Scanners are quite useful if you're doing any amount of digital photograph editing or storage. Although you can shoot new photos with a digital camera, the only way to get your old photos into digital format is to scan them. In fact, many camera buffs still prefer to shoot with a 35-millimeter (mm) film camera and then scan the photo prints into their computer for digital editing, rather than com promise initial quality with a low-performance digital camera.

Scanners are also useful for scanning documents into computer files. Legal documents, credit card bills, monthly bank statements, you name it—you can use a scanner to make a hard copy electronic

Connecting a scanner to your system is relatively easy, especially if you have a newer computer sys tem, a newer scanner, and a recent version of Windows. (It's easiest with Windows XP, which includes a Scanner and Camera Wizard to handle most of the configuration for you.) Scanners are also fairly reliable machines, with most of their moving parts enclosed to reduce maintenance.

In this chapter, I'll discuss pretty much all you need to know about scanners—how to connect them, configure them, and troubleshoot them.

QuickSteps: Connecting a Flatbed Scanner

The following are the basic steps for connecting the most popular type of scanner—the flatbed scanner. For in-depth coverage on how to troubleshoot scanner-related problems, refer to the later sections of this chapter.

BE PREPARED

Before you start, there are some things you may need on hand. These include the following:

◆ Scanner documentation or user manual

◆ Scanner software or drivers ready to install, if required

◆ A cable for connecting the scanner to the computer

◆ Your new flatbed scanner

To connect a flatbed scanner, follow these steps:

1. If you're installing via a parallel or Small Computer System Interface (SCSI) port, turn off your computer. If you're installing via a Universal Serial Bus (USB) port, leave your computer on.

2. Plug your new scanner into a power source, and then connect it to the appropriate port (USB, parallel, or SCSI) on the back of your computer. If your scanner shares a parallel port with your printer, power off your printer and connect the printer to the scanner to your PC, as directed in the scanner's instructions. If you're connecting via SCSI, you'll probably need to install a separate SCSI card in your computer and connect the scanner to that board. If you're connecting a SCSI scanner to an existing SCSI board, see Chapter 11, "Understanding and Installing SCSI Devices," for help configuring the SCSI ID and termination settings.

3. Turn your computer on, and then turn on your scanner.

TIP   Some scanners have a lock to protect the Charge Coupled Device (CCD) from getting damaged during shipping. If your unit has such a lock, don't forget to unlock the CCD before you first use the scanner. It's probably a switch on the bottom of the back of the scanner.

4. Windows should recognize the new scanner and install the appropriate drivers. You may be prompted to insert the scanner's installation disk or CD at this step.

5. If your scanner came with its own software (most scanners typically come with some graphics program or another), install that software now.

TIP   Some high-end scanners might require a manual calibration on installation. This is typically done by scanning a special shaded card that comes with the scanner and then configuring various settings on the scanner's software control panel.

Types of Scanners and How They Work

A scanner works a little like a traditional office photocopier—except that the final result is a digital computer file, not a printed copy.

Scanner Types

You can install several types of scanners on your system. There's little or no difference in how each interacts with the computer; each uses one of the standard interface types (USB, parallel, or SCSI), and each is recognized as a scanner in Windows. However, there's a difference in their physical dimensions and arrangement and operation of the physical parts inside:

Flatbed scanners The most popular type of scanner for home use is the flatbed, or desktop, scanner. You can buy flatbed scanners, such as the one in Figure 18.1, for as little as $50; they make it easy to scan papers, books, and any other item that you can lay flat between a glass bed (plate) and the scanner's top cover. The image is scanned via a scan head that moves across the face of the original document.

Sheet-fed scanners Sheet-fed scanners are like flatbed scanners, except the scan head is fixed and the original document moves across the head like in a fax machine. Whereas flatbed scanners can scan just about any item that can fit on the glass plate, including three-dimensional objects, sheet fed scanners can scan only flat pieces of paper. Sheet-fed scanners were popular in the late 1990s but today are rarely seen.

Combination scanner/printer/fax A popular option in home offices and small offices is the "all-in-one" machine that scans, prints, faxes, and copies. (It doesn't make coffee, though…) These units, popularized by Hewlett-Packard (HP), effectively merge a flatbed or sheet-fed scanner with an inkjet or laser printer and a fax machine. Such a unit may have its own proprietary integrated software that drives it through Windows rather than relying solely on separate Windows drivers for each component.

NOTE In the early days of scanners, some inexpensive models were handheld. They were somewhat like the bar code readers you may see in retail stores, but wider (about 5 inches across, usually). You'd drag them across a page to scan it, a half page at a time, and then software would "knit" the two halves together. They never worked all that well and are now obsolete.

Film scanners/slide scanners There are specialty scanners available that scan from 35mm negatives and/or 35mm slides. Because the originals are so small, such scanners must scan at a high resolution to produce an acceptable quality output—usually 3000 to 4000 dots per inch (dpi). One of these is an indispensable piece of equipment for many professional graphic design businesses and magazine publishers, but the average consumer would look elsewhere.

TIP You can purchase many higher-end flatbed scanners with film negative and/or slide scanning attachments and adapters for the occasional casual film scanning job, so you don't need to buy a film scanner just to scan a few negatives.

Drum scanners   If you want high-quality black-and-white or color scans, such as the kinds required by the magazine, newspaper, and book publishing industries, you need to go all the way up to an expensive drum scanner. This type of scanner mounts the original document on a rotating glass cylinder, called a *drum*. At the center of the cylinder is a sensor that splits light bounded off the document into three beams. Each beam is then sent through a color filter into a *photomultiplier tube*, where the light is changed into an electrical signal. Drum scanners are much more expensive than consumer-quality flatbed scanners (I've seen them as high as $15,000), and they typically connect to a computer system via a SCSI.

In this chapter, I'll spend more time on the flatbed scanners than any of the other technologies because they're the most prevalent in the average technician's work environment. Just be aware that the other types do exist, in case you should encounter one at some point.

FIGURE 18.1
Low-priced flatbed scanners—such as this model from Visioneer—are part of many home computer systems.

How a Scanner Scans

As shown in Figure 18.2, most flatbed scanners are composed of the following parts:

- Glass bed (or plate), on which the source document is placed facedown
- Lamp, used to illuminate the source document
- Mirrors, used to reflect the image of the source document
- Filters, which adjust the image of the source document
- Lens, used to focus the image of the source document onto the CCD array
- CCD array, used to turn reflected light into an electrical charge

- Scan head, which contains the CCD array, mirrors, lens, and filter
- Stabilizer bar, to which the scan head is attached
- Belt, attached to the stepper motor and used to advance the stabilizer bar
- Stepper motor, used to drive the stabilizer bar
- Cover, used to provide a uniform background for the scanned document—and to keep you from being blinded by the scanner lamp

FIGURE 18.2
The major parts of a flatbed scanner

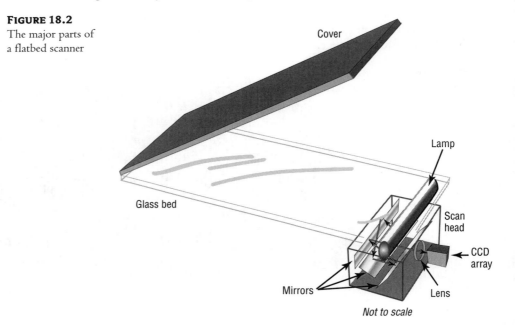

You prepare for a scan by placing the source document facedown on a glass plate. You then close the scanner's cover, which provides a uniform background that the scanner software can use as a reference point for determining the size of the scanned document.

When you press the button to start the scan, the lamp lights to illuminate the source document and the stabilizer bar rolls from one end of the document to the other. As the scan head—which is attached to the stabilizer bar—travels across the face of the document (in what is called a *pass*), light is reflected off the document through a series of mirrors, filters, and lenses, and then onto the CCD array. Some scanners will do a "draft" pass first to send preliminary info to the scanner software that can be used to indicate the image area if desired.

NOTE *Older scanners used a standard fluorescent lamp, but most newer scanners use either a Cold Cathode Fluorescent Lamp (CCFL) or xenon lamp.*

The CCD is actually a collection of light-sensitive diodes, called *photosites*. The photosites convert the reflected light into an electrical charge; because each photosite is sensitive to slight variations in light, the brighter the light that hits a photosite, the greater the electrical charge generated.

Most consumer-grade scanners use a single pass to scan the original document, but some higher-end models use a three-pass method. In the single-pass method, the lens splits the image into three identical versions of the original. These images are then passed through three color filters (red, green, and blue) to separate sections of the CCD and combined to create a single full-color image. In the three-pass method, each pass of the scan head uses a different color filter (red, green, or blue) between the lens and the CCD array; assembling the three filtered images results in a single full-color image.

Some inexpensive flatbed scanners use a Contact Image Sensor (CIS) instead of a CCD array. The CIS replaces the entire CCD/mirror/filter/lens/lamp mechanism with rows of red, green, and blue Light-Emitting Diodes (LEDs). The image sensor is placed very close to the glass plate, and the LEDs combine to provide a bright white light. The illuminated image is then captured by the same sensors.

NOTE   *Although CIS scanners are smaller, lighter, and less expensive than similar CCD scanners, they don't deliver the same image quality as their higher-priced CCD siblings. Look in the scanner's specifications before you buy to see if it's CIS or CCD.*

Scanner/Computer Interface

Three main interfaces connect scanners to personal computers: USB, parallel (on older models only), and SCSI:

USB   The USB interface is the easiest way to connect a consumer-grade flatbed scanner. Just connect a cable from your scanner's USB output to a USB input on your PC. Because USB is a "hot" interface, you don't have to turn off your computer to make your connection, and Windows should recognize the new device as soon as it's plugged in and turned on. A scanner can support either USB 1.1 or USB 2.0 as its standard. If connecting to a PC that also supports USB 2.0, there's a big speed difference in the data transfer with a 2.0 scanner interface. However, the mechanical parts of the scanner are also a speed bottleneck—usually more so than the USB connection.

Parallel   Before USB became popular, parallel was the interface of choice for consumer-grade scanners of all types. It has disadvantages over USB, however, and is rapidly waning in popularity as more and more PCs are equipped (hardware and operating system) to support USB. Because the parallel port may also be supporting a printer, the two devices must share it. This is achieved with a pass-through or Y-splitter that typically comes with the scanner. This type of connection can be problematic, especially if you try to use the scanner and printer at the same time. (You can't.)

SCSI   The faster SCSI interface is used for the high data transfer rates inherent with drum scanners. Most drum scanners include a dedicated SCSI card you have to install in your computer, but many also let you use a standard SCSI controller. Some high-end flatbed scanners are also SCSI.

If you plan to buy a typical inexpensive flatbed scanner and you have a choice, go with a USB model. They're the easiest to hook up and don't interfere with other peripherals in your system (such as your printer).

Image Quality Measurement

Even the lowest-quality scanners today deliver a resolution of at least 1200 × 1200dpi. The highest-quality scanners today can exceed 4800 × 4800 dpi. The dpi is determined by the number of sensors in a single row of the CCD or CIS array (which determines the x-direction sampling rate) and by the precision of the stepper motor (which determines the y-direction sampling rate).

For example, a scanner with 10,200 sensors in each horizontal row delivers an x-direction sampling rate of 1200. (10,200 sensors divided by 8.5 inches = 1200 sensors/inch). If the stepper motor can move the stabilizer bar in increments of 1/1200th of an inch, the y-direction sampling rate is also 1200—resulting in a 1200 × 1200dpi resolution.

Resolution can be artificially enhanced by the scanning software used by the scanner. Some software programs *interpolate* extra pixels between the actual pixels, thus increasing the apparent resolution. For example, software that puts one extra pixel between each real pixel turns a 1200 × 1200dpi scanner into a virtual 2400 × 1200 scanner. Interpolation works by averaging the values of two adjacent pixels and inserting an extra pixel between them that's halfway between the two. When a scanner's resolution is advertised as *optical resolution*, that number is the actual number of sensors on the CCD. Optical resolution is "real" resolution. Resolution advertised as *enhanced* or *digital* is interpolated.

The other factor in image quality is the sharpness of the image. Sharpness is determined primarily by the quality of the lens optics and the brightness of the light source. The higher quality the lens and the brighter the light, the sharper the scan.

Color fidelity is measured in terms of bit depth. Almost all color scanners deliver 36-bit color, and some higher-priced models promise 40- or 48-bit color. Although these higher-bit scanners process colors with the higher bit depth, they still output in 24-bit color, so you might not notice any measurable difference in the color of your scans. The extra bits are used for on-the-fly color correction. The scanner selects the best 24 bits it gets from the scan and sends them on to the computer; the other bits are discarded.

TIP *You can control which bits are kept by adjusting the gamma correction setting in the scanning software.*

When scanning in grayscale mode, no scanner on the market today can produce more than 256 levels, even if it boasts up to 48-bit color scanning. To understand why, you need to realize that color scanning outputs in 24-bit color with 8 bits of red, 8 bits of green, and 8 bits of blue—in other words, 256 levels of each of those colors. With grayscale, you've got only one color (black), so you're limited to 8-bit output for it (256 levels).

Working with a Scanner in Windows

How you interact with the scanner through Windows depends largely upon whether your version of Windows directly supports your scanner.

Windows Me and Windows XP support a technology called Windows Image Acquisition (WIA) for some scanner models. If you have one of these Windows versions and your scanner is compatible with WIA for that version, you don't have to install the software that comes with the scanner. You just plug it in and go, and use the Windows Image Acquisition (WIA) through the Scanner and Camera Wizard to do your scanning. If there's not direct support, you must install the scanning software for the scanner and interact with it through some scanning application (usually third-party) via the TWAIN driver. (More shortly on both TWAIN and WIA.)

TIP   Need a quick yes or no answer on a specific model and a specific operating system version? See Microsoft's Hardware Compatibility List (`www.microsoft.com/hcl`).

Especially with Windows Me, there have been some glitches noted where Windows detects the scanner automatically and appears to be installing a driver for it, but then the scanner doesn't work through the Windows Scanner and Camera Wizard interface. This spotlights an important fact: *Plug and Play doesn't equal WIA necessarily.* Even though Windows may be able to detect a scanner, it doesn't necessarily mean that the scanner will work with WIA.

This business of having to use the scanner's own software is really no big deal. That's how it's always been throughout the history of scanning, before WIA was invented. So don't panic if you've got a scanner that isn't on the Hardware Compatibility List; just download the latest drivers for it for your operating system from the manufacturer's Web site, and it should work just fine.

TWAIN

There are hundreds (thousands, even) of new and old scanner models out there, and each one is a little different. So how is it that they can all communicate with Windows applications? In a word: TWAIN.

TWAIN is a universal software interface driver that acts as an interpreter between the scanner and any TWAIN-compliant applications on your computer, such as a graphics program with a scanning capability. When you install the software that comes with your scanner, you install the TWAIN driver and a TWAIN-compliant graphics program, and the two of them work together to enable you to scan.

NOTE   TWAIN is that rare computer term that isn't an acronym. (It actually comes from the phrase "never the twain shall meet" because the driver sits between the software and the scanner.) For those of you who are acronym inclined, however, feel free to use the following pseudo-acronym for TWAIN: Technology Without An Interesting Name.

If you have Windows XP or Me and your scanner is on the Hardware Compatibility List for your operating system version, you don't need TWAIN because Windows supports the scanner directly through WIA. However, you're still free to install the scanner's software, including the TWAIN driver, and use it if you prefer it.

NOTE   There is a less-popular competitor to TWAIN called Image and Scanner Interface Specification (ISIS) that you may occasionally encounter support for in some applications. It allows not only image scanning but also image handling and processing. ISIS drivers for most scanners are available at `www.scannerdrivers.com`.

Don't confuse the TWAIN driver with the image-editing software that comes with most scanners. The editing software may be TWAIN compliant (and probably is), but the ability to acquire images directly from the scanner is a function of the TWAIN driver, not of the image-editing program.

Windows Image Acquisition (WIA)

As I mentioned earlier, Windows Me and XP support an Application Programming Interface (API) called Windows Image Acquisition. It works with both scanners and digital cameras and allows users to connect supported devices without TWAIN, ISIS, or any other special software. I'll bring it up again in Chapter 22, "Digital Imaging," too.

When you scan with a scanner's own software through TWAIN, the interface and options vary from scanner to scanner and even from version to version of the software. Therefore, if you work with several different scanners, there's a learning curve involved. With WIA, however, every scanner can be accessed through the same Scanner and Camera Wizard interface in Windows, so you know exactly what you're doing at all times. Figure 18.3 shows the Scanner and Camera Wizard from Windows XP at work with a HP multifunction device that includes scanning capability, for example.

FIGURE 18.3
Windows Image Acquisition offers a consistent Scanner and Camera Wizard interface for all scanners

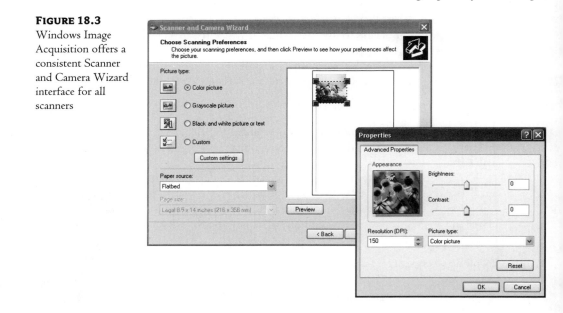

NOTE   *WIA was new in Windows Me and was still getting the bugs worked out. You'll find that it works much more smoothly and with a much wider variety of hardware under Windows XP and higher.*

Optimizing Scan Size and Image Quality

As you're scanning, you'll have a choice of the resolution at which the scan occurs (for example, in Figure 18.3 it's set to 150 dpi) and of the file format in which the scanned file will be saved. These are both important decisions. For the best scans possible, you may have to change the resolution, the file type, and perhaps some other settings in the scanning application as well.

Select an Appropriate Resolution

If you shelled out extra money for a scanner with a very high maximum resolution (dpi), you may be tempted to always use the highest available resolution setting. After all, more is better, right?

Well, sort of. Higher resolution may result in a better quality scan, but it also results in a huge file that takes up many megabytes on your hard disk, is awkward or impossible to distribute to others via e-mail, and takes forever to download when placed on a Web site. And when viewed on a computer monitor, the higher resolution is completely wasted because the average monitor displays at 72 dpi.

You might want a high-resolution scan if you're scanning something that'll eventually be placed in a professional-quality publication and printed. In a case like that, you'll want to match the resolution of the picture to the maximum resolution of the printer on which you'll be printing. For example, if you're going to be printing to a commercial-grade full-color printer that prints at 1200 dpi, then scanning at 1200 dpi might produce a noticeably better image than, say, 300 dpi.

However, if you're scanning something that'll eventually be placed on the Web, you want to keep resolution as low as possible without noticeably degrading the image. People visiting the Web page will (or should) thank you for keeping the image size small so that they don't have to go get a cup of coffee while the page is loading. For an image that will be viewed only on-screen, 75 dpi is adequate. If I weren't absolutely sure that I was never going to print the image on paper, however, I'd probably play it safer and scan it at 150 dpi—a compromise.

Select an Appropriate File Type

The file type in which you save the image also makes a big difference in the file size. Avoid using BMP format because it's bloated and not particularly stellar in any way. TIF is great for high-resolution images where printed quality is important, but it results in large file sizes. For Web use, go with the JPG format, which is quite compact and results in decent-quality images good enough for on-screen viewing.

Crop Images

If you don't need the whole image, don't scan the whole image. The Scanner and Camera Wizard (WIA) and most TWAIN-compatible scanner interfaces allow you to preview the image before doing the "official" scan, and after the preview, you can adjust crop marks so that only part of the scanner glass is scanned. If that's not possible, then use the Crop feature in your image editing software to cut it down to size. Cropping only what you need from an image not only makes the file size smaller but also makes for a better-looking picture in many cases.

Choose an Appropriate Image Mode

Most scanner interfaces enable you to choose between at least three settings: Color, Grayscale, and Black and White (line art). This is an important decision with implications for both image size and image quality:

Color   This is the default usually. It scans in full color and results in the largest file size.

Grayscale   This scans in 256 or more levels (shades) of gray. This results in a smaller file size than color. It's useful when you know you're going to output to black-and-white media (such as a black-and-white printed newsletter or newspaper).

Black and White   This scans in only one color: black. It results in the smallest image size, but all shades and colors are converted to either black or white, resulting in something like a fax. This is useful for line art but very poor for photos.

Optical Character Recognition

Many scanners also include Optical Character Recognition (OCR) software, which enables you to convert scanned text into computer-based text. This way you can scan a document and import it directly into a word processor (such as Microsoft Word) as editable text, rather than as a graphic.

Most current OCR software does a fairly good job of translating printed characters to digital characters, but you'll still need to clean up any misinterpretations. The cleaner the scan, the better the job the OCR software does, so start with a clean original and make sure you take a good, high-contrast scan. (Also be sure the original document is centered and level on the glass bed and has no creases or blemishes.)

NOTE   Some advanced OCR software—sometimes referred to as page-recognition software—also captures fonts and page layout from the source document.

TIP   OCR software works best when capturing black-and-white images. All the extra information in a color image only serves to confuse the software.

Scanner Maintenance

Scanners don't require a lot of maintenance. (Unlike printers, scanners don't use up any consumables, such as paper or ink.)

The main thing is to keep your scanner clean and as dust-free as possible. Use a soft cloth and glass cleaner to clean the scanner's glass bed. Take particular care to keep the glass free from smudges and scratches, both of which can affect the quality of your scans. You may also need to disassemble the unit to clean the *underside* of the glass, which can also get dusty. (Be aware that doing so will probably void the warranty, however.)

As to mechanical maintenance, most consumer-level scanners don't have too many moving parts to which you have easy access. Depending on your scanner, even the light source (typically a lamp or small light bulb) may or may not be serviceable. Many manufacturers now use sealed lamps that can't be replaced by the user.

If you have a sheet-fed scanner (or an all-in-one unit that includes a sheet-fed scanner function), make sure the paper path is clean and free from jams and paper bits. Don't inadvertently jam the paper path by force-feeding paper that's too thick to fit.

The truth is, given the low price of today's scanners, if it breaks, you'll probably be tempted to just replace it.

Common Problems and Solutions

Before the dawn of USB, most scanner problems came from trying to share a parallel port with the printer. If you have a USB scanner, you automatically have an easier installation and fewer subsequent problems.

Beyond the parallel port problem, other common scanner problems include the inability to scan and poor-quality results.

Check the Connections

As with any peripheral device connected to your system, there are some basic things you need to check if you're having trouble with your scanner.

First, make sure the scanner is plugged into a live power supply and is turned on. You should see a light below the glass bed when the scanner is turned on and operational.

Second, make sure the scanner is properly connected to the correct port on your PC. Check both ends of the cable, just in case.

Finally, many scanners ship with their CCD and stabilizer arm locked down for transport. The scanner won't do much scanning if the stabilizer arm can't move, so check the manufacturer's instruction manual to make sure you've unlocked the CCD properly. A horrible grinding or clicking noise the first time you try to use the scanner is a good indicator of a locked CCD.

Give It a Test

When you're trying to track down a problem with your scanner, it helps to follow a step-by-step troubleshooting approach. For that reason, the first thing you should do (after you have the scanner connected and powered up) is perform a comprehensive test of your scanner to determine the nature of the problem.

TIP   Many scanners have a "self-test" mode that you can run to check out the unit's operation. In addition, some scanners come with software-based diagnostic utilities.

Here's what you need to do:

1. Turn on your scanner, and launch the scanner's image acquisition utility or software, or in Windows Me or XP (with a compatible scanner) run the Scanner and Camera Wizard from the Accessories menu.

2. Place a black-and-white photo *facedown* on the glass bed. (If you're using a sheet-fed scanner, insert a black-and-white document into the sheet feed—and make sure it's facing the correct direction!)

3. Acquire the image with the scanning software.

4. If the scanned image is blank (either all black or all white), make sure the original photo or document was either placed facedown or inserted proper-side-up into the sheet feeder. (You could be scanning the back of the photo!)

5. If the acquired image is blurry or distorted, make sure the original photo or document was set firmly in place and that the cover of the scanner was closed. You may also need to select a particular type of scan in the scanning software. (You'll probably have choices such as B/W Photo, Color Photo, Line Art, and so on.) Choose the most appropriate image type.

6. Once you get a good preview image, save the scan to disk. Experiment with scanning the document at different resolutions and image settings.

7. Now it's time to check the TWAIN driver (if you're even using TWAIN; you might not be if you have Windows Me or XP). Close the scanner's software and open another graphics program—one that you know is TWAIN compliant. Select File ➤ Open or File ➤ Acquire, and select your scanner from the Select Source option. Choose to acquire the image, and see if the graphics program actually acquires the image from your scanner.

8. If you can't acquire an image via the graphics program, you should check several things. First, make sure the program is TWAIN compliant; if not, use another program. Second, if your scanner doesn't appear on the Acquire Source menu, you may not have installed the TWAIN driver; try reinstalling the driver and testing again.

TIP   If, no matter how hard you try, you can't acquire scanned images from within your graphics program, you can always default to saving the images to disk using your scanner's acquisition software and then opening or importing those files into your graphics-editing program as normal.

Check the Port—and the Configuration

If you've connected your scanner via a parallel port, make sure your port is configured as an Enhanced Parallel Port (EPP) or Extended Capabilities Port (ECP). Many scanners require EPP/ECP operation, which utilizes high-speed, bidirectional data transfer to send data back and forth to your computer.

If Windows isn't recognizing your new scanner, your best course of action is to rerun the play. That is, unhook the scanner and try reinstalling it. (You may want to uninstall it before you reinstall it, but this isn't always necessary.) If Windows doesn't recognize the scanner when you reconnect it, try uninstalling the scanner, turning off your computer, and then reconnecting and rebooting. Windows should recognize the new device when it starts up again.

If Windows *still* doesn't recognize your scanner, run the Scanner and Camera Wizard (in Windows XP) or the Add New Hardware Wizard (in any version of Windows). Either of these options should let you install the scanner driver manually.

With some scanners, an even better approach is to install the unit from the scanner's installation CD. Some scanners include a robust installation program that'll do everything from installing the drivers to configuring your system to installing the scanner's graphics-editing software.

TIP   When in doubt, read the scanner's manual for the recommended installation method—or visit the manufacturer's Web site for the latest drivers, installation instructions, and advice.

If your system recognizes your scanner after installation but doesn't recognize it on subsequent use, you may have a configuration that requires your scanner to be powered up *before* Windows starts. That is, Windows won't recognize your scanner if you turn it on after Windows is up and running. Power down your computer, turn on your scanner, and then power up your computer again. When Windows loads, it should recognize the already-running scanner.

A related problem occurs when your scanner is set too far away from your computer. You should never use a cable longer than the one supplied with your scanner; long cable runs will not only degrade the image quality but will also cause your computer not to recognize the signals coming from the scanner. Don't, under any circumstances, use an extension cable to lengthen the cable from your scanner to your PC.

With a USB scanner, if you're having problems connecting through a USB hub, try connecting directly to the USB port on the PC. It shouldn't make a difference with a powered USB hub, but with an unpowered one (such as a USB extension port on a USB keyboard), it might.

Allocate Necessary Resources

Scanners can be resource hogs. Not only do scanned images take up a lot of disk space, scanners also use a lot of memory and processing power when they're acquiring images.

If you find your system slowing down or hanging when you try to make a scan, consider the following options:

◆ Close down any unnecessary applications while you're scanning.

◆ Add more Random Access Memory (RAM) to your system.

◆ Make sure you have plenty of hard disk space available because most scanners take full advantage of your system's swap file; you can also increase the size of your Windows swap file to better handle large scanned images.

If you still run into performance problems, try scanning at a lower resolution. (Smaller pictures use fewer resources.)

Troubleshoot Parallel Port Sharing Problems

When a scanner and a printer share a parallel port, there are some inherent issues. Thankfully, this is a less common situation than it was in the past because most scanners are USB nowadays. But I'll tell you about it anyway because as you know, there's always the occasional client who is still working with old equipment.

If you try to use both devices at once, you'll either slow down both devices or freeze up one or both of them. You should avoid scanning while printing (and vice versa) or just install a switch box that only lets you feed one device at a time to your PC's parallel port.

You should also consider the order in which you power up each device. You should always turn the printer on first, then the scanner, and then your computer. Many manufacturers require that your scanner be switched on and connected for the printer to work.

Finally, your printer might not be configured to share your PC's parallel port. Open the printer configuration utility and look for a setting like Use Port Exclusively—then turn that setting off. Also, deactivate any Use Bidirectional Printing setting. Changing these settings will allow other devices (such as your scanner) to share the parallel port with the printer. You might also try some different parallel port mode settings in Basic Input/Output System (BIOS) Setup.

If you happen to have a spare parallel port Input/Output (I/O) board, you can install that in your system to give yourself an LPT2. That way the devices don't have to share. I wouldn't buy a parallel port I/O board for this purpose, however, because for $50 you can buy a cheap USB scanner and avoid the issue entirely.

Fix Problems with Scan Quality

If a scan isn't quite what you expected—if it's too light or too dark, crooked, or *whatever*—you don't have to rescan the image. You can fix many simple problems via the scanner's graphics-editing software or in any graphics-editing program.

If your scan is too dark or too light, simply adjust the brightness and contrast in the graphics editor. If the scan is crooked (a common problem), use your graphics editor to rotate the image a few degrees. If the scanned image is off-center, crop the unnecessary portion of the image in the graphics editor. In other words, you can correct many scanning mistakes after the fact. (Or, as my musician friends like to say, you can "fix it in the mix!")

If, on the other hand, you see vertical streaks in your scanned image, your problem is with the scan, and it must be fixed there. These streaks are caused when your scanner scans a dust or dirt particle along with the original document. To eliminate this type of image streaking, make sure the glass bed is clean (on a flatbed scanner) or that the paper path is clear (on a sheet-fed model).

If you see circular diffraction patterns in your scans, you probably have a moisture problem with the original item—particularly if you're scanning a slide or film negative. These "Newton rings" are created when the scanner's light hits the moisture on the original item. You can eliminate the rings by eliminating the moisture or by using a film or slide holder to lift the original off the scanner's glass surface.

Another common problem is the presence of a moiré pattern over halftone or patterned areas of the image. This is caused when the dots used to create the original printed picture are smaller than the pixel size of your scanner. You can fix this problem by increasing your scanner's resolution (thus making the pixels smaller) or by shrinking the scanned image, which makes the pixels more closely match the original image's dot size.

TIP *If a scanned image doesn't look right on your monitor, it may not be a problem with your scanner. If you have your monitor set for a low bit-rate display—256 color, for example—you might think that you're viewing a bad scan, when in fact it's your monitor that's causing the apparent problem. That's because your scans are probably made with 24-bit color and thus don't reproduce well on your monitor if it's set for a lower bit rate. (The colors get dithered on-screen, which isn't an accurate representation of the original colors.) To fix this problem, open Windows' Display Properties dialog box and increase the bit rate of your monitor to 24 bits or more.*

Troubleshooting Tips

The following is a summary of troubleshooting tips for your scanner:

◆ If your scanner is connected via the parallel port and isn't communicating with your computer (or if your scanner and printer are interfering with each other), check the order in which everything is powered up (scanner first, printer second, PC third) or consider installing a parallel port switch or a second parallel port card (LPT2).

◆ If your scanner's stabilizer arm isn't moving, unlock it. (The lock is typically located on the bottom of a flatbed scanner.)

- If you can't acquire images from your scanner, reinstall the scanner's TWAIN driver.

- If your scans are slow—and you're connecting via the parallel port—make sure the port is configured as either an EPP or ECP.

- If your scans are slow (no matter how you're connected), consider increasing the size of your PC's swap file or adding more RAM to your system.

- If your scans are coming out blank, make sure you're placing the original facedown on a flatbed scanner or in the appropriate direction in a sheet-fed scanner.

- If the scanned image is blurry or distorted, make sure the original document is placed firmly in or on the scanner and that the flatbed scanner's cover is closed.

- If the quality of your scans is poor, make sure your scanner or scanner software is set to the appropriate setting for the type of image you're trying to scan.

- If you find minor errors in your scan—it's crooked, off-center, or too dark or too light—use your scanner software or graphics-editing software to fix the errors in the scanned image.

In general, here's what you want to remember: if you can, connect your scanner via USB instead of the parallel port. Make sure the item to be scanned is in good condition and centered on the glass bed or in the sheet feeder. (While you're at it, make sure the glass surface is clean and the sheet feeder is clear.) Set your scanner or scanner software to the appropriate setting for the original image type. Then use your scanner software or image-editing software to edit any little mistakes that pop up in the scan.

Follow that general advice, and you'll minimize the opportunity for scanner-related problems. In the next chapter, I'll discuss keyboards and mice.

Chapter 19

Keyboards and Mice

- ◆ QuickSteps: Installing a Keyboard, Mouse, or Trackball
- ◆ Types of Keyboards and How They Work
- ◆ Keyboard Maintenance
- ◆ Types of Mice and How They Work
- ◆ Wireless Input Devices
- ◆ Troubleshooting Your Keyboard and Mouse

Introduction

Every personal computer has a keyboard—and, with the near-universal acceptance of Graphical User Interfaces (GUIs), practically every PC has some kind of pointing device.

When it comes to keyboards, they all have pretty much the same keys, though there are some differences. You have the traditional IBM-type keyboard, the newer split ergonomic keyboards, and even wireless keyboards that let you do your typing from your easy chair. They're all the same to trouble shoot, however.

Turning to pointing devices, I've tried trackballs, electronic stylus devices, light pens (I wanted to call this chapter "Of Mice and Pens," but I couldn't really justify it), and even a Headmouse that tracks the way you're facing. Still, the most popular pointing device seems to be the mouse (either the traditional ball type or the newer optical and/or wireless). Mice can be more of a pain than keyboards, however, so I'll tell you how to handle them, too, in this chapter.

QuickSteps: Installing a Keyboard, Mouse, or Trackball

Installing a new keyboard, mouse, or trackball is among the easiest installations you'll encounter.

BE PREPARED

Before you start, there are some things you may need on hand. These include the following:

- ◆ Documentation that came with the product to ensure proper installation
- ◆ Software or drivers ready to install, if required
- ◆ Your new keyboard, mouse, or trackball

To install a keyboard, mouse, or trackball, follow these steps:

1. Turn off your computer if the device you're installing isn't a Universal Serial Bus (USB) model.

NOTE   *USB devices are* hot-swappable *and shouldn't require you to turn off your computer or reboot.*

2. Unplug the old device (keyboard, mouse, or trackball).

3. Plug your new device into the appropriate port (keyboard, mouse, or USB) on the back of your computer.

4. Turn your computer on (if it's off).

5. Windows will detect almost all keyboards and mice and allow them to function at a basic level. If desired, install the software that came with the device to add additional functionality.

Keyboard Types and Components

With all of its moving parts, the keyboard has many potential sources of problems. Understanding those sources requires understanding the types of keyboards and their parts; here's a look at them.

Keyboard Types

There are a number of ways to distinguish one keyboard from another, but the most obvious way is the number and arrangement of keys.

You'll first look at a couple of keyboards you're *not* likely to see anymore. The XT keyboard and the AT keyboard were introduced with the IBM PC and the IBM PC-AT, respectively.

The XT keyboard had 83 keys, and the function keys and numeric keypad were at the right of the other keys. There was no separate set of arrow keys; you had to press Num Lock to enable the numeric keypad as an arrow pad.

Improvements of the AT keyboard over the XT keyboard include a larger Enter key and the addition of a SysReq (or SysRq) key intended for use with OS/2 (IBM's attempt at an operating system of that era). It also has 10 function keys either along the top or on the left side of the keyboard (labeled F1–F10).

The main difference inside the XT and AT keyboards is that the XT keyboard puts the keyboard microprocessor in the keyboard, and the AT keyboard assumes that the keyboard microprocessor is on the system board. They're generally incompatible: you can't use an XT keyboard on an AT, or vice versa. Clone keyboards generally get around this by putting an XT/AT switch on the keyboard.

Both XT and AT keyboards are long obsolete, replaced in the marketplace by the *enhanced keyboard*. It's compatible with all other keyboard interfaces (AT an XT), but you might need to use an adapter plug to change the pins/size of the connector to make it fit. The enhanced keyboard layout has at least 101 keys. The extra keys come from adding two more function keys (F11 and F12) and adding a separate arrow keypad. Figure 19.1 shows an enhanced keyboard.

So-called Windows keyboards add three keys to the standard 101-key keyboard, typically on the same row as the spacebar. The new keys are two Windows keys (one on either side of the spacebar) that open the Windows Start menu and an Application key that displays the same context menus you get when you right-click an item.

NOTE *Many newer keyboards have additional keys that can speed up your productivity. Some keyboards provide a large number of specialized keys that help you connect to and browse the Internet and even operate your CD and multimedia applications. Some keys, through the help of drivers and special software, can be configured to perform your favorite tasks or to work with programs of your choosing; these are called* hot keys.

FIGURE 19.1
Enhanced keyboard

The "broken" keyboard designs (also called ergonomic keyboards), such as the Microsoft Natural Keyboard, look like a 101-key keyboard to the PC hardware. Figure 19.2 shows what they look like to the user. Because they're compatible with the existing hardware, they're easy to install, and although they take a little getting used to, they're easier on the wrists than standard keyboards. People who do a lot of typing might prefer these.

FIGURE 19.2
Microsoft Natural Keyboard

Keyboard Interfaces

A keyboard can have three possible interfaces: AT (DIN), PS/2 (mini-DIN), and USB.

The motherboard will have either a PS/2 or AT-style keyboard connector built into it. (That's the case as of this writing, but manufacturers will soon be phasing out the inclusion of any keyboard interface because they assume consumers will be switching to USB keyboards.) The keyboard interface depends on the motherboard form factor; AT motherboards have the AT interface, and ATX motherboards have the PS/2.

Another name for the AT keyboard connector is DIN. It's a large round plug with five big pins. The PS/2 style is also called mini-DIN, and it has six small pins. Figure 19.3 shows both. Pay attention when buying a replacement keyboard to which type your motherboard has. You can buy an adapter that'll switch between them for a few dollars, and some new keyboards come with the adapter.

In recent years, USB has become the interface of choice for keyboards (and mice). The Microsoft Natural Keyboard and several Microsoft mice are examples of devices that are USB by design, but some versions may include a USB-to-PS/2 adapter with the product. USB devices have several benefits, which mostly derive from USB being a newer, faster technology. A USB connection is faster than the other, older Input/Output (I/O) ports on your computer, such as COM and parallel ports. In addition, a USB device doesn't require special device drivers for it to operate. (A driver is required, but USB drivers cover a wide range of devices, so, for example, a USB pointing device driver covers mice, touchpads, and writing boards.) You simply plug the device in, and it works (ideally, that is). USB devices also require no conflict resolution for competing resources such as COM ports, which require Interrupt Requests (IRQs) and other precious system resources to operate.

About the only drawback to using a USB device is backward compatibility. Although Windows 98 and higher are USB "aware," Windows 95 and NT 4 aren't and are therefore incompatible with USB devices.

FIGURE 19.3
An old-style DIN keyboard connector with five pins (top) and a more current PS/2 mini-DIN keyboard connector with six pins (bottom)

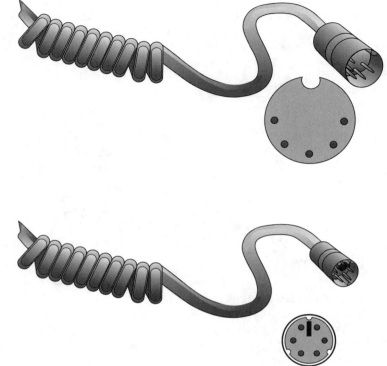

Wireless Keyboards

A wireless keyboard frees you of the tether between the PC and the keyboard, so you can sit back in your recliner and type on your large-screen monitor from across the room. It's a techie dream!

NOTE   Nearly everything I'm about to tell you about wireless keyboards also applies to wireless mice.

They work like this: you get a receiver with the wireless keyboard that plugs into your computer, usually through the keyboard or USB port. This cabled receiver then sits on top of your monitor (in the case of infrared systems) or anywhere within 30 feet or so of your keyboard or mouse—for Radio Frequency (RF) models.

Some of these devices use InfraRed (IR) frequencies to transmit data, meaning that they have high bandwidth (not really an issue with something that transmits as little data as a keyboard or mouse does) and are pretty much immune to outside interference. Use a cordless telephone or other infrared devices (such as a TV remote control) in the same room, and it'll have no effect at all. For the infrared frequencies to communicate, however, the receiver (on your PC) and transmitter (on your mouse or keyboard) have to be within the line of sight.

More common are radio-controlled wireless keyboards. Newer wireless devices operate in the 900 megahertz (MHz) frequency band and have a range of about 30 feet. Because RF signals pass through most objects, your mouse and keyboard don't have to be within the line of sight of the receiver—a big advantage over IR devices.

If you're using an RF device, there's a slight risk of interference with other wireless devices (such as cordless phones) that also use the 900MHz band. Practically, however, this isn't much of an issue; if you do experience interference, just put a little distance between the two devices, and the problem will probably fix itself.

Generally, wireless devices are more expensive than wired devices, and input devices are no exception. Although one manufacturer's advertising extols wireless keyboards as a wonderful way to reduce cabling needs, the lack of one or two cables doesn't make up the price difference. You can find the cheapest keyboards for under $10, with wireless models starting at around $40.

Personally, I've grown to like wireless input devices. I've been using a Logitech wireless keyboard and mouse for about a year now, and I like being able to lean back in my chair, put my feet up on my desk (not good for my back, I know), and type away with my keyboard in my lap, not worrying at all about whether the cord will reach. If you don't mind replacing batteries every few months (and also don't mind the higher initial cost), doing away with the cords is a good thing.

Keyboard Maintenance

The major aspect of maintenance for keyboards is *abstinence*—abstinence, that is, from spilling things into the keyboard. Protecting keyboards with plastic covers was discussed in Chapter 4, "Avoiding Service: Preventive Maintenance"; this is one approach. Another is just to be careful.

Some people like to clean their keyboard by pulling the keytops off and cleaning them individually, plus cleaning underneath them. Do it if you want (but make sure you can put them back in the right places!), but personally I don't do this. I clean my keyboard by doing the following:

1. Turn the PC off, and disconnect the keyboard.

2. Turn it upside down and shake it so that all the debris falls out onto the floor. (What? I didn't say, "Put down a towel to shake it over"? I should have.)

3. Use a can of compressed air to blow out any remaining particles of gunk under the keys.

4. Clean the key tops with a paper towel dampened with a cleaning solution for computers. If you have to remove some keys to get them cleaned, do so, but personally I try not to do so.

Why don't I like to disassemble a keyboard? Mainly because I had a bad experience once, about 15 years ago, trying to get an old XT keyboard back together again. But basically it's a question of effort versus money. Say my time is worth $60 an hour—do I really want to spend a whole hour meticulously scrubbing the keys on a $20 keyboard? I think not.

In extremis, you can soak a sticky keyboard in water overnight or even run it through your dishwasher (in the top rack only)—but make sure it's completely dry before you try using it. I wouldn't put water on a keyboard unless it was really gross, though—like if I had spilled a can of sugared soda on it.

What to Do When a Keyboard Fails You

Because most keyboards are so inexpensive (with the exception of some ergonomic and wireless keyboards), you may want to view the keyboard as disposable. There are some simple things you can do before throwing out a keyboard, however.

Make Sure It's Plugged In

On the back of computers that use PS/2-type connectors are two identical ports: the mouse port and the keyboard port. Make sure you've plugged the keyboard into the correct port. You'll get an error when turning on the computer if the mouse and/or keyboard are connected to the wrong port.

Make Sure BIOS and Windows See It

If there's a keyboard failure, you should see a message when your computer boots up. A PS/2-style or AT-style keyboard will be detected as a "legacy keyboard." Pay close attention, and if you see the message, try checking the connection first before you move on to more drastic measures.

If the BIOS doesn't display any errors on-screen (such as `Keyboard not present` or `Keyboard failure`) when you boot up, make sure Windows recognizes your keyboard by checking Device Manager. You can access Device Manager in Windows by opening the Control Panel and double-clicking the System icon. Select the Device Manager tab in the System Properties dialog box. Your keyboard should be listed in the Keyboard category. If it's listed, make sure it's the proper make and model.

To access Device Manager in Windows 2000, open the Control Panel and double-click Administrative Tools. Next, double-click Computer Management, and expand the System Tools category to find Device Manager. Your keyboard should be listed in the Keyboards category.

NOTE *If a USB keyboard doesn't work at a command prompt (prior to Windows boot), check to see whether there's a Legacy USB setting in Basic Input/Output System (BIOS) Setup that you can enable. This will help the system recognize USB input devices outside of Windows.*

Fix Bent Pins

Check your PS/2-type connector that plugs into the motherboard for any bent or missing pins. This often happens if someone (usually children, but adults can do this too if they aren't paying attention) tries to force the connection in the wrong orientation. What happens is that the pins that aren't lined up with the correct holes on the motherboard connector get bent back as you force the connection. There's simply no place for them to go but sideways. If your pins are bent, carefully straighten them with a pair of slim, needle-nosed pliers. Be careful not to break off the pins as you straighten them.

Connect It to Another Computer

If you're fortunate enough to have more than one computer in your home (most businesses have several), you can try swapping keyboards with a machine that you know isn't suffering keyboard problems. If the keyboard that you suspect is having trouble doesn't work on the "good" computer, you know that keyboard is bad. If the new keyboard doesn't work on the machine you're testing, you may have a faulty keyboard connection on the motherboard. Unfortunately, there's not much you can do about this yourself. If your computer or motherboard is under warranty, or you have a maintenance agreement, you might be able to send your computer to the manufacturer and let them replace the keyboard connection. If you're doing the work yourself, you may have to replace the motherboard.

TIP   A good workaround for a faulty keyboard connector is to purchase a low-cost PCI card with a built-in keyboard connector; this is a good way to get a new keyboard connector without going to the cost and trouble of replacing the entire motherboard. (Similarly, you can just buy a new USB keyboard and connect it to your PC's USB port—bypassing the keyboard connection completely.)

Check the Keys

If only one key is malfunctioning, check the spring under the key to see whether it springs up and down, as a key should. Remove the key by grabbing it with your fingers and pulling up. For the tough keys, fashion a hook from a paper clip or, again, use a chip puller. You'll see a spring under the key. Replace the keytop, and see whether the problem goes away. If not, try pulling the spring out *just a little*. Then replace the keytop.

Some keyboards use rubber cups instead of springs. Either way, the cup or spring is designed to keep the keys from being "on" all the time.

Test Pin Voltages

The voltage between pin 4 and each of the other pins should be in the range of 2–5.5 volts Direct Current (DC). If any of these voltages are wrong, the problem probably lies in the PC—the system board in particular. If they're okay, the problem is probably in the keyboard. Note that the pins aren't numbered consecutively for either a DIN or a mini-DIN.

If you hold a DIN so that the pins are at the top and count from left to right, the pins are numbered 1, 4, 2, 5, and 3; the 2 pin is at the top-center point. Holding a mini-DIN with the single groove in the connector at the top and starting from the bottom left and moving clockwise, the pins are numbered 1, 3, 5, 6, 4, and 2; the groove is between pins 5 and 6.

Check the Cable Continuity

Next, test the continuity of the cable. Turn the keyboard upside down so that the cable is coming out of the back of the keyboard to the right. Remove the two screws. The bottom plate will swing back and up for removal.

You'll now see that the cable splits to a single wire, which is grounded to the bottom plate. You'll also see a cable with a flat-jaw connector. Push apart the jaws of the connector to release. You can then use an ohmmeter to test each of the five wires for continuity. An *ohmmeter* is a device that electricians (and computer technicians) use to test electrical circuits for power and detect short-circuits.

Replace the Keyboard

If you've gotten this far and have had no luck, don't despair. Many keyboard problems can't be fixed and the things aren't that expensive anyway. As you're shopping for a new keyboard, consider these factors:

◆ How it feels when you type on it (in-store displays will help!)

◆ Connector type

◆ Wired or wireless

◆ Special keys such as volume control, shortcuts to e-mail, and so on

◆ Split keyboard (ergonomic) or traditional

Mouse Types and Components

Mice are in some ways simpler devices than keyboards; after all, most have only two or three buttons and maybe a wheel as compared to the standard keyboard's 101 keys. (Some new mice do have up to six buttons.) But most mice have some moving parts that can go seriously wrong.

Buttons and Wheels

All mice for PCs have at least two buttons: left and right. (You may occasionally find a very old Mac mouse with a single button.) You can't go wrong choosing a two-button mouse, but a number of more modern mice have extra buttons and wheels to make scrolling, zooming, and selecting much easier. Microsoft's IntelliMouse Explorer (see Figure 19.4) has five programmable buttons that can be used with standard programs and Internet-related applications; it also has a small wheel (located between the left and right mouse buttons) that zooms in and out or scrolls.

FIGURE 19.4
Microsoft
IntelliMouse
Explorer

Mouse Positioning Methods

Basically, mice work in this way: you move them, they figure out somehow how much you've moved them, and then they transmit that information to the computer. The "how they figure out how much you moved them" and the "transmit the data to the computer" parts are how mice vary.

The older type of mice are mechanical, meaning that they use some mechanical method for detecting motion. On most mice, the primary mechanical part is a ball on the bottom of the mouse. Take the mouse apart (remove the retaining ring, turn the mouse over, and the ball falls out, generally rolling under something), and you'll see three little wheels that turn when the ball moves against them.

Two of those wheels are monitored electronically; when they turn, they transmit to the computer how much they turned. The two wheels are perpendicular to each other, so one tracks X-axis motion and one tracks Y-axis motion. The third wheel just balances the first two.

An alternative kind of positioning mechanism is in the optical mouse, sold by Microsoft, Logitech, and others. This type of mouse has no moving parts. The mouse has optical sensors instead of a physical mouse ball, and can be used on any surface.

I recently purchased a Microsoft optical mouse for my laptop and simply love it. I can use the laptop downstairs while sitting on my living room couch and use the couch as a mouse pad or travel in the car and use my leg. (Even better—there are no moving parts to get clogged up!)

NOTE *Don't confuse an optical mouse with a wireless mouse. A mouse can be one or the other, neither, or both. An optical mouse is one that lacks a ball—it uses optical sensors for tracking. A wireless mouse is one that lacks a cord and uses either IR or RF signal to communicate with the PC.*

Optical mice operate by using a red Light-Emitting Diode (LED) that takes 1500 snapshots per second of the surface below it. By comparing the images dynamically, they can determine speed, direction, and distance. You can use these mice on top of just about any surface that's relatively flat. However, you'll want to avoid using these optical mice on surfaces with solid color or on glass or reflective surfaces. You'll also want to avoid patterns that are highly repetitive.

NOTE *The new Microsoft optical mice are a boon to gamers. In addition to having precise positioning, they're all USB mice. Normal mice operate at 40MHz (the frequency their position is updated by Windows) because of the interface, but USB mice operate at 120MHz. With frame rates of some games shooting at more than 40MHz, having a mouse that can keep up with your game is a must.*

For those of you who like to navigate by feel, Logitech offers the iFeel mouse. This new little critter provides tactile feedback as you scroll around a Web page or desktop. You'll feel a gentle vibration when you roll over a menu or dialog box, almost as if your virtual computer desktop was physically real. Naturally, this type of enhancement increases the cost of the mouse—and introduces a new element to wear out or break down at a later date.

Alernatives to Mice

Trackballs are pointing devices that have the ball (normally located underneath and inside of a mouse) on the top of the unit. Instead of moving a mouse around, you move the trackball with your finger. It's just like the trackballs on some arcade machines—or like using an upside-down mouse, if you want to think of it that way.

Many people prefer trackballs to standard mice because you have fine control over the position of the cursor and don't have to move anything around on your desktop. Trackballs are ideal for certain professions, such as architects and graphic artists, who need a high degree of pointing precision as they work. Trackballs are also an attractive alternative for young children and people with certain disabilities because they often find them easier to use than mice. Some laptops even use this technology as their primary pointing device.

Another mouse alternative is a touchpad, popular on notebook computers. A touchpad is a touch sensitive rectangular pad. You move your finger over the pad to move the pointer on-screen.

Mouse Interfaces

A mouse can connect to the PC using USB, PS/2, legacy serial port, or a proprietary bus interface. That list is in order of modernity, from newest to oldest. You'll probably never encounter a proprietary bus interface mouse and very seldom a legacy serial one.

Mouse and Trackball Cleaning

On a mechanical mouse or trackball, the little wheels get gunk stuck to them or hair wrapped around them, so you must clean them. Just remove the mouse ball and examine the wheels. I've used rubbing alcohol, a toothpick, and a cotton swab to get the gunk off the wheels. You may also need to clean the ball with a bit of alcohol. Clean the mouse about twice a year—or more if your desk is covered with dirt or dust, which is just gunk in its fetal stages.

On an optical mouse, all you have to do is clean the sensors; you can often just polish them with a soft cloth.

What to Do When Your Mouse Fails You

You can troubleshoot a mouse by following these steps:

1. Make sure your mouse is plugged in securely.

2. Check the driver. Is the mouse driver set up correctly? Is it there in the first place?

3. Clean the mouse, and shake any debris off the mouse pad.

4. Check the interface at the end of your mouse cable and at the motherboard to see whether it's USB, PS/2, or the serial port. See if there are any obvious problems such as bent pins (for PS/2 and serial port mice only) that can be straightened.

5. Ensure that Windows recognizes the mouse and that it's listed in Device Manager as properly installed.

If all this fails, and your computer isn't the culprit, you'll need to replace your mouse. Fortunately, mice are quite affordable; standard mice run around $10, with the fancy optical models starting at around $20.

Keyboard and Mouse Adjustments in Windows

When a keyboard or mouse isn't working optimally, you can sometimes get relief by adjusting its settings in Windows through the Control Panel.

Keyboard settings you can change in the Keyboard applet include these:

Repeat Delay This is the amount of time between holding down a key and having it start to repeat rapidly in typing.

Repeat Rate This is the speed at which a key repeats after the delay time has passed.

Cursor Blink Rate In applications that accept text, you may see a blinking vertical cursor showing where the text will appear; this setting controls the blink speed.

Mouse settings you can change in the Mouse applet include the following:

Pointer Speed This is the amount that the pointer moves across the screen in relation to the amount you move the mouse. Sometimes this is called *pointer sensitivity*.

Pointer Scheme This controls the look of the various mouse pointers. You might switch to a large pointer set for someone with limited vision, for example.

Switch Primary and Secondary Buttons Left-handed users may prefer to use the mouse with the left hand and to switch button functionality so that the primary button is under the index finger.

Double-Click Speed This controls how close together the two clicks in a double-click need to be to be perceived as a double-click rather than two separate clicks. A beginner having trouble double-clicking might benefit from having this setting turned down.

It's important to note that the options described pertain to the default drivers for keyboards and mice in Windows. If you install the special software that comes with your keyboard or mouse, the Properties box for Keyboard or Mouse in the Control Panel may display very different options and probably will offer more sophisticated options and settings.

Troubleshooting Tips

The following is a summary of troubleshooting tips for your keyboard:

- Make sure that the keyboard is plugged in and the connection is secure.
- Ensure that there are no BIOS warnings at bootup and that Windows recognizes the keyboard.
- Check the cable connector for any bent or missing pins.
- Swap the keyboard you suspect is malfunctioning with one that you're sure works to see if the problem lies with the computer and not the keyboard.

- Check the keys for proper functionality. They should all spring back to their original state when you press and release them.

- Test pin voltages on the keyboard cable.

- Check for cable continuity within the keyboard housing.

- Disassemble the keyboard and check all internal parts.

- Replace the keyboard if none of the previous tips work and your computer isn't at fault.

And here are a few things to try when your mouse isn't working correctly:

- Ensure that the mouse is plugged in securely.

- Check the mouse driver in Windows to make sure it's correctly installed.

- Clean your mouse to remove built-up gunk.

- Check for bent pins on the cable.

- Replace your mouse if nothing else works.

In this chapter, you learned all about mice and keyboards. In the next chapter, you'll learn about video adapters and displays.

Part 4

Multimedia

Chapter 20

Video Adapters and Displays

- ◆ QuickSteps: Shopping for a Video Card
- ◆ QuickSteps: Installing a New Video Card
- ◆ How a Video Board Works
- ◆ Video Board Characteristics
- ◆ Understanding and Comparing Monitors
- ◆ Troubleshooting Tips

Introduction

Why do people buy computers? Well, there are a lot of reasons. Some of the more common ones are to play games, browse the Web, send e-mail, and take care of personal and professional business needs. One of the things that all of these reasons have in common, whether you're flying the best fighter plane in the world or managing your checkbook, is that you need to see what you're doing. And even if you can't see, there are devices that'll read the screen to you.

Because of what we do with computers, it makes sense that the display on a computer is the primary output device. Your personal comfort when using a PC is wrapped up in the display, from the colors and background to your favorite screen saver. Video taste tends to be a personal kind of thing. But what's behind the screen? How can you choose the best equipment for you? And how much can you fix when it fails?

This chapter will help you select and install a video card. You'll also look at the parts of a video board, as well as their image resolution, color depth, vertical frequency, and 3D capability. In addition, you'll look at the device used to display your video—the monitor. Because even if you have the latest and greatest video card available, it won't do you much good if you have a cheap old 14-inch monitor that only displays 256 colors.

QuickSteps: Installing a New Video Card

Here's a quick overview of the items you'll need and the steps you should take to install a new video card.

BE PREPARED

Before you start, there are some things you may need on hand. These include the following:

- A container for screws
- The manual for your computer

To install a video card, follow these steps:

1. Begin with a clear tabletop so you have room to work.

2. Make sure your computer and peripherals are turned off, and ground yourself by touching something metallic.

3. Unplug all the connecting cables, including the power.

4. Remove the screws that hold the outer case of the computer, put them in your container, and carefully remove the case.

5. If you're replacing an old video card, find the old card inside your computer and remove the screw that attaches it to the computer chassis.

NOTE If you have a system with onboard video circuitry (you can tell if you do because the monitor will plug into the motherboard rather than to an expansion card), you must disable the onboard video system before an add-on card will work. This usually involves disabling it through the Basic Input/Output System (BIOS) during setup, but some older computers have you move a jumper on the motherboard. For computers that use jumpers, your computer's manual should have a jumper diagram that'll tell you how to do this.

6. Gently but firmly, ease the old video card out of the slot on the motherboard and remove the card from your computer.

7. Insert the new card into an open, compatible slot (AGP or PCI) on your motherboard:

   - If the slot is the same as the card you just took out, you can insert the new card into the slot you just vacated on your motherboard.

   - Alternatively, if your new card requires a different slot, you may need to remove a metal plate that covers an expansion card opening at the back of your computer. Unscrew the plate, remove it, and cover the opening that's left by the card you removed.

8. Mount the card securely by screwing the video card's rear plate into the computer's chassis.

9. Put the cover back on your computer, and screw it on.

10. Reattach all the external cables.

11. Turn your computer and peripherals back on.

12. When Windows boots up, it should detect that you have a new video card, and attempt to install the proper drivers. You should have the drivers (on CD, but sometimes floppy disk) that came with the card handy at this stage. If Windows fails to detect your new video card, you should install the drivers manually. Either way, read through the manual that came with the video card for instructions about how to ensure the drivers are installed correctly.

QuickSteps: Shopping for a Video Card

Follow these steps when buying a video card:

1. Decide what your needs are—business, entertainment, gaming, or general purpose.

2. Budget yourself. Today's prices range from about $30 for a low-end Peripheral Component Interconnect (PCI) Video Graphics Array (VGA) card to about $400 for a high-end Accelerated Graphics Port (AGP) consumer 3D card. And if you want to get really crazy, you can spend in excess of $1000 for a card with more features than you'll ever need.

3. Pick your favorite 3D Application Programming Interface (API), if necessary for gaming. Many games support multiple APIs (DirectX, OpenGL, and Glide), but some will specialize in one over the others. Check the requirements of the games you have or want to buy, and look for a card that supports those APIs.

4. Choose a manufacturer such as Asus, ATI, Matrox, or PNY. Check out online or magazine reviews of different cards to see how they match up.

5. Decide on the card you want. It's usually best to get the most memory you can afford, but general-purpose and business-computing video memory needs are less demanding. In addition, be sure to pay attention to the standard supported by your card (and by your motherboard). For example, if your motherboard only supports AGP 2, then there's no real point in spending extra money for an 8 card.

How a Video Board Works

The parts of the board you must understand to see how video works and how it can be tuned up include the following:

◆ The system Central Processing Unit (CPU)

◆ The system bus and its interface to the video board

◆ The video memory on the video board

◆ The video imaging chip on the video board

◆ The Digital-to-Analog Converter (DAC) on the video board

Consider this: how does the CPU get an image onto the computer's display? I'll start from the CPU and end up at the monitor in this explanation.

A basic video board looks like the one shown in Figure 20.1.

The CPU and Video Images

The primary objective of a video board is to take information from the CPU and display it on a monitor. When a program wants to display data, it does so by telling the CPU to store data in the video board. Exactly *how* a CPU does that varies. There are two basic kinds of video boards: dumb frame buffers and coprocessor/accelerator boards. Pretty much everything you see today will be of the coprocessor/accelerator variety. I'll take up those two types in a bit, but for now just understand that the CPU controls the video board.

What that implies, for anyone trying to speed up a video subsystem, is that a faster CPU will make for faster video, all other things being equal.

FIGURE 20.1

A video board

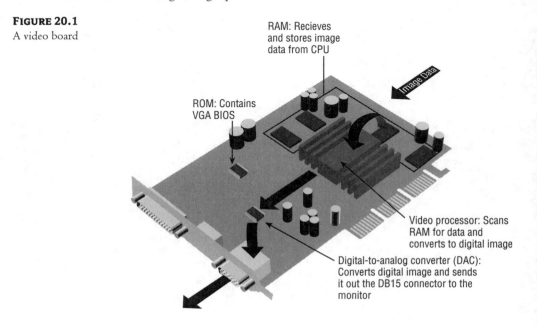

RAM: Recieves and stores image data from CPU

Image Data

ROM: Contains VGA BIOS

Video processor: Scans RAM for data and converts to digital image

Digital-to-analog converter (DAC): Converts digital image and sends it out the DB15 connector to the monitor

The System Bus

The CPU is connected to the video board through the system's bus. The speed of that bus can constrain how fast the video system can update. What's the fastest rate at which data might be zapped into a video board? Well, the video system doesn't need to update the picture on the screen much more often than 72 times per second because you probably can't perceive images much faster than that. High-quality video boards have up to 256 megabytes (MB) of Random Access Memory (RAM) on them, so the maximum amount of data that a video board might have to work with would be 72×256, or 18,432MB per second. By contrast, a PCI bus runs at 33MHz and is 32 bits wide, so the maximum video data throughput for PCI video cards is 133MB per second. What does all that mean? Simply this: the faster your bus interface, the better for your video board. This suggests that when you buy a video board, you should buy a video board that uses an AGP bus. If your motherboard doesn't have AGP, it's time for a motherboard upgrade as well.

NOTE   *If your motherboard has an AGP slot that goes bad, you only have two choices. You can either go with a PCI video card, or buy a new motherboard.*

Why use AGP? For starters, it uses a 66 megahertz (MHz) clock and a 64-bit bus, which dramatically increases its speed over PCI. The AGP 3.0 specification, which defines AGP 8, provides an impressive 2.1 gigabytes per second (GBps) of video bandwidth. Aside from its increased speed, the most distinguishing characteristic of an AGP bus is that an AGP video card can use system memory as an extension of its own local frame buffer memory.

All AGP cards have a clock speed of 66MHz; the difference between AGP speeds isn't the card's clock speed but how many transfers the card makes during a cycle. AGP 1 makes a single transfer per cycle for a maximum data transfer rate of 266MBps—about twice as fast as the 33MHz PCI slot. AGP 2 makes two transfers per cycle, making its maximum data transfer rate 533MBps. AGP 4 has maximum data transfer rate of 1066MBps, and as mentioned earlier, AGP 8 doubles that. Obviously, when you're dealing with 3D animations or any other full-motion video environment, faster data transfer is better. AGP 8 is able to move data between the video card and your CPU at *four times* the rate of AGP 2, and *sixteen times* faster than PCI. So, if you need quick crisp video (3D action games, anyone?), you do the math. In fact, the peripheral that probably benefits the most from a fast bus is the video board.

NOTE   *A quick historical note for you: it wasn't too long ago (well, okay, 10 years or so) that we were using Industry Standard Architecture (ISA) video cards. An ISA bus slot can only transfer data 16 bits at a time, at 8MHz, for a blazing throughput of 16MB per second. Compare that with your new AGP 8 board!*

To fully take advantage of AGP 8, you need an AGP 8 video card and an AGP 8-compatible motherboard, a CPU and memory modules that support 133MHz system bus speeds, and Windows 98 or a later operating system.

NOTE   *AGP 8 is expected to be the last AGP standard developed. That's because in early 2004 the industry is expecting to transition to a PCI Express–based serial graphics standard. High-end PCI Express cards promise bidirectional transmission speeds of about 8GBps.*

The Video Memory

The video image is then stored in the video memory. As with all memory, faster is better and more is better. (Why is more better? I'll discuss video resolution and color depth later, but the answer is, briefly, the more dots you want to put on your screen and the more colors you want to be able to use for them, the more memory your video board needs.) But video memory has some special needs in that it's usually addressed in blocks, and it's addressed simultaneously by several chips—in particular, the CPU and the video imaging chip.

DUAL-PORTED MEMORY: VRAM

Let's look at that second characteristic first. Ordinarily, a RAM chip is addressed by the CPU and no other chip, unless there's a Direct Memory Access (DMA) operation going on—and when that happens, the CPU doesn't access the memory.

In contrast, memory on a video chip has no choice but to talk to two chips at the same time; the CPU shovels image data into the video memory, and the imaging chip pulls it out. On video boards with normal RAM, this presents a performance problem; normal RAM can only address one chip at a time. Video boards with normal RAM just make the CPU and the imaging chip take turns, slowing things down.

Some older video boards used a special kind of memory originally called Dual-Ported RAM but which most people called VRAM, for Video RAM. There's nothing intrinsically video-ish about this RAM; it's just that its most logical application is in video boards.

DUAL-PORTED, BLOCK-ADDRESSABLE MEMORY: WRAM

But another thing about memory is its blocky nature. Modern graphical user interfaces tend to address memory in large blocks, rather than on a byte-by-byte basis. For example, to draw a colored background, the CPU must say to a whole large block of memory, "Store value X," where X is the value that sets the desired background color. A CPU does that by arduously working on several locations one at a time.

Window RAM (WRAM) made that task easier by allowing blocks, or "windows," of memory to be addressed in just a few commands. WRAM was a bit more expensive, but it was also considered a good buy in video boards.

NEWER VIDEO MEMORY: MDRAM, SGRAM, AND DDR

Multibank DRAM (MDRAM) is aimed at the cost-conscious user who still wants good performance. MDRAM allows you to add memory in 32-kilobyte (KB) chunks, which lets you calculate exactly how much you need and install just that much. You therefore aren't wasting money on excess video memory that you may not need. MDRAM is much faster than VRAM and WRAM.

Synchronous Graphics RAM (SGRAM) operates at higher speeds than other video memory. It's capable of operating at speeds between 66MHz and 80MHz.

The most common video memory you'll see today is Double Data Rate Synchronous Dynamic RAM (DDR SDRAM), or DDR for short. DDR doesn't increase the memory clock speed, but it does move twice as much memory per clock cycle, thereby doubling the rate at which video data is moved.

The Video Imaging Chip

Once the image is in the VRAM, that image must be converted into a digital video image format. That's done by the *display chip*, or video chip or imaging chip," depending on who's talking about it. Over the years, there have been many different imaging chips. Nowadays, however, the main question to answer when looking at video chips is this: is it a dumb frame buffer or an accelerator/coprocessor of some kind?

FRAME BUFFER CHIPS

Most video chips in the PC world before 1992 were frame buffers. *Frame buffer* means that the board is populated with memory chips, as you've just learned, and the memory chips hold an image that closely resembles what shows up on the screen. Each dot (*pixel*) on the screen has a corresponding location on the video memory. Set it to one numeric value, and one color appears on the pixel. Another value, and another color, appears in its place.

The problem with frame buffers is that every one of those pixels must be arranged by the CPU. That can be a lot of work for one CPU, and it's incredibly slow. That's where accelerators and coprocessors come in.

SMARTER VIDEO CHIPS

Current video chips take some of the burden off the main processor and put it on themselves. These kinds of chips are coprocessors called *video accelerators*.

Back in Chapter 2, "Inside the PC: Core Components," you learned about numeric coprocessors, special-purpose CPUs that are particularly good at a small group of jobs. Video coprocessors are just another kind of special-purpose CPU. As you'd expect, they're designed to shove pixels around quickly.

Accelerators typically include VGA circuitry onboard; coprocessors typically complement a VGA, requiring that you have both a VGA board and a coprocessor in your system. Coprocessors require that you link them to a normal video board via a "feature connector," a pin header or edge connector that you'll commonly see on video boards.

Related to a coprocessor is a less-expensive alternative called an *accelerator*. The difference is that a coprocessor is a full-fledged microprocessor that's programmable to do just about any task that the main CPU can do. An accelerator, on the other hand, isn't a general-purpose CPU but rather a special-purpose chip that knows how to do a few particular graphical tasks quickly. Most accelerators are good at something called *bitblitting*. As you probably know, a term commonly used by GUI users for pictures is *bitmaps*. Windows wallpapers are bitmaps, screen captures are bitmaps, and any picture created with Paintbrush is a bitmap. Much of what slows Windows down is placing bitmaps on the screen, either transferring them from memory to screen or moving them from one part of the screen to another part of the screen. Moving a bitmap is technically referred to as a *bitmap block transfer*, which is abbreviated *bitblt*. A number of inexpensive Windows accelerators are just VGA boards with a bitblitter chip onboard. The large number of bitblt operations that Windows does makes this combination of VGA and hardware bitblt support very cost-effective. Accelerators may also know how to build simple geometric shapes such as lines or circles.

The fact that accelerators are a one-board approach in contrast to the video-board-and-coprocessor approach may make an accelerator a better buy. It's certainly a cheaper option, but be aware that an accelerator board's dual nature means that it has both generic VGA circuitry and accelerator circuitry, and the two circuits are unrelated. It's quite common to see incredibly fast accelerator chips paired with painfully slow VGA circuits, and the result is that running Windows is quite fast (the accelerator is at work) but games run very poorly because the slower VGA circuit is now active. When looking at benchmark results for an accelerator, look for times for both the VGA circuit and the accelerator.

DIGITAL-TO-ANALOG CONVERTER (DAC)

The video board's work is almost done; the digital image has been produced by the imaging chip. Only one more thing to do—convert the image from digital to analog. That's done with a special chip called the Digital-to-Analog Converter (DAC).

About all there is to say about the DAC is that it comes in varying abilities to produce color. The 15-bit DAC produces 32,768 colors; the 16-bit DAC produces 65,536 colors; and the 18-bit DAC produces 262,144 colors. The 24-bit and 30-bit DACs produce 16 million and 1 billion colors, respectively.

You usually can't upgrade DACs; whatever your vendor built in is what you're stuck with.

Video Board Characteristics

Now that you know the parts of a video board, how do you choose between video boards? RAM type, bus attachment, and video chip are all important, but so are image resolution, color depth, vertical frequency, and 3D capability. You'll learn about those next.

NOTE   If your needs are more specialized than for general computing or playing games, look for a video board that has a TV-out (S-Video) or digital flat-panel connection, video capture, or TV-tuner capabilities. Others support dual-monitor connections and may come with DVD software.

Resolution and Colors

Resolution on a video display is the number of horizontal and vertical dots that make up the picture. For example, the most basic resolution today is 640 × 480, which means that the image is 640 dots wide by 480 dots high. Most VGA boards nowadays are Super VGA boards, even the cheap clones. You can pick up a no-name VGA board for about $15–$30, and in addition to standard VGA, it'll probably support 800 × 600 mode. The more expensive the board, generally the higher the resolution that it supports. For example, many high-end boards today support 2048 1536. More resolution means more dots on the screen, which means that the video board needs more memory.

NOTE   Just because your graphic card and monitor can support high resolution doesn't mean you should use high resolution. For example, if you use 1024 768 on a 14-inch monitor, everything on the screen will look microscopic. Even if you own a huge monitor, beware of setting the resolution too high when playing certain games. Most of the games expect lower resolutions (for example, 800 600) and may result in a fuzzy-looking game. Of course, with some of the games, it may be difficult to tell if the display is distorted.

A video board's memory requirements are determined by two things: its resolution and the number of colors it can display. For instance, a simple VGA may be able to display a resolution of 320 × 200 with 256 colors, but when in the higher 640 × 480 resolution, it might only be capable of displaying 16 colors. Most new cards have enough memory that this isn't a problem like it used to be, but you'll still occasionally run into video boards that don't perform quite like you'd like them to perform. And even if the video card does support the resolution and number of colors you want, it might not do it well. Setting video too high on cheap cards can cause incredibly slow system performance. And of course, you need to keep in mind what your monitor will support as well.

Table 20.1 shows a summary of resolutions available for common video boards throughout PC history.

TABLE 20.1: VIDEO BOARD RESOLUTIONS

BOARD TYPE	RESOLUTIONS SUPPORTED	COLORS SUPPORTED
Color Graphics Array (CGA)	320 × 200	4
	640 × 200	2
Enhanced Graphics Array (EGA)	CGA resolutions	
	640 × 350	16
Video Graphics Array (VGA)	CGA and EGA	
	320 × 200	256
	640 × 480	16
Super VGA	CGA, EGA, VGA	
	640 × 480 up to 2048 × 1536	256, 32K, 64K, or 16 million+ (ranges from 4-bit to 32-bit color)

Resolutions such as 1024 × 768 with 16 million colors obviously require more memory than does 800 600 with 256 colors. That's why you see ads for video cards touting how much memory they have on the board. In today's computers, if you have anything less than 32MB of video memory, you really have a dinosaur. Many video cards have 256 or 512MB, and the size of video memory keeps growing just like the size of system RAM.

How much video memory do you need? Well, if you're only using simple graphics (the most intense game you play is Solitaire), then go with a cheap card—you could probably get away with 16MB of video memory if you can find a card with that little on it. But if you want cutting-edge technology (and you don't want to become obsolete quite as fast), then you need to spend some money on a card with at least 128MB of DDR.

Although the memory on your video card determines the resolutions and color depth that it supports, resolution schemes are typically classified by their standards. That's why everyone still refers to VGA and SVGA, even though these standards may seem ancient. It should be explained that IBM did create several new video standards after VGA, which received *very* limited acceptance in the market—mainly because they were implemented on cards that used IBM's proprietary Micro Channel Architecture (MCA), which received *no* acceptance in the market. These weren't included in most of the tables. Still, you may run across these acronyms from time to time (especially when looking at sales on old equipment), so here's a brief summary of these oldies-but-not-so-goodies:

8514/A   This "professional" standard was actually introduced about the same time as standard VGA. It provided both higher-resolution/color modes and some limited hardware acceleration capabilities as well. By today's standards the 8514/A is quite primitive, supporting 1024 × 768 graphics in 256 colors but only at 43.5Hz (interlaced) or 640 × 480 at 60Hz (noninterlaced). You watch such a screen for prolonged periods, and your friends will begin to call you *blinky*.

XGA This acronym stands for Extended Graphics Array. XGA cards were used in later PS/2 models; they can do bus mastering on the MCA bus and use either 512KB or 1MB of VRAM. In the 1MB configuration, XGA supports 1024 × 768 graphics in 256 colors or 640 × 480 at high color (16 bits per pixel).

XGA-2 This graphics mode improves on XGA by extending 1024 × 768 support to high color and also supporting higher refresh rates than XGA or 8514/A.

Vertical Scan Frequencies: Interlacing and 72Hz

Having a video board that supports high resolutions and millions of colors only benefits you if your monitor supports them. That statement might sound a bit obvious, but it's a factor that people often overlook. In fact, it's not always that obvious. While it's apparent that your old monochrome monitor isn't going to display more than one color, how is your four-year-old monitor going to handle your new, snazzy video adapter? To know the answer, you should understand a bit about how monitors interface with the video card.

Standard Cathode Ray Tube (CRT) monitors display information by projecting a narrow beam of electrons onto a phosphor-covered glass panel—your monitor screen. Wherever the beam hits, the phosphor becomes excited and the phosphor lights up for a brief period and then fades out. Because it fades very quickly—in hundredths of seconds—the electron beam must retrace its path constantly to keep the image on the screen. How often must it travel across the screen? Well, the electron beam in the back of a video monitor must repaint or *refresh* the screen at least 60 times per second, or your eye will probably perceive flicker. (Why *probably*? Hang on for a sentence or two.) And that brings me to a story about the IBM 8514 video system.

INTERLACING AND THE 8514

As mentioned earlier, the 8514 was an early IBM high-resolution (1024 × 768) video system; as a matter of fact, the 8514 video system is important because it was the first mass-market PC-based video system to support a resolution of 1024 × 768. But, in order to save money on the monitor, IBM cut a corner on the system. Now, to get high-resolution images, you need a high-quality (read: expensive) monitor. One way to get higher resolution out of a cheaper screen is to refresh it less often. The 8514 doesn't refresh 60 times per second but rather 43 times per second.

This isn't the first time you've seen this less-than-60-refreshes-per-second approach to high resolution; it's called *interlacing*. What was significant was that IBM did it, so the practice of interlacing became acceptable.

But, you see, interlacing *isn't* acceptable, at least not from a quality standpoint. The result of interlacing is a flickering screen and eyestrain headaches. That's why you used to have to be careful when buying a system that supported higher resolutions. The only real way to go, and what everyone supports today, is called *noninterlaced*. If someone tries to sell you something that only supports interlaced higher resolutions, run away.

By the way, if you do have an interlaced monitor, you can do a few things to reduce the effects of flicker. Several factors affect flicker. You see flicker better with your peripheral vision because the center of your vision is built around low-resolution color receptors called *cones* on your retina. Surrounding the cones are high-resolution monochromatic receptors called *rods*.

Peripheral vision images fall on the rods. Sailors know this because when searching for a ship on the horizon, they don't look right at the horizon—they look below it, so the horizon falls on the high-resolution rods. In any case, the closer you are to your monitor, the more of its image falls on the cones, which are less flicker-prone. You can demonstrate this with any monitor. Stand so that your monitor is about 60 to 80 degrees to your left: If the direction you're facing is 12 o'clock, the monitor should be at about 10 o'clock. Hold a piece of paper in front of you and read the text on it. You'll notice that you're seeing the monitor out of the corner of your eye, and that it's flashing. This also suggests that you should buy a small monitor—a large image will end up falling more on your rods—but 1024 × 768 on a 12-inch screen is, well, suboptimal. Antiglare screens will also reduce flicker. Another antiflicker tactic is to keep your room bright. When the ambient light is bright, your pupils contract, which has the side effect of reducing the amount of light that gets to the peripheral rods. You'll also find that certain color combinations exaggerate the flicker—black and white is one problem combination—so play around with the Windows colors to make the screen more readable.

The Benefits of Fast Vertical Refresh Rates

Because I've brought up the subject of video with low refresh rates, it's worthwhile looking at the opposite end of the spectrum—video systems that refresh at more than 60 screens per second. The more common use of larger monitors means that more people notice flicker on default 60Hz settings. Furthermore, people nowadays use their computers all day, so anyone who has even the slightest sensitivity to flicker will get some eyestrain. As a result, modern video cards generally put out much higher vertical refresh rates. Indeed, 72Hz, 80Hz, and 120Hz cards are commonly available. Investing in the highest refresh rate you can afford is well worth it. My eyes rest much more easily on an 80Hz screen than a 60Hz screen.

There are, of course, a few caveats. First, you need a *monitor* that can handle the vertical refresh rate you want. If you're buying a used monitor, this might be an issue. But all newer monitors can handle 80Hz or higher. Still, check the monitor's documentation to make sure it supports the resolution you want at the refresh rate you want. The second caution is actually kind of funny or sad, depending on how you look at it. Every computer I've set up in the past several years had a video system that came out of the box configured for a lower refresh rate than it could actually handle. In other words, the video card was set to 60Hz (which is common), but the card could easily handle 75Hz or more. Now, reconfiguring the video for a faster refresh rate usually isn't any harder than just running a short program that comes with the video board (or right-clicking your Desktop, choosing Properties, selecting the Settings tab, and then changing the settings), so it's not like I unlocked some hidden feature of the video board. It's just plain inexplicable why a computer company would sell a superior video product as part of its PC but wouldn't take the two minutes to utilize those features.

So, if you've a recently purchased computer, take a close look at the video documentation that came with it. I've been able to bring more than a few surprised smiles to the faces of owners of PCs by running the video setup programs that were sitting right on their hard disks.

3D Video Boards

Three-dimensional graphics are where it's at today, especially in the gaming world. Although these video boards are also very important to a segment of the computer-aided design and graphics industry, it's through gaming that they've enjoyed their vast popularity.

Quite simply, 3D-capable video adapters are made for gamers. If you don't play games, you'll see little to no improvement in the video displayed on your computer after investing several hundred dollars in one of these jewels. What's the draw of these expensive cards? They're able to make you believe you're seeing action in three dimensions in real time. They do this through the illusion of adding depth to a scene, creating powerful lighting effects, mapping textures to polygons, and other special effects.

Although they share a common overall objective, there are different types of 3D video boards that implement 3D in substantially different manners. Each video board manufacturer relies on special chipsets, which are in turn created by other manufacturers. It's the video chipset that has the greatest effect on the 3D capabilities of the card. The prominent chipset manufacturer today is nVidia, which produces the TNT, TNT2, and GeForce series of chipsets. Back in December 2000 they bought out their major competitor, 3Dfx, which produced the Voodoo line of chipsets. Another popular 3D chipset is the Radion series, manufactured by ATI.

NOTE *Because of the perception that every user needs a 3D graphics card, it's becoming increasingly difficult to find 2D video cards on the market. But if you don't play games, or are purchasing a video card for a corporate workstation, you can generally save money by buying a 2D video card instead of a 3D one—provided that you can find one, of course.*

In addition to the chipset, the 3D API is also important. The top three APIs are DirectX, OpenGL, and Glide. DirectX is a 3D graphics API that was created by Microsoft for computers running Windows. DirectX was a latecomer to the 3D party but now vies with OpenGL as the standard 3D API for Windows-based 3D applications. OpenGL, originally created by Silicon Graphics, is a 3D API supported by an independent industry consortium that's compatible with other operating systems besides Windows. Glide is a proprietary API that was used by 3Dfx's Voodoo line of chipsets.

Video Monitor Characteristics

Now that you have a board, what monitor goes with it? Monitors aren't as complex as video boards, but there are a few terms you need to know.

Perhaps the most important thing to understand about the monitor/board partnership is that the video board calls the tune, and the monitor dances—if it can. Virtually all computers (except for some older laptops) have video circuitry that can produce at least 1024 × 768 signals, but that kind of resolution won't work unless your monitor supports it. In addition, having 120Hz is nice, but both the video board and the monitor must support it.

Monitor Mumbo Jumbo: Horizontal Scan Frequency

As I explained earlier, a Cathode-Ray Tube (CRT) monitor works by directing a beam of electrons against the inside of its screen. Phosphors on the inside of the screen become "excited" and glow. Making phosphors glow or not glow defines images on the screen. From a computer's point of view, a video display is just an array of pixels. *Resolution* is the number of dots that can be put on the screen. The electron beam sweeps across the tube, painting lines of dots. CGA uses 200 lines top to bottom, EGA used 350, and VGA uses 480. Because it uses higher resolutions, Super VGA uses even more lines.

Consider the number of horizontal lines that a monitor must draw per second. In a basic VGA, each screen has 480 lines, and there are 60 screens per second. So 480 times 60 is 28,800 lines per second. That's called the *horizontal scan frequency*; it's the number of times that the beam sweeps horizontally per second. It too is measured in hertz (Hz) or kilohertz (kHz)—thousands of hertz. Actually, a VGA has a somewhat higher horizontal scan rate than 28,800Hz (28.8kHz) because the monitor has extra lines that you can't see (they're called *overscan*). How *many* extra lines a monitor has varies from video mode to video mode. A CGA has a horizontal scan frequency of 15,750Hz, or 15.8kHz. EGA uses 21.8kHz, and VGA uses 31.5kHz. So, the horizontal scan frequency your monitor needs to serve your board is determined in part by two important factors: the number of horizontal lines on the screen and the screen's refresh rate.

Dot Pitch

Some monitor ads tout *0.25mm dot pitch*. What are they talking about?

You've seen that more resolution means more dots (pixels) on the screen. The distance between the centers of the dots on the monitor is the monitor's *dot pitch*, and it's measured in millimeters (mm). The smaller the dots, the closer together they can be and the higher the resolution that a monitor can show in a crisp and readable manner. A larger monitor can have a larger dot pitch without sacrificing resolution simply because the monitor's screen is larger.

In reality, you'll see many different dot pitches for VGA monitors, including ancient standards such as 0.34mm and 0.31mm, to modern 0.21mm and 0.20mm. Any new monitor you purchase will have at least a 0.26mm dot pitch.

Monitor Size

Monitors range in size from small 14-inch models to more professional-caliber monitors that have a display of 21 inches or more. Although 17-, 19-, and 21-inch monitors are pretty standard today, the factors you should weigh when choosing the right monitor for you are price, space, and use.

It almost goes without saying that the larger the monitor, the more money it'll cost. Generally, you can expect to pay between $150 and $1000 for a monitor, with the smaller monitors available at the low end of this spectrum. Seventeen-inch monitors fall in the middle, and 19- and 21-inch monitors can go off this scale.

In addition to price, space can be an important consideration. The larger monitors take up more desktop space (called a *footprint*)—sometimes much more. Of course, the width of a 21-inch monitor will be larger than a 15-inch model, but the depth is of much more concern because of the size of the cathode ray tubes used in larger monitors. If your computer desk space is limited, consider a flat-panel display, discussed in the following section.

Finally, how you plan to use your computer is an important factor in determining the right monitor to buy. If the primary role of your computer is general computing, you can get by with a 15- or 17-inch monitor, but if you spend much time with graphics, a larger monitor will help greatly. In some cases, you should use two monitors, which I'll cover in more detail later in this chapter.

Another important point to remember when you choose a monitor is that the size of the screen you can actually use will be smaller than what's advertised. A 17-inch monitor, for example, may only have a viewable dimension of approximately 16 inches. This is caused in part by the fact that monitor sizes are based on the measurement of the CRT diagonally from one corner to the opposite and also because computer monitors underscan. Underscanning creates an image that's smaller than the overall size of the CRT and leaves a black frame around your picture.

Flat-Panel Displays

Flat-panel Liquid Crystal Display (LCD) monitors (also called digital monitors) have become quite popular for desktop computers as their prices have dropped in recent years. Their main benefit is their space-saving nature. Based on the technologies that power laptop displays rather than the traditional CRTs used in everyday monitors, flat-panel LCD displays take up significantly less desktop space.

These displays differ from their CRT counterparts in several ways. First, the dot pitch is determined by the physical size of the LCD elements that make up the LCD panel, rather than the size of the aperture grill or shadow mask of the CRT. Some flat-panel displays have a larger dot pitch than most CRTs. Another important difference is how the monitor size is measured. With CRTs, manufacturers must list the diagonal size of the CRT as well as the viewable area. This is because the geometry of the CRT curvature prevents the monitor from displaying information to the extreme corner edges. For example, a 19-inch CRT monitor may have only a 17.5-inch viewable area. Flat-panel displays don't have the same issues as the CRT, so a 15-inch diagonal LCD display has a viewable diagonal area of 15 inches. Flat-panel displays are still more costly than CRT monitors, however. Even though the cost of the displays is still dropping, you can still expect to pay anywhere from $50 to $200 more for a comparably sized flat-screen device.

Multifrequency Monitors

The last monitor feature is *multisyncing*, the ability to handle multiple resolutions automatically. Recall that the horizontal frequency that you need to display an image is determined by the refresh rate (the vertical frequency) and the horizontal resolution. Until 1986, monitors were fixed-frequency in both the horizontal and vertical directions. When you bought a CGA monitor, it could only do one set of frequencies: 15.75kHz horizontal, 60Hz vertical. The EGA monitor had to be able to do double duty—it could be attached to either CGA or EGA boards and so had two sets of frequencies: 15.75kHz/60Hz for CGA boards and 21.8kHz/60Hz for EGA boards. The VGA knows of three sets of frequencies: one for CGA modes, one for EGA modes, and 31.5kHz/60Hz for its native standard VGA mode. So a "vanilla VGA" monitor is a fixed-frequency monitor that only supports CGA, EGA, and VGA—no Super VGA modes.

In 1986, NEC changed the PC world with its MultiSync monitor. The MultiSync could detect and synchronize with any horizontal frequency from 15kHz to 31.5kHz and with any vertical frequency from 50Hz to 70Hz. That meant that a single monitor could work on any kind of video board that was out at the time. More important, when IBM introduced the VGA standard in April 1987, the Multi-Sync was ready—it could handle VGA's 31.5kHz horizontal frequency with no problem.

Pretty much every monitor vendor offers their own MultiSync-like monitors: they're generically called Variable Frequency Monitors (VFMs). NEC doesn't sell the original MultiSync anymore, but they have MultiSync models from the 3FGX (31.5–38kHz horizontal, 50–80Hz vertical) to the 6FGX (30–66kHz horizontal, 50–90Hz vertical). The biggest advantage to most multisync-style monitors is that they generally size themselves. You don't need to play with size controls if you change the resolution or refresh frequency of your display.

Multiple Displays

No matter how large your display is, it never seems large enough to let you see everything without scrolling or panning. The size of the monitors seems to have peaked at 21 to 22 inches (even though larger monitors are available) for several reasons. First, when you get a monitor larger than 21 inches, there's precious little room left on your desk. The second reason has to do with proper viewing distance. If you have a monitor with a 24-inch screen, you should view it from a distance of 6 feet! These are good for those users who are vision-impaired, but not for most people. The solution that has been gaining in popularity since the late '90s has been to have two or more displays hooked to the same computer. If this is the first you have heard of this, you might think that sounds a little weird. But it's popular enough that most major graphic card vendors offer dual-display support on their products. You will pay a little more for the video card, but the upside is huge.

So, how can you get your computer to use more than one display at the same time? There are two approaches, and both involve additional hardware and support from the operating system. One approach involves adding one or more additional graphic cards and monitors to your computer. If using Windows 98/Me/2000/XP, the computer will recognize the additional card and allow you to set up one as the primary display and the other as the secondary. From here it's possible to configure the monitors so that your desktop is spread between the two or more displays. This can be a very inexpensive solution when you consider that a decent used VGA monitor sells for around $50 and a new video card can be purchased for under $20.

The other solution is to either remove your existing graphic card or disable the integrated one in your motherboard and install a new graphic card that supports dual displays.

Having dual monitors can increase productivity of you deal with a lot of information at once. For example, an accountant can have a ledger open on one side, with input data on the other side. My all-time favorite is the ability to have my photo-editing application open on both displays and to zoom in to do touch-up while the image in the secondary display remains at its original zoom level. This saves zooming back and forth, which is a common issue with photo retouching.

Issues Installing Multiple Display Cards

With the multiple-display support feature in Windows, you need to install the new graphic adapter(s) and monitor. The monitors and graphic adapters can be different—quite different. One of the systems I just tested had an AGP card as well as a PCI video card. Each monitor was set for a different color depth and screen resolution. One monitor serves as the primary display and will show the logon dialog box when you start your computer. In addition, most programs, when you open them, will display windows on the primary. The first time this happens, Windows will attempt to detect and install the drivers for the new graphic cards. Depending on the graphic card, it may reboot, so if you've added more than two graphic cards (you animal!), you may end up rebooting several times. If successful, all of the display adapters should appear in System Properties.

To configure the settings for multiple monitors, open Display Properties in Control Panel or right-click the Windows Desktop and choose Settings. In Windows XP, right-click the Desktop and choose Properties, and then click the Settings tab in the Display Properties dialog box. You'll see the icon of the monitors, and at the bottom there will be an Extend My Windows Desktop onto This Monitor check box. Checking this will open a Compatibility Warning dialog box that essentially warns you that if your application doesn't support multiple displays, you should probably turn this feature off. Please be aware that not all graphic cards are supported—only those that work with Windows 98/Me/2000/XP/2003. A good rule of thumb is if the driver works with Win9x/Me/2000/XP/2003, it most probably was shipped with your operating system. When in doubt, check with the Microsoft Web site for a detailed list. When configuring the display settings, you drag the monitor icons so that the monitors are configured in Windows the same way they're physically aligned on your desktop.

Troubleshooting Tips

Once you have a system in place, how do you attack video problems? The following are a few suggestions.

Some of the dumbest monitor problems are the easiest to resolve:

◆ Is it turned on?

◆ Is the brightness or contrast turned down?

◆ Is everything plugged in? Is it plugged into the right place?

◆ Did you hear one long and two short beeps indicating a bad video card?

◆ If the display is dead, do you hear the power supply fan? There are nonvideo reasons for a display "malfunction," such as when the power supply has killed the computer.

◆ If the computer is okay but the display is bad, you'll see the drive light come on. Use a sound-emitting program to see if the computer is functioning.

The quickest test is a monitor swap. If that does nothing, swap the display cards. *Don't* try to service the monitor. As I've said before, you can hurt yourself doing that.

If the display is rolling and you can't see enough to check the video modes, restart the computer in Windows Safe mode (press the F8 key when you reboot and you'll be given a menu with Safe Mode as one of the options). This will start Windows in standard 640 × 480 in 16 colors, so you can use almost any card and monitor to test your system.

Speaking of drivers, sometimes you'll see a case where you reboot your operating system only to lose synchronization—the screen turns into moving bands. That probably means that you told your video board to exceed the capabilities of the monitor. Drop back a bit in resolution, and you'll be okay.

Now that I've talked about what you can see, let's talk about what you can hear on your computer. The next chapter is all about sound.

Chapter 21

Play It Loud: Sound Cards

◆ How Sound Synthesis Works

◆ Sound Card Characteristics

◆ Choosing the Right Speakers

◆ Installing a Sound Card

◆ Troubleshooting Sound Problems

Introduction

In the early days of personal computing, the only way a PC could make noise was with its built-in speaker. Even the best PC speaker is tinny, however, and the best you could hope for were squeaks, squawks, and the occasional boom (though even that was more like a crackle). One ambitious 1984 program called PC Parrot attempted to make the PC speak, but it was limited by the sound equipment possibilities.

That's not true anymore, of course, and it hasn't been for many years. Sound equipment on the PC is so good that millions of computer users are now using their PCs to burn MP3 files to CDs, listen to Internet radio stations, play audio-intensive PC games, and mix and record digital audio files. Although the standard sound card (or built-in sound support on the motherboard) that came with your PC might be adequate for office work and day-to-day Internet browsing, these special applications sometimes require a little more punch in the audio department, which a higher-end or more specialized sound card can deliver.

Sound Characteristics

First I'll discuss what sound *is*. Sound consists of a set of waves of varying pressure created in the air by vocal cords, musical instruments, or natural forces. A picture of a sound is called a *sonogram,* and you can see one in Figure 21.1. It's a sonogram of the word *hello* being spoken (by me, in this case).

FIGURE 21.1

A sonogram of the word *hello*

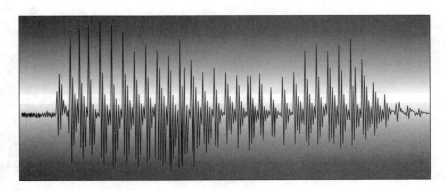

The dimensions of this signal are called *amplitude* and *frequency.* Amplitude and frequency probably conjure up visions of trigonometry and physics, but—I promise!—there's nothing tough about this.

Sine Waves

To discuss signals in a bit more detail, I have to talk about another potentially scary topic—sine waves. Take a look at Figure 21.2.

FIGURE 21.2

Sine waves

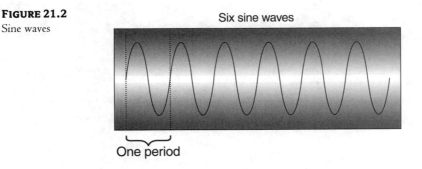

Six sine waves

One period

A wave starts anywhere, makes one upturn and one downturn (unless you start later in the signal, in which case it makes one downturn, *then* one upturn), and then ends up at the same height at which it started. That's one wave. But what does this have to do with data communications?

The imagery of waves works to describe signals because of the up-and-down (*periodic* is the more exact term) nature of waves. It turns out the sine wave is the building block of *all* waves.

What do I mean by *building block*? A mathematician by the name of Fourier proved that *any* wave phenomenon could be built by adding together the right series of waves. Finding the right series of waves to build any one signal isn't a simple task—it's called a *Fourier decomposition*—but it *can* be done with the right tools (read: computing power). I won't do Fourier decompositions in *this* book; I just want you to understand why sine waves are so important to any study of signals. To see an example of sine waves adding up to a signal, look at Figure 21.3, which shows many sine waves superimposed on one another.

FIGURE 21.3
Several sine waves
superimposed upon
one another

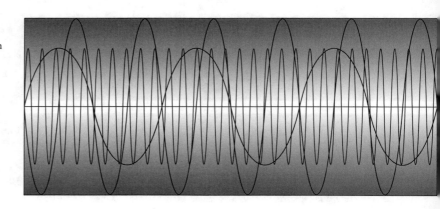

Notice that some jump up and down more quickly, some reach higher or lower, and some stretch a bit farther left and right, but they're all sine waves. In Figure 21.4, you can add them all together.

FIGURE 21.4
Sum of the sine
waves in Figure 21.3

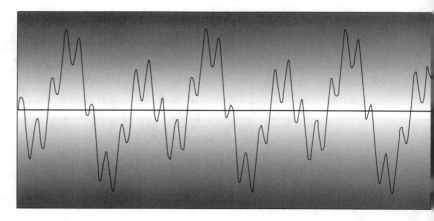

The sum is no longer anything like a sine wave. Any signal, no matter how bizarre, can be broken down into sine waves, which is why they're so important to a good understanding of signaling limitations. With that in mind, you'll now look at two aspects of a sine wave—amplitude and frequency.

Amplitude

This should be a familiar concept because we talk about amplitude all the time—it's just called *loudness* or *volume*.

In human voice communications, volume carries meaning, such as urgency, or it may be used so that a voice will carry far. From a sine wave's perspective, *amplitude* means *height*. Take a look at Figure 21.5.

FIGURE 21.5
Amplitudes of
sine waves

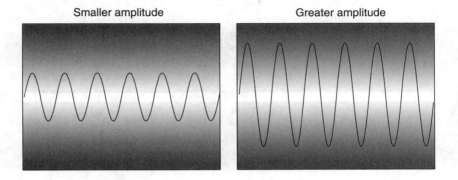

Smaller amplitude   Greater amplitude

In signals, amplitude also relates to *power* used for transmission. When transmitting data, communications engineers must overcome the fact that transmitting data over a distance reduces a signal's amplitude, weakening it or *attenuating* it. You can partially restore a signal by *amplifying* it; all an amplifier does is try to boost the amplitude of the signal.

Communications systems use power, or amplitude, to describe two things:

- The raw transmission power of the communications medium

- Perhaps more important, the *clarity* of the communications medium—a ratio of the power of the noise to the power of the signal, known as the *signal-to-noise ratio*

Frequency

The other sine wave characteristic is its frequency. *Frequency* describes how often a wave goes up and down in a given time. You can see this in Figure 21.6.

In this figure, you see two waves diagrammed over the course of one second. The top wave goes up and down 12 times in that second, the bottom one only 6 times. That means that the top wave has a higher frequency.

Frequency is measured in *cycles per second*, which is abbreviated CPS, or, more commonly, the term *hertz* is used. Hertz is a unit that means, as you'd guess, "cycles per second" and is named after Heinrich Hertz, who was a German physicist. Hertz is usually abbreviated as Hz. Look back at Figure 21.5, and you'll see that the two waves in that picture have the same frequency. Conversely, the two waves in Figure 21.6 have the same *amplitude* but different frequencies.

Frequency corresponds to *pitch* in the sounds you hear. Higher frequencies sound like higher pitches. If you say that someone has a high-pitched voice, you mean that person has a voice that produces a range of frequencies whose average is somewhat high, as human voices go.

FIGURE 21.6

Comparative frequency of two sine waves

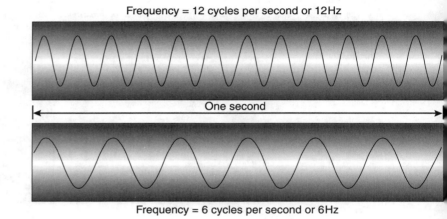

Frequency = 12 cycles per second or 12Hz

One second

Frequency = 6 cycles per second or 6Hz

Signals to Bits: Sampling

For your sound card to use a sound, the sound has to be converted from its analog self into a more bit-friendly format. The main method of converting analog sounds into digital is called *sampling*. (Before I learned how this was done, I called it *digitizing* the audio. I've since learned that expert types always say *sampling*, so file that in your list of good-stuff-to-know-at-cocktail-parties, and *never* say *dig itizing*.) It's done with a method called Pulse Coded Modulation (PCM).

Suppose you're trying to convert the simple analog signal shown in Figure 21.7 into digital.

Under PCM, the signal is sampled many times per second, and the height of the wave is recorded. (Actually, what's recorded is the *logarithm* of the height—remember that sound volume is perceived logarithmically.) You can see an example of sampling in Figure 21.8.

The lines represent the height of the signal at various times. It's impossible to measure the height of the signal at all times, so you can measure only a limited number of samples per second—hence the *sampling* name.

That doesn't seem like a lot of information about the signal in Figure 21.8, and it isn't. To get a better picture of how to reconstruct the original audio signal, you'd do better to get more samples in the same time period, as you see in Figure 21.9.

This underscores an important point, which is emphasized in Figure 21.10: more samples mean a higher-quality signal once reproduced. At the top of Figure 21.10, you can see an original signal for a second's duration. Below that is the result of sampling it 20 times in that second and the result of sampling it 40 times per second.

FIGURE 21.7
A simple analog
signal

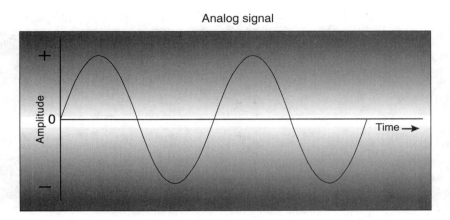

FIGURE 21.8
Sampling a signal

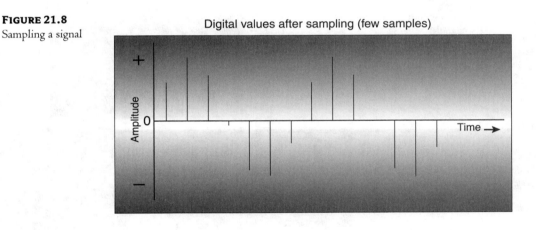

There are more values in the more frequently sampled signal, so the reconstructed signal will be of higher quality.

How many samples do you need per second? For the answer to that, you need to turn to Nyquist's theorem. It says that to completely capture a signal, you've got to have N samples, where

$$N = 2 \times \text{signal bandwidth}$$

FIGURE 21.9
Reconstructing the original audio signal by getting more samples

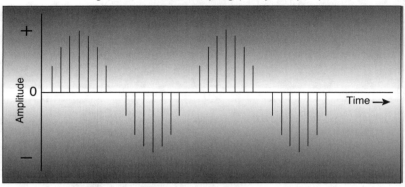

Digital values after sampling (many samples)

FIGURE 21.10
Having more samples equals a higher-quality reproduction of the signal.

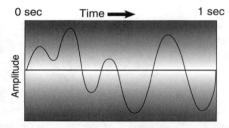

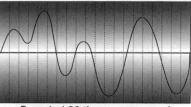

Sampled 20 times per second

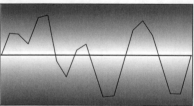

Sampled 20 times per second

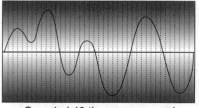

Sampled 40 times per second

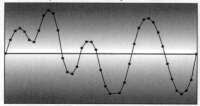

Sampled 40 times per second

The bandwidth of our ears is considered to be well within a 22,050Hz range. Twice that would be 44,100 samples per second, which is the sampling rate of a music CD. Higher sampling means more data must be stored per second. Sampling rates are expressed in kilohertz, so you would typically see that sampling rate expressed as 44.1 kilohertz (KHz). Sampling rate is sometimes called *frequency* in some specifications and reference books, but it's a different meaning of the word than earlier in the chapter. In this case, it refers to the number of times per second that the sound is sampled, not the pitch of the sound itself.

But that's not all there is to sampling with PCM. Suppose the recorded values can range from −127 to +128, and they can be only integers. Because the total possible number of values is only 256, each signal value is encoded with 8 bits.

Why not use 16 bits per sample? Using 16 bits would allow for many more nuances of sound—65,536 values for 16 bits compared to 256 for 8 bits—but it doubles the amount of data needed to store a given audio signal. Of course, with the size of today's hard disks, there's little stopping you from using 16-bit encoding, at least as far as space goes. You can see the difference in bit sample sizes in Figure 21.11.

Music CDs sample 16 bits per sample, or 44,100 samples per second. For most voice and music uses, 16 bits is fine, which yields about as much quality as the human ear can directly perceive. High-end sound cards can sample up to 24 bits per sample, at a sampling rate of up to 96KHz.

FIGURE 21.11

The difference in bit sample sizes

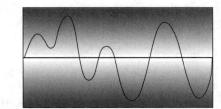

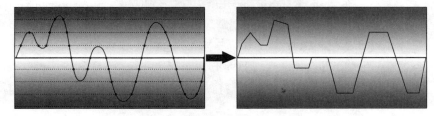

8-bit: ranges from −127 to +128

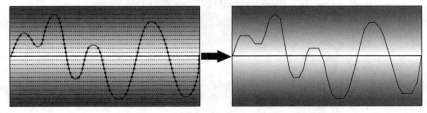

16-bit: ranges from −32707 to +32708

NOTE *It's typical of a high-end card to be able to play back (that is, convert digital to analog) at a higher sampling rate than it records (that is, converts analog to digital). For example, a card that records in 24/96 (that is, 24-bit at 96KHz) may be able to play back at up to 192KHz in stereo mode.*

Sound Card Characteristics

Sound cards vary according to many factors, including the number of bits used for sampling, the maximum sampling rate, the wavetable synthesis, quality measurements such as harmonic distortion and signal-to-noise ratio, and the internal and external ports they offer. This section explains those options

Number of Bits

First, I'll clear up a bit of confusion (no pun intended!). All Peripheral Component Interconnect (PCI) sound cards use the 32-bit PCI interface, and in that sense they all are 32-bit cards. However, this isn't what I mean when I talk about the number of bits of a sound card!

Instead, the number of bits when talking about sound cards refers to the number of bits used to record each sample. As you learned earlier in the chapter, 8-bit recording has only 256 possible values for each sample, which isn't as good as the more modern default of 16-bit recording (65,536 possible values). High-end sound cards today offer 24-bit sound, which provides more than 16.8 million possible values.

Maximum Sampling Rate

The more times per second an analog waveform is sampled, the more accurate the digital representation of it will be. Turn back to the section "Signals to Bits: Sampling" section earlier in the chapter for a reminder if needed.

Modern sound cards can sample analog recordings at rates of up to 96KHz, but you probably won't want to record at that frequency often because of the huge file sizes produced. More likely, you'll choose one of the preset sampling rates in your recording software such as the following:

CD quality   44,100Hz sampling rate, 16 bits per sample

Radio quality   22,050Hz sampling rate, 8 bits per sample

Telephone quality   11,025Hz sampling rate, 8 bits per sample

FM and Wavetable Synthesis

Sampling works well for recording sounds from analog sources, but to assemble entirely new sounds through an all-digital interface such as a MIDI device, the PC needs a way to tell a sound card, "Play an *A* as it would sound on a harpsichord." The oldest method is to use Frequency Modulation (FM) synthesis.

I'm simplifying here, but the idea behind FM synthesis is that musical sounds follow a four-part cycle, as you see in Figure 21.12.

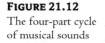

FIGURE 21.12

The four-part cycle of musical sounds

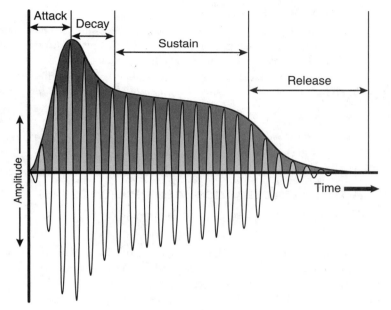

The notion in FM synthesis is to describe an instrument's waveform in terms of the size of the Attack, Decay, Sustain, and Release (ADSR) parts of the cycle. These four elements are generally the basis for sound in terms of waveforms. *Attack* is the speed at which a sound begins. *Decay* describes how the sound begins to release. *Sustain* describes the actual length of the sound. And finally, *release* describes when the note is "turned off."

FM synthesis does an imperfect job of reproducing actual instrument sounds and has been eclipsed in the past decade by a newer, better method called *wavetable synthesis*. Modern sound cards avoid having to artificially reproduce instrument sounds by storing actual waveform sound clips of various instruments playing various notes. When a piece of digital music calls for a certain instrument to play a certain note, the corresponding sound clip loads from the sound card's Read-Only Memory (ROM) and plays through the speakers.

Nowadays all sounds cards—even the really cheap ones—have some wavetable synthesis support. The main differentiating factors are hardware versus software clips and the number of simultaneous voices.

Hardware versus Software Wavetable Recordings

Sound cards that support wavetable synthesis store at least 1 megabyte (MB) of sound clips on ROM chips on the card itself. This is *hardware wavetable* support. In addition, the sound card may come with software that, when installed, stores additional wavetable clips on the hard disk and uses the operating system's driver for it to channel them through to the sound card when needed. This is called *software wavetable* support. On a fast, modern computer, software wavetable support is perfectly adequate.

Number of Voices

A *voice* is a single note from a single instrument (or simulation of an instrument). For example, if the sound card is reproducing a three-note chord on a piano through a MIDI clip, that's three voices. If a cello is also playing at the same time, that's a total of four voices. If a whole orchestra is also playing at the same time, that's many more voices—perhaps 50 or more. Modern sound cards support 64 simultaneous voices (also called *64-voice polyphony*). Older sound cards supported only 32.

NOTE *There was some confusion when the SoundBlaster 64 sound card first hit the market, offering 64 voices. Because its predecessor was called the SoundBlaster 16, and the 16 referred to the number of bits, some people wrongly assumed that the SoundBlaster 64 was a 64-bit card.*

Audio Performance Measurements

There are three main measurements of a sound card's performance to be used in comparing one card to another:

Frequency response   This is the range of pitches that the sound card can support. Cards don't need to support sounds outside of a human's range of hearing, but some of the better ones do anyway. Human range is between 16Hz and 20,000Hz, and a high-end sound card might support a range of 10Hz to 46,000Hz.

Harmonic distortion   This is the measurement of the accuracy of sound reproduction. It has to do with the nonchipset parts of the sound card; a more cheaply manufactured card might have more harmonic distortion than a better-quality one, even if they both used the same chipset. It's measured in percentages; a high-end sound card might have a measurement of about 0.004 percent.

Signal-to-noise ratio   This is the measurement of how little (or much) noise you get (that is, hiss or static) in relationship to the volume of the output. A high-end card should have a high ratio (more than 100 decibels). Lesser cards will have a lower number.

Inputs and Outputs

What types of input and output ports do you want on your sound card? "The right ones!" is the obvious answer. In other words, you want the ones that happen to correspond to the devices you want to hook up to it. High-end cards will have more ports, of course, and ports that correspond to higher-end external equipment.

If you plan to hook up an external stereo system to your sound card, be aware that most of the entry-level sound cards use ⅛-inch stereo minijacks for line-level audio input and output, and most stereo systems use RCA jacks. That means that hooking the two systems together will involve an adapter cable from your stereo's left and right RCA jacks to your PC's single stereo minijack. Some sound cards have separate left and right minijacks so you can run separate cables from stereo to sound card for the two channels.

High-end sound cards support more ports than will fit on that little backplate on the card, so they include an extra set of ports either on an add-on circuit board that connects to the sound board or (more commonly today) on a panel that mounts in a 5¼-inch drive bay in the PC and then connects to the sound card via a cable. Another alternative is represented by the SoundBlaster Extigy box, which takes over the entire functionality of a sound card in an externally connected box that has more different kinds of Input/Output (I/O) ports than you probably knew existed, including all the ports you'll need for direct connection to a stereo system.

One of the ports that's becoming increasingly common on mid-to-high-end sound cards is Sony/Philips Digital Interface Format (S/PDIF), a digital interface found both as input and output jacks. Using digital input and output produces much higher-quality sound than the sound that has to be converted (on your audio card) from native digital to analog—and then, depending on the other device, back again. Digital jacks can be either coax (using an RCA jack and 75-ohm cable) or optical (using a TOSLink connector and fiber-optic cable); most cards opt for the lower-cost coax connectors. You can run the S/PDIF output and input to and from MiniDisc (MD) and Digital Audio Tape (DAT) recorders; if your PC includes a DVD player, you can also use the digital outputs to send surround-sound signals to a home theater system equipped with Dolby Digital surround processing. (Most stand-alone CD players, for copy-protection purposes, don't include any digital outputs.)

TIP   *If you want to use the S/PDIF digital connections, make sure that your sound card includes the same type of jack (either coax or optical) used by your other audio equipment. Not all sound cards include both types of S/PDIF jacks.*

If you want your PC to play and record music (or feed sequenced music to synthesizers and other musical instruments), then you'll probably want a sound card that includes MIDI In and MIDI Out jacks. Low-end sound cards interface with MIDI devices through the joystick port. (In fact, on many of these the joystick port is labeled Joystick/MIDI). The joystick port is a 15-pin female D-sub connector on the sound card. At the higher end, a sound card will include a separate 5-pin DIN connector for MIDI.

To play sound from an audio CD-ROM through the PC's speakers, you must connect the CD-ROM drive to the sound card directly with an audio cable. This is typically a small round cable with a Berg connector on it, as in Figure 21.13. This has nothing to do with the operating system, Random Access Memory (RAM), or the Central Processing Unit (CPU)—it's a direct bypass that feeds audio from the CD directly to the sound card and from there to the speakers.

FIGURE 21.13
Berg connector
on a cable

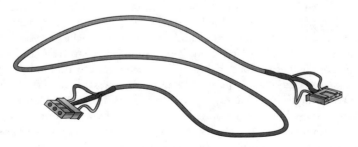

TIP   *If you want to play an audio CD through the speakers but you don't have an audio cable, or you can't open up the PC's case for some reason, you can fake it by running a cable from the headphone jack on the front of the CD drive to the Line In input on the sound card.*

Speaker Systems

All this sound stuff is of no value unless you have some speakers through which to hear it. You *can* run some sound cards through the internal PC speaker, but *don't*: most built-in speakers are monaural and of low quality.

Low-end add-on speakers you buy will most likely be a set of two stereo speakers. They can either be externally powered or run off the sound card's output, but try to get the externally powered ones if possible. Unpowered speakers won't produce much volume. Low-end powered speakers that run on batteries are available for less than $20; better ones that run on Alternating Current (AC) power start at $20 and go up from there.

WARNING   *Don't place speakers near the PC that aren't designed for computer usage because they're probably unshielded speakers. In other words, the magnets inside the speakers may interfere with magnet-sensitive components such as monitors and disks.*

Many speaker systems that come with mainstream PCs these days also include a *subwoofer*, which is a separate amplifier box into which the smaller speakers connect. The subwoofer connects to the sound card and then parcels out the sound signals to the individual stereo speakers.

Of course, if you're interested in a true surround-sound experience (especially nice if you're playing games that utilize so-called 3D audio or watching DVD movies that include surround-sound soundtracks), you need more than two speakers. Just as a surround-sound system for a home theater system includes at least four speakers (plus a separate subwoofer), surround-sound systems for PCs include two front and two rear speakers, plus a subwoofer—and possibly a fifth center-channel speaker, for movie surround-sound. If you decide to go this route, make sure your sound card has a S/PDIF digital output and that you can figure out an efficient way to run cabling from the front to the rear of your computer workspace. Speaker sets are available that support Dolby Digital 4.1, 5.1, 6.1, and 7.1 for computer systems. (Make sure your sound card supports the corresponding technology.)

For the ultimate in sound reproduction, consider routing the sound from your PC to a separate, free-standing audio or home theater system. Look for sound cards that have the appropriate line-level RCA jack outputs (or relegate yourself to using an RCA-to-miniplug adapter) and then connect these to a free set of inputs on your stereo or audio/video receiver. (Make sure your cables are long enough to run from one unit to the other!) Alternately, if your sound card has an S/PDIF digital output, you can funnel this signal to the digital input on any audio/video receiver with Dolby Digital surround-sound decoding. Although Windows' bleeps and bloops don't necessarily need this deluxe treatment, it's a joy to hear CDs and audio files in a way that only a full-sized system can deliver.

Sound quality isn't the only thing to consider when shopping for speakers. Today's computers come in a range of shapes and colors, and the same is true of speaker sets. You'll now see a variety of shapes and sizes that are more visually appealing and less "boxy" than the speakers of old. You'll find materials from clear to opaque and in an assortment of colors. Shapes range from streamlined and smooth to more artistic and sculptured.

Installation Tips

Installing a sound card isn't particularly tricky. Insert it in a PCI slot, the same as any other PCI expansion board. The trickiest part can be hooking up the cables to its I/O ports (that is, figuring out what plugs in where), but the card instructions and color-coding should guide you.

If you're installing an Industry Standard Architecture (ISA) sound card, there may be some issues with resource assignment if you have a full system already. An ISA card will require at least one Direct Memory Access (DMA) channel, for example, as well as at least two Interrupt Requests (IRQs). If it's a Plug and Play (PnP) card, motherboard, and operating system, the resource assignments should happen automatically, but if one or more components of PnP are lacking, you might need to set jumpers on the card. Chapter 23, "Hardware Management via Software Solutions," covers resource issues in detail.

If you're installing a very old sound card or installing a new sound card in an older version of Windows (such that the card is newer than the Windows version), you might need to run the Setup software for the sound card to complete its installation. Windows may detect the card imperfectly or not at all, necessitating a "jump start" that the Setup program will provide with its driver install.

Selecting Among Multiple Sound Devices

Normally a PC will have only one sound card (or built-in support on the motherboard for sound and no actual sound card at all). If you install a new sound card, you'll typically remove the old one, or if it's built-in, you'll disable it in Basic Input/Output System (BIOS) Setup.

However, there may be cases where removing or disabling the old sound system isn't possible or desirable. In such cases, you can install a second (or more) sound card without removing or disabling the first one. However, if you do that you must tell Windows which one you want to use for various tasks. You do this through the sound controls in the Control Panel.

The exact name of the applet in the Control Panel where you select the sound devices varies depending on the Windows version:

- **Windows 95 and 98**: Multimedia

- **Windows Me and 2000**: Sounds and Multimedia

- **Windows XP and 2003 Server**: Sounds and Audio Devices (or Sounds, Speech, and Audio Devices in Category view)

Figure 21.14 shows Windows XP. Notice that there are separate tabs for Audio and Voice, each with their own separately selectable preferred devices for input and output. Open the drop-down lists, and select the preferred device for each activity.

FIGURE 21.14
Select the preferred sound device for various sound activities through the Control Panel.

Troubleshooting Sound

Having problems with your sound system? The following sections offer some advice.

Installation Problems

So you've installed your new sound card, and it's not working. This is actually no big surprise; in my experience, sound cards are one of the more persnickety components to install.

PHYSICAL CONNECTIVITY AND POWER

The first thing to do—as you should with any new card you install in your PC—is to double-check all the connections. Make sure the card is seated properly and that all connections, both internal and external (to your speakers, for example), are solid. Also make sure you have the speakers plugged into the correct plug! On color-coded sound cards, the speaker plug is usually black or green. Next, make sure the speakers are plugged in (if powered by AC) or have good batteries in them (if battery-powered), they're turned on, and the volume is turned up.

DRIVER INSTALLATION AND RESOURCE USAGE

Check whether your computer system is configured properly for your sound card. Make sure you have the correct drivers installed and that you're using the latest, most up-to-date versions of those drivers. (When in doubt, check the manufacturer's Web site for new drivers, patches, and other utilities.) In Windows versions prior to XP, and with off-brand sound cards, it's common for Windows not to fully accept the sound card until you run the Setup software that came with it to install a driver. Windows may partly recognize the card, or might see it as an "Unknown Device," but the driver installation is required to make it start working. So much for PnP, huh?

To test a sound card, force it to make a sound. An easy way to do this: go into the Sound properties in the Control Panel, and go to the Sounds tab. Select one of the sounds and try to play it by clicking the Play button (the right-pointing triangle). If, after these basic checks, you're still having sound problems, chances are that you have some sort of port, IRQ, or DMA conflict with your sound card. Conflict problems are tough to track down, but the tools discussed in Chapter 24, "Using the Internet for Hardware Support," can help you find and fix any resource-related conflicts.

Performance Problems

Let me preface this section by saying, "You get what you pay for." In other words, if you buy a $19 sound card, you're not allowed to complain too bitterly if it doesn't sound very good. However, there are some adjustments you can make to improve a "bad sound" situation in some cases.

BUZZING OR FEEDBACK

Cheap sound cards aren't always the best-shielded cards available. This means that high-frequency interference from other components in your system can be a problem, in the form of an annoying buzz or hum. If you're experiencing this sort of problem, try repositioning the cards in your computer to separate the sound card from another card or another component generating the interference. (If you have the space, leave empty the slots on either side of your sound card.) You may even want to place a thin strip of aluminum sheeting around your sound card (being careful not to touch any other component with the sheeting) to better shield the card from interference. Of course, spending a few more bucks on a higher-quality sound card will also fix this problem.

OVERALL POOR QUALITY

Poor quality audio can also be the result of cheap speakers. The greatest sound card in the world isn't going to give you the sound you want if you hook up some cheap unpowered speakers to it. Match the sound card and the speakers in quality level to avoid wasting the capabilities of either one.

VOLUME TOO SOFT

Volume comes from the "powered" part of the powered speakers equation. No power means less maximum volume. Some speakers will work with either AC or DC power. Such speakers usually work better on AC than on batteries, so use the AC adapter whenever possible. And of course, if the speakers will work in powered or unpowered modes, you always want to use powered.

CD AUDIO WON'T PLAY

If system sounds are fine but audio CDs don't play, you probably forgot to install the audio cable between the sound card and the CD-ROM drive.

CERTAIN INPUT PORTS SEEM DEAD

On some systems, the Mic input or other input ports are set to Off or Mute by default. If you aren't getting anything from a microphone, check to make sure it's attached to the proper port, then open the Volume control in Windows, and choose Options ➤ Properties. In the dialog box that appears, choose Recording and click OK. You'll see the volume levels for inputs then, and you can make a note of whether there's a checkmark in the Select check box for the microphone (or other input device you're trying to use).

BAD SOUND IN CERTAIN PROGRAMS ONLY

This is usually a game-related issue. Perhaps system sounds in Windows are fine, but when you try to play a particular game, you get crackling and hissing or no sound at all. This is probably an issue with the sound API. If it's using Microsoft DirectSound, the DirectX Troubleshooter utility may be helpful. Choose Start ➢ Run, type **DXDIAG**, and click OK, and then on the Sound tab, click Test DirectSound and follow the on-screen prompts.

Summary

In this chapter, you learned how PCs and sound work together and how to select, install, and troubleshoot a sound card. In the next chapter, you'll look at the other side of the coin, moving from sound to pictures. Chapter 22, "Digital Imaging," discusses digital imaging, including interfacing with digital cameras and managing digital images in Windows.

Chapter 22

Digital Imaging

Introduction

These days digital cameras are rivaling traditional 35 millimeter (mm) cameras in popularity; it seems like everyone from the local antique shop staff to my neighbor's great grandmother is snapping digital pictures. With this explosion in the popularity of digital imaging devices, there's a loud clamoring for convenient ways to store these images and transfer them from camera to PC. One of the most innovative and popular solutions to emerge is Flash RAM. (Flash RAM is actually used in many other types of devices besides cameras, but that's the most popular use in the consumer mainstream.)

This chapter begins by explaining how Flash RAM works and the various formats in which you'll find it for sale, both for digital cameras and for other types of devices. Then the chapter covers digital camera features and operation, and it explains how to manage digital camera interaction with a PC and how to troubleshoot any problems you may encounter.

QuickSteps: Connecting a Digital Camera

Most digital cameras today have either a Universal Serial Bus (USB) or FireWire (IEEE 1394) interface and connect quickly and easily to a PC for transferring their data. The process is so easy that you probably don't need these steps, but this section will confirm your thinking. For in-depth coverage on how to troubleshoot problems with different types of flash memory devices, refer to the section "Common Problems and Solutions" later in this chapter.

BE PREPARED

Before you start, there are some things you may need on hand. These include the following:

◆ Camera documentation or user manual

◆ Flash memory card (in camera) containing the pictures you've taken

◆ USB or FireWire cable (which probably came with the camera)

To connect a digital camera, follow these steps:

1. Connect the cable to the camera. Refer to the camera's manual if needed.

2. Turn on the camera.

3. If needed, flip any switches or press any buttons on the camera that put it into a PC interface mode. Refer to the camera's manual if needed.

4. Connect the cable to the PC, either to the USB or the FireWire port as appropriate.

5. Windows should recognize the camera's Flash RAM card as a new drive and assign it a drive letter. Double-click that drive letter in My Computer to browse the pictures.

6. Use the My Computer interface to transfer the pictures to your hard disk or other disk on your system.

7. Optionally, delete the pictures from the camera. (Delete them from the camera's "drive letter.")

8. Disconnect the camera from the PC. Press any buttons or flip any switches on the camera needed to put it back into normal camera mode. Then turn it off.

Flash RAM Basics

Flash RAM (also called flash memory) is the primary means by which digital cameras store their pictures. Flash RAM technology stores data on tiny, nonvolatile chips and cards that can easily be transported from one device to another.

Flash RAM is a type of Static RAM (SRAM). Unlike the Dynamic RAM (DRAM) used as the main memory in a PC, SRAM retains whatever is placed in it until it's changed. This gives it the stability of Read-Only Memory (ROM) but the changeability of DRAM. It takes very little electricity to read and write from Flash RAM, and because it has no moving parts, it isn't subject to physical failure as disks are.

The nonvolatile nature of flash memory makes it ideal for long-term data storage in portable electronics devices. When you take a picture with your digital camera, for example, that file is stored on a flash memory device, typically a CompactFlash or SmartMedia card. The data stays on the card, even when you turn off your camera or remove the card from the camera. When next you use the camera, or when you plug the card into a card reader (attached to your PC), the digital file is still there, ready to use.

NOTE   *All erasable memory, including flash memory, is limited to a finite number of write/erase cycles. Early designs were only good for tens of thousands of cycles; today's flash memory can be written and erased more than a million times without a degradation in data integrity.*

How Flash RAM Stores Data

Flash memory is actually a variation of electrically Erasable Programmable Read-Only Memory (EEPROM). The big difference between the two is that EEPROM can be erased and rewritten at the byte level; flash memory can erase or reprogram blocks of bytes, not individual bytes.

Like all RAM, flash memory stores its data in cells within a memory chip. As you can see in Figure 22.1, a flash memory chip has a grid of columns and rows; each intersection is a cell, and each cell contains two transistors, separated from each other by a thin oxide layer. The first transistor, called the *floating gate*, accesses a row (called a *wordline*) via the second transistor, called the *control gate*.

FIGURE 22.1
Changing the value of a flash memory cell

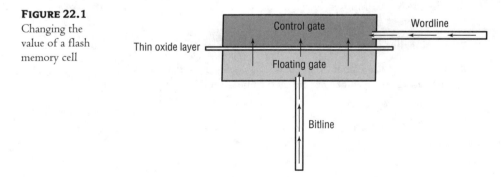

The default value of an empty cell is 1. Changing this value is done through a process called *Fowler-Nordheim tunneling*. In this process, a small electrical charge, about 10–13 volts (v), is applied to the floating gate. This charge (which comes from the column, or *bitline*) causes the floating gate to act like an electron gun and direct a flow of negatively charged electrons to the other side of the oxide layer. These electrons effectively act as a barrier between the control gate and the floating gate, breaking the connection (closing the gate) and changing the cell's value to 0. A cell's value can be returned to 1 by the application of a higher-voltage charge. This is how the pixels of a digital image are stored in flash RAM.

NOTE   *The memory cells in a flash memory device can be arranged in either a serial or a parallel fashion. The serial arrangement is called NAND flash memory; the parallel arrangement is called NOR.*

Another defining characteristic of flash memory is that it's erased and reprogrammed in large chunks, called *blocks*. (Other types of memory are erased at the byte level.) That's where the name comes from, by the way; you erase one of these memory chips "in a flash" by working with large blocks of data. Erasing large blocks is faster than erasing individual bytes.

Why Not Replace *All* Disks with Flash RAM?

By storing large amounts of memory—anywhere from several megabytes to 1 gigabyte (GB)—on a single chip, flash memory is starting to rival hard disks for sheer storage capacity. And because it's all done electronically, access times are typically faster for memory-based storage than they are for disk-based storage—and the amount of physical space required is significantly less.

So if flash memory can store data like a hard disk—but faster, and in a smaller physical space— why not replace your computer's hard disk with a flash memory device?

The answer is simple. It's because of the price.

Today's super-big hard disk drives cost less than $0.01 per megabyte of storage. A typical flash memory device, such as a CompactFlash or SmartMedia card, costs between $0.60 and $0.90 for that same megabyte of storage. So you *could* use flash memory as your primary storage medium, but it would cost you dearly.

That said, the cost of flash memory is acceptable when you need to store lots of data in a small physical space—such as in a digital camera, a Personal Digital Assistant (PDA), or a portable MP3 player. You can't put normal hard disks in these devices (both because of size and because of ruggedness), but you can use flash memory.

And, in fact, it's in these portable devices that flash memory really shines.

NOTE   *Although normal hard disks are much bigger than flash memory cards, IBM's Microdrive is an honest-to-goodness hard drive that's the approximate size of a CompactFlash card. (The drive itself is just 1 inch in diameter.) Storage capacities range from 340MB to 1GB; you can buy the 1GB Microdrive for less than $300.*

Types of Flash RAM Devices

Several different types of storage media utilize flash memory technology. These media have several factors in common, including small physical size, low voltage requirements, and extreme portability and durability.

Most digital cameras use removable CompactFlash or SmartMedia cards to store pictures. This is useful because you can swap out the card with a blank one to keep taking pictures after your camera fills up; you don't need to take the camera back to the PC and dump off the pictures to the hard disk before taking more pictures.

Because of the removable nature of the flash RAM from the camera, various types of card readers have sprung up that'll enable you to read (and sometimes write) the Flash RAM card without the camera. You can also use the camera itself as a reader, though, by hooking up the camera directly to the PC via cable (as in the QuickSteps for this chapter).

There's a whole other category of Flash RAM devices that are self-contained, such as memory sticks. The Flash RAM is built into some little portable device that has a USB dongle on it that plugs into the USB port on any PC. Essentially it's an ultra-portable small drive that can replace a floppy drive's functionality.

In the following sections, I'll tell you about the various packaging for Flash RAM, including both the ones that are commonly found in digital cameras and the ones that stand alone.

BIOS Chip

Although the concept of using flash memory for large data storage is a relatively new one, flash memory has been used in personal computers almost from the dawn of the PC era. The computer's Basic Input/Output System (BIOS) code is held in flash memory, which is how your computer holds its settings even when it's powered off.

Flash memory makes updating your computer's BIOS chip relatively easy. When you make changes to your computer's settings, the new settings are "flashed" onto the BIOS, with the new data blocks overwriting the old data blocks in the chip's flash memory.

CompactFlash

CompactFlash (CF) cards are small, thin, square flash memory cards used in a variety of electronics devices, including portable PCs, handheld PCs, PDAs, digital cameras, digital voice recorders, set-top television boxes, and so on. Unlike SmartMedia, which is designed primarily for portable devices, CF is used in a variety of nonportable devices that need small, removable, high-capacity storage devices. Figure 22.2 shows a typical CF card from SanDisk Corporation, one of the primary manufacturers of flash memory devices.

Introduced in 1994, CF is fully compatible with the PC Card/PCMCIA format, so it can be used anywhere a PC Card can be used (with the proper physical adapter, of course). The original CF cards used an 8MB flash memory chip. Subsequent releases have expanded CF capacity all the way up to 2GB, with even higher capacity devices on the horizon. CompactFlash cards have a higher maximum transfer rate than many of the other types of cards, too—up to 20 megabytes per second (MBps) to and from the Flash RAM and up to 16MBps to and from the host.

Like SmartMedia cards, CF cards are widely used in digital cameras, as well as in various types of handheld PCs. CF cards differ from SmartMedia (discussed next) in that they're slightly larger and thicker, and they utilize a built-in controller chip.

FIGURE 22.2
A Compact
Flash card from
SanDisk—no bigger
than a couple
of tacks (photo
courtesy of SanDisk
Corporation)

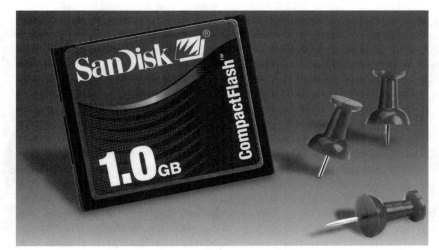

SMARTMEDIA

SmartMedia cards are small, lightweight, flash memory cards that are designed for portable digital devices. You can find SmartMedia cards used in digital cameras, portable MP3 players, PDAs, and other similar devices. SmartMedia cards are available in sizes ranging from 2MB to 128MB. Figure 22.3 shows a typical SmartMedia card. Not only does SmartMedia have a smaller maximum capacity than CompactFlash, but it also is slower—only about 2MBps maximum burst transfer from the Flash RAM.

SmartMedia cards also conform to the PC Card/PCMCIA format used by all of today's portable computers—which means you can use a simple PC Card adapter to insert a SmartMedia card into your laptop's PC Card slot.

NOTE *The original name for SmartMedia was Solid State Floppy Disk Card (SSFDC). The new name, SmartMedia, is a much better name, for marketing purposes, anyway. (It's also a registered trademark of Toshiba.)*

DIRECTV AND FLASH RAM

If you have a DIRECTV satellite system, your satellite receiver unit (the box that sits on top of your TV) has a slot for a CF card. It's a credit card–sized access card with an embedded Flash RAM chip. It stores your DIRECTV account information and must be inserted in the box before you can activate your system. (You can also take your card with you to another DIRECTV box—and take all your personal information with you.)

FIGURE 22.3
A SmartMedia card, used in digital cameras and other portable devices (photo courtesy of SanDisk Corporation)

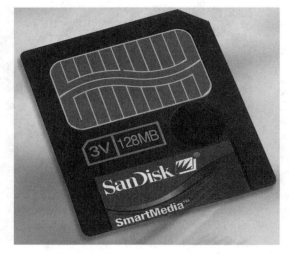

There are two different types of SmartMedia cards, operating at different voltages. Some equipment supports the 3.3v SmartMedia cards, other equipment supports 5v cards, and some devices support both. You can tell the voltage requirement of a SmartMedia card by the notch at the top of the card. If the notch is on the left side, it's a 5v card. If the notch is on the right, as in Figure 22.3, the card requires 3.3v.

The most popular use of SmartMedia technology today is in digital cameras. Although some cameras use CompactFlash cards (and Sony still clings to the memory stick format for most of its cameras), the majority of cameras today use SmartMedia cards to store their digital photos.

MEMORY STICK

The *memory stick* is a flash memory device used almost exclusively by Sony in its many different portable digital devices—digital cameras, portable MP3 players, CLI... handheld PCs, and so on. A memory stick is about the size and shape of a pack of chewing gum and can range in capacity from 16MB to 1GB.

Figure 22.4 shows a typical memory stick.

MULTIMEDIACARD

The MultiMediaCard (MMC) is a postage stamp–sized flash memory card, originally targeted at the mobile phone and pager markets. (It was, in fact, codeveloped by Siemens, one of the world's largest mobile phone manufacturers.) Because of its relatively high storage capacity, extremely small size, and miserly power consumption, it has found popularity in a variety of other devices, including digital video cameras, global positioning systems, portable MP3 players, and some newer PDAs. Figure 22.5 shows a typical MMC.

MultiMediaCards are available with capacities in the 8MB to 128MB range.

FIGURE 22.4
A memory stick storage device, used primarily in Sony electronics equipment (photo courtesy of SanDisk Corporation)

SECURE DIGITAL CARD

Secure Digital (SD) Cards build upon the MMC format with additional capacity and a digital copyright security scheme. As you can see in Figure 22.6, an SD Card has the same form factor as an MMC, except that it's a little thicker. (The extra thickness enables the security features.) SD Cards are finding widespread popularity in handheld PCs, such as the PalmPilot and the Compaq iPAQ.

The big thing about SD Cards is the built-in cryptographic security for the protection of copyrighted data. Because SD Cards comply with both current and future Secure Digital Music Initiative (SDMI) requirements, the SD Card is the favored storage format of the large music companies. Cards are available with capacities ranging from 8MB to 256MB.

All SD Card devices will accept existing MultiMediaCards, but the opposite isn't true; the thicker SD Card can't fit into the thinner MMC slots.

FIGURE 22.5
A MultiMediaCard, about the size of a postage stamp (photo courtesy of SanDisk Corporation)

FLASH USB DRIVES (PEN DRIVES)

The latest implementation of flash memory technology is in so-called flash USB drives. These "drives" are actually flash memory devices designed to function like removable disk storage. They're also called pen drives because they're elongated like a pen.

As you can see in Figure 22.7, these devices are small enough to be carried in your pocket or hung on your keychain, and they connect directly to the USB port on your computer. Flash USB drives typically weigh less than an ounce, and many are instantly recognized as a new disk drive by WindowsXP and other Plug and Play (PnP)–compatible operating systems. (Some of these devices require the installation of a software driver to work; others don't.)

FIGURE 22.6
An SD Card—which looks almost exactly like an MMC (photo courtesy of SanDisk Corporation)

FIGURE 22.7
Big disk storage in a small memory device—JMTek's Flash USBDrive

Some of the more popular of these miniature storages devices include the Q Drive (Agatè Technologies), Flash USBDrive (JMTek), DiskOnKey (M-Systems), FlashDio (FlashDioUSA), EasyDisk (EasyDisk USA), and ThumbDrive (TREK). These drives are currently available in 8MB–1GB sizes, priced from les than $30 to more than $500, depending on capacity. Many users find them a good substitute for the bulkier Zip drive or other removable storage.

PC CARD FLASH

Although most of the flash attention is on the smaller storage devices (CF, MMC, and so on), the *original* flash memory device came in the form of a larger PC Card (formerly PCMCIA). The advantage of PC Card flash, of course, is that you can use it in any device with a PC Card slot—which means in most laptop PCs and even some desktops. The extra size also enables larger storage capacities, so you can find PC Card flash cards with up to 5GB of storage.

TIP *You can also purchase PC Card adapters for CF cards. These devices enable you to use your CF cards in your computer's standard PC Card slot.*

CHOOSING A FLASH MEMORY TYPE

With so many flash memory options around, which format is right for your needs? Although the type of card you use is probably dictated by what slots your computer or other device has, you can also get a feel for the typical uses of each card from Table 22.1.

TABLE 22.1: TYPES OF CARDS

CARD TYPE	MAX. CAPACITY	DIMENSIONS (WIDTH HEIGHT × THICKNESS, IN MM)	TYPICAL USES
SmartMedia	128MB	37 × 45 × 0.76	Digital cameras, PDAs, MP3 players
MultiMediaCard	128MB	24 × 32 × 1.4	Mobile phones, pagers, digital cameras, MP3 players, PDAs
Secure Digital Card	256MB	24 × 32 × 2.1	Digital cameras, PDAs, MP3 players
Memory stick	1GB	21.5 × 50 × 2.8	Sony digital cameras, laptop PCs, PDAs
CompactFlash	2GB	43 × 36 × 3.3	Digital cameras, PDAs, MP3 players
Flash USB drive	1GB	Varies	Desktop and laptop computers
PC Card flash	5GB	54 × 85.6 × 3.3 (Type I), 5.0 (Type II), or 10.5 (Type III)	Laptop PCs

NONCOMPUTER USES FOR FLASH MEMORY

Obviously, flash memory—in the form of CompactFlash, SmartMedia, MultiMediaCards, and other media—is used in a variety of noncomputer devices. From digital cameras and camcorders to cordless phones and answering machines, flash media is an essential part of many of today's consumer electronics devices.

A future use of flash memory technology is the *Personal Tag* (P-Tag). Developed by SanDisk, the P-Tag is a removable electronic card capable of storing information about the person carrying it. Designed to be about the size of a quarter, the P-Tag could be used to store medical information about the wearer for hospitals and emergency medical personnel to use. (In fact, the P-Tag was originally developed for use by the U.S. military as a kind of universal ID card for military personnel.)

The brings us to the concept of the *smart card*. The smart card is a device that looks like a standard credit card but that actually contains an embedded microprocessor and/or flash memory chip. The card can thus be programmed to contain various types of data—your personal ID information, the balance in your checking account, and so on.

Although smart cards haven't caught on yet in the United States, they're big in Europe. The smart-card industry claims to have shipped more than one billion cards per year since 1998 for purposes as wide ranging as accessing pay phones, managing banking transactions, and providing identification for health-care services.

The data on a smart card can be read and written to via contact or contactless methods. A contact smart card requires insertion into a smart-card reader; a contactless smart card contains a small, embedded antenna and transfers data via a wireless connection.

The flash memory in most smart cards is typically small—no more than 256 kilobytes (KB). But that's enough to contain the basic numbers in a checking or credit account or your name, address, and other personal information.

By the way, the national ID card concept that's been tossed around in the wake of the 2001 terrorist attacks on the World Trade Center would utilize this type of smart-card device. If some people get their way, we'll all be carrying flash memory around in our pockets—or maybe even embedded under our skin!

Troubleshooting Flash RAM Devices

Because flash memory devices have no moving parts, there's not a lot of maintenance required to keep them operating in tip-top shape. Just make sure the contacts are clean and that you don't bend or break them.

That's not to say you can't run into problems with these devices. Let's take a quick look at some of the common problems you're likely to encounter when working with flash memory.

WORKING WITH DRIVERS

Most flash memory problems are driver related. Either the wrong drivers get installed, the drivers become corrupted, or somehow Windows doesn't recognize the device and its drivers. Fortunately, the latest generation of flash devices relies less heavily (or not at all) on drivers, being more fully PnP.

If you think you have a driver-related problem, the first thing to do is reinstall the original driver software. These files should be located on the installation disk or CD that came with your flash memory device. You can also check for updated versions of these drivers on the manufacturer's Web site.

Recognizing the Device

Some flash memory devices—flash USB drives, especially—are supposed to operate without the need to preinstall software drivers; Windows, theoretically, recognizes the device every time it's plugged into your PC. This USB-enabled device recognition actually works, sometimes. If you're finding that your system *isn't* recognizing your flash memory device, you'll probably need to consult the device's instruction manual and install the drivers anyway. (Also know that this automatic device recognition works only with newer operating systems, such as Windows XP; if you're using Windows 95, you'll definitely need to install drivers. And remember that Windows 95B and earlier don't support USB.)

NOTE *The vast majority of non-PC devices that use flash memory (digital cameras, MP3 players, and so on) have built-in support for the type of media they're designed for—no separate driver installation necessary.*

If you have all the correct drivers installed and your system *still* doesn't recognize your device, make sure you're connecting it correctly. It's not uncommon for users to insert SmartMedia or Compact-Flash cards upside down—and your system definitely won't recognize an upside-down device. (And it should go without saying that you need to insert the memory card firmly—but not forcefully—into the card reader or card slot; poorly seated cards are also a common problem.)

Formatting Cards

SmartMedia and CompactFlash cards need to be formatted before use—although most cards come preformatted from the factory. (You can also format a card to "quick clean" the existing data.) However, it's possible for the format on a card to become corrupted, which can cause the card to appear to malfunction. This can happen when the following occurs:

- A card is removed from a camera or other device before the camera has finished writing to the card.

- A camera is turned off before it has finished writing to the card.

- A camera's batteries run low or go dead.

- The wrong batteries are used in a camera or other device.

WARNING *Low batteries in a portable device (digital camera, MP3 player, and so on) will often result in flash memory devices not being recognized. Trying to use the device with low batteries could result in corrupted formatting or corrupted data on the memory device.*

When a card is unformatted, formatted incorrectly, or has a corrupted format, that card probably won't be recognized by your PC or other electronic device. Sometimes the card will be recognized but will be inaccessible; other times the card will cause some sort of warning light or error message to appear. In any case, when you have a problem accessing or reading a flash memory card (and all your other cards work fine), then you probably have a formatting problem.

If you suspect that a card's format has become corrupted, reformat the card according to the device's instructions. If the card is connected to your PC (via a card reader or while inserted into a PC Card slot), use My Computer to right-click the drive letter for that card and then select Format from the context menu.

It's also possible that your old card reader doesn't read the newest, highest-capacity cards. For example, suppose you have a very old MMC reader that has a 4MB card that works perfectly with it. You replace the card with a 128MB card, but it doesn't work. The problem may not be the card but that the card reader is unequipped to support that capacity. Check with the device manufacturer to find out what it supports. In some cases, there may be a driver update or a firmware patch for the reader that will increase its capabilities.

NOTE *You might get a little confused when you go to check the capacity of your new flash memory card. It's not unusual for the actual reported capacity to be a little less than the promised capacity. For example, a 64MB card might report 60.9MB of free space. Where did the other 3.1MB space go? In this instance, it's a matter of definitions. Remember that a megabyte is actually 1,048,576 bytes—not 1,000,000 bytes. However, most flash memory manufacturers count a megabyte as an even million bytes, which results in the discrepancy. (Divide the advertised 64MB by 1,048,576 and you get 60,972,656 bytes—or the reported 60.9MB.)*

Dealing with Multiple Flash Memory Devices

Not all devices use the same formatting for their flash memory cards. For example, Diamond Rio's MP3 players use SmartMedia cards but use a proprietary formatting for the flash memory—which means you can't take a card from your MP3 player and use it in your digital camera without reformatting or adapting it first.

SimpleTech provides a free utility to convert Rio-adapted SmartMedia cards back to the standard SmartMedia format. Go to `www.simpletech.com/support/drivers/Photo_Readers/rio-diag.exe` to download the file.

If you want to transfer data from one type of flash memory device to another, you *could* copy it to your hard disk first and then move the data to the second device. A more eloquent solution is presented by Addonics Technologies, which produces a neat little unit called the Pocket DigiDrive. This device connects to a single USB port on your PC and contains slots for most current types of flash devices—CompactFlash, SmartMedia, and memory sticks. You can plug in multiple flash devices and use the DigiDrive to copy data from one device to another, just as if they were separate drives on your computer system.

You might also want to strategize your equipment purchases around a specific type of flash card. Because these little buggers are pricey, it's nice if you can use the same cards in multiple devices—in your PDA, camera, and MP3 player, for example. That way, you can reuse your stash of cards and not have to make duplicate purchases in multiple formats.

Digital Cameras

Now that you're fully versed in Flash RAM technology, you'll turn your attention to the device that has done more than any other to bring Flash RAM usage into popular usage: the digital camera.

A digital camera works on basically the same principles as a scanner (see Chapter 18, "Understanding and Troubleshooting Scanners"). A Charged Coupler Device (CCD) measures the amount of light bouncing back into the lens when it's pointing at a particular location and records those varying amounts of light as digital values. For a color camera, it applies a color filter that makes it possible to separately record the red, green, and blue values.

Camera Features and Specifications

A quick trip down the digital camera aisle at your local electronics superstore will reveal scores of different models, ranging in price from less than $50 to more than $3000. What makes one different from another?

Resolution   The number of unique cells in the CCD in the camera form its maximum resolution. This determines the maximum number of total pixels in the image the camera produces. Very early digital cameras had resolutions of only about 640×480, but today's digital cameras can have maximum resolutions of 2048×1536 or more. The resolution of a digital camera is described in *mega pixels*, or millions of pixels. The megapixel number for a camera is derived by multiplying the maximum width by the maximum height. So, for example, a camera with 2048×1536 maximum resolution would have a total of 3,145,728 pixels, or 3.1 megapixels.

Lenses and zoom   High-end digital cameras have detachable lenses like regular 35mm cameras, so you can change lenses as desired. There are two kinds of zoom lenses found in digital cameras: optical and digital. Optical zoom is "real" zoom that uses a zoom lens. Digital zoom is simulated zoom through interpolation (that is, interjecting pixels between two existing ones by averaging their values) and isn't as good.

Storage media   Nearly all digital cameras today use some form of Flash RAM as their primary storage medium. A few cameras (mostly the older Sony Mavicas) use floppy disks rather than Flash RAM, but because floppies can hold less than 2MB of data, it's not an ideal method.

Traditional camera features   A high-end digital camera will have many of the features that photography experts associate with regular 35mm cameras, including adjustable aperture, focus, and exposure controls.

Interface to PC   Nearly all digital cameras are either USB or FireWire in their interface to the PC. If it's a USB interface, it could be either USB 1.1 or USB 2.0; as you learned in earlier chapters, USB 2.0 is faster (rivaling FireWire), but both the computer and the camera must support it or the interface will revert to USB 1.1 standards. Most PCs have a USB port, but if you've got a FireWire interface camera, you'll need a FireWire Input/Output (I/O) board.

Communicating with a Digital Camera in Windows

The way you interact with your camera through Windows depends upon the version of Windows you have.

With older versions of Windows, you may need to install software (which comes with the camera) that enables the camera to interface with Windows. There may be a step-by-step wizard to help you transfer the pictures to your hard disk, but it'll vary by camera manufacturer.

With Windows Me and Windows XP, there's a Scanner and Camera Wizard, which you also saw in Chapter 18 when I discussed scanners. You can use it to automate the process of browsing and transferring your photos through a standard interface that's the same no matter what kind of camera you have. You can browse the pictures on the camera, transfer selected ones to a disk, and then delete or retain the pictures on the camera.

Depending on the camera model, you might also be able to directly access the camera's "drive" (that is, its Flash RAM) from the My Computer window. Open My Computer, and if the camera is connected and Windows sees it, there may be a drive icon there for it. If so, you can open a file management window as if it were a regular drive and copy or move the picture files from it.

Image Management in Windows

This section applies no matter where your pictures came from—scanner, camera, downloads, or whatever. The newer versions of Windows make it much easier to browse pictures through the Windows Explorer/My Computer interface than previous versions did. Windows XP in particular is very strong. It has a Filmstrip view; in it, you can see a rather large preview of the selected image so you can browse picture files without opening them (see Figure 22.8).

FIGURE 22.8

Image management in Windows XP through the Filmstrip view

NOTE *Filmstrip view doesn't appear on the View menu for all folders; the folder has to be designated in Windows as a Photo Album—that is, as containing photos. To set this up for a folder, choose View ➤ Customize This Folder. Open the Use This Folder Type as a Template list, choose Photo Album, and then click OK.*

Windows 2000 isn't quite as strong as Windows XP for image management, but it does have an Image Preview mode that provides a preview pane for the selected picture to appear. It isn't enabled by default, but you can enable it by choosing View ➤ Customize This Folder and running the Customize This Folder Wizard. When prompted by the wizard to choose or edit a template, do so and select Image Preview as the template.

Windows 95 and 98 have no graphics-viewing modes. Windows Me has a graphics-viewing mode somewhat like the one in Windows 2000 but slightly more feature-rich. The procedure for setting it up under Windows Me are the same as that for Windows 2000.

Troubleshooting Camera Connectivity Problems

Most camera problems are connectivity problems. The camera works fine, and the PC works fine, but they can't communicate. The following are some tips for resolving those problems:

◆ Check cable connections for snugness (of course).

◆ Make sure Windows is able to recognize devices through the port you're trying to use. For example, if using a USB port, try some other USB device in that port to see if it works. If this is the first USB device you've ever used on this PC, make sure that Windows knows it has a USB port. Check in Device Manager (see Chapter 23, "Hardware Management via Software Solutions") to make sure the USB root hub is available. And remember, Windows 95B and earlier don't support USB.

◆ If you have a USB-aware version of Windows but your USB port doesn't show up in Device Manager, check BIOS Setup to make sure the USB port hasn't been disabled. Some people disable it to free up the Interrupt Request (IRQ) on a system that uses no USB devices.

◆ Some cameras have a button or switch that places them in a special mode for communicating with the PC. Check the camera instructions to find out.

◆ Most cameras must be powered on when connected to the PC in order to be seen. Some of them turn themselves on automatically when you connect them to a computer; others require you to manually power them on.

If the problem is the camera itself—that is, if it won't turn on, won't take pictures, and so on, consult the documentation for the camera and/or check the manufacturer's Web site. Troubleshooting at the PC end won't do you much good if you've got yourself a dead camera. The most common cause of a "dead camera" is a dead battery, so check the camera battery first before you go jumping to any conclusions.

In this chapter, you learned about Flash RAM and the many forms it takes in portable devices. You also learned about one of the most popular device types that employs Flash RAM—digital cameras. This chapter focused on the still type of camera—that is, ones that take still, static images. Next, we'll look into managing and troubleshooting hardware with software.

Part 5

Hardware Management and Troubleshooting

Chapter 23

Hardware Management via Software Solutions

- ◆ QuickSteps: Adding Hardware in Windows
- ◆ Installing Device Drivers
- ◆ Updating a Device Driver
- ◆ Understanding System Resources
- ◆ Working with Device Manager

Introduction

The hardware and software of a computer system are mutually dependent on each other. For a new piece of hardware to work, your software (in particular, your operating system) must be aware of the new device and must be configured appropriately. This means that whenever you're working on your system's hardware, you're also interfacing with the operating system—which introduces an extra level of complexity to the operation.

Because of this interrelationship between hardware and software, you need to be aware of and know how to use various configuration and system management utilities that are built into your operating system. If you know what you're doing, you can use these built-in Windows utilities to manage the installation and operation of your hardware and to track down any hardware-related problems that may develop.

QuickSteps: Adding Hardware to Windows

Adding hardware to Windows is usually fairly simple thanks to Plug and Play. Follow these steps.

BE PREPARED

Before you start, here are some things you may need on hand:

◆ Setup CD for the hardware device being installed

◆ Windows CD (might or might not be needed)

To add the hardware, follow these steps:

1. Install the new hardware physically, and start the computer. Windows may detect the new device automatically. If so, you're done.

2. If Windows doesn't detect the new device, run the software on the Setup CD that came with the device or download setup software from the manufacturer's Web site and run it. If Windows detects the new device, you're done.

3. If you're not sure whether Windows has detected the device, look for the device in Device Manager (from the System applet in the Control Panel). In Device Manager, double-click the device to view its properties and check its status:

   ◆ If the status shows the message *This device is working properly*, then you're done.

   ◆ If the device status reports a conflict, troubleshoot the resource conflict (as described later in this chapter).

   ◆ If the device doesn't appear in Device Manager, recheck its physical installation, including any jumpers or switches. Consider also the possibility of a physically defective device or an incompatibility with your version of Windows.

   ◆ If the new device replaces a removed device of the same type but the old device still appears in Device Manager, delete it from there (select it and press Delete).

4. If you can't make the device work, consult the manufacturer's Web site for driver updates and troubleshooting information.

Installing Device Drivers

Any piece of computer hardware is just a useless hunk of circuitry unless it can communicate with your PC's operating system. That communication happens through a *device driver*, which is a piece of software designed to serve as a translator interface between the operating system and the hardware. So, for example, if a certain piece of hardware is "Windows XP compatible," it means there's a Windows XP driver available for it.

Any hardware can work with Windows, given an appropriate driver and a way of physically connecting them and assigning system resources. Heck, you could even hook up your refrigerator to a PC and talk to it if the connectors and drivers were present. (You laugh, but that day is coming, sooner than you think.)

Okay, so what do I mean by *the right driver*? Two things:

♦ The driver is written for the exact make/model of device you have.

♦ The driver is written for the exact version of Windows you have.

Sometimes you can kludge your way through with a driver that doesn't meet both of these criteria, but not always.

So, when I talk about installing a piece of hardware in Windows, what I'm really talking about is installing the correct driver for it. Plug and Play (PnP) makes the process simple in many cases; in the rare cases where PnP doesn't work, you can fall back to manual techniques.

Understanding Plug and Play

PnP is a hardware identification system that enables the Basic Input/Output System (BIOS) and the operating system to immediately see new hardware and assign resources to it. In addition, if a driver is available for the device, PnP will try to install it in the operating system.

PnP requires three things to work:

♦ The BIOS on the motherboard must support PnP. Most motherboards made since 1995 or so do.

♦ The device itself must support PnP. Again, most made since 1995 or so do.

♦ The operating system must support PnP. Windows 98 and higher do; Windows 95 and NT 4 don't.

For a device to work in Windows, it has to have a compatible driver, of course, and this is a separate issue from whether it's PnP-capable. However, Windows (especially the recent versions) has built-in drivers (or drivers readily available on its Setup CD) for thousands of devices, so it may seem as if PnP is also providing a driver. It isn't. The PnP process looks for the driver and automates its installation if found, but it doesn't actually provide the driver.

Therefore, during the PnP detection process for new hardware, you might be prompted to insert a CD containing the needed driver. If Windows has a suitable driver built-in, it installs it; otherwise, it prompts you.

Installing New Hardware in Windows

When PnP works flawlessly, you start up the PC, and Windows detects the device, it installs a driver for it, and the device works. When it doesn't…well, see the following sections.

RESPONDING TO A PROMPT FOR A DRIVER

When a prompt appears for a driver, it means Windows doesn't have one for the device. You have three choices:

◆ You can insert a disk or CD containing the needed driver. If it can't find the file, a message will appear, and you might need to browse the disk or CD to locate the driver. For example, the CD that came with a device might have separate folders for each operating system version, and you might need to navigate to the correct folder.

◆ If you *can't* insert a disk or CD and click OK, a message will appear telling you that it still can't find the driver and allowing you to enter a path or browse for one. Browse to a location on your hard disk or other disk or CD that contains the needed driver. This works well when you've downloaded a driver to use.

◆ You can click Cancel to abort the PnP installation of the device and then run the setup software that came with the device. This is the best choice for devices that came with special software you need or want to use, such as a multifunction printer that has its own scan/fax/copy/print utility.

WARNING   The best driver for an older device might not be the one that came with it on CD. If there's a newer one on the manufacturer's Web site, you should use it instead. It doesn't hurt to check for one before installing a device. You can update the driver later if you prefer, as I'll explain later in the chapter.

SIGNED DRIVERS

A few years ago, one of the most common ways Windows could get screwed up was with third-party hardware to come with its own drivers that hadn't been tested well with all Windows versions. Windows 2000 and higher attempt to prevent such problems by preferring signed drivers. A *signed driver* is one that has a digital signature that certifies it has been tested with certain versions of Windows and proved to work, and that it hasn't been altered since the signature was granted. By installing only signed drivers, you can virtually eliminate driver-based system problems.

When you attempt to install a certain driver in Windows 2000 and higher, Windows checks to see if it's signed. If it is, the installation proceeds. If it's not, you see a warning box. You have the option of allowing the unsigned driver to be installed or aborting. (That is, unless your network administrator has clamped down on your security settings and made it impossible to install unsigned drivers.)

If you're installing an unsigned driver for a noncritical device such as a printer, scanner, or modem, it's no big deal. Prefer the signed driver, but if you don't have one, try the unsigned driver. It'll probably work. However, if you're installing an unsigned driver for some critical component such as the video card, beware. Back up your Registry first (using System Restore in Windows Me or XP or the Registry Editor in other versions), and don't do the install at all if there's any way you can possibly get your hands on a signed driver instead.

To control Windows' behavior in the face of an unsigned driver, do the following (these steps are for Windows XP, but Windows 2000 is similar):

1. From the Control Panel, double-click System.

2. Click the Hardware tab.

3. Click the Driver Signing button.

4. Choose a warning level, as in Figure 23.1.

5. Click OK.

FIGURE 23.1
Changing the warning level for unsigned drivers

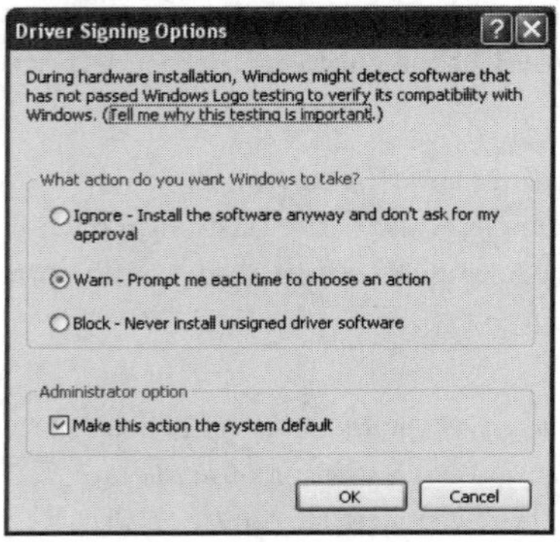

DON'T HAVE A DRIVER?

Earlier in the chapter I told you that the ideal driver is written for exactly your model of hardware *and* for exactly your Windows version. And ideally you'll have the latest one on a Setup CD that came with the device.

The ideal doesn't always happen. So the following are some ways around a no-driver situation, in order of preference:

◆ Go to the device manufacturer's Web site and download the correct driver, making sure you get the latest one for your operating system and your hardware model. Unpack and install it as recommended by the manufacturer. (It might be a Zip file, but it'll probably be a self-extracting EXE or an EXE Setup program.)

◆ Check other Web sites that might have the driver you need, such as WinDrivers (www .windrivers.com). Chapter 24, "Using the Internet for Hardware Support," is devoted to finding hardware support on the Internet.

NOTE   *Before going on to the next thing to try, I strongly recommend you do a backup of your Registry. In Windows XP and Me you can use System Restore; in other versions, you can go into the Registry Editor (regedit) and back up through there.*

◆   Look for a driver that's for this exact hardware device but the previous operating system version. Make sure you stay in the same operating system family. For example, if there's no Windows XP driver, try a Windows 2000 one (or even Windows NT 4 if it's your only hope). If there's no Windows Me driver, try a Windows 98 or 95 one.

◆   Look for a driver that's for the exact operating system version and for a similar hardware device. For example, if you're looking for a driver for a device with a model number of PXD387n, you might try a driver for model number PXD387 or PXD387a. Some model numbers change for certain retail channels; the hardware may be identical to some other model but happens to have a slightly different model number. See if you can find information about such variations at the manufacturer's Web site.

◆   As a last resort, look for a driver for the exact operating system (or one in the same family) for a device that uses the same chipset as your device. The chipset on the main board of the device determines its internal workings, and often multiple manufacturers will buy the same chipset and slap their own brand on the device. For example, S3 is a popular manufacturer of video card chipsets, and almost any video card that uses that chipset will be able to function at least at a basic level with a driver designed for any of the other S3-based video cards.

Notice the words *last resort* in that last bulleted item. Don't go there unless you're out of other options. Trial and error can be messy. It's not so bad with noncritical components such as scanners, printers, and modems, but when you're experimenting with video drivers not designed specifically for your hardware, you can really whack things out and have to go back to a Registry backup to get things back to normal.

When PnP Doesn't Happen

Today's PnP is pretty good. If the device is there, Windows will usually notice it right away. So if that doesn't happen, either your system doesn't support PnP or there's some kind of problem with the installation. Unless it's a *really* old system or device, it's probably the latter.

One way to nudge Windows into looking for new devices is to run the New Hardware Wizard from the Control Panel. The applet's name varies slightly among Windows versions; it's called the Add New Hardware Wizard in older versions and the Add Hardware Wizard in newer ones. No matter.

I don't mean to be a pessimist, but except under the original version of Windows 95 (which had a few PnP bugs in it), I've never seen a case where PnP didn't detect a PnP-compatible device but the Add New Hardware Wizard found the device and installed it successfully. In my experience, when PnP doesn't work, *there's a reason*, and just running the wizard isn't going to cure it. However, the Add Hardware Wizard can be useful when installing non-PnP devices or when installing on a system where the BIOS doesn't support PnP.

If you've installed a new board in your system and Windows didn't notice, double-click Add New Hardware (or Add Hardware) to open a wizard that'll walk you through the installation. Figure 23.2

shows the Windows XP version's opening screen. Note the warning in bold letters on it, and heed it. You should always prefer the Setup CD that came with a piece of hardware to running this wizard.

FIGURE 23.2
Accessing the Add
New Hardware
Wizard

WARNING *In versions prior to Windows XP, sometimes the New Hardware Wizard will find the wrong things, such as a stray port that you haven't been using—perhaps a built-in controller on the motherboard that isn't connected anything or perhaps the PS/2 mouse port when you've been using a Universal Serial Bus (USB) mouse. So before you allow it to install the drivers and assign resources for the devices it finds, you should review the list. If it found the wrong thing, click Cancel.*

If the wizard doesn't find the device, your next stop should be Device Manager, where you'll see whether any trace of the device appears and figure out why Windows doesn't like it. I'll explain that process later in this chapter.

GIVING PnP A LITTLE HELP

Sometimes Windows can detect that a new device is present, but it has no clue as to what type of device it is or what driver might be appropriate. One indicator of this would be the device showing up in Device Manager (covered shortly) as Unknown Device. When that happens, all you need to do is run the Setup program that came with the device. This tells Windows the device's make and model and installs a driver.

INSTALLING NON-PnP HARDWARE

The main thing about non-PnP hardware that's different is that Windows can't assign resources to it automatically. For example, if the device needs an Interrupt Request (IRQ), you must set the jumpers on the device to a particular IRQ. Windows has no say in the matter; it merely reads the IRQ setting on the device and then tries to shuffle around all the automatic assignments for other devices to accommodate it. If that's possible—great. If not, one or more devices may not work until you make some manual resource adjustments in Device Manager.

The best way to integrate a non-PnP device into a system is to let it have first pick of the resources. Install it first, and then boot into Windows and run the Add Hardware Wizard to cause Windows to detect it and read its resource claims. After the device is working, then install the PnP devices (which ostensibly can use whatever resources are left).

If you're installing a non-PnP device into a system that already has lots of PnP devices, you might save some time by trying the non-PnP device without removing anything. It might work. If not, you can take a fallback position of removing PnP devices that are currently using the resources it wants and then reinstalling them later.

Updating a Device Driver

Hardware manufacturers periodically release new versions of their drivers for various operating systems, both to patch bugs and to introduce new features. You can check the manufacturer's Web site periodically and download whatever is available.

NOTE   *Some hardware makers will let you register to receive e-mail notification whenever a new driver is available for a certain hardware model.*

Once you get that new driver, it'll be in one of these formats:

◆   Executable installation file with an EXE extension

◆   Executable self-extracting Zip file with an EXE extension

◆   Zip file (requires unzipping) containing the files needed to run a Setup utilit

◆   Zip file containing bare files (such as DRV and INF) requiring manual installation

If you get an executable file, run it. If a Setup program runs—great. Use it. If a WinZip self-extractor appears, extract the files to some temporary location on your hard disk and then check out what you got. If there's a Setup.exe file in there somewhere, run it.

The same goes for getting a ZIP file, except you'll need an unzipping utility such as WinZip to extract the files (unless, of course, you have Windows XP or higher, with built-in ZIP support.) Place the files in some temporary location on your hard disk, and again, check out what you've got. Run the SETUP.EXE if there is one.

I've saved the hardest possibility for last—no Setup utility, just a bunch of files with obvious way of installing them. If that's what you've ended up with, you'll need to do the following:

1.   Open Device Manager. For Windows 95/98/Me, open the Control Panel, double-click System, and click the Device Manager tab. For Windows 2000/XP/2003, open the Control Panel, double-click System, click the Hardware tab, and click the Device Manager button.

2.   In the list of device types, click the plus sign next to the type of the desired device. That device's name appears on the expanded list (see Figure 23.3).

FIGURE 23.3
Accessing Device
Manager in
Windows XP

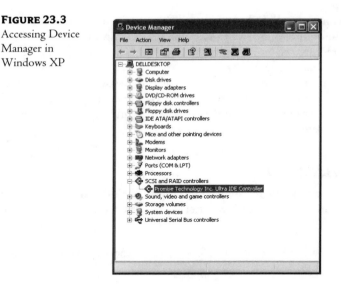

3. Double-click the device name to see its Properties box.

4. Click the Driver tab (see Figure 23.4).

5. Examine the details of the current driver, noting the date and whether it's signed. Proceed only if the driver you're replacing it with is a better one (in other words, a more recent one or signed when the current one isn't).

6. Click the Update Driver button. The Hardware Update Wizard runs. Follow its prompts to install the new driver. (It'll ask you for the location at some point; browse for it.)

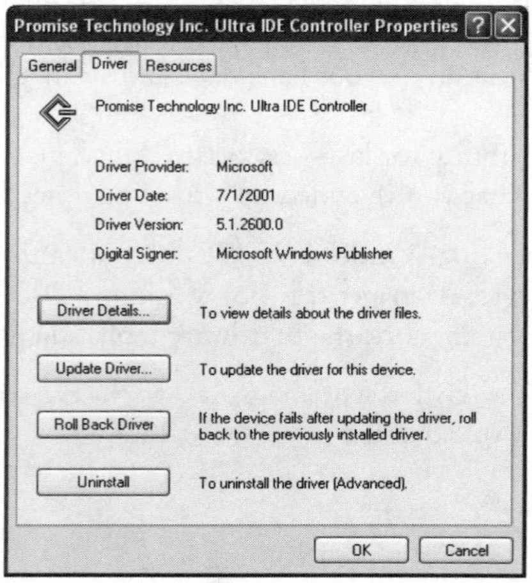

FIGURE 23.4
Viewing the Driver
tab in a device's
Properties box

Rolling Back a Driver Update

After updating a driver, you can revert to the earlier version with the Roll Back Driver feature:

1. Open Device Manager and display the Properties box for the device. (See the preceding steps for more detailed instructions.)

2. On the Driver tab (Figure 23.4), and click the Roll Back Driver button. Then follow the prompts.

Understanding System Resources

Each hardware device that interacts with the central processing unit (CPU) needs resources assigned to it. Different devices have different resource requirements, but they all need at least one of these types:

IRQs   IRQs are signaling lines between the CPU and the device. The devices use the IRQ line to signal to the CPU that it wants to have a conversation. IRQs are numbered 0 through 15. Some devices—for example, Industry Standard Architecture (ISA) boards—require their own reserved IRQ; others—for example, Peripheral Component Interconnect (PCI) boards—can share.

Memory addresses   These are areas of Random Access Memory (RAM) set aside for the device to use. Some devices need a range of memory preassigned to them; others can take from the general pool as needed.

I/O addresses   Input/Ouput (I/O) addresses are also areas of RAM, but these are reserved for the transfer of data to and from the device.

DMA channels   Direct Memory Access (DMA) channels are less commonly needed on modern devices. Keyboards and sound cards used to need them, but not so much anymore. They're pathways that allow the device to read and write directly from memory, bypassing the CPU. They were helpful back in the days when the CPU wasn't very fast, but nowadays they're not that important.

Many of the most common device types have certain resources preallotted to them by default. For example, the legacy serial port COM1 has IRQ4 and I/O address 3F8-3FF. The PnP portion of the BIOS does these preassignments at startup, and then when Windows starts up, it accepts them. If you take the A+ Certification exams, you'll want to memorize the default assignments, but it isn't necessary otherwise.

When two or more devices want the same resource, a conflict occurs. This is a real possibility if you have multiple non-PnP devices, but most of the PnP devices are flexible enough to accept whatever resources happen to be free. If a conflict among defaults does occur, Windows works out compromises among all PnP devices so that every device is satisfied. This all happens automatically and invisibly for the most part.

However, situations may arise where Windows is unable to handle resource assignments completely independently, and that's where you come in. You can use Device Manager to straighten it all out.

Working with Device Manager

Device Manager is a list of all the hardware that Windows recognizes as installed on the system, broken down by category. You can select any device and view its status and properties from there, as well as manually change its resource assignments in some cases.

To access Device Manager, use these steps:

- For Windows 95/98/Me, in the Control Panel, double-click System, and then click the Device Manager tab. Device Manager appears as a tab in the dialog box (see Figure 23.5).

- For Windows 2000/XP/2003 Server, in the Control Panel, double-click System, and then click the Hardware tab. On the Hardware tab, click the Device Manager button. Device Manager appears as a separate window (see Figure 23.6).

TIP A shortcut for displaying the System Properties is to right-click My Computer and choose Properties.

Because everyone's computer is a little different, chances are your list won't look exactly like this one, but it'll have most of the same device types. The information in the list is organized like an outline, listing categories of devices. The devices themselves appear within each category. To see the devices, click the plus sign beside the category.

FIGURE 23.5

Viewing the Device Manager tab under Windows 9x

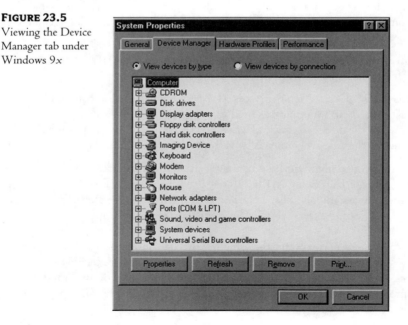

FIGURE 23.6

Viewing Device
Manager under
Windows XP

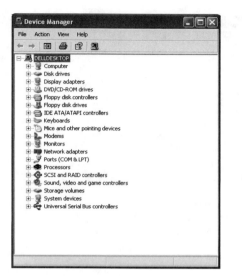

NOTE *Figures 23.5 and 23.6 were captured from two different computers; that's why they don't have the same devices. If you were to view the same computer through the Device Managers of the two different Windows versions, the lists of devices would be identical.*

Troubleshooting Device Problems with Device Manager

If a device is installed and working properly, it should show up on the Device Manager list as a name and icon. Double-clicking it to display its properties should show a message of *This device is working properly* on the General tab, as in Figure 23.7.

If you don't see that message, then perhaps you have one of these situations:

Device doesn't appear on the list   The device is not installed properly, defective, or not PnP-compatible, or your BIOS isn't PnP-compatible.

Device appears in the Unknown category with a question mark as its icon   You need to run the setup software that came with the device to complete its driver installation.

Device has an X on its icon   The device has been disabled. Re-enable it in its Properties box. (See "Disabling a Device" later in this chapter.)

Device has an Exclamation Point on its Icon   There's a resource conflict or a problem with the device. View the status on the General tab of the device's Properties box for details.

FIGURE 23.7
A device that's
working properly
in Windows

Manually Changing a Device's Resource Assignments

Especially on older PCs and in older Windows versions, conflicts may occur between two or more devices that want the same resource. Symptoms of this include the following:

- One or both of the devices aren't working.

- One or both of the devices show an exclamation point on its icon in Device Manager.

- For one or both devices, the device status on the General tab of the device's Properties box reports a conflict.

- When you view the device's Resources tab in its Properties box, a conflict shows.

To resolve a resource conflict, change the resource assignment for one of the devices as follows:

1. Open the Properties box for one of the devices, and display the Resources tab. In the Conflicting Device List window, note the other device involved in the conflict.

2. Clear the Use Automatic Settings check box.

3. Open the Settings Based On drop-down list, and choose a different setting. Keep doing this until No Conflicts appears in the Conflicting Device List window, as in Figure 23.8.

4. Click OK.

NOTE   *I'm showing a device in Windows 98 in Figures 23.8 and 23.9 because it's in those lower 9x-based Windows versions that you're most likely to need to do this. Windows 2000 and XP manage resources very well, so it's unlikely that you'll ever need to do this in one of those versions.*

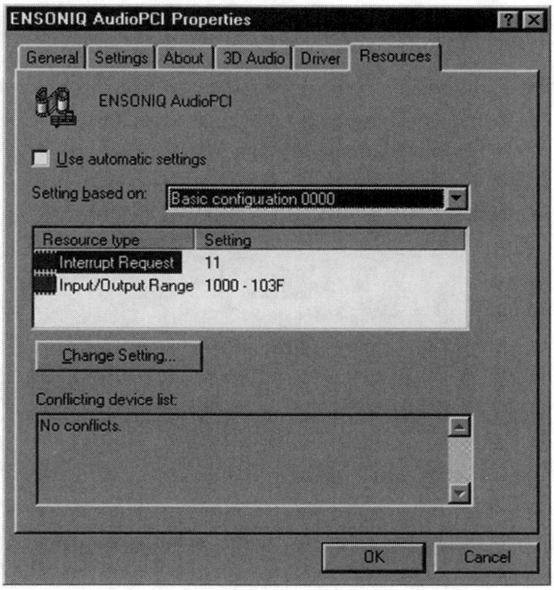

FIGURE 23.8
This device now has
no conflicts.

If none of the choices in step 3 resolve the conflict, you can try manually configuring a particular resource. For example, if the Conflicting Device List window reports that the problem is an I/O address conflict, double-click Input/Output Range in the Resource Type list (Figure 23.8), opening a dialog box where you can choose a different range to use (see Figure 23.9).

What's actually more likely to happen on a modern system, however, is that an error message will appear when you try to change the resource assignments saying that the resource setting can't be modified. In that case, refer to the Conflicting Device List window to determine what other device is involved and then try approaching the conflict from that device's properties.

WHY CAN'T I CHANGE THE RESOURCE ASSIGNMENTS?

Most newer systems today support Advanced Power and Configuration Interface (ACPI) standards. You probably know about ACPI's power management features, but you might not have given much thought to the *Configuration* portion of that acronym. When ACPI is in effect on a system, it takes over most of the resource assignments, with the result that the resources for individual devices aren't manually adjustable through Device Manager. On the plus side, however, ACPI does a good job managing resources, such that you shouldn't have any conflicts to resolve in the first place.

FIGURE 23.9
Manually change a
resource assignment
if needed.

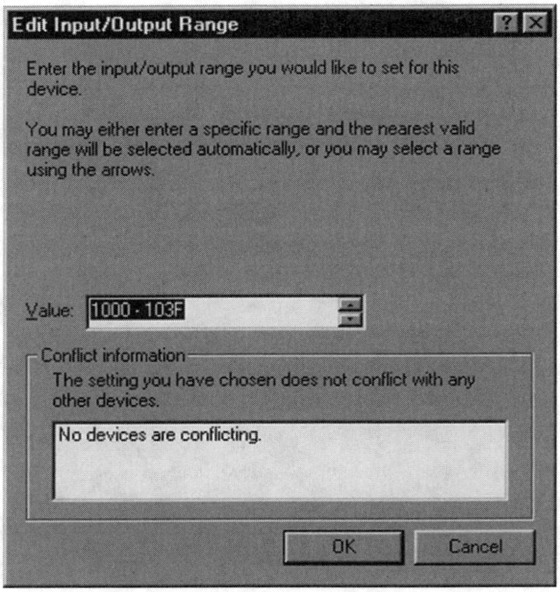

Removing a Device Driver

After you physically remove a device from the system, its driver might still appear in Device Manager. This could be harmless, or it could cause problems with devices of the same type. For example, if you removed an old modem and installed a new one, the fact that the old modem's driver is still installed can cause problems with some applications recognizing the new modem.

To remove a device driver, delete it from Device Manager:

1. Select the device on the list.

2. Press Delete.

3. Click OK.

Another way to delete a driver (Windows 2000/XP only) is to select it and then click the Remove Device button on the toolbar. It's the one that looks like a computer with a red X on it.

You can delete the device drivers for hardware that's still physically present, but Windows will redetect the device and reinstall the driver at its first opportunity. One way to possibly resolve a problem with a device is to remove its driver and then redetect hardware (see the next section).

Redetecting PnP Hardware

While in Device Manager, you can force Windows to rescan for PnP hardware, thereby refreshing the Device Manager's list. To do this, follow this step depending on your operating system:

- In Windows 9*x*/Me, click the Refresh button in Device Manager.
- In Windows 2000/XP, Choose Action ➢ Scan for Hardware Changes.

Disabling a Device

Suppose you want to delete a device from Device Manager that's still physically present in the system, perhaps something built into the motherboard, but it keeps coming back like a bad penny. To end the cycle, disable it instead of deleting it. When a device is disabled, it appears in Device Manager with a red X through its icon, and it uses no resources.

The procedures are different for disabling a device in different Windows versions:

- In Windows 9*x*/Me, display the device's Properties box, and on the General tab, mark the Disable in This Hardware Profile check box to disable the device.
- In Windows 2000/XP, display the device's Properties box and on the General tab, set the Device Usage drop-down list to Do Not Use This Device (Disable). Or, from the Device Manager list, select the device and then click the Disable button on the toolbar. (It's the one that looks like a computer with a red circle and diagonal line on it.)

Disabling a device can be an effective troubleshooting technique. If Windows won't start up normally but it'll start in Safe mode, you've got a bad driver somewhere. A good way to troubleshoot this is to disable hardware devices one by one from Device Manager until you find the one that's causing the problem.

This chapter covered Windows hardware resource management, focusing on Device Manager as the primary tool for controlling devices and their drivers. The next chapter continues this discussion by examining ways you can find help on the Internet for working with hardware.

Chapter 24

Using the Internet for Hardware Support

Introduction

There's only one place where you can obtain help for your computer-related problems, find the latest drivers for your hardware and peripherals, and learn about the latest developments in the technology field. That place is the Internet—and it should be an essential component of your information and support strategy.

Going online gives you the tools you need to master the PC—from the hardware to the operating system to the software—as well as tips on future technology that you need to prepare for now to handle tomorrow.

I just spent one hour on the Web and quite literally solved a week's worth of PC hardware concerns. In that hour, I grabbed two updated drivers for devices I use, researched the pros and cons of a motherboard I'm planning to buy, read a couple of articles on Peripheral Component Interconnect (PCI) Extended, arranged to beta-test some new diagnostic software, looked up technical notes on configuring my wireless router, exchanged messages with a friend at 3Com who pointed me to a solid Digital Subscriber Line (DSL) modem for my new office, and performed a bandwidth test to see whether my current connection is operating at optimal speed. That's a lot of necessary ground to cover in an hour, all made possible because of the phenomenal amount of material available on the Internet today.

QuickSteps: Getting Online Help

Gathered from the information presented in this chapter, the following are the steps for getting online help for problems you may experience with your PC.

Before you start, there are some things you may need on hand. These include the following:

◆ Paper and a pen/pencil for taking notes and for keeping information you need handy (or maybe you already have these things stored in a database or text file on another PC).

◆ Basic information about your PC—the type of Central Processing Unit (CPU) and mother-board video card chipset used, exact version of your operating system—so that you can provide these necessary details when posting or calling to get assistance.

◆ Short synopsis of the problem (for example, what you may have installed, removed, or modified just before the problem cropped up; exact symptoms you're seeing; what you've already tried and what behavior changes, if any, you saw as a result) so that you can report it when posting or calling for technical assistance.

◆ Product registration information and/or the model and serial number of the malfunctioning device to give to the manufacturer if you're reporting the device (especially if you need to return it for a working one).

◆ The problem PC or device nearby when you conduct research, post a message online, or call for support so that you can double-check settings and walk through a set of steps. Trouble-shooting is a lot harder when you don't have the system right there.

To find help online, follow these steps:

1. Connect to the Internet as you normally do.

2. Select one of the resources mentioned in this chapter—CNET, for example.

3. Search the site for relevant information—in Frequently Asked Questions (FAQs), via interactive troubleshooters, or in previous messages on forums or message boards.

4. To post your own question to a forum or message board, prepare your post by giving the necessary information about the problem you're having, including exact error messages and relevant background information about your PC (such as which operating system and version you have, recent changes you've made to the configuration, and your type of PC). Post your message on the board, wait a few hours (or perhaps a few days, on less-busy sites), and then check back to see what responses you may have—and respond appropriately.

5. Analyze the information you've received and proceed with your troubleshooting.

Problems with Traditional Support

Getting the information you need through traditional means can be difficult—or, at times, virtually impossible. You have problems to solve, new drivers to track down and acquire, newer and fancier hardware to install, and new software versions to understand. Where do you turn?

If you're looking for technical or industry information, many good trade magazines are available—and some are free to computer professionals—but these periodicals give you too much to peruse. It's easy for me to accumulate a dozen magazines and journals in a week while I'm out of town. How can I read all of that and pull out the information I need in time to get through the next lot when they show up the following week?

Magazines can't solve most problems anyway. A lot of knowledgeable people read them and write for them, but the problem is the time lag. If I'm installing a new board, and it's not working no matter what I do, I want to know how to make it work *now*, not weeks or months from now. Writing a letter to an advice columnist at my favorite computer magazine, waiting for the letter to be published, and then waiting for a reply isn't going to help me.

Another option is to call the board manufacturer's technical support line, but that approach is problematic as well. First, the manufacturer might not have a support line—or the line might not be available during hours convenient to you. Second, even if a support line is available, it's probably not free—you might have to foot the bill for the call (ever notice how few technical support lines these days are toll-free numbers?), or you may even have to pay the manufacturer to get a response (by purchasing a service contract). If you do happen to get through to a real person (after listening to the all-Muzak version of "Raindrops Keep Falling on My Head" for an hour or more), that person might not have the answer you need, or may have to "check it out and get back to you." Good luck with that one.

Then there's the problem of acquiring updated drivers, software patches, hardware documentation that the maker assumed you wouldn't need, and just new product information. Working with computers often involves a fair amount of isolation and not a lot of free time, and it's hard to keep up with all that stuff. I need a way to throw questions into the ether for anyone and everyone to answer, to acquire drivers without waiting for the manufacturer to get around to sending me a CD, and to learn about new products.

The following sections highlight some examples of the frustrating situations you can run into when trying to get information you need *now*. At the least, these are some reasons why *I* learned to use online services for getting technical support and getting software.

Journey into Faxback Hell

In concept, faxback services are a nice way of answering common customer questions. Why hire staff to run a telephone line when 75 percent of the people who call have the same question? It's much simpler to prepare documents that answer the most frequently asked questions and then make those documents available via fax to those who request them.

The catch is that you usually have to know exactly what you want before these services work and be able to provide a document number for it. No document number, no fax. Even if you get one of the rare faxback services in which real people handle telephone questions, that real human probably doesn't know which document you need. Usually, the only way to get a document number is to order the catalog from the faxback service, at which point you have a list of titles with document numbers next to them. In other words, you still can't be sure you're ordering the document you need.

One major computer company (which shall remain nameless) that I worked with had a faxback service. One of their faxback documents was about how to troubleshoot your fax modem if it wasn't working. I don't think I was the only one who saw the irony in this. How in the blazes is the customer supposed to receive the fax if their fax modem isn't working?

Facing the Muzak: Technical Support Lines

I don't want to pick on those who staff technical support lines. Technical support has to be one of the most thankless jobs around. Callers are stressed out from worrying about their problem, probably snappish from being kept on hold, and prone to ask what sound like stupid questions because the technical support representative has answered the same one six times already that day. (See where faxback services come from?)

But technical support lines aren't usually any fun for the caller, either. Many people have a hard time explaining a particular chain of events to someone they can't see. Others wait on hold for 20 minutes (or longer!) to hear a technical support person tell them, "Gee, I've never heard of that problem before—can you hold on a minute (or 2, or 10) while I get my supervisor?"

Having to "upgrade" your problem to the next level is also annoying. The folks on the first line of support (the so-called level-one reps) often have limited technical knowledge. These are the folks who tell you to defrag your hard disk when you're actually experiencing some sort of interrupt conflict (as if defragging your disk is the magic solution to all possible computer problems!). If you want *real* technical support, you need to ask for a level-two rep, who might—if you're lucky—have some technical experience and access to the company's technical support database.

To make matters worse, the handful of phone lines that feed into the tech support department—unlike the large number of sales lines available for taking orders—are often not toll-free, which means that if you're at work, you may have to explain to the business manager all those long-distance charges on your code, or if you're at home, you have to swallow the long-distance bill yourself. In addition, far too many tech support lines are 9-to-5 propositions, which means that weekend warrior types can be stuck until Monday if they have a problem.

And then there's that period of being on hold. I'm never sure whether it's more annoying to hear violin renditions of "Purple Haze" or a comforting voice repeatedly assuring me that my patience is appreciated. (How do they know that I'm being patient? Maybe I'm grinding my teeth smooth while waiting to get back to something productive.)

True story—during one recent patch of dismal service from my DSL provider, who shall remain nameless, users were forced to wait on hold for *more than two hours* before getting connected to a tech support rep. I know one user who was so fed up over this intolerable wait that he decided to cancel his service—and then had to wait on hold for another hour to reach an account representative in the customer support department!

Finally, there are the tech support lines that won't even talk to you until you've given them $250. I ask you—what other industry ships such a large percentage of shoddy, barely working products and then charges you even more money to restore the products to what should have been a normal working condition?

The *idea* of a tech support line is wonderful—that a company will provide a team of experts to answer your questions on demand. The reality is often less wonderful, for both the caller and the tech support person.

Making Friends and Influencing People

Often, one of the best ways to answer a question is to find someone who has more experience than you do. Unfortunately, this is sometimes easier said than done. You may not have anyone around to ask (often the case for home PC-ers), or *you* may be the person with the most experience. Sometimes your circle of personal resources just doesn't have experience where you need it—or they may profess a great deal more expertise than they actually have, and some of the poorest PC tech support is done over the watercooler. If you've been a NetWare person all your life, and all the people you know are NetWare people, then you could be stuck when setting up that Windows Server 2003 machine and something obscure goes wrong. At this point, you need more friends and work associates.

Then, too, friends don't always give you written instructions when answering your questions. Either you try to remember what they told you or you write it down yourself, but there's always the possibility of misinterpreting or forgetting what they told you. I leave it to your imagination to envision how ugly *that* can get.

Fortunately, there's a way around having to write things down when friends answer your questions. Windows XP and Windows 2003 include a Remote Assistance feature that allows a trusted friend or associate to connect directly to your computer over the Internet, and he or she can actually help you fix your PC remotely. In fact, you can even connect directly with a Microsoft technical representative. Basically, you send out an invitation to this person to connect to your computer, and he or she accepts the invitation. Once the connection is established, your friend or associate can control your Desktop as if he or she is sitting right at your side.

Read All about It

As I noted at the beginning of this section, the computer industry produces too much information for one person to keep up with—hundreds of pages show up on my doorstep every week. Then there's the problem of money. Not all these magazines come cheap, especially if you can't demonstrate that you work in the industry (not difficult to do, but a consideration) and therefore warrant a professional courtesy rate. And some magazines require you to pay full price, no matter who you are. Even if the subscriptions are tax deductible for you, it adds up.

Advantages of Online Support

So if obtaining technical support through traditional methods is so problematic, what do you do? Fortunately, many companies have turned to the Internet to provide technical support for their customers—and many third-party sites now offer much better (and easier-to-find) information than what has been historically available in the "real world."

What's Out There?

One of the advantages of going online is the massive amount of information that's available. So what help can you get from cyberspace? Take a look at the kinds of support you can find.

New Product Information

Not surprisingly, there's a lot of new product information on the Web. You've certainly heard of e-commerce, and it's likely you've heard of it because it has been force fed to you. Most reputable manufacturers provide detailed product specs online for your pre- or post-purchase perusal—and if the manufacturer's information is lacking, it's likely that one of the many online e-tailers for that product will have the facts you need. Finding this type of information online is a lot easier than trying to appropriate a much-coveted and exceedingly rare product brochure from your local PC retailer!

PRODUCT DOCUMENTATION

Complete product docs aren't *always* available in cyberspace, but manufacturers are more frequently posting this information online for anybody to read. Because a lot of hardware is sold without documentation (as if you didn't need the documentation to set up the hardware?), going online is often the easiest—and sometimes the *only*—way to get it. Many times, too, documentation updates will be posted online, covering ground missed in the original docs—or features documented incorrectly. Going online is often the only way to get this updated information.

REVIEWS

Product reviews—both professional and real-user anecdotes—are available everywhere on the Internet, often ahead of similar reviews in traditional print journals. The lack of printing delay means the reviewers are working with the latest versions or drivers, especially when reviewing a product in testing. When new hardware, a new driver, or a patch debuts, you don't have to be a guinea pig by being the first to buy and try it. Instead, you can take a few days to read about the response the item is getting from users posting to newsgroups and Web-based message boards—before you invest your money and/or time.

WHITE PAPERS AND BACKGROUND INFORMATION

White papers are wholly different from short question-and-answer help and quick troubleshooting pieces: they're sort of the mini-thesis or novella of the tech world. They take a specific topic (the effect of older analog phone lines and wiring on a modem's dial-up connection speed or the configuration of Windows NT/2000/XP/2003 for optimal security, for example) and explore it in some detail. Sometimes such papers include an industry-wide perspective, and sometimes they provide in-depth comparisons of different chipsets or features.

Typically authored by an expert in the field (a senior project manager, a senior product developer, and so on at a company responsible for the product or issue being discussed), they can provide quite a bit of background that several short technical articles or product information churned out by a company's marketing department don't provide.

FREQUENTLY ASKED QUESTIONS (FAQs)

Because certain topics come up as questions again and again ("How do I update a driver?" or "How do I get this device to work under Windows XP?"), one Internet information resource stable is FAQ pages, listing the most common questions about a product along with their answers.

TIP *If you're having problems with a device or piece of software, FAQs are generally the best place to start looking for an answer. They're usually categorized appropriately to help you narrow your search, and they're a lot quicker to go through than a detailed white paper.*

TECHNICAL SUPPORT DATABASES

Chances are that you're not the first user experiencing this specific problem with this particular product. If the manufacturer is on its toes (and not all are...), they've kept a record of previously reported problems and assembled them into a searchable technical support database. (One terrific example of a technical support database is Microsoft's Knowledge Base—an indispensable resource for anyone using a Microsoft product— located at `search.support.microsoft.com`.) Searching for your problem in a database of problems is often the best and easiest way to find the "official" solution.

INTERACTIVE TROUBLESHOOTERS

Many manufacturers have automated the question-and-answer format of a typical tech support phone call and put it online in the form of an interactive troubleshooter. Answer the branching questions posed by the troubleshooter, and the troubleshooter will present what it thinks is the appropriate solution to your problem.

ADVICE

Today on the Internet, many sites provide step-by-step how-tos and advice for hardware installation and troubleshooting. One big advantage to these sites is that you can often learn from people who use a product much like you do. The downside tends to be that there are a lot more so-called experts than people who can actually fix a PC. One tip is to look around such sites for people who seem to be well respected and able to explain things clearly. A good technician tends to have a big following, so with a little reading, it often becomes clear which "experts" you should listen to and which ones you should ignore.

WARNING   Advice you'll get from other Internet users isn't any more universally accurate than advice you get from people you run into in the "real world." Check your sources before doing anything drastic based on anyone's posting!

DEVICE DRIVERS AND UTILITIES

The Internet is the primary resource for the latest versions of these necessary files. Device drivers are crucial to getting your hardware to work with your software. For instance, when Windows XP first came out, some peripherals wouldn't work with the old drivers, so users eagerly awaited the arrival of new Windows XP drivers from their hardware manufacturers—which were promptly made available for downloading at the manufacturers' Web sites. The same story is true when almost any new operating system comes out. Shareware and freeware PC utilities are also commonly available on the Web.

Why Online Support Is Better

Now that you know what types of resources you can find on the Internet, let's look at why you'd want to use online support—instead of the traditional phone-and-paper support.

IT'S OFTEN CHEAPER

There are two types of costs: money you *spend* and money you *lose*—or, as old-country economists would have it, explicit and implicit costs. Let's assume you have a telephone and a modem (or a fast Internet connection) and compare what you'll find online with what you typically receive via phone-based support.

If you call technical support with your problem, the process goes like this:

1. Call the technical support line (almost certainly long distance), probably between 9 A.M. and 5 P.M. (*their* time zone, not necessarily yours) when phone rates are the highest.

2. Wait on hold. (Get a cup of coffee, order a pizza, do a crossword puzzle, hum along to Montovani…)

3. Talk to the technical support person.

4. Possibly wait on hold again while the technical person looks up the problem or consults with someone else (the old level-1 to level-2 upgrade).

5. If all goes well, get the answer.

Not only is the process time consuming, but every single bit of that process occurs while the meter—*your* meter!—is ticking.

To find the answer to your problem online, on the other hand, the process is more like this:

1. Go to the manufacturer's Web site.

2. Search the support section of the site for your particular problem—this can include searching preprepared FAQs, using interactive troubleshooters, or browsing through previously posted messages on the site's message boards.

3. If the answer to your question hasn't been previously addressed, go to the site's message board (sometimes called a *forum*) and post your question as a new message. Optionally, you can ask your question of the site's technical support staff via a Web-based form (if available) or an email message (if email support is offered).

4. If you don't receive a direct response to your question (via a return email from company support staff), return to the site's message board to read any responses to your question.

None of this costs you anything above the monthly service charge for your Internet Service Provider (ISP), which you're paying for anyway (it's what economists call a *sunk cost*). And at no time do you have to sit on hold and listen to elevator music or some inane greeting.

IT'S CONVENIENT

One of the biggest hassles of technical support lines is the time spent on hold. If you have something else you could be doing, it's annoying to have to wait, tied to the telephone, for someone to answer your call. If instead you seek support at the manufacturer's Web site or post your question to a newsgroup or forum, then you can do something else while waiting for an answer—assuming you can't find a solution on your first trip online.

NOTE *If you need an answer now, posting a question to a newsgroup may not be good enough—you may get the answer you need in 10 minutes, tomorrow, next week, or never. (It all depends on whether other users see your question and have an appropriate answer.) But if it's something you want to know but don't have to know right this second, newsgroups and similar forums are great.*

Another aspect to the convenience of the Internet is that it runs on a 24-hour clock. People are online all the time, not just from 9 to 5. For instance, I've found that one of the best times to post a question to a newsgroup is after the normal workday. This may have something to do with geography—on the East Coast, 5 P.M. comes earlier than it does to most of the country. But it's also because a lot of techies check into their newsgroups (or Web-based message boards) when they get home from work or late at night. If you post a question at 5 P.M. Eastern Standard Time (EST), then by morning you often have a collection of answers.

The Internet's 24/7 convenience isn't limited to question-and-answer sessions, either. Want to see what applications are out for Windows 2003/XP, but it's 3 A.M.? How about looking up the technical specifications on Advanced Micro Devices' latest CPU—on Christmas Day? You can often find this type of information listed at the manufacturer's Web site, or you can use a search engine to search the Web for other sites containing information about the subject at hand. You can also download drivers and evaluation software at your convenience, not at the convenience of someone else.

Initial Results May Be Better

One of the nasty truths about today's very inexpensive (relative to the past) hardware, coupled with the burgeoning population of first-time PC users, is that a lot of technical companies have had to scale back some of their support services, or at least not beef them up as much as might be needed to handle a high volume of user phone calls. (Kind of counterintuitive, isn't it—just when they need to provide *more* support, they provide *less* of it!)

As one cost-saving measure, many manufacturers *outsource* their first-tier product support, meaning they hire an outside support firm to handle initial calls from users. Additional follow-up, if such a thing exists, is provided by more experienced technicians supplied by the manufacturer.

This means that during your first call for support, it's possible you won't reach someone employed by the manufacturer. In some cases, you may not even reach someone who has ever used the product for which you need help. Heck, the person you talk to may be more of an operator than a technician. Many agencies use script books or computer databases to look up your question and offer an answer based on the closest match they can find. Throw them a question not in the script, and you may be in for a long wait or several calls.

However, when you access support resources on the Internet, you can go right to the good stuff—no level 1 techs here! Some manufacturers provide public access to a database of known issues and problems, and some even provide very detailed technical documents and white papers. If you need this higher-level information, you can go right to it, without having to pass through several levels of technical support personnel first.

Follow-up Is Often Better

One of the best aspects of the Internet's many newsgroups and forums is that those people who answer your questions are generally doing it not because they're getting paid for it but because they're trying to help you. I've found that that translates to good follow-up. Until you post a message saying that all is well with your problem, you can almost certainly count on people trying to help you through the process if you're polite and respond to messages posted to you.

For example, on one occasion I was helping a friend figure out how best to deliver Microsoft PowerPoint (a PC application) to people in a largely Unix-oriented office. We were trying to decide whether it'd be better to provide the users with individual machines that could run the application, set up a PowerPoint workstation or two for those times when they needed it, use some kind of PC emulation on the SPARC 5s and 20s that the users already had, or what. (For those of you raising your eyebrows at the thought of buying users a second computer just to run an application, this office was an intelligence shop that had some money to spend on the project.) I posted a message outlining the situation on a couple of relevant forums, one for the PowerPoint side of the problem and one for the organizational side of the problem. The answers I received about the organizational aspects of the problem sparked some new questions, which I asked, and then some other people got into the question and raised some more issues. By the time things wound down a couple of days later, I had what I needed and far more background besides.

Using the World Wide Web for Support

Originally a method devised by a Swiss think tank to make its papers on physics available to other scientists, the World Wide Web has become the most-used portion of the Internet. (In fact, to many users, the Web is synonymous with the Internet.) The graphical side of the Internet, the Web offers papers you can read online, files you can download, and links you can follow to related sites. In short, the Web offers you the world—at the click of a hyperlink.

Clicking and Linking

I don't need to tell you how to use a Web browser (such as Internet Explorer) to navigate the Web. I'll point out, however, that there may be more uses for your browser than you currently know.

For example, you know that clicking a hyperlink will jump you to the Web page referenced in the hyperlink. But did you know that hyperlinks don't always link to other pages? Web developers can use hyperlinks to link to pictures, sound files, video files, and any type of file you might want to download.

On most manufacturers' Web sites you can find lists of drivers, patches, and other programs for downloading. If the developer of the site has done his or her work well, when you click the link for one of these files, that file will automatically download to your hard disk. (Actually, you'll see a dialog box asking you if and where you want to save the file, but you know what I mean.)

If clicking the link doesn't download the file (if, for example, clicking a link to a graphics file simply displays the graphic in a new window), you can still use your browser to download the file. Just right-click the link to display the pop-up menu, then select the Save or Save to Disk option. This will display the old familiar Save As dialog box, which will enable you to save the linked file to your hard disk.

Your Web browser can also be used to access and download files from File Transfer Protocol (FTP) sites; you'll learn more about that later.

NOTE *Many drivers and other utilities are relatively small files, easily downloadable via a 56Kbps modem. However, some manufacturers package drivers and utilities together in larger files and make you download the whole shebang just to get the little driver you need. Some of these files can be huge (several megabytes) and are easier to deal with if you have a high-speed (DSL or cable) Internet connection.*

Finding Useful Web Sites

The Web is big—really, really big. Out of all the millions and millions of pages in cyberspace, how do you find the ones you need to solve your PC hardware problems?

I've put together a list of the best technical Web sites, which I'll get to in a minute. But before you hit these general sites, it's probably a good idea to go to the source of your problem—the hardware or software manufacturer.

FINDING MANUFACTURER WEB SITES

A good rule of thumb when seeking support via the Internet is to go to the manufacturer's Web site first, learn everything you can, and then expand your search to related sites (technical sites with reviews of a product or sites where users may be asking questions and getting help with that product and newsgroups. You should hit the manufacturer first because—in theory, anyway—that's where the most accurate and most up-to-date information will reside.

NOTE   *The relevancy—in terms of both applicability and timeliness—of technical information on manufacturers' Web sites varies. Some manufacturers take Web-based support seriously and update their sites daily. Others view the Web as more of a marketing tool and let their Web support pages languish unattended for weeks and months. As with all things Internet-related, some sites are better than others.*

You have several ways to find the Uniform Resource Locator (URL) for a specific manufacturer. Many manufacturers list their Web address (and email address, for direct contact) in their product documentation. If the address isn't listed there, try typing the manufacturer's name into the middle of a URL, surrounded by a `www.` and a `.com`—for example, if the manufacturer is IBM, you would give `www.ibm.com` a try. (This one happens to work!) Finally, you can use a Web search engine (which I'll discuss in a moment) to search for the manufacturer's Web site; Yahoo! is particularly good at this type of manufacturer search.

Sometimes it's quicker to go to unofficial Web sites that link to the official ones, rather than going to the opening page of an official site and then wandering through a maze of linked pages. For example, if you need Hewlett-Packard (HP) scanner drivers, you might go first to a third-party site that contains links to a bunch of different manufacturers' scanner download sites. When you click the HP link on that page, you'll jump immediately to the specific part of the HP site where drivers are stored.

On some occasions, the manufacturer's site might not contain the documentation or the drivers you need. For example, when I needed documentation for an Adaptec Small Computer System Interface (SCSI) host adapter, I went first to the official Adaptec site. Unfortunately, all that was available on the site was a phone number I could call to order the docs—not exactly what I was looking for. My response was to use one of the Web search engines to search for *Adaptec documentation*, which led me to the Memory Lane Computers site, which had the documentation I wanted, online and immediately accessible. My point is that when a manufacturer's site doesn't contain the documentation you need, a third-party site might.

TIP   *Two of the best sites to find updated drivers and related information are Drivers.com (`www.drivers.com`) and DriverGuide.com (`www.driverguide.com`).*

Using Search Engines and Directories

If you don't know the exact URL for the Web site you want—or don't even know what site you're looking for—then your best bet is to use one of the Web's many search sites. Hundreds of search sites are available, of which a dozen or so generate the bulk of the overall traffic.

There are two types of search sites—search engines and directories. A *search engine* uses high-powered software to automatically crawl the Web and compile huge indexes of available sites; when you search a search site, you're actually searching the millions of pages currently listed in that index. A *directory* consists of a smaller number of handpicked (by human beings!) listings, often organized into easy-to-navigate categories.

Google, Northern Light, HotBot, Excite, Lycos, and AltaVista are all search engines.

Which type of search site should you use—a search engine or a directory? In general, a search engine delivers *more* results, and a directory delivers *more targeted* results. Many users prefer directories because of their organization; other users prefer the quantity of results delivered by search engines. It's really a matter a personal taste.

TIP   To generate more efficient results, enter precise search criteria. For example, if you need a driver for a particular video card, enter the vendor's name plus the word driver. *Most search engines offer advanced search results that allow you to search for specific strings, use Boolean operations such as "and" or "or" conditions, and put quotes around several words to search for a phrase.*

That said, the following are some of the features I find desirable in a search site:

A report of the total number of hits generated from a search   Although a smaller number of hits are easier to read through, a larger number of hits may yield a lot more information for you. A Web search engine that generates only a few hits on a major topic may not be a robust search engine.

A large number of hits displayed simultaneously   I find it faster to scroll down a page than to move to another page to see the next 10 hits. This parameter can be adjusted on many sites.

As little extraneous text surrounding the hits as possible   This is so that the links are easy to see. An option is the capability to customize the query results to show more or less surrounding information.

NOTE   Before deciding that a particular topic isn't referenced on the Web, make sure you've tried more than one search site. Different search engines and directories index different parts of the Internet (or index the Internet using different criteria), so an identical search might generate totally different results at different search sites.

The following search sites, although a small subset of what's available, happen to be the ones I've used most or like best:

Google   Google (`www.google.com`) is one of the best search engines—and my current favorite. In my experience, it produces the most accurate results of any search engine and delivers those results faster than any other site. Unlike the Excites and Lycos of the world, Google has resisted the urge to become a bloated "portal"; the only thing Google does is search, and it does that exceedingly well.

Interestingly, Google uses a slightly unusual method to rank the pages in its index. Whereas other search engines tend to rank their results on the frequency or predominance of the search term on the page, Google ranks results based on how many other pages link to that page. This sounds kind of like a popularity contest, but it works—you're more likely to find the official manufacturer site listed at the top of a Google results page than you are with other search engines. Chances are good that when you enter the search term and click the I'm Feeling Lucky button, you'll get there.

Northern Light   Northern Light (`www.northernlight.com`) is a hidden gem. Not only does it have one of the largest indexes of any search engine, it also features a "special collection" of additional documents (available for a fee) that you just can't find on any other site. I also like how Northern Light automatically categorizes its results into folders and subfolders.

AltaVista and HotBot   AltaVista (`www.altavista.com`) and HotBot (`www.hotbotcom`) are both big, powerful search engines. Both provide lots of search options, including advanced Boolean operations that you can use to refine your search. As a bonus, AltaVista also offers specific searches for Usenet postings and multimedia files. They're both good, general search sites, worthy of everyday use.

Yahoo!   Yahoo! (`www.yahoo.com`) is one of the most popular search sites on the Internet—and one of the most popular sites on the Web, period. Yes, it offers the fewest results (it's a directory, not a search engine), but those results are typically high quality and well organized. If all you're looking for is the URL for a specific manufacturer's site, Yahoo! is the place to go.

The Best Web Sites for Technical Information

Because the Internet was born on a computer and initially populated by computer enthusiasts, it makes sense that many Web sites focus on topics of interest to computer users. Some of these sites offer news and reviews, and others incorporate discussion forums where you can post questions, get answers, and maybe even help someone else. Still more sites offer drivers and utilities for downloading, deliver online tutorials and how-tos, or provide free or fee-based technical support from experts (both real and self-professed).

That said, the following is a short list (organized alphabetically) of some of the better technical sites on the Web. The next time you need help or information, check them out.

WARNING   *Web sites and other Internet resources tend to come and go—which means any specific URL listed in this book may, at some point in time, go dead. Also, the character of existing groups or Web sites may change over time. This information isn't guaranteed.*

The following are the sites:

Active-Hardware   As you can tell from its name, Active-Hardware (`www.active-hardware.com`) is a PC hardware-oriented site, complete with technical news and reviews. The site also includes a robust section of downloadable drivers.

AnandTech   This site (`www.anandtech.com`) focuses on hardware news and reviews and includes a number of discussion forums.

CMPnet   CMPnet (`www.cmpnet.com`) offers a multitude of resources for technical professionals, culled from the CMP magazine group.

CNET   The CNET family of sites (`www.cnet.com`) is a true one-stop shop for computer industry news and technical information. This technical portal includes links to other full-service sites that offer technical news, file and driver downloads, hardware and software reviews, and how-to and help information. It's a key site for anyone serious about computing.

Computer Hope   If you're having problems with your computer, there is hope—Computer Hope, that is. Computer Hope (`www.computerhope.com`) offers free computer help, questions and answers about common problems, listings of hardware and software vendors, and quick links to computer magazines and a computer dictionary.

Computing.Net   Computing.Net (`www.computing.net`) bills itself as "the industry's first technical support site." I don't know about being first, but it's one of the best; Computing.Net does a good job of centralizing technical support for all operating systems and types of computers. The support forums, which organize information by operating system (Windows 9*x*, Windows 2000/XP/2003, Linux, and so on), are the best part of the site. Also useful are the numerous FAQs that contain answers to the most common questions asked in the forums, a huge listing of downloadable hardware drivers, a number of how-tos for solving common problems, and a section just for novices.

DriverGuide.com   DriverGuide.com (`www.driverguide.com`) is *the* place to look for updated device drivers. The site consists of a massive database (compiled by the site's users) of drivers and related resources. Follow the links from this site to download and install the latest drivers for your system. The site also includes discussion boards, utilities, and helpful tutorials.

EarthWeb   EarthWeb (`www.earthweb.com`) is a network of sites targeting Information Technology (IT) professionals. It includes individual portals for IT management, networking and communications, Web development, hardware and systems, and software development.

Expertcity.com   Although Expertcity.com (`www.expertcity.com`) offers some free assistance, most of the help on this site comes from experts who "bid" to help you—for a fee. You ask your question and then choose your expert and price.

Experts Exchange   Experts Exchange (`www.experts-exchange.com`) is billed as "the number-one professional collaboration network." It works on a type of bonus system—you answer questions on a topic for another user and then earn points toward getting *your* questions answered by other experts.

HardwareCentral   HardwareCentral (`www.hardwarecentral.com`) is a terrific source for in-depth computer hardware information. It includes news, reviews, previews, opinions, tips, and tutorials—as well as a discussion section and a variety of driver and utility downloads.

HotHardware   HotHardware (`www.hothardware.com`) is another hardware-oriented site, based on the following claim: "Only the hottest PC hardware tested and burned in." The site includes news, reviews, and a user discussion forum.

Karbo's Guide   Karbo's Guide (`www.karbosguide.com`) offers hundreds of illustrated guides and tutorials for all manner of technical topics, from adapters to Zip drives. It's a terrific resource for learning about any new computer-related technology.

Microsoft Personal Support Center   This site (`support.microsoft.com/`) serves as the gateway to all of Microsoft's support services, including the indispensable Microsoft Knowledge Base. If you're having any sort of problem on a Windows-based machine, chances are a Microsoft product is somehow involved—which means this site should be at the top of your Favorites list. You can also find a ton of FAQs, service releases, patches, and updates in the Microsoft Download Center accessible from the main Support Center page (or you can go there directly at `www.microsoft.com/downloads/`).

The PC Guide   The PC Guide (`www.pcguide.com`) offers step-by-step how-tos, discussion forums, and tips on a variety of hardware-related topics.

PC Mechanic   This site (`www.pcmech.com`) offers articles, columns, and tutorials for various technical topics.

PC911   As the site's name implies, it provides help for computer problems in plain English. It contains a lot of how-tos, reviews, and freeware; you can find it at `www.pcnineoneone.com`.

PCsupport.com   PCsupport.com (`www.pcsupport.com`) bills itself as "the leader in e-support solutions." This translates into a combination of automated online support tools, searchable "knowledge directories" of more than 2200 hardware and software products, and 24/7 live support from certified technical experts. Some of this is free; some is fee-based. (Note that PCsupport.com acquired MyHelpDesk, another top-rated tech support site, and integrated that site's content and services into the PCsupport.com site.)

Protonic.com   Protonic.com (`www.protonic.com`) is an online community that provides free technical support to computer users. You can ask questions directly to site personnel or visit the site's many discussion boards.

SelfHelpDesk   SelfHelpDesk (`www.selfhelpdesk.com`) is run by Unisys and offers a variety of free online technical support, targeted primarily at corporate computing.

TechTutorials.com   This site (`www.techtutorials.com`) contains a huge directory of more than 1500 free computer and networking tutorials and white papers, targeted at IT professionals.

TechWeb   TechWeb (`www.techweb.com`) offers news and downloads for IT professionals. Use this site's Advanced Search option to investigate various computing topics—and check out the links to related sites at the bottom of the home page. (TechWeb is associated with CMPnet.)

Tom's Hardware Guide   Tom's Hardware Guide (`www.tomshardware.com`) is one of the best PC hardware sites on the Internet and includes plenty of information you can use to either troubleshoot or soup up your system.

VirtualDr   VirtualDr (`www.virtualdr.com`) offers technical support and information for all major operating systems, as well as many types of hardware. Also included are numerous discussion groups and online tutorials.

WebTechGeek   WebTechGeek (`www.webtechgeek.com`) presents news and guides on a variety of technical topics, including PCs, Personal Digital Assistants (PDAs), MP3s, and digital cameras.

WinDrivers.com   The main feature of this site (`www.windrivers.com`) is a huge library of downloadable Windows device drivers from practically every vendor in existence. It also features Windows-related hardware support.

ZDNet   ZDNet (`www.zdnet.com`) is a high-tech portal that combines all the technology news and information from *PC Magazine, Macworld,* and other Ziff-Davis magazines. It includes news, product reviews, online help, how-tos, and lots of useful downloads.

NOTE   *No doubt that I've left out dozens of useful sources of information, but this is meant to be a starting point, not a definitive guide of every single technical resource available online. If you know of a newsgroup, forum, or Web site that I haven't mentioned here but you think could be helpful to those repairing or upgrading their PCs, please don't email me with the information. I'll find it.*

Using FTP Sites for Support

FTP sites are dedicated servers, connected to the Internet, that hold collections of files available for downloading. Although Web sites are now the most common places to find files for downloading, many Web sites link to FTP sites for their file storage and downloading—and FTP sites are still good places to find software, utilities, and drivers.

DOWNLOADING PATCHES, DRIVERS, AND UTILITIES

You can find drivers, utilities, and patches available for downloading at any number of Web and FTP sites, as well as in newsgroups devoted to binary files. In addition to driver-only sites (such as DriverGuide.com and Drivers.com), almost all hardware and software vendors that have a Web site have some sort of Support link on their home page and a relatively easy way to locate driver downloads.

When downloading files, keep these things in mind:

◆ It's rare that a virus is uploaded to a moderated forum or commercial Web site, but it can happen. Before running any program on your system, it's a good idea to virus-check it first. (PC viruses, recall, can exist only in executable files or Microsoft Office documents containing macros, so other binary files and message threads don't need to be checked for viruses.)

◆ Downloading large files can take a long time, and if there's an error in your connection during the download, you may have to repeat it. Therefore, if you're connecting to the Internet over a phone line that has call-waiting activated, you may want to disable that feature before you connect by prefacing the phone number with *70.

◆ Shareware isn't freeware. If you use a shareware product, then you're implicitly agreeing to pay the shareware's author for the software once the evaluation period has expired.

◆ Copyright laws apply to electronic documents. You can't, for example, download a white paper that someone has written, remove their name, and substitute your own.

Downloading via FTP

FTP is an Internet protocol that predates the World Wide Web. In essence, an FTP site is a server optimized for file downloading using either specialized FTP client software or a Web browser. This is as opposed to the Hypertext Transfer Protocol (HTTP), which is used by what everyone thinks of as the Web. (Because HTTP supports more than FTP, such as pictures, it tends to be a little bulkier and slower than FTP for downloads.)

When you use your Web browser to access an FTP server, the directories and subdirectories on the server are displayed in a directory tree in the browser's main window. You turn your browser into a de facto FTP client by entering the address of the FTP site into the address box in your browser—but with *FTP* (instead of *HTTP*) in front of the address. For example, the full address of the Megatrends FTP server looks like this: `ftp://ftp.megatrends.com`. (For the curious, you can download utilities and Windows NT information from this site.)

Unless you have an account on the FTP server you're trying to reach—if you're not sure, you probably don't—you'll have to log in anonymously, providing your email address for a password. (Supplying your email address isn't always necessary, but it's polite because that lets the FTP administrator know who's been there.) Not all sites support anonymous login, but most of the ones you're likely to need do.

NOTE *When you use a Web browser to FTP, you're automatically connected to FTP sites with anonymous login—no extra steps required. If a site doesn't support anonymous login, then you'll know it: you'll be prompted for a password you won't have and will have to cancel in disgrace.*

NOTE *Incidentally, if you do have a username and password to log into an FTP site, you need to know the syntax to use in Internet Explorer (unless you use another FTP client). The syntax is* `ftp://username:password@ftp.site.com`.

Finding Useful FTP Servers

There are two ways to find FTP sites: through the lists of sites built into popular FTP clients and through Web-based FTP search engines and directories.

If you want to use a dedicated FTP client for downloading, check out CuteFTP (downloadable from `www.cuteftp.com`) or LapLinkFTP (downloadable from `www.laplinkftp.com`). These programs include comprehensive lists of public and corporate FTP servers, built right into the software.

If you prefer to access FTP sites from your Web browser, you can find directories of FTP sites (categorized by topic) at TILE.NET/FTP (`tile.net/ftp`) and at the LapLinkFTP Web site.

NOTE *As the Web continues to become more popular, the number of FTP sites is decreasing—so don't be surprised if you run into a dead link or two on any list of FTP servers.*

The Best FTP Servers for Downloading Files

As a kind of head start for your quest for online support, the following is a short list of FTP servers that have plentiful archives of drivers, utilities, and other downloadable software programs:

- ◆ FUNET (`ftp.funet.fi`)
- ◆ Megatrends (`ftp.megatrends.com`)

- ◆ Microsoft (`ftp.microsoft.com`)

- ◆ Universitat Duisburg Archive (`ftp.uni-duisburg.de`)

- ◆ University of Illinois Archive (`ftp.cso.uiuc.edu`)

- ◆ University of North Carolina/ibiblio Archive (`ibiblio.org/pub/`)

- ◆ Washington University Archives (`wuarchive.wustl.edu`)

In addition, most hardware and software vendors maintain their own corporate FTP servers. Try accessing these sites by adding an `ftp` to the company name and `.com`. For example, the address for 3Com's server is `ftp.3com.com`.

TIP *When you're navigating through FTP sites, you're most likely to find downloadable files in the* `Pub` *or* `Files` *directories.*

Using Usenet Newsgroups for Support

Newsgroups are discussion groups that are part of a service called *Usenet*. (Usenet, like the World Wide Web, is part of the larger Internet.) Newsgroups are available on all kinds of topics, from bicycle maintenance to cat stories to problems associated with configuring hard drives to…you name it. If you haven't found a group that covers the topic you want to discuss, either you should look a little harder or one will probably pop up soon enough.

NOTE *An unspoken rule of the technical Internet is that in exchange for getting help from those more knowledgeable than you, you in turn help someone else less experienced than you are.*

Understanding Usenet

Usenet (also called NewsNet and NNTP) is similar in many ways to email except that you don't have a dedicated address and you don't exchange messages on a one-to-one basis. Instead, you *post* messages (called *articles*) into a forum for all other users to read and perhaps respond to.

In essence, each Usenet newsgroup (and there are tens of thousands of them) is a collection of topic-related messages that are stored on special NNTP servers. You access the messages using an NNTP-compliant client, such as Outlook Express. Usenet groups have names similar to Web site domain names, but they're often longer and, hence, more descriptive. An example of a Usenet newsgroup name is `comp.os.ms-windows.apps.compatibility.win95`, a group dedicated to discussing application compatibility issues with Windows 95. Other newsgroup names can get quite silly, such as the obvious dislike for a beloved purple dinosaur shared by the list members of `alt.barney.dinosaur.die.die.die`.

Because of their interactive nature, newsgroups are good places to get problem-solving advice. (Message boards on computer-oriented Web sites are also good sources for this type of advice.) Sometimes you can get lucky and find that someone else has asked a similar question before you did, but most of the time it's easiest if you go ahead and ask anyway.

TIP *If the forum or newsgroup in which you plan to post a question has a list of FAQs, read the FAQ before posting to make sure your solution isn't in it.*

NOTE *Although newsgroups are great sources for advice, they're not really good sources for downloadable utilities. That's because newsgroups don't archive information; most messages remain "live" for only a few days or weeks before they're cleared away to make space for newer postings. However, there's a way you can take a trip down memory lane. Check out Google Groups (`http://groups.google.com`), which lets you search through a complete 20-year Usenet Archive of more than 700 million Usenet messages. In addition to finding threads of a more technical nature, imagine finding such items as the first Usenet mention of Microsoft (28 May 1981, `net.general`), MTV (22 March 1982, `net.music`), or Madonna (13 July 1983, `net.audio`)! You'll learn more about Google Groups later in this chapter.*

How Newsgroups Work

Most newsgroups are unmoderated, meaning that no one's watching the message content to ensure that subject discussions stay on track, that people are polite (or even not downright obscene) to one another, or that people don't post totally irrelevant messages in the wrong forums (called *spamming* considered to be impolite). Although there's a lot of garbage in newsgroups (on the order of offers of nude celebrity pictures or discounted prices on your next order of Viagra), newsgroups have been around for a long time and are good places to find people with lots of technical experience. Technical newsgroups, after all, are frequented by those interested enough in talking shop to do it online.

WARNING *Know that Usenet is frequently used by unscrupulous individuals to pass material with mature content and/or illicit and illegal information, including child pornography. Newsgroups that carry this type of information often have descriptive names with sex in the title. If you're careful, you'll never see such material, but be aware that it's out there (the Internet is anonymous, remember—especially Usenet). Also remember that many people cross-post (distribute the same message to a number of other groups) and send such material to groups that don't dwell on those things.*

Normally, your access to newsgroups works like this: your ISP maintains a news server that stores as many of the postings in all or selected newsgroups as possible. (Note that this means you may not have access to all available newsgroups—if a group isn't on your news server, you can't reach it.) Rather than connecting directly to Usenet, then, you connect to the news server and read the messages posted there. Any messages that you post to a newsgroup will be uploaded from the news server to Usenet itself and then propagated to other Usenet servers across the Internet.

NOTE *The more traffic a newsgroup or forum experiences (that is, the more new messages are posted each time you visit), the more likely it is that someone will see your posting and reply to it.*

Newsgroup Hierarchies

More than 30,000 newsgroups are on Usenet (although not all may be available on your ISP's server, as noted earlier). Browsing through this many newsgroups takes more time and energy than even I have, so there has to be a way to organize the groups. There is, of course, because all news group names adhere to a simple hierarchy. You start with one of several major domains (the part of the name to the left of the first period) and then move down through the hierarchy (much as you'd move down through a list of folders and subfolders) as you move past each additional period in the name.

The major newsgroup domains include the following:

`alt.`   This stands for *alternative*—the discussions here are probably a little weird, as just about anything goes in these groups.

`biz.`   These newsgroups are host to discussions about various business products and services.

`comp.`   These newsgroups are, broadly speaking, computer-based. They may be computer-related humor or Sound Blaster installation hints. The exact nature of the discussion depends on which group you're talking about, but the discussions should in some way touch on computers (even if it's about how evil they are). This is probably the best domain to browse through for computer-related information and help.

`humanities.`   This is the place to discuss literature, fine arts, and other humanities (but *not* popular entertainment—see the `rec.` domain for that!).

`k12.`   This domain includes education-related discussions about kindergarten through grade 12.

`misc.`   Hard to fit into any particular category, these groups might cover such topics as good techie books, militia activity, and home schooling.

`news.`   These newsgroups generally cover network- and newsgroup-related technical issues.

`rec.`   These groups are recreation oriented, covering just about any topic that you could think of for recreation.

`soc.`   These groups deal with social and cultural issues.

`sci.`   This is where you'll find science-related discussions, for both professionals and laypersons.

`talk.`   These groups are for those who like debate. Whatever you feel like arguing about, it's probably covered here.

NOTE   *There are also many regional and company-specific Usenet domains. (For example, the* `japan.` *domain contains Japanese-oriented newsgroups, and the* `microsoft.` *domain includes newsgroups about Microsoft products.) Some of the larger regional domains include hierarchies that resemble the overall Usenet hierarchy in their complexity.*

There's a lot of crossover between domains. If you're so inclined, you can probably start a flame war on a `comp.` newsgroup that would do credit to an `alt.` newsgroup. (Just post an "NT is better than Linux!" message to see what I mean.) That said, the previous domains represent how the usual topic hierarchies shake out, more or less.

Finding Useful Usenet Newsgroups

Even if you browse Usenet by hierarchy, you still have tens of thousands of individual newsgroups to sift through. That's a lot of list scrolling, so it's useful to have a newsgroup reader that includes a search function (most do).

NETIQUETTE

This chapter is about research, not manners, but manners can play a significant role in determining whether your research results pay off. Remember, no one *has* to answer your questions.

◆ DON'T WRITE IN ALL CAPITAL LETTERS. THIS IS CONSIDERED SHOUTING AND IS RUDE.

◆ Be specific in message headers. "Help!" is too vague to grab my attention; "Need to restore hard disk configuration information" is more effective.

◆ Explain your situation briefly, but completely, at the beginning of the message. If it's a troubleshooting question, describe what you've done so far and any relevant parts of your configuration. People are more likely to reply to your posts if they know the background.

◆ Don't make posts longer than they need to be. First, reading on-screen is harder than reading hard copy, and paging through messages is wearisome. Second, people are paying to download and read your messages—don't give them junk.

◆ Don't post a question in more than one section in an online forum or in more than one newsgroup. If it's in the wrong section of a forum, the forum sysop (system operator) will move it to the correct one. Posting the same question to more than one newsgroup is sometimes acceptable if the groups aren't too similar in topic and the question fits into more than one category, but keep it to a minimum.

◆ Be polite. The people who are replying to your posts are doing *you* a favor. For heaven's sake, don't be rude to them, even if you disagree with their conclusions. Everyone can see your posts, not just their intended recipient.

◆ If you encounter anyone breaking these rules, don't lecture them about it. If the forum or newsgroup is moderated, the moderator will do so. If it isn't, I assure you that someone else will take care of it and you won't have to look like a scold.

As an example, searching for the word *computer* generates a list that includes a lot of newsgroups in the `comp.` or `news.` domains—as well as groups *not* in those domains. It's also important to note that the results of this search don't include some newsgroups that I know (from personal experience) are computer related because those newsgroups don't have the word *computer* in their names. In other words, don't assume that if the keywords you enter to find information about your particular DSL modem don't net anything, then no one is talking about your DSL modem. You just need to start surfing the groups themselves to see what people are talking about.

When you need help with a problem and you don't know where to start looking, think about key words associated with your difficulty. In your newsreader, you can see how newsgroups are named. Based on that naming scheme, identify the parts of your problem that might be in the name of a newsgroup. For instance, if you want to ask advice about choosing a SCSI controller to work with your system running Windows XP Professional, that gives you several good potential keywords: *SCSI, XP,* and *configure.* (In this case, I'd probably start with SCSI because that's really what your question is about.)

From the results of this keyword search, you can choose a newsgroup that looks likely (perhaps `comp.periphs.scsi`), go to it, and read a little of the message traffic already posted to see whether people are talking about subjects related to your problem.

If no SCSI newsgroups seem to fit the bill, you can try *XP* instead. There's a trick to this one, though: newsreaders aren't case sensitive, and most don't let you distinguish between searching for whole words only and searching for part of a word. Therefore, if you search for *xp* only, you'll get the XP hits, but you'll also get any other newsgroups with names that have *xp* in any form. (Obviously, this point doesn't apply to just XP but to any combination of letters that have significance on their own but can also be part of a word.) So this time, if you search for *.xp* (note the period before the *xp*), you'll get a more targeted list of results.

TIP *If you post to a newsgroup using your real email address, you're likely to find yourself on multiple mailing lists for get-rich-quick schemes—even ones having nothing to do with what you posted about. The quick-and-dirty workaround for this little problem is to use a phony address for your Usenet postings. (Some users insert the term* nospam *somewhere in their real address; any thinking human being who wants to respond directly to you will see the nospam and remove it, thus revealing your real address.)*

As I've discussed, tens of thousands of newsgroups are available. Not all of them will be available from your news server (some servers subscribe to only a limited number of groups, and there's not much you can do about that), but there are enough that you should be able to get help with almost anything.

SEARCHING NEWSGROUP ARCHIVES AT GOOGLE GROUPS

Because there are so many newsgroups, a server that subscribes to all the groups may be able to store only a few days' worth of traffic at a time. To keep current with a newsgroup, then, you'll need to check in fairly regularly.

What do you do if you want to read messages that were posted more than a few days ago—messages that are no longer available on your ISP's newsgroup server? When this need arises, it's time to access the Usenet archives, which are available on the Google Groups Web site (`http://groups.google.com`).

For several years, a full archive of postings from all Usenet newsgroups was maintained by Deja.com (formerly called DejaNews). Early in 2001, Google, the search engine site, acquired the Deja.com site and all its archives. So now you can search the Usenet archive at Google Groups in any number of ways—including, if you click the Advanced Groups Search link, by keyword, by newsgroup name, by date, by username, and so on. (If you want to avoid the nasty stuff, you can also choose to filter out all adult-oriented newsgroups from your search.)

Google Groups is *the* site for serious newsgroup research. Not only can you search multiple newsgroups with a single query, you can also view all the messages in related threads—or even read all messages from a specific user. If it's ever been posted to a newsgroup, chances are that you can find it at Google Groups.

The Best Newsgroups for Technical Information

The following is a short list of individual newsgroups and newsgroup hierarchies that might be of interest if you need technical computer information or support. A wildcard (*) at the end of a name indicates that some or all of the groups in that particular hierarchy might be worthwhile:

- `alt.comp`
- `alt.comp.hardware.*`
- `alt.comp.periphs.*`

- ◆ `alt.computer`
- ◆ `alt.sys.pc-clone.*`
- ◆ `comp.misc`
- ◆ `comp.os.linux.*`
- ◆ `comp.os.ms-dos.*`
- ◆ `comp.os.ms-windows.*`
- ◆ `comp.periphs.*`
- ◆ `comp.sys.ibm.pc.hardware.*`
- ◆ `comp.sys.intel`
- ◆ `microsoft.public.*`
- ◆ `misc.forsale.computers.*`

TIP   Some of the best computer troubleshooting groups seem to have the word hardware *in them. This keyword nets you a plethora of useful newsgroups. Why* hardware *and not more specific words? Traffic levels, mostly. Newsgroups devoted more specifically to particular hardware questions—such as Input/Output (I/O) transfer—seem to have too little traffic to do much good.*

Using E-Mail Mailing Lists for Support

Similar to Usenet newsgroups are email mailing lists. The major differences are that newsgroups are public and unmoderated (generally), and mailing lists are mostly private (by invitation only, in some cases) and often moderated. The result, typically, is a more focused forum with less extraneous "noise" from off-topic posts.

How Mailing Lists Work

E-mail mailing lists operate through the convenience of email. Members of the mailing list send email messages to the list moderator; those messages are then re-sent (either individually or combined into a more manageable daily *digest*) to other members of the list. This means, of course, that you have to *subscribe* to the list and provide the list moderator with your email address. Some lists allow just about anyone with an inbox to subscribe, and other lists have more stringent membership requirements—necessary, in some cases, to keep out the riffraff and improve the quality of the list.

TIP   If you're uneasy about giving out your private email address (and you should be, given the huge quantities of unsolicited spam that result from public address postings), consider opening a separate email account solely for mailing list use. Hotmail, Yahoo!, and other free email services are worth considering for this sort of "buffered" email account.

Although different mailing lists have different methods of subscribing (and some even have their own Web sites for both subscription and archival purposes), most use some sort of automated email registration. The way it typically works is that you send a blank email message to the designated address, with the single word *subscribe* in the subject line. Unsubscribing is usually the reverse: you send a blank email with the word *unsubscribe* in the subject line.

Using a mailing list to obtain advice and information is similar to using a Usenet newsgroup. You begin by sending an email message containing your question or comment to the list moderator. Your message is then immediately sent to the other list subscribers—or, for those lists that offer digest services, combined with all other messages received that day and then sent as one large message to the digest subscribers. When other subscribers choose to respond, they send a reply to the list moderator; that reply is then sent to all other subscribers or added to the daily digest. Naturally, if a fellow subscriber chooses to make their email address public, you can bypass the rest of the list and reply directly to that individual.

Finding Useful Mailing Lists

Because many mailing lists are run by individuals (or by individual organizations), where can you find a list of all the lists that are available?

One good listing of mailing lists is Topica, formerly Liszt (`www.liszt.com`). You can use this Web site to search for mailing lists by keyword, or you can browse through Liszt's hierarchical directory of topics. To give you an example of what you'll find, if you go to the Computers & Internet topic, you'll find listings for nearly 40 subcategories, with several lists in each subcategory. (The Technical Support subcategory, at time of writing, included 61 mailing lists.)

Another good source of mailing lists is Yahoo! Groups (`http://groups.yahoo.com`), which serves as a hosting service for tens of thousands of lists. As with Liszt, you can search through Yahoo! Groups' mailing lists or browse through their organized categories. (Yahoo! Groups' Hardware category, at time of writing, included more than 1000 mailing lists.)

The Best Mailing Lists for Technical Information

To give you a head start on your hunt for the perfect mailing list, the following are lists to consider for computer hardware help and support:

1PCBuilder   Contains a list for people who build, upgrade, or repair their own PCs. See `http://groups.yahoo.com/group/1PCBuilder/` for more information.

compuhelp   Provides help for hardware and operating system problems. Contact `compuhelp-owner@lists.spunge.org` for more information.

computertalkshop   Provides a general computer discussion list. See `http://www.computertalk-shop.com/` for more information.

pchelp   Provides help on computer hardware and software issues. See `http://groups.yahoo.com/group/pchelp/` for more information.

pchelp4u   Specializes in help for hardware and Windows-related problems. See `http://groups.yahoo.com/group/pchelp4u/` for more information.

survpc   Provides a list for users of older DOS and Windows-based PCs. See `http://groups.yahoo.com/list/survpc/` for more information.

TIP   *Using Liszt and Yahoo! Groups, you can also find mailing lists devoted to specific vendors or types of equipment. Just search by vendor name.*

Using Internet Relay Chat for Support

If you can't wait the hours or days it might take to generate a response from a question posted to a newsgroup or mailing list, you have a real-time alternative: Internet Relay Chat (IRC).

Chatting with IRC

IRC is that part of the Internet that facilitates real-time text-based conversation between groups of like-minded users. Think of IRC as being kind of like CB radio; different *channels* are dedicated to specific topics, and once you're in a channel, you're talking publicly with everybody else who is currently in the channel. It's also possible to hold private conversations with other users logged on to a specific IRC network; these conversations aren't visible to other users in a channel.

NOTE   *IRC operates on a traditional client/server model. You (and your software) are the* client, *and the IRC computer you and other clients connect to is the* server.

IRC is a collection of individual chat networks, all connected to the main Internet backbone. To participate in IRC, you have to connect to an IRC *server* dedicated to a specific IRC *network*; you can connect to only one network at a time. (You'll often find similar channels on different networks; these channels operate independently from each other, however.)

You can find a complete list of available IRC networks (and their associated servers) at www.mirc.com/servers.html. The most popular IRC networks include ChatNet, DALnet, EFnet, Galaxynet, IRCnet, NewNet, Starlink, and Undernet.

Because each IRC network is composed of multiple servers, you connect to a specific server that is itself connected to the larger network. (You access the server over the Internet, of course.) You have to log on to the server with a unique *nickname* (of your own creation), and then you can access specific channels on that network.

To use IRC, you need a piece of software called an *IRC client*. The most popular IRC client is mIRC, a shareware program you can download from www.mirc.com. mIRC enables you to connect to any IRC server (and includes a full list of servers for all major IRC networks) and then chat in multiple channels simultaneously.

NOTE   *IRC is one of the largest and most accessible forms of online chat on the Internet. You can also find similar-working chat rooms on proprietary online services (such as America Online) and on many individual Web sites. (For example, Yahoo! has a thriving chat section.) Web-based chat can be either Hypertext Markup Language (HTML) or Java-based and typically requires no other software beyond your Web browser.*

Finding Useful IRC Channels

The best place to search for IRC channels is the same place you search for email mailing lists: Liszt (www.liszt.com/chat/). Liszt lets you search for specific topics and then lists channels that match those topics—and the specific IRC networks where you can find those channels.

WARNING   *Of all the flaky components of the Internet, IRC is the most flaky. IRC channels come and go with the wind, and you never know what's going to be there from one day to the next. Take any lists of IRC channels (including the one coming up next) with a grain of salt—there are no guarantees with IRC!*

The Best IRC Channels for Technical Information

There are tens of thousands of IRC channels, devoted to everything from general chat to kinky sex to local sports teams. Naturally, you're interested in those channels where the best and the brightest computer gurus hang out, so you can learn from their expertise.

The first thing to do is to identify those IRC networks with the most traffic because more traffic equals more people chatting equals more of a chance that you'll get your questions answered. For hardware support purposes, those channels are DALnet, EFnet, and Undernet.

What follows is a short list of the busiest hardware support channels on those three networks. Obviously, other channels touch on the topic at hand, but these channels are probably the best places to start if you need a quick answer to a problem:

DALnet   The best hardware-related channel on the DALnet network is `#computers`.

EFnet   There are three good support-oriented channels on the EFnet network: `#computerhelp`, `#computers`, and `#hardware`.

Undernet   On Undernet, the busiest hardware and support channels are `#computerhelp`, `#computers`, and `#hardware`.

NOTE   *All IRC channels start with a #.*

Cautions about Online Support

Throughout this chapter I've talked about how the Internet can be a marvelous help to you when you're trying to research something related to your computer or to get help with a problem. Now it's time for some cautions to go along with the cheerleading. (Most of this stuff will probably seem really obvious, but bear with me.)

Don't Believe Everything You Hear

There's a lot of misinformation in the PC world. It's not actual lying, but it's stuff that's misheard, or corrected later, but the person telling you missed the correction or misunderstood because the listener didn't have enough background to remember the information correctly. The trouble is that a lot of this misinformation gets repeated until it has a life of its own. Some is harmless, such as an assertion I saw repeated that Microsoft was responsible for changing the PCMCIA card's name to the PC Card (they weren't), but some isn't.

If someone suggests a drastic measure in response to a problem that you've posted a question about, I suggest you hang on for a little while and see whether you get any other responses. Surely you've met people in person who claim to know more than their experience covers; well, they exist in cyberspace, too—and they're harder to strangle when you follow their suggestion and something goes desperately wrong.

When in Doubt, Check for Viruses

A dose of reality: viruses aren't a problem for most commercial sites. FTP sites, for example, rarely allow anonymous logins to upload files to their sites. Manufacturer-supported Web sites provide

PROPRIETARY ONLINE SERVICES AND SUPPORT

All the resources listed so far in this chapter are available to anyone with an Internet connection. In addition to these public sources of information, several proprietary sources of online information are available to you—providing you subscribe to the services that supply the information, that is.

The largest source of proprietary online information is America Online (AOL). With more than 27 million users, AOL is the world's largest ISP—and the largest provider of proprietary online content.

Unfortunately, AOL doesn't develop a lot of its own content but rather licenses content from other sources. For example, much of the content on AOL's Computing channel comes from CNET—and mirrors what you can find for free on CNET's regular Web site. (You can check out some of AOL's computing content for free on the AOL Web site at www.aol.com/webcenters/computing/.)

The second-largest proprietary online service is MSN (The Microsoft Network). Unlike AOL, most of MSN's computer-related content is freely accessible over the Web, and it includes a good deal of unique information—including news, reviews, downloads, forums, and so on. You can access MSN Computing Central at http://computingcentral.msn.com.

MSN Computing Central maintains more than two dozen computing forums, running through a range of operating systems (not just Microsoft based: Unix, Linux, and OS/2, too), telephony and PC communications, games, and safe computing (virus and network security). For the purpose of researching how to upgrade and maintain your PC (check the title of this book), Computing Central's Hardware forum is probably your best bet; it has an active membership, and a variety of question topics and skill levels are represented. (I haven't seen anyone laughed at for asking a newbie question yet.) In fact, one very basic question about what Random Access Memory (RAM) was got some people out of the woodwork admitting that they didn't know either and thanks for asking. The traffic there isn't as heavy as some hardware-related Usenet newsgroups, but it's not bad.

The third proprietary online service, CompuServe, used to be *the* online service to join if you were into computers or wanted access to the people shaping the computer industry. A decade ago, it was pretty easy to join a whole host of computer forums (available exclusively on the CompuServe service) and rub elbows with top decision-makers and senior support brass at companies such as Microsoft, Novell, Lotus, and Digital Equipment Corporation (DEC). You paid for the privilege, too; for a very long time, you paid a hefty monthly subscription fee—in addition to hourly connection fees (as high as $24 per hour!).

Today's CompuServe, however, is a pale image of what used to be—and CompuServe's supremacy in online technical material has faded considerably. CompuServe is now owned by America Online, and its technical content has become somewhat limited. Most of the old CompuServe contingent of experienced professionals—those folks who could answer almost any computer question—have migrated to the World Wide Web. Today, you can still join and participate in computer forums and download files, but it's usually easier to locate the same—or better—material on the Web.

official files (and only official files) for downloading and go to the extra effort of virus-checking those files. No company wants the public relations nightmare of being responsible for a virus infection.

That said, you should be careful of sites that aren't related to a particular company or that cater to those who might enjoy a little rule breaking before breakfast. If you come across a site that offers to let you download games and (possibly) pirated software, or quite openly caters to hackers, it's a good idea to check the files that you download before running them. Once again, only executable files can contain PC viruses, so you needn't worry about document files (with the exception of Office documents that have macros in them) or messages.

NOTE *Macro viruses are both cross-platform and capable of being contained in a document. This class of virus is discussed in more detail in Chapter 29, "Viruses and Other Nasty Bugs."*

Don't Give Out Personal Information

When posting in public areas such as newsgroups or forums, don't give out any personal information you don't want the world to know, such as your home address, your telephone number, your credit card or checking account information, or the like. This information isn't impossible to find or figure out (especially for those who have a little time on their hands and nothing better to do), but that doesn't mean you have to make it easy for them.

Troubleshooting Tips

Getting assistance from a remote source always presents some degree of difficulty, just because the person who is helping you can't see your system. This puts the responsibility squarely on your shoulders to present your problem as clearly as possible, erring on the side of offering too much rather than too little information.

In a recent informal survey of several managers who run online technical support forums for MSN Computing Central, almost all reported the same thing: users often don't give enough information when first presenting their problem to get useful help.

These are real examples taken from just one morning's online help requests:

"Help. I'm getting an error message. What do I do?" is all one user writes, not mentioning *which* error message, let alone where it was observed, or what might have happened as a result.

"Why doesn't the drive I just added work?" writes another, failing to provide even basic details about what kind of drive, how it was prepared and configured, or what operating system is being used.

"My PC beeps. What do I do to stop it????? Also, why does it crash when I use my favorite program??? Huh???? That's really dumb!!!!!!!!!!!!!!!!!!"

"Why couldn't I install Windows 2000 or Windows XP???" types another person. All PCs beep unless they're dead, but because no information is provided, you don't know if it's beeping unusually. You don't know what program is causing the user's PC to crash or whether the user is getting any error messages before the crash that might give an indication of what's wrong. As for why Windows 2000/XP wouldn't install, you're left wondering here, too, because there's no information on what happened when the person tried to install. Finally, this exemplifies a common myth about online technical support: that more punctuation—such as exclamation marks to highlight frustration—will take the place of providing details about the PC and its problem. Sadly, they don't.

If you find someone able and willing to help you, the last thing you want to do is force the person into a position of having to pull teeth to extract information from you—it's a waste of their time and yours, and you probably want to solve this sooner rather than later. So present basic details about your system and the problem at hand when you post the first time, and if you reply, reference the previous messages. You don't have to write a book, but you need to offer basic facts. Important details to include are the following:

- Type of machine, such as Pentium 4, and a quick overview of what you have installed—that is, 256 megabytes (MB) of RAM, 40 gigabytes (GB) hard drive with 15GB free, and so on.

- Operating system used—check your version and report it. (And yes, Windows 98 Second Edition is distinct from the original Windows 98; Windows XP Home is also distinct from Windows XP Professional.)

- If receiving an error message, provide the *exact* wording and whether it can be reproduced when it occurs.

- The last thing(s) you were doing before noticing and reporting the problem, including any hardware, software, or upgrades installed or removed.

- Exact steps you've taken already to try to resolve the problem (important in case something you tried was in error, and a second problem could mask the solution of the original problem).

- Any other relevant information, such as noting a Light-Emitting Diode (LED) power indicator not on when it should be, your machine's failing to boot, or the PC beeping a specific number of times on bootup.

That's about all there is to obtaining support online. At this point, you should have a good idea of the tools available to you and how to find what you need. Just remember these basic rules:

- The answer is probably out there somewhere. Don't give up too easily.

- Most people like nothing more than to give advice, so never be afraid to ask.

So have fun out in cyberspace—I'll see you there! Now armed with the resources you need to research the solution to computer problems, it's time to move on to troubleshooting hardware issues, which is the topic of the next chapter.

Chapter 25

Troubleshooting PC Problems

Introduction

Okay, suppose you dust out your PC fortnightly. You clean and adjust your disk drives semiannually. You have a robot that zaps anyone carrying food or drink within 50 feet of your PC. But, one day, Microsoft Word refuses to print your purple prose. How do you proceed?

You might say that this is a chapter about religion. I want you to develop a process for dealing with computer repairs that you follow as dutifully as a zealot follows a religion.

Why get religious? Because people who fix PCs day in and day out—people who fix *anything* day in and day out, for that matter—have learned to do it by following some repeatable step-by-step procedures. That isn't the only approach you can take, of course; the alternative method is to attack each problem in a haphazard way.

Now, I'm somebody who's tried both the religious way and the haphazard way. As such, you might say I'm qualified to offer you some advice on how to choose which approach to take.

If you find you're plagued with too much free time, time you have to spend with the spouse and kids; if you just can't sleep at night and need something to fill those insomniac hours; if Saturdays and Sundays are painful tedium broken only by the occasional *Three Stooges* rerun—then, by all means, adopt the haphazard method. You'll be able to tackle all kinds of fascinating problems, most of which you created yourself while messing around trying to fix the original problem. And, because the true haphazard fixer never takes notes, you'll get to experience the joy of problem-solving over and over, even when it's the same problem.

If, on the other hand, you want to do something with your days other than futzing around with balky PCs, then think about getting religion.

Don't get me wrong: there's nothing wrong with futzing around with a PC—you'll get some of your deepest insights and "ohhh...*that's* how it works" kind of knowledge through that kind of experimentation. All I'm saying is keep the experimenting and the fixing as separate as possible. And when you *must* experiment, make sure all your experiments are repeatable ones; taking notes should be gospel.

QuickSteps: Troubleshooting PC Problems

The following are the key steps you should take in troubleshooting most PC problems (while remembering to stay calm and positive). Several of these steps occur before you ever power down and remove the case.

BE PREPARED

Before you start, there are some things you may need on hand. These include the following:

- Documentation for your PC and/or its separate components (including warranty information)
- Container for placing screws between removal and reinstallation
- Appropriate screwdriver(s), such as a Phillips-head
- Antistatic wrist strap
- Boot disk and operating system installation CD (just in case)
- Connector cleaner or hard, white artist's eraser
- Diagnostic utilities

To diagnose PC problems, always follow these steps:

1. Check for operator errors—commands or configurations you may have done wrong, software or hardware you may have set up incorrectly, or instructions you may have reversed (for example, reversing a cable or putting a jumper on opposite from the way it needs to go).
2. Check to make certain that everything that should be plugged into either a direct power source or the PC itself is plugged in correctly and that the connection is secure.
3. Check the software, including program files and drivers, to make sure you have the most current versions installed—and configured properly.
4. Check for external signs of trouble, such as flickering Light-Emitting Diode (LED) power indicators or those that don't come on at all, strange sounds or lack of sound, and lack of display.
5. Run appropriate diagnostic programs.
6. Only when all else fails, disassemble the PC. Shut it down, disconnect all power, remove the case, ground yourself, and go inside to check cable and power connections, the proper seating of expansion boards and memory modules, and anything out of the ordinary.
7. Reseat connectors as necessary. If your sound card doesn't work, for example, unplug it and plug it back in, making sure the connection is secure. Often times, reseating a flaky device can make it magically work again.

TIP *Windows NT/2000/XP/2003 operating systems have an Event Viewer application that logs system errors. Checking this log can help you track down system issues related to hardware as well as software.*

General Troubleshooting Rules

The following rules have kept me out of trouble for a long time. I know they'll be of use to you.

PC TECHNICIAN'S CREED

◆ Remember: don't panic, and you will win.

◆ Wait…and repeat.

◆ Write everything down.

◆ Do the easy stuff first.

◆ Reboot and try again.

◆ Simplify, simplify, simplify!

◆ Draw a picture, separate into components, and test.

◆ Never assume.

◆ Trust no one: the documentation sometimes lies.

◆ Observe like Sherlock Holmes.

Although some of these suggestions are a bit tongue-in-cheek, there's a nugget of advice in every one, and they're all part of the philosophy of troubleshooting.

Remember: Don't Panic, and You Will Win

You have to have confidence in yourself as a troubleshooter. Look, this stuff isn't that hard. My technical training is as a Ph.D. economist rather than as a computer scientist or engineer, I have 10 thumbs, and people pay *me* to fix machines. If I can do it, you can do it, too. There's not that much to these machines. When it comes right down to it, the only thing you really can't replace for (at most) a hundred dollars or so is your data, and you can protect that with frequent backups.

If you don't go in there *knowing* you're going to win, you're going to get beaten—these machines can *smell* fear. A former girlfriend, a black belt in Tae Kwon Do, told me once that an important tenet of Tae Kwon Do is to "have an indomitable spirit." Sounds good to me—practice some *Tech* Kwon Do, and don't forget that indomitable spirit.

Wait…and Repeat

It's a simple fact that the vast majority of "computer" problems are actually caused by human error. (That means you!) If something goes wrong when you're using your PC, stop what you're doing, take a few deep breaths, and then try it again. Chances are you hit the wrong key, clicked the wrong button, or just plain zigged when you meant to zag. There's a lot to be gained by having a little patience and perhaps going a little slower, so you don't repeat your mistakes.

Write Everything Down

If you read Chapter 3, "Taking Apart and Rebuilding the PC" (and if you didn't, go do it), then you've already learned about the hazards of not documenting. I tend not to write things down when I'm pretty sure the operation will be simple (it almost never is) or when it's sufficiently traumatic that I'm certain I couldn't forget (there's always another, bigger trauma waiting). I've found I'm more likely to write down important notes if I keep my notebook—the paper kind—handy. These notes might include, for example, special location information or notations about a problem, such as a bent pin or the actual layout being the reverse of how it appears in the manufacturer's diagram. As a bonus, writing things in your notebook means you'll be able to find them later.

TIP   Some technicians now take digital photographs of hardware setups (hardware location, cable runs, switches, etc.) to make their troubleshooting easier. This is just another example of technology replacing the paper-and-pencil way of doing things.

Do the Easy Stuff First

I am, by nature, a lazy person. That's why I got interested in computers: they were machines that could free me from some drudgery. The *inexperienced* and lazy troubleshooter tries to save time by not making notes, by acting before thinking, and by *swapping* components or configuration information when he ought to be *stopping*. . .stopping to consider his next move.

What I've eventually figured out is that well-planned laziness is a virtue. An *experienced* lazy person looks ahead and says, "Oh, heck, what if I *can't* fix this thing? I don't want to create any more trouble for myself than necessary." And so the lazy person keeps diagrams and writes down everything that she does so she doesn't have to tear out her hair trying to put the PC back together.

The *experienced* lazy person does the easy stuff first; if it's a video problem, and it's not software, then four things could be swapped: the motherboard, the video board, the cable, or the monitor. What gets swapped first? The easy thing: the cable.

Reboot and Try Again

Your computer is affected by fluctuations in the power supply as brief as four milliseconds. This means that if your power disappeared for only $1/200$ of a second, you wouldn't see the lights flicker, the microwave would still work, and the TV wouldn't skip a beat—even the digital clocks wouldn't start blinking. But several bytes of your computer's memory (not a lot of the memory, or you'd see a memory error message of some kind) get randomized. The result is that a program that has always worked pretty well all of a sudden stops dead. You'll never find out why it locked up that one time in a thousand. Maybe everybody in the building was running their photocopiers at the same time. Maybe radiation from a solar storm assaulted your memory chips (yes, that can happen, but it's unlikely; when a technician blames something on "cosmic rays," she's being facetious). It doesn't matter; the quick answer to this problem is just to start over and reboot the machine.

Now, don't get too trigger-happy with the reboot if you're in the middle of an application. It's usually a really bad idea to do a hard reboot (the Ctrl+Alt+Del kind) out of Windows—try everything you can to get the machine to respond and let you do a graceful shutdown. If you reboot in the middle of an application, the application may leave files "open," and those files will be lost. Such half-finished files lead to a phenomenon you may have seen called lost clusters.

GETTING THE REMOTE USER TO REBOOT — WITHOUT INSULTING THEIR INTELLIGENCE!

When troubleshooting other peoples' computers, we technicians frequently tell them to reboot. As we know, rebooting solves a lot of computer "problems." Unfortunately, end users see our advice as insulting their intelligence, and often we'll get the, "I've already done that," whether they have or not. Sometimes they actually have rebooted, but we really don't have any way of knowing.

Here's a little trick. Tell them that you need to try a troubleshooting step. Have them reboot into Windows Safe Mode (when the computer reboots, generally tapping the F8 key will bring up the menu with the choice to boot into Safe Mode). After the system is into safe mode, have them perform a normal shutdown and restart. Yes, it's just a reboot. But you have accomplished two things. One, you've rebooted the computer. Two, you've avoided "insulting their intelligence" by telling them to do something they might otherwise find menial.

Simplify, Simplify, Simplify!

The average PC has about a bazillion screensavers, applications, background communications programs (such as fax receive programs), and of course driver programs for sound boards, network cards, video boards, and the mouse, to name just a few. Determining the source of a problem is really hard when there are innumerable interactions between hardware and software.

That means it's a good idea to eliminate as much as you can from a PC before trying to diagnose it. For example, boot without the network. If you're running Windows 95/98/Me, wait for the `Starting Windows` message and press F8. That gives you the chance to boot Windows in Safe mode. In Windows NT/2000/XP/2003, you can choose a configuration with a simple video driver at startup and then use Control Panel, under Services (or Control Panel ➢ Performance and Maintenance ➢ Services in Windows XP and 2003), to stop the loading of any unnecessary drivers or programs.

I've seen this happen over and over again. Programs or drivers or *whatever* that are loaded into your computer's memory—often without your knowledge—bump into other programs or drivers or whatever, causing a major conflict that can freeze up your entire system. Check out *everything* that gets loaded when Windows launches (don't forget to look in the StartUp program group) and eliminate those things that don't need to be there. Software troubleshooting is just like hardware troubleshooting: divide and conquer. Each piece of software you're running is a piece of the system, and you want to minimize the number of pieces you have to deal with.

Draw a Picture, Separate into Components, and Test

This is a true story: a friend was once a PC troubleshooter for a county government in Virginia, where I live. She tells this story about another PC troubleshooter—let's call him Ignatz. One day, their help desk got a phone call.

"Ignatz," the caller said, "Microsoft Word isn't printing with the new laser printer!"

Now, an experienced lazy person listens and says, "Gosh—how can I fix this without leaving my chair?" Many of us would probably zero in on that word, *new*. As in "*new* laser printer." The next questions might be something such as, "What kind of printer did you have before the new laser printer?" "Have you ever seen Word print on this laser printer before?" (Probably not.) "Have you reconfigured Windows for the laser printer?" (A confused "What?" is the probable answer.)

Ignatz, on the other hand, attacked the problem by first swapping the motherboard on the PC that was attached to the laser printer.

Yes, that's right—you read that correctly. It even kind of fixed the problem because Iggie figured he'd reload the user's software while he was at it. Yeah, you can observe that Ignatz is, umm, shall I say, "a couple sandwiches short of a picnic" when it comes to troubleshooting. But I see people do less extreme (but just as unnecessary) things all the time. Heck, I still do a lot of dumb things myself, playing Macho Man with a Screwdriver. But I hope to get better at remembering to be lazy when troubleshooting.

Now, if old Ig had stopped to think, then he could have diagrammed the whole system. Simplified, you could say that the laser printer is attached to a cable, which attaches to a parallel port, which is connected to the motherboard, which runs the software. That kind of divides the problem into: laser printer, cable, parallel port, motherboard, and software. Each of those components can then be isolated and tested. *Testing* most hardware just means swapping it because most of us lack the expensive equipment needed to test hardware. But software can be played with in many ways, the most fruitful of which is usually in its setup and configuration. I'd look at the software first. I always look at the software before I go after the hardware. Why? Simple: I have a much better chance of finding the answer in software.

Never Assume

It's far too easy to assume that something is blameless. "How could the problem be the new version of PowerQuick? It's been clean for the last five versions!" Subject everything to your scrutiny, *including* the documentation. And while I'm on the subject…

Trust No One: The Documentation Sometimes Lies

Many years ago, I bought my first Video Graphics Adapter (VGA) board. It was made by Compaq Computer Corporation, and it wasn't cheap, but I bought it from Compaq because I knew they made a compatible, high-quality product. Because it was in the early days of the VGA, many clones were kinda wobbly compatibility-wise, so I was playing it safe.

When I went to install the board, I took the time to read the documentation. About half of the booklet that came with the board discussed installation. In particular, several pages outlined how to properly set the three jumpers that were clearly marked and even illustrated in black-and-white photos. Before even removing the board from its antistatic bag, I studied the documentation and figured out how to set the three jumpers. Donning my antistatic wrist strap, I removed the board from its bag.

But it had only one jumper on it.

I looked and looked and *looked*, but there was only one jumper on the %$#@! thing. I picked up the manual again—and a lone piece of paper fluttered from between its pages. It basically said, "Your VGA is a new-and-improved model. It has only one jumper. Set it like this." Frustrating, yes, but at least Compaq provided the right documentation, albeit hidden. I've often wondered if the documentation's author didn't have a sense of humor, however: this 3-by-8-inch piece of paper is *copyrighted*.

Jumpers are usually not the real nightmare, however; the documentation is. Almost every one of these things is badly translated from some Pacific Rim nation's language to English and, worst of all, it's usually wrong. The jumper setting for the parallel port is usually off, and I've seen incorrect documentation for the serial port jumpers as well. If you're wondering, by the way, how I figure out the correct settings when the documentation is wrong, then I'm afraid there's no single trick I can share with you. When I run into one of these boards, I check my notes to see whether I've run into this particular model before. If I have, great; if not, all I can do is work by trial and error.

Today, more and more information about PC hardware (and software) is available from the manufacturers' Web sites. If you haven't tapped this resource yet, refer to Chapter 24, "Using the Internet for Hardware Support," where you'll get a taste of some of the technical help riches on the Net.

Observe Like Sherlock Holmes

In Arthur Conan Doyle's tales of the great detective, Sherlock Holmes sometimes exclaims about some new piece of evidence. He's obviously excited about it, but when Dr. Watson asks him *why* he's excited, Holmes gives nothing away. "Not yet, Watson," he demurs. "It's too early for theories."

What Holmes knew was that problem solving entails making theories and then proving or disproving the theories with facts. But suppose Holmes had advanced an early theory aloud, perhaps in the company of the beleaguered Inspector Lestrade? Lestrade would like nothing better than to witness his harasser Holmes brought down by a faulty theory. Now, Holmes also knows that, so he has a subconscious aversion to finding any facts that disprove this ill-uttered supposition. By keeping his mouth shut until he has enough facts, he can offer a theory he feels confident about.

You'll see this in your everyday troubleshooting life. Someone stands over your shoulder as you peer inside a disemboweled PC carcass. "What do you think it is?" he asks.

This is a crucial moment. Learn to say automatically, "I don't know—there's not enough information yet." Otherwise, you'll find that now the game you're playing is no longer "fix the machine"; unconsciously, you're now playing a game called "prove you're right." So hang onto the theories until you have the facts.

When you open up a machine, you expose the machine to a certain risk that you'll do something dumb to it. PC troubleshooting differs from, say, automotive troubleshooting, in that the thing that's most commonly broken is the user. If you separate out the "user is broken" stuff (they forgot to turn it on, for example), software is the next most common problem. Honest-to-goodness hardware problems are actually quite uncommon compared to user and software problems. That leads me to the six specific troubleshooting steps.

Six Steps to Troubleshooting Success

The smart troubleshooter makes the troubleshooting job tractable by breaking down problems into individual steps. Don't panic, and remember to be methodical; otherwise, you'll thrash helplessly about and get frustrated. Once you're frustrated, you're *lost*, and you start creating new problems.

The following is the method I use. It looks a lot like methods suggested by other people, but it's not the only method. You certainly don't have to use *my* method, but find one you like and stick to it—even for the small or seemingly easy jobs. It's the "this'll take only five minutes" repairs that get me in trouble. (You know—like when someone gives you directions, saying, "You can't miss it." I *know* I'm in trouble then.) I'll assume for this discussion that you're interacting with someone else (the person with the PC problem), but you can just as easily interview yourself.

Before opening up the computer, do the following:

1. Check the nut behind the keyboard.

2. Check that everything is plugged in: power, monitor, phone lines, printer, modem, and so on.

3. Check the software.

4. Check external signs. Make notes of them.

5. Run an appropriate diagnostic utility. Only then, if you still haven't solved the problem, go to the next step.

6. Disassemble the machine, clean the connectors, push the socketed chips back into their sockets (reseat connections), and put the machine back together.

Notice that the first five steps *aren't* hardware steps; let's take a closer look at all six.

TIP *If you're running Windows Me, XP, or 2003 and experience a problem after installing a new piece of software or hardware, consider using the new System Restore feature to effectively "undo" the installation and return your system to its previous (that is, working) condition. Once your system is back up and working properly, you can analyze what went wrong—and consider trying the installation again.*

Check for Operator Error

Operator error is responsible for 93.3 percent of PC failures. (That's a made-up statistic. But it got your attention and probably isn't far from the truth.) There are lots of things that an operator can do wrong. But one real statistic from the PC retail industry is that up to 75 percent of hardware purchases returned as defective aren't defective and worked fine on retesting.

Regardless of how inflated that statistic may or may not be, that means a lot of folks aren't installing their hardware properly. Sure, some of it can be blamed on bad instructions, but many people flat-out admit they never look at any documentation packed with the device they're trying to install—or read it after the first three to four times a device won't install "instantly."

And because the accompanying paperwork often ends up in the trash can with the packaging from the hardware, you can end up feeling isolated and uninformed a few months later, when the device stops working. Remember the old saying about how desperate people do desperate things?

There are three main sources of problems for PCs: hardware, software, and users. Guess which one is the most likely? Users. Software is second. Hardware is a distant third.

That begs the question of why the computer industry has so many people problems. In my opinion, it's mainly because the user interfaces still stink—even the "good" ones.

Frequently, people will ask me how to prepare a new hard disk to use in their PCs. I'll go through all the steps and usually point them to a Web site or two that spells out the steps again for them so they have something in print they can stare at. All too many times, however, one of these folks will come back to tell me, "It didn't work."

"What didn't work?" I'll ask.

The answer will come back, "I can't access my CD drive to install Windows" or "I followed all the instructions, but the hard drive won't boot up!"

Invariably, I find that they didn't follow one—or more—of the steps. They either didn't use FDISK or FORMAT (necessary to prep the drive), so it's not really ready for use, or they decided they didn't need to go to the trouble of installing a DOS CD driver on their boot disk, so they can't access their CD drive to install their operating system.

You see, computers are made up of hardware, and hardware for the most part is a pretty logical beast. Turn something one way, and a device becomes available for use. Turn it another way, and a device doesn't respond to you. You can't see a list of 10 steps and decide which 5 you might like to follow because all 10 steps are likely required to get the result you want.

Still, the language of computers confuses people. You've heard the stories about users doing goofy things; well, they're true. I've seen them. Back in the old days of personal computing, I once watched a user follow the dBase III installation instructions: "Insert System Disk 1 in drive A, and close the door." He inserted the disk in the drive, then got up (looking a little puzzled, I'll give him that), and closed the door to his office. If I hadn't been there to see it, I probably wouldn't have believed it. But before you giggle too loudly, consider: where was the "door"? Have you seen a door on a floppy drive lately? No, there's never been one, really—although old 5¼-inch drives did have a little latch across the drive opening. I mean, if you hired me to put a door on your house and instead I installed a little plastic latch, then you'd sue me, and you'd *win*.

I teach quite a few computer classes, and now and then I've had some guy staring at the keyboard in puzzlement.

"What's wrong?" I'd ask.

"I'm looking for a key," he'd reply.

"Which one? I'll point it out," I'd offer.

"The Any key," he'd say, still puzzled. I'd look at the screen, where the software program was prompting `Press any key to continue`. I had just finished with my "pay attention to what the computer is doing" lecture, so this poor soul was trying his hardest to follow my directions. (Nowadays, there's an answer for the Any key searchers. You can buy an Any key kit: it's a keytop sticker that says, "ANY KEY." You install it on…well, any key.)

I've seen users "copy a floppy" with a photocopier. I once saw a bank organize their backup floppies by punching holes in them so they'd fit into a small binder. True stories, all of them.

A friend at Microsoft tells the story of being called by someone who couldn't get Windows to do anything. "I've got my foot on the pedal," he said, "and it's not doing anything!" Well, mice are often found on the floor, but still…

Even worse, sometimes users will (horrors!) prevaricate slightly. "I didn't do anything. It just stopped working." Please note: I'm not one of those techie types whose motto is, "Assume that the user is lying," but sometimes it happens. More often, it's not that users lie. It's just that they don't know what's important, or they're embarrassed to tell you what they really did.

People feel defensive calling a support person (such as you). You want to collect as much information as possible. If you make them feel defensive, they'll misremember or withhold information. Here's a trick that telemarketers are told: smile when you're on the phone with someone. It works. (As the late Sam Kinison once said, "It creates the illusion you care.") Being a support person can be wearing. There's a tendency to think, "These people must get up early in the morning to think up dumb things to ask," but you can't let it get you down. Remember, these folks can't be too dumb—after all, the same company that hired them hired you, too. (Heh, heh.)

Again, think *lazy*. How can you collect enough information while on the phone to fix the problem right over the phone? The key is to not act like so many support people, the ones who don't even let you get your question out before they break in with, "Are you sure your computer is plugged in?" Stop and think about how idiotic this phrasing is. Who's going to answer "no"? It's roughly equivalent to saying, "Oh! Look at that. It's not plugged in. I *am* an idiot. Sorry to bother you."

Now, don't get me wrong: you have to ask the question—that's why it's step 2 in my six steps. But there's a right way and a wrong way. One right way is the "bureaucracy" approach: "I'm sorry that's happening to you. That must be really frustrating; I'll do whatever I can for you. But first, you know how it is here at XYZ Corp.; we have a form for everything. Forgive me, but I have to ask some dumb-sounding questions. Can you just double-check for me that the PC is plugged in...." Another good approach is to couch it in a self-deprecating way: "My asking you if the PC is plugged in reminded me of something dumb I did the other day. The PC was plugged into the surge protector, and the surge protector was plugged into the wall. It took me 15 minutes to figure out that the surge protector was turned off! Can you believe that I did something that stupid?" If the next sound you hear is, "Ummm, can I call you back? Someone just walked into my office," then you can be pretty sure you've just engineered another fixed PC.

Best of all, however, is that your *user* just fixed that PC. He's now had a success, so he'll remember that particular problem/solution combination. (Psychology tells us that people learn better with positive reinforcement than with negative reinforcement.) He'll probably end up feeling more capable, more likely to tackle the problem himself next time. "Success is a habit," said Vince Lombardi.

Another source of operator error stems from inexperienced operators. The PC isn't exactly the simplest thing in the world to master. The author of the book *Computer Wimp: 166 Things I Wish I Had Known Before I Bought My First Computer* observes that learning to use a computer system may be the most difficult learning endeavor that people will undertake in their post-school life. (Things like raising kids are undoubtedly tougher, but they're different kinds of learning experiences.) It doesn't take a genius to recognize that most PC hardware and software manuals aren't the easiest things to comprehend. The answer? Good education. There are tons of good books, videos, college courses, and professional seminars on PCs, one for every budget. "If you think education is expensive," they say, "try ignorance."

Make Sure Everything Is Plugged In—Correctly

I know this sounds stupid, but we've all done it. A friend bought a modem and couldn't get it to work. It accepted commands all right but couldn't dial out. The phone line was tested with a regular phone and worked fine. He was quite puzzled until he realized he'd plugged the phone line into the *out* jack in the modem instead of the *in* jack. (The out jack is intended to be connected to the phone itself—not the phone line—so that the line can be shared between the modem and the phone).

As I just said, when you ask the user, "Is it plugged in?" be diplomatic. (Don't you hate it when technical support people ask *you* that question?) But don't be afraid to ask for firm answers to the following questions:

- Is the PC plugged into some kind of multi-outlet strip?

- Is the strip on? Did the user kick off the power switch?

- Can the user actually see that the power strip is plugged into the wall?

◆ Are the other devices that are plugged into the power strip working? Try having the user plug a desk lamp or fan into the power strip to see whether it works.

◆ If the PC or peripheral is plugged into an outlet controlled by a wall switch, is the switch turned on?

◆ Are the peripherals plugged in? Are they plugged *into the computer*? Are they plugged into the proper ports or connectors on the computer?

I know of a large communications company that kept sending technicians to try to determine why a Local Area Network (LAN) server kept dying at strange hours of the night. They'd set up the software at the user site, leave it running, and then eventually get called back to the site because after a day or two all kinds of files had been trashed. The technicians would always ask, "Has this been turned off in the middle of an operation?" The users would solemnly (and annoyingly—this tech guy wasn't going to weasel out of fixing his company's buggy software *that* easily, they thought) shake their heads no. Finally, this large company sent its SuperTech—the guy who'd seen it all. He looked over the server and listened to the users' stories.

Now, this guy *knew* from the symptoms that the server was getting shut down improperly. (Remember that indomitable spirit. On the other hand, save the spirit for the machine—don't get snotty with the users.) So he looked for easy ways to turn off the machine accidentally. Noticing two light switches on the wall and only one fluorescent ceiling panel, he flipped both switches. You guessed it—the server was plugged into a switched outlet. The security staff, in making the rounds each night, would shut off the lights.

When you're checking whether peripherals are plugged in, you also need to make sure they're in *tight*. Multiple-pin connectors slowly bend under gravity unless the mounting screws are tightened. As someone stretches their legs under the desk, a loose power cord could be moved enough to disconnect it or to disconnect and reconnect it. Connectors on the floor take a lot of abuse.

I think people don't properly secure connectors because it often can't be done without one of those small straight-slot screwdrivers that are smaller than the one you have in the kitchen tool drawer but larger than the one you use to adjust the screws in your glasses. (Of course, true PC repair warriors are never without small screwdriver with the pocket clip and the logo of some company on its side, but normal humans...) Nowadays, you can find a remedy: many cables are sold with big plastic screws that are easily hand-turnable. (Many folks call those screws *thumbscrews*, and I guess it's as good a term as any, but I find it a bit medieval.) Whenever possible, get cables with hand-turnable screws. They'll pay for themselves in the long run.

I'm one of the worst offenders in the cable screws department. Because I install and reinstall various PC components a lot, I tend to just push my serial and video cables into their sockets, not bothering with the screwdriver. (I don't have the little screwdriver with the pocket clip when I don't happen to have my pocket protector around. You know, sometimes I want to work undercover, so I leave the pocket protector behind.) A few years ago, I had myself convinced that my serial port or modem was fried because I was getting terrible error rates on my communications sessions all of a sudden. Because I'd just finished giving a lecture on lightning damage to serial ports, and it was T-storm season in Washington, I figured ruefully that I'd just lost a serial port. "But," I thought, "who knows? Maybe when lightning toasted the port, it burned up some chips—I can at least take some pictures." So I got ready to take my PC apart. Of course, one of the first things I did was to remove the cables, and that's when I noticed that the serial cable just about fell off the back of the PC when I touched it. So I returned the cables to their interfaces—making sure they were secured tightly—and, as you've already guessed, the problems went away.

Check the Software

Remember I said that more problems are software problems than hardware problems? Software problems arrive in several guises:

◆ Operator error

◆ Keyboard/screen/disk/timer conflicts with memory-resident software

◆ Software that doesn't clean up after itself

◆ Software that requires hardware that isn't connected or activated

◆ Buggy applications

◆ Buggy driver programs

Software troubleshooting could be a book in itself. In fact, most of the books about supporting Windows, Linux, Novell NetWare, and the like are software-troubleshooting books. But let's tackle some of the broad causes of software problems.

VIRTUAL DEVICE DRIVERS AND DYNAMIC-LINK LIBRARIES

Modern operating systems, including Windows, are built in a kind of layer-cake fashion. The application programs (such as word processing, email, and spreadsheet programs) sit atop the cake—they're the frosting. Your applications are supported by layers of cake and filling, which are layers that they need in order to work—heck, frosting all by itself is a bit much, right?

The bottom layer of the cake is the hardware. Application programs need services (such as printing, communicating with a network server, or saving files) done for them by the hardware (the printer, the network card, or the hard disk). How do applications communicate with hardware? How does your system prioritize and handle multiple requests without exploding?

Enter the operating system. If every application tries to use a piece of hardware at the same time, nothing works. What you need is a kind of traffic cop between the apps and the hardware. The operating system is that cop, the piece that routes hardware requests between applications and hardware, keeping traffic jams to a minimum and "crashes" nonexistent (well, in theory, anyway). The operating system acts as a "traffic cop" layer between your hardware and your applications.

Also between your hardware and applications are two components that applications rely on to operate correctly. They're called Virtual Device Drivers (VxDs) and Dynamic-Link Libraries (DLLs). Both act as filling between the layers, hidden from external view but key to the structure of the cake. I'll discuss DLLs in a minute, but first I'll talk about drivers.

The lowest level of system software is the set of programs called *drivers*, which are customized to particular pieces of hardware. Drivers attach in a modular fashion to the main body of the operating system (called the *kernel*). For example, to get Windows to recognize and use your Hewlett-Packard (HP) LaserJet model 5P, you must load a driver for that printer, adding it to the Windows system software.

Drivers can pose a bit of a problem for software stability. Most of the operating system is designed by a close-knit software development team; for example, most of the code in Windows 2003 was written by a handful of individuals working together at Microsoft. But most Windows drivers aren't written by Microsoft. Instead, the burden of writing driver programs usually falls to the hardware vendors: Diamond Multimedia writes drivers for its video boards, HP writes drivers for its laser printers, and so on. Programmers working at these companies don't get the same kind of support (in terms of information, resources, and time) they'd have if they were working at Microsoft, so as a result they can't always write driver programs that are well integrated into an operating system. This isn't a slap at programmers at Diamond, HP, or any other hardware vendor; it's just a reality that the guy on Microsoft's Windows programming team who writes the Calculator code probably plays softball on the same team as the programmer who writes the Windows kernel code. And that has to mean he'll get better answers to sticky programming questions than would someone from outside Microsoft.

Because of the way that drivers work in modern operating systems, they're usually called *virtual device drivers*. V*x*Ds are sometimes designed to plug into a particular operating system (which means, for example, that you might not want to waste your time trying to use a Windows 95 V*x*D under Windows XP or Windows 2003, unless you know that the driver will work in both of those operating systems).

The bottom line is that driver programs are often a weak link in an operating system. Windows may run fine for weeks, and then you install a new version of the driver for your video card. You try to enter Print Preview mode from your favorite word processor, and something happens, whether it's an outright lockup or some garbage on the screen. The problem is most likely to be that new driver.

Although this isn't gospel, most operating system designers do much of their initial development on "lowest common denominator" hardware, such as VGA for video. Keep those vanilla drivers around and use them when possible as a kind of "known good" baseline configuration.

And a final tip about device drivers: when a new version comes along, *keep the old one around for a while!* "Latest" isn't always "greatest" when it comes to drivers.

TIP If you're running Windows Me, XP, or 2003, you can use the System Restore feature to return your system to its previous state after you install a bad or incorrect driver. See Chapter 23, "Hardware Management via Software Solutions," for more information.

I recommend you do what a friend of mine does and use the baby food method of testing new drivers. The first time she mentioned this to me, I was puzzled.

"The *baby food* method?" I asked her. (I'm an excellent straight man.)

"Sure," she replied. "When a baby starts eating solid food, you don't know what he's going to be allergic to. So, suppose you want to see if he's allergic to carrots. You start feeding him carrots; if a few days go by and he hasn't swollen up, then carrots are probably okay.

"I do that with device drivers. I just pop 'em into the system, try out all my applications to make sure that none of them break, and then just live with the thing for a week to see if anything new and unpleasant happens to my system. If not, I keep the driver. If I have problems, then I document the problems, restore the old device driver, and see if those problems go away."

Good advice. But I'd add one thing to it. When you swap drivers on a piece of hardware, be sure to power down the system completely before restarting it. Some video drivers in particular don't work quite right unless you shut down the PC and restart after installing them

Another term you'll see turn up when troubleshooting software is DLL, short for *dynamic-link library*. A *library* is a file containing a bunch of small programs that get a particular task done. It's called a *library* for two reasons: first, there are usually many of those small programs in a particular library, and, second, the library file resembles a library in that it's publicly available; the programs in it are available to any application. For example, the program that tells Windows how to change the color of a part of the screen is almost certainly part of a library.

Now, the way a program finds a library is called *linking*. For most of the history of computer programming, libraries have become linked when a program called the *link editor* makes a copy of the desired library routines and incorporates those routines directly into the program. This is called *static linking*. Static linking is bad for two reasons: first, if you're running three programs that all know how to print (for example), then you're wasting Random Access Memory (RAM) because you now have three copies of the print routine resident in memory, and second, if the way that the operating system wants an application to print (to continue the example) changes, then every application would have to be rebuilt.

Operating systems in use since the early '80s incorporate a different kind of linking, called *dynamic linking*. Under dynamic linking, a DLL is relinked every time the application calls for one of its library routines. Taking the example of printing, a program using static linking gets the whole library program inserted into it. A program linked dynamically to a library contains only a note that says, in essence, "When you need this routine, go out to PRINT.DLL, load it up, and link the routine before going any further." A DLL can also be shared; once one program has PRINT.DLL in memory, any other program needing PRINT.DLL gets the one copy that's already in memory, rather than loading another one.

What's this got to do with troubleshooting? Well, sometimes an incorrectly installed program may crash, complaining of a lack of a DLL. That may be fixable by reinstalling the program or by editing the Windows Registry to include the correct path for the DLL. Or the DLL may have been accidentally erased. Or it could have been replaced.

Whenever you select File ➢ Open in any Windows program, your program calls up a DLL that contains a routine that knows how to put an Open dialog box on the screen. (In Windows, the DLL is called COMMDLG.DLL.) Now and then, I've installed programs that replaced the comes-in-the-Windows-box version of COMMDLG.DLL with their own "improved" versions.

How do you find out whether you have a cowbird DLL in the nest? One simple way is to just compare the dates of the *other* DLLs that shipped with the operating system to the suspect one. Or, as is more frequently the solution, you can simply reinstall the operating system; it often saves more time than poking through DLLs looking for the "pretender."

ILL-BEHAVED SOFTWARE

A number of mysteries can be linked to software that doesn't recover well from disabled or nonexistent hardware. The following are some common problems:

- Trying to print to a nonexistent printer

- Trying to print a non-PostScript formatted file to a PostScript printer—or vice versa

- Trying to print to a printer that's offline

- Trying to display high-resolution graphics data on a low-resolution monitor

- Trying to run a program that needs more memory than the PC contains

- Trying to install a program that insists on using your modem to dial into the mothership to register itself before it finalizes the installation—even if you don't have a modem connected to your system

These aren't really problems with the software—the problems all have something to do with the hardware—but the real issues arise because the software doesn't deal well with the hardware problem. The easy fix, however, is on the hardware side; you can't recode the program, but you *can* make simple hardware fixes.

FAULTY SOFTWARE

Sometimes the problem *is* just plain buggy software. Even the most popular programs can misbehave when faced with a full disk, insufficient memory, or some situation that the designer didn't anticipate or didn't test.

If you experience a problem with software, try to note exactly when the behavior occurs. Perhaps it always fails when you're trying to save to a network drive, but not to a local hard drive. Or maybe the software always crashes when system resources on the desktop run below 50 percent. Or maybe the software will run on any PC except one with an AMD Central Processing Unit (CPU). Any behavior like this that you can reproduce can be helpful to a team trying to debug a program.

If you have some experience with software and compiler/decompilers, you can sometimes check out the source code used to design the program and spot where an error might be (such as an incorrect command issued). Normal human beings can dismiss this possibility.

Finally, you can try uninstalling the suspect program to see whether that sorts things out. It always amazes me how often an uninstall/reinstall will fix even the most persnickety problems.

Check External Signs

If the computer has indicator lights, what do they indicate? Are all the lights glowing on the modem? Does the printer indicate "ready"? Is the hard disk squealing or grinding? Does the monitor image look bent? Your drives and other peripherals produce hums, whirrs, and clicks. After a while, these noises become familiar, and any variation in them signals a problem. Pay attention to these signs.

The first step in successful troubleshooting is to isolate the problem component. These signs can point the way.

It's important to document any signs here. Write down what lights are on and off, the positions of switches, and so forth.

Run a Diagnostic Utility

There's lots of help out there for your hardware problems—in the form of diagnostic software. Some computers ship with diagnostic programs that can help pinpoint various problems. Windows itself comes with a variety of diagnostic utilities, and other diagnostic programs are available from third parties or via downloading from freeware/shareware software archives.

Diagnostic programs can be quite valuable in helping to track down and fix both hardware and software problems—but only if your computer is up and running. If your computer is dead as a doornail, having a copy of the latest and greatest diagnostic program won't do you a lick of good, unless you want to use the CD as a drink coaster. (And by this point, having a refreshing drink might seem appealing!)

Of course, if your computer is up and running, you might question the value of running a diagnostic program. After all, what must be functioning for you to run one of these programs? Well, the system board must be running, the video must be running so you can see the screen, the keyboard must be active to accept commands, and the floppy disk or CD drive must be working so the program can load. Merely loading the diagnostic program (or any other program, for that matter) tells you some things about your system.

Then there's the additional bonus that most diagnostic programs are visually impressive—they look technical as heck. My friend Dave Stang says that if nothing else, running a diagnostic on a customer's machine buys you a few minutes to think about what's actually wrong.

A Diagnostic Wish List

When assembling a set of tools to help you diagnose and fix hardware-related problems, you should consider the following types of utilities:

System inventory These programs display and inventory what they can detect in your system. This can be useful not as inventory in and of itself; its greater value is in cataloging what the system can *see*. If you know darn well that you installed the mouse interface but it doesn't show up on the system inventory, then you have a problem. Before looking *too* hard for the answer, however, ask yourself first: is the driver for the mouse loaded? Diagnostic programs, such as the operating system itself, usually can't detect an unusual piece of hardware unless the driver for that program is loaded.

Burn-in When you first get a computer, it's a good idea to *burn it in*. This means to run it continuously for at least three days, running some kind of diagnostic software over and over again. Some PC manufacturers even offer a burn-in when buying a new PC.

Simple diagnostics are no good for this kind of process—for two reasons. First, most simple diagnostics insist on informing you of any errors and then *requiring* you to press a key to acknowledge you've seen the error message. Higher-quality diagnostic programs allow you to run the diagnostic in a *logging* mode, whereby any error messages are saved to a file, and don't require confirmation of an error. Second, simple diagnostics tend to be of the "run-once" variety; good programs let you run the diagnostic in a *continuous* mode, meaning it runs over and over and over until you tell it to stop.

Burn-in is an important step, so don't ignore it! Of the last 10 computers I've installed, two didn't fail until after four days of continuous testing. If I hadn't done a burn-in on them, I probably would've ended up with a mysterious error appearing at a no-doubt inopportune time. (Mr. Murphy and his law seem to have taken up residence in my office.)

Interrupt/DMA/input/output address summary As you learned in Chapter 5, "Installing New Circuit Boards," the hardest thing about installing a new circuit board is adjusting the input/output port address, the Direct Memory Access (DMA) channel, the Interrupt Request (IRQ) level, and the Read-Only Memory (ROM) address. The reason you adjust these settings is to make sure they don't conflict with the port/DMA/IRQ/ROM of any other boards. For example, if you're putting a board in the system and that board must use either IRQ5 or IRQ7, but there's already a board in your system that uses IRQ7, then you can't let the new board use IRQ7. But the question arises, how do you find out what interrupts are in use on your system? Diagnostic procedures *try* to report this information. I say *try* because they unfortunately can't be trusted in this task, not because of inadequacies on the part of their programmers but because of a simple fact: there's no way to reliably detect ports, DMAs, IRQs, or ROM addresses. How *do* you find out this information? You can look at the devices in your system by launching the System applet in Windows' Control Panel.

Hardware testing   A good diagnostic program should provide your hardware with a workout. It'll test your computer's memory thoroughly, test every possible data pattern on your hard disk, and run your serial port at its maximum speed—in short, a good diagnostic program should be a sort of cybernetic boot camp for your computer.

Setup   Some of these programs do things associated more with setup responsibilities than diagnostic ones. For example, most of these programs will low-level format a hard disk, an important step in setting up an older type of hard disk. Others may have a built-in system setup program that sets up the CMOS chip in a computer. (CMOS stands for Complementary Metal Oxide Semiconductor.)

If you read these items carefully, you no doubt noticed a lot of *shoulds*, as in "a good diagnostic program should…." All this equivocation has a purpose, believe me: most diagnostic programs are junk. Look carefully before you spend the ton of money that you can easily spend on a diagnostic package.

THIRD-PARTY DIAGNOSTIC SOFTWARE

There's an entire subset of the computer software industry dedicated to providing software and hardware diagnostic utilities. Between the commercial publishers and the freeware/shareware publishers, you can find literally dozens of utilities, each designed to provide a variety of diagnostic functions.

It's said that one time the science fiction author Theodore Sturgeon was approached by a literary critic who said, "Ted, you write such good stuff; why do you waste your time writing science fiction?" Sturgeon asked, "What's wrong with science fiction?" The critic answered, "90 percent of science fiction is crap." (Well, he didn't actually say *crap*, but this book is rated for general audiences.) Sturgeon is reported to have replied archly, "90 percent of *everything* is crap." I'm afraid that this truism, dubbed *Sturgeon's Law* by generations of science fiction fans, applies well to the diagnostics world. Let me then not waste ink beating up on this chaff; let's look at the wheat.

Technical Hardware–Only Diagnostics

The first diagnostics to consider are those that focus exclusively on hardware-related problems. These are often quite technical in nature and sometimes include hardware (such as loopback plugs) to facilitate the testing of various hardware components. (Some of them are also quite expensive—the most comprehensive packages will cost you anywhere from $200 to $400.) They are as follows:

CheckIt   This is a fairly useful, extremely comprehensive set of hardware diagnostics from Smith Micro Software (formerly Touchstone Software). Actually, there are several different versions of CheckIt; for the most detailed diagnostics, you want the Professional Edition. Note that CheckIt doesn't include some of the hardware accessories you need to do a thorough system check, such as loopback plugs for external port testing. (Smith Micro does have loopback plugs available as an extra-cost option, however.) That's not meant as a negative assessment; I like CheckIt and use it quite a bit. It has a good set of motherboard checkout routines (DMA, timer, IRQ, and the rest) as well as one of the better memory testers available. See `www.smithmicro.com/checkit/` for more information.

PC-Technician   This is an industrial-strength package from Windsor Technologies. I first looked at PC-Technician back in 1988, and I must truthfully say I didn't think much of it then. But it's matured into a decent, general, inventory/setup/deep diagnostic routine. The full package includes the test disks, the loopbacks, a nice manual, and a carrying case for your tools. (Just make sure you don't put any magnetic screwdrivers next to the disks in the case!) Windsor also sells a program that'll put your PC printer through its paces, as well as a plug-in BIOS POST code. The features I like best about PC-Technician are the memory test—again, a good one in the same league as CheckIt's—and the serial and parallel tests. All in all, PC-Technician is the best all-in-one tester. See `www.windsortech.com/pctech.html` for more information.

DisplayMate   This is a utility from DisplayMate Technologies (formerly Sonera Technologies) that checks only one thing—your display. But it does an extremely thorough job, testing aspects of your monitor you probably didn't know were testable—*pincushioning*, for example. The accompanying manual is a tutorial on monitor problems and solutions. It won't test your memory or your printer, but it deserves a place on your diagnostics shelf. See `www.displaymate.com` for more information.

General Hardware/Software Diagnostics

The second class of utilities to consider includes those that perform both hardware and software diagnostics. These programs typically aren't as technical as the hardware-only diagnostics and therefore aren't as rigorous in their testing. They are, however, more consumer-friendly and thus easier for the average user to use.

I discuss these system tools—such as Norton Utilities and McAfee Utilities—in Chapter 23; turn there if you want to learn more.

WARNING   Some diagnostic programs—such as McAfee First Aid and Norton CrashGuard—are promoted as crash-prevention tools, meant to help prevent problems with your PC or with Windows. However, these programs require you to run them all the time; they attempt to create a buffer, or a shield, between the errors you might make and the machine itself. Although this type of software can keep you from making a fatal mistake, it also may interfere as you troubleshoot PC problems—the software may not allow you to make the changes you need to make. Over time, you may also find that the rescue program isn't working as effectively—perhaps because it's configured wrong or perhaps because you overrode it when it suggested you do or not do something. When this happens, whole new sets of problems can crop up that may affect booting your PC or Windows' proper operation. Thus, using this protection software may leave you needing protection from it. Use judiciously.

As I've suggested, you can spend a *lot* of money on diagnostic programs, so it's a good idea to take advantage of the option that many computer dealers provide today whereby you can buy software and return it within a few weeks if it fails to live up to expectations or doesn't work properly with your PC setup. Better yet, check to see if there's a free 30- or 45-day trial of the program you can download and try and then buy the full package if it works well for you.

Windows Diagnostics

Although not focused exclusively on hardware issues, all versions of Windows since Windows 98 include a set of diagnostic system tools (accessed via Start ➢ Programs ➢ Accessories ➢ System Tools) that can help you track down many types of system problems. For example, ScanDisk enables you to perform either a surface or thorough scan of your drives and tries to fix errors it finds; Disk Defragmenter defragments and reorganizes your hard drive to make it run more efficiently.

Microsoft's System Information tool provides a host of indispensable data about various components of your system and (via its Tools menu) serves as a gateway for several more "hidden" utilities. These utilities include the Dr. Watson logging tool, which keeps track of operations performed and error messages generated; System File Checker, which seeks out missing or damaged essential files and attempts to replace them; and the System Information Utility (a.k.a. MSCONFIG), which enables you to set up a troubleshooting bootup mode and select which items you really want to load at Windows startup.

These diagnostics aren't available directly within Windows 95 or Windows NT 4. Windows 95 (as well as all later versions) does include Device Manager, one of the tabs available under the System icon in the Control Panel. Although it's not a diagnostic checker, vital information gets reported there that you need to check when you're having a problem. You may see an exclamation mark or red x on a device, indicating a device in conflict or disabled entirely. Or you may notice a needed device driver isn't present when it should be. Or you may find a note on your hard drive indicating that the drive is running in MS-DOS compatibility mode (meaning Windows feels the drive isn't set to run properly in Windows, so it's running in a slower mode compatible with MS-DOS).

I talk about all these Windows utilities—as well as some of the third-party diagnostic programs—in Chapter 23.

NOTE   *Windows XP and 2003 also provide several hardware troubleshooters that help you diagnose and repair hardware- or driver-related problems. A series of questions ask what the problem is and suggest solutions for you to try. For a complete list of these troubleshooters, search for the "List of Troubleshooters" help topic in the Windows Help and Support Center.*

Look Under the Hood

Assuming you've worked through steps 1 through 5—and especially availed yourself of the appropriate troubleshooting utilities built into the Windows operating system—it's possible, if your troubles persist, that you may actually have a problem inside your PC's system unit. Fortunately, you can handle many internal hardware problems simply and without any fancy equipment. Step 6 just says this:

- ◆ Take the PC apart.

- ◆ Clean any connectors with an artist's eraser or connector cleaner.

- ◆ Push all socketed chips back into their sockets.

- ◆ Reassemble the PC.

As you saw in Chapter 4, "Avoiding Service: Preventive Maintenance," edge connectors become dirty and make circuit boards fail. Sometimes "dead" boards will do the Lazarus trick if you clean their edge connectors.

If you examine most circuit boards, you'll see that most chips are soldered right onto the board. *Soldering* is a process whereby the chip is bonded to the printed circuits on the board by heating a mixture of tin and lead to the point that it's molten, allowing the tin/lead mixture to flow over the printed circuit and chip leg and finally solidifying. Soldering is a great technique for mass-producing electronic components. The downside is that when you must fix soldered components, you must *first* de-solder the components. This isn't much fun, and most people don't have soldering skills. Besides, it's far more cost effective to simply replace the part these days.

Not all chips are soldered to boards, however. Some are put in *sockets*. A typical board might have 30 soldered chips and 4 socketed ones. Chips are socketed either because they've been voted "most likely to fail," because the designer wanted to put off a decision until the last minute, or because the chip will likely have to be replaced periodically because it contains software that changes over time—remember ROM? So socketing chips makes your job as a troubleshooter easier.

On the other hand, heating and cooling systems make these socketed chips creep out of their sockets. That's why you should push socketed chips back into their sockets when inspecting a board for whatever reason. One particularly persnickety technician I know takes the socketed chips out of their sockets, cleans their chip legs with connector cleaner, and *then* puts the chips back in the sockets.

This should be obvious, but let me point it out anyway: don't push *soldered* chips. The best it can do is nothing. The worst it can do is damage a board and maybe a chip. When you push socketed chips back into a board, be sure you're supporting the *back* of the board. If you just put a board on a table and then push down on the chips, you can end up bending and damaging the board.

I know this kind of advice—"take it apart, clean the connectors, push the chips back in the sockets, and reassemble"—doesn't sound very dazzling. But, darn it, *it works!* Buying a board to replace a defective one is a pretty rare event for me as a troubleshooter, and I don't do much soldering. And besides, it impresses the people whose machines you're fixing—all they see you do is basically touch the boards. Eventually, you get the reputation as a person who can just "lay hands upon the board…and make it *whole!*" (Apologies to the evangelists in the crowd.)

When All Else Fails…

Don't feel ashamed if you can't diagnose every single problem you encounter. Even the best of us get stumped from time to time. When you've checked all your cables, run all the diagnostics, and disassembled/reassembled your entire system—and the darn thing *still* doesn't work!—it's time to turn to the experts for help.

One level of expert, of course, can be found on the Internet. A number of tech support sites are available on the Web, and most hardware and software vendors maintain technical support sections on their official Web sites. As I discuss in Chapter 24, it's likely that your problem has already been reported and documented *somewhere*, and the information available online might keep you from reinventing the wheel.

If the online help isn't any help, then you need to drop back 10 and punt—and call the vendor's official technical support line. This might cost you a bit, but at least you'll be getting advice from the horse's mouth. (Know that although some vendors still offer toll-free—and fee-free—tech support, others have eliminated 800 numbers and even make you pay them a fixed amount per call.) Although email support is preferred by most vendors—and, in fact, is usually more effective—sometimes there's nothing like talking to a real human being in your quest to get your system back up and running.

Before you call tech support, make sure you've done your homework and have the following in front of you:

The vendor's tech support phone number   Don't laugh—you can't look up the number on the vendor's Web site if you can't start your PC!

The make and model number of your PC   Include other pertinent information—processor speed, amount of RAM installed, other peripherals attached, and so on.

A detailed description of your problem   Note the operations you were performing just before the problem occurred.

A list of what other steps you've taken to track down the problem   There's no sense doing the same thing twice.

A good book or a big, thick magazine   You'll probably be on hold for a long, long time!

When you finally get through to a support technician, keep calm, cool, and collected and be as polite as possible. As frustrated as you may be with your particular problem, the technician on the other end of the phone has already listened to dozens of complaining customers today. If you're nice to them, they'll be nice to you—and do whatever they can to help you find and fix your problem.

Common Problems—and Solutions

Enough with the theory and advice—let's get down to practical matters! This section looks at some of the more common hardware-related problems you may be unfortunate enough to encounter and offers the most-likely causes of those problems.

Your Computer Won't Start

This is perhaps the scariest problem you can encounter. Nothing at all happens, you hear a few familiar or unfamiliar sounds, or even see a blinking light or two, but it all leads to a big fat zero. What can cause your entire system not to work? The following are some things to look for:

◆   Make sure the power cable is connected, both to your PC and to either a power strip/surge suppressor or wall outlet. If the cable is connected to a power strip/surge suppressor, make sure the strip is turned on—and that other devices plugged into the strip are working. (The strip itself could be bad.) Make sure that the wall outlet has power. (Flip that wall switch—and check that circuit breaker—just to be sure.)

◆   Check to see whether the power cable itself is bad. If you have a spare cable or one from another PC, try swapping it for the current cable.

◆   If your system unit lights up and makes noise but nothing appears on-screen, make sure that the computer monitor is turned on and getting power and that it's connected properly and securely to the monitor output on your system unit. If you suspect you actually have a monitor problem rather than a system unit problem, try connecting your PC to a different monitor.

◆ If your computer starts up but you receive an error message telling you that you have a non-bootable or invalid or nonsystem disk, you've accidentally left a floppy in the A: drive. Remove it.

◆ If your system *tries* to start but then locks up, it's possible you have some type of damage to your main hard disk. You could've a damaged boot sector, an internal connection may have worked loose, or your key system files might have become corrupted. Try restarting with an emergency boot disk (or the Windows Startup disk) and then use ScanDisk to check for hard disk errors.

NOTE *ScanDisk is not available with Windows XP or 2003.*

◆ If your system appears to start but then generates a series of beeps (with nothing showing on your video display), it's possible you have a problem with your video card. (Consider this a *probability* if you've just installed a new video card!) Make sure the video card is seated firmly in its slot and that you've switched the appropriate switches on your motherboard (if necessary) to recognize the new card. Try uninstalling the new card and reinstalling your old one—it's possible the new card is defective.

◆ A beeping-and-not-starting scenario can also be caused by incorrect settings in your system's CMOS setup. Check the video and memory settings. Another possible cause is a bad memory chip or faulty memory installation. A weak or dead CMOS battery can also cause this problem.

◆ If nothing turns on—no power lights light, no disk drives whirr, nothing—it's possible that the power supply transformer in your system unit is bad.

Your Computer Locks Up

In terms of causing extreme user panic, a frozen system is second only to a completely dead system. What can cause your system to freeze up? The following are some of the most likely causes:

◆ It's possible that it's not your entire system that's locked up—it could be your keyboard or mouse. Check the connections for both these devices, and make sure both cables are firmly plugged into the appropriate ports. If you're using a wireless keyboard or mouse, replace your batteries.

◆ Misbehaving software problems are, perhaps, the greatest cause of frozen systems. If a program is stalled, try switching to another open program, either by using the Windows Taskbar or by pressing Alt+Tab to shuttle through all open programs. If things are still frozen, press Ctrl+Alt+Del (the old "three-fingered salute") to display the Close Program dialog box (or the Security dialog box to get to Task Manager); highlight the program that isn't responding and click the End Task button. If, after trying all these actions, your system is *still* frozen, you'll have to reboot completely—press Ctrl+Alt+Del *twice* to shut down and then restart your entire system. If even this doesn't shut things down, you'll have to use the Power button on your system unit—or, in the worst of all possible cases, unplug the system unit from its power source.

WARNING *Shutting down your PC by any method other than the standard Windows shutdown procedure runs the risk of damaging any currently open files—and, under some circumstances, of altering some of your system's display and operational settings.*

◆ Many computer lockups are caused by too many programs trying to use more memory than is available. It's possible that you'll get a kind of warning before a total lockup; if your computer starts to slow down in the middle of an operating session, it's a sure sign of an upcoming memory-related failure. If the problem recurs, try closing a program or two to free up system memory—or upgrade the amount of memory in your system unit.

◆ Because Windows uses free hard disk space to augment random access memory, too little disk space can also cause your system to slow down or freeze. Make sure you've gone through your folders and deleted any nonessential or unused files—especially TMP files in the \WINDOWS\ TEMP\ directory.

Finally, any time something weird happens with your system, consider whether the problem could have been caused by a computer virus. Make sure you're running some sort of antivirus program—especially when downloading files from the Internet or opening email attachments—and run a full system sweep if you start experiencing performance problems.

A New Piece of Hardware Won't Work—or Messes Up Your System

It happens to the best of us. You install a new card or external peripheral, and all of a sudden your system either starts working funny or stops working completely. Obviously, something in the new installation caused the problem—but what?

◆ Make sure the new hardware is properly installed. If you installed a new internal board, make sure the board is fitted properly in its slot, that any additional wires or cables are connected properly, and that any switches are set appropriately. If you installed a new external peripheral, make sure that it's plugged into the right port, that the cable is firmly connected, and that the device is hooked up to and is receiving external power (if that's required).

◆ Some new devices require you to reset specific jumpers or switches on your system's motherboard. Check the item's installation instructions, and make sure you've performed this vital step.

◆ Check your system configuration. It's possible that Windows Plug and Play (PnP) didn't recognize your new device, didn't recognize it properly, or installed the wrong driver. Try uninstalling both the hardware and its associated software and then reinstalling. Use the Add New Hardware Wizard to override the standard PnP operation.

◆ Make sure you have the latest version of the item's device drivers. Go to the vendor's Web site and download updated drivers, if necessary. (While you're there, check the online support facilities to see whether any documented problems exist between this peripheral and your specific system.)

- Look for an interrupt conflict, which could occur if the new device tries to use the same IRQ as an older device. This happens a lot with COM ports—not only is sharing the same port a problem, but some devices (such as mice and modems) don't like to share even- or odd-numbered ports. (This means you may have a conflict between COM1 and COM3 that could be fixed by moving one of the devices to COM2 or COM4.) If worse comes to worst, try reassigning the IRQ for your new piece of hardware.

- It's possible that your system's CMOS settings need to be changed. This is most common when you upgrade or change memory or disk drives. Enter the CMOS configuration utility on system startup and change the settings appropriate to the new hardware you added.

Your Hard Disk Crashes

Any problem you may encounter with your hard disk is a major problem. That's because everything—from your system files to your program files to your data files—resides on your hard disk. If you can't access your hard disk, your multithousand-dollar computer system is just that much more junk.

What are the most common causes of hard disk problems? The following are a few to look for:

- If your system can't access your hard disk at all, you'll need to reboot using a system disk or the Windows Startup disk. Run ScanDisk (it's built into the Windows Startup disk) or a third-party hard disk utility from a floppy to check drive C: for defects and then fix any found damage.

- If the hard disk utility doesn't get your hard disk spinning again, call in an expert. Even if your hard disk is seriously damaged, it may be possible for a professional technician to "rescue" the data on the damaged hard drive and transfer it to another disk. This generally costs quite a bit of money, however.

- If you encounter frequent disk write errors, it's possible you have some physical damage on your hard disk. Run the hard disk utility to check and fix any defects.

- If your disk is working but running slower than normal, it probably needs to be defragmented. Run a good disk defrag program (such as Windows' Disk Defragmenter) to get all those non-contiguous clusters lined up properly.

- If you experience a lot of disk write errors or your system runs much slower than normal, and if you're using DriveSpace for disk compression, the problem is probably in DriveSpace. DriveSpace gives your system a pretty good workout and can cause lots of different types of problems. You may find that disk compression is more trouble than it's worth; if so, uncompress the drive! (In these days of cheap hard drives, you're probably better off to install a second hard disk drive than you are to use DriveSpace or some similar disk compression utility.)

To avoid catastrophic hard disk crashes, make sure you perform all the activities outlined in Chapter 4. I know it's a cliché, but an ounce of prevention is certainly worth a pound of cure, especially where the valuable data on your hard disk is concerned.

Your Monitor Doesn't Display Properly

If your computer is working but your monitor isn't, look for these possible causes:

◆ Make sure the monitor is plugged in, turned on, and firmly connected to your PC.

◆ Try to determine whether it's a monitor problem or a video card problem. If you have a spare one handy, plug a different monitor into your PC; if it works, your old monitor has a problem. If it doesn't, the problem is most likely in your video card.

◆ Make sure your system is configured properly for your video card/monitor combination. Right-click anywhere on the Desktop and select Properties to display the Display Properties dialog box; use the Settings tab to select the correct hardware and configuration settings.

◆ If your monitor suddenly goes blank and emits a high-pitched whine, turn off your monitor—*immediately!* Leaving the monitor on in this condition could damage it. Now check the settings on your video card (or in Windows' Display Properties dialog box); chances are the configuration is set to a higher resolution than your monitor is capable of displaying. Reconfigure the settings for a lower-resolution display, and you should be fine.

◆ If your monitor pops and crackles and maybe even starts to smell (like something's burning), turn it off and go check the credit line on your nearest charge card. Although it's possible that all this hubbub is caused by dirt building up inside your monitor, it's more likely that something major—like the power supply—has gone bad and that it's time to invest in a new monitor.

Your DSL, Cable, or Old-Fashioned POTS Modem Won't Connect

In this interconnected world, we all need the Internet to survive. What do you do if your Digital Subscriber Line (DSL) or cable modem won't let you connect? Try the following tips:

◆ Check your cables! If you're using an external modem, make sure it's firmly connected to the correct port on your PC and that it's plugged into and receiving power from a power strip or wall outlet. If you're using an internal modem, make sure the card is firmly seated. For all modems, make sure that it's connected to a working phone line—and that you have the cable connected to the *in* jack on the modem, not the *out* jack!

◆ Make sure your modem is configured correctly. If you're using Windows 98, Me, XP, or 2003, use the Modem Troubleshooter to track down potential problems. Otherwise, go to the Control Panel, start the Modems applet, and then run the diagnostics in the Modem Properties dialog box. If problems persist, try uninstalling and then reinstalling the modem on your system—and then check whether an updated driver is available from the modem vendor.

◆ Check your dial-up configuration. Make sure you have the right phone numbers listed, that you've entered the correct username and password, and that any Internet Service Provider (ISP)-specific information—such as Domain Name Service (DNS) numbers—is entered properly.

◆ Check your system network or Transmission Control Protocol/Internet Protocol (TCP/IP) settings. This isn't so much a problem with Windows 98/Me/2000/XP/2003, but it can be an issue with Windows 95/NT and other operating systems.

Also, remember that just because you can't connect to your ISP doesn't mean you have a modem problem. Many ISPs try to connect too many users through too few phone lines, resulting in busy signals, slow connections, dropped connections, or similar problems. See whether your connection problems ease up at different times of the day (the after-dinner period is a typical "rush hour" for most ISPs) or if your ISP has different numbers you can use to connect. If the problem persists, consider changing ISPs.

Your Printer Won't Print

Printer problems are quite common—especially after you've just hooked up a new printer to your old system. The following are a few things to look for:

- It sounds so simple as to be insulting, but make sure that your printer is plugged in and has power and that it's connected properly to your PC. A loose printer cable can cause all sorts of bizarre problems.

- Along the same lines, make sure that your printer isn't out of paper and that it's online and not experiencing any type of paper jam.

- Make sure that Windows recognizes your printer—and that it recognizes the *correct* printer. (Recognizing a similar model from the same manufacturer doesn't cut it.) Make sure that Windows has the correct printer driver installed. You may even want to check with the manufacturer to make sure you have the latest-and-greatest version of the printer driver.

- If you have more than one printer installed on your system or network (including faxes and devices that your system sees as printers), check the Print dialog box to make sure you have the correct printer selected.

- Check for device conflicts. Fax machines and printers frequently interfere with each other, but any two devices, if not configured properly, can cause conflicts.

- Make sure you have enough free disk space to print. Windows will use temporary hard disk space (called a *cache*) to store data while a print job is in process. Try deleting old and unused files (including TMP files in the `\WINDOWS\TEMP\` folder) to free up additional disk space.

Troubleshooting Tips for an Emergency

There really is a reason why I caution you to stay calm and not do anything desperate when you hit a snag. When people get scared, they do things they wouldn't even think about doing when their minds are clearer. If you lose your cool, you could end up having to fix several problems you created when trying to fix the first one.

Try to remember these considerations when troubleshooting a PC emergency:

Have an emergency kit handy.   Your kit should include a good screwdriver, a good flashlight, a boot disk or two (including the Windows Startup disk if you're running Windows), a floppy-based copy of a virus scanner, and some key diagnostic utilities.

In addition, if you want to be incredibly prepared, you can include a 10/100 Ethernet NIC, a cheap CD-ROM drive, a floppy drive, a PCI video card, a mouse, and replacement cables in your toolkit.

Have your operating system installation CD ready. Many problems—both hardware and software—require you to have the installation CD to reinstall or fix components. This is especially true with the Windows operating system though not entirely unique to it.

When you see the problem, stop! At this point, you need to take a moment to shift gears from working to troubleshooting.

Ask yourself, "What's the last thing I did?" Understanding the steps you just took to get you into the problem can help you identify the steps necessary to get you back out of it.

Do a first analysis of the "damage" before you try to change anything. The first thing you spot wrong might not be the only thing wrong, and you need all the information you can gather to make a smart choice about how to proceed.

If you find yourself getting frustrated, take a break. A good rest helps you keep your wits about you when you return to the computer.

When you finally put your hands on the PC to begin correcting the problem, take it one step at a time. Try one procedure, and see whether it fixes the problem. If not, undo it and try the next. Do too many things at once, and you'll start to forget what you tried or what your results were.

If you have another PC available, get on the Internet. Use the resources talked about in Chapter 24 to look for help.

Ask yourself why you have no backup system in place. (Apologies extended if you're one of the statistical minority who regularly backs up their files...or even thinks about doing so before they've lost data they sorely need.) Then, ask yourself whether the time you're going to waste doing work over again is better than the time you thought you'd waste making a backup. If backups are taking too long, the answer isn't fewer backups but faster, more capable backup hardware.

Make sure you have the tech support number of your hardware manufacturer handy. Always have the number handy—just in case everything else you try fails!

In this chapter we looked at how to troubleshoot some hardware problems, and troubleshooting advice in general. Next, we'll dive into how to set up and configure computer networks.

Part 6

Networking, Mobile Computing, and the Internet

Chapter 26

Networking Concepts and Hardware

- ◆ QuickSteps: Installing a New Network Card
- ◆ Basic Networking Concepts
- ◆ Understanding Networking Hardware and Software
- ◆ Network Connectivity Devices

Introduction

Okay, you're convinced—it seems like everyone you know has their own network. Your colleagues, your family, and even your technically challenged friends who have problems finding the Send button in e-mail seem to have multiple systems wired together. Because you figure that everyone else has done it, it's about time you set up a network yourself. After all, you want to be part of the cool crowd, don't you? Besides bringing you back into the "in" crowd, linking your computers has fringe benefits such as sharing files, applications, peripherals (printers and scanners), and Internet connections.

You already have the computers—what else do you need to make them start talking to one another? First, you'll need to understand some basic networking concepts. That's where this chapter comes in. Second, once you understand the basics, I'll tell you about all the components needed to set up your network—from network cards to cabling—and how to make them work.

If you've already set up a network, don't just skip this chapter. I'll tell you what you need to extend your network or to link it to another one.

QuickSteps: Installing a New Network Card

If you have already installed any other type of card, installing a network card is straightforward.

BE PREPARED

Before you start, there are some things you'll need to perform the operation. These include the following:

◆ Antistatic wrist strap.

◆ Container to hold screws.

◆ CD (or floppy disk) with software drivers that shipped with your card.

◆ Inventory of used Interrupt Requests (IRQs) and Input/Output (I/O) address spaces, just in case you come up with a system conflict after installation. Plug and Play (PnP) should set up the card just fine (provided of course you have a modern operating system), but it's a good idea to have this information just in case. You can obtain this inventory by accessing Control Panel ➢ System ➢ Device Manager and double-clicking Computer at the top of the list.

If you're removing another card to insert the new one, follow these steps:

1. Power down your PC, open the computer case, and identify the card you want to remove.

2. Make sure the card is disconnected from any outside cables.

3. Unscrew the small screw attaching the card to the PC case and lay it aside.

4. Pull gently on the card, using both hands to wiggle it back and forth slightly to disengage it from the connectors.

5. After you've pulled the card out, wrap it in its original sheath if you plan to use the card again. Don't touch the gold connectors on the card; the oils in your skin can corrode the gold and degrade connectivity.

To install a new networking card, follow these steps:

1. Power down the PC, open the computer case, and find a slot in the PC that's free and fits your specific network card. Most network cards are Peripheral Component Interconnect (PCI), so you're looking for a white PCI slot. Try to choose a slot that's not next to another card to maintain a good airflow.

2. Install your new card by first unwrapping the card, being careful not to touch the gold connectors, and setting it aside.

3. Unscrew the plate that covers the slot's opening to the rear of the computer and set the plate and screw aside. (You may need the plate later, and you'll need the screw in just a minute.)

4. Align the card with the slot in the PC and push gently but firmly to seat the card in its slot. You may need to push fairly hard, which can be somewhat intimidating if you're not used to inserting cards. If you have the right slot and push straight in, then the card should snap into place.

5. Using the screw that you set aside in step 3, screw the card in to hold it in place. This extra step will keep the card from sagging or working loose.

6. Close the case and, if the cables are already in place, connect them to the card.

7. Install the network card's drivers. The process for installing drivers depends on your operating system. If you have a PnP-compatible operating system (which you should), the operating system should detect the card automatically and begin the installation process. Follow the instructions that come with the network card.

TIP *Check the manufacturer's Web site to make sure you have the most recent drivers for your card!*

Basic Networking Concepts

Before you get started on making your computers talk to each other, you need to get some introductory material out of the way. There's no sense in trying to set up something unless you understand what you're trying to accomplish. In this section, I'll explain what a Local Area Network (LAN) is and discuss some advantages of networking, just in case you're not convinced yet.

Networks Defined

By now, you know what a network is. It's two or more computers connected for the purpose of communicating. That's the easy definition. But when you dive into it, there are several other ways you can classify networks. These classifications can depend on the size and location of the network, as well as the roles computers play on the network.

LANs AND WANs

Strictly speaking, a LAN is a group of computers connected within an enclosed area, such as a building. LANs can vary greatly in size. They can consist of two Windows PCs in your basement or several hundred workstations spread out over several floors in an office building. Historically, LANs were defined as groups of computers that shared a high-speed (10 megabits per second or higher) connection. But with current networking speeds blowing this figure out of the water, and remote connection speeds approaching this number, you'll find people who like to argue this definition. So, a safe way to go is to say that all the computers on the LAN are connected and in the same location.

Most LANs use some sort of cable to connect the computers. However, as I'll discuss in Chapter 27, "Installing and Troubleshooting Networks," wireless connections are becoming more popular, and networks can even be linked via telephone or power lines (although these last two options are rare).

Once you extend beyond the basic LAN, you start driving into WAN territory. A *Wide Area Network (WAN)* is simply a collection of two or more LANs. For example, a remote sales office permanently connected to the local main office would be considered a WAN. WANs are usually connected through phone lines and often use the Internet as a backbone. WANs can also be connected via radio transmissions or satellite, but these methods are usually prohibitively expensive. The Internet itself is a WAN—a really big WAN.

CLIENT/SERVER AND PEER-TO-PEER NETWORKS

When you look at the computers themselves on the network, you can classify them as serving in one of two roles (or sometimes both): a *client* and a *server*. A server is a powerful computer that answers client requests and is usually locked in a closet somewhere. Servers must have strong processors (plural), oodles of Random Access Memory (RAM) and hard disk space, and fast network connections. One network can have several servers, but their numbers are significantly fewer than clients. A client computer makes requests of the server and is generally what the network users use.

A *client/server* network is composed, as you might have guessed, of clients and servers. Once again, servers are pretty much dedicated to servicing requests for resources from other computers on the network. Clients utilize the services provided by the server. Can one computer be both a client and a server? Sure, but it depends on what the computer is doing and the computer's operating system. For example, if your computer is running Windows Server 2003, what is it? Most likely it's a server. How about Windows XP

Professional? It's probably a client. But XP Professional is also capable of sharing resources, making it a server as well. Still, XP Professional isn't intended to run as a long-term server.

A *peer-to-peer* network is a simpler type of network. In this type of network—often used in home and small office environments—there's no designated server. Each computer is essentially on the same level as every other computer; they can all share resources and use resources from each other. Does this mean that all computers must be running the same operating system? Absolutely not. You can have Windows XP Professional on one, Windows 98 on another, and Windows for Workgroups 3.11 on a third system and have a peer-to-peer network. In a peer-to-peer environment, each PC is connected to the other computers primarily for file sharing, peripheral sharing, and (if you're into it) gaming.

Advantages of Networking

Although setting up a network can be a time-consuming experience, there are many benefits to be gained by hooking all your computers together—benefits that far outweigh the hassles of configuring and maintaining the network.

SHARING APPLICATIONS

When all your computers are connected to a LAN, you gain the multiple advantages that come from application sharing. The way application sharing works is that one (and only one) copy of a software program is installed on the network server. When a client PC connects to the server, a copy of the application is loaded into the client computer's memory. As the client interacts with the program, it interacts with the copy stored in its own memory, not the one on the server, so that more than one client can access the same application simultaneously.

One major advantage gained by sharing applications in this fashion is that less disk space is needed on the individual client computers than if the application were installed on every PC. This is no small consideration in a world where the full installation of Microsoft Office now requires 2 gigabytes (GB) or more of disk space—before you create a single memo or spreadsheet! Even though large disks are common nowadays, you won't necessarily have those large hard disks installed in every computer in your network.

Another advantage is that installing and upgrading applications is much easier if you can install the program files on a single point instead of on all computers in the network. Although this doesn't work for all applications or in all situations, when application sharing is feasible, it can save a lot of time and energy.

Finally, some applications are just meant to be shared—games in particular. Many of today's popular PC games come with multiple-player capabilities, which can be utilized only if you're connected to a network (or, in some cases, to the Internet). If you have two PCs, two avid gamers, and the right cards and cables, it's easy to set up an exciting Quake III contest.

NOTE   *One word of caution, however: installing applications on an application server for use by the rest of the network doesn't mean you have to buy only one license for that application. Typically, you must buy one license for each user of the application, whether concurrent or total. (The requirements differ depending on the application.) If you don't have proper licensing for all your applications, you're guilty of software piracy, which is a federal crime. You don't think that anyone will know or care? Think again. The sole purpose of the watchdog organization called the Software and Information Industry Association (SIIA) is to care about piracy issues, and it'll prosecute violations against its member organizations.*

SHARING PERIPHERAL DEVICES

A *peripheral* (or *peripheral device*) is any piece of hardware that attaches to your computer. Most of the time, peripherals are considered to be external to the computer case. Not all peripherals can be shared, but if you can do it, peripheral sharing is a great way to make these devices available to everyone on the network. For example, rather than having people line up at the PC with the printer attached, they can send print jobs to the printer as though it were attached to their machine and pick up those jobs at their leisure.

Sharing peripheral devices can save network users both time and money. It's true that even without a network, you don't have to buy printers or CD-RW drives for every computer you own. One or two devices distributed throughout the office can work just as well if demand isn't high or people don't mind standing in line to use them. However, if people must waste time waiting for a device to be free, then the money saved by not having a printer at every desk may be spent in lost productivity.

Another advantage of peripheral sharing is the ability to connect multiple computers to a single high-speed Internet connection. If you have Digital Subscriber Line (DSL) or cable Internet service feeding into your house or small office, you can share all that Internet bandwidth with all the computers you've networked.

Note that you don't have to make all shared peripheral devices available to everyone on the network or give each user the same level of control. Thus, you can share that color printer (you know, the one that uses the really expensive cartridges) on the network, but you can protect it so that only the graphics people can access it—and keep all the other workers from using up those expensive cartridges by printing out rough drafts of their memos and to-do lists.

ENHANCING OFFICE INTERACTION

As offices get larger, it can be hard to keep people apprised of important events and to get them together all in one place. Networks can help encourage office cohesion by using email and group scheduling software.

Group scheduling was once probably one of your office manager's favorite ways of accumulating gray hair. It can be made much easier with the use of a network and some specialized scheduling software. Without these tools, organizing departmental meetings can be a nightmare as the organizer tries to sort through everyone's schedules to find a compatible time to meet. Group scheduling software can make this task much more approachable. The idea is this: everyone enters their schedules into a calendar program. Only they or selected people can see their own schedules, but the times are stored in a central database. When you want to call a meeting, you enter the names of the people you want to be present and then pick a time. If all the people listed are free at that time, the scheduling software will notify you. If not, it'll notify you that there's a conflict and with whom, and (depending on the package) it may be able to suggest the first time when all the people listed will be free. Once a time has been set, you can use the scheduling program to email everyone invited to the meeting, telling them of the date and time.

Speaking of email, it's useful for a lot more than just scheduling office meetings. In fact, email is probably the most ubiquitous networking application today. And, because most email systems permit you to attach files to email messages, email becomes another useful way to share files. Sending files via email is like sharing the file with the network, but it has four main advantages (for some applications):

◆ You can explain anything confusing about the data in the email message or emphasize the importance of the information.

◆ You can ensure that the recipient is getting the intended file, and you don't have to worry that they'll open the wrong one by mistake.

◆ You don't have to worry about setting the proper permissions on the file or muck around with passwords because only the recipient of the email message will get a copy of the file you send

◆ You can send files to people with whom you don't share a LAN connection, such as those you can access only through email via the Internet.

In short, the amalgamation of LANs into offices is one of the best things to ever happen to office communication and information sharing. Now that you understand the basics of what you can do with a LAN, you're ready to take a look at the pieces of the backbone that make all of this possible.

Understanding Networking Components

You've got the basics down, and you're convinced. Networking your computers isn't only a good idea, it's morally imperative that you do so. Now you need more details. Although networking isn't the hardest thing to do, it can seem that way if you don't understand what you need to make it work. The "what you need" part can be divided into two general categories: hardware and software. These categories probably aren't earth-shattering groupings to you because pretty much everything in a computer can be labeled this way, but, remember, a network is just extending your computer.

The next sections discuss the hardware and software needed to make your computer aware of the network and how to play nice with other computers on the network. If your computer doesn't know the rules and can't play nice, then it has to sit alone in the corner.

Networking Hardware

To create a simple network, you'll need hardware to connect your computers: network cards, some sort of cabling, and connectors to affix the cables to the cards inserted in each PC. I'll explain each of these items in turn.

DOOR TO THE OUTSIDE WORLD: NETWORK CARDS

The Network Interface Card (NIC), also known as the network board or adapter, is the add-in card you'll plug into the motherboard of your computer to provide an interface to the network. A network card really isn't fundamentally different from any other PCI card: it plugs into a slot on the motherboard, requires certain resources in order to operate, and has a built-in port into which you can plug the network connection. If this were a sound card, you'd plug in speakers to produce sound. Because it's a network card, you plug in a network cable to produce connectivity.

You can divide NICs into categories in a few different ways. First, there's the type of network they support. The main type of LAN is Ethernet, but others such as Token Ring, Fiber Distributed Data Interface (FDDI), and Asynchronous Transfer Mode (ATM) exist (but generally aren't used in home networks). Second, there's the type of cable the cards support. The jack on the back of the card must be of a type into which you can plug the cable you want to use. Older Ethernet cards supported coaxial cables as well as Unshielded Twisted-Pair (UTP) cables in a single card. For example, Figure 26.1 shows a 3Com network card that includes ports for both types of interfaces, as well as an Attachment, or Adapter, Unit Interface (AUI) port.

FIGURE 26.1

A 3Com 3C509B-C network card. It has BNC, AUI, and RJ-45 connectors

These types of cards were called *combo cards* because they had a combination of connectors. Note that you could only have a cable attached to one of the transceivers at a time, though. Nowadays, if you're using cables to connect your computers, you'll use either UTP or fiber-optic cable.

Third, there's the card's bus type, which governs how fast the NIC can talk to the motherboard. Most modern cards for desktop machines utilize either PCI or Universal Serial Bus (USB). You'll occasionally run across some old Industry Standard Architecture (ISA) NICs, but they're few and far between.

NOTE   *For laptops, you generally have three choices. The first is to get a built-in network adapter (which usually has a wireless antenna built into the case, as well as an RJ-45 port for wired connections). The second is to get a PC Card NIC, and the third is to get a USB network device. Combining laptops with wireless technology is the wave of the present and the future and will be discussed more in Chapter 30, "Notebook/Laptop Computers."*

Fourth, there's the external data transfer rate, typically measured in megabits per second (Mbps). The data transfer rate that the network card you choose can support isn't the only factor that determines network speed, but it's one of them. Ethernet runs at 10Mbps (regular Ethernet), 100Mbps (Fast Ethernet), or 1Gbps (Gigabit Ethernet). Although you can plug a PC with a 10Mbps card into a 100Mbps network, for example, the speed of the PC's connection to the LAN will be determined by the speed of the card connecting it to the LAN—or by the speed of the LAN, whichever is slowest. Most NICs operate at 100Mbps. Some of the older cards work at 10Mbps as well and are identified by the designation of 10/100.

The fastest version of Ethernet, Gigabit Ethernet, supports transmission speeds of up to 1 billion bits per second (Gbps). The NICs designed for Gig Ethernet are more expensive than Fast Ethernet cards, and are generally marketed for use in servers. As the price of these cards continues to drop, you will see more and more gigabit connections to the desktop.

NOTE   *External data transfer rates are typically described in terms of bits per second (bps), and internal data transfer rates are typically described in terms of bytes per second (Bps). Remember, 1 byte equals 8 bits, and one ASCII character can be expressed in 1 byte.*

THE SILVER LINK, THE SILKEN TIE: NETWORK CABLING

Sir Walter Scott may not have been talking about network cables when he wrote of these bonds, but the description fits: network cables are indeed the sometimes almost invisible but essential pieces for tying together a network. The types of information that'll be sent between computers (text, complex graphics, video, or audio), the distance between computers, the kind of network you want to create and the environment in which those cables must operate are all determining factors for the type of cable you'll need to use.

What are the options? There are several, divided between copper wire and fiber optic. Each of them is designed to solve, in a different way, one of the most nagging problems facing any kind of transmission: interference, radio frequency (RF) noise (terms you may remember from Chapter 4, "Avoiding Service: Preventive Maintenance"). Copper wire was originally chosen as a medium for network transmissions because it conducts signals well, but that same capability makes it susceptible to interference from other sources of electrical signals, thus endangering the integrity of the original transmission. To get around this, copper cables have protection to insulate the wire from outside interference.

The less susceptible cabling is to interference, the faster it is because transmission speed along analog channels (such as copper wire) is a function of frequency. Before your eyes glaze over, understand that this is important. Copper cables are sometimes described in terms of the frequencies they can support, so if you don't understand what this means, then you're not going to understand those descriptions.

Frequency describes the rate at which electrical impulses travel through a certain area. Frequency is expressed in hertz, or cycles per second, with the cycles being how fast the pulses can be created. They can be illustrated as sine waves (see Figure 26.2). In other words, a signal that runs at 8 megahertz (MHz) can run 8 million cycles in one second. The higher the frequency, the faster the data is traveling because more 1s and 0s are being packed into a single second.

Higher frequencies are more susceptible to interference than lower frequencies because more data is compressed into a given instant. If you're unsure why this is so, take a look again at Figure 26.2. Suppose that something interfered with both the low-frequency signal and the high-frequency signal for a $1/2$ second (a long time, but this is to make the point, not to show precise measurements). During that $1/2$ second, the data transmitted along those channels would be corrupted and lost. In the case of the higher-frequency signal, you've lost a larger proportion of the data because more data was crammed into that $1/2$ second. The lower-frequency signal lost much less data.

The maximum frequency supported by a given cable doesn't imply that the data transfer rate of that cable always uses that frequency, but it indicates only what the physical medium of the cable is theoretically capable of supporting, if undamaged and installed correctly. For example, Category 5 UTP (discussed in the following section) operates at a maximum frequency of 100MHz; but to support speeds of 100Mbps, a frequency of only 62.5MHz is required. That's just how fast the cable could transmit data under ideal conditions if the data were pushed through it that quickly.

FIGURE 26.2

The more bumps of a sine wave in a given time period, the higher the frequency

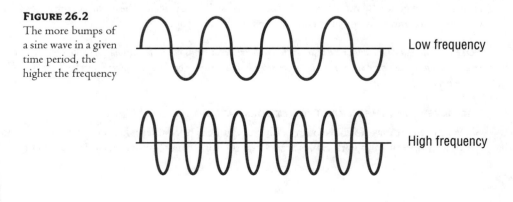

Low frequency

High frequency

INTERFERENCE VERSUS ATTENUATION

Although interference and attenuation have similar effects on data transmission (they're not good for it), they're not the same. *Interference* is a stray electronic signal that distorts the signal being transmitted, possibly corrupting the data being carried by adding extra humps in the sine wave or otherwise interfering with the signal. *Attenuation* is the increasing weakness of a signal as it travels. Just as a sound loses power from the time it leaves its source but may still be audible at a given distance from its source, all signals experience attenuation. The problem arises when the signal is so severely attenuated (because it has traveled farther than it was meant to) that the fading signal can distort the data.

Interference is like the problem you run into when a lot of people are all talking at once and it's difficult to sort out who said what or even to distinguish the sound of one voice as it gets overrun by the sound of another. Attenuation is the problem you run into when someone is too far away for you to hear their voice properly and you may misunderstand them. Interference problems are resolved by shielding out other "conversations"; attenuation problems are resolved by boosting the signal.

Another variable in physical cable types is their reach. When reading the descriptions of the cable types, you'll notice that they vary in their maximum functional length. That's mostly because of attenuation. Some cables are more susceptible to attenuation and interference than others. The good news is that devices, such as repeaters, can rebroadcast the signal on long cables so they can run for longer distances.

Twisted-Pair Cable

By far the most common cable type used today is *twisted-pair cable*. It's cheap and fairly reliable, and it's easy to connect. If you can plug in a phone, you can plug in a twisted-pair cable.

If you wrap one good conductor around another one, they form an electromagnetic field that protects the conducting wires from RF noise. That's the approach taken by twisted-pair cable. There are two types of twisted-pair cable: UTP and Shielded Twisted-Pair (STP).

These two types differ in two ways. First, modern UTP has four pairs of wires, and STP has two. Second, and the key to the difference in their names, is that STP has an extra conducting layer surrounding the twisted wires to give the cable an extra level of protection from interference. This doesn't necessarily imply that STP is always better protected from RF noise than UTP but only that the two cable types take different approaches.

The theory with UTP is that the two wires wrapped around each other individually conduct noise but cancel out each other's noise. STP was designed with the idea that the conductors are best protected with an additional layer of conducting wires rather than the two conductors being wrapped around each other. This extra layer of protection stiffens the cable, making STP harder to work with, and makes the cable more expensive to produce. In addition, if the shielding on an STP cable becomes torn or cut, the cable becomes ineffective. Figure 26.3 shows the physical difference between UTP and STP.

NOTE *UTP is used in Ethernet and Fast Ethernet networks. STP cable is commonly used in Token Ring networks, which used to be popular in the 1980s but are now somewhat rare.*

FIGURE 26.3
Sections of UTP
(top) and STP
(bottom)

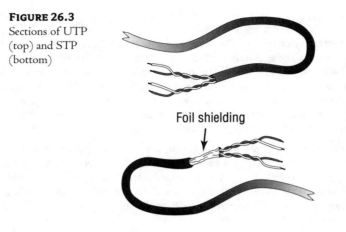

Foil shielding

UTP Standards UTP cabling is classified by how much data it can transmit. The higher the category number, the better the cable is, and the more data it can handle. The most common type of cable sold over the past several years is Category 5 UTP, also known as Cat-5. Cat-5 cable has been available since 1991 and can handle 100Mbps Fast Ethernet traffic without problems. Older cable, called Cat-3, can only handle 10Mbps Ethernet, so you don't want to buy it if you see it. The maximum functional distance for Cat-5 cable is 90 meters.

There are two other categories of UTP you might hear about. They're enhanced Category 5 (Cat-5e) and Cat-6. Cat-5e was approved as a standard in 1999, and as the name implies, it's an enhancement to existing Cat-5. It's rated for 100Mbps as well but can handle faster transmissions if your Cat-5 just isn't cutting it for you anymore.

Cat-6 has a higher frequency (250MHz) than Cat-5 or 5e (100MHz), as well as lower attenuation—19.8 decibels (dB) versus 22 dB at 100MHz. Cat-6 is also backward compatible with Cat-3 and Cat-5. What does all of this mean? Basically, it can handle faster transmissions, which is required if you're going to run Gigabit Ethernet, and you don't want to switch to fiber-optic cables.

UTP Connectors Most UTP cable uses RJ-45 connectors, which look like chunkier versions of the connectors used to plug your telephone into the wall (see Figure 26.4). (Phone plugs are RJ-11 connectors.) The RJ-45 connectors are attached to both ends of the cable; one end plugs into your network card, and the other plugs into a hub or a switch (a central connectivity device).

FIGURE 26.4
Each end of UTP
network cable has
an RJ-45 connector
on it.

A lot of people wonder, "Do I need to buy a hub or a switch? Can't I just plug two computers in to each other?" The answer is "yes," you can plug two computers directly in to each other. What you'll need is a special type of cable called a *crossover cable*.

A "regular" UTP cable (called a *drop cable* or a *patch cable*), one used to connect your computer to a hub, uses two sets of pairs to transmit and receive data. Pins 1 and 2 are used to transmit, and pins 3 and 6 are used to receive data. And, of course, your network card is wired to understand this as well. So imagine your two computers are directly lined with a Cat-5 cable. If one computer sends a message (outgoing on pins 1 and 2), then the other computer is going to get the signal on pins 1 and 2. Unfortunately, those leads on your network card don't know how to receive data, so they can't talk.

A crossover cable switches pins 1 and 2 with pins 3 and 6 on one end. In other words, the cable delivers the signal from my pin 1 to your pin 3 (receive), from my pin 2 to your pin 6 (receive), and vice versa. Now, when my computer sends you a message, it hits your receive ports instead of your send ports. Mission accomplished.

STP Connectors Although it's unlikely you'll run into STP cable (because they're typically used on Token Ring networks only), it's a good idea to know what the connectors look like just in case you do. On the computer end, you'll use a D-shell connector (see Figure 26.5), and on the hub end, you'll see an androgynous IBM Data Connector (Figure 26.6).

WARNING *You may notice that the D-shell connector used to connect to a Token Ring card is the same one that's used to connect to a video card. Be careful not to plug the network cable into your monitor.*

Twisted-pair networks typically link each NIC to a centrally located connectivity area: either a hub or a switch. I'll talk about hubs and switches in the "Extending Your Network" section of this chapter.

FIGURE 26.5

A D-shell connector connects the cable to the machine's network card.

FIGURE 26.6

An IBM Data Connector connects the cable to the hub.

WHAT IS ETHERNET?

One of the biggest sources of confusion for people when discussing networks is, "What is Ethernet, really?" Is it where the Ether Bunny lives? (I have bad jokes for all occasions, folks.)

Ethernet is a contention-based communications standard, based on a method called Carrier Sense Multiple Access with Collision Detection (CSMA/CD). In plain English, it's the communications rules for computers on a network. In an Ethernet network, a computer that wants to communicate listens for traffic on the line (carrier sense). If it doesn't hear any traffic, it figures that the line is free, and it transmits its data. Of course, all other computers on the network can do the same thing (multiple access). When two or more computers send a message at the same time, the messages collide (think of two trains on the same track—not good), and the computers detect that (collision detection). If a collision happens, each sender waits a random amount of time (a few milliseconds) and then retransmits.

It might sound a bit barbaric or even inefficient at best. But it works, and it's a cheap transmission technology to build.

Other communications standards are available, and they each use slightly different rules to communicate. In Token Ring, which has been mentioned a few times in this chapter, a computer can only communicate if it has the token, which is a blank data packet that circles the network. This method ensures that there are no collisions because you can only talk when you have the token. Another token-granting method is FDDI, which is generally only used with servers. Yet another communications standard is ATM, which uses a continuous transmission stream of fixed-length (53-byte) data packets.

Even with these other methods available, you'll probably go with Ethernet at home or for small offices. The key is to make sure that all hardware you purchase—network cards, hubs, switches, routers, and so on—are Ethernet compatible. You might get a great deal on that Token Ring card from the pawn shop, but don't expect to use it on your Ethernet network!

Coaxial Cable

Coaxial cable, often referred to as *coax* or *thinnet,* is made of a single copper wire encased in insulation and then covered with a layer of aluminum or copper braid that protects the conducting wire from RF noise. As you can see in Figure 26.7, coaxial cable has four parts:

◆ The central wire, called the *inner conductor*

◆ A layer of insulation, called the *dielectric,* which surrounds the inner conductor

◆ A layer of foil or metal braid, called the *shield,* which covers the dielectric

◆ The final layer of insulation (the part you can see), called the *jacket*

NOTE   *There's a second kind of coaxial cable known as* thicknet, *which is used in older networks but is rarely installed new today. This cable can stretch for longer distances than can thinnet cable, but it's much harder to work with. One contractor I know who used to have to work with thicknet refers to it as "frozen yellow garden hose" because of its stiffness. Thicknet doesn't actually connect to the PCs themselves but forms a backbone to the network that the PCs connect to with short patch cables.*

FIGURE 26.7
Coaxial cable

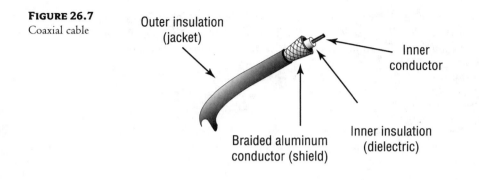

Coax Specifications   If you think that coax cable looks a lot like the cable used for cable TV, you're right, it does. They do use different levels of resistance, though; networking coax needs 50 ohms of resistance, and cable TV uses 75 ohms. So don't ever use cable TV cable for a computer and vice versa.

   With a top data transfer rate of 10Mbps, coaxial cable is slow by modern standards, but it's got a couple of advantages over UTP for some installations. First, it can extend for longer runs. The top length for UTP cable runs is 90 meters, but coaxial cable can extend for more than 800 meters. However, after 185 meters you'll have to boost the signal with a device called a *repeater*, which I'll describe later in the chapter.

   The second advantage is that you can use coaxial cables to connect more than two PCs directly to each other (rather than to a central hub) in a daisy-chain effect. This can be handy for those who have only three or four computers in the same room to connect and don't want to go to the expense of a hub. And using coax usually requires less cable than UTP, so you're likely to save a little cash there (but not much).

Coax Connectors   Three types of connectors are associated with coaxial cable:

   ◆   T connectors

   ◆   BNC connectors

   ◆   Terminators

   T connectors (see Figure 26.8) plug into network cards, where they stick out the back of the PC and provide an interface for plugging in the BNC connector or the terminator.

FIGURE 26.8
A T connector cre-
ates the interface into
which you plug the
BNC connector.

BNC connectors are at the ends of the coax cable (see Figure 26.9) and plug into the T connector attached to the NIC. This links the card and the cable, with the cable forming the crossbars of the *T* (see Figure 26.10), and may also be used to link sections of coaxial cable.

FIGURE 26.9

The BNC connector may link coaxial cables to each other or to T connectors.

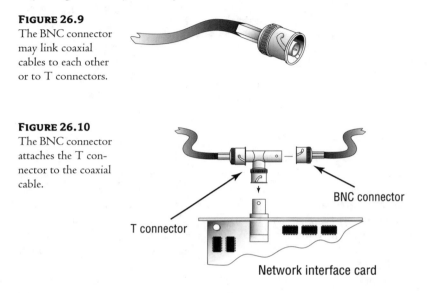

FIGURE 26.10

The BNC connector attaches the T connector to the coaxial cable.

BNC connector

T connector

Network interface card

The terminators are the final piece of the coaxial puzzle; they're used to define the ends of the cable. If you don't have terminators at each end of a coaxial segment, then the signal will "echo" from the end of the cable and *shadow packets* will result. Shadow packets slow down network speed by increasing traffic and may corrupt data if confused with real packets. Terminating the segments ensures that packets will be destroyed when the signal reaches the end of the segment. So, if you don't have another computer to connect, place a terminator on the terminal end of the T connector.

WARNING *Terminators are made for either 50ohm or 75ohm cable. Make sure to get a 50ohm terminator for use with computers! Using a 75ohm terminator can fry your network card.*

Fiber-Optic Cable

One of the fundamental problems with copper wiring is that it's susceptible to Electromagnetic Interference (EMI). Cable designers have found ways to reduce the effects of EMI, but those effects can't be completely eliminated. So, how do you solve this problem? The one way of making a cable EMI resistant is to use another transmission method: light. That solution is called *fiber-optic cable*.

Fiber-optic cable is indifferent to RF noise because of the difference in its conductive medium; rather than using electronic pulses to send data, it uses light. The light is conducted through a hairlike glass or plastic fiber that's covered with a thin insulating layer called *cladding*. The cladding is then surrounded with a plastic jacket to protect the delicate fiber. You can see a drawing of fiber-optic cable in Figure 26.11.

FIGURE 26.11

Fiber-optic cable

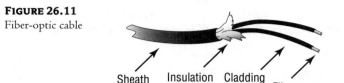

Sheath   Insulation   Cladding   Fiber core

As you'd expect, the fibers are the crucial element of data transmission. At each end of the fiber is a device called a *codec*, or coder/decoder. The codec is responsible for encoding the data into light pulses and then decoding them back into the electronic impulses that a computer can understand. To transmit data, a Light-Emitting Diode (LED) or a laser at one end of the fiber sends signals along the cable. When those signals reach the other end, they're decoded into their original form.

NOTE   *Astute readers will note from earlier chapters that I defined the term codec as meaning compression/decompression. You'll find it both ways, but generally the coder/decoder form is used to describe a hardware device, and the compression/decompression form refers to software used to encode and decode audio and video.*

Generally, fiber-optic cable isn't used for installations that need less than 155Mbps; just use copper. Fiber-optic can easily handle several gigabits of data per second.

Fiber-Optic Types   It might sound as though traffic through a fiber-optic cable is limited to a single path of data, but this isn't true for a couple of reasons. First, fiber-optic cable may have more than one fiber in it, meaning that multiple data pathways exist. The more fibers a cable has, the more data can pass through it at once, just as a four-lane highway can carry more traffic than a single-lane road. Second, there are two types of fiber-optic cable:

Single-mode fiber   Sends transmissions along a single path, like a flashlight. This beam of light is concentrated, so single-mode fiber can carry more data for longer distances than can multimode fiber. Single-mode fiber has a maximum distance of about 2 kilometers (km).

Multimode fiber   Allows multiple modes (signals) to pass through the cable at once. There are two kinds of multimode fiber: step index and graded index. In *step index fiber-optic cable,* the light beams bounce around inside the cable in a zigzag pattern. *Graded index cable* has a more rounded pattern to the light movement, like a sine wave.

NOTE   *A mode is a ray of light entering a fiber at a particular angle.*

Both kinds of multimode fiber-optic cable are prone to *modal dispersion*—spreading of the received light impulse—because of the number of light beams traveling through the cable. When the signal spreads, it moves more slowly, so single-mode cable transmits faster than multimode cable. To understand this behavior, try imagining what would happen if you threw a ball down a pipe. If you threw just one ball and it went through without hitting the walls of the pipe, it would move faster and more accurately than if it bounced off the walls of the pipe. Just as bouncing off the walls of the pipe slows down the ball's travel speed, bouncing off the walls of the cable slows down the light signal.

NOTE   *Single-mode cable is more expensive than multimode and can extend farther without requiring the signal to be boosted. Multimode cable is more often used within buildings; single-mode is reserved for inter-building use.*

Fiber has had notable success as a LAN backbone, combined with UTP taps to each workstation, for those with high-traffic networks and deep pockets. Fiber isn't often run to the desktop for a couple of reasons:

◆   Fiber cable is more expensive than copper cable.

◆   The connectivity devices required for fiber-optic transmissions are significantly more expensive than their copper-based counterparts.

◆   Fiber generally requires more expertise to properly install.

◆   Fast Ethernet speeds (100Mbps) are generally fast enough for the corporate desktop or home user, and the cost of fiber isn't justifiable.

Of course, to any story, there are two sides. The following are reasons why fiber-optic is used:

◆   It's fast. Very fast.

◆   It's resistant to EMI.

◆   Fiber-optic can transmit for longer distances than copper can.

◆   There are no worries about wire corrosion, as with copper.

◆   Fiber-optic is more secure because it's virtually impossible to tap into, as opposed to copper wires, which "leak" signals.

The price of fiber-optic cable and its connectivity devices have dropped in recent years. In addition, higher transmission speeds are continually being required for some applications. Fiber optic is certainly used more than it was a few years ago, and it's possible that in a few years fiber optic will obviate copper network cabling all together. But by then, everyone will want wireless networking anyway, right?

To summarize fiber optic, it's fast and expensive. Do you need it in your house? That depends. If you're Bill Gates's neighbor, then most certainly you need it. But for most of us, copper wiring is plenty fast and a lot cheaper and easier to set up.

Fiber-Optic Connectors   Unlike copper-wire cables, in which the transmission medium is the biggest source of signal loss, fiber-optic cable is most susceptible to signal dispersion at its connectors. Fiber-optic cables can use several different kinds of connectors, including FC, LC, SC, ST, MT-RJ, and VF-45. Figure 26.12 shows an ST connector, which is one of the most popular types.

FIGURE 26.12
An ST connector
and a connector
cover

CONNECTING A NETWORK—WITHOUT CABLE

Although the vast majority of office networks are connected via some type of cable, there are other ways to connect your computers without running all that wire. These alternate types of "wiring" are particularly popular in home networks, where it's often impractical to run long lengths of cable through walls and ceilings.

Power line networks enable you to send Ethernet packets over the electrical lines in your house. Power line networking uses Frequency Shift Keying (FSK) to send data back and forth. Two frequencies are used, one for 1 and one for 0; a transceiver unit attached between each computer and the nearest power outlet performs the frequency modulation. Although a power line network is extremely convenient and easy to set up, it's also very slow and prone to disruptions from other electrical devices in your home. Data transfer can be as low as 50 kilobits per second (Kbps)—compared to Fast Ethernet's 100Mbps.

Telephone line networks provide a similar level of convenience, but with higher data transfer rates (a minimum of 1Mbps) and greater reliability. With telephone line networking (commonly referred to as Home-PNA, based on the specifications developed by the Home Phone Networking Alliance), you connect each computer to an adapter that plugs into a standard phone jack. Then, utilizing a technology known as Frequency Division Multiplexing (FDM), data signals are sent through the adapter into your home phone line and picked back up by another adapter and PC elsewhere on the network. Each adapter on the network sends its signal at a different frequency within the available band—enabling your computer network to effectively share the phone line with other voice and data traffic.

Finally, it's possible to connect a computer to a network without using any wires whatsoever. *Wireless networks* operate on the same principle as do wired networks but without wires. Because of the importance of wireless, it gets its own section in Chapter 27.

Networking Software

For data to get from point A to point B on the LAN, you don't need only hardware but also networking software to package that data for transmission. That networking software consists of three main parts, which work in tandem with the file system drivers of your operating system:

Redirector   Sends requests to the network instead of the local hard disk

Network card drivers   Provides communications between the operating system and the network card

Networking protocols   The language of networking, so computers know how to speak to each other

So, for example, if Fred tries to save a Microsoft Word file from his computer to a shared drive on the network file server, the following happens:

1. Fred clicks Save and chooses to save the document to his drive G:, which is in reality a network connection to a physical drive shared from the file server.

2. The redirector examines the request to save, notes that drive G: isn't locally available, and redirects the request to a part of the operating system called the *network file system driver.*

3. The file system driver passes the request to the network card driver.

4. The network card driver passes the request—and the data—to the network card.

5. The network card packages the data for transmission across the network and sends it.

6. The file server's network card notes that a package has arrived for it and receives it.

At this point, the process is reversed: the server's network card driver passes the request to the file system driver in the operating system and writes the file to the local drive.

If you're building a network in an office, chances are excellent that sooner or later the network you create will be connected to another network in some manner or other. After all, that's how the Internet itself got started; local networks were given the means to connect to each other in a larger whole. Most networks grow in stages, rather than emerging full-blown in their final form, so they often include a hodgepodge not only of hardware but of network operating systems and communications needs as well. This, in turn, means that the network needs more than one type of redirector, must use more than one type of network protocol, and that not all the cards use the same driver. In short, sometimes even with careful planning, it can be a bit of a mess as networks grow and merge. In this section, I'll discuss the various software components involved in the networking process so you can better understand what you're dealing with when it comes to managing networking software.

THE ROLE OF REDIRECTORS

From the perspective of the PC initiating a network request, the first actor in the networking process is the *redirector*. Its role is to fool an application on the local machine into thinking that it's getting data from a local drive, rather than from a network drive. The point is that it shouldn't matter where the file being requested is stored; it should be accessible in the same way, no matter what.

For example, what happens if you're running Word and open a file stored on a network drive? From Word's point of view, there *is* no network. It knows only that there are one or more disk drives available with names consisting of a letter and a colon, as in A:, C:, D:, H:, and so on. Like many other applications, Word wasn't built to accommodate storage devices that aren't on the local machine. Thus, there must be a layer of software (placed just below Word) whose job it is to present a common drive-letter interface to Word when supplying data stored on the network. Word thinks that it's addressing local drives, but its requests for information from network drives must be *redirected* to other devices (or computers) on the network. So, if you tell Word to get the data from the directory DOCS on the server named BIGDOG, the redirector software initiates the request.

NOTE *Redirectors are often referred to as* clients *(as in, the Client for NetWare Networks or Client for Microsoft Networks) because they're a required part of a client machine.*

Therefore, before you can join a network, you must install a redirector that's compatible with the network type. Not all network operating systems use the same redirectors, so you must install the one that corresponds to the operating system on the network to which you're connecting. For example, Microsoft networks use Server Message Blocks (SMBs) to pass data back and forth, so they need a redirector that can phrase things in terms of SMBs. Novell networks use NetWare Control Protocols (NCPs) for the same job. So, to make requests of a NetWare server, you must use a redirector that can phrase requests in terms of NCPs. Note that having a transport protocol such as TCP/IP in common isn't enough—you must have a redirector that works with the operating system to which you're connecting. The good news is that redirector support can overlap several operating systems. Thus, if you're using Windows XP Professional, you can use the SMB-supporting Client for Microsoft Networks to connect to any operating system that supports SMBs.

FILE SYSTEM DRIVERS

The redirector is the piece on the end of the connection that's making the request. Its counterpart on the end of the connection that's complying with that request is the *file system driver*.

REDIRECTORS AND APIS

Most user applications are unaware of the network or networks they use. But some, such as email or groupware programs, must be cognizant of the network and exist only *because* of the network. They need to be able to "plug in" and communicate with other programs running on other machines in the network.

Programmers build network-aware programs to be tailored to sets of commands that a network offers to applications programs. Those sets of commands are Application Programming Interfaces (APIs). Think of an API as being somewhat like the dashboard of a car. Your car's dashboard is the interface you see, and you must learn to use it to operate the car. You have no idea while you're driving about what's under your car's hood—you just push down on the accelerator, and the car goes faster.

Thus, you don't have to know precisely how a car works to drive it. Not only that, but once you know how to drive one car, you can drive just about any car because the controls—the API—are the same.

(I discovered while driving a friend's Volkswagen one night that Volkswagens don't use the same API for "reverse" that other manual-shift cars do, but this analogy generally works.)

A dashboard consists of just a few primitive commands: brake the car, accelerate the car, shift the car's transmission, and so on. There's no command for "back the car out of the driveway," and yet you can still back a car out of a driveway by just assembling a number of the primitive commands into the actual action of backing a car out of a driveway. You have, in a sense, built a program with your car's dashboard controls arranged in a certain order.

Your computer's API functions in pretty much the same way. Your network services, like the redirector, can sit on top of different transport protocols. Without an API, the programmers of your network software would have to develop one redirector program to connect Windows Server 2003 to Internet Package Exchange/Sequence Package Exchange (IPX/SPX) and a different redirector program to connect Windows Server 2003 to Transmission Control Protocol/Internet Protocol (TCP/IP). It's the same redirector; it's just talking to different transport protocols. The way to avoid this is to provide a common "dashboard" for all the network services. Thus, the redirector service isn't written to a protocol but rather is written to an API. One example is NetBIOS. NetBIOS can sit on top of IPX/SPX, NetBEUI, and TCP/IP. This means that the transport protocol can change, but you don't have to rewrite your network service because it's written to the API (NetBIOS).

Sockets are a well-known type of API. They're temporary communication channels set up for passing information between a client program and a server program. These programs can be running either on the same machine or across the network. There are three network APIs you'll probably come across in the networking world:

◆ Novell sockets

◆ NetBIOS

◆ TCP/IP sockets

The API will take your network request and perform the task through the proper transport protocol.

File system drivers aren't used just for networking but are part of any request for access to storage media. In Windows XP, for example, the network file system driver is one of the supported file systems: FAT, NT File System (NTFS), Compact Disc File System (CDFS), and the network.

In general, the role of *any* file system driver is to organize and retrieve data on the storage media with which it's used. To take a commonly used disk drive file system that you're already familiar with, FAT numbers each cluster and notes which files are stored in which cluster. If a file's data requires more than one cluster to hold it all, then each cluster will also include a pointer to the next cluster on the disk that's used to store that data; the final cluster has an end-of-file marker so the FAT file system knows when to stop looking. How does the file system know where the clusters are? When you format a disk, you're cataloging the space on it with the file system you use.

When you ask to retrieve a file, the FAT file system is in charge of finding the data you want and making sure that all of it is retrieved (as chances are excellent that not all of the data will be in the same cluster). Similarly, when you attempt to save a file to disk, the FAT file system finds the first free space on the disk and stores the data associated with that file in those clusters, marking the clusters to point to the next one used as required.

NOTE *Depending on where disk space is available, those clusters may not be contiguous. The file system doesn't look for the first group of unused clusters that's large enough to store the file; it looks for the first unused cluster, period. If all the file's data won't fit into that space, then the file system will store the remaining data in the next free cluster, wherever that cluster happens to be on the disk.*

The network file system is just one more interface for reading disk space. The only difference is that it's used for network access instead of local access as are the other file systems. Thus, the process works as follows: the client makes the file request, which is intercepted by the network redirector. The network redirector passes on the request to the server, which receives the request and forwards it to the appropriate local file system driver. The disk is accessed—retrieve data, store a file, or whatever—and if data needs to be returned to the client, the reverse of this process happens. Back to the file system driver, network redirector, and the client's file system driver.

There are two important aspects to all of this. The first is that the user doesn't need to know if the file is local or remote; the computer will figure it out, and accessing the file is the same to the user either way. The second is that the network file system makes the local format of the server's hard disk immaterial to the client. Even if the client doesn't support the file system on which the remote file is stored (say, Windows 98 connecting to a Windows Server 2003 NTFS hard disk), it doesn't matter because the client's file system driver isn't the one used to access the file. As long as the client can talk to the server, the server will interpret the file system for the client.

THE ROLE OF NETWORK CARD DRIVERS

Now you know how a request gets from the application to the operating system or is satisfied on the operating system side. How does that request get to the network? That's the role of a piece of software called a *network card driver*.

As you know, any device driver is a piece of software that lets an operating system and a piece of hardware talk to each other. Network drivers are responsible for managing any extra-computer communications, including those required to access the Internet. One network driver is installed for each model of card used. Thus, for example, if you have a PC with a cable modem connection to the Internet and a network connection, you'll need two drivers installed. If you have more than one network card installed (perhaps if your PC is acting as a router) and they're different kinds, you'll have one driver installed for each. However, if you have two network cards of the same type installed, you'll have to install only the one driver.

Network Binding Interfaces

Modern drivers use a tool to bind the network cards to the transport protocols. (I'll explain transport protocols more fully in the next section.) In general terms, this tool is called the *network binding interface*. It serves as the interface between a NIC driver and a collection of protocols called a *transport stack*.

For a network card to use a communications protocol, they must be bound together. If you've ever skied or snowboarded, you're familiar with the concept of binding. Bindings on skis and boards hold you to the device you need to get down the hill. Without bindings, you won't stay on your device. The same idea holds true for computers: the NIC needs to be bound to the protocol.

There's no limitation to the number of protocols that can be bound to an adapter or the number of adapters that can share a protocol. In other words, your one network card can have four protocols if you want (although it's not a good idea because it causes more work for your card), and the four network cards in your computer (hey, you're really cool) can all use TCP/IP.

The Ties That Bind

Your network card has three protocols bound to it. Which one does it use first? The answer depends on the order in which the transport protocols were bound. You can edit the binding order to place the protocol that'll be used most often first so as to reduce the number of retries required to find the protocol needed to access a particular server. If your computer is responding to another computer's request, you'll use the protocol that the other computer used first. In other words, assume that both of us speak English and Spanish. If I ask you a question in Spanish, you'll respond in kind.

If you want to cut off communication to a server that's using a particular protocol, you don't have to uninstall it—just remove it from the list of protocols bound to the network card.

There are two competitors for the title of world standard network binding interface: Novell's Open Datalink Interface (ODI) and Microsoft's Network Driver Interface Specification (NDIS). These two binding interfaces have a lot in common in terms of what they do and how they do it. The main difference between them is that ODI-compliant drivers operate in real mode. As you know, this means that they must use memory in the first 640KB of the memory installed in your machine and that they can't cooperate with other drivers that may be installed in the system. NDIS-compliant drivers, in contrast, run in protected mode so they can multitask with other drivers and don't use scarce conventional memory.

Why use ODI-compliant drivers if they can't run in protected mode? Mostly because your redirector sometimes requires them. Not all redirectors will work with the NDIS-compliant drivers. If you're not sure, check the documentation for your operating system to find out the requirements of your particular redirector. Generally speaking, both NDIS and ODI work with all transport protocols; any limitation is on the driver side.

NETWORK TRANSPORT PROTOCOLS

Sneakily, throughout this part of the chapter I've been referring to transport protocols without ever really explaining what they are. Now's the time for the explanation.

I'll start with the concept of protocols. A *protocol*, quite simply, is a standard or set of rules. You're confronted with protocols in various aspects of your daily life. For example, if your phone in your house rings, you pick it up and say, "Hello?" Why do you say "hello" first? Why doesn't the caller identify himself first? The answer is that it's a tradition. It's the custom in the United States that the person answering the phone should respond first. In other words, this is the American protocol for answering the phone. If you were in mainland China, you'd pick up the telephone and wait for the other person to say, "Wei," to signal they were there. When you meet someone, do you hug, kiss, or shake hands? Once again, the answer is determined by protocol.

How does this apply to networks? *Network transport protocols* determine how data is transmitted across the network and how that data is packaged and addressed. For two computers on the same network to communicate, they must be using the same transport protocols because the protocols used determine how the data is packaged and delivered. Another way to think about it is that it's the language, as well as the rules, that computers use to communicate. If I don't speak your language, we're not going to have much of a conversation.

The good news is that modern operating systems can simultaneously support more than one protocol, so you can use one for each type of connectivity you need. The bad news is that not all operating systems support all transport protocols; in fact, they tend to specialize, and even some like-named protocols aren't usable across all platforms. However, today there's enough overlap that some degree of communication and interoperability is possible across all major operating systems.

TIP   Loading more than one network transport protocol uses up RAM, so even though it's possible to load more than one transport protocol with modern operating systems, it's a good idea to install support for only the ones you need.

Please be aware that the following sections are *introductions* to the three main protocols used in PC networking and aren't complete. TCP/IP, for one, is an enormously complex protocol; you could write several books about it alone. What's here is simply intended to help you understand the basics of how each of these protocols work.

NetBEUI

Back when IBM first started marketing their PC network, they needed a basic network protocol. They had no intention of building large networks, just small workgroups of a few dozen computers or less.

Out of that need grew the Network Basic Input/Output System (NetBIOS). NetBIOS is just 18 commands that can create, maintain, and use connections between PCs on a network. IBM soon extended NetBIOS with the NetBIOS Extended User Interface (NetBEUI), which is basically a refined set of NetBIOS commands. Over time, however, the names NetBEUI and NetBIOS have taken on different meanings. NetBEUI is the transport protocol, and NetBIOS is the set of programming commands that the system can use to manipulate the network; it's actually an API.

NetBEUI is one of the fastest protocols you can use in terms of its speed when slapping data into packets for transmittal and unwrapping said data on the receiving end. It's also beautifully simple to set up: you install it and bind it to a network driver, and it works. No configuration is required, and the address of the computer is an easy-to-remember name that you assign.

NOTE   Computer names on a network using NetBEUI are actually NetBIOS names. They can be up to 16 characters long and are not case sensitive.

However, there's one problem with NetBEUI, which really limits its usefulness: you can't route it. In other words, if your needs are larger than those of a single segment, you can't use it to transport data beyond your local segment. (A *segment* is a piece of a network that can operate on its own or that has been subdivided simply for better management purposes. For example, within a network comprising several floors of a building, a segment might be on one floor.)

It's also supported only by some Microsoft operating systems and OS/2, so if you planned to communicate with the Unix file server or NetWare print server, well, you're out of luck.

Today, NetBEUI's usefulness is extremely limited. First, Microsoft (who has traditionally been NetBEUI's biggest supporter) isn't installing NetBEUI on the newer releases of its operating systems. With every operating system since (and including) Windows 2000, NetBEUI must be manually installed off the CD. Second, TCP/IP is faster than it used to be, so NetBEUI doesn't have the performance advantage it did at one time. As Internet access becomes ever more ubiquitous, you need TCP/IP anyway because it's the protocol required to use that network.

In short, NetBEUI's is small and fast, but its usefulness is limited to small, single-site networks that don't need Internet connectivity, and there aren't a lot of those around.

IPX/SPX

IPX/SPX, Novell's proprietary transport protocol, is actually two protocols—IPX and SPX. IPX is a network-layer connectionless protocol. It's responsible for finding the best path for packets to take to reach their destination or for picking them up when they arrive. SPX is a transport layer protocol that provides connection-oriented services between two nodes on the network.

NOTE *Some Microsoft operating systems refer to the IPX/SPX protocol as NWLink.*

Packet addressing and routing are handled by the IPX protocol. So, logical network addresses (as opposed to the hardware ones that are burned into the network card at production) are assigned at the IPX level. An IPX address consists of a 4-byte (32-bit) network number and a 6-byte (48-bit) node number.

What do these numbers mean? The *network number,* also called the external network address, identifies the physical segment to which the computer is attached. If two or more servers are on the same network segment, then they'll all use the same external address.

NOTE *External network addresses are assigned only to NetWare servers. Client machines on a NetWare network inherit their external network addresses from the server they log into.*

The *node number,* or internal network address, is usually the hardware address of the network card inside the PC. This is handy because it means that no translation has to take place from software-assigned names to hardware-assigned names. When installing a Novell NetWare server, you're asked to accept or change the internal IPX number. It then becomes that server's ID number. If you type **slist** from a workstation, you'll see this ID for each server listed.

NOTE *With the release of Netware 5, Novell made a drastic shift in philosophy. No longer was IPX/SPX the default protocol, TCP/IP was. Does this mean the end of IPX/SPX? Not yet, but perhaps in the near future.*

TCP/IP

TCP/IP is an industry-standard suite of networking protocols. It's safe to say that TCP/IP is the most widely used protocol in existence. Does that mean that it's the fastest or the most efficient? No. But everyone uses it because of one thing: the Internet.

TCP/IP is a suite of protocols, meaning that there are several parts working together to ensure that your computers can communicate. Internet Protocol (IP) provides a standard set of rules for addressing computers and routing packets. Transmission Control Protocol (TCP) is responsible for several things, the most important being the guaranteed delivery of data packets. The rest of the protocol suite consists of several dozen protocols with specific functions. There are too many to list here and cover adequately, but if you want to see how an interesting puzzle works, you might want to look more into TCP/IP. The more I've learned about networking, the more amazed I am that people thought of this stuff.

You can tell how good TCP/IP is at its job by its current task. It's the transport protocol for the Internet, the system that connects thousands of individual computers and networks across the world. Although originally designed for use by universities and the military, TCP/IP is becoming more popular for business applications. It can be used to connect LANs, Unix hosts, DEC VAX minicomputers, Macs, and many other kinds of computers. Today, if a commercial computer platform doesn't support TCP/IP, it won't be around for very long.

Configuration Requirements for TCP/IP

One catch to TCP/IP is that it can be difficult for novices to set up because there are so many addresses and servers to assign. As I've discussed already in this chapter, NetBEUI and IPX/SPX are pretty simple to set up. In the case of NetBEUI, you assign a computer name, and in the case of IPX/SPX, you assign a network identifier and let the system assign its own node identifier based on the hardware address of the PC's network card. However, TCP/IP can require a whole slew of addresses, including these:

- A local IP address.

- A subnet mask that identifies the network segment to which your computer is attached.

- The default gateway (that is, the portal to the next network segment), which is required for Internet access. This is also a router.

- The IP address of the Domain Name Service (DNS) server, which translates an easy-to-remember name, such as `computer.company.com`, into an IP address, such as `192.168.0.100`.

- A Windows Internet Naming Service (WINS) server, which translates NetBIOS names into IP addresses on networks running Windows NT.

The only required configuration parameters are an address and a subnet mask. All of the others are optional but can make your networking experience much more enjoyable. In addition, a wonderful service called Dynamic Host Configuration Protocol (DHCP) can automatically assign TCP/IP configurations to client computers.

If you've spent any time on the Internet at all, you're probably familiar with the concept of IP addresses. Simply put, they're a 32-bit number that identifies a computer on the network. This is the logical (software) address of the PC, as opposed to the hardware address burned into the network card. In its binary form, an IP address might look something like this:

```
11000000 01101010 01111110 11000001
```

It's not exactly easy to read by anyone but a programmer or a computer, so for the convenience of humans, IP addresses are written in what's called *dotted decimal* format, converting each byte of the 32 bits into a number using the base-10 system, as shown here:

```
192.106.126.193
```

That's much easier to read and remember, isn't it? Each number in the example is an octet, so each IP address has four octets.

Each network card attached to a TCP/IP network has a unique IP address that identifies it on the network—not just the physical segment to which it's attached, but the entire network.

Where does this IP address come from? How do you know what numbers to include in it? The answer depends on the scope of your network. If you're creating IP addresses for a local TCP/IP network that'll never have any contact with the Internet whatsoever, then you can more or less make them up if you want to, just as long as each network card has a unique IP address. However, if you want to connect to the Internet, you'll need to get unique IP addresses (Internet-scale now), and that's where an organization called the InterNIC comes in.

The InterNIC, simply put, is an organization in charge of assigning Internet addresses to companies and organizations that request them. In broad terms, it assigns groups of IP addresses to organizations, based on their sizes, by assigning specific numbers for the first octet (or first two or first three) and then letting the organization use any numbers they like for the remaining octets. So, for example, if you requested a set of Internet addresses from the InterNIC, they might give you the set `192.106.X.X`. This would mean that all your IP addresses would have to start with the `192.106.` prefix but that you could assign numbers (from 0 to 255) as you choose for the final two octets of the address. The parts assigned by the InterNIC are called the *network* portion of the address, and the parts assigned internally are called the *host* portion.

A key part of Internet addressing lies in identifying not just a specific computer, but identifying the *subnet*, or part of a network, to which it belongs. That's done not with an external network number, as with IPX/SPX addresses, but with the subnet mask. Really, the subnet mask defines your true network address (it's not necessarily just the address given to you by InterNIC). When your computer wants to send a message to another computer, it looks at both computer's addresses and its (your) subnet mask to determine the network address. If the network addresses match, your computer assumes that the other computer is on the same network. If the network addresses are different, then your computer assumes that the other computer is on a different network.

It's easy for two computers on the same subnet to communicate with each other; TCP/IP sends out the data, and the computer with the destination address that matches the one in the IP packet picks up the data. If a computer on one subnet wants to communicate with a computer on another subnet, then the request must go to the router that connects the two subnets. The address of the router is configured as the default gateway.

The router looks at the network address of the destination address, decides whether that address is on the local subnet, and, if it isn't, forwards the packet to the next subnet. Then that router examines the destination IP address, decides whether the address is on *that* subnet, and either broadcasts the message for pickup or forwards the packet again to the next subnet. This procedure continues until the correct subnet is found.

When a packet arrives at its destination, a protocol called the Address Resolution Protocol (ARP) resolves the IP address to the network card's hardware address. ARP is also responsible for translating the addresses for outgoing data.

Multiple Transport Stacks

With the popularity of TCP/IP and the regression in popularity of the other protocols, most people choose to run just TCP/IP. But, you might have a reason to run more than one protocol. For example, you might have an older NetWare server that requires IPX/SPX, or you might want to use Net-BEUI locally and TCP/IP to get on the Internet.

Remember two things, though. First, don't load a protocol unless you absolutely need it. Second, if you do load multiple protocols, optimize the binding order to use your most used protocol first.

Connecting and Extending the Network

So far, all I've talked about are the things your computer needs to get on the network. Of all of the topics discussed to this point, the most important you need to worry about are the network card, drivers, cables, and protocols. It's not like you have to worry about APIs or file system drivers; those just take care of themselves.

But now, it's time to move on to connecting two or more computers together. This section will start off with the basic hardware needed to connect computers on a LAN and move toward extending your network into a WAN.

Hubs: Connecting the Dots

Hub is a catchall term for a device that connects networked devices to each other. The term is used most often to apply to devices used in Ethernet networks. Token Ring networks use Multistation Access Units (MAUs), which, like the network itself, function differently from the Ethernet hubs. However, both hubs and MAUs serve the same basic function of joining PCs together on a LAN.

TYPES OF HUBS

Most hubs come in one of three forms:

◆ Stand-alone

◆ Stacked

◆ Modular

Stand-alone hubs are what they sound like—powered or (rarely) unpowered devices that may or may not include the capability to connect to other hubs with a short run of cable, perhaps fiber or twisted-pair, in which case they're *stacked*. Stand-alone hubs, in stacked form, are shown in Figure 26.13.

TIP   *Unmanaged stand-alone hubs are generally pretty inexpensive (you can likely find a four-port Ethernet 10/100 hub for around $20), but hubs get more expensive as more ports and features are added. If you don't need management capabilities, buying two stand-alone hubs and linking them may be cheaper than buying one big one.*

Modular hubs are built with a backplane that hub cards can plug into, as shown in Figure 26.14.

FIGURE 26.13
Stand-alone hubs may be used alone or linked to other hubs.

FIGURE 26.14
Modular hubs look like add-in cards plugging into a motherboard.

Add-in card for additional ports

If built to be "intelligent" (I'll explain that further in just a moment), the hubs in a modular or stacked design may be managed by one hub that's the Master, while the rest are Slave hubs. Why choose a modular or stacked hub? Mostly, it'll depend on how your network will grow. You can add modules to a hub chassis, or you can get stackable hubs to distribute them throughout your building, wherever they happen to be needed.

SOME HUBS ARE MORE EQUAL THAN OTHERS

Hubs come in a variety of forms, ranging from extremely simple designs that act as a cable interface to those that offer some advanced management techniques. You can basically divide hubs into three categories:

- ◆ Passive
- ◆ Active
- ◆ Intelligent/managed (two terms for the same thing)

Passive hubs are unpowered devices, such as patch panels, that provide an interface for cables to transfer data back and forth. They're appropriate for some applications, such as wiring a house for a network, but you're more likely to find an active and/or managed hub in most LANs.

NOTE *All completely passive devices are unpowered. Powered hubs regenerate the signal and are therefore active.*

An *active hub*—that is, any powered hub—has repeating qualities, repackaging and regenerating the signal (as described in the upcoming section on network repeaters). Otherwise, active hubs serve the same functions as passive hubs, blindly making sure that data put on the network is broadcast to each connected segment so that whomever the data is for can pick it up. One advantage that most powered hubs have is *status lights*. If a PC's connection to the network is working, then the light for the port it's plugged into comes on. If the PC isn't connected to the network, then the light is out. Another status light on one hub I have shows a scary-looking red light whenever collisions take place, but recall that some collisions are a normal and expected part of Ethernet operations.

Intelligent, or *managed, hubs* have a module that allows them to do a bit more than just shove data along the network; they can be used to help you troubleshoot or keep tabs on your network. If you see a hub sold with a Managed Device Interface (MDI), it's an intelligent hub.

Management protocols, such as the Simple Network Management Protocol (SNMP), have two parts. A monitor runs on a management server, and an agent runs on the managed devices. The monitor and the agent can communicate. In the case of SNMP, the most common generic management protocol, the monitor queries the agent and collects information from it, perhaps including the following:

- ◆ Hub and/or port-level status and activity information
- ◆ Performance statistics on a per-port basis
- ◆ Network mapping of all SNMP-capable hardware on the network
- ◆ Event logging of network errors and activity

You can also use management software to do things to managed devices, such as the following:

◆ Change network security by denying unauthorized people access to the hub.

◆ Set tolerances for activity, error levels, and performance so that you know if those tolerances are exceeded.

NOTE *This is a sample of the kinds of information that may be available with managed hubs, not a complete list or one that'll apply to all managed hubs. The precise information that the management software delivers depends on the agent installed and may vary with the model.*

Managed hubs aren't always necessary. If your network has only a single hub and this hub is easy to get at, you can probably check it out in person as easily as you can call up diagnostic software. The more PCs that are on the network and the harder the hub is to get at, the more complicated troubleshooting gets. What's simple with one hub becomes a nightmare when you have 10 hubs with 16 ports each. In that case, some kind of management software can help you keep your sanity when it comes time for troubleshooting.

HUB ARCHITECTURE

At its most basic level, a hub is a device that offers an electrical connection for cables that can't be hooked into each other directly. *Ports,* or the little holes you stick the cables in to connect them, are relevant to the definition of any hub because they determine the following:

◆ The cable type or types the hub supports

◆ The number of PCs that may be connected with a single hub

◆ Whether the hub is expandable and may be remotely managed when the network is down

Like network cards, hub ports are designed to accommodate only particular kinds of cable connectors. For example, coaxial cable and UTP require different ports, and both of them are completely different from those used by fiber-optic cables. Some hubs have ports for various sorts of cables. This allows them to connect to more than one type of cable so that you can physically connect, say, a server with a fiber NIC to the rest of your PC-based 100Base-T LAN.

Those ports won't do you any good unless there's some mechanism to connect them internally so that packets from one cable may be passed to the rest of the network. To let ports—and thus the nodes plugged into those ports—communicate, there's an internal bus system inside the hub providing each port with a receiving connection and a sending connection. The way that data is sent to each port depends on the type of network involved. For example, Ethernet networks broadcast data to all parts of the network, leaving it to the individual devices to sort out whether a packet is intended for them or should be ignored. Thus, data coming into a hub from a PC on a 100Base-T Ethernet network is broadcast to all segments plugged into the hub, as illustrated in Figure 26.15.

Some intelligent hubs note the physical address of the network card associated with a particular port. These hubs either may be preprogrammed with a static list of address-hub mappings, or they may create mappings through discovery. Static address mappings can be used to keep unauthorized people off the network. As shown in Figure 26.16, if a hub is given a static list of port-address mappings, and a PC with a physical address not found in that list attempts to connect to the network, a smart hub can isolate that port. Once isolated, the unauthorized PC can't connect to any of the other PCs plugged into the hub.

The internal bus of the hub operates at the same speed as the network, or, more precisely, the speed of the network is determined in part by the speed of the hub. Therefore, if you want to run a 100Mbps network, you'll need a hub with an internal bus that supports that speed.

Not all the ports in a hub are for plugging in computers. Some hubs have an uplink port to connect to other hubs, and others have an AUI port, which can let you connect the hub to another hub or to another device such as a bridge or router, as shown in Figure 26.17.

Models with AUI ports typically list the number of ports like this: 5 + 1, meaning that the hub has five ports for PCs to plug into and one AUI. The type of cable that plugs into the AUI port depends on the hub; fiber and RJ-45 are common.

FIGURE 26.15

Data sent on a 100Base-T network is broadcast to each PC plugged into a hub via the ports.

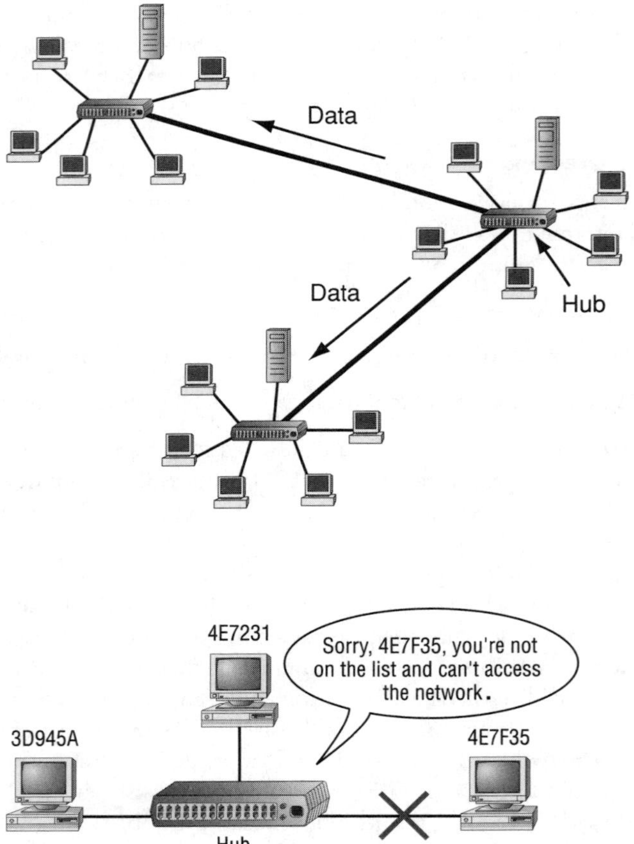

FIGURE 26.16

Intelligent hubs can use static lists of authorized physical addresses to keep unauthorized PCs off the network.

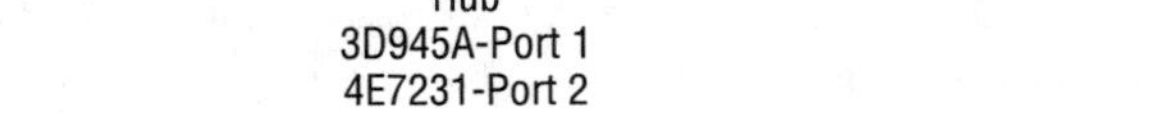

FIGURE 26.17

Use the extra port to link hubs to each other or to internet-working devices.

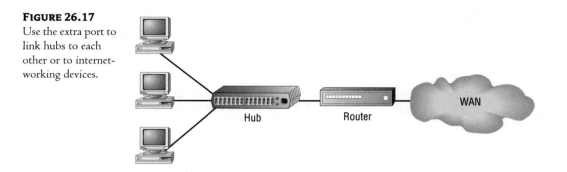

In addition to their uplink or AUI ports, some hubs will have a serial port interface. This interface enables you to connect the hub to a PC or modem and remotely manage the device. This is handy if the network has crashed, but the crash wasn't related to the hub itself. Such management is referred to as *out of band* management because it takes place independent of ordinary network transmissions.

Switches: The More Intelligent Cousin

Switches basically perform the same task that hubs perform: they connect multiple devices on a LAN. Switches just do it a lot better.

You'll notice that some smart hubs don't just blindly shove data onto all the segments of the network that are plugged into them. Instead, they notice the Media Access Control (MAC) or hardware addresses of the network cards associated with each port and can discriminate based on those addresses. Switches carry this capability somewhat further to identify the destination's MAC address and forward the packet only to the segment on which that address is located.

The distinction between an ordinary hub and a switching hub is the difference between the office switchboard operator paging the intended recipient to pick up a call and calling a specific office and patching through the call directly. Figure 26.18 illustrates this concept.

Why bother switching the signal instead of broadcasting it? One major reason is traffic control. If every time there's a telephone call into the office, the switchboard operator makes everyone listen to the page and then decide whether to pick up, that's more of an interruption to the office than it is to directly notify the call's target. Similarly, when a hub broadcasts all frames to all segments attached to it, then every PC on the network has to stop and "listen" and can't "talk" unless they want to cause a collision. If the signal is switched only to the part of the network where it needs to go, then the rest of the network isn't bothered. It can transmit data on the other segments without interfering with the first transmission.

Switching also makes it possible to reserve more bandwidth for high-traffic applications. With ordinary hubs or repeaters on a 100Mbps network, all ports share the same 100Mbps pipe. With switching, each port can have its own 100Mbps pipe, unencumbered by traffic from other ports. Switching makes it possible to connect multiple LANs to get all the advantages of being linked without the disadvantages of sharing bandwidth.

FIGURE 26.18
Switching the signal (top) versus broadcasting the signal (bottom)

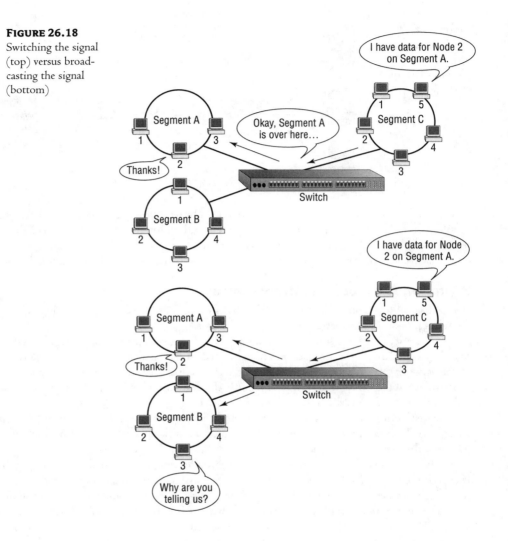

Repeaters: Extending the Network's Reach

Repeaters are devices that regenerate an electronic or photonic signal to increase the distance that the signal can travel—basically, to boost it at some point after its original transmission. All repeaters do is strengthen the signal by repackaging and rebroadcasting; they don't connect disparate networks, filter packets, or route data to other subnets.

The sole purpose of a repeater is to reduce the effects of attenuation. As you may recall, that's the tech-ese for "signals get weaker as they travel." As signals get weaker, they're more easily corrupted by other signals. This shouldn't be news to anyone who's ever used a radio while on the road. Say you're driving along, listening to Bela Fleck. As your drive approaches the end of the broadcast area,

Bela doesn't immediately disappear but has a disturbing habit of suddenly breaking off and sounding like the Bee Gees because the radio station in the new broadcast area is having a "Best of Disco" show. Bela fades out, and the Bee Gees fade in. What happens with radio also happens to networks; no matter what type of signal it is, how well it's shielded, or how immune to interference, sooner or later it'll fade to the point at which it's no longer intelligible at its destination.

You can take two approaches when it comes to solving the problem of attenuation. First, you can boost the signal with increased voltage, which is what your radio station is doing when they start boasting about getting a new transmitter. The new transmitter will have no effect on the signal's quality for the original broadcast area. However, it'll improve it on the outer edges of the broadcast area and extend it to new areas. Sooner or later, the signal will still fade, but with the stronger original signal, it'll travel farther before doing so.

The second approach, and the one taken by networks and inherent in repeater design, is to repeat the signal to start it out fresh again.

Bridges: Spanning the Gap

Bridges are connectivity devices like hubs and switches, but they add more intelligence. A bridge connects multiple segments within a network and provides some traffic-filtering capabilities. Although you'd use a hub or a switch to connect multiple PCs, you could use a bridge to connect multiple hubs or switches.

A bridge filters traffic based on computers' physical (MAC) address. After the bridge is powered up, you can enter in a list of addresses and their location, or you can allow the bridge to discover the addresses on its own. When the bridge receives an incoming packet, it forwards it to the appropriate segment of the network only, making it so other segments don't have to see the unnecessary data.

Sounds a lot like a managed switch, doesn't it? They work the same way, but as I said in the last paragraph, bridges are usually a bit more intelligent, and they're also generally capable of handling more traffic than a switch can.

Routers: Connecting Multiple Networks

Routers are used to connect two or more separate networks as well as to connect multiple computers on a network to a single shared unit, such as a DSL or cable modem. Whereas bridges forward data packets *within* a network, routers forward data packets *between* networks.

Routers operate based on specific protocols (such as TCP/IP or IPX/SPX) and are independent of the technology used for the network itself (such as Ethernet or Token Ring). Because of this, routers can easily interconnect networks that employ different topologies. This capability to "bridge" different networking technologies has led to the widespread deployment of routers throughout the Internet.

NOTE *Because a router is a logical boundary for the network—Ethernet data doesn't cross a router unless instructed to do so by the router itself—a router can also be used to divide a single network into two logically separate networks.*

If you're responsible for only a single network, the only router you're likely to encounter is the one between your network and the Internet. If you're responsible for multiple networks, you'll have routers between each network.

REPEATERS VERSUS EXTENDERS

It's a given that repeaters don't just repeat but actually repackage. There *is* a device that just repeats; it's called a LAN *extender*, and this device fulfills the function you'd expect from something called a *repeater*. Extenders function similarly to repeaters in that they permit you to have longer networks without increasing the chances of collisions, but they don't add to your repeater count. What's repeater count? You can have up to only four repeaters in a single network, and the number you have is called your *repeater count*.

There's no reason to *not* use a repeater in place of an extender, except that you can use only so many repeaters in a network, and you're not limited in the number of extenders you can use.

When data arrives from one network, the router decides—based on its *routing table*—where to forward that data. Whereas bridges and switches move traffic based on physical address, routers forward traffic based on logical (IP) addresses. A routing table contains information on which connections lead to particular groups of addresses, priorities for connections to be used, and rules for handling both routine and special types of traffic. In small routers, a routing table might contain only a half-dozen lines of instructions. In large routers handling significant amounts of Internet traffic, routing tables can be staggering in their size and complexity.

NOTE *If you're interested in how many routers are involved in a typical bit of Internet traffic, use the Traceroute utility (included with most versions of Windows). Go to the MS-DOS prompt, change to the* WINDOWS *directory, and type* tracert www.sitename.com *(where the second part of the command is a specific site name). Traceroute will return a list of the routers that were utilized to get from your computer to that site, along with their addresses and the time (in milliseconds) it took a packet of information to move from one router to another. Don't be surprised to see dozens of routers involved in even the simplest connections!*

Routers are also responsible for optimizing, as much as possible, the routing paths for internetworked data. A router uses a routing algorithm to determine the optimal path to a destination, attempting to reduce the number of hops and delays between the originating point and the destination point. However, because network data travels in packets—and because the optimal route between two points is in constant flux, especially over the Internet—different packets from the same message might travel completely different routes. This route determination, on a packet-by-packet basis, is made by each router the packet encounters on its trip.

Also understand that, unlike bridges, routers deal only in networks, not in individual hosts. Even though the IP address of a host contains both the host's network address and the host's specific number on that network, a router will extract only the network address—and decide, based on the network address, where to transfer the data being routed.

One additional responsibility of the router is to keep unwanted visitors and data *out* of the network to which it's connected. Most routers have rules limiting how computers from outside the network (either from another LAN or from the Internet) can connect to computers inside the network. In addition, rules within the router will determine how your network appears to the outside world, as well as execute various security functions.

Gateways: Language Translators

The final connectivity device you need to know about is a *gateway*. Gateways function at a higher networking level than do routers, and as such, most gateways can do everything a router can and then some. Consequently, they often cost more.

The primary function of a gateway is to connect networks that use different protocols together. For example, imagine that a company has a NetWare network using the IPX/SPX protocol exclusively. It acquires another company that has an existing network running TCP/IP exclusively. It could take a lot to switch one or the other of the company's networks to match, so one solution is a gateway. The gateway could take TCP/IP packets from one network and translate them into IPX/SPX packets for computers on the other network. This process can be a slow and tedious one, but it's an available solution if you need it.

Now that you understand the basics of networking, as well as the hardware and software involved in networking, it's time to move on. In the next chapter, you'll learn how to choose the right network type for you, as well as install the network, handle network security, and troubleshoot network problems.

Chapter 27

Installing and Troubleshooting Networks

Introduction

Now that you've read the exciting technical data and structure of networking, you're ready to implement your own, right? Or did you just skip the previous chapter with all of the technical mumbo-jumbo? If you did, do yourself a favor and go back over it. The details presented there can save you a lot of headaches in the long term, even if they cause your eyes to glaze over in the short term.

But here you are, ready to plug that Network Interface Card (NIC) in and get in the fast lane of the information superhighway. I appreciate your enthusiasm.

In this chapter, the first thing I'll talk about is selecting the type of network you need. Yes, you learned all of the technical stuff in the previous chapter, but this chapter allows you to integrate all those ideas into a workable networking plan. Once the plan is established, *then* you can purchase the needed hardware (unless you already have it) and start your installation. I've said before that you need to plan things out with computers (such as troubleshooting in an orderly fashion); otherwise, things can go very wrong. In networking, this concept is especially true. Remember diagramming? Networks are the perfect thing to draw. A network plan without a diagram is like a...well, it's a really bad thing.

After getting your network all set up, you'll look at some network security issues. Security is one of those things you really need to think about *before* you install, but in a chapter like this it logically flows after the installation. Finally, I'll discuss troubleshooting network problems. I can't possibly cover resolutions for all network problems you might encounter, but like other troubleshooting sections in this book, I hope to at least point you in the right direction.

QuickSteps: Planning a Network

Planning a network configuration isn't always the most exciting task. But, if you don't plan ahead, you can't realistically expect your network to work like you want it to work. It might still work, but that would be more a function of luck than anything else. Personally, I'd rather not chance my network to luck.

BE PREPARED

Before you start, there are some things you'll need to perform the operation. These include the following:

- Pen and paper.
- Building floorplan (or an approximation).
- Overview of general network functionality and goals.

Follow these steps when planning a network:

1. Determine the number of computers (and other devices, such as networked printers) that'll be on the network.

2. Decide if you'll need a dedicated server. If you will, then you need to designate one computer (or more) as a server and make sure you have the right operating system (say, Windows Server 2003) for that computer. If not, then you'll be running a peer-to-peer network.

3. Choose a communications method. Most choices will boil down to wired (Ethernet, most likely) and wireless. Wireless has a higher initial cost, but if you can't run cables, what choice do you have?

4. Diagram what your network will look like. Include locations, computer names, Internet Protocol (IP) addresses (if you're going to assign them manually), and services provided (if applicable).

5. Review your diagram and your plans to ensure that the design meets your needs and is feasible to implement.

6. Purchase the necessary hardware for your network. This includes network cards, cables (unless you're going wireless), and hubs or switches. If you're going for a really big network, you might need routers as well. But if you're going to do that, then you better read more than this chapter for a networking background. Sybex has a lot of great books that can help, such as the Network+ Study Guide, by Groth, Lammle, and Tedder.

7. Grab your screwdriver and get ready to install!

Choosing a Network

Now that you know how a network works, how do you choose the type of network to use? If you're in a traditional office, your choice is simple—you'll use an Ethernet network, perhaps with wireless capability for specific users. If you're building a home network, however, the choices are more numerous. Do you go with a more complex and costly (although faster and more reliable) Ethernet network, or do you embrace one of the non-Ethernet technologies, such as wireless or phone-based connections? This section will help you make the right choice.

Office Networking Options

When installing a Local Area Network (LAN) in a corporate environment, your big choices will be the transfer speed to support—and whether you want to include wireless accessibility.

ETHERNET NETWORKING

If you're installing a network in a medium or large office, Ethernet is the LAN of choice. Only a cabled connection provides the security and speed you need for an effective corporate network. In addition, phone-line and power-line networks are impractical if you share a large building with other businesses; it's too easy for your packets to get mixed in with those of another business using the same technology.

The most common type of Ethernet connection used in most corporations is 100Base-T, which transmits data at 100 megabits per second (Mbps). 10Base-T is still used in some cases, but 10Mbps feels incredibly sluggish by today's standards, especially if you have a lot of users connected to the network. Conversely, if you have a large network (and a big budget) you may want to splurge for the 1 gigabits per second (Gbps) speed of a Gigabit Ethernet.

WIRELESS NETWORKING

If your employee base includes telecommuters or outside sales reps who often stop by the office (and want to use their laptops while they're there), consider adding wireless capability to your network. Each remote PC must be outfitted with a wireless LAN card, and you need to add wireless access points to your network hardware installation. Wireless access points can vary in their looks, but common ones look like a two-foot section of white plastic polyvinylchloride (PVC) pipe, which is basically an antenna. The antenna connects to a hub, and the rest of the "background" of the network is usually wired. Common wireless connection speeds are 11Mbps and 54Mbps, which is indeed slower than Ethernet. But to get convenience, sometimes you have to sacrifice speed. Several vendors offer a variety of wireless access products, including 3Com, LinkSys, NETGEAR, Intel, and Proxim.

Several standards for wireless networking have been developed over recent years. Two of the ones you'll hear a lot about are the IEEE 802.11 standards and Bluetooth. One of the other up-and-coming wireless candidates, HomeRF, probably won't make it because its working group disbanded in January 2003.

IEEE 802.11 Standards

The Institute of Electrical and Electronics Engineers (IEEE) has their acronym spread across a variety of networking concepts. For example, the Ethernet standard, which you read about earlier, is defined by the IEEE 802.5 specification and Token Ring by the IEEE 802.3 spec. The IEEE standard making the most waves today, though, is the series of 802.11 standards, which define wireless communications.

Originally developed in 1997, IEEE 802.11 offered 1Mbps–2Mbps in the 2.4 gigahertz (GHz) frequency range. In 1997, wired LANs were all running at 10Mbps or higher, and the wireless alternatives at the time were comparatively expensive. So, wireless didn't exactly take the world by storm.

Over the next few years, two 802.11 standards developed independently: 802.11a and 802.11b. Designed to be backward compatible with the original 802.11 specification, the 802.11b standard also operated in the 2.4GHz range but offered speeds up to 11Mbps. And because 802.11b has been pretty much the de facto standard for the past several years, most people associate 11Mbps with wireless networking. The 802.11a standard used a higher frequency (5.2GHz) and a multicarrier modulation technique, so it wasn't compatible with 802.11 or 802.11b. It did promise a bandwidth of 54Mbps, however.

There would be several new 802.11x proposals made over the next few years, but the one that gained the most momentum was 802.11g. It's basically an upgrade to 802.11b: it operates at the same 2.4GHz frequency, uses single carrier modulation, and offers 54Mbps data speeds. Of course, there are other improvements, such as greater reliability, range, and security as well. But those details are for another time and place. The single biggest advantage to 802.11g? Yes, it's faster, but it's backward compatible with your existing 802.11b devices.

NOTE   *Another name for the IEEE 802.11b standard is WiFi. It might be more marketing than anything else, but it's a cooler name than IEEE 802.11b.*

So to summarize, if you're going to go wireless, many people would recommend going with WiFi or its faster 802.11g cousin (maybe they'll call it Fast WiFi?). It seems to be the strongest standard at the moment, but Bluetooth still has a solid market share.

Bluetooth

The major competitor to WiFi is Bluetooth, developed by the Bluetooth Special Interest Group (SIG). SIG supporters include 3Com, Agere, Ericsson, IBM, Intel, Microsoft, Motorola, and Toshiba, among others.

Bluetooth is a specification designed for small profile electronics, such as laptops, cell phones, and Personal Digital Assistants (PDAs). In addition, some car manufacturers, namely Daimler Chrysler, BMW, Audi, and Saab are introducing Bluetooth capabilities in their cars. So with your Bluetooth-enabled cell phone, you can make hands-free phone calls and hear your caller through your car stereo speakers. Of course, integrating devices such as Bluetooth-enabled Global Position System (GPS) functionality is also part of the plan.

Okay, enough of the introductory stuff. You want to know the bottom line: how fast is it? You should be able to get 10Mbps data transfers without any problem, and one Bluetooth radio can support up to seven Bluetooth devices. Bluetooth also operates in the 2.4GHz frequency range.

Which One Do I Use?

That's a good question. The focus of each standard is slightly different. Although they compete with each other in some arenas, I think they're trying to go different directions.

WiFi is specifically designed for wireless Ethernet. And with the 802.11g specification, its connection speeds are faster than what Bluetooth currently offers. Bluetooth, on the other hand, offers devices that are Internet-ready but is trying to replace several small portable devices, such as cell phones, PDAs, headsets, speakers, and digital cameras.

So if all you want is wireless networking, WiFi is probably the answer. But if you want to integrate several of your small electronics devices, then you might want to try Bluetooth.

Can you use both? Sure, but just remember one key point: because the two are competing standards, they won't interoperate with each other. And because they operate at the same frequency, the potential for interference between devices is possible. So it's probably best to go with one or the other (based on your needs), but don't try to mix the two.

Home Networking Options

When you're setting up a network for your home (or home-based office), you have the same options available as you would in a corporate environment—plus a few more. Whereas speed and security are the two main considerations for a corporate LAN, ease of setup is probably the main concern for most home networkers—especially the ease of cabling. Let's face it—unless you had the prescience to have Ethernet cabling strung when your home was under construction, the prospect of running long lengths of cable from room to room (and through walls!) might be a tad daunting. In this likelihood, implementing an easier-to-set-up phone-line or wireless network might have greater appeal.

VIRTUAL PRIVATE NETWORKING

Something else to consider when setting up your corporate network is how to provide access to the network to employees not in the office. Traditionally, remote users had to use a modem and dial into a server located on the company's internal network. This type of connection is called Remote Access Service (RAS) and has been in place for many years. Of course, it's limited in speed (because it's a dial-up modem), but it worked fairly well. Basically, users dialed in just as someone would dial up to an Internet Service Provider (ISP).

A newer networking technology, called Virtual Private Networking (VPN), has been becoming more popular since 2000. With virtual private networking, employees working from home (or away on a business trip) can still dial into your corporate network and access their office computers, as well as other resources on the network, but they can also use higher-speed connections.

In addition, VPNs provide considerably more robust security options than standard RAS. A typical VPN consists of authenticated and encrypted "tunnels" through a shared data network—in most cases, the Internet.

To enable this type of extra-LAN access, VPN uses what's called a *tunneling protocol*, such as Point-to-Point Tunneling Protocol (PPTP), Layer 2 Tunneling Protocol (L2TP), or Layer 2 Forwarding (L2F). When one of these protocols is installed on your network, any remote client can configure their Dial-Up Networking connection with the proper information specific to your network (including IP addresses and passwords) and then gain secure access to the corporate network.

ETHERNET NETWORKING

Yes, you can build an Ethernet-based home network. An Ethernet network is still the fastest, most reliable, most cost-effective network you can construct—and most new PCs have built-in Ethernet capability. In fact, 100Mbps is more bandwidth than most home users could ever consume, unless you throw LAN parties and invite friends over for several hours of fragging. But the cost difference between 10Mbps and 100Mbps cards is so miniscule, there's no sense in buying the slower ones. You'd probably have a hard time finding just a 10Mbps card anyway.

NOTE   *Many Ethernet cards are billed as 10/100. This means they're capable of Fast Ethernet's 100Mbps transmission rate but can also operate at the slower speed if connected to a 10Mbps hub.*

Note, however, that hooking up an Ethernet network requires a small degree of technical know-how—expertise that not all home users may possess. Not only do you need to install an Ethernet card in each PC, you also have to install a hub or a switch to physically connect the machines. Although this isn't necessarily costly or complex, you do have to know what you're doing. Plus, you have to physically run the Ethernet cabling between the machines, which, depending where your PCs are located, may or may not be a piece of cake—and could require complex and costly installation.

POWER-LINE NETWORKING

Connecting your computers via your home's power grid is one cableless option—although probably not a practical one. This technology has always been relatively slow—around 50 kilobits per second (Kbps—but newer products from NETGEAR now transfer data at speeds of up to 14Mbps. Even with this speed improvement, power-line networking is still considered slow. The other major downside is that power-line networks are susceptible to power fluctuations, which happen a lot more than you might realize.

Power-line networking products should adhere to the HomePlug 1.0 specification. This specification has a theoretical maximum throughput of 14Mbps, but you're only likely to get about half of that. Most power-line devices also offer encryption features, which is always a good idea for increasing security.

TELEPHONE-LINE NETWORKING

An easier way to construct a cableless network is by using your home's phone lines. Phone-line networking (called HomePNA) is based on specifications produced by the Home Phone Networking Alliance (HPNA). Even though you use the phone lines to transmit data on your home network, your telephones can still function without interfering with the network. HomePNA networks haven't enjoyed huge success because the original equipment could only transfer data at an unacceptably slow rate of 1Mbps. The HPNA 2 specification raised that to 10Mbps, and HPNA 3 should support speeds up to 128Mbps.

NOTE   *There's been a battle between power-line networking and HPNA for the past several years. Basically, Home-Plug 1 and HPNA 2 will deliver about the same performance. The devices are also similarly priced. So there has been no clear-cut winner, and wireless networking threatens to send them both to the deep, dark pits of computer obsolescence.*

Several HomePNA products are on the market, most for less than $100 per PC. The standard HomePNA adapter plugs into a parallel or Universal Serial Bus (USB) port on your PC and then connects to the nearest phone line (no hub necessary). It's about that easy—and the software bundled with these products makes setting up the network a snap. (If you don't want to tie up an external port on your PC, there are HomePNA PCI cards, as well.)

HomePNA hasn't been as successful as its creators envisioned, but it hasn't been because lack of effort. The advantages of HomePNA have been overshadowed by wireless network solutions that cost about the same amount of money, offer better data rates and higher reliability, and don't require the installation of phone wires.

WIRELESS NETWORKING

Wireless networking has made an incredible metamorphosis in recent years. Once the stuff of science fiction, technology improvements first made it a luxury, and now wireless is at the forefront of networking technologies. Intel even designed a mobile processor chipset package (Centrino) with built-in wireless networking capabilities.

The same information that was in the "Office Networking Options" section about wireless apply here as well. WiFi is probably the way to go, and if you can get devices that support IEEE 802.11g, then that's the best bet. If not, then go with 802.11b.

Wireless networking will still you a bit more than wired networking, and you won't get the same transmission rates. But you save the hassle of running cables throughout your house.

SHARING A BROADBAND INTERNET CONNECTION

One of the most popular uses of a home network is to connect multiple computers to a single broadband—Digital Subscriber Line (DSL) or cable modem—Internet connection. If this is your goal, you may have several options available to you.

If you're using a DSL connection, note that some DSL modems also function as network routers. To use a DSL modem/hub to connect multiple PCs, you'll have to connect each computer to the modem/router via an Ethernet connection. (Many DSL modems can also be connected via a USB or parallel port, but you can't use these ports for multiple-PC connections.) If your DSL supplier offers this hardware and service, it's an easy-to-use option. If not, then you can usually run your DSL cable to a separate router and then just plug in your computers to the router.

The other option, of course, is to connect all your computers to some sort of home network (Ethernet, phone line, power line, or wireless). One computer will connect to your DSL or cable modem, and then all the other computers on the network will also have access to that connection.

Because of the growing popularity of broadband Internet, a feature called Internet Connection Sharing (ICS) was added to Windows 98 Second Edition, Me, 2000, XP, and 2003. With ICS, it's relatively easy to configure one PC to be the ICS computer and then route Internet access from other networked computers through this lead PC.

With ICS, the only computer on your network that's visible to the Internet is the ICS computer, which provides private IP addresses and name resolution services for all the other computers on your network. When an individual PC accesses the Internet, that computer's private IP address is transmitted to the ICS computer, which then translates it to the IP address of the ICS computer and sends it out to the Internet. Translation back to the initiating PC is made when information is downloaded from the Internet to that PC.

Setting Up Your Network

Now that you understand the technology behind networking and have decided on the type of network you want to install, let's get to it!

Installing Cables

Most of what I'll talk about here concerns how to prepare for a contractor's help and what you need to know about your physical installation before the cabling process begins. This isn't a complete tutorial in cable installation. First, I don't have room. Second, it's difficult to tailor such instructions when you can't see the environment in which the cable will be installed. Third, complex cabling is often a specialist's job. Therefore, I'll talk about the basics—what you need to know them for simple cabling jobs or for overseeing someone else doing a more complex one. After reading this, you'll be better prepared to instruct the cable installer in what you need done. Outsourcing this kind of work isn't cheap, and the meter's always ticking, so it's best to be prepared.

PLAN AHEAD

This is one of those really obvious but easily overlooked hints: don't just think about what your needs are now, think about what they'll be five or ten years down the line. Cabling a building isn't so much fun that you're going to want to do it twice, so plan ahead.

First, know your situation. Get the blueprints for the building you're in and study them. Where's the ductwork? Where's the electrical wiring, and how is it shielded? Are there any surprises waiting to happen? What are the fire codes for your area? What do they say about where you can use PVC-coated cable and where you must use plenum?

Get the fastest cable you can afford. Even if you don't need it now, the chances are excellent that sooner or later you'll use it when your company starts implementing databases or video to the desktop or some such thing. Buy that Cat-5e or Cat-6 now, or even fiber if you can justify it, and you'll save yourself money later when you don't have to pay for two cabling installations.

GIVE YOURSELF SOME SLACK

Don't plan your cabling needs to the last foot, but anticipate quite a bit of extra cable. First, you'll need this because you can't just plug PCs into the network on top of each other.

Second, the extra room will give you flexibility. If you have just enough cable for your needs, then sooner or later Joe User is going to want to move his PC five feet to the left, and that's going to completely throw off your entire network because your plan has no flexibility built into it. When running the cable along the ceiling or floor, leave a few loops (six to eight) at each corner, each doorway, or anywhere there's a permanent physical feature in the building so you can find it again. Secure the loops with electrical tape to keep them neat and out of the way. When you need a little more length in your cable, you'll have it.

Otherwise, you'll have two options: splicing the cable yourself or paying someone else to do it. Contractors typically charge not only for the length of the cable they run but also for the number of terminations they must do. Splicing the cable means paying for two useless terminations that don't do anything but give you more length that you could've had from the beginning with a little planning. Similarly, when running drops from a backbone or hub, give yourself a spare 10 to 15 feet so that you can move the PC later if you need to do so.

WARNING   *If you haven't planned for flexibility and need to extend your cable, splice it rather than attempting to stretch it. Stretching can damage cable—especially stranded cable—and damaged cable is far more prone to interference.*

Giving yourself elbow room applies to conduit, too. In big installations with high security needs, you'll often have a central backbone run in a large duct, with smaller conduits branching off from it. This is an expensive configuration, and larger conduits will make it more expensive yet. Regardless, you should seriously consider getting conduit a little larger than you need now. For example, if the $1/2$-inch variety will let you run two taps from the backbone, get the $3/4$-inch variety so that you can run three or four taps if you need to do so. Once again, even if it's more expensive up front, giving yourself room to grow will save you money down the road, when you don't have to buy new conduit, pay to have it installed, and scrap the stuff you already paid for.

NEATNESS COUNTS

Keep in mind you're going to have to deal with this cable at some point after it's installed, so make it as easy to get at as possible. When it comes to ceiling installations, you may be tempted to just throw the cables across the "floor" of the ceiling because it's less work. It's true; this is less work initially, but when you have to work up in that ceiling later, you're not going to like it if you have to trip over cable snaking across the floor. To avoid this, tie the cables to something such as the supports of the drop ceiling; clamps are made for the purpose, or you can use the plastic snap ties. You may also want to consider attaching the cables to air conditioning or heating ductwork.

As a last resort, leave all the cables on the floor of the ceiling, but bundle and tie them so they're out of the way. That way, if you have to move them, you have to move only one lump, not six individual cables all tangled up together.

NOTE   *Not all drop ceilings can support cable, so you may have to tie the cables to the supports or ductwork to make this work.*

Running cables under the floor requires similar planning. Again, lay the cables neatly so they're easy to reach. If you have the money, consider getting ductwork to run the cables in so they stay in one place. Also, put the cables somewhere you can get to them *after* the furniture has been put into the room. It might look neater to have the cables running along the wall, but chances are excellent that cubicles or an extremely heavy table will be along the wall. The middle of the room, where there's less likely to be furniture, is a better bet.

If you're running cable *on* the floor, then the rules are a little different. In that case, you'll do well to keep the cables against the wall and out of harm's way. That way, people will be less likely to trip over them (injuring themselves and/or the network in the process). Also, the janitorial staff is less likely to damage them with enthusiastic cleaning. Tape down cables as best you can to avoid the chances of them being tripped on or wandering away. Buying cable protectors (they look like rubber speed bumps lying on the floor) is a great way to protect cables running across doorways or other high-traffic areas. And they look a lot better than tape.

Finally, label *everything*. And I mean *everything*. At troubleshooting time, you're going to want to know which cables go where without doing this routine: "Okay, Karen, when I say 'Go,' shake the cable so I can tell which one it is." That exchange is typically followed by this routine: "Okay, it wasn't that cable. When I say so, shake the one next to it."

To avoid this, you can use different colors of electrical tape wrapped around the ends of the cables, little adhesive numbers, or (if you have deep pockets) color-coded cables themselves. These make it easier to tell which cable you have at the end and also make it possible to tell which cable you're holding when you're crouched in the ceiling. I don't recommend hand-printed labels because they can be hard to read. Unless you have a really complicated cabling system that requires extensive description, symbols are probably the way to go. You can identify them at a glance and don't have to decipher someone else's handwriting or turn the cable over to read the whole thing. A little more than 10 percent of the male population can't tell red from green, so consider using symbols or avoiding green and red cables.

TIP   *Keep a legend of cable codes around so people can tell what they're looking at even if you're out of the office.*

PLAY WELL WITH OTHERS

Finally, think about what's going to be running in the same place as your network cable. Got lots of interference-producing devices around? Consider cable with extra shielding, such as coaxial or Shielded Twisted-Pair (STP), or, better yet, fiber that's immune to Radio Frequency Interference (RFI).

TIP   *Fluorescent lights emit a lot of Electromagnetic Interference (EMI), so don't run cables over the top of them.*

Are electrical cables already in place? Don't run your network cables parallel to them, particularly if you're looking at big bundles, such as those leading up to a fuse box. If new electrical cables are going in after the network has been installed, avoid introducing new interference problems by asking for armored cable (run in a metal sheath) rather than the ones enclosed in the plastic sheath. Once again, it'll cost more up front, but these extra precautions may save you money later.

USE WALL PLATES

If you can, run your cables through the wall and then use wall jacks. They look a little like phone jacks, and they come in several varieties (one, two, four, and eight connections are common). It requires a bit more to install these because you need a punch-down tool to get the cable to fit into the backside of the wall plate. But once they're installed, they can make your life so much easier. Now when you move a computer, instead of yanking on a 100-foot run of cable (and stretching who knows what along the way), you can just replace the 6-foot cable that went to the wall with a 12-foot cable. Easy.

THINGS TO KNOW AHEAD OF TIME

I've talked about some of the specifics you need to be aware of before the cabling process begins. The following are some questions for your contractor. Figuring out these details early in the process can save you time, money, and lots of headaches:

Do you have wiring conduits?   Many buildings provide you with built-in places in the walls and ceilings where you can run your cable. Often, these wiring conduits are themselves plenum-rated. This means you *may* be able to use a cheaper PVC cable.

How are you testing your cables?   You'll want to know the precise method that's being used to test the cables after they're installed. Common sense reigns supreme on this issue. (Keep in mind that common sense really isn't that common.) Make sure you get a written description of the testing method and follow the testing logic from start to finish to ensure that it makes sense for installation.

How are you documenting your cables?   Make sure the cables are being documented and labeled according to your company's set standard. If your company hasn't set one, then it should do so. You want to be sure that the labeling system makes sense to you, so I recommend your company set the labeling standard, not the contractor.

What's the repair policy for the cable installation?   You'll want at least a 24-hour on-site response from your contractor. Many contractors say they have a 24-hour response to cable problems, when what they mean is, "We'll call you back within 24 hours, and it may take us up to a week to get there." You don't want that; you want the contractor at your site in 24 hours or less. Cable problems are mission-critical problems.

Can you get at least three local references from the contractor?   You'll want three local references from your contractor so that you can personally see the quality of their work and documentation of it. Most companies won't mind taking you on a tour of their cable systems if they're happy with the work the contractor has done. Don't forget to reciprocate when prospective clients call you to come see your expertly designed and installed cable system.

Are you following building and fire code requirements?   To ensure the safety of all your employees, follow all local building and fire codes. You want to select a contractor who can demonstrate by experience and references that they're well versed in the local regulations. When in doubt, call the city or county offices and ask questions.

Do you need to notify anyone else in your building or locale of your plans?   You may need to check with other tenants in your building to make sure that the cable installation won't conflict with their workflow. This is usually more of a courtesy than a requirement. Often, if you notify building management, they'll notify all the other tenants in your building.

How long is the guarantee on the cable installation valid?   Verify the length of time the contractor will guarantee their labor and the cables. A one-year service contract is advisable. Reasonable costs for an annual service contract shouldn't exceed 12 percent of the overall cable installation cost.

Preparing a Wireless Network

Preparing for a wireless network, or a wireless portion of a wired network, isn't significantly different from preparing for a wired one. You still have to think about environmental factors and how the data is going to get from point A to point B.

Two kinds of wireless networking are used in LANs. Most common are the RF wireless networks, which can be used to connect PCs and servers over a fairly wide area—even though some have relatively low transmission speeds (sometimes as low as 1Mbps, but the 10Mbps range is common with 54Mbps readily available). More specialized applications, such as wireless printers and keyboards, use infrared (IR) technology to create a high-speed, short-range link.

Interference is the biggest problem you're likely to encounter with wireless networks. Infrared communications have an extremely high frequency, so in order to use them, the sender and receiver must be close and in the line of sight. If you can't stretch a piece of string between the sending device and the receiving one, they can't communicate. Therefore, if you have an IR printer, it's a good idea to place it somewhere that IR notebook users can access it without people walking between the two devices.

RF devices are less prone to interference because their lower frequencies mean that the signal can more or less go around obstacles instead of being blocked by them. For this reason, although IR devices are confined to the room in which they operate, RF wireless devices can roam up to about 100 to 150 feet away from their source if indoors, or 800 to 1000 feet away if outdoors. Thick walls or metal barriers will interfere with the signal, but otherwise they're pretty flexible.

Installing and Configuring Network Cards

The cables are in. Now, you're ready to attach them to something. If you're not familiar with cable installation and configuration, read on. You'll learn how to get the card in the box in the first place and how to make it work with the other cards in the box once it's in there.

INSTALLING NETWORK CARDS

If you have any experience installing cards in a PC, the mechanics of installing a network card are pretty straightforward. Power down the PC, don your antistatic strap, open the computer case, and find a slot in the PC that's free and fits the kind of card you have.

TIP   *If you can, choose a slot that's not next to another card to keep the airflow inside the PC's box as open as possible.*

If you're removing another card to insert the new one, follow these steps:

1. Make sure the card is disconnected from any outside cables.

2. Unscrew the small screw attaching the card to the PC case, and lay it aside.

3. Pull gently on the card, using both hands to wiggle it back and forth slightly to disengage it from the connectors. This may take a little tugging, but if the card doesn't come fairly easily, stop and make sure that the card is indeed fully disconnected from the PC.

4. After you've pulled the card out, set it aside. Wrap it back up in its original sheath if you kept it and plan to use the card again. Don't touch the gold connectors on the card; the oils in your skin can corrode the gold and thus reduce the card's connectivity.

Installing a card is much the same process, in reverse:

1. Unwrap the card, being careful not to touch the gold connectors, and set it aside.

2. Power down the PC, and open it up.

3. Find an open slot on the motherboard. You will most likely be looking for an open Peripheral Component Interconnect (PCI) slot.

4. Unscrew the plate that covered the open slot's opening to the rear of the computer, and set the plate and screw aside. You may need the plate later, and you'll need the screw in just a minute.

5. Align the network card with the slot in the PC, and push gently but firmly to seat the card in its slot. You may need to push fairly hard for this to work, which can be somewhat intimidating if you're not used to inserting cards. If you have the right slot and push straight in, then the card should snap into place.

6. Using the screw that you set aside in step 4, screw the card into the little hole in the case to hold it in place. If the card is in all the way, this extra step won't affect the card's positioning all that much, but it'll keep it from sagging or working loose.

7. Replace the case and, if the cables are already in place, connect them to the card.

INSTALLING NETWORK CARD DRIVERS

The process for installing the drivers for the card depends on your operating system. Most operating systems today will autodetect the Plug and Play (PnP) network card and begin to install it for you the first time you boot with the card inserted. Like other add-in cards, most network cards come with a CD or floppy disk containing drivers. To install these drivers, follow the instructions that come with the network card. And if you need more assistance, read the documentation for the card included in the package or (often) on the manufacturer's Web site.

TIP   The operating system may include drivers for the card, but if the operating system is more than a year old, the drivers that come with the card itself are likely to be newer, with the drivers on the manufacturer's Web site being the best option.

Any responsible company will prominently display the date that the drivers were released. Compare the dates listed on the site with the dates of the drivers on the floppy disk to determine whether there are more recent versions of the drivers for your particular card. This tip about downloading drivers from the Internet applies not only to network cards but also to any device you're installing. Not all device drivers are frequently updated, but it's always worth looking.

CONFIGURING CARD RESOURCES

Now that the card is in, you need to make sure it's configured properly. Every Windows-based operating system from Windows 95 on will automatically detect and configure your card. Isn't PnP great?

But if you're having resource conflicts, check the IRQ and I/O address settings in Device Manager. A lot of times, network cards will want IRQ7, which is used by the parallel port (but you should have a USB printer anyway, right?), or IRQ5, which is a favorite of a lot of sound cards.

In Device Manager, your network card will show up under the Network Adapters category, as shown in Figure 27.1.

Right-clicking the network card and choosing the Resources tab will show you which resources are being used by the card, as shown in Figure 27.2.

FIGURE 27.1
Device Manager

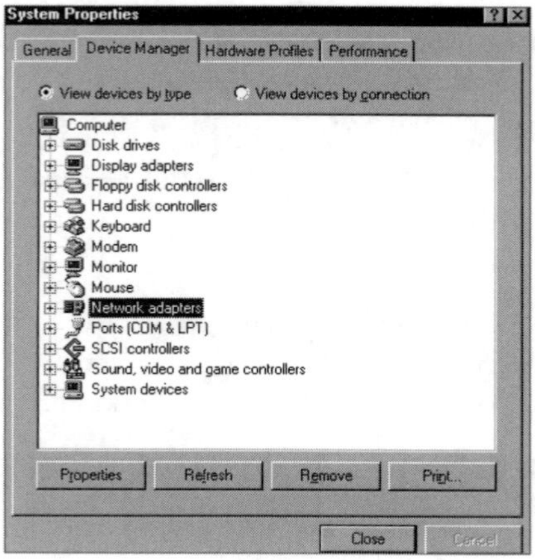

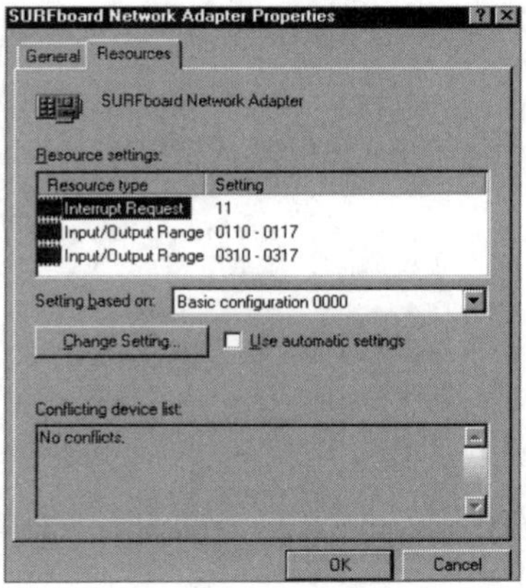

FIGURE 27.2

The properties of a network card

And finally, Device Manager is kind enough to warn you if your device is conflicting with another device or if the drivers aren't installed properly. If you look at Figure 27.3, you can see an exclamation point over the network card's icon. This means there's a problem. Right-click the device to see what that problem is. You might need to reassign a resource or reinstall the driver. If it still gives you problems, remove the device and hit the F5 key to force Windows to detect it again.

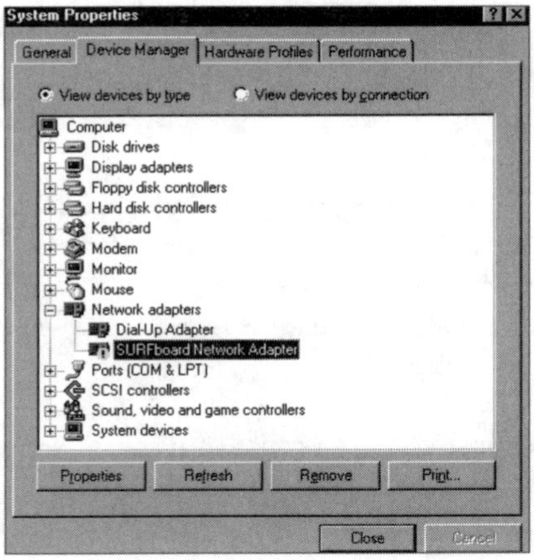

FIGURE 27.3

Exclamation points aren't good things in Device Manager.

Networking Security

Anytime you connect two or more computers (or connect a single computer to that global network called the Internet), you run the risk of unauthorized access. In an ideal world, a computer will be accessed only by its designated user; in the real world, the possibility exists for any given computer to be accessed by users who don't have appropriate authorization.

The only surefire way to keep the data and programs on a computer safe from unauthorized access is to never connect that computer to a network—including the Internet. Of course, in today's networked world, that sort of isolation is impractical, if not impossible. That means that, at some level, you have to apply some degree of security measures to the computers on your network. Of course, too much security makes the computer inconvenient to use; too little security opens the computer to potential unauthorized use. Like most things in life, networking security becomes a game of risk versus reward—with the safety of your programs and data in the balance.

General Security Tips

Whenever you have valuable data stored on a network, you should take certain commonsense precautions, just in case something bad happens:

- Keep backups—off the network, if not completely offsite!—of all your important files.

- If data doesn't have to be accessed by the network, don't store it on the network—store it on a non-networked computer instead.

- Make sure you're up-to-date with recent operating system updates and patches—these updates often patch holes that allow unauthorized access.

- For greater security, keep your server and other key equipment locked up in a separate room; the fewer people who have access to the hardware, the less likely it is that your hardware will be vandalized.

Beyond these basic advisories, let's look at some more-specific security measures you probably should be evaluating.

Passwords

Within the boundaries of a LAN, the biggest security concern is the illicit access by one user of another user's computer. This is why every user of the network should be assigned a password and every computer on the network should be password protected. Theoretically, if a computer can be accessed only by a specific password, and that password is known only to a single user, unauthorized access should pretty much be shut down.

Unless a password is stolen.

Stolen passwords are the most common cause of network security breaches. That's because the human beings who use your network are sometimes careless.

Sometimes users have a password that's too easily guessed. (Birthdates, Social Security numbers, children's names, and pet's names are common ones.) You can combat this problem by requiring passwords to be a certain length (the longer, the better) and to contain a combination of letters and numbers. In short, the more complex the password, the harder it is to crack.

Sometimes users leave their password lying around for prying eyes to see. (Really—take an after hours walk around the office and observe how many passwords you see attached to computer monitors via Post-It notes, under keyboards, or in top drawers.) You can try to combat this problem by yelling at the offending parties—a lot of good that will do!—or by requiring users to change their passwords on a frequent basis. (This doesn't eliminate sloppiness or prying eyes but does minimize the amount of time a "borrowed" password is usable.)

Sometimes users can use their password to access parts of the network they really shouldn't be accessing. This, of course, is your problem, not theirs. Make sure the computers, drives, or folders that contain sensitive data are designated as off-limits for all but the most essential personnel. Not everyone needs access to everything; only grant the access that's absolutely necessary. The fewer people who have access to your most sensitive data, the less likely your data will be compromised.

One last thing you can do to improve your network's password security is to limit the number of tries a user has to enter a password. Password-cracking software exists that keeps feeding (at a rapid clip) hundreds and thousands of different combinations into a password field in an attempt to guess the password; limiting the number of retries effectively defeats this type of software.

Firewalls

When you open your network to the Internet (or to any external network), your security concerns multiply by several orders of magnitude. Just look at the types of security threats you can potentially encounter:

Viruses and Trojans   A computer *virus* is a piece of malicious code that can infect your computer system. A Trojan (as in Trojan horse) is a type of virus, such as NetBus or Black Orifice, that's planted on your network and surreptitiously takes control of the host computer. Trojans can be programmed to do just about anything to your system—such as change the computer's IP address, install destructive scripts or programs, and so on. This is particularly damaging if the computer accessed is the network server because any damage inflicted could affect the entire network.

Denial-of-Service (DoS) attacks   These easy-to-launch attacks involve sending more requests to a computer or network than it can handle. If, for example, a host computer is capable of answering 25 requests per second, and an attacker sends (via automated programs) 40 requests per second, the host will be unable to service all the attacker's requests—let alone any legitimate requests. In essence, the host computer (and often the host computer's network) gets overloaded.

E-mail bombs   Similar to a DoS attack, this type of attack is caused by someone sending you the same email hundreds or thousands of times until your network's email system can't accept anymore messages.

Redirect bombs   This type of attack changes the path that information takes by sending it to a different router—essentially letting hackers erase their steps by using computers on your network to do their dirty work.

IP spoofing   A spoof occurs when the attacker's computer claims to have the IP address of another computer, thus enabling the attacker to gain access and execute operations based on the authority of the spoofed computer.

IP session hijacking   This sophisticated type of attack enables the attacker to take over and control individual computers on your network. Whatever the user is doing at the point of the hijack is visible to the hijacker; it's a great way to read confidential email and other information. When a computer is hijacked, the user sees only that their session has been dropped; more often than not, they'll log back in, even as the hijacker (still logged in as the hijacked user) continues poking around the network, typically unnoticed.

Data theft One of the more common results of unauthorized access is the "stealing" of confidential data. This might not sound like a big thing, but industrial espionage is big business—and trade secrets are meant to be kept secret.

Data diddling Even worse than data theft, data diddling occurs when an unauthorized user accesses confidential data—and changes it. Think of the repercussions if someone broke into your network and moved a few decimal points in the master spreadsheet or transposed some of the digits in the numbers used in the automatic payroll system. Not only is the data changed, but you might not notice the change until something *really* bad results!

Data destruction Some attackers just want to cause damage—and deleting and corrupting files are particularly high-tech forms of vandalism.

Short of disconnecting your Internet connection, how do you guard against these types of unwanted intrusions?

The best protection against Internet-based attacks is to install a *firewall* between your network and the Internet. A firewall is simply a collection of components (software, hardware, or both) that forms a barrier between two networks (such as your network and the Internet) and selectively filters the information that's passed between the networks. Hardware-based firewalls typically take the form of routers with built-in filtering capabilities. Software-based firewalls can be installed on any computer with the proper Internet connection.

NOTE *A firewall (software-based) is also recommended for any home computer connected to a constant Internet connection—such as that provided by a DSL, cable, or Integrated Services Digital Network (ISDN) modem. Many personal firewall products are cheap and easy to install for home users.*

The most obvious place to install a firewall is where your network connects to the Internet—typically a T1 or T3 line. (If you have multiple T1/T3 lines, you'll need to install a separate firewall at each access point.) If your company utilizes several LANs (one for each department or floor, for example), you may also want to install firewalls between the individual networks.

Firewalls use one or more of three methods to control traffic flowing in and out of the network.

Proxy service A proxy essentially serves as a "middleman" between computers on your network and the Internet. Instead of data being sent from the Internet to an individual PC, the data is sent to the firewall (proxy), where it's *cached*. Users on your network thus access the cached data on the proxy server instead of actually going out to the Internet.

Packet filtering In this scheme, individual data packets are fed through a set of administrator-assigned filters. Packets that pass the filtering are sent to the requesting system, and packets that don't pass the test are discarded.

Stateful inspection This method doesn't examine the contents of each packet but instead compares certain key parts of the packet to a database of trusted information. If the comparison results in a match, the information is allowed through. Nonmatching data is discarded.

Almost all types of firewalls are customizable to one degree or another. In essence, you can add or remove filters based on IP addresses, domain names, protocols, ports, and specific words and phrases

(In the last instance, the firewall will *sniff* each packet of information looking for an exact text match; you can program this type of filter to block packets that contain the word *dork*, for example.)

TIP *You can assess the vulnerability of your network to outside attacks by availing yourself of an online security service. These services—such as NetIQ's Security Analyzer—essentially try to hack into your network (via the Internet) and then report back to you where your weaknesses are.*

If you value the information stored on your network, you'll take the appropriate steps to protect that information—by protecting the security of your network. Strict password management and firewalls are your two best defenses against unauthorized access and should be part of the arsenal of any network administrator—no matter how large or how small the network!

Network Troubleshooting

You've got the cables installed, you've got the NICs inserted, and everything is plugged in. You've set up passwords. You've installed a firewall. But you don't have any network connectivity. What went wrong? That's a good question.

I'll end this networking discussion with some troubleshooting tips because occasionally things *do* go wrong. A thorough network troubleshooting exposition would take several hundred, if not thousand, pages. I'll point you in the right direction to find problems.

Check the Easy Stuff First

As always, check the easy stuff first. Lazy is good, remember? This means checking your connections. Are they plugged in and powered on? Most network cards and connectivity devices (hubs, switches, routers, and so on) have lights on them when they have a live connection. If a cable is plugged in and there's no light, it's possible that the cable is unplugged at the other end. Or it's possible that the cable is bad. Most wireless cards have a light on when they're receiving a signal.

If you think it's a bad cable, swap cables. If you don't have an extra, it's time to get a spare. Cables are cheap.

The Network Card

Is the network card installed properly? Check the drivers first in Device Manager. If the card doesn't even show up, is it seated properly in the computer? Remember, getting into the case is an option, but you want to exhaust all other options first.

TCP/IP Specifics

Transmission Control Protocol/Internet Protocol (TCP/IP) is the most complex of the three commonly used protocols, so it's no wonder that every once in a while people have problems with it. Remember that your computer must have two configuration items:

◆   A unique IP address for your network.

◆   A subnet mask.

Additionally, if your network connects to other networks, your computer will need a default gateway address (which is the address of the near side of your router). To check your IP address, use the `ipconfig` or `winipcfg` commands. It's impossible for me to tell you which addresses are valid for your network, but I can tell you one that's not `0.0.0.0`. If you have this address, then you have a problem.

If you're assigning IP addresses manually, this means you didn't assign an address to this computer. If you usually get addressing information from a Dynamic Host Configuration Protocol (DHCP) server (from your network people or your ISP), then for some reason you're not connecting to it at the moment. At a command prompt, you can try typing **`ipconfig /release`**, and then after it returns another prompt, type **`ipconfig /renew`**. If you still get `0.0.0.0`, you're definitely not connecting to the DHCP server.

Web Problems

You try to go to your favorite Web site only to get an error that the site can't be found. Can you get to other sites? It's possible your favorite site is temporarily down. If you can't get to other sites, check your IP address.

If your IP address looks okay, then you might want to try the `ping` command, which is a great little connectivity tester. For example, you could type **`ping 192.168.0.44`** (or whatever IP address you know works) or **`ping www.sybex.com`**.

If the `ping` command tells you that the request timed out, it looks like you have a connectivity problem. If you can ping addresses by number or get to Web sites by placing their IP address in your Address window of your Internet browser, but you can't get to the same sites with their name, then you have a Domain Name Service (DNS) problem. If you'll recall from previous chapter, DNS resolves friendly names (such as `www.sybex.com`) to IP addresses, which computers need to communicate.

Make sure your computer has the address of a DNS server (again, `ipconfig` or `winipcfg`). If not, you might want to contact your network administrator or ISP.

Other Connectivity Problems

When troubleshooting networking, the first question you always need to ask is, "What can I do, and what can't I do?" And the second question should be, "Is it only affecting me?"

As an example of the first question, assume that your IP address is `0.0.0.0`. I can tell you now that running `ping` won't do you any good because you need an IP address to do that. Or, if you can get to any Web site except for one specific site, chances are that the site you're trying to get to is the problem.

As for the second question, who is affected? If no one on your network can get to the server, then maybe it's the server or maybe it's the switch. But if no one can get to the server (not just you), then what's the sense in checking your network cable?

Well, this concludes the little network troubleshooting discussion. In the next chapter, I'll stick with the networking theme but from a little more distance. Up next are modems and other Internet connectivity devices.

Chapter 28

Modems and Other Internet Connection Devices

- ◆ How Analog Modems Work
- ◆ Migrating to Broadband Connections
- ◆ Installing and Configuring ISDN, DSL, Cable, and Satellite Modems
- ◆ Troubleshooting Tips

Introduction

Broadband is the buzzword on the Internet scene today—cable, Digital Subscriber Line (DSL), and satellite. If you don't have broadband access, you're probably planning to get it in the near future.

Not everyone has broadband yet, though; you'll probably have some clients who are still limping by on a dial-up modem for many years to come. That's unfortunate for several reasons. Obviously it's frustrating for the user trying to surf the Internet with a 56 kilobytes per second (Kbps) modem, but it's also frustrating for the technician supporting them because modems have far more problems than broadband connection equipment. Therefore, even though you'll probably work with modems less and less as time goes by, I'll still devote the first chunk of this chapter to their installation and trouble shooting. Until everyone is up-and-running on broadband, you'll still need the information. Of course I'll also address the various broadband access methods here, including the pros and cons of each and what can go wrong.

Selecting a Modem

The Internet owes much of its tremendous popularity to the humble modem. Even though there are faster and better ways to achieve Internet connection these days, the modem remains a common piece of hardware, especially in home systems.

Modem stands for *modulator-demodulator*. The modem at one end converts digital data into a series of analog signals for transmission over the analog telephone lines, and the modem at the other end does the opposite, converting analog signals into digital data.

You'll now look at some of the ways in which one modem is different from another.

Maximum Transmission Rate

All modern modems have a maximum data transfer rate of 56Kbps. This hasn't always been the case, of course; early modems transmitted as little as 300 bits per second. But for the past eight years or so, 56Kbps has been the standard. Digging around in some old hardware bins you might occasionally run into a 33.6Kbps or even 9600bps or 2400bps model. Run away. Quickly. The modern 56Kbps is bad enough for Internet use; don't even try anything slower.

NOTE *56Kbps is a theoretical maximum; it isn't actually achieved. The most you can hope for in real usage is a consistent 50.6Kbps, with peaks of 53Kbps. Why? Ask your local telephone company. Existing current (electrical, that is) limitations prevent telephone companies from extending beyond 53Kbps in total analog bandwidth per connection.*

Internal versus External

An *internal* modem fits into an expansion slot inside your PC's system unit. An *external* modem connects to your PC via one of its serial ports (COM1 or COM2, an older technology) or via its Universal Serial Bus (USB) port (the newer technology).

In today's market, internal modems are much more common than the external type. One reason is that they tend to be cheaper. It costs more to manufacture an external modem because there has to be a plastic case with Light-Emitting Diodes (LEDs) and a separate power supply. An internal modem, on the other hand, is just a Peripheral Component Interconnect (PCI) or Industry Standard Architecture (ISA) circuit board. The desk space required for an external modem is another drawback, as is the need for a power outlet. Still anther disadvantage of an external modem is that it needs to connect to the computer, so it occupies a port. This was much more of an issue when modems were using serial ports because there was typically only one or two of them. With USB, it's not a problem because you can have many USB devices on a single PC.

The main advantage of an external modem is that you don't have to take the cover off the PC and install anything. That makes them attractive for technophobes and novices.

Hardware Modem versus Winmodem

The cost of a modem ranges from $30 for the really cheap off-brand ones to more than $120 for the full-featured name-brand models. That's a pretty big range, considering they all do basically the same thing at the same speed.

The main difference between the high- and low-end modems is whether they're software-assisted modems, a.k.a. *Winmodems*.

So what's this Winmodem thing? Well, back in the heyday of modem popularity, some vendors went through this train of thought:

◆ People want a low-priced modem.

◆ Modems cost a lot to manufacture because the modem has a heavy responsibility in translating between analog and digital and compressing/decompressing the data. Each modem must have chips that do all that.

◆ Software could be developed that would take over some of the modem's functions. The modem hardware could then be much cheaper to manufacture because most of its duties would be handled through the software.

◆ For such software to work, it'd have to be designed for a specific operating system; the modem couldn't be platform independent as "real" modems are.

◆ Most people use Microsoft Windows.

You can guess where all this reasoning ended up. A cheap modem was created that worked only within Windows and that required special software to be installed to support it. *Voilà*, the Windows Modem, or Winmodem.

Nowadays most internal modems are Winmodems. And to be fair, Winmodems have gotten a lot better over the past decade. (There were troubleshooting and installation nightmares in the early days.) However, I still won't buy one, even though I run only Microsoft Windows as an operating system. I always spring for the more expensive "hardware modem," given a choice, for two reasons. One is performance. Any time extra software runs on a computer, performance suffers. A Winmodem uses Random Access Memory (RAM) and Central Processing Unit (CPU) time that a hardware modem doesn't. The other is the assurance that installation will go smoothly; Winmodems can be quirky, especially the off-brands. If I'm buying a modem for a client, I'd rather spend $50 more for a brand name hardware modem than charge him $100 more in installation labor.

Store clerks are often not very well educated about hardware modems versus Winmodems, so you have to read the packaging carefully when shopping. Look for a modem that doesn't mention that it requires Windows. It may have the word *performance* in the name or *controller-based*. (Winmodems are sometimes called *controllerless*.)

NOTE *Everyone has an opinion as to the best modem brand, and here's mine: U.S. Robotics. You can't go wrong with them. Even their Winmodems are okay.*

Technology Standards

Modems are designed to follow certain standards so that they can communicate with other modems. These standards define not only the speed at which a modem may operate but also determine how, exactly, a modem compresses data and performs its error control. The most common standards over the years—the so-called V-dot standards—are ratified by the Comité Consultatif International Télégraphique et Téléphonique (CCITT) and the International Telecommunications Union (ITU).

As with all technology standards, modem standards have evolved over the years. The initial V.22bis standard (2.4Kbps) evolved into the V.32 standard (9.6Kbps), which evolved into the V.32bis standard (14.4Kbps) and then the V.34 standard (28.8Kbps), which was upgraded in 1996 to the slightly faster V.34+ standard (33.6Kbps).

The next standard, V.90, was the result of a contentious protocol war that erupted in the late 1990s. At that time, two distinct technologies developed by two industry groups, X2 and k56flex, brought speeds up from their previous 33.5Kbps limit. After a bit of a spat, X2 disappeared and was replaced in 1998 by the V.90 standard—which has backward compatibility to k56flex, the apparent winner in the previously mentioned V.90 war.

The most recent attempt at standardizing, V.92, was instituted in late 2000. The V.92 standard includes several enhancements beyond those defined by the more established V.90 standard, including the following:

Modem on Hold   Suspends your online session for incoming calls and returns to your previous activity—without redialing—after the conversation ends.

Quick Connect   Remembers line conditions from your last session to reduce the dial-up connection time (to about a third of what it was with V.90).

PCM Upstream   Boosts the maximum upstream data rate between you and your Internet Service Provider (ISP), from 33.6Kbps to 48Kbps, to reduce upload times for large files and email attachments.

As with all standards, both modems on a connection (yours and your ISP's) must support V.92 to take advantage of these new features.

Installing and Testing a Modem

Modems install just like any other circuit board, hardware-wise. Almost all are PCI these days, but ISA models are still available for use in older systems.

Some modems come with a Setup CD that has some dire warning on it such as "Run This Before Installing the Modem!" This may be necessary for a Winmodem (you can try not doing it first if you're up for an experiment), but for a controller-based modem it's not necessary.

And speaking of the Setup CD that comes with the modem, it probably contains a lot of software that you don't need—perhaps a terminal application or some "helpful links" to Web sites (that coincidentally have paid a marketing fee to the modem manufacturer). The only things you really need off that Setup CD are the driver for the modem and the software that does the Winmodem thing (if applicable).

Installing an Internal Modem

The following are the steps for installing an internal modem:

1. If installing a Winmodem and the instructions say so, run the Setup software that came with it.

2. Shut down the PC, and take all necessary precautions to avoid static discharge. If you have an antistatic wrist strap, wear it.

3. Open the PC case, and locate a free slot (PCI or ISA depending on the modem's needs). Remove its backplate cover if needed.

4. Insert the modem. Tighten it down with a screw.

5. Close up the PC case, and start the PC. Windows will probably detect it automatically at startup.

6. If prompted to insert a disk containing a driver for the modem, insert its Setup CD. If a message comes back saying it can't find the driver, click Browse to browse the CD and locate it. (It may be in a folder named for a specific Windows version, such as WIN98 or WINXP.)

7. Check for the modem in Device Manager to confirm that it is correctly installed. (Refer to Chapter 23, "Hardware Management via Software Solutions" for help if needed.)

Installing an External Modem

External modems are easy to install because you don't have to open the case. The only thing to remember is that with a serial port connection, you must shut down the PC. With a USB connection, you don't need to shut it down. Follow these steps:

1. If installing on a legacy serial port, shut down the PC.

2. Connect the modem's power supply to the wall outlet and to the modem.

3. Connect the cable between the modem and the PC, and turn the modem on.

4. Start up the PC. Windows will probably detect the modem automatically at startup.

5. If prompted to insert a disk containing a driver for the modem, insert its Setup CD. If a message comes back saying it can't find the driver, click Browse to browse the CD and locate it. (It may be in a folder named for a specific Windows version, such as WIN98 or WINXP.)

6. Check for the modem in the Device Manager to confirm that it's correctly installed. (Refer to Chapter 23 for help if needed.)

Testing the Modem

Testing the modem in Windows doesn't require a telephone line, so you can do it anytime. When a modem isn't working correctly within an application (such as America Online (AOL), for example, or Windows Dial-Up Networking), the first thing I do is check it out through Windows.

Step 1 is to look for the modem in the Device Manager and make sure it reports a status of This Device Is Working Properly. If you don't get that status, then the modem isn't installed correctly, is physically defective, or has a resource conflict. See Chapter 23 for details.

Step 2 is to run the modem's diagnostics. This varies depending on your Windows version. In Windows 9x/Me, follow these steps:

1. Open the Control Panel, and double-click Modems.

2. Click the Diagnostics tab.

3. Click the COM port for the modem (or USB connection if applicable).

4. Click More Info. The test results appear in a separate dialog box, as in Figure 28.1. If at least some of the lines report OK or Success, the modem is communicating with the PC. If instead of results you get an error message, the modem is having a problem; see the "Troubleshooting a Modem" section later in the chapter.

FIGURE 28.1

A successful
modem test under
Windows 98

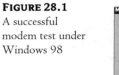

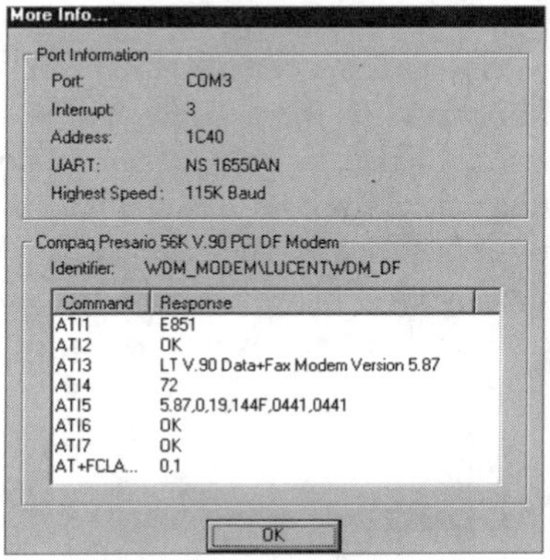

NOTE *The diagnostic test sends various codes to the modem, including ATI1 through ATI7, and then reports back the modem's response. Different modem chipsets may have different meanings for these codes, but on all modems ATI3 provides modem information such as the chipset and firmware revision.*

In Windows 2000/XP, follow these steps:

1. Open the Control Panel, and double-click Phone and Modem Options.

2. Click the Modems tab.

3. Click the modem, and click the Properties button.

4. Click the Diagnostics tab.

5. Click the Query Modem button. The test results appear in a window on the Diagnostics tab. If at least one command reports OK or Success, the modem is working, as in Figure 28.2. If an error appears, see the "Troubleshooting a Modem" section later in the chapter.

FIGURE 28.2

A successful
modem test under
Windows XP

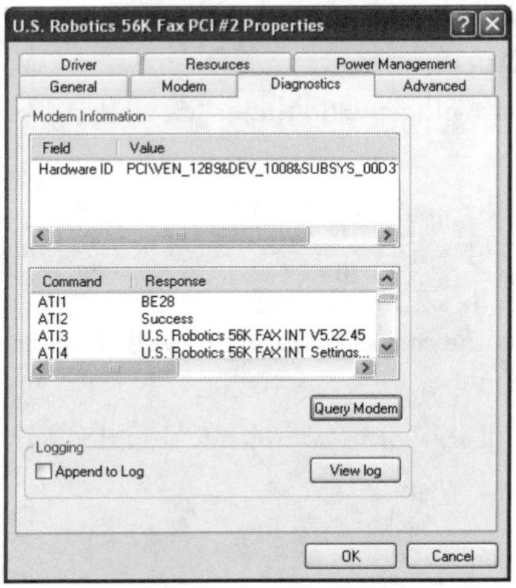

Connecting the Phone Line

If the modem successfully passes its diagnostic tests, you're ready to hook up a phone line to it.

Modern modems have two phone jacks on them. They may be labeled *Line* and *Phone,* or they may have little pictures on them along those lines. *These two jacks aren't interchangeable.* One's an "in" (the Line jack) and one's an "out" (the Phone jack) for connecting a telephone to share the phone line.

If you accidentally switch the cords such that the phone line from the wall is coming into the Phone (out) jack, the modem might work—sort of. You'll probably hear some static in the connection, at the minimum. Some modems make an annoying buzzing or honking sound when you connect with the wrong jack used.

Troubleshooting a Modem

What can go wrong with a modem? Plenty. The following sections address some of the most common problems with modems.

Doesn't Appear At All in the Device Manager

The modem is either not physically installed properly (maybe it's not seated in its slot?) or is defective, isn't a Plug and Play (PnP) device, or isn't being installed in a PnP-compatible system.

Try running the software that came with the modem. If it can't find the modem either, you've probably got yourself a defective modem. See Chapter 23 for details on troubleshooting hardware that won't show up in the Device Manager.

TIP   If an external modem isn't recognized, make sure that the port to which it's attached can be seen in the Device Manager. Check Basic Input/Output System (BIOS) Setup to see whether the port has been disabled if applicable.

Appears as Unknown Device in Device Manager

This is most often the result of failing to run the Setup software that came with the modem on a Winmodem (controllerless modem). The Setup software should make everything okay. If you don't have it, you can probably download it from the manufacturer's Web site.

Fails Diagnostic Testing

If the Device Manager sees the modem and thinks it's working, but the modem fails testing, try the following procedure:

1. Did you replace an older modem with this newer one? If so, remove the older modem's driver from the Device Manager. (See Chapter 23.) Then try the diagnostic test again.

2. Disconnect the phone line from the modem, and then try the test again. The test should work even without a phone line connected, and this will eliminate false errors on the test caused by the phone line being in use.

3. Do a cold reboot. In other words, completely shut down the computer and restart it. Try the diagnostic test again.

4. If it still doesn't work, remove the modem from the Device Manager and then reinstall it using the Setup CD that came with the modem (if possible).

5. If it still doesn't work, reposition the modem in a different slot in the motherboard.

Lots of Static

When the modem picks up the phone and starts to dial, do you hear a lot of static over the top of the normal dialing noises? A staticky phone line can result from any of these things:

◆ Phone line plugged into the wrong jack on the modem

◆ Poor-quality residential phone lines

◆ Bad telephone cable

◆ Overly long telephone cable

◆ Electromagnetic interference

◆ Other telephony devices connected to the same line (fax machines, and so on)

Fails to Stay Connected

A failure to stay connected is often the result of a staticky phone line (see the previous section).

There's one other possibility: if the modem has never been able to stay connected to your ISP for more than a few seconds, check to make sure that Transmission Control Protocol/Internet Protocol (TCP/IP) is installed in the network connection properties. You must have TCP/IP installed to communicate with most ISPs.

Slow Modem Connection Speed

First of all, don't expect a 56Kbps connection from a 56Kbps modem. It's not going to happen. The maximum you can possibly get is around 53Kbps, and you'll be lucky to achieve 50Kbps. Somewhere between 33Kbps and 44Kbps is average.

The speed depends almost entirely on the quality of the phone line. That's because the connection speed is negotiated at the beginning of the call by the two modems that are communicating. If the line between them can't support the highest rates, they keep dropping down incrementally to lower speeds until they find one at which they can reliably communicate. That's what all those connection noises are about. The longer the connection noises go on, the more negotiation is being done and the lower the speed you're probably going to end up with when they're finished. See the "Lots of Static" section earlier for reasons why the line might not be clear.

One other possible bottleneck might be the modem at the other end of the connection. In the early days of ISPs, this was a major problem; few ISPs had installed 56.6Kbps modems, even though that speed had become standard on most new PCs. The result of a 56.6Kbps modem connecting to a 33.6Kbps modem is a 33.6Kbps connection; the transmission speed defaults to the speed of the slowest modem. So if you're using a dial-up service such as AOL, make sure the access number you're calling is a 56Kbps number.

NOTE *In the early days of 56Kbps connectivity, there were two standards: k56flex and X2. Both were replaced by V.90. It's possible that some access numbers for some online services might be X2 only or k56flex only, but it's not likely. Any modern V.90 or V.92 modem will connect to either, but an X2 modem won't connect at full speed to a k56flex modem and vice versa.*

Broadband Internet Connectivity

We all know one thing about the modem connection to the Internet—*it's slow!* Especially if you visit media-rich Web sites, download large files, or receive emails embedded with large JPEG pictures of your Uncle Jake's vacation to Myrtle Beach. Every little thing you look at or listen to online has to travel down that pipe to your PC, and the more things there are—and the bigger they are—the slower the Internet appears to be.

What's the solution to this World Wide Wait? A faster connection, of course.

If you're using a traditional analog modem connected to a standard phone line, you're stuck downloading your bits and bytes at 53Kbps. However, if you have a digital broadband connection—via DSL, cable, or satellite—you can now receive data at 10 to 20 times that of your old analog speed. With broadband access, using the Internet is actually tolerable!

Choosing a Digital Technology

So you want a faster Internet connection than your old dial-up modem, do you? (You're not alone...) Unfortunately, it's not as simple as calling your current ISP and saying, "Speed it up!" No, you'll probably have to choose a new provider, based on the type of broadband technology you want to embrace. Some ISPs offer both dial-up and broadband, and in some cases even multiple types of broadband (such as EarthLink, for example), but most specialize in one type.

FIVE TYPES OF BROADBAND

For consumer and small business users, five main types of digital broadband connections are available. Each have their pluses and minuses, as follows:

Integrated Services Digital Network (ISDN) ISDN was the first digital connection technology, offering speeds double that of existing analog modems. Unfortunately, ISDN technology is unwieldy, unreliable, and costly. In most areas, ISDN has been supplanted by the lower-cost, higher-performance DSL technology.

DSL DSL is a digital connection that piggybacks on your standard phone lines. Costing not much more than a second phone line, DSL provides speeds that approach that of a T1 line (a long-established, very fast digital connection typically used by large businesses). T1 happens to cost about $400–500 a month, which makes it prohibitive in cost and maintenance fees for the average Internet user. In comparison, a DSL connection at a minimum of 384Kbps downstream will run you about $30–$50 a month—including full ISP service.

Digital cable Cable modems work just as you'd think they would, providing digital Internet access over the same cable that brings you your cable television programming. Because it has to handle all those channels, it's a big pipe to work with—and typically provides download speeds comparable to DSL, at approximately the same prices.

Digital satellite   The advent of these pizza box–sized satellite dishes opened up another interesting opportunity beyond crystal-clear television signals. The same type of satellite that delivers hundreds of channels of TV programming can also deliver high-speed data from the Internet. (In fact, some dishes can receive both TV and PC data.) There are two subtypes of this: one-way and two-way. The one-way type uses the satellite dish only for downloading; it uses a regular modem for uploading.

Broadband wireless   Also known as fixed-wireless connections, wireless systems use microwave technology to transmit and receive Internet data at broadband speeds. You'll need a special antenna on your roof, of course, but the link between your antenna and the Internet source is completely wireless.

PROS AND CONS

With all these broadband options, which is the best for you? The following are some factors to consider:

Availability   Not all types of broadband are available in all areas. If your cable company offers cable modems but your phone company doesn't offer DSL, the choice is easy. Likewise, if no land-based options are available, the satellite option is always there if you have a clear view of the southern sky. (Broadband wireless is likely to be the least-available option—and probably not available at all in your area.)

Reliability   Will the connection be available 24 hours a day? It depends on the ability of your ISP to keep it up-and-running. DSL and cable typically have few problems with temporary outages; satellite (especially two-way) is more prone to them. A friend of mine who has two-way satellite Internet estimates that he's without service about six hours a month on the average because of weather conditions, sun spots, and problems with the ISP's equipment.

Faster—and easier—installation   Cable access is a snap to set up—many cable companies provide customer self-installation kits, and you can typically complete the entire procedure in an hour or less. DSL is typically not much harder. Satellite Internet access typically requires professional installation of the dish, especially with the two-way type.

Download speed   Even the best DSL connection is slightly slower than the same-priced cable connection (except during high network volume, as discussed in a few paragraphs). If you live far enough from the central office, you might find available DSL speed to be unacceptable. If this is the case, go with cable. Satellite is nowhere near as fast as cable and DSL, but it's still better than dial-up. Speed for two-way satellite typically ranges from 120Kbps to 400Kbps depending on network traffic and weather conditions.

Upload speed and latency   Most broadband connections are asynchronous—in other words, the upload is slower than the download. Usually this is okay because you send less data to the Internet (requests for certain URLs and so on) than you retrieve from it. If, however, you send a lot of email messages (or very large messages) or upload big files to File Transfer Protocol (FTP) servers or newsgroups, you'll discover that many cable companies are using a narrow band for return signaling, below all the space allocated for TV channels. This band is prone to Radio

Frequency (RF) interference and is very limited in capacity—with the result of delivering slow upstream speed or high latency (slightly delayed) uploads. This can be a major problem if you're participating in any real-time activities, such as multiplayer games, video conferencing, and the like. Satellite is similarly subject to slow uploading (around 120Kbps) and latency issues. If upload speed and latency are an issue, go with DSL.

Shared network traffic   One of the downfalls of cable broadband is that you share a network connection with many other users in your neighborhood. The more people using the network at the same time, the less bandwidth available for each individual user—and the slower the connection speed. You'd think this would be an easy fix (the cable company installs more network routers), but it remains a significant issue with some providers, so much so that connecting during prime time results in some very slow connections for users in highly connected neighborhoods. So check with your neighbors—if they're complaining about their cable connections slowing down, go with DSL instead. With satellite, all traffic goes through the same satellites and ISP, so network traffic is somewhat of an issue as well.

Making the ISDN Connection

As I've said, the first type of digital connection available to home and small business Internet users was ISDN. For several years it was the *only* digital option—although it has been supplanted both in speed and cost by DSL and digital cable connections.

How ISDN Works

ISDN is a high-speed digital telephone line. ISDN utilizes two data channels that can each transmit 64Kbps, or the two channels can be combined for a single-channel throughput of 128Kbps. Not too shabby, especially when compared to the 53Kbps throughput of today's fastest analog modems. If you keep the channels separate, you can run two conversations (or two data sessions) via the same telephone connection. For example, you can use a single ISDN line to talk on the telephone while also using your modem.

ISDN is still available in most (but not all) areas of the United States. The cost of an ISDN connection varies significantly from state to state—so significantly, in fact, that it's difficult to quote usual charges with any amount of accuracy. Most often, the charges are based on a flat monthly fee plus a per-minute connection time charge. If you're connecting two places within the same calling zone or are able to wrangle a deal with your ISDN provider, you *may* have to pay only a flat monthly fee. If you can get such a deal, I highly recommend it; it'll probably save you money if you're the kind of person who goes online enough to need a high-speed connection. In any case, you're probably looking at monthly ISDN bills in the $50–$100 range and probably toward the high end of that range.

Besides being able to afford the connection, you'll need to make sure your ISP has its own ISDN connection. Just as you can't make a 56.6Kbps connection unless the modems on both ends of the connection support speeds that high, you can't dial up using ISDN unless there are ISDN devices on both ends of the connection. (Really, it's a bit more complicated than that—an analog modem wouldn't know what to do with a digital signal if you did call it—but the end result is still the same: unless your provider offers an ISDN connection to the Internet, you can't have one.) These can be a little tricky to come by even if you live in an area that offers ISDN, so you may have to shop around a bit for a provider.

The bottom line is that ISDN is expensive and often difficult to obtain. Most users are better off investigating the availability of DSL, cable, or satellite broadband.

INSTALLING AN ISDN CONNECTION

Assuming that you have an ISDN line and an Internet provider with an ISDN line, you'll need an ISDN modem (typically called a *terminal adapter*). This will let your analog modem use a digital line. (In the early days of ISDN, you would've needed another device called an NT1 to plug the terminal adapter into, but many new models are including the NT1 in the adapter itself.)

NOTE *If you intend to use additional devices, such as a telephone, on an ISDN line, you'll either need digital versions of the device or a converter. Converters are about $150. Considering that your analog phone is probably worth about that much, save some money by making sure the ISDN line is dedicated.*

If you plan to upgrade, you can replace your old modem with an ISDN model. These aren't cheap, but their cost is proportional to the increase in speed that you see. Some ISDN modems have more features than others do. Most ISDN modems have user-controlled band allocation so that you can combine the two data channels to get 128Kbps. If the telephone rings while you're connected, however, the channels will separate so that you can answer the telephone while keeping the original connection; they'll recombine once you hang up.

To recap, here's what you'll need to use ISDN:

◆ An ISDN telephone line

◆ Someone with an ISDN telephone line and associated equipment to call

◆ An ISDN modem and/or telephone or a converter that you can plug analog equipment into

Although this will get you up and running with ISDN, you should also investigate the other digital broadband options—all of which provide much faster connections, often at a much lower cost, than what you can get with ISDN.

Going Faster with DSL

DSL technology transforms a traditional phone line into a high-speed digital connection. Even the slowest DSL speeds are typically four to five times that of ISDN, or close to 10 times that of a traditional analog modem. And you get all this, plus traditional ISP services, for about $30 a month—cheaper than what it'd cost you to add a second phone line and subscribe to a traditional ISP and cheaper than ISDN.

Because of the average Internet user's need for speed, DSL has become a hot technology—so hot that DSL providers have had trouble keeping up with the demand. There's also been a problem with DSL providers (especially the smaller players) staying in business. The result is that the biggest issue with DSL is availability. Still, although not all areas of the country have access to DSL service, the rollout continues. If you can't get DSL today, chances are you'll have access soon.

How DSL Works

DSL is very cool, and it doesn't work much differently from ISDN—it's just a whole lot faster.

All forms of DSL are based on the ability to split existing phone lines into two or three frequency bands. This is called a *frequency spectrum*. If there are two frequency bands, one band is used to provide upstream data flow and the other is used to provide downstream data flow. If there are three bands the third "channel" is used for standard voice. Plain Old Telephone Service (POTS) takes up only a small portion of the total capacity of the available bandwidth, so adding this is trivial.

Physically, there has to be a connection between the provider and you. It's relatively easy enough for your local telephone company to pipe a T1, T3, or faster connection into your location, but they also need to add what's called a DSLAM, or DSL access multiplexer (just another fancy name for splitter). The Internet connection goes into the DSLAM, and the POTS lines pass through it. If there's no terminal adapter, your DSL modem on the other end of the DSLAM does nothing and simply acts as a fancy wire holder for the POTS lines.

On the other hand, if you *do* have a DSL modem, an Asynchronous Transfer Mode (ATM) link which a very high-speed protocol link, is established.

It's in the so-called Last Mile that most of the problems with DSL can occur. The Last Mile, which is owned by the big telcos (such as Verizon, SBC Communications, Bell Canada, and Pacific Bell), is essentially just a simple POTS line, also known as twisted-pair, run from the switching facility—called a Central Office (CO)—nearest to your home. It's this stretch of POTS line that creates a distance limitation for DSL service. Copper wire can retain only so much cohesion for so long. After a certain point, the signal begins to degrade and it's no longer usable—which means that the further you are from a CO, the slower your DSL speed will be.

NOTE   *It's worth noting that you don't always deal directly with the telco for your DSL service—even though they provide (and service) your POTS line. In many areas, you deal with a DSL service provider, who deals with the telco—typically through an intermediary called a Competitive Local Exchange Carrier (CLEC). The CLEC bundles large volumes of DSL service to multiple service providers; your individual service provider provides you with your Internet access. With the recent shakeout in the DSL market, however, a lot of service providers and CLECs went out of business—including two of the biggest, Northpoint and Rhythms. For many users, this leaves their telco as the sole available DSL provider. And, of course, the telco functions both as the CLEC and the service provider.*

Types of DSL

There are several types of DSL to choose from, each with its own advantages and disadvantages. Not all types are available in all areas or from all providers. The most common types of DSL are the following

ADSL   Asymmetric Digital Subscriber Line (ADSL), also known as ADSL Full Rate or G.dmt where upstream speed (from your modem to the ISP) is slower than downstream speed (from your ISP to you). With ADSL, downstream speeds can hit 8.5 megabits per second (Mbps), with upstream speeds capped at 1.5Mbps. This type of pure ADSL is rather high-priced and targeted more at business users than home users.

ADSL Lite   Also called G.Lite, DSL-Lite, consumer DSL (CDSL), or universal ADSL (UADSL) this is a "notched-down" version of ADSL for the home market. ADSL Lite has a maximum downstream speed of 1.5Mbps and a typical upstream speed of 384Kbps. Chances are if a company advertises home DSL service, they're talking about some version of ADSL Lite.

HDSL   High-bit-rate DSL (HDSL), the original DSL technology. It uses four copper wires (two pairs) and delivers speeds of 1.5Mbps or so both upstream and downstream. HDSL was originally developed as a lower-cost alternative to T1 lines for large businesses.

IDSL   IDSL stands for ISDN Digital Subscriber Line, and it's an ISDN service based on ISDN technology. It's slower than other types of DSL (144Kbps both upstream and downstream) but can be used over longer distances. Because IDSL uses ISDN transmission coding, it can go just about anywhere that ISDN can go—36,000 feet or more from a CO. If distance is a problem in obtaining ADSL-based service, IDSL is often a reasonable alternative. (I've heard, however, that some IDSL customers encounter a number of distance-related issues; the increased distance from the CO tends to result in a weaker signal, which is more difficult to keep in sync.)

RADSL   Rate-Adaptive DSL (RADSL)—which means that the speed dynamically varies according to line conditions. When a RADSL modem first starts up, it tests the line and fixes the operating speed at the fastest rate the line can handle.

SDSL   Symmetric DSL (SDSL), which is also called HDSL-2, is an enhanced version of HDSL that works with only one pair of wires. It typically delivers speeds of 1.1Mbps in both directions.

VDSL   Very high-bit-rate DSL (VDSL), which is also called BDSL, is targeted at companies with high access demand, typically delivered over fiber-optic networks. Offers typical speeds of 34Mbps in both directions.

NOTE   *"Generic" DSL is sometimes referred to as xDSL to embrace all the other leading acronyms.*

Table 28.1 compares the features of the various types of DSL. Two caveats: first, if you're at the far end of the distance range, expect your speeds to be substantially slower than the maximum. Second, the workable distance for each type of DSL varies considerably from provider to provider; the figures given here are reasonable averages.

TABLE 28.1: TYPES OF DSL

DSL TYPE	TYPICAL UPSTREAM SPEEDS	TYPICAL DOWNSTREAM SPEEDS	MAX. DIST. FROM CO
ADSL	1.5Mbps	8.5Mbps	18,000 feet (9000 feet for maximum performance)
ADSL Lite	384Kbps	1.5Mbps	18,000 feet
HDSL	1.5Mbps	1.5Mbps	12,000 feet
IDSL	144Kbps	144Kbps	36,000 feet
RADSL	Variable	Variable	18,000 feet
SDSL	1.1Mbps	1.1Mbps	20,000 feet
VDSL	34Mbps	34Mbps	4500 feet
V.90 modem (comparison)	33.6Kbps	53Kbps	N/A

The most common type of DSL currently available is ADSL—or, for the home, ADSL Lite. ADSL's slower upstream speed is acceptable to most users, who download more than they upload, and enables the DSL provider to cram more users into their system.

Although ADSL Lite is the most popular DSL for home use, some companies also offer home SDSL (which is preferable if you need a fast upstream rate) and ISDL (which is an option if you're too far from a CO for ADSL service) for home users. For business users, the faster (and higher-priced) ADSL Full Rate, HDSL, RADSL, and VDSL are popular options.

SPEED IS RELATIVE (TO DISTANCE)

Even if your area has DSL service, your particular location might not qualify. That's because your distance from your local telephone company's CO directly affects the speed of your DSL connection. The further you are from the CO, the slower the connection—and if you're too far away, you can't get service at all.

WARNING   The quality of your existing phone wiring will also affect your DSL connection. Even if you live close enough to the CO to get a fast connection, deteriorating wiring in your home or office may cause your DSL to either slow down or cease working. If this happens to you, see if your telco can clean or "condition" your line. You may also need to install a filter on your phone line so that your DSL connection doesn't interfere with your normal voice service.

Table 28.2 shows what types of DSL service are available, depending on your distance from the CO. (Because ADSL distance is dependent on speed, many service providers deliver a reduced-speed version for customers further out from the CO; therefore, I've included columns for both maximum speed and reduced-speed ADSL.)

TABLE 28.2: DSL SERVICE BY DISTANCE FROM CO

DISTANCE (IN FEET)	VSDL	ADSL (MAXIMUM SPEED)	HDSL	ADSL (REDUCED SPEED)	ADSL LITE	RADSL	SDSL	ISDL
<5000	X	X	X	X	X	X	X	X
5000–9000		X	X	X	X	X	X	X
9000–12,000			X	X	X	X	X	X
12,000–18,000				X	X	X	X	X
18,000–20,000							X	X
20,000–36,000								X
>36,000								

INSTALLING AND CONFIGURING DSL

DSL requires professional installation in most cases because there are several steps involved in checking your location for suitability and setting up the service. Further, because DSL service is a cooperative effort among multiple players in most cases, troubleshooting it can sometimes be an exercise in corporate finger pointing.

The first thing you do is call a DSL service provider—such as Yahoo! DSL or EarthLink—or your local telco, and order service appropriate to your price range and needs. Most providers offer ADSL Lite service (1.5Mbps maximum downstream, but actual speeds may be slower than that) for $30 or less a month, often with a free modem and installation.

TIP   *To obtain a list of DSL providers in your area—and to confirm that your location qualifies for DSL service of any kind—visit the DSL Reports Web site at* `www.dslreports.com`. *This site is a fount of information about DSL in general and also offers tips and tweaks you can use to get the maximum performance from your DSL connection.*

Your DSL service provider will then contract with a CLEC (sometimes called a *partner*), such as Covad, which then makes arrangements with whichever telco owns your phone line. (Remember, if your telco is your DSL service provider, it's also your CLEC.) For those of you counting, that's a three-step process: service provider to partner to telco—which means that if you run into installation or service problems, you may end up dealing with three separate companies, each of which will undoubtedly point the finger at one of the other two companies.

Once you've placed your order, a representative of your local telco comes to your office or domicile to test the line to see if the "loop" is good. This means they're checking the telephone lines to see whether they can handle the connection and will pass clean data.

NOTE   *As mentioned earlier, DSL is limited to the distance from the CO and that CO's installed DSLAM. If that distance is exceeded, you can't have DSL. If it were installed despite the long distance, it'd be unreliable or not work at all.*

The CLEC that provides the DSL access is then notified by the telco that the line was tested and informed of its condition. If your line is acceptable, the process moves onward, and a technician from the CLEC makes an appointment to complete your installation. The telco marks the specific line tested for DSL, which is typically an existing phone line. The installer (from the CLEC) finds the line and prepares it, installs an RJ-45 jack at the wall plate you specify, and plugs it in to test it.

The installer will bring a DSL modem, unless you made arrangements to provide your own. They'll also need to plug into your Network Interface Card (NIC). What? You don't have a network card in your PC? Don't panic—you may have other options available.

First, you could just go out and buy a NIC. (If you opt to go this route, make sure you buy and install the NIC before your DSL installer arrives.) Some DSL providers offer an internal DSL modem card (also known as a PCI DSL modem), which eliminates the need for a NIC. Another option is a DSL modem that connects through your PC's USB port (good) or serial port (not so good). Choose the option that works best for you—but know that the traditional Ethernet connection often works best, with the least installation and operational hassles.

Anyway, once the installer has the modem connected and everything appears to be working correctly, it's time to configure. You'll need a few things, which should be provided either by your
installer or your DSL service provider:

◆ A static IP number (if your service provider provides static IP service—see the "Static IP versus PPPoE" sidebar for more information)

◆ A gateway IP number

◆ At least two Domain Name Service (DNS) IP numbers

◆ Your Post Office Protocol version 3 (POP3) and Simple Mail Transfer Protocol (SMTP)
  server IP numbers

Now, write all these down and put the list in a safe place. Repeat this three times. Even fast mind
such as yours can get all in a twist and remember only one clever and crafty hiding place at a time, so
it's best to hedge one's bets.

Now you can get to the configuration (this procedure assumes you're working with Windows 95
98/Me/XP):

1. Go to Start ➤ Settings ➤ Control Panel, and open Network. (In Windows XP, select the Create a New Connection task.)

2. Enter the appropriate information. Don't activate WINS.

3. Click OK.

4. Restart the machine.

5. Enjoy your speedy connection.

SECURING WINDOWS WITH A STATIC IP

As I've said, there's one big negative about DSL with a static IP: crackers. And, no, I don't mean the
Ritz kind—I'm referring to the kind of mean and nasty people who use various technological mean
to "crack" into your system. (You've probably heard them called hackers, but *hacker* actually means
someone who enjoys working with computers "very close to the metal." Hackers aren't mean and
malicious; crackers are.) Crackers like to gain access to systems that aren't their own and destroy data
take things, or just leave evidence of their illicit presence.

To do this, they need what are called *exploits*, or shortcomings, in the system that allow them to ge
around established security measures. Windows is very, *very* bad in this respect (bad, *bad* operating system...bad!) in that it practically broadcasts its presence. So, how do you prevent this from happening
Easy. Follow this very complicated list of instructions:

1. Turn off file sharing.

There is no step 2.

Obviously, this is a simplistic answer to a potentially complex problem, but if you have only one
computer connected to the DSL, there's absolutely no need whatsoever to share your files with the
world. Of course, there are more factors in real life and, hence, more options.

STATIC IP VERSUS PPPOE

One of the early advertised benefits to DSL was an *always-on* connection (also called a persistent connection). Unlike connections via analog modem, where each session has to be started by dialing in and connecting to your ISP, a persistent connection is always there, always connected, with no dialing in or connecting to required. (And I can tell you from my experience, having the Internet *always there* is a huge benefit.)

To deliver a persistent connection, a DSL provider must assign a static IP number to your computer. Think of a static IP as a permanent street address—it's a unique number, and it's always yours, no changing.

However, in the quest to maximize the use of their bandwidth, many DSL providers have quietly ceased offering static IPs. The reasoning is simple—if you have a static IP, your PC is always connected, and you're always using a set amount of bandwidth, even when you're not surfing the Net. If, on the other hand, you were assigned an IP address only when you were physically using your connection, that would free up additional bandwidth that the DSL provider could then allocate to other users. It's a more efficient use of their pipe, if you want to think of it that way.

The alternative, then, to a static IP is something called Point-to-Point Protocol over Ethernet (PPPoE). With PPPoE, you don't have a constant address—and you don't have a persistent connection. Instead, you have to log onto the DSL network each time you turn on your PC, and you're assigned a new and temporary IP address at that time, for the current session only. Not only is this a hassle (your Internet won't always be there, waiting patiently for you), it also eliminates the possibility of you hosting your own Web server (which you can if you have a static IP).

As much as most users hate PPPoE, it does have one distinct end user advantage—it's more secure than static IP. If your IP address is constantly changing, it's less likely that crackers will find their way into your system.

That slight benefit (which can be obviated via the use of firewall software) is, in most users' opinions, negated by the lack of an always-on connection. For that reason, if you have the choice between a provider offering static IP and another offering PPPoE, it's an easy decision to choose the static IP provider.

To turn file sharing off under Windows 9*x*/Me, go to Start ➤ Settings ➤ Control Panel and open the Network item. Click the File/Print Sharing button in the lower half of the dialog box, and deselect both items. You're done. To do it under Windows 2000/XP, go into the properties for your network connection (select Start ➤ Connect To ➤ Show All Connections, right-click the connection, and choose Properties), and on the General tab, delete File and Printer Sharing for Microsoft Networks. This would prevent you from sharing files and printers on your home network, however.

In Windows XP there's a better solution: just make sure that the Internet connection firewall is enabled for the Internet connection. To do this, display the properties for the connection (select Start ➤ Connect To ➤ Show All Connections, right-click the connection, and choose Properties), and on the Advanced tab, mark the Internet Connection Firewall check box.

Digital Cable Internet

The primary competitor to DSL is high-speed digital cable. The advantages are many: cable broadband is faster, easier to install, and—in many cases—more widely available than DSL. Depending on the deal offered by your local cable company, cable broadband may also be slightly cheaper than comparable DSL service. (Prices in the $35–$40/month range—if you're also a cable TV subscriber—are common.)

I recently switched from DSL to cable. My experience is that cable is much easier to install, the cable company is easier to deal with and more willing to please than my old DSL provider, and the service itself is both faster and more reliable. (I was getting about 600Kbps downstream with my DSL connection; now I'm averaging close to 2Mbps with cable.)

How Internet Over Cable Works

Cable broadband works a little differently from either ISDN or DSL. Whereas ISDN and DSL piggy-back over your copper phone lines, cable Internet occupies a *tunnel* within the cable signal that's sent via the cable company's fiber-optic or coaxial cable.

Internet signals are typically assigned a 6MHz slot within the cable signal, and they deliver download speeds that can theoretically reach 5Mbps. (More common speeds are between 500Kbps and 2Mbps.) Upstream signals are assigned a smaller subset of that slot, resulting in slower upstream rates—typically in the 128–384Kbps range.

Some cable companies offer only one-way access. In this type of system, all upstream requests are sent via analog phone lines and are limited to 33.3Kbps. As you can no doubt ascertain, this is a much inferior way of doing things, and you should opt for two-way cable (where both downstream and upstream access are via digital cable) whenever possible.

Fortunately, most cable companies support the Data Over Cable Service Interface Specification (DOCSIS). Any DOCSIS-compatible cable modem will work on any DOCSIS-compatible cable system—which means you can probably take your cable modem with you if you move. You can find cable modems from a variety of manufacturers, including Cisco Systems, Thomson Consumer Electronics (RCA), Motorola, Samsung, and others.

NOTE *Just because you have cable TV in your home doesn't mean you have access to cable Internet. Not all cable systems support data service—in fact, if your system is an older one, chances are it doesn't offer Internet access. More modern systems, or older systems that have been upgraded to offer digital cable, are more likely to offer Internet access to their subscribers.*

Installing and Configuring Cable Access

Although some cable companies still offer installation by a professional installer (and often charge you $50–$100 for the service!), many companies now provide self-installation kits. These kits include installation software, a USB-enabled cable modem, and enough instructions for you to figure out how it all fits together.

With this sort of self-install kit, the basic installation goes something like this:

1. Connect a coaxial cable from your cable outlet to your cable modem. (You may need to install a low-cost splitter so that the single outlet can feed both your PC and your television and some type of filter to keep the signals separate.)

2. Connect your cable modem to your computer's USB port or an Ethernet card (depending on the model).

3. Use the cable company's installation software to configure Windows' network settings to recognize the new connection.

And that's that.

NOTE *Your cable company might not yet offer USB-capable cable modems. In that instance, you'll need to install a 10/100Base-T Ethernet card in your computer and connect an Ethernet cable from this card to your cable modem. It's a trickier installation but no worse than what you have with a typical DSL setup.*

THE ONE DOWNSIDE TO CABLE ACCESS—YOUR NEIGHBORS!

When you connect to your cable company's Internet service, you're connecting to a very large network. Because you're now a client on this giant client/server system, you're sharing various network services—which isn't necessarily a good thing.

Too Many Neighbors = Slower Speed

Although cable access is supposed to deliver much faster download speeds than DSL, in actuality the speed you receive on your connection is affected by the number of other users in your neighborhood. This is because your cable company provides a single 27Mbps connection to each node on its network. Because each node serves multiple homes, the more people accessing the Internet at any given time, the slower each connection will be. (Do the math—two users sharing a 27Mbps connection will have much higher transmission speeds than 10 users—or 100!—sharing the same connection.)

Of course, the cable company can alleviate this problem by installing more nodes and connecting fewer households per node. Nodes come in various sizes and can be combined differently for downstream and upstream use. Although the typical cable company today creates 1500-user nodes, there's nothing stopping them from reconfiguring to just 500 users per node (nothing except the quest for higher profits, of course!).

Unfortunately, there's no way of knowing how many people your cable company assigns to a node, so it's impossible to know what to expect when you subscribe. (You can ask your cable representative what to expect, but they probably won't know.) The only sure thing is that your service *will* slow down during peak usage periods—typically during the early evening hours. If it gets too slow, you can always complain, but the results of such constructive feedback are, unfortunately, variable.

The shared network issue, however, might not be as bad as it once was. The latest version of the DOCSIS standard—DOCSIS 1.1—provides for modems with security enhancements and improved quality of service. Among these improvements is the ability to tie a specific data rate or percentage of total bandwidth to each user on the network. This enables cable companies to assign minimum bandwidth to users, if they so desire, which *should* help to alleviate the current bandwidth-sharing problem.

Nosy Neighbors in the Network Neighborhood

The fact that you're sharing a network with your neighbors creates another type of problem—that of security. Unless you take proper security precautions, it's relatively easy for nosy neighbors to peek at the folders and files on your computer. Because you're all on one big network together, all nearby computers will show up in Windows' Network Neighborhood. Clicking a neighbor's computer will display the contents of their hard disk—and, in some cases, provide access to all the programs and data stored there.

To eliminate unwanted sharing, you want to disable Windows' file- and print-sharing features, as I explained how to do in the DSL discussion. You probably also want to install some type of firewall software, which won't only keep out your neighbors but will also discourage more dedicated crackers from breaking into your system. (Like most DSL systems, many cable broadband systems utilize static IP addresses, or dynamically assigned addresses, that don't change for years on end.)

In addition, most cable providers are now managing the network security issue from their end. System software is used to isolate your connection from your neighbors on the network so that you can't go peering into your neighbors' systems (or vice versa). Check with your cable provider to see how they manage this particular issue.

Using a Satellite for Broadband Connections

If you're too far away from your telco's CO for a DSL connection, and your cable company isn't so state-of-the-art that it doesn't yet offer cable modems, there's still one broadband solution available to you—Internet via digital satellite.

Internet over satellite offers downstream rates of 400Kbps or so, about what you'd expect with a slower DSL connection—which is about eight times faster than analog dial-up connections. (It's much slower than typical cable access, however.) Upstream rates are capped at either 128Kbps or 256Kbps, depending on your service plan—or even slower (33.3Kbps) if you choose a one-way system that uses a standard analog phone line for all upstream transmissions.

The largest provider of satellite Internet access is Hughes Network Systems, the company behind the popular DIRECTV system. For Internet users, Hughes offers the DIRECWAY system (formerly called DirecPC), where Internet data is received by a 24-inch by 36-inch oval dish at 400Kbps speeds. The installation package (including dish and modem) will set you back about $500, with subscription fees in the $60–$70 range. Consult the DIRECWAY Web site (`www.direcway.com`) for more details.

NOTE The basic DIRECWAY dish can't receive DIRECTV signals, and you can't receive DIRECWAY data on a DIRECTV dish. If you want to avail yourself of both services, Hughes offers the DirecDuo system, which uses a single dish for both Internet access and television programming. Aside from the sharing of the dish, all other aspects of DirecDuo are identical to that of DIRECWAY.

How Satellite Internet Works

The bits and bytes that make up the Internet's data don't have to travel to you via some sort of cable—they can also be beamed through the air. This, in essence, is how satellite Internet works—by beaming Internet data off an orbiting satellite down to a satellite dish that's connected to your PC. The data's the same as what you get via DSL or cable; it just travels a longer distance (about 22,000 miles from your dish to the satellite!).

Older satellite systems use the satellite to transmit data downstream but rely on traditional phone lines (and a normal analog modem) to transmit data upstream. Newer two-way systems also let you send data upstream from your dish to the satellite, so you get the same transmission speed upstream and down. (This effectively makes you a satellite broadcaster—which sounds kind of cool, doesn't it?

You'll now look at how the two-way DIRECWAY system operates. When you access a Web page, the request to view that page travels is sent up from your dish to the DIRECWAY satellite (22,000 miles up) and then down (another 22,000 miles) to DIRECWAY's Network Operations Center (NOC) in Maryland. The NOC sends a request to the Web page's server, and the data that makes up that page is then sent from that server back to DIRECWAY's NOC. (This request and fulfillment is all handled over multiple T3 lines.) The NOC then beams the data for the Web page up to the DIRECWAY satellite (22,000 miles up, again); the signal bounces off the satellite back down to your DIRECWAY dish (another 22,000 miles) at 400Kbps. The signal then travels from your dish to your PC.

Because of the huge distances involved, there's some delay (called *latency*) in the receipt of the requested page. Typical latency is around 0.5 seconds, with ping times averaging between 400 milli-seconds (ms) and 600ms. This latency is virtually unnoticeable when you're dealing with typical Web viewing or email communications, but it could be a problem when you're playing real-time multiple-player online games.

Still, the entire process—as complicated as it is—takes place in about a half-second. Not bad for an 88,000-mile trip!

DIRECWAY signals—as with any satellite signals—need direct line-of-sight from satellite to dish. If something gets in the way—even something as small as a leaf on a tree—the signal can be interrupted. In addition, heavy precipitation, in the form of either rain or snow, can disrupt the sat-ellite signal. This can be an issue if you live in an area prone to heavy storms, such as southern Florida in the summertime.

Installing and Configuring Satellite Access

Setting up satellite access requires installing a satellite dish (outside your house) and installing a PCI card modem (inside your PC). You'll start by looking at the dish installation.

Installing a DIRECWAY dish is no different from installing any other of the pizza box–sized dishes currently on the market. DIRECWAY recommends using a professional installer (and if free installation is offered, I recommend you take it) for one-way satellite service and requires pro-fessional installation for the two-way because of Federal Communications Commission (FCC) regulations regarding transmitters.

For one-way installation, it's easy enough that if you're relatively handy with a screwdriver, you can probably tackle it yourself. You have to find a southern-facing space, not obscured by trees or other objects, and then mount the dish in a secure fashion. Following the instructions provided by DIRECWAY, you then aim the dish at the satellite; some dishes come with an LED indicator that lights up when you're on target. The better your aim, the stronger the signal; the stronger the signal, the more reliable your Internet connection.

Now you run a special coaxial cable from the dish back inside your house, where it connects to an external receiver box. If you have two-way satellite, there's a separate transmitter box that connects to a separate cable from the transmitter unit on the satellite dish. The two boxes are then connected to one another with a short DB25 male/male cable. A power supply connects to the receiver, which then feeds power to the transmitter box.

The receiver box connects to the PC via a USB cable. The PC has special DirecWay software that runs in the background under Windows and talks to the transmitter and receiver.

NOTE   You must also have a normal analog modem—either internal or external—connected to your computer for the DIRECWAY service to work. DIRECWAY doesn't supply an analog modem with its system. Further, it must be a hardware modem—not a Winmodem—according to the documentation, but I'd be tempted to try using a Winmodem first before going out and buying a hardware modem just for this purpose.

Wireless Connections via Microwave

Broadband Wireless Access (BWA) provides wireless Internet connections—the only cable involved is from the microwave antenna to the back of your PC. This technology is probably the least-used of all broadband technologies, however; it's available only in a limited number of cities. You have to be within 35 miles of a microwave-transmitting tower to connect to the service.

Like most other broadband technologies, BWA is an "always on" connection. You'll find typical connection speeds to be between 512Kbps and 1.5Mbps downstream, with upstream rates in the 256Kbps neighborhood.

The problem with BWA is that it just isn't competitive with DSL or cable broadband—and it costs too much for the providers to roll out on a large scale. The largest provider of wireless broadband, Sprint, recently put a moratorium on signing new users and announced that it wouldn't be rolling out its service to any new markets.

Dead in the water, in other words.

How Broadband Wireless Access Works

BWA uses a technology called *fixed wireless*. This technology is similar to cellular phone technology in that it uses cell towers to transmit and receive signals via microwaves. The microwave signals are received by a stationary antenna, called a *transceiver*. The transceiver is a diamond-shaped antenna about 13.5 inches by 13.5 inches. You point it at the nearest microwave transmission tower and then connect it to your PC via a modem and network card.

Installing and Configuring Broadband Wireless Access

Installation of broadband wireless is typically done by a professional installer employed by your broadband service provider. The installer will mount the transceiver on the outside of your house (on the roof, typically) and precisely aim it at the nearest transmission tower. The installer then runs a cable from the transceiver to your computer and connects it to an external broadband modem. This modem is connected to your PC via an Ethernet card (yours to provide).

All you have to do is run the installation software to complete the connection.

Downsides to Wireless Broadband

Like cable broadband, BWA is a shared bandwidth technology. This means that when more users log on in your neighborhood, your download speeds will drop.

Like satellite broadband, BWA depends on a clear line of sight to the transmission source. Although physical objects (like trees) don't obstruct microwave signals, you still have to aim the antenna carefully. If it's more than a few degrees off-center, it'll miss the signals coming from the transmission tower.

Of course, the biggest downside is that the BWA infrastructure costs too much to roll out, with the result that it isn't widely available. Unless you're a current subscriber, you probably don't have wireless broadband as an option where you live.

Sharing the Internet Connection

There are two ways to share an Internet connection on a home network:

- ◆ You can connect the Internet directly to one PC and then use Internet Connection Sharing through Windows (which requires Windows 98 Second Edition or higher).

- ◆ You can install a router between the broadband connection device and the PC and have all PCs connect to the router.

To set up connection sharing from Windows 98SE or Windows Me, run the Internet Connection Sharing wizard. In Windows 2000 or XP, the Internet Connection Wizard or New Connection Wizard will ask you about sharing and set it up automatically. The main drawback to this sharing method is that the main computer must remain up-and-running whenever any other computer needs the Internet. Another drawback is that heavy Internet usage by one of the sharing PCs can bog down the main PC.

The router alternative costs more—$100 or more for a router. Further, it works only with cable and DSL; you can't share a satellite or wireless connection that way. However, it does allow each computer to be an equal Internet participant, and it doesn't rely on—or slow down—any one computer.

In this chapter, you learned about modems and other Internet connection methods, including how to purchase, install, and troubleshoot them. Up next in Chapter 29, "Viruses and Other Nasty Bugs," is a discussion of the viruses, worms, and other nasties that you can potentially encounter in your Internet adventures and how to prevent them from hurting your system.

Chapter 29

Viruses and Other Nasty Bugs

◆ Types of Viruses and How They Work

◆ Virus Hoaxes

◆ How to Protect Your PC from Viruses

◆ Antivirus Software and Other Resources

◆ How to Know if Your PC Is Infected

◆ Troubleshooting Tips

Introduction

Writing most of this book is a lot of fun. Fixing things is like putting together a puzzle—it's challenging and provides rewards in the end (a completed puzzle or a recovered hard disk). In either case, your biggest opponents are bad electrical power, buggy software, or (if you're supporting others) inattentive users.

Viruses are a whole different story. With viruses, you actually have a human opponent and sometimes a competent one.

Computer viruses are increasing at an alarming rate. In 1986 there was one known computer virus; three years later, that number had increased to six, and by 1990 the total had jumped to 80. Beginning in 1991, viruses were being discovered at the rate of one per week. As of the last quarter in 2002, approximately 1200 viruses (including variants) were being processed per month, and the total number of known viruses topped 80,000 in early 2003. Although most of these new nasty viruses are variations of original viruses, they're nasty just the same.

A humorous anecdote came in the form of a technical support call I received a while back from a woman who claimed her computer had 50,000 viruses. When I questioned how she knew this, she said she had just installed the latest Norton AntiVirus program and that was what it told her. As it turned out, she was reading the splash screen that appeared when she launched the program, which proudly announced that it could detect more than 50,000 viruses—sigh.

People often ask at this point, "Why do people write viruses?" I wish I didn't have to answer this question. The answer is, viruses are written by computer criminals. Some people just plain get their jollies making other people's lives difficult, and they think it's clever to write viruses. They're just childish. Virus authors exploit not cleverness but rather trust. Most viruses attack PCs via portals that exist because of *trust* in the computer community, not stupidity on the part of users. It's rather like this: suppose you lived in a community where everyone knew everyone else, so folks didn't lock their doors. How clever need one be in order to be a thief? Not very—the thief *knows* it's easy to get into any house. Would you applaud or be impressed with the skill of such a thief? Of course not. That's what today's virus authors are—mere children screaming for attention.

And that brings us to the topic of "ScriptKiddies." Instead of socializing with school friends, they're home wreaking havoc on the Internet. They use freely available virus-maker programs to modify existing viruses and code, which could translate into more attacks such as the ILOVEYOU and Melissa viruses. They also scan networks to find computers they can compromise. Once they find a target, they have no respect for privacy. They gain control of your machine through Trojan programs that have been installed on your machine (which are usually installed when you run unscanned executable files that you downloaded or received via email). Once they get in, ScriptKiddies get their kicks by crashing your machine, playing with your CD drive door or your mouse, or stealing your password files so that they can crack them later.

There *are* people who get their kicks this way, and that's why antivirus software can be a nice support tool. It does the job that you and I have neither the time nor the knowledge for—monitoring the PC for common viruses and suspicious virus-like behavior. Good antivirus software should be able to prevent, detect, and remove viruses without destroying valuable data. It must also be easy to update because new viruses are created every day, and software that can detect and clean every virus except the one you've currently got is less than useless. Good software, combined with educated users and regular backups, can make virus attacks less likely—and less serious.

This chapter provides an overview of viruses, including the most common terminology, the most common ways a virus enters your system, and tips on how to prevent and detect a virus.

Types of Viruses

What's a computer virus? A *virus* is a program that has been designed to replicate and spread on its own, preferably without a user's knowledge. *Virus* has come to be a generic term that people use these days to describe any of a group of programs designed to replicate themselves and spread (much like life, if you think about it). Some are pranks and do no damage, and others are intentionally destructive computer programs. Not all viruses are malicious or even intentional. While I was doing some contract work for IBM in the late 1990s, a virus shut down the entire IBM global network for the better part of a working day. What was this killer virus? It was a badly written program that was supposed to post a single Christmas greeting on everyone's computer screen in a single work area. Unfortunately, it wasn't written very well, and it posted thousands of copies of the greeting on every terminal in the entire IBM worldwide network. By definition, it was a virus.

This section outlines various types of viruses, how they enter your computer, and the type of damage they do once they've infected your machine. You'll explore the following:

◆ File infectors and boot-sector viruses

◆ Macro viruses

◆ Worms

◆ Web applet viruses

◆ Spyware

NOTE *Myth: viruses can't harm your hardware—they affect only the data stored on your computer. Truth: a few viruses can and do attack the Basic Input/Output System (BIOS) of a computer, rendering the computer useless and requiring that a new BIOS be installed.*

In the past, classifying viruses was much simpler than it is today. The two most common types of viruses a few years ago were file infectors and boot-sector viruses. But just as life continues to get more complicated as technology evolves, so do viruses. These days, a virus can be classified as, for example, a file-infector macro virus or a polymorphic stealth Web applet virus. Table 29.1 breaks down the types of known viruses (courtesy of `www.sophos.com`).

Virus creators are constantly reinventing the wheel to develop the killer, undetectable virus. I'll cover how to protect your system from viruses later, but for now you'll look at the types of viruses and their techniques.

TABLE 29.1: VIRUS TYPES

TYPE	PERCENTAGE OF KNOWN VIRUSES
Macro virus	26.1
Trojan horse	26.1
Executable	19.2
Scripts	6.8
Other (Unix, boot sector, Internet worms, Macintosh, multipartite)	21.8

File Infectors and Boot-Sector Viruses

File infectors begin their dirty work whenever the executable file to which they're attached is run. They may proceed directly to certain areas of the disk where specific files sit (such as the partition tables or `COMMAND.COM`) or hide in memory for just the right moment. (File infectors are also called program infectors or parasitic viruses.)

Another strain of file infector is made up of two split programs. One is the top program that won't register as a virus when a virus scanner runs, and the other contains an algorithm that, once the first program is resident, changes part of the first program's code to make it a virus.

The following lists the file types susceptible to viruses:

- EXE
- COM
- BIN
- DLL
- SYS
- DRV
- OVL
- VXD

Boot-sector viruses aren't as common as they used to be. They infect your system when it reads an infected drive or floppy disk. Today, floppies are declining as a major source of virus infection, accounting for 68 percent of all reported infections in 1998, some 38 percent in 1999, and less than 2 percent today. This probably has to do with the fact that fewer and fewer people use floppies today.

These types of viruses generally prefer hard drives, but a minority, including the Stoned virus, infect floppies. They're loaded into memory when the PC is booted from a drive that contains an infected disk. You're probably wondering, "What if the disk isn't really bootable (in other words, it has no `COMMAND.COM` file) and the screen displays the message `Non-system disk error`?" That doesn't stop anything, unfortunately. Once the computer attempts to boot from the infected disk, it's too late—the PC has to read the boot sector of the floppy to know it isn't bootable. During the read, the virus wakes up and springs into action.

Macro Viruses: Melissa Isn't the Girl Next Door

Macro viruses are one of the most widespread viruses. Infections that spread through email attachments—the source of macro viruses—increased from 32 percent in 1998 to 56 percent in 1999. Email attachments are the biggest source of macro viruses, and floppies are the typical carrier for boot-sector viruses. You can infect your system simply by opening a document with a macro virus attached. As their name implies, macro viruses reside as macros in a document.

How do macro viruses work? Macro viruses are written in the macro language of an application. Applications that currently permit the use of macros, such as word processing programs and spreadsheet programs, are at risk not only of infection but also of infecting others. Macro viruses spread when infected documents are transferred. Most of the macro viruses around right now are designed to infect Microsoft Word and Microsoft Excel.

Many macro viruses do nothing or almost nothing: they spread, but that's about all. Some people believe that these relatively unobtrusive examples of macro viruses aren't the product of hackers at all but are mutations that first appeared as the result of random bit scrambling in somebody's download and wound up propagating, unseen and unnoticed, as time passed. On the other hand, there are destructive macro viruses that overwrite data, modify the contents of documents, and even send documents via email.

Melissa, Concept, DMV, and Nuclear are names of some macro viruses. Melissa, which infected Microsoft Word 97 and Word 2000 documents, was so widespread that it brought computer viruses to the evening news. Once an infected document was opened, the virus attempted to locate the user's Microsoft Outlook address book, and if it found one, it emailed a copy of the infected document to up to 50 people. Microsoft included security against macro viruses in Word 2000, but Melissa was intelligent enough to disable those security dialog boxes, so users wouldn't be aware that the document they were trying to open was infected.

NOTE *Melissa was not only a macro virus; she was a worm, too. To understand more about worms, see the section "Worms Wiggle Their Way through Email," later in this chapter.*

Concept and DMV worked in pretty much the same way: they forced you to save documents as templates and replicated themselves to your other documents. The main difference between the two is that DMV used the AutoClose macro to install itself in the Normal template, and Concept used AutoOpen. Nuclear could be destructive, however. On April 5, it deleted `COMMAND.COM` and zeroed out `MSDOS.SYS` and `IO.SYS` so that not only would your system fail to boot because it had no command shell, it wouldn't tell you what the problem was because the SYS files were missing.

That's the bad news. The good news is that Microsoft got on the ball and created the Word Macro Virus Protection Tool (available from `www.microsoft.com`) to alert you of the presence of macros in your documents (not macro viruses, just macros) and allow you to open documents without activating the macros. Once they're open, you can look at the list of attached macros. If you see anything called Insert Payload or Payload, you've got the Nuclear virus. AAAZAO and AAAZFS indicate the presence of the Concept virus. Other tools can clean the viruses from your system.

Worms Wiggle Their Way through Email

The major trait of a worm virus is its ability to propagate itself via email. Although viruses technically need another transportation method, worms can transport themselves. A worm program can be sent as an email attachment. Once you open the attachment, the worm locates your email address book and sends out the infected attachment. You can imagine how quickly this type of virus can spread, considering how many of us rely on email as a means to send documents, whether personal or work related.

As you learned previously in this chapter, our friend Melissa was a worm—she propagated by locating Microsoft Outlook address books and sending herself, infected Word document that she was, to your friends and colleagues. But alas, poor Melissa, she lost her place as the most popular worm. Another famous worm was the Love Bug virus. In the simplest terms, thousands of people received emails with the subject line "ILOVEYOU." Thousands of people threw caution to the wind

A DAY IN THE LIFE OF A MACRO VIRUS

Here's a relatively benign example of how a macro virus works: ShareFun is a Microsoft Word macro virus that attempts to spread over email attachments. Every time somebody opens an infected file in Word, the chance of the virus becoming activated and spreading is one in four. You might open the document once, twice, or even a hundred times and you might luck out, but your odds each time are one in four that the virus will activate. If it does, and if Microsoft Mail is running at the same time, the virus will try to send email messages to three people randomly selected from the local MSMail alias list. (It's harmless if you're not running MSMail.) The subject of the messages is always the same: "You have GOT to see this!" The message is empty of text, but it contains a link to a file attachment called DOC1.DOC, which is infected by the virus. If recipients double-click the attachment, they'll get infected by the virus and could spread the infection further with their own MSMail. The virus does nothing destructive; it merely propagates and only when the circumstances are there for it. (Incidentally, this virus isn't technically an "email virus" because the recipients don't literally get infected from your email; rather, they get infected by trying to open the attachment.)

ShareFun also has code to protect itself: if you try to analyze the virus in Word for Windows by looking at the "macro" using either Tools ➤ Macro or File ➤ Templates, the virus will execute and infect your Word NORMAL.DOT template.

---

when they read the subject line and opened the attachment. Oooops. The ILOVEYOU worm went right to work, wiggling its way into users' Outlook Express address books and propagating itself. (At least it wasn't propagation without love.) Not only did the Love Bug virus propagate via email, but it scanned users' PCs for passwords, which were sent back to the originator of the virus. It also copied itself over numerous file types, including MP3, JS, and JPEG.

The number of complex, high-level worms is on the rise. One of the most notable was Nimda (the reverse of Admin). It spread itself in multiple ways: by email, by open network shares, and by vulnerable Microsoft Internet Information Services (IIS) Web servers. Once a server was compromised, Nimda would create a local account with administrator privileges and copy itself to multiple locations. It used JavaScript to modify files with .htm, .html, and .asp extensions. When visitors browsed the infected pages, they were presented with a file named readme.eml, which then spread itself through Outlook Express as an email attachment without the users' knowledge. And once the attachment reached the recipient, what made Nimda so dangerous was that a simple *preview* of the infected message could cause it to spread even further! As a result, the worm spread like wildfire and affected servers worldwide.

WARNING *A good way to avoid worms is to never open any file attachments from unknown sources and to listen to, or read, the national news. You can also visit the bug alert sites mentioned in this chapter. Viruses and their creators have been getting a lot of attention in the press lately. Press reports alerted computer users about the Love Bug and so limited the damage it caused.*

One of the fastest worms was the Sapphire/Slammer SQL worm. In January 2003, it hit with a vengeance. It's reported that Slammer spread worldwide within 10 minutes of its introduction into the wild. Some other interesting statistics were that at its peak, Slammer was doubling in size (the number of compromised hosts) every 8¹/₂ seconds and scanning 55 million Internet Protocol (IP) addresses (looking for more to infect) per second, and it infected more than 75,000 victims.

So what was Slammer's nasty payload? It allowed for the attacker to execute arbitrary (and likely malicious) code on SQL servers. But although that was important to know, the process of the worm scanning the Internet at the rate of 55 million addresses per second was enough to crash some of the Internet backbone. Not all viruses or worms have malicious code. Some just want to consume all the bandwidth they can to cause network crashes. And if someone can bring down the entire Internet, they will.

A recent worm that has caused a lot of consternation is the Sobig worm (`W32/Sobig.f@MM`). Using its own Simple Mail Transport Protocol (SMTP) engine, it propagates itself in attempts to fill up mailboxes.

Blaster (`W32.Msblast.A`, `W32.Lovsan.worm`, and other variants) has also shown its ugly face recently. It's a worm that exploits a vulnerability in Windows' Distributed Component Object Modem (DCOM) Remote Procedure Call (RPC) interface. In clearer language, it allows a hacker to execute code on your system, which is something you never want. Microsoft has a patch to guard against it, and if you're running Windows NT/2000, Windows XP, or Windows 2003, you had better download and install the patch.

Real-Time Messaging Viruses

As if email viruses aren't enough, you also have to worry when you're talking with your friends in real-time. If you're fond of Instant Messaging (IM) services such as MSN Messenger, AOL Messenger, or ICQ, you'll probably notice an increase in viruses and worms there, too. If you see a flood of emoticons (smiley or winky faces and so on) and then receive a message that prompts you to open a file, don't open it!

MSN Messenger was attacked in May and June of 2001 by two worms. The first was the W32/Hello worm, which was triggered when you received a message from another MSN Messenger user or when you added another MSN Messenger user to your contact list. The worm attempted to spread itself by sending a message that read, "I have a file for u. its real funny." If you opened the HELLO.EXE file, the worm installed itself on your system and continued to spread. Soon afterward, MSN Messenger users began to see the Choke worm, which operated in a similar manner. Its attachment was an executable file named with antipolitical overtones.

Fortunately, these two introductory IM worms did not do anything damaging—they only propagated themselves. But what they did do was open the door to using IM services as yet another vehicle for virus distribution (as if there weren't enough vehicles already).

Web Applet Viruses

Danger, Will Robinson—browsing the Web may be hazardous. A newer type of virus can exist in three popular Web scripting languages: ActiveX, JavaScript, and Java. Although these languages allow for much of the gee-whiz features of the Web, such as 3D animation, it's possible for these languages to transfer virus programs to your system. The transfer is triggered by you simply opening a Web page that contains infected ActiveX controls or Java/JavaScript code. Once the virus makes its way into your system, it may corrupt files or directories or do other types of damage—what happens depends on the actual virus.

To date there hasn't been a large-scale outbreak of a Web applet virus. However, as more consumers log on to the Internet, it's a safe bet that you'll be hearing more about this type of virus in the future.

NOTE *For information about how to protect yourself from Web applet viruses, see the section "Tips for Protecting Your PC Against Viruses" later in this chapter.*

Spyware

Spyware is a newer form of malicious software designed to ruin people's computing experiences. Spyware literally spies on you as you surf the Internet, and reports your travels back to someone else. Some spyware applications can even take over your computer. If you get popup ads even when your browser is closed, chances are you have spyware installed on your computer. In a nutshell, here are some of the things that spyware programs are capable of:

◆ Stealing information from your computer, such as credit card numbers, email addresses, and Web surfing habits

◆ Spamming your email account

◆ Sending unwanted pop-up ads to you

◆ Slowing down and/or crashing your system

VIRUS NAMING CONVENTIONS

How are viruses named? First, you'll see a prefix, such as W97M. This is normally the platform where the virus operates. W97M is a Word 97 macro virus. Next, you'll see the virus family name, such as Melissa. Sometimes you'll see a suffix, such as .a. This indicates the variant of the virus. In certain situations, a virus will have an alias that's more commonly known than the official name. W32/Ska, also known as Happy99, is one such virus.

Here's a list of some common virus prefixes:

A97M Microsoft Access macro viruses native to Microsoft Access 97.

AOL America Online (AOL) Trojans.

Java Viruses written in Java.

Trojan/Troj Trojan horses.

W32 32-bit Windows viruses.

W95 Microsoft Windows 95 viruses. These may affect Microsoft Windows 98, too.

W97M Microsoft Word macro viruses native to (and applicable only to) Microsoft Word 97.

WNT 32-bit Windows viruses that can infect Microsoft Windows NT.

X97M Excel Macro viruses native to Microsoft Excel 97.

VBS Viruses written in Visual Basic Script.

I'm guessing that you haven't downloaded any files that claim to be spyware, just as you haven't ever seen any files that say "hey, download this great new virus." What happens is that programmers build a spyware applet into another application you download. When you install the application, the spyware is installed as well, without your knowledge or consent. And whenever you turn your computer on, it runs silently in the background, watching… waiting.…

Spyware is often bundled with popular Internet programs. Examples are KaZaA, GATOR, Grokster, NetPal, and DoubleClick. Spyware writers pay the distributors of these software programs (and others) to include their spyware. Why? It's a great marketing research tool. If a business knows which Web sites you frequent, it can send you targeted popup ads, hoping to get you to make online purchases.

Another way you can get spyware is just by visiting a Web site that is designed to download it automatically on to your system. Using Internet Explorer's Active X installation option, Web sites can automatically install spyware on your computer the moment you visit the site. And of course, you won't even know.

Worried that you have spyware installed? Most anti-virus programs won't detect spyware. Here's a few sites that can help:

◆ www.spykiller.com

◆ www.enigmasoftwaregroup.com

◆ www.spywareinfo.com

◆ www.spywareguide.com

It's not enough anymore to have a good antivirus program. It seems like you now need an anti-spyware applet too. I recommend scanning and protecting your system now, before your annoying popup ad problem turns into a stolen credit card number.

Techniques of Attack

Virus creators get their kicks from tricking you—the more complex the virus, the longer it takes investigators to figure out how it works and how it spreads. A virus may use one or several sneaky modes of operation covered in the following sections.

Polymorphic Viruses

A *polymorphic* virus changes, or mutates, so that it can't be detected by antivirus software. For example, back in 1998 a polymorphic macro virus named Excel8_Extras appeared. It created an infected spreadsheet in the Microsoft Excel startup directory and then added a *randomly generated* macro and module name to infected documents. Because the virus was able to randomly generate new names, it took longer for investigators to pinpoint the virus.

Multipartite Viruses

Just to make things maximally confusing, some viruses have a boot-sector portion *and* a program-infector portion; these are called *multipartite* viruses. For example, researchers discovered that the Hare virus was a polymorphic, multipartite virus that infected COM and EXE files as well as Master Boot Records (MBRs) on hard drives and boot sectors of floppy disks. Upon execution, the virus infected the MBR and became resident, infecting any COM or EXE file that executed.

Stealth Viruses

Some viruses are said to be *stealth* viruses. A stealth virus attempts to hide itself by keeping a copy of the parts of the disk that it infected, *before* it infected the disk. Then, when it detects that a virus scanner is looking for it, it shows the scanner the uninfected copy of the file, as if to say, "Nobody here but us chickens." Now, note that the stealth feature of a virus works only if the virus is active in memory, which won't be the case if you've first booted from a clean, write-protected DOS floppy. Always do that before running an important virus scan.

WARNING   Many program infectors (and all boot sector viruses) become Terminate and Stay Resident (TSR) programs—which is a good reason to install a TSR scanner that can constantly monitor your system for viruses. TSRs take system memory, which tips you off that you may have a virus. If your system memory doesn't add up to 640KB, then you might have a virus.

Trojan Horses

A *Trojan horse* program acts like the Trojan horse of Greek mythology. A malevolent program is hidden inside another, apparently useful, program. While the "useful" program is running, the malevolent part does something nasty, such as erase your File Allocation Table (FAT) and directory structure.

The only good thing about Trojans is that they're self-limiting: once an evil Trojan erases your hard disk, it has erased itself as well. Today, instead of running on private email systems such as bulletin board systems as they did in the past, Trojans (which now typically have a replication component) are finding their way to the Internet and the World Wide Web.

Pure Trojans seem to have gone out of style. Trojans instead show up in the virus world as the initial source of infection for some viruses. A virus that injects itself into COM or EXE files is also a Trojan because it's waiting for you to run that formerly useful program: once you run an infected copy of any application, you're waking the virus up.

Time Bombs and Logic Bombs

Then there's the bomb. There are *time bombs* and *logic bombs*. The *bomb* is a piece of code embedded in a program or the operating system itself that waits for a particular event to occur. When that event occurs, the logic bomb "goes off," doing some kind of damage.

Logic bombs have been around nearly since the beginning of computing. An early one showed up in a mainframe payroll program. The program's creator had inserted a clause in the payroll program that said, "If you find I'm not on the payroll, erase all payroll files."

Bombs show up as the more destructive part of viruses. They include instructions such as, "If it's Friday the 13th, erase the hard disk" or "If the worm has succeeded in making 10 copies of itself, erase the hard disk."

An Example of a Virus at Work

By now you know that a virus can use a combination of approaches in attacking your data. A virus might work in the following way:

1. Assume that you double-clicked one of those animated holiday cards sent to you in an email as an EXE file—an executable program. The virus is then introduced to your system via the infected EXE file (an example is a Trojan horse). Either this Trojan is hidden in an application program that has been doctored by the virus creator or it's the Trojan portion of a virus that's injected into a program file or the boot record by the worm portion.

2. Once the program with the Trojan is activated by a certain event, such as your running a particular application, the virus is awakened. It installs itself in the operating system as a logic bomb, waiting for an opportunity to activate the worm and/or activate the destructive portion of itself.

3. The logic bomb activates the worm portion whenever an acceptable host presents itself. Some viruses replicate only onto floppies from the hard disk. Other viruses infect any program file that gets activated, whether on the floppy disk or the hard disk. Every time the worm copies itself onto another disk or program, it activates a built-in counter that keeps track of how many copies it has made.

4. Eventually, the destructive part of the virus may be activated, either by an event, such as running a program, by a date occurring (such as Friday the 13th), or by a certain number of replications. When the destructive portion activates, the virus may do something as innocuous as flashing a message on the screen or as damaging as erasing the hard disk.

Virus Hoaxes

As if viruses and the very real threat they pose to computer users everywhere aren't enough to cause you concern, there's a cottage industry springing up that's intended to cause panic and anxiety: hoaxes. Hoaxes are just that. They're fake virus warnings initially transmitted by a malicious person who relies on the likelihood that people will send them to everyone they know thinking they're doing a good deed. Sadly, no threat is averted, no virus is exposed, and no one is helped. What actually happens is a great deal of wasted time, confusion, and higher blood pressure.

In fact, virus hoaxes can be just as destructive as viruses themselves. In many cases, the hoax is helpful enough to include the resolution to remove a virus. The tip will tell you to go to your `C:\Windows\System` folder (or some other folder) and look for a file named *whatever.exe*. If you see that file, you know you're infected, so you must delete that file immediately! But, the problem is that the file is a legitimate file, and in most cases it's needed to run some aspect of Windows. So once you've deleted the file (and emptied your Recycle Bin for good measure), you've just messed up your system.

To avoid falling into this trap, if you get a virus warning from anyone, you should first check with an authoritative antivirus Web site and research whether the message you're reading is about a real virus or a hoax. (See the "Resources: Stay Informed" section later in this chapter for a list of helpful Web sites.) If it's a hoax, please pass that onto the person who sent you the message and inform them of this tragic misuse of the Internet.

Tips for Protecting Your PC Against Viruses

The most effective way to avoid catching viruses is to shut off your computer...permanently. Don't like that idea? How about just removing your floppy disk drives, disconnecting from your network, and never connecting to the Internet?

Effective as those means are, they're not much good in the real world. Never opening emails so as not to catch viruses is sort of like cutting off your hand so as not to get a hangnail. Sure, it prevents what you were trying to prevent, but it doesn't give you much good use of your hand—or your computer. In the real world, what can you do about viruses?

Purchase virus-protection software, install it on your system, and use it. See the "Antivirus Software" section later in this chapter for a list of the best virus-protection/detection software.

Be sure to update your virus-protection software. Most antivirus software will automatically link to the vendor's site and download detection code for the newest viruses. Or you can check the vendor's site from time to time to make sure your software is up-to-date. However you do it, do it often.

Don't open email attachments from people you don't know. This is critically important because many newer viruses spread by sending infected files over the Internet as email attachments. Sometimes, this includes people you do know, who may be unwittingly passing on an infected file to you. It's important to note that simply opening an email with an infected attachment won't introduce the virus into your system.

Don't download files from the Internet unless you have virus-protection software that scans them for viruses. Also, think twice about the site you're considering downloading from. Is it a company with its reputation at stake or an unknown individual?

Consider disabling your browser's ability to handle pages that contain JavaScript, Java code, or ActiveX controls. This doesn't necessarily mean that you won't be able to view the page—just the parts that contain ActiveX controls or Java/JavaScript. You can always reset your browser to handle those components if you need to do so.

If you don't want to disable your browser for ActiveX, Java, and JavaScript, consider the source before entering a site. If you know nothing about the site, think twice before entering. There are a lot of people out there who have Web sites, a lot of time on their hands, and nothing to lose.

Keep up with the news. Major outbreaks are reported on national, even local (depending on where you live) news, in newspapers, and on Web sites such as www.cnet.com.

Back up your data frequently. I've already said this: viruses are scary, but not backing up regularly is scarier. Any of a large number of random external events—flood, fire, power surges, vibration—could destroy data on your hard disk, and it could happen at any time. Backing up regularly is more important than keeping up-to-date on the latest virus-buster programs.

If you're managing a network, centralize your applications. Install all programs used in the department on one computer (preferably one not used as a workstation) and then back up all the application software from that computer. Protect this computer from virus infection with your life. If you get a virus, you can use either the files from the computer or backup floppies to restore applications to the newly cleaned computer.

Don't use pirated software, especially games. First of all, it's not nice to use commercial software that you didn't pay for. Most software companies are fairly small operations, no more than 10 to 15 people. These aren't large, faceless corporations that "deserve" (in the eyes of some people) to be taken down a peg or two. Most software operations are mom-and-pop operations that just barely get by. Using copies of software you didn't buy is just plain theft. People who use illegal copies are thieves, plain and simple—and cowardly thieves, to boot. There's good, cheap software in all areas, so "just say no" when someone offers you a copy of a program. More relevant to the present discussion, many virus attacks I've heard of seem to have come from pirated software— another good reason not to use copies.

Don't assume bundled CD-ROM software is safe. Although you might think all software distributed on CD-ROM is virus-free and safe to use, there have been cases where companies inadvertently distributed a virus on their CD. Microsoft Word macro viruses are a particular problem, so be sure to scan those files before opening them.

Avoid Web sites that cater to self-proclaimed "hackers." These sites tend to mainly have pirated games anyway, and the software generally isn't screened. The same idiots who think it's okay to crack the copy protection on a game and give it away free also think it's okay to insert a virus in the cracked game. In some odd Robin Hood manner, they view it as "just punishment" for anyone *else* who uses illegally copied software.

Be wary of shareware programs without documentation. If they don't tell you how to use it, maybe you shouldn't! Don't run the program.

Stick to big shareware download sites such as Tucows or PC Magazine and Web sites that register their users. Most reputable Web sites these days ask that you register when you go there. Then they don't let you upload files until they've checked that you're who you say you are. That way, if you upload a virus, they can come after you. This makes people less likely to upload viruses.

Write-protect any floppy that you put in your drive if possible. Floppy disk drives are becoming less common, but they're still used enough to cause virus problems. Get in the habit of leaving the floppy drive empty. Boot-sector viruses can't get at your hard disk it you don't boot from an infected floppy. You can read and write data on a floppy with an infected boot record for years and never be infected. But boot from the floppy—even if it's not a bootable floppy—and you've got the virus. If you're not careful, you'll find that now and then you try to reboot the machine with a floppy in drive A:. Keep the drive empty, and it won't happen.

Antivirus Software

Quite a few antivirus software packages are available that'll search your PC for viruses and alert you if incoming files are infected. The following products are well worth considering:

- Command AntiVirus (from Command Software Systems at `www.authentium.com`)

- F-Secure Anti-Virus (from F-Secure at `www.datafellows.com`)

- McAfee Internet Guard Dog (from McAfee at `www.mcafee.com`)

- McAfee VirusScan for Windows (from McAfee at `www.mcafee.com`)

- Norton AntiVirus (from Symantec at `www.symantec.com`)

- PC-cillin (from Trend Micro at `www.antivirus.com`)

- AVG Anti-Virus (from Grisoft at `www.grisoft.com`)

Resources: Stay Informed

You should understand that you're on shaky ground here. There are really no totally reliable sources of data on virus prevalence. As I said earlier, the people doing most of the yelling about what a big danger viruses pose to life on Earth are generally the people who stand to gain the most from the panic—vendors of antivirus products. Personally, I'm concerned about viruses, but I haven't panicked and I don't advise panic on your part.

The following URLs provide current lists of the top viruses, as well as virus descriptions and recent news about viruses, including hoaxes:

- McAfee AVERT Virus Information Library: `vil.nai.com/villib/alpha.asp`

- Symantec: `www.symantec.com/avcenter/`

- The WildList Organization International: `www.wildlist.org/WildList/`

- F-Secure: `www.f-secure.com/virus-info/`

- ICSA, division of TruSecure: `www.icsalabs.com/html/communities/antivirus/index.shtm`

- Virus Bulletin: `www.virusbtn.com`

Virus Hoax Lists

When you receive a warning in your email to be on the lookout for the "latest and greatest" virus and you can't find any information about it in the virus lists mentioned in the section "Resources: Stay Informed," it could be a hoax. The following are some sites you can check for the latest virus hoaxes:

- McAfee: `vil.nai.com/VIL/hoaxes.asp`

- Symantec: `www.symantec.com/avcenter/hoax.html`

- Trend Micro: `www.antivirus.com/pc-cillin/vinfo/hoaxes/hoax.asp`

- F-Secure Hoax Warnings: `www.f-secure.com/virus-info/hoax/`

- Virus Hoax Listings: `www.virusbtn.com/Hoax/hoaxlist.html`

Viral Symptoms

How can you tell if your PC is infected with a virus? The following are some of the most common symptoms:

- Files or programs become corrupted or aren't working properly. For example, a Microsoft Word document that was fine an hour ago now includes text or formatting that you didn't insert.

- New programs or files appear mysteriously in a directory.

- Odd warning messages, error messages, or random dialog boxes appear on-screen.

- A drive name has been renamed.

- Programs or files suddenly disappear from directories.

- Memory problems occur—for example, not enough memory when you should have no problem running the applications and files you're running.

- Visual elements appear; distortions of the screen and strange visual effects can suddenly start appearing on your screen.

Troubleshooting Tips

The following procedures have been helpful to me in coping with a virus attack. I recommend you make a form for yourself from this list, arranging the list in two columns so that you've got one side free for checking things off and for your notes.

1. Calm down.

2. Grab a pen and pad so you can write out the diagnostic steps you take. It might be hard to believe that you could forget important details, but under the stress caused by a virus attack, anyone could be subject to bouts of amnesia. To keep from forgetting anything, make two lists. The first list should record what you've done in the recent past that may have allowed entry, such as opening an executable file from a friend of a friend. The second list should detail the steps you take to detect, isolate, and (you hope) destroy the virus. To remember what you've done as the hunt continues, you'll want to reread your notes for the next few days—or months. Writing down what you're about to do also forces you to think about the next step. That mental pause may prevent you from taking an unnecessary step or making a dangerous error.

3. If you haven't already powered down the computer, record all information being displayed on-screen inside the virus dialog box: the type of virus reported, in which files it is contained, and the exact Windows message.

4. Note your most recent actions and computer symptoms (leaving the screen on for this step may help your memory).

5. In the rare case that your PC was infected by a floppy disk, note the names of all floppy disks lying around and whether you received disks from anyone recently (if so, did you insert them in the floppy drive?) or gave disks to anyone else recently. Remove all floppies from drives and remember to discard all the floppy disks that were around the infected PC.

6. If you must save your on-screen data, save it to an empty floppy and mark the disk *immediately* as "Potentially Infected."

7. If at all possible, access the Internet on another system and look up the most recent virus list. Compare the reported symptoms with those manifested by the computer.

8. If there's a match, determine whether your antivirus software needs updating to detect the viru infecting your PC.

9. Power down (just rebooting may not oust the virus). Then reboot from the hard drive and ru your antivirus software. Download the latest virus detectors from your antivirus software ver dor's site.

10. Write down all files reported as infected. If no backups or hard copies exist for infected files consider making copies to another floppy. If you make backups, mark those floppies as "Potentially Infected."

11. Rescan the hard drive with your antivirus program.

Don't let fear of viruses destroy your use and enjoyment of your PC. The analogies between saf sex and safe computing, although now trite, are very accurate. Have a good time, but use protection At the minimum, use antivirus software and back up data regularly. Don't put original program flop pies in your PC's drives unless they have write-protect tabs on them. On a final note: if you know someone who's a virus author, report her to the authorities.

In the next chapter, you will learn about laptop and notebook computers.

Chapter 30

Notebook/Laptop Computers

- ◆ QuickSteps: Upgrading and Maintaining Your Laptop
- ◆ Upgrading Your Memory
- ◆ Upgrading Your Hard Disk
- ◆ Recharging and Replacing Batteries
- ◆ Maintaining and Protecting Your Laptop
- ◆ Syncing Data with Your PC or PDA
- ◆ Troubleshooting Tips

Introduction

It used to be that laptops were considered either luxury toys or necessary evils in the computing world. There were only two classes of people that owned them: those who had the money to burn on the new toy and those who absolutely had no other choice because they needed mobile computing for their job. Not anymore.

Over the past several years, laptops are being sold more and more in lieu of desktops, and laptops have overtaken desktops in sales volume. The primary reason for this shift is that technology has gotten better, allowing laptops to become more convenient (lighter and smaller) and narrowing the gap between desktop and laptop performance. In addition, prices have fallen, and many computer manufacturers have decided to market convenience as a feature. After all, if you could get on the Internet from anywhere without using cables, why wouldn't you?

In some respects, upgrading and maintaining your laptop or notebook computer is much simpler than taking care of a desktop machine. On one hand, the jobs you can take care of on your own usually are plainly indicated in your owner's manual and often require nothing more than unplugging an old module and plugging in a new one. On the other hand, you must leave some things in the hands of experts with specialized equipment. Again, your task is simple: put your laptop in a box, ship it off, and pay the nice people who are taking care of you.

Between these two clear extremes are upgrades and fixes that require taking the laptop apart and doing the kind of minor surgery that, with a little instruction, you can typically handle on your own. In this chapter, I'll identify which types of upgrades and fixes fall into each of the previously mentioned categories and give you instructions for accomplishing them. The following are some examples of all three classes of upgrade:

- You want to add a modem. For most laptops, the process is simple: you locate the PC Card slot on your laptop, open the cover, and slide in your new credit card–sized modem. Okay, you might need to install the drivers too, but with PC Cards it's almost automatic.

- You've decided to install a larger hard disk or more memory. These are two tasks you *can* handle yourself, but both entail opening a system that might not have been designed to be taken apart easily. If you're adventurous, handy with small tools, and want to save some money, you can do the job. If you have a lot invested in your laptop and don't feel that experimenting is such a good idea, companies that specialize in laptop upgrades will do the job quickly and for relatively little money, and they will usually guarantee their work.

- You want to upgrade your Pentium III laptop to a Pentium 4 Mobile processor. This you can't do on your own. The reason is that laptop Central Processing Units (CPUs) are generally surface mounted rather than socket mounted. You can't remove a surface-mounted laptop CPU on your own. It takes special tools and expert skills.

I'll be spending time in this chapter on the first and second categories in the preceding list. Let me also reiterate that such items as hard drives and memory modules, although designed to be easily replaced, do involve opening your system.

WARNING   You should read and reread the terms and conditions of any service agreements and/or warranties that came with your laptop. In some cases, opening your laptop and tinkering with its innards can void such agreements.

Whenever you do your own upgrading, be mindful of several important factors:

◆ Depending on which brand of laptop you have, opening the system could mean removing the screen and/or the keyboard before you can get to the object of your replacement tasks. Getting from point A to point B in a laptop usually requires a detour or two, so don't get frustrated. Plan your moves carefully, but expect to be sidetracked.

◆ Refer to your owner's manual early and often. If you've lost it, check for documentation on the manufacturer's Web site or write to the manufacturer and get a new one.

◆ In all cases, be even more aware than usual of cleanliness and antistatic precautions. Real estate inside a laptop is cramped; loose bits of dust, crumbs, and pet fur really need to be kept out. Not only can they cause components to not fit right, they can cause electrical shorts and trap and hold excess heat. You can get away with a little dust in a big desktop box; there's usually enough room to let the system fan work and enough space to dissipate the heat. Laptops don't give you that luxury.

◆ Always assume that cables and connectors have no slack. Again, space is so tight inside a laptop that everything has been measured down to the last millimeter. Never tug, bend, or twist anything.

◆ Never handle new parts anywhere but along the edges, if possible (and, if there's a choice, handle them along the plastic edges instead of the metal edges). Latex hospital gloves are really handy as well as cheap; consider wearing one glove for basic moves such as picking up objects and taking them out of a bag, and keep your other hand free for performing the moves that require more dexterity.

◆ Go out and buy the correct tools if you don't already have them. A set of jeweler's screwdrivers with rotating barrel bodies will save you more grief than you can even guess, and for $5 or $10 a set, you don't have to break the bank to add them to your toolbox.

Modern laptops have been purposely designed to keep those of us who love to tinker firmly in the back seat. The parts you can mess with are clearly marked. The parts that are off-limits should be scrupulously avoided. In a lot of respects, these are delicate, precision instruments, and the best way to really screw one up is to start hacking around with the assumption that you can make something fit by pushing just a *little* bit harder.

QuickSteps: Upgrading and Maintaining Your Laptop

These QuickSteps summarize how to upgrade your laptop's memory, install a new hard drive, and replace your battery.

Upgrading Your Memory

These steps will help you upgrade your memory quickly.

BE PREPARED

Before you start, there are some things you may need on hand. These include the following:

- ◆ Small Phillips-head screwdriver for removing the cover over the memory panel on the laptop
- ◆ Documentation for the laptop to tell you where and how to insert the memory
- ◆ (Optional) Antistatic wrist strap to guard against static electricity damage
- ◆ Memory purchased from laptop manufacturer or reputable third-party vendor

To upgrade your memory, follow these steps:

1. Turn off the laptop, and unplug the power cord.

2. Consult the laptop documentation to find out where the memory goes.

3. Open the computer to gain access to the memory. On many laptops, there's a panel on the bottom that you remove by sliding off a small plastic cover or unscrewing a few small screws. On some others, you must remove the keyboard and place the memory underneath.

4. Remove the old memory, if needed. Consult the documentation; the procedure varies from system to system.

5. Insert the new memory. Again, see the documentation.

6. Put everything back together, replacing any components or panels you removed to get access to the memory.

7. Turn on the PC. It should detect the new memory automatically.

Upgrading Your Hard Disk

These steps will help you upgrade your hard disk quickly.

BE PREPARED

Before you start, there are some things you may need on hand. These include the following:

- Bootable floppy disk to restart the PC after installing the new hard disk.
- Documentation for the laptop to tell you where and how to insert the hard disk.
- Small Phillips-head and flat-head screwdrivers to remove screws on access plates (if necessary) and mounting hardware (if necessary).
- Needle-nosed pliers in case you drop something into the system and need to fish it out.
- Pencil and paper to write or sketch the current physical layout of cables and connectors.
- (Optional) Antistatic wrist strap to guard against static electricity damage.
- Hex or Torx screwdriver on some computers to remove screws on access plates (if necessary) and mounting hardware (if necessary).
- Software to partition and format the new drive if you have bought what's known as a *bare* drive, which hasn't been partitioned and formatted by the manufacturer.
- Hard disk designed to work with your laptop. (Consult the manufacturer to find out what you need.)

To upgrade your hard disk, follow these steps:

1. Back up your important data on your hard disk.
2. Open your laptop's case. Refer to the laptop documentation to find out what you need to remove for access to the hard disk.
3. Remove the existing hard drive. The exact method varies; the documentation should tell you how.
4. Install the new hard drive.
5. Boot from your floppy startup disk, and partition/format the new drive.
6. Install your operating system.

Replacing Batteries

These steps will help you replace your batteries.

BE PREPARED

You don't usually need any special tools to install a battery because on a laptop batteries are designed for quick swapping in and out. But before you start, there are some things you'll need to perform the operation. These include the following:

◆ New battery, specifically chosen to work with your laptop. (There are many kinds out there but only a few will work with any one particular laptop.)

◆ The documentation for the laptop to tell you where the battery is located and how to access it.

1. To replace your batteries, follow these steps:

2. Turn off the computer.

3. Disconnect it from the Alternating Current (AC) adapter, and remove any cables to printers, modems, networks, and so on.

4. Find out where your battery is located by checking the laptop documentation, and remove any panel or flip open any hatch needed to access it.

5. Pull the old battery out.

6. Insert the new battery.

7. Close up the laptop.

8. If this is a new battery, keep the machine off and connect the AC adapter. Fully charge the battery before you turn on the computer.

Memory Upgrades

Upgrading the computer's memory is probably the most common improvement that people make, as well as one of the easiest to accomplish. Most laptops come with specific instructions on how to do it and provide the specifications for exactly what kind of memory to buy.

Early laptops used proprietary memory modules, rather than standard Single Inline Memory Modules (SIMMs) or Dual Inline Memory Modules (DIMMs). This meant you had to buy very carefully and only after consulting your laptop documentation and/or its manufacturer. Now, most laptops use a standardized Small Outline DIMM (SO-DIMM) form factor, which has been responsible for reducing the price and availability of Random Access Memory (RAM) for laptops. For most laptops, you can order a memory module from a company that specializes in various brands of memory, but as a fallback plan you can order it from the laptop's manufacturer.

Many laptops use a modular system for memory. A certain amount of memory is built into the system, and you can't remove it. On modern laptops it's usually some basic amount such as 32 megabytes (MB). Then there's an expansion socket into which you can plug one additional memory module of whatever size you want. So, for example, suppose your current PC has 128MB of memory—64MB built in and a 64MB expansion module. You'll need to remove the 64MB expansion and replace it with a higher-denomination expansion module to increase your overall memory.

Preparing for the Upgrade

As long as you follow some basic, preliminary precautions, you should have little to worry about when it comes time to upgrade the memory on your laptop.

BACK UP YOUR IMPORTANT DATA

Making sure you back up your important data on your hard disk before you do any work on your computer is always a good idea. The chances that you'll do some damage are slight, but you have to lose everything only one time to understand the value of backups.

PREPARE YOUR WORKSPACE

Before you start, clear off your workspace. The kitchen table will do just fine (wipe it down first). Have a flat surface to work on with plenty of room to lay things out. You don't want your screwdriver rolling onto the floor just when you need it. I like to work on a clean, white towel (not a terry-cloth towel, though—you don't want to introduce lint). The color provides contrast, and the softness reduces ricochets and adds a little traction for fast-moving, small items such as screws. Lay out your tools (a small flat-blade screwdriver, small- and large-head Phillips screwdrivers, and maybe small needle-nosed pliers just in case). Some systems require little hex-head screwdrivers, but most don't. The tools will vary; just make sure you've got your toolkit close at hand. You may want an antistatic strap that you can wrap around your wrist or ankle to keep static from building up while you work, but for a short job such as this, you probably won't need one.

DISCONNECT EVERYTHING

When installing any kind of internal components in your laptop, including memory modules, always double-check that the computer is turned off and disconnected from the AC adapter. Remove the battery pack from the computer. Remove all cables to components such as printers, external modems, and so on, as well as any PC Cards.

Ground Yourself

Make sure that you are well grounded and always touch something metal before you touch the del cate stuff inside the laptop. That way, if you've collected any static, you'll discharge it onto the meta object instead of into your computer. Those little blue sparks that come off your fingers can have hundreds or even thousands of volts, and that's definitely not good for electronic components tha run on 2.2–5 volts. Filing cabinets, light fixtures, and door frames are good things to touch to see i you're sparking.

Also, please make sure that none of your tools are the magnetized kind. They're good for fishin lost screws out of the sink, but you don't want them anywhere near your computer.

Keep It Clean

So, touching some things is good to get rid of static. On the other hand, there are other things you never want to touch at all. For example, do not touch the metal conductors on the memory modules Even minute amounts of dust, grit, skin oils, and sticky crud left over from lunch can be a real prob lem. Also, try not to touch cables, wires, and other components you're not working on. Maybe it's picky, but the fewer things you mess with, the fewer things you'll have to check later if the system doesn't work the way it's supposed to. Remember the latex gloves I mentioned earlier? This is a goo time to take them out and put them on.

Making a Map

With some laptops, you may need to unplug something else (such as a hard drive or a battery) befor you can get to the memory module adapter, or slot. If you do, sit back for a minute, grab a pencil an paper, and make a sketch of what plugs into what before you start pulling things apart. Don't worr about making it pretty or exactly to scale; just make sure everything in the sketch is accurately ider tified and labeled. This is especially important for any wires you need to move out of the way. You can't rely on your remembrance of things past to make sure they'll go back exactly the way they nee to go back. With bigger machines, such as desktop computers or car engines, you can get away witl tagging wires with masking tape. You won't have that kind of room inside a laptop, and you really don't want gummy tape glue inside your system.

Get Motivated!

At this point, you may be asking yourself whether you really want to do this kind of upgrade on your own. You may think that all these precautions signal something difficult or dangerous. That is really not the case. All I'm trying to do is point out that you need to take your time and proceed in a careful, well-planned manner.

Look at it this way—installing memory in your laptop will take you 10 to 15 minutes. These things are made to be upgraded, after all. Now, if you pay people at the local computer store to do the upgrade for you, it'll take them the same 10 or 15 minutes to do the job. It'll also cost you about $85. That's the going hourly rate for most PC repair jobs, and you'll pay for a full hour regardless of how little time the upgrade really takes.

At the least, you should try doing the installation yourself, and if you get to a place where you really don't want to go any further, then take it down to the shop. But first give it a shot yourself. You'll be surprised at how easily most of these systems come together—and you can use the $85 you save to treat yourself to dinner and a movie.

Performing the Installation

Increasing the memory on your laptop is probably the easiest upgrade option available. The following sections detail the steps involved.

ACCESS THE MEMORY MODULE

The first thing you have to do is open up the computer so you can get at the memory modules. Most laptops have access hatches that you open from the bottom, so close the screen, turn the laptop over, and work from the bottom of the laptop system unit. Sometimes you have to unscrew a cover plate to open the memory hatch; with other laptops, you push small locking tabs and lift the cover plate away from the body of the machine. In either case, the correct hatch should be marked with something that indicates which is the correct one. It might say *memory*, it might have a stylized drawing of a memory module, it might have something arcane, such as the term *exp*, but it'll usually have something to indicate that this is where the memory lives. If there are other hatches, they too will be marked. You're smart—you'll figure it out.

Some older laptops require you to remove or simply lift up the keyboard to access the memory area. For these systems, open the screen, unlatch the keyboard (by sliding the unlocking latches on the side or at the back), and work on the system from the top.

The top-access systems usually still have the memory modules down at the bottom of the system, so you may also have to move the disk drive or hard drive to get at the memory. If you have to move a drive, it'll usually come equipped with a plastic tab that you use as a handle. Always use the tabs or handles they give you. Don't put a screwdriver under the drive and try to lever it out. Look before you pull. There may be little plastic or metal devices that the manufacturer used to hold the drive in place. There may be small screws that hold it down. Refer to your owner's manual to see whether you need to remove any of these things or whether the whole unit should slide out as a single piece.

Even on systems you access from the bottom, you may still have to move something else out of the way before you can reach the memory area. Some laptops, for example, require that you remove the hard drive by sliding it out of its socket and removing it from the machine.

LOOK AROUND

Once you've exposed the memory area, you'll want to stop for a minute and study what's in front of you. Does your system have slots that accept SO-DIMM memory modules, or is it the kind that uses prepackaged proprietary memory modules? By the way, this is a question you should've asked before you bought your RAM anyway. But now that you're inside the case, it's a good idea to make sure everything looks right.

Do you have empty slots, or are all of them filled? If you have empty slots, you can go ahead with the addition of your new memory. If your slots are all filled, you'll have to empty one or more of them so you have a place to put your new memory.

OUT WITH THE OLD

If you have to remove memory, look for something that indicates which slot has the highest number (for example, there might be a small 0 or 1 printed on the board next to the slot). You'll usually want to replace existing memory starting with the highest numbered slot. (This is where your owner's manual or the company's technical support people can be most helpful by giving exact instructions if you can't find a clear indicator just by looking at the slots.)

To remove any memory modules you have to get rid of, look for the locking latches on both edge of the socket. Unhook the latches from the module by pressing them away from the module. These latches can sometimes be fairly tight, but don't get carried away and apply too much force; you don't want to snap them off. Just a gentle push outward should be enough. Once the latches are released from the edges of the module, you can tilt the module upward and slide it out. Don't touch the gold or tin connectors.

Set aside any modules you've removed and save them for possible future use. You never know when they might come in handy. You may be able to sell your old memory. My local computer store has a bulletin board for people to advertise old parts they want to sell or buy, including used chips. Failing that, try giving them to a school. Taxpayer revolt being what it is, schools are probably pretty desperate for any charity you care to offer, and you can probably take a tax break by deducting the value (or a percentage of it) when April rolls around. (Ask your tax preparer just to be sure.)

IN WITH THE NEW

If you have empty slots and don't have to take anything out before you add the new memory, or if you've freed some room by following the previous instructions, pick up your new module by the edge and slide it into the socket. It will go in at an angle and then pivot down until it locks into place. Make sure it's fully seated in the slot before you pivot it down.

Most memory modules are keyed by having little notches cut into the side so they'll fit into the slot only one way. If you have any doubts (for example, if the module seems really hard to fit into the connector), take it out and try it the other way. (This is also why you took a few minutes to sketch what things looked like before you started.) Never try to cram something into a place where it doesn't seem to want to go. It might be misaligned, something might be blocking the way, or it might be upside down. These things slide in easily. If yours doesn't, it's the wrong way around. Turn it and try again: dust it off, line it up, and make sure it goes in straight; just don't force it.

PUT EVERYTHING BACK

Once you have the new memory correctly installed by whichever method your laptop requires, replace whatever you took out, or off, in exactly the same way you removed it. Replace the drives, battery packs, and access covers in reverse order from the way they came off. Reconnect any cables you disconnected, and turn the machine on. It'll go through its normal boot cycle; only this time you should see a bigger number on your screen when it does the memory check. If all goes well, you're done. For example, if you installed a 64MB module in a computer that already had 32MB of memory, the boot sequence should confirm that all went well by showing that you now have 96MB of memory.

If you get an error message or if the amount of memory the computer recognizes doesn't match the amount you should now have, don't worry about it just yet. Sometimes the BIOS will be a bit confused. Just enter the Basic Input/Ouput System (BIOS) program, and then exit it, and everything should be fine from then on.

If you continue to get BIOS error messages regarding the memory at startup, however, you'll have to turn off the machine and go through the installation process again. If you have to reopen the computer and do it all again, it'll probably be because the new memory module isn't fully inserted into the slot. Make sure it's straight and fully seated, so the locking tabs snap into the notches on the module. If that doesn't work, then now might be a good time to make sure that the memory you bought is compatible with your system. Again, you should have done this before purchasing the memory, but we all make mistakes. Finally, if you just can't get it to work, it's possible that you have defective memory. Get it tested, or send it back.

Hard Disk Upgrades

As I'm sure you're aware by now, space has always been an issue with laptops. And when you think of devices that are space dependent, hard disks come to mind. First, they tend to be one of the bigger components in a computer. Second, a small hard disk means you don't have space for the stuff you want to store.

It used to be that the common way to increase the capacity of your laptop's hard disk drive was to install a compression program, such as Microsoft's DriveSpace. It'd effectively double the amount of space you had but at the expense of precious system resources (memory and processor time). That, and if for some reason the compression utility had problems—and invariably that always happened to me—then you'd lose all of your data.

A better solution is to increase your storage space, but once again, you have to deal with the physical space issue. You have these options:

◆ You can attach a removable media drive, such as a Zip drive or CD-RW drive, via your laptop's Universal Serial Bus (USB) or parallel port.

◆ You can slip a PC Card hard drive into your laptop.

◆ Memory sticks are convenient and small. Some of them have a USB connector, and most memory sticks have a proprietary 10-pin connector. They're shaped like a piece of gum and can easily slip into your pocket.

◆ Many laptops have modular bays that'll let you swap the floppy disk drive or CD-ROM drive with a second hard disk.

◆ You can remove your current hard drive and completely replace it with a new, higher-capacity model.

All of these solutions have good and bad points. External removable media drives force you to carry extra gear and, although they're good for special occasions such as hauling around huge graphics files, they tend to be cumbersome and somewhat slow.

PC Card hard drives are handy and work quite well, but using one means giving up, at least temporarily, access to PC Card modems and other devices that use the same slot or slots. Memory sticks are great and very popular. About the only problem with them is that they're easy to lose, and you need to purchase a memory card reader if your system doesn't already have one.

Replacing your floppy drive or CD-ROM with a second hard drive is a tempting solution, and some people are happy to trade their floppy for something bigger. However, some people still rely on their floppies to load new files and programs or need to keep their CD-ROMs for the large reference works they have in their CD libraries. Additionally, not all laptops have controllers capable of supporting a second hard drive. If you have one that will, such as an IBM ThinkPad, I'll go into that upgrade option shortly. For now, though, you'll look at what you need to do to replace your current hard drive with a new one.

Finding the Right Hard Disk

The only real trick in replacing your hard drive is getting a new one that'll work with your laptop—and that isn't really much of a trick. Almost all laptop computers use $2^1/_2$-inch, $9^1/_2$-millimeter (mm) high hard drives. If your laptop was made before 1996, it probably has a *full-height* hard drive, about 18 millimeters high.

A newer slim hard drive will usually work in an older (pre-1996) laptop, but a full-height drive won't fit in a laptop made for 11mm or $9^1/_2$-mm drives. If you find a really good deal on a full-height drive but aren't sure whether it'll fit into your newer laptop, the best way to check is to remove your current drive (see "Taking Out the Old Hard Drive" later in this chapter) and take a ruler to its height. Just measure the height of the drive, not its supporting brackets. If it's 18mm, you can use a new drive that's 18mm or smaller. If it's 11mm or 9.5mm, you need to specify the same (a slim-line model) for your new drive, too.

VERIFYING THE BIOS

Another factor you have to watch out for is the kind of BIOS you have. If you have an older laptop, the BIOS chip might not let you have a hard drive larger than 540MB, 4 gigabyte (GB), or 8.4GB, depending on the BIOS version. If you have an outdated BIOS, you can get a software BIOS *extender* (software that enables the BIOS to recognize larger hard drives) for your notebook/laptop, or you'll need to send your laptop to an upgrade company that'll update your firmware BIOS.

The good news is that most mail-order sources either will include the BIOS upgrade software as part of the price or will upgrade your firmware BIOS if you send them the computer. The bad news is that if you have to send your laptop away to be upgraded, you're going to be without it for a few days. Generally speaking, however, most laptops will do just fine with a software BIOS extender, and you won't have to send your machine out into the cold, cruel world on its own.

OBTAINING MOUNTING HARDWARE

Finally, some laptop hard drives are manufactured with their supporting brackets built right into the drive itself. If you have this kind of hard drive, you'll need to get new mounting hardware along with your hard drive, and you may have to hunt to find it. A lot of retailers don't carry a large variety of brackets. Your best bet in such a case is to call your laptop's manufacturer, or the hard drive vendor, and find out where you can get the hardware you need to attach the new drive to the laptop. It seems like such a minor item, but details such as these can give you the biggest headaches.

NOTE *Need some pointers on how to locate a source for laptop hard drives? Again, the best way to find one quickly is to use one of the search engines on the Internet. Just run a search for* **laptop + hard drive.**

Backing Up Your Data

Things can go wrong—remember Murphy's law? It's always better to be safe than sorry when messing around with your hard-earned data. Don't remove your old hard drive until it's entirely backed up, either on the new hard drive or by some other means.

TIP *On laptops and notebooks, CD-R/RW drives are a particularly convenient way to back up your data.*

To back up your data, you have a number of options, as presented in the following sections.

NETWORK BACKUP

If you have access to a network, the easiest way to back up your hard disk is to copy everything from your laptop to the server and keep it there until you have finished installing your new hard drive. You'll need to make sure you have all your configuration software on a floppy disk, however, or your machine won't be able to access the network to let you download all your files when you're ready for them.

EXTERNAL DRIVE

If you have an external tape drive, a CD-R/RW drive, or a Zip drive, you can use the backup program that comes with your version of Windows or a third-party backup application to move all your files to the external drive and then restore them to the new hard drive after you finish installing it.

SECOND LAPTOP OR DESKTOP COMPUTER

You can use a commercial program such as LapLink to copy all your files to another machine and then restore them to the new hard drive after you finish installing it.

SECOND HARD DRIVE

If you have a laptop that'll accommodate two hard drives (by removing the floppy disk drive or CD-ROM, for example), you can install the new hard drive, copy everything from the old drive to the new drive, remove both drives, install the new drive in place of the old drive, and finally, reinstall the floppy drive or CD-ROM. This is a lot of work, but sometimes you have to get creative if you want to get something such as this done.

Alternatively, you can use the Seagate FileCopy program. FileCopy will make an exact, bootable duplicate of the original hard drive on another hard drive that has as large or larger capacity.

Programs such as Norton Ghost and Drive Copy make complete copies of your hard disk content onto whatever media you choose (another hard disk, a CD-R/RW, and so on). That way, you can back up everything just as it is and then "transplant" it onto the new drive later. Such a program can save you hours in reinstalling Windows and all your Windows programs and recopying all your files.

Preparing for the Hard Drive Upgrade

You've got the hard drive and mounting hardware. You've backed up all your files. You have a bootable floppy disk at hand and another floppy with all your network access software. If you've backed up your old hard drive to a server and removed all boisterous children and pets to another room, you're all set to begin. Before you start, however, make sure you have all the necessary tools handy. Refer back to the QuickSteps at the beginning of this chapter for a list of what you might need.

Installing the New Hard Drive

You're all ready to go. You have your hard drive. You have your laptop. You have a flat, clean surface on which to work. Your tools are all laid out where you can reach them. You've grounded yourself. Let's get started.

OPENING THE LAPTOP

Some laptops need to be completely opened up to get to the hard drive. With others, you may just have to lift off the keyboard by unsnapping it. And some have drives that simply slide out (my favorite).

First, make sure you know the location of the hard drive.

You may be lucky and have a drive caddy that slides out from the computer with no screws required. Another easy replacement job is for machines in which the keyboard or other piece unsnaps or lifts up to reveal the hard drive. Only slightly more involved are laptops in which a top or bottom piece is unscrewed and removed to get to the hard drive. More difficult are the laptops that have a top or bottom piece that's unscrewed and removed and then require that one or more components be removed to get to the hard drive. The hardest type is the kind of laptop in which a top or bottom piece is unscrewed and removed, and most components, including the system board, are removed to get to the hard drive.

If you have a computer that comes with a hard drive caddy, you can ignore most of this information because you just slide out the old drive and slide in the new one.

Second, work slowly and carefully. Don't try to pry apart your computer once the screws are removed. Many of the notebook computers have extremely thin plastic snaps that align the top and bottom and help to hold them together. In addition, some types of notebooks also require you to remove a keyboard mask, and others may have this keyboard mask built into the top cover piece. Slowly pull away the plastic cover while carefully looking for connecting cables. If you find any, you'll need to disengage them before you can completely open the system.

Finally, many laptops have quite a bit of mounting hardware, which has to be removed before you can gain access to the drive.

TAKING OUT THE OLD HARD DRIVE

Once you can see the hard drive, find the proper screwdriver among the tools you've thoughtfully laid out within reach and unscrew the mounting bracket. Remove the mounting bracket along with the drive.

Be sure to carefully detach the drive interface from the interface connector, and remember which way the drive was positioned. Consider drawing a sketch to help you remember the proper position.

Remove the hard drive from its mounting bracket. It'll probably just slide out, but you may have to push it a little. Never push at an angle, and be careful not to push too hard. If you don't detect any movement while applying moderate force, check it for small screws or plastic tabs that may be holding it in place.

PUTTING IN THE NEW HARD DRIVE

First, install the new hard drive in the mounting bracket. Next, carefully place the new hard drive (in its mounting bracket) into the same spot where the old one was positioned. Pull out the sketch you made when removing the old drive, and make sure you're putting the new one in the same way the old one came out. Also, be extra careful that the drive interface pins are properly aligned with the cable or connector to which they attach. These parts are really small and often quite delicate, and it's easy to wind up with the top row of pins in the bottom row of the connector.

That's really all there is to it. Carefully align and replace any covers, keyboard masks, plastic snaps, and so on in the same order you removed them, but don't try to permanently close the system just yet. Make sure any screws you do install go in all the way, but don't overtorque them. You shouldn't have any pieces left over. If you drop a screw and it rolls down into the system, get it out before you do anything else. These are small machines—it didn't go very far. Pick the system up and roll it from side to side (like one of those kid's toys with little ball bearings that you try to roll into the clown's nose). The little screw will eventually rattle into a place where you can see it and grab it with your nonmagnetized needle-nosed pliers or grabbing device. Dental picks and hemostats are also handy for this kind of work, but they're usually not things most people have in their toolboxes, and they're too expensive unless you do this kind of thing a lot.

Finally, while you have everything open, you could spray it with a can of compressed air to get out any dust. Don't try to wipe away the dust with a cloth or a paper towel, though—you'll likely scratch something or leave lint or paper fibers behind. Also, don't blow on the inside of your laptop. Your breath may be minty fresh, but it's also very humid.

TESTING THE NEW HARD DISK

Now, before you put the system completely back together, put the battery pack back in and turn on the laptop. If the system runs through its memory test, you can breathe a sigh of relief. If the system won't run the memory test, the most likely culprit is the hard drive interface or one of the other connections. Check all the connections. If you don't find anything obvious, try replacing the old drive and try again. If this works, something is wrong with the new hard drive.

If the memory test succeeds, you'll probably get an error message such as `HDD Configuration Error`. Don't worry. You want it to say this. Your BIOS is looking for the hard drive you took out and just doesn't recognize the new one yet. Get into your BIOS setup routine (by pressing one or more keys while the system is booting; it'll tell you how on your screen), and set the hard drive to the correct type as indicated by the information that came with the new unit. You might have to identify it by number, and you may need to fill in several parameters, such as number of heads, number of cylinders, and number of sectors. All this information should be in with the packing slip and the bubble wrap in the new drive's shipping box. Most of the time, though, you probably won't need to do anything except reboot.

Now that there's nothing on your hard drive, you'll need to boot your computer from your bootable floppy disk (a floppy that has `COMMAND.COM` on it) or bootable CD-ROM. For example, most full versions of Windows installation CD-ROMs are bootable and will format your hard disk and install Windows for you. After you've formatted the drive, you should be able to boot right from the new hard drive.

NOTE   *In addition to installing the operating system, some laptops require special drivers to get all devices, such as the touch pad or USB ports, to work properly. Generally, these drivers are provided by the laptop manufacturer on a CD. After installing the operating system, look to install additional drivers as needed.*

CLOSING UP

Once everything seems to be working, you can close your computer. Put the keyboard back in place, and screw down any access hatches you had to remove. If you haven't installed your operating system already, you'll need to do that now. Boot to your boot disk or Windows installation CD-ROM, and begin the installation process. You might also need to connect your laptop to the network, Zip drive, external tape drive, or whatever you used to hold all of your backup files and restore your precious data from that location.

Installing a Second Hard Drive

By now, you've read several hundred pages about computer parts, upgrades, and of course, my great jokes. One of the things you should have learned by now is that when a technology is new, every manufacturer that jumps on it does its own thing. And doing their own thing doesn't necessarily equate to convenience for the customer. Laptops and their expandability are a prime example.

Early laptops were hard to upgrade, and I've already talked a little bit about why this is. A big reason is that the components in a laptop are so crammed into a tiny little space, and not knowing what you're doing (or not being careful) can be very dangerous. And another reason is related to size as well. Laptops are supposed to be portable, and early on, the reasoning was that the manufacturer would put whatever they thought you needed into it, and you didn't need to upgrade it. Hence, you didn't need to be in the case.

But as technologies mature, the manufacturers get a little more comfortable with their designs and make improvements on the way. Somewhere along the timeline of laptop history, someone had a brilliant idea: "Hey, why don't we make interchangeable devices? That way, we could put a CD-ROM or floppy drive or hard disk or extra battery into the same slot." That little stroke of genius (whoever the engineer was, I'm sure they didn't get enough of a raise for that one) takes us to where we are today with laptop expandability. So now you might ask me, "Great, thanks for the history. But what does this have to do with installing a hard drive?"

On most laptops today, you can replace the floppy drive or CD drive with a second hard disk. All you do is remove the modular device you want to replace and slide the new hard drive in. The one thing to keep in mind is that these modular bays aren't compatible with other manufacturer's bays. For example, if you have an IBM ThinkPad, its bay is different from that of a Sony VAIO or a Dell Latitude C-series. For that matter, the Dell Latitude C-series uses different modules than a Latitude D-series. In the case of a hard drive upgrade, you can often purchase an "empty" module to put a standard laptop hard drive in and then slide your module into the case. This makes it so the new hard drive doesn't just rattle around in there.

If your laptop doesn't have modular bays, then you might need to remove a device to add your new hard disk. If this is the case, you'll probably need to put the hard disk into a caddy or mounting bracket of some sort. When you put your secondary hard drive into its caddy, make sure that any slots, connectors, or projections on the hard drive match the corresponding slots, connectors, and projections on the caddy. Then press it firmly into the caddy until you hear it click into place. If it doesn't seem to be going in after you've applied a moderate amount of force, don't keep pushing. It's probably not lined up right. Take it out, and reinsert it. You may have to wiggle it a little to make sure everything is lined up correctly.

Next, remove the old disk drive or CD drive. On laptops that have removable keyboards, this requires the following steps:

1. Make sure no disks or CDs are in the drive you're taking out.

2. Turn off the power.

3. Disconnect the AC adapter.

4. Unplug any cables that attach to printers and modems.

5. Unlatch the keyboard, and swing it up out of the way.

6. Remove the battery.

7. Use the attached handles, tabs, or straps to remove the CD drive or disk drive.

If you're replacing a disk drive with a hard drive, you'll have a hole in the front of the laptop where you used to insert disks. You can cover this with a shaped piece of plastic called a *bezel*. Remember the baggie with all that unidentifiable stuff from when you brought your laptop home and unpacked it? Your bezel is in there. If you saved the box, go rummage around in the closet until you find it. If you threw the box away, you can usually get a bezel at your local computer store. Generally, they ship with new hard drives, but you might make a note to ask just to be sure. Some bezels are installed from the inside of the computer while the drive bay is empty. Others are designed to be pushed into place from the outside. Either way, make sure you cover the hole in the front or side of your laptop. Holes like that are invitations to all sorts of problems.

If you're replacing a CD drive with a hard drive, you can usually just slide the new hard drive into the space vacated by the old, unwanted CD drive. If that space was previously unoccupied, you may have to remove a bezel so you can see the front of the hard drive from the outside (so you can see the drive's activity light) and then finish up with the following steps:

1. Firmly press the new hard drive holder until it clicks into the connector.

2. Replace the battery.

3. Reattach the keyboard and reconnect the AC adapter and whatever cables you just took off.

Installing PC Card Drive Cards

PC Card hard drives, sometimes also called hard cards or credit-card hard drives, offer an extremely simple way to add storage capacity to your laptop. They generally come in the size known as a Type 3 PC Card, which means they take up two card slots in your laptop and can store 20GB, 40GB, or more. You can get Type 1 and Type 2 PC Card hard drive cards, which take up only one slot but tend to be small in terms of capacity. For example, IBM offers a series of Microdrives in the Type 2 format that have a capacity of up to 1GB. Although they were primarily designed for use in digital cameras, they can be used in most laptops. And these drives tend to be a bit expensive (upwards of $400 for 1GB of storage space).

Installing a PC Card hard drive requires nothing more than making sure you've installed the device driver software that comes on a disk with the card and that you have the card pointed the right way. Make sure the notched edge on the card goes in first. Press the card firmly into the connector. Usually, there will be an Eject button either inside the PC Card opening or on the side of the computer next to the card slot. You'll know when the card is fully installed because the Eject button will pop out. On some laptops—the IBM ThinkPad, for example—you then pull the Eject button out a little bit and fold it toward the front of the laptop. If you need to eject a PC Card while the laptop is operating, you should ensure that a PC Card manager program isn't running. If a program is running, eject the card using the program before physically removing it.

Memory Sticks

Memory sticks are a great example of where the computer industry takes common convention and throws it out the window. I've said before, and so have a lot of other people, to avoid confusion, you should use the term *memory* for stuff such as RAM and use *storage* or *disk space* for more permanent storage. When you hear *memory stick*, it sounds like something to augment your RAM, right? Wrong.

The memory stick started out as a proprietary interface built by Sony but is now pretty much an industry standard. The idea is simple and beautiful: a small device, about the size of a stick of gum (or half that size, for newer sticks), can store digital data even if it doesn't have power. It's small, portable, and convenient. Plus, memory sticks can be used in a variety of devices, including digital cameras, cell phones, Personal Digital Assistants (PDAs), printers, and of course, laptops.

If you want actual measurements, the memory stick is 21.5mm wide, 2.8mm thick, and 50mm long—as long as an AA battery. Figure 30.1 shows you a standard-sized memory stick, as well as the smaller Memory Stick Duo.

FIGURE 30.1
Memory stick (left)
and Memory Stick
Duo (right)

Size: 50x21.5x2.8mm   MagicGate Memory
Weight: 4g   Stick Duo Media

Memory sticks come in a variety of storage sizes, from several megabytes to several gigabytes. The new Memory Stick PRO standard (with the same physical size as the original standard) has a theoretical maximum capacity of 32GB. As far as the price goes, these devices are more expensive than standard hard disk space, but you should expect that for the convenience.

To use memory sticks, you need a reader. They're fairly cheap (usually around $20) and connect to your system through a USB port. Most memory stick readers will accept other types of removable stick media in addition to the memory stick, such as Compact Flash (CF), Multimedia Cards (MMC), and Smart Media (SM).

Other Kinds of Upgrades

I've covered upgrading memory and hard drives, but what if you want to upgrade your laptop in different ways? Say you want to increase its utility in the office instead of just using it at home or on the road. The following sections go into some of the other things you can do to put more life in your laptop.

DVD Drives

This is my favorite upgrade because my job requires long flights to the Far East, and there's nothing like watching movies on your laptop to make the time fly by. If you're looking to justify the expense, remember that you can use the DVD drives for reading reference DVDs (such as Microsoft's Encarta) as well as watching movies.

There are two ways to add a DVD to your laptop: installing an internal DVD drive (which replaces your CD drive) and attaching an external DVD to the laptop using a USB port. The latter is cumbersome (involving a lot of external stuff), and the internal solution must be made specifically for the laptop. Regardless of which type of DVD drive you have, there are a few other considerations.

Once you've resolved the inny or outy (internal/external) question, your next decision is whether to get a DVD that has hardware decoding or software decoding. Hardware decoding places no performance burden on the CPU but costs more. Software decoding uses the laptop's CPU to do the decoding. If CPU in your laptop is slower than 266 megahertz (MHz), you should consider hardware decoding. If your laptop already has a DVD drive that uses software decoding and you discover that your CPU is really having difficulty doing the job, you can get a hardware decoder that plugs into the PC slot. MARGI makes an excellent decoder called DVD-to-Go, which I use in my Dell Inspiron 7000 to watch movies.

As you're having wonderful warm fuzzy thoughts of long flights with endless movies, remember that watching a movie on your laptop puts a continuous load on your battery; you might be surprised how quickly it can dissipate your laptop's battery. The solution is to either bring several (heavy) batteries or invest in an airline/car power adapter. Most airlines now have power outlets available (even in coach). In fact, on my last flight to Greece, when I was selecting a seat I specifically requested one with a power outlet. It took the reservations representative a while to figure it out, but I ended up with my favorite films on the 12-hour flight.

Laptop LAN Adapters

You can connect your laptop to the company network by connecting a Local Area Network (LAN) adapter to the laptop. Some adapters connect via the parallel or USB ports of your laptop, but the most common way today is by inserting a LAN adapter card into your PC Card slot. Cards today generally have telephone jack–type connectors (RJ-45) for Ethernet connections. Prices can range from about $30 to $100, depending on the type of network you have and which vendor you choose. Also, prices change rapidly, as with everything else involving computers, so be sure to get the most recent price quotes from whomever you choose.

One of the more popular options is to get a card that has both LAN and modem capabilities. Figure 30.2 shows a Xircom combo card.

You can find dozens of resources on the Internet that make information about LAN adapters easy to find. Computer Shopper has a wonderful set of utilities that enable a person to select, compare, and choose which system they want peripherals for. CNET has similar information, as does ZDNet and dozens of other sites, both retail and editorial.

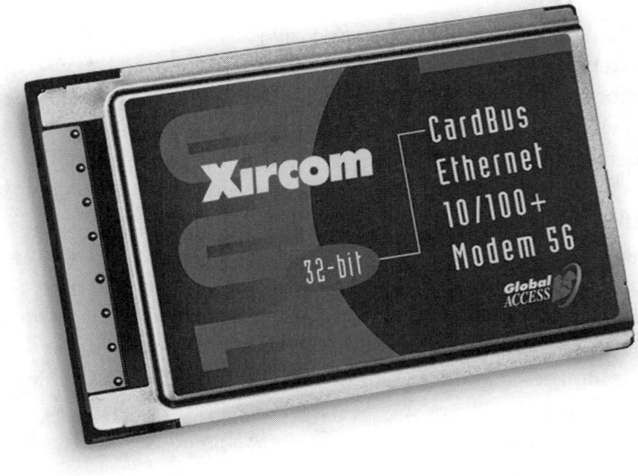

FIGURE 30.2
Xircom network
adapter/modem
combo PC Card

Wireless LAN Cards

If you're the type of person who thinks it's more than a little pointless to have a walkabout computer that's shackled to a desk by its LAN connection, you can upgrade to a wireless LAN card. These cards are more expensive than the ones discussed in the preceding section, but they do give you more mobility.

The most common wireless communications standard, and the one you'll want to make sure that your card supports, is Wireless LAN (IEEE 802.11x), which is also called WiFi. Chapter 27, "Installing and Troubleshooting Networks," has information on the wireless standards, but here's a quick recap:

- IEEE 802.11b is the most common standard, and it supports 11 Megabits per second (Mbps).

- IEEE 802.11g is the newest standard, is backward compatible with 802.11b, and supports speeds up to 54Mbps (as well as other features).

- IEEE 802.11a does boast speeds up to 54Mbps, but *isn't* compatible with the other two. And it seems as though this standard is getting squeezed out.

Another standard is IEEE 802.15, better known as Bluetooth. Bluetooth is designed more for several types of devices, not specifically mobile networking.

As mentioned earlier, your best source for current and accurate information about wireless LAN cards is the Internet because technology and pricing change so rapidly.

Working with Laptop Batteries

When you're on the road, without access to AC power, your laptop battery is your lifeline. Without it, your laptop is just another seven-pound paperweight. The following sections look at charging, replacing, and extending the life of the battery's charge.

Battery Care

Most laptops come with specific instructions on how to deal with their batteries. They're not all the same. In general, however, you'll have a recharger and/or AC adapter you can use when your battery power runs low. The AC adapter will recharge the battery at the same time it provides power to keep your laptop running. Some batteries will fully recharge no matter when you plug in the AC adapter. Others will not. Older NiCad batteries had problems with having a "memory." In other words, if you periodically only drain it halfway, it'd eventually lose the rest of the capacity. The newer Lithium Ion batteries don't have that problem.

Always be especially careful that the adapter you use with your laptop is the one that came with the computer or is a replacement specifically recommended by the manufacturer. The plug from your cordless electric drill's adapter may very well fit your computer, but there's little chance that the voltage and amperage requirements will match as well, and you'll be really sorry if you use it to recharge your laptop.

WARNING *A battery isn't just something that can hurt your computer. It's something that can hurt you. Batteries can and do explode if you handle them carelessly—such as throw them in a fire or use a battery charger that wasn't designed for the type of battery you're charging.*

Keep these tips in mind when handling your laptop battery:

◆ Keep the battery away from fire.

◆ Keep the battery away from water.

◆ Never try to take it apart.

◆ Don't drop it, throw it, or bang it on the table.

◆ Always use only the battery designed especially for your particular make and model.

Something else to pack into your carrying case is a small, one- or two-socket surge protector. If you're going to be using your laptop from hotel rooms, conference centers, airport lounges, and other such places, you'll need one. You can't be any more confident of the quality of the electricity out there than you can back in the office—and you've got a surge protector on the floor under your desk, right?

Finally, it's a good idea to have more than one battery for your laptop. You never know when you might need it.

Charging a Battery

Keep your battery healthy by following the manufacturer's guidelines for first use and for when and how to recharge it. For example, the battery pack in many computers will be low or "dead" when you first buy it. You have to plug in the AC adapter and let it take a charge before you can use it.

NiCad batteries are old, and you'll rarely see them anymore, but they work best when they're completely discharged before you recharge them. NiMH and Lithium Ion batteries couldn't care less. Most laptops come with advanced power management features to both manage power use and to notify you of the power left in your battery.

TIP   When purchasing a laptop, longer battery life is definitely something to look for. You might pay a bit more for it, but if you can get battery life of three hours or more, it's well worth your investment.

Replacing a Battery

Regardless of how well you care for your battery, there will come a time when you have to take it ou and put in a new one. Because this is one of the things most people will have to do fairly routinely most laptops make it pretty easy. Follow these steps:

1. Turn off the computer.

2. Disconnect it from the AC adapter and remove any cables to printers, modems, networks, and so on.

3. Find out where your battery is located. On some laptops, you'll access it through a hatch or the bottom or the front of the computer. Generally, the hatch will simply slide out, but in some cases you'll need to take out some screws or release a locking mechanism. On other laptops, you reach the battery from the top by first lifting off the keyboard. Check your owner's manua if you're not sure how the keyboard comes off.

4. The battery is usually right on top. Once you get the hatch or access panel off, the battery is the first thing you see. Make sure, however, that you don't need to remove something else before you go to work on the battery. If your laptop has a CD drive, for example, you may have to remove it before you can pull the power pack.

5. Some batteries have plastic tabs or handles that you use to pull them away from their sockets before lifting them out. Others are unplugged simply by sliding them out of the connectors by hand. If yours has tabs or handles, use them.

6. Don't pull out the battery and then go home for the evening. Put the new one in right away Some laptops depend on their batteries to hold their Complementary Metal Oxide Semicon ductor (CMOS) configurations for more than a few minutes or seconds.

7. Close up the laptop in the reverse order you opened it.

8. If this is a new battery, keep the machine off and connect the AC adapter. Fully charge the bat tery before you turn on the computer. Also, you may have to completely discharge and then recharge the battery a few times before the battery will operate at maximum capacity.

Buying a New Battery

Sometimes the information printed on the side of the battery can be confusing or obscure. The Inter net has a plethora of information about batteries for just about every laptop and notebook available One site you might want to check out is **www.batteries.com**. And of course, you can always check your manufacturer's Web site.

NOTE   Several good online sources are available on the Internet for finding more information about batteries for your laptop. Just run a search on **laptops + battery.**

Conserving Battery Power

Virtually every laptop now has power-management functions, either built into the BIOS, operating from within Windows, or available by using special drivers. These functions monitor whether the system is on and whether anybody is using it. After prescribed periods of no input from the keyboard or mouse, the laptop "goes to sleep." It doesn't turn itself off but slumbers until you wake it up. The advantage is that power-consuming features of the unit, such as the screen display, are no longer drawing down the charge in the battery. Preserving the life of the battery is obviously preferable to replacing it, so there are several things you can do to make sure you get the most use out of yours.

Most laptops today have power-management features in the BIOS that work hand-in-hand with Windows settings. When you enable power management, you allow the laptop to help you save battery power by shutting itself off in various degrees when you leave it running without AC power. Various degrees of power management are often available, such as Max Performance, Balanced Power Saving, and Max Power Saving. They control when and if the hard disk will stop spinning, the display will turn off, and so on. The Windows power management feature, located in the Power or Power Management icon in the Windows Control Panel, is shown in Figure 30.3.

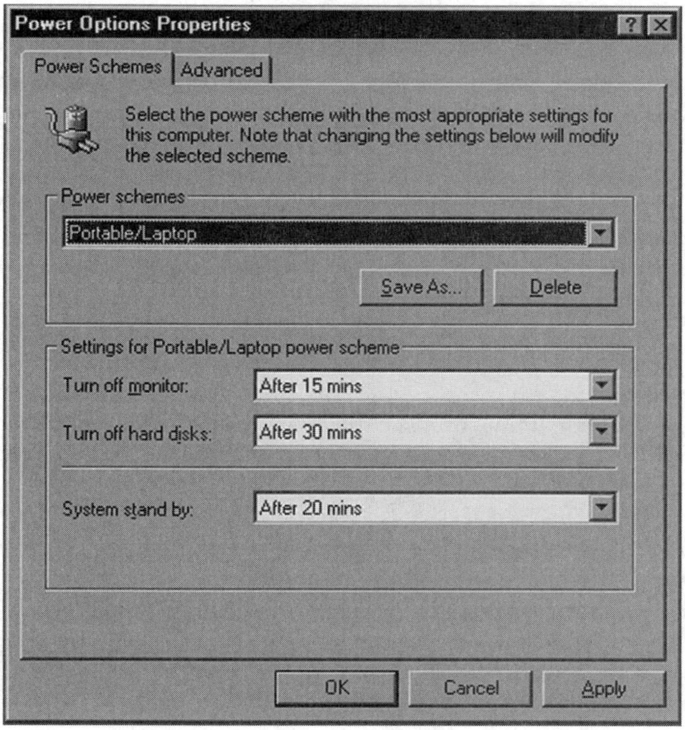

FIGURE 30.3

Windows power management

Laptop Maintenance Issues

Although keeping your laptop in good condition requires many of the same considerations as a desktop machine (for instance, keep it clean and dry, and feed it high-quality electricity), its portability adds a few factors to the equation and makes some of the ordinary issues especially important.

One of the most important things you can do to keep your laptop in good shape is to make sure you have a good carrying case. It might sound trivial, but it's not. Your laptop is a traveling companion, and as with any situation where you leave a secure, controlled environment, it'll be subject to the same bumps and knocks as you.

Modern carrying cases are especially designed to save you and your notebook lots of grief, and it's well worth the investment to get one you can count on. I don't necessarily mean you have to spend hundreds of dollars for one of those aluminum suitcases. A good padded shoulder bag will give you all the protection you'll usually need; also, it'll make it easier for you to get through doors, into cars and onto airplanes, and it'll keep you from having to reinvest in new laptops.

So, don't carry your laptop outside without a case. It may look power-chic in a TV commercial, but it's probably the worst thing you can do. People drop things, even important things, and no ordinary laptop will survive a tumble onto concrete.

When you're looking at carrying cases, check that it's made of a nonporous material. Even if you like the look of a canvas-type bag, make sure there's some kind of inner liner that will keep it from transferring moisture to the inside. Raindrops on the outside are okay. When they soak through and fizzle your laptop, they're not okay.

Check the hardware between the bag and the carrying strap. If the connection is a simple spring latch, never pick up the bag with the computer inside without first making sure the "tongue and groove" pieces are straight before pulling on the strap. Sideways pressure on many of the latches that I've had experience with will cause most of them to release. You'll find out how much a new case (or perhaps a new computer) costs when the case opens and the computer lands on one of its corners or slams into something hard (such as airport steps).

You also want to make sure that the case you get has separate compartments for things you carry with you. Pens, pencils, mice, and modems rattling around and bumping into your machine can cause damage.

Make sure the outer walls of the case are well padded. The padding doesn't have to be extremely thick, but you want something between the case walls and your computer to distribute the shock of accidental bumps.

Finally, don't put anything in your case that doesn't belong there. I know people who have packed socks, toothbrushes, and candy bars into their carrying cases and treated them as overnight bags for emergency business trips. These people also tend to buy more new laptops than my other acquaintances. Putting anything in the bag that's damp, pointy, or crumbly is always a bad idea.

The weakest link on your laptop is the hinge that flips the screen up and down. It's not that the hinges are designed badly; it's just that they get the most exercise, and unlike with people, exercise makes them weaker instead of stronger. Unfortunately, the only thing you can do to keep a hinge from croaking before its time is just don't fool with it too much:

- Never pick up the laptop by the open screen.
- Don't slam it shut because you're in a hurry.

◆ Don't yank it open and bend it too far.

◆ Don't open and close it repeatedly as a way to ease nervous tension.

Generally, you shouldn't oil the hinges. They really weren't made for that kind of maintenance, and oil is a tremendous attractor of dust, grit, and pollen, all of which will only gum things up even worse.

The other areas you have to watch are the openings in your laptop's case. The floppy drive has a latch, flap, or door that closes when there's no disk in the drive. If this gets stuck in the "open" position, you'll collect lots of dust and your floppy drive, at least, could be ruined. On many laptops, the floppy drive flap is pretty flimsy and can be quite easily pushed aside (which is another good reason to have a laptop carrying case that gives you separate compartments for business cards, paper clips, and pencils). You don't want a stick of chewing gum wedging into your floppy drive after you've packed up your laptop for a business trip.

The other area that exposes the inside of your laptop to the outside world is the bay with your PC Card slot openings. Your computer probably came with plastic covers to seal up any slots that are not in use. Or it may have hinged flaps that come down when the slot is empty. Make sure these slots are closed or sealed. The connectors inside the slots are especially tiny, and even minute amounts of foreign material can cause big problems.

When it comes to the monitor screen, there are only a couple of precautions you have to keep in mind. First, when you clean it, use a soft, lint-free cloth. Dry is best; very slightly damp is okay if you have really sticky garbage caked onto the screen; wet is never recommended. Try not to use paper towels—the cheap kind can scratch. Second, don't twist the monitor, which means don't grab it when you want to swivel the computer around to show somebody what's being displayed. You can damage the screen as well as the hinges that hold it to the computer. If your computer uses one of the film technologies for display (such as a thin-film transistor display), then pushing, hitting, or twisting the screen can warp the film. Screens aren't repairable items. If yours gets broken, you have to replace it.

PC-to-Laptop Syncing

Most people who have a laptop also have a desktop PC. Keeping files updated between them can be a real challenge.

If both PCs are on a network together, you can transfer files between PCs using the network connection. If not, you can connect them directly with a null modem cable (basically a straight pass-through serial cable) and then use special software to manage the connection. Windows comes with a Direct Cable Connection utility that does the job just fine. Null modem cables are incredibly slow, though, and investing in a small network is a much better option.

Windows also comes with a synchronization feature called My Briefcase that's specifically designed for keeping files matched up between your desktop and your laptop PCs. For example, suppose you're working on a report at work, and you want to take the latest draft home with you over the weekend. You copy the report from your desktop computer to the Briefcase on your laptop (using either a disk or your LAN). Then, you work on the report at home, and when you return to the office, you synchronize your Briefcase, copying the latest version back to the desktop to overwrite the older version.

You can use My Briefcase either with a floppy disk or on a network. To do it on a floppy, firs copy the files on your main PC into the My Briefcase icon on your Desktop in Windows. Then dra the My Briefcase folder onto the floppy drive icon to move it there. On a network, start at the remo PC (the laptop) and access the files on the main PC through Network Neighborhood (or My Ne work Places, depending on the Windows version you have). Drag them to the My Briefcase icon o the remote PC to copy them there.

Then, to sync the files from a floppy, copy the My Briefcase folder back to the desktop from th floppy disk. Then open the My Briefcase window and click the Update All button. Or, on a networl make sure both PCs are connected to the network and open the My Briefcase folder on the remot PC. Then click Update All to update the copies on the main PC.

Syncing Data with PDAs

Many people these days use PDAs, made by Palm, Handspring, Sony, Toshiba, Hewlett-Packard, and other well-known companies. You have two choices in PDA operating systems. The original an popular Palm OS is available on the Palm, Handspring, and Sony devices. Models running the Microsoft Pocket PC operating system include the iPAQ, Cassiopeia, and Jornada. Both operating systems are "Windows-compatible" and are capable of synchronizing with desktop PCs.

The primary purpose of a PDA is to store addresses, appointments, and task lists in a portable easy-to-update format. You can use a PDA as a stand-alone tool, but it's most effective when com bined with a computer. You can enter and update your data on the computer and then transfer it t the PDA by syncing. *Syncing* updates the information on both sources—the PDA and the computer— by comparing the dates of various additions, edits, and deletions and placing the most current infor mation in both places.

Palm OS–based PDAs come with their own operating system, called Palm Desktop. You can us it to store and edit your information if you like, or you can use any of a variety of other programs instead if you prefer. The PDAs work with Microsoft Outlook, Lotus Notes, and several other popula programs through special drivers called *conduits*. Most Palm OS–based models come with conduits fo popular applications that you can install when you run the setup software for the device on your PC. Pocket PCs ship with ActiveSync, which lets the device synchronize with Microsoft Outlook.

To sync a PDA, simply place it in its cradle (which is attached to the PC via a serial or USB port and press the button on the cradle. (There's only one button; you can't miss it.) You can also initiat a sync from the PC by clicking the Synchronize button in the program you have set the device up t sync with. In Outlook, for example, installing the conduit places a Synchronize icon on Outlook's toolbar, and you can click that icon to begin the sync.

Troubleshooting Tips

Troubleshooting laptops and handheld computers involves some techniques similar to those you'c use for a desktop computer, but there are some important differences. The similarities (at least for laptops) lie mainly with the operating system and software you use. The version of Windows runnin on a laptop is the same operating system that you have on your desktop. The main difference is tha all your components are connected together internally, and you have an internal power supply (tha is, your battery). You don't really have to check cable connections or mess with add-in cards as you do for a desktop model. Instead, the trouble might have to do with configuration and battery issues.

If your computer won't turn on and is unplugged, your battery may be dead. Try plugging in the laptop's A/C adapter so you know you have power and try it again. Most of the time, that's the problem. If your laptop still won't turn on, it may already be on, but it might be in a power-saving sleep mode. Try pressing a key on the keyboard to wake it up or move your mouse/cursor around a bit (or touch your finger on the touchpad). In some cases, you may have to press and hold the power button down for a few seconds to get it to wake up.

As with desktop computers, make sure all your drivers are updated. On my Dell Latitude C840, I regularly check for updates at the Dell Web site for my major components:

- Integrated video system
- DVD-ROM drive
- Touchpad drivers
- Modem/network adapter PC Card
- Sound card

Laptops are the computer of choice for more and more people every day because of their unique combination of features and convenience. Now that you know how to keep yours in good repair and to care for it properly, you're ready to join the ranks of the computing road warriors.

Glossary

Numbers and Symbols

See asterisk.

See slash.

/

See double slash.

See colon.

See question mark.

See at symbol.

See backslash.

¹⁄₂-inch cartridge

See quarter-inch cartridge.

10/100

A term used to indicate that a device can support both Ethernet (at a data transfer rate of 10Mbps) and Fast Ethernet (at a data transfer rate of 100Mbps).

10Base-T

A version of the Ethernet networking standard that uses unshielded twisted-pair cable and RJ-45 connectors.

10Base-T cable

A popular Ethernet cable that uses unshielded twisted-pair wiring and RJ-45 connectors at each end. You should use Category 3 10Base-T cable with 10Mbps Ethernet networks.

10Base-TX cable

A popular Ethernet cable that uses unshielded twisted-pair wiring and RJ-45 connectors at each end. You should use Category 5 10Base-TX cable with 100Mbps Ethernet networks.

10Mbps

An abbreviation for 10 megabits per second, the standard Ethernet network data rate.

100Mbps

An abbreviation for 100 megabits per second, the standard Fast Ethernet network data rate.

1000Mbps

An abbreviation for 1000 megabits (1 Gigabit) per second, also known as Gigabit Ethernet.

1394

See IEEE 1394.

23B+D

A common abbreviation for Primary Rate ISDN, which has 23 B or bearer channels and one D or data channel.

24/7

An abbreviation for round-the-clock availability, implying that the service is available 24 hours a day for seven days per week.

24-bit color

A color display in which the level of each of the primary colors is represented by 8 bits of information. A 24-bit color image can contain more than 16 million separate colors.

2B+D

A common abbreviation for Basic Rate ISDN, which has 2 B or bearer channels and one D or data channel.

A

a-b box

A switching box that allows a peripheral device such as a printer to be shared between two or more computers. It can be switched manually or through software.

AC adapter

A small external power supply that converts main electrical power to the low-voltage DC required for a laptop or notebook computer or other device needing its own power supply.

Accelerated Graphics Port

Abbreviated AGP. A specification developed by Intel to support high-speed, high-resolution 3D graphics and video images.

AGP uses a dedicated point-to-point connection between main memory and the graphics controller so that images can be displayed faster and more smoothly than when they have to travel across the main system bus. AGP runs at 66MHz and supports data transfer rates of up to 533Mbps.

accelerator board

An add-in, printed circuit board that replaces or augments the main processor with a higher-performance processor. Using an accelerator board can reduce upgrading costs substantially because you won't need to replace the monitor, case, keyboard, and so on. However, the main processor isn't the only component that affects the overall performance of your system. Other factors, such as disk-access time and video speed, contribute to a system's performance.

access

To use, write to, or read from a file, or to log in to a computer system or network.

access time

The period of time that elapses between a request for information from disk or memory and the arrival of that information at the requesting device.

Memory-access time refers to the time it takes to transfer a character between memory and the processor. Disk-access time refers to the time it takes to place the read/write heads over the requested data. Random Access Memory (RAM) may have an access time of 80ns or less, and hard disk access time would be less quicker than 10ms.

ACPI

See Advanced Configuration and Power Interface.

active hub

A device that amplifies transmission signals in a network, allowing signals to be sent over a much greater distance than is possible with a passive hub.

An active hub may have ports for coaxial, twisted pair, or fiber-optic cable connections, as well as LEDs to show that each port is operating correctly.

active-matrix display

A high-quality, liquid-crystal display used in laptop and notebook computers with a wide viewing angle and narrow depth. This is also known as a Thin-Film Transistor (TFT) display.

active termination

A technique used to terminate a Small Computer System Interface (SCSI). Active termination reduces electrical interference in a long string of SCSI devices.

adapter

A printed circuit board that plugs into a computer's expansion bus to provide added capabilities.

Common adapters include video adapters, joystick controllers, and Input/Output (I/O) adapters, as well as other devices, such as internal modems, CD-ROM and Network Interface Cards (NICs). One adapter can often support several different devices. Some modern PC designs incorporate many of the functions previously performed by these individual adapters on the motherboard.

ddress

, The precise location in memory or on disk where a iece of information is stored. Each byte in memory nd each sector on a disk has its own unique address. , The unique identifier for a specific node on a net-ork. An address may be a physical address specified y switches or jumpers on the network interface card ardware or a logical address established by the net-ork operating system. 3. To reference or manage a orage location. 4. Information used by a network or ne Internet to specify a specific location in the form f `username@hostname`, where `username` is your user-ame, logon name, or account name or number and ostname is the name of the Internet Service Provider SP) or computer system you use. The `hostname` may onsist of several different parts, each separated from ne next by a period.

ddress bus

he electronic channel, usually from 20 to 64 lines ide, used to transmit the signals that specify loca-ons in memory.

The number of lines in the address bus determines ne number of memory locations that the processor can ccess because each line carries one bit of the address. 20-line address bus (used in early Intel 8086/8088 rocessors) can access 1MB of memory, a 24-line ddress bus can access 16MB, and a 32-line address us can access more than 4GB. A 64-line address bus n access 16EB.

DSL

e asymmetric digital subscriber line.

dvanced Configuration and Power Interface

bbreviated ACPI. An interface specification devel-ped by Intel, Microsoft, and Toshiba for controlling ower use on the PC and all other devices attached to ne system. A BIOS-level hardware specification, CPI depends on specific hardware that allows the perating system to direct power management and stem configuration.

Advanced Power Management

Abbreviated APM. An API specification from Microsoft and Intel intended to monitor and extend battery life on a laptop computer by shutting down certain system components after a period of inactivity.

Advanced SCSI Programming Interface

Abbreviated ASPI. A programming standard that defines how Small Computer System Interface (SCSI) devices work together and with the other components that make up the PC.

Advanced Technology Attachment

Abbreviated ATA. The ANSI X3T10 term for the disk drive interface standard known as Integrated Drive Electronics (IDE).

Advanced Technology Attachment Packet Interface

Abbreviated ATAPI. An interface standard used to connect a CD-ROM drive to an Enhanced IDE adapter.

aftermarket

The market for related hardware, software, and peripheral devices created by the sale of a large number of computers of a specific type.

alphanumeric

Consisting of letters, numbers, and sometimes special control characters, spaces, and other punctuation characters.

AGP

See Accelerated Graphics Port.

American Standard Code for Information Interchange

Abbreviated ASCII, pronounced "as-kee." This is a standard coding scheme that assigns numeric values to letters, numbers, punctuation characters, and con-trol characters to achieve compatibility among dif-ferent computers and peripheral devices. In ASCII, each character is represented by a unique integer value from 0 to 255.

analog

Describes any device that represents changing values by a continuously variable physical property, such as a voltage in a circuit. Analog often refers to transmission methods developed to transmit voice signals rather than high-speed digital signals.

anonymous FTP

A method used to access an Internet computer with FTP that doesn't require you to have an account on the target computer system. Simply log on to the Internet computer with the username *anonymous* and use your email address as your password. This access method was originally provided as a courtesy so that system administrators could see who had logged on to their system, but now it's often required to gain access to an Internet computer that has FTP service.

You can't use anonymous FTP with every computer on the Internet; only with those systems that are set up to offer the service. The system administrator decides which files and directories will be open to public access, and the rest of the system is considered to be off-limits and can't be accessed by anonymous FTP users. Some sites only allow you to download from them; as a security precaution, you're not allowed to upload files to them.

antistatic device

Any device designed to minimize electrical shocks caused by a build-up of static electricity, including special floor mats, wrist bands, even sprays and lotions.

antivirus program

A program that detects or eliminates a computer virus. Some antivirus programs can detect suspicious activity on your computer as it happens; others must be run periodically as part of your normal housekeeping activities.

An antivirus program locates and identifies a virus by looking for characteristic patterns or suspicious activity in the system, such as unexpected disk access or EXE files changing in some unusual way. It recognizes the virus by comparing information from the system against a database of known viruses, which is kept on disk.

API

See application programming interface.

APM

See Advanced Power Management.

application programming interface

Abbreviated API. The complete set of all operating system functions that an application can use to perform such tasks as managing files and displaying information.

An API provides a standard way to write an application, and it also describes how the application should use the functions it provides. Using an API is quicker and easier than developing functions from scratch and helps to ensure some level of consistency among all the applications developed for a specific operating system.

In operating systems that support a graphical user interface, the API also defines functions to support windows, icons, pull-down menus, and other components of the interface. In network operating systems, an API defines a standard method that applications can use to take advantage of all the network features.

application-specific integrated circuit

Abbreviated ASIC. A computer chip developed for specific purpose, designed by incorporating standard cells from a library rather than created from scratch. Also known as a gate array, ASICs are found in all sorts of appliances, including modems, security systems, digital cameras, even microwave ovens, and automobiles.

architecture

1. The overall design and construction of all or part of a computer, particularly the processor hardware and the size and ordering sequence of its bytes. 2. The overall design of software, including interfaces to other software, the operating system, and the network.

archive

. To transfer files to some form of long-term storage, such as magnetic tape or large-capacity disk, when the files are no longer needed on a regular basis but must be maintained for periodic reference. 2. On the Internet, a site containing a collection of files available via anonymous FTP. 3. A compressed file.

archive file

. single file that contains one or more files or directories that may have been compressed to save space. Archives are often used as a way to transport large numbers of related files across the Internet.

arrow keys

Any of the four keys labeled with arrows pointing down, up, left, and right, which are used to move the on-screen cursor.

ASCII

See *American Standard Code for Information Interchange.*

ASCII extended character set

The second group of characters, from 128 to 255, in the ASCII character set. The extended ASCII character set used in the PC includes mathematical symbols and characters from the PC line-drawing set.

ASCII file

. file that contains only text characters from the ASCII character set. An ASCII file can include letters, numbers, and punctuation symbols but doesn't contain any hidden text-formatting codes. Also known as a text file or an ASCII text file.

ASCII standard character set

. character set that consists of the first 128 (from 0 to 127) ASCII characters. The values 0 to 31 are used for nonprinting control codes, and the range from 32 to 127 is used to represent the letters of the alphabet and common punctuation symbols. The entire set from 0 to 127 is referred to as the standard ASCII

character set. All computers that use ASCII can understand the standard ASCII character set.

ASIC

See *application-specific integrated circuit.*

ASPI

See *Advanced SCSI Programming Interface.*

assembly language

A low-level programming language in which each program statement must correspond to a single machine language instruction that the processor can execute.

Assembly languages are specific to a given microprocessor or microprocessor family and, as such, aren't portable; programs written for one type of processor must be rewritten before they can be used on another type of processor.

asterisk

You can use the asterisk (*) as a wildcard character to represent one or more unknown characters in a filename or filename extension.

asymmetric digital subscriber line

Abbreviated ADSL. A high-speed data transmission technology originally developed by Bellcore and now standardized by ANSI as T1.413 that delivers high bandwidth over existing twisted-pair copper telephone lines. Also called asymmetric digital subscriber loop. ADSL supports speeds in the range of 1.5 to 9Mbps in the downstream direction (from the network to the customer) and upstream speeds in the range of 16 to 640Kbps, hence the term *asymmetric.*

Asynchronous Transfer Mode

Abbreviated ATM. A method used for transmitting voice, video, and data over high-speed LANs and WANs. ATM uses continuous bursts of fixed-length packets called *cells* to transmit data. The basic packet consists of 53 bytes, 5 of which are used for control functions and 48 for data.

ATM is a connection-oriented protocol, and two kinds of connection are possible: Permanent Virtual Circuits (PVCs), in which connections are created manually, and Switched Virtual Circuits (SVCs), in which connections are made automatically. Speeds of up to 2.488Gbps have been achieved in testing.

ATM will find wide acceptance in the LAN and WAN arenas as a solution to integrating disparate networks over large geographical distances. Also known as cell relay.

asynchronous transmission

A method of data transmission that uses start bits and stop bits to coordinate the flow of data so the time intervals between individual characters don't need to be equal. Parity may also be used to check the accuracy of the data received.

ATA

See Advanced Technology Attachment.

ATAPI

See Advanced Technology Attachment Packet Interface.

at symbol

The separating character (@) between the account name and domain name in an Internet email address.

Athlon

A family of microprocessors introduced by AMD in 1999. The Athlon, also known as the K7 processor, represents the successor of the K6 family of microprocessors and adds several notable features, including much improved FPU power. The original Athlon had 22 million transistors, a 200MHz bus, and a 512KB half-speed L2 cache. An addition to the Athlon family was the faster Thunderbird. The Thunderbird has 37 million transistors on a smaller die as well as a full-speed 256K L2 cache.

attenuation

The decrease in power of a signal with increasing distance. Attenuation is measured in decibels, and it increases as the power of the signal decreases. The best cables (those exhibiting the least attenuation) are fiber-optic lines, and the worst cables are unshielded untwisted-pair lines, such as the silver, flat-satin cable used in short-run telephone and modem lines.

In a LAN, attenuation can become a problem when cable lengths exceed the stated network specification; however, the useful length of a cable may be extended by the use of a repeater.

ATM

See Asynchronous Transfer Mode.

attribute

1. A file attribute is a technique for describing access to and properties of files and directories within a file system. You may see the term *attribute* used interchangeably with the term *property*. 2. A screen attribute controls a character's background and foreground colors, as well as other characteristics, such as underlining, reverse video, and blinking. 3. In operating systems, a characteristic that indicates whether a file is read-only file, a hidden file, or a system file or whether the file has changed in some way since it was last backed up.

auto-answer

A feature of a modem that allows it to answer incoming calls automatically.

auto-dial

A feature of a modem that allows it to open a telephone line and start a call. To auto-dial, the modem sends a series of pulses or tones that represents a stored telephone number.

B

backslash

1. Used to separate directory or subdirectory names in a path statement or when changing to another directory from a command prompt. 2. A shorthand name for the root directory. Sometimes called the reverse slash or backslant. It goes from the upper left to the lower right (\).

backup

An up-to-date copy of all your files. Your decision when or how often to make a backup depends on how frequently important data on your system changes. If you rely on certain files always being available on your system, it's crucial that you make regular, consistent backups.

backward compatibility

Full compatibility with earlier versions of the same application or computer system.

bad sector

An area on a hard disk or floppy disk that can't be used to store data because of a manufacturing defect or accidental damage.

Some operating systems will find, mark, and isolate bad sectors. Almost all hard disks have some bad sectors, often listed in the bad track table. Usually, bad sectors are a result of the manufacturing process and not a concern; the operating system will mark them as bad, and you're never even know they're there.

bad track table

A list of the defective areas on a hard disk, usually determined during final testing of the disk at the factory. Some disk-preparation programs ask you to enter information from this list to reduce the time that a low-level format takes to prepare the disk for use by the operating system.

bandwidth

1. In communications, the difference between the highest and lowest frequencies available for transmission in any given range. 2. In networking, the transmission capacity of a computer or a communications channel, stated in megabits per second (Mbps).

Basic Rate ISDN

Abbreviated BRI. An Integrated Services Digital Network (ISDN) service that offers two 64Kbps B channels used for data transfer and one 16Kbps D channel used for signaling and control information.

Each B channel can carry a single digital voice call or can be used as a data channel; the B channels can also be combined into a single 128Kbps data channel.

baud rate

In communications equipment, a measurement of the number of state changes (from 0 to 1 or vice versa) per second on an asynchronous communications channel.

Baud rate is often assumed to correspond to the number of bits transmitted per second, but baud rate and bits per second (bps) aren't always the same. In modern high-speed digital communications systems, one state change can be made to represent more than one data bit.

BEDO DRAM

See Burst Extended Data Out DRAM.

binary

Any scheme that uses two different states, components, conditions, or conclusions.

In mathematics, the binary or base-2 numbering system uses combinations of the digits 0 and 1 to represent all values. The more familiar decimal system has a base of 10 (0–9).

Unlike computers, people find binary numbers that consist of long strings of 0s and 1s difficult to read, so most programmers use hexadecimal (base-16) or octal (base-8) numbers instead.

Binary also refers to an executable file containing a program.

BIOS

Acronym for basic input/output system, pronounced "bye-ose." In the PC, the BIOS is a set of instructions that tests the hardware when the computer is first turned on, starts to load the operating system, and lets the computer's hardware and operating system communicate with applications and peripheral devices, such as hard disks, printers, and video adapters. These instructions are stored in ROM Read-Only Memory (ROM) as a permanent part of the computer.

As new hardware is developed, new BIOS routines must be created to service those devices. For example, BIOS support has been added for power management and for ever-larger hard disks.

If you're experiencing problems accessing such devices after adding them to an existing system, your computer's BIOS may be out-of-date. Contact your computer supplier for information about BIOS updates.

bit

Contraction of binary digit. A bit is the basic unit of information in the binary numbering system, representing either 0 (off) or 1 (on). Bits can be grouped to form larger storage units; the most common grouping is the 8 bits, called a *byte*.

bit rate

The rate at which bits are transmitted over a communications channel, described in terms of bits per second (bps).

bits per inch

Abbreviated bpi. The number of bits that a tape or tape cartridge can store per inch of length.

bits per second

Abbreviated bps. The number of binary digits, or bits, transmitted every second during a data transfer procedure. Bits per second is a measurement of the speed of operation of equipment, such as a computer's data bus or a modem that connects a computer to a communications circuit.

BNC connector

A small connector with a half-turn locking shell for coaxial cable, used with thin Ethernet and RG-62 cabling.

boot

To load an operating system into memory, usually from a hard disk although possible from a floppy disk or CD-ROM. Booting is generally an automatic procedure that begins when you turn on or reset your computer.

A set of instructions contained in Read-Only Memory (ROM) begins executing. The instructions run a series of Power-On Self Tests (POSTs) to check that devices such as hard disks are in working order, then locate and load the operating system, and finally pass control over to that operating system.

boot sector virus

A virus that infects the master boot record of a computer by overwriting the original boot code with infected boot code. This kind of virus is usually spread to a hard disk by using an infected floppy disk as a boot disk.

bootable disk

Any disk capable of loading and starting the operating system. Bootable floppy disks are becoming less common because operating systems are growing larger. In some cases, all the files needed to start the operating system won't fit on even the largest-capacity floppy disk, which makes it impossible to boot from a floppy disk.

bpi

See bits per inch.

bps

See bits per second.

brain damaged

An expression used to describe any poorly designed program or piece of hardware that doesn't include those features most users would consider essential. The implication is that the designer should have known better than to leave those features out of the product.

breakout box

A small device that can be connected into a multicore cable for testing the signals in a transmission. Small LEDs in the breakout box indicate when a signal is transmitted over one of the lines. Switches or short jumper cables can be used to reroute these signals to other pins as required for troubleshooting.

RI

ee Basic Rate ISDN.

rownout

short period of low voltage, often the result of an nusually heavy demand for power, that may cause our computer to crash. If your area experiences fre uent brownouts, consider using a Uninterruptible ower Supply (UPS) as a battery backup system.

uffer

n area of memory set aside for temporary storage of ata. Often, the data remains in the buffer until some xternal event finishes. A buffer can compensate for e differences in transmission or processing speed etween two devices or between a computer and a eripheral device, such as a printer or modem.

Buffers are implemented in a variety of different ays, including First-In-First-Out (FIFO) used for pes and last-in-last-out used for stacks and circular uffers such as event logs.

ug

logical or programming error in hardware or soft are that causes a malfunction of some sort. If the roblem is in software, it can be fixed by changes to e program. If the fault is in hardware, new circuits ust be designed and constructed. Some bugs are tal and may cause a program to stop responding or ause data loss; others are just annoying, and many ren't even noticeable.

urned-in address

he hardware address on a network interface card. his address is assigned by the manufacturer of the iterface card, which ensures that every card has a nique address.

urst Extended Data Out DRAM

bbreviated BEDO DRAM. A type of EDO dynamic AM that manages data in bursts of four items at a me to increase speed. This approach takes advantage f the fact that memory requests usually refer to a eries of sequential addresses.

bus

An electronic pathway along which signals are sent from one part of a computer to another.

bus mastering

A technique that allows certain advanced bus archi tectures to delegate control of data transfers between the Central Processing Unit (CPU) and associated peripheral devices to an add-in board. This technique gives greater system bus access and higher data transfer speeds.

In the PC, bus mastering is supported by all of the common architectures except for the older Industry Standard Architecture (ISA).

byte

Contraction of binary digit eight. A group of bits. In computer storage terms, a byte usually holds a single character, such as a number, letter, or symbol. A byte usually contains 8 bits, but on some older computer systems, a byte may only have 7 bits or may have as many as 11.

Because bytes represent a small amount of storage, they're usually grouped into kilobytes (1024 bytes), megabytes (1,048,576 bytes), and gigabytes (1,073,741,824 bytes) for convenience when describing hard disk capacity or computer memory size.

C

cable modem

A modem that sends and receives signals through a coaxial cable connected to a cable television system rather than through conventional telephone lines. Cable modems, with speeds of up to 500Kbps, are faster than current conventional modems but are sub ject to performance changes as system load increases. Theoretical data rates are much higher than those achieved with conventional modems; downstream rates of up to 36Mbps are possible, with 3Mbps to 10Mbps likely, and upstream rates up to 10Mbps are possible.

cache

Pronounced "cash." A special area of memory, managed by a cache controller, which improves performance by storing the contents of frequently accessed memory locations and their addresses.

A memory cache and a disk cache aren't the same. This entry describes a memory cache, which is implemented in hardware and speeds up access to memory. A disk cache is software that improves hard disk performance.

When the processor references a memory address, the cache checks to see if it holds that address. If it does, the information is passed directly to the processor, so Random Access Memory (RAM) access isn't necessary. A cache can speed up operations in a computer whose RAM access is slow compared with its processor speed because cache memory is always faster than normal RAM.

cache memory

Pronounced "cash memory." A relatively small section of fast memory (often static RAM) reserved for the temporary storage of the data or instructions likely to be needed next by the processor.

Cache memory integrated directly onto the microprocessor is called *primary cache* or L1 cache, and cache memory located in an external circuit is known as *secondary cache* or L2 cache.

carrier signal

A signal of chosen frequency generated to carry data, often used for long-distance transmissions. A carrier signal doesn't convey any information until the data is added to the signal by modulation and then decoded on the receiving end by demodulation.

cascading

A technique used to connect two Ethernet hubs when expanding the network; sometimes called daisy chaining. Cascading usually requires a special cable.

Category 1

For Unshielded Twisted-Pair (UTP) telephone cable. This cable may be used for voice but isn't suitable for data transmissions.

Category 2

For UTP cable for use at speeds up to 4Mbps. Category 2 cable is similar to IBM Cabling System Type 3 cable.

Category 3

For UTP cable for use at speeds up to 10Mbps. Category 3 cable is the minimum requirement for 10Base-T and is required for token ring. This cable has four pairs of conductors and three twists per foot.

Category 4

For the lowest acceptable grade of UTP cable for use with 16Mbps token ring.

Category 5

For 100-ohm, four-wire twisted-pair copper cable for use at speeds up to 100Mbps with Ethernet or ATM. This cable is low capacitance and shows low crosstalk when installed according to specifications.

Category 1–5

The Telecommunications Industry Association and Electronics Industry Association (TIA/EIA) 586 cabling standards, sometimes abbreviated Cat 1–5.

CAV

See constant angular velocity.

CCD

See charge-coupled device.

CD-R

See CD-recordable.

CD-recordable

Abbreviated CD-R. Using CD-R, you can write to the disc just once; after that, the disc can only be read from and not written to.

From a functional point of view, a CD-R and a CD-ROM are identical; you can read CD-Rs using most any CD-ROM drive, but the processes that create the discs are slightly different. Low-cost CD-R drives are available from several manufacturers, including Kao, Kodak, Mitsui, Phillips, Ricoh, Sony, TDK, 3M, and Verbatim.

CD-rewritable

Abbreviated CD-RW. A CD format that can be written to and erased up to 1,000 times.

From a functional point of view, a CD-RW drive and a CD-ROM drive are identical, but not all CD-ROM drives can read CD-RWs. Low-cost CD-RW drives are available from several manufacturers, including Kodak, Mitsui, Phillips, and Sony.

CD-ROM

Acronym for Compact Disc Read-Only Memory. A high-capacity, optical storage device that uses the same technology used to make ordinary music discs to store large amounts of information. A single 4.72-inch disc can hold up to 650 megabytes.

CD-ROMs are important components of multimedia applications. They're also used to store encyclopedias, dictionaries, and other large reference works, as well as libraries of fonts and clip art for desktop publishing. CD-ROMs have replaced floppy disks as the distribution mechanism for software packages, including network operating systems and large applications, so you can load the whole package from a single compact disc and an operating system from a set of discs.

A CD-ROM uses the constant linear velocity data-encoding scheme to store information in a single, spiral track, divided into many equal-length segments. To read data, the CD-ROM disk drive must increase the rotational speed as the read head gets closer to the center of the disk and decrease as the head moves back out.

CD-ROM drive

A disk device that uses compact disc technology for information storage. Many CD-ROM disk drives also have headphone jacks, external speaker jacks, and a volume control.

CD-ROM disk drives designed for computer use are more expensive than audio CD players are because CD-ROM disk drives are manufactured to much higher tolerances. If a CD player misreads a small amount of data, the human ear probably won't detect the difference; if a CD-ROM disk drive misreads a few bytes of a program, the program won't run.

The two most popular CD-ROM drive interface cards are Small Computer System Interface (SCSI) and Advanced Technology Attachment Packet Interface (ATAPI). ATAPI is part of the Enhanced IDE specification introduced by Western Digital in 1994.

CD-ROM Extended Architecture

Abbreviated CD-ROM/XA. An extension to the CD-ROM format developed by Microsoft, Phillips, and Sony that allows for the storage of audio and visual information on compact disc, so you can play the audio at the same time you view the visual data. CD-ROM/XA is compatible with the High Sierra specification, also known as ISO standard 9660.

CD-ROM/XA

See CD-ROM Extended Architecture.

CD-RW

See CD-rewritable.

Celeron

A low-cost version of Intel's Pentium microprocessor line. The Celeron includes an integrated 128KB L2 cache, supports Intel's MMX technology, and is available in a wide range of speeds.

charge-coupled device

Abbreviated CCD. A device in which the semiconductor elements are connected so that the electrical output from one provides the input to the next. CCDs are used in the light-detection circuitry in digital and video cameras.

chassis

The metal frame into which the PC's components, including power supply, printed circuit boards, and fan, are mounted.

checksum

A method of providing information for error detection, usually calculated by summing a set of values. The checksum is usually appended to the end of the data that it's calculated from so that they can be compared. A checksum can't detect all possible errors and can't be used to correct an error in the data.

chip

A slang expression for integrated circuit.

chipset

A group of integrated circuits designed to perform as a unit.

CISC

See complex instruction set computing.

Class A certification

An FCC certification for computer equipment, including mainframe computers and minicomputers destined for industrial, commercial, or office use, rather than for personal use at home. The Class A commercial certification is less restrictive than the Class B certification for residential use because it assumes that most residential areas are more than 30 feet away from any commercial computer equipment.

Class B certification

An FCC certification for computer equipment, including PCs, laptops, and portables destined for use in the home rather than in a commercial setting. Class B levels of Radio Frequency Interference (RFI) must be low enough so that they don't interfere with radio or television reception when there's more than one wall and 30 feet separating the computer from the receiver. Class B certification is more restrictive than the commercial Class A certification.

Clear to Send

Abbreviated CTS. A hardware signal defined by the RS-232-C standard that indicates that the transmission can proceed.

clock

An electronic circuit that generates regularly spaced timing pulses at speeds up to millions of cycles per second. These pulses are used to synchronize the flow of information through the computer's internal communications channels.

clock speed

The internal speed of a computer or processor, normally expressed in megahertz (MHz) or gigahertz (GHz). Also known as clock rate.

The faster the clock speed, the faster the computer will perform a specific operation (assuming the other components in the system, such as disk drives, can keep up with the increased speed).

The Intel 8088 processor used in the original IBM PC had a clock speed of 4.77MHz—painfully slow when compared with speeds used by modern processors, which can run at clock speeds of a gigahertz or more.

clone

A computer that contains all the same hardware elements as a name-brand system but that is usually cheaper.

cluster

The basic unit of data storage recorded onto a hard or floppy disk during a low-level format. It usually contains two or more sectors.

clustering

In networking, the grouping of several servers in a way that allows them to appear to be one server from the point of view of network clients. Clustering improves data security, increases network capacity, and provides live backup in the event a server fails.

CLV

See constant linear velocity.

CMOS

See complementary metal-oxide semiconductor.

coaxial cable

A high-capacity cable used in networking that contains a solid inner copper core surrounded by plastic insulation and an outer braided copper or foil sheath. Depending on the diameter of the cable, it may be known as *thinnet* (thin Ethernet, used for office installations) or *thicknet* (thick Ethernet, used for facility-wide applications).

codec

1. Acronym for coder/decoder. A device that converts analog signals (such as voice or video) into a digital bit stream suitable for transmission and then converts those digital signals back into analog signals at the receiving end. 2. Acronym for compression/decompression. A general term to describe the hardware and software used in processing animation, digital video, and stereo-quality audio.

cold boot

The computer startup process that begins when you turn on power to the computer. You're doing a cold boot when you first turn on your computer. A cold boot might also be necessary if a program or the operating system crashes and freezes entirely. If your keyboard is operational, a warm boot may suffice.

collision

An attempt by two computers on the network to send a message at the same instant; Ethernet automatically resends both messages but with altered timing so they don't collide and they're received properly.

colon

The symbol used after the protocol name in a Universal Resource Locator (URL).

command line

An interface between the user and the command processor that allows you to enter commands from the keyboard for execution by the operating system.

command processor

The part of the operating system that displays the command prompt on the screen, interprets and executes all the commands and filenames you enter, and displays error messages when appropriate. Also called the command interpreter. The command processor also contains the system environment.

command prompt

A symbol (character or group of characters) on the screen that lets you know that the operating system is available and ready to receive input.

command-line argument

A parameter that alters the default mode of a command. In many operating systems, a command-line argument is one or more letters or numbers preceded by the slash (/) character. With some commands, you can group several arguments together. Sometimes called a command-line switch.

communications parameters

Any of several settings required to allow computers to communicate successfully. In asynchronous transmissions, commonly used in modem communications, the settings for baud rate, number of data bits, number of stop bits, and parity parameters must all be correct.

communications protocol

1. A standard way of communicating between computers or between computers and terminals. Communications protocols vary in complexity, ranging from Xmodem, a simple file-transfer protocol used to transfer files from one PC to another, to the seven-layer OSI reference model used as the theoretical basis for many large, complex computer networks. 2. A hardware interface standard, such as RS-232-C.

compact disc

Abbreviated CD. A nonmagnetic, polished, optical disk used to store large amounts of digital information. A CD can store approximately 650MB of information, equivalent to more than 450 floppy disks. This storage capacity translates into approximately 300,000 pages of text or 72 minutes of music, all on a single 4.72-inch disc.

Digital information is stored on the compact disc as a series of microscopic pits and smooth areas that have different reflective properties. A beam of laser light shines on the disc so that the reflections can be detected and converted into digital data.

compatibility

The extent to which a given piece of hardware or software conforms to an accepted standard, regardless of the original manufacturer.

In hardware, compatibility is often expressed in terms of widely accepted models—this designation implies that the device will perform in the same way as the standard device.

In software, compatibility is usually described as the ability to read data file formats created by another vendor's software or the ability to work together and share data.

complementary metal oxide semiconductor

Abbreviated CMOS, pronounced "see-moss." A type of integrated circuit used in processors and for memory.

CMOS devices operate at very high speeds and use little power, so they generate little heat. In the PC, battery-backed CMOS memory is used to store operating parameters, such as the hard disk type and the date and time, when the computer is switched off. CMOS is easily damaged by static electricity, so take appropriate precautions.

complex instruction set computing

Abbreviated CISC, pronounced "sisk." A processor that can recognize and execute more than 100 different assembly-languages, or low-level instructions. CISC processors can be powerful, but the instructions take a high number of clock cycles to execute.

This complexity is in contrast to the simplicity of Reduced Instruction Set Computing (RISC) processors, in which the number of available instructions has been cut to a minimum. RISC processors are common in workstations and can be designed to run up to 70 percent faster than CISC processors.

COM port

The device name used for a serial communications port.

compressed file

A file that has been processed by a special utility so that it occupies as little hard disk space as possible. When the file is needed, the same program decompresses the file back into its original form so that it can be read by the computer.

Popular compression techniques include schemes that replace commonly occurring sequences of characters by tokens that take up less space. Some utilities use Huffman coding to shrink a file, and others use adaptive Lempel-Ziv coding.

connection speed

The speed of a data communications circuit. Some circuits are symmetrical and can maintain the same speed in both directions, and others are asymmetric and use a faster speed in one direction, usually the downstream side.

constant angular velocity

Abbreviated CAV. An unchanging speed of rotation. Hard disks use a CAV encoding scheme. The constant rate of rotation means that sectors on the disk are at the maximum density along the inside track of the disk. As the read/write heads move outward, the sectors must spread out to cover the increased track circumference, and therefore the data transfer rate falls off.

constant linear velocity

Abbreviated CLV. A changing speed of rotation. CD-ROM drives use a CLV encoding scheme to make sure that the data density remains constant. Information on a compact disc is stored in a single, spiral track, divided into many equal-length segments. To read the data, the CD-ROM drive must increase the rotational speed as the read head gets closer to the center of the disc and decrease as the head moves back out.

control character

A nonprinting character with a special meaning. Control characters, such as a carriage return, line feed, bell, or escape, perform a specific operation on a terminal, printer, or communications line. They are grouped together as the first 32 characters in the ASCII character set.

You can type a control character from the keyboard by pressing and holding the Ctrl key while you simultaneously press another key. For example, if you press and hold the Ctrl key and then press C, you generate Ctrl+C.

corona wire

In a laser printer, the wire that applies an electrostatic charge to the paper.

crash

1. An unexpected program halt, sometimes because of a hardware failure but most often because of a software error, from which there's no recovery. You usually need to reboot the computer to recover after a crash. 2. A disk drive failure, sometimes called a head crash, which leaves the hard disk unusable.

CRC

See cyclical redundancy check.

cross-linked clusters

Clusters on a hard or floppy disk allocated to more than one file because of a storage error.

crosstalk

In computer communications, any interference from a physically adjacent channel that corrupts the signal and causes transmission errors.

Ctrl+Alt+Del

A three-key combination used to reset the machine and reload the operating system. By pressing Ctrl+Alt+Del, you initiate a warm boot, which restarts the computer without going through the Power-On Self Tests (POSTs) normally run when the computer goes through a cold boot.

In Windows 98/2000/XP, the sequence opens a dialog box from which you can either end a task or shut down the computer. Sometimes called the three-finger salute.

Ctrl key

A key on the keyboard that, when pressed at the same time as another key, generates a nonprinting control character.

CTS

See Clear to Send.

cursor

A special character displayed on a monitor to indicate where the next character will appear when it's typed. In text or character mode, the cursor is usually a blinking rectangle or underline. In a graphical user interface, the mouse cursor can take many shapes depending on the current operation and its screen location.

cursor-movement keys

The keys on the keyboard that move the cursor, also called cursor-control keys. These keys include the four arrow keys and the Home, Page Up, End, and Page Down keys.

On full-sized keyboards, cursor-movement keys are often found on the numeric keypad; laptops and notebooks often have separate cursor-movement keys.

cut through

A technique used by some Ethernet hardware to speed up packet forwarding. Only the first few bytes of the packet are examined before it's forwarded or filtered. This process is much faster than looking at the whole packet, but it does allow some bad packets to be forwarded.

cyclical redundancy check

Abbreviated CRC. A complex calculation method used to check the accuracy of a digital transmission over a communications link or to ensure the integrity of a file stored on a hard disk.

The sending computer uses one of several formulas to calculate a value from the information contained in the data, and this value is appended to the message block before it is sent. The receiving computer performs the same calculation on the same data and compares this number with the received CRC. If the two CRCs don't match, indicating a transmission error occurred, the receiving computer asks the sending computer to retransmit the data.

This procedure is known as a redundancy check because each transmission includes extra or redundant error-checking values as well as the data itself.

As a security check, a CRC may be used to compare the current size of an executable file against the original size to determine if the file has been tampered with or changed in some way.

D

D channel

The data channel in Integrated Services Digital Network (ISDN), which is used for control signals and customer data. In the Base Rate ISDN (BRI), the D channel operates at 16Kbps; in the Primary Rate ISDN (PRI), it operates at 64Kbps.

daisy chaining

See cascading.

DAT

See Digital Audio Tape.

data bits

In asynchronous transmissions, the bits that actually make up the data. Usually, 7 or 8 data bits are grouped together. Each group of data bits in a transmission is preceded by a start bit and followed by an optional parity bit as well as one or more stop bits.

Data Carrier Detected

Abbreviated DCD. A hardware signal defined by the RS-232C standard that indicates the modem is ready to transmit.

data compression

Any method of encoding data so that it occupies less space than it did in its original form, thus allowing that data to be stored, backed up, retrieved, or transmitted more efficiently.

Data compression is used in fax and many other forms of data transmission, CD-ROM publishing, and in still- and video-image manipulation.

Data Set Ready

Abbreviated DSR. A hardware signal defined by the RS-232-C standard that indicates the device is ready to operate.

3 connector

ny of several types of cable connectors used for par-
el or serial cables. The number following the letters
B (for data bus) indicates the number of pins that
e connector usually has; a DB25 connector can have
 to 25 pins, and a DB9 connector can have up to 9.
 practice, not all the pins (and not all the lines in the
ble) may be present in the larger connectors. If your
uation demands that all the lines be present, make
re you buy the right cable.

CD

e Data Carrier Detected.

DR SDRAM

e Double Data Rate syncDRAM.

ecibel

bbreviated dB. One-tenth of a bel, a unit of mea-
rement common in electronics that quantifies the
udness or strength of a signal. A decibel is a relative
easurement derived by comparing a measured level
ainst a known reference.

ecimal

he base-10 numbering system that uses the familiar
umbers 0–9; also known as the base-10 radix or the
ecimal radix.

efragmentation

he process of reorganizing and rewriting files so that
ey occupy one large area on a hard disk rather than
veral smaller areas.

When a file on a hard disk is updated, it may be
ritten into different areas all over the disk. This out-
ome is particularly likely when the hard disk is con-
nuously updated over a long period of time. This
le fragmentation can lead to significant delays in
ading files, but you can easily reverse its effect by
organizing and rewriting the file.

defragmenter

Any utility that rewrites all the parts of a fragmented
file into contiguous areas on a hard disk. A defragmenter (such as the Microsoft Windows utility Disk
Defragmenter) can restore performance lost because
of file fragmentation.

demand paging

A common form of virtual memory management in
which pages of information are read into memory
from disk only when required by the program.

demodulation

In communications, the process of retrieving the
data from a modulated carrier signal; the reverse of
modulation.

Desktop Management Interface

Abbreviated DMI. A standard API for identifying
desktop workstation hardware components automatically, without intervention from the user.

At a minimum, DMI identifies the manufacturer,
component name, version, serial number (if appropriate), and installation time and date of any component installed in a networked workstation. This
information is designed to help network administrators resolve configuration problems quickly and easily
and to indicate when and where system upgrades should
be applied. PCs, Macintosh computers, and Unix systems are all covered by DMI.

DMI is backed by Digital Equipment Corporation
(DEC), IBM, Intel, Microsoft, Novell, Sun, and more
than 300 other vendors.

desktop video

The combination of video capture hardware and
application software that controls the display of video
or television pictures on a desktop PC.

Desktop video is becoming increasingly important
with the sharp increase in video-conferencing applications now available.

device

A general term used to describe any computer peripheral or hardware element that can send or receive data. Some examples are modems, printers, serial ports, disk drives, cameras, and game ports. Some devices require special software, or device drivers, to control or manage them; others have built-in intelligence.

device dependence

The requirement that a specific hardware component be present for a program to work. Device-dependent software is often difficult to move or port to another computer because of its reliance on specific hardware.

device driver

A small program that allows a computer to communicate with and control a device. Each operating system contains a standard set of device drivers for the keyboard, the monitor, and so on. When you add specialized peripheral devices, such as a network interface card, you must install the appropriate device driver so that the operating system knows how to manage the device.

device independence

The ability to produce similar results in a wide variety of environments without requiring the presence of specific hardware.

The Java programming language and the PostScript page-description language are examples of device independence. Java runs on a wide range of computers, from the PC to a Cray; PostScript is used by many different printer manufacturers.

diagnostic program

A program that tests computer hardware and peripheral devices for correct operation. Some faults, known as *hard faults*, are relatively easy to find, and the diagnostic program will diagnose them correctly every time. Other faults, called *soft faults*, can be difficult to find because they occur under specific circumstances rather than every time the memory location is tested.

Most computers run a simple set of system check when the computer is first turned on. The PC tests are stored in Read-Only Memory (ROM) and are known as Power-On Self Tests (POSTs). If a POST detects an error condition, the computer will stop an display an error message on the screen.

differential backup

A backup of a hard disk that includes only the information that has changed since the last complete backup was made.

A differential backup assumes that a full backup already exists, and in the event of an accident, this complete backup will be restored before the differential backup is reloaded.

differential SCSI

A Small Computer System Interface (SCSI) bus wiring scheme that uses two wires for each signal on the bus. One wire carries the signal, and the other carries its inverse. Differential SCSI minimizes the effects of external interference, so it allows longer SCSI cable lengths to be used.

digital

Describes any device that represents values in the form of binary digits or bits.

Digital Audio Tape

Abbreviated DAT. A method of recording information in digital form on a small audio tape cassette, originally developed by Sony and Hewlett-Packard The most common format is a 4mm, helical-scan drive, which can hold more than 3GB of information DATs can be used as backup media; however, like a tape devices, they're relatively slow.

digital signal processing

Abbreviated DSP. An integrated circuit used in high speed data manipulation. You'll find DSP chips integrated into sound cards, modems, and video conferencing hardware where they're used in communication image manipulation, and other data-acquisition applications.

digital subscriber line

bbreviated DSL. A high-speed data transmission
chnology originally developed by Bellcore that
elivers high bandwidth over existing twisted-pair
opper telephone lines.

There are several different DSL services, providing
ata rates from 16Kbps to 52Mbps. The services can
e symmetrical, with the same data rate in both
pstream and downstream directions, or asymmet-
cal, with the downstream capacity greater than the
pstream capacity. Asymmetric services are particu-
rly suitable for Internet users because more informa-
on is downloaded than is uploaded.

As DSL data rates increase, the distance over which
e service is provided decreases; certain users who are
cated too far from the telephone company's central
ffice may not be able to obtain the higher speeds or, in
me cases, may not be able to receive the service at all.

digital versatile disc

e digital video disc.

digital video disc

bbreviated DVD; sometimes called digital versatile
sc. A compact disc format. A standard single-layer
ngle-sided disc can currently store 4.7GB of infor-
ation; a two-layer standard increases this to 8.5GB,
d eventually double-sided discs are expected to
ore 17GB per disc. DVD drives can also read
onventional compact discs.

digital video disc–erasable

bbreviated DVD-E. An extension to the digital
deo disc format to allow multiple rerecordings.

digital video disc–recordable

bbreviated DVD-R. An extension to the digital
deo disc format to allow one-time recording.

digital video disc–ROM

bbreviated DVD-ROM. A computer-readable
orm of digital video disc with either 4.7GB or 8.5GB
f storage per side.

DIMM

See Dual Inline Memory Module.

DIP

See Dual Inline Package.

DIP switch

A small switch used to select the operating mode of a
device, mounted as a dual inline package. DIP switches
can be either sliding or rocker switches, and they're
often grouped together for convenience. They're used
in printed circuit boards, printers, modems, and many
other peripheral devices.

direct memory access

Abbreviated DMA. A method of transferring information directly from a mass-storage device, such as a
hard disk, into memory without the information
passing through the processor. Because the processor
isn't involved in the transfer, DMA is fast. An alternative data transfer method known as *programmed
input/output* moves data between a hard disk and
memory via the processor and is much slower.

direct-mapped cache

A location in the cache corresponds to several specific
locations in memory, so when the processor calls for
certain data, the cache can locate it quickly. However,
because several blocks in RAM correspond to that same
location in the cache, the cache may spend its time
refreshing itself and calling main memory. *See also cache.*

directory

In a hierarchical file system, a convenient way of organizing and grouping files and other directories on a
disk. Sometimes called a *folder*.

The beginning directory is known as the *root directory*,
from which all other directories must branch. Directories inside another directory are called *subdirectories*.

You can list the files in a directory in a variety of
different ways: by name, by creation date and time, by
file size, or by icon.

disk cache

Pronounced "disk cash." An area of computer memory where data is temporarily stored on its way to or from a disk.

When an application asks for information from the hard disk, the cache program first checks to see if that data is already in the cache memory. If it is, the disk cache program loads the information from the cache memory rather than from the hard disk. If the information isn't in memory, the cache program reads the data from the disk, copies it into the cache memory for future reference, and then passes the data to the requesting application.

disk controller

The electronic circuitry that controls and manages the operation of floppy and hard disks.

A single disk controller may manage more than one hard disk. Many disk controllers also manage floppy disks and compatible tape drives. In the PC, the disk controller may be a printed circuit board inserted into the expansion bus, or it may be part of the hard disk drive itself.

disk drive

A peripheral storage device that reads and writes magnetic or optical disks. When more than one disk drive is installed on a computer, the operating system assigns each drive (or logical drive) a unique name.

Several types of disk drive are in common use: floppy disk drives, hard disk drives, compact disc drives, digital video disc drives, Zip drives, and magneto-optical disk drives.

disk optimizer

A utility that rearranges files and directories on a disk for optimum performance. By reducing or eliminating file fragmentation (storage in pieces in different locations on the hard disk), a disk optimizer can restore the original level of performance of your disk system.

Also, it is usually easier to undelete, or recover, an unfragmented file than a fragmented one.

Many disk optimizers won't only rewrite files as contiguous files but will also place specific unchanging files in particular locations on the disk, optimize directories, and even place specific applications on the disk so they load more quickly.

DLL

See dynamic-link library.

DMA

See direct memory access.

DMI

See Desktop Management Interface.

docking station

A hardware system into which a portable computer fits so that it can be used as a full-fledged desktop computer.

Docking stations vary from simple port replicator that allow you access to parallel and serial ports and mouse to complete systems that give you access to network connections, CD-ROMs, and even a tape backup system. The portable computer and docking station are designed as two parts of the same system you can't swap computers and docking stations from different manufacturers or even from different models from the same manufacturer.

Double Data Rate syncDRAM

Abbreviated DDR SDRAM. A variation of SDRAM that maximizes output by using both the leading and following edge of the clock tick to perform operation

double slash

Notation used with a colon to separate the communications protocol from the host computer name in a Universal Resource Locator (URL) as in *http://www.sybex.com.*

wnload

In communications, to transfer a file or files from
he computer to another over a network or using a
odem. 2. To send information, such as font informa-
on or a PostScript file, from a computer to a printer.

RAM

e dynamic RAM.

rive letter

designation used to specify a PC disk drive. For
:ample, the first floppy disk drive is usually referred
 as drive A:, and the first hard disk drive is usually
ferred to as drive C:.

SL

e digital subscriber line.

SP

e digital signal processing.

SR

e Data Set Ready.

ual Inline Memory Module

bbreviated DIMM. A group of memory chips
ounted on a small circuit board. DIMMs have two
ts of connectors that connect to different circuits,
d they have a 64-bit data path.

ual Inline Package

bbreviated DIP. A standard housing constructed of
rd plastic commonly used to hold an integrated cir-
it. The circuit's leads are connected to two parallel
ws of pins designed to fit snugly into a socket; these
ns may also be soldered directly to a printed circuit
ard.

uplex

 asynchronous transmissions, the ability to transmit
d receive on the same channel at the same time; also
ferred to as full duplex. Half-duplex channels can
ansmit only or receive only.

DVD

See digital video disc.

DVD-E

See digital video disc—erasable.

DVD-R

See digital video disc—recordable.

DVD-ROM

See digital video disc—ROM.

dynamic-link library

Abbreviated DLL. A program module that contains executable code and data that can be used by applications or
even by other DLLs in performing a specific task.
DLLs are used extensively throughout the family of
Microsoft Windows products. DLLs may have filename extensions of `.dll`, `.drv`. or `.fon`.

The DLL is linked into the application only when
the program runs, and it's unloaded again when no
longer needed. If two DLL applications are running
at the same time and both perform a particular function, only one copy of the code for that function is
loaded for more efficient use of limited memory.

Another benefit of using dynamic linking is that
the EXE files araren'tnot as large as they'd be without
DLLs because frequently used routines can be put
into a DLL rather than repeated in each EXE file that
uses them. A smaller EXE file means saved disk space
and faster program loading.

dynamic RAM

Abbreviated DRAM, pronounced "dee-ram." A
common type of computer memory that uses capacitors and transistors storing electrical charges to represent memory states. These capacitors lose their
electrical charge, so they need to be refreshed every
millisecond, during which time they can't be read by
the processor.

DRAM chips are small, simple, cheap, easy to make,
and hold approximately four times as much information as a Static RAM (SRAM) chip of similar complexity. However, they're slower than SRAM.

E

E

See exa-.

EB

See exabyte.

ECP

See extended capabilities port.

EDO RAM

Abbreviation for Extended Data Out RAM. A type of Random Access Memory (RAM) that keeps data available to the processor while the next memory access is being initialized, thus speeding up overall access times. EDO RAM is significantly faster than conventional dynamic RAM.

EIDE

See Enhanced IDE.

EISA

See Extended Industry Standard Architecture.

electromagnetic interference

Abbreviated EMI. Any electromagnetic radiation released by an electronic device that disrupts the operation or performance of another device.

EMI is produced by many sources commonly found in an office environment, including fluorescent lights, photocopiers, and motors such as those used in elevators. EMI is also produced by natural atmospheric or solar activity.

electrostatic

A term used to describe an electrical charge that isn't flowing along a conductor. Electrostatic charges are used in laser printers and in copiers to attach particles of toner to a photoconducting drum as a part of the printing process.

electrostatic discharge

Abbreviated ESD. A discharge of static electricity, often from human hands, onto an integrated circuit which usually results in severe damage to the integrated circuit.

ELF

See extremely low-frequency emission.

EMI

See electromagnetic interference.

encode

1. To compress a video file using a codec so that th file can be transmitted in the shortest possible time. 2 To convert a binary file into a form suitable for dat transmission.

Enhanced IDE

Abbreviated EIDE, contraction of enhanced and Integrated Drive Electronics (IDE). An extension to the IDE standard, EIDE supports larger hard disks allows you to connect four drives to your PC rathe than just two, allows data transfer rates of up to 13.3MBps, and also supports the ATAPI interface, which connects CD-ROM drives, optical discs, and tape drives.

enhanced parallel port

Abbreviated EPP. A parallel port specification, developed by Microsoft and Hewlett-Packard, that allow for high-speed, two-way communication between the computer and a peripheral other than a printer or scanner. EPP is used with external drives, is a part o the IEEE 1284 standard for advanced parallel ports and can provide data rates in excess of 1Mbps.

EPP

See enhanced parallel port.

error

The difference between the expected and the actual

In computing, the way that the operating system reports unexpected, unusual, impossible, or illegal events is by displaying an error number or error message. Errors range from trivial (such as an attempt to write a file to a disk drive that doesn't contain a disk) to fatal (such as when a serious operating system bug renders the system useless).

In communications, errors are often caused by line noise and signal distortion. Parity or Cyclical Redundancy Check (CRC) information is often added as overhead to the data stream, and techniques such as error detection and correction are employed to detect and correct as many errors as possible.

error detection and correction

A mechanism used to determine whether transmission errors have occurred and, if so, to correct those errors.

Some programs or transmission protocols simply request a retransmission of the affected block of data if an error is detected. More complex protocols attempt to both detect and determine at the receiving end what the correct transmission should have been.

error handling

The way that a program copes with errors or exceptions that occur as the program is running.

Good error handling manages unexpected events or wrongly entered data gracefully, usually by opening a dialog box to prompt the user to take the appropriate action or enter the correct information. Badly written programs may simply stop running when the wrong data is entered or when an unanticipated disk error occurs.

error message

A message from the program or the operating system that contains information about a condition that requires some human intervention to solve.

Error messages can indicate relatively trivial problems, such as a disk drive that doesn't contain a disk, as well as fatal problems, such as when a serious operating system bug renders the system useless and requires a system reboot.

error rate

In communications, the ratio between the number of bits received incorrectly and the total number of bits in the transmission, also known as Bit Error Rate (BER). Some methods for determining error rate use larger or logical units, such as blocks, packets, or frames. In these cases, the measurement of error rate is expressed in terms of the number of units found to be in error out of the total number of units transmitted.

ESD

See electrostatic discharge.

Ethernet

A popular network protocol and cabling scheme with a transfer rate of 10Mbps, originally developed by Xerox in 1970 by Dr. Robert Metcalf. Ethernet uses a bus topology, and network nodes are connected by either thick or thin coaxial cable, fiber-optic cable, or twisted-pair cable.

Ethernet uses Carrier Sense Multiple Access/Collision Detection (CSMA/CD) to prevent network failures or collisions when two devices try to access the network at the same time.

The original Digital Equipment, Intel, Xerox (DIX), or Blue Book, standard has evolved into the slightly more complex IEEE 802.3 standard and the ISO's 8802.3 specification.

Ethernet address

The address assigned to a network interface card by the original manufacturer or by the network administrator if the card is configurable.

This address identifies the local device address to the rest of the network and allows messages to reach the correct destination. Also known as the Media Access Control (MAC) or hardware address.

Ethernet packet

A variable-length unit in which information is transmitted on an Ethernet network.

An Ethernet packet consists of a synchronization preamble, a destination address, a source address, a type code indicator, a data field that can vary from 46 to 1500 bytes, and a Cyclical Redundancy Check (CRC) that provides a statistically derived value used to confirm the accuracy of the data.

exa-

Abbreviated E. A prefix meaning one quintillion or 10^{18}. In computing, the prefix means 1,152,921,504,606,846,976, or the power of 2 closest to one quintillion (260).

exabyte

Abbreviated EB. One quintillion bytes, or 1,152,921,504,606,846,976 bytes.

extended capabilities port

Abbreviated ECP. A parallel port specification, developed by Microsoft and Hewlett-Packard, that allows for high-speed, two-way communication between the computer and the peripheral attached to the port, usually a printer or scanner. ECP is a part of the IEEE 1284 standard for advanced parallel ports.

Extended Industry Standard Architecture

Abbreviated EISA. A 32-bit bus standard introduced in 1988, now mostly eclipsed by the PCI bus.

extremely low-frequency emission

Abbreviated ELF. Radiation emitted by a computer monitor and other common electrical appliances.

ELF emissions fall into the range of 5Hz to 2000Hz and decline with the square of the distance from the source. Emissions aren't constant around a monitor; they're higher from the sides and rear and weakest from the front of the screen. Low-emission models are available, and laptop computers with an LCD display don't emit any ELF fields.

F

fading

In both electrical and wireless systems, a decrease in a signal's strength.

Fading may be because of physical obstructions or the transmitter or receiver, distance from the source of the transmission, or some form of external interference from other signals or from atmospheric conditions.

fall back

A technique used by modems to adjust their data rate in response to changing line conditions.

far-end crosstalk

Abbreviated FEXT. Interference that occurs when signals on one twisted-pair are coupled with another pair as they arrive at the far end of a multipair cable system.

FEXT becomes a problem on short loops supporting high-bandwidth services such as Very high bit-rate Digital Subscriber Line (VDSL) because of the high carrier frequencies used.

Fast Ethernet

A term applied to the IEEE 802.3 Higher Speed Ethernet Study Group proposals, which were originally developed by Grand Junction Networks, 3Com, SynOptics, Intel, and others. Also known as 100Base-T, Fast Ethernet modifies the existing Ethernet standard to allow speeds of 10Mbps, 100Mbps, or both and uses CSMA/CD access method.

Fast IR

A 4Mbps extension to the Serial Infrared Data Link Standard that provides wireless data transmission between IrDA-compliant devices.

fast page-mode RAM

See page-mode RAM.

ast SCSI

version of the SCSI-2 interface that can transfer
ata 8 bits at a time at data rates of up to 10MBps.
he Fast SCSI connector has 50 pins.

ast/Wide SCSI

version of the SCSI-2 interface that can transfer
ata 16 bits at a time at data rates of up to 20MBps.
he Fast/Wide SCSI connector has 68 pins.

AT

e file allocation table.

AT16

Microsoft Windows, a file allocation table that
es a 16-bit cluster addressing scheme that restricts
e maximum hard disk size to 2.6GB. Also, FAT16
inefficient in disk-space utilization because the
fault cluster size can be as large as 32KB.

AT32

Microsoft Windows 95 (release 2) and later ver-
ons of Windows, a file allocation table that uses a
2-bit cluster addressing scheme to support hard
sks larger than 2.6GB, as well as a default cluster
ze of as small as 4KB. FAT32 can support hard
sks of up to 2 terabytes in size.

x modem

n adapter that fits into a PC expansion slot pro-
ding many of the capabilities of a full-sized fax
achine but at a fraction of the cost.

The advantages of a fax modem include ease of use
d convenience; the main disadvantage is that the
aterial you want to fax must be present in digital
rm in the computer. Unless you have access to a
anner, you can't fax handwritten notes, line art, or
rtain kinds of graphics. Most faxes sent directly
om a PC using a fax modem are text files.

CC certification

pproval by the Federal Communications Commis-
on (FCC) that a specific computer model meets its

standards for Radio Frequency Interference (RFI)
emissions.

FDDI

See Fiber Distributed Data Interface.

female connector

Any cable connector with receptacles designed to
receive the pins on the male connector.

Fiber Distributed Data Interface

Abbreviated FDDI. The ANSI X3T9.5 specification
for fiber-optic networks transmitting at a speed of up
to 100Mbps over a dual, counter-rotating, token ring
topology.

FDDI's 100Mbps speed is close to the internal
speed of most computers, which makes it a good
choice to serve as a superbackbone linking two or
more LANs or as a fiber-optic bus connecting high-
performance engineering workstations. FDDI is
suited to systems that require the transfer of large
amounts of information, such as medical imaging,
three-dimensional seismic processing, and oil reservoir simulation.

The FDDI-II version of the standard is designed
for networks transmitting real-time full-motion video
(or other information that can't tolerate any delays) and
requires that all nodes on the network use FDDI-II;
otherwise, the network automatically reverts to FDDI.

An FDDI network using multimode fiber-optic
cable can include as many as 500 stations up to 2 kilometers (1.25 miles) apart; with single-mode fiber, run
length increases up to 60 kilometers (37.2 miles)
between stations. This type of network can also run
over shielded and unshielded twisted-pair cabling—
known as Copper Distributed Data Interface
(CDDI)—for shorter distances.

fiber-optic cable

A transmission technology that sends pulses of light
along specially manufactured optical fibers.

Each fiber consists of a core, thinner than a human
hair, surrounded by a sheath with a much lower refrac-
tive index. Light signals introduced at one end of the

cable are conducted along the cable as the signals are reflected from the sheath.

Fiber-optic cable is lighter and smaller than traditional copper cable, is immune to electrical interference, offers better security, and has better signal-transmitting qualities. However, it's more expensive than traditional cables and is more difficult to repair.

file

A named collection of information that appears to the user as a single entity and is stored on disk.

A file can contain a program or part of a program, just data, or a user-created document. Files may actually be fragmented or stored in many different places across the disk. The operating system manages the task of locating all the pieces when a request is made to read the file.

file allocation table

Abbreviated FAT, pronounced "fat." A table, maintained by the operating systems, that lists all the blocks of disk space available on a disk.

The FAT includes the location of each block, as well as whether it's in use, available for use, or damaged in some way and therefore unavailable. Because files aren't necessarily stored in consecutive blocks on a disk, the FAT also keeps track of which pieces belong to which file.

file compression

A technique that shrinks program or data files so that they occupy less disk space. The file must then be extracted or decompressed before use. Some types of files, such as word processor documents, can be compressed by 50 percent or more. Recompressing an already compressed file usually makes the file slightly larger because of the compression overhead.

File compression can be automatic and performed by the operating system, or it can be manual and be performed by a file-compression program.

file format

A file structure that defines the way information is stored in the file and how the file appears on the screen or on the printer.

The simplest file format is a plain ASCII file. Some of the more complex formats are Document Content Architecture (DCA) and Rich Text Format (RTF), which include control information for use by a printer, Tagged Image File Format (TIFF) and Encapsulated PostScript (EPS), which hold graphics information, and Xbase Database File (DBF) and DB (Paradox file), which are database formats. Word processing programs, such as Microsoft Word, also create files in special formats.

file fragmentation

Storage of files in pieces scattered on a disk. As files grow on a hard disk, they can be divided into several small pieces. By fragmenting files, the operating system makes reasonable use of the disk space available.

The problem with file fragmentation is that the disk heads must move to different locations on the disk to read or write to a fragmented file. This process takes more time than reading the file as a single piece. To speed up file operations, you can use a disk optimizer or defragmenter.

file transfer protocol

Abbreviated FTP. The TCP/IP protocol used when transferring single or multiple files from one computer system to another.

FTP uses a client/server model, in which a small client program runs on your computer and accesses a larger FTP server running on an Internet host. FTP provides all the tools needed to look at directories and files, change to other directories, and transfer text and binary files from one system to another.

file-infecting virus

Any virus that infects files on disk, usually executable files with filename extensions of .com, .exe, and .ovl. An unexpected change in the file size may indicate an infection. In certain cases, the original program is replaced with a new file containing an infected program.

filename

The name of a file on a disk used so that both you and the operating system can find the file again. Every file a directory must have a unique name, but files in different directories can share the same name.

FireWire

See IEEE 1394.

firmware

Any software stored in a form of Read-Only Memory (ROM), Erasable Programmable Read-Only Memory (EPROM), or electrically Erasable Programmable Read-Only Memory (EEPROM) that maintains its contents when power is removed.

flash memory

A special form of Read-Only Memory (ROM) that can be erased at signal levels commonly found inside the PC.

This ability allows the contents to be reprogrammed without removing the chips from the computer. Also, once flash memory has been programmed, you can remove the expansion board it's mounted on and plug it into another computer without loss of the new information.

flat-panel display

A thin video display that doesn't use CRT technology. Flat-panel displays were originally used in laptop and other portable computers, but now they're available as desktop units.

flow control

1. In communications, control of the rate at which information is exchanged between two computers over a transmission channel. Flow control is needed when one of the devices can't receive the information at the same rate as it can be sent, usually because some processing is required on the receiving end before the next transmission unit can be accepted. Flow control can be implemented either in hardware or in software. 2. In networking, control of the flow of data throughout the network, ensuring that network segments aren't congested. A router controls data flow by routing around any trouble spots.

FM synthesis

Abbreviation for frequency modulation synthesis. A method used by a sound board to simulate musical instruments. FM synthesis is cheaper than wavetable synthesis but is also of lower quality.

footprint

The amount of desktop space or floor space occupied by a computer, printer, or monitor.

forced perfect termination

A technique used to terminate a Small Computer System Interface (SCSI). Forced perfect termination actively monitors the bus to ensure that no signal reflection occurs.

formatting

The process of initializing a new, blank floppy disk or hard disk so that it can be used to store information.

forward error correction

A technique used to control errors that insert extra or redundant bits into the data stream. The receiving device uses the redundant bits to detect and, if possible, correct the errors in the data.

four-wire circuit

A transmission system in which two half-duplex circuits, consisting of two wires each, are combined to create one full-duplex circuit.

fps

See frames per second.

frame

1. A block of data suitable for transmission as a single unit, also referred to as a packet or block. Some media can support multiple frame formats. 2. In digital video, one screen of information, including both text and graphics.

frames per second

Abbreviated fps. The number of video frames displayed each second. Although 24fps is considered the slowest frame rate that provides convincing motion to the human eye, most Internet video runs at between 5fps and 15fps.

free memory

Any area of memory not currently in use. Often refers to the memory space remaining for applications to use after the operating system and the system device drivers have been loaded.

fried

A slang expression for burned-out hardware, especially hardware that has suffered from a power surge. Also applied to people, as in "My brain is fried; I haven't slept since last weekend."

FTP

See file transfer protocol.

ftp

A command used to transfer files to and from remote computers using the file transfer protocol. You can use ftp to log in to an Internet computer and transfer text and binary files.

When you use ftp, you start a client program on your computer that connects to a server program on the Internet computer. The commands that you give to ftp are translated into instructions that the server program executes for you.

The original ftp program started life as a Unix utility, but versions are now available for all popular operating systems; ftp is also built into all the major Web browsers.

full backup

A backup that includes all files on a hard disk or set of hard disks. A network administrator must decide how often to perform a full backup, balancing the need for security against the time taken for the backup.

full-duplex

Abbreviated FDX. The capability for simultaneous transmission in two directions so that devices can be sending and receiving data at the same time.

full-page display

Any monitor capable of displaying a whole page of text. Full-page displays are useful for graphical art and desktop publishing applications, as well as medical applications.

fully associative cache

A cache in which information from RAM may be placed in any free blocks in the cache so that the most recently accessed data is usually present; however, the search to find that information may be slow because the cache has to index the data to find it. *See cache.*

function keys

The set of programmable keys on the keyboard that can perform special tasks assigned by the current application.

Most keyboards have 10 or 12 function keys (F1 to F10 or F1 to F12), some of which are used by an application as shortcut keys. For example, many programs use F1 to gain access to the Help system. In some programs, using function keys is so complex that special plastic key overlays are provided as guides for users.

G

G

See giga-.

gauge

A measurement of the physical size of a cable. Under the American Wire Gauge (AWG) standards, higher numbers indicate thinner cable.

GB

See gigabyte.

nder changer

special intermediary connector for use with two
bles that each have only male connectors or only
male connectors.

ga-

prefix meaning 1 billion, or 10^9.

gabit

breviated Gb or Gbit. Usually 1,073, 741,824
nary digits or bits of data. Sometimes used as equiv-
nt to 1 billion bits.

gabit Ethernet

1Gbps (1000Mbps) extension of the IEEE 802.3
hernet standard, also known as 1000Base-X.
  This standard has been developed by the IEEE
2.3z Task Group and a number of interested com-
nies collectively known as the Gigabit Ethernet Alli-
ce. Gigabit Ethernet runs over multimode fiber-optic
ble and is intended for use as a backbone and a way
 connect high-speed routers, switches, and hubs.

gabyte

breviated GB. Strictly speaking, 1 billion bytes;
wever, in computing, in which bytes are most often
unted in powers of 2, a gigabyte becomes 230, or
073,741,824 bytes.

323

videoconferencing standard defined by the Interna-
nal Telecommunication Union (ITU) that defines
deoconferencing from the desktop over LANs,
tranets, and the Internet.
  H.323 specifies techniques for compressing and
nsmitting real-time voice, video, and data between
air of videoconferencing workstations. It also
scribes signaling protocols for managing audio and
deo streams, as well as procedures for breaking data
to packets and synchronizing transmissions across
mmunications channels.

half-duplex

Abbreviated HDX. In asynchronous transmissions,
the ability to transmit on the same channel in two
directions but only in one direction at a time.

handshaking

The exchange of control codes or particular characters to maintain and coordinate data flow between
two devices so that data is only transmitted when the
receiving device is ready to accept the data.
  Handshaking can be implemented in either hardware or software, and it occurs between a variety of
devices. For example, the data flow might be from one
computer to another computer or from a computer to
a peripheral device, such as a modem or printer.

hang

1. When a program waits for an event that never
occurs, as in, "The program hangs waiting for a character from the keyboard." 2. A slang expression used
when attaching a new piece of hardware to a system,
usually an external device attached by one or more
cables, as in, "I'm going to hang a new tape drive on
the server this afternoon."

hard disk

That part of a hard disk drive that stores data, rather
than the mechanism for reading and writing to it.
Sometimes called a platter.

hard disk controller

The circuitry used to control and coordinate a hard
disk drive.
  Many hard disk controllers are capable of managing
more than one hard disk, as well as floppy disks and
tape drives. On some PCs, the hard disk controller is
built into the motherboard, and in others, the controlling circuitry is mounted on the drive itself, eliminating
the need for a separate controller.

hard disk drive

A storage device that uses a set of rotating, magnetically
coated disks called *platters* to store data or programs.

In everyday use, the terms *hard disk*, *hard disk drive*, and *hard drive* are used interchangeably because the disk and the drive mechanism are a single unit.

A typical hard disk platter rotates at several thousand revolutions per minute, and the read/write heads float on a cushion of air from 10 to 25 millionths of an inch thick so that the heads never come into contact with the recording surface. The whole unit is hermetically sealed to prevent airborne contaminants from entering and interfering with these close tolerances.

Hard disks range in storage capacity from a few tens of megabytes to several terabytes. The more storage space on the disk, the more important your backup strategy becomes. Hard disks are reliable, but they do fail, usually at the most inconvenient moment.

hard disk interface

A standard way of accessing the data stored on a hard disk. Several different hard disk interface standards have evolved over time, including ST506 Interface, Enhanced Small Device Interface (ESDI), Integrated Drive Electronics Interface (IDE), and Small Computer System Interface (SCSI).

hard disk type

A number stored in a PC's CMOS RAM memory area that defines certain hard disk characteristics, such as the number of read/write heads and the number of cylinders on the disk. This number isn't accessible directly from the operating system. Some PCs require a special configuration program to access the hard disk type; others permit access via the computer's built-in ROM BIOS Setup program.

hard reset

A system reset made by pressing the computer's reset button or by turning the power off and then on again. A hard reset is used only when the system has crashed so badly that pressing Ctrl+Alt+Del to reboot doesn't work.

hardware

All the physical electronic components of a computer system, including peripheral devices, printed-circuit boards, displays, and printers. If you can stub your toe on it, it must be hardware.

hardware address

The address assigned to a network interface card by the original manufacturer or, if the interface card is configurable, by the network administrator.

This address identifies the local device address to the rest of the network and allows messages to find the correct destination. Also known as the physical address, Media Access Control (MAC) address, or Ethernet address.

hardware compatibility list

A list of all the hardware devices supported by Microsoft Windows NT and Windows 2000/XP. Items on this list have actually been tested and verified to work properly with Windows.

hardware dependent

The requirement that a specific hardware component be present for a program to work. Hardware-dependent software is often difficult to move or port to another computer.

hardware independent

The ability to produce similar results in a wide variety of environments, without requiring the presence of specific hardware. The Java programming language and the PostScript page-description language are both examples of hardware independence. Java runs on a wide range of computers from the PC to a mainframe; many printer manufacturers use PostScript.

hardware interrupt

An interrupt or request for service generated by a hardware device, such as a keystroke from the keyboard or a tick from the clock. Because the processor may receive several such signals simultaneously, hardware interrupts are usually assigned a priority level and processed according to that priority.

DSL

e high-bit-rate digital subscriber line.

ertz

bbreviated Hz. A unit of frequency measurement; Hz equals one cycle per second.

exadecimal

bbreviated hex. The base-16 numbering system that es the digits 0 to 9, followed by the letters A to F, hich are equivalent to the decimal numbers 10 rough 15.

Hex is a convenient way to represent the binary umbers computers use internally because it fits neatly to the 8-bit byte. All the 16 hex digits 0 to F can be presented in 4 bits, and two hex digits (one digit for ch set of 4 bits) can be stored in a single byte. This eans that 1 byte can contain any one of 256 different hex numbers, from 0 through FF.

dden file

ny file that has the hidden attribute set, which indites to the operating system that information about e file shouldn't appear in normal directory listings. here may also be further restrictions on a hidden e, and you may not be able to delete, copy, or disay the contents of such a file.

gh Sierra specification

specification for CD-ROM data that served as the sis for the International Organization for Standardization (ISO) 9660 standard. It's called High erra because it was defined at a meeting held near ke Tahoe, California, in November 1985.

gh-bit-rate digital subscriber line

bbreviated HDSL. A high-speed data transmission chnology originally developed by Bellcore that livers high bandwidth over existing twisted-pair pper telephone lines.

HDSL is the most common Digital Subscriber ne (DSL) service and provides T1 data rates of 544Mbps over lines of up to 3.6 kilometers

(12,000 feet) in length. HDSL is symmetric, providing the same data rate in each direction.

The service isn't intended for residential purposes but is used in the telephone company's own private data networks, Internet servers, and interexchange connections.

hooked vector

An intercepted interrupt vector that now points to a replacement Interrupt Service Routine (ISR) rather than to the original service routine.

hub

A device used to extend a network so that additional workstations can be attached. Active hubs amplify transmission signals to extend cable length and ports. Passive hubs split the transmission signal, allowing additional workstations to be added, usually at a loss of distance. In some star networks, a hub is the central controlling device.

Huffman coding

In data compression, a method of encoding data on the basis of the relative frequency of the individual elements. Huffman coding is often used with text files, where the coding is based on the frequency of occurrence of each letter, because it's a lossless compression method. Huffman coding is used in fax transmissions.

Hz

See hertz.

I

IC

See integrated circuit.

IDE

See Integrated Drive Electronics.

IEEE 1394

An IEEE standard for a digital Plug-and-Play bus, originally conceived by Apple Computer in 1986.

IEEE 1394 supports up to 63 nodes per bus and up to 1023 buses.

Three speeds for device connections are available: 100Mbps, 200Mbps, and 400Mbps.

All devices are hot-pluggable, and both self-powered and bus-powered devices can be attached to the same bus. Also known as FireWire, IEEE 1394 uses six-pair shielded twisted-pair cable and is intended for high-end applications such as digitized video.

impedance

An electrical property of a cable that combines capacitance (the ability to store an electrical charge), inductance (the ability to store energy in the form of a magnetic field), and resistance (the ability to impede or resist the flow of electric current), measured in ohms.

Impedance can be described as the apparent resistance to the flow of alternating current at a given frequency. Mismatches in impedance along a cable cause distortions and reflections. Each transmission protocol and network topology specifies its own standards for impedance.

incremental backup

A backup of a hard disk that consists of only those files created or modified since the last backup was performed.

infection

The presence of a virus or Trojan horse, which may be active in memory or present on the hard disk.

An infection may remain hidden from the user for a considerable time. Some viruses are triggered by specific dates or by particular events on the system. Many macro viruses act immediately when you open an email attachment containing a virus.

Infrared Data Association

Abbreviated IrDA. A trade association of more than 150 computer and telecommunications hardware and software suppliers, including Hewlett-Packard,

Apple Computer, AST, Compaq, Dell, IBM, Intel, Motorola, Novell, and others.

IrDA is concerned with standards definitions for products that use wireless communications.

infrared transmission

A method of wireless transmission that uses part of the infrared spectrum to transmit and receive signals. Infrared transmissions take advantage of a frequency range just below that of visible light, and they usually require a line of sight connection between transmitter and receiver.

Infrared transmission can be used to send documents from portable computers to printers, to transmit data between portable computers, to exchange information between computers and cellular telephones and faxes, and to connect to home entertainment systems. Almost every manufacturer of portable devices is implementing infrared communications at some level.

inkjet printer

A nonimpact printer that sprays a mist of liquid ink through tiny jets in the print head to form characters or graphics on the page.

inoculate

To protect a file against attack from a virus by recording characteristic information about it and then monitoring any changes.

input/output

Abbreviated I/O. The transfer of data between the computer and its peripheral devices, disk drives, terminals, and printers.

input/output bound

Abbreviated I/O bound. A condition in which the speed of operation of the input/output port limits the speed of program execution. Getting the data into and out of the computer is more time-consuming than actually processing that same data.

install

To configure and prepare hardware or software for operation.

Many application packages have their own installation programs, which copy all the required files from the original distribution disks into appropriate directories on your hard disk and then help to configure the program to your own operating requirements. Microsoft Windows programs are installed by a program called Setup.

instruction set

The set of machine-language instructions that a processor recognizes and can execute.

An instruction set for Reduced Instruction Set Computing (RISC) may only contain a few instructions; a computer that uses Complex Instruction Set Computing (CISC) may be able to recognize several hundred instructions.

integrated circuit

Abbreviated IC; also known as a chip. A small semiconductor circuit that contains many electronic components.

integrated Drive Electronics

Abbreviated IDE. A hard disk interface that removes the need for a separate disk controller card by integrating the required circuitry onto the drive itself or into the motherboard; no expansion slot is needed.

integrated Services Digital Network

Abbreviated ISDN. A standard for a worldwide digital communications network originally designed to replace all current systems with a completely digital, synchronous, full-duplex transmission system.

Computers and other devices connect to ISDN via simple, standardized interfaces. They can transmit voice, video, and data, all on the same line.

interface

The point at which a connection is made between two hardware devices, between a user and a program or operating system, or between two applications.

In hardware, an interface describes the logical and physical connections used, as in RS-232C and is often considered to be synonymous with the term *port*. A user interface consists of the means by which a program communicates with the user, including a command line, menus, dialog boxes, online help systems, and so on.

Software interfaces are Application Program Interfaces (APIs) and consist of the codes and messages used by programs to communicate behind the scenes.

interleaved memory

A method of speeding up access by dividing Dynamic RAM (DRAM) into two (or more) separate banks.

DRAM requires that its contents be updated at least every thousandth of a second, and while this update is taking place, it can't be read by the processor. Interleaved memory divides available memory into banks so that the processor can read from one bank while the other is cycling, so it doesn't have to wait.

internal modem

A modem that plugs into the expansion bus of a personal computer or into the PC Card connector of a laptop computer.

Internet

The world's largest computer network, consisting of millions of computers supporting tens of millions of users in hundreds of countries.

The Internet was originally established to meet the research needs of the U.S. Defense industry, but it has grown into a huge global network serving universities, academic researchers, commercial interests, government agencies, and private individuals in the United States and the rest of the world.

The Internet uses TCP/IP protocols, and Internet computers run many different operating systems, including many variations of Unix, VMS, and Microsoft Windows.

internet

Abbreviation for internetwork. Two or more networks using different networking protocols, connected by means of a router. Users on an internetwork can access the resources of all connected networks.

Internet address

An address on the Internet. An Internet address usually takes the form *someone@abc.def.xyz*, where *someone* is a user's name or part of a user's name, *@abc* is the network computer of the user, and def is the name of the host organization. The last three letters denote the kind of institution the user belongs to: edu for educational, com for commercial, gov for government, mil for the military, org for nonprofit organizations, and net for Internet administrative organizations.

Internet Protocol

Abbreviated IP, IP version 4, and IPv4. The protocol that regulates packet forwarding by tracking addresses, routing outgoing messages, and recognizing incoming messages in TCP/IP networks and the Internet.

Internet service provider

Abbreviated ISP. A company that provides commercial or residential customers access to the Internet via dedicated or dial-up connections. An ISP will normally have several servers and a high-speed connection to an Internet backbone. Some ISPs also offer Web site hosting services and free email to their subscribers.

Internetwork Packet Exchange

Abbreviated IPX. Part of Novell NetWare's native protocol stack, used to transfer data between the server and workstations on the network. IPX packets are encapsulated and carried by the packets used in Ethernet and the frames used in Token Ring networks.

interprocess communication

Abbreviated IPC. A term that describes all the methods used to pass information between two programs running on the same computer in a multitasking operating system or between two programs running on a network, including pipes, shared memory, message queues, sockets, semaphores, and Object Linking and Embedding (OLE).

interrupt

A signal to the processor generated by a device under its control, such as the system clock, that interrupts normal processing.

An interrupt indicates that an event requiring the processor's attention has occurred, causing the processor to suspend and save its current activity and then branch to an Interrupt Service Routine (ISR).

interrupt handler

Special software located in the operating system kernel that manages and processes system interrupts. Also known as an interrupt service routine.

When an interrupt occurs, the processor suspends and saves its current activity and then branches to the interrupt handler. This routine processes the interrupt, whether it was generated by the system clock, keystroke, or a mouse click. When the ISR is complete, it returns control to the suspended process.

Each type of interrupt is processed by its own specific interrupt handler. A table, called the *interrupt vector table*, maintains a list of addresses for these specific interrupt handlers.

interrupt request

Abbreviated IRQ. Hardware lines that carry a signal from a device to the processor.

A hardware interrupt signals that an event has taken place that requires the processor's attention. The interrupt may come from the keyboard, the network interface card, or the system's disk drives.

terrupt vector table

list of addresses, maintained by the operating
stem kernel, for specific software routines known as
terrupt handlers.

tranet

private corporate network that uses Internet soft-
are and TCP/IP networking protocol standards.
Many companies use intranets for tasks as simple
distributing a company newsletter and as complex as
sting and updating technical support bulletins to
rvice personnel worldwide. An intranet doesn't
ways include a permanent connection to the
ternet.

O

input/output.

O bound

input/output bound.

Internet Protocol.

address

he unique 32-bit number that identifies a computer
the Internet or other Internet Protocol network.
An IP address is usually written (in decimal) as
ur numbers separated by dots or periods and can be
vided into two parts. The network address is made
from the high-order bits in the address, and the
st address comprises the rest. In addition, the host
rt of the address can be further subdivided to allow
r a subnet address.
These numbers are difficult for most people to
member, so humans tend to refer to computers by
eir domain names instead.

X

Internetwork Packet Exchange.

DA

Infrared Data Association.

IRQ

See interrupt request.

ISDN

See Integrated Services Digital Network.

J

Joint Photographic Experts Group

Abbreviated JPEG. An image-compression standard
and file format that defines a set of compression
methods for high-quality images such as photographs,
single video frames, or scanned pictures; JPEG doesn't
work very well when compressing text, line art, or
vector graphics.
JPEG uses lossy compression methods that result
in some loss of the original data; when you decom-
press the original image, you don't get exactly the
same image you started with although JPEG was specifically designed to discard information not easily
detected by the human eye.
JPEG can store 24-bit color images in as many
as 16 million colors; files in Graphics Interchange
Format (GIF) form can only store 256 colors.

JPEG

See Joint Photographic Experts Group.

jumper

A small plastic and metal connector that completes a
circuit, usually to select one option from a set of several user-definable options. Jumpers are often used to
select one particular hardware configuration from a
choice of configurations.

K

K

See kilo-.

Kb

See kilobit.

KB

See kilobyte.

Kbit

See kilobit.

Kbps

See kilobits per second.

Kbyte

See kilobyte.

kernel

The most fundamental part of an operating system. The kernel stays resident in memory at all times, often hidden from the user, and manages the system memory, the file system, and the disk operations.

The kernel also runs processes and provides interprocess communications between those processes, including synchronization of events, scheduling, message passing, management of input and output routines, and memory management.

keystroke

The action of pressing and then releasing a key on the keyboard to initiate some action or enter a character.

kilo-

A prefix indicating 1000 in the metric system. Because computing is based on powers of 2, kilo usually means 2^{10}, or 1024. To differentiate between these two uses, a lowercase k is used to indicate 1000 (as in kHz), and an uppercase K is used to indicate 1024 (as in KB).

kilobit

Abbreviated Kb or Kbit. 1024 bits (binary digits).

kilobits per second

Abbreviated Kbps. The number of bits, or binary digits, transmitted every second, measured in multiples of 1024bps. Used as an indicator of communications transmission rates.

kilobyte

Abbreviated K, KB, or Kbyte. 1024 bytes.

L

L1 cache

See level 1 cache.

L2 cache

See level 2 cache.

LAN

See local area network.

laptop computer

See notebook computer.

laser printer

A printer that's based on the same technology as tha used by photocopiers.

A laser and a rotating mirror create an image of th page on a rotating photosensitive drum. This image converted into an electrostatic charge that attracts an holds the toner. Electrostatically charged paper is rolled against the drum, and the toner is transferred t the paper and fused to the paper using heat. The las step is to remove the electrostatic charge from the drum and collect any excess toner.

latency

The time it takes for the area of a hard disk containing the required information to rotate to a posi tion under the read/write head. The faster the har disk platter rotates, the lower the latency.

LBA

See logical block addressing.

LCC

See leadless chip carrier.

adless chip carrier

bbreviated LCC. A method used to mount inte-
rated circuits onto a board. Although similar in
ppearance to the cheaper plastic leadless chip carrier
PLCC), LCCs are made from a ceramic material, and
he two chip carriers are incompatible.

vel 1 cache

bbreviated L1 cache. A primary cache built into
icroprocessors to increase speed. The L1 cache can
read in a single clock cycle, so it's always tried first.
he Intel Pentium contains two separate 512KB L1
ches, one each for data and instructions. Also called
primary cache.

vel 2 cache

bbreviated L2 cache. A secondary cache located
etween the L1 or primary cache and the rest of the
stem. A level 2 cache is often larger than the pri-
ary cache, and it's usually slower. Also called a sec-
idary cache.

ne analyzer

ny device that monitors and displays information
out a transmission on a communications channel. A
ie analyzer is used for troubleshooting and load
onitoring.

cal area network

bbreviated LAN. A group of computers and associ-
ed peripheral devices connected by a communica-
ons channel, capable of sharing files and other
sources between several users.

gic bomb

sabotage attack on a system timed to go off some
ne in the future; essentially a Trojan horse with a
ner.

A logic bomb goes off at a certain time or when
ggered by a certain event and then performs some
peration. It might release a virus, delete files, or send
mments to a terminal. An unhappy programmer

may plant a logic bomb on a system timed to go off
long after they've left the company to avoid suspicion.

logical block addressing

Abbreviated LBA. An element of the Enhanced IDE
standard that allows a hard disk to store more than
8.4GB of information.

logical drive

The internal division of a large hard disk into smaller
units. One single physical drive may be organized into
several logical drives for convenience, with each
appearing to the user to be a separate drive.

logical unit number

Abbreviated LUN. The logical address of a Small
Computer System Interface (SCSI) device when several devices are attached to a single SCSI device ID.
The LUN is usually set to zero, unless the SCSI
adapter supports multiple LUNs on a single SCSI
device ID.

loopback

A troubleshooting test in which a signal is transmitted
from a source to a destination and then back to the
source again so that the signal can be measured and
evaluated or the data contained in the signal can be
examined for accuracy and completeness.

lossless compression

Any data compression method that compresses a file
by rearranging or recoding the data that it contains in
a more compact fashion.

With lossless compression, there's no loss of original data when the file is decompressed. Lossless compression methods are used on program files and on
images such as medical X-rays when data loss can't be
tolerated, and they can typically reduce a file to 40
percent of its original size.

Many lossless compression programs use a method
known as the Lempel-Ziv-Welch (LZW) algorithm,
which searches a file for redundant strings of data and

converts them to smaller tokens. When the compressed file is decompressed, this process is reversed.

lossy compression

Any data compression method that compresses a file by discarding any data that the compression mechanism decides isn't needed.

Original data is lost when the file is decompressed. Lossy compression methods may be used for shrinking audio or image files when absolute accuracy isn't required and the loss of data won't be noticed; however, this technique is unsuitable for more critical applications in which data loss can't be tolerated, such as with medical images or program files. Lossy compression can typically reduce a file to as little as 5 percent of its original size.

LPT ports

The device name used to denote a parallel communications port, often used with a printer.

LUN

See logical unit number.

M

M

See mega-.

m

See milli-.

machine language

The native binary language used internally by the computer; also known as machine code.

Machine language is difficult for humans to read and understand. Programmers create applications using high-level languages, which are translated into a form that the computer can understand by an assembler, a compiler, or an interpreter. Whichever method is used, the result is machine language.

macro virus

An executable program that attaches itself to a document created in Microsoft Word or Excel or to an email created in Outlook. When you open the attachment and execute the macro, the virus runs and does whatever damage it was programmed to do. Both the Melissa and ILOVEYOU viruses were Visual Basic programs distributed as email attachments.

male connector

Any cable connector with pins designed to engage the sockets on the female connector.

map

1. To direct a request for a file or service to an alternative resource. For example, in a virtual memory system, an operating system can translate or map a virtual memory address into a physical address; in a network, drive letters are assigned to specific volumes and directories. 2. An expression of the structure of an object. For example, a memory map describes the use and layout of physical memory.

mask

A binary number that's used to remove bits from another binary number by using one of the logical operators (AND, OR, NOT, XOR) to combine the binary number and the mask. Masks are used in IP addresses and file permissions.

MB

See megabyte.

Mb

See megabit.

Mbps

See megabits per second.

mean time between failures

Abbreviated MTBF. The statistically derived average length of time for which a system component operates

:fore failing. MTBF is often expressed in thousands
: tens of thousands of hours, also called Power-On
ours (POH).

.ean time to repair

:bbreviated MTTR. The statistically derived average
ngth of time it takes to repair a component.

.eg

common abbreviation for megabyte.

.ega-

:bbreviated M. A prefix meaning one million in the
etric system. Because computing is based on powers
`2, mega usually means 2^{20} or 1,048,576; the power of
closest to 1 million.

.egabit

:bbreviated Mb or Mbit. Usually 1,048,576 binary
gits or bits of data. Often used as equivalent to 1
illion bits.

.egabits per second

:bbreviated Mbps. A measurement of the amount of
formation moving across a network or communica-
ns link in one second, measured in multiples of
048,576 bits.

.egabyte

:bbreviated MB. Usually 1,048,576 bytes. Mega-
·tes are a common unit of measurement for com-
iter memory or hard disk capacity.

.egahertz

:bbreviated MHz. One million cycles per second.
processor's clock speed is often expressed in
egahertz.

The original IBM PC operated an Intel 8088 pro-
ssor running at 4.77MHz, a Pentium processor
ns at 800MHz, and modern systems are capable
running at more than 1000MHz or 1GHz.

memory

The primary physical Random Access Memory
(RAM) installed in the computer. The operating
system copies applications from disk into memory,
where all program execution and data processing
takes place, and then writes the results back to disk.
The amount of memory installed in the computer can
determine the size and number of programs that it can
run, as well as the size of the largest data file.

memory address

The exact location in memory that stores a particular
data item or program instruction.

memory board

A printed circuit board containing memory chips.
When all the sockets on a memory board are filled
and the board contains the maximum amount of
memory that it can manage, it's said to be "fully
populated."

memory cache

An area of high-speed memory on the processor that
stores commonly used code or data obtained from
slower memory, eliminating the need to access the
system's main memory to fetch instructions.

The Intel Pentium contains two separate 512KB L1
or primary caches, one each for data and instructions.

memory chip

A chip that holds data or program instructions. A
memory chip may hold its contents temporarily, as in
the case of Random Access Memory (RAM), or permanently, as in the case of Read-Only Memory).

memory leak

A programming error that causes a program to
request new areas of computer memory rather than
reusing the memory already assigned to it. This causes
the amount of memory in use by the program to
increase as time goes on. In a worst case, the application may consume all available memory and stop the
computer.

memory management

The way in which the operating system handles the use of memory, usually as a combination of physical memory and virtual memory.

When applications are loaded, they're assigned space in which to run and store data. As they're removed, the memory space they occupied is released for use by the next program to run.

memory management unit

Abbreviated MMU. The part of the processor that manages the mapping of virtual memory addresses to actual physical addresses.

In some systems, such as those based on early Intel or Motorola processors, the MMU was a separate chip; however, in most modern systems, the MMU is integrated into the processor.

memory map

The organization and allocation of memory in a computer. A memory map will indicate the amount of memory used by the operating system, as well as the amount remaining for use by applications.

memory-resident

Always located in the computer's memory and available for use; not swapped out.

MHz

See megahertz.

microcode

Low-level instructions that define how a particular microprocessor works by specifying what the processor does when it executes a machine-language instruction.

micron

A unit of measurement. One millionth of a meter, corresponding to approximately $1/25000$ of an inch. The core diameter of fiber-optic cable for networks is often specified in terms of microns; 62.5 microns is a common size.

microprocessor

A central processor unit on a single chip, often referred to as the processor. Intel developed the first microprocessor in 1969.

MIDI

See Musical Instrument Digital Interface.

milli-

Abbreviated m. A prefix meaning one thousandth i the metric system, often expressed as 10–3.

millisecond

Abbreviated ms or msec. A unit of measurement equ to one thousandth of a second. In computing, hard disk and CD-ROM drive access times are often described in terms of milliseconds; the higher the number, the slower the disk system.

millivolt

Abbreviated mv. A unit of measurement equal to or thousandth of a volt.

mirroring

The process of duplicating stored information in re time to protect vital data from unexpected hardwa failures.

MJ

See modular jack.

MMU

See memory management unit.

mobile computing

1. The everyday use of a portable computer as a normal part of the workday. 2. Techniques used to establish links to a network by employees who mov from one remote location to another, such as mem bers of a sales staff or telecommuters who work fro home. Once the connection is made, users log in an access network resources as easily as if they were working from a computer in the corporate office.

modem

Contraction of modulator/demodulator, a device that allows a computer to transmit information over a telephone line.

The modem translates between the digital signals that the computer uses and analog signals suitable for transmission over telephone lines. When transmitting, the modem modulates the digital data onto a carrier signal on the telephone line. When receiving, the modem performs the reverse process to demodulate the data from the carrier signal.

modular jack

Abbreviated MJ. The jack used to connect telephone cables to a wall-mounted face plate.

modulation

In communications, the process used by a modem to add the digital signal onto the carrier signal so that the signal can be transmitted over a telephone line. The frequency, amplitude, or phase of a signal may be modulated to represent a digital or analog signal.

Moore's law

Moore's law states that the number of transistors on a chip of a given size doubles approximately every 18 months. Named for Intel's Gordon Moore, who first made this statement in 1965.

motherboard

The main printed circuit board in a computer, containing the central processing unit, appropriate coprocessor and support chips, device controllers, and memory. It may also include expansion slots to give access to the computer's internal bus.

Motion Picture Experts Group

Abbreviated MPEG. A set of image-compression standards and file formats that defines a compression method for desktop audio, animation, and video.

MPEG is a lossy compression method that results in some data loss when a video clip is compressed. Standards include MPEG1 through MPEG4.

mouse

A small input device with one or more buttons used with graphical user interfaces. As the mouse moves, an on-screen mouse cursor follows; all movements are relative. Once the pointer is in the correct position on the screen, you press one of the mouse buttons to initiate an action or operation.

MPEG

See Motion Picture Experts Group.

MPEG1

The original MPEG standard, designed for CD-ROM use, with a bandwidth of 1.5Mbps, two audio channels, and noninterlaced video.

MPEG2

An extension to MPEG-1 designed for broadcast television, including High-Definition Television (HDTV), with a bandwidth of up to 40Mbps, five audio channels, interlaced video, and a wider range of frame sizes.

MPEG3

A standard designed for HDTV until it was discovered that MPEG-2 covered HDTV. This standard is no longer used.

MPEG4

A standard designed for video phones and multimedia applications, with a bandwidth of up to 64Kbps.

ms

See millisecond.

MTBF

See mean time between failures.

MTTR

See mean time to repair.

multimedia

A computer technology that displays information using a combination of full-motion video, animation, sound, graphics, and text, with a high degree of user interaction.

multimode fiber

A fiber-optic cable with a wide core that provides multiple routes for light waves to travel. Its wider diameter of between 25 to 200 microns prevents multimode fiber from carrying signals as far as single-mode fiber because of modal dispersion.

multipart virus

A form of virus that infects both the boot sector of a hard disk and executable files. Multipart viruses are difficult to detect because they use stealth and polymorphic techniques to avoid detection.

multiple zone recording

Abbreviated MZR. A method of increasing the storage capacity of a hard disk by using Constant Angular Velocity (CAV) techniques. CAV allows for the storage of additional data on the disk's outer edges, which would otherwise not be filled to their full capacity.

Musical Instrument Digital Interface

Abbreviated MIDI. A serial interface standard and communications protocol that defines the connections between a computer and a synthesizer. MIDI devices can be used to create, record, and play back music.

mv

See millivolt.

MZR

See multiple zone recording.

N

n

See nano-.

name resolution

The process of translating the appropriate numerical IP address, which is required by a computer, into a name that's more easily understood and remembered by a person.

In the TCP/IP environment, names such as www.sybex.com are translated into their IP equivalents by the Domain Name Service (DNS). In a Microsoft Windows NT/2000 Server environment, NetBIOS names are resolved into IP addresses by Windows Internet Naming Service (WINS).

nano-

Abbreviated n. A prefix meaning one billionth in the American numbering scheme and one thousand millionth in the British system.

nanosecond

Abbreviated ns. One billionth of a second. The speed of computer memory and logic chips is measured in nanoseconds.

narrow SCSI

A Small Computer System Interface (SCSI) or SCSI-interface capable of transferring only 8 bits of data at a time.

NAT

See Network Address Translation.

National Television Standards Committee

Abbreviated NTSC. The standards-setting body for television and video in the United States. Most European and Asian countries use a different standard known as Phase Alteration Line (PAL). The two standards are incompatible.

ear-end crosstalk

bbreviated NEXT. Any interference that occurs ose to a connector at either end of a cable. NEXT usually measured near the source of the test signal.

etBEUI

bbreviation for NetBIOS Extended User Interface, onounced "net-boo-ee." A network device driver pplied with Microsoft's LAN Manager, Windows r Workgroups, Windows NT, Windows 98, and indows 2000. NetBEUI will work with Windows XP, but you must manually install it from the stallation CD. NetBEUI communicates with the twork interface card via the Network Driver Interce Specification (NDIS).

NetBEUI is a small protocol with no networking er and therefore no routing capability. It's suitable ly for small networks; you can't build internetorks using NetBEUI, and so it's often replaced th TCP/IP.

Microsoft added extensions to NetBEUI in indows NT to remove the limitation of 254 ssions per node and calls this extended NetBEUI e NetBIOS Frame (NBF).

etBIOS

cronym for network basic input/output system, onounced "net-bye-ose." A session-layer network otocol, originally developed in 1984 by IBM and tek, to manage data exchange and network access. etBIOS provides an API with a consistent set of mmands for requesting lower-level network serces to transmit information from node to node, thus parating applications from the underlying network erating system. Many vendors provide either their vn version of NetBIOS or an emulation of its comunications services in their own products.

tiquette

contraction of network etiquette. The set of written rules governing the use of email and other mputer and network services.

Like any culture, the online world has its own rules and conventions, and if you understand and observe these conventions, you can take your place in the online community without problems.

Examples of netiquette include remembering that if you wouldn't make the comment to someone's face, don't post it in your email, not posting messages in uppercase because it's the email equivalent of YELLING (to add emphasis, place an asterisk before and after a word), avoiding flaming or mounting personal attacks on other users, checking your grammar and spelling before posting, and sharing your knowledge with others.

network

A group of computers and associated peripheral devices connected by a communications channel capable of sharing files and other resources between several users.

A network can range from a peer-to-peer network connecting a small number of users in an office or department to a LAN connecting many users over permanently installed cables and dial-up lines to a Metropolitan Area Network (MAN) or WAN connecting users on several different networks spread over a wide geographic area.

network adapter

See network interface card.

Network Address Translation

Abbreviated NAT. A term used to describe the process of converting between IP addresses on an intranet or other private network and Internet IP addresses.

network device driver

Software that controls the physical function of a network interface card, coordinating between the card and the other workstation hardware and software.

Network Driver Interface Specification

Abbreviated NDIS. A device-driver specification, originally developed by Microsoft and 3Com in

1990, that's independent of both the underlying network interface card hardware and the protocol being used. NDIS also allows multiple protocol stacks to be used at the same time in the same computer.

network interface card

Abbreviated NIC. In networking, the PC expansion board that plugs into a personal computer or server and works with the network operating system and the appropriate device drivers to control the flow of information over the network. Novell NetWare documentation uses the term *network board*, and some Microsoft documentation uses *network adapter*.

The network interface card is connected to the network media (twisted-pair, coaxial, or fiber-optic cable) and is designed for a specific type of network such as Ethernet, token ring, FDDI, or ARCnet.

network operating system

Abbreviated NOS. In typical client/server architecture LANs, the NOS consists of two parts. The largest and most complex part is the system software running on the file server. This system software coordinates many functions, including user accounts and network access information, security, resource sharing, administrative functions, UPS and power monitoring, data protection, and error detection and control. A much smaller component of the NOS runs on each of the networked PCs or workstations attached to the network.

In peer-to-peer networks, a part of the NOS is installed on each PC or workstation attached to the network and runs on top of or as a part of the PC operating system. In some cases, the NOS may be installed on one PC designated as a file server, but this PC isn't dedicated to the file server function; it's also available to run applications.

network printer

A printer attached to and accessible from the network. A network printer may be attached to a file server or a printer server, or it may have its own direct connection to the network.

network protocol

A formal specification that defines the procedures t follow when transmitting and receiving data over th network. Protocols define the format, timing, sequenc and error checking used on the network. TCP/IP, NetBEUI, and IPX/SPX are three of the most common protocols in use.

newsgroup

A Usenet email discussion group devoted to a singl topic. Subscribers to a newsgroup post articles that can be read by all the other subscribers.

Newsgroup names fit into a formal structure in which each component of the name is separated from the next by a period. The leftmost portion of the name represents the category of the newsgroup, and the name gets more specific from left to right.

The major top-level newsgroup categories includ alt, comp, misc, news, rec, sci, soc, and talk.

Private newsgroups are often available on corpo rate intranets, where the system administrator decide the organization, structure, and subject matter.

newsreader

An application used to read articles posted to Usene newsgroups. Newsreaders are of two kinds: *Threade* newsreaders group the posts into threads of related articles, and *unthreaded* newsreaders present articles i their original order of posting without regard for th subject. Of the two, threaded newsreaders are muc easier to use and are available in most popular We browsers.

NEXT

See near-end crosstalk.

NIC

See network interface card.

noise

In communications, extraneous signals on a transmi sion channel that degrade the quality or performanc of the channel. Noise is often caused by interferenc om nearby power lines, electrical equipment, or ikes in the AC line voltage.

minal velocity of propagation

ie speed at which a signal moves through a cable, pressed as a percentage or fraction of the speed of ht in a vacuum. Some cable testers use this speed, ong with the time it takes for a signal to return to e testing device, to calculate cable lengths.

tebook computer

small, portable computer that's light enough to ry comfortably, with a flat screen and keyboard at fold together.

Advances in battery technology allow notebook mputers to run for many hours between charges. Some odels can mate with a docking station to perform as ull-sized desktop system back at the office, and iny portable computers allow direct connection to e network via a Network Interface Card (NIC).

nanosecond.

SC

National Television Standards Committee.

ll

character that has all the binary digits set to zero SCII 0) and therefore has no value.

In programming, a null character is used for several ecial purposes, including padding fields or serving delimiter characters. In the C programming lan- age, for example, a null character indicates the end a character string.

ll modem

short serial cable that connects two personal com- ters so that they can communicate without the use modems.

The cable connects the two computers' serial rts, and certain lines in the cable are crossed over so at the wires used for sending by one computer are ed for receiving data by the other computer.

O

OCR

See optical character recognition.

octet

The Internet's own term for a unit of data containing exactly 8 bits. Some of the computer systems attached to the Internet have bytes with more than 8 bits, hence the need for this term.

OEM

See original equipment manufacturer.

offline

Describes a printer or other peripheral device that isn't in ready mode and is therefore unavailable for use.

online

1. Most broadly, any work done on a computer instead of by more traditional manual means. 2. Any function available directly on a computer, such as an application's help system. 3. Describes a peripheral device, such as a printer or modem, when it's directly connected to a computer and ready to operate. 4. In communications, describes a computer connected to a remote computer over a network or a modem link.

online service

A service that provides an online connection via modem for access to various services. Online services generally refer to Internet Service Providers (ISPs) but can also include commercial services and spe- cialist databases such as such as the Dow Jones News/Retrieval, and Lexis-Nexis.

operating system

Abbreviated OS. That software responsible for allo- cating system resources, including memory, processor time, disk space, and peripheral devices such as printers, modems, and monitors. All applications use the oper- ating system to gain access to these resources as necessary. The operating system is loaded into the computer as it boots, and it remains in memory until the computer is turned off.

optical character recognition

Abbreviated OCR. The computer recognition of printed or typed characters. OCR is usually performed using a standard optical scanner and special software, but some systems use special readers. The text is reproduced just as though it had been typed. Certain advanced systems can even resolve neatly handwritten characters.

optical mouse

A mouse that must be used on a mouse pad containing a special grid. The mouse shines a small beam of light on the grid that conveys mouse movements back to the computer.

original equipment manufacturer

Abbreviated OEM. The original manufacturer of a hardware subsystem or component. For example, Canon makes the print engine used in many laser printers, including those from Hewlett-Packard (HP); in this case, Canon is the OEM and HP is a Value-Added Reseller (VAR).

output

Computer-generated information that's displayed on the screen, printed, written to disk or tape, or sent over a communications link to another computer.

P

P

See peta-.

paged memory management unit

Abbreviated PMMU. A specialized chip designed to manage virtual memory. High-end processors, such as the Motorola 68040 and the Intel Pentium, have all the functions of a PMMU built into the chip itself.

page-mode RAM

A memory-management technique used to speed up the performance of Dynamic RAM (DRAM).

In a page-mode memory system, the memory is divided into pages by specialized DRAM chips. Consecutive accesses to memory addresses in the same page result in a page-mode cycle that takes abo half the time of a regular DRAM cycle.

Palm

The hand-held computer from 3Com Corporatio which has proved to be extremely popular.

parallel communications

The transmission of information from computer t computer, or from computer to peripheral device, which all the bits that make up the character are tra mitted at the same time over a multiline cable.

parallel port

An Input/Output (I/O) port that manages inform tion 8 bits at a time, often used to connect a parall printer.

parity

In communications, a simple form of error checkir that uses an extra or redundant bit after the data bi but before the stop bit or bits. Different types of parity used include odd, even, mark, space, and nor The parity settings used by both communicating computers must match. Most online services, such America Online, use no parity and an 8-bit data wor

parity bit

An extra or redundant bit used to detect data trans mission errors.

parity checking

A check mechanism applied to a character or series characters that uses the addition of extra or redunda parity bits.

Parity checking is useful for a variety of purpose including asynchronous communications and computer memory coordination.

arity error

mismatch in parity bits that indicates an error in ansmitted data.

artition

portion of a hard disk that the operating system eats as if it were a separate drive. In Windows, a rd disk can be divided into several partitions. A pri-ary partition, generally assigned the drive letter C:, ight contain files that start the computer running. ou could also set up a non-Windows partition to be ed by a different operating system.

artition table

n area of storage on a hard disk that contains infor-ation about the partitions the disk contains. This formation is usually recorded during the initial reparation of the hard disk before it's formatted.

assive termination

method used to terminate a Small Computer System terface (SCSI) chain of devices. Passive termination a simple termination method that works best with ur or fewer devices on a SCSI daisy chain.

assword

security method that identifies a specific authorized er of a computer system or network by a unique ring of characters.

In general, passwords should be a mixture of pper- and lowercase letters and numbers and should longer than six characters.

Passwords should be kept secret and changed fre-uently. The worst passwords are the obvious ones: eople's names or initials, place names, phone num-ers, birth dates, and anything to do with computers *Star Trek*. There are a limited number of words in e English language, and it's easy for a computer to y them all relatively quickly.

B

e petabyte.

PC Card

A term that describes plug-in cards that conform to the Personal Computer Memory Card International Association (PCMCIA) standard. A PC Card is about the size of a credit card and uses a 68-pin con-nector with longer power and ground pins that'll always engage before the signal pins engage.

Three versions of the standard have been approved by PCMCIA, and they differ by card thickness.

In theory, each PC Card adapter can support 16 PC Card sockets (if there's enough space), and up to 255 adapters can be installed in a PC that follows the PCMCIA standard; in other words, PCMCIA allows up to 4080 PC Cards on one computer.

The majority of PC Card devices are modems, Ethernet and Token Ring network adapters, dynamic RAM, and flash memory cards, but mini-hard disks, wireless LAN adapters, and SCSI adapters are also available.

PC Card slot

An opening in the case of a portable computer, intended to receive a PC Card; also known as a PCMCIA slot.

PC Memory Card International Association

Abbreviated PCMCIA. A nonprofit association, formed in 1989, with more than 320 members in the computer and electronics industries, that developed a standard for credit card–sized plug-in adapters designed for portable computers.

PCI local bus

Abbreviation for Peripheral Component Intercon-nect local bus. A specification introduced by Intel in 1992 for a local bus that allows up to 10 PCI-com-pliant expansion cards to be plugged into the com-puter. One of these expansion cards must be the PCI controller card, but the others can include a video card, network interface card, SCSI interface, or any other basic function.

The PCI controller exchanges information with the computer's processor, either 32 or 64 bits at a time, and allows intelligent PCI adapters to perform certain tasks concurrently with the main processor by using bus-mastering techniques.

PCI is compatible with ISA, EISA, and MCA expansion buses for backward compatibility with older technologies. PCI can operate at a bus speed of 32MHz and can manage a maximum throughput of 132MBps with a 32-bit data path or a rate of 264MBps with a 64-bit data path. PCI also supports Plug and Play.

PCI-X

A revision to the PCI standard proposed by IBM, Hewlett-Packard, and Compaq that increases the bus width to 64 bits, the bus speed to 133MHz, and the maximum throughput to 1GBps. Several vendors also offer hot-plug PCI slots that allow you to replace a failed component without a system reboot.

PCMCIA

See PC Memory Card International Association.

PCMCIA slot

See PC Card slot.

PDA

See personal digital assistant.

peer to peer

A network architecture in which two or more PCs can communicate with each other directly without the need for any intermediary devices. In a peer-to-peer system, a PC can be both a client and a server.

peer-to-peer network

A LAN in which drives, files, and printers on each PC can be available to every other PC on the network, eliminating the need for a dedicated file server. Each PC can still run local applications.

Peer-to-peer networks introduce their own system management problems, including administration and responsibility for system backup, reliability, and security. Peer-to-peer systems are often used in relatively small networks, with two to ten users.

Pentium

A family of microprocessors introduced by Intel in 1993. The Pentium represents the continuing evolution of the 80486 family of microprocessors and adds several notable features, including instruction code and data caches and a built-in floating-point processor and memory management unit. It also has a superscalar design and dual pipelining (which allow the Pentium to execute more than one instruction per clock cycle), a 32-bit address bus, and a 64-bit data bus. The Pentium is equivalent to 3.1 million transistors, more than twice that of the 80486.

Pentium II

A family of microprocessors from Intel. The Pentium II includes several notable features, including integrated L1/L2 caches of up to 2MB, which can be accessed at the full clock speed, and a built-in floating-point processor and memory management unit. It also has superscalar design and dual pipelining, which allow the Pentium II to execute more than one instruction per clock cycle.

Available in a whole range of clock speeds, the Pentium II can use a 100MHz system bus and is equivalent to 7.5 million transistors, more than twice that of the Pentium.

Pentium III

A family of microprocessors introduced by Intel in 1999. The Pentium III includes 50 new floating-point instructions and 8 new registers to speed up floating-point calculations in scientific and engineering calculation, along with 12 new multimedia instructions to increase MPEG2 performance and speech recognition. The most controversial feature is the processor serial number, designed to increase network and online shopping security but feared by many as a threat to privacy.

Available in a whole range of clock speeds, the Pentium III can use the Pentium II 100MHz system bus and is equivalent to 9.5 million transistors.

ntium 4

family of microprocessors introduced by Intel in
00. The Pentium 4 is based on the all-new Net-
rst micro-architecture. It features Hyper-pipelined
hnology, a rapid execution engine, an execution
ce cache, enhanced floating point/multimedia
structions, and the second generation of Internet
eaming Single Instruction, Multiple Data (SIMD)
tensions.

Available in a range of clock speeds starting at
3GHz, the Pentium 4 uses a 400MHz system bus
d is equivalent to 42 million transistors.

ntium Pro

family of microprocessors introduced by Intel in
995. The Pentium Pro is optimized for the execu-
on of 32-bit software and is available with clock
eeds from 150 to 200MHz. With a 32-bit data bus
nning at 60 or 66MHz, it supports superscalar
chitecture and pipelines and contains the equivalent
5.5 million transistors.

Dynamic execution (a combination of branch pre-
ction and speculative execution) allows the pro-
ssor to anticipate and schedule the next instructions
r execution. Pentium Pro offers up to 1MB of level 2
che that runs at the same speed as the processor.

eriod

he . character; pronounced "dot." Used to indicate
e name of the current directory in a pathname and
ed to separate the different elements in a domain
me, as in www.sybex.com.

eripheral Component Interconnect

e *PCI local bus.*

ermanent swap file

swap file that, once created, is used over and over
ain. This file is used in virtual memory operations,
here hard disk space is used in place of RAM.

personal digital assistant

Abbreviated PDA. A tiny, pen-based, battery-powered computer that combines personal organization
software with fax and email facilities into a unit that
fits into your pocket. PDAs are available from several
manufacturers.

peta-

Abbreviated P. A metric system prefix for one quadrillion, or 10^{15}. In computing, based on the binary system,
peta has the value of 1,125,899,906,842,624, or the
power of 2 (2^{50}) closest to 1 quadrillion.

petabyte

Abbreviated PB. Usually 1,125,899,906,842,624
bytes (2^{50}) but may also refer to 1 quadrillion bytes
(10^{15}).

PGA

See pin grid array.

PhotoCD

A standard for storing 35mm photographs taken with
an ordinary (nondigital) camera onto CD-ROM.

physical device

An item of hardware, such as a disk drive or a tape
drive, that's physically separate from other devices.

physical drive

A real device in the computer that you can see or
touch, as opposed to a conceptual or logical drive.
One physical drive may be divided into several logical
drives, which are parts of the hard disk that function
as if they were separate disk drives.

pin grid array

Abbreviated PGA. A method of mounting integrated
circuits onto boards. PGA is often used with integrated circuits that have a large number of pins.

pinouts

The configuration and purpose of each pin in a multipin connector.

PIO

See programmed input/output.

pipeline burst cache

A secondary or L2 cache associated with a microprocessor that allows fast data transfer rates. Pipeline burst cache requires RAM chips that can synchronize with the microprocessor's clock.

pipeline stall

A microprocessor design error that leads to delays in the processing of an instruction.

pipelining

In processor architecture, a method of fetching and decoding instructions that ensures that the processor never needs to wait; as soon as one instruction is executed, the next one is ready.

plastic leadless chip carrier

Abbreviated PLCC. A method used to mount integrated circuits onto a board. Although similar in appearance to the more expensive Leadless Chip Carrier (LCC), which is made from a ceramic material, the two chip carriers are incompatible.

PLCC

See plastic leadless chip carrier.

Plug and Play

Abbreviated PnP. A standard from Compaq, Microsoft, Intel, and Phoenix that defines techniques designed to make PC configuration simple and automatic. A user can plug in a new device, and the operating system will recognize it and configure it automatically when the system is next started.

PnP adapters contain configuration information stored in nonvolatile memory, which includes vendor information, serial number, and checksum information.

The PnP chipset allows each adapter to be isolated one at a time, until all cards have been properly identified by the operating system.

The PnP-compatible BIOS isolates and identifies PnP cards at boot time, and when you insert a new card, the BIOS performs an autoconfiguration sequence enabling the new card with appropriate settings.

PMMU

See paged memory management unit.

PnP

See Plug and Play.

Point-to-Point Protocol

Abbreviated PPP. A TCP/IP protocol used to transmit data over serial lines and dial-up telephone point-to-point connections.

PPP allows a PC to establish a temporary direct connection to the Internet via modem and appear to the host system as if it were an Ethernet port on the host's network.

PPP provides an automatic method of assigning an Internet Protocol (IP) address so that mobile users can connect to the network at any point.

polymorphic virus

A form of virus that can change its appearance to avoid detection. The virus encrypts itself using a special formula each time an infection occurs. Virus detecting software uses special scanning techniques to find and remove polymorphic viruses.

POP

See Post Office Protocol.

port

1. The point at which a communications circuit terminates at a network, serial, or parallel interface card, usually identified by a specific port number or name. 2. A number used to identify a connection point to a specific Internet protocol.

port number

The default identifier for a TCP/IP or Internet process. For example, FTP, HTML, and Telnet are all available at preassigned unique port numbers so that the computer knows how to respond when it's contacted on a specific port; Web servers use port 80, and SMTP email is always delivered to port 25. You can override these defaults by specifying different values in a URL, but whether they'll work depends on the configuration on the target system.

port replicator

A device containing standard computer ports used to avoid constantly connecting and disconnecting peripherals from a portable computer.

A port replicator duplicates your computer's ports and may even add a Small Computer System Interface (SCSI) port or a second Universal Serial Bus port. The external monitor, full-sized keyboard, and mouse you use in the office are connected to the port replicator; when it's time to take the portable computer on the road, you just unplug the port replicator, leaving everything attached to the replicator for your return.

portal

A large Web site that acts as a gateway to the Internet and may also offer search facilities, free email, online chat, and instant messaging, as well as other services including hard news, sports, and personal finance. Many portals make money by selling advertising space.

POST

See Power-On Self Test.

post

An individual article or email message sent to a Usenet newsgroup or mailing list, rather than a message sent to an individual.

Post Office Protocol

Abbreviated POP. An Internet mail server protocol that also provides an incoming mail storage mechanism.

POP works with Simple Mail Transfer Protocol (SMTP), which actually moves the email from one system to another, and the latest version of the standard is POP3.

When a client connects to a POP3 server, all the messages addressed to that client are downloaded; there's no ability to download messages selectively. Once the messages are downloaded, the user can delete or modify messages without further interaction with the server.

In some locations, POP3 is being replaced by another standard, Internet Mail Access Protocol (IMAP) version 4.

PostScript

A page-description language from Adobe Systems that offers flexible fonts and high-quality graphics. PostScript uses Englishlike commands for page layout and to scale fonts and is used with high-quality printers.

power conditioning

The use of protective and conditioning devices to filter out power surges and spikes and to ensure clean power. The three main types of power conditioning devices are suppression devices, regulation devices, and isolation devices.

power supply

A part of the computer that converts the power from a wall outlet into the lower voltages, typically 5 to 12 volts Direct Current (DC), required internally in the computer. PC power supplies are usually rated in watts, ranging from 90 to 300 watts. If the power supply in a computer fails, nothing works—not even the fan.

power surge

A sudden, brief, and often destructive increase in line voltage. A power surge may be caused by an electrical appliance, such as a photocopier or elevator, or by power being reapplied after an outage.

Power-On Self Test

Abbreviated POST. A set of diagnostic programs loaded from Read-Only Memory (ROM) before any attempt is made to load the operating system, designed to ensure that the major system components are present and operating. If a problem is found, the POST firmware writes an error message in the screen, sometimes with a diagnostic code number indicating the type of fault located.

PPP

See Point-to-Point Protocol.

primary cache

See level 1 cache.

Primary Rate ISDN

Abbreviated PRI. An Integrated Services Digital Network (ISDN) service that provides 23 B (bearer channels), capable of speeds of 64Kbps, and one D (data channel), also capable of 64Kbps. The combined capacity of 1.544Mbps is equivalent to one T1 channel.

printer emulation

The ability of a printer to change modes so that it behaves like a printer from another manufacturer. For example, many dot-matrix printers offer an Epson printer emulation in addition to their own native mode. Most laser printers offer a Hewlett-Packard LaserJet emulation.

programmed input/output

Abbreviated PIO. A method of moving data between a hard disk and memory via the processor. An alternative data transfer method known as Direct Memory Access (DMA) bypasses the processor and moves data directly between the hard disk and memory.

protocol stack

The several layers of software that define the computer-to-computer or computer-to-network protocol.

Several companies have developed important proprietary protocol stacks, including Novell NetWare IPX/SPX, but the trend these days is moving toward more open systems such as TCP/IP.

Q

QIC

See quarter-inch cartridge.

quarter-inch cartridge

Abbreviated QIC. A set of tape standards defined by the Quarter-Inch Cartridge Drive Standards Association, a trade association established in 1987. Several standards are in use today.

question mark

A wildcard character (?) used in many operating systems to represent a single character in a filename or filename extension.

R

radio frequency interference

Abbreviated RFI. Many electronic devices, including radios, televisions, computers, and peripherals, can interfere with other signals in the radio frequency range by producing electromagnetic radiation. The use of radio frequencies is generally regulated by government agencies.

RAID

See Redundant Array of Inexpensive Disks.

RAM

See random access memory.

AM chip

semiconductor storage device, either dynamic
AM or static RAM.

ndom access

escribes the ability of a storage device to go directly
the required memory address without needing to
ad from the beginning every time data is requested.
a random-access device, the information can be
ad directly by accessing the appropriate memory
dress. There's nothing random or haphazard about
ndom access; a more precise term is *direct access*.

ndom access memory

bbreviated RAM. The main system memory in a
mputer, used for the operating system, applica-
ns, and data.

te-adaptive digital subscriber line

bbreviated RADSL. An Asymmetric Digital Sub-
riber Line (ADSL) service with a provision for
sting the line length and quality before starting the
rvice and adjusting the line speed accordingly.

ad-after-write verification

method of checking that data is written to a hard
sk correctly. Data is written to the disk and then
ad back and compared with the original data still
ld in memory. If the data read from the disk
atches, the data in memory is released. If the data
esn't match, that block on the disk is marked as
d, and another attempt is made to write the data
sewhere on the disk.

EADME file

plain-text file containing information about the
ftware, placed on the distribution disks by the
anufacturer.

The filename may vary slightly; it might be `READ.ME`,
EADME`.1ST`, `README.TXT`, or `README.DOC`, for example.
EADME files may contain last-minute, important
formation that's not in the program manuals or
nline help system.

You should always look for a README file when
installing a new program on your system; it may contain information pertinent to your specific configuration. You can open a README file in any word
processor or text editor because the file doesn't contain embedded formatting commands or program-
specific characters.

read-only

Describes a file or other collection of information
that may only be read; it may not be updated in any
way or deleted.

Certain important operating system files are designated as read-only files to prevent accidental deletion.
Also, certain types of ROM and some devices such as
archive backup tapes and CD-ROMs can be read
from but not changed.

read-only memory

Abbreviated ROM. A semiconductor-based memory
system that stores information permanently, retaining
its contents when power is switched off. ROMs are
used for firmware, such as the BIOS used in the PC.
In some portable computers, applications and even
the operating system are stored in ROM.

reboot

To restart the computer and reload the operating
system, usually after a crash.

In some cases, you may be able to restart the computer from the keyboard; in more severe crashes, you
may have to turn the computer off and then back on
again.

reduced instruction set computing

Abbreviated RISC, pronounced "risk." A processor
that recognizes only a limited number of assembly-
language instructions.

RISC chips are relatively cheap to produce and debug
because they usually contain fewer than 128 different
instructions. RISC processors are commonly used in
workstations, and they can be designed to run up to
70 percent faster than processors that use Complex
Instruction Set Computing (CISC).

Redundant Array of Inexpensive Disks

Abbreviated RAID. Also seen as Redundant Array of Independent Disks. In networking and mission-critical applications, a method of using several hard disk drives (often SCSI or Integrated Drive Electronics, or IDE, drives) in an array to provide fault tolerance in the event that one or more than one drive fails.

There are several different RAID levels, and the appropriate level of RAID for any particular installation depends on network usage. RAID levels 1, 3, and 5 are available commercially, and levels 3 and 5 are proving popular for networks.

Registry

In the Microsoft Windows family of operating systems, a system database containing configuration information.

The operating system continually references the Registry database for information on users and groups, the applications installed on the system and the types of document each can create, what hardware is available and which ports are in use, and property sheets for folders and application icons.

Changes to the Registry are usually made automatically as configuration information is changed using Control Panel applications or the Administrative Tools; however, knowledgeable users can make changes directly using the Windows Registry Editor.

restore

To copy files from a backup or archival storage to their normal location, especially when the files are being copied to replace files lost by accident.

retensioning

A maintenance operation required by certain tape drives to ensure correct tape tension; retensioning fast-forwards and then rewinds the entire tape or tape cartridge.

RFI

See radio frequency interference.

RISC

See reduced instruction set computing.

RJ-11

A commonly used modular telephone connector. R 11 is a four-wire (two-pair) connector most often used for voice communications.

RJ-45

A commonly used modular telephone connector. R 45 is an eight-wire (four-pair) connector used for data transmission over Unshielded Twisted-Pair cable (UTP) and leased telephone line connections

ROM

See read-only memory.

RS-232C

A recommended standard interface established by the Telecommunications Industry Association and the Electronic Industries Association (TIA/EIA). Also known as TIA/EIA-232.

The standard defines the specific electrical, functional, and mechanical characteristics used in asynchronous transmissions between a computer, which a Data Terminal Equipment (DTE) and a peripheral device, which is a Data Communications Equipment (DCE). RS is the abbreviation for recommended standard, and the C denotes the third revision of the standard. RS-232C is compatible with the CCITT V.24 and V.28 standards, as well as with ISO IS211

RS-232C uses a 25-pin or 9-pin DB connector and is used for serial communications between a computer and a peripheral device, such as a printer, modem, or mouse. The maximum cable limit of 15.25 meters (50 feet) can be extended by using high quality cable, line drivers to boost the signal, or short haul modems.

g

short-term drop in line voltage to between 70 and
) percent of the nominal voltage.

AN

e Storage Area Network.

:SI

cronym for small computer system interface, pro-
ounced "scuzzy."

A high-speed parallel interface defined by the
NSI X3T9.2 committee. SCSI is used to connect a
mputer to peripheral devices using just one port.
evices connected in this way are said to be "daisy
ained" together, and each device must have a
ique identifier or priority number.

SCSI is often used to connect hard disks, tape
ives, CD drives, and other mass storage media, as
ell as scanners and printers.

:SI-1

commonly used name for the first Small Computer
ystem Interface (SCSI) definition, published in
186 with an 8-bit parallel interface and a maximum
ta transfer rate of 5MBps.

:SI-2

1994 extension to the Small Computer System
terface (SCSI) definition.

This standard broadened the 8-bit data bus to 16 or
2 bits (also known as Wide SCSI), doubling the
ta transfer rate to 10 or 20MBps (also known as
ist SCSI). Wide SCSI and Fast SCSI can be com-
ned to give Fast-Wide SCSI, with a 16-bit data
is and a maximum data transfer rate of 20MBps.
:SI-2 is backward compatible with SCSI-1, but for
aximum benefit, you should use SCSI-2 devices with
SCSI-2 controller.

SCSI-2 also adds new commands, and although
e connector is physically smaller, it uses 68 pins
ther than the 50 in SCSI-1. Higher data transfer

rates are achieved by using synchronous rather than
asynchronous transfers.

SCSI-3

An extension to the Small Computer System Interface
(SCSI) standard.

This definition increased the number of connected
peripherals from 7 to 16, increased cable lengths,
added support for a variety of interfaces including a
serial interface, a Fibre Channel interface, an IEEE
1394 interface, and support for Serial Storage Architecture and several packet interfaces.

Data transfer rates depend on the hardware implementation, but data rates in excess of 160MBps are
possible.

SCSI bus

Another name for the Small Computer System Interface (SCSI) interface and communications protocol.

SCSI terminator

The Small Computer System Interface (SCSI) interface must be correctly terminated to prevent signals
echoing on the bus.

Many SCSI devices have built-in terminators that
engage when they're needed. With some older SCSI
devices, you must add an external SCSI terminator
that plugs into the device's SCSI connector.

SDRAM

See synchronous DRAM.

SDSL

See single-line digital subscriber line.

search engine

A special Web site that lets you perform keyword
searches to locate interesting Web pages.

To use a search engine, you enter one or more keywords or, in some cases, a more complex search string
such as a Boolean expression. The search engine
returns a list of matching Web pages, newsgroups,
and FTP archives taken from its database, usually

ranked in some way, containing the expression you're looking for, along with a brief text description of the material.

Searching this database is much faster than actually searching the Internet, but the accuracy and relevance of the information it contains depends on how often the data is updated and what proportion of the Web is actually searched for new content.

secondary cache

See level 2 cache.

sector

A portion of one of the concentric tracks recorded on a hard or floppy disk during a low-level format, usually capable of storing 512 bytes of information.

seek time

The time it takes to move a disk drive's read/write head to a specific location on the disk.

Sequenced Packet Exchange

Abbreviated SPX. A set of Novell NetWare protocols implemented on top of IPX to form a transport-layer interface.

SPX provides additional capabilities over IPX. For example, it guarantees packet delivery by having the destination node verify that the data was received correctly. If no response is received within a specified time, SPX retransmits the packet. If several retransmissions fail to return an acknowledgment, SPX assumes that the connection has failed and informs the operator. All packets in the transmission are sent in sequence, and they all take the same path to their destination node.

sequential access

An access method used by some storage devices, such as tapes, that requires them to start at the beginning to find a specific storage location. If the information you're looking for is toward the end of the tape, access can take a long time.

serial communications

The transmission of information from computer to computer, or from computer to peripheral device, or bit at a time.

Serial communications can be synchronous and controlled by a clock or asynchronous and coordinated by start and stop bits embedded in the data stream. The sending and receiving devices must both use the same baud rate, parity setting, and other communication parameters.

Serial Line Internet Protocol

Abbreviated SLIP. A protocol used to run Internet Protocol over serial lines or telephone connections using modems.

SLIP allows a computer to establish a temporary direct connection to the Internet via modem and appear to the host system as if it were a port on the host's network.

SLIP is being replaced by Point-to-Point Protocol (PPP).

serial port

A port on the computer that supports serial communications in which information is processed one bit at a time.

RS-232C is a common protocol used on serial ports when communicating with modems, printers, mice, and other peripherals; Universal Serial Bus (USB) is replacing RS-232C.

set-associative cache

A cache in which information from RAM is kept in sets, and these sets may have multiple locations, each holding a block of data; each block may be in any of the sets, but it'll only be in one location within that set. Search time is shortened, and it's less likely that frequently used data will be overwritten. A set-associative cache may use two, four, or eight sets. *See cache.*

SGRAM

See Synchronous Graphics RAM.

shielded cable

Cable protected against electromagnetic and Radio Frequency Interference (RFI) by metal-backed Mylar foil and plastic or PVC.

shielded twisted-pair cable

Abbreviated STP. Cable with a foil shield and copper braid surrounding the pairs of wires.

The wires have a minimum number of twists per foot of cable length; the greater the number of twists, the lower the crosstalk. STP offers high-speed transmission for useful distances, and it's often associated with Token Ring networks, but its bulk quickly fills up wiring conduits.

short circuit

Often abbreviated to short. A circuit that's accidentally completed at a point too close to its origin to allow normal or complete operation. In cabling, a short circuit often occurs when two stripped wires touch.

SIMM

See Single Inline Memory Module.

Simple Mail Transfer Protocol

Abbreviated SMTP. The TCP/IP protocol that provides a simple email service and is responsible for moving email messages from one email server to another. SMTP provides a direct end-to-end mail delivery, which is rather unusual; most mail systems use store-and-forward protocols.

The email servers run either Post Office Protocol (POP) or Internet Mail Access Protocol (IMAP) to distribute email messages to users.

Single Inline Memory Module

Abbreviated SIMM. A group of memory chips mounted on a small circuit board. SIMMs have one set of connectors, and they have a 32-bit data path.

Single Large Expensive Disk

Abbreviated SLED. The traditional alternative to Redundant Array of Inexpensive Disks (RAID), which is used by most networks.

single-line digital subscriber line

Abbreviated SDSL; sometimes called symmetrical digital subscriber line. A symmetrical, bidirectional digital subscriber line service that operates on one twisted-pair wire.

SDSL can provide data rates of up to the T1 rate of 1.544Mbps over a cable length of up to 1,000 feet, and because it operates above the voice frequency, voice and data can be carried on the same connection at the same time.

single-mode fiber

Narrow diameter fiber-optic cable in which lasers rather than LEDs are used to transmit signals through the cable.

Single-mode fiber allows only one route for a light wave to pass through, and it can transmit signals over considerable distances. For this reason, it's often used in telephone networks rather than in LANs.

slash

The / character. Used to separate command-line switches that alter the default settings for an operating system command.

SLED

See Single Large Expensive Disk.

SLIP

See Serial Line Internet Protocol.

Small Computer System Interface

See SCSI.

SMTP

See Simple Mail Transfer Protocol.

spike

A short, transient electrical signal, often of very high amplitude.

SPX

See Sequenced Packet Exchange.

SRAM

See static RAM.

start bit

In asynchronous transmissions, a start bit is transmitted to indicate the beginning of a new data word.

static RAM

Abbreviated SRAM, pronounced "ess-ram." A type of computer memory that retains its contents as long as power is applied; it doesn't need constant refreshment, as required by Dynamic RAM (DRAM) chips. An SRAM chip can store only about $1/4$ of the information that a DRAM chip of the same complexity can hold. However, SRAM is much faster than DRAM and is often used in caches.

stealth virus

A form of virus that attempts to hide from antivirus software and from the operating system by remaining in memory.

stop bit

In asynchronous transmissions, a stop bit is transmitted to indicate the end of the current data word. Depending on the convention in use, one or two stop bits are used.

Storage Area Network

Abbreviated SAN. A method used to physically separate the storage function of the network from the data processing function.

SAN provides a separate network devoted to storage and so helps to reduce network traffic by isolating large data transfers such as backups. Most of

the SAN vendors, including StorageTek and Compaq use a Fibre Channel–based SAN system, but IBM ha proposed a proprietary architecture.

store-and-forward

A method that temporarily stores messages at inter mediate nodes before forwarding them to the next destination. This technique allows routing over net works that aren't available at all times and lets user take advantage of off-peak rates when traffic and costs might be lower.

STP

See shielded twisted-pair cable.

straight-tip connector

Abbreviated ST. A fiber-optic cable connector that maintains the perfect alignment of the ends of the connected fibers, required for efficient light transmission.

streaming tape

A high-speed tape backup system designed to optimiz throughput; the tape isn't stopped during a backup To use streaming tape, the computer and backup software must be fast enough to keep up with the tape drive.

stripe set

A single volume created across multiple hard disk drive and accessed in parallel to optimize disk-access tim

subdirectory

A directory contained within another directory. Th root directory is the top-level directory, from which all other directories must branch. In common use, subdirectory is synonymous with directory or folde

subnet

A logical network created from a single IP address. A mask is used to identify bits from the host portion o the address to be used for subnet addresses.

subnet address

The subnet portion of an IP address. In a subnetted network, the host part of the IP address is divided into a subnet portion and a host portion by a subnet mask.

subnet mask

A number, or more correctly, a bit pattern, that identifies which parts of an IP address correspond to the network, subnet, and host portions of the address. Also referred to as an address mask.

superpipelining

A preprocessing technique used by some microprocessors in which two or more execution stages (such as fetch, decode, execute, or write back) are divided into two or more pipelined stages, giving considerably higher performance.

superscalar

A microprocessor architecture that contains more than one execution unit, or pipeline, allowing the processor to execute more than one instruction per clock cycle.

For example, the Pentium processor is superscalar, with two side-by-side pipelines for integer instructions. The processor determines whether an instruction can be executed in parallel with the next instruction in line. If it doesn't detect any dependencies, the two instructions are executed.

surge

A short, sudden, and often destructive increase in line voltage. A voltage-regulating device, known as a *surge suppressor*, can protect computer equipment against surges.

surge suppressor

A voltage-regulating device placed between the computer and the AC line connection that protects the computer system from power surges; also known as a surge protector.

swap

To temporarily move a process from memory to disk so that another process can use that memory space. When space becomes available again, the process is swapped back into memory. This allows more processes to be loaded than there's physical memory space to run them simultaneously.

swap file

On a hard disk, a file used to store parts of running programs that have been swapped out of memory temporarily to make room for other running programs. A swap file may be permanent, always occupying the same amount of hard disk space even though the application that created it may not be running, or temporary, created as and when needed.

In Windows 2000 documentation, the swap file is called the *paging file*.

swapping

The process of exchanging one item for another. In a virtual memory system, swapping occurs when a program requests a virtual memory location that isn't currently in memory. Swapping may also refer to changing floppy or compact disks as needed when using a single disk drive.

symmetrical digital subscriber line

See single-line digital subscriber line.

synchronous DRAM

Abbreviated SDRAM or syncDRAM. A high-speed memory technology, faster than EDO RAM, used in high-end systems and servers. SDRAM runs at higher speeds than conventional DRAM by using a technique that attempts to predict the location of the next memory address to be accessed.

Synchronous Graphics RAM

Abbreviated SGRAM. A type of high-speed dynamic RAM used in video adapters.

T

T

See tera-.

T.120

A group of communications and applications protocols that support real-time, multipoint data communications over LANs, ISDN, dial-up, and Internet connections. T.120 became well known after Microsoft incorporated it into the NetMeeting package.

tape cartridge

A self-contained tape storage module, containing tape much like that in a video cassette. Tape cartridges are primarily used to back up hard disk systems.

tape drive

A computer peripheral device that reads from and writes to magnetic tape.

The drive may use tape on an open reel or from an enclosed tape cartridge. Because tape management software must search from the beginning of the tape every time it wants to find a file (a process called *sequential access*), tape is too slow to use as a primary storage system; however, tapes are frequently used to back up hard disks.

TB

See terabyte.

TCP

See Transmission Control Protocol.

TCP ports

In a TCP/IP network when a computer connects with another computer to access a specific service, an end-to-end connection is established and a socket is set up at each end of the connection. This socket is created at a particular port number, depending on the application in use.

TCP/IP

See Transmission Control Protocol/Internet Protocol.

Telnet

A terminal emulation protocol, part of the TCP/IP suite of protocols, that provides remote terminal-connection services.

The most common terminal emulations are for Digital Equipment Corporation (DEC) VT-52, VT-100, and VT-220 terminals, but many companies offer additional add-in emulations.

temporary swap file

A swap space that's created every time it's needed. A temporary swap file can consist of several discontinuous pieces of hard disk space. A temporary swap file doesn't occupy hard disk space if the application that created it isn't running.

tera-

Abbreviated T. A prefix meaning 10^{12} in the metric system, or 1,000,000,000,000; commonly referred to as 1 trillion in the American numbering system and million million in the British numbering system.

terabyte

Abbreviated TB. In computing, usually 2^{40}, or 1,099,511,627,776 bytes. Terabytes are used to represent extremely large hard disk capacities.

terminal emulation

A method of operation or software that makes a PC act like a terminal attached to a mainframe, usually for the purpose of telecommunications. Communications programs often include popular emulations, such as ANSI, VT-52, VT-100, VT-200, and TTY.

terminator

A device attached to the last peripheral device in a series or the last node on a network.

For example, the last device on a SCSI bus must terminate the bus; otherwise, the bus won't perform.

roperly. A 50-ohm resistor is placed at both ends of
1 Ethernet cable to prevent signals reflecting and
1terfering with the transmission.

ext mode

mode in which the computer displays characters on
1e screen using the built-in character set but doesn't
1ow any graphics characters or a mouse pointer. Also
1own as character mode.

FT display

e active-matrix display.

1ick Ethernet

1onnecting coaxial cable used on an Ethernet net-
1ork; also known as thicknet.

The cable is 1-centimeter (0.4 inch) thick, almost
1 thick as your thumb, and can be used to connect
1etwork nodes up to a distance of approximately
1006 meters (3300 feet). Thick Ethernet is primarily
1ed for facility-wide installations.

1icknet

e thick Ethernet.

1in Ethernet

1onnecting coaxial cable used on an Ethernet net-
1ork; also known as thinnet.

The cable is 5-millimeters (0.2 inch) thick, about
1 thick as your little finger, and can be used to con-
1ct network nodes up to a distance of approximately
1.5 meters (500 feet). Thin Ethernet is primarily
1ed for office installations.

1in film transistor display

e active-matrix display.

1innet

e thin Ethernet.

thrashing

An excessive amount of disk activity that causes a virtual memory system to spend all its time swapping
pages in and out of memory and no time executing the
application.

Thrashing can be caused when poor system configuration creates a swap file that's too small or when
insufficient memory is installed in the computer.
Increasing the size of the swap file or adding memory
are often the best ways to reduce thrashing.

thread

1. A concurrent process that's part of a larger process
or program. In a multitasking operating system, a
single program may contain several threads, all running at the same time. For example, one part of a program can be making a calculation while another part
is drawing a graph or chart. 2. A connected set of
postings to a Usenet newsgroup. Many newsreaders
present postings as threads rather than in strict chro-
nological order.

throughput

A measure of the data transfer rate through a complex
communications or networking scheme.

Throughput is considered to be an indication of
the overall performance of the system. For example, the
throughput of a server depends on the processor type,
operating system in use, hard disk capacity, network
interface card in use, and the size of the data transfer
buffer.

In communications, throughput is usually measured as the number of bits or packets processed each
second.

TIA/EIA 586

A standard, jointly defined by the Telecommunications Industry Association and the Electronic Industries Association (TIA/EIA), for telecommunications
wiring used in commercial buildings. TIA/EIA 586
applies to all unshielded twisted-pair wiring that
works with Ethernet, Token Ring, ISDN, and other
networking systems.

TIA/EIA structured cabling standards

Standards specified by the Telecommunications Industries Association and the Electronics Industry Association (TIA/EIA).

Token Ring network

IBM's implementation of the token ring network architecture, which uses a token-passing protocol transmitting at 4Mbps or 16Mbps.

Using standard telephone wiring, a Token Ring network can connect up to 72 devices; with Shielded Twisted-Pair (STP) wiring, each ring can support up to 256 nodes. Although it's based on a closed-loop ring structure, a Token Ring network uses a star-shaped cluster of up to eight nodes, all attached to the same wiring concentrator or Multistation Access Unit (MAU). The MAUs are then connected to the main ring circuit.

A Token Ring network can include personal computers, minicomputers, and mainframes. The IEEE 802.5 standard defines token ring networks.

token ring network

A LAN with a ring structure that uses token passing to regulate traffic on the network and avoid collisions.

On a token ring network, the controlling network interface card generates a token that controls the right to transmit. This token is continuously passed from one node to the next around the network.

When a node has information to transmit, it captures the token, sets its status to busy, and adds the message and the destination address. All other nodes continuously read the token to determine if they're the recipient of a message. If they are, they collect the token, extract the message, and return the token to the sender. The sender then removes the message and sets the token status to free, indicating that it can be used by the next node in sequence.

top-level domains

On the Internet, the highest category of host name, which either signifies the type of institutio or the country of its origin.

In the United States, the most common top-lev domains include com, edu, gov, int, mil, net, and or Most countries also have unique domains named aft their international abbreviations; for example, ca re resents Canada, uk represents Great Britain, and jp represents Japan.

topology

The map of a network. *Physical* topology describes where the cables are run and where the workstation nodes, routers, and gateways are located. Networks are usually configured in bus, ring, star, or mesh topologies. *Logical* topology refers to the paths that messages take to get from one user on the network t another.

TP

See twisted-pair cable.

track

One of the concentric data areas recorded onto a har or floppy disk during a low-level format.

trackball

A device used for pointing, designed as a space-savin alternative to the mouse.

A trackball contains a movable ball that you rotat with your fingers to move the cursor on the screen. Because it doesn't need the area of flat space that a mouse needs, trackballs are popular with users of po table computers; Microsoft has released a small trac ball that clips onto the side of a laptop computer, an IBM has developed a dual-button, touch-sensitive pointing stick called the TrackPoint.

Transmission Control Protocol

Abbreviated TCP. The transport-level protocol use in the TCP/IP suite of protocols. It works abov IP in the protocol stack and provides reliable data delivery over connection-oriented links.

TCP adds a header to the datagram that contain the information needed to get the datagram to its de tination. The source port number and the destinatio port number allow data to be sent back and forth t correct processes running on each computer. A quence number allows the datagrams to be rebuilt the correct order in the receiving computer, and a ecksum verifies that the data received is the same as e data sent.

ansmission Control Protocol/Internet Protocol

breviated TCP/IP. A set of communications pro- cols first developed by the Defense Advanced esearch Projects Agency (DARPA) in the late 70s. The set of TCP/IP protocols encompasses edia access, packet transport, session communica- ns, file transfer, email, and terminal emulation.

TCP/IP is a widely published open standard, d, although completely independent of any specific rdware or software company, it's supported by a ge number of vendors and is available on many dif- ent computers, from PCs to mainframes, running ny different operating systems. Many corporations, iversities, and government agencies use TCP/IP, d it's also the basis of the Internet.

TCP/IP is separated from the network hardware d will run over Ethernet, token ring, X.25 net- orks, and dial-up connections. It's a routable pro- col, so datagrams can be sent over specific routes, d it has reliable and efficient data-delivery mecha- sms. TCP/IP uses a common expandable addressing heme, so any system can address any other system, en in a network as large as the Internet, and new net- orks can be added without service disruptions.

The popularity that the TCP/IP family of proto- ls enjoys today didn't arise just because the protocols re available or even because the U.S. government andated their use. They're popular because they're bust, solid protocols that solve many of the most fficult networking problems and do so in an elegant d efficient way.

ansmission medium

he physical cabling used to carry network informa- n, such as fiber-optic, coaxial, Shielded Twisted- ir (STP), or Unshielded Twisted-Pair (UTP) bling.

Trojan horse

A type of computer virus that pretends to be a useful program, such as a game or a utility program, to entice you to use it, when in reality it contains special code that'll intentionally damage any system onto which it's loaded.

twisted-pair cable

Abbreviated TP. Cable that comprises two or more pairs of insulated wires twisted together, at six twists per inch.

In twisted-pair cable, one wire carries the signal and the other is grounded. The cable may be shielded or unshielded. Telephone wire installed in modern buildings is often twisted-pair wiring.

Type 1–9 cable

IBM Cabling System specifications. Each type refers to a specific category of cable, such as type 2, which is two-pair, shielded cable with solid conductors and a braided shield, and type 9, which is shielded, dual- pair, plenum cable with solid or braided conductors and a fire-resistant outer coating, for use between floors in a building.

U

UART

See Universal Asynchronous Receiver/Transmitter.

UDP

See User Datagram Protocol.

Ultra SCSI

An extension of the SCSI-2 standard that increases the data transfer rate to 20Mbps independent of the bus width. Ultra SCSI supports four to eight devices depending on cable type and length.

Ultra Wide SCSI

An extension of the SCSI-2 standard that increases the data transfer rate to 80Mbps over a 16-bit bus. Ultra2 SCSI supports up to 16 devices.

Ultra2 SCSI

An extension of the SCSI-2 standard that increases the data transfer rate to 40Mbps over an 8-bit bus. Ultra2 SCSI supports up to eight devices.

uncompress

The process of restoring a compressed file to its original form.

Uniform Resource Locator

Abbreviated URL. An address for a resource on the Internet.

URLs are used as a linking mechanism between Web pages and as an access method for Web browsers to access Web pages.

A URL specifies the protocol to be used to access the resource (such as HTTP or FTP), the name of the server where the resource is located (as in `www.sybex.com`), the path to that resource (as in `/catalog`), and the name of the document to open (`/index.html`).

uninterruptible power supply

Abbreviated UPS, with the letters pronounced just like the shipping company. An alternative power source, usually consisting of a set of batteries, used to power a computer system if the normal power service is interrupted or falls below acceptable levels.

A UPS system is usually applied only to the most critical devices on the network, such as servers, routers, gateways, and independent hard disks. A UPS can be continuously online and monitor and modify the power flowing through the unit, or it can be a standby UPS, which monitors the AC level, but only switches in when the power drops below a preset level.

Universal Asynchronous Receiver/Transmitter

Abbreviated UART; pronounced "you-art." An electronic module that combines the transmitting and receiving circuitry needed for asynchronous communications over a serial line.

Universal Serial Bus

Abbreviated USB. A standard from Intel and Microsoft for a high-speed peripheral bus designed to remove the need for almost all the connectors on the back of a personal computer.

USB defines the ports and bus characteristics with data transfer rates of up to 12Mbps over a single cable of up to 5 meters (16 feet) long. USB is capable of supporting up to 63 devices, such as external CD drives, printers, external modems, mice, and the keyboard, without rebooting the system, and also supplies power to some devices so there's no need for separate power cords or batteries. Most personal computers will have two USB ports.

unshielded cable

Any cable not protected from electromagnetic interference or Radio Frequency Interference (RFI) by an outer foil shield.

unshielded twisted-pair cable

Abbreviated UTP. Cable that contains two or more pairs of twisted copper wires.

The greater the number of twists, the lower the crosstalk. UTP is offered in both voice grade and data grade. The advantages of UTP include ease of installation and low cost of materials. Its drawbacks are limited signaling speeds and shorter maximum cable segment lengths.

UPS

See uninterruptible power supply.

UPS monitoring

The process that a server uses to make sure that an attached Uninterruptible Power Supply (UPS) system is functioning properly.

URL

See Uniform Resource Locator.

USB

See Universal Serial Bus.

senet newsgroups

he individual discussion groups within Usenet.

Usenet newsgroups contain articles posted by ternet and Usenet subscribers; very few of them tually contain hard news.

Most newsgroups are concerned with a single sub-ct, and the range of subjects throughout Usenet is nply phenomenal; if people are interested in a topic, u'll find a newsgroup for that topic.

ser Datagram Protocol

bbreviated UDP. The connectionless, transport-vel protocol used in the TCP/IP suite of protocols, ually bundled with IP-layer software. Because UDP oesn't add overhead, as does connection-oriented CP, UDP is often used with Simple Network Man-ement Protocol (SNMP) applications.

Multicast applications such as Mbone and the eal-time Transport Protocol that deliver audio and deo streams use UDP as their delivery mechanism cause the acknowledgment and retransmission ser-ces offered by TCP aren't needed and add too much erhead. If a packet of audio data is lost, retransmis-on is neither practical nor desirable.

TP

e unshielded twisted-pair cable.

.90

modem standard; also known as the 56K modem andard. V.90 describes an asymmetric connection, th theoretical speeds of up to 56Kbps downstream d an upstream connection rate of up to 33.6Kbps. .90 modems attain their high speed by assuming the rcuit is a digital circuit and reducing the number of alog-to-digital conversions they perform, except r the conversion that takes place for outbound affic at your modem.

Whether you actually achieve these rates depends 1 the quality of the phone line and the distance to e local telephone company central office. If the other end of the connection isn't digital, the modem switches into full analog mode at 28.8 or 33.6Kbps.

To reduce crosstalk between adjacent lines, the FCC has placed restrictions on maximum signal strength levels, so 54Kbps is the theoretical maximum data rate.

vaccine

A utility program designed to protect files from viruses. By adding a small amount of code to an existing file, the vaccine program causes an alert to be generated if a virus does attack.

VBScript

A version of Microsoft Visual Basic used as a scripting language in the Microsoft Internet Explorer Web browser.

very high-bit-rate digital subscriber line

Abbreviated VDSL. A higher-speed version of Asymmetrical Digital Subscriber Line (ADSL).

VDSL is asymmetrical with a higher downstream data transfer rate than its upstream rate. Upstream rates can be from 1.6Mbps to 2.3Mbps, and downstream rates range from 12.96Mbps to 51.84Mbps, depending on the distance involved.

very low-frequency emission

Abbreviated VLF. Radiation emitted by a computer monitor and other common household electrical appliances, such as televisions, hair dryers, electric blankets, and food processors.

VLF emissions range from 2 to 400kHz and decline with the square of the distance from the source. Emissions aren't constant around a computer monitor; they're higher from the sides and rear and weakest from the front of the screen.

Sweden is the only country to have defined a set of standards for monitor emissions. In 1990, Mat Oct Provadet (MPR), the Swedish National Board for Meterology and Testing, revised its guidelines for acceptable VLF emissions as less than or equal to 25 nanoTesla (nT). A nanoTesla is a unit of measurement for small magnetic fields.

video adapter

An adapter that provides the text and graphics output to the monitor. Some video adapters, such as the SVGA, are included in the circuitry on the motherboard rather than as separate plug-in boards.

video conferencing

A method used to allow people at remote locations to join a conference and share information. Originally done with analog video and expensive satellite links, video conferencing is now performed with compressed digital video transmitted over a LAN or the Internet.

From an application standpoint, video conferencing has gone way beyond looking at a picture of a person; users can look at and update charts, make drawings or sketches on a chalkboard, update spreadsheets, and so on, all online.

video RAM

Abbreviated VRAM, pronounced "vee-ram." Special-purpose RAM with two data paths for access (conventional RAM has just one). These two paths let a VRAM board manage two functions at once: refreshing the display and communicating with the processor. VRAM doesn't require the system to complete one function before starting the other, so it allows faster operation for the whole video system.

virtual memory

A memory-management technique that allows information in physical memory to be swapped out to a hard disk if necessary.

This technique provides applications with more memory space than is actually available in the computer. True virtual-memory management requires specialized hardware in the processor for the operating system to use; it isn't just a matter of writing information out to a swap area on the hard disk at the application level.

In a virtual memory system, programs and their data are divided into smaller pieces called *pages*. When more memory is needed, the operating system decides which pages are least likely to be needed soon (using an algorithm based on frequency of use, most recent use, and program priority), and it writes these pages out to disk. The memory space that they used is now available to the rest of the system for other applications. When these pages are needed again, they're loaded back into real memory, displacing other pages.

virus

A program intended to damage a computer system without the user's knowledge or permission.

A virus clones itself from disk to disk or from system to system over a network. Numbers are hard to come by, but certain authorities claim that there are approximately 30,000 known viruses, with 400 new ones appearing each month.

A virus may attach itself to another program or to the partition table or boot track on a hard disk. When a certain event occurs, a date passes, or a specific program executes, the virus is triggered into action. Others, including the ILOVEYOU virus, take advantage of the trusting relationship that exists between Microsoft Office applications and run as scripts as soon as an email attachment is opened.

VLF

See very low-frequency emission.

VRAM

See video RAM.

W

wait state

A clock cycle during which no instructions are executed because the processor is waiting for data from memory.

Static RAM chips and paged-mode RAM chips can store information without being constantly refreshed by the processor, thus eliminating the wait state. A computer that can process information without wait states is known as a zero-wait-state computer.

AN

wide area network.

arm boot

reboot performed after the operating system has en running for some period of time by pressing rl+Alt+Del rather than cycling the power to the mputer.

avetable synthesis

method used by a sound board to simulate musical struments. Wavetable synthesis uses digitized mples of real orchestral instruments, which are ited and mixed to produce music. FM synthesis is eaper than wavetable synthesis but is also of much wer quality.

eb browser

client application that lets you look at hypertext cuments, follow links to other HTML documents, d download files on the Internet or on a corporate ranet.

When you find something that interests you as u browse through a hypertext document, you can ck that object, and the system automatically takes e of accessing the Internet host that holds the doc-ient you requested; you don't need to know the IP dress, the name of the host system, or any other tails. A Web browser will also display the graphics a Web page, play audio and video clips, and execute all Java or ActiveX programs called *applets*.

Netscape Navigator and Microsoft Internet plorer are examples of popular Web browsers.

eb page

formation placed on a Web server for viewing with Web browser. A Web page may contain text, aphics, audio or video clips, and links to other eb pages.

eb server

hardware and software package that provides ser-es to client computers running Web browsers.

Clients make requests in the form of HTTP mes-sages; the server responds to these messages, returning Web pages or other requested documents to the client. Most Web servers run one of the versions of Unix or Microsoft Windows 2000 Server.

Web site

A group of HTML documents and associated scripts supported by a Web server on the World Wide Web. Most Web sites have a home page used as a starting point or index into the site, with other Web pages or even other Web sites connected by links. To connect to a Web site, you need an Internet connection and a Web browser.

Webcam

A low-cost video camera used to capture live images for display on a Web site. Webcams are used to dis-play traffic information, activity inside a person's apartment, fish tanks, scenic views, and street scenes.

wide area network

Abbreviated WAN. A network that connects users across large distances, often crossing the geographical boundaries of cities or states.

Wide SCSI

A version of the SCSI-2 standard that provides data transfer rates of up to 20MBps over a 16-bit data bus.

Wide Ultra SCSI

A version of the SCSI-2 standard that provides data transfer rates of up to 40MBps over a 16-bit data bus.

Wide Ultra2 SCSI

A version of the SCSI-2 standard that provides data transfer rates of up to 80MBps over a 16-bit data bus.

wildcard character

A character that represents one or more unknown characters. In many operating systems, a question mark (?) represents a single unknown character in a filename or filename extension, and an asterisk (*) represents any number of unknown characters.

Windows Internet Naming Service

Abbreviated WINS. A Microsoft Windows NT Server and Windows 2000 Server service that maps NetBIOS computer names used in Windows networks to IP addresses used in TCP/IP-based networks. WINS is almost completely automated; it builds its own database and manages updates to the database.

WINS

See Windows Internet Naming Service.

Wintel

A contraction of Windows and Intel that refers to an Intel-based computer that runs Microsoft Windows.

wireless communications

A method of connecting a node or a group of nodes into the main network using a technology other than conventional cabling. Infrared and radio frequencies are commonly used in wireless communications.

Wireless LANs aren't always completely wireless. They may be used to replace the cabling on certain network segments or to connect groups of networks that use conventional cabling.

World Wide Web

Abbreviated WWW, W3, or simply the Web. A huge collection of hypertext pages on the Internet. World Wide Web concepts were developed in Switzerland by the European Laboratory for Particle Physics (known as CERN), but the Web isn't just a tool for scientists; it's one of the most flexible and exciting tools in existence.

Hypertext links connect pieces of information (text, graphics, animation, audio, and video) in separate HTML pages located at the same or at different Internet sites, and you explore these pages and links using a Web browser such as Netscape Navigator or Microsoft Internet Explorer.

You can also access a Web resource directly if you specify the appropriate Uniform Resource Locator (URL).

World Wide Web traffic is growing faster than most other Internet services, and the reason for this becomes obvious once you try a capable Web browser; it's very easy and a lot of fun to access World Wide Web information.

write-back cache

A technique used in cache design for writing information back into main memory.

In a write-back cache, the cache stores the changed block of data but only updates main memory under certain conditions, such as when the whole block must be overwritten because a newer block must be loaded into the cache or when the controlling algorithm determines that too much time has elapsed since the last update. This method is rather complex to implement but is much faster than other designs.

write-through cache

A technique used in cache design for writing information back into main memory.

In a write-through cache, each time the processor returns a changed bit of data to the cache, the cache updates that information in both the cache and in main memory. This method is simple to implement but isn't as fast as other designs; delays can be introduced when the processor must wait to complete write operations to slower main memory.

WWW

See World Wide Web.

X

XON/XOFF

In asynchronous transmissions between two PCs, a simple method of flow control.

The receiving PC sends an XOFF control character (ASCII 19, Ctrl+S) to pause the transmission of data when the receive buffer is full and then sends an XON character (ASCII 17, Ctrl+Q) when it's ready to continue the transmission.

R

Zone Bit Recording.

o insertion force socket

breviated ZIF socket. A specially designed chip
ket that makes replacing a chip easier and safer.
To change a chip in a ZIF socket, you raise a lever
side the socket to free the original chip's pins from
socket. Then slide the old chip out and slide in the
lacement chip, taking care to align the pins and
es. Finally, lower the lever again. A ZIF socket
nimizes damage to the delicate pins that connect
chip to the rest of the system.

F socket

zero insertion force socket.

Zip drive

A popular removable storage device from Iomega Corporation, capable of 100MB or 250MB of storage on relatively cheap, portable, 3$^1/_2$-inch disks.

Zip drives have emerged as the de facto standard personal computer backup device.

ZIP file

A file whose contents have been compressed by one of the popular file-compression utilities, such as PKZIP, WinZip, or other comparable program; the filename extension is `.zip`.

A ZIP file can contain a single compressed file or a whole collection of archives. A file compressed in this way is said to have been "zipped."

To uncompress a ZIP file, use the same utility that compressed it originally. Some ZIP files are self-extracting and can uncompress themselves when you click their icons.

Zone Bit Recording

Abbreviated ZBR. A Seagate Technologies term for multiple zone recording.

Index

Note to the reader: Throughout this index **boldfaced** page numbers indicate primary discussions of a topic. *Italicized* page numbers indicate illustrations.

B

U

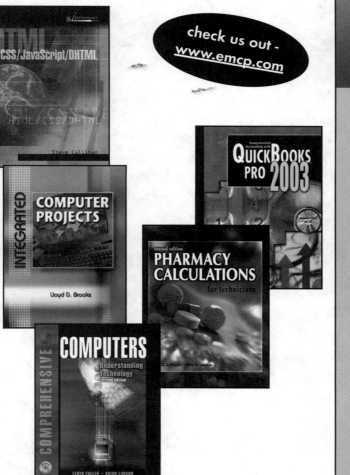